The
Good Beer
Guide to
Great
Britain

A CAMRA/STOREY BOOK

*The mission of Storey Communications is to serve our customers
by publishing practical information that encourages
personal independence in harmony with the environment.*

North American edition published in 1998 by Storey Books.
United Kingdom edition published in 1998 by CAMRA Books.

Edited by Jonathon Preece and Jill Adam (CAMRA);
  Brad Ring (Storey Books)
Cover design by Rob Johnson, Johnson Design
Front cover photograph © Doug Franga
Back cover photograph © Herb Swanson/SWANPIX
Text design by Stephen Stafford
Typesetting by Anne Braley
Database design and DTP transfer by Yvonne Cavaller,
  Pentactive, Kingston-upon-Thames
Maps by Perrott Cartographics, Machynlleth

CAMRA Campaigns team: Mike Benner, Iain Loe,
  Caroline Mozley, Mel Taylor, Ben Wardle
CAMRA Administration: Cressida Feiler, Gary Fowler,
  Malcolm Harding, Jean Jones, Karen Lynch, Abi Maddock,
  Steve Powell, Anna Romano, Kirk Winkler

  The information in this book is true and complete to the best of
our knowledge. All recommendations are made without guarantee on
the part of the editor or Storey Books. The editor and publisher dis-
claim any liability in connection with the use of this information. For
additional information please contact Storey Books, Schoolhouse
Road, Pownal, Vermont 05261.

  Storey Books are available for special premium and promotional
uses and for customized editions. For further information, please call
Storey's Custom Publishing Department at 1-800-793-9396.

Printed in Canada by Webcom Limited
10 9 8 7 6 5 4 3 2 1

ISBN 1-58017-101-X

CONTENTS

How to use the Good Beer Guide   4

Editorial

The campaigning year   5
Who owns our pubs?   8
Pub Design Awards   11
Real pub fires   14
This brewing life   16
The not-so free house   18
The good pint guide   20
The craft of brewing   22
A beer style guide   24
Champion Beers of Britain   25
Go to a beer festival!   26
Beer festival calendar   29
Great historic pubs: CAMRA's National Inventory   30

The Pubs

England   34
Wales   372
Scotland   400
Northern Ireland   425
Channel Islands   427
Isle of Man   429

The Breweries

Independent breweries   431
New breweries   534
The nationals   536
Pub groups   545
Beers index   553

How to use the Good Beer Guide

Selection criteria
• A pub is selected for the *Guide* because it serves good beer: cask conditioned real ale, traditionally well kept, without the application of life-extending gases. Unless the beer is first class, a pub will not be chosen.

•A pub which indulges in anti-consumer practices, such as deliberately short-measuring its customers, is unlikely to find favour.

• The use of deliberately misleading dispense equipment, such as fake handpumps which make you think you're getting real ale or real cider but which only dispense keg versions, is another reason why pubs are not chosen.

How the *Guide* is organised
• Pubs are listed in areas which largely follow the county/local authority system. In some instances, where the new authorities are small they have been amalgamated into larger regions. There have been many changes of boundary areas over the years, and to keep up with them all would mean wholesale and ongoing revisions of all areas within the CAMRA branch and regional network, and this would take resources – all of which are provided voluntarily at branch level – away from the campaign. This arrangement is the best compromise at present.

• The county maps pinpoint the pub location as well as independently-owned breweries. Breweries and brewpubs owned by the national brewers are not included.

The pub listings
• Pubs are listed by location, then alphabetically within each location.

• The beers are listed alphabetically by brewery. Where more than one beer from a brewery is given, they are listed by order of strength. Seasonal beers, such as winter ales, are included, but are clearly available only at certain times of the year.

• Opening times confirm the hours in operation for most of the week, followed by the hours on which they different from the norm. Sunday hours are individually stated. Each section of time is separated by a semi-colon.

• The pub's key facilities are listed according to the symbols printed on the inside front cover.

• For meals and accommodation, no assessment of quality is made unless mentioned in the pub description.

• Evening meals are assumed to be available until 9pm, unless otherwise stated.

• Some pubs welcome drinkers with dogs, some do not. If you are planning a long trek, it would be advisable to phone ahead before taking Bonzo to the boozer.

Removing pubs from the *Guide,* and complaints
• Pubs are removed from the *Guide* on an ongoing basis as part of CAMRA's drive to maintain quality. The licensee may have left, the pub have been sold or taken over. Deletions from the *Good Beer Guide* are listed in *What's Brewing*, CAMRA's monthly newspaper.

• Readers' complaints about pubs are passed on for review to the local branch, since it is the branches who choose the pubs which are listed in this *Guide* – no one else, as this ensures the integrity of the information.

The campaigning year

It was the best of times, it was the worst of times... **Mike Benner**, Head of Campaigns and Communications, gives you reasons to be cheerful – and reasons to campaign

Over 26 years the *Good Beer Guide* has seen the real ale scene and the industry change massively. And it doesn't stop – if anything, it is more frenetic.

The choice of beers you can drink is now huge, but you rarely get a chance to try more than a few in the average pub. Look at the *Guide*'s brewery section: hundreds and hundreds of great ales – but all you can see over a bar is what you see over so many other bars: a choice from half a dozen beers, which include lagers, nitrokegs and keg beer. We don't want to see pubs with slow or variable turnover selling too many real ales at the same time, as this can mean a poor quality pint, but a more imaginative choice of revolving beers would be a welcome step forward for most pubs.

We are continually told that the demand for cask ale is in decline. That depends on which corporate plan is in operation at any one time. According to Whitbread, 51.6 per cent of drinkers prefer ale, and 45.2 per cent prefer lager, and by 2002 lager's market share will be 54.8 per cent and ale's 45.2 per cent. But 20 years ago Whitbread said that by the late 1990s lager would account for more than 80 per cent of beer sales.

On the other hand, we were assured by brewers in the early 1990s that the future lay with cask. But Bass blamed the closure of its Cardiff and Sheffield breweries on the steep decline in sales of cask-conditioned ales. Yet it is Bass and other national brewers which are to blame for the fall in consumption of real ale. They have the power to determine the shape and style of the beer market. In the mid-90s they began to push nitrokeg beers into the market, because the truth is that big brewers have a declining interest in the cask ale market, even though it accounts for about 22 per cent of all draught beers consumed in Britain.

In reality the big brewers have lost some power in the market to the larger non-brewing pub chains. As exclusive supply agreements, signed after the Beer Orders came into force in 1990, come to an end these companies are buying their beer from a variety of brewers. This is making life a little tougher for the brewers and each is fighting to become the lowest-cost producer with the most appealing 'must have' brands. They are achieving this by closing breweries, axing regional beers and pouring their marketing millions into a handful of brands which they feel have 'national appeal'.

Fullers, Batemans and other regional brewers report that they have bucked the trend of decline and are selling more cask beer. There has never been so much choice and diversity in the real ale sector of the beer market.

MP Alan Duncan joins the protest against the closure of Ruddles.

But such is the grip of the nationals that if their sales decline then the overall line on the graph will point downwards.

They see the answer as expansionism. Bass wanted to buy Carlsberg-Tetley. Refused permission by the government, the group is now hell bent on paring down its brewing and pub divisions so as to concentrate on big-profit brands and outlets. It recently sold almost all of its leased pubs to a new pub company.

This expansionism encroaches on the markets of the small brewers. In the past seven years, the regional brewers' share of the beer market has fallen from 22 per cent to less than 15 per cent. The microbrewer's contribution, important as it is as a result of the diversity it has brought, is a minute 1.5 to 2 per cent of the market. That's good news for the corporations, but bad news for choice.

Whitbread has axed nine regional real ale brands over the last year or so and announced the closure of Castle Eden and Flowers, both important real ale breweries.

Carlsberg-Tetley has announced the closure of its Alloa brewery and the famous Wrexham Brewery, the longest-established traditional lager brewery in Britain. Bass is to close breweries in Cardiff and Sheffield, and Scottish Courage closed Websters and Home Breweries in 1997.

This vandalism is not limited to the big brewers. The management at Morrells in Oxford are abandoning over 200 years of brewing tradition and selling the business, lock, stock and barrel to the highest bidder. That bidder is unlikely to keep this town-centre brewery open. Short-term profits from turning it into residences or offices will prevail, rather than a long-term plan to make the business work. As I write, a 'white knight' could still be on the horizon.

Morland of Abingdon bought the Ruddles brewery and brands last year and intends to close the brewery and brew Rutland's favourite in Oxfordshire.

The Campaign for Real Ale is not sitting idly by and watching all this happen: action groups are working hard to combat important brewery closures, and we are turning our attention to getting the real ale message across to today's drinkers – who don't always drink ale, or lager, or wine, but choose different products at different times.

We have to sell the benefits of including real ale in people's drinking repertoires. Effectively, it will fall to us to market real ale as a genre.

What kind of pubs do you want?

With reduced choice of beer comes reduced choice of pubs – perhaps between Flann 0'Flunkey's Beyond the Pale Irish Bar or Ned Kelly's Outback Experience...

But there could be good news for you, the drinker, since there is a drift back to old-fashioned values which typify the traditional tenancy. That's the view of Oxfordshire's tiny Hook Norton Brewery, nationally known for distinctive brews such as Old Hooky. Company director James Clarke says: 'Most pubs in our estate are typical village pubs and we find customers like them. Some are turning away from theme bars and returning to the local.'

This means that the city-centre superpub's days are numbered. There is anecdotal evidence that young people, especially students, are beginning to desert the brash, noisy, overcrowded and overpriced town centres in favour of more traditional locals.

There's no doubt that the market for town-centre theme pubs is saturated. Standing in an average high street, you can hardly turn your head without being affronted with the lurid facade of a theme pub. The economic tide looks set to run against giant managed houses and expensively-refurbished theme pubs, according to Graham Page, consultant with research agency AC Nielsen. 'It takes six years on average to recoup the investment, but by then it's time for another change,' he said.

But the success of Wetherspoons, Whitbread's Hogshead chain, and Tut 'n' Shive alehouses prove there's a vibrant market for real ale.

Putting the case for the pub tie in Brussels: Mike Benner (CAMRA), with MEPs Simon Murphy and Tony Cunningham, Ben Wardle (CAMRA) and CAMRA director Terry Locke.

Open all hours

CAMRA continues with its call for more sensible licensing hours and we are making progress. The government has now committed itself to a ground-up review of the existing archaic and unfair system. But when this will be is anyone's guess.

Threat to community pubs?

While town pubs get turned into fun/pub discos, country pubs get turned into private homes. Recent research commissioned by CAMRA shows that 81 per cent of people believe that a pub is essential to a rural community.

It's time the government recognised the pub as an essential service and offered it the same status as the village shop when being considered for mandatory rate relief, charitable status or other support initiatives.

There's a clear message for the pub companies, too. Rather than pouring £1 million into the latest superpub, why not give the people what they want and invest to improve the amenity levels in rural and community pubs? Imagine what 50 marginal pubs could each do with £20,000...

Beer tax

Calls for moves towards a harmonisation of beer duty with our European neighbours are still falling on deaf ears. This is despite the fact that the Treasury's own economic model has been used to show that a 20 per cent cut in tax would be self-financing within two years. There would be no losers – except for the gangs making millions from selling cheap French beer to teenagers. It's a growing problem, and if tax is not cut we can expect some 20 per cent of beer drunk over here to be brewed over there by 2006. That means pubs and breweries will close.

The guest beer

The universally popular 'guest beer law', introduced in 1991, has been extended to include a bottle-conditioned beer, as well as a draught real ale.

But the guest beer remains under threat. The legislation applies only to tenanted or leased pubs owned by the national brewers. Most of these are being sold to pub companies – where guest beers are being removed.

CAMRA is in discussions with the authorities, as we believe the law should be extended to pub companies which have supply agreements with the national brewers.

Honest pints

Eighty per cent of pints sold in pubs are short. That's the hard fact. Despite this, 84 per cent of people think you should get a full liquid pint. Step in Dennis Turner MP, whose private member's bill, the Weights and Measures (Beer and Cider) Bill, made it to the Commons in July after much support and help from CAMRA. That would have guaranteed you a full measure plus consumer protection.

But it was talked out of the Commons by a single Conservative MP.

Despite this setback the Campaign for Real Ale continues to work with the DTI and the new Consumer Affairs Minister to get you what you pay for – a full pint every time.

Who owns our pubs?

That olde-style pub may mask a corporate giant waiting to theme it. **Steve Cox** looks at how the brewing industry works and how it affects you, the drinker.

Most people think they understand the beer industry – they use pubs, after all. But few people really grasp the enormous changes that have taken place in the last ten years.

Who owns our pubs?

Four big national companies produce most of our beer: Bass, Carlsberg-Tetley, Scottish & Newcastle and Whitbread brew around eight out of every ten pints drunk. Their beers are everywhere. But you'll be surprised to hear how few pubs they actually own.

On the other hand, companies who aren't brewers own a third of all pubs. These pub retailers really took off after the 1989 Monopolies Commission report; some were brewers who had sold their breweries, some bought chunks of pubs sold off by existing companies, and others just grew by building their own pubs from scratch. If you look up the ten largest pub owners in Britain, only four of them are brewers.

Some pub companies are easy to spot: every Wetherspoons has a distinctive design, no music, a cheap beer policy, a reasonable real ale range, and so on.

Others are very difficult to spot: a pub selling mostly Bass beer might be owned by Bass, or it might be a free house, or it might be a pub from any one of 50-plus retailers who stock Bass!

Who brews our beer?

The *Good Beer Guide* lists nearly 600 brewers. These fall roughly into three groups: the national companies mentioned above, the long-established regional and local brewers, and the new-wave brewers – the small companies set up since 1971. The long-established companies have their own pub estates, and vary in size from 1,000 pubs down to 20.

The new-wave brewers include a few management buyouts of long-established firms, but – this is an enormous generalisation – they are small companies relying largely on the free trade.

Two-thirds of all beer is drunk in pubs, clubs, restaurants and so on, and one-third is consumed at home. And there is a mad scrap to sell into those places where you can. Obviously, a single publican is very different from a big retailing group, but they do have two things in common: they want the best price, and they like to have heard of the beer. The biggest brewers offer enormous discounts and spend heavily on advertising to make sure that is the case. Big guys squeeze out the small and medium-sized brewers, and then take the lion's share of what's left.

% of all pubs owned	
National brewers	20
Pub companies	34
Regional brewers	20
Free houses	26

The retailing revolution

The emphasis is now on retailing – that is, selling you on the type of pub rather than the type of beer it sells. Think of supermarkets, which sell pretty similar product ranges. Companies which own breweries talk just as much about retailing as those who don't.

Pub food is now around a third of turnover. It is predicted to grow steadily. People are drinking less in pubs, and that's one reason why companies promote 'premium' – that is, more expensive – products.

Currently a third of pub customers are women, but the industry expects that to grow to a half within a decade.

Beer – all types together – is still the majority of what pubs sell. And, of course, within the current pub trade, there are plenty of traditional beer-drinkers' pubs.

That is the point – there are now vast numbers of types of pub aimed at different audiences.

Are you an affluent 18–24-year-old on the pull, who needs to be dazzled with ever-changing concepts? Or are you a portly family person who is looking for a foodie pub with a family feel?

You have been allocated your slot. I hope you like it.

Why the high street is full of newly tarted-up pubs

The larger companies are spending money like mad on new concepts and also on doing up existing pubs in good locations. The industry spent £1.5 billion on pubs in 1997. A brand new pub costs, on average, £1.6 million; converting an old bank or post office to a pub costs £1.2 million. But if the company gets it right, it can make 30+ per cent profit in the first year on that sum, and get the lot back in five years. These developments have higher prices and attract a high-spending crowd.

There's been particular emphasis on pubs on the high street aimed at the wandering bands of young people (spending lots of time in 'circuit' pubs) and concepts aimed at families and those eating out (who spend money when they do get out). For example, Allied Domecq has Firkin (aimed at students) and the Big Steak Pubs (food and families).

These sort of branded concepts were less than a third of Allied's managed pubs in 1995 – they are now more than half.

Why? Because these branded pubs generate more profit – even more profit than an unbranded refurbishment.

Every substantial company, more or less, is stepping up investment. Wetherspoons alone plans to build 90 new pubs in 1998-99, each with up to six times the turnover of the typical community tenancy. No wonder 1,000 small pubs close every year.

Some of this investment raises standards and meets a need: cleaner pubs, cleaner air, disabled access, decent toilets, proper cellar cooling. Some of the concepts widen choice. But much of the expenditure is wasted – spending half the money well would have looked just as good. And which pubs get urgently needed investment depends on where they fit in the corporate plan.

A pub which met the standards of 1971 could now look backward and unwelcoming. But some great pubs have been ripped apart in the pursuit of 'earnings per share'. The constant rise in beer prices is suddenly more understandable... the industry is spending the equivalent of 22 pence a pint.

It seems likely that 1999 will be the year when some companies hit the rails. The ten largest companies spent 80 per of their profits on doing up and building pubs. Many analysts believe that some of the very latest developments will flop.

THAT'S IT! A SKATEBOARD THEME PUB!

People

Pubs remain places where you go to drink, perhaps to eat, and to meet people – above all to have a good time. That hasn't changed. Surveys show time and again that what makes a good pub in the round is the warmth, the welcome and the atmosphere. This comes down to the people working there, in particular the publican, who has a positive or a baleful effect on the staff.

Are tenancies and free houses better than managed houses?

In theory, pubs run by individuals should be better than those rolled out from corporate HQ. The publican should be more motivated, the pub more individual, and so on. In practice, most customers probably don't notice the difference.

Pubs have long since ceased to be places where if the publican opened on time people drifted in – and the guv'nor made money. Customers have many many places to spend their dosh, and the average tenant pays much more just for the right to run the pub. The very best pubs will probably always be those run by committed individuals with a long-term stake in the business – what is best at delivering a reasonable average is another question.

TRADE BODIES
It's not CAMRA who argues for quality standards: these trade bodies also do, too.

Brewers and Licensed Retailers Association (BLRA)
Represents brewers from multi-nationals down to small family firms, and some pub companies.
'Lobbies government and runs occasional industry promotions, provides statistics, careers information and briefings on various industry issues.'
Relations with CAMRA like a sunny March day – surprisingly warm but sudden frosty patches.
(0171) 486 4831

Independent Family Brewers of Britain (IFBB)
Represents 36 family-owned members of the BLRA.
'We run two main campaigns: to lower beer duty and to retain the traditional tied tenancy.'
(01483) 202050

Society of Independent Brewers (SIBA)
Represents around 250 new-wave brewers set up since 1971, and gives realistic advice to those interested in doing so, and so on. 'Desperately keen to hear from anyone who wants to set up a small brewery.'
Contact via Ballard's Brewery (01730) 821301.

Association of Licensed Multiple Retailers (ALMR).
'We represent 83 pub companies with 13,000 pubs between them. We lobby government and provide networking opportunities.'
Some common membership with BLRA.
(0181) 813 2800

British Institute of Innkeeping (BII)
'Provides information, skills and qualifications to help its 15,000 individual members run the best pubs in the country.'
The BII seeks to raise professional standards, it accredits

training courses and is responsible for the National Licensee Certificate, now demanded by many licensing benches for all new licensees.
(01276) 684449

Local Licensed Victuallers Associations
Represents publicans, in particular tenants. There is no national body, but the various regional federations co-operate closely. The FLTA, the Yorkshire and North body, publishes a useful pack on some pitfalls about entering the licensed trade.
(01484) 710534

Cask Marque is a new industry initiative to raise the quality of real ale. Individual pubs will be accredited and given a plaque after independent inspection... It has already produced some depressing research. Write to Cask Marque, MDA, Waterfall Mill, Queen Victoria St, Millhill, Blackburn, Lancs BB2 2QG.

Pub Design Awards

Dr Steven Parissien, chairman of the judges, looks back at the best of the 1997 Pub Design Awards, awarded by CAMRA in conjunction with English Heritage.

It may be premature to call for general rejoicing over the state of pub design in Britain, but in many ways 1997 gave all those interested in the future of the British pub something to shout about.

The judges' campaign to persuade designers and their clients to reinterpret the pub for the 1990s – instead of churning out grotesque parodies of the Good Old Days of the 1890s – appears to have borne fruit. At last we are seeing the creation of high-quality pub interiors which are contemporary, but whose vibrance and individuality is harnessed to the elements which define the pub as a uniquely British institution: warmth, friendliness and informality.

But a depressingly large proportion of the entries submitted to the 1997 Pub Design Awards were bedecked with overfamiliar 'heritage' paraphernalia. Most evocations of 'Victorian' pubs are as authentic as Dick Van Dyke's cockney accent; they may have an admirably restrained pub facade but there are Heritage Horrors inside.

Conversion to pub use

1997 was also the Year of the Bank, and many of the bank-to-pub conversions of 1997 were carried out with great panache and sensitivity. One of these, Frazer's Bar in Edinburgh, is the recipient of the Conversion to Pub Use category award. Ian Whyte's triumphal resurrection of the former office of the Royal Bank of Scotland in George Street, the heart of Edinburgh's historic New Town, enthusiastically and deftly exploited the building's full potential. The site is already impressive: the new pub is in the former bank offices (the banking hall itself is adjacent) of the muscular, temple-fronted edifice built by David Rhind in 1874.

After the bank left their listed premises in 1992, the building fell into decay. But it has been brought back from the dead in an exciting

Bread and Roses, Clapham: pub refurbishment award winner.

11

yet carefully thought-out manner by entrepreneur Whyte – a previous Pub Design Award winner in 1993.

The pub blends the highest quality new materials – Mr Whyte says '17 different woods have been used for the parqetry bar front – with the architectural features of Rhind's bank. The design of the bar, the wall decoration and the impressive. Dutch-made lighting evokes a 1930-ish Art Deco feel, while at the same time remaining unmistakably contemporary.

Every new element of the interior is designed to be as attractively functional as possible; a good example of this is the colourful Marmoleum lino on the floors, which combines practicality with flair in a manner which makes a welcome change from Victorian carpet or sawdust-strewn floor-boards.

At Frazer's Bar, Ian Whyte has shown that good design, combined with a simplicity of touch and a recognition of the importance of the building, can work extremely well – at relatively little cost. Pub owners who throw tens of thousands of pounds at over-elaborate and inappropriate schemes would do well to come and see for themselves.

However, in other instances pub owners and their architects prefer to treat the building simply as a shell whose interior needs to be completely reinvented. The misconception that a historic building is nothing more than four walls and a roof seems an especially ingrained one.

Also worthy of mention is Wetherspoons' conversion of a former hotel, The Imperial on St David's Hill in Exeter. Here the vast, semi-circular conservatory bar, lit by a huge lunette window and supported curved iron beams, provided an exuberant and enjoyable contrast to the building's restrained Late Georgian facade. While the boldness and execution of this approach was applauded, however, on the whole it did not match the impressively high standard set by last year's runaway winner, Wetherspoons' own Commercial Rooms in Bristol.

Encouragingly, a surprising number of entries in the Conversion to Pub Use category were couched in a refreshing modern idiom. *Bargo* in Glasgow's Albion Street was certainly one of best of these, yet it failed to qualify for an award since it does not to serve any cask or bottle-conditioned beer.

The Refurbishment category

The popular Refurbishment category included a number of schemes which eschewed the tired old cliches of pseudo-Victoriana or fake Oirish in favour of a bold, contemporary approach to the traditional pub concept.

The overall winner of the Refurbishment category avoided the usual tired design solutions, employing an inspired, but sensitive, contemporary approach to revitalise a run-down urban pub. Bread and Roses in Clapham Manor Street (just off Clapham's busy High Street), in London SW4, arose from the ashes of Allied's Bowyer Arms, a building of the 1840s which 150 years later was in a decidedly poor condition.

The pub was remodelled by architect Andrew Wong and building co-operative ARC for the trades union-backed Workers' Beer Company; its name comes from a song written during a long and bitter strike by 20,000 women textile workers in the USA in 1911 ('Give us bread but give us roses'). It now serves both adults and (accompanied) children in an atmosphere which, like most much-loved pubs, is welcoming and informal.

At the outset the architect sensibly chose not to 'create a pastiche of a Victorian pub'; instead the overall impression is, in the words one judge, 'of a well-lit, open, light space, with a sense of order and calm – the complete antithesis of many pubs. The flooring is of wide planks of blonde wood – not a saw-dusted board or a floral carpet to be seen – while the interesting dichroic lamps provide an effective but subtle and reflective light.

The internal colour scheme of purple, sage green and cream (with more lurid hues in the toilets) works very well. It also makes a subtle political statement which dovetails nicely with the origin of the pub's new name and the aspirations of building's current owners: purple, green and silver were the colours of the Suffragette movement, at its British peak when 'Bread and Roses' was being penned.

The cream terrazzo bar top, with a stainless-steel leaning rail, is a robust alternative to the usual timber bar counter. And the dramati-

Frazer's Bar in Edinburgh, winner of the Conversion to Pub Use award.

cally-glazed, steel-framed conservatory neatly complements the existing Victorian brickwork.

Even the wall decoration is classy and quietly confident; instead of the usual sepia prints there are high-quality black and white photographs, carefully-selected modern art, and a prominent photo of Nelson Mandela visiting nearby Brixton (the colour of his shirt fortuitously matching that of the wall).

The result is a pub with attitude which is also relaxed and friendly, and it has been enthusiastically received by locals (and the area's trades union branches), as well as by English Heritage, who have applauded the sensitive juxtaposition of new and old.

Bread and Roses, together with the commended Tavern on the Green in Grattons Drive, Crawley, Sussex, appear to represent the way forward for new pub design. No plagiarism, no fakes, no boring repetition. Just good, confident, modern design, carefully melded with the demands of the trade, the history of the building and the wishes of the customers.

Disappointments

The judges were once more unable to present any award in the New-build category. Several entries impressed: Judge Gill Associates' excellent work at the *Nowhere,* in Manchester's Deansgate, was one – but it doesn't serve real ale.

The judges also felt unable to make an award in the prestigious Conservation category. Indeed, while good, modern pub design appears to have turned the corner, the discrepancy between the resources put behind the refurbishment of historic pubs and the poor standards achieved seems to be widening.

Last year, millions were spent on revamping or recreating Britain's pubs. However, with hindsight, much of this money seems to have been unwisely spent.

The refurbishment or restoration of old pubs is often quite unnecessary and more often than not is unduly heavy-handed. The principles of conservation – recognising and celebrating the importance of the building, instead of imposing the latest marketing theme and making reversible changes with sympathy and care – have, it, seems, been completely ignored.

Dr Steven Parissien is assistant director of the Paul Mellon Centre for Studies in British Art

Stop where you see this sign:

Real ale and a real fire. Few things go together better. This year's *Good Beer Guide* features over 2000 pubs that know how the waves of warmth and flickering flames of a real **fire** can draw in the customers. Look for the open **fire** symbol – .

Keep the Homefire burning

Homefire, sponsor of the *Good Beer Guide*, has been a favourite smokeless fuel in homes for over thirty years and is now growing in popularity in pubs, too. Specially made for open fires and multi-fuel stoves, Homefire combines all the traditional qualities of a coal fire with the easily controllable, high heat output and long-burning qualities expected of a modern solid fuel.

Being smokeless, Homefire is cleaner to burn and cleaner to use than coal. Each briquette burns efficiently to give maximum heat and minimum waste and yet retains all the joy of a glowing **fire**.

Good health!

According to the Asthma Council, solid fuels are less drying than other forms of heat – they introduce moisture into the air which makes breathing easier.

Homefire's companion brand, Homefire Ovals, is made from a blend of anthracite and other coals to give exceptional value for money. Both are made by CPL Products, Britain's largest manufacturer of solid fuel, to conform to the latest environmental standards.

Other fuels in the CPL range suit-

A real fire. The natural fit for real ale.

14

able for pubs and homes include Phurnacite and Ancit, ideal smoke-less fuels for closed-in appliances such as roomheaters, boilers and cookers.

All CPL fuels are available in bulk, or in handy pre-packed bags, from leading coal merchants country-wide.

Your guarantee of quality

CPL British Fuels and CPL Charringtons are the two largest merchants giving nationwide service. Like most merchants they operate a Code of Practice known as the Approved Coal Merchant Scheme. This ensures members take all reasonable steps to meet customers' needs – a high-quality service to match high-quality products.

Your nearest Approved Merchant can be found by calling the Freephone CPL Customer Helpline number: 0800 716 626.

The Good Fuel Guide – it's good and it's free

The CPL *Good Fuel Guide* describes a range of solid fuels suitable for open **fires,** multi-fuel stoves, roomheaters, boilers and cookers. In full colour and illustrated, it also contains tips on lighting a fire, getting the best out of appliances and sources of further information. To get your free copy, write to David Burnhope, whose address is on this page.

Warmth and comfort in a takeaway bag.

You can stop where you see this sign, too.

THE GOOD FUEL GUIDE

Send for your free copy today.

David Burnhope
CPL Industries
Mill Lane
Wingerworth
Chesterfield S42 6NG
E mail:
corporate@cplindustries.co.uk
Or telephone our Freephone number above.

This brewing life

Small brewers have big problems. **Robin Loxeley** looks at the highs and the lows of the brewer's life.

Why couldn't the Brewer of the Year sell his beer in his own town? Sean Franklin runs Rooster's brewery in Harrogate – just one of over 300 new brewers set up since 1971. The Tap & Spile chain used to sell over a thousand beers, and Rooster brewed three out of their top 20 best-sellers nationwide. 'Drinkers in the Tap & Spile, Harrogate, voted Rooster's Cream their favourite beer two years in a row,' Franklin said. But in March Tap & Spile nationally stopped selling his beer, and Sean Franklin had no regular outlets in Harrogate.

This story could be repeated again and again: small brewers can brew beer that customers like – they just can't get their beers into pubs.

The number of free houses fell by a third between 1993 and1996. Many of those remaining had taken out loans from big brewers, shutting them off to small brewers.

The guest beer law allowed tenants of national brewers to stock one beer bought from a brewery of their choice. When the law was passed in 1989, over 10,000 tenants were eligible, and the result was a small brewery boom. Now the number of eligible pubs may be as low as a couple of thousand.

Big brewers are constantly battling to keep their market share in free houses, clubs and the guest beer market. As a result, they offer beer at cutthroat prices. Small brewers who match these prices might as well pour the beer down the drain for the profit they'd make.

What about independent retailers? Most of them could buy smaller brewers' beers if they wanted to. It turns out their bosses want well-known beers at bargain basement prices. True, some companies experiment with speciality pubs offering a wider range, and smaller brewers slip in here. But they can be 'taken off the list' when head office so decides.

Tap & Spile used to sell a lot of small brewers' beers. They claimed problems with logistics, quality and image made them change and use a centralised list of suppliers. But also, the beers they are selling now are cheaper to buy and if customers stay, the company makes money.

So who can we sell to?

So where do small brewers sell their beer? Answer: the same group of independent free houses and guest beer outlets that everyone else wants to use. A regularly changing guest beer might be nice for you, the customer, but selling one cask of beer every two years does not make a brewer rich.

If this litany of problems is not enough, remember that regional and local brewers produce well-known beers with a long history, and a pub can sell a reasonably good range of beers simply by going to the family brewers.

'I hate griping about commercial problems,' said Sean Franklin. 'There is usually a way around the problem.' With a fair amount of legwork he has won back as many sales as he lost in the Tap & Spile decision. And the good news is that Tap & Spile has relented, following pressure from pub managers and customers. Selected microbreweries are being allowed to supply, directly, in their immediate area. Rooster's beer is now on sale in the Tap & Spile outlets in Harrogate and York and is extremely happy with the arrangement.

Wetherspoons is also giving its managers a freer hand with selecting beers.

So why not buy pubs?

Owning pubs has several advantages for any brewer. You control the quality of the product, you showcase your beers, and you get immediate income.

Relying on the precarious free trade, on the other hand, gives you loads of problems. Outlets change hands or change minds and you have to run just to stay still.

But pubs are expensive, and bigger companies can pay more for them. Building a new pub can be even more expensive.

The best way to set up a small brewery is to be a millionaire to start with, and to buy a few pubs outright with it.

Why worry about pubs at all? Why not bottle your beer and sell it to the take-home trade? Here you run into familiar problems: supermarkets want big volumes, reliable quality, and low prices. Nethergate, Wychwood, St Peter's and Cottage are just some of the brewers who do get their bottled beer into supermarkets and off-licences.

Generally, of course, supermarkets go for the well-known regional brewers. Microbrewers need to be long-established and well known.

But no one ever got rich on it, and few companies would survive on that alone.

So, what's the future?

Some smaller brewers are doing well, and aren't so small – they may even be bigger than the small family brewers. There is a Premier Division of companies who started at the right time, are well run, have good products, and by now have got themselves known everywhere. No one expects them to disappear.

Small brewers innovate and they give us choice. Their beers constantly win CAMRA awards because they taste good, not out of sentiment. If their business was profitable, they could make the investment they need in the future. They need laboratories and better equipment to stay ahead in the constant fight for consistency and quality.

One solution is progressive excise duty. In other words, you acknowledge the problems smaller brewers face, and ask them to pay a lower rate of tax. Various schemes are used in most European countries and the United States, and we could do this under European law if we wanted to.

What would brewers do with the money saved? They could invest in equipment, take on staff, improve quality, and compete properly in the free trade. More small brewers surviving, more choice, more competition, and, probably, more tax in the long run for the Treasury. They could even get into the pub business.

A generous scheme would cost half a per cent of the current excise duty bill. Or, we could scrap the Millennium Dome and have sliding scale for the next 57 years. But the political obstacles are enormous.

The not-so free house

That free house sign outside a pub may indicate that it's anything but free. The pub could be in thrall to a national company, but you'd never know it, says **James Corbett**.

It used to be so simple. If a pub was owned by a brewery, it sold that brewer's beer. Other pubs were generally owned by the person behind the bar. Free houses were those where the licensee had a free choice of what beers to sell.

Nowadays if you see the sign 'Free House' over a pub, it probably means very little. A big pub in the high street is probably owned by some national combine, which not only decides what beers are sold and tells its managers what to do, but which probably designs the food menus, too. 'Free house' as a term has a marketing advantage, and so companies use it. Less sophisticated observers would call this lying.

One of the most absurd cases is the Firkin Brewery, a national chain of pubs run by Allied Domecq. These pubs offer standard Allied products and beers brewed by the one-third of the pubs which actually brew. They are no more free houses than laundrettes. Even that stalwart company, Wetherspoons, stretches the point somewhat. Their pubs offer a wider choice of beers than many, but it is still from a nationally determined list.

Nor is the individually owned and run free house as free as it might seem. Suppose a licensee wants to expand the kitchen or build an extension. The brewers will offer a substantial low-interest loan: all the publican has to do is sign an agreement to buy so much beer each year from them. The industry vehement-ly denies that this is a 'tie' – it is easy to get another loan from another brewer and switch suppliers, and many loan-tied publicans do this every year. The point is, however, that most of Britain's brewers don't have the cash to offer loans, so this is a game which only the largest companies can win.

Reliable figures are limited. However, many small owner-occupied free houses have closed in recent years – and well-known successful free houses are often bought out by expanding brewers. The number of individually-owned free-houses fell by a third between 1993 and 1996, according to Merrill Lynch.

Look at the brewery section at the back of the book. Most of these breweries rely heavily on genuine free trade – genuine free houses and those pubs able to take a genuine independent guest beer. Both markets are being slowly closed off.

What about pub companies not owned by brewers? These chains now own more than a third of our pubs. Chains generally like to buy their beer as cheaply as possible, so most chains prefer to buy from nationals and large regional brewers. They may have a specialist ale-house division which might buy a broader range, but this is hardly a big guaranteed market.

What it means

Free house
Grossly abused term. Should mean: the publican can buy beer from anyone they want to. Often means: this pub is owned by a national chain, with a buying policy decided 300 miles away; some bright spark in the marketing department thought customers should be conned by putting 'Free House' over every door.

Free trade
Outlets which can, in theory, buy beer from anyone they want.

Loan tie

A genuine free house publican takes a low-interest loan from a brewer, say, to do up the kitchen. In return he buys most of his beer from that brewer for the next few years. This squeezes out smaller brewers who can't afford to provide the loan or to buy it out. CAMRA argues such a pub is not genuinely 'free' while the loan stands.

Managed house

The owner of the pub puts a salaried employee in to manage it. The advantage to the company is that they control the outlet and get higher profits if all goes well. The manager gets a regular income, and if the pub goes bust it isn't his problem.

A good manager will be well-paid, well-trained and perfectly capable of running a good pub – but you do run into the time-servers and drudges, too.

Tenanted pub

The owner of the pub leases it to an individual publican, who pays rent, but runs the actual business themselves. Most pubs run like this are tied: that is, there is an agreement dictating who the publican must buy their beer from. The publican gets to run their own pub without having to buy a building, they keep their profit, and if they don't go bankrupt they might do rather well. Longer leases are a similar principle.

Guest beer

A genuine independent guest beer is one which the publican has chosen to buy themselves from a different brewer. The 1989 guest beer law allowed tenants of brewers with more than 2,000 pubs to buy one beer outside their tie agreement. Pub sell-offs and companies quitting brewing mean that fewer and fewer pubs qualify.

'Guest beer' is widely used as a marketing tool to refer to beers – possible even brewed by the owning brewery – that appear on the bar for a short while. Mind you, any variation and choice is better than none. Many companies now distribute other brewers' beers to their own estates.

Retail branding

With Boots or McDonald's you know what you are going to get from 100 yards away.

Retail branding in the pub world is about delivering a consistent offer – whether it's a mock-Irish pub, a student bar or a genteel dining pub aimed at the grey-haired.

This means a company manual and staff trained in that particular style of operation, with design, beer, food, promotions all 'by the book'.

Once a few have been tried in places such as Fulham and Sutton, the 'concept' can be 'rolled out' – that is, duplicated everywhere from Aberdeen to Torquay.

The good pint guide

What makes a good pub for beer brings together the skill of the brewer, the way the pub is run and the skill of the cellar staff, explains **Mike Campbell**.

Cask beer needs skill to look after, but this should not be beyond the abilities of the majority of pubs.

To start with the basics, decent hygiene is absolutely essential, and a good, deep, cool cellar is also ideal. Beer that gets warm becomes flat, cloudy and unappetising. Real ale kept too cold will develop a haze and you won't be able to taste the full flavour. Modern technology allows most cellars to be kept cool even in a hot summer, and there are even ways of keeping cask beer cool behind the bar itself.

A cask of beer needs time to condition. Several things happen: the rough edges come off the flavour, the beer settles so that it is clear, and the extra fermentation produces enough carbon dioxide to make the beer lively without being fizzy.

Pubs are under pressure to sell beer as soon as they can. In fact, many beers benefit from a bit of waiting around: a beer might become clear in a day but still benefit in flavour from four days' conditioning.

The cellar staff can adjust the liveliness of the beer by releasing and retaining the natural gas. They do this by swapping a porous and a non-porous peg in the cask: the first lets carbon dioxide out, the second keeps it in. If your pint is flat, the staff have mucked this up (or kept the beer too warm).

Keg beers start sterile and are kept sterile; as such they last for months. Cask beer is very different. Once the cask is broached, it is exposed to air, and various ageing processes begin. The metaphorical clock starts ticking: a cask must be sold within a certain time before it starts to go off (the stronger the beer, the more robust it is). If the cask is drunk in the right time, every customer gets a good pint. If the beer goes really slowly, most of them might get rubbish.

Pubs could sell lots of real ales only if they guarantee that each of them is good. If each cask is drunk dry in a suitable time, then there's no problem; if that does not happen, some customers will get elderly beer or even vinegar.

So, here is another piece of skill. The licensee must judge the right number of beers to sell, and order the right amount, so that, on the one hand, he has enough beer and, on the other, there's never too much hanging around.

Real ale has to be drawn from the cask. The most usual method is by a tall handpump (the symbol Ⓗ is used in this *Guide*).

An electric meter looks like a keg dispenser but it just uses mechanical power instead of the staff's muscles (the symbol Ⓟ).

Beer can be poured directly out of the cask (Ⓖ), or, in Scotland and occasionally elsewhere, pushed to the bar by air pressure (Ⓐ). If in doubt, always ask for cask beer.

Into your glass

Real ale is not supposed to be warm, cloudy, or flat; nor is it supposed to have bits in it. It should:
• be served well under room temperature
• be clear and attractive
• have sufficient sparkle in the mouth.

The means of dispense also affects the pint. Southern beers are pulled by handpump, with a relatively large hole at the end of the spout. The beer is agitated and aerated a bit, but not enough to create a large head.

Northern beers, in general, are the same until they reach the hand-pump, but are forced through a tight nozzle with very small holes (a sparkler). This agitates and aerates the beer a great deal, and a creamy head of foam emerges. The hop flavours in the beer are volatile, and these are driven into the head – so there is more bitterness in the head, and less in the body of the beer.

This is a sweeping generalisation: some beers suit a sparkler dispense, while many other do not. In the breweries section, preference is indicated by the symbol for a sparkler (☺) or no sparkler (☒).

Beer poured directly from the cask is agitated least of all and it tastes heavier than the hand-pumped beer. Increasingly, beers are dispensed via a sparkler, regardless of the wishes of the brewer or customer. It is a counsel of perfection, but the perfect pub for beer would sell each type of beer in its own style. Some pubs will remove the sparkler

from the dispense if you ask them.

When you discuss quality, two different issues tend to run together. A beer should clearly be free of all technical faults; it should be clear, cool, consistent, and have no off-putting taints or smells. But a beer can be perfect in that sense, and also very boring. The perfect pub for beer will look after its beer well, but it will also choose beers that tickle the taste-buds. That is not the same as saying every beer must be extreme or peculiar, it does say that flavour matters too.

Bar tips

Finally, a few more points for the perfect pub: a clean, cool glass; staff who know at least what brewery brews each beer they are selling; and one member of staff who can answer more complex questions.

Even the best brewery or the best licensee makes mistakes, and not every pint is perfect. No one brings beer back to the bar for the hell of it. The perfect pub replaces every pint with a smile, even if the licensee thinks the customer is barking mad.

The craft of brewing

How beer is made is an ancient art and has changed little over the centuries. Here's a brief explanation of making ale – and why it beats the socks off ghastly keg beer.

What is beer?

All beer – ale or lager – starts with barley malt, hops, water and yeast. Yeast is a marvellous little organism which ferments sugars into alcohol and carbon dioxide. Each brewery preserves its own yeast variety, which gives its own individual taste to the beers.

Malt and barley

Barley from the field is mostly made of starch which yeast cannot digest. Malting that barley turns starch into digestible sugars, which allows yeast to work.

Different malts add their own flavours: sweetness, chewiness and body.

Malt also gives the colour of the beer: heavily roasted dark malts produce a darker beer; pale malts a lighter colour.

Adding the hops

Hops add both bitter taste and flowery aroma to the beer. Again, different varieties have distinctive flavours and smells. The same hops added at the start of brewing will mostly tend to add bitterness; added at the end will produce far more aroma. Whole hops, or compact hop pellets, give a more complex and palatable flavour than chemical extracts and essences of hop.

Water and other factors

The finest beer in the world is still mostly water. Brewing towns grew up where there was suitable water, but now any water can be treated to be used.

Brewers use a lot of other ingredients, which they are not obliged to declare. Purists dislike the use of cheaper sugars and starches to cut costs, but it is probably legitimate to use other ingredients in moderation to improve appearance, or fine tune the flavour.

Brewers may use other grains – such as wheat, to produce a distinctive lemony flavour – or to produce exotic beers with ingredients as diverse as chilli, vanilla, ginger, fruit, honey or chocolate.

How beer is brewed

The brewing process is not particularly difficult to understand, though it is littered with its own jargon.

Everyone should visit a brewery to see beer being made. One clear advantage of the more traditional brewery is that most of the process is visible from start to finish.

Malt is ground into a coarse powder and mixed with boiling water. The resulting porridge is left to steep, so all the goodness of the malt is dissolved.

A sweet malt liquid is run off. This is boiled with hops for flavour, and then allowed to cool.

Yeast is added. The liquid is warm, wet and full of sugar, and the yeast grows energetically, making alcohol.

The type of fermentation broadly decides whether the beer is ale or lager. Ale yeasts prefer a warmer, faster and more vigorous fermentation, where the yeast will froth up in the fermenting vessel (which will be uncovered in the older style of brewery). Ale yeasts give fruity, rich flavours to their beers. Lager yeasts have a longer, cooler fermentation, where the yeast sinks to the bottom of the fermenter, and where the lager should have a long period of cold conditioning. This produces a cleaner flavour.

For an ale, after several days fermentation, sufficient sugar has been turned to alcohol. The beer is still too rough to drink, but it is what happens now which determines whether this is to be 'real ale' or not.

Why keg beer is dead beer

Beer can be denatured (sterilised, or killed) to give it a long shelf life. It will be pasteurised and filtered – processes which remove flavour and aroma, and add odd flavours of their own. Sparkle will have been knocked out of the beer, and gas will be added to restore it.

All cans, most bottles and most UK lagers are this dead beer, as are keg ales and stouts.

Old-fashioned dead beers were made fizzy with carbon dioxide. Guinness – and now many ales – are stored under a mixture of nitrogen and carbon dioxide. These 'nitrokegs' are more creamy and frothy, and less fizzy, than old-style keg beer. However, the manufacturing processes involved make them bland and they are normally served too cold to taste.

Like the supermarket tomato, appearance is terrific, flavour is at best disappointing.

Cask ale lives!

Real ale – the term brewers use for cask conditioned beer – is very different.

The beer isn't pasteurised or filtered, but continues to ferment in the cask. The secondary fermentation provides extra character and development.

Cask beer gives you beer that is fresh, untampered with, full of all the flavours intended by the brewer. It brings out all the subtle choices of malt, hops, yeast, water and the like made by the brewer.

Support your living pint

This is why there is a Campaign for Real Ale. It is not that all real ale is automatically wonderful beer – a badly kept pint is awful, and some brands of real ale are still dull. It is that a good pint of real ale gives you beer at its best. If we kegged all our beer, there would be much less difference between the best and the dreadful.

Fermentation bubbling away.

A beer style guide

There is no Academy of Beer laying down what a particular beer name means. Some people would prefer such a style guide; some brewers would rather go on brewing how they choose.

Mild means, simply enough, milder in flavour – that is, less hoppy. The classic dark mild is dark, sweet and rounded, bringing you back for more. Light milds are more like a bitter in colour. Good mild is worth seeking out.

Mild is in decline, for a mixture of reasons. Some brewers who do brew it are reluctant to call it mild any more, and it can be hard to find outside Wales, the Midlands and some of the North. CAMRA's National Mild Day is there to reverse the trend and put mild back on the map.

Bitter can have a soft rural burr or a sharp urban tang. It is easier to brew something intriguing at ABV 4.8%; what takes skill is the moreishness of a mere ABV 3.7%.

India Pale Ale, IPA used to refer to a splendidly clear, hoppy, strong ale brewed for export – the grandfather of modern bitters. Some revivals might qualify. Where standard drinking-strength beers are called IPA, one at least hopes for a clean, hoppy character. Partly we are the victim of a century of high tax, which has driven down the average strength of beer by over a third.

Porter, stout The very first porters tasted like a blend of young and aged beers. By Victorian times porter was a dark, characterful beer, perhaps best described as a stout, only less so.

Indeed **stout** is the stoutest – that is

the strongest – porter. Stouts can be sweet or dry, and if all you have drunk are the rather anodyne keg products, try a real cask conditioned stout with a real head.

Roasted barley gives bitterness, and microbrewed stouts often have real hop character, or rounded smoothness.

Lager There is nothing wrong with a good lager, one of the great beer styles of the world. Brewed to a sufficient strength and well conditioned, it can be remarkable beer. Much British lager is poor stuff, and even if you pay for a strong one it may not be up to much in flavour terms. There may be some exciting beers lurking among the imported bottles, though.

Premium means one you are charged a premium for; it is therefore stronger, imported, or just more expensive anyway. **Special** doesn't mean much, either.

Old Ale used to be specially aged, but nowadays Old is just added to any old name. Expect a dark strong beer. **Winter ales** were specially brewed to last through the festive season; they are powerful stuff, and can develop in richness and character over several weeks. At this strength they can have enormous amounts of hop and still a strong sweetness.

Summer ales are really a new invention. Typically golden in colour, moderate in strength and with a good lager hop character, they are intended to wean lager drinkers back to ale in the summer months. Modern cellar cooling has made this possible.

Barley wine is not wine, but a strong, rich ale, to be sipped slowly. At high strength ale develops a wine-like character, hence the name. Use a taxi if you intend to drink it.

Champion beers of Britain

BEST BITTERS
Adnams Extra
Brakspear Special Bitter
Caledonian 80/-
Cheriton Best Bitter
City of Cambridge Hobsons Choice
Dark Tribe Galleon
Everards Tiger
Exe Valley Dobs Best Bitter
Fuller's London Pride
Goff's Jouster
RCH Pitchfork
Rooster Scorcher
Taylor Landlord
Whitbread Castle Eden Ale

STRONG BITTERS
Batemans VictoryAle
Cheriton Diggers Gold
Dent Kamikaze
Hopback Summer Lightning
Jolly Boat Plunder
Mordue Radgie Gadgie
Wolf Granny Wouldn't Like It

SPECIALITY BEERS
Daleside Morocco Ale
Dark Horse Fallen Angel
Freeminer Shakemantle Ginger Ale
Harvieston Schieghallion
Heather Froach
Hopback Thunderstorm
Nethergate Umbel Magna

MILDS
Batemans Dark Mild
Harveys Sussex XX Mild
Elgoods Black Dog
Goachers Real Mild Ale
Highgate Mild
Moorhouse Black Cat
Taylors Golden Best

BITTERS
Archers Village
Coniston Bluebird
Dent Aviator
Eccleshall Slaters Bitter
Goachers Fine Light

Highwood Tom Wood Best Bitter
Itchen Valley Godfathers
Maclay's Broadsword
Oakham JHB
Otter Bitter
RCH PG Steam
Reepham Granary
Rooster Special
Woodforde's Wherry Best Bitter

OLD STRONG MILD
Adnams Old
Branscombe Vale Old Stoker
Daleside Monkey Wrench
King & Barnes Old
Sarah Hughes Ruby Mild

STOUTS/PORTERS
Batemans Salem Porter
Hanby Shropshire Stout
Hopback Entire Stout
McGuinness Tommy Todd's Porter
Nethergate Old Growler
Ringwood XXXX Porter
Shepherd Neame Original Porter
Wickwar Station Porter

BARLEY WINES
Adnams TallyHo
Cottage Norman's Conquest
Exmoor Beast
Lees Moonraker
Marston's Owd Rodger
Robinson's Old Tom
Woodforde's Headcracker

GUARDIAN BOTTLE-CONDITIONED ALE AWARDS
Fuller's 1845
Gale's Prize Old Ale
Hopback Summer Lightning
King & Barnes Festive Ale
Shepherd Neame Spitfire

Champion Beer of Britain:
Coniston Bluebird
Champion Winter Beer of Britain:
Nethergate Old Growler

Go to a beer festival!

CAMRA beer festivals are one of the best ways to sample a huge range of cask ales (plus ciders, perries, real lagers). **Steve Cox** takes you round the Cambridge Beer Festival.

Strange as it might seem, the idea was new, and pretty much untested. Twenty-five years ago the Campaign for Real Ale branch in Cambridge decided to put on a beer festival. CAMRA members wanted to show the drinking public the range of tasty real ales available from all over the country. This was in the dire days of the early Seventies, when keg flowed from every tap, when local brewers were giving up the ghost, and finding decent real ale was a real effort.

That event was the start of something big. It led to the Great British Beer Festival, an annual extravaganza serving over 300 different real ales – and to the 140 different local festivals CAMRA runs every year.

Each event is run by unpaid volunteers, doing it for the love of it.

Festivals still show off the best of real ale. In that sense, anyway, nothing has changed.

On a given Friday in May, I could have been drinking real ale, served by CAMRA volunteers, at all sorts of places: an arts centre in Colchester, the Drill Hall in Lincoln, Alloa Town Hall, Frodsham Community Centre, or on the playing fields at the Mount School, Newark. In fact, I took a trip to Cambridge City football ground, to the 25th Cambridge Festival.

Inside a beer festival

So, what is a modern beer festival like? Each one is different, but certain things always come through. There is the friendly atmosphere, the hubbub of conversation and, of course, the beer.

Whatever the stocking policy, it will favour independent brewers and distinctive, tasty beers.

There'll be food and, probably, live music.

The venue will not have lush carpet, satellite TV, and piped Europop.

It will be informal, perhaps even basic by the standards of the modern pub. What you get, in short, are hundreds of men and women enjoying decent beer, and having a good time without theming, fruit machines, bouncers and nitromuck.

Live at Cambridge

Cambridge this year was run under a big L-shaped marquee. There was green grass underfoot, and you had the rest of the pitch as a beer garden. One side of the marquee contained tables and chairs and the food stall – food was farm cheese and a pub barbecue run outside. The other side of the marquee had the beer. Casks stood on two-tier scaffolding, cooled by nothing more sophisticated than wet cloth. Children were allowed in the non-beer end of the marquee.

The crowd on Friday lunchtime was mixed, laid back and friendly. Men in suits, pensioners, small groups of women and a few families were tucking into their beer. You could spot 'late office lunch', 'not planning to go back' and 'on holiday' fairly easily. It was pub drinking: pints and halves, rather than sip and spit like a wine fair. That evening was expected to be extremely hectic.

This is the fifth year that Bruce Law has organised the festival. He works in the printing trade, and first got involved as a St John's Ambulance volunteer in 1982 He said that the rows of real ale casks are 'silent campaigning: that is still what it is all about'.

The festival serves 95 different

beers from all over the country, has a traditional cider bar showing off East Anglian ciders, and a good range of foreign bottle-conditioned beers. Despite the cost of the site, the festival still undercut local pubs with its prices. The branch expected 9,000 people over the week.

'The atmosphere's brilliant,' Bruce said, 'and we never have any trouble. We get a real mix of people, a good cross-section, and that helps'

CAMRA festivals try to use their own people as stewards, which creates a much better atmosphere than paid 'bouncers'. A mixed clientele, mellow drinkers and mellow staff produce an event that is safe and friendly.

No such thing as a typical ale drinker

Jane, a probation officer, brought Joseph (two months), who is sleeping through the proceedings, and a friend. 'I like drinking beer, and it's just round the corner,' she said. 'I've been a couple of times – it's easy to bring the baby.'

Her friend complains that pubs are too smoky. The festival, with the canvas rolled up, has pleasantly clear air. 'We don't expect a bouncy castle and a creche,'

Beer festivals attract a wide range of people of all ages.

she said. In fact, they are both pretty down on the chain family pubs, as lacking any character: 'Horrible food, horrible beer.' The female-friendly drive by big companies is 'patronising'. A beer festival, however, seems to be just the ticket.

Tom, Christian and Neil are working their way through the beers. When I interrupt them they

have just decided that Hop Back brewery deserves further exploration. An adman might peg them as the lager generation; indeed, they drink lager, too, but they also frequent the local Hogshead. 'It sells 23 guest beers!'

They can see through the real ale stereotypes. 'People think it is all hats, beards and pipes, but that's a fallacy. You can find someone like that if you look for them.' The festival has a broader range of people than the pubs. 'OK, a pub has pool, fruit machines, today's music – but here you get a good laugh and a bit of chat. There are plenty of young people around, and they don't find it offputting.'

The festival has brought in beers from breweries threatened with closure; posters talk about rural pub closures; the blandness of beer; and *full* measure. But campaigning as such is not high profile. There's the sense that CAMRA takes stands, but the main emphasis is on trying the beer. Recruitment is similarly low key.

Whether you like a festival depends in part what you are looking for. Most have a cheerful, basic feel, with no pretensions – you get a decent pint and a good night out. Most throw in entertainment for free – everything from steel bands to brass bands, from classical quartets to rock.

Festivals are a major part of what CAMRA does. CAMRA recruits around half its new members from them, and they give the local branch a shot of publicity each year. Thousands of local drinkers get reminded what good beer tastes like and why CAMRA is still needed. But no one goes out of duty or political correctness – they go because festivals are fun!

Behind the bar

But why work at an event? Isn't the day job enough? Rob Allen travels round the country with a small group of friends. Simply, it is part of his social life. He has worked at the Great British Beer Festival, and a number of local events, but this is the first time at Cambridge. To be honest, just before closing he is a bit rushed. Peterborough branch have a twinning arrangement, sending branch volunteers to reinforce Cambridge on Friday night.

Win a prize! CAMRA's fundraising tombola stalls are always a good bet for a fun bet!

There's a network of volunteers across the country, helping each other out, and keeping the festivals going.

People enjoy getting their hands dirty; there are a wide variety of jobs to do and you have a real sense of achievement. People run festivals to campaign, to recruit but, above all, because they are fun to go to and fun to work at. That's what Cambridge started all those years ago.

Some common questions answered...

'Why isn't the beer free?'
Because, of course, CAMRA has to pay for the venue, the bar, and the beer, and takes the whole risk if the event loses money. Long gone are the days when councils gave halls for free. Brewers give all sorts of

support, but they are rarely asked to give CAMRA the beer for nothing. Any profits fund the local branch and CAMRA's central work. In fact, most festivals charge too little, and prices are highly competitive.

'Why isn't every beer available every session?'
If you open a cask of real ale, it must be drunk before it goes off. It would be simplicity itself to have every beer on at every session – the festival would just order, say, 50 per cent more than it needed and then have to throw dozens of casks of unused beer away at the end. Needless to say, this would raise the price to the punter enormously. Every festival juggles to keep the variety as good as possible. Don't go expecting and demanding a particular beer to be on at a particular instant – it is unreasonable.

'Where do I get more information'
CAMRA members get *What's Brewing*, which lists the forthcoming events for the next couple of months; ring CAMRA on (01727) 867201 if you want more information. The Great British Beer Festival, in London in August, is particularly interesting. It offers over 300 different real ales, one of the widest choices of traditional cider in the country, and a splendid selection of foreign beers.

It is open for five days and the atmosphere has to be felt to be believed.

Incidentally, most CAMRA festivals offer a discount on entry to CAMRA members.

'Do other people run beer festivals?'
Indeed, though a big local festi,tal will usually be a CAMRA event. Pubs, breweries and the Society of Independent Brewers run regional beer festivals, too. *What's Brewing* carries ads for many of these.

Beer festival calendar

CAMRA beer festivals provide wonderful opportunities for sampling beers not normally found in the locality. Festivals are staffed by CAMRA members on a voluntary basis and offer a wide range of interesting real ales from breweries all over the country, plus live entertainment and much more. The biggest event is the Great British Beer Festival in August, where over 500 different beers can be enjoyed. For further details of this and the major regional events outlined below, together with precise dates and venues, *What's Brewing* provides a comprehensive monthly round-up. Or contact CAMRA on (01727) 867201, or see your local press.

JANUARY
Atherton
Exeter

FEBRUARY
Basingstoke
Battersea
Bradford
Burton-upon-
  Trent
Dorchester
Dover
Durham
Falmouth
Fleetwood
Merseyside
Plymouth
Rugby
Sussex

MARCH
Camden(London
  Drinker)
Darlington
Dukeries (Notts)
Ealing
Eastleigh
Gosport
Leeds
Walsall
Wigan

APRIL
Bury St
  Edmunds
Castle Point
Chippenham
Coventry
Dunstable
Farnham
Huddersfield
Mansfield
Newcastle-

upon-Tyne
Oldham
Perth

MAY
Alloa
Barnsley
Cambridge
Chester
Cleethorpes
Colchester
Dewsbury
Doncaster
Dudley
Frodsham
Lincoln
Northampton
Ongar
Oxford
Paisley
Reading
Sudbury
Wolverhampton
Woodchurch
Yapton

JUNE
Barnsley
Catford
Exeter
Leighton
  Buzzard
Salisbury
Stockport
Surrey
Thurrock
  (Grays)

JULY
Ardingly
Canterbury
Chelmsford
Cotswolds

Derby
Grantham
Larling
Lewes
Milton Keynes
Southampton
Tameside
  Canals
Woodcote

AUGUST
**Great British
  Beer Festival**
Birmingham
Clacton
Peterborough
Portsmouth

SEPTEMBER
Belfast
Burton-upon-
  Trent
Camarthen
Chappel (Essex)
Chichester
Darlington
Durham
Feltham
Galsgow
Harbury
Ipswich
Keighley
Letchworth
Maidstone
Northampton
Norwich
St Ives
  (Cambs)
Severn Valley
  Railway
Sheffield
Shrewsbury
Tamworth

OCTOBER
Alloa
Bath
Bedford
Cardiff
East Lancs
Edinburgh
Falmouth
Guernsey
Holmfirth
Hull
Keighley
Loughborough
Middlesbrough
Newton Abbot
Norwich
Nottingham
Overton
Rhyl
St Albans
Scunthorpe
Stoke-on-Trent
Swindon
Wakefield
Westmorland

NOVEMBER
Aberdeen
Bury
Dudley
Jersey
Luton
Mid Wales
Rochford
Wirral
Woking
York

DECEMBER
East London
  (Pig's Ear)
More details in
What's Brewing

Great historic pubs

These pubs are of outstanding historic interest and as such are on CAMRA's National Inventory of intact or little altered heritage pubs. Those which appear in the *Guide* are marked ☆; the full list is given here as well as the full address of each outstanding pub.

ENGLAND

BEDFORDSHIRE
Broom: Cock, 23 High Street

BERKSHIRE
Aldworth: Bell, Bell Lane (off B4009)
Frilsham: Pot Kiln (Yattendon–Bucklebury road)

CHESHIRE
Alpraham: Travellers Rest, Chester Road (A51)
Barthomley: White Lion, Audley Road
Gawsworth: Harrington Arms, Congleton Road
Macclesfield: Castle, Churchwallgate
Stockton Heath: Red Lion, London Road
Wheelock: Commercial, Game Street

CORNWALL
Falmouth: Seven Stars, The Moor

CUMBRIA
Broughton Mills: Blacksmiths Arms
Kendal: Ring O'Bells, 39 Kirkland

DERBYSHIRE
Brassington: Gate Inn, Well Street
Derby: Old Dolphin, Queen Street
Elton: Duke of York, West End
Kirk Ireton: Barley Mow, Main Street
Wardlow Mire: Three Stags Heads (at A623/B6465 jct)

DEVON
Drewsteignton: Drewe Arms, The Square

Holsworthy: Kings Arms, Fore Street
Luppitt: Luppitt Inn
Topsham: Bridge, Bridge Hill
Widecombe-in-the-Moor: Rugglestone Inn (¼ mile S of village)

DORSET
Worth Matravers: Square & Compass (off B3069)

DURHAM
Durham City: Shakespeare, 63 Saddler Street
Victoria, 86 Hallgarth Street

GLOUCESTERSHIRE & BRISTOL
Ampney St Peter: Red Lion (on A417)
Bristol: Kings Head, 60 Victoria Street
Cheltenham: Bath Tavern, 68 Bath Road
Duntisbourne Abbots: Five Mile House, Gloucester Road (A417)
Purton: Berkeley Arms
Willsbridge: Queens Head, 62 Bath Road

HAMPSHIRE
Steep: Harrow, Harrow Lane

HEREFORDSHIRE
Kington: Olde Tavern, 22 Victoria Road
Leintwardine: Sun Inn, Rosemary Lane
Risbury: Hop Pole ('Bert's'), on Pencombe road

KENT
Cowden Pound: Queens Arms, Cowden Cross (on B2026)
Ightam: Old House, Redwell Lane
Snargate: Red Lion, (on B2080)

LANCASHIRE
Brierfield: Waggon & Horses, Colne Road
Great Harwood: Victoria, St John Street
Overton: Ship Hotel, 9 Main Street
Preston: Black Horse, 166 Friargate

Waddington: (Lower) Buck, Church Road

LEICESTERSHIRE & RUTLAND
Medbourne: Horse & Trumpet, Old Green

GREATER LONDON
EC1 Hatton Garden: Old Mitre, Ely Court, 9 Ely Place
EC4 Blackfriars: Black Friar, 174 Queen Victoria Street
WC1 Holborn: Cittie of York, 22 High Holborn
Princess Louise, 208 High Holborn
WC2 Covent Garden: Lamb & Flag, 33 Rose Street
Salisbury, 90 St Martins Lane

E14 Poplar: Grapes, 76 Narrow St

N4 Finsbury Park: Salisbury, 1 Grand Parade, Green lanes
N6 Highgate: Flask, 77 Highgate West Hill
N8 Hornsey: Gt Northern Railway, 67 High Street

NW3 Hampstead: Holly Bush, 22 Holly Mount
NW6 Kilburn: Black Lion, 274 Kilburn High Road
NW8 St Johns Wood: Crockers, 24 Aberdeen Place

SE1 Southwark: George Inn, 77 Borough High Street
SE21 Dulwich: Crown & Greyhound, 73 Dulwich Village

SW1 Belgravia: Antelope, 22 Eaton Terrace
Nags Head, 53 Kinnerton Street
Paxtons Head, 153 Knightsbridge
SW1 St James's: Red Lion, 2 Duke of York Street

W1 Marylebone: Barley Mow, 8 Dorset Street
W1 Soho: Argyll Arms, 18 Argyll Street
W6 Hammersmith: Dove, 19 Upper Mall
W9 Maida Vale: Prince Alfred, 5a Formosa Street
Warrington Hotel, 93 Warrington Crescent

GREATER MANCHESTER
Altrincham: Railway, 153 Manchester Road, Broadheath

Bolton: Howcroft, Clarence Court
Eccles: Grapes, 439 Liverpool Road
Lamb, 33 Regent Street
Royal Oak, Barton Lane
Gorton: Plough, Hyde Road
Heaton Norris: Nursery Inn, Green Lane (off A6)
Manchester: Britons Protection, 50 Great Bridgewater Street
Circus Tavern, 86 Portland Street
Crown & Kettle, Oldham Road
Hare & Hounds, 46 Shudehill
Mr Thomas's, 52 Cross Street
Peveril of the Peak, 127 Great Bridgewater Street
Marple: Hatter Arms, Church Lane
Middleton: Old Boars Head, Long Street
Mossley: Colliers Arms, Broadcarr Lane
Rochdale: Cemetery Hotel, 470 Bury Road
Stalybridge: Station Buffet, Railway Station
Stockport: Alexandra, 195 Northgate Road
Arden Arms, 23 Millgate
Queens Head, 12 Little Underbank
Swan with Two Necks, 36 Princes Street
Wigan: Springfield Hotel, 47 Springfield Road

MERSEYSIDE
Birkenhead: Stork Hotel, 41-43 Price Street
Liverpool: Lion, 67 Moorfield
Philharmonic, 36 Hope Street
Prince Arthur, 93 Rice Lane, L9
Vines, 81 Lime Street
Lydiate: Scotch Piper, 347 Southport Road

NOTTINGHAMSHIRE
Nottingham: Olde Trip to Jerusalem, 1 Brewhouse Yard, Castle Road
Stag & Pheasant, 245 Parliament St
Vale Hotel, Thackeray's Lane, Woodthorpe, Arnold
West Bridgford: Test Match Hotel, Gordon Square, Gordon Road

NORTHUMBERLAND
Berwick upon Tweed: Free Trade, Castlegate
Netherton: Star Inn

OXFORDSHIRE
Banbury: Wine Vaults, 5 & 6 Parson Street

Checkendon: Black Horse, Burncote Lane (off A4074)
Christmas Common: Fox & Hounds (off B480/B481 and B4009)
Steventon: North Star, 2 Stocks Lane
Stoke Lyne: Peyton Arms (off B3069)
Stoke Row: Crooked Billet, Nottwood Lane
Stoke Talmage: Red Lion
Wantage: Shoulder of Mutton, 38 Wallingford Street

SHROPSHIRE
Halfway House: Seven Stars (on A458)
Sleattyn: Cross Keys, (on B4579)
Shrewsbury: Loggerheads, 1 Church Street

SOMERSET
Appley: Globe
Bath: Old Green Tree, 12 Green St
Star, 23 The Vineyards
Crowcombe: Carew Arms (off A258)
Faulkland: Tuckers Grave Inn, Wells Road (A366)
Huish Episcopi: Rose & Crown ('Eli's'), by Pounsell Lane
Midsomer Norton: White Hart, The Island
Norton St Philip: George, The Plan
Witham Friary: Seymour Arms (off B3092)

STAFFORDSHIRE
High Offley: Anchor, Old Lea (by canal)

SUFFOLK
Brent Eleigh: Cock, Lavenham Road
Bury St Edmunds: Nutshell, 17 The Traverse
Ipswich: Golden Hind, Nacton Road
Margaret Catchpole, Cliff Lane
Laxfield: Kings Head ('Low House'), Goram's Mill Lane
Pin Mill: Butt & Oyster, The Quay

SUSSEX (East)
Berwick: Cricketers Arms (off A27)

SUSSEX (West)
The Haven: Blue Ship (at Rudgwick, off A281)

TYNE & WEAR
Newcastle-upon-Tyne: Crown Posada, 31 The Side

WARWICKSHIRE
Five Ways: Case is Altered, Case Lane, off Fiveways Lane
Long Itchington: Buck & Bell, Green End

WEST MIDLANDS
Birmingham: Anchor, 308 Bradford St, Digbeth
Barton Arms, 152 High Street, Aston
Bellefield, 36 Winson Street, Winson Green
Black Horse, Bristol Road, Northfield
Britannia, 287 Lichfield Road
British Oak, Pershore Road, Stirchley
Market Tavern, 210 Moseley Street, Digbeth
Red Lion, Soho Road, Handsworth
Rose Villa Tavern, Warstone Lane
Samson & Lion, Yardley Green Road, Small Heath
Sherwood, Highfield Road, Yardley Wood
Three Magpies, Shirley Road, Hall Green
White Swan, 276 Bradford Street, Digbeth
Woodman, 106 Albert Street, Digbeth
Villa Tavern, 307 Nechells Park Road, Nechells
Boxwich: Turf Tavern, 13 Wolverhampton Road
Dudley: Shakespeare, Stone Street
Rushall: Manor Arms, Park Road, Daw End
Sedgley: Beacon, 129 Bilston Street
Smethwick: Waterloo Hotel, Shireland Road

WILTSHIRE
Easton Royal: Bruce Arms (on B3087)
Salisbury: Haunch of Venison, 1 Minster Street

WORCESTERSHIRE
Breforton: Fleece, The Cross
Deffod: Monkey House (on A4104, Woodmancote)

YORKSHIRE (East)
Beverley: White Horse ('Nellie's')
Hull: Olde White Harte, 25 Silver St

Skerne: Eagle Inn, Wandsford Road

YORKSHIRE (North)
Beck Hold: Birch Hall Inn (1 mile N of Goathland)
Boroughbridge: Three horse Shoes, Bridge Street
Harrogate: Gardeners Arms, Bilton Lane
Saxton: Greyhound, Main Street
York: Blue Bell, 53 Fossgate

YORKSHIRE (West)
Bradford: Cock & Bottle, 93 Barkerend Road
New Beehive, 171 Westgate
Heath: Kings Arms, Heath Common
Leeds: Adelphi, 1 Hunslet Road
Cardigan Arms, 364 Kirkstall Road, Burley
Garden Gate, 37 Waterloo Road, Hunslet
Rising Sun, 290 Kirkstall Road, Burley
Whitelocks, Turks Head Yard, Briggate
Wakefield: Redoubt, 28 Horbury Road

WALES

GWENT
Abergavenny: Hen & Chickens, 7-9 Flannel Street
Grosmont: Cupid's Hill Tavern (on B434)

MID WALES
Hay on Wye: Three Tuns, 4 Broad Street
Llanfihangel-yng-Ngwynfa: Goat
Welshpool: Grapes, Salop Road

WEST WALES
Llandovery: Red Lion, 2 Market Square
Pontfaen: Dyffryn Arms (off B4313)

SCOTLAND

THE BORDERS
Ancrum: Cross Keys, the Green

FIFE
Kirkaldy: Feuars Arms, 66 Commercial Street
GRAMPIAN
Aberdeen: Grill, 213 Union Street

THE LOTHIANS
Dirleton: Castle, Manse Road
Edinburgh: Abbotsford, 3-5 Rose Street
Bennets Bar, 8 Leven Street
Cafe Royal, West Register Street
Kenilworth, 152-154 Rose Street
Leslie's Bar, 45 Ratcliffe Terrace
Oxford Bar, 8 Young Street

STRATHCLYDE
Glasgow: Horseshoe Bar, 17-19 Drury Street
Old Toll Bar, 1-3 Paisley Road West
Lochgilphead: The 'Comm', Lochnell Street
Paisley: Bull, 7 New Street
Shettleston: Portland Arms, 1169 Shettleston Road
Uddingstone: Rowan Treet, 60 Old Mill Road

TAYSIDE
Dundee: Clep, 92-98 Clephington Road
Speedwell, 165-7 Perth Road

NORTHERN IRELAND

COUNTY ANTRIM
Ballycastle: House of McDonnell, 71 Castle Street
Ballyclare: Carmichael's, 16 Ballyeaston Village
Bushmills: Charles H Callaghan, 72-74 Main Street
Cushendun: Mary McBride's, Main Street

COUNTY ARMAGH
Portadown: McConville's, West Street

BELFAST
Dan Magennis's ('Bradan Bar'), May Street
Crown Liquor Saloon, 49 Great Victoria Street

COUNTY FERMANAGH
Enniskillen: Blake's Bar, 6 Church Street

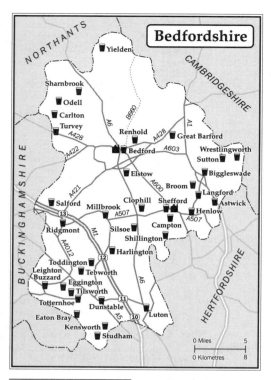

Bedfordshire

NORTHANTS

CAMBRIDGESHIRE

BUCKINGHAMSHIRE

HERTFORDSHIRE

Yielden
Sharnbrook
Odell
Carlton
Turvey
Renhold
Bedford
Great Barford
Wrestlingworth
Sutton
Biggleswade
Elstow
Broom
Langford
Astwick
Salford
Clophill
Shefford
Henlow
Millbrook
Campton
Ridgmont
Silsoe
Shillington
Harlington
Toddington
Leighton Buzzard
Tebworth
Eggington
Tilsworth
Totternhoe
Dunstable
Luton
Eaton Bray
Kensworth
Studham

0 Miles 5
0 Kilometres 8

ASTWICK

TUDOR OAKS
1 Taylors Road (A1)
☎ (01462) 834133
11-11; 12-3, 7-10.30 Sun
Beer range varies Ⓗ
A very friendly, inviting bar, boasting a glowing fire in winter. Real cider and perry are kept cool; excellent food plus six different weekly beers. Very large car park - walk through the patio and into the bar and be amazed.
🏨 ❀ ⇄ ◖ 🅳 🍺 ♣ ⇨ P 🏮

BEDFORD

DE PARYS HOTEL
45 De Parys Avenue (continue N from High St, A6)
☎ (01234) 352121
11-11; 12-10.30 Sun
Wells Eagle; guest beers Ⓗ
Nicely appointed, comfortable, medium-size hotel on the edge of the town centre. Its delightful gardens are used for barbecues and occasional beer festivals. Children's certificate.
🐕 ❀ ⇄ ◖ P

FLEUR DE LIS
12 Mill Street, (off A6, High St)
☎ (01234) 211004
10.30-11; 12-10.30 Sun
Wells Eagle; guest beer Ⓗ
One-bar, town-centre pub with a mix of clientele. Live music Thu

eve and Sun afternoons. It can get smoky when busy, and parking difficult in office hours. In every edition of this *Guide*. No food Sun.◖

BIGGLESWADE

BROWN BEAR
29 Hitchin St
☎ (01767) 316161
12-3, 6.30-11; 11-11 Thu-Sat; 12.30-3, 7-10.30 Sun
Beer range varies Ⓗ
Licensees try not to repeat the same beer twice, serving 120 beers in the first 120 days: friendly, it draws a cross-section of customers. Live music Fri eve. Eve meals by arrangement. Children welcome until 9pm.
❀ ◖ ⇌ ♣

WHEATSHEAF
5 Lawrence Road (near library)
☎ (01767) 222220
11-3.30, 7-11; 12-11 Sat; 12-10.30 Sun
Greene King XX Mild, IPA Ⓗ
A little one-bar gem hidden in a residential street away from the town centre. There's not many pubs like this left - no food, no pretensions, just beer, cards and dominoes. A traditional, friendly, workingman's pub.
❀ ⇌ ♣

Try also: Golden Pheasant, High Street (Wells)

BROOM

COCK ☆
23 High Street ☎ (01767) 314411
11-3, 6-11; 11-11 Sat; 12-10.30 Sun
Greene King IPA, Abbot, seasonal beers Ⓖ
A rural gem, worth seeking out, just off the A1 near Biggleswade. In every edition of the *Guide*, it has no bar, but many small rooms off a central corridor, with beer served from cellar door straight from casks. Excellent food, especially the game.
🏨 ❀ ◖ 🅳 🅰 ♣ P

CAMPTON

WHITE HART
Mill Lane (off A507)
☎ (01462) 812657
12-3, 6.30-11; 11-11 Sat; 12-3, 7.10.30 Sun
Hook Norton Best Bitter; Morland Old Speckled Hen; Theakston Best Bitter, XB; guest beers Ⓗ
300-year-old, Grade II listed brick and beam pub with quarry-tiled floors and inglenooks. Live folk music Wed. Petanque played, and good play equipment in the garden. Weekday lunches.
🏨 ❀ ◖ 🅳 ♣ P

CARLTON

ROYAL OAK
Bridge End (N of A428 at Turvey)
OS956558
☎ (01234) 720441
12-3; 11-11 Fri & Sat; 12-10.30 Sun
Wells Eagle; guest beer Ⓗ
Traditional, friendly, village local with facilities for families indoors and out. Near the country wildlife park. 🏨 🐕 ❀ ◖ 🅳 ♣ P

CLOPHILL

STONE JUG
Back Street (off A6)
☎ (01525) 860526
11-3, 6-11; 11-11 Sat; 12-10.30 Sun
B&T Shefford Bitter; John Smith's Bitter; guest beers Ⓗ
Popular village free house a *Guide* regular, convenient for the Greensand Ridge walk. Check before arriving with children as the family room is used for functions. Lunches Mon-Sat.
🏨 Q 🐕 ❀ ◖ ♣ ⇨ P 🏮

DUNSTABLE

VICTORIA
69 West Street
☎ (01582) 662602
11-11; 12-10.30 Sun
Tetley Bitter; guest beers Ⓗ
Friendly, one-bar town-centre local, strong on pub games and televised sports. It has a house beer from Tring, plus three ever-changing guest beers and occasional beer festivals. South Beds

CAMRA *Pub of the Year* 1996 and
'97. Good value lunches. 🕮 ◖ ♣

Try also: Star & Garter, High St
South (Courage)

EATON BRAY

HOPE & ANCHOR
63 Bower Lane
☎ (01525) 220386
11-3, 5-11; 12-5, 7-10.30 Sun
**Tetley Bitter; Vale Notley Ale,
Wychert Ale; guest beer** ⊞
Old, low-beamed village inn,
refurbished and extended gaining
recognition to combine a large
restaurant and an urban-style
main bar. Popular with locals.
Supper licence until 1am. Live
music some Sats.
🕮 ◖ ♿ ♣ P

EGGINGTON

HORSESHOES
High Street ☎ (01525) 210282
12-2.30, 6-11; 12-10.30 Sun
**Theakston Best Bitter;
Wadworth 6X; guest beer** ⊞
Picture-postcard village pub with
an upstairs gallery. An imaginative range of food is on offer (not
served Mon), also an extensive
wine list.
🕮 Q 🕮 ◖ ♣ P

ELSTOW

SWAN
High Street
☎ (01234) 352066
11.30-3, 6-11; 12-4, 7-10.30 Sun
Greene King IPA, Abbot ⊞
Old village pub near Elstow
Abbey and Moot Hall: one
L-shaped room plus a restaurant.
Local clientele, mainly from this
village associated with John
Bunyan. Good reputation for Sun
lunches (no food Sun eve or
Mon).
🕮 🕮 ◖ ♣ P

GREAT BARFORD

GOLDEN CROSS
2-4 Bedford Road, (A421)
☎ (01234) 870439
12-3, 5-11; 12-11 Fri & Sat;
12-10.30 Sun
**Greene King IPA; Wells Eagle;
guest beers** ⊞
Traditional pub with a Chinese
restaurant attached. Up to three
guest beers.
🕮 ◖ ⊞ ♣ P

HARLINGTON

CARPENTERS ARMS
Sundon Road
☎ (01525) 872384
12-11; 12-10.30 Sun
**Banks's Bitter; Marston's
Pedigree; Theakston Best
Bitter** ⊞
17th-century village inn featuring
a low-lit, low-beamed lounge
with copper-topped tables and a

small snug. The public bar has
pool and darts. Good food in the
bar and upstairs restaurant (no
meals Sun
eve). 🕮 🕮 ◖ ▶ ⊞ ⇌ ♣ P

HENLOW

ENGINEERS ARMS
66 High Street
☎ (01462) 812284
3 (11 Fri & Sat)-11; 12-10.30 Sun
**Adnams Bitter; Everards Tiger;
Exmoor Gold; Marston's Pedigree,
HBC; Taylor Landlord** ⊞
A real community pub with its
own football team. Many unusual
beers are served alongside the
regular selection. Loads of breweriana; the lounge bar has no
music or fruit machines.
🕮 🕮 ⊞ ♣ 🗂

KENSWORTH

FARMERS BOY
216 Common Road
☎ (01582) 872207
11-11; 12-10.30 Sun
**Fuller's London Pride, ESB, sea-
sonal beers** ⊞
Friendly village pub with a small
public bar, a comfortable lounge
and a dining area (excellent
home-cooked food). A children's
certificate applies in the lounge
and dining areas; play area in the
garden.
🕮 🕮 ◖ ▶ ⊞ ♣ P

LANGFORD

RED COW
60 High Street
☎ (01462) 700642
11-11 (may vary); 12-3, 7-10.30 Sun
Greene King IPA ⊞
Village local where all are welcome; very games oriented,
including cricket. Summer barbecues are held most weekends.
🕮 🕮 ♣ P

LEIGHTON BUZZARD

HUNT HOTEL
19 Church Road, Linslade (opp
station)
☎ (01525) 374692
11-3, 6-11; 11-11 Sat; 12-3,
7-10.30 Sun
**Draught Bass; Fuller's London
Pride; Tetley Bitter; guest
beers** ⊞
Ochre-coloured hotel with a generally quiet bar (live music Fri
nights). Two ever-changing guest
beers are available (at a price!).
Wheelchair access is via the rear
entrance. Children welcome during the day.
Q 🛏 🖼 ◖ ▶ ♿ ⇌ P

STAG
1 Heath Road (A418, ½ mile N
of centre)
☎ (01525) 372710
12-2.30, 6-11; 12-3, 7-10.30 Sun
**Fuller's Chiswick, London Pride,
ESB, seasonal beers** ⊞

Triangular, ex-Allied house
appealing to drinkers of all ages.
Food oriented, with special
theme nights (for example,
Valentine's, Hallowe'en), but
there is no food on Sun.
Tiny car park.
Q ◖ ▶ ♣ P

LUTON

BIRD & BUSH
Hancock Drive, Bushmead
☎ (01582) 480723
12-11; 12-10.30 Sun
**Draught Bass; Fuller's London
Pride; guest beer** (occasional) ⊞
Modern estate pub with attractive Yorkshire flagstone and
quarry-tiled floors. Good bar food
includes vegetarian options (no
food Sun eve).
🕮 ◖ ▶ ♿ ♣

BRICKLAYERS ARMS
14-16 Hightown Road (100 yds N
of station)
☎ (01582) 611017
12-2.30, 5-11; 12-11 Fri & Sat;
12-10.30 Sun
**Bateman Mild; Everards Beacon,
Tiger; guest beers** ⊞
Friendly, unpretentious town pub.
Basic furnishings include old
casks scattered about, some of
which come from the short-lived
Mickles microbrewery. It can
be busy on Luton Town FC
match days.
🕮 ⇌ ♣ P

MOTHER REDCAP
80 Latimer Road
☎ (01582) 730913
11-3, 5-11; 11-11 Fri & Sat; 12-3,
7-10.30 Sun
**Greene King IPA, Abbot, season-
al beers** ⊞
Well-renovated one-bar pub with
a games area separated from the
lounge by a chimney breast. No
food Sun.
◖ P

TWO BREWERS
43 Dumfries Street
☎ (01582) 616008
12-11; 12-10.30 Sun
**B&T Shefford Bitter,
Dragonslayer, SOS, seasonal
beers; guest beers** ⊞
Friendly, back-street local with a
good mix of customers, offering
good value beer in no-frills surroundings.
🕮 🕮 ♣

WHEELWRIGHTS ARMS
34 Guildford Street
☎ (01582) 759321
10.30-11; 12-10.30 Sun
**Flowers IPA; Fuller's London
Pride, ESB, seasonal beers** ⊞
Lively, one-bar, town-centre free
house, which is close to the bus
and rail stations and the Arndale
Centre. Early birds may like to
known that it opens at 7am for
breakfasts.
🕮 🖼 ◖ ▶ ⇌ 🥂

MILLBROOK

CHEQUERS
☎ (01525) 403835
11.30-2.30, 6-11; 12-3, 7-10.30 Sun
Adnams Broadside; Banks's Mild; Wadworth 6X; Wells Eagle ⊞
Popular pub overlooking Marston Vale, near Ampthill; frequented by testers from the nearby vehicle proving track. The restaurant area serves a wide variety of meals including Sun roasts (no eve meals Sun). ◖ ▶ ♣ P

ODELL

BELL
Horsefair Lane ☎ (01234) 720254
11-2.30, 6-11 (11-11 Sat spring & summer); 12-3, 7-10.30 Sun
Greene King IPA, Abbot, seasonal beers ⊞
Thatched multi-roomed village pub serving good food. The large garden near the River Great Ouse boasts an aviary of unusual birds. A riverside footpath leads into Harrold-Odell Country Park. Sun lunches 12-2; no food Sun eve in winter. ⇔ ⊛ ◖ ▶ P

RENHOLD

THREE HORSESHOES
42 Top End (1 mile N of A421)
☎ (01234) 870218
11-2.30, 6-11; 11-11 Sat; 12-10.30 Sun
Greene King XX Mild, IPA, Abbot ⊞
Traditional country pub giving a friendly welcome. Good value, home-cooked food includes fresh steaks and fish. No food Sun, or Tue eve. Abbot is sometimes replaced by a guest beer. ⇔ Q ⊛ ◖ ▶ P

RIDGMONT

ROSE & CROWN
89 High Street
☎ (01525) 280245
10.30-2.30, 6-11; 12-4, 7-10.30 Sun
Adnams Broadside; Mansfield Riding Bitter; Wells Eagle, Bombardier ⊞
Popular, welcoming pub, recently altered to connect the two comfortably furnished bars and provide dining areas in each. Loosely Rupert Bear themed (note the Nutwood Ales sign). Extensive grounds offer camping and caravanning facilities. In every edition of this Guide.
⇔ ⊛ ◖ ▶ ▲ P

SALFORD

RED LION COUNTRY HOTEL
Wavendon Road (main Cranfield-Woburn Sands road)
☎ (01908) 583117
11-2.30, 6-11; 12-2.30, 7-10.30 Sun
Wells Eagle, Bombardier ⊞

350-year-old building with a comfortable lounge bar and a popular restaurant. The accommodation boasts four-poster beds in some rooms. There is a good garden for children, but the pub has no children's certificate.
⇔ Q ⊛ ⇌ ◖ ▶ ℒ P

SHARNBROOK

SWAN WITH TWO NICKS
High Street
☎ (01234) 781585
11-3, 5-11; 11-11 Sat; 12-10.30 Sun
Wells Eagle, Bombardier; guest beers ⊞
Friendly village local with a small patio. Home-cooked food includes daily specials and a vegetarian choice.
⇔ ⊛ ◖ ▶ ⊟ ♣ P

SHEFFORD

BREWERY TAP
North Bridge Street
☎ (01462) 628448
11-11; 12-10.30 Sun
B&T Shefford Bitter, Dragonslayer, seasonal beers; guest beers ⊞
Timber-clad, wooden-floored, friendly local, B&T's brewery tap. Children and well behaved dogs welcome. Filled rolls are usually available (no food Sun), and there is live music Fri eve. Bar billiards is played.
⊛ ◖ ♣ P

SHILLINGTON

MUSGRAVE ARMS
18 Apsley End Road (Shillington-Pegsdon road)
☎ (01462) 711286
12-3, 5-11; 12-4.30, 7-10.30 (12-10.30 summer) Sun
Greene King XX Mild, IPA, Abbot
Low-beamed, one-bar country pub: a raised 'public' end, with scrubbed wooden tables, is popular with domino players. Good food (not served Mon eve). The large garden features petanque and there is also children's play equipment.
⇔ Q ⊛ ◖ ▶ ♣ P

SILSOE

STAR & GARTER
14-16 High Street
☎ (01525) 860250
11-3, 5.30-11; 12-3, 6-10.30 Sun
B&T Shefford Bitter; Boddingtons Bitter; Flowers IPA; Wadworth 6X ⊞
Dating in part from the 16th century: a large, comfortable lounge bar with a raised restaurant area and a smaller, more traditional, public bar adjoining. Families welcome.
⇔ ⊛ ◖ ▶ ⊟ ♣ P

STUDHAM

RED LION & STUDHAM
Church Road
☎ (01582) 872530
11-3, 5.30-11; 11-11 Sat; 12-10.30 Sun
Adnams Bitter; Greene King Abbot; Marston's Bitter; Taylor Landlord; guest beer ⊞
Well-furnished, comfortable pub facing the village common, with an L-shaped lounge bar, a dining room and a snug. Popular with walkers, it is convenient for Whipsnade Zoo.
⇔ Q ⊛ ◖ ▶ ♣ P

SUTTON

JOHN O'GAUNT
30 High Street
☎ (01767) 260377
12-3, 7-11; 12-3, 7-10.30 Sun
Greene King IPA, Abbot ⊞
Attractive, rural pub close to the village ford, offering an interesting range of bar meals (no food Sun eve). The floodlit petanque court and Northamptonshire skittles are well used by local leagues.
⇔ Q ⊛ ◖ ▶ ⊟ ▲ ♣ P

TEBWORTH

QUEENS HEAD
The Lane
☎ (01525) 874101
11-3, (3.30 Sat), 6 (7 Sat)-11; 12-3, 7.30 Sun
Adnams Broadside Ⓖ**; Wells Eagle** ⊞
Fine village local with a welcoming atmosphere. The two small bars are popular with locals and visitors alike. Good value food (not served Sun). Quiz night Thu; live music Fri.
⇔ ⊛ ◖ ▶ ⊟ ♣ P

Try also: Plough, Wingfield (Free)

TILSWORTH

ANCHOR
1 Dunstable Road
☎ (01525) 210289
11-11; 12-10.30 Sun
Marston's Bitter, Pedigree, HBC ⊞
Lively, welcoming, one-bar village local, due for alterations and an increased beer range. The large garden has play equipment; families are welcome at all times.
⇔ Q ⊛ ◖ ▶ ▲ ⇔ P

TODDINGTON

ANGEL
1 Luton Road
☎ (01525) 872380
11-11; 12-10.30 Sun
Banks's Mild; Marston's Bitter, Pedigree, HBC ⊞
Attractive pub, dating in part from the 16th century, with two lounge bars, two restaurant

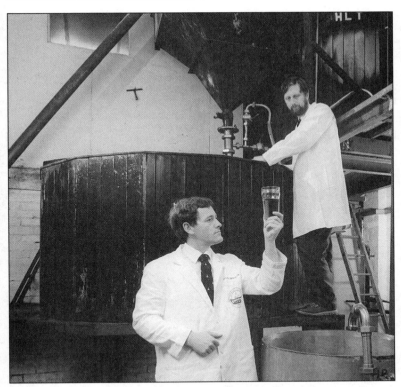

Checking out the quality at the Shefford brewery of B&T. Founded in 1981 it was rescued from receivership in 1994 and continues to brew its award-winning ales. B&T is one of the many craft breweries who create tasty ales and who should be supported.

areas and a large patio for summer drinking. Children's certificate. Live jazz Sun lunch. Popular for cream teas.
🏠 🍂 🌓 🍺 P ✄

SOW & PIGS
19 Church Square
☎ (01525) 873089
11-11; 12-10.30 Sun
Greene King IPA, Abbot, seasonal beers Ⓗ
19th-century commercial inn, with a long, narrow bar and a decor strong on pigs. The 'Sow' has appeared in every edition of this Guide, and despite superficial changes the atmosphere and character remain unaltered.
🏠 Q 🍂 ♣ P

TOTTERNHOE

OLD FARM
16 Church Road
☎ (01582) 661294
12-3 (4 Sat), 6 (5 Fri)-11; 12-5, 7-10.30 Sun
Fuller's London Pride, ESB, seasonal beers Ⓗ
Old village pub with a popular public bar, featuring a low boarded ceiling. The no-smoking dining room boasts a large inglenook.
🏠 Q 🍂 🌓 🍺 ♣ P

TURVEY

THREE CRANES
High Street
☎ (01234) 881305
11-2.30, 6-11; 12-3, 7-10.30 Sun
Courage Best Bitter, Directors Fuller's London Pride; Ruddles County; guest beers Ⓗ
17th-century coaching inn serving an excellent range of food in both the bar and restaurant (vegetarian meals available). Regular theme nights are arranged throughout the year - the fish night is a must!
🏠 🍂 🛏 🌓 🍺 P

WRESTLINGWORTH

CHEQUERS
43 High Street
☎ (01767) 631256
11.30-3, 6-11; 12-3, 7-10.30 Sun
Greene King XX Mild, IPA, Abbot Ⓗ
A real village local with a strong community feel decorated with

lots of brasses. Central carvery. Very friendly. Very good food (not served Sun eve).
🏠 🍂 🌓 🍺 ♣ P

YIELDEN

CHEQUERS
High Street
☎ (01933) 356383
12-2.30, 5.30-11; 12-11 Sat; 12-10.30 Sun
Flowers IPA; Fuller's London Pride; guest beers Ⓗ
Large, single bar with a family/skittles room and a restaurant (open Wed-Sun) plus a large garden. The village is on the Three Shires Way walkers' route and boasts some impressive earthworks of a Norman castle. 🏠 🐕 🍂 🌓 🍺 ♣ P

INDEPENDENT BREWERIES

B&T:
Shefford
Wells:
Bedford

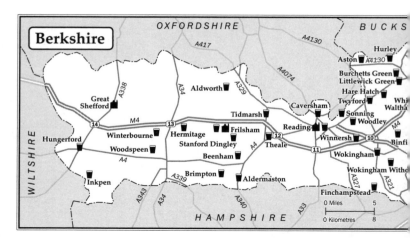

ALDERMASTON

HIND'S HEAD
Wasing Lane
☎ (0118) 971 2194
11-2.30, 5-11 Mon-Sat; 12-3,
7-10.30 Sun
**Courage Best Bitter; Fuller's
London Pride; Guest Beer** Ⓗ
Imposing, red-brick inn, popular
as an overnight stop for business
travellers. It offers a varied and
ever-changing menu of good
food. Evidence of a former brewery can be seen and the inn even
has its own lock-up, last used in
1865. ⚏ Q ✿ ➡ ◖ ▶ P

ALDWORTH

BELL INN
Off B4009, NE of Newbury
OS556797 ☎ (01635) 578272
11-3, 6-11 Tue-Sat; 12-3, 7-10.30
Sun; closed Mon
**Arkell's 3B, Kingsdown;
Morrells Bitter, Mild; West
Berkshire Old Tyler** Ⓗ
Regional CAMRA *Pub of the Year*
1998. An unspoiled country pub;
open outside gents and a central,
windowed bar. Family-run for
over two centuries, it stands next
to the cricket ground and one
mile from Ridgeway Path.
⚏ Q ✿ ◖ ▶ ⊞ ♣ P

ASTON

FLOWER POT HOTEL
Ferry Lane (via Aston Lane, off
A423) ☎ (01491) 574721
11-3, 6-11; 12-2.30, 7-10.30 Sun
**Brakspear Mild, Bitter, Old,
Special** Ⓗ
Wonderful old two-bar inn, a
short walk from its own landing
stage on the Thames. The public
bar has wooden floors and a col-
lection of stuffed fish.
Comfortable lounge and a large
garden. No food Sun eve.
⚏ Q ⛺ ✿ ⊞ ➡ ◖ ▲ ♣ P ⛁

BEENHAM

STOCKS INN
1 mile off A4, E of Thatcham
☎ (0118) 971 3127
12-2 (2.30 Sat), 7-11 Mon-Sat;
12-3, 7-10.30 Sun
**Archers Village; Hook Norton
Best Bitter; Shepherd Neame
Spitfire; Wells Bombardier;
guest beer** Ⓗ
18th-century pub of Flemish
bonded brick: a comfortable
lounge serving splendid Sunday
roasts; darts played regularly in
the public bar. Landlord's WWII
and pipe collections displayed
beneath old farm implements.
⚏ Q ✿ ⊞ ◖ ♣ P

Try also: Six Bells, (Free)

BINFIELD

VICTORIA ARMS
Terrace Road North
☎ (01344) 483856
11.30-3, 6 (6.30 Sat)- 11; 12-3,
7-10.30 Sun
**Fuller's Chiswick, London Pride,
ESB, seasonal beers** Ⓗ
Attractive village pub, well used
by locals, hosting summer barbecues in the pleasant garden. An
extensive bottled beer collection
is housed in the rafters. No food
Sun eve. ✿ ◖ ▶ ♣ P ⛝

BRIMPTON

THREE HORSESHOES
Brimpton Lane (1¼ miles off A4,
E of Thatcham)
☎ (0118) 971 2183
11-3, 6-11; 12-3, 7-10.30 Sun
**Fuller's London Pride, ESB;
Wadworth 6X; guest beer** (occasional) Ⓗ
170-year-old former Mays of
Basingstoke pub serving traditional, good value meals. Photos
of the pub dating back to 1911
are displayed in a wood-panelled

lounge whilst the pleasant public
bar offers pool, darts, jukebox
and TV. No food Sun.
Q ✿ ◖ ⊞ ♣ P

BURCHETTS GREEN

RED LION
Apple House Hill, Hurley (A423)
☎ (01628) 824433
11-3, 6-11; 12-3, 7-11 Sun
**Brakspear Bitter, Special, sea-
sonal beers** Ⓟ
Friendly, 18th-century coaching
inn hosted by a parrot in the
front bar. The listed cellar is built
over the original cellar which
dates back to the *Domesday
Book*. Eve meals Tue-Sat.
⚏ Q ✿ ◖ ▶ ⅋ ♣ P

CAVERSHAM

BARON CADOGAN
22-24 Prospect Street (A4155)
☎ (0118) 947 0626
11-11 Mon-Sat; 12-10.30 Sun
**Courage Directors; Theakston
Best Bitter; guest beers** Ⓗ
New, open-plan Wetherspoon's
pub – a great asset to the area.
Q ◖ ▶ ⅋ ⛝ ⛁

CLIFTON ARMS
12 Gosbrook Road (off A4155)
☎ (0118) 947 1775
11-11; 12-10.30 Sun
**Brakspear Bitter, Special, sea-
sonal beers** Ⓗ
Smart saloon bar with a restau-
rant-cum-meeting room to the
rear. Good home cooking. (Sun
meals 12-6).
Q ✿ ◖ ▶ ⊞ ⅋ ♣ P

COOKHAM

COOKHAM TAVERN
Lower Road ☎ (01628) 529519
11.30-2.30, 5.30-11; 11.30-11
Fri-Sat; 12-10.30 Sun
**Brakspear Bitter; Young's
Special; guest beer** Ⓗ

Welcoming, comfortable local by the station. No food Mon.
🏚 🌺 ◖❶ ⇌ P

DATCHET

ROYAL STAG
The Green
☎ (01753) 548218
11-11; 12-10.30 Sun
Ind Coope Burton Ale; Tetley Bitter; guest beer Ⓗ
An alehouse since the mid 17th century; panelling in the older part is made from champagne boxes. A ghostly child's handprint appears in the window next to the churchyard.
🏚 🌺 ◖❶ 🍺 ⇌ ♣ P

ETON

WATERMANS ARMS
Brocas Street (off High St)
☎ (01753) 341001
11-2.30 (3 Sat), 6-11; 12-3, 7-10.30 Sun
Brakspear Bitter; Courage Best Bitter; Directors; Morland Old Speckled Hen; Ushers Best Bitter; Wadworth 6X Ⓗ
Popular riverside local dating back to the 16th century. An extensive menu is served in the covered restaurant (previously the courtyard) where families are welcome. No food Sun eve. The no-smoking room has a boating theme.
🏚 Q ◖❶ ⇌ (Windsor/Eton Riverside) ♣ ⊁

Try also: Hogshead, High St (Free)

FINCHAMPSTEAD

QUEENS OAK
Church Lane (off B3016)
☎ (0118) 973 4855
11-2.30, 6-11; 11.30-3 (4 summer), 6.30-11 Sat; 12-3, 7-10.30 Sun

Brakspear Bitter, Old, Special, seasonal beers Ⓗ
Great country pub. The well-equipped large garden hosts barbecues and Aunt Sally is played. No food Sun eve.
Q 🌺 ◖❶ 🍺 ♣ P ⊁

FRILSHAM

POT KILN ☆
1½ miles S of Yattendon Church OS552731 ☎ (01635) 201366
12-2.30 (not Tue), 6.30-11; 12-3, 7-10.30 Sun
Arkell's 3B; Morland Original; West Berkshire Brick Kiln Bitter, Dr Hexter's Healer Ⓗ
Regional CAMRA *Pub of the Year* 1997, a secluded 18th-century pub set amongst beech-woods near a former brick-works. It features four small rooms, a large garden, good home-cooked food (filled rolls only Sun, no food Tue) and a variety of non-electronic games. The landlord is always ready for a chat.
🏚 Q 🐴 🌺 ◖❶ 🍺 ♣ P ⊁

HARE HATCH

QUEEN VICTORIA
Blakes Lane (off A4)
☎ (0118) 940 2477
11-2.30 (3 summer), 5.30-11; 12-10.30 Sun
Brakspear Bitter, Old, Special Ⓗ
An oasis of calm civility just yards from the busy A4. The original building is 300 years old. Walkers and well-behaved children are welcome. An extensive menu makes it popular for food. 🌺 ◖❶ ♣ P ⊁

HERMITAGE

LAMB
Long Lane (B4009)
☎ (01635) 200348
11 (11.30 Sat)-2.30, 6 (5.30 Fri)-11; 12-3, 7-10.30 Sun
Flowers IPA, Original; Wadworth 6X; guest beer Ⓗ
This area was noted for fine brickmaking and this building is an attractive example of local Flemish bond. The three bars have been knocked into one comfortable lounge, but the atmosphere is determinedly a village local. 🌺 ◖❶ P ⊁

HOLYPORT

BELGIAN ARMS
Holyport Street
☎ (01628) 634468
11-3, 5.30-11; 12-3, 7-10.30 Sun
Brakspear Bitter, Special Ⓗ
Unspoilt village pub, very popular with locals and families. The garden overlooks the duck pond. It was known as the Prussian Eagle

before WWI. An excellent spot for a bar lunch or a relaxing summer pint. No food Sun eve.
🏚 Q 🌺 ◖❶ 🛏 P

HUNGERFORD

HUNGERFORD CLUB
3 The Croft, (off Church St, then turn right after rail bridge)
☎ (01488) 682358
12-3 (not Mon-Fri), 7-11 (10.30 Sun)
Morland Original; Ruddles Best Bitter; guest beers Ⓗ
A sports and social club overlooking the croft green where tennis and bowls are enjoyed in the summer. Visitors will find reasonably priced beer including a regularly changing guest. Show this *Guide* or CAMRA membership to be signed in. 🌺 ⇌ ♣ P

Try also: Railway, Station Rd (free)

HURLEY

DEW DROP INN
Batts Green, Honey Lane (off minor road, between Burchetts Green and Hurley)
☎ (01628) 824327
12-3, 6-11; 12-3, 7-10.30 Sun
Brakspear Bitter, Special, seasonal beers Ⓗ
Famously hard to find, picturesque pub in woodland, popular all year round with walkers, especially the large garden in summer.
🏚 Q 🐴 🌺 ◖❶ P

INKPEN

SWAN INN
Lower Inkpen (Hungerford-Combe road) OS359643
☎ (01488) 668326
11-2.30, 7-11; 12-3, 7-10.30 Sun
Adnams Bitter; Butts Bitter, Barbus Barbus; Hook Norton Mild Ⓗ
Recently renovated village inn, popular with walkers, boasting its own organic farm shop and restaurant (organic beef dishes a speciality).
🏚 Q 🐴 🌺 🛏 ◖❶ P ⊁

LITTLEWICK GREEN

CRICKETERS
Littlewick Green (off A4 near the Shire Horse Centre)
☎ (01628) 822888
11-3, 5.30-11; 11-11 Sat; 12-10.30 Sun
Brakspear Bitter; Fuller's London Pride; guest beers Ⓗ
Popular local overlooking the village green and cricket ground, frequented by ramblers on local walks. The main bar is dominated by a large real fire and a railway clock. 🏚 Q 🌺 🛏 ◖❶ ♿

MAIDENHEAD

VINE
20 Market St ☎ (01628) 782112
11-11 Mon-Sat; 12-10.30 Sun
Brakspear Bitter, Special, seasonal beers Ⓗ
Friendly, popular town-centre pub, with a pleasant local atmosphere. ❀ ◖ ▶ ⇌

Try also: Pond House, 55 Bath Rd (Free)

OAKLEY GREEN

OLD RED LION
Oakley Green Road (off A308)
☎ (01753) 863892
12-3, 5.30-11; 12-10.30 Sun
Draught Bass; Flowers IPA; Tetley Bitter Ⓗ
400-year-old coaching inn retaining many original features. The restaurant boasts an extensive menu of home-cooked food (Sun meals 12-7). Aunt Sally is played in the garden in summer.
Q ❀ ◖ ▶ P

OLD WINDSOR

JOLLY GARDENERS
92-94 St Lukes Road
☎ (01753) 865944
11-11; 12-5, 7-10.30 Sun
Courage Best Bitter; Ushers Founders, seasonal beers Ⓗ
Traditional village pub, notable for the games which are popular with the regulars, including chess, shove-ha'penny and Shut-the-Box. ❀ ♣

OXFORD BLUE
Crimp Hill Road ☎ (01753) 861954
11-11; 12-10.30 Sun
Fuller's London Pride; Tetley Bitter; Wadworth 6X Ⓗ
Pub established in 1802 by a retired soldier who named it after his regiment. Split into a number of areas, it also has two conservatories, one of which functions as a family room, and one as a restaurant (food all day). Note the large collection of aircraft memorabilia.
Q ☎ ❀ ⇌ ◖ ▶ ♣ P

READING

BACK OF BEYOND
108 Kings Road (½ mile E of centre) ☎ (0118) 959 5906
11-11; 12-10.30 Sun
Archers Golden; Courage Directors; Fuller's London Pride; Theakston Best Bitter; guest beers Ⓗ
Typical Wetherspoons conversion of a former warehouse; very comfortable with a no-smoking area to the rear. Up to five guest beers. A riverside terrace for outdoor drinking.
Q ❀ ◖ ▶ ⅙ ⇌ ⅋ �🇗

BUTLER
89-91 Chatham Street (near centre, off inner distribution road)
☎ (0118) 939 1635
11-11; 12-3, 7-10.30 Sun
Fuller's London Pride, ESB Ⓗ
A 20-year-old pub taking its name from the wine merchants who formerly occupied the premises. A recent refurbishment has enhanced its character. Outside drinking area in front of the pub. No food Sun eve.
❀ ◖ ▶ ⇌ ♣ P

FISHERMAN'S COTTAGE
224 Kennetside, (canal bank, E of centre, off Orts Rd, near college)
☎ (0118) 957 1553
11.30-3, 5.30-11; 11-11 Fri-Sat; 12-3, 7-10.30 (12-10.30 summer) Sun
Fuller's Chiswick, London Pride, ESB, seasonal beers Ⓗ
Extended pub by Blakes Lock on the Kennet & Avon canal, a pleasant walk from the town centre. Very popular in summer with a rear garden and front terrace overlooking the canal. Good food.
🏖 Q ❀ ◖ ▶ P

HOBGOBLIN
Broad Street
☎ (0118) 950 8119
11-11; 12-10.30 Sun
Beer range varies; guest beer Ⓗ
Do not be put off by the exterior - behind the green door lies a real ale drinker's heaven: three beers from the Wychwood range plus five ever-changing guests. Do not confuse with the other Hobgoblin in Oxford Road.⇌ ▱

HOP LEAF
163-165 Southampton Street (A33 one-way system, towards town centre) ☎ (0118) 931 4700
12 (4 Mon)-11; 12-10.30 Sun
Hop Back GFB, Crop Circle, Entire Stout, Summer Lightning, Thunderstorm; Reading Lion seasonal beers Ⓗ
This one is a must, on the outskirts of the town centre, a friendly local serving the full range of Hop Back beers plus Reading Lion ales brewed on site. Satellite sports in back room.
🏖 ♣

HORSE & JOCKEY
120 Castle Street (A4155, just W of inner ring road, near police station)
☎ (0118) 959 0172
11-11; 12-10.30 Sun
Archers Village; guest beers Ⓗ
Friendly one-bar pub, local CAMRA *Pub of the Year* 1996 and '97, serving ever-changing guest beers often from small independent breweries, plus excellent home cooked-food at reasonable prices (not served Sun eve).
🏖 ◖ ▶ ♣ ▱ 🇗

RETREAT
8 St John's Street (E of centre, near Kings Rd/Queens Rd jct.)
☎ (0118) 957 1593
11-11; 12-10.30 Sun
Flowers IPA; Marston's Pedigree; Wadworth 6X; guest beers Ⓗ
Cosy, friendly pub, aptly named, away from Reading's bustle. Sing-songs on Thu nights. 🗗 ♣

SWEENEY & TODD
10 Castle Street (off St Marys Butts)
☎ (0118) 958 6466
11-10.30; closed Sun
Adnams Bitter; Hardy Royal Oak; Wadworth 6X; guest beer Ⓗ
Tiny bar squeezed between the home-made pine shop at the front and dining areas to the rear and below. Pricey.Q ◖ ▶

Try also: Hope Tap, Friar St (Weatherspoons)

SLOUGH

MOON & SPOON
86 High Street (opp library)
☎ (01753) 531650
11-11; 12-10.30 Sun
Courage Directors; Fuller's London Pride; Greene King IPA; Theakston Best Bitter; guest beer Ⓗ
Large Wetherspoons pub converted from a building society premises in 1995. Attracting a good mix of clientele, it can get very crowded on Fri and Sat eve.
Q ◖ ▶ ⅙ ⇌ ⅙ 🇗

ROSE & CROWN
312 High Street, (E end)
☎ (01753) 521114
11-11; 12-10.30 Sun
Brakspear Bitter; guest beer Ⓗ
Small friendly, two-bar pub built around 1690 and first licensed 1820. Karaoke Fri eve. The guest beer comes from the Whitbread portfolio ❀ ▶

WHEATSHEAF
15 Albert Street
☎ (01753) 522019
11-11; 12-10.30 Sun
Fuller's Chiswick, London Pride, ESB, seasonal beers Ⓗ
Single-bar pub attracting mainly 'thirty-somethings'. The garden, which features a red phone box, is tended over in winter. Try the pies made with beer. Live music weekend eve. ❀ ◖

SONNING

BULL
High Street (next to church)
☎ (0118) 969 3901
11-3, 5.30-11; 12-3, 7-10.30 (12-10.30 summer) Sun
Gale's Best Bitter, IPA, HSB, seasonal beers Ⓗ

Old-worlde former church house, now an upmarket pub/hotel, boasting oak beams and award-winning hanging basket displays on the patio. Food oriented, but there is a separate bar for drinkers. 🏚 🕮 🛌 🌑 🍴 🍺 P

STANFORD DINGLEY

BOOT INN
S of River Pang, on road to Chapel Row OS576714
☎ (0118) 974 5213
11-3, 6-11; 12-3, 7-10.30 Sun
Archers Best Bitter; Brakspear Bitter, Special; guest beers ⊞
A brick-built inglenook draws the attention of diners in the main bar of this comfortable restaurant and pub.
🏚 Q 🍴 🕮 🌑 🍴 P

BULL
200 yds S of church OS576716
☎ (0118) 974 4409
12-3 (not Mon), 7-11; 12-3, 7-10.30 Sun
Draught Bass; Brakspear Bitter; West Berkshire Skiff, Good Old Boy; guest beers ⊞
An original wattle and daub wall is visible in this small, 15th-century two-bar inn, where you can play Ring the Bull — if diners permit. 🏚 Q 🛥 🍴 🌑 🍴 ♣ P

SUNNINGDALE

NAG'S HEAD
28 High Street (off A30 or A329)
☎ (01344) 622725
12-3, 5-11; 11-11 Fri & Sat; 12-10.30 Sun
Harveys XX Mild, BB, Armada, seasonal beers ⊞
Friendly, two-bar local with an award-winning garden. Rare outlet for Harveys' beers in the area. Good value food (not Sun or Mon eves). 🍴 🌑 🍴 ♣ P

SUNNINGHILL

DUKES HEAD
Upper Village Road (near B3020)
☎ (01344) 626949
11-11; 12-10.30 Sun
Greene King IPA, Abbot; Marston's Pedigree; guest beers ⊞
Very friendly pub hidden in a village back street, offering a good range of quality food. Children are allowed in the no-smoking area. Difficult to find but worth the effort. No meals Sun eve.
🛥 🍴 🌑 🍴 P ✂

THEALE

FALCON
31 High Street (old A4)
☎ (0118) 930 2523
10.30-11; 12-10.30 Sun
Archers Best Bitter; Courage Best Bitter; guest beers ⊞

16th-century coaching inn; unmodernised but neat. Wheelchair access is good but there are no special facilities. Guest beers are from the Inntrepreneur portfolio.
🏚 Q 🍴 🌑 🍴 ♿ 🍺 P

LAMB
22 Church Street (old A4)
☎ (0118) 930 2216
12-3, 6-11; 12-10.30 Sun
Courage Best Bitter; guest beer ⊞
Recently extended family pub with a large garden and a genteel lounge bar. Wheelchair WC (but a 2ft step up).
🏚 Q 🍴 🍴 🌑 🍴 ♿ 🍺 P

VOLUNTEER
Church Street (old A4)
☎ (0118) 930 2489
11-3, 5.30-11; 11-3, 7-10.30 Sun
Fuller's Chiswick, London Pride, ESB ⊞
Extended pub with bars knocked through to form one large bar. Low ceilings and mock beams make for a cosy atmosphere amongst horse racing mementoes. 🍴 🌑 🍴 ♣ P

TIDMARSH

GREYHOUND
The Street (A340 Pangbone & Theale Road nr M4 jct 12)
☎ (0118) 984 3557
11-3.30, 5.30-11; 11-11 Sat; 12-10.30 Sun
Brakspear Bitter; Courage Best Bitter; Fuller's London Pride; Wadworth 6X; West Berkshire seasonal beers ⊞
Twelfth-century inn with a thatched roof, very handy for M4 travellers who want a change from motorway service area food as the main focus is on meals.
🏚 🍴 🌑 🍴

TWYFORD

DUKE OF WELLINGTON
High Street ☎ (0118) 934 0456
11.30-2.30 (3 Sat), 5-11; 12-3, 7-10.30 Sun
Brakspear Mild, Bitter, Old, Special, seasonal beers ⊞
Comfortable, smart, friendly, 16th-century village pub with a busy public bar and a quieter lounge, and a large garden. Within easy reach of the station.
Q 🍴 🌑 🕮 🍺 P

GOLDEN CROSS
38 Waltham Road
☎ (0118) 934 0180
11-11; 12-10.30 Sun
Brakspear Bitter; Fuller's London Pride; guest beer ⊞
Smart, comfortable, two-area pub convenient for the station.

Home-cooked food (not served Sun or Mon eves). Plenty of seating, plus an outdoor drinking area. 🍴 🛌 🌑 🕮 🍺 ♣ P

WHITE WALTHAM

BEEHIVE
Waltham Road ☎ (01628) 822877
11-2.30 (3 Sat), 5.30-11; 12-3, 7-10.30 Sun
Brakspear Bitter; Flowers IPA, Original; guest beers ⊞
Thriving village local opposite a cricket pitch and near the airfield. A tasteful refurbishment has retained two bars, with good value food served in the lounge. A wide variety of social events staged; games include petanque. Real cider in autumn and winter.
🏚 🍴 🌑 🍴 🕮 ♣ 🅰 P

WINDSOR

PRINCE CHRISTIAN
11 Kings Road ☎ (01753) 860980
11-3, 6-11; 12-2.30, 7-10.30 Sun
Brakspear Bitter; Fuller's London Pride ⊞
Free house just off the tourist trail, somewhat Irish in flavour. Popular with staff from nearby council offices. Basic weekday lunches. 🌑 🍺

SWAN
9 Mill Lane, Clewer Village (off A308, nr A332 jct)
☎ (01753) 862069
12-3, 6-11; 12-3, 7-10.30 Sun
Boddingtons Bitter; Courage Best Bitter; Fuller's London Pride ⊞
Haunted 16th-century pub. The function room was once a court house with mortuary attached (now the kitchen). Small and friendly YHA hostel nearby.
🍴 🛌 🅰 ♣ P

VANSITTART ARMS
105 Vansittart Road
☎ (01753) 865988
11-11; 12-10.30 Sun
Fuller's Chiswick, London Pride, ESB, seasonal beers ⊞
Comfortable pub away from the centre offering a good range of reasonably priced food. It can get very crowded.
🏚 🍴 🌑 🍴 ♣

WINKFIELD

OLD HATCHET
Hatchet Lane (A330) OS922713
☎ (01344) 885545
11-11; 12-10.30 Sun
Draught Bass; Hancock's HB; guest beers ⊞
Attractive country pub of character enhanced by superb real fires in winter. Excellent, good value food is available in the bar or restaurant, served until 10 (9 Sun). 🏚 🍴 🌑 🍴 P

Make the tea, make the mash, make the beer, make a living wage: it's a tough life being a small brewer, but Chris Butts is enjoying himself as he concocts another craft ale.

WINNERSH

WHEELWRIGHTS ARMS
Davis Street (B3030, opp Dinton Pastures Country Park entrance)
☎ (0118) 934 4100
11-3, 5.30-11; 11.30-11.30 Sat; 12-10.30 Sun
Wadworth IPA, 6X, Summersault, Farmers Glory; guest beers H
Upmarket, food-oriented pub with somewhat pricey guest beers (albeit in top condition). One of Wadworth's few houses in the area. The garden has playthings for children.
ﷺ Q ❀ ◖ ▶ ꝸ P

WINTERBOURNE

WINTERBOURNE ARMS
OS455722
☎ (01635) 248200
11.30-3 (not Mon except Bank Hols), 6-11; 12-3, 7-10.30 Sun
Brakspear Bitter; Flowers Original; West Berkshire Gold Old Boy; Young's Special; guest beers H
Village pub and restaurant. The garden leads to a stream.
ﷺ ❀ ◖ ▶ ♣ ⅍ P

WOKINGHAM

DUKES HEAD
Denmark Street (main road to Finchampstead)
☎ (0118) 978 0316
11.30-3 , 5.30 (5 Fri, 6 Sat)-11; 12-3, 7-10.30 Sun
Brakspear Bitter, Special H
Popular town pub opposite the new library, serving good lunches. It boasts a skittle alley and a wonderful array of hanging baskets in summer.
❀ ◖ ⇌ ♣ P

QUEEN'S HEAD
23 The Terrace (A329, opp Station Rd)
☎ (0118) 978 1221
11-3, 5.30-11; 12-3, 7-10.30 Sun
Morland IPA, Original, Tanners Jack, Old Speckled Hen, seasonal beers; Ruddles Best Bitter H
Originally a 15th-century barn and one of only seven cruck-framed buildings in Berkshire, this charming pub stands on a terrace above the busy main road. It has a hidden rear garden where Aunt Sally can be played. No food Sun.
Q ❀ ◖ ⇌ ♣

RED LION
Market Place
☎ (0118) 978 0319
11-3, 5.30-11; 12-3, 7-10.30 Sun
Brakspear Bitter, Special H
Two-bar pub with a Thai restaurant upstairs (open eves except Sun); pub food served lunchtime.
◖ ▶ ⇌ P

Try also: Ship, Peach St (Fuller's)

WOKINGHAM WITHOUT

CROOKED BILLET
Honey Hill (off Nine Mile Ride)
OS826667
☎ (0118) 978 0438
11-11; 12-10.30 Sun
Brakspear Bitter, Special, seasonal beers H
Excellent, unspoilt country pub offering a friendly welcome. A small restaurant serves good value food (no meals Sun eve). Beware of the ford if approaching from the north-east.
ﷺ Q ❀ ◖ ꝸ ♣ P

WOODLEY

INN ON THE PARK
Woodford Park, Haddon Drive (through park gates, and follow road to sports centre)
☎ (0118) 962 8655
11-2.30, 6-11; 11-11 Fri-Sat; 12-3, 6-10.30 Sun
Draught Bass; Brakspear Bitter, Special; guest beers H
Modern bar in a sports centre. Guest beers come mainly from nationals, but independents sometimes feature. ❀ ꝸ P

WOODSPEEN

FIVE BELLS
Lambourn Road (2 miles NW of Newbury) OS451687
☎ (01635) 48763
12-2.30, 6-11; 12-3, 7-10.30 Sun
Ruddles Best Bitter; guest beers H
One-bar rural pub with a dining area separate from a small, friendly drinking area. Ideally situated for exploring the picturesque Lambourne Valley or for visiting the famous Watermill Theatre nearby. No meals Sun or Mon eves. Wheelchair WC.
Q ❀ ⌂ ◖ ▶ ꝸ ♣ P ⅍

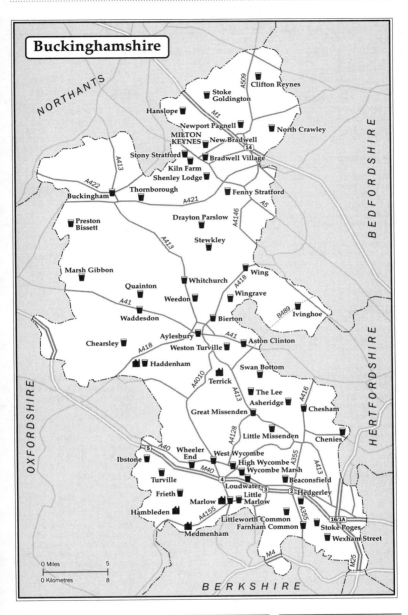

Buckinghamshire

ASHERIDGE

BLUE BALL
1½ miles NW of Chesham
☎ (01494) 758263
12-2.30, 5.30 (4 Fri)-11; 12-11
Sat; 12-4, 7.30-10.30 Sun
Beer range varies Ⓗ
Set in beautiful countryside, this
family-run pub is a true free
house with a range of four, constantly changing beers. Try the
home-made soup. Own campsite
and large garden hosting barbecues. ❀ ◖ ▲ ♣ P

ASTON CLINTON

ROTHSCHILD ARMS
82 Weston Road (off A41,
Weston-Turville Road)
☎ (01296) 630320
12-2.30, 6-11; 12-11 Fri & Sat;
12-3, 7-10.30 Sun
**Tetley Imperial; Worthington
Bitter; guest beer** Ⓗ
Barbecues in summer and occa-
sional live music Fri eve. No food
Sun. Guest beers are from the
Tapster's Choice range.
🏕 ❀ ⇔ ◖ ▯ ♿ ♣ P

AYLESBURY

QUEEN'S HEAD
1 Temple Square
☎ (01296) 415484
11-3, 5.30-11; 12-3, 7-10.30 Sun
**Greenalls Bitter, Original;
Shipstone's Bitter; guest beer** Ⓗ
Village-style pub (circa 17th century) in the old part of Aylesbury:
two bars and a recently enlarged
dining area. A collection of water
jugs hangs from beams in the
back bar. ❀ ⇔ ◖ ▯ ≈

43

SHIP

59 Walton St ☎ (01296) 421888
11.30-2.30, 5.30-11; 11.30-11 Fri
& Sat; 12-3, 7-10.30 Sun
**Greene King Abbot; Tetley
Bitter; guest beer** Ⓗ
Cosmopolitan, warm and friendly
town pub situated by the canal
basin at the end of the Aylesbury
arm of the Grand Union Canal.
Discos Thu. Award-wining out-
door drinking area.
✿ ◖ ⛓ ⇌ ♣ P

BEACONSFIELD

GREYHOUND

33 Windsor End
☎ (01494) 673823
11-3, 5.30-11; 12-3, 7-10.30 Sun
**Courage Best Bitter; Fuller's
London Pride; Wadworth 6X;
guest beers** Ⓗ
Originally a drovers' inn, this pub
now has a popular beamed
lounge bar and a restaurant area
(no eve meals Sun). No mobile
phones permitted.
Q ✿ ◖ ▶

BIERTON

BELL

191 Aylesbury Road
☎ (01296) 436055
11-3, 6-11; 11-11 Sat; 12-3,
7-10.30 Sun
**Fuller's Chiswick, London Pride,
ESB, seasonal beers** Ⓗ
Small, two-bar pub within easy
reach of Aylesbury. It enjoys a
thriving food trade – all meals
home-prepared. Live jazz last Sun
of each month. ✿ ◖ ▶ ♣ P

BUCKINGHAM

WHALE

14 Market Hill
☎ (01280) 815537
11-11; 12-10.30 Sun
**Fuller's Chiswick, London Pride,
ESB, seasonal beers** Ⓗ
Traditional, town-centre pub;
welcoming and friendly, with a
split-level bar.
🏨 ✿ ⇌ ◖ ♣

Try also: New Inn, Bridge St
(Greene King)

CHEARSLEY

BELL INN

The Green ☎ (01844) 208077
12-2.30 (not Mon except Bank
Hols), 6-11; 12-3, 7-10.30 Sun
**Fuller's Chiswick, London Pride,
seasonal beers** Ⓗ
An attractive, cottage-style,
thatched, one-bar local overlooking the village green, warmed by
open fires at both ends. A large,
secure garden play area for children is home to chickens, ducks
and rabbits. Eve meals Tue-Sat.
🏨 ✿ ◖ ▶ Å P

CHENIES

RED LION

(Off A404) ☎ (01923) 282722
11-2, 5.30-11; 12-3, 7-10.30 Sun
**Benskins BB; Vale Notley Ale;
Wadworth 6X** Ⓗ
Friendly, busy village free house,
which attracts drinkers and diners. Look for the snug to the rear
of the dining room. No chips with
any meals and no bookings
taken. The house beer is brewed
by Rebellion. Q ✿ ◖ ▶ P

CHESHAM

KING'S ARMS

1 King Street ☎ (01494) 774466
11-2.30, 5.30-11; 12-4, 7-10.30 Sun
**Brakspear Bitter, Marston's
Pedigree; guest beer** Ⓗ
Traditional old pub also serving
Hoegaarden white beer on
draught, close to the football and
cricket grounds. ✿ ◖ ▶ ⊖ ♣

QUEEN'S HEAD

120 Church Street, Old Chesham
☎ (01494) 783773
11-2.30, 5-11; 11-11 Sat; 12-3,
7-10.30 Sun
**Brakspear Bitter, Special;
Fuller's London Pride, seasonal
beers** or **guest beers** Ⓗ
Traditional, popular pub which
can be very busy, with a Thai
restaurant upstairs. English food
is available lunchtime.
🏨 Q ✿ ◖ ▶ ⊖ ♣ P ✕

Try also: Last Post, Broadway
(Wetherspoons)

CLIFTON REYNES

ROBIN HOOD

Signed off A509 at Emberton
OS902512 ☎ (01234) 711574
12-2.30, 6.30-11; 12-2.30,
7-10.30 Sun
Greene King IPA, Abbot Ⓗ
16th-century pub with two bars
plus a conservatory; the large
garden has a pets corner. Caters
for locals due to its remoteness
and is popular with walkers (no
muddy boots in the bars). No
food Mon or Sun eve. Note the
Greene King leaded window.
🏨 Q ⛴ ✿ ◖ ▤ ♣

FARNHAM COMMON

YEW TREE

Collinswood Road (A355, 1 mile
N of village) ☎ (01753) 643723
11-11; 12-10.30 Sun
**Morland IPA, Old Speckled Hen;
Ruddles County** Ⓗ
Deservedly popular, 300-year-old
country local: a small, basic
public bar and a larger, food-
dominated saloon serving award-
winning pies. Opens at 7am for
breakfast Mon-Sat. No-smoking
dining area. 🏨 ◖ ▶ ▤ Å ♣ P

FRIETH

PRINCE ALBERT

Moors End (100 yds from Lane
end to Frieth Road) OS798906
☎ (01494) 881683
11-3, 5.30-11; 12-4, 7-10.30 Sun
**Brakspear Mild, Bitter, Old,
Special, seasonal beers** Ⓗ
One of the best pubs in the
Thames Valley, and a regular
entry in the *Guide*. It offers a
superb atmosphere, location and
hospitality. Josie's platefuls are a
bonus at lunchtime (Mon-Sat).
🏨 Q ✿ ◖ ♣

GREAT MISSENDEN

CROSS KEYS

40 High Street
☎ (01494) 865373
11-3, 5-11; 12-3, 7-10.30 Sun
**Fuller's Chiswick Bitter, London
Pride, ESB, seasonal beers** Ⓗ
400-year-old pub with a high-
back settles in the bar area.
Meals only served in the restaurant eves, thus preserving a good
atmosphere elsewhere.
Q ✿ ◖ ▶ ⇌ ♣ P

HADDENHAM

RED LION

Church End
☎ (01844) 291606
11.30-3, 6-11; 12-10.30 Sun
**ABC Best Bitter; Ansells Mild,
Bitter; Marston's Pedigree** Ⓗ
Straightforward, two-bar local
overlooking the village duckpond.
The long-serving landlord has
recently re-introduced mild which
is rare in this part of the county.
🏨 Q ✿ ◖ ▤ ♣ P

RISING SUN

9 Thame Road
☎ (01844) 291744
11-3, 5.30-11; 11-11 Fri & Sat;
12-10.30 Sun
Wells Eagle; guest beers Ⓗ
Small, friendly, one-bar village
local. It offers an interesting
range of guest beers and occasional mini-beer festivals. No
lunches on Sun. Real cider in
summer.
✿ ◖ ⇌ ♣ ⌣

HANSLOPE

GLOBE

58 Hartwell Road, Long Street
(unclassified road to Hartwell)
☎ (01908) 510336
12-2.30 (11-3 Sat), 6-11; 12-3, 7-
10.30 Sun
Banks's Bitter Ⓗ**P**; **guest beers** Ⓗ
Classic country pub with an
award-winning cellar – one of
Banks's best. Quality food in the
restaurant and a cheaper bar
menu (no food Tue). A friendly,
very community-oriented public
bar, a good lounge and games

room. The garden has a play area. Children's certificate.
🏚 Q ❀ ◑ ▶ 🍴 ♣ ⌂ P ⊟

Try also: Watts Arms, Castlethorpe Road (Wells)

HEDGERLEY

ONE PIN
One Pin Lane ☎ (01753) 643035
11-3, 5.30-11; 12-10.30 (closed 2 hrs in afternoon) Sun
Courage Best Bitter, Directors; guest beers (summer) Ⓗ
200-year-old traditional coaching inn with two bars. The lounge bar is busy throughout the week with diners sampling the varied Thai menu (no food Sun). The public bar is popular with locals.
🏚 Q ❀ ◑ ▶ 🍴 ♿ ♣ P

WHITE HORSE
Village Lane ☎ (01753) 643225
11-3, 5.30-11; 11-11 Sat; 12-10.30 Sun
Greene King IPA; guest beers Ⓖ
Traditional, family-owned free house, popular with visitors and locals alike. A comfortable lounge bar and a stone-floored public bar create a relaxing atmosphere. Six guest beers and a beer festival held spring bank holiday. An excellent starting/finishing point for ramblers. Eve meals Fri-Sat.
🏚 Q ❀ ◑ ▶ 🍴 ♿ ♣ ⌂ P

HIGH WYCOMBE

ROSE & CROWN
Desborough Road
☎ (01494) 527982
11.30-3, 5-11; 11-11 Fri & Sat; 12-10.30 Sun
Courage Best Bitter; Gales HSB; Marston's Pedigree; Wadworth 6X; guest beers Ⓗ
Wycombe's most interesting selection of beers in an L-shaped corner pub with a busy lunchtime office trade (no food weekends).
◑ ≠ ♣

WYCOMBE WINES
20 Crendon Street
☎ (01494) 437228
10-10; 12-2, 7-10 Sun
Adnams Broadside; Brakspear Special; Fuller's ESB; Hook Norton Old Hooky; guest beer Ⓖ
Popular off-licence with five or six beers and more at weekends; English bottle-conditioned beers are a speciality.≠

IBSTONE

FOX
The Common (off M40 jct 5)
OS752939 ☎ (01491) 638289
11-3, 6-11; 12-3, 6-10.30 Sun
Brakspear Bitter; Fuller's London Pride; guest beers Ⓗ

A popular pub offering high quality hotel accommodation and food in both bar and restaurant; also a large garden in superb countryside.
🏚 Q ❀ ⇌ ◑ P ⊁

IVINGHOE

ROSE & CROWN
Vicarage Lane (right opp church, then first right)
☎ (01296) 668472
12-2.30 (3 Sat), 6-11; 12-3, 7-10.30 Sun
Adnams Bitter; Greene King IPA; Morrells Mild; guest beer Ⓗ
Hard-to-find, street-corner local with a comfortable lounge and a lively atmosphere in bars on different levels. High quality food is reasonably priced (no meals Wed lunch or Sun eve).
🏚 Q ❀ ◑ ▲ ♣

LITTLE MARLOW

KING'S HEAD
Church Road ☎ (01628) 484407
11-3, 5.30-11; 11-11 Sat; 12-10.30 Sun
Brakspear Bitter; Flowers Original; Fuller's London Pride; Wadworth 6X; guest beers Ⓗ
Village pub of much character. Varied, home-cooked meals always available, along with six ales. Families welcome. Wheelchair WC.
🏚 ❀ ◑ ▶ ♿ P ⊁

LITTLE MISSENDEN

CROWN
Off A413
☎ (01494) 862571
11-2.30, 6-11; 12-3, 7-10.30 Sun
Adnams Broadside; Morrells Varsity; Hook Norton Best Bitter; guest beer Ⓗ
Fine, traditional pub with a genuine welcome; in the same family for nearly 100 years. Good wholesome food with prompt service. Occasionally has a beer on gravity dispense. There is a large garden.
🏚 Q ❀ ◑ ♣ P

LITTLEWORTH COMMON

BLACKWOOD ARMS
Common Lane OS936861
☎ (01753) 642169
11-2.30, 5.30-11; 11-11 Fri & Sat; 12-10.30 Sun
Beer range varies Ⓗ
A beer drinker's oasis on the fringes of Burnham Beeches – well worth the search. Renowned for selling over 1,000 real ales in a year; the present landlord keeps up the tradition. Good value food means it is a very popular pub all the year round.
🏚 Q ❀ ◑ ▶ ⌂ P

LOUDWATER

DEREHAMS INN
5 Derehams Lane OS903907
☎ (01494) 530965
11-3, 5.30-11; 12-3, 7-10.30 Sun
Brakspear Bitter; Fuller's London Pride; Taylor Landlord; Wadworth 6X; Young's Bitter; guest beers Ⓗ
Cosy pub, recently extended. Hard to find so mainly geared to a local trade. Small car park. Weekday lunches.
❀ ◑ ♣ P

MARLOW

CARPENTERS ARMS
15 Spittal Street
☎ (01628) 473649
11-11; 12-10.30 Sun
Morrells Bitter, Varsity Ⓗ
Thriving workingman's local of considerable character. Acquired by Morrells in 1992. A variety of fresh home-made sandwiches always available.
🏚 ❀ ≠ ♣

CLAYTON ARMS
16 Oxford Road, Quoiting Square
☎ (01628) 478620
11-3, 5.30-11; 11-3.30, 6-11 Sat; 12-3.30, 7-10.30 Sun
Brakspear Bitter, Special, seasonal beers Ⓗ
Genuine local, unspoilt by its refurbishment. The public bar atmosphere has been retained (darts at one end); the function room doubles for families and a no-smoking area for lunchtime food. (No Sun meals in winter.)
🏚 Q ❀ ◑ ≠ ♣

PRINCE OF WALES
1 Mill Road
☎ (01628) 482970
11-11; 12-10.30 Sun
Brakspear Bitter; Fuller's London Pride; guest beers Ⓗ
Friendly, back-street local with two connecting bars: comfortable public and a lounge with a dining area (families welcome). No food Sun eve. Constantly changing range of four real ales.
❀ ◑ ▶ ≠ ♣ P

MARSH GIBBON

GREYHOUND
West Edge ☎ (01869) 277365
12-3.30, 6-11; 12-4, 7-10.30 Sun
Fuller's London Pride; Greene King IPA, Abbot; Hook Norton Best Bitter Ⓗ
Listed building, probably of Tudor origin, with 17th-century brickwork, rebuilt after a fire in 1740, it still bears the fire plaque of Sun Insurance. Specialising in Thai cuisine, it is also popular for steaks and quick business lunches.
🏚 Q ❀ ◑ ▶ P ⊟

MILTON KEYNES: BRADWELL VILLAGE

PRINCE ALBERT
Vicarage Rd ☎ (01908) 312080
11-3, 5.30-11; 12-3, 7-10.30 Sun
Wells Eagle, Bombardier; guest beers ⊞
Large, comfortable bar on two levels; a Victorian building in an older village with a warm, friendly atmosphere and children's outdoor play area. No food Sun.
❀ ◖ ▶ P

FENNY STRATFORD

BRIDGE INN
12-14 Watling Street
☎ (01908) 373107
11-11 (midnight Wed, 1am Fri & Sat); 12-10.30 Sun
B&T Shefford Bitter; Boddingtons Bitter; Wells Eagle, Bombardier ⊞
Welcoming canalside pub: an open-plan lounge-style bar area. An outside terrace offers access to canalside seating and moorings. The conservatory is also used for meetings. Good food (no eve meals Sat-Sun); book Sun lunch. Disco Wed, Karaoke Fri-Sun, live bands Sat. Over 20's only. ♨ ❀ ◖ ▶ ₰ ♣ P

NEW BRADWELL

NEW INN
Bradwell Rd ☎ (01908) 312094
11.30-11; 12-10.30 Sun
Adnams Broadside; Morland Old Speckled Hen; Wells Eagle, Bombardier; guest beer ⊞
Popular, two-bar canalside inn. The large bar menu offers daily specials. Pets' corner in garden.
❀ ◖ ▶ ⊞ ₰ (Wolverton) P

SHENLEY LODGE

OLD BEAMS
Paxton Crescent, off Clegg Square (off Fulmer St, Faraday Drive) ☎ (01908) 201054
11-3, 5.30-11; 11-11 Fri & Sat; 12-10.30 Sun
Courage Directors; McMullen AK, Gladstone, seasonal beers ⊞
Old extended farmhouse with a good atmosphere, soon to be surrounded by new houses. Very good restaurant; bar meals as well. The large garden, with ponds and trees, is popular on weekends. ♨❀◖▶♿P⊁

Try also: Burnt Oak, Egerton Gate, Shelley Brook End (Banks's)

STONY STRATFORD

FOX & HOUNDS
87 High Street ☎ (01908) 563307
12-2.30, 5-11; 11-11 Fri & Sat; 12-2.30, 7-10.30 Sun

Courage Directors; guest beers ⊞
Friendly community pub in this historic market town High Street. Darts and local skittles played. Live blues, folk and jazz Thu and Sat. Offers 'international' dinners twice-monthly; no food Sun.
Q ❀ ◖ ⊞ ₰ P ⛨

VAULTS BAR (BULL HOTEL)
64 High Street ☎ (01908) 567104
12-11; 12-10.30 Sun
Draught Bass; Eldridge Pope Royal Oak; Fuller's London Pride; Wadworth 6X; Worthington Bitter; guest beers ⊞
Traditional market town drinking den, sports oriented; it forms part of a larger complex with various restaurants including Spanish and Mexican.
❀ ⇔ ◖ ▶ ♣ P

NEWPORT PAGNELL

BULL
33 Tickford Street (between Iron Bridge and Aston Martin motorworks) ☎ (01908) 610325
11.30-2.30, 5.15-11; 11.30-3, 6.15-11 Sat; 12-3, 6-10.30 Sun
Guest beers ⊞
Splendidly unmodernised, very popular free house. A permanent beer festival. The house beer, Life's a Bitch, is from Morrells. Two smallish bars and a smaller pool room – can get very crowded. Good value varied menu (no meals Sun eve). Cider in summer.
Q ❀ ⇔ ◖ ▶ ⊞ Ⓐ ♣ ⟲ P

GREEN MAN
92 Silver Street (down Station Rd, off High St)
☎ (01908) 611914
12-11; 12-10.30 Sun
Banks's Mild (occasional), **Bitter; guest beers** ⊞
Marvellously traditional workman's back-street boozer where no-one's a stranger for long. Family-owned and run: a rumbustious public bar with lots of games, the quiet lounge has two coal fires and a fascinating clutter of clocks and bric-à-brac. Well worth finding.
♨ Q ⇔ ⊞ Ⓐ ♣

Try also: Cannon, 50 High Street (Free)

NORTH CRAWLEY

COCK INN
16 High Street ☎ (01234) 391222
11-3, 6-11; 12-3, 7-10.30 Sun
Adnams Broadside; Morland Old Speckled Hen; Wells Eagle ⊞
Traditional village inn, the large lounge bar includes a restaurant. Selection of paintings by local

artists for sale.
♨ Q ❀ ⇔ ◖ ▶ ⊞ ♣ P

PRESTON BISSETT

OLD HAT
Main Street ☎ (01280) 848335
11.30-2 (2.30 Sat), 6 (5 Fri)-11; 12-2.30, 7-10.30 Sun
Hook Norton Mild, Best Bitter; guest beers (summer) ⊞
Part-thatched, single bar, 16th-century village pub, very friendly. Home-cooked lunches (no meals Sun). ♨ Q ❀ ◖ ♣ ⟲ P

QUAINTON

WHITE HART
4 The Strand ☎ (01296) 655234
12-2, 5.30-11; 12-3, 7-11 Sat; 12-3, 7-10.30 Sun
ABC Bitter; Fuller's London Pride; guest beer ⊞
1930s ex-Chesham and Brackley two-bar village pub, featuring transport memorabilia behind the bar and a vintage bus in the car park. North Bucks Way long distance footpath goes through the garden. No food Mon or Thu eves.♨ ❀ ⇔ ◖ ▶ P

STEWKLEY

SWAN
High Street North
☎ (01525) 240285
12-3, 6-11; 12-3, 7-10.30 Sun
Courage Best Bitter, Directors; guest beer ⊞
Fine Georgian village pub, enjoying a good atmosphere in an old beamed interior with a separate dining area (no food Sun eve). Monthly live music on Sun eve.
❀ ◖ ▶ ♣ P

STOKE GOLDINGTON

LAMB
20 High Street ☎ (01908) 551233
12-3, 5-11; 12-3, 7-10.30 Sun
Draught Bass; Fuller's London Pride; Hook Norton Best Bitter; ⊞
Comfortable free house in a very attractive village: a youth-oriented public bar, a relaxed lounge and a dining area. The trapdoor to the cellar is in front of the lounge bar – it can be disconcerting when it suddenly opens at your feet! No food Sun eve.
♨ Q ⚲ ❀ ◖ ▶ ⊞ ♣ P

STOKE POGES

ROSE & CROWN
Hollybush Hill ☎ (01753) 662148
11-3, 5.30-11; 11.30-3, 7-11 Sat; 12-4, 7-10.30 Sun
Adnams Broadside; Morland Original, Old Speckled Hen, seasonal beers ⊞
Cosy, welcoming, pre-war pub with two bar areas, frequented mainly by locals. ❀ ◖ ♣ P

SWAN BOTTOM

OLD SWAN
OS902055
☎ (01494) 837239
12-3, 6-11; 12-11 Sat; 12-10.30 Sun
Adnams Bitter; Brakspear Bitter; Fuller's London Pride; guest beer Ⓗ
Old country pub, tucked away in the Chilterns in a lovely setting; large garden. Opening times may vary. ⚄ Q ⚘ ◖▶ ♣ P

THE LEE

COCK & RABBIT
Signed off A413
☎ (01494) 837540
12-2.30 (3 Sat), 6-11; 12-3, 7-10.30 Sun
Fuller's London Pride; Morland Old Speckled Hen; Ruddles Best Bitter; guest beer Ⓗ
Large pub with a snug and friendly public bar, set in a picturesque Chiltern village. Try the Italian food. The house beer is from an unnamed brewer.
⚄ Q ⚘ ◖▶ ♿ ♣ P ⌧

THORNBOROUGH

LONE TREE
Bletchley Road (A421, 2 miles E of Buckingham)
☎ (01280) 812334
11.30-3, 5.30-11; 12-4, 5-10.30 Sun
Black Sheep Bitter; Adnams Beechwood Bitter; Hook Norton Best Mild, guest beers Ⓗ
17th-century, one-bar pub, popular with diners, it gets very crowded. Stocks a good range of bottled beers.
⚄ Q ⚘ ◖▶ ♣ ⌂ P ⌧ ☗

TURVILLE

BULL & BUTCHER
Off M40 jct 5, (through Ibstone, right at foot of hill) OS768911
☎ (01491) 638283
11-3, 6-11; 12-3, 7-10.30 Sun
Brakspear Mild, Bitter, Old, Special, seasonal beers Ⓗ
Welcoming, unspoilt country pub in most attractive countryside, first licensed in 1617. The extensive menu includes vegetarian dishes; meals are cooked to order. HQ of the local MG Car Club. ⚄ Q ⚘ ◖▶ ▣ ♣ P

WADDESDON

THE LION
High Street ☎ (01296) 651227
12-2.30, 5.30-11; 12-3, 7-10.30 Sun
Draught Bass; Fuller's London Pride; guest beer Ⓗ
Free house specialising in quality meals, served at a leisurely pace. Ample portions and plenty of elbow room at the large wooden tables (no meals Sun eve).
⚄ Q ⚘ ◖▶ P

WEEDON

FIVE ELMS
Stockaway ☎ (01296) 641439
12-2.30 (3.30 Sat), 6-11; 12-4, 7-10.30 Sun
Ansells Bitter; Greene King IPA; Wadworth 6x; guest beer Ⓗ
Charming, 16th-century house with small bars and a fire in each. The pub's history has been published in a 40-page book. Handy for walkers on the Aylesbury Ring. No meals Sun, or Tue eve. ▶ ◖ ⚘ ☞ Q ⚄

WEST WYCOMBE

GEORGE & DRAGON
☎ (01494) 464414
12-2.30 (3 Sat), 5.30-11; 12-3, 7-10.30 Sun
Courage Best Bitter; guest beers Ⓗ
18th-century coaching inn with original timbered bar. Two of its bedrooms have four-poster beds. Noted for its food. Excellent garden.⚄ Q ☞ ⚘ ⇔ ◖▶ P

WESTON TURVILLE

CHANDOS ARMS
Main Street ☎ (01296) 613532
11.30-11; 12-10.30 Sun
Benskins BB; Flowers Original; Tetley Bitter Ⓗ
Friendly local at the western end of the village, with three distinct areas: a lower bar with dartboard and main bar leading to a newly extended dining area. Limited parking.⚘ ◖▶ P

WEXHAM STREET

PLOUGH
N of Wexham Park Hospital OS989835 ☎ (01753) 663814
11-11; 12-10.30 Sun
Benskins BB; Greene King Abbot; Marston's Pedigree; guest beer Ⓗ
Originally three cottages, circa 17th century, with a listed frontage. Children are welcome in restaurant for meals (no food winter Sun eve). Roadside tables provide outdoor drinking.
⚄ ⚘ ◖▶ ♣ P ⌧

WHEELER END

CHEQUERS
Bullocks Farm Lane OS806926
☎ (01494) 883070
11-2.30 (not Mon), 5.30-11; 11-11 Sat; 12-10.30 Sun
Adnams Broadside; Draught Bass; Brains Dark; Brakspear Bitter; Fuller's London Pride; Greene King IPA Ⓗ
350-year-old country pub just over the motorway from Lane End; difficult to find but worth buying a map for. Try Patsy's platefuls Tue-Sat lunchtimes.
⚄ Q ⚘ ◖▶ ♣ P

WHITCHURCH

WHITE SWAN
10 High Street ☎ (01296) 641228
11-11; 12-3, 7-10.30 Sun
Fuller's Chiswick, London Pride, ESB, seasonal beers Ⓗ
Attractive, part-thatched 16th-century pub with a large mature garden. It boasts distinctive wood panelling in the lounge bar; small dining/meeting room (no meals Sun eve).
⚄ Q ⚘ ◖▶ ▣ ♣ P

WING

COCK
High Street ☎ (01296) 688214
11.30-3, 6-11; 12-3.30, 7-10.30 Sun
Courage Directors; Theakston Best Bitter; guest beers Ⓗ
Former coaching inn, partly dating back to the 16th century. It stocks six ales with a bias towards microbreweries. Seasonal beer festivals are held. The restaurant offers an extensive menu. ⚄ Q ⚘ ◖▶ ♿ ♣ P

WINGRAVE

ROSE & CROWN
The Green ☎ (01296) 681257
11.30-3, 5.30-11 (11.30-11 Sat); 12-10.30 Sun
ABC Best Bitter; Adnams Bitter; Marston's Pedigree; guest beer Ⓗ
Excellent, unspoilt, early 17th-century, three-bar local with a stone-flagged public bar, a small snug and a lounge. No meals Sun eve. ⚄ Q ◖▶ ▣ ♣ P

WYCOMBE MARSH

GENERAL HAVELOCK
114 Kingsford Road OS889915
☎ (01494) 520391
11-2.30, 5.30-11; 11-3, 5-11 Fri; 12-4, 7-10.30 Sun
Fuller's Chiswick, London Pride, ESB, seasonal beers Ⓗ
Traditional family pub, smart and friendly, noted for its lunches. Evening meals served until 9 Fri and Sat (can be booked other days). ⚄ ⚘ ◖▶ ♣ P

INDEPENDENT BREWERIES

Chiltern:
Aylesbury
Rebellion:
Marlow
Trueman's:
Medmenham
Vale:
Haddenham

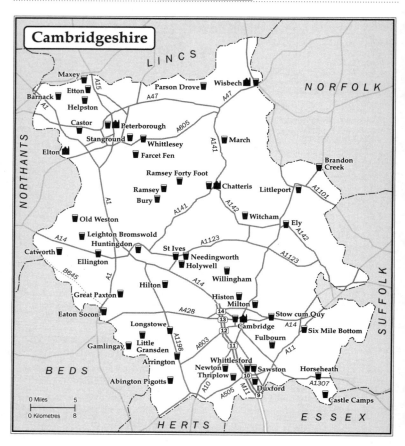

Cambridgeshire

L I N C S

NORFOLK

NORTHANTS

SUFFOLK

BEDS

HERTS

ESSEX

Maxey
Etton
Barnack
Helpston
Castor
Stanground
Elton
Peterborough
Whittlesey
Farcet Fen
Parson Drove
Wisbech
March
Brandon Creek
Ramsey Forty Foot
Ramsey
Bury
Chatteris
Littleport
Old Weston
Witcham
Ely
Leighton Bromswold
Huntingdon
Catworth
Ellington
St Ives
Needingworth
Holywell
Willingham
Hilton
Histon
Milton
Great Paxton
Stow cum Quy
Eaton Socon
Longstowe
Cambridge
Six Mile Bottom
Gamlingay
Little Gransden
Fulbourn
Arrington
Whittlesford
Newton
Thriplow
Sawston
Horseheath
Abington Pigotts
Duxford
Castle Camps

0 Miles 5
0 Kilometres 8

ABINGTON PIGOTTS

PIG & ABBOT
High Street (off A505 towards Litlington, follow the signs to the village)
OS530244
☎ (01763) 853515
12-3, 7-11; 12-10.30 Sun
Tetley Bitter; guest beers Ⓗ
Superb, welcoming village pub saved from closure when it was bought in October 1997 by the villagers. Guest beers are mostly from small micros and the house beer is brewed by Mansfield. Well worth finding. Lunches Wed-Sun, eve meals Wed-Sat.
🏚 ❀ ◖ ▶ ♣ P

ARRINGTON

HARDWICKE ARMS
Ermine Way (A1198)
☎ (01223) 208802
11-3, 7-11; 12-3, 7-11 Sun
Adnams Bitter; Greene King IPA; Hook Norton Old Hooky Ⓗ
Warm, comfortable hotel bar in a roadside inn. Popular with local and passing trade alike.
Q ➰ ⇌ ◖ ▶ P ⽊

BARNACK

MILLSTONE
Millstone Lane (lane opp Hills and Hollows Common)
☎ (01780) 740296
11-2.30, 5.30-11; 12-4, 7-10.30 Sun
Adnams Bitter; Everards Tiger, Old Original; guest beer Ⓗ
Friendly local, celebrating its 24th year in this *Guide*. This 300-year-old pub features horse brasses and yokes and attractive floral displays above the fire. It offers country wines and an extensive restaurant menu.
Wheelchair WC
Q ➰ ❀ ◖ ▶ ⅆ P ⽊

BRANDON CREEK

SHIP
On A10 ☎ (01353) 676228
11-3, 6-11; 12-3, 7-10.30 Sun
Beer range varies Ⓗ
Smart, friendly riverside inn, where the six handpumps often feature local brews; cider in summer. The opening hours are subject to seasonal variations.
🏚 ❀ ◖ ▶ ⇪ P

BURY

WHITE LION
Upwood Road (B1040, E end of village) ☎ (01487) 813452
12-2.30, 5-11; 12-4, 7-11 Sat & Sun
Courage Directors; John Smith's Bitter; Webster's Yorkshire Bitter; guest beers Ⓗ
Traditional village local, just outside Ramsey, with a restaurant (no food Mon or Tue). Noted for interesting guest ales.
🏚 Q ❀ ◖ ▶ ⅆ ♣ P ⽥

CAMBRIDGE

CAMBRIDGE BLUE
85-87 Gwydir Street (off Mill Rd)
☎ (01223) 361382
12-2.30 (4 Sat), 6-11; 12-3, 7-10.30 Sun
Nethergate IPA, Bitter, Golden Gate, Old Growler; guest beers Ⓗ
Characterful, terraced pub where a no-smoking bar, a tiny snug and conservatory complement the main bar. The large garden features a model railway. Children's certificate. Guest beers always include a mild.
🏚 Q ➰ ❀ ◖ ▶ ⇌ ♣ ⇪ ⽊

CASTLE
38 Castle Street
☎ (01223) 353194
11.30-3, 5(6.30 Sat)-11; 12-3,
6.30-10.30 Sun
**Adnams Bitter, Extra, Broadside;
Draught Bass; Marston's
Pedigree; Wadworth 6X; guest
beers** Ⓗ
Adnams' western flagship is a
superb example of sensitive
renovation. There are five drinking areas on the ground floor and
more upstairs. The patio is a real
sun trap.
🏚 ➔ 🅦 ◖ ▶ ✖

COW & CALF
14 Pound Hill
☎ (01223) 576220
12-3, 5-11; 12.30-3, 7-11 Sat;
12-3, 7-10.30 Sun
**Elgood's Cambridge; Mauldons
Moletrap; Nethergate Bitter;
York Yorkshire Terrier; guest
beers** Ⓗ
A traditional pub atmosphere
prevails in one of the city's few
true free houses, which is also
inhabited by four pub cats. There
are good value lunches (not
served Sat or Sun).
🏚 🅦 ◖ ♣

ELM TREE
42 Orchard Street
☎ (01223) 363005
12-3, 4.30-11; 11-11 Fri; 12.30,
7-10.30 Sun
**Adnams Broadside; Badger
Tanglefoot; Wells Eagle,
Bombardier** Ⓗ
Relaxed, old-fashioned, living-
room atmosphere complete with
a large fish tank, at this popular
local. Live jazz Thu. New patio
garden. Filled rolls and baguettes
at lunchtime.
🅦 ċ ♣

EMPRESS
72 Thoday Street (off Mill Rd)
☎ (01223) 247236
11-2.30, 6.30-11; 12-2.30,
7-10.30 Sun
**Castle Eden Ale; Flowers
Original; Marston's Pedigree;
guest beers** Ⓗ
Thriving back-street pub: surprisingly large, it has three distinct
drinking areas plus a space for
games. Conversation prevails
over the jukebox.
🅦 ♣ ċ

FREE PRESS
Prospect Row
☎ (01223) 368337
12-2.30, 6-11; 12-3, 7-10.30 Sun
**Greene King XX Mild, IPA,
Abbot** Ⓗ
Unspoilt back-street gem, completely no-smoking and with a
very snug snug. Food includes
unusual vegetarian options; eve
meals finish at 8.30.
🏚 Q 🅦 ◖ ▶ ✖

JUG & FIRKIN (OFF LICENCE)
90 Mill Road
☎ (01223) 315034
10.30-10; 10-10.30 Sat; 12-2.30,
7-9.30 Sun
Beer range varies Ⓖ
Off-licence offering a staggering
selection of bottled beers (many
bottle-conditioned) plus at least
five real ales and various ciders.
➤ ċ

LIVE & LET LIVE
40 Mawson Road (off Mill Road)
☎ (01223) 460261
11.30 (12 Sat)-2.30; 5.30 (6 Sat)-
11; 12-2.30, 7-10.30 Sun
**Adnams Bitter; B&T Edwin
Taylor's Extra Stout; Bateman
Mild; Everards Tiger; Nethergate
Umbel Ale; guest beers** Ⓗ
Cosy, friendly, gas-lit back-street
pub, popular with regulars, students and tourists. Brunos Bitter
is brewed specially by B&T. Live
music most Sun eves.
🏚 Q 🅦 ◖ 🅖 ✖ ➤ ċ ✖

ST RADEGUND
129 King Street
☎ (01223) 311794
12-2.30, 5.30-11; 12-11 Sun;
6-10.30 Sun
**Adnams Bitter; Fuller's London
Pride; Shepherd Neame Spitfire;
guest beer** Ⓗ
Proof that size isn't everything;
quiet at lunchtime, boisterous
eves, this pub is welcoming
always. Swap your traveller's
tales with the landlord and
locals.

WRESTLERS
337 Newmarket Road
☎ (01223) 566554
12-3, 5-11; 12-3, 7-10.30 Sun
**Adnams Broadside; Badger
Tanglefoot; Morland Old
Speckled Hen; Wells Eagle,
Bombardier, Fargo** Ⓗ
Lively and accommodating town
pub. Very green, following a sympathetic refurbishment which
gives more comfort without loss
of essential character. Thai food
is cooked to order by Thai chefs
and served at tables lit by
candlelight. Annual 'Hash Run'
in November.
🏚 ◖ ▶ ċ

CASTLE CAMPS

COCK
High Street
☎ (01799) 584207
12-2, 7-11; 12-11 Sat; 12-3,
7-10.30 Sun
**Greene King IPA, Abbot;
Nethergate Bitter; guest beer** Ⓗ
Well worth a diversion off the
beaten track to find this friendly,
two-bar local. Monthly folk
nights.
🏚 🅦 ◖ ▶ 🅖 ♣ P

CASTOR

ROYAL OAK
24 Peterborough Road
☎ (01733) 380217
12-2.30 (3 summer), 5-11; 11-11
Fri & Sat; 12-10.30 Sun
**Ind Coope Burton Ale; Tetley
Bitter; guest beers** Ⓗ
Rural, 17th-century thatched pub
with a cosy atmosphere generated by the open fires, low,
beamed ceilings and maze of
passages and rooms. Lunches
served Tue-Sat.
🏚 Q 🅦 ◖ 🅖 P

CATWORTH

RACEHORSE
High Street (B660, off A14)
☎ (01832) 710262
11-3, 6-11; 11-11 Sat; 12-10.30
Sun
**Marston's Pedigree; Theakston
Best Bitter; Wadworth 6X; guest
beer** Ⓗ
Smart village pub with a restau-
rant serving unusual food. Chess
and bridge nights held.
🏚 Q 🅦 ◖ ▶ 🅖 🄰 ♣ P

CHATTERIS

HONEST JOHN
24-26 South Park Street
☎ (01354) 692698
11-2.30, 5.30-11; 12-2.30,
5.30-10.30 Sun
Marston's Bitter; guest beers Ⓗ
Former labour exchange, now a
comfortable pub with a large,
well-divided main room and a
dining area. The landlord is interested in foreign beers. Bar billiards played.
🅦 ◖ ▶ ♣ P

DUXFORD

PLOUGH
St Peters Street
☎ (01223) 833170
11-3, 5.30-11; 11-11 Sat; 12-3,
7-10.30 Sun
**Adnams Bitter; Everards Tiger,
Old Original, seasonal beers;
guest beers** Ⓗ
17th-century thatched village
local, convenient for the Aircraft
Museum. Food at reasonable
prices (eve meals Tue-Sat).
🏚 🅦 ◖ ▶ P

EATON SOCON

MILLERS ARMS
38 Ackerman Street (off Gt North
Rd, B1428)
☎ (01480) 405965
11-3, 5-11; 11-11 Fri & Sat;
12-10.30 Sun
**Greene King XX Mild, IPA,
Abbot, seasonal beers** Ⓗ
Small pub on the larger of Eaton
Socon's greens. The spacious
garden boasts many children's

facilities and a petanque court; barbecues with live jazz held in summer. Popular with boat-owners from the nearby river. No eve meals Sun.
🏾 Q ⊛ ◖ ▮ ♣

ELLINGTON

MERMAID
High Street (off A14)
☎ (01480) 891450
12-2.30, 7-11; 12-3, 7-10.30 Sun
Draught Bass; guest beer Ⓗ
Unspoilt, single room village pub with a friendly welcome.
Q ⊛ 🛏 ◖ ♣

ELY

FOUNTAIN
1 Silver Street
☎ (01353) 663122
5-11 (closed lunch) Mon-Fri; 12-2, 6-11 Sat; 12-2, 7-10.30 Sun
Adnams Bitter, Broadside; Fuller's London Pride; Woodforde's Wherry; guest beer Ⓗ
Well refurbished local, handy for the Cathedral. CAMRA Cambridgeshire *Pub of the Year* 1997. Children's certificate.
🏾 Q ⊛ ⇌

PRINCE ALBERT
62 Silver Street
☎ (01353) 663494
11.30-3.30, 6.30-11; 12-3.30, 7-10.30 Sun
Greene King XX Mild, IPA, Abbot, seasonal beers Ⓗ
Classic town local with the emphasis on good ale and chat. You can bring your own food into the delightful garden as long as drinks are bought. Public car park opposite. No lunches Sun.
Q ⊛ ◖ ⇌

WEST END HOUSE
16 West Fen Road
☎ (01353) 662907
11-2.30 (3 Sat), 6-11; 12-3, 7-10.30 Sun
Courage Directors; Marston's Pedigree; Ruddles Best Bitter; Theakston XB; Webster's Yorkshire Bitter Ⓗ
An unspoilt tumble of drinking areas with low ceilings, beams and brasses. The cat declined to be interviewed.
🏾 ⊛ 占 ♣

ETTON

GOLDEN PHEASANT
1 Main Road (next to A15 – take turn for Helpston then first right)
☎ (01733) 252387
11.30-11; 12-10.30 Sun
Greene King IPA; Taylor Landlord; Woodforde's Wherry; guest beers Ⓗ
Large, 19th-century manor house with a comfortable lounge dis-

playing paintings for sale. It also has a family room and restaurant, a large garden with a play area, aviary and a permanent marquee for functions.
🏾 Q 🛋 ⊛ 🛏 ◖ ▮ 占
🄰 ♣ P ♒

FARCET FEN

PLOUGH
Milk and Water Drove, Ramsey Road
☎ (01733) 844307
11-4, 6-11; closed Tue & Wed; 12-10.30 Sun
Bateman or **Elgood's Mild; John Smith's Bitter; guest beer** Ⓗ
Isolated fenland pub with a welcoming interior. Its new owners have expanded the adjoining restaurant (no food is available in the bar).
🏾 ⊛ ♣ P ♒

FULBOURN

SIX BELLS
9 High Street
☎ (01223) 880244
11.30-2.30, 6-11; 12-11 Sat; 12-10.30 Sun
Flowers IPA; Ind Coope Burton Ale; Young's Bitter; guest beer Ⓗ
Buoyant village pub, the centre of local activity. A cosy, smaller bar features an internal window; live jazz (Wed) and blues bands (Fri/Sat) in the main bar. The restaurant has been refurbished in cottage style for greater intimacy (no food Sun eve or Mon).
🏾 ⊛ ◖ 🄰 🄰 ♣ P

Try also: Bakers Arms, Hinton Rd (Greene King)

GAMLINGAY

COCK
25 Church Street
☎ (01767) 650255
11.30-3, 5.30-11; 11.30-11 Sat; 12-4, 7-10.30 Sun
Greene King IPA, Abbot; guest beer Ⓗ
Timber-framed pub of some interest: both bars have extensive wood panelling. Popular for food at weekends (eve meals Tue-Sat).
🏾 🛋 ⊛ ◖ ▮ 🄰 ♣ P

GREAT PAXTON

BELL
High Street
☎ (01480) 472265
11.30-2.30, 6-11; 11.30-11 Sat; 12-3, 7-10.30 Sun
Greene King IPA, Abbot, seasonal beers Ⓗ
Small village pub dating from the 19th century. No eve meals available on Sun.
🏾 ⊛ ◖ ▮ ♣ P

HELPSTON

BLUEBELL
10 Woodgate (200 yds off B1443)
☎ (01733) 252394
11-3, 6-11; 12-3, 7-10.30 Sun
Bateman XB; Draught Bass; John Smith's Bitter; guest beer Ⓗ
Stone-built, 17th-century free house near John Clare Cottage. A simple, traditional bar and a quiet, comfortable lounge boasting a large collection of teapots and toby jugs. The house beer, JC's Writer's Cramp, is brewed locally. A mini beer festival is held each year.
🏾 Q ⊛ 🄰 ♣ ◠ P ♒

HILTON

PRINCE OF WALES
Potton Road (B1040)
☎ (01480) 830257
11 (12 winter)-2.30 (3 Sat; closed Mon), 6 (7 winter Sat)-11; 12-3, 7-10.30 Sun
Adnams Bitter; Elgood's Black Dog, Mild; guest beer (occasional) Ⓗ
Welcoming two-bar village local with a large log fire. Good accommodation. No food Mon or winter Sun eve.
🏾 ⊛ 🛏 ◖ ▮ 🄰 占 ♣ P ♒

HISTON

RED LION
27 High Street
☎ (01223) 564437
11.30-3, 5-11; 11-11 Sat; 12-5, 7-10.30 Sun
Adnams Extra; Bateman Mild; Everards Tiger; guest beers Ⓗ
Bustling, characterful free house offering a choice between a comfy, newly-extended lounge and a boisterous public.
🏾 Q ⊛ ◖ 🄰 ♣ P

HOLYWELL

FERRYBOAT INN
(1 mile from Needingworth village, on the river)
☎ (01480) 463227
11-3, 6-11 (11-11 summer); 12-3, 7-10.30 Sun
Draught Bass; Nethergate IPA; guest beers Ⓗ
Claimed to be the oldest in England, now a sprawling, frequently extended, riverside inn with good food. Moorings, marina and a caravan park are nearby. Four guest beers usually available. Q 🛋 ⊛ 🛏 ◖ ▮ P ♒

HORSEHEATH

OLD RED LION
Linton Road
☎ (01223) 892909
11-11 ; 12-3, 7-10.30 Sun

Courage Directors; Ruddles County or John Smith's Bitter; Younger IPA; guest beer Ⓗ
Welcoming, stone-flagged inn, heavily timbered with lots of nooks and crannies. A blackboard menu describes the guest beer in detail; extensive newspaper table. The warm, splendid restaurant is replete with lamps, brasses and beams; six different specials to chose from at each meal (no food Sun eve).
🚪 ❀ 🍴 ◑ 🍺 ♣ P

HUNTINGDON

OLD BRIDGE HOTEL
1 High Street
☎ (01480) 452681
11-11; 12-10.30 Sun
Adnams Bitter; City of Cambridge Hobson's Choice; guest beer Ⓗ
Sumptuous splendour in this relaxing hotel bar with highly rated wine and beer. This handsome 18th-century, ivy-clad building was originally a bank.
🚪 Q ❀ 🚪 ◑ 🍺 ⇌ P

LEIGHTON BROMSWOLD

GREEN MAN
37 The Avenue
☎ (01480) 890238
12-3 (not Mon-Thu), 7-11 (not Mon); 12-3, 7-10.30 Sun
Fuller's London Pride Ⓗ; Nethergate IPA Ⓖ; Shepherd Neame Spitfire; guest beer Ⓗ
Welcoming, genuine, village free house with a relaxing atmosphere and a firm focus on good interesting beers. Also popular for food, Fri and Sat (no eve meals Sun). Northants skittles and bar billiards played.
🐌 ❀ ◑ ♣ P

LITTLE GRANSDEN

CHEQUERS
71 Main Road
☎ (01767) 677348
12-2, 7-11; 11-11 Sat; 12-3, 7-10.30 (maybe all day) Sun
Adnams Bitter; guest beer Ⓗ
This friendly, welcoming rural pub is well worth searching for. A rare, rustic gem.
🚪 🐌 ❀ 🚪 ♣ P

LITTLEPORT

CROWN INN
34 Main Street
☎ (01353) 860202
12-2.30, 5-11; 11-11 Sat; 12-3, 7-10.30 Sun
Adnams Bitter; Boddingtons Bitter; Courage Directors; guest beers Ⓗ
Pleasantly appointed, one-bar pub with a dining area (no food Mon).
🐌 ❀ ◑ 🚪 ⇌ ♣ P ⚖

GEORGE & DRAGON
13 Station Road
☎ (01353) 862639
11-2 (not Wed), 4.30-11; 12-11 Sat; 12-3, 7-11 Sun
Badger Dorset Best; guest beers Ⓗ
Now boasting three rooms following refurbishment, this enterprising establishment continues to offer a relaxed, friendly atmosphere.
❀ 🚪 ◑ 🚪 ⇌ ♣ P

LONGSTOWE

GOLDEN MILLER
53 High Street
☎ (01954) 719385
12-2.30, 6.30-11; 12-3, 7-10.30 Sun
Adnams Bitter, Broadside; guest beer Ⓗ
Homely, family-run, free house. Home-cooked food to order can be eaten in the bar or restaurant - booking advisable Fri and Sat. A duck pond and aviary enliven the garden. Named after the 1934 Grand National Winner.
❀ ◑ 🍺 P 🍺

MARCH

ROSE & CROWN
41 St Peters Road
☎ (01354) 652879
12-2.30 (not Wed), 7-11; 12-3, 7-10.30 Sun
Beer range varies Ⓗ
Friendly, 150-year-old, traditional two-roomed pub, the only true free house in March. Always a good range of guest ales; the cider varies. Pool and darts in the bar.
Q ❀ ♣ ⌂ P ⚖ 🍺

MAXEY

BLUE BELL
37-39 High Street
☎ (01778) 348182
5.30-11; 12-5, 7-11 Sat; 12-5, 7-10.30 Sun
Fuller's London Pride; Marston's Bitter, Pedigree; guest beers Ⓗ
Imposing, 300-year-old building of local limestone. A pub for the last 100 years. The small front bar (no smoking) has hatch service and there is a larger, low-ceilinged beamed bar. Enthusiastic cask ale licensees have transformed this pub into a popular village local.
🚪 Q ❀ 🅰 ♣ P ⚖ 🍺

MILTON

WAGGON & HORSES
39 High Street ☎ (01223) 860313
12-3, 5-11; 12-11 Sat; 12-10.30 Sun
Bateman XB; guest beers Ⓗ
Offering five hand-pulled guest beers, five ciders from the cellar

and over 30 malt whiskies, this pub also has a no-smoking dining area. Occasional live music at weekends. Limited parking.
🚪 ❀ ◑ 🍺 ♣ ⌂ P ⚖

Try also: Lion & Lamb, High St (Whitbread)

NEEDINGWORTH

QUEENS HEAD
30 High Street (off A1123)
☎ (01480) 463946
12-11; 12-3, 7-10.30 Sun
Marston's Pedigree; Woodforde's Wherry; guest beers Ⓗ
Friendly, two-bar village local, with a strong dominoes following. Typically stocking a range of four guest beers, the handpumps are in the public bar. No food Wed, Sat lunch or Sun eve.
🚪 ❀ ◑ 🍺 ♣ P

NEWTON

QUEENS HEAD
☎ (01223) 870436
11.30-2.30, 6-11; 12-2.30, 7-10.30 Sun
Adnams Bitter, Broadside, seasonal beers Ⓖ
Unchanging as ever, one of the few 1950s pubs left in the country. Chess is more popular than dominoes at the moment. Outside drinking area is the village green.
🚪 Q ❀ ◑ 🍺 ♣ ⌂ P

OLD WESTON

SWAN
Main Street (B660, off A14)
☎ (01832) 293400
Closed lunch Mon-Fri, 6.30-11; 12-3, 7-11 Sat; 12-3, 7-10.30 Sun
Adnams Bitter, Broadside; Greene King Abbot; Hook Norton Old Hooky; Ruddles Best Bitter, County; guest beers Ⓗ
Characterful and welcoming village pub where the impressive beer range often includes a mild. Hood skittles played. Good value food. 🚪 Q 🐌 ❀ ◑ 🅰 ♣ P

PARSON DROVE

SWAN
Main Road (B1166/B1187 jct)
☎ (01945) 700291
12-3 (not Tue or Thu), 7-11; 12-3, 7-10.30 Sun
Elgood's Black Dog Mild, Cambridge; guest beer Ⓗ
Dating from 1541, this pub is largely unspoilt with a bar room, a small lounge and a dining room. Various games are played, including table billiards. Phone for accommodation and dining details as these can vary by season.
🚪 Q ❀ 🚪 ◑ 🍺 🚪 ♣ P

PETERBOROUGH

BLUE BELL
6 The Green, Werrington (½ mile
off A15)
☎ (01733) 571264
11-11; 12-3, 7-10.30 Sun
Elgood's Cambridge,
Greyhound Ⓗ
Attractive white building, circa
1890 (extended in 1985): a
friendly public bar and a very
comfortable lounge. Fresh food
is home-cooked daily by the
landlord who is fiercely
proud of the quality of his beer
and the presentation of his
meals (no food Wed eve).
The best pub in
Werrington.
❀ ◖ ▶ ⌺ ♣ P

BLUE BELL
Welland Road, Dogsthorpe
(1 mile off A15)
☎ (01733) 554890
11-3, 6-11; 12-3, 7-10.30 Sun
Elgood's Cambridge, Pageant
Ale, Golden Newt, Greyhound,
seasonal beers; guest
beers Ⓗ
One of the oldest pubs in
Peterborough, converted from a
farmhouse in 1665: two large
rooms with real fires; the
lounge has an oak panelled
snug. Five cask ales always
available, maybe more – the
best pint of Elgood's in
Peterborough.
🚶 ❀ ◖ ⌺ ♣ P ⊟

BOGARTS
17 North street (opp Queensgate
Shopping
complex)
☎ (01733) 703599
11-11; closed Sun
Draught Bass; Hop Back
Summer Lightning; Oakham
JHB; guest beers Ⓗ
The city's last remaining
Victorian building still in use as a
pub; six ales on offer for discerning drinkers. Small suntrap garden. No pool or jukebox, just
good ale.
❀ ◖ ⇌ ⊟

CHARTERS CAFE BAR
Town Bridge (S bank of river,
down steps)
☎ (01733) 315700
12-11; 12-10.30 Sun
Draught Bass; Everards Tiger;
Fuller's London Pride; Oakham
JHB, Bishops Farewell; guest
beers Ⓗ
Real ale flagship: a large converted Dutch barge. Its 12
handpumps served over 500
beers in 1997. Oakham Ales
Brewery's main outlet.
Restaurant on the upper deck.
The large garden is frequented
by hordes of rabbits.
❀ ◖ ▶ ⇌ ⊟

CHERRY TREE INN
9-11 Oundle Road, Woodston
(near town bridge)
☎ (01733) 703495
12-2, 6-11; 12-11 Sat; 12-10.30 Sun
Draught Bass; Marston's
Pedigree; Morland Old Specked
Hen; Tetley Bitter; guest beer Ⓗ
Refurbished pub which retains a
good community standing locally.
A varied food menu complements
the beer range. A popular weekend music venue with live bands.
🚶 ⇌ ❀ ◖ ▶ P

COACH & HORSES
39-41 High street, Fletton
☎ (01733) 343400
11.30-3, 5-11; 11-11 Fri & Sat;
12-10.30 Sun
Draught Bass; Morland Old
Speckled Hen; John Smith's
Bitter; Wadworth 6X; guest
beers Ⓗ
Friendly, two-roomed community
pub attracting all ages. Large
garden. 🚶 Q ❀ ◖ ▶ ⌺ ♣ P ⊟

HAND & HEART
12 Highbury Street (off Lincoln
Rd, A15) ☎ (01733) 707040
10.30-11; 12-4, 7-10.30 Sun
Bateman Mild, XXXB; John
Smith's Bitter, Magnet; Taylor
Landlord; guest beers Ⓗ
Classic, 2-roomed back-street
local. A 1930s pub with some
original features retained; note
the Warwicks windows. A lively
bar and a snug smoke room.
🚶 ❀ ⌺ ◖ ◠ ⊟

PALMERSTON ARMS
82 Oundle Road, Woodston
(½ mile from town bridge)
☎ (01733) 565865
11-11; 12-10.30 Sun
Bateman XB; Hopback Summer
Lightning; guest beers Ⓖ
Small, stone-built, two-roomed
local, serving an ever-changing
range of beers from small brewers, all direct from the cask. The
cider varies. Friendly atmosphere, worth finding; local
CAMRA *Pub of the Year* 1997.
Bottle-conditioned beers are a
new feature. Q ⌺ ◠

RAMSEY

JOLLY SAILOR
43 Great Whyte (B1040)
☎ (01487) 813388
11-3, 5.30 (7 Sat)-11; 12-3,
7-10.30 Sun
Flowers Original; Ind Coope
Burton Ale; Tetley Bitter; guest
beers Ⓗ
An absolute classic: good beer
and good conversation in a pub
full of copper, brass and pewter.
Friendly and unspoilt, it has no
food, music or other distractions
in any of the three bars. The
street door to the bar is extremely narrow. 🚶 Q ❀ ⌺ P ⊟

RAMSEY FORTY FOOT

GEORGE INN
11 Ramsey Road, Forty Foot
Bridge (3 miles NE of Ramsey on
B1096)
☎ (01487) 812275
12-4, 6-11; 12-2.30, 7-10.30 Sun
Beer range varies Ⓗ
Fen village free house with a
cosy, friendly atmosphere; a single room with inglenook and cosy
corners. Handy for anglers and
boaters on the Forty Foot Drain.
🚶 ❀ ♣ P

ST IVES

ROYAL OAK
13 Crown Street
☎ (01480) 462586
11-11; 12-4, 7-10.30 Sun
Benskins BB; Ind Coope Burton
Ale; Marston's Pedigree; Tetley
Bitter; guest beers Ⓗ
Popular Festival Alehouse with
two bars and up to 10 beers on
sale (sparklers removed on
request). Cheaper beer is available in two-pint jugs 5-7pm daily.
Regular beer festivals.
🚶 ◖ ♣ P

SAWSTON

GREYHOUND
2 High Street
☎ (01223) 832260
11-3, 5-11; 12-3, 7-10.30 Sun
Boddingtons Bitter; Flowers IPA,
Original; Fuller's London Pride;
Wadworth 6X; guest beer Ⓗ
Large, comfortable pub (the oldest in Sawston) with a spacious
conservatory-cum-dining area.
Children's garden. No food Sun
eve. 🚶 ❀ ◖ ▶ P

SIX MILE BOTTOM

GREEN MAN
London Road
☎ (01638) 570373
11.30-11; 4.30-7 Mon; 12-6 Sun
Adnams Bitter; Bateman Mild;
Belhaven 60/-; guest beers Ⓗ
Loyal local following attracted by
the random charm and easy-
going bustle at this genuine free
house. The beer choice reflects a
majority of driver customers. No
food Sun eve or Mon. Has a new
petanque pitch.
🚶 ❀ ◖ ▶ ♣ P

STANGROUND

WOOLPACK
29 North Street
☎ (01733) 554417
11-3, 5-11; 11-11 Fri & Sat;
12-10.30 Sun
Boddingtons Bitter; Brains
Bitter; Wadworth 6X; guest
beer Ⓗ
18th-century building on a much
older site. A locals' pub with its

Beers festivals are one of the best ways of sampling a wide range of ales – and are proving more and more popular. All over the country, and all year round, branches of the Campaign for Real Ale organise local festivals. Go along to one – you'll be hooked!

own moorings, making it popular with boaters. See the collection of old photos and militaria.
Q ⌛ ✿ ◖ ▶ ⊟ ♣

STOW CUM QUY

WHITE SWAN
Main Street
☎ (01223) 811821
11-3, 5.30-11; closed Mon. 12-3, 7-10.30 Sun
Adnams Bitter; Fuller's London Pride; Greene King IPA; Nethergate Bitter; guest beer Ⓗ
Fine village local, at the heart of the community. Doms and crib arouse strong feelings; no boring background music to detract from the nattering. Outstanding home-cooked meals are served in the bar or adjoining no-smoking restaurant.
✿ ◖ ▶ ♣ P

THRIPLOW

GREEN MAN
2 Lower Street (½ mile from A505 overlooking village green)
☎ (01763) 208855
12-2.30, 6-11; closed Tue; 12-3, 7-10.30 Sun
Taylor Landlord; guest beers Ⓗ
Newly refurbished village free house owned by West End musical director Roger Ward, and frequented by farmers, yachtsmen and artists. The large, landscaped garden features a chessboard. Catch the annual toad race (April). No meals Sun eve.
⚏ Q ✿ ◖ ▶ ⅙ P

WHITTLESEY

BRICKLAYERS ARMS
9 Station road
☎ (01733) 202593
11-3, 6.30-11; 12-3, 7-10.30 Sun
John Smith's Bitter; Theakston XB; Webster's Yorkshire Bitter; guest beer Ⓗ

Large bar, frequented by locals of all ages. Friendly atmosphere; strong language not tolerated. Also a small, quiet lounge. Close to the local council boat moorings.
⚏ Q ✿ ⊟ ⅙ ⇌ ♣ P ⊟

HERO OF ALIWAL
75 Church Street
☎ (01733) 203736
12-3 (not Mon), 7-11; 12-3, 7-10.30 Sun
Adnams Bitter; guest beer Ⓗ
Town pub, named after local hero Sir Harry Smith. A large locals' bar with a pool table and a newly extended restaurant. Petanque played.
Q ✿ ⇥ ◖ ▶ ⊟ ⅙ ⚑ ♣ P

WHITTLESFORD

BEES IN THE WALL
36 North Road (1½ miles off A505 towards Shelfords)
☎ (01223) 834289
12-2.30 (not Mon-Fri), 6-11; 12-4, 7-10.30 Sun
Draught Bass; City of Cambridge Hobson's Choice; Shepherd Neame Spitfire; Wadworth 6X; guest beers Ⓗ
Friendly village pub on the village outskirts, with large gardens. There really are bees in the wall.
⚏ ✿ ⊟ ♣ P

WILLINGHAM

THREE TUNS
Church Street
☎ (01954) 260437
11-2.30, 6-11; 12-2.30, 7-10.30 Sun
Greene King XX Mild, IPA, Abbot, seasonal beers Ⓗ
Unchanging epitome of the English village local. Basic lunchtime snacks are available.
Q ✿ ♣ P ⊟

WISBECH

ROSE TAVERN
53 North Brink
☎ (01945) 588335
12-2.30, 6 (5.30 Thu & Fri)-11; 12-3, 7-10.30 Sun
Butterknowle Banner Bitter; Everards Beacon; guest beers Ⓗ
Cosy, one-roomed pub on the riverside. A listed 200-year-old building close to Elgood's brewery and gardens. A May Bank Holiday beer festival is held in an outbuilding.
✿ ♣

WITCHAM

WHITE HORSE
7 Silver Street
☎ (01353) 778298
12-3 (not Mon), 6.30-11; 12-3, 7-10.30 Sun
Greene King IPA; Nethergate IPA; guest beers Ⓗ
Run with panache, this pub has gained a well-deserved reputation for both its food and ale. No meals Sun eve.
✿ ◖ ▶ ♣ P ⅙

INDEPENDENT BREWERIES

City of Cambridge:
Cambridge

Elgood's:
Wisbech

Fenland:
Chatteris

Oakham:
Peterborough

Rockingham Ales:
Elton

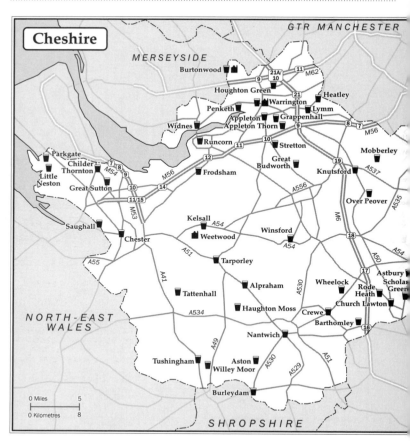

CHESHIRE ALPRAHAM

TRAVELLER'S REST ☆
Chester Road (A51)
☎ (01829) 260523
12-3 (not Mon-Fri), 6-11; 12-3,
7-10.30 Sun
**McEwan 70/-; Tetley Mild,
Bitter** Ⓗ
'Time-warp' pub whose interior
has remained unchanged since
the 1960s. One of the longest
listed pubs in this *Guide,* it has
won the local CAMRA *Pub of the
Year* award yet again. Bowling
green to the rear.
Q ❀ & ♣ P

APPLETON

BIRCHDALE HOTEL
Birchdale Road (off A49 at
London Bridge)
☎ (01925) 263662
6 (8.30 Fri & Sat)-11; 8.30-11 Sun
Boddingtons Bitter; guest beer Ⓗ
Quiet residential hotel with a
large comfortable lounge, a small
games/TV room and a large garden. A pleasant oasis an an area
dominated by themed Greenall's
outlets. Q ❀ 🛏 ♣ P ⛉

APPLETON THORN

APPLETON THORN
VILLAGE HALL
Stretton Road
☎ (01925) 261187
8.30-11 (not Mon-Wed);
8.30-10.30 Sun
Beer range varies Ⓗ
Increasingly popular, former
school converted to a village hall.
CAMRA *Club of the Year* 1995.
Also opens 12-3 alternate Suns.
It stocks six guest beers, usually
including a mild. Q ❀ & P

ASTBURY

EGERTON ARMS
Audley Road (off A34)
☎ (01260) 273946
11.30-11; 12-3, 7-10.30 Sun
Robinson's Best Bitter Ⓟ,
Frederics Ⓗ
Comfortable, roomy 14th-century
pub. It has six bedrooms and a
menu of home-cooked food in the
restaurant, including good vegetarian options. Children will enjoy
the play area in the garden,
which is fenced and safe.
🏚 Q 🛏 ❀ 🛏 ◖ ▶ P

ASTON

BHURTPORE INN
Wrenbury Road (off A530)
OS610469
☎ (01270) 780917
12-2.30 (3 Sat), 6.30-11; 12-3,
7-10.30 Sun
Hanby Drawwell; guest beers Ⓗ
A beer paradise in south
Cheshire: at least nine guest
cask ales, three changing
draught Belgian beers and a
huge range of bottled beers.
Food is high quality with all
main courses freshly made (curries a speciality). A good atmosphere and comfortable surroundings.
🏚 Q ❀ ◖ ▶ 🛏 & ⇌
(Wrenbury) ♣ ⌂ P

BARTHOMLEY

WHITE LION ☆
Audley Road (off B5078, ½ mile
from M6 jct 16)
☎ (01270) 882242
11.30 (5 Thu)-11; 12-10.30 Sun
**Burtonwood Bitter, Forshaw's,
Top Hat, Buccaneer** Ⓗ
Thatched half-timbered pub

dated 1614. A Grade II listed building opposite the village church, the scene of a Civil War massacre. Bunkhouse accommodation available – bring your own sleeping bag.
🏚 Q 🍺 ❀ ➡ ◖ 🍴 ♣ P

BOLLINGTON

MERIDIAN
48 Palmerston Street
☎ (01625) 573883
12-11; 12-10.30 Sun
Boddingtons Bitter; Theakston Mild; Wilson's Bitter ℍ
Wonderful, multi-roomed pub which time forgot, popular with all ages. Skittles played.
🏚 ♣

QUEENS
40 High Street
☎ (01625) 573068
2 (12 Fri & Sat)-11; 12-3, 7-10.30 Sun
Robinson's Hatters Mild, Best Bitter ℍ
Solidly built, stone pub. Set back slightly from the rest of the terrace and modernised in typical

Robinson's style. Very popular. Pavement tables. ❀ ◖ 🍴

Try also: Cotton Tree, Ingersley Rd (Vaux)

BURLEYDAM

COMBERMERE ARMS
On A525, ½ mile from A530 jct
☎ (01948) 871223
11 (12 winter)-11; 12-10.30 Sun
Draught Bass; Worthington Bitter; guest beers ℍ
Large country pub dating from the 16th century. Food is served all day Sat and Sun. There is a huge indoor play area for children. 🏚 Q 🍺 ❀ ◖ 🍴 ♣ P

BURTONWOOD

BRIDGE INN
Phipps Lane
☎ (01925) 225709
11.30-11; 12-10.30 Sun
Burtonwood Mild, Bitter ℍ
Four-roomed pub, a centre for a dozen local sports and games teams, with souvenirs of the licensee's RL days on display. The garden has a bowling green and a small play area for children, who may also go in the conservatory. Meals Mon-Fri.
🍺 ❀ ◖ ♣ P

CHESTER

ALBION
Albion Street
☎ (01244) 340345
11.30-3, 5.30-11 (11.30-11 Fri); 12-2.20, 7-10.30 Sun
Cains Bitter; Greenalls Mild, Original; guest beers ℍ
WWI themed pub: cosy, quiet, with three small rooms, one with an open fire. A long-standing *Guide* entry. Good, traditional food is served in a candlelit room (not Mon eve). 🏚 Q ◖ 🍴 ⌸

CENTURION
1 Oldfield Drive, Vicars Cross (off A51, 1 mile from city)
☎ (01244) 347623
11.30 (11 Sat)-11; 12-10.30 Sun
Jennings Bitter; Marston's Pedigree; Robinson's Best Bitter; Tetley Dark Mild, Bitter; guest beer ℍ
Friendly, two-roomed local, winner of Cheshire's *Community Pub of the Year* award. Holds beer festivals and numerous charity events. No food Sun eve. Guest ales are from the Tapster's Choice range. ❀ ◖ 🍴 ⌸ ♣ P

MILL HOTEL
Milton Street (opp ring road)
☎ (01244) 350035
11-11; 12-10.30 Sun
Boddingtons Bitter; Cains Bitter; Weetwood Best Bitter, Eastgate Ale; guest beers ℍ

The primary attraction of this lively, welcoming hotel bar is the extensive and ever-changing range of ales, most of which are from independents; the house beer comes from Coach House. Good choice of reasonably priced food. Small canalside drinking area. ❀ ➡ ◖ 🍴 ⇌ P

OLDE CUSTOM HOUSE
Watergate Street
☎ (01244) 324435
11-11; 12-10.30 Sun
Banks's Mild; Marston's Bitter, HBC ℍ
Cosy, city-centre pub near the racecourse. Three drinking areas cater for a diverse clientele. Note the impressive fireplace and carvings in the bar. Supports many sports teams. Marston's only city house. Parking difficult but there's a bus to Chester station. ❀ ◖ 🍴

TALBOT
33 Walter Street, Newtown
☎ (01244) 317901
11-11; 11-5, 7-11 Sat; 12-5, 7-10.30 Sun
Burtonwood Mild, Bitter ℍ
Traditional back-street pub with a friendly local atmosphere: two rooms both providing games, including bagatelle. ⌸ ⇌ ♣

UNION VAULTS
Egerton Street
☎ (01244) 322170
11-11; 12-10.30 Sun
Plassey Bitter; Greenalls Bitter ℍ
Friendly local, hosting many events, including a regular folk club (Sun eve). 🍺 ❀ ⇌ ♣

Try also: Harkers Arms, Russell St (Free)

CHILDER THORNTON

WHITE LION
New Road (off A41)
☎ (0151) 339 3402
11.30-3, 5-11; 11.30-11 Fri & Sat; 12-4, 7-10.30 Sun
Thwaites Best Mild, Bitter ℍ
Small, friendly unspoilt two-roomed country pub, popular with the whole community. Families welcome in the snug lunchtime. No food Sun.
🏚 Q ❀ ◖ P

CHURCH LAWTON

LAWTON ARMS
Liverpool Road West (A50/A5011 jct)
☎ (01270) 873743
11.30-3, 5.30 (6.30 Sat)-11; 11.30-11 Fri; 12-3, 7-10.30 Sun
Robinson's Hatters Mild, Best Bitter ℗
Two-roomed pub with a dining room offering four daily specials

at all sessions. It has a strong dominoes following. The best pint of Robinson's in south Cheshire.
❀ ◖ ◗ ⊟ ♣ P ⊓

CONGLETON

Moss Inn
140 Canal Road
☎ (01260) 273583
11-11; 12-10.30 Sun
Bateman Mild; Marston's Bitter, Pedigree H
Warm and welcoming cosy pub whose walls are laden with interesting artefacts. A thriving local trade is boosted by cyclists, walkers and 'boaters' from the canal (100 yards). It has an extensive smoke filter and extraction system. Eve meals 6-8, Tue-Fri. ❀ ◖ ◗ ♿ ⇌ ♣ P

Rams Head
Rood Hill (follow Manchester signs from the centre)
☎ (01260) 273992
11-11; 12-10.30 Sun
Highgate Mild; Tetley Bitter; guest beer (occasional) H
Small, busy, urban neighbourhood pub, the last of its kind in the town. Two rooms and an enclosed, half-covered outside area that is a pleasure to drink in on balmy eves. ♞ ⊟ ♣ P

Waggon & Horses
Newcastle Road, West Heath (A34/A54/A534 jct)
☎ (01260) 274366
11-11; 12-10.30 Sun
Bateman Mild; Marston's Bitter, Pedigree H
Large, well established inn, on the western edge of town. The tables outside in the summer with the pub's situation (at the confluence of three main roads) make it somewhat akin to sitting in the middle of a roundabout. No food Sun. ♨ ◖ ♣ P

CREWE

Albion
1 Pedley Street (Mill St jct)
☎ (01270) 256234
7 (2 Fri, 12 Sat)-11; 12-3, 7-10.30 Sun
Tetley Mild, Bitter; guest beers H
Traditional, unspoilt two-roomed welcoming local with the emphasis on real ale from small brewers (more than 1,000 beers since December 1994). Railway memorabilia in the lounge. Occasional traditional ciders. No food.
⊟ ⇌ ♣ ⌓

Cheshire Cheese
332 Crewe Road, Gresty
☎ (01270) 500304
11-11; 12-10.30 Sun
Boddingtons Bitter; Greenalls Original; Tetley Bitter; guest beers H

Friendly 'Millers Kitchen' which attracts a wide range of clientele, including families. Well-kept garden; kids club every Tue; food served all day.
❀ ◖ ◗ ♿ ♣ P

Kings Arms
56 Earle Street
☎ (01270) 584134
11.30-11; 12-10.30 Sun
Boddingtons Bitter; Chester's Mild; Whitbread Trophy H
Four-roomed, friendly, town-centre pub, Victorian in origin. See the collection of miniatures in the lounge. ❀ 🛏 ⊟ ♣

DISLEY

Albert Hotel
75 Buxton Road
☎ (01663) 763175
12-11; 12-10.30 Sun
Vaux Samson, Waggledance; Ward's Best Bitter H
Small, but imposing redbrick pub situated on the A6, just to the east of the village centre. Popular with all ages due to its welcoming atmosphere.
♨ ❀ ◖ ⇌ ♣

Dandy Cock Inn
15 Market Street
☎ (01663) 763712
12-11; 12-10.30 Sun
Robinson's Hatters Mild, Best Bitter H
Once a home for cock fighting, this traditional local sits in the heart of the village on the busy A6. The cosy lounge bar and the restaurant area, serving quality food, create a good mix. Other Robinson's beers are often available. ❀ ◖ ◗ ⇌ P

Try also: Ploughboy, Buxton Old Road (Vaux)

EATON

Plough
Macclesfield Road
☎ (01260) 280207
12-3, 7-11; 12-3, 7-10.30 Sun
Banks's Bitter; Beartown Bearskinful; Marston's Pedigree H
Village pub, revitalised in recent years by ex-brewer Clive Wincle. Much emphasis is on food and it can get busy as a consequence. This does not detract from the welcoming atmosphere; a new extension has just been added for diners. ♨ ❀ 🛏 ◖ ◗ ♣ P

FRODSHAM

Netherton Hall
Chester Road (A56)
☎ (01928) 732342
12-11; 12-10.30 Sun
Marston's Pedigree; Tetley Bitter; guest beers H

Former farmhouse now a large, open-plan pub, serving excellent food. Set in a good walking area for Frodsham and Helsby Hills, it caters for everyone's needs. Excellent guest beer range.
❀ ◖ ◗ ♿ ♣ P ⊓

Queens Head
92 Main Street (A56)
☎ (01928) 733289
11 (11.30 Tue & Wed)-11; 11.30-3, 6.30-11 Mon; 12-10.30 (12-2.30, 7-10.30 Jan-Mar) Sun
Greenalls Mild, Bitter; guest beer H
Popular 16th-century pub with various rooms, excellent for pub games. A folk club is held in the stables at the rear Fri eves. Located on the main street, it gets very busy on market day (Thu). The guest is from Greenalls' list.
◖ ⇌ ♣ P

GRAPPENHALL

Grappenhall Community Centre
Bellhouse Farm, Bellhouse Lane
☎ (01925) 268633
7.30-11; 12-5, 7.30-11 Sat; 12-5.30, 7.30-10.30 Sun
Ruddles Best Bitter; guest beers H
Large, busy private club and social centre in an old farmhouse and barn, supporting a wide range of activities. Extended in 1998, cask ales are now also available in the old barn function room. CAMRA membership card allows admission.
Q ❀ ♿ ♣ P

Parr Arms
Church Lane
☎ (01925) 267393
11.30-3, 5.30-11; 11.30-11 Sat; 12-10.30 Sun
Greenalls Bitter, Original, guest beer H
Traditional pub in a cobbled village, close to the Bridgewater Canal. A central bar area serves a public bar and two lounges; strong emphasis on food. The guest is from Greenalls' list.
❀ ◖ ◗ ♣ P ⚟

GREAT BUDWORTH

George & Dragon
High Street (off A559)
☎ (01606) 891317
11.30-3, 6-11; 11.30-11 Fri & Sat; 12-10.30 Sun
Tetley Bitter; guest beers H
Comfortable, friendly village local opposite the church in a picturesque village with a recently refurbished restaurant. Two guest beers are always available in this former local CAMRA *Pub of the Year.*
Q ♞ ❀ ◖ ◗ ⊟ ♣ P

GREAT SUTTON

White Swan
Old Chester Road
☎ (0151) 339 9284
11.30-11; 12-10.30 Sun
Burtonwood Mild, Bitter; guest beers H
Two-roomed pub whose landlord always seeks to serve guest beers from independent brewers. Pictures of old Ellesmere Port adorn the walls. No food Tue.
❀ ◑ ▶ ♣ P

HANDFORTH

Railway
Station Road
☎ (01625) 523472
11-3, 5.30-11; 12-3, 7-10.30 Sun
Robinson's Hatters Mild, Best Bitter, Frederics H, **Old Tom** G
Large, multi-roomed pub facing the station. This thriving local is popular with all.
Q ◑ 🍴 ⇌ ♣ P

HAUGHTON MOSS

Nags Head
Long Lane (between Bunbury and Burland on back roads) OS561580
☎ (01829) 260265
11-3 (not Mon), 6-11; 12-3, 7-10.30 Sun
Marston's Bitter, Pedigree; guest beer H
Attractive black and white country pub with a friendly atmosphere and good food. A bowling green and good gardens make this a very nice place in the summer, with an outside play area for children.
🏨 ❀ ◑ ▶ ⊼ ♣ P

HEATLEY

Railway
Mill Lane (B5159)
☎ (01925) 752742
12 (11.30 Sat)-11; 12-10.30 Sun
Boddingtons Bitter; Taylor Landlord; guest beer H
Large, traditional pub by the Trans-Pennine Trail, a focus for the local community and home to many societies. It boasts many different rooms and a large garden; folk club Thu. No food Sun. The guest beer is from Greenall's list. 🏨 Q 🍴 ❀ ◑ 🍴 ♣ P

HIGHER HURDSFIELD

George & Dragon
61 Rainow Road
☎ (01625) 424300
12-3 (not Sat), 7-11; 12-3, 7-10.30 Sun
Guest beers H
Small, friendly pub built of local stone, set back off the main road. Part of the pub is 400 years old. Bus stop outside. ◑ ♣

HOUGHTON GREEN

Plough Inn
Mill Lane
☎ (01925) 815409
11.30-11; 12-10.30 Sun
Boddingtons Bitter; Greenalls Mild, Bitter, Original; guest beer H
Popular pub, expanded in the early 1990s to cater for a large residential area. Strong emphasis on food; live music Tue; quiz night Thu. Bowling green at the back. The guest beer is from Greenalls' list — can be pricey.
❀ ◑ ▶ ♿ P

KELSALL

Boot Inn
Boothsdale (1 mile from A54 Kelsall bypass)
☎ (01829) 751375
11-3, 6-11; 11-11 Sat; 12-10.30 Sun
Greenalls Bitter; Worthington Bitter; guest beer H
Attractive, traditional, 19th-century village pub in a picturesque area, known locally as Little Switzerland. Quality fresh food includes mouthwatering specials. No music. The varied clientele receive a warm welcome. Donkeys in the garden.
🏨 Q ❀ ◑ ▶ P

KNUTSFORD

Builders Arms
Mobberley Road
☎ (01565) 634528
11.30-3, 5.30-11; 12-2, 7-10.30 Sun
Banks's Mild; Marston's Bitter, Pedigree H
Delightful pub in an attractive terrace on the outskirts of the town centre. A former Taylors Eagle Brewery pub, it is busy, with a keen games emphasis. Best approached from the road opposite the Legh Arms.
Q ❀ 🍴 ⇌

Cross Keys
King Street
☎ (01565) 750404
11.30-3, 5.30 (7 Sat)-11; 12-3, 7-10.30 Sun
Boddingtons Bitter; Taylor Landlord; guest beers H
18th-century coaching inn, now a friendly, lively town-centre pub. The lounge and vault are separated by an unusual wood and glass partition. Knutsford's only free house, it offers accommodation and a restaurant.
🛏 ◑ ▶ 🍴 ⇌ P

Legh Arms
Brook Street ☎ (01565) 633420
11-3, 5-11; 11-11 Fri & Sat; 12-10.30 Sun
Banks's Mild; Marston's Bitter, Pedigree, HBC H
Smart, friendly pub on the outskirts of town; the Art Deco-style interior features wood panelling and an impressive copper fire canopy at the end of the bar. Bowling green at the rear. Previous names of this pub were Sword & Serpent and Snig & Skewer (snig was an old name for an eel).
❀ ◑ ▶ ⇌ ♣ P ✂

LITTLE NESTON

Harp Inn
19 Quayside
☎ (0151) 336 6980
11-11; 12-10.30 Sun
Chester's Mild; Flowers IPA; Taylor Landlord; Whitbread Trophy H
Delightful, two-roomed, ex-miners' pub served by a single bar. The superb public bar has a real fire and low beams. It may be difficult to get to, but it's a joy to find. Beware high tides! Eve meals finish at 7.30 (not served Sun eve).
🏨 Q 🍴 ❀ ◑ ▶ 🍴 P

LYMM

Star
Star Lane, Statham
☎ (01925) 753715
3 (12 Fri & Sat)-11; 12-10.30 Sun
Boddingtons Bitter or **Worthington Bitter; Greenalls Mild, Bitter; guest beer** H
Warm, welcoming community local,which is close to both the Bridgewater Canal and the Trans-Pennine Trail. The guest is from Greenalls' list.
❀ ▶ P

MACCLESFIELD

Baths
40 Green Street (behind station)
11-4 (not Mon-Fri), 6.30-11; 12-3, 7-10.30 Sun
Banks's Hanson's Mild, Bitter; Boddingtons Bitter; H
Small, but thriving local, just off the A537, Buxton road, a few minutes' walk uphill from the station. A local bowling green inspired its original name — Bowling Green Tavern and later a public bath. The pub has outlived both.
🍴 ⇌ ♣

Boarhound
37 Brook Street (off Silk Rd)
☎ (01625) 421200
11-11; 12-10.30 Sun
Robinson's Hatters Mild, Best Bitter H
Originally called the Commercial, this large, brick local is a few minute's walk from Waters Green. Recently refurbished, its large upstairs meeting room is popular with many groups.
❀ ⇌ ♣

GEORGE & DRAGON
Sunderland Street
☎ (01625) 421898
11-4 (3 Tue & Wed), 5.30-11;
11-11 Fri; 11-5, 7-11 Sat; 12-3,
7-10.30 Sun
**Robinson's Hatters Mild, Best
Bitter** P
Friendly pub serving good value
food early eve. Pool, darts and
skittles played. Close to both bus
and rail stations. 🍴 🍺 ♣ ♣

QUEENS
5 Albert Place ☎ (01625) 422328
11-11; 12-10.30 Sun
Holt Mild, Bitter H
Large, Victorian inn opposite the
station. The original brickwork
has been restored by Holt. Now
an honest drinking house selling
very cheap beer. 🍺 ≈ ♣

RAILWAY VIEW
Byrons Lane ☎ (01625) 423657
12-3 (not Mon-Fri), 6-11; 12-3,
7-10.30 Sun
**Bateman Mild, XXXB;
Boddingtons Bitter; guest
beers** H
Pleasant pub, 100 yards from the
main London road. Excellent
range of guest beers plus a
house beer from Coach House.
Q ▶ ♣

WATERS GREEN TAVERN
96 Waters Green
☎ (01625) 422653
11.30-3.30, 5.30-11; 12-3, 7-11
Sat; 12-3, 7-10.30 Sun
**Mansfield Riding Bitter; guest
beers** H
Close to bus and rail stations,
this pleasant pub was originally
three storeys; the half-timbered
frontage is false. Popular at
lunchtime (good food); excellent
range of guest beers.
◑ ≈ ♣

MOBBERLEY

ROEBUCK
Town Lane (off B5085)
☎ (01565) 872757
11-11; 12-3, 7-10.30 Sun
**Boddingtons Bitter; Hydes Anvil
Bitter; Marston's Bitter,
Pedigree; guest beers** H
Opposite the Bulls Head, this also
has a cobbled frontage and
impressive wisteria-strewn
walls. Catering well for the food
trade, this large pub serves
meals on Sun from 12-8.30.
🍺 🍴 ◑ ▶ ≈ ♣ P

Try also: Bulls Head, Town
Lane (Tetley)

NANTWICH

BLACK LION
39 Welsh Row ☎ (01270) 628711
11-11; 12-10.30 Sun
Weetwood Best Bitter, Old Dog H

Very small, old black and white
half-timbered pub: downstairs is
all nooks and crannies; and
there is also an upstairs room.
Live music features at
weekends.
🍴 🍺 🍴 ≈ ♣

VINE INN
42 Hospital Street
☎ (01270) 624172
12-3 (not Mon), 5.30-11; 12-2.30,
7-10.30 Sun
**Draught Bass; Worthington
Bitter; guest beer** H
Old pub in a picturesque, winding
street. Most of it is below street
level, so watch the slope as you
go in. Eve meals available
Wed-Sat.
◑ ▶ ≈ ♣

NEWBOLD

HORSESHOE
Fence Lane
☎ (01270) 272205
11-3, 6-11; 12-3, 7-10.30 Sun
Robinson's Best Bitter P;
Frederics (summer) H
Isolated country pub, formerly
part of a farmhouse and which
still enjoys a farming atmosphere. Although it is difficult to
find it is well worth the effort.
Good local trade and a welcome
for walkers and canal-users.
There is also a superb children's
play area.
🍴 Q 🍴 🍴 ♣ P

OVER PEOVER

PARKGATE
Stocks Lane
☎ (01625) 861455
11-11; 12-4, 7-10.30 Sun
Samuel Smith OBB H
Very smart, ivy-clad old pub with
several small, wood-panelled
rooms, including a tap room.
Stages an annual Gooseberry
Competition (Aug) and has occasional visits from local Morris
dancers.
🍴 Q 🍴 ◑ ▶ 🍺 ♣ P

PARKGATE

RED LION HOTEL
The Parade
☎ (0151) 336 1548
12-2.30, 5-11; 12-11 Fri, Sat &
summer; 12-10.30 Sun
**Ind Coope Burton Ale; Tetley
Bitter; Walker Mild, Bitter** H
Wirral CAMRA *Pub of the Year*
1996: there is a traditional
lounge and bar which enjoys a
superb view of the Welsh hills
across the Dee estuary and
marsh (which is famous for
birdlife). Local numbers are
swelled by many summer visitors. Nelson, the parrot, guards
the bar.
🍴 Q ◑ 🍺 ♣

PENKETH

FERRY TAVERN
Station Road (off A562, follow
signs to yacht haven)
☎ (01925) 791117
12-3.30, 5.30-11; 12-11 Sat &
summer; 12-10.30 Sun
**Courage Directors; Ruddles
County; Webster's Yorkshire
Bitter; guest beers** H
Atmospheric pub situated by the
River Mersey. There is a wide
range of bar food served (but
which are not available Sun or
Mon eves); children are welcome
for meals and there is a play
area and pets corner. The pub
serves three regularly changing
guest ales.
🍴 🍴 ◑ ▶ 🍺

PRESTBURY

ADMIRAL RODNEY
New Road
☎ (01625) 828078
11-3, 5.30-11; 11-11 Fri & Sat;
12-3, 7-10.30 Sun
**Robinson's Hatters Mild, Best
Bitter** H
Popular inn situated in an attractive village terrace, a Grade II
listed building. The original front
door became the back door when
the new road was built through
the village.
🍴 Q ◑ ≈ P

RAINOW

HIGHWAYMAN
Whaley Bridge Road (B5470)
☎ (01625) 573245
11-3, 7-11; 12-3, 7-10.30 Sun
Thwaites Bitter H
This remote, windswept inn,
uwas formerly known as the
Blacksmith's Arms until 1949
and locally as the Patch.
Breathtaking views from the
front door; inside there is a
maze of connecting rooms with a
small tap room in the far
corner. There are three blazing
open fires in winter.
🍴 Q ◑ ▶ 🍺 P

RODE HEATH

ROYAL OAK
41 Sandbach Road (A533)
☎ (01270) 875670
12-3 (not Mon), 5.30 (5 Fri)-11;
12-11 Sat; 12-10.30 Sun
Titanic Premium H
Two-roomed pub separated by a
partition, served by a single bar.
The bar is a games room with TV.
The lounge is comfortable, divided into two parts, one section
mainly for food. Cask breathers
are used on all the real ales,
except the Titanic Premium.
Lunches Tue-Sun. Eve meals
Wed-Sat.
Q 🍴 ◑ ▶ 🍺 🍴 ✂

RUNCORN

MASONIC
Devonshire Place
☎ (01928) 576163
12-11; 12-10.30 Sun
Boddingtons Bitter; Cains Mild, Bitter Ⓗ
Two-roomed local community pub in Runcorn old town; a basic and lively meeting place hosting regular entertainment. ⌸ ⇌

SAUGHALL

GREYHOUND
Sea Hill Road ☎ (01244) 880205
11-3, 5.30-11; 11-11 Sat; 12-3, 7-10.30 Sun
Boddingtons Bitter; Castle Eden Ale; guest beer Ⓗ
Unpretentious local by the Welsh border — one bar serves three areas. Outdoor children's play area. The guest beer is from Whitbread's list. Eve meals finish at 8 (not served Sun).
Q ⊛ ◑ ▶ ⌸ P

SCHOLAR GREEN

RISING SUN
112 Station Road (off A34, road to Mow Cop) ☎ (01782) 776235
12-3 (not Mon-Fri Jan-Mar), 7-11; 12-3, 7-10.30 Sun
Marston's Bitter, Pedigree, HBC (occasional) Ⓗ
Comfortable, three-roomed pub: one main room with a central bar, offering traditional games and Sky TV; a dining room and a children's room. All food is freshly prepared on the premises and is reasonably priced (eve meals Wed-Sun). ⇞ ⌇ ◑ ▶ ♣ P

STRETTON

RING O'BELLS
Northwich Road, Lower Stretton (A559, off M56 jct 10)
☎ (01925) 730556
12-3, 5.30 (7 Sat)-11; 12-4, 7-10.30 Sun
Greenalls Mild, Bitter; guest beer Ⓗ
Once a row of cottages, this pub has one main and two side rooms: Friendly and comfortable — a rare survivor of a rural local.
⇞ Q ⊛ P

TARPORLEY

FORESTERS ARMS
94 High Street (A51)
☎ (01829) 733151
11.30-11; 12-10.30 Sun
Greenalls Mild, Bitter; guest beer Ⓗ
Very cosy pub close to the Sandstone Trail. Good value Sun lunch is served in the dining area. The guest beer is from Greenall's list.
⇞ ⊛ ⇄ ◑ ▶ ⌸ ♣ P

RISING SUN
38 High Street (A51)
☎ (01829) 732423
11.30-3, 5.30-11; 11.30-11 Sat; 12-10.30 Sun
Robinson's Hatters Mild, Best Bitter Ⓗ
This authentic old pub scores heavily on almost all fronts and is the only Cheshire pub to have appeared in all 26 editions of this Guide. Meals in the lounge bar and dining room are renowned for quality and value, but one bar is reserved for drinkers. Children welcome at lunchtime (and eves in the restaurant). TV for sport.
Q ⊛ ◑ ▶ P

TATTENHALL

SPORTSMANS ARMS
High Street ☎ (01829) 770233
11-11; 12-10.30 Sun
Thwaites Best Mild, Bitter Ⓗ
Unassuming village pub, serving good value food, where a large collection of jugs hangs from the ceiling. Pool and darts room; small outdoor children's play area. ⊛ ◑ ▶ ♣ P

TUSHINGHAM

BLUE BELL INN
Signed Bell 'o t'Hill from A41, 4 miles N of Whitchurch
☎ (01948) 662172
12-3, 6-11; 12-3, 7-10.30 Sun
Hanby Drawwell; guest beers Ⓗ
Welcoming, 17th-century inn with original beams and artefacts. Guest beers usually come from small independents.
⇞ Q ⇞ ⊛ ◑ ▶ P

WALKER BARN

SETTER DOG
Buxton Road
☎ (01625) 431444
11.30-3, 6 (7 Sat)-11; 12-3, 7-10.30 Sun
Draught Bass; guest beers Ⓗ
Small rural pub on a sharp bend on the Buxton road, 1158ft above sea level, affording excellent views over Macclesfield and beyond. The pub used to be a quarryman's local in the days when the quarries were a thriving local industry.
⇞ Q ⊛ ◑ ▶ P

WARRINGTON

BULLS HEAD
33 Church Street
☎ (01925) 635680
12-11; 12-10.30 Sun
Draught Bass; Flowers Original; Greenalls Mild, Bitter; guest beer Ⓗ
Rambling 17th-century community pub: the modest frontage conceals not only five rooms but also a bowling green and a function

room. An understandably popular pub which sets a standard for all other Greenalls' pubs.
⊛ ◑ ⇌ (Central) ♣

LORD RODNEY
67 Winnick Road
☎ (01925) 234296
12-11; 12-10.30 Sun
Cains Bitter; Tetley Bitter; guest beers Ⓗ
Tetley Festival Alehouse with regularly changing guest beers (about 10 a week). Live music Fri and Sat eves (can be very loud). Weekday lunches.
◑ ⇌ (Central) ♣

LOWER ANGEL
27 Buttermarket Street
☎ (01925) 633299
11-4, 7-11; 12-3, 7-10.30 Sun
Ind Coope Burton Ale; Walker Mild, Bitter; guest beer Ⓗ
Popular town-centre pub concentrating on beer, not food. A long, narrow lounge and a bar with a collection of odd and old bottled beers. Resident ghost.
⌸ ⇌ (Central) ♣

OLD TOWN HOUSE
Buttermarket Street
☎ (01925) 242787
11.30-11; 12-10.30 Sun
John Smith's Bitter; Theakston XB; guest beers Ⓗ
Single-bar pub, set back from the main road. Up to four guest beers at any one time (usually from micros) although at the time of writing (July 1998) the adventurous guest beer range is under threat by owners, Grand Pub Company. Guest ciders are served by gravity. Local CAMRA Pub of the Year 1998. Eve meals weekdays.
⊛ ◑ ▶ ⇌ (Central) ♣ ⌣

WHEELOCK

COMMERCIAL HOTEL
Game Street (off A534, near Bridge 154, Trent & Mersey Canal) ☎ (01270) 760122
8-11; 12-2, 8-10.30 Sun
Boddingtons Bitter; Marston's Pedigree; Thwaites Bitter; guest beer Ⓗ
Listed Georgian building, a former home brew pub. A finely restored games room boasts a full-sized snooker table, and table skittles. Spontaneous folk music Thu eves, when a guest beer is sold. ⇞ Q ⌸ ⌣ ⊁

WIDNES

EIGHT TOWERS
Weates Close ☎ (0151) 424 8063
11-11; 12-10.30 Sun
Banks's Mild Ⓟ**, Bitter** Ⓗ
Modern pub on the outskirts of town: a bar and a comfortable lounge, close to Fiddlers Ferry

Out *Inn* CHESHIRE
The definitive guide to all the county's pubs

Featuring:
- best inns for meals
- home cooked food
- child-friendly pubs
- disabled facilities
- beer gardens
- non-smoking rooms
- unspoilt pubs

and
the Best of British Beer!

Includes articles on:
- cycling
- walking
- canals

With full details of

CAMPAIGN FOR REAL ALE

OPENING HOURS

with Foreword by Martin Bell M.P.

One of the latest local guides, this 144-page paperback features all Cheshire's pubs, including the flagship 100, as well as town maps and photos. Price £4.95, available from CAMRA.

power station, notable for its eight cooling towers. Large garden with a play area and a sports pitch. Sun meals 12-6.

HORSE & JOCKEY
18 Birchfield Road (next to Victoria Park entrance)
☎ (0151) 420 2966
11.30-11; 12-10.30 Sun
Greenalls Bitter; Tetley Bitter; guest beers Ⓗ
Comfortable, friendly, one-roomed local community pub. Bar snacks available daily until 7pm. Live music and quiz nights and an annual beer festival held in August.
☀ ⇄ (Farnworth) P

WILLEY MOOR

WILLEY MOOR LOCK
Tarporley Road (off A49, opp wildfowl sanctuary) OS534452
☎ (01948) 663274
12-2.30 (3 summer), 6-11; 12-3, 7-10.30 Sun
Theakston Best Bitter; guest beers Ⓗ

Converted lock-keeper's cottage by Willey Moor lock on the Llangollen Canal. The Sandstone Trail runs alongside. Admire the collection of over 150 teapots. A good choice of guest beers. This friendly, family-run pub gets very busy on summer weekends; food may finish early.
☀ Q ❀ ◑ ▶ P

WILMSLOW

SWAN
2 Swan Street
☎ (01625) 522528
12-11; 12-3, 7-10.30 Sun
Boddingtons Bitter; Taylor Landlord; guest beers Ⓗ

Open-plan pub in the centre of Wilmslow, stocking the best selection of guest beers in town.
☀ ⇄ P

WINCLE

SHIP
Off A54, near Danebridge
☎ (01260) 227217
12-3, 7-11 (closed winter Mon); 12-4, 7-10.30 Sun
Boddingtons Bitter; guest beers Ⓗ
Attractive 16th-century, sandstone village inn, overlooking the scenic Dane Valley, the thick stone walls are designed to withstand the rigours of local winters. The sign above the door is of the 'Nimrod', the ship in which Shackleton sailed to the Antarctic. Popular with walkers; good food.
☀ Q ⛺ ❀ ⇄ ◑ ▶ ♣ P

WINSFORD

PRINCES FEATHERS
281 Station Road (½ mile from new A54)
☎ (01606) 594191
11-3, 6-11; 11-11 Fri & Sat; 12-10.30 Sun
Cains Bitter; Chester's Mild; Weetwood Old Dog; guest beers Ⓗ
Traditional, two-roomed town pub, offering cask promotions Tue eve. Boxing memorabilia features in the bar. Local CAMRA *Pub of the Year* 1996. Traditional hot pub snacks.
☀ Q ❀ A ⇄ ♣ P

Don't let it happen! Stop brewery and pub closures!

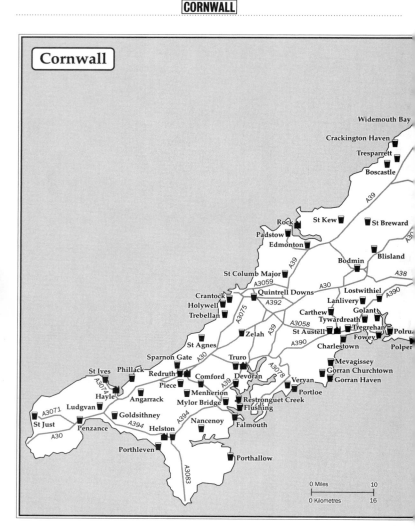

ALTARNUN

RISING SUN
1 mile N of village on Camelford road OS825215 ☎ (01566) 86332
11-3, 5.30-11; 11-11 Sat; 12-3, 7-10.30 Sun
Boddingtons Bitter; Flowers Original; Sharp's Doom Bar Bitter; guest beers Ⓗ
Up to six ales offered at this 16th-century, granite-built farmhouse which has been a pub for over 150 years. Three fireplaces, a clome oven, a slate-flagged floor, low, beamed ceiling and a proper underground cellar.
🚪 ⏰ 🕷 ⛺ ◖ ▶ Å ♣ P

ANGARRACK

ANGARRACK INN
32 Steamers Hill (off A30 at Loggans Mill roundabout)
☎ (01736) 752380

11-3, 6-11; 12-3, 7-10.30
St Austell Bosun's, Tinners, HSD Ⓗ
Attractive, welcoming and comfortable village pub with an extensive range of good value home-cooked food (not served winter Mon eves). 🚪 🕷 ◖ ▶ Å P

BLISLAND

BLISLAND INN
The Green (2 miles off A30 E of Bodmin) ☎ (01208) 850739
11.30-3, 6-11; 11-11 Fri-Sat summer; 12-4.30, 7-10.30 (12-10.30 summer) Sun
Worthington Best Bitter; guest beers Ⓗ Ⓖ
Set on the only village green in Cornwall, this popular granite free house offers up to five guest ales (200 per year) plus a house beer from Sutton Brewery. It boasts a knowledgeable landlord, good food and atmosphere and a

large family room. The cider changes regularly.
🚪 Q ⏰ 🕷 ◖ ▶ 🕮 ♣ ◔ P

BODMIN

WHITE HART (TAP & BARREL)
Pool Street ☎ (01208) 79080
12-11; 12-10.30 Sun
Beer range varies Ⓖ
A separate bar at the rear of the pub on two levels with granite walls. A convivial place to enjoy a pint and a game of backgammon (Wed eve). All beers racked behind the bar with an extensive collection of pump clips. Cider on gravity. 🚪 🕷 ◖ ▶ Å ♣ ◔ P

BOSCASTLE

COBWEB
The Bridge ☎ (01840) 250278
11-3, 6-11 (11-midnight Sat, 11-

quiet village near Saltash. Outside boules pitch. Inch's cider. ⚑ Q ✿ ⚐ ♣ ⌕ P

CARTHEW

SAULS ARMS
On A391, 3 miles N of St Austell
☎ (01726) 850317
11-11; 12-10.30 Sun
St Austell Bosun's, XXXX Mild, Tinners, Ⓗ **Winter Warmer** Ⓖ
Friendly local situated in a small hamlet close to the china clay museum. Genuine Cornish landlord. Eve meals served.
⚑ Q ✿ ◖▶ ♣ P

CHARLESTOWN

RASHLEIGH ARMS
☎ (01726) 73635
11-11; 12-10.30 Sun
Draught Bass; Ruddles County; St Austell Tinners; Sharp's Doom Bar Bitter or Own; Tetley Bitter; Wadworth 6X; guest beers Ⓗ
Large, friendly inn overlooking the famous port, comprising two large bars and a family room. The port is a popular location for films. ⚐ ✿ ⊨ ◖▶ ⚇ ⚐ ♣ P

COMFORD

FOX & HOUNDS
On A393 ☎ (01209) 820251
11-3, 6-11 (varies summer); 12-3, 7-10.30 Sun
Draught Bass; St Austell Tinners, HSD Ⓖ
Comfortable country pub ; the garden is a blaze of colour in summer. All ales served from casks behind the bar. An excellent restaurant specialises in home-cooked food. Look for the frieze in the snug. ⚑ ✿ ◖▶ ⚐ ♣ P

CRACKINGTON HAVEN

COOMBE BARTON INN
☎ (01840) 230245
11-3, 6-11 (11-11 summer); 12-3, 7-10.30 (12-10.30 summer) Sun
Dartmoor Best Bitter; Sharp's Doom Bar Bitter; guest beers Ⓗ
Spacious 300-year-old hotel overlooking the beach, set in a steep valley with exceptional geology on show in cliff faces. Two bars with a dining area and large family room. ⚐ ✿ ⊨ ◖▶ ⚐ ♣ P

CRAFTHOLE

LISCAWN INN
Off B3247, E of village
☎ (01503) 230863
11-3, 6-11 (11-11 summer); 12-3, 7-10.30 (12-10.30 summer) Sun
Draught Bass; Wells Bombardier; Theakston Old Peculier; guest beer (summer) Ⓗ
In a forgotten corner of Cornwall, this charming, family-run 14th-century inn is set in 8 acres of

grounds with Dartmoor views. Families and pets welcome. Extensive menu, function room and friendly, attentive owners.
⚑ Q ⚇ ✿ ⊨ ◖▶ Ⓖ

CRANTOCK

OLD ALBION
Langurroc Road ☎ (01637) 830243
12-11; 12-10.30 Sun
Courage Best Bitter; John Smith's Bitter; Skinner's Betty Stogs Bitter; guest beer Ⓗ
Thatched pub by the church gate, steeped in smuggling history and close to a safe sandy beach. Sunday lunches are popular with food to suit all tastes. Guest beers a regular feature.
⚑ ⚇ ✿ ◖▶ ⚐ ⌕ P

DEVORAN

OLD QUAY INN
St Johns Terrace (off A39)
☎ (01872) 863142
11.45-2.30, 6-11; 12-3, 7-11 Sun
Draught Bass; Flowers IPA; guest beers Ⓗ
Welcoming pub with fine views over Devoran quay and creek, offering ever-changing guest ales. Good home-cooked food. Home to many village sports teams. Tiny car park.
⚑ ✿ ⊨ ◖▶ ♣ P

EDMONTON

QUARRYMAN
Off A39 at Whitecross
☎ (01208) 816444
12-11; 12-10.30 Sun
Sharp's Doom Bar Bitter; guest beers Ⓗ
Pleasant, 18th-century pub, handy for the Royal Cornwall Showground and the Camel Trail. Part of a holiday and sports complex. Popular with sports followers. British beef steaks a speciality. ⚑ Q ✿ ⊨ ◖▶ ⚐ ♣ P

FALMOUTH

QUAYSIDE INN
41 Arwenack Street
☎ (01326) 312113
11-3, 7-11 (11-11 summer and upstairs bar); 12-10.30 Sun
Courage Directors; Flowers Original; Ruddles County; Sharp's Doom Bar Bitter; Tetley Bitter; guest beers Ⓗ Ⓖ
Pub where the bar at street level has comfortable surroundings and is popular for lunches, while the bar at quay-level has bare floors. The downstairs bar serves beer, cider and wine only.
✿ ◖▶ ⇌ (The Dell) ⌕

SEVEN STARS ☆
The Moor
☎ (01326) 312111
11-3, 6-11; 12-3, 7-10.30 Sun

11 Fri & summer); 12-3, 7-10.30 (12-10.30 summer) Sun
Draught Bass; St Austell Tinners, HSD; Ⓗ **guest beers** Ⓗ Ⓖ
Thriving pub full of character featuring worn slate floors and live music Sat eves (hence late licence). Many strange objects hang from the beamed ceilings.
⚑ Q ⚇ ✿ ◖▶ ⚏ ♣ P

Try also: Wellington Hotel Old Rd (Free)

BOTUS FLEMING

RISING SUN
½ mile off A388, near Saltash
☎ (01752) 842792
12-4 (not Mon-Thu), 7-11; 12-3.30, 7-10.30 Sun
Draught Bass; Worthington Bitter; guest beers Ⓗ
Unchanged for 40 years, this rural gem is tucked away in a

Draught Bass⑤; Morland Old Speckled Hen Ⓗ;Sharp's Own ⑤
Pub whose unspoilt interior has remained unchanged for five generations: a lively tap room and quiet snug. The present landlord is an ordained priest. Q ❀ ⊞

FLUSHING

ROYAL STANDARD
St Peters Hill (off A393 at Penryn, or foot ferry from Falmouth) ☎ (01326) 374250
11-2.30 (3 Fri & Sat); 6.30-11; 12-3, 7-10.30 Sun (varies winter)
Draught Bass; Flowers IPA; Sharp's Doom Bar Bitter Ⓗ
Friendly local, run by the present landlord for over 30 years, with fine views of the Penryn River from the front patio. Home-made pasties and apple pies are a speciality. Takeaway service available for lunches. ☖ ❀ ◑ ▶ ♣

FOWEY

GALLEON
12 Fore Street ☎ (01726) 833014
11-11; 12-10.30 Sun
Draught Bass; Flowers IPA; Sharp's Cornish Coaster; guest beers (summer) Ⓗ
400-year-old riverside pub, well refurbished, enjoying fine views from lounge and patio. A wide range of bar meals available with fish a speciality. Trad jazz Sun lunch and live music Fri eve. ☖ ❀ ◑ ▶ ⅙ ▲ ♣

GOLANT

FISHERMAN'S ARMS
Fore Street (off B3269)
☎ (01726) 832453
11-11 (12-3, 6-11 winter); 12-4, 7-10.30 Sun
Ushers Best Bitter, Founders Ale, seasonal beers Ⓗ
Charming village pub in a lovely waterside setting with views across the River Fowey. Beware of being cut off by the tide. Good food served all day. Very small car park. ☖ ⛵ ❀ ◑ ▶ ♣ P

GOLDSITHNEY

CROWN
Fore Street ☎ (01736) 710494
11-3, 6-11 (11-11 summer); 12-10.30 Sun
St Austell XXXX Mild, Tinners, HSD Ⓗ
Attractive, comfortable village pub, popular for meals. ☖ ❀ ◑ ▶

GORRAN CHURCHTOWN

BARLEY SHEAF
☎ (01726) 843330
12-2, 7-11 (12-3, 6-11 summer); 12-3.30, 7-10.30 (12-3, 6-10.30 summer) Sun

Draught Bass; guest beers Ⓗ
Built in 1837 by a local landowner, this two-bar pub was haunted until 1987 when it was exorcised and featured on TV. One mile from Heligan Gardens. Excellent ale and food.Q ⛵ ❀ ◑ ▶ ⊞ ⅙ P

GORRAN HAVEN

LLAWNROC INN
Shute Lane ☎ (01726) 843461
12-3, 7-11 (12-4, 6-11 summer); 11-11 Sat; 12-10.30 Sun
Beer range varies Ⓗ
Two-bar hotel, two miles from Heligan Gardens, overlooking village and St Austell Bay. Features a fisherman's bar with log fire and lounge bar with family room. Very good home-cooked food and usually two local beers are served by friendly staff in a good atmosphere. ☖ Q ⛵ ❀ ◑ ▶ ⅙ P

GUNNISLAKE

RISING SUN INN
Calstock Road ☎ (01822) 832201
11-3, 5-11; 11-11 Sat; 12-3, 7-10.30 Sun
Draught Bass; St Austell HSD; Sharp's Cornish Coaster, Own; guest beers Ⓗ
Friendly inn with pleasing decor, serving an excellent choice of mainly Cornish beers and superb food. Helpful bar staff. The garden overlooks the Tamar Valley. ☖Q ❀ ◑ ▲ ⇌ ♣ P

HELSTON

BLUE ANCHOR
Coinagehall St ☎ (01326) 562821
11-11; 12-10.30 Sun
Blue Anchor Middle, Best, Special, Extra Special Ⓗ
The flagship of pub breweries; a rambling, unspoilt 15th-century granite building with a thatched roof and its own brewery at the rear. Good home-cooked food served 12-4. ☖ Q ⛵ ❀ ◑ ⊞

HOLYWELL

TREGUTH
Holywell Bay, NewQuay
☎ (01637) 830248
11.30-11 (winter varies); 12-10.30 Sun
Courage Best Bitter; John Smith's Bitter; Skinner's Betty Stogs, Skilliwidden; guest beers Ⓗ
13th-century thatched pub on route to a scenic, sandy beach. Popular in summer, close to army training camp. Excellent food available. Local scrumpy on gravity. ☖ ⛵ ❀ ◑ ▲ ⌂ P

KILKHAMPTON

LONDON INN
On A39 ☎ (01288) 321665
12-3.30, 6-11; 12-3.30, 7-10.30 Sun

Sharp's Doom Bar Bitter, Own; guest beer Ⓗ
Coaching inn dating from 1785 next to the church. Lounge, snug and public bar, with a separate dining room. Strong darts and euchre teams. Accommodation is in two self-contained cottages. ☖ ⛵ ❀ ⊨ ◑ ▶ ♣

Try also: New Inn, A39 (Free)

KINGSAND

RISING SUN
The Green ☎ (01752) 822840
11-11 (11-3, 6-11 winter); 12-10.30 Sun
Draught Bass; Courage Best Bitter; guest beer Ⓗ
Popular, quiet and cosy pub: a former customs house in a village of narrow streets on the coastal path. Friendly hosts. Parking for four cars. Excellent food (served all day Sat-Sun). ☖ Q ❀ ⊨ ◑ ▲ ♣ P

LANLIVERY

CROWN
Off A390, 2 miles W of St Austell
☎ (01208) 872707
11-3, 6.30-11; 12-3, 6.30-10.30 Sun
Draught Bass; Sharp's Own; Worthington Bitter Ⓗ
12th-century, listed pub with two restaurants, one no-smoking. Lovely surroundings, friendly staff. The accommodation is adapted for wheelchair users. ☖Q ⛵ ❀ ⊨ ◑ ▶ ⊞ ⅙ ▲ ♣ P

LAUNCESTON

BAKERS ARMS
Southgate St ☎ (01566) 772510
11-11; 12-10.30 Sun
Courage Directors; John Smith's Bitter; guest beers Ⓗ
Well patronised town-centre pub next to the ancient Southgate Arch. Wood-panelled lounge and a games-oriented public bar. ☖ Q ⊨ ◑ ⊞ ♣

Try also: White Horse, Newport Sq (Free)

LOSTWITHIEL

ROYAL OAK
King Street (off A390 at traffic lights) ☎ (01208) 872552
11-11; 12-10.30 Sun
Draught Bass; Fuller's London Pride; Sharp's Cornish Coaster; guest beers Ⓗ
Busy, historic 13th-century inn in the old capital of Cornwall. A stone-floored public bar contrasts with a comfortable lounge and restaurant; very good food. ☖Q ⛵ ❀ ⊨ ◑ ⊞ ▲ ⇌ ♣ P

Try also: Globe Inn, North St (Free)

LUDGVAN

WHITE HART
Signed W of Crowlas on A30
☎ (01736) 740574
11-2.30, 6-11; 12-3, 7-10.30
Sun
**Draught Bass; Flowers IPA;
Marston's Pedigree** Ⓖ
14th-century pub by village
church. Small, unspoilt rooms,
beams, rugs on the bare floor,
old prints and photographs, and
many old tables and chairs. Good
local reputation.
🏠 Q ✿ ◖ ▶ ♣ P ✄

MENHERION

GOLDEN LION
Off B3297 by Stithians Lake
OS709372
☎ (01209) 860332
12-2, 7-11 (may extend summer);
12-3, 7-10.30 Sun
St Austell Tinners, HSD Ⓗ
Old granite pub with good food
and a friendly atmosphere.
Superbly situated by Stithians
Reservoir with its watersports.
Accommodation in a self-catering
cottage.
🏠 Q ✿ 🚲 ◖ ▶ ♿ ▲ P

MEVAGISSEY

FOUNTAIN INN
Small turning off Fore Street
☎ (01726) 842320
11.30-11; 12-10.30 Sun
**St Austell Tinners, HSD,
Trelawny's Pride, Winter
Warmer** Ⓗ
Friendly, two-bar olde-worlde inn
with slate floors, beams and his-
toric photos. The upstairs restaur-
ant is open Mar-Oct.
🏠 Q 🚲 ◖ ▶ ▲ ♣

MYLOR BRIDGE

LEMON ARMS
Off A393 at Penryn
☎ (01326) 373666
11-3, 6-11; 12-3, 7-10.30 Sun
**St Austell Bosun's, Tinners,
HSD** Ⓗ
Friendly one-bar village-centre
pub, popular with village sports
teams. Good food.
🏠 ✿ ◖ ▶ ▲ ♣ P

NANCENOY

TRENGILLY WARTHA INN
Off B3291 OS731282
☎ (01326) 340332
11-3, 6.30-11 (may vary summer); 12-3, 7-10.30 Sun
Sharp's Cornish Coaster; Ⓗ
guest beers Ⓖ
Pleasant country pub/hotel with
a restaurant offering a range of
constantly changing guest ales
from independent breweries. Can
get busy in summer.
🏠 Q 🚲 ✿ 🚲 ◖ ▶ P

PADSTOW

OLD SHIP HOTEL
Mill Square ☎ (01841) 532357
11-3, 7-11 (11-11 summer), 12-3,
7-10.30 (12-10.30 summer) Sun
**Draught Bass; Brains SA;
Flowers IPA;** Ⓗ **guest beers** Ⓗ Ⓖ
Pleasant hotel in a popular holiday resort set back off the road
with outdoor drinking area in
front. Wood-panelled front bar,
decorated with a nautical flavour.
Regular live music. En-suite
accommodation.
Q 🚲 ✿ 🚲 ◖ ▶ ♿ ♣ P

Try also: London Inn, Lanadwell
St (St Austell)

PENZANCE

GLOBE & ALE HOUSE
Queens Square
☎ (01736) 64098
11-11; 12-10.30 Sun
**Draught Bass; Sharp's Doom Bar
Bitter;** Ⓗ **guest beers** Ⓖ
Very friendly, well-appointed
Greenalls conversion, with a
wide choice of real ales on pump
and gravity. Q ◖ ▶ ≠

MOUNT'S BAY INN
The Promenade, Wherry Town
☎ (01736) 63027
11-3, 5.30-11; 12-3, 7-10.30 Sun
**Draught Bass; Worthington
Bitter; guest beers** Ⓗ
Deservedly popular, small free
house on the seafront towards
Newlyn. Very friendly landlord
serving a great choice of real
ales. 🏠 Q 🚲 ◖ ▶

Try also: Turks Head, Chapel St
(Free)

PHILLACK

BUCKET OF BLOOD
14 Churchtown Road
☎ (01736) 752378
11-2.30, 6-11; 12-4, 7-10.30 Sun
**St Austell Bosun's, XXXX Mild,
HSD** Ⓗ
Historic, low-beamed, friendly
pub close to Hayle beaches; its
name is derived from a gory legend! Meals in summer.
🏠 🚲 ◖ ▶ ♣ ⌂ P

PIECE

COUNTRYMAN
On Fourlanes-Pool road
☎ (01209) 215960
11-11; 12-10.30 Sun
**Courage Best Bitter, Directors;
Morland Old Speckled Hen;
Sharp's Own; Theakston Old
Peculier; guest beers** Ⓗ
A former count house, this wel-
coming, popular, country pub
provides good food and regular
entertainment. Quiz Tue eve.
🏠 🚲 ✿ ◖ ▶ ♿ ▲ ♣ P

POLPERRO

BLUE PETER
The Quay
☎ (01503) 272743
11-11; 12-10.30 Sun
**St Austell Tinners, HSD; Sharp's
Doom Bar Bitter; guest beers** Ⓗ
Small pub on the coastal path
reached by a flight of steps at
end of the quay; very lively and
friendly, hosting live music Sat
and Sun lunchtime. No food, but
customers can bring their own
sandwiches. 🏠 ▲ ♣ ⌂

OLD MILL HOUSE HOTEL
Mill Hill
☎ (01503) 272362
11-11; 12-10.30 Sun
**Draught Bass; Exmoor Gold;
guest beer** Ⓗ
Welcoming inn, tastefully refurbished three years ago. Extensive
bar area and separate bistro
offering superb home-cooked
food; fish a speciality. Families
welcome, as are dogs. Excellent
accommodation. Guest beers usually at a special low price.
🏠 🚲 🚲 ◖ ▶ ♣ ⌂

Try also Crumplehorn Inn, The
Old Mill (Free)

POLRUAN

LUGGER
The Quay ☎ (01726) 870007
11-11; 12-10.30 Sun
**St Austell Bosun's, XXXX Mild,
Tinners, Trelawny's Pride, HSD** Ⓗ
Fine riverside pub with two bars,
boasting nautical decor and a
friendly atmosphere. Can be
reached on foot ferry or
Boddinick car ferry from Fowey.
Q ◖ ▶ ♿ ♣

PORTHALLOW

FIVE PILCHARDS
☎ (01326) 280256
12-2.30, 7-11; 12-2.30, 7.30-10.30
Sun (not winter Sun & Mon eve)
**Greene King Abbot; Sharp's
Doom Bar Bitter; guest beers**
(summer) Ⓗ
Friendly one-bar pub next to the
beach with fine views across
Falmouth Bay. Parking nearby.
🏠 Q ✿ ◖ ▶

PORTHLEVEN

ATLANTIC INN
Peverell Terrace
☎ (01326) 562439
12-11; 12-10.30 Sun
**Boddingtons Bitter; Brakspear
Bitter; Fuller's London Pride;
Wadworth 6X; Whitbread
Fuggles IPA; guest beers** Ⓗ
Friendly, strong community local
overlooking the harbour. Live
music.
🏠 🚲 ✿ ◖ ▶ ▲ ♣ ⌂ P

PORTLOE

SHIP INN
☎ (01872) 501356
11.30-2.30, 6.30-11 (11-11 summer); 12-3, 7-10.30 (12-10.30 summer) Sun
St Austell XXXX Mild, Tinners, Trelawny's Pride Ⓗ
Friendly, welcoming, two bar local in small fishing village featuring old village photos. Good home-cooked food. Convenient for scenic coastal walks.
🏨 Q 🍺 🛏 ◑ 🍻 ⌂ P

QUINTRELL DOWNS

TWO CLOMES
East Road (A390) ☎ (01637) 871163
12-3, 7-11 (12-11 summer); 12-3, 7-10.30 (12-10.30 summer) Sun
Sharp's Doom Bar Bitter; guest beers Ⓗ
Named after the two fireside ovens, this 18th-century free house offers excellent beers to accompany home-cooked food. Conveniently situated on the main route into Newquay and close to camp sites.
🏨 ❀ ◑ ▶ ▲ ⇌ P

REDRUTH

TRICKY DICKIE'S
Tolgus Mount (off old Redruth bypass) ☎ (01209) 219292
11-3, 6-11 (midnight Tue & Thu); 12-3, 7-10.30 (may vary) Sun
Flowers IPA; Sharp's Own, Special; guest beer Ⓗ
Renovated old tin mine smithy, offering an extensive bar and restaurant plus adjoining rooms. Live jazz Tue; other entertainment Thu. The emphasis is on meals. Children welcome.
🏨 ❀ ◑ ▶ ♿ ⇌ P

RESTRONGUET CREEK

PANDORA INN
Restronguet Hill, near A39
OS814371 ☎ (01326) 372678
12-2.30, 7-11 (11-11 summer); 12 (11 summer)-11 Sat; 12-10.30 Sun
Draught Bass; St Austell Bosun's, Tinners, Trelawny's Pride, HSD Ⓗ
13th-century waterside thatched pub, reached by road or water. Bar snacks and à la carte restaurant upstairs.🏨 Q 🍺 ❀ ◑ ▶ ▲ P

RILLA MILL

MANOR HOUSE INN
N of Liskeard on B3254, right at Upton Cross OS295731
☎ (01579) 362354
12-3, 7(6.45 Sat)-11; 12-3, 7-10.30 Sun
Draught Bass; guest beers Ⓗ
Very busy, comfortable 17th-century inn and restaurant in the

Lynher Valley. Two guest beers are offered, plus cider in summer. Excellent food.
Q 🍺 ❀ 🛏 ◑ ▶ ⌂ P ✄

ST AGNES

DRIFTWOOD SPARS
Trevaunance Cove
☎ (01872) 552428
11-11 (midnight Fri-Sat); 12-10.30 Sun
Draught Bass; Ind Coope Burton Ale; Sharp's Own; Skinner's Betty Stogs Bitter; guest beers Ⓗ
Rambling 17th-century hotel with a nautical theme in an old tin mining area. Live entertainment at weekends.
🏨 🍺 ❀ 🛏 ◑ ▲ ⌂ P

ST AUSTELL

CARLYON ARMS
Sandy Hill (1 mile E of town on Bethel road) ☎ (01726) 72129
11-11; 12-10.30 Sun
St Austell Tinners, Trelawny's Pride, HSD Ⓗ
Friendly local serving good home-cooked food. Regular live music. On hopper bus route. Eve meals Tue-Sat. 🏨 ❀ 🛏 ◑ ▶ ♿ ⇌ 🍻 P

Try also Duke of Cornwall, Victoria Rd (St Austell)

ST BREWARD

OLD INN
Churchtown ☎ (01208) 850711
11-2.30 (3 Sat), 6-11; 12-3, 7-10.30 Sun
Draught Bass; Ruddles County; Sharp's Doom Bar Bitter, Special Ⓗ
11th-century granite moorland pub next to the highest church in Cornwall. A slate flagstone floor and large open fireplace are features. 🏨 Q 🍺 ❀ ◑ ▶ 🍻 P

ST CLEER

STAG INN
Fore Street
☎ (01579) 342305
12-11; 12-10.30 Sun
Draught Bass; Greene King Abbot; Sharp's Cornish Coaster, Doom Bar Bitter, Own; guest beers Ⓗ
Welcoming inn on the edge of Bodmin Moor, offering a good range of beers and regular events. A family room is available when the pub is not too busy. The restaurant offers a wide and varied menu.
🏨 Q 🍺 ❀ ◑ ▶ 🍻 P

ST COLUMB MAJOR

COACHING INN
13 Bank Street
☎ (01637) 881408
12-11; 12-10.30 Sun

Draught Bass; Fuller's London Pride; Skinner's Cornish Knocker Ale, Skilliwidden; Worthington Bitter; guest beer Ⓗ
Built in 1661, retaining gas lighting, this pub radiates atmosphere. The landlords have developed a reputation for excellent food and great theme nights, eg beach parties with sand and apres ski with real snow! Family room upstairs.
🏨 🍺 ◑ ▶ ♿ ▲ 🍻 P ✄

RING O'BELLS
3 Bank Street
☎ (01637) 880259
12-3, 5-11; 12-4, 7-10.30 Sun
Draught Bass; Sharp's Cornish Coaster, Own; Ⓗ guest beers Ⓖ
A narrow frontage belies the extensive three-bar interior of this pub which caters for all tastes, from loud rock to an intimate restaurant (supper licence until midnight).
🏨 ❀ ◑ ▶ ▲ P

ST IVES

SLOOP INN
The Wharf
☎ (01736) 796584
11-11; 12-10.30 Sun
Courage Best Bitter; Morland Old Speckled Hen; Ruddles County; John Smith's Bitter; Theakston XB, Old Peculier Ⓗ
One of Cornwall's oldest and most famous inns, dating from 1312. It is situated on the harbour front, and is popular with locals, fishermen, artists and tourists all year. Seafood is a speciality. Beware the low ceilings.
Q 🍺 ❀ 🛏 ◑ ▶ ⇌ 🍻

ST JUST

STAR INN
Fore Street
☎ (01736) 788767
11-3, 6-11 (11-11 summer); 12-10.30 Sun
St Austell XXXX Mild, Ⓗ **Tinners, HSD** Ⓖ
Old, atmospheric one-bar local where beer is served from the wood.
🏨 🍺 ❀ ◑ ▶

ST KEW HIGHWAY

RED LION
Off A39
☎ (01208) 841271
11-3, 6-11; 11-11 Sat; 12-3, 7-10.30 (12-10.30 summer) Sun
Draught Bass; Sharp's Doom Bar Bitter Ⓗ
Comfortable 17th-century pub with two bars and a dining area. Large games area in public bar.
🏨 Q 🍺 ❀ ◑ ▶ 🍴 🍻 P

SPARNON GATE

CORNISH ARMS
On old Portreath road
☎ (01209) 216407
12-2.30, 4.30 (5 summer)-11;
12-3, 7 (6.30 summer)-10.30 Sun
**Sharp's Doom Bar Bitter,
Own;** Ⓗ **guest beer**
17th-century, unspoilt free house
with welcoming owners. One bar
is small and intimate, the other
larger and popular with locals. It
boasts stone walls, beams, log
fires, brasses and mining
photos. Good home-cooked food
served. 🏚 Q ❀ ◖ 🗗 ♿ 🅰 P

STRATTON

KING'S ARMS
Howells Road ☎ (01288) 352396
12-2.30, 6.30-11; 12-11 Fri & Sat;
12-10.30 Sun
**Sharp's Cornish Coaster, Own;
guest beers** Ⓗ
Busy, 17th-century village pub.
Two bars with slate flagstone
floors and a games room. Cider
in summer.
🏚 Q ❀ 🚃 ◖ 🗗 ♣ 🍺 P

TORPOINT

KING'S ARMS
Fore Street ☎ (01752) 812882
11-11; 12-10.30 Sun
**Courage Best Bitter, Directors;
guest beers** Ⓗ
Large, one-bar pub by the ferry.
Very relaxing, overlooking HM
dockyard. 🏚 🛏 ◖ 🅰 ⇌ ♣

TREBELLAN

SMUGGLERS DEN
Off A3075 towards Cubert then
first left ☎ (01637) 830209
11-11 (12-2, 6-11 winter, hours
may extend); 12-10.30 Sun
**Fuller's London Pride; Sharp's
Doom Bar Bitter;** Ⓗ **guest
beers** Ⓗ Ⓖ
16th-century thatched country
inn with smuggling history. Close
to good beaches, coarse and sea
fishing. See the food specials
board for meals to suit all tastes.
Many camping and caravan sites
nearby. Family room not always
open. 🏚 🛏 ❀ ◖ 🗗 🅰 🍺 P

TREGREHAN

BRITANNIA
Tregrehan Par (on A390, 3 miles
E of St Austell) ☎ (01726) 812889
11-11; 12-10.30 Sun
**Draught Bass; Fuller's London
Pride; Morland Old Speckled
Hen; St Austell Tinners; Sharp's
Own; guest beers** Ⓗ
Large 16th-century inn, open all
day for food. Safe garden and
play area, large car park. Meals
served all day.
Q 🛏 ❀ ◖ 🗗 ♿ 🅰 ♣ P

TRESPARRETT

HORSESHOE INN
☎ (01840) 261240
12-3, 6.30-11 (11-11 summer); 12-
3, 7-10.30 (12-10.30 summer) Sun
**Sutton Knickadroppaglory; guest
beers** Ⓗ
200-year-old building with a flagstone floor and beamed ceiling.
Excellent gourmet eves Sat.
Strong following for darts and
pool. Guest beers usually from
Sutton Brewery, who brew the
house beer, 'Hosspiss'.
🏚 ❀ ◖ 🗗 ⇌ P

TRURO

CITY INN
Pydar Street (B3284, signed
Perranporth) ☎ (01872) 272623
11-11; 12-10.30 Sun
**Courage Best Bitter, Directors;
Skinner's Best Bitter, Betty
Stogs Bitter, Cornish Knocker
Ale; guest beers** Ⓗ
Popular local with friendly atmos-
phere and excellent value food.
Large garden. ❀ 🚃 ◖ 🗗 ♣

OLD ALE HOUSE
7 Quay Street
☎ (01872) 271122
11-11; 12-10.30 Sun
Draught Bass; Ⓗ Ⓖ **Boddingtons
Bitter; Courage Directors; Sharp's
Doom Bar Bitter,** Ⓗ **Own;** Ⓖ
guest beers Ⓗ Ⓖ
Popular, busy ale-house 'theme'
pub where sawdust and peanuts
abound. Loud live music Mon,
Wed, Thu and Sat eves.
Pleasantly quiet lunchtimes and
other eves. No food Sun. ◖ 🗗

TYWARDREATH

NEW INN
Fore Street ☎ (01726) 813901
11.30-3.30, 6-11; 11.30-11 Sat;
12-4, 7-10.30 Sun
Draught Bass Ⓖ; **St Austell
Tinners; HSD** Ⓗ
Popular, classic village local near
the coast; secluded garden and a
games/children's room. Eve
meals finish 8pm. Limited parking.
🏚 Q 🛏 ❀ ◖ 🗗 ♿ 🅰 ⇌
(Par) ♣ 🍺 P

UPTON CROSS

CARADON INN
Near Liskeard ☎ (01579) 362391
11-3.30, 5.30-11; 12-4, 7-10.30 Sun
Draught Bass; Ⓖ **Boddingtons
Bitter; Flowers Original; St
Austell HSD; Sharp's Own** or
Doom Bar Bitter Ⓗ
Friendly, 17th-century country
inn, with a reputation for good
beer and good value food. Pool
and juke box in the public bar;
quieter lounge. Cider in summer.
Near Sterts Open Air Theatre.
🏚 Q ❀ ◖ 🗗 ♿ 🅰 ♣ 🍺 P

WIDEMOUTH BAY

BAY VIEW INN
Marine Drive
☎ (01288) 361273
11-3, 6-11 (11-11 summer); 12-3,
6-10.30 (12-10.30 summer) Sun
**Sharp's Cornish Coaster, Own;
guest beers** Ⓗ
Friendly, small pub overlooking a
surfing beach, home to the
Widemouth frog. Note the extensive collection of pump clips.
Separate dining room. Gravity-
dispensed cider in summer.
🛏 ❀ 🚃 ◖ 🗗 🔲 ♣ 🍺 P ⚥

VERYAN

NEW INN
☎ (01872) 501362
11.30-3, 6.30-11; 12-3, 7-10.30
Sun
St Austell Tinners, HSD Ⓖ
Beautiful pub on the Roseland
Peninsula, in a village famous for
its round thatched cottages. Ales
are served from the wood behind
the bar. Good range of food.
Superb beaches and walks close
by. 🏚 Q ❀ 🚃 ◖ 🗗

ZELAH

HAWKINS ARMS
High Road
☎ (01872) 540339
11-3, 6-11; 12-3, 7-10.30 Sun
**Draught Bass; Dartmoor Best
Bitter; Greene King Abbot;
Tetley Bitter; guest beers** Ⓗ
Popular village local off the A30,
offering ever-changing guest ales
(over 1,000 to date) plus real
cider, excellent home-cooked
meals and good value B&B. No-
smoking dining area.
🏚 🛏 ❀ 🚃 ◖ 🗗 ♿ ♣ 🍺 P 🍴

INDEPENDENT BREWERIES

Bird in Hand:
Hayle

Blue Anchor:
Helston

Keltek:
Redruth

St Austell:
St Austell

Sharp's:
Rock

Skinner's:
Truro

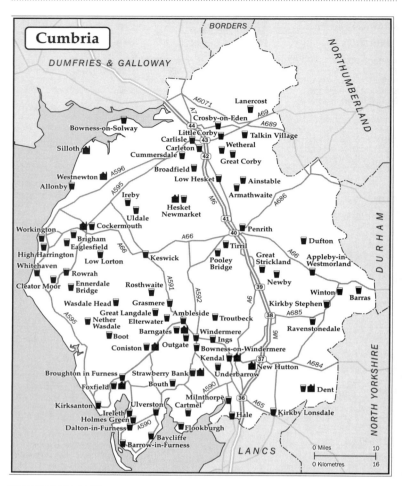

AINSTABLE

NEW CROWN INN
SE of Carlisle off A6
☎ (01768) 896273
12-3 (not Mon-Fri), 5-11; 12-3,
7-10.30 Sun
**Jennings Cumberland Ale;
Tetley Bitter; guest beers** H
Cosy village local with separate
dining room. Worth visiting.
🏨 Q 🕸 🛏 ◖ 🍴 ♣ P

ALLONBY

SHIP INN
☎ (01900) 881017
12-3, 7-11, (12-11 summer Sat);
12-11 Sun
**Yates Bitter, Premium, seasonal
beers; guest beers** H
Peaceful, comfortable seaside
village hotel on the beautiful
Solway coast, with stunning sunsets and amazing views. The only
Yates tied house. A 10% discount
on B & B for CAMRA members.
🏨 Q 🛏 🕸 🛏 🍺 ♠ P

AMBLESIDE

GOLDEN RULE
Smithy Brow (100 yds off A591
towards Kirkstone)
☎ (015394) 32257
11-11; 12-10.30 Sun
**Robinson's Hatters Mild, Old
Stockport, Hartleys XB, Best
Bitter** H
Well known for its lack of frills
such as juke box and fancy menu
(just good filled rolls and pork
pies), the 'Rule' has a bar area
with a cracking good atmosphere, two side rooms and a suntrap patio at the back.
🏨 Q 🕸 ♣

QUEENS HOTEL
Market Place
☎ (0153 94) 32206
11-11; 12-10.30 Sun
**Boddingtons Bitter; Jennings
Bitter; Theakston XB; guest
beers** H
Village centre hotel with a com-
mendable guest beer policy - a

blackboard indicates those available and those coming next. It
has a dining room and restaurant with a different menu. Both
are no-smoking.
🏨 🕸 🛏 ◖ ▶

APPLEBY-IN-WESTMORLAND

ROYAL OAK INN
Bongate
☎ (0176 83) 51463
11-11; 12-10.30 Sun
**Black Sheep Best Bitter; John
Smith's Bitter; Theakston Best
Bitter; guest beers** H
Civilised edge of town inn with
two wood panelled bars in which
to enjoy the wide choice of guest
ales, often from small Scottish
brewers. Also has a fine selection of malt whiskies. The house
beer is brewed by Hesket
Newmarket. Westmorland
CAMRA *Pub of the Season* spring
1998. 🏨 Q 🕸 🛏 ◖ ▶ 🍺 P

ARMATHWAITE

FOX & PHEASANT
SE of Carlisle, off A6
☎ (016974) 72400
11-11; 12-10.30 Sun
Hesket Newmarket Doris's 90th Birthday Ale; Mitchell's Lancaster Bomber Ⓗ
17th-century coaching house with a small hotel at the front, featuring an oak-beamed lounge and a slate-floored stable bar. Good food. The village is on the Settle-Carlisle Railway Line.
🏨 Q 🕸 🚪 ◖ ▮ 🕭
⇌ (Armathwaite) ♣ P

BARNGATES

DRUNKEN DUCK
Barngates, Ambleside
☎ (0153 94) 36347
11.30-3, 6-11; 12-3, 6-10.30 Sun
Barngates Chesters, Cracker; Jennings Bitter; Theakston Old Peculier; Yates Bitter Ⓗ
Isolated but very popular, with mountain views. No juke box, TV, machines etc. Good quality meals with imaginative vegetarian choices. Home of the Barngates brewery. 🏨 Q 🕸 🚪 ◖ ▮ ♣ P ✄

BARRAS

SLIP INN
Barras, Kirkby Stephen
OS834121 ☎ (0176 83) 41054
11 (7 Mon)-11; (7-11 winter Mon -Fri except bank hols); 12-10.30 Sun
Heather Fraoch Heather Ale; guest beer Ⓗ
A warm welcome awaits those who find this remote, cosy pub offering good value pub grub at all reasonable hours. No juke box or machines, this is a classic, genuine rural pub. Separate games room with pool table.
🏨 Q 🕸 🚪 ◖ ▮ 🕭 ▲ ♣ P

BARROW-IN-FURNESS

ALBION HOTEL
29 Dalton Road
☎ (01229) 820089
11-3, 6-11; 12-11 Fri & Sat; 12-3, 7-10.30 Sun
Caledonian Deuchars IPA; Ruddles Best Bitter; Theakston Best Bitter; guest beer Ⓗ
Friendly local close to the new shopping centre with two rooms offering enough variety to appeal to all. Good value pub lunches available Mon-Fri.
🕸 🚪 ◖ ▮ ⇌ ♣

KING'S ARMS
Quarry Brow, Hawcoat (100 yds W of Hawcoat Lane near Barrow Golf Club) ☎ (01229) 871303
7-11; 11-4, 7-11 Sat; 12-4, 7-10.30 Sun

Robinson's Best Bitter, Old Stockport, Hatters Mild, Hartleys XB Ⓗ
Pleasant traditional two-roomer with a friendly regular clientele. Quiz alternate Sun.
Q 🕸 🚪 🐀 ♣ ▯

BAYCLIFF

FARMERS ARMS
☎ (01229) 869382
12-3 (not Wed), 7.30-11; 11-11 Sat; 12-10.30 Sun
Robinson's Hartleys XB Ⓗ
Cosy pub set back from the coast road. The licensee is enthusiastic about beer and food. Traditionally warm atmosphere and climate. Weekday lunches; eve meals Fri-Sun.
🏨 Q 🕸 ◖ ♣ P

BOOT

BURNMOOR INN
☎ (01947) 23224
11-3, 5-11; 12-3, 5-10.30 Sun
Jennings Bitter, Cumberland Ale Ⓗ
Charming inn set in beautiful scenery in a fold of the hills near the foot of Scafell, close to the La'al Ratty narrow gauge steam railway. Perennially popular; families welcome. Austrian cooking is a speciality
🏨 Q 🕸 🚪 ◖ ▮ ▲
⇌ (Dalegarth (R & E) P

BOUTH

WHITE HART
☎ (01229) 861229
12-2 (not Mon), 6-11; 12-3, 6-11 Sat; 12-3, 6-10.30 Sun
Boddingtons Bitter; Jennings Bitter; guest beers Ⓗ
Set in a pleasant, unspoilt area on the fringe of the south lakes, this pub features old lakeland photos and paintings as well as hunting trophies and memorabilia. The mild varies.
🏨 🐀 🚪 ◖ ▮ ▲ ♣ P

BOWNESS ON SOLWAY

KINGS ARMS
☎ (016973) 51426
7-11; 1-3, 7-11 Sat; 1-3, 7-10.30 Sun
Jennings Bitter Ⓗ
At the western end of Hadrian's Wall, this village pub features old photographs and a real fire.
🏨 Q ▲ ♣

BOWNESS-ON-WINDEMERE

VILLAGE INN
Lake Road ☎ (0153 94) 43731
11-11; 12-10.30 Sun
Boddingtons Bitter; Castle Eden Ale; Jennings Cumberland Ale; Marston's Pedigree; guest beer Ⓗ

Busy, town-centre pub near the lake steamer piers, built as the Manse to the parish church opposite. Good value meals (served all day in summer) and separate no-smoking restaurant. Guest beer is often from a micro-brewery.
🕸 ◖ ▮ ♣ P

BRIGHAM

LIME KILN
Low Road
☎ (01900) 825375
12-3, 6.30-11; 12-3, 7-10.30 Sun
Hartley's XB Ⓗ
Pleasant, two-roomed village local, popular for meals. No food Mon, except bank holidays. Children welcome.
Q 🕸 🚪 ◖ ▮ ▲ ♣ P

BROADFIELD

CROWN
4 miles S of Carlisle racecourse
☎ (0169 74) 73467
12-3, 6.30-11; 12-3, 7-10.30 Sun
Theakston Best Bitter; guest beer Ⓗ
Roadside country pub featuring three rooms knocked into one. A friendly welcome and excellent meals assured.
🏨 🕸 ◖ ▮ ♣ P ▯

BROUGHTON-IN-FURNESS

MANOR ARMS
The Square
☎ (01229) 716286
12-11; 12-10.30 Sun
Draught Bass; Butterknowle Banner Bitter; Coniston Bluebird Bitter; Yates Bitter; guest beers Ⓗ
Busy, friendly, 18th-century family-run free house in a quiet, pleasant village square. A focal point of the community. Accommodation discounts for CAMRA members. All rooms ensuite. 🏨 Q 🕸 🚪 ♣ ▯

Try also: Old Kings Head, Church St (Whitbread)

CARLISLE

BIDDY MULLIGAN'S LITTLE SAUSAGE FACTORY
79 Milbourne Street
☎ (01228) 532459
11-11 (Jan-Feb); 12-10.30 Sun
Jennings Bitter, Cumberland Ale, seasonal beers Ⓗ
Jennings' only tied house in Carlisle, formerly 'The Woolpack' - a regular in this before it fell on bad times. Now revamped and much improved as an Irish theme pub. Cumberland sausage and Cumbrian ales. Live music.
🕸 ◖ ▮ ⇌ P

BOARDROOM
Paternoster Row (opp Cathedral)
☎ (01228) 527695
11-11; 12-2, 7-10.30 Sun
**Theakston Mild, Best Bitter, XB;
Younger Scotch; guest beers** Ⓗ
Old pub, nestling alongside the
11th-century cathedral near the
city centre; popular with students
and office workers.
◑ ▶ ⇌

CALEDONIAN CASK HOUSE
17 Botchergate (near station)
☎ (01228) 530460
11-11; 12-10.30 Sun
**Boddingtons Bitter; Marston's
Pedigree; guest beers** Ⓗ
Large one-room city-centre pub,
busy at weekends. Several regu-
larly-changing guest beers.
Lunches served 12-5. ◑ ♿ ⇌

CARLISLE RUGBY CLUB
Warwick Road
☎ (01228) 521300
7 (5.30 Fri, 6 Sat)-11 (12.30-11
Sat in football season); 12.30-3,
7-10.30 Sun
**Tetley Bitter; Yates Bitter; guest
beer** Ⓗ
Welcoming club with a cosy
lounge and large bar; often
crowded when Carlisle Utd are at
home. Show this *Guide* or CAMRA
membership to be signed in.
⚌ ⚓ ☸ ♣ P

CROWN INN
Scotland Road, Stanwix (on old
A7, 1 mile N of city centre)
☎ (01228) 512894
11-11; 12-10.30 Sun
**Theakston Best Bitter; guest
beers** (occasional) Ⓗ
Popular local standing on the line
of Hadrian's Wall, a pleasant
walk from the city centre across
River Eden. Retains some nice
wood-panelling from State
Management days. Guest beers
are from the S&N range.
☸ ◑ ▶

HOWARD ARMS
Lowther Street (next to Lanes
shopping centre)
☎ (01228) 532926
11-11; 12-10.30 Sun
Theakston Best Bitter, XB Ⓗ
A regular *Guide* entry; partitions
in this busy pub give a multi-
roomed effect. Unchanged for
many years it bears evidence of
the State Management scheme.
☸ ◑ ⇌

CARLTON

CARROW HOUSE HOTEL
On A6, off M6 jct 42
☎ (01228) 532073
11-11; 12-10.30 Sun
**Banks's Bitter; Marston's
Pedigree** Ⓗ
One of the Milestone chain of
restaurants and taverns, part of

a much-extended house. Large
lounge bar in the now familiar
pub chain style. Ideal stopping-
off point for a journey on the M6.
Meals served all day.
⚌ ☸ ◑ ▶ ♿ ♣ P ⅍ 🍴

CARTMEL

CAVENDISH ARMS
☎ (015395) 36240
11.30-11; 12-10.30 Sun
**Draught Bass; Cartmel Pride,
Lakeland Gold; guest beer** Ⓗ
Large, old inn with central bar -
diners one side, drinkers the
other. Good varied menu with
unusual specials. Can get busy
and consequently smoky.
⚌ Q ☸ 🛏 ◑ ▲ ♣ P

CLEATOR MOOR

NEW VICTORIA
Ennerdale Road
☎ (01946) 811345
11-5, 7-11; 11-11 Thu-Sat;
12-10.30 Sun
**Boddingtons Bitter; Jennings
Bitter; guest beer** Ⓗ
Comfortable pub on the main
street of this small town.
Excellent enclosed beer garden.
Strong community atmosphere
with a welcome for all. ☸ ♣

COCKERMOUTH

BITTER END
15 Kirkgate (just off main street)
☎ (01900) 828993
12-2.30, 6-11; 11-3, 6-11 Fri &
Sat; 12-3, 7-10.30 Sun
**Bitter End Cockersnoot; Derwent
Mutineer; Jennings Bitter;
Theakston Best Bitter, XB, Old
Peculier; guest beers** Ⓗ
Interesting brewpub created out
of a derelict shell by licensees
with a proven commitment to
real ale and good food. Own
beers brewed weekly in a small
room visible from the lounge.
Children welcome at mealtimes
(eve meals served until 8.30).
⚌ Q ◑ ▲

BUSH HOTEL
Main Street
☎ (01900) 822064
11-11; 12-10.30 Sun
**Jennings Mild, Bitter,
Cumberland Ale, Cocker Hoop,
Sneck Lifter, seasonal beers;
guest beers** Ⓗ
The nearest thing to a brewery
tap, this popular pub has a loyal
following. Winner of a local
CAMRA award; now selecting
rarer guest ales.
⚌ ◑ ▶

SWAN INN
Kirkgate
☎ (01900) 822425
11.30 (11 Sat)-3, 7.15-11; 12-2,
7-10.30 Sun

Jennings Bitter Ⓗ
Traditional friendly local in a
Georgian cobbled area of town.
Strong community spirit. A large
choice of whiskies.
Q ▲ ♣

CONISTON

BLACK BULL HOTEL
Yewdale Road
☎ (015394) 41668
11-11; 12-10.30 Sun
**Coniston Bluebird Bitter, Old
Man Ale, seasonal beers;
Theakston Old Peculier; guest
beers** Ⓗ
Sprawling 16th-century coaching
inn at the heart of Coniston. One
room has a children's certificate. The house beers now number three regulars and one winter warmer, Blacksmith's Ale.
Tours of the brewery by
appointment.
⚌ Q ☸ 🛏 ◑ ▶ P

SUN HOTEL AND
COACHING INN
200 yds up steep hill off A593
☎ (015394) 41248
11-11; 12-10.30 Sun
**Jennings Cumberland Ale;
Tetley Bitter; guest beer** Ⓗ
16th-century coaching inn with a
more modern hotel added.
Beams, horse brasses and an
open fire in the main bar welcome climbers and ramblers.
Note the Donald Campbell memorabilia. Very busy at peak
times. Children allowed in bar
until 9pm.
⚌ ☸ 🛏 ◑ ▶ ▲ P ⅍

CROSBY ON EDEN

STAG INN
☎ (01228) 573210
12-3, 6-11; 12-3, 6.30-10.30 Sun
**Jennings Bitter, Cumberland
Ale, Sneck Lifter** Ⓗ
Superb olde-worlde pub in
bypassed village with low-
beamed ceilings and stone-
flagged floors. Good value home-
cooked food is served in the bar
and the upstairs restaurant. Well
worth a detour.
Q ☸ ◑ ▶ ♣ P

CUMMERSDALE

SPINNERS ARMS
Off B5299, on outskirts of
Carlisle
☎ (01228) 532928
12-3, 7-11; 12-11 Sat; 12-10.30
Sun
**Theakston Best Bitter, Black Bull
Bitter; guest beers** Ⓗ
Village local designed (like other
State Management pubs) by
Harry Redfern, with an
L-shaped bar and a small lounge
area.
⚌ ☸ ◑ ▶ ♣

DALTON-IN-FURNESS

MASONS ARMS
101 Market Street
☎ (01229) 462678
10.30-11; 12-10.30 Sun
Mansfield Classic; guest beer Ⓗ
Cosy, friendly, unassuming main
road pub. Live music Fri-Sun.
🏚 ⬖ ⇌ ♣ P

Try also: Red Lion, Market St
(Free)

DENT

SUN INN
Main Street
☎ (015396) 25208
11-2.30, 7-11; 11-11 Sat &
summer; 12-10.30 Sun
**Dent Bitter, Kamikaze, T'owd
Tup; Younger Scotch** Ⓗ
Unspoilt, traditional pub on the
main street of this delightful
Dales village. Reasonably priced
meals in the quiet bar with a no-
smoking annexe (no eve meals
winter Mon-Fri). Separate games
room. Dent brewery's other pub,
the George & Dragon, almost
next door, is also recommended.
🏚 Q 🏚 ⇌ ⬖ ▶ Å P ⅍

DUFTON

STAG INN
☎ (0176 83) 51608
11-3 (not winter Mon), 6-11; 11-
11 Sat & summer; 12-10.30 Sun
**Black Sheep Best Bitter; Castle
Eden Ale** (summer)**; Flowers IPA**
(winter)**; guest beer** Ⓗ
Traditional local in this charming
village at the foot of the
Pennines. There is an impressive kitchen range in one of the
three rooms - ideal on winter
evenings. Also has a self-catering cottage.
🏚 🏚 ⇌ ⬖ ▶ Å ♣ P

EAGLESFIELD

BLACK COCK
☎ (01900) 822989
11-3, 6-11; 12-4, 7-10.30 Sun
Jennings Bitter Ⓗ
A gem of a pub run by a gem of a
landlady; well worth a detour.
Unspoilt and unaltered it stands
in a delightful village with a
history.
🏚 Q 🏚 🏚 ♣

ELTERWATER

BRITANNIA INN
☎ (0153 94) 37210
11-11; 12-10.30 Sun
**Coniston Bluebird; Dent Aviator;
Jennings Bitter; guest beers** Ⓗ
Very popular village pub on the
green with stunning surroundings with a bar, dining room and
back room (formerly a bar).
🏚 Q 🏚 ⬖ ▶ Å

ENNERDALE BRIDGE

SHEPHERDS ARMS
☎ (01946) 861249
11-11; 12-10.30 Sun
**Theakston Best Bitter, XB; guest
beer** Ⓗ
Small hotel with an informal and
relaxed atmosphere on the Coast
to Coast footpath and close to
tranquil Ennerdale Water. A good
place to relax after a day's walking in this less-frequented part of
the Lakes. Boots and backpacks
OK; children's certificate.
🏚 Q 🏚 🏚 ⇌ ⬖ ▶ Å P

FLOOKBURGH

CROWN
45 Market St ☎ (0153 95) 58248
12-4, 7-11; 12-4, 7-10.30 Sun
**Robinson's Old Stockport,
Hartleys XB Best Bitter;** Ⓗ
Bustling and friendly, roomy vil-
lage local.
🏚 🏚 🏚 ⇌ Å ⇌ (Cark &
Cartmel) ♣ P

FOXFIELD

PRINCE OF WALES
☎ (01229) 716238
5-11 (not Mon & Tue); 12-11 Sat;
12-10.30 Sun
Beer range varies Ⓗ
Pleasant, welcoming, open-
roomed pub with views of
Duddon Estuary and the Fells.
Local CAMRA *Pub of the Year*
1997. A house-brewed Foxfield
beer will often be available and
there is usually a mild.
🏚 Q ⇌ ♣ P ⬚

GRASMERE

TRAVELLERS REST
☎ (015394) 35604
11-11; 12-10.30 Sun
Jennings Mild (summer)**, Bitter,
Cumberland Ale, Sneck Lifter;
Marston's Pedigree** Ⓗ
Family-run roadside pub near the
Coast to Coast walk. Cosy bar
with log fire, games room and
no-smoking dining room (food all
day in summer). Also has two
nearby cottages to let.
🏚 🏚 ⇌ ⬖ ▶ Å ♣ P

GREAT CORBY

CORBY BRIDGE INN
Off A69 E of Carlisle, next to rail-
way crossing ☎ (01228) 560221
12-11; 12-4, 7-10.30 Sun
Tetley Mild, Bitter; guest beers Ⓗ
Grade II listed building of archi-
tectural and historic interest.
One room with three distinct
drinking areas. The landlady is
enthusiastic about her beers.
🏚 Q 🏚 ⇌ ⬖ ▶ Å
⇌ (Wetheral) ♣ P

Try also: Queen Inn (Free)

GREAT LANGDALE

OLD DUNGEON GHYLL
☎ (0153 94) 37272
11-11; 12-10.30 Sun
**Jennings Mild, Cumberland Ale;
Theakston XB, Old Peculier;
Yates Bitter; guest beer** Ⓗ
Ever-popular, atmospheric bar
looking after the liquid, solid and
drying needs of walkers. No juke
box, TV or machines. Book for
dining in the hotel lounge bar.
🏚 Q 🏚 ⇌ ⬖ ▶ Å ⟲ P

GREAT STRICKLAND

STRICKLAND ARMS
☎ (01931) 712238
12-3 (not Wed), 6-11; 12-10.30 Sun
**Ind Coope Burton Ale; Jennings
Bitter; Tetley Bitter; guest beer**
(occasional) Ⓗ
Welcoming two-bar village pub
with a separate games room.
Freshly-cooked meals are excellent value plus snacks until closing time. Large, safe garden with
play area.
🏚 Q 🏚 ⇌ ⬖ ▶ Å ♣ P

HALE

KINGS ARMS
On A6
☎ (0153 95) 63203
11-3, 6-11; 12-10.30 Sun
**Mitchell's Original, Lancaster
Bomber** Ⓗ
Traditional roadside pub with
L-shaped bar, pool room and
family/function room upstairs
(children's certificate). Bowling
green for hire. Beer range may
extend in summer.
🏚 🏚 🏚 ⇌ ⬖ ▶ Å ♣ P

HESKET NEWMARKET

OLD CROWN
1 mile SE of Caldbeck OS341386
☎ (0169 74) 78288
12-3 (not Mon-Fri except school
hols), 5.30-11; 12-3, 7-10.30
Sun
**Hesket Newmarket Great
Cockup, Blencathra, Skiddaw
Special, Doris's 90th Birthday
Ale, Catbells Pale Ale, Old
Carrock, Pigs Might Fly** Ⓗ
Superb fellside village pub, offering fine food. Hesket Newmarket
brewery is in the converted barn
at the back. Eve meals finish 8.30
(not served Sun or Mon, except
bank hols).
🏚 Q 🏚 ⬖ ▶ Å ♣

HIGH HARRINGTON

GALLOPING HORSE
Main Road
☎ (01900) 830083
12-3, 7-11; 12-3, 7-10.30 Sun
Jennings Mild, Bitter Ⓗ
Large, comfortable pub with several rooms, including a large

games room. Tasty, reasonably-priced meals include a renowned steak pie. Children's certificate until 9.30pm.
Q ☜ ☸ ◖ ◑ ♣ P ⊁

HOLMES GREEN

BLACK DOG INN
Broughton Road (between Ireleth, Marton and Dalton-in-Furness) ☎ (01229) 462561
11-11, 12-10.30 Sun
Coniston Opium; Yates Bitter; guest beers Ⓗ
Cosy country retreat with a friendly atmosphere, serving good value home-cooked food until 9pm. Popular with the farming community. Local CAMRA *Pub of the Year* 1998. Cider varies. Children's certificate.
♨ Q ☜ ☸ ⇌ ◖ ◑ ♣ ○ P ⊁ ☗

INGS

WATERMILL INN
☎ (01539) 821309
12-2.30, 6-11; 12-3, 6-10.30 Sun
Black Sheep Special; Coniston Bluebird; Lees Moonraker; Theakston Best Bitter, XB, Old Peculier; guest beers Ⓗ
Deservedly popular, two-bar, family-run pub offering the widest selection of guest ales in Cumbria. The cellar can be viewed through a cartwheel window. A story teller visits first Tues in the month. West Pennines CAMRA *Pub of the Year* 1997.
♨ Q ☸ ⇌ ◖ ◑ ♿ ♣ ○ P ⊁

IREBY

PADDY'S BAR
The Square
☎ (0169 73) 71460
11-11; 5.30-11 Wed & Sat; 12-3, 7-10.30 Sun
Jennings Bitter; Yates Bitter; guest beers Ⓗ
Irish character pub serving as village shop and post office, situated on the old market square. This is not a theme pub. Eve meals served Tue-Sun.
♨ Q ◑

IRELETH

BAY HORSE INN
Ireleth Brow
☎ (01229) 463755
7-11; 12-3, 7-11 Wed-Sat; 12-3, 7-10.30 Sun
Jennings Mild, Bitter, Cumberland Ale Ⓗ
Impressive 18th-century local on the brow of a hill. Jennings' only tied real ale outlet in the area. Small car park.
♨ Q ⇌ (Askam-in-Furness) ♣ P ⊁

KENDAL

CASTLE INN
Castle Street
☎ (01539) 729983
11-11; 12-10.30 Sun
Tetley Bitter; Theakston Best Bitter; guest beers Ⓗ
Popular two-roomer, busy with office staff at lunchtime, a genuine local at night. Good value lunches. See the rare Duttons window framed on an inside wall.
♨ ☸ ⇌ ◖ ♣ ♠

RING O' BELLS ☆
Kirkland
☎ (01539) 720326
12-3 (not Tue), 6-11; 12-3, 7-10.30 Sun (may vary)
Vaux Lorimer's Best Scotch, Bitter, Samson; Ward's Best Bitter; guest beer Ⓗ
Two-bar pub with a gem of a snug between a cosy front bar and a back lounge. Probably unique in standing on consecrated ground. Good value home-made meals. On CAMRA's inventory of historic pub interiors.
♨ ☸ ◖ ◑ ▣ ♣

KESWICK

BANK TAVERN
Main Street
☎ (0176 87) 72663
11-11; 12-10.30 Sun
Jennings Bitter, Cumberland Ale, Sneck Lifter Ⓗ
Town pub with a village atmosphere, a strong focus on the community and charity fundraising. Early King Kong arcade table in the family area.
☜ ◖ ◑ Å

LAKE ROAD INN
Lake Road
☎ (0176 87) 72404
12-3, 6-11 (11-11 Sat & summer); 12-10.30 Sun
Jennings Bitter, Cumberland Ale, Cocker Hoop, Sneck Lifter Ⓗ
Cosy, attractive town pub, popular with visitors and locals. Stunning flower baskets in summer. Children's certificate.
♨ Q ☜ ◖ ◑ Å ♣

KIRKBY LONSDALE

SNOOTY FOX
Main Street
☎ (0152 42) 71308
11-11; 12-10.30 Sun
Robinson's Hartleys XB; Taylor Landlord; Theakston Best Bitter Ⓗ
Well appointed two-bar pub with unusual memorabilia. Dining area at the front and part-flagstoned back bar with juke box. Quality meals served.
♨ Q ☸ ⇌ ◖ ◑ ▣ Å P

KIRKBY STEPHEN

WHITE LION
4 Market Street
☎ (017683) 71481
12-3 (4 Sat), 6-11 (may vary); 12-4, 7-10.30 Sun
Jennings Bitter, Cumberland Ale Ⓗ
Refurbished two-bar town-centre pub on Coast to Coast walk, popular with locals and visitors. Beer range from Jennings may extend in summer. ◖ ◑ ⇌ ⊕

KIRKSANTON

KING WILLIAM IV
2 miles N of Millom on Whitehaven road.
☎ (01229) 772009
11-3, 7-11 (extension on bank hols); 12-3, 7-10.30 Sun
Jennings Cumberland Ale; guest beers Ⓗ
18th-century country pub with stone-flagged floor and beamed ceiling. Roaring log fire. Community spirit where everyone is welcome (including children until 9pm).
♨ Q ☜ ☸ ⇌ ◖ ◑ Å ♣ P ☗

LANERCOST

ABBEY BRIDGE INN (BLACKSMITH'S BAR)
2 miles from Brampton, off A69
☎ (0169 77) 2224
12-2.30, 7-11; 12-2.30, 7-10.30 Sun
Adnams Extra; Shepherd Neame Spitfire; guest beers Ⓗ
An absolute gem. The split-level bar area has a spiral staircase leading to a restaurant. Close to Lanercost Priory and Hadrian's Wall. ♨ Q ☸ ⇌ ◖ ◑ ♣ P

LITTLE CORBY

HAYWAIN
Off A69
☎ (01228) 560598
7-11; 11-11 Sat; 11-10.30 Sun
Robinson's Hartleys XB, Best Bitter, Frederics Ⓗ
Homely village pub with a lounge, a bar and a snug. A warm welcome, good food and live entertainment await. ☸ ◖ ◑ ♣ P

LOW HESKET

ROSE & CROWN
On A6, 3 miles S of M6 jct 42
☎ (0169 74) 73346
11.30-3, 6-11; 12-3, 7-10.30 Sun
Jennings Mild, Bitter, Cumberland Ale Ⓗ
Comfortable village pub with a friendly atmosphere and good value food, including a vegetarian option from a varied menu (no food Mon eve except bank hols). One of the few real mild pubs in the area. ♨ Q ☸ ◖ ◑ ♣ P

LOW LORTON

WHEATSHEAF
Near Cockermouth
☎ (01900) 85268
12-3, 6-11 (11-11 summer); 12-3,
7-10.30 (12-10.30 summer) Sun
**Jennings Bitter, Cumberland Ale,
Cocker Hoop, Sneck Lifter** H
Pleasant country pub with superb
food (restaurant and bar meals),
a children's certificate and
enclosed garden. Interesting
artefacts, maps and books on
display, plus an extensive collection of teddies.
Q ⛺ ✿ ◑ ▶ ▲ ♣ P

MILNTHORPE

COACH & HORSES
Haverflatts Lane
☎ (0153 95) 63210
11-3, 6-11; 11-11 Fri & Sat;
12-10.30 Sun
Mitchell's Mild, Original H
Popular, spacious, traditional
local just off the village square.
Sponsors local sports teams and
charities. Good value pub grub.
Handy for Levens Hall.
🏠 ✿ ◑ ▶ ♣ P

NETHER WASDALE

SCREES HOTEL
☎ (0194 67) 26262
12-2.30, 6-11; 12-3, 6-10.30 Sun
**Jennings Bitter, Cumberland
Ale; Theakston Best Bitter, Old
Peculier; Yates Bitter; guest
beers** H
Homely hotel with split-level
bars, set in a delightful hamlet
with superb views from the garden, a mile west of Wastwater;
much loved by walkers, campers
and climbers. Regular live music
and guest ale nights.
🏠 Q ⛺ ✿ 🛏 ◑ ▶ ▲ ♣ P

NEWBY

NEWBY HALL HOTEL
☎ (01931) 714456
12-3, 7-11; 12-3, 7-10.30 Sun
Beer range varies H
The impressive bar in this former
manor/farmhouse which dates
from 1642 is dominated by a
huge fireplace. Usually has a
Jennings and a guest beer.
Separate dining room with different menu. No eve meals Sun.
🏠 ✿ 🛏 ◑ ▶ ▲ ♣ P

OUTGATE

OUTGATE INN
Nr Hawkshead
☎ (0153 94) 36413
11-3 (12-2.30 winter), 6-11; 12-3,
6-10.30 Sun
**Robinsons Hartley's XB, Best
Bitter, Frederics** (summer) H
Friendly traditional rural pub,
popular for meals. Traditional

jazz music every Fri eve (alternate weeks winter). Get there
early for a seat in summer.
🏠 Q ⛺ 🛏 ◑ ▶ ♣ P ✖

PENRITH

AGRICULTURAL HOTEL
Castlegate (200 yds from railway
station towards town centre)
☎ (01768) 62622
11-11; 12-10.30 Sun
**Jennings Mild, Bitter,
Cumberland Ale, Sneck Lifter** H
Comfortable town pub, recently
extended. Handy for the station.
🏠 ✿ 🛏 ◑ ➤ P ✖

POOLEY BRIDGE

SUN INN
☎ (0176 84) 86205
12-11; 12-10.30 Sun
**Jennings Bitter, Cumberland
Ale, Sneck Lifter** H
Traditional, village centre pub
with a panelled lounge bar, separate dining room and downstairs
public bar with a jukebox and
pool (winter).
🏠 ✿ 🛏 ◑ ▶ 🍴 ▲ ♣ P

RAVENSTONEDALE

BLACK SWAN
☎ (0153 96) 23204
11.30-3, 6-11; 11-11 Fri & Sat;
12-10.30 Sun
**Black Sheep Best Bitter;
Theakston XB; Younger Scotch;
guest beer** (summer) H
Stylish Victorian hotel with a
locals bar and a well-appointed
lounge. The separate no-smoking
dining room has a different
menu. The large garden has a
stream and wood.
Accommodation includes ground-
floor bedrooms suitable for
wheelchair-users.
🏠 Q ✿ 🛏 ◑ ▶ 🍴 ♿
▲ ♣ P

ROSTHWAITE

SCAFELL HOTEL RIVERSIDE BAR
☎ (0176 87) 77208
11-11; 12-10.30 Sun
**Theakston Best Bitter, XB, Old
Peculier** H
Real ale bar at the rear of a
country hotel in a beautiful valley. Popular for outdoor pursuits.
Walkers, campers (boots and all)
and well-behaved children welcome.
🏠 Q ⛺ ✿ 🛏 ◑ ▶ ▲ P

ROWRAH

STORK HOTEL
On A5086 ☎ (01946) 861213
11-3, 6-11; 12-5, 7-10.30 Sun
**Boddingtons Bitter; Jennings
Bitter** H
Family-run local, near go-kart

track and Coast to Coast
walk/cycleway.
🏠 Q ⛺ ✿ 🛏 🍴 ♣ P

STRAWBERRY BANK

MASONS ARMS
OS413895
☎ (0153 95) 68486
11.30-3, 6-11; 11.30-11 Fri, Sat &
summer; 12-10.30 Sun
**Strawberry Bank Damson Ale;
guest beers** H
Extremely popular lakeland inn,
famous for its vegan/vegetarian
cuisine and enormous range of
bottled beers from around the
world. Strawberry Bank and
Barnsley beers plus two others
are usually available, plus a Kriek
beer. Accommodation is self-
catering. Cider available in
summer.
🏠 Q ⛺ ✿ 🛏 ◑ ▶ ▲ ⌒ P

TALKIN VILLAGE

HARE & HOUNDS
From B6413 take village (not
Tarn) turn
☎ (0169 77) 3456
12-2.30 (school & bank hols),
7-11; 12-11 Sat; 12-10.30 Sun
**Jennings Bitter, Cumberland
Ale; guest beers** (summer) H
Charming two-roomed village
inn with beams, stone fire-
places, etched glass and bags of
atmosphere, close to the lovely
Talkin Tarn.
🏠 Q ✿ 🛏 ◑ ▶ ▲ ♣ P

TIRRIL

QUEENS HEAD
☎ (01768) 863219
12-3, 6-11(12-11 Sat & bank
hols); 12-10.30 Sun
**Black Sheep Best Bitter;
Jennings Cumberland Ale; guest
beers** H
New owners have rapidly gained
a reputation for quality beer and
food. Both bars have flagstone
floors, the back one has pool
and a jukebox. Separate no-
smoking dining room. Cumbrian
beer and sausage festival held
in August.
🏠 Q ✿ 🛏 ◑ ▶ 🍴 ♣ P

TROUTBECK

QUEENS HEAD HOTEL
Townhead
☎ (0153 94) 32174
11-11; 12-10.30 Sun
**Boddingtons Bitter; Mitchell's
Lancaster Bomber; Tetley Bitter;
guest beers** H
Award-winning pub, noted for
fine meals, a four-poster bed
frame bar and upstairs Mayor's
parlour. Guest beers, though not
cheap, are usually from local
small breweries.
🏠 ✿ 🛏 ◑ ▶ ▲ ♣ P ✖

ULDALE

SNOOTY FOX
☎ (0169 73) 71479
12-3, 6.30-11; 12-11 Sat;
12-10.30 Sun
Theakston Best Bitter H
Inn nestling in a peaceful village
in the northern fells, within the
Lake District National Park. Uld
Ale comes from Hesket
Newmarket.
Q ✿ ⊨ ◖ ▮ ⅏ ♣ P

UNDERBARROW

PUNCHBOWL INN
☎ (0153 95) 68234
12-3.30 (not Tue except after a
bank hol, 4 Sat); 6-11; 12-4,
7-10.30 Sun
**Draught Bass; Jennings
Cumberland Ale; guest beer** H
Intimate lakeland inn whose
interesting features include a
priest's hole behind the bar. The
menu board in the adjoining room
lists good value, home-made
meals. Games/function room up
a few steps.
🏨 ✿ ◖ ▮ ♣ P

ULVERSTON

FARMERS ARMS
Market Place
☎ (01229) 5844469
10-11; 11.30-10.30 Sun
**Theakston Best Bitter; guest
beers** H
Comfortable town-centre local
with separate dining/lounge
area. Newspapers always available. Coffee only served until
10.30am. Children welcome until
9pm. 🏨 ➹ ✿ ◖ ▮ ⇌

Try also: Kings Head, Queen St
(Free)

STAN LAUREL INN
The Ellers
☎ (01229) 582814
12-3, 7-11; 12-3, 7-10.30 Sun
**Tetley Dark Mild, Bitter; guest
beers** H
Friendly local featuring Laurel &
Hardy memorabilia. Lounge,
bar/games room and a dining
room that doubles as a function
room. Six guest beers include
Carlsberg-Tetley Tapsters'
Choice. ➹ ✿ ◖ ▯ ⇌ ♣ P

WASDALE HEAD

**WASDALE HEAD INN
(RITSON'S BAR)**
☎ (0194 67) 26229
11-11; 12-10.30 Sun
**Derwent Mutineer; Jennings
Cumberland Ale, Sneck Lifter;
Theakston Best Bitter, Old
Peculier; guest beers** H
A nine-mile walk (or drive) down
a single-track road, through stun-
ning mountain and lakeside

scenery is rewarded by the interesting Ritson's bar. The wide
range of local and Cumbrian
brewed beers includes a house
beer from Yates. Adjacent campsite is useful for May and Sept
beer festivals. CAMRA West
Pennines *Pub of the Year* 1991.
Eve meals until 8pm winter.
Q ✿ ⊨ ◖ ▮ ▯ ⅏ ▮ P ✄

WETHERAL

WHEATSHEAF
☎ (01228) 560686
12-2.30, 5-11; 12-11 Sat;
12-10.30 Sun
**Greenalls Bitter, Original; guest
beers** H
One-roomed local offering good
food. The village is on the bank of
the River Eden and there is excellent local walking and fishing.
🏨 ✿ ◖ ▮ ⇌ ♣ P

Try also: Crown, Station Rd
(Thwaites)

WHITEHAVEN

JUBILEE INN
Low Road
☎ (01946) 692848
12-3, 6.30-11; 11-11 Sat;
12-10.30 Sun
Jennings Bitter H
Friendly and unpretentious local
known as 'The Canteen', with a
'clubby' atmosphere. Very sport
oriented, nearest real ale outlet
to RLFC ground. Base for CAMRA
quiz team.
Q ➹ ✿ ▯ ⇌ (Corkickle) ♣ P

WINDERMERE

**GREY WALLS HOTEL
(GREYS INN)**
Elleray Road
☎ (0153 94) 43741
11-11; 12-10.30 Sun
**Theakston Best Bitter, XB; guest
beers** H
Very popular pub with a strong
local and visitor following. Family
room, games area with pool and
large-screen TV for sports. No
smoking area in the bar until
9.30pm. Meals served all day Sun
(also Sat Easter to Nov). Regular
quiz nights.
🏨 ➹ ✿ ⊨ ◖ ▮ ⇌ ♣ P ✄

WINTONS

BAY HORSE
☎ (0176 83) 71451
12-3 (not Winter Mon & Tue),
7 (6 summer)-11; 12-3, 7-10.30 Sun
**Theakston Best Bitter; Younger
Scotch** H
Traditional two-bar local overlooking the village green.
Comfortable lounge and stone-
flagged bar. Separate games
area. Guest beers usually from
small independent brewers.
🏨 Q ✿ ⊨ ◖ ▮ ▯ ♣

WORKINGTON

GEORGE IV
Stanley Street
☎ (01900) 602266
11-3, 7-11; 12-2, 7-10.30 Sun
Jennings Bitter H
End of terrace, cosy, quiet,
friendly local, on probably the
oldest street in town. Convenient
for football and greyhound stadia
and next to an attractive harbour
development. 🏨 Q ➹ ♣

INDEPENDENT
BREWERIES

Barngates:
Barngates

Bitter End:
Cockermouth

Cartmel:
Kendal

Coniston:
Coniston

Dent:
Dent

Derwent:
Carlisle

Foxfield:
Broughton in Furness

Hesket Newmarket:
Hesket Newmarket

Jennings:
Cockermouth

Lakeland:
Kendal

Old Cottage:
New Hutton

Strawberry Bank:
Cartmell Fell

Yates:
Westnewton

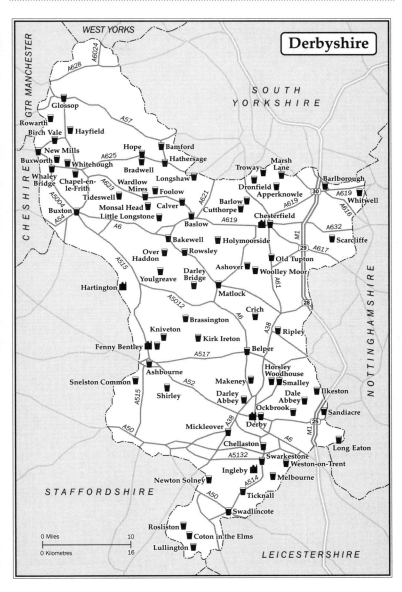

Derbyshire

(Map showing locations including Glossop, Rowarth, Birch Vale, Hayfield, New Mills, Buxworth, Whitehough, Buxton, Whaley Bridge, Chapel-en-le-Frith, Tideswell, Monsal Head, Little Longstone, Hope, Bamford, Hathersage, Bradwell, Longshaw, Wardlow Mires, Foolow, Calver, Baslow, Bakewell, Over Haddon, Rowsley, Darley Bridge, Youlgreave, Hartington, Matlock, Brassington, Crich, Kniveton, Kirk Ireton, Ripley, Fenny Bentley, Belper, Ashbourne, Snelston Common, Shirley, Makeney, Horsley Woodhouse, Smalley, Ilkeston, Darley Abbey, Dale Abbey, Sandiacre, Ockbrook, Mickleover, Derby, Chellaston, Long Eaton, Swarkestone, Weston-on-Trent, Ingleby, Melbourne, Newton Solney, Ticknall, Swadlincote, Rosliston, Coton in the Elms, Lullington, Troway, Marsh Lane, Dronfield, Apperknowle, Barlborough, Whitwell, Barlow, Cutthorpe, Chesterfield, Scarcliffe, Holymoorside, Old Tupton, Ashover, Woolley Moor)

APPERKNOWLE

YELLOW LION
High Street
☎ (01246) 413181
12-3, 6-11; 12-3, 7-10.30
Sun
**Draught Bass; Greene King
Abbot; Stones Bitter; guest
beers** Ⓗ
Stone-built village free house
with a large lounge and a no-
smoking restaurant. It also holds
a regular beer festival in early
summer. A pub that has been a
Guide entry since 1977.
Q ✿ 🛏 🕪 ▶ P 🍴

ASHBOURNE

BOWLING GREEN
2 North Avenue (A515)
☎ (01335) 342511
11-3, 5-11; 11-11 Thu & Sat;
12-10.30 Sun
**Draught Bass; Mansfield Old
Baily; Marston's Pedigree;
Worthington Bitter; guest
beer** Ⓗ
Spacious bar and a smaller
lounge housing oriental artefacts. Wide food choice - all
home-cooked - fresh fish is a
speciality; children welcome in
the restaurant. There is always a

mild on tap.
🛏 🕪 🍴 🛏 ▲ ♣ P

Try also: White Lion, Buxton Rd
(Free)

ASHOVER

CRISPIN INN
Church Street ☎ (01246) 590591
12-3 (not Tue & Thu); 12-11 Sat;
12-10.30 Sun
**Mansfield Riding Mild, Riding
Bitter, Bitter** Ⓗ
One of the oldest and most historic inns of the area, it has been
added to many times since 1416.

A comfortable and welcoming village local. Deakins and Old Baily are on cask breather.
Q ☎ ❀ ⇄ ◖ ▶ ⊕ ♣ P

BAKEWELL

PEACOCK
Market Place
☎ (01629) 812994
11-11; 12-10.30 Sun
Ward's Best Bitter; guest beer Ⓗ
Busy, town-centre pub where visitors are made welcome. Eve meals summer.
🏠 Q ❀ ◖ ▶ ♣ P

BAMFORD

DERWENT HOTEL
Main Road (A6013)
☎ (01433) 651395
11-11; 12-10.30 Sun
Stones Bitter; Ward's Best Bitter; guest beer Ⓗ
Sturdy hotel, built with the coming of the railway in 1890, enjoying a strong local trade, and a warm welcome for visitors. Now rather a period piece with many original furnishings. Good home-cooked food.
❀ ⇄ ◖ ▶ ⊕ ▲ ⇌ ♣ P

BARLBOROUGH

ROSE & CROWN
High Street (near M1 jct 30)
☎ (01246) 810364
12-3, 6-11; 12-3.30, 7-10.30 (12-10.30 summer) Sun
Hardys & Hansons Best Bitter, seasonal beer Ⓗ
Village pub with two bars and a restaurant area, set behind an historic Norman cross. Popular for food (no lunch Mon; eve meals served Wed-Sat).
❀ ◖ ▶ ⊕ ♣ P

BARLOW

HARE & HOUNDS
32 Commonside Road (off B6051) ☎ (0114) 289 0464
11-11; 12-4, 7-10.30 Sun
Draught Bass; Stones Bitter Ⓗ
Warm, friendly multi-roomed village local; the lounge offers splendid panoramic views of the Cordwell valley. 🏠 Q ❀ ♣ P

BASLOW

ROBIN HOOD
Chesterfield Road (A619/B6050 jct, 1½ miles E of village)
☎ (01246) 583186
11.30-3.30, 6.30-11; 11.30-11 Sat; 12-3, 7-10.30 (12-10.30 summer) Sun
Mansfield Riding Mild, Riding Bitter, Bitter, Old Baily Ⓗ
Excellent venue for walkers as well as the local trade. Dogs are welcome in the 'hikers' den'. Children's certificate. Note:

Riding Mild is served under cask breather in Jan if necessary.
🏠 ❀ ⇄ ◖ ▶ ⊕ ▲ ♣ P
✂ 🏠

BELPER

QUEENS HEAD
29 Chesterfield Road
☎ (01773) 825525
12-11; 12-10.30 Sun
ABC Best Bitter; Ind Coope Burton Ale; Tetley Bitter; guest beers Ⓗ
Lively, multi-roomed local hosting live music. Weekend lunches.
🏠 ◖ ⊕

BIRCH VALE

VINE
Hayfield Road (A6015, New Mills-Hayfield road)
☎ (01663) 741021
12-2.30, 6-11; 12-3, 7-10.30 Sun
Robinson's Hatters Mild, Best Bitter Ⓗ
Traditional stone pub on the edge of the Peak District, near the Sett Valley Trail. Good value food and pleasant views over the Sett Valley from the lounge. A warm welcome always assured. Limited parking. 🏠 ☎ ◖ ▶ ♣ P

BRADWELL

VALLEY LODGE
Church Street ☎ (01433) 620427
12-3 (not Mon-Fri), 7-11; 12-3, 7-10.30 Sun
Barnsley Bitter; Stones Bitter; guest beers Ⓗ
Large, brick-built 1930s pub in a limestone village: a basic tap room with its own entrance, a small foyer bar and a large lounge. Wide and ever varying range of guest beers.
🏠 Q ❀ ⇄ ◖ ▶ ⊕ ♣ P

BRASSINGTON

GATE INN ☆
Well Street ☎ (01629) 540448
12-2.30 (3 Fri & Sat), 6-11; 12-3, 7-10.30 Sun
Marston's Pedigree, HBC Ⓗ
Traditional village pub of considerable character, with an enormous inglenook range, wooden settles and scrubbed-top tables. Interesting choices of fresh cooked food. 🏠 Q ❀ ◖ P

BUXTON

BAKERS ARMS
26 West Road (near Fiveways traffic lights) ☎ (01298) 24404
12-3, 6-11; 12-3, 7-10.30 Sun
Ind Coope Burton Ale; Tetley Bitter; guest beer Ⓗ
Unspoilt, two-roomed alehouse, previously owned by Samuel Allsopp's brewery.
Q ❀ ▲ ♣ P

DUKE OF YORK
123 St Johns Road, Burbage
(1 mile from centre, on Macclesfield–Leek road)
☎ (01298) 24006
12-3, 5-11; 12-11 Sat & summer; 12-10.30 Sun
Marston's Pedigree; Tetley Mild, Bitter; Younger No. 3 Ⓗ
Old coach house: two large rooms served by a central bar. In the heart of the Peak District, it is popular with locals and walkers. Q ◖ ▶ ▲ P

SWAN HOTEL
41 High Street ☎ (01298) 23278
11-11; 12-10.30 Sun
Marston's Bitter; Tetley Bitter; guest beer Ⓗ
Nice three-roomed local. One room devoted to Scotland (with a selection of 100+ whiskies) and another to the RAF. Q ▲ ⇌ P

Try also: London Road, London Rd (Tetley)

BUXWORTH

NAVIGATION INN
Brookside Road (off B6062, by canal basin) ☎ (01663) 732072
11-11; 12-10.30 Sun
Marston's Pedigree; Taylor Landlord; Webster's Yorkshire Bitter; guest beer Ⓗ
Dating from pre-1795, this excellent multi-roomed pub with extensive restaurant is well worth seeking out. Partially stone-flagged with a nostalgic canal theme, it is popular with locals and hikers. Located alongside the only remaining UK canal/tramway interchange. Cider in summer.
🏠 Q ☎ ❀ ⇄ ◖ ▶ ⊕ ♣ ⌣ P

CALVER

BRIDGE INN
Calver Bridge, Hope Valley (A623) ☎ (01433) 630415
11.30-3 (4.30 Sat), 5.30-11; 12-4.30, 7-10.30 Sun
Hardys & Hansons Best Bitter, Classic; Stones Bitter Ⓗ
Cosy village local with a large lounge and a tap room with a games area. Good collection of local guide books. No food Mon eve or winter Sun eve.
Q ❀ ◖ ▶ ⊕ ♿ ▲ ♣ P ✂ 🏠

CHAPEL EN LE FRITH

ROEBUCK INN
Market Place ☎ (01298) 812274
11-11; 12-10.30 Sun
Tetley Mild, Bitter; guest beer Ⓗ
Thriving market place pub in a Peak District town. One bar serves the large, airy interior. Note the set of medieval stocks opposite. Meals served 12-6 Sun and bank hols. 🏠 Q ◖

CHELLASTON

CORNER PIN
Swarkestone Rd
☎ (01332) 705715
11-11; 12-10.30 Sun
Ind Coope Burton Ale; Marston's Pedigree; Ruddles County; guest beer Ⓗ
Early 19th-century roadside inn with a Cruck-built parlour.
Q ❀ ◖ ▶ ⊞ ▲ ♣ P ⊁

CHESTERFIELD

BOYTHORPE INN
Boythorpe Road, Boythorpe (opp Chesterfield Sports Centre)
☎ (01246) 235280
12-11; 12-10.30 Sun
Hardys & Hansons Best Mild, Best Bitter, Classic, seasonal beers Ⓗ
Large, friendly pub on the edge of the town centre, close to Queens Park and county cricket ground. Bowling green at the rear. Big screen satellite TV.
⛺ ❀ ◖ ⊞ ♣ P ⊟

DERBY TUP
387 Sheffield Road, Whittington Moor ☎ (01246) 454316
11.30-11 (11.30-3, 5-11 Mon & Tue); 12-4, 7-10.30 Sun
Bateman XXXB; Everards Tiger; Greene King Abbot; Marston's Pedigree; Theakston Old Peculier Ⓗ
Superb, unspoilt, corner free house with three rooms, offering multiple guest beers weekly, usually from independents. Eve meals end 7.30pm.
Q ◖ ♣ ⌂ ⊁

MARKET HOTEL
95 New Square
☎ (01246) 273641
11-11; 12-2, 7-10.30 Sun
Ind Coope Burton Ale; Marston's Pedigree; Tetley Bitter; guest beer Ⓗ
Busy Tetley Festival Ale-house with an excellent range of guest beers and beer festivals three times a year. No meals Sun.
◖ ⇌ ♣

RED LION
570 Sheffield Road, Whittington Moor ☎ (01246) 450770
12-4, 6-11; 12-3, 7-10.30 Sun
Old Mill Bitter, Old Curiosity Ⓗ
Pleasant local with a small lounge and larger public bar on either side of a central bar area. Weekday lunches.
Q ❀ ◖ ⊞ ♣ P

ROYAL OAK
43 Chatsworth Road, Brampton (A619, op. B&Q)
☎ (01246) 277854
11-11; 12-10.30 Sun
Marston's Pedigree; Ruddles Best Bitter; Theakston Best Bitter, Old Peculier; guest beers Ⓗ

Busy local, hosting regular live music. Nine cask ales include a guest from Townes, plus bottle-conditioned and Belgian beers. There is a children's playground in the garden.
⛺ ⛬ ❀ ◖ ⊞ ⇌ ♣ P

RUTLAND ARMS
16 Stephenson Place
☎ (01246) 205857
11-11; 12-10.30 Sun
Boddingtons Bitter; Marston's Pedigree; Castle Eden Ale; guest beer Ⓗ
Open-plan Hogshead Tavern, popular with all ages, stocking a wide choice of guest ales and bottle-conditioned beers. Eve meals finish at 6pm.
❀ ◖ ▶ ⇌ ♣ ⌂

VICTORIA INN
21-23 Victoria Street West, Brampton (off A619)
☎ (01246) 273832
12-4 (5 Sat), 7-11; 12-5, 7-10.30 Sun
Vaux Samson; Ward's Thorne BB, Best Bitter; guest beer Ⓗ
Friendly, two-roomed traditional local, hosting occasional live music and a charity quiz Mon eve.
⛺ ❀ ⊞ ♣

COTON-IN-THE-ELMS

BLACK HORSE INN
17 Burton Road ☎ (01283) 763614
12-11; 12-10.30 Sun
Banks's Mild; Marston's Pedigree, HBC Ⓗ
Friendly, village pub opposite the duck pond; it sells a selection of Hartington cheeses, also duck eggs. Its big fried breakfast is well known in the district.
⛺ ❀ ◖ ▶ ♣ P ⊟

CRICH

CLIFF INN
Cromford Road Town End
☎ (01773) 852444
11-3, 6-11; 12-3, 7-10.30 Sun
Hardys & Hansons Best Mild, Best Bitter, Classic or **seasonal beer** Ⓗ
Cosy, popular two-roomed stone pub near the Tramway Museum.
⛺ Q ◖ ▶ ▲ P

CUTTHORPE

GATE INN
Overgreen
☎ (01246) 276923
11.30-3, 6.30-11; 12-3, 7-10.30 Sun
Bateman XB; Flowers Original; guest beer Ⓗ
Comfortable village pub with fine views. Excellent food served lunchtimes and Wed-Sat eves in the pleasant restaurant and the bar. Note the Mansfield may be on a cask breather.
⛺ ◖ ▶ ▲ P ⊟

DALE ABBEY

CARPENTERS ARMS
Dale Lane (½ mile off A6096)
☎ (0115) 932 5277
12-3, 6 (7 Sat)-11; 12-4, 7-10.30 Sun
Ansells Bitter; Ind Coope Burton Ale; Marston's Pedigree; guest beer Ⓗ
Popular, food-oriented pub off the beaten track in a pretty hamlet.
⛺ ⛬ ❀ ◖ ▶ ⊞ ▲ ♣ P

DARLEY ABBEY

ABBEY
Darley Street (near river)
☎ (01332) 558297
11.30-2.30, 6-11; 12-10.30 Sun
Samuel Smith OBB Ⓗ
15th-century ecclesiastical building, skilfully rescued from dereliction and now the focal point of this conservation area. A wealth of interesting features includes a stone-flagged floor.
⛺ ❀ ◖ ♣ P

DARLEY BRIDGE

THREE STAGS'S HEADS
Main Road
☎ (01629) 732358
12-3, 6.15-11; 12-11 Sat; 12-3, 7-10.30 Sun
Hardys & Hansons Best Mild, Best Bitter, seasonal beers Ⓗ
Busy, 18th-century village pub, which is handy for both the moors and riverside walks. Boules played.
⛺ ❀ ◖ ▲ ♣ P

DERBY

ALEXANDRA HOTEL
203 Siddals Road
☎ (01332) 293993
11-11; 12-3, 7-10.30 Sun
Bateman XB; Castle Rock Hemlock; Marston's Pedigree; guest beers Ⓗ
Friendly, two-roomer with an excellent bottled beer and whisky selection. At least seven guest beers including a mild and two changing imported draught beers. Discounted accommodation for CAMRA members. No food Sun.
Q ⛬ ⇌ ◖ ⛬ ⇌ ⌂ P

BRUNSWICK INN
1 Railway Terrace
☎ (01332) 290677
11-11; 12-10.30 Sun
Brunswick Recession, Second Brew, Railway Porter; Marston's Pedigree; Taylor Landlord Ⓗ
Traditional railwaymen's pub with an on-site brewery and 17 handpumps selling its own beers and a countrywide selection of independent brews.
Q ⛺ ❀ ◖ ⛬ ⇌ ♣ ⌂ ⊁

DRILL HALL VAULTS
1 Newland Street
☎ (01332) 298073
11-11; 12-2.30, 7-10.30 Sun
Marston's Pedigree H
Friendly, multi-sectioned, single-roomed, back-street pub. No food Sun. ⚌ ◖ ♣

FALSTAFF TAVERN
74 Silverhill Road, Normanton
☎ (01332) 342902
11-11; 12-10.30 Sun
Marston's Pedigree; guest beers H
Richly decorated brick and terra-cotta corner house: three rooms include a lively curving bar, wooden settles and tables. A portrait of Barry McGuighan hangs in the games room.
⚌ Q ❀ ⌖ ♣

FLOWERPOT
25 King Street
☎ (01332) 204955
11-11; 12-10.30 Sun
Draught Bass; Marston's Pedigree; guest beers H G
Lively, extended pub, offering at least ten beers (always including a mild), some on gravity dispense. Live music in the function room.
Q ❀ ◖ ⚴ ♣

FRIARGATE
114 Friargate
☎ (01332) 297065
11-11; 12-3, 7-10.30 Sun
Draught Bass; Marston's Pedigree; G **guest beers** H G
Unspoilt, popular, city-centre bar with a wide range of ever-changing guest beers and the occasional real cider. Wheelchair entrance at the rear.
◖ ⚴ P

NEW ZEALAND ARMS
2 Langley Street (off Ashbourne Rd)
☎ (01332) 370387
12-2.30, 5.30-11; 12-11 Sat; 12-10.30 Sun
Marston's Pedigree; Tetley Bitter; H **guest beers** H G
Festival Ale House featuring wood panelling and stone floors; good value food (Tue-Sat) regular beer festivals. Bar billiards played.
◖ ⚴ ♣ P

ROWDITCH INN
246 Uttoxer New Road
☎ (01332) 343123
12-2, 7-11; 12-3, 7-10.30 Sun
Mansfield Riding Bitter, Old Baily; Marston's Pedigree; guest beer H
Friendly roadside pub on the outer edge of the city. It hosts occasional quiz and food nights. A real gem, and well worth seeking out.
⚌ ❀ ♣ ✁

STATION INN
Midland Road ☎ (01332) 608014
11.30-2.30, 5.30-11; 11.30-11 Fri; 12-3, 7-10.30 Sun
Draught Bass
Single-room pub opposite the mail sorting office. Good quality food is served in the bar or back room. ◖ ▶ ⚴ ♣ ⊟

SMITHFIELD
Meadow Road ☎ (01332) 370249
11-11; 12-10.30 Sun
Draught Bass; Marston's Pedigree; Whim Hartington Bitter, seasonal beers; guest beers H
Bow-fronted, riverside pub with a big bar and two smaller rooms, one with table skittles. The ten handpumps frequently feature Derbyshire breweries. Food is served until 3pm.
⚌ Q ⚘ ❀ ◖ ⚴ ♣ P

Try also: Old Spa Inn, Abbey St (Ind Coope)

DRONFIELD

OLD SIDINGS
91 Chesterfield Rd
☎ (01246) 410023
12-11; 12-10.30 Sun
Draught Bass; Highgate Mild; Stones Bitter; guest beer (occasional) H
Enterprising pub, popular with all ages and well known locally for its food (downstairs restaurant). Decorated with railway memorabilia. It serves as a training school for new licensees.
❀ ◖ ▶ ⚴ ♣ P ✁

VICTORIA
5 Stubley Lane ☎ (01246) 412117
12-2, 4.30-11; 12-11 Thu & Fri; 11-11 Sat; 12-10.30 Sun
Banks's Bitter; Marston's Pedigree H
Genuine local with a comfortable L-shaped lounge and darts area. No food Sun. ❀ ◖ ⚴ ♣ ⊟

FENNY BENTLEY

BENTLEY BROOK INN
On A515 ☎ (01335) 350278
11-11; 12-10.30 Sun
Leatherbritches Goldings or Ashbourne Ale; Mansfield Riding Bitter; Marston's Pedigree H
Imposing country house, the home of Leatherbritches Brewery. Skittle alley outside.
⚌ ❀ ⚴ ◖ ▲ ♣ P

COACH & HORSES
On A515 ☎ (01335) 350246
11.30-3, 6.30-11; 12-3, 6.30-10.30 Sun
Draught Bass; Black Bull Dovedale, Best Bitter H
Charming pub and restaurant featuring low ceilings and panelled walls. ⚌ ❀ ◖ ▶ ▲ P

FOOLOW

BULL'S HEAD INN
☎ (01433) 630873
12-3 (not Mon), 7 (6.30 summer)-11, (closed winter Mon eve); 12-3 (closed eve) Sun
Black Sheep Best Bitter; Ward's Best Bitter; guest beers H
Smart pub in an attractive limestone village with a pond. The drinking area and restaurant flank a stone-flagged central bar.
⚌ Q ❀ ⚴ ◖ ⚴ ▲ P ⊟

GLOSSOP

BULLS HEAD
102 Church Street
☎ (01457) 853291
2-11; 12-11 Sat; 12-10.30 Sun
Robinson's Old Stockport, Best Bitter, Old Tom H
Listed, 16th-century roadside inn at the foot of the Pennines, renowned for its Indian/Balti cuisine. It boasts a traditional northern tap room. Sun meals served 2-10.30. ⚘ ❀ ▶ ⚴ ♣

CROWN INN
142 Victoria Street
☎ (01457) 862824
11.30-3, 5-11; 11.30-11 (Fri & Sat); 12-10.30 Sun
Samuel Smith OBB H
Friendly local in the Whitfield area of Glossop. It has a central curved bar, with three rooms off: a large games room and two small, comfortable snugs (one no-smoking). The cheapest pint in the area.
⚌ Q ⚴ ⚴ ⚴ ♣ ✁

FRIENDSHIP
3 Arundel Street
☎ (01457) 855277
12.30-3 (4 Sat), 5 (7 Sat)-11; 12-3, 7-10.30 Sun
Robinson's Hatters Mild, Best Bitter H
Stone street-corner local with a wood-panelled interior. The semi-circular bar is an attractive feature of the open-plan lounge. The back tap room is served by a hatch. Families welcome.
⚌ Q ⚴ ⚴ ⚴ ♣

GROUSE INN
Chunal (2 miles outside Glossop on Hayfield Road)
☎ (01457) 852603
11-11; 12-10.30 Sun
Thwaites Bitter, Chairman's H
Pleasant, homely pub on the edge of Kinder Scout in the Peak District. One large room divided into four areas. ⚌ ❀ ◖ ▶ P ⊟

STAR INN ALE HOUSE
2 Howard Street (by station)
☎ (01457) 853072
12-11; 12-10.30 Sun
Boddingtons Bitter; guest beers H
Recently refurbished town-centre

alehouse of polished wood and tiled floors. Up to four guest beers; Quiz night Tue.

🍺 ≈ ♣ P

HATHERSAGE

SCOTSMAN'S PACK
School Lane ☎ (01433) 650253
12-3, 6-11; 12-11; 12-10.30 Sun
Burtonwood Bitter, Forshaw's, Top Hat, seasonal beers Ⓗ
Comfortable village pub with three lounge areas served by a central bar. A recent brewery award-winner, it enjoys a strong local and visiting trade.
Q ❀ 🛏 ◖ ▲ ≈ ♣ P ✂

HAYFIELD

ROYAL HOTEL
Market Place
☎ (01663) 742721
12-11; 12-10.30 Sun
Marston's Pedigree; John Smith's Bitter; guest beers Ⓗ
Former vicarage by the River Sett and the village church and cricket ground. Original oak panels and pews are features which give a relaxing atmosphere. Regular live music, e.g. jazz Sun afternoons.
🏠 Q ❀ 🛏 ◖ ▶ ♿ ▲ P

SPORTSMAN
Kinder Road
☎ (01663) 741565
12-3 (not Mon), 7-11; 12-3, 7-10.30 Sun
Thwaites Best Mild, Bitter, Chairman's, seasonal beers Ⓗ
Long, stone-built pub above the River Sett. An ideal base for fell walking. It has a wide range of malt whisky on optics.
🏠 Q ❀ 🛏 ◖ ▶ ▲ ♣

HOLYMOORSIDE

LAMB INN
16 Loads Road
☎ (01246) 566167
12-3 (not Mon-Thu), 7-11; 12-3, 7-10.30 Sun
Draught Bass; Home Bitter; Theakston XB; guest beer Ⓗ
Cosy, two-roomed village pub close to the Peak District National Park. Up to four guest ales, including one from Adnams.
🏠 Q ❀ ♣ P

HOPE

CHESHIRE CHEESE
Edale Road ☎ (01433) 620381
12-3 (not winter Mon), 6.30-11; 12-11 Sat; 12-4 (12-10.30 summer) Sun
Ward's Best Bitter; guest beers Ⓗ
This 16th-century free house has cosy rooms and interesting split-level layout. Guest beers are from the Ward's guest list. Limited parking.
🏠 Q ❀ 🛏 ◖ ▶ ▲ P

HORSLEY WOODHOUSE

OLD OAK INN
176 Main Street
☎ (01332) 780672
5.30-11; 12-3, 6-11 Sat; 12-3, 7-10.30 Sun
Everards Tiger; Mansfield Bitter; Marston's Pedigree; guest beer Ⓗ
Two-roomed village local in traditional style. No food available Tue.
🏠 Q ❀ ▶ ♣ P

ILKESTON

ANCHOR
7 Market Street (off Market Place)
☎ (0115) 944 4385
11-11; 11-5, 7-12 Fri & Sat; 12-3, 7-10.30 Sun
Mansfield Bitter; Marston's Pedigree; guest beer Ⓗ
Busy, two-roomed local with a comfortable family/function room. The garden has a play area with a bouncy castle in summer. Wheelchair access at the rear.
Q 🚲 ❀ ♣ 🍴

DEWDROP INN
Station Street (off A609, near railway)
☎ (0115) 932 9684
11.30-3 (not Sat), 7-11; 12-4, 7-10.30 Sun
Vaux Mild Waggle Dance; Ward's Best Bitter; guest beers Ⓗ
Welcoming, traditional, multi-roomed boozer. TV and pool in the bar and a sociable lounge with impromptu pianists. CAMRA Mildands *Pub of the Year* 1997. It offers a fine whisky selection and doorstep butties; supports local micros.
🏠 Q 🚲 ❀ 🍺 ♣

DURHAM OX
25 Durham Street
☎ (0115) 932 4570
11-11; 12-10.30 Sun
Vaux Mild, Waggle Dance; Ward's Best Bitter; guest beer Ⓗ
Open-plan but cosy, back-street local which used to be a prison. Skittle alley.
🏠 ♣

SPRING COTTAGE
1 Fulwood Street
☎ (0115) 932 3153
11-3 (4 Fri), 6-11; 11-5, 7-11 Sat; 12-3, 7-10.30 Sun
Draught Bass; guest beers Ⓗ
Genuine, traditional back-street local with a relaxing lounge. The sociable bar has Sky TV and pool. Excellent value home-cooked food (not served Sat eve or Sun); innovative guest beer selection.
🏠 🚲 ❀ ◖ ▶ 🍺 ♣ 🍴

KIRK IRETON

BARLEY MOW ☆
Main Street
☎ (01335) 370306
12-2, 7-11; 12-2, 7-10.30 Sun
Hook Norton Best Bitter, Old Hooky; guest beers Ⓖ
Tall, gabled, Jacobean building with a rambling interior. Multi-roomed, it features low-beamed ceilings, well-worn woodwork and slate tables made from a snooker table. Beers are still-aged behind the bar.
🏠 Q ❀ 🍺 ▲ ♣ ○ P

KNIVETON

RED LION
Wirksworth Road
☎ (01335) 345554
12-2 (not winter Thu), 7-11; 12-3, 7-10.30 Sun
Black Bull Bitter; Burton Bridge Bitter; guest beer Ⓗ
Stone-built community pub with an open-plan interior, plus a dining room. Close to Carsington reservoir.
🏠 ❀ ◖ ▶ ♣ P

LITTLE LONGSTONE

PACKHORSE INN
Main Street
☎ (01629) 640471
11.30-3 , 5 (6 Sat)-11; 12-3.30, 7-10.30 Sun
Marston's Bitter, Pedigree Ⓗ
Unspoilt village local; a pub since 1787 comprising three small rooms, one doubling as a dining room. Ramblers are welcome and there is also a strong local trade.
🏠 Q ❀ ◖ ▶ ▲ ♣

LONG EATON

HOLE IN THE WALL
Regent Street
☎ (0115) 973 4920
10.30-3, 5.45-11; 10.30-11 Fri & Sat; 12-4.30, 7-10.30 Sun
Draught Bass; Worthington Bitter; guest beers Ⓗ
Excellent, two-roomed local: a bar with TV and pool, a lounge, plus an off-sales hatch. The garden has a skittle alley and a barbecue. Guest beers and ciders are changed weekly. Lunches Mon, Wed and Fri. An award-winning town-centre pub.
❀ ◖ 🍺 ≈ ♣ ○

LONGSHAW

GROUSE INN
On B6054
☎ (01433) 630423
12-3, 6-11; 12-3, 7-10.30 Sun
Vaux Waggle Dance; Ward's Best Bitter; guest beer Ⓗ
Isolated pub, popular with walkers and climbers on the nearby Froggatt Edge. A lounge, tap

room and conservatory. The guest beer is from the Ward's guest list. Eve meals Wed-Sun.
🏚 Q ⇞ 🏵 ◖◗ ⊟ ♣ P 🏮

LULLINGTON

COLVILE ARMS
Coton Road
☎ (01827) 373212
12-3 (not Mon-Fri), 7-11; 12-3, 7-10.30 Sun
Draught Bass; Marston's Pedigree; guest beer 🅷
Popular, 18th-century free house in a pleasant village: a basic, wood-panelled bar, a smart lounge plus a second lounge/function room. Bowling green in the garden. 🏚 🏵 ⊟ ♣ P

MAKENEY

HOLLYBUSH INN
Holly Bush Lane OS352447
☎ (01332) 841729
12-3, 5-11; 11-11 Fri & Sat; 12-10.30 Sun
Marston's Pedigree; Ruddles County; guest beers 🅷
Old pub with many rooms in a Grade II listed building. Some of the beers come from the cellar in jugs: the house beer is from Brunswick. 🏚 Q ⇞ 🏵 ◖ ♣ P

MARSH LANE

GEORGE INN
46 Lightwood Road (off B6056)
☎ (01246) 433178
12-4, 7-11; 12-3, 7-10.30 Sun
Stones Bitter; Ward's Best Bitter; guest beer 🅷
Popular, traditional local with good views over the Rother Valley. Two guest beers, one is often from the local brewer, Townes. Q 🏵 ⊞ ♣ P 🏮

MATLOCK

THORN TREE
48 Jackson Road, Matlock Bank (N of town, behind County Hall)
☎ (01629) 582923
12-2.30 (not Mon or Tue), 7-11; 12-3, 7-10.30 Sun
Marston's Pedigree; Mansfield Bitter, Old Baily; Whim Hartington Bitter 🅷
Welcoming, 18th-century local with two cosy rooms enjoying extensive views across the valley. Lunches served Wed-Sun.
Q 🏵 ◖ ♣

MELBOURNE

RAILWAY HOTEL
22 Station Road (E edge of town, 1 mile from Donington Park)
☎ (01332) 862566
6-11; 12-10.30 Sun
Marston's Pedigree; guest beers 🅷
Traditional pub and restaurant

with wood floors and tiling. The house beer is brewed by Townes of Chesterfield. Sun lunch available plus eve meals Fri-Sun.
🏚 Q 🏵 🛏 ◖ ⅄ Å ♣ P

MICKLEOVER

HONEYCOMBE
Ladybank Road
☎ (01332) 515600
12-2.30 (3 Sat), 6.30-11; 12-3, 7-10.30 Sun
Everards Beacon, Tiger, Old Original; guest beer 🅷
Popular, modern honeycomb-shaped pub on two levels. Lunches Tue-Sat. 🏵 ◖ ♣ P

MONSAL HEAD

MONSAL HEAD HOTEL
On B6465 ☎ (01629) 640250
11-11; 12-10.30 Sun
Courage Directors; Theakston Old Peculier; Whim Hartington Bitter; guest beers 🅷
Real ales are available in the Stable Bar at the rear of the hotel. This has the original floor and is appropriately decorated. The house beer is from Lloyds.
🏚 Q 🏵 🛏 ◖ ⅄ Å ♣ P

NEW MILLS

MASONS ARMS
High Street ☎ (01663) 744292
11-11; 12-10.30 Sun
Robinson's Hatters Mild, Old Stockport 🅷, **Best Bitter** 🅿
Traditional local, tucked away in a quiet part of the market street shops, but only a step from the market street shops and a few minutes' walk from the Sett Valley Trail.
🏵 ⇌ ♣ P 🏮

Try also: Beehive, Albion St (Free)

NEWTON SOLNEY

UNICORN
Repton Road (B5008)
☎ (01283) 703324
11.30-3, 5-11; 11.30-11 Sat; 12-3, 7-10.30 Sun
Draught Bass; Marston's Pedigree; guest beer 🅷
Lively village local featuring a variety of pub games. It has a restaurant (no food Sun eve) and the accommodation has recently been doubled to eight rooms.
🏵 🛏 ◖ ⅄ ⅃ ♣ P

OCKBROOK

ROYAL OAK
Green Lane ☎ (01332) 662378
11.30-2.30, 7-11; 12-2.30, 7-10.30 Sun
Draught Bass; Worthington Bitter; guest beers 🅷
Lively, friendly village local with small cosy rooms. Good value

lunches; children's play area.
🏚 Q 🏵 ◖ ♣ P

OLD TUPTON

ROYAL OAK
Derby Road (A61, Chesterfield-Clay Cross road)
☎ (01246) 862180
12-3, 5-11; 12-11 Fri & Sat; 12-7-10.30 Sun
Home Bitter; Morland Old Speckled Hen (weekend)**; John Smith's Bitter; Wells Bombardier; guest beer** 🅷
100-year-old three-roomer with ample bar space. Popular, as the village regulars enjoy the beers kept by a master cellarman. Eve meals Fri and Sat. Boules and skittles are played outside.
Q 🏵 ◖◗ ♣ P 🏮

OVER HADDON

LATHKIL HOTEL
½ mile S of B5055 at Burton Moor OS206665
☎ (01629) 812501
12-3 (4 Sat), 7-11 (12-11 summer Sat); 12-4, 7-10.30 (12-10.30 summer) Sun
Ward's Best Bitter; Whim Hartington Bitter; guest beers 🅷
Free house in an idyllic setting with views over Lathkill Dale Nature Reserve with a fine oak-panelled bar. Excellent home-cooked food (not Sun eve).
🏚 Q ⇞ 🏵 ◖ ⅄ ♣ P 🏮

RIPLEY

PRINCE OF WALES
107 Butterfly Hill
☎ (01773) 743499
12-3.30, 6.30-11; 11-11 Sat; 12-10.30 Sun
Marston's Bitter, Pedigree; guest beers 🅷
Multi-sectioned locals at the foot of the hill; popular, especially with young people. 🏵 ◖ ⊟ ♣ P

Try also: Three Horseshoes, Market Place (Ward's)

ROSLISTON

BULLS HEAD
Burton Road ☎ (01283) 761705
12-2.30, 7-11; 12-3, 7-11 Sun
Draught Bass; Marston's Pedigree; guest beer 🅷
Turn-of-the-century village local with a public bar and a cosy lounge. 🏚 ◖ ⊟ ⅃ ♣ P

ROWARTH

LITTLE MILL INN
Off Siloh Rd ☎ (01633) 743178
11-11; 12-10.30 Sun
Banks's Bitter; Camerons Strongarm; Hardys & Hansons Best Bitter; Marston's Pedigree; guest beer 🅷

Large, multi-roomed pub of character, boasting a fully working waterwheel. Children's adventure playground. Food available all day. ♨Q❀⌂◑❿ⓖⰅ▲P❒

ROWSLEY

GROUSE & CLARET
Station Road (A6)
☎ (01629) 733233
11-11; 12-10.30 Sun
Mansfield Riding Bitter, Old Baily, guest beer Ⓗ
Large, comfortable pub with excellent facilities; it retains a good public bar where hikers are welcome. Good food, a well equipped garden and a family room are added attractions. ♨Q☎⌂◑❿ⓖ▲♣P✆

SANDIACRE

BLUE BELL
36 Church Street
☎ (0115) 939 2193
12-2 (3 Fri & Sat), 6-11; 12-4, 7-10.30 Sun
Ind Coope Burton Ale; Marston's Pedigree; John Smith's Bitter; guest beers Ⓗ
Friendly local in a converted 300-year-old farmhouse with exposed beams, displaying brewery and brewing memorabilia around the walls. ♨❀♣P

SHIRLEY

SARACENS HEAD
Church Lane ☎ (01335) 360330
12-3, 7-11; 12-3, 7-10.30 Sun
Draught Bass; Hoskins & Oldfield Supreme; Marston's Pedigree; guest beer Ⓗ
Attractive pub, dating from 1791 an open lounge format with a small snug area, offering a good range of home-cooked food (not served Sun eve). Children are welcome if dining. This is a good walking and cycling area. ♨Q❀⌂◑❿▲♣P

SMALLEY

BELL INN
Main Road ☎ (01332) 880635
11.30-2.30, 6-11; 12-2, 7-10.30 Sun
Marston's Pedigree; Ruddles County; Whim Hartington Bitter, Hartington IPA, Magic Mushroom Mild Ⓗ
Two-roomed local, popular with diners and a champion of Whim Brewery ales. ♨Q❀⌂◑❿ⒼP

SNELSTON COMMON

QUEEN ADELAIDE
1 mile off A515
☎ (01335) 324222
7-11; 12-2, 7-10.30 Sun
Marston's Pedigree Ⓗ

Not so much a pub as a farmhouse that has beer: very plain and the more pleasant for being so. May open at lunchtime for groups of ramblers by prior appointment. ♨Q❀P

SWADLINCOTE

SPRINGFIELD
25 North St ☎ (01283) 221546
11-11; 12-4, 7-10.30 Sun
Draught Bass; Marston's Pedigree Ⓗ
Friendly, popular two-roomed local. No food Sun. ❀◑Ⓖ♣P

SWARKESTONE

CREW & HARPER
On A514
☎ (01332) 700641
11-11; 12-10.30 Sun
Marston's Bitter, Pedigree, seasonal beers Ⓗ
Popular, 200-year-old coaching inn displaying Bonnie Prince Charlie memorabilia, including a monument in the large garden on the bank of the River Trent. Meals are served all day in the dining area. Children's indoor play area. ☎◑❿ⓖP

TICKNALL

CHEQUERS INN
27 High Street
☎ (01332) 864392
12-2.30, 6-11; 12-3, 7-10.30 Sun
Marston's Pedigree; Ruddles Best Bitter, County; guest beer Ⓗ
Small, stone, two-roomed local with an inglenook and beams. ♨Q❀♣P

TIDESWELL

GEORGE HOTEL
Commercial Road
☎ (01298) 871382
11-3, 7-11; 12-3, 7-10.30 Sun
Hardys & Hansons Best Bitter, Classic, seasonal beers Ⓗ
Substantial stone-built hotel next to the church - the 'Cathedral of the Peak': a large L-shaped lounge, a snug and a contrasting tap room, popular with local youth. ♨Q❀⌂◑❿Ⓖ▲♣P✆

TROWAY

GATE INN
Main Road
☎ (01246) 413280
12-3, 7-11; 12-3, 7-10.30 Sun
Burtonwood Bitter, Forshaw's, Top Hat Ⓗ
Well-preserved, family-run pub overlooking the Moss Valley; a cosy village local. Children welcome. ♨Q❀Ⓖ♣P❒

WHITWELL

JUG & GLASS
13 Portland Street
☎ (01909) 720289
11-3, 6.30-11; 12-3, 6.30-10.30 Sun
John Smith's Bitter, Magnet Ⓗ
Two-roomed local in an ex-mining community. A listed building, it features a wooden bar and open fires; full of community spirit encouraged by the convivial, long-established landlord. ♨Q❀Ⓖ♣P❒

WARDLOW MIRES

THREE STAGS' HEADS ☆
On A623/B6465 jct
☎ (01298) 872268
7-11; 11-11 Sat; 12-10.30 Sun
Abbeydale Matins, Absolution, Black Lurcher; Springhead Bitter; Ⓗ **guest beer** Ⓖ
Carefully restored farmhouse pub with two small rooms and a stone-flagged floor, the local CAMRA *Pub of the Year* 1997. It has many canine residents (and visitors). No draught lager. Substantial meals served. ♨Q❀◑❿▲P

WESTON-ON-TRENT

COOPERS ARMS
Weston Hall
☎ (01332) 690002
11.30-3, 6-11; 11.30-11 Sat; 12-10.30 Sun
Draught Bass; Marston's Pedigree; Worthington Bitter ⒽPⒼ
17th-century former mansion house set in its own grounds by a lake. Multi-roomed, it boasts lots of character and many original features including oak panelling and fireplaces. ♨❀◑❿ⓖ♣P✆

WHALEY BRIDGE

GOYT INN
8 Bridge Street (opp station)
☎ (01663) 732840
11-11; 12-10.30 Sun
Vaux Bitter, Samson; Ward's Best Bitter Ⓗ
Small, two-roomed local: a bar in the lounge area, plus a vault area with darts. ♨◑⇌♣❒

SHEPHERD'S ARMS
7 Old Road
☎ (01663) 732384
11-3, 5.30-11; 12-3, 7-10.30 Sun
Banks's Mild; Marston's Bitter, Pedigree Ⓗ
Ageless local, near the High Peak canal terminus. The lounge is quiet, the vault is lively and convivial, with scrubbed tables and a flagged floor. ♨Q❀Ⓖ⇌♣P

Beer festivals aren't just about sampling the finest ales: often entertainment is laid on, and there will also be a selection of stalls selling food, t-shirts and suchlike as well as CAMRA books and goodies. All the CAMRA events are run entirely by volunteers, which goes a long way to making the atmosphere fun, relaxed and friendly.

WHITEHOUGH

ODDFELLOWS
Whitehead lane
☎ (01663) 750306
12-3 (not winter Mon-Fri), 5-11;
12-11 Sat; 12-10.30 Sun
Bateman Mild; Marston's Bitter, Pedigree Ⓗ
Classic stone conversational pub in a picturesque Peak District village near Chinley. Three small rooms cluster around the bar creating a homely atmosphere. Eve meals end 8pm. ✿ ◖ ▶

WOOLLEY MOOR

WHITE HORSE INN
Badger Lane (1½ miles W of A61 at Stretton) OS367614
☎ (01246) 590319
11.30-3, 6-11; 12-3.30, 5-10.30 Sun
Draught Bass; guest beer Ⓗ
Award-winning, 17th-century village pub and restaurant. A new conservatory extension complements the large gardens with views over the Amber Valley. Three guest beers.
Q ➳ ✿ ◖ ▶ ⊟ ఉ ▲ ♣ P ⊁

YOULGREAVE

GEORGE HOTEL
Church Street
☎ (01629) 636292
11-2.30, 6.30-11; 11-11 Sat;
12-10.30 Sun
John Smith's Bitter; Theakston Mild; guest beer Ⓗ
Large, lively local opposite a fine church. Hikers welcome. Good range of home-cooked food.
Q ✿ ⊟ ◖ ▶ ⊟ ▲ ♣ P

INDEPENDENT BREWERIES

Black Bull:
Ashbourne
Brunswick:
Derby
Leatherbritches:
Ashbourne
Townes:
Chesterfield
Whim:
Buxton

Support independent brewers!

Eighty per cent of of Britain's beer is brewed by four companies. The national companies can brew good beers, sometimes. But their main emphasis has to be nationally promoted, nationally available brands.

They talk about 'low-cost high-volume production units' rather than breweries.

Independent brewers for choice

The 400 or so independent brewers keep local tastes, local history, and local choice alive. They brew over 1,200 real ales.

The Independent Family Brewers of Britain represents 38 traditional companies; they estimate that three-quarters of their production is real ale. Members of SIBA, the Society of Independent Brewers, sell an even higher proportion. SIBA represents around 300 new brewers set up since 1971.

If you're interested in beer rather than marketing, innovation comes from the bottom up. It is new, small brewers who revived porters and stouts, invented summer beers, tried out brewing with weird and wonderful ingredients. Larger companies may copy, but it is the diversity at the other end of the market which really drives the cask beer world.

Since the Campaign for Real Ale was founded in 1971 an astonishing brewing revival, from Orkney to the Channel Islands, has quadrupled the number of brewers.

Keeping brewers independent

Takeovers mean broken promises, closed breweries, lost beers and local tastes denied. Beers are moved to other plants, recipes changed, and national brands take their place in pubs.

If the ex-independent has a well-known beer, it might become available in more pubs – but often blander and brewed at more than one site.

CAMRA campaigns against takeovers, alerting shareholders and the public to the inevitable destruction of the local brewing heritage that mergers involve. We highlight the deception where a name has been bought and the beer changed.

Double whammy: tax and duty

British brewers and pubs are under threat from a flood of cheap foreign booze. Over a million pints a pour into Britain, brought back from the Continent. And the price difference comes down to tax – six times the French beer duty. CAMRA wants UK tax slashed to save brewery jobs and the local pub.

The tax system is a particular burden on the smallest brewers. Many countries run a 'sliding scale' system of duty, which gives smaller brewers a lower tax rate. This encourages local employment and diversity in brewing. Such a tax system was recommended by the Monopolies Commission in 1989, but the British Government simply refuses to introduce it.

Tied houses and guest beers

The guest beer law was one of CAMRA's triumphs. We want to widen the guest beer law to include non-brewing pub operators, which aren't currently covered, and ensure that mass market lagers don't push small brewers out of pubs.

CAMRA wants independent brewers to retain the right to tie their pubs. This gives them guaranteed markets, and allows them to compete against national advertising and the heavy discounts of big companies. Abolition would allow the big companies to gobble up most of the beer market. We want an end to local monopolies in pub ownership, whether from big or small companies.

Campaigning for Independents

There are two ways to help independent brewers:
• Ask for their beers and drink them!
• Join the Campaign for Real Ale – it's an investment in the future of real beer and independent brewers.

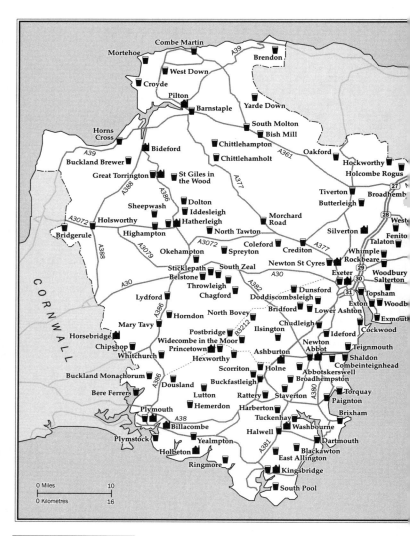

ABBOTSKERSWELL

TWO MILE OAK
Totnes Road (A381)
☎ (01803) 812411
11-3, 5-11 (11-11 summer); 12-3,
7-10.30 (12-10.30 summer) Sun
**Draught Bass; G Eldridge Pope
Royal Oak; Flowers IPA** G H
Pub with a superb public bar with
bare floorboards, where the beer
is served on gravity if you ask.
There's also a well established
bar menu and a restaurant.
Taunton Traditional cider.
🏨 Q 🕸 🌓 🍴 🛆 ♣ P 🍷

AXMOUTH

SHIP INN
Church Street
☎ (01297) 21838
11-2.30, 6-11; 12-2.30, 7-10.30 Sun

**Draught Bass; Flowers IPA;
guest beer** H
In every edition of this *Guide*.
The public bar is a Guinness
museum, while the lounge has a
huge display of dolls in national
costume. The garden houses a
convalescent home for owls. (No
eve meals Tue, winter.)
🏨 Q 🐎 🕸 🌓 🍴 🗄 🛆
▲ ♣ P

BARNSTAPLE

CHECK INN
14 Castle Street (opp old town
station, near cattle market)
☎ (01271) 375964
11-11; 12-10.30 Sun (may vary)
Beer range varies H P
Friendly town pub serving a wide
range of beers. Thatcher's cider.
Live jam sessions on Thu eves.

Super League darts played. Eve
meals on request. North Devon
CAMRA *Pub of the Year* 1998.
🏨 🌓 🛆 ⇌ ♣ 🍷

CORNER HOUSE
108 Boutport Street
☎ (01271) 343528
11-3, 5 (7 Wed)-11; 11-11 Fri &
Sat; 12-3, 7-10.30 Sun
Draught Bass; G guest beers H
Traditional, unspoilt popular
town-centre local with wood-panelled interior and L-shaped bar.
Good range of beers. Yearly beer
festivals.
Q ⇌ ♣

REFORM INN
Reform Street, Pilton
☎ (01271) 323164
11.30-2.30, 5-11; 11.30-11 Fri &
Sat; 12-4, 7-10.30 Sun

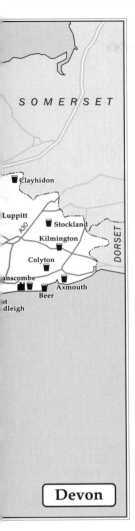

**Barum Original; Flowers
Original; guest beer** (summer) H
Originally three cottages converted into a pub with two bars, one
having a nautical theme. Brewery
at rear. Friendly town pub with
live music every month. Taunton
Tradional cider. 🏚 🏵 ♣ ⌂

Try also: Rolle Quay, Rolle's
Quay (Free)

BEER

ANCHOR INN
Beer, nr Seaton ☎ (01297) 20386
11-2.30, 5.30-11 Mon-Thu, 11-11
Fri, Sat & summer; 12-10.30 Sun
Otter Bitter, Ale; guest beers H
A pub for over 100 years in this
picturesque fishing village. The
separate garden overlooks the
bay. Q 🏵 🏚 ◖ ▶ P

BELSTONE

TORS
2 miles SE of Okehampton
OS619936 ☎ (01837) 840689
11.2.30, 6-11; 12-5, 7-10.30 Sun
Otter Bitter, Ale; guest beer
(summer) H
Large, granite building in an
unspoilt village on the northern
edge of Dartmoor, situated on
the Tarka Trail. A good base for
country walks. The accent is on
Devon Ales and home-cooked
food. 🏚 🏚 ◖ ▶ ♣

BERE FERRERS

OLD PLOUGH
☎ (01822) 840358
12-3 (closed Mon Nov-Feb), 7-11;
12-3, 7-10.30 Sun
Draught Bass; Flowers IPA; H
guest beers G
16th-century village inn with an
outstanding view over the River
Tavy at the rear. Situated in an
area of natural beauty. Friendly
atmosphere. Cider in summer.
🏚 🏵 ◖ ▶ ≈ ♣

BISH MILL

MILL INN
From S Molton take B3137 to
Tiverton ☎ (01769) 550944
12 (11 summer)-3, 6.30-11 (all
day if busy); 12-3, 7-10.30 Sun
Cotleigh Tawny; guest beer H
17th-century inn with a warm and
friendly atmosphere. Separate
restaurant area with large
games room where children are
welcome. Opens at 7.30am in
summer for breakfast.
🏚 🐎 🏵 🏚 ◖ ▶ ▲ ♣ P

BLACKAWTON

GEORGE INN
1 mile off A3122 ☎ (01803) 712342
11-11; 12-10.30 Sun
Beer range varies H G
This traditional village pub has a
very good atmosphere and a regularly changing beer list. Mini-
beer festivals are held throughout the year. Redaways cider is
served, and there is a large
selection of foreign beers. House
beer is Princetown IPA (ABV 4%).
South Devon *Pub of the Year*
runner-up 1998.
🏚 Q 🐎 🏵 🏚 ◖ ▶ 🏕 ▲ ♣
⌂ P 🖂

BRANSCOMBE

FOUNTAIN HEAD
☎ (01297) 680359
11.30-2.30, 6.45-11 (11-3, 6-11
summer); 12-2.30, 7-10.30 (12-3,
6-10.30 summer) Sun
**Branscombe Vale Branoc,
Summa That** H
14th-century pub: the lounge was
formerly a blacksmith's forge.
Wood-panelled walls and stone-
flagged floors are features. Good
value food served. The house
beer comes from Branscombe
Vale. Green Valley cider.
🏚 Q 🏵 🏚 ◖ ▶ ▲ ♣ ⌂ P

OLDE MASONS ARMS
☎ (01297) 680300
11-11; 12.-10.30 Sun
**Draught Bass; Otter Bitter, Ale;
guest beers** H
This 14th-century pub has hosted
many people over the years,
including smugglers, but now
serves good beer and food — its
speciality is spit roasts.
🏚 Q 🏵 🏚 ◖ ▶ P 🖂

BRENDON

ROCKFORD INN
4 miles from Lynmouth OS756478
☎ (01598) 741214
12-11; 12-3, 7-10.30 Sun
**Barum Original; Cotleigh Tawny,
Barn Owl; guest beers** H G
Set by the East Lyn River, in the
stunning Brendon Valley, this pub
takes some finding but is worth
it. The atmosphere is instantly
welcoming and the trout fishing
on the river is as good as the ale!
🏚 Q 🐎 🏵 🏚 ◖ ▶ ▲ ♣ P

BRIDFORD

BRIDFORD INN
OS815866 ☎ (01647) 252436
12-2.30, 7 (6.30 Sat)-11; 12-3,
7-10.30 Sun
Draught Bass H**; guest
beers** H G
Traditional, family-run village pub
with single large bar area and a
family room. The 17th-century
building was converted to a pub
in 1968. Local farm ciders in
summer.
🏚 Q 🐎 🏵 ◖ ▶ 🏕 ▲ ⌂ P 🖂

BRIDGERULE

BRIDGE INN
☎ (01288) 381316
12-2, 6.30-11 (12-2, 4.30-11 during football season); 12-4,
7-10.30 Sun
Flowers original; guest beer H
The only Devon pub west of the
Tamar. Dating from the 17th century, this friendly pub features an
aviary at the rear by the garden.
The main bar's fireplace is set
almost in the middle of the bar,
making the space behind like a
snug. 🏚 🐎 🏵 ◖ ▶ ▲ ♣ P

BRIXHAM

BLUE ANCHOR
83 Fore Street (at the bottom of
main shopping street)
☎ (01803) 859373
11-11; 12-3, 7-10.30 Sun
**Blackawton Bitter; Ind Coope
Burton Ale; guest beers** A

This is 16th-century former sail loft is popular with locals and tourists alike. Live music on certain nights and reasonably priced food (eves 7-9, not Sun). ⚏ Q ◖ ▮

BROADHEMBURY

DREWE ARMS
☎ (01404) 841267
11-2.30, 6-11; 12-2.30, 7-10.30 Sun
Otter Bitter, Ale, Bright, Head; seasonal beers Ⓗ
Popular village pub in an idyllic setting of white-washed thatched cottages. Its menu has a reputation for interesting fish dishes (no food Sun eve). Bollhayes cider. ⚏ Q ❀ ◖ ♣ ⌂ P

BROADHEMPSTON

COPPA DOLLA INN
On Ippleton Road out from village centre OS807664
☎ (01803) 812455
11.30-3, 6.30-11; 12-3, 6.30-10.30 Sun
Dartmoor Best; Marston's Pedigree; Morland Old Speckled Hen; Wadworth 6X Ⓗ
Traditional country inn situated within 15 minutes of Dartmoor, featuring beamed ceilings and stone walls. Caravans allowed on campsite. ⚏ Q ❀ ⌷ ◖ ▮ ▲ P

BUCKFASTLEIGH

WHITE HART
2 Plymouth Road
☎ (01364) 642337
11.30-11; 12-10.30 Sun
Dartmoor Best; Greene King Abbot; Teignworthy Beachcomber; guest beer Ⓗ
Pleasant pub with an open-plan lounge and bar with Dartmoor stone walls and a separate dining area. Inch's cider.
⚏ ⛴ ❀ ◖ ▮ ▲ ⌂

BUCKLAND BREWER

COACH & HORSES
Village sign from Landcross Chapel off A386
☎ (01237) 451395
12-3, 6-11; 12-3, 7-10.30 Sun
Fuller's London Pride; Flowers Original; guest beer Ⓗ
13th-century thatched village inn with low ceilings and two bars. In the Middle Ages the pub was used as the village court.
⚏ Q ❀ ⌷ ◖ ▮ ♣ P

BUCKLAND MONACHORUM

DRAKE MANOR INN
☎ (01822) 853892
11.30-2.30 (3 Sat), 6.30-11; 12-3, 7-10.30 Sun
John Smith's Bitter; Ushers Best Bitter, Founders, seasonal beers Ⓗ

16th-century local in a picturesque village. It serves over 70 whiskies and offers a varied menu with home-cooked specials. ⚏ Q ❀ ◖ ▮ ⊞ P

BUTTERLEIGH

BUTTERLEIGH INN
☎ (01884) 855407
12-3, 6 (5 Fri)-11; 12-2.30, 7-10.30 Sun
Cotleigh Tawny, Barn Owl; guest beers Ⓗ
Friendly, unspoilt village inn with accommodation. Popular for food (no reservations taken).
⚏ Q ❀ ⌷ ◖ ▮ ♿ ♣ P

Try also: Silverton Inn, Silverton (Free)

CHAGFORD

GLOBE INN
High Street ☎ (01647) 433485
11-3, 7-11 (11-11 Sat); 12-3, 7-10.30 Sun
Courage Best Bitter, Directors; guest beers Ⓗ
Friendly, 16th-century, two-bar coaching inn in the centre of a delightful country town, just off the moors. Cider in summer.
⚏ Q ⌷ ◖ ▮ ⊞ ▲ ⌂ 🍺

CHIPSHOP

CHIPSHOP INN
Off A384, 3 miles W of Tavistock OS437751 ☎ (01822) 832322
12-2.30, 5-11; 12-11 Sat; 12-10.30 Sun
Draught Bass; Exmoor Ale; guest beers Ⓗ
Welcoming, one-bar pub on a remote crossroads. Free, popular skittle alley. It boasts a notable collection of mirrors. Good selection of reasonably priced pub food. ⚏ Q ◖ ▮ ▲ P

CHITTLEHAMHOLT

EXETER INN
Take B3226 to Crediton from South Molton, 4 miles then right
☎ (01769) 540281
11.30-2.30, 6-11; 12-3, 7-10.30 Sun
Dartmoor Best; Ⓖ **Greene King Abbot; Tetley Bitter** Ⓗ
Cosy, 16th-century thatched coaching inn with an interesting collection of matchboxes and bank notes on the beams. Popular and friendly. Good food; Inch's cider.
⛴ ❀ ⌷ ◖ ▮ ▲ ♣ ⌂ P

CHITTLEHAMPTON

BELL INN
The Square (off B3227, between South Molton and Umberleigh)
☎ (01769) 540368
11-3, 6-11; 11-11 Sat; 12-3, 7-10.30 Sun

Draught Bass; Greene King Abbot; guest beers Ⓗ
Lively village pub in a picturesque square. It has a good community focus and supports local sports and charities. Over 120 whiskies displayed in the bar. Excellent collection of pump clips. Look out for pot-bellied pigs!
❀ ◖ ♣ ⌂

CHUDLEIGH

BISHOP LACY
Fore Street
☎ (01626) 854585
11-11; 12-10.30 Sun
Boddingtons Bitter; Ⓗ **Fuller's London Pride;** Ⓗ **Princetown Jail Ale;** Ⓖ **guest beers** Ⓖ
Former church house, now a bustling village local. At least three guest beers available, all on gravity. Seasonal beer festivals held. Good value food is served in a no-smoking room. South Devon CAMRA *Pub of the Year* 1998.
⚏ Q ❀ ◖ ▮ ⊞ ♣ P

CLAYHIDON

HALF MOON INN
☎ (01823) 680291
12-2.30, 7-11; 12-3.30, 7-10.30 Sun
Cotleigh Tawny; Otter Bitter Ⓗ
Popular village local set on the Blackdown Hills. Good value, home-cooked food in the restaurant. Superb views across the Culm Valley. No food Mon. Bolhayes cider.
⚏ Q ⛴ ❀ ◖ ▮ ♿ ▲ ♣ ⌂ P

COCKWOOD

ANCHOR
On A379 ☎ (01626) 890203
11-11; 12-10.30 Sun
Draught Bass; Eldridge Pope Royal Oak; Marston's Pedigree; Morland Old Speckled Hen; Wadworth 6X; Whitbread Fuggles Imperial Ⓗ
16th-century inn, originally opened as a seaman's mission, situated on a beautiful inlet overlooking the railway line. Very good food, with fish a speciality.
⚏ Q ❀ ◖ ▮ ⌂ P

COLEFORD

NEW INN
☎ (01363) 84242
12-2.30, 6-11; 12-2.30, 7-10.30 Sun
Badger Best; Otter Ale; Wadworth 6X; guest beer Ⓗ
Large, well-appointed pub, with one bar in a 13th-century, Grade II listed, thatched building. Friendly atmosphere, talkative parrot, and a pleasant garden by a stream. Separate dining area with excellent food at restaurant prices. ⚏ ❀ ⌷ ◖ ▮ P

COLYTON

GERRARD ARMS
St Andrews Square
☎ (01297) 552588
11-3, 6-11; 11-11 Sat; 12-3,
7-10.30 Sun
**Draught Bass; Otter Ale; guest
beers** Ⓗ
Welcoming, recently refurbished
local. A drinker's pub which also
serves good quality, good value
food. Intermittently talkative parrot. Summer hours may vary.
Local scrumpy served.
❀ ◖ ▮ ⚹ ♣ ⌂

COMBEINTEIGNHEAD

WILD GOOSE
Between Newton Abbot and
Shaldon on road S of Teign
estuary ☎ (01626) 872241
11.30-3, 6.30-11; 12-3, 7-10.30 Sun
Beer range varies Ⓗ
Traditional, 17th-century free
house in a quiet village with a
constantly varying choice of six
ales, including brews from Exe
Valley, Princetown and
Teignworthy. Excellent, home-
cooked food and Thelma's
renowned puddings. Trad jazz
every Mon. South Devon CAMRA
Pub of the Year 1996.
♨ Q ❀ ◖ ▮ ▲ ♣ P

COOMBE MARTIN

CASTLE
High Street ☎ (01271) 882706
11-11; 12-10.30 Sun
**Draught Bass; Worthington
Bitter; guest beers** Ⓗ
This genuine local is a delight for
dedicated beer drinkers. The
landlord serves one of the finest
lines in ales from independent
breweries. A wonderful place to
stop.
☎ ❀ ▰ ◖ ▮ ▲ ♣ P

CREDITON

CREDITON INN
28a Mill Street (on the Tiverton
road) ☎ (01363) 772882
11-11; 12-2, 7-10.30 Sun
Draught Bass; guest beers Ⓗ
Friendly and welcoming free
house just off the town centre,
serving three ales in a convivial
atmosphere. A modest menu of
cooked meals and a skittle alley
feature. ❀ ◖ ▮ ⇌ ♣ P

CROYDE

THATCHED BARN INN
14 Hobbs Hill ☎ (01271) 890349
11-11; 12-10.30 Sun
**Draught Bass; St Austell HSD;
Tetley Bitter; guest beers** Ⓗ
Spectacularly popular pub with
locals and visitors alike.
Impressive points are that
although it's renowned for great

food it has avoided turning into a
restaurant; the bar staff are bril-
liantly efficient, no matter how
busy. ☎ ❀ ▰ ◖ ▮ ⚹ ▲ ♣ P

DARTMOUTH

CHERUB
11 Higher St ☎ (01803) 832571
11-2.30, 5.30-11 (11-11 summer);
12-3, 5.30-10.30 (12-10.30 summer) Sun
**Morland Old Speckled Hen;
Wadworth 6X; guest beers** Ⓗ
Dartmouth's oldest building is
700 years old and Grade II listed.
The bustling bar is very atmospheric; the restaurant is upstairs.
Good bar food features
many dishes using the wealth of
local seafood. The house beer
comes from Summerskills.
Addlestones cider. ◖ ▮ ⌂

DODDISCOMBLEIGH

NOBODY INN
☎ (01647) 252394
12-2.30, 6-11; 12-3, 7-10.30 Sun
Draught Bass Ⓖ**; Branscombe
Vale Branoc; guest beers** Ⓗ
Popular village pub with an interi-
or to match its age, which is 15th
century. Nobody Bitter is brewed
by Branscombe. Beers tend to be
dwarfed by the 900 wines, 250
whiskies and extensive menu.
♨ Q ❀ ▰ ◖ ▮ ⌂ P ✄

DOLTON

UNION INN
Fore Street (B3220 from Great
Torrington, then B3217)
☎ (01805) 804633
12-2.30, 6-11; 12-2.30, 7-10.30 Sun
**Dartmoor Best Bitter, St Austell
HSD; seasonal beers** Ⓗ
16th-century Devon cob longhouse with two bars, a cosy
restaurant and a function room
opening out on to a courtyard
garden. No food Wed.
♨ Q ❀ ▰ ◖ ▮ ▲ ♣ P

DOUSLAND

BURRATOR INN
☎ (01822) 853121
11-11; 12-10.30 Sun
**Draught Bass; Flowers IPA; St
Austell HSD; Wadworth 6X;
guest beer** Ⓗ
Victorian country inn near
Burrator Reservoir. The large
restaurant serves good value
food. ♨ ☎ ❀ ▰ ◖ ▮ ⚹ ♣ P

DUNSFORD

ROYAL OAK
☎ (01647) 252256
12-2.30, 6 (7 Mon)-11; 12-2.30,
7-10.30 Sun
**Greene King Abbot; Flowers
Original, London Pride; guest
ales** Ⓗ

Attractive old pub set in a beautiful village on the edge of
Dartmoor. The main bar leads to
the dining and games areas.
♨ Q ❀ ▰ ◖ ▮ ▲ ♣ ⌂ P

EAST BUDLEIGH

ROLLE ARMS
☎ (01395) 442012
11-2.30, 6-11; 12-3, 7-10.30 Sun
Flowers IPA Ⓗ
Typical small village pub serving
excellent food. Popular with
nearby agricultural college students. House beer comes from
Branscombe Vale. Broad Oak
cider. Q ☎ ❀ ▰ ◖ ▮ ▲ ⌂ P

EAST ALLINGTON

FORTESCUE ARMS
Left off A381 from Totnes
☎ (01548) 521215
11-2.30, 6-11; 11-11 Fri, Sat &
summer; 12-3, 7-10.30 (12-10.30
summer) Sun
**Badger Dorset Best; Palmers
IPA; guest beer** (summer) Ⓗ
Wonderful, original 19th-century
pub down from the church,
named after a local landowner.
Flagstone floor in the bar with a
collection of brewery memorabilia adorning the walls. Separate
lounge/dining room.
♨ Q ❀ ▰ ◖ ▮ ⊟ ⚹ ▲ ♣
⌂ P ✄

EXETER

BROOK GREEN
Well Street (near St James's
Park football ground)
☎ (01392) 203410
12-2.30 (3 Sat), 6-11; 12-3,
7-10.30 Sun
Beer range varies Ⓗ
Basic, no-frills, back-street pub
with a pleasing atmosphere. The
regular Whitbread beer may be
kept under gas, but all four guest
beers are served without cask
breathers. Very keen pricing on
some guest beers.
◖ ⇌ (St James's) ♣ P

CITY GATE
Iron Bridge, North Street.
☎ (01392) 495811
11-11; 12-10.30 Sun
Draught Bass; guest beers Ⓗ
Ex-Courage pub (the Crown &
Sceptre) recently bought as a
free house and extensively refurbished. The main bar has a very
civilised decor and atmosphere;
the cellar bar is more lively.
Plans for accommodation in 1999.
♨ ❀ ◖ ▮ ⇌ (St David's/Central)

COWICK BARTON
Cowick Lane, St Thomas
☎ (01392) 270411
11-3, 6-11; 12-3, 7-10.30 Sun
**Draught Bass; Courage Best
Bitter; guest beers** Ⓗ

87

A converted Elizabethan manor house on the edge of the city with olde worlde charm. Large selection of country-style wines. Good value food in the restaurant.
♔ ❀ ◖ ◗ ⊟ P

Double Locks Hotel
Canal Banks (follow lane next to incinerator over canal and turn right) OS932900
☎ (01392) 256947
11-11; 12-10.30 Sun
Adnams Broadside; Ⓖ
Everards Old Original; Smiles Golden Brew, Best, Heritage; Ⓗ
guest beers Ⓖ
Large, canalside pub with spacious grounds where there are barbecues in the summer. Usually ten cask ales available; Greys cider. Good value food served. Popular with all; two rooms available for families.
♔ ♞ ❀ ◖ ◗ ♿ ▲ ♣ ⌓ P

Exeter Community Centre
17 St David's Hill (near iron bridge)
☎ (01392) 255188
5.30-10.50 (11 Fri); closed Sun
Ind Coope Burton Ale; guest beers Ⓗ
Situated between the rail stations, this friendly bar is open eves only. Temporary day membership available on production of CAMRA membership card or this *Guide*. Difficult access to car park at rear.
Q ♞ ❀ ≡ (St Davids/Central) ♣ P ⊁ ⊔

Great Western
St David's Station Approach
☎ (01392) 274039
11-11; 12-10.30 Sun
Draught Bass; Fuller's London Pride; guest beers Ⓗ
Comfortable hotel/pub serving up to six cask beers at any one time and good value food. Friendly staff and a manager who is extremely enthusiastic about real ale. Children allowed.
♔ Q 🛏 ◖ ◗ ≡ ♣ P

Imperial
New North Road
☎ (01392) 434050
11-11; 12-10.30 Sun
Draught Bass; Courage Directors; Exmoor Gold, Stag; Theakston Best Bitter; guest beers Ⓗ
Sympathetic Wetherspoons conversion of a former hotel, just outside the city centre, retaining many original features, including the orangery. The pub divides into a number of separate drinking areas, including a large no-smoking section. Popular with all.
Q ❀ ◖ ◗ ♿ ≡ (St David's/Central) ⌓ P ⊁ ⊔

Jolly Porter
St David's Hill
☎ (01392) 254848
11-11; 12-10.30 Sun
Courage Best Bitter, Directors; John Smith's Bitter; guest beers Ⓗ
Long, narrow pub with a low-level bar and high-level seating areas. Forceful guest ale policy – the landlord serves beers as the brewer recommends or as he deems suitable. Popular with students and older people alike.
◖ ◗ ≡ (St David's) ♣ ⌓

Royal Oak
31 Fore Street, Heavitree
☎ (01392) 254121
11-3, 6-11; 11-11 Fri; 11-3.30, 7-11 Sat; 12-3, 7-10.30 Sun
Castle Eden Ale; Flowers IPA; Wadworth 6X Ⓗ
The military hardware on show is no reflection of the welcome you will receive here. A Grade II listed building, it has been a pub since 1761. Mini traffic lights behind the bar help to call last orders. Good value food. Quiz night Wed. ❀ ◖ ◗ ♣ P ⊁

Welcome Inn
Haven Banks (at jct of River Exe and Exeter ship canal)
☎ (01392) 254760
12-2.30, 6.30-11; 12-2.30, 7-10.30 Sun
Beer range varies Ⓗ
Aptly named pub situated on the quay where the canal joins the Exe. This is Exeter's last remaining unspoilt pub, boasting gas lighting and furniture made by the landlord in the 1960s. Popular at lunchtimes with people from the local industrial estate. Q ❀ ◖ ♣

Well House
Cathedral Close
☎ (01392) 319953
11-11; 7-10.30 Sun
Draught Bass; guest beers Ⓗ
Small bar opposite the cathedral, offering five guest beers, both local and unusual. This pub is deservedly popular, and runs its own real ale appreciation society. Very busy during the tourist season. Local byelaws restrict outside drinking and opening hours. (Accommodation in hotel next door.)
🛏 ◖ ◗

EXMOUTH

County House Inn
Withycombe Village Road
☎ (01395) 263444
10.30-11; 12-10.30 Sun
Draught Bass; Boddingtons Bitter; Flowers Original Ⓗ
Very friendly suburban local, formerly a blacksmith's. Excellent food at very good prices, Mon-Sat lunchtimes and Fri & Sat eves (booking advisable). Summer barbecues beside the stream. Skittle alley and a games room available. ❀ ◖ ◗ ♣

Grove
The Esplanade ☎ (01395) 272101
11-3, 5.30-11 winter; 11-11 Sat & summer; 12-10.30 Sun
Boddingtons Bitter; Brakspear Special; Flowers Original; Waworth 6X; guest beers Ⓗ
Friendly, family seafront pub near the docks. Good value food includes specials autumn and winter; mini-beer festivals are held in the winter. Safe play area for children. Live music Fri. Wheelchair WC.
♞ ❀ ◖ ◗ ♿ ≡ P

EXTON

Puffing Billy Inn
Station Road (by station)
☎ (01392) 873152
12-3, 6-11 (12-11 summer Sat); 12-10.30 Sun
Draught Bass; Branscombe Vale Branoc; guest beer (occasional) Ⓗ
15th-century village inn with a good atmosphere; close to the estuary. Boules played in fine weather. Interesting food.
♔ Q ❀ ◖ ◗ ♿ ≡ ♣ P

FENITON

Nog Inn
Sidmouth Junction (opp station)
☎ (01404) 850210
11-3, 6-11; 12-3, 7-10.30 Sun
Cotleigh Tawny; guest beers Ⓗ
Friendly village pub, by Feniton station on the Waterloo-Exeter line, selling mostly local ales. Large function/skittles room at rear. ♔ ❀ 🛏 ⊟ ≡ ♣ P

GREAT TORRINGTON

Black Horse Inn
The Square ☎ (01805) 622121
11-3, 5.30-11; 11-11 Sat; 12-4, 7-10.30 Sun
Courage Best Bitter, Directors; John Smith's Bitter; guest beer Ⓗ
Town-centre Tudor inn with strong links with the Civil War. There is a lively main bar with local support and a quieter lounge; the restaurant is at the rear. ♔ 🛏 ◖ ◗ ♣

Try also: Newmarket Inn, South St (Free)

HALWELL

Old Inn
Follow A381 from Totnes to Kingsbridge ☎ (01803) 712329
11-2.30, 6-11; 11-11 Sat; 12-3, 6-10.30 Sun
Beer range varies Ⓗ

Friendly, family-run village pub with a warm atmosphere, next to a beautiful Norman church. There has been an inn on this site since 1104. Oriental food a speciality.
Q ☎ ✿ ⊨ ◖▶ ♣ ⌣ P

HARBERTON

CHURCH HOUSE INN
Off main Totnes to Kingsbridge Road, in village centre
☎ (01803) 863707
12-3, 6-11; 12-3, 7-10.30 Sun
Draught Bass; Courage Best Bitter; guest beers Ⓗ
13th-century pub with one large room, heavily beamed, with the bar at one end and a dining area at the other. There is an additional small room. Churchwards cider.
🏛 Q ☎ ✿ ⊨ ◖▶ ⌣ P ✕

HATHERLEIGH

GEORGE HOTEL
Market Street
☎ (01837) 810454
11-11 (hours sometimes shorter in winter); 12-3, 7-10.30 Sun
Draught Bass; Dartmoor Best, Bitter; St Austell HSD; guest beer Ⓗ
Thatched hotel with three bars and a central cobbled courtyard, popular with farmers on market days. Note the interesting wooden panel on the seat by the main bar. Inch's cider.
🏛 Q ✿ ⊨ ◖▶ ♣ ⌣ P

Try also: Tally Ho! Country Inn & Brewery (Free)

HEMERDON

MINERS ARMS
OS563574
☎ (01752) 343252
11-2.30, 5.30-11; 12-3, 7-10.30 Sun
Draught Bass Ⓗ Ⓖ **Boddington Bitter; Sutton XSB; Ushers Best Bitter; guest beers** Ⓗ
Traditional, former tin-miners' pub overlooking Plympton whose landlord is of the third generation. 🏛 Q ☎ ✿ ⊟ ♣ P

HEXWORTHY

FOREST INN
Signed off the B3357 Twobridges to Bartmeet road OS654728
☎ (01364) 631211
12-3, 6-11 (may be longer in summer); 11-11 Sat; 12-10.30 Sun
Teignworthy Reel Ale; guest beer Ⓗ
Isolated, attractive inn on Dartmoor. A haven for walkers, horse riders and fishermen. Extremely comfortable, with chesterfield sofas in the lounge area.
🏛 ✿ ⊨ ◖▶ ♣ ⌣ P

HIGHAMPTON

GOLDEN INN
☎ (01409) 231200
11.30-3, 6.30-11; 12-3, 7-10.30 Sun
Butcombe Bitter; Fuller's London Pride; guest beer Ⓗ
16th-century inn with a low-beamed ceiling and a hop-stewn bar. Good atmosphere. Campsite in pub grounds accepts caravans.
🏛 ✿ ◖▲ ♣ P

HOCKWORTHY

STAPLE CROSS INN
☎ (01398) 361374
12-3 (not Mon - Thu), 6.30-11; 12-10.30 Sun
Cotleigh Tawny; guest beers Ⓗ
Unspoilt, 400-year-old country pub on the Somerset border with two bars, both having traditional stone floors. Eve meals by arrangement only; cider in summer.
🏛 Q ✿ ◖⊟ ♿ ▲ ♣ ⌣ P

HOLCOMBE ROGUS

PRINCE OF WALES
☎ (01823) 672070
11.30-3 (not Tue; or Wed - Thu winter), 6.30-11; 12-3, 7-10.30 Sun
Cotleigh Tawny; Otter Bitter Ⓗ
Pleasant country pub, not far from the Grand Western Canal. Note the cash-register hand-pumps. Cider in summer.
🏛 Q ✿ ◖▲ ♣ ⌣ P

HOLNE

CHURCH HOUSE INN
OS706696
☎ (01364) 631208
12-3, 7-10.30 (11.30-3, 6.30-11 summer); 12-3, 7-10.30 Sun
Butcombe Bitter, Wilmot's; Dartmoor Best Bitter; Morland Old Speckled Hen Ⓗ
Grade II listed, 14th-century inn situated in the centre of the village, located in the Dartmoor National Park. Two bars and a dining area. Grays Farm Cider.
🏛 Q ☎ ✿ ⊨ ◖▶ ▲ ♣ ⌣ P ✕

HOLSWORTHY

KINGS ARMS ☆
The Square
☎ (01409) 253517
11-11; 12-3, 7-10.30 Sun
Draught Bass; Sharp's Doom Bar Bitter Ⓗ
Three-bar town pub unaltered since it was built early this century. A snob screen separates the main bar from the snug. Wooden floors and a cellar-level pool room feature. Lunches in summer.
🏛 Q ◖⊟ ▲ ♣

HORNDON

ELEPHANTS NEST INN
Off A386, 1½ miles E of Mary Tavy OS517800
☎ (01822) 810273
11.30-2.30, 6.30-11; 12-2.30, 7-10.30 Sun
Boddingtons Bitter; Palmers IPA St Austell HSD; guest beers Ⓗ
Picturesque, 16th-century moorland pub with a relaxed atmosphere, serving a varied menu. Excellent garden and moorland views.
🏛 Q ☎ ✿ ◖▶ ⌣ P

HORNS CROSS

HOOPS INN
On A39, 6 miles W of Bideford
☎ (01237) 451222
11-11; 12-10.30 Sun
Beer range varies Ⓗ Ⓖ
Real gem of a coaching inn, built in the 13th century. Cosy atmosphere with log fires at both ends of the main bar. It was once a smugglers' haunt. Usually serves South-West independent ales such as Cottage. Inch's cider in summer.
🏛 ☎ ✿ ⊨ ◖▶ ♣ ⌣ P

IDDESLEIGH

DUKE OF YORK
On B3217
☎ (01837) 810253
11-11; 12-10.30 Sun
Adnams Broadside; Cotleigh Tawny; Sharp's Doom Bar Bitter; guest beers Ⓖ
12th-century thatched village pub which has a superb inglenook fireplace with rocking chairs. Freshly prepared food available all day. Local CAMRA *Pub of the Year* 1996. Thatchers cider.
🏛 Q ✿ ⊨ ◖▶ ♣ ⌣

IDEFORD

ROYAL OAK
2 miles off A380
☎ (01626) 852274
12-3, 7-11; 12-3, 7-10.30 Sun
Draught Bass; Flowers IPA Ⓗ
Small, unspoilt, thatched country pub, full of wartime marine souvenirs.
🏛 Q ✿ P

ILSINGTON

CARPENTERS ARMS
☎ (01626) 661215
11-2.30, 6-11; 12-3, 7-10.30 Sun
Flowers IPA Ⓖ; **Morland Old Speckled Hen** Ⓗ
Old village pub with a friendly local atmosphere, used mainly by local farmers and villagers. Churchward's cider.
🏛 ✿ ◖▶ ⌣

KILMINGTON

NEW INN
The Hill ☎ (01297) 33376
11-3, 6-11;12-3, 7-10.30 Sun
Palmers BB, IPA Ⓟ
Friendly village pub with a large,
safe garden where there are regular summer barbecues. This
14th-century building has been a
pub since at least 1800. In every
edition of the *Guide*.
🏚 Q ❀ ◖ Ⅾ 🍴 ᗡ ᴧ ♣ P

KINGSBRIDGE

SHIP & PLOUGH
The Promenade ☎ (01548) 852485
11-11; 12-10.30 Sun
Blewitts Head Off; guest beer Ⓗ
Lively, town-centre pub offering
home-brewed beers and food at
reasonable prices. Dating from
the 18th-century, it boasts
beamed ceilings and other historic features. Cider in summer.
🏚 ❄ ❀ ◖ Ⅾ ᴧ ♣ ᗡ

LOWER ASHTON

MANOR INN
☎ (01647) 252304
12-2.30, 6 (7 Sat)-11 (closed
Mon); 12-2.30, 7-10.30 Sun
**RCH Pitchfork; Teignworthy
Reel Ale; Theakston XB;** Ⓗ
Wadworth 6X; Ⓖ **guest beers** Ⓗ
Country gem in deepest Devon.
Over 1,000 beers have been
served in the past five years.
Food is popular, but does not
dominate. Local CAMRA *Pub of
the Year* 1998. Gray's cider.
🏚 Q ❀ ◖ Ⅾ 🍴 ᴧ ♣ ᗡ P

LUTTON

MOUNTAIN INN
Old Church Lane (off Cornwood to
Sparkswell road, up steep hill)
OS596594 ☎ (01752) 837247
11-3, 7 (6 Fri & Sat)-11; 11-3,
7-10.30 Sun
Sutton XSB; guest beers Ⓗ
Traditional village pub, with a
large fireplace, popular with
locals. Food is recommended.
House beer brewed by Summer-
skills. Cider in summer only.
Plymouth CAMRA *Pub of the Year*
1997.🏚 Q ❄ ❀ ◖ Ⅾ ♣ ᗡ P

LYDFORD

MUCKY DUCK INN
Next to White Lady Falls
☎ (01822) 820208
11.30-3, 6-11; 12-3, 7-10.30 Sun
**Sharp's Cornish Coaster, Own;
guest beers** Ⓗ
Accomodating inn with slate
floors and exposed stone walls,
featuring a display of many
ducks. A large family room and
and a pool area supplement the
bar area. No food Mon.
🏚 Q ❄ ❀ 🍴 ◖ Ⅾ P

MARY TAVY

MARY TAVY INN
On A386, 4 miles from Tavistock
☎ (01822) 810326
11.45-3, 6-11; 12-3, 7-10.30 Sun
**Draught Bass; St Austell XXXX
Mild; guest beer** Ⓗ
Cosy, friendly, two-bar pub on
the edge of Dartmoor. Good
value food.
🏚 Q ❄ ❀ 🍴 ◖ Ⅾ ᴧ ♣ P

MORCHARD ROAD

STURT ARMS
On A377
☎ (01363) 85102
12-3, 5.30-11; 12-3, 7-10.30 Sun
Banks's Mild; guest beers Ⓗ
Pleasant roadside pub with a
friendly atmosphere. Good range
of meals in a separate dining
area. Banks's Mild is a permanent feature, plus at least one
guest. House beer is brewed by
Branscombe Vale. Inch's Harvest
cider. The station is a request
stop only.
🏚 Q ❀ ◖ Ⅾ ᴧ ⇌ ♣ ᗡ P ⚹

MORTEHOE

CHICHESTER ARMS
☎ (01271) 870411
12-3, 6.30-11 (11-11 summer);
12-3, 7-10.30 (12-10.30 summer)
Sun
**Courage Directors; Badger
Tanglefoot; Shepherd Neame
Bishops Finger; Ushers Best
Bitter; guest beer** Ⓗ
Welcoming village local, popular
with visitors, too. Around 400
years old and still lit by gas
lamps.
Q ❄ ❀ ◖ Ⅾ ᴧ ♣ P

NEWTON ABBOT

GOLDEN LION
4 Market Street
☎ (01626) 367062
11-3 (4 Sat), 5.30 (6 Sat)-11;
12-3, 7-10.30 Sun
**Teignworthy Reel Ale; guest
beers** Ⓗ
The oldest pub in town, with a
single, long bar, plus a large
games room. The first pub to sell
Teignworthy beers. It holds mini-
beer festivals.
❀ 🍴 ◖ Ⅾ ᗡ ⇌ ♣ P

LOCOMOTIVE INN
35 East Street (main Totnes-
Torquay through road)
☎ (01626) 365249
11-11; 12-10.30 Sun
**Draught Bass; Flowers Original;
guest beers** Ⓗ
Three-roomed, 17th-century inn,
with a railway theme. Very popular with locals. Warm atmosphere; open fire in the main bar.
Separate pool room. Bar snacks
throughout. 🏚 Q ᗡ ♣

NEWTON ST CYRES

BEER ENGINE
Station Road (follow directions
to station from A377)
☎ (01392) 851282
11-11; 12-10.30 Sun
**Beer Engine Rail Ale, Piston
Bitter, Sleeper Heavy, seasonal
beers** Ⓗ
Friendly, popular pub by the station (limited rail service), serving
good value food with an emphasis on local produce. The brewery
may be viewed when the downstairs bar is open.
🏚 Q ❄ ❀ ◖ Ⅾ ⇌ ♣ P ⚹

NORTH BOVEY

RING OF BELLS
1 mile SW of Mortenhampsted
OS741839 ☎ (01647) 440375
11-3, 6-11 (11-11 summer); 12-
10.30 Sun
**Butcombe Bitter; Teignworthy
seasonal beers; Wadworth 6X;
guest beers** Ⓗ
13th-century, thatched village inn
offering first-class accommodation and excellent home-cooked meals.
Ideally situated for walking, hiking
and cycling. Will serve on gravity if
asked. Grays Farm cider.
🏚 Q ❄ ❀ 🍴 ◖ Ⅾ 🍴 ᴧ ♣
ᗡ P ⚹

NORTH TAWTON

FOUNTAIN INN
Exeter Street
☎ (01837) 82551
11-3 (not Mon-Tue), 7-11; 12-4,
7-10.30 Sun
**Flowere Original; Sharp's
Cornish Coaster, Doom Bar
Bitter; Shepherd Neame
Spitfire; guest beers** Ⓗ
Lively pub in a central position,
attracting all ages. Constantly
changing guest beers, food
theme nights and Thatchers cider
feature. The pub is the HQ of the
Flat Earth Society.
🏚 🍴 ◖ Ⅾ ♣ ᗡ ⚹ 🗌

RAILWAY INN
Whiddon Down Road (1 mile S of
village) ☎ (01837) 82789
12-2 (not Mon), 6-11; 12-3,
7-10.30 Sun
Beer range varies Ⓗ
Converted, 19th-century farmhouse, but still part of a working
farm, next to North Tawton railway station; the bar decor recalls
the station in past years.
🏚 ❀ 🍴 ◖ Ⅾ ᴧ ♣ P

OAKFORD

RED LION
Rookery Hill ☎ (01398) 351219
5.30-11; 11-11 Sat; 12-10.30 Sun
Juwards Bitter; guest beers Ⓗ
17th-century, Grade II listed, former coaching inn with a single

bar and a warm welcome. Close to Exmoor for walkers. Lunchtime food in summer; Sun lunches only in winter. Occasional cider. Limited parking.
🏠 Q ⇔ ◖ ㊎ ⅄ ♣ P

OKEHAMPTON

PLYMOUTH INN
26 West Street
☎ (01837) 53633
12-3, 7-11; 11-11 Sat; 12-10.30 Sun
Beer range varies Ⓖ
Old coaching inn that brings the welcome and atmosphere of a country pub to the centre of an old market town. Accent on South-Western beers.
🦮 ㊛ ◖ ▶ ♣

PAIGNTON

DEVONPORT ARMS
43 Elmbank Road
☎ (01803) 558322
11-11; 12-10.30 Sun
Blackawton seasonal beers; guest beers Ⓗ
Back-street local, near the zoo, well worth finding.
🏠 Q ㊛ ㊛ ◖ ▶ ㊐ ⇌ ⌂ P

POLSHAM ARMS
35 Lower Polsham Road
☎ (01803) 558360
11-11; 12-10.30 Sun
Boddingtons Bitter; Castle Eden Ale; Wadworth 6X; guest beers Ⓗ
All are made welcome in this delightful, two-bar pub, just off the main road. A quiet lounge bar and pool and music in the other.
🏠 Q ㊛ ◖ ▶ ㊐ ㊎ ⅄ ⇌ ♣ P

PLYMOUTH

BUTCHERS ARMS
160 Cremyll Street, Stonehouse
☎ (01752) 660510
11-11; 12-6 (10.30 summer) Sun
Courage Best Bitter; Sutton XSB Ⓗ
Small and friendly local worth seeking out, opposite the entrance to the Grade I listed King William victualling yard (due to be turned into a factory outlet). Wonderful views of the River Tamar. Cider in summer.
Q ㊛ ◖ ♣ ⌂ 🍺

CLIFTON
35 Clifton Street, Greenbank
☎ (01752) 266563
5-11; 11-11 Fri & Sat; 12-10.30 Sun
Draught Bass; Flowers IPA; Summerskills Indiana's Bones; guest beers Ⓗ
A house beer, Clifton Classic, is brewed by Summerskills for this warm, friendly pub, said to be the luckiest pub in the UK since three Lottery millionaires drink here. Unusual guest beers. The clock is correct twice a day! ⅄ ⇌ ♣

DOLPHIN HOTEL
14 Barbican
☎ (01752) 660876
10-11 (fisherman's licence); 12-10.30 Sun
Draught Bass; guest beer (occasional) Ⓖ
The last unspoilt pub on the historic Barbican, opposite the Dartington glass factory. Frequented by fishermen, artists and actors. 🏠 Q

FORTESCUE
37 Hutley Plain
☎ (01752) 660673
11-11; 12-10.30 Sun
Badger Tanglefoot; Tetley Bitter; Wadworth 6X; guest beers Ⓗ
A Carlsberg-Tetley Festival Ale House with a friendly atmosphere; used by both locals and students. The atmospheric cellar is also open at times.
◖ ▶ ⇌ (North Rd)

LIBRARY
15 Wyndham Street East (off North Rd West)
☎ (01752) 266042
11-11; 12-10.30 Sun
Draught Bass; Federation Buchanan's Best Bitter; guest beer Ⓗ
Claimd to be Plymouth's first students pub, hidden away in a back-street terrace. A real ale oasis. Good for sport.
◖ ▶ ⇌ (North Rd) ♣

PRINCE MAURICE
3 Church Hill, Eggbuckland
☎ (01752) 771515
11-3, 7 (6 Fri)-11; 11-11 Sat; 12-3, 7-10.30 Sun
Badger Tanglefoot; Draught Bass; Courage Best Bitter; Summerskills Best Bitter, Indiana's Bones; guest beers Ⓗ
Cosy, two-roomed pub in a village swallowed up by the expansion of Plymouth. A house beer, Royalle, is brewed by Summerskills. Plymouth CAMRA Pub of the Year in 1994 and '95.
🏠 ㊛ ♣ P 🍺

PROVIDENCE
20 Providence Street, Greenbank
☎ (01752) 228178
12-11; 12-5, 7-10.30 Sun
Ind Coope Burton Ale; Tetley Bitter; guest beers Ⓗ
Cosy, one-bar street-corner local in a terraced residential area near the city centre. ◖ ⇌ ♣

PYM ARMS
16 Pym Street, Devonport (behind flats in Albert Road, bordering Devonport Park)
☎ (01752) 561823
11-11; 12-10.30 Sun
Princetown Jail Ale; St Austell HSD; guest beers Ⓗ
Traditional Devonport local, fre-

quented by locals, students and dockyard workers. Sells Bass badged as Pym's own. Devonport.
◖ ⇌ ♣ ⌂

SHIPWRIGHT'S
18 Sutton Road, Coxside
☎ (01752) 665804
11-3, 6 (5.30 Fri)-11; 12-3, 7-10.30 Sun
Courage Best Bitter, Directors Ⓗ
Small local which is cosy and friendly, within walking distance of the National Aquarium and Barbican. 🏠 ㊛ ◖ ⅄ ♣ P

TAP & SPILE
21 Looe Street, Barbican
☎ (01752) 662488
11.30-3, 5-11; 11-11 Sat; 12-10.30 Sun
Beer range varies Ⓗ
Bordering the historic Barbican and within walking distance of the National Aquarium and Arts Centre, this refurbished and enlarged venue is popular for offering up to eight varying beers. Good value meals. Inch's Harvest cider.
㊛ ◖ ▶ ⅄ ♣ ⌂

THISTLE PARK TAVERN
32 Commercial Road, Coxside
☎ (01752) 204890
11-11; 12-10.30 Sun
St Austell HSD; Sutton Dartmoor Pride, XSB; guest beers Ⓗ
Popular with locals and students, this friendly pub is situated near the fish market and the National Aquarium. It offers a range of beers from the adjacent Sutton Brewery. ㊛ ◖ ♣ ♣

PLYMSTOCK

BORINGDON ARMS
Boringdon Terrace, Turnchapel
☎ (01782) 402053
11-11; 12-10.30 Sun
Butcombe Bitter; RCH Pitchfork; Summerskills Best Bitter; guest beers Ⓗ
Friendly, 18th-century popular local with up to five varying guest beers, set in a terrace in a waterside village close to the South-West Coastal Footpath. It hosts a bi-monthly beer festival. All day food; cider in summer.
🏠 Q ㊛ ⇔ ◖ ▶ ㊐ ㊎ ♣ ⌂

NEW INN
Boringdon Road, Turnchapel
☎ (01752) 402765
12-3 (not Mon-Thu), 6-11; 12-11 Sat; 12-10.30 Sun
Draught Bass; Sharp's Doom Bar Bitter; guest beers Ⓗ
Excellent views over the Cattewater and Marina, beers fine food (including local fish) make this recently refurbished village local worth visiting.
🏠 ◖ ▶ ♣

POSTBRIDGE

WARREN HOUSE INN
On B3212 between Postbridge
and Mortonhampstead
☎ (01822) 880208
11-3, 6-11; 11-11 Fri, Sat & summer); 12-3, 6-10.30, (12-10.30
summer) Sun
**Badger Tanglefoot; Butcombe
Bitter; Gibbs Mew Bishop's
Tipple; guest beer** Ⓗ
The third highest pub in England,
islotated in high Dartmoor. A
haven for both walkers and visitors. A friendly welcome to a
granite building hewn from the
moor itself. A log fire has been
burning continuously since 1845.
🏚 Q ☕ ❀ ◖▌ A ♣ ⌐ P

PRINCETOWN

PLUME OF FEATHERS INN
The Square (opp visitors centre)
☎ (01822) 890240
11-11; 12-10.30 Sun
Draught Bass; St Austell HSD Ⓗ
Princetown's oldest building
(1785) with copper bars, slate
floors and granite walls. A busy
pub with a good atmosphere and
friendly people. It has very good
facilities for the disabled.
Feathers beer is brewed by Bass.
🏚 ☕ ❀ ⌂ ◖▌ ⊞ ﾟ A ♣ ⌐ P

PRINCE OF WALES
Tavistock Road (opp primary
school) ☎ (01822) 890219
11.30-3, 6.30-11; 12-3, 7-10.30 Sun
**Draught Bass; Princetown
Dartmoor IPA, Jail Ale;** Ⓗ
Comfortable, village inn which
has a children's certificate. The
brewery tap for the adjacent
Princetown Brewery.
🏚 ◖▌ ﾟ ⌐ P

RAILWAY
2 Bridges Road (opp visitors
centre)
☎ (01822) 890232
11-11; 12-10.30 Sun
Draught Bass; guest beer Ⓗ
A friendly pub, decorated with
memorabilia from the old
Plymouth-Princetown branch line.
The house beer is 4410, brewed
by Skinner's of Cornwall.
Occasional cider.
🏚 ☕ ❀ ⌂ ◖▌ ﾟ ♣ ⌐ P

RATTERY

CHURCH HOUSE INN
☎ (01364) 642220
11-2.30, 6-11 (6.30-10.30 winter
Mon-Thu); 12-2.30, 7-10.30 Sun
**Dartmoor Best Bitter; Greene
King Abbot; Marston's
Pedigree** Ⓗ
Historic, Grade II star listed inn
beside the church. Originally
used to house the monks who
built it in 1028, it has a long, single, low-beamed bar, with two

inglenooks and a good reputation
for food. Luscombe cider in summer. 🏚 ❀ ◖▌ ⌐ P

RINGMORE

JOURNEYS END
☎ (01548) 810205
11.30-3, 6-11; 12-10.30 Sun
Adnams Broadside; Ⓖ **Exmoor
Ale;** Ⓗ **Otter Ale; guest
beers** Ⓖ
Wonderful, 13th-century friendly
village inn where nothing is too
much trouble. The main bar is
wood panelled; the snug has
flagstones. Children welcome.
Stancombe cider in summer.
🏚 Q ☕ ❀ ⌂ ◖▌ ⊞ ♣ ⌐ P

ROCKBEARE

JACK IN THE GREEN INN
On A30, 5 miles from Exeter
☎ (01404) 822240
11-3, 6-11; 12-3, 7-10.30 Sun
**Draught Bass; Cotleigh Tawny;
Otter Ale; guest beer** Ⓗ
A roadside inn on the busy A30; it
can be too quickly passed, but it
is well worth stopping to sample
the selection of local beers and
the good food, including local
cheeses, at competitive prices.
🏚 Q ☕ ❀ ◖▌ ♣ P

ST GILES IN THE WOOD

CRANFORD INN
On B3227, 3 miles from
Torrington
☎ (01805) 623309
12-2.30, 6-11; 12-3, 7-10.30 Sun
Beer range varies Ⓖ
Food-oriented country inn with a
warm atmosphere, converted
from a farm. Holiday accomodation is situated in the former stables and other farm buildings.
❀ ◖▌ ♣ P

SCORRITON

TRADESMAN'S ARMS
☎ (01364) 631206
12-3, 7-11; 12-3, 7-10.30 Sun
**Draught Bass; Princetown IPA;
guest beer** Ⓗ
Attractive, quiet, 300-year old
pub set in a very small village. A
good atmosphere, popular with
walkers. Good food, no-smoking
family room. Luscombe cider. No
food Mon eve.
🏚 Q ☕ ❀ ⌂ ◖▌ A ⌐ P
✂

SHALDON

CLIFFORD ARMS
34 Fore Street
☎ (01626) 872311
11-3, 5-11; 11-11 Sat; 12-3,
7-10.30 Sun
**Draught Bass; Young's Bitter;
guest beers** Ⓗ

One of Devon's prettiest pubs,
this 18th-century gem is much
photographed for its fabulous
summer floral display. Olde-
worlde atmosphere and excellent
food. Family room available in
summer only.
☕ ❀ ◖▌ A

SHEEPWASH

HALF MOON INN
The Square (1½ miles from
Highampton on Hatherleigh-
Holsworthy road, A3072)
☎ (01409) 231376
11-2.30, 6-11; 12-2.30, 7-10.30
Sun
**Courage Best Bitter; Jollyboat
Mainbrace; Marston's
Pedigree** Ⓗ
Old village inn with a long bar,
stone floor and huge log fire.
Ideal for fishing breaks.Has been
in the same family since 1958.
Restaurant food only eves; must
book.
🏚 Q ❀ ⌂ ◖▌ ♣ P ⊟

SOUTH MOLTON

GEORGE HOTEL
Broad Street
☎ (01769) 572514
12 (11 Thu & Sat)-2, 6-11; 12-2,
7-10.30 Sun
**Barum Original; Jollyboat
Mainbrace** Ⓗ
Originally a 16th-century posting
inn, tastefully refurbished over
the years. The public bar at the
rear serves local beers and regularly hosts folk and jazz
evenings.
🏚 ☕ ⌂ ◖▌ ♣ P

SOUTH POOL

MILLBROOK INN
(Left off A379 at Chillington)
☎ (01548) 531581
12-2.30, 7-11 (11-2.30, 5.30-11
summer); 12-3, 7-10.30 Sun
Draught Bass; Ⓖ **Ruddles Best;
Wadworth 6X; guest beer** Ⓗ
Charming, 17th-century, two-
room pub set by a stream with
pet ducks. Well supported by
local clientele; it gets very busy
at high tide. Cottage to let.
🏚 Q ☕ ❀ ⌂ ◖▌ ⌐

SOUTH ZEAL

OXENHAM ARMS
☎ (01837) 840244
11-2.30, 6-11; 12-2.30, 7-11 Sun
Princetown Dartmoor IPA, Ⓖ
Jail Ale Ⓗ
12th-century inn (first licensed
in 1477), described by one novelist as 'the stateliest and most
ancient abode in the hamlet'.
Still a fair description – though
the hamlet has grown into a
village.
🏚 Q ☕ ❀ ⌂ ◖▌ A ♣ P

SPREYTON

TOM COBLEY TAVERN
☎ (01647) 231314
12-2 (not Mon), 6 (7 Mon)-11;
12-3 , 7-10.30 Sun
Cotleigh Tawny; guest beers Ⓗ
Quiet village local with a superb
function/family room. All food is
home-cooked. There is a fine
view of Dartmor tors from the
splendid garden. No food Mon.
▲ Q ⊃ ❀ ⇔ ◖ ▶ ♣ P

STAVERTON

SEA TROUT INN
Off A384
☎ (01803) 762274
11-3, 6-11; 12-3, 7-10.30 Sun
Draught Bass; Ⓖ **Dartmoor Best
Bitter; Wadworth 6X; guest
beer** Ⓗ
15th-century pub close to the
River Dart. Large pub with two
bars and a restaurant.
▲ Q ❀ ⇔ ◖ ▶ ⊞ P

STICKLEPATH

DEVONSHIRE INN
☎ (01837) 840626
11-11; 12-3, 7-10.30 Sun
**Draught Bass; St Austell XXXX
Mild** (summer)**, Tinners HSD** Ⓖ
Unspoilt,16th-century thatched
local in a north Dartmoor village.
Water flowing through the leat
by the back wall helps to keep
the stillage cool as well as pow-
ering water wheels in the
foundry museum next door. Eve
meals by arrangement. Camping
barn in the village.
▲ Q ⊃ ❀ ▶ ⚹ Å ♣ P

STOCKLAND

KINGS ARM
☎ (01404) 881361
12-3, 6.30-11;12-3, 7-10.30 Sun
**Exmoor Ale; Otter Ale; John
Smith's Bitter; Theakston XB** Ⓗ
Carefully enlarged and mod-
ernised, Grade II listed free
house, with a friendly atmosphere.
Excellent menu; no food Sun lunch.
Lyme Bay Jack Rat cider.
▲ ⊃ ❀ ⇔ ◖ ▶ ⊞ ♣ ⌂ P ⊟

STOKENHAM

TRADESMANS ARMS
☎ (01548) 580313
12-3, 6-11 (closed Mon-Thu winter eves); 12-3, 6-10.30 (12-3
winter) Sun
Beer range varies Ⓗ
14th-century thatched pub in a
pretty village. Seafood is a speciality, local steaks are served
and there is traditional curry on
Sun. The range of three varying
beers may be reduced in winter.
Ask to see the traditional pub
slate. Dogs welcome.
▲ ❀ ◖ ▶ Å ⌂ P

TALATON

TALATON INN
☎ (01404) 822214
12-3, 7-11; 12-3, 7-10.30 Sun
**Fuller's London Pride; Otter
Bitter; guest beers** Ⓗ
Friendly, family-run village local.
Good range of freshly-cooked
food at reasonable prices.
▲ Q ❀ ◖ ▶ ♣ P

TEIGNMOUTH

GOLDEN LION
85 Bitton Park Road
☎ (01626) 776442
12-4, 6-11 ; 12-11; 12-4, 7.30-
10.30 Sun
Beer range varies Ⓗ
Two-roomed local overlooking
the docks. At least three guest
beers are available, all at reasonable prices. Pool and darts are
popular. ⊞ ⚹ ♣ P

Try also: Blue Anchor, Teign St
(Free)

THROWLEIGH

NORTHMORE ARMS
Wonson (2½ miles SW of A30 jct
at Whiddon Down) OS674897
☎ (01647) 231428
11-11; 12-10.30 Sun
**Adnams Broadside; Cotleigh
Tawny; Exe Valley Dob's Best
Bitter** Ⓖ
Welcoming, traditional country
local on the northern edge of
Dartmoor. Ideally situated for
walks. Cider in summer.
▲ Q ❀ ⇔ ◖ ▶ Å ♣ ⌂ P

TIVERTON

RACEHORSE
Wellbrook Street
☎ (01884) 252606
11-11; 12-10.30 Sun
**Webster's Yorkshire Bitter;
Banks's Mild; guest beers** Ⓗ
Popular local with a large function room/skittle alley at the
rear. Food served all day. There
is a children's play area and pets
area in the garden. Limited parking. ▲ ⊃ ❀ ◖ ▶ ♣ ⌂

TOPSHAM

BRIDGE INN ☆
Bridge Hill
☎ (01392) 873862
12-2, 6-10.30 (11 Fri & Sat); 12-2,
7-10.30 Sun
**Adnams Broadside; Badger
Tanglefoot; Branscombe Vale
Branoc; Exe Valley seasonal
beers; Otter Ale; guest beers** Ⓖ
Well known 16th-century Grade
II listed pub, unchanged for most
of the century and in the present
family for over 100 years. This
was where the Queen paid her
first official to a pub in March

1998. The barn bar was once a
maltings and brewery, but the
original building was a lodging
house for cathedral masons.
Sandwiches and ploughmans
available.
▲ Q ❀ ⇌ P

GLOBE HOTEL
34 Fore Street
☎ (01392) 873471
11-11; 12-3, 7-10.30 Sun
**Draught Bass; Hancock's HB;
Worthington Bitter; guest beer**
(occasional) Ⓗ
16th-century Grade II listed
coaching house boasting many
original beams and exuding an
olde-worlde atmosphere. Good
food available.
⊃ ⇔ ◖ ⚹ ⇌ ♣ P

TORQUAY

CHELSTON MANOR HOTEL
Old Mill Road
☎ (01803) 605142
12-3, 6-11; 12-3, 7-10.30 Sun
**Boddingtons Bitter; Flowers IPA,
Original; guest beers** Ⓗ
17th-century pub well known
locally for its fine range of ales
and excellent food.
Q ⊃ ❀ ⇔ ◖ ▶ ⚹ ⇌ P

CROWN & SCEPTRE
2 Petitor Road, St Marychurch
☎ (01803) 328290
11-3 (4 Sat), 5.30 (6.30 Sat)-11;
12-3, 7-10.30 Sun
**Courage Best Bitter, Directors;
Marston's Pedigree; Morland
Old Speckled Hen; Ruddles
County; Young's Bitter; guest
beers** Ⓗ
South Devon CAMRA *Pub of the
Year* 1997: a 200-year-old stone
coaching house with a very
friendly atmosphere. Popular
with the locals and visitors. Well
worth a visit for the ceiling decor.
No food Sun.
▲ Q ⊃ ❀ ◖ ⊞ ⚹ Å ♣ P

DEVON DUMPLING
108 Shiphay Lane, Shiphay
☎ (01803) 613465
11-2.30 (3 Fri), 5.30-11;
11-11 Sat; 12-3, 7-10.30 Sun
**Courage Best Bitter, Directors;
John Smith's Bitter** Ⓗ
An attractive, popular local serving a wide range of home-cooked
food. The 'Dumpling' house beer
is brewed by Branscombe Vale.
▲ Q ⊃ ❀ ◖ ▶ P

TUCKENHAY

MALTSTERS ARMS
Bow Creek (off A381 Totnes-
Dartmouth)
☎ (01803) 732350
12-3, 6-11; 11-11 Sat & summer;
12-3, 7-10.30 Sun
**Draught Bass; Princetown
Dartmoor IPA; guest beer** Ⓗ

A delightful waterside pub overlooking Bow Creek, ideal for riverside walking and with ample parking space for cars and boats. A good selection of traditional ales and a warm, friendly welcome. Several guides and books for browsing.
🏨 Q 🐾 🚗 ◁ ▶ P

WESTCOTT

MERRY HARRIERS
On B3181, 2 miles S of Cullompton
☎ (01392) 881254
11.30-2.30, 6-11 ; 12-3, 7-10.30 Sun
Draught Bass Ⓗ
Friendly, family-run pub with a restaurant offering excellent, good value home-cooked cuisine.
🏨 Q 🐾 ◁ ▶ ♿ ▲ ♣ P

WEST DOWN

CROWN
The Square
☎ (01271) 862790
12-3, 7 (6 summer)-11; 12-3, 7 (6 summer)-10.30 Sun
Marston's Pedigree; Wadworth 6X; Ⓗ **guest beers** Ⓗ Ⓖ
This lovely village pub is a real gem, with one of the finest gardens you're likely to find. Friendly, real-ale drinking regulars make it a must for beer fans. Thatcher's cider is available in summer.
🏨 Q 🎠 🐾 ◁ ▶ ▲ ♣ ○ P

WHIMPLE

NEW FOUNTAIN INN
Church Road (turn off A30 at Hand & Pen, signed Whimple, 1 mile on left)
☎ (01404) 822350
12-2.30, 6.30-11; 12-2.30, 7-10.30 Sun
Branscombe Vale Branoc; Teignworthy Reel Ale; guest beers Ⓗ
Welcoming, family-run village pub serving a good range of reasonably priced beer. Well-behaved children welcome: the garden has rabbits, chickens and goats as well as swings and a climbing frame. Inch's traditional cider. 🏨 Q 🐾 ◁ ▶ 🍴 ⇄ ♣ ○ P

WHITCHURCH

WHITCHURCH INN
Church Hill
☎ (01822) 615383
11-3, 5 (6 Tue & Thu)-11; 11-11 Sat; 12-4, 6-10.30 Sun
Draught Bass; Worthington Bitter; guest beer Ⓗ

Village pub and restaurant near the moor; a single bar boasting exposed beams and a large fireplace with a built-in bread oven. Friendly atmosphere.
Q ◁ ▶ ♣ P

WIDECOMBE IN THE MOOR

RUGGLESTONE INN ☆
¼ mile S of village, OS721766
☎ (01364) 621327
11-2.30 (3 Sat), 6 (7 winter)-11; 12-3, 7-10.30 Sun
Butcombe Bitter; Dartmoor Best Bitter Ⓖ
Unspoilt, cosy little pub in a splendid Dartmoor setting, named after a local 'logan' stone. No children under 14 allowed in the bar, but across the stream is a large garden and a shelter for use in bad weather. Much of the food is home-cooked.
🏨 Q 🐾 ◁ ▶ ▲ ○ P

WOODBURY

WHITE HART
Church Stile Lane
☎ (01395) 232221
10.30-2.30, 6-11; 10.30-11 Sat; 12-3, 7-10.30 Sun
Draught Bass; Otter Ale Ⓗ
14th-century Grade II listed pub. The pleasant garden overlooks the church and village green; entertainment is provided by the cockatiels in the aviary. Very good food.
🏨 Q 🐾 ◁ ▶ ▲ ♣ P

WOODBURY SALTERTON

DIGGERS REST
☎ (01395) 232375
11-2.30, 6.30-11; 12-2.30, 7-10.30 Sun
Draught Bass; Dartmoor Best Bitter Ⓗ
14th-century Grade II listed thatched pub. Unusual handpumps dispense the beer. A skittle alley at the rear doubles as a family room in summer.
🏨 Q 🎠 ◁ ▶ ▲ P

YARDE DOWN

POLTIMORE ARMS
Off A399 OS725357
☎ (01598) 710381
12-2.30, 6.30-11; 12-2.30, 7-10.30 Sun
Cotleigh Tawny; guest beer Ⓖ
Situated on the edge of Dartmoor, you will find this fine country pub frequented by tourists and locals enjoying a friendly atmosphere and a selec-

tion of good ales and home-cooked food.
🏨 Q 🐾 ◁ ▶ ▲ P

YEALMPTON

VOLUNTEER
Fore Street (A379, 8 miles E of Plymouth)
☎ (01752) 880463
11-3, 5-11; 11-11 Fri & Sat; 12-10.30 Sun
Draught Bass; Courage Best Bitter; John Smith's Bitter; Summerskills Best Bitter Ⓗ
Friendly, two-bar village local. The lounge bar features paintings by a local artist; the public bar has a very large collection of ship's crests on the beams, including the Summerskills logo. Very good and unusual food.
🏨 🐾 ◁ ▶ 🍴 ♣

INDEPENDENT BREWERIES

Barum:
Barnstaple
Beer Engine:
Exeter
Blackawton:
Totnes
Blewitts:
Kingsbridge
Branscombe Vale:
Branscombe
Jollyboat:
Bideford
Mildmay:
Plymouth
Otter:
Honiton
Princetown:
Princetown
Royal Inn:
Tavistock
St Giles in the Wood:
Great Torrington
Summerskills:
Plymouth
Sutton:
Plymouth
Tally Ho!:
Hatherleigh
Teignworthy:
Newton Abbot

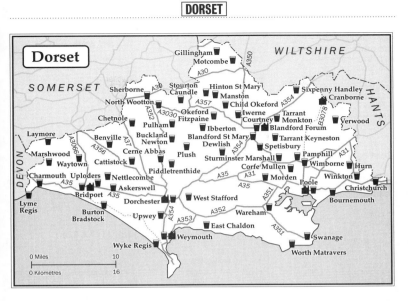

ASKERSWELL

SPYWAY
☎ (01308) 485250
10.30-2.30, 6-11 (closed Mon);
12-3, 7-10.30 Sun
**Adnams Bitter; Branscome Vale
Branoc; Morland Old Speckled
Hen; guest beers** H
Three-room rural pub, popular
with diners and ramblers at
lunchtime; the food is excellent
value. Two rooms have traditional character. Children (and dogs)
welcome in the garden only.
🏚 Q 🕷 🌓 ▶ P

BENVILLE

TALBOT
Off A356, towards Evershot
☎ (01935) 83381
11.30-2.30, 6.30-11; 12-3, 7-11 Sun
Guest beer H
Small, friendly village local with
impressive views over the
Somerset border.
🏚 Q 🕷 🌓 ▶ 🔥 ♣ P

Try also: Acorn Hotel, Evershot
(Free)

BLANDFORD FORUM

DAMORY OAK INN
Damory Court Street
☎ (01258) 452791
11-11; 12-2.30, 7-10.30 Sun
Badger Dorset Best, Tanglefoot H
Friendly local with a two-roomed
bar, displaying many trophies for
darts and pool.
🏚 🕷 ♣

DOLPHIN
42 East Street
☎ (01258) 456813
11-3, 6-11; 11-11 Fri & Sat; 12-3,
7-10.30 Sun
**Draught Bass; Gibbs Mew
Wiltshire, Salisbury, Deacon,
Bishop's Tipple; guest beers** H
Friendly, small, town pub, comfortably refurbished and well laid
out. Good value food (not served
Sun eve). 🏚 🌓 ▶

NELSON CHEESE & ALE HOUSE
77 Salisbury Street
☎ (01258) 451468
11.30-3, 5-11; 11.30-11 Fri & Sat;
12-3, 7-10.30 Sun
Flowers Original; H **Ringwood
Best Bitter, True Glory;** G **John
Smith's Bitter; guest beers** H
Lively, popular bar, featuring a
low, beamed ceiling, a sawdust
covered floor and comfortable
armchairs. Good food . 🌓 ▶ ♣

BLANDFORD ST MARY

STOUR INN
5 Dorchester Road
☎ (01258) 451276
11-2.30, 6-11; 12-3, 7-10.30 Sun
Badger IPA, Dorset Best H
Cosy, friendly one-bar pub, set
back from the road in an attractive terrace, close to the banks of
the River Stour and the Hall &
Woodhouse brewery. 🏚 Q 🕷 ♣

BOURNEMOUTH

COTTONWOOD HOTEL
82 Grove Road (East Cliff,
between the two piers)
☎ (01202) 553183
11.30-3, 5-11; 12-10.30 Sun
**Draught Bass; Ringwood Best
Bitter** H
Lounge bar of an hotel, open to
non-residents. The outdoor balcony overlooks the bay. Pianists
Thu and Sun eves; swing band Fri
eve. 🕷 🛏 🌓 P

DEAN COURT SUPPORTERS' CLUB
Kings Park, Boscombe (by AFC
Bournemouth ground)
☎ (01202) 398313
11-3, 7-11; (11-11 Sat match
days); 12-10.30 Sun
**Wadworth 6X; Worthington
Bitter; guest beer** H
Large, two-roomed club with an
interesting guest beer list and an
occasional cider. Show this *Guide*
or CAMRA membership to be
signed in (limited admittance
match days). 🔥 ♣ 🍺 P

GOAT & TRICYCLE
27-29 West Hill Road
☎ (01202) 314220
12-3, 5.30 (7 Sat)-11; 12-3,
7-10.30 Sun
Beer range varies H
Split-level comfortable pub, near
the town centre. One part of the
pub is dedicated to games.
Covered patio outside. Good
value food. 🏚 Q 🕷 ♣

MOON IN THE SQUARE
4-6 Exeter Road
☎ (01202) 314940
11-11; 12-10.30 Sun
**Courage Directors; Ringwood
Fortyniner; Theakston Best
Bitter; guest beers** H
Large, popular Wetherspoons
pub in the town centre which
good, tasty pub grub is served all
day. Sometimes runs beer festivals, with excellent prices for a
pint. Q 🕷 🌓 🍽

PORTERHOUSE
113 Poole Road, Westbourne
☎ (01202) 768586
11-11; 12-3, 7-10.30 Sun
**Ringwood Best Bitter, True
Glory, Fortyniner, XXXX Porter,
Old Thumper; guest beer** H

Local CAMRA *Pub of the Year* 1996, and the best example of a proper pub in Bournemouth. Very good value food; varying guest cider.
Q ◁ ♣ ⌣

PUNCH & JUDY
32 Poole Hill
☎ (01202) 290016
11-3, 5-11; 11-11 Sat; 12-3, 7-10.30 Sun
Marston's Bitter, Pedigree, Owd Rodger, HBC Ⓗ
Friendly, popular pub with a disco Fri & Sat. A short walk from Bournemouth Square. Good value food. ◁ &

BRIDPORT
HOPE & ANCHOR
13 St Michaels Lane
☎ (01308) 422160
11-3, 6-11; 12-3, 7-11 Sun
Beer range varies Ⓗ
Busy local, offering two cask beers, usually from West Country breweries. It hosts live folk music and holds a beer festival in summer.
🏨 🏵 & 🛆 ♣ ⌣

BUCKLAND NEWTON
GAGGLE OF GEESE
☎ (01300) 345249
12-2.30, 6.30-11; 12-3, 7-10.30 Sun
Badger Dorset Best; Draught Bass; Ringwood Best Bitter; Ⓗ **guest beers** (summer) Ⓖ
Large, traditional village pub serving good food. It holds a goose auction May and Sept. Popular with ramblers on the 'Hardy Way'.
🏨 Q 🏵 ◁ ▶ 🛆 ♣ P

BURTON BRADSTOCK
ANCHOR
High Street
☎ (01308) 897228
11-2.30, 7-11; 12-3, 7-10.30 Sun
Ushers Best Bitter, Founders, seasonal beers Ⓗ
Two-bar pub at the village centre, popular for food. Welcoming and friendly.
🏨 Q 🏵 ◁ ▶ 🛆 ♣ ⌣ P ☂

CATTISTOCK
FOX & HOUNDS INN
Duck Street
☎ (01300) 320444
12-2, 5.30-11; 11.30-11 Sat; 12-3, 7-10.30 Sun
Fuller's London Pride; Oakhill Best Bitter Ⓗ
Three-roomed village local. Formerly an old longhouse, featuring large fireplaces and flagged floors.
🏨 Q ◁ ▶

CERNE ABBAS
RED LION
Long Street
☎ (01300) 341441
11.30-3, 6.30-11; 12-3, 7-10.30 Sun
Wadworth IPA, 6X; guest beer Ⓗ
Pub with an interesting Victorian frontage in the centre of a pretty village below the famous giant. Comfortable and welcoming, it serves excellent food, including local game and good vegetarian dishes.
🏨 Q 🏵 ◁ ▶ 🛆 🛆 ♣

CHARMOUTH
GEORGE
The Street
☎ (01297) 560280
11-3, 7-11; 12-3, 7-10.30 Sun
Otter Bitter; Ruddles Best Bitter; John Smith's Bitter Ⓗ
Busy pub at the village centre, attracting a mainly young clientele at weekends. 🏨 ◁ ▶ ♣

CHETNOLE
CHETNOLE INN
☎ (01935) 872337
11-2.30, 6.30-11; 12-3, 7-10.30 Sun
Otter Ale; Palmer's IPA; guest beers Ⓗ
Two-roomed local, set in a quiet village with always three guest beers and excellent food. Beer festival at Easter. Local CAMRA *Pub of the Year* 1998.
🏨 Q 🏵 ◁ ▶ 🛆 & 🛆 ⇌ ♣ ⌣ P

CHILD OKEFORD
SAXON INN
Gold Hill
☎ (01258) 860310
11.30-2.30 (12-3 Sat), 7-11; 12-3, 7-10.30 Sun
Butcombe Bitter; Hook Norton Old Hooky; guest beer Ⓗ
Quiet, friendly, two-roomed whitewashed inn converted from two cottages in 1949. The garden is home to a pot-bellied pig. Parking can be difficult. No eve meals Tue or Sun.
🏨 Q 🏵 ◁ ▶ & 🛆 ♣ P

CHRISTCHURCH
OLDE GEORGE INN
2a Castle Street
☎ (01202) 479383
10.30-2.30 (3 Sat), 6 (7 Sat)-11; 12-3, 7-10.30 Sun
Flowers Original; Ringwood Fortyniner; guest beers Ⓗ
Friendly, former Tudor coaching inn featuring two low-ceilinged bars and a covered courtyard which admits children. The meeting-cum-music room hosts jazz Thu eve and occasional folk/blues music Wed. 🏵 ◁ P

CORFE MULLEN
COVENTRY ARMS
Mill Street (A31, 2 miles W of Wimborne) ☎ (01258) 857284
11-2.30 (3 Sat), 5.30-11; 12-3, 5.30-10.30 Sun
Ringwood Best Bitter, Fortyniner, Old Thumper; guest beers Ⓖ
Pub dating back to 1426, built on a site mentioned in the *Domesday Book*. It is famous for its 500-year-old mummified cat. A large riverside garden, up to six guest beers and excellent food add to its attractions.
Q 🏵 ◁ ▶ & 🛆 ♣ P

DEWLISH
OAK AT DEWLISH
☎ (01258) 837352
6-11; 12-3, 7-10.30 Sun
Cottage Golden Arrow; Ⓖ **Flowers Original;** Ⓗ **Wadworth 6X** Ⓖ
Two-roomed village pub in the heart of the Dorset countryside.
🏨 🏵 ◁ ▶ &

DORCHESTER
BLUE RADDLE
8 Church St ☎ (01305) 267762
11.30-3, 7-11; 12-3, 7-10.30 Sun
Greene King Abbot; Otter Bitter; guest beers Ⓗ
Lively, side-street local serving constantly changing guest beers plus an excellent range of good value food (not served Mon eve) ◁ ▶ ⇌ (South/West)

TOM BROWNS
47 High East St ☎ (01305) 264020
11-11; 12-3, 7-10.30 Sun
Goldfinch Tom Brown's, Flashman's Clout, Midnight Blinder Ⓗ
The Goldfinch brewery tap; a basic local with a single bar and wooden floors.
🛏 ◁ ▶ ⇌ (South/West)

EAST CHALDON
SAILORS RETURN
1 mile from A352
☎ (01305) 853847
11-2.30, 6.30-11; 12-2, 7-10.30 Sun
Flowers IPA; Fuller's London Pride; guest beers Ⓗ
Well-extended, thatched pub with a stone-flagged floor, two bars and a restaurant serving good value food in large portions. Very busy in summer.
🏵 ◁ ▶ & 🛆 ♣ ⌣ P

GILLINGHAM
BUFFALO
Lydfords Lane, Wyke (100 yds from B3081 road to Wincanton)
☎ (01747) 823759
12-2.30, 5.30 (7 Sat)-11; 12-2.30, 7-10.30 Sun

Badger Dorset Best; Wells
Eagle Ⓗ
One-bar country pub on the outskirts of town; the locals'
favourite. Stone built, old-fashioned and friendly, it hosts occasional live music (piano). No food
Sun. 🏾 ⊛ ⟨ 🖡 ᕦ ♣ P

HINTON ST MARY

WHITE HORSE
200 yds from B3092
☎ (01258) 472723
11.30-2.30, 6.15-11; 12-3,
7-10.30 Sun
Beer range varies Ⓗ
Popular and friendly village pub,
the heart of the community. It
runs a wide range of social events.
🏾 Q ⟿ ⊛ ⟨ 🖭 Å ♣ ᕦ P

HURN

AVON CAUSEWAY HOTEL
Off B3073 ☎ (01202) 482714
11-11; 12-10.30 Sun
Beer range varies Ⓗ Ⓟ
Formerly Hurn railway station,
now a large bar area and railway
carriage restaurant, staging murder mystery nights Fri and Sat;
jazz on Tue. Skittle alley available. Bar meals available until
9pm Mon-Fri.
⟿ ⊛ ᕦ ⟨ 🖡 ᕫ Å P ⅄

IBBERTON

CROWN
Church Lane (4 miles SW of
A357) OS788077
☎ (01258) 817448
11-2.30, 7-11 (11-11 summer);
12-3, 7-10.30 (12-10.30 summer)
Sun
Draught Bass; M&B Brew XI;
guest beer Ⓗ
Idyllic country pub nestling below
Bulbarrow Hill. The bar features
an original flagstone floor, an
inglenook and photos of bygone
village life. The guest beer is
from the Cottage Brewery range.
🏾 Q ⊛ ⟨ 🖡 ᕫ ♣ ᕦ P

IWERNE COURTNEY

CRICKETERS
½ mile W of A350, near Shroton
☎ (01258) 860421
11.30-2.30, 7(6.30 summer)-11;
12-3, 7-10.30 Sun
Beer range varies Ⓗ
Village pub with an excellent
restaurant, handy for walkers,
enjoying glorious scenery around
the Iron Age hill fort on
Hambledon Hill.
Q ⊛ ⟨ 🖡 ᕫ ♣ P ⅄

LAYMORE

SQUIRREL
800 yds from B3165 jct
OS387048 ☎ (01460) 30298
11.30-2.30, 6-11; 12-3, 7-10.30 Sun

Crewkerne Crookhorn; Oakhill
Yeoman; Wadworth 6X Ⓗ
Unexpected pub in the middle of
nowhere, enjoying a good local
trade. Classical background
music does not intrude. Beer festival in summer.
🏾 Q ⊛ ⟨ 🖡 Å ♣ ᕦ P

NAG'S HEAD
Silver Street
☎ (01297) 442312
11-3, 6-11; 11-11 Tue & Sat;
12-10.30 Sun
Wells Bombardier; guest beers Ⓗ
Friendly free house offering a
wide range of guest beers and
local games. Very good traditional food (not served Thu) in an
upstairs restaurant with sea
views. It holds three beer festivals a year.
🏾 ⊛ ᕫ ⟨ 🖡 ᕫ ♣

VICTORIA HOTEL
Uplyme Road
☎ (01297) 444801
11-3, 6-11 (11-11 summer); 12-3,
7-10.30 Sun
Marston's Pedigree; Otter Bitter;
Wadworth 6X Ⓗ
Café/bar ambience in a traditional building. High quality à la carte
food (fresh ingredients) and bar
snacks always available, also
wines. ⊛ ᕫ ⟨ 🖡 Å P

VOLUNTEER INN
31 Broad Street
☎ (01297) 442214
11-3, 7-11; 12-3, 7-10.30 Sun
Draught Bass; Ⓗ Branscombe
Vale Branoc; Ⓖ Fuller's
London Pride; guest beer Ⓗ
Welcoming single bar and dining
room (children welcome). The
house beer (Donegal Ale) is from
Branscombe Vale.
⟨ 🖡 ᕫ Å ♣

MANSTON

PLOUGH
Shaftesbury Road (B3091)
☎ (01258) 472484
11.30-2.30, 6.30-11; 12-3,
7-10.30 Sun
Smiles Golden Brew; Ⓗ guest
beers Ⓗ Ⓖ
Originally a cider house, then a
Hall & Woodhouse tenancy, now
free of tie. Note the unusual plas-
terwork in the bar, including,
allegedly, fertility symbols.
🏾 Q ⊛ ⟨ 🖡 ᕫ ♣ P

MARSHWOOD

BOTTLE
On B3165 near Devon border
☎ (01297) 678254
11-2.30, 6-11; 12-3, 7-10.30 Sun
Morland Old Speckled Hen;
Otter Bitter; Wadworth 6X; guest
beers (occasional) Ⓗ
Classic postcard thatched country pub, boasting beamed rooms,

both with a fireplace, served by a
single bar. Popular with walkers.
🏾 Q ⊛ ⟨ 🖡 Å ♣ P

MORDEN

COCK & BOTTLE
B3075, off A35
☎ (01929) 459238
11-2.30, 6-11; 12-3, 7-10.30 Sun
Badger IPA, Dorset Best,
Tanglefoot Ⓗ
Friendly, 400-year-old village pub
in a rural setting, with a sympathetic restaurant extension serving a range of good value food.
🏾 ⊛ ⟨ 🖡 ᕫ ♣ P

MOTCOMBE

COPPLERIDGE INN
Off Mere Road OS842266
☎ (01747) 851980
11-3, 5-11; 11-11 Sat; 12-10.30 Sun
Butcombe Bitter; Hook Norton
Best Bitter; guest beer Ⓗ
Converted 18th-century farmhouse affording extensive views
and many facilities, including
cricket, tennis, a nature trail and
an adventure playground. The
menu is interestingly varied.
🏾 Q ⟿ ⊛ ᕫ ⟨ 🖡 ♣ P ⅄

NETTLECOMBE

MARQUIS OF LORNE
☎ (01308) 485236
11-2.30, 6.30 (6 summer)-11;
12-3, 7-10.30 Sun
Palmers BB, IPA Ⓗ, 200 Ⓖ
Excellent pub at the heart of
West Dorset's countryside, offering several eating and drinking
areas, with an adventurous menu
at reasonable prices. Well worth
finding. 🏾 ⊛ ᕫ ⟨ 🖡 ♣ P ⅄

NORTH WOOTTON

THREE ELMS
☎ (01935) 812881
11-2.30, 6.30 (6 Fri & Sat)-11;
12-3, 7-10.30 Sun
Butcombe Bitter; Fuller's
London Pride; Shepherd Neame
Spitfire; guest beers Ⓗ
Popular pub serving eight ales
and a wide range of good food
(especially vegetarian). Over
1100 model vehicles are on
show. Three Elms Traditional is
Ash Vine Bitter rebadged.
Q ⊛ ᕫ ⟨ 🖡 ♣ ᕦ P

OKEFORD FITZPAINE

ROYAL OAK
Lower Street
☎ (01258) 861561
12-3, 5.30-11; 12-11 Sat; 12-3,
7-10.30 Sun
Ringwood Best Bitter; Wadworth
6X; guest beer Ⓗ
Friendly, thriving village local,
offering a comfortable lounge
and a flagstoned bar with an

upstairs skittle alley. Good value home-cooked food (not served Sun eve).
🏭 Q 🕸 ⬤▌ ⏚ ♣ 👄 P

PAMPHILL

VINE INN
Vine Hill (off B3082) OS995003
☎ (01202) 882259
11-2.30, 7-11; 12-3, 7-10.30 Sun
Fuller's London Pride; guest beer ℍ
Good pub for walkers, owned by the NT and a focal point for local activities; near Kingston Lacey House. This former E Dorset CAMRA *Pub of the Year* has two small bar areas and a games room upstairs. Q 🕸 ⬤ 👄 P 🍺

PIDDLETRENTHIDE

PIDDLE INN
☎ (01300) 348468
11.30-2.30, 6.30-11; 11.30-11 Sat; 12-3, 7-10.30 Sun
Draught Bass; Ringwood Best Bitter; Wadworth 6X ℍ
Traditional village pub with a garden on the bank of River Piddle. Licensed since 1770, it boasts a collection of 160 chamber pots.
🏭 🏕 🕸 ⬤▌ ⚷ ♣ 👄 P

PLUSH

BRACE OF PHEASANTS
Off B3143 ☎ (01300) 348357
12-2.30, 7-11; 12-2.30, 7-10.30 Sun
Fuller's London Pride; guest beer ⅁
Friendly, traditional, thatched pub in a quiet village, extremely popular for its extensive range of good food and regularly changing guest beers.
🏭 Q 🕸 ⬤▌ ⚷ ♣ P

POOLE

BERMUDA TRIANGLE
10 Parr Street, Lower Parkstone
☎ (01202) 748087
12-2.30, 5.30-11; 12-4, 6-11 Sat; 12-10.30 Sun
Beer range varies ℍ
Superb, comfortable free house offering four ales. It bears a nautical theme, based on the Bermuda Triangle. Good selection of foreign bottled beers.
⬤ ⇌ (Parkstone)

BLUE BOAR
29 MarketClose
☎ (01202) 682247
11-3, 5-11; 12-3, 7-10.30 Sun
Courage Best Bitter, Directors; Cottage Southern Bitter; guest beers ℍ
Former merchants house in the old town, sympathetically converted: a comfortable ground-floor lounge and an extensive cellar, admitting children lunchtimes (closed Sun lunch).

Live bands perform Thu and Sun. No meals Sun. ⬤ ⇌ ♣

BREWHOUSE
68 High St ☎ (01202) 685288
11-11.30; 11-5, 7-11.30 Sat; 11-11.30 Sun
Poole Best Bitter, Bosun ℍ
Lively, basic pub, an ideal spot after shopping, selling probably the cheapest beer in Dorset. The home of Poole Brewery. ⇌

SANDACRES FREE HOUSE
3 Banks Road, Sandbanks
☎ (01202) 707244
11-3, 6-11; 12-3, 7-10.30 Sun
Poole Bosun; Ringwood Best Bitter, Old Thumper; Wadworth 6X; guest beer ℍ
Popular free house, handy for Sandbanks beach, affording spectacular views over Poole Harbour. A large comfortable lounge often shows Sky sports; a games room with pool tables and amusement machines allows children until 9pm. ⬤ ▌ ⚷ ♣ P

PULHAM

HALSEY ARMS
☎ (01258) 817344
11.30-2.30 (not Wed), 6-11; 12-3, 7-10.30 Sun
Courage Best Bitter; Ringwood Best Bitter; guest beers ℍ
Very popular, traditional village pub with a friendly atmosphere, good food and an excellent choice of beers and ciders.
🏭 Q 🏕 🕸 ⬤▌ ⚷ ♣ 👄 P 🍺

SHERBORNE

DIGBY TAP
Cooks Lane ☎ (01935) 813148
11-2.30, 5.30-11; 12-2.30, 7-10.30 Sun
Beer range varies ℍ
Basic, traditional drinking house featuring stone-flagged floors, wood panelling, old photos and a good atmosphere. No food Sun. It stocks over 20 different beers a week. ⬤ ⇌ ♣

SKIPPER'S
1 Terrace View, Horsecastles
☎ (01935) 812753
11-2.30, 5.30-11; 12-3, 7-10.30 Sun
Adnams Bitter; Wadworth IPA, 6X, Farmers Glory, seasonal beers; guest beer ℍ
Refurbished former cider house displaying naval pictures.
🕸 ⬤▌ ⇌ ♣ P

SIXPENNY HANDLEY

ROEBUCK
22 High Street ☎ (01725) 552002
11-2.30 (not Mon), 6.30-11 (closed winter Mon); 12-3, 7-10.30 Sun
Ringwood Best Bitter, XXXX Porter, Fortyniner, guest beers ℍ

Aesthetically pleasing and comfortable single-bar village free house with a fireplace, piano and old village photos. Separate pool room; excellent, innovative food served (not Mon).
🏭 Q 🏕 🕸 ⬤▌ Å ♣ P

SPETISBURY

DRAX ARMS
High Street (A350)
☎ (01258) 452658
11.30-2.30, 7 (6.30 Fri, Sat & summer)-11; 12-3, 7-10.30 Sun
Badger Dorset Best, Tanglefoot ℍ
Popular pub rebuilt in 1926: two communicating bars, one with darts and a shove ha'penny board. No meals Mon eve. 🕸 ⬤▌ ♣ P

STOURTON CAUNDLE

TROOPER
☎ (01963) 362405
12-2.30 (not Mon); 7-11; 12-3, 7-10.30 Sun
Beer range varies ℍ
Attractive old village centre pub, with two small bars, a skittle alley and remarkable collection of old farm implements. No menu, but good sandwiches always available.
Q 🕸 ⏚ ⚷ Å ♣ 👄 P

STURMINSTER MARSHALL

RED LION
Church Street (1 mile E of A350)
☎ (01258) 857319
11-2.30, 6-11; 12-3, 6-10.30 Sun
Badger Dorset Best, Tanglefoot ℍ
Well-appointed village pub opposite the church, winner of many local awards. The skittle alley doubles as a family no-smoking area. 🏭 🏕 🕸 ⬤▌ ♣ P ✄

SWANAGE

CROWS NEST INNE
11 Ulwell Road ☎ (01929) 422651
12-2.30, 6-11; 12-10.30 Sun
Ringwood Best Bitter; Flowers IPA; guest beer ℍ
Comfortable pub with a dining area, offering a good value menu (including vegetarian choices). Popular with all ages; note the opening times vary in winter. Limited parking. 🏕 🕸 ⬤▌ P

RED LION
63 High St ☎ (01929) 423533
11-11; 12-10.30 Sun
Flowers Original; ℍ **Ringwood Best Bitter, Fortyniner** ⅁
Popular, down-to-earth, two-bar pub: the public bar adjoins the ground floor cellar from where the beers are dispensed; a lounge leads to a large garden and children's room. Eve meals Fri and Sat. 🏕 🕸 ⬤▌⏚ ♣ 👄 P

TARRANT KEYNESTON

TRUE LOVERS KNOT
On B3082
☎ (01258) 452209
11-2.30, 7 (6.30 Fri & Sat)-11;
12-3, 7-10.30 Sun
Badger Dorset Best ⊞
Ivy-clad, one-bar inn set at a crossroads in the picturesque Tarrant Valley. The large garden has a children's play area. No meals Mon eve.
🏠 Q ❀ ◑ ▶ ♿ ▲ ♣ P

TARRANT MONKTON

LANGTON ARMS
Off A354
☎ (01258) 830225
11.30-3, 6-11; 11.30-11 Sat; 12-3,
7-10.30 Sun
Ringwood Best Bitter; guest beers ⊞
Local CAMRA *Pub of the Year* 1997. This 17th-century country pub serves three ever-changing ales in the lounge (and on request in the public bar). Plenty of facilities to suit all tastes. A beer festival is held at Easter.
🏠 Q ⛺ ❀ ⇔ ◑ ▶ ⊞
♿ ♣ P

UPLODERS

CROWN INN
☎ (01308) 485356
11-3, 6-11; 12-3, 7-10.30 Sun
Palmers BB, IPA, 200 ⊞
Single-bar village pub and restaurant where there's a warm welcome from the regulars
🏠 Q ❀ ◑ ▶ ♣ P

UPWEY

ROYAL STANDARD
200 Dorchester Road
☎ (01305) 812558
11-3, 6-11; 11-11 Sat; 12-10.30 Sun
Eldridge Pope Pope's Traditional, Hardy Country, Royal Oak ⊞
Unspoilt local on the main road to Weymouth, one of the few EP houses not to use sparklers.
🏠 ⊞ P

VERWOOD

ALBION INN
Station Road
☎ (01202) 825267
11-2.30, 5 (6 Sat)-11; 12-2.30,
7-10.30 Sun
beer range varies ⊞
Superb, cosy pub built in 1866 as Verwood railway station. Good value food. ❀ ◑ ▶ P

WAREHAM

QUAY INN
The Quay ☎ (01929) 552735
11-3, 7-11 (11-11 summer); 12-3,
7-10.30 Sun

Boddingtons Bitter; Fuller's London Pride; Greene King Abbot; Ringwood Best Bitter; guest beer ⊞
Lovely old pub in a market town serving good value food. Sit outside by the river.
🏠 ❀ ⇔ ◑ ▶ ⇌ ♣

WAYTOWN

HARE & HOUNDS
☎ (01308) 488203
11.30-2.30, 6.30-11; 12-3,
7-10.30 Sun
Palmers BB, IPA, 200 ⊞
Unspoilt country pub midway between Bridport and Beaminster. Serving good food, it can get busy in summer.
🏠 Q ⛺ ❀ ◑ ▶ ⊞ ♣ ⌂ P

WEST STAFFORD

WISE MAN
☎ (01305) 263694
11-3, 6-11; 12-3, 7-10.30 Sun
Draught Bass; Ringwood Best Bitter ⊞
Attractive, ivy-draped, thatched pub in a quiet village. This 400-year-old pub has retained its public and lounge bars; note the fine display of toby jugs. A nitro-keg free zone.
🏠 ❀ ◑ ▶ ⊞ ♿ ♣ ⌂ P

WEYMOUTH

KINGS ARMS
15 Trinity Rd ☎ (01305) 770055
10-11; 12-10.30 Sun
Greenalls Original; Quay Weymouth JD; Ringwood Best Bitter; Wadworth 6X ⊞
Traditional harbourside pub, haunt of local fishermen, whose menu features fresh fish from the quay. No food Sun or winter Mon-Tue. 🏠 ◑ ▶ ⊞ ⌂

WEATHERBURY
7 Carlton Road North
☎ (01305) 786040
11-2.30, 5.30-11; 11-11 Fri & Sat;
12-10.30 Sun
Draught Bass; guest beers ⊞
Very popular pub set in a residential area, always stocking four guest beers. It holds a beer festival (20 plus beers) in summer. Limited parking.
❀ ⇔ ◑ ▶ ⇌ ♣ P

WIMBORNE

CROWN & ANCHOR
Walford Bridge
☎ (01202) 841405
10.30-2.30, 6-11; 12-3, 7-10.30 Sun
Badger Dorset Best ⊞
Superb, friendly, local with a garden alongside the River Allen, handy for the craft centre at Walford Mill. Good selection of good value food.
🏠 Q ❀ ◑ ▲ P

WINKTON

LAMB INN
Burley Road ☎ (01425) 672427
11-2.45, 5.30-11; 11-11 Sat;
12-10.30 Sun
Fuller's London Pride; Young's Special; guest beers ⊞
Cheerful two-roomer set amongst green fields with a children's play area in the garden.
🏠 ❀ ◑ ▶ ⊞ ▲ ♣ P

WORTH MATRAVERS

SQUARE & COMPASS ☆
Off B3069 OS974777
☎ (01929) 439229
11-3, 6-11; 11-11 Sat; 12-3,
7-10.30 Sun
Ringwood Best Bitter, Badger Tanglefoot; guest beers Ⓖ
Run by the Newman family for over 90 years, this ancient stone pub boasts flagstone floors, serving hatches and views of medieval field patterns and the sea. The only pub in Dorset to be in every edition of this *Guide*.
🏠 Q ❀ ◑ ▲ ♣ ⌂ P

WYKE REGIS

WYKE SMUGGLERS
76 Portland Road
☎ (01305) 760010
11-2.30, 6-11; 12-3, 7-10.30 Sun
Boddingtons Bitter; Flowers Original; Ringwood Old Thumper; Young's Special; guest beers ⊞
Dart players' paradise between Weymouth and Portland, busy most evenings, serving at least two guest ales. Note: its popularity plus a small cellar can result in restricted beer choice near closing time. ❀ ♿ ♣ ⌂ P

INDEPENDENT BREWERIES

Badger:
Blandford Forum

Cranborne:
Cranborne

Goldfinch:
Dorchester

Hardy:
Dorchester

Palmer's:
Bridport

Poole:
Poole

Quay:
Weymouth

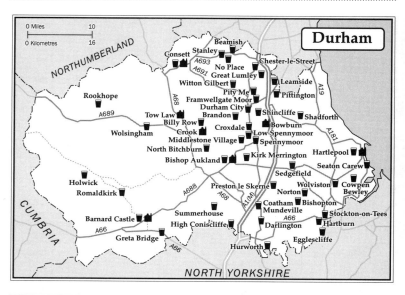

Durham

BARNARD CASTLE

THREE HORSE SHOES
Galgate
☎ (01833) 638774
11-11; 12-10.30 Sun
Draught Bass or Tetley Bitter; Worthington Bitter Ⓗ
Lively, 17th-century, town-centre pub with a good traditional feel and a fine collection of old local railway photos.
🌂 ❀ ◑ ♣

Try also Old Well, The Bank (Free); Charles Dickens, Market Place (John Smith's)

BEAMISH

BLACK HORSE
Red Row, off A6076
☎ (01207) 232569
12-3, 7-11; 11-3, 6-11 Sat; 12-3, 7-10.30 Sun
Vaux Waggledance; Ward's Best Bitter Ⓗ
Traditional alehouse dating from the 17th century. Very cosy and welcoming, but it can take some finding. Until recently the beer was brought direct from the cellar. Note the unusual collection of matchboxes. Handy for the Beamish Museum.
🏚 Q ❀ ♣ P ⟐

BEAMISH OPEN AIR MUSEUM

SUN INN
Old Industrial Town Centre, Beamish Open Air Museum, Stanley ☎ (01207) 231811
11-6 (or Museum closing time); 12-4 off season; 12-6 Sun
Theakston Best Bitter, XB; guest beer Ⓗ

Taken stone by stone from Main Street, Bishop Auckland and rebuilt in the Beamish North of England Open Air Museum. A faithful reconstruction of a traditional North-Eastern industrial area pub. Best visited on a quiet day time before it fills up.
🏚 Q 🐂 ❀ ◑ ◗ ⊟ ⅙ ⇌ P

BILLY ROW

DUN COW (COW'S TAIL)
Old White Lea ☎ (01388) 762714
12-2 (not Mon-Fri), 7-11; 12-2, 7-10.30 Sun
Butterknowle Banner Bitter; Hodge's Original; guest beers Ⓗ
Unspoilt gem well off the beaten track, but worth a visit. A two-roomed pub with open fires and range. One of the few original inns left in the county; owned by the same family since 1830, the present landlord has been behind the bar for 40 years. Guest beers come from Darwin.
🏚 Q ❀ ♣ P ⅙

BISHOP AUCKLAND

TUT 'N' SHIVE
68 Newgate Street
☎ (01388) 603252
11-11; 12-10.30 Sun
Boddingtons Bitter; Castle Eden Ale; Flowers Original; Whitbread Trophy; guest beers Ⓗ
Town-centre bar, always offering good basic beers but look out for seasonal and guest beers. One room with two distinct areas - a games area at front and more comfortable seating at the back. Very popular at the weekends. No food Sun.
◑ ⇌ ♣

BISHOPTON

TALBOT
The Green
☎ (01740) 630371
11-3, 5.30-11; 12-3, 7-10.30 Sun
Camerons Strongarm; Tetley Bitter; guest beers Ⓗ
Cosy village local, in this *Guide* for 25 consecutive editions under the same landlord. A choice of spaces: a flagged bar area with a raised lounge to one side and a small 'snug' to the other. Strong emphasis on meals (upstairs restaurant).
🏚 Q ❀ ◑ ◗ ♣ P

BRANDON

BRAWN'S DEN
Winchester Drive (300 yds from A690)
☎ (0191) 378 1687
11-3, 7-11; 12-3, 7-10.30 Sun
Tetley Bitter; guest beer Ⓗ
Modern estate pub on the outskirts of Durham City by the Brandon to Bishop Auckland Walk; walkers and cyclists are always welcome.
❀ ⅙ ♣ P

CHESTER-LE-STREET

BUTCHERS ARMS
Middle Chare
☎ (0191) 388 3605
11-3, 6.30-11; 12-3, 7-10.30 Sun
Camerons Bitter, Strongarm; Marston's Pedigree Ⓗ
Traditional one-roomed town pub with a side snug area. It always smells of cooking. Popular with all ages.
🛏 ◑ ♣

SMITHS ARMS
Brecon Hill, Castledene (off B1284)
☎ (0191) 385 6915
4 (12 Sat)-11; 3, 7-10.30 Sun
Draught Bass; Courage Directors; M&B Brew XI; guest beer Ⓗ
Brass and china adorn the walls of this traditional country-style pub comprising two rooms plus a games room. Relaxed and comfortable, it is miles from anywhere, minutes from everywhere. Guest beer at weekends.
ᐄ Q ✿ ⊟ P

Try also: Market Tavern, Market Place (Whitbread)

COATHAM MUNDEVILLE

FORESTERS ARMS
Brafferton Lane (A167 near A1(M) jct)
☎ (01325) 320565
11-3, 4.45-11; 11-11 Fri & Sat & summer; 12-10.30 Sun
John Smith's Magnet Ⓗ
Welcoming pub with a strong Irish flavour, serving well-prepared food (no meals Sun eve). Occasional live music. Two rooms: a bar and a dining room; children welcome for meals.
ᐄ ✿ ◖ ▶ P

CONSETT

GREY HORSE
115 Sherburn Terrace (off A692)
☎ (01207) 502585
12-5, 7-11; 11-11 Sat; 12-10.30 Sun
Derwent Rose, Mutton Clog, Steel Town Bitter, Red Dust, Swordmaker, Coast to Coast, Derwent Deep Ⓗ
Ex-coaching inn, now a brewpub, with a traditional bar, a pool room and a cosy lounge hosting popular organ music and singaround Fri night. Six real ales available, all brewed on site; occasional 'specials' are brewed and customers asked for suggestions.
ᐄ Q ✿ ◖ ⊟ ♿ ♣

COWPEN BEWLEY

THREE HORSE SHOES
☎ (01642) 561541
12-3, 5.30 (6 Sat)-11; 12-3, 7-10.30 Sun
Camerons Strongarm; Marston's Pedigree Ⓗ
A homely village pub at one end of the green. A pub has been on this site for 550 years; the present building was opened in 1955 and inherited the earlier building's helpful ghost who cools the cellar in hot weather.
ᐄ ✿ ◖ ▶ ⊟ ♿ ♣ P ⊟

CROXDALE

DALESIDE ARMS
Front Street (B6288)
☎ (01388) 814165
2-5.30, 7-11; 11-11 Sat; 12-4, 7-10.30 Sun
Mordue Workie Ticket; guest beers Ⓗ
Small, cosy bar next to a larger restaurant. In a short time this former guest house has built a good reputation for its wide-ranging guest ales.
ᐄ ⊟ ♣ P ⊟

DARLINGTON

BINNS DEPARTMENT STORE (OFF-LICENCE)
1-7 High Row ☎ (01325) 462606
9-5.30 (6 Sat); closed Sun
House of Fraser department store with an impressively-stocked bottled beer selection in the basement. Over 250 quality beers, including dozens of British and Belgian bottle-conditioned ales, also a good selection of special glasses. ⇻

BRITANNIA
Archer Street
☎ (01325) 463787
11.30-3, 5.30-11; 12-3, 7-10.30 Sun
Camerons Strongarm; Tetley Imperial; guest beer Ⓗ
Relaxed, uncomplicated old local, on the fringe of the town centre but a million miles from the hectic weekend 'circuit'. A bastion of cask beer for 140 years, it is still recognisable as the private house it once was. Guest beers from the Tapster's Choice range. Q ⇻ ♣ P

CENTRAL BOROUGH
12 Hopetown Lane (near Railway Museum, off A167)
☎ (01325) 468490
11-11; 12-10.30 Sun
Camerons Strongarm Ⓗ
Classic street-corner local in an area of terraced housing. Three rooms: a bar, lounge and a tiny front 'parlour'. A loyal clientele. Nearby, the town Railway Museum is housed in one of the world's oldest stations on the original Stockton and Darlington Railway.
⊟ ⇻ (North Rd) ♣ ⊟

GOLDEN COCK
5 Tubwell Row
☎ (01325) 468843
11-11; 12-10.30 Sun
John Smith's Magnet Ⓗ
18th-century, town-centre local, popular with all ages who enjoy the pool, darts and dominoes in a friendly atmosphere. Well behaved children welcome. Good food available at reasonable prices. ◖ ▶ ♣ ♣

NUMBER TWENTY-2
22 Coniscliffe Road
☎ (01325) 354590
11-11; closed Sun
Hambleton Nightmare; Ind Coope Burton Ale; Village White Boar, Bull, Old Raby; guest beers Ⓗ
Very popular, classy, new pub in a former restaurant, NE CAMRA *Pub of the Year* 1997 and '98. Huge curved windows and a high ceiling give it an airy spaciousness even when packed. Catering for 'thirtysomethings' it turns over 15-plus independent ales per week. No spirits.
Q ◖ ♿ ⇻ ⊡ ⊟

OLD YARD (TAPAS BAR)
98 Bondgate
☎ (01325) 467385
11-2.30, 7-11; 11-11 Fri & Sat; 12-2, 7-10.30 Sun
John Smith's Magnet; guest beers Ⓗ
A Mediterranean style taverna with a range of real ales. Traditional Spanish Tapas and Greek Mezes are always available, also a specials menu. It's perfectly acceptable to come in just for a beer. ◖ ▶ ⇻

RAILWAY TAVERN
8 High Northgate (A617, 1/2 mile N of centre)
☎ (01325) 464963
11-11; 12-10.30 Sun
Beer range varies Ⓗ
Possibly the first 'railway' pub in the world, taking its name from the nearby 1825 Stockton and Darlington line. A friendly two-roomed local where children are welcome. Live music Fri eves and most Sats. A Whitbread leasehold, but guests come from independent brewers.
ᐄ ✿ ⊟ ⇻ (North Rd) ♣ P

WHITE HORSE HOTEL
North Road, Harrowgate Hill (A167) ☎ (01325) 382121
11.30-3, 6-11; 11.30-11 Sat & Bank Hols; 12-10.30 Sun
Camerons Strongarm; Tetley Imperial; guest beer Ⓗ
Three-star hotel on the north side of town: a public bar and a lounge with a log fire. Hot food available in the bars or restaurant. Children welcome.
ᐄ Q ✿ ⊟ ◖ ▶ ⊟ ♿ ♣ P

Try also: Tap & Spile, Bondgate(Free)

DURHAM CITY

DUN COW
37 Old Elvet (opp jail)
☎ (0191) 386 9219
11-11; 12-10.30 Sun
Boddingtons Bitter; Castle Eden Ale; guest beer Ⓗ
Pub with a tiny bar and outside

WC, popular with regulars and sports-oriented Sunday lunchtime locals. A strong student contingent in the lounge; in termtime it boasts the highest cask sales of Castle Eden Ale in the country.
Q ◁ ⍾ ⅋ ♣ ✦

HALF MOON
New Elvet (opp. County Hotel)
☎ (0191) 386 4528
11-11; 12-10.30 Sun
Draught Bass; Worthington Bitter; guest beer ⓗ
Nicely redecorated old inn; a split-level crescent-shaped bar gives the pub its name. It draws a mixture of locals, tourists and students. Particularly busy Fri eves. The guest beer comes from Durham Brewery. ◁

OLD ELM TREE
12 Cross Gate (behind bus station, via Neville St)
☎ (0191) 386 4621
12-3, 6-11; 12-11 Sat; 12-3, 7-10.30 Sun
Vaux Samson, Waggledance, seasonal beers; Ward's Best Bitter; guest beer ⓗ
Built in 1601, this old coaching inn is an open, friendly pub well used by all ages. Lively (but not noisy) at weekends. Note the old elm tree in the bar. Durham CAMRA *Pub of the Year* 1998.
🚶 Q ⊛ ⍾ ◁ ⅋ ≱ ♣ ○ P

SHAKESPEARE
63 Saddler Street (between Market Place and Cathedral)
☎ (0191) 386 9709
11-11; 12-10.30 Sun
Courage Directors; McEwans 80/-; Theakston Best Bitter; Webster's Yorkshire Bitter ⓗ
Listed building with an interesting snug (ex-auction room). A lunchtime drinking club, it is popular with university students and the cathedral choir. Q ◁

VICTORIA
86 Hallgarth Street
☎ (0191) 386 5269
11-3, 6-11; 12-2, 7-10.30 Sun
Hodge's Original; Marston's Pedigree; Theakston Best Bitter; guest beer ⓗ
Attractive, city-centre pub boasting authentic Victorian fixtures, fittings and furnishings. Differing decor in the bar, snug and lounge; no TV or jukebox. Its traditional warm atmosphere is enjoyed by locals and students.
🚶 Q ⌂ ◁ ⍾ ⅋ ♣

EGGLESCLIFFE

POT & GLASS
Church Road ☎ (01642) 651009
12-3, 5.30-11; 12-10.30 Sun
Draught Bass; guest beer (occasional) ⓗ
Historic village pub of character:

two bars and a function/children's room. The ornate bar fronts were made by a previous licensee from old country furniture. Many have heard the ghostly nuns! Booking essential for eve meals. Fields its own cricket team.
Q ⌕ ⊛ ◁ ▶ ⍾ ♣ P ⊟

FRAMWELLGATE MOOR

TAP & SPILE
27 Front Street (off A167 bypass) ☎ (0191) 386 5451
11.30-3, 6 (5 Fri)-11; 12-3, 7-10.30 Sun
Tap & Spile Premium; guest beers ⓗ
Two main rooms, one of which is no-smoking, in basic 'Tap & Spile' decor. The rear room is a partitioned games/family room. Up to nine beers available.
Q ⌕ ♣ ○ ⌿

Try also: Marquis of Granby, Front St (Samuel Smith)

GREAT LUMLEY

OLD ENGLAND
Front Street
☎ (0191) 388 5257
11-11; 12-10.30 Sun
Beer range varies ⓗ
Busy bar, popular with younger drinkers; the lounge is quieter and more comfortable, attracting older clientele and diners. A good and widely varying range of guest beers (usually three on tap).
Q ◁ ▶ ⍾ ♣ P

GRETA BRIDGE

MORRITT ARMS HOTEL
Off A66
☎ (01833) 627232
11-11 (Sir Walter Scott Bar opens at 8pm); 12-10.30 Sun
Butterknowle Conciliation Ale; Taylor Landlord; Tetley Bitter; Theakston Best Bitter ⓗ
Two very different hostelries exist here, in a fine, secluded setting. The main bar, in the magnificently traditional country house hotel, has Dickens murals by 'Guinness artist' John Gilroy. The detached Sir Walter Scott bar serves the local trade with Conciliation only.
🚶 Q ⌕ ⊛ ⌂ ◁ ▶ ⍾ ♣ P

HARTBURN

MASHAM HOTEL
87 Hartburn Village
☎ (01642) 580414
11-11; 12-3, 7-10.30 Sun
Draught Bass; Black Sheep Special; guest beers (occasional) ⓗ
Unspoilt Grade II listed pub in a

tree-lined village street, offering a choice of drinking areas.
Q ⊛ ⌂ ♣ P ⊟

HARTLEPOOL

BLACKSMITHS ARMS
Stockton Street (A689 next to Camerons Brewery)
☎ (01429) 274762
11-11; 12-10.30 Sun
Camerons Strongarm ⓗ
Impressive, whitewashed, multi-room pub which would not look out of place in a rural setting: a small bar and a smoke room plus a large lounge and a games room.Q ◁ ⍾ ≱ ♣ P ⊟

NURSERY
Hart Lane
☎ (0142) 268994
12 (11.30 Sat)-11; 12-10.30 Sun
Camerons Strongarm ⓗ
Large, well refurbished three-room pub with a strong community focus. It won the 1994 Hartlepool Civic Society *Conservation Award*.
⊛ ⍾ ♣ P ⊟

OLD WEST QUAY
Maritime Avenue
☎ (01429) 890115
11-11; 12-10.30 Sun
Boddingtons Bitter; Castle Eden Ale; guest beer ⓗ
New 'Brewer's Fayre' with a smart, split-level drinking area served by an L-shaped bar. It enjoys an impressive setting in the marina development of the old docks area. 'Fun Factory' for children with an adventure play area.
⌕ ⊛ ⌂ ◁ ▶ ⍾ ≱ P ⌿

TAP & SPILE
66 Church street
☎ (01429) 222400
12-3, 6-11; 12-3, 7-10.30 Sun
Camerons Strongarm; guest beers ⓗ
Fine restoration of a 19th-century ale house, featuring an internal balcony. Situated in one of the town's main drinking areas, it is close to award-winning museums and art gallery.
◁ ⍾ ≱ ♣ ○

HIGH CONISCLIFFE

DUKE OF WELLINGTON
On A67
☎ (01325) 374283
11-3, 6-11; 12-3, 7-10.30 Sun
Camerons Strongarm; Theakston Best Bitter; guest beer ⓗ
One-roomed village local in a pleasant setting near a scenic stretch of the River Tees. Good garden and children's play area; quoits played. The guest beer is from the Tapster's Choice range.
🚶 ⊛ ◁ ♣ P ⊟

HOLWICK

STRATHMORE ARMS
Off B6277
☎ (01833) 640362
12 (7 Mon)-11; 12-10.30 Sun
Ruddles Best Bitter; Theakston Best Bitter; guest beers (summer) H
17th-century stone-built inn near the Pennine Way. A cosy, unspoilt bar and an upstairs bar for functions (regular live music). Families welcome. A camping field lies to the rear, beneath the magnificent Holwick Scar. The pub has a smokehouse for curing its own food. No meals Mon eve.
🏭 Q ❀ ⇔ ◖ ▲ ♣ P

HURWORTH

EMERSON ARMS
32 Church View
☎ (01325) 720695
11-11; 12-10.30 Sun
Draught Bass; guest beer H
Neat village local named after Hurworth's most famous son, the 18th-century mathematician, William Emerson. Two lounges, the front one is favoured by more mature regulars, the other attracts the young set and diners. Fine pastoral views from the attractive riverside patio.
❀ ◖ ▶ ⊟ ♣ P

HURWORTH PLACE

STATION
8 Hurworth Road
☎ (01325) 720552
11-3, 5.30-11; 11-11 Sat; 12-10.30 Sun
John Smith's Bitter, Magnet H
Charmingly idiosyncratic local with a warm welcome. The main room is the final resting place of a number of horned animals - a huge moose-head bears a sailor's hat; also much other ephemera. Small pool room to the rear. Q ♣ P

KIRK MERRINGTON

HALF MOON INN
Crowther Place (B6282, 1 mile W of Ferryhill)
☎ (01388) 811598
11-11; 12-10.30 Sun
Beer range varies
Busy village local with two real fires stocking an ever-expanding range of guest beers. Can get busy at weekends. 🏭 ◖ ▶ ♿ P ☖

LEAMSIDE

THREE HORSE SHOES
Pittington Lane (off A690)
☎ (0191) 584 2394
12-3 (not Mon-Wed), 7 (5 summer)-11; 12-3, 7-10.30 Sun
Theakston Best Bitter; guest beers H

Friendly country inn where visitors are made welcome: a large bar with a lounge and a family room. Occasional music nights are staged by locals. Snacks available lunchtime.
🏭 Q ⇔ ❀ ▶ ▲ ♣ P

LOW SPENNYMOOR

FROG & FERRET
Coulson Street (½ mile from A167) ☎ (01388) 81312
11-11; 11-4.30, 7-11 Sat; 12-3, 7-10.30 Sun
Boddingtons Bitter; Camerons Strongarm; Courage Directors; Theakston XB; guest beers H
Small, former Durham CAMRA *Pub of the Year* deserving of its reputation for beer choice; often sells a guest beer from the Durham brewery. Not suitable for families. Q

MIDDLESTONE VILLAGE

SHIP INN
Low Row
☎ (01388) 810904
12-3, 5-11; 12-11 Fri & Sat; 12-10.30 Sun
Vaux Samson; Ward's Best Bitter; guest beers H
The Ship, which was closed by Vaux and then re-opened after a vigorous campaign by local CAMRA members, offers a warm welcome to all. Restaurant and bar meals complement the ever-changing range of guest ales.
▶ ▲ ♣ P

NO PLACE

BEAMISH MARY INN
Front Street (600 yds from A693)
☎ (0191) 370 0237
12-3, 6-11; 12-11 Fri & Sat; 12-10.30 Sun
Black Sheep Best Bitter; Courage Directors; guest beer H
Close to Beamish Museum and popular with locals and visitors. Good atmosphere; live music three times a week, plus a beer festival in Jan. CAMRA National *Pub of the Year* in 1995. Well worth a visit. The house beer comes from Big Lamp.
🏭 Q ⇔ ❀ ◖ ▶ ♿ ♣ P

NORTH BITCHBURN

FAMOUS RED LION
North Bitchburn Terrace
☎ (01388) 763561
12-3, 7-11; 12-3, 7-10.30 Sun
Greene King Abbot; Marston's Pedigree; Tetley Bitter; guest beers H
Friendly, traditional village pub with a welcome as warm as its open fires. Very popular for its excellent meals and wide range of guest beers, a regular guest is

Mane Brew, brewed for the pub by Hambleton. CAMRA regional *Pub of the Year* 1995.
🏭 ❀ ◖ ♣ ⇔ P ☖

NORTON

UNICORN
High Street ☎ (01642) 643364
11.30-3, 5.30-11; 11.30-11 Fri; 11-11 Sat; 12-3, 7-10.30 Sun
John Smith's Magnet H
Friendly, old, street-corner village local with a basic but welcoming bar and several characterful side rooms in which families are welcome. Known locally as 'Nellie's'.
Q ⇔ ◖ ⊟ ♣

PITTINGTON

VILLAGE TAVERN
Hallgarth Manor Hotel
☎ (0191) 372 1188
11-11; 12-10.30 Sun
Tetley Bitter; Vaux Samson; guest beers H
Popular bar in the busy Hallgarth Manor Hotel, used by villagers and hotel guests. Stylish and comfortable decor, featuring a cast iron cooking range. The hotel menu is also available in the bar. Q ❀ ⇔ ◖ ▶ ♿ ♣ P

PITY ME

LAMBTON HOUNDS
62 Front street (off A167 roundabout)
☎ (0191) 386 4742
11-11; 12-10.30 Sun
Vaux Lorimer's Best Scotch, Ward's Best Bitter; guest beer H
250-year-old coaching inn on the Great North Road. A basic bar, a lounge (children welcome), a comfortable snug with bell service and a restaurant. Minor alterations have not affected the character of the pub. Quoits played in summer.
🏭 Q ⇔ ❀ ⇔ ◖ ▶ ⊟ ♣ P

PRESTON-LE-SKERNE

BLACKSMITH'S ARMS
Ricknall Lane
(1 mile E of A167, on Aycliffe-Gt Stainton Road)
☎ (01325) 314873
12-11 (12-3, 7-11 winter); 12-10.30 (12-3, 7-10.30 winter) Sun
Black Sheep Bitter; John Smith's Magnet; guest beer H
Locally known as the 'Hammers', this family-run free house offers home-cooked meals and supports local microbreweries through its choice of guest ales. The large garden features a children's play area and free-roaming farm birds, peacocks and guinea fowl. No food Sun eve.
Q ❀ ◖ ♣ ♣ P

CAMRA's fight to save Castle Eden

Durham is a county of contrasts; a rural heartland surrounded by industrial towns and the university city of Durham. The problems faced by the licensed trade are typical of many such counties in the UK. The decline of heavy industry has left only a handful of real ale pubs in many Durham towns. In the country the widespread nature of the pubs makes access difficult.

There are now, however, a number of breweries in the county (Old Barn and the prize-winning ales of Durham Brewery and Butterknowle) which are able to supply the pubs with fine cask beer.

The main question concerning CAMRA in Durham for the last decade however has been: when will Whitbread decide to close Castle Eden Brewery?

Formerly brewers of Nimmos beers, this brewery is housed in a listed building in a rural setting in the constituency of Prime Minister Tony Blair.

The axe is now threatening to fall on Castle Eden in October 1998. Whitbread announced in April that they were looking for a buyer in the next six months or Castle Eden would be closed and the brands brewed elsewhere.

The campaign to save the brewery has taken many forms. CAMRA has maintained a watching brief throughout the 1990s. A local Castle Eden Action Committee was set up in 1991 when Whitbread announced the brewery was 'safe for five years' and the brewery, which has great local affection, has been treated in many ways as if it were still independent. The 1998 announcement took nobody by surprise, but is perhaps an opportunity for Castle Eden to regain its independence. Conversely it might be the beginning of the end for this historic establishment.

Possibly by the time of publication of this *Guide* the matter will have been settled.

In the meantime CAMRA is pursuing an active Keep Castle Eden Brewing campaign. CAMRA has raised public awareness with a petition and pledge cards; CAMRA has mobilised support through a series of meetings with interested parties and has pursuing an active media campaign. The campaign will, of course, go on until the fate of Castle Eden is decided.

'We will be pleased to support CAMRA's campaign to keep this brewery open,' said John Burton, Mr Blair's agent.

As the *Good Beer Guide* went to press, the fate of Castle Eden was hanging in the balance. A consortium of local businessmen had made a bid for the site. If successful, brewing will continue there. Whitbread confirmed that it was pursuing the sale of the brewery as a going concern. Mandy Atkinson, who is spearheading CAMRA's campaign to save the brewery, said, 'Let's hope Whitbread honours that.'

ROMALDKIRK

KIRK INN
The Green
☎ (01833) 650260
12-2.30 (not Tue), 6-11; 12-3,
7-10.30 Sun

Boddingtons Bitter; Castle Eden Ale; guest beers Ⓗ
Charming single-room pub situated on the village green, with a welcoming atmosphere. It doubles as a part-time post office. Excellent meals are produced by the chef/landlord. The guest beers are generally from Black Sheep, Hambleton, High Force or Rudgate breweries.
🏾 Q ✿ ◖ ▶ P

ROOKHOPE

ROOKHOPE INN
☎ (01388) 517215
12-3 (not winter), 7-11; 12-3,
7-10.30 Sun

Butterknowle Bitter; Hexamshire Devil's Water; Four Rivers Gladiator; guest beers Ⓗ
Pleasant country village pub on the Coast to Coast cycleway in Weardale. Hikers and locals are welcomed. Paved area for outside drinking. Good food available and basic B & B. the beer range expands in summer.
🏾 ✿ 🛏 ◖ ▶ ♣ P

SEATON CAREW

SEATON HOTEL
Church Street
☎ (01429) 266212
11-11; 12-10.30 Sun

Boddingtons Bitter; Castle Eden Ale; guest beers Ⓗ
Splendid seafront pub dating from 1792, reputedly haunted. The lounge is decorated with photographs of old Seaton. It draws a mixture of locals and tourists.
◖ ▶ ♣ ⌂ 🍺

SEDGEFIELD

DUN COW
43 Front St ☎ (01740) 620894
11-3, 6-11; 12-3, 7-10.30 Sun
Theakston Best Bitter, XB; guest beers Ⓗ
Well-established, country-style pub in the village centre. It can be a little over-popular for meals but this only shows how good its reputation is. Ever-changing list of guest beers, mostly from small brewers.
Q 🛏 ◖ ▶ P 🍺

SHADFORTH

PLOUGH INN
South Side (B1283 at Sherburn Hill) ☎ (0191) 372 0375
12-5, 6.30-11; 12-4, 7-10.30 Sun
Draught Bass; guest beers Ⓗ

18th-century village inn and coaching house, renovated to keep separate bar and lounge areas. The two guest ales change weekly. Durham CAMRA *Pub of the Year* 1996.
🏾 Q ✿ ◖ ▶ ♣ P

SHINCLIFFE

ROSE TREE
On A177 by river
☎ (0191) 386 8512
11-3, 7-11; 11-11 Sat; 12-4,
7-10.30 Sun

Vaux Lorimer's Best Scotch, Samson, Waggledance Ⓗ
Friendly pub, supported by village locals, students and tourists, it has recently extended the beer range. Outdoor drinking area with playground for young children. Good food.
Q ➤ ✿ ◖ ▶ ⊞ ♿ ♣ P

SEVEN STARS
On A177, between river and High Shincliffe
☎ (0191) 384 8454
12-2.30, 6.30-midnight; 12-3,
7-10.30 Sun

Vaux Samson, Waggledance; Ward's Best Bitter Ⓗ
Comfortable, small hotel catering to village regulars, hotel diners and residents. A warm welcome and usually a quiet atmosphere.
Q ✿ 🛏 ◖ ▶ ♿ ♣ P

Try also: The Avenue (Vaux)

SPENNYMOOR

ASH TREE
Carr lane, Greenways Estate (½ mile from centre)
☎ (01388) 814490
12-2 (not Mon, Thu or Fri), 6-11;
11-11 Sat; 12-10.30 Sun
Vaux Samson, Double Maxim; guest beers Ⓗ
Hub of the local community, the pub has sold cask beer since it opened in 1980. Tries to cater for all tastes, whilst eager, friendly bar staff help create a good atmosphere.
✿ ♣ P 🍺

PENNY GILL
Cheapside (town centre precinct)
☎ (01388) 812420
11.30-4; 11.30-11 Fri & Sat; 12-3,
7-10.30 Sun
Vaux Samson; guest beers Ⓗ
Large, friendly free house with an ever-changing selection of guest beers. A welcome retreat in the town centre beer desert. Live music Sat in the lounge bar. Has had many names before reverting to the original.
◖ ⊞ ♣

Try also: Hillingdon, Clyde Terrace (Bass)

STANLEY

BLUE BOAR
Front Street (near Civic Centre)
☎ (01207) 231167
11-3, 7-11; 11-11 Thu-Sat; 12-10.30 Sun
Draught Bass; Stones Bitter; guest beers Ⓗ
Restored coaching inn, a busy, open-plan pub with a friendly atmosphere, well used by locals. Popular with diners lunchtime and eves.
🏾 ◖ ▶ ♿

STOCKTON-ON-TEES

CLARENDON
72 Dovecoat Street
☎ (01642) 873303
11-11; 12-10.30 Sun
Camerons Strongarm Ⓗ
Classic, two-roomed, back-street boozer with a basic public bar and a comfortable lounge. Usually bustling and full of life.
⊞ ⇌ ♣ P

FITZGERALD'S
9-10 High Street
☎ (01642) 678220
11.30-3 (3.30 Fri, 4 Sat), 6.30-11;
7-10.30 (closed lunch) Sun
Draught Bass; Taylor Landlord; Younger IPA, No. 3 or **Theakston Old Peculier; guest beers** Ⓗ
The imposing stone facade looks much too grand for a pub. Open-plan, split-level interior with typical Fitzgerald's touches. Holds regular beer festivals.
◖ ⇌ ♣

SENATORS
Bishopton Road West, Fairfield (by Whitehouse Farm shopping centre)
☎ (01642) 672060
11-3, 7-11; 11-11 Sat; 12-4,
7-10.30 Sun
Vaux Double Maxim, seasonal beers; Ward's Thorne BB; guest beer Ⓗ
Smart, modern pub with split-level drinking and eating areas around a single bar. Packed on Tue eve for the free quiz. May open longer on demand. Booking advised for Sun lunch; no eve meals Tue or Sun.
✿ ◖ ▶ P

SUN INN
Knowles Street (off High St)
☎ (01642) 623921
11-4, 5.30-11; 11-11 Wed, Fri & Sat; 12-10.30 Sun
Draught Bass Ⓗ
Classic town-centre pub with an unswerving commitment to real ale; it boasts the UK's largest sales of Draught Bass which comes as no surprise to those who've sampled it. Folk club on Mon.
⊞ ⇌

TRADERS
Blue Post Yard
☎ (01642) 675718
11-11; 12-10.30 Sun
Wadworth 6X; guest beers Ⓗ
Old hotel in a yard off Stockton High Street, much modernised and altered. The lively clientele like TV sport but there's good commitment to real ale.
🏵 & ≈ (Thornaby)

SUMMERHOUSE

RABY HUNT
On B6279
☎ (01325) 374604
11.30-3, 6.30-11; 12-3, 7-10.30 Sun
John Smith's Magnet; Theakston Black Bull; guest beer Ⓗ
Neat, welcoming old stone free house in a pretty whitewashed hamlet. A homely lounge and a locals' bar. Good home-cooked lunches (Mon-Sat).
🏚 Q 🍺 🏵 ① ⊞ & ♣ P

WITTON GILBERT

GLENDINNING ARMS
Front Street
☎ (0191) 371 0316
12-4, 7-11; 12-4, 7-11 Sun;
Vaux Samson; guest beer Ⓗ
Locals and visitors enjoy the friendly atmosphere of this traditional village pub. Two rooms: a basic bar featuring racing memorabilia and a comfortable lounge.
🏚 Q 🏵 ⊞ ♣ P

INDEPENDENT BREWERIES

Butterknowle:
Bishop Auckland
Camerons:
Hartlepool
Darwin:
Crook
Durham:
Bowburn
Grey Horse:
Consett
High Force:
Barnard Castle
Middleston's:
Bishop Auckland

TRAVELLERS REST
Front Street
☎ (0191) 371 0458
11-3, 6-11; 12-3, 7-10.30 Sun
Courage Directors; Theakston Best Bitter, XB; guest beers Ⓗ
Popular village pub, particularly busy with diners lunch and eves. Boules is a popular summer activity in the outdoor recreation area. 🏚 Q 🍺 🏵 ① ▮ & ♣ P

WOLSINGHAM

BAY HORSE
Main Street (B6296)
☎ (01388) 527220
11-11; 12-10.30 Sun
Ruddles County; Tetley Bitter Ⓗ
19th-century pub with later extensions in an attractive rural setting. The bar has two linked rooms; the restaurant is open all day (children welcome).
🏵 🛏 ① ▮ ⊞ 🅰 ♣ P

WOLSINGHAM

MILL RACE
Front Street ☎ (01388) 526551
11-11; 12-10.30 Sun
Courage Directors; McEwan 80/-; Theakston XB; guest beers Ⓗ
Warm, friendly, family pub where food is served all day.
🏚 Q 🍺 🏵 🛏 ① ▮ & ♣ P

WOLVISTON

SHIP
50 High Street
☎ (01740) 644420
12-3, 6-11; 12-3, 7-10.30 Sun
Black Sheep Best Bitter; guest beer Ⓗ
Smartly refurbished village inn with a strong emphasis on food. Built in the 1890s, on the site of an earlier pub, it still has the original stables at the rear.
🏵 ① ▮ ♣ P ⌿ 🖵

Great books on beer!

AINGERS GREEN

ROYAL FUSILIERS
Aingers Green Road (1 mile S of
Gt Bentley Green) OS119204
☎ (01206) 250001
11-2.30 (3.30 Sat), 5.30-11; 12-4,
7-10.30 Sun
Beer range varies Ⓗ
Friendly free house featuring
beams and brick in both bars.
Pool and darts are away from the
bar area. Cider in summer.
🏚 Q 🕸 ♣ ➪ P

ALTHORNE

HUNTSMAN & HOUNDS
Green Lane (near B1018)
OS906004 ☎ (01621) 740387
12-3, 5-11; 12-11 Sat; 12-3,
7-10.30 Sun
**Greene King IPA, Abbot; guest
beer** Ⓗ
Picturesque country pub dating
back to the 16th century with a
wealth of oak beams. Large field
at the side for campers and caravans (with showers).
🏚 🕸 ◑ ▶ Å ♣ ➪ P

ARKESDEN

AXE & COMPASSES
OS483344
☎ (01799) 550272
12-2.30, 6-11; 12-2.30, 7-10.30 Sun
Greene King IPA, Abbot Ⓗ
Partly thatched, 17th-century village local with award-winning
food and a very friendly atmosphere in a beautiful location; a
restaurant, lounge and a
public bar. 🏚 Q 🕸 ◑ ▶
🍺 ♣ P

BANNISTER GREEN

THREE HORSE SHOES
Between Gt Leighs and Felstead,
near B1417
☎ (01371) 820467
12-2.30, 6-11; 12-3, 7-11 Sat;
12-3, 7-10.30 Sun
Ridleys IPA, ESX, Rumpus Ⓗ
Cosy, beamed 15th-century pub
on the village green. Its two bars
have low-beamed ceilings and a
welcoming atmosphere.
Reputedly haunted.
🏚 Q 🕸 ◑ ▶ 🍺 Å ♣ P

BASILDON

MOON ON THE SQUARE
1-15 Market Square (near A176)
☎ (01268) 520360
11-11; 12-10.30 Sun
**Courage Directors; Theakston
Best Bitter; guest beers** Ⓗ
Attractive Wetherspoons pub
converted from a former bakery,
popular with all ages, very busy
eves and weekends.
Q ◑ ▶ 🕭 ⇌ ⚥ 🛏

BELCHAMP OTTEN

RED LION
Fowes Lane (6 miles W of
Sudbury)
OS798415
☎ (01787) 277537
12-3 (not winter weekdays),
7-11; 12-3, 7-10.30 Sun
Greene King IPA; guest beer Ⓗ
Friendly village local, which is
also popular with walkers and
hikers. No music or machines.
Weekend lunches; no meals
Mon eve.
🏚 Q 🕸 ◑ Å ♣ P ⚥

Essex

```
...ford
...anningtree        A120        Harwich
        Little                  Little Oakley
        Bentley      A133
        Aingers Green  Tendring
                        Little
...ightlingsea        Clacton   Walton-on-
        Great                   the-Naze
        Clacton
```

0 Miles   10
0 Kilometres   16

whiskies, quality bar food and an extensive restaurant. No gimmicks. 🏚 Q ❀ ◖ ▶ 🏚 ♣

BOCKING

ANGEL
36 Bocking End (B1053)
☎ (01376) 321549
11-3, 5.30-11; 12-10.30 Sun
Beer range varies Ⓗ
Lively, 15th-century pub in a conservation area, the friendly landlord runs a beer club, hence the range of beers on offer. Sport oriented; live football matches shown. ❀ ◖ P

RETREAT
42 Church Street (near B1053)
☎ (01376) 347947
12-3, 7-11; 12-3, 7-10.30 Sun
Ridleys IPA; Ⓗ **guest beers** ⒽⒼ
Originally three cottages, converted in 1910, giving two bars on different levels. Families welcome. ❀ 🛏 ◖ ▶ & ♣ P ⌿

BRAINTREE

KING WILLIAM IV
114 London Road (by B1053/A120 jct)
☎ (01376) 330088
11-3, 6-11; 12-11 Sat; 12-3, 7-10.30 Sun
Ridleys IPA Ⓖ
Cosy, friendly two-bar local where darts and quizzes are popular. Award-winning flower displays in summer. 🏚 ❀ 🏚 ♣ P

BRENTWOOD

SWAN (HOGSHEAD)
123 High Street (A1023)
☎ (01277) 211848
11-11; 12-10.30 Sun
Boddingtons Bitter; Flowers IPA; Fuller's London Pride; Mighty Oak Burntwood; Greene King Abbot; Whitbread Abroad Cooper; Ⓗ **guest beers** ⒽⒼ
1930s-style pub which dates back to the 15th century, with extensive wood panelling and a recent garden bar extension. Up to 12 cask beers (including four on gravity). A good atmosphere is encouraged by staff and friendly management. Car park open eves. 🏚 Q ❀ ◖ ⇌ P

BRICK END (BROXTED)

PRINCE OF WALES
Midway between Broxted and Molehill Green, 1 mile off B1051
OS573259 ☎ (01279) 850256
12-3, 6-11; 12-3, 7-10.30 Sun
Friary Meux Best Bitter; guest beers Ⓗ
Comfortable, extended pub in the small hamlet of Brick End, near Stansted Airport. Popular with families; the family conservatory

is the no-smoking area. Good quality food. 🏚 ❀ ◖ ▶ P ⌿

BRIGHTLINGSEA

RAILWAY TAVERN
58 Station Road (near B1029)
☎ (01206) 302581
5 (3 Fri, 12 Sat)-11; 12-3, 7-10.30 Sun
beer range varies Ⓗ
This was the local CAMRA *Pub of the Year* 1997 and maintains that excellent quality. It retains two bars and is convenient for walks along the promenade. A good locals' boozer offering five beers, always with a mild or dark ale. Cider festival in May.
🏚 Q 🏚 ❀ 🏚 & ▲ ♣ ⌂

BROADS GREEN

WALNUT TREE
1 mile W of B1008 OS694125
☎ (01245) 360222
11.30-2.30, 6.15-11; 12-2.30, 7-10.30 Sun
Ridleys IPA Ⓖ
Traditional Essex village pub facing an attractive green: an unspoilt public bar and snug, with a more recently added saloon bar. A warm welcome awaits.
🏚 Q ❀ ◖ ▶ 🏚 ♣ P

BURNHAM-ON-CROUCH

ANCHOR HOTEL
The Quay (near B1010)
☎ (01621) 782117
11-11; 12-10.30 Sun
Adnams Bitter; Greene King IPA; Crouch Vale Millennium Gold Ⓗ
16th-century riverside inn on the tidal reaches of the River Crouch. Ferry boat trips to a local seal colony start here. Cider in summer. ❀ 🛏 ◖ ▶ ⌂ P

SHIP INN
52 High Street (B1010)
☎ (01621) 785057
11-3, 7-11; 12-3, 7-10.30 Sun
Adnams Bitter, Broadside, seasonal beers Ⓗ
Cheerfully refurbished town-centre local: three bar areas each with its own nautical theme: excellent food and friendly service. Children welcome if eating. The furthest Adnams tied house from the brewery. Wheelchair WC. 🏚 ❀ 🛏 ◖ ▶ & P

BURTON END (STANSTED)

ASH
Take airport road from M11 jct 8, then signed
OS532237 ☎ (01279) 814841
11-11; 12-10.30 Sun
Greene King IPA; Abbot, seasonal beers Ⓗ
15th-century thatched pub in a

BILLERICAY

COACH & HORSES
36 Chapel Street (near B1007)
☎ (01277) 622873
10-11; 12-3.30, 7-10.30 Sun
Greene King IPA, Abbot; Shepherd Neame Master Brew Bitter; guest beers Ⓗ
Friendly, comfortable one-bar pub off the High Street, appealing to all ages with a common interest in good beer and conversation. The collection of jugs and elephants are impressive. No food Sun.
🏚 ❀ ◖ ⇌ ♣ P

BIRDBROOK

PLOUGH
The Street (1 mile off B1054 in village) OS706411
☎ (01440) 785336
12-3, 6-11; 12-3, 7-10.30 Sun
Adnams Bitter; Greene King IPA; guest beer Ⓗ
16th-century, thatched traditional village pub offering a friendly welcome, a large range of malt

109

tiny hamlet near Stansted Airport, with a rural atmosphere. It has been extended to provide a lounge bar/dining room, but the public bar retains character.
🚶 ❀ ◖ ▶ P

CASTLE HEDINGHAM

RISING SUN
71 Nunnery Street (300 yds off A1017)
☎ (01787) 460355
11-2.30, 7-11; 12-3, 7-10.30 Sun
Greene King IPA, Abbot Ⓗ
Friendly two-bar local with a cosy public bar and beams throughout. A secluded garden and play area at rear gives views of the historic village home of the Earls of Oxford. ❀ ◖ ▶ 🍽 ▲ ♣ P

CHELMSFORD

ENDEAVOUR
351 Springfield Road (B1137)
☎ (01245) 257717
11-11; 12-2.30, 7-10.30 Sun
Greene King XX Mild, IPA, Abbot; Shepherd Neame Spitfire; guest beers Ⓗ
Friendly, quiet, three-roomed Gray's pub serving good home-cooked food (not served Sun). The GK Mild, rare for the area, is always on top form. Note the unusual pub sign. A mobile phone-free zone, unless you wish to donate to the charity box.
🚶 Q ◖ ▶ ♣

ORIGINAL PLOUGH
28 Duke Street (near A138)
☎ (01245) 250145
11-11; 12-10.30 Sun
Greene King IPA; Tetley Bitter; guest beers Ⓗ
Festival Ale House offering a choice of six guest ales, popular with students and commuters. It hosts occasional live music and beer festivals.
❀ ◖ ≈ ♣ P

PARTNERS
30 Lower Anchor Street (150 yds from B1007) ☎ (01245) 265181
11-3, 5.30-11; 11-11 Sat; 12-10.30 Sun
Crouch Vale Best Bitter; Greene King IPA; guest beers Ⓗ
Friendly, one-bar local with a large family/pool room, offering an ever-changing range of guest beers (at least three). No food Sun. Close to the county cricket ground.
🐾 ❀ ♣ P

WHITE HORSE
25 Townfield Street (near A138)
☎ (01245) 269556
11-3, 5.30 (7 Sat)-11; 12-10.30 Sun
Otter Bitter; Wards Thorne BB; guest beers Ⓗ
This one-bar back-street local is

deservedly renowned for its range and quality with up to ten beers on offer, usually including a mild. Bar billiards and big screen TV for sports.
◖ ≈ ♣

COLCHESTER

BRICKLAYERS ARMS
27 Bergholt Road (B1508/A134 jct) ☎ (01206) 852008
11-3, 5.30-11; 11-11 Sat; 12-3, 7-10.30 Sun
Adnams Bitter, Broadside, seasonal beers; guest beers Ⓗ
Pub with a refurbished split-level saloon bar and a public bar run by a CAMRA award-winning landlord. Good value Sunday lunch; eve meals Wed-Sat.
❀ ◖ ▶ 🍽 ≈ (North) ♣ P

BRITISH GRENADIER
67 Military Road
☎ (01206) 791647
11-2.30 (3 Fri & Sat), 7-11; 12-3, 7-10.30 Sun
Adnams Bitter Ⓗ, **seasonal beers** ⒽⒼ
The highest pub in town, a two-bar friendly local with strong dart teams; pool also played.
🍽 ≈ (Town) ♣

DRAGOON
82 Butt Road (B1026)
☎ (01206) 573464
11-2.30, 5.30-11; 12-3, 7-10.30 Sun
Adnams Bitter, Broadside; guest beers Ⓗ
Pleasant local with an L-shaped bar near the barracks and the football ground. Try the chilli.
❀ ◖ ≈ (Town) ♣

KINGS ARMS (HOGSHEAD)
61-63 Crouch Street (near A134)
☎ (01206) 572886
11-11; 12-10.30 Sun
Boddingtons Bitter; Whitbread Abroad Cooper Ⓗ; **guest beers** ⒽⒼ
Very well refurbished, open-plan pub with a central bar, stocking a good range of guest beers. The menu includes Thai dishes; eve meals 5.30-7. Beer fests every bank holiday. Quiz night Sun eves.
🚶 ❀ ◖ ▶ ≈ (Town) ⌂ P

LEATHER BOTTLE
Shrub End Road (B1022)
☎ (01206) 766018
11-2.30 (3 Fri), 5.30-11; 11-11 Sat; 12-10.30 Sun
Adnams Bitter; Tetley Bitter; guest beers Ⓗ
Attractive pub with a large fire in the middle of the lounge bar; popular with locals. The garden has a children's play area. No-smoking dining area available.
❀ ◖ ▶ 🍽 ♣ P

ODD ONE OUT
28 Mersea Road (B1025)
☎ (01206) 578140
4 (11 Fri & Sat)-11; 12-10.30 Sun
Archers Best Bitter; Ridleys IPA; guest beers Ⓗ
The first free house and arguably still the best in town: five real ales are always changing, plus two real ciders. A friendly atmosphere in this all-round excellent boozer with low, low prices.
🚶 Q ❀ ❀ (Town) ♣ ⌂ 🚭

ROSE & CROWN HOTEL
51 East Street (on A137 by level crossing) ☎ (01206) 866677
11-2.30, 6.30-11; 11-11 Sat; 12-3.30, 7.30-10.30 Sun
Adnams Broadside; Tetley Bitter Ⓗ
Tasteful 17th-century hotel bar; lots of heavy beams and ironwork and a central fireplace. Renowned for good food and accommodation. Claims to be the oldest inn in the oldest recorded town in England. The house beer is from Tolly Cobbold 🚶 Q 🛏 ◖ ▶ P

STOCKWELL ARMS
18 West Stockwell Street (near A1124) ☎ (01206) 575560
10.30-11; 10.30-4, 6.30-11 Sat; 12-4, 7-10.30 Sun
Courage Best Bitter, Directors; Greene King IPA; Marston's Pedigree; Nethergate Bitter; Theakston Best Bitter; Wells Bombardier Ⓗ
600-year-old historic Dutch Quarter local with a village pub feel. A *Colchester in Bloom* floral award-winner. The landlord is a dedicated charity fundraiser, a *Man of the Year* winner. Book for Sun roast. ❀ ◖ ≈ (North) ♣

COXTIE GREEN

WHITE HORSE
173 Coxtie Green Road
☎ (01277) 372410
11-3, 5.30-11; 12-4, 7-11 Sat; 12-3, 7-10.30 Sun
Fuller's London Pride; Woodforde's Wherry; guest beers Ⓗ
Small cosy, welcoming country pub usually stocking six beers. The large garden has some children's play equipment. Annual beer festival (July). No food Sun.
Q ❀ ◖ ▶ 🍽 ♣ P

DEBDEN

PLOUGH
High Street OS558333
☎ (01799) 541899
12-3, 6-11; 12-3, 7-10.30 Sun
Greene King IPA, Abbot; guest beers Ⓗ
Friendly local meeting place, whose landlord is a real ale enthusiast. No food Mon.
🚶 ❀ ◖ ♣ P 🚭

EARLS COLNE

BIRD IN HAND
Coggeshall Road (B1024)
☎ (01787) 222557
12-2, 6-11; 12-2, 7-10.30 Sun
Ridleys IPA; H guest beer H G
Good, traditional country pub
with two bars and an off-sales
hatch, popular with retired air-
men as this pub was almost on
the runway (they had to lower
the roof in WWII). The guest
beer is from Ridleys.
🏰 Q 🏡 ◖ ▶ Å ♣ P

EAST HANNINGFIELD

WINDMILL TAVERN
The Tye OS771012
☎ (01245) 400315
11-11; 12-10.30 Sun
**Boddingtons Bitter; Crouch Vale
Best Bitter; Marston's Pedigree;
guest beers H**
Popular free house opposite the
village green; roomy and welcoming, with an excellent restaurant (open Thu-Sat eves and Sun
lunch).
🏰 🏡 ◖ ▶ ♣ P

EASTHORPE

HOUSE WITHOUT A NAME
Easthorpe Road (1½ miles off
A12)
☎ (01206) 213070
11-3, 6-11; 11-11 Sat; 12-10.30
Sun
Greene King IPA; guest beers H
Attractive, 16th-century, split-
level country pub featuring a
large double-sided fire at its centre, plus a restaurant (food
served all day Sat and Sun).
🏰 🏡 ◖ ▶ ♣ P

ELSENHAM

CROWN
High Street (B1051)
☎ (01279) 812827
11-2.30, 6-11; 12-3, 7-10.30 Sun
**Shepherd Neame Best Bitter;
guest beers H**
Deservedly popular, friendly, village pub with a pargetted
exterior, a wealth of beams, an
inglenook and a reputation for
good food. Roast lunch only Sun,
no eve meal.
🏰 ◖ ▶ 🍺 ♣ P

EPPING

FOREST GATE
111 Bell Common (off B1393, Ivy
Chimneys Road OS451011
☎ (01992) 572312
10-3, 5.30-11; 12-3, 7-10.30 Sun
**Adnams Bitter, H Broadside; G
Ridleys IPA, H ESX; guest
beers G**
On the edge of Epping Forest, a
single-bar, traditional, 17th-cen-
tury pub which has been run by

the same family for many years.
The guest beers come from local
independent brewers. A
renowned turkey broth is sold
lunchtime.
🏰 Q 🏡 ◖ ♣ ⌒ P

FEERING

SUN INN
3 Feering Hill (B1024)
☎ (01376) 570442
11-3, 6-11; 12-3, 6-10.30 Sun
**Courage Directors; guest
beers H**
Heavily-beamed with real log
fires, this quiet, friendly local
offers good value, home-made
food. It hosts beer festivals (Aug
and May bank hols.)
🏰 Q 🏡 ◖ ▶ ⇌ (Kelvedon) ⌒

FINCHINGFIELD

RED LION
6 Church Hill (B1053)
☎ (01371) 810400
11.30-3, 5.30-11; 11.30-11 Fri &
Sat; 12-10.30 Sun
Ridleys IPA, Rumpus H
Friendly pub in one of the most
picturesque villages in Essex,
attracting both locals and visitors. Food is available in the bar
and the congenial restaurant. A
third Ridleys beer is usually
stocked.
🏰 🏡 🍺 ◖ ♣ P

FORD STREET

COOPERS ARMS
On A1124, 3 miles W of
Colchester
☎ (01206) 241177
12-3, 5-11; 12-3, 7-10.30 Sun
**Greene King IPA; Woodforde's
Wherry; guest beers H**
A Tardis of a pub - the small
frontage conceals a long pub,
half serving as a restaurant (a
good vegetarian selection). Cosy
bar with leather sofas to relax in;
a nice friendly pub in an attractive village.
Q 🏡 ◖ ♣ P

FYFIELD

QUEEN'S HEAD
Queen Street (off B184)
☎ (01277) 899231
11-3, 6-11; 11-11 Sat; 12-3,
7-10.30 Sun
**Adnams Bitter; Mansfield Bitter;
Smiles Best Bitter; guest
beers H**
Genuine free house; a focal
point in the village, popular with
all ages. The long bar has spacious alcoves. Guest beers are
always from small independents.
The garden looks out on to the
River Roding. Kitchen facilities
recently upgraded (no meals Sat
eve).
🏰 🏡 ◖ ▶ ♣ P

GRAYS

GRAYS ATHLETIC FC
Bridge Road
☎ (01375) 377753
5 (3 Thu, 12 Fri & Sat)-11; 12-3,
7-11 Sun
Beer range varies H
Social club of Grays Athletic
Football Club with admission for
card-carrying CAMRA members
on production of this *Guide*. The
bar overlooks an indoor five-a-
side pitch. Snacks available.
Limited parking. ⇌ ♣ P

THEOBALD ARMS
141 Argent Street
☎ (01375) 372253
10.30-3 (4 Sat), 5.30-11; 11-11
Fri; 12-10.30 Sun
**Courage Best Bitter; guest
beers H**
Traditional, family-run, two-bar
pub in an area currently undergoing regeneration. Try the unusual
revolving pool table in the public
bar. Good value food.
🏡 ◖ 🍺 ♿ ⇌ ♣ P

GREAT CHESTERFORD

CROWN & THISTLE
High Street (near B1383)
☎ (01799) 530278
12-3 (4 Sat), 6-11; 12-4, 7-10.30
Sun
Greene King IPA; Tetley Bitter H
Very old village pub with a wel-
coming atmosphere and an
inglenook. No food Sun or
Mon eve.
🏰 Q 🏡 🍺 ◖ ▶ 🍺 Å ⇌ ♣ P

GREAT CLACTON

PLOUGH
1 North Road (near B1032)
☎ (01255) 429998
11-11; 12-6, 7-10.30 Sun
**Flowers Original; Greene King
IPA; Tetley Bitter H**
One large bar caters for pub
bands and the local youth at
weekends; a smaller lounge bar
provides a quiet area for gossip
and meetings; a gem.
🏰 🏡 ◖ ▶ 🍺 Å ♣

GREAT SALING

WHITE HART
The Street (2 miles N of A120)
OS701254
☎ (01371) 850341
12-3.30, 5.30-11; 12-11 Sat;
12-10.30 Sun
Ridleys IPA, Rumpus H
Superb, 16th-century, beamed
Tudor pub, with a raised timbered gallery. A speciality is the
Essex Huffer - a large roll with a
choice of fillings (which the pub
claims to have invented). The
restaurant is in a restored bake-
house at the rear.
🏰 Q 🏡 🍺 ◖ ▶ 🍺 P

GREAT TEY

CHEQUERS
The Street (1½ miles N of A120)
☎ (01206) 210814
11-3, 6.30-11; 12-4, 7-10.30 Sun
Greene King XX Mild, IPA, Abbot; guest beers Ⓗ
16th-century pub with a low beamed ceiling and a no-smoking restaurant, one end of the lounge bar. Note the tiled floor in the public bar. A pleasant garden affords a view of the village church. No food Mon eve.
🏚 🌸 ◖ ▶ 🚪 ♣ P ⅙

GREAT WAKERING

ANCHOR
23 High Street (B1017)
☎ (01702) 219265
11-11; 12-10.30 Sun
Fuller's London Pride; Ridleys IPA; guest beers Ⓗ
Friendly, family-run pub with two bars, very popular with all ages, offering regular guest beers and good value food (not served Mon). Note the collection of walking sticks above the bar.
🏚 Q 🌸 🛏 ◖ ▶ 🚪 ♣ ⌂ P

GREAT YELDHAM

WAGGON & HORSES
High Street (A1017)
☎ (01787) 237936
11-11; 12-10.30 Sun
Greene King IPA, Abbot; guest beers Ⓗ
Village pub with strong local support and a friendly welcome. It boasts a wider, more interesting range of food than most pubs, but at lower prices than many.
🌸 🛏 ◖ ▶ 🚪 ♣ P

HADSTOCK

KINGS HEAD
Linton Road (B1052)
☎ (01223) 893473
11.30-2.30, 6-11; 12-3, 7-10.30 Sun
Friary Meux BB; guest beers Ⓗ
Comfortable village pub with distinct drinking areas, close to Linton Zoo. Happy hour and meals on Fri eve; bar billiards played. Occasional cider.
🏚 Q 🌸 🛏 ♣ ⌂ P

HALSTEAD

DOG INN
37 Hedingham Road (A1124)
☎ (01787) 477774
12-2.30, 6-11; 12-3, 7-10.30 Sun
Adnams Bitter; Nethergate Bitter; guest beer Ⓗ
Friendly, 17th-century local, offering reasonably priced en-suite accommodation and bar meals. Close to the town centre.
🏚 Q 🛏 🌸 🛏 ◖ ▶ ☂ P

HARWICH

ALMA
25 Kings Head Street (off the Quay) ☎ (01255) 503474
11.30 (11 Sat)-3, 7-11; (11-11 Fri & Sat summer); 12-3, 7-10.30 (12-10.30 summer) Sun
Flowers Original; Greene King IPA, Abbot Ⓗ
Quiet pub, just off the quay, imbuing a strong nautical feel from the various artefacts around the single bar with its portholes. Good value food (eve meals Tue-Sat). 🏚 🌸 ◖ ▶ ⇌ ♣

HANOVER INN
65 Church Street
☎ (01255) 502927
10.30-2, 6-11; 12-3, 7-10.30 Sun
Ridleys IPA, Witchfinder; Tolly Cobbold Mild Ⓗ
One of Harwich's historic pubs: lively, vibrant house, catering for its community. Its darts, pool and crib teams all feature at the top of their leagues. An ideal base for exploring the Tendring Peninsula. 🏚 🛏 ⇌ ♣ ⌂

HATFIELD BROAD OAK

COCK INN
High St (B183) ☎ (01279) 718273
12-3, 6-11; 12-3, 7-11 (may vary) Sun
Fuller's London Pride; Greene King IPA; guest beers Ⓗ
Friendly village local with bare boards and walls decorated with old theatre programmes. Guest beers come from independent breweries. Private dining room available (no meals Sun eve). Former local CAMRA *Pub of the Year*. 🏚 Q 🌸 ◖ ▶ ♣ ⌂ P ⅙

HELIONS BUMPSTEAD

THREE HORSESHOES
Water Lane OS650414
☎ (01440) 730298
11.45-2.30, 7-11; 12-2.30, 7-10.30 Sun
Greene King IPA; guest beer Ⓗ
Fine, friendly, remote pub boasting superb award-winning gardens. No food Mon/Tue eve or Sun. 🏚 Q 🌸 ◖ ▶ 🚪 🅰 ♣ P

HERONGATE

GREEN MAN
11 Cricketers Lane (near A128)
☎ (01277) 810292
11-3, 6-11; 12-10.30 Sun
Adnams Bitter; Ind Coope Burton Ale; Marston's Pedigree; Tetley Bitter; guest beer Ⓗ
Pleasant main bar with several rooms set back; darts and shove ha'penny played. Guest beer comes from the 'Tapsters Choice' range. Occasional beer festivals held. Children's play area in the garden. 🏚 🛏 🌸 ◖ ▶ ♣ ⅙

OLD DOG INN

Billericay Road (1 mile E of A128) OS641910
☎ (01277) 810337
11 (12 Sat)-2.30, 6-11; 12-3.30, 7-10.30 Sun
Beer range varies Ⓗ Ⓖ
Friendly, low-beamed country pub, stocking beers from independent and microbreweries including Mauldons, Mighty Oak and Ridleys. 🐕 🌸 ◖ ▶ 🚪 ♣ P

HEYBRIDGE

MALTSTERS ARMS
Hall Road ☎ (01621) 853880
11.30-3.30, 6.15-11; 12-3, 7-10.30 Sun
Greene King IPA, Abbot Ⓖ
Good, down-to-earth, back-street local with a friendly welcome. The gravity dispense, together with a formica-topped counter and old till create a 1960s atmosphere. ♣

HORNDON-ON-THE-HILL

BELL INN
High Road (signed from Stanford le Hope jct of A13)
☎ (01375) 673154
10-2.30, 6-11; 11-3, 6-11 Sat; 12-3, 7-10.30 Sun
Draught Bass Ⓖ; **Fuller's London Pride; Greene King IPA; Mighty Oak Burntwood** Ⓗ; **Thwaites Daniels Hammer** Ⓖ; **guest beers** Ⓗ Ⓖ
Busy, 15th-century coaching inn in an attractive old village, now bypassed. Award-winning restaurant; bar food also served. Draught Bass is served cool.
🏚 Q 🌸 🛏 ◖ ▶ P

HOWE STREET

GREEN MAN
Dunmow Road (near A130)
☎ (01245) 360203
12-3, 5.30-11; 11.30-11 Sat; 12-10.30 Sun
Ridleys IPA, ESX Ⓗ
Two-bar, 14th-century roadside pub with a welcome log fire in the lounge bar. Good bar food with 'blackboard specials' and a restaurant.
🏚 🌸 ◖ ▶ 🚪 🅰 P

HUTTON

CHEQUERS
213 Rayleigh Road (A129)
☎ (01277) 224980
12 (11 Sat)-11; 12-10.30 Sun
Draught Bass; Fuller's London Pride; guest beer Ⓗ
Pub with a small, cosy beamed lounge bar and a public bar. The guest beer is usually from an independent brewery not normally available locally (including Mighty Oak). 🌸 ◖ 🚪 ♣ P

INGATESTONE

STAR
High Street (B1002)
☎ (01277) 353618
11-2.30, 5.45-11; 12-3, 6.45-10.30 Sun
Greene King IPA, Abbot G
Cosy, one-bar pub with a huge fire in winter. Regular live country or folk music.
🏚 Q 🐎 ❀ ≈ ♣ P

LANGLEY LOWER GREEN

BULL
OS436345
☎ (01279) 777307
12-2.30, 6-11; 12-3, 7-10.30 Sun
Adnams Bitter, Broadside; Greene King IPA H
Classic, Victorian rural pub in one of the smallest Essex villages with a local clientele. A pitch-penny game is concealed under a bench in the saloon bar.
🏚 Q ❀ 🍺 ♣ P

LAWFORD

MANNINGTREE STATION BUFFET
Station Road (near A137)
☎ (01206) 391114
10.30-11; 12-3 (closed eve) Sun
Adnams Bitter; Shepherd Neame Spitfire; guest beers H
Small, one-bar pub in a listed 19th-century station building, where friendly staff welcome locals and rail travellers alike. Two, often interesting, guest beers are normally on offer. Breakfast from 8 until lunchtime. Booking for restaurant advised eves and Sun lunch.
❀ ◖ ▮ ≈ (Manningtree)

LEIGH-ON-SEA

BROKER
213-217 Leigh Road
☎ (01702) 471932
11-3, 6-11; 12-3, 7-10.30 Sun
Shepherd Neame Spitfire; Tolly Cobbold Original; guest beers H
Friendly, family-run, free house serving a varied range of beers and bar or restaurant meals (not served Sun eve). Children welcome until 7.30 in a sectioned-off, no-smoking area of the bar.
🐎 ❀ 🍺 ◖ ▮ ≈ (Chalkwell)

CROOKED BILLET
51 High Street (Old Town)
☎ (01702) 714854
12-11; 12-10.30 Sun
Adnams Bitter; Friary Meux BB; Ind Coope Burton Ale; guest beers H
Excellent, unspoilt, listed 16th-century pub situated between the railway and the cockle sheds.

The atmosphere is redolent of fishermen and smugglers in this well-preserved 'Heritage' pub.
🏚 Q ❀ ◖ ≈

ELMS
1060 London Road (A13)
☎ (01702) 474687
10-11; 12-10.30 Sun
Courage Directors; Theakston Best Bitter; guest beers H
Old, large, rambling building refurbished by Wetherspoons, but more like a local than their usual outlets.
Q ❀ ◖ ▮ ⚅ P ⊁ 🍺

LITTLE BENTLEY

BRICKLAYER'S ARMS
Rectory Road (near A120)
☎ (01206) 250405
12-3, 6.30-11; 12-3, 7-10.30 Sun
Greene King IPA; H **Mauldons Squires** G
Comfortable rural pub, full of fascinating artefacts, the only outlet for gravity ale in Tendring; also first rate food at realistic prices. A centre for the local community.
Q ❀ ◖ ▮ ♣ P

LITTLE CLACTON

APPLE TREE
The Street (B1441)
☎ (01255) 861026
11-11; 12-10.30 Sun
Fuller's ESB; Wells Eagle; guest beers H
New young owners have extended the range of beers on handpump and indeed the whole range of drinks. A leading venue for pub bands in the area; the RNLI benefited from its novel Beaujolais Nouveau and beer festival. Valuable sponsors of the CAMRA Clacton beer festival.
❀ ◖ ▮ ♣ P

LITTLE HALLINGBURY

SUTTON ARMS
Stortford Road, Hall Green (by A1060) ☎ (01279) 730460
11-2.30, 6-11; 12-11 Sat; 12-10.30 Sun
B & T Shefford Bitter; Ind Coope Burton Ale; Tetley Bitter; guest beer H
Village pub with a well deserved reputation for food, very busy at weekends. The public bar is used by locals. The guest beer is from the 'Tapster's Choice' range
🏚 ❀ ◖ ▮ ⚅ ▲ ♣ P

LITTLE OAKLEY

OLDE CHERRY TREE
Clacton Road (B1414)
☎ (01255) 880333
11-2.30, 5-11; 12-3, 7-10.30 Sun
Adnams Bitter, Broadside; Wells Eagle; guest beers H
17th-century, single-bar pub,

with Tardis-like dimensions. In winter it offers a bleak panorama of the North Sea which is countered by the large wrought iron cradled open fire. Whatever the weather this pub is a haven for real ale drinkers from far and wide.
🏚 ❀ ◖ ▮ ♣ P

LITTLE TOTHAM

SWAN
School Road (near B1022)
☎ (01621) 892689
11-11; 12-10.30 Sun
Adnams Bitter; Greene King IPA; guest beers H G
Two-bar village local, heavily beamed, with a walled garden. The landlord strongly supports microbreweries and hosts a beer festival in June. Gravity beers and cider are fetched from the temperature-controlled cellar.
🏚 ❀ ◖ ▮ 🍺 ▲ ⌂ P 🍺

LITTLEY GREEN

COMPASSES
Off B1417, at Ridleys Brewery)
OS699172
☎ (01245) 362308
11.30-3, 6-11; 12-3, 7-10.30 Sun
Ridleys IPA, ESX, Witchfinder, Spectacular, Rumpus, Winter Ale G
This Victorian cottage-style pub is difficult to find, but well worth the effort. Its bar food speciality is the Essex Huffer (a very large bap). Good range of whiskies. A real gem.
🏚 Q ❀ ◖ ▮ ♣ P

MANNINGTREE

CROWN HOTEL
51 High Street (B1352)
☎ (01206) 396333
11-11; 12-10.30 Sun
Greene King XX Mild, IPA, Abbot, seasonal beer H
A 16th-century, three-bar coaching inn, which affords panoramic views over the River Stour from the restaurant. Artefacts about the place reflect Manningtree's history. No food Mon.
🐎 ❀ 🛏 ◖ 🍺 ⚅ ≈ ♣ P

MATCHING TYE

FOX INN
The Green OS516113
☎ (01279) 731335
12-3, 7-11 (closed Mon); 12-3, 7-10.30 Sun
Shepherd Neame Spitfire; guest beers H
Three-bar pub (one bar is used for food). The large garden has a petanque piste. Warm welcome from friendly locals.
🏚 Q ❀ ◖ ▮ 🍺 ♣ P

MILL END GREEN

GREEN MAN
1 mile E of B184 OS619260
☎ (01371) 870286
12-3, 6-11; 12-3, 7-10.30 Sun
**Adnams Bitter; Greene King IPA;
Ridleys IPA** Ⓗ
This friendly, 15th-century oak-
studded, low-beamed country
pub features in TV's *Lovejoy*
series. Superb gardens and outdoor area. Good value food (not
served Sun eve).
🏚 🕸 🚲 ◖ ▶ 🅰 P

MILL GREEN

VIPER
Mill Green Road OS641018
☎ (01277) 352010
12-2.30 (3 Sat), 6-11; 12-3,
7-10.30 Sun
Ridleys IPA; guest beers Ⓗ
Only pub of this name in the
country, appropriately in a pretty,
wooded area. The tap room bar
is an unspoilt rural gem. A quiet,
relaxing atmosphere, all too rare
nowadays, can be enjoyed. Local
CAMRA *Pub of the Year* 1997 and
'98. 🏚 Q 🕸 🏠 ♣ P

MORETON

NAGS HEAD
Church road (from A414 take
Moreton Rd) ☎ (01277) 890239
12-3 (not Mon), 6.30-11; 12-3,
6.30-10.30 Sun
**Brakespear Bitter; Hook Norton
Best Bitter; Tolly Cobbold
Original; guest beer** Ⓗ
Large, split-level free house
which featured in TV's *Lovejoy*.
The guest beer changes regular-
ly. Good quality menu.
Q 🕸 ◖ ▶ P

MOUNTNESSING

PRINCE OF WALES
199 Roman Road (B1002)
☎ (01277) 353445
11-3, 6-11; 12-3, 7-10.30 Sun
**Ridleys Mild, IPA, ESX,
Witchfinder, Rumpus, seasonal
beers** Ⓗ
Popular, old, beamed pub, opposite the windmill, serving home-
cooked food (no food Mon eve).
Local CAMRA *Pub of the Year*
1996.🏚 🕸 ◖ ▶ 🏠 ♣ P

Try also: Plough, Roman Road
(Free)

NEWPORT

COACH & HORSES
Cambridge Rd (B1383)
☎ (01799) 540292
11-11; 12-10.30 Sun
**Flowers Original; Young's Bitter;
guest beers** Ⓗ
Warm, welcoming, 16th-century
coaching inn with an excellent
restaurant and bar food.
Pleasant garden.
🏚 🕸 🚲 ◖ ▶ 🚲 ♣ P 🍴

NORTH FAMBRIDGE

FERRY BOAT INN
Ferry Road
☎ (01621) 740208
12 (11 Sat & Summer)-3, 7 (6.30
Sat, 6 summer)-11; 12-4, 7-10.30
(12-10.30 summer) Sun
**Flowers IPA; Morland Old
Speckled Hen; Wadworth 6X** Ⓗ
15th-century beamed inn by the
River Crouch with a warm, inviting atmosphere. Nautical bric-à-
brac abounds.
🏚 🚲 🕸 ◖ ▶ 🚲 ♣ P

NORTH SHOEBURY

ANGEL INN
Parsons Corner (A13/B1017 jct)
☎ (01702) 589600
11-3, 5.30-11; 12-3, 7-10.30 Sun
**Fuller's London Pride; Greene
King IPA, Abbot; guest beers** Ⓗ
Superb restored group of 17th-
century, timber-framed buildings
(Grade II listed) to form a truly
traditional pub with a thatched
restaurant. Note the genuine
flagstones and carved bar with
angels. Meals Tue-Sat and Sun
lunch. Q 🕸 ▶ 🚲 P

ORSETT

FOXHOUND
18 High Road (B188)
☎ (01375) 891295
11-3.30, 6-11; 11-11 Sat; 12-3.30,
7-10.30 Sun
**Courage Best Bitter; Crouch
Vale Woodman IPA, Best Bitter;
Morland Old Speckled Hen** Ⓗ
Village pub with many signs of
history, still a natural meeting
place for all.Q 🕸 ◖ ▶ 🏠 ♣ P

ORSETT HEATH

FOX
176 Heath Road (near A1013)
OS639800 ☎ (01375) 373861
11-11; 12-10.30 Sun
**Crouch Vale Best Bitter; guest
beers** Ⓗ
Quiet two-bar pub set in an
award-winning garden. Eve
meals Fri and Sat: pizzas and
seafood. 🏚 🕸 ◖ ▶ 🏠 🚲 P

PEBMARSH

KING'S HEAD
The Street (1½ miles E of A131)
OS851335
☎ (01787) 269306
12-2, 7 (5 Fri)-11; 12-3, 7-10.30
Sun
Greene King IPA; guest beers Ⓗ
15th-century village local with an
oak-beamed interior. Three constantly changing guest beers are
dispensed from the bar where

pumpclips from 300 plus beers to
date feature; beer festival in
October. Skittles and table football played.
🏚 Q 🚲 🕸 ◖ 🅰 ♣ P

PLESHEY

WHITE HORSE
The Street OS663143
☎ (01245) 237281
12-3, 7-11; 11-11 Sat; 12-10.30 Sun
Beer range varies Ⓗ
Attractive, old, beamed pub with
a new drinkers' extension (usually two or three beers available).
Extensive menu. 🏚 🕸 ◖ ▶ 🅰 P

PURLEIGH

BELL
The Street (near B1010)
OS841020
☎ (01621) 828348
11-3, 6-11; 12-3, 7-10.30 Sun
**Adnams Bitter; Benskins BB;
Greene King IPA; guest beer** Ⓗ
Spacious country pub with a
wealth of exposed beams and a
large inglenook, on a hilltop with
views over the Blackwater estuary. No music but a relaxing
atmosphere. No food Tue eves.
🏚 Q 🕸 ◖ ▶ ♣ P

ROUNDBUSH
Roundbush Road (by B1010 jct)
OS858019
☎ (01621) 828354
Lunchtime varies, 6-11; lunchtime
varies, 7-10.30 Sun
**Greene King IPA, Abbot; guest
beer** Ⓖ
Classic country pub, a gem. The
adjoining cafe is open from
8.30am. Probably the only
Roundbush in the country. Eve
meals Thu-Sat.
🏚 Q 🕸 ◖ ▶ ♣ P

RADLEY GREEN

CUCKOO
500 yds off A414 OS622054
☎ (01245) 248356
12-2, 7 (6 Sat)-11 (closed Tue eve
winter); may vary Sat; 12-4,
7-10.30 Sun
Ridleys IPA, seasonal beers Ⓗ
Formerly the Thatchers Arms,
this welcoming pub is surrounded
by extensive grounds and farmland. Popular with caravanners.
The menu caters for children.
🏚 Q 🕸 ◖ ▶ 🅰 ♣ P

RADWINTER

PLOUGH
Sampford Road (B1053/B1054
jct) ☎ (01799) 599222
11.30-3 (12-3.30 Sat), 6.30-11;
12-3.30, 7-10.30 Sun
**Greene King IPA; Hook Norton
Old Hooky; Woodforde's Wherry;
guest beers** Ⓗ
Grade II listed building, originally

an ale house with beams and studding; quiet atmosphere. Home-made specialities feature on the à la carte menu.
🏨 Q 🐴 🐾 🚗 ◖ ▶ ♣ P ✂

RICKLING GREEN

CRICKETERS ARMS
½ mile W of B1383
OS511298 ☎ (01799) 543210
12-3, 6-11; 12-3, 6.30-10.30 Sun
Flowers IPA; guest beers Ⓖ
Extended old village pub overlooking a historic cricket green. Guest beers usually include a mild or dark beer. The imaginative menu specialises in mussels. Quality accommodation; handy for Stansted Airport. 🏨 🐴 🐾 🚗 ◖ ▶ 🍺 ♣

RIDGEWELL

WHITE HORSE
Mill Road (A1017)
☎ (01440) 785532
11-3, 6-11; 12-3, 7-10.30 Sun
Adnams Bitter, Broadside, Regatta; guest beers Ⓗ
Low-ceilinged bar with a games room, fielding local league teams. Note the unusual arm wrestling table. Many guest beers stocked. Walkers and cyclists welcomed.
🏨 🐾 ◖ ▶ ▲ ♣ ⌣ P

ROCHFORD

GOLDEN LION
35 North Street
☎ (01702) 545487
12-11; 12-10.30 Sun
Elgood's Cambridge; Fuller's London Pride; Greene King Abbot; Theakston Old Peculier; guest beers Ⓗ
300-year-old ex-tailor's shop. Although a bit run down, it has a good atmosphere, serving a good selection of guest ales; a real cider is always available.
🐾 ◖ 🚃 ♣ ⌣

OLD SHIP
12-14 North St ☎ (01702) 544210
11-11; 12-10.30 Sun
Marston's Pedigree; Morland Old Speckled Hen; guest beers Ⓗ
Large traditional pub serving a good range of beers (including a house bitter) and good value food (Mon-Fri). This old coaching inn dates from the 15th century.
🐾 ◖ 🚃 ♣ P

ROWHEDGE

WALNUT TREE
Fingringhoe Road (1 mile E of B1025) OS021216
☎ (01206) 728149
8 (7.30 Fri)-11; 12-3, 7-11 Sat; 12-3, 7.30-10.30 Sun
Beer range varies Ⓗ
Friendly, cosy yet lively pub on

the outskirts of Colchester. Good value food featuring a Cheese Club Fri. The vinyl juke box is great. Check opening times and meet Nutty the one-horned goat who shares the garden with chickens and an aviary.
🐾 ◖ ▶ ♣ P

SAFFRON WALDEN

AXE
60 Ashdon Road
☎ (01799) 522235
12-2.30, 6-11; 12-10.30 Sun
Greene King IPA, Abbot Ⓗ
Popular town local in an extended Victorian building. It has a dining room for meals and meetings (good pub food Mon-Sat lunch and Wed-Sat eve).
🐾 ◖ ▶ P

Try also: Kings Head, Market Hill (Free)

SHALFORD

GEORGE INN
The Street (B1053)
☎ (01371) 850207
12-3, 6.30-11; 12-3.30, 7-10.30 Sun
Adnams Broadside; Greene King IPA; guest beer Ⓗ
Friendly, open-plan beamed local with a large inglenook; no fruit machines. Good value pub grub with a spacious, no-smoking dining area. 🏨 Q 🐾 ◖ ▶ ▲ P ✂

SOUTH FAMBRIDGE

ANCHOR HOTEL
Fambridge Road
☎ (01702) 203535
11-3, 6-11; 12-10.30 Sun
Greene King Abbot; Nethergate Porters Suffok Bitter; guest beers Ⓗ
Welcoming olde-worlde pub near the river. Good food. 🐾 ◖ ▶ 🚃 P

SOUTHEND ON SEA

CORK & CHEESE ALE HOUSE
10 Talza Way (below Victoria Plaza shopping centre)
☎ (01702) 616914
11-11; closed Sun
Beer range varies Ⓗ
Pub which specialises in independent and microbrewers' beers. A real cider is always available. Very reasonable prices.
🐾 ▶ 🚃 (Victoria/Central) ♣ ⌣

LAST POST
5 Weston Road
☎ (01702) 431682
10-11; 12-10.30 Sun
Courage Directors; Theakston Best Bitter; guest beers Ⓗ
Massive, town-centre Wetherspoons pub on the site of a former post office. Popular with

all ages and very busy at weekends.
Q ◖ ▶ 🚻 ♿ 🚃 (Central/Victoria) ✂ 🍴

LIBERTY BELLE
10-12 Marine Parade
☎ (01702) 466936
10-11; 12-10.30 Sun
Courage Best Bitter, Directors; guest beers Ⓗ
Large, 1903 pub that stands out from the rest; much improved decor with darts, pool and a family room. See the blackboard above the bar for guest beers and real cider.
🚃 🐾 ◖ ♿ 🚃 (Central) ♣ ⌣

Try also: Pipe of Port, 84 High St (Free)

SOUTHMINSTER

STATION ARMS
39 Station Road (near B1020/ B1021 jct) ☎ (01621) 772225
12-2.30, 6 (5.30 Thu & Fri)-11; 12-11 Sat; 12-4, 7-10.30 Sun
Crouch Vale Best Bitter; Fuller's London Pride; guest beers Ⓗ
Friendly, weather-boarded pub hosting regular beer festivals. East Anglian CAMRA *Pub of the Year* 1997 & '98. Good value home-cooked food in the restaurant or bar, Thu-Sat eves and winter Sun lunch. 🏨 Q 🐾 ▶ 🚃 ♣ ⌣

STANFORD RIVERS

WOODMAN
155 London Road (A113)
☎ (01277) 362019
11-11; 12-10.30 Sun
Nethergate Bitter; Shepherd Neame Spitfire; Woodforde's Wherry; guest beers Ⓗ
Traditional country pub with low-beamed ceilings and two open fireplaces. The patio area overlooks the large garden which leads down to a river. Excellent home-cooked meals. Occasional beer festivals. Local CAMRA *Pub of the Year* 1998. 🏨 🐾 ◖ ▶ P

STANSTED MOUNTFITCHET

QUEENS HEAD
3 Lower Street (B1051)
☎ (01279) 812458
11-3, 5.30 (7 Sat)-11; 12-3, 7-10.30 Sun
Draught Bass; Flowers IPA; Wadworth 6X; guest beers Ⓗ
Bright, comfortable pub at the village centre. An eclectic collection of brass and old agricultural implements adorns the walls. No food sun. Bar billiards played.
🐾 ◖ 🚃 ♣

Try also: Rose & Crown, Bentfield End (Free)

115

STAPLEFORD TAWNEY

MOLETRAP
Tawney Common, Theydon Mount
(from A414 take Toot Hill road for
approx 3 miles) OS501014
☎ (01992) 522394
12-3, 6 (7 winter)-11; 12-10.30 Sun
Beer range varies Ⓗ
Low-beamed, friendly rural local,
difficult to find but worth the
effort, especially as the pub has
recently been enlarged but still
retains its character. Cider and a
fourth real ale in summer. Local
CAMRA *Pub of the Year* 1997.
🏚 Q ❀ ◖ ▶ ⌣ P

STISTED

DOLPHIN
Coggleshall Road (A120, 2 miles
E of Braintree)
☎ (01376) 321143
11-3, 6-11; 12-3, 7-10.30 Sun
Ridleys IPA, ESX Ⓖ
Traditional old beamed pub with
two bars. No meals Tue eve.
🏚 Q ❀ ◖ ▶ ♣ P

STOCK

HOOP
21 High Street (B1007)
☎ (01277) 841137
10-11; 12-10.30 Sun
Adnams Bitter; guest beers ⒽⒼ
Very popular, small, timber-
framed pub with usually six ales
from independent brewers, often
including a mild, plus a cider and
often a perry. A good selection of
home-made food is available all
day. Famed for its May beer festival in the large garden.
Q ❀ ◖ ▶ ♣ ⌣

STOW MARIES

PRINCE OF WALES
Woodham Road (near B1012)
OS830993
☎ (01621) 828971
11-11; 12-10.30 Sun
Beer range varies Ⓗ
Beautifully restored, with a working Victorian bakery and a changing range of five or six beers and
a selection of Belgian beers.
Special events include a now-
famous firework display. Winner
of numerous awards. Good
home-cooked food (not served
Mon eve).
🏚 Q ⛴ ❀ ◖ ▶ ▲ ⌣ P

TENDRING

CHERRY TREE
Crow Lane (B1035)
☎ (01255) 830340
11-3, 6-11; 12-8 (10.30 summer)
Sun
**Adnams Bitter; Greene King IPA,
Abbot; guest beers** Ⓗ
Former 17th-century cider house,
now catering for a wider clien-

tele. Food is paramount at the
weekends. Locals discuss field
sports eves and real ale buffs
come to enjoy a good pint.
🏚 ❀ ◖ ▶ ▲ P

THAXTED

ROSE & CROWN
31 Mill End (B184)
☎ (01371) 831152
12-3, 6-11; 12-3, 7-10.30 Sun
Ridleys IPA; guest beers Ⓗ
Friendly local in an historic town
with a famous church, guildhall
and windmill. Said to be on the
site of a monastic hostelry. A
cosy dining room offers excellent
food (book Sun lunch).
🏚 ❀ ⇚ ◖ ▶ ⌸ ▲ ♣ P

Try also: Swan, The Bullring
(Old English Inns)

THORNWOOD COMMON

CARPENTERS ARMS
Carpenters Arms Lane (B1393, 2
miles from M11 jct 7)
☎ (01992) 574208
11-3, 6-11; 11-11 Fri & Sat;
12-10.30 Sun
**Adnams Broadside; Courage Best
Bitter; Crouch Vale Best Bitter,
SAS; McMullen AK; guest beers** Ⓗ
Popular village pub, playing a
strong role in the social life of
the aircrews at nearby North
Weald Airfield since WWII.
Guest beers come from indepen-
dent breweries. No food Sun.
Essex CAMRA *Pub of the Year*
1998.
❀ ◖ ⌸ ⊖ ♣ ⌣ P ⊖ (Epping)

TILLINGHAM

CAP & FEATHERS
8 South Street (B1021)
☎ (01621) 779212
11.30-3, 6-11; 12-4, 7-10.30 Sun
**Crouch Vale Dark, IPA, Best
Bitter, Millennium Gold; guest
beer** Ⓗ
Unspoilt, 15th-century pub with a
wide range of Crouch Vale beers
and excellent home-cooked food.
Traditional games played in a
warm friendly atmosphere.
🏚 Q ⛴ ❀ ◖ ◖ ▶ ♣ ⌣ P ⌸

TOOT HILL

GREEN MAN
Off A414, Blake Hall Road on to
Toot Hill Road for 2 miles
OS515025
☎ (01992) 522255
11-3, 6-11; 12-3, 7-10.30 Sun
Crouch Vale IPA; guest beers Ⓗ
Early 19th-century rural inn.
Guest beers come from indepen-
dent breweries. Can get busy at
weekends.
🏚 Q ❀ ◖ ▶ ⅙ P ⅍

WALTON-ON-THE-NAZE

ROYAL MARINE
3 Old Pier Street (near B1034)
☎ (01255) 674000
11-11; 12-10.30 Sun
**Adnams Bitter; Marston's
Pedigree; guest beers** Ⓗ
Small, snug lounge bar and a
larger adjoining bar speak volumes about this pub's history.
Involvement with the RNLI and
participation in the local folk festival make it an ideal community
pub. 🏚 ◖ ▶ ⇌ ♣

WARLEY

BRAVE NELSON
138 Woodman Road (off B186)
☎ (01277) 211690
12-3, 5.30-11; 12-11 Sat; 12-4,
7-10.30 Sun
**Nethergate Bitter; Webster's
Yorkshire Bitter; guest beer** Ⓗ
Comfortable friendly local, bearing a nautical theme. A rare local
outlet for Nethergate beer. The
safe garden for children hosts
summer barbecues and petanque
games. No food Sun.
❀ ◖ ⌸ ♣ P

WENDENS AMBO

BELL
Royston Road (B1039)
☎ (01799) 540382
11.30-2.30, 6-11; 12-3, 7-10.30 Sun
Adnams Bitter; Ansells Mild; Ⓗ
guest beers ⒽⒼ
Splendid, welcoming, traditional
village pub at the heart and soul
of its community. An unusual outlet for mild in the area. The
extensive garden houses goats.
No food Mon eve. Convenient for
Audley End station.
🏚 ❀ ◖ ▶ ⇌ ♣ P

WESTCLIFF-ON-SEA

CRICKETERS INN
228 London Road (A13)
☎ (01702) 343168
11.30-11; 12-10.30 Sun
**Greene King IPA, Abbot; guest
beer** Ⓗ
Gray's south-eastern outpost.
Recently refurbished; good food.
⛴ ◖ ▶ ⅙ ⇌ ♣ ⌣ P

HAMLET
54 Hamlet Court Road (near A13)
☎ (01702) 391752
11-11; 12-10.30 Sun
**John Smith's Bitter; Courage
Directors; Greene King Abbot;
guest beers** Ⓗ
Former bank, now a one-bar pub
offering table service, popular
with drinkers of all ages. Regular
beer festivals are held. Opens for
breakfast from 10 Mon-Sat.
Limited parking.
◖ ▶ ⇌ ♣ P ⅍

WITHAM

WOOLPACK
7 Church Street (near B1018)
☎ (01376) 511195
11.30-11; 12-10.30 Sun
Guest beer Ⓗ
500-year-old community local in
the old part of Witham. The
house beer is usually from Tolly
Cobbold. Note a cask breather is
used occasionally on Greene King
IPA. 🏚 🍺 ⇌ ♣

WIVENHOE

HORSE & GROOM
55 The Cross (B1028)
☎ (01206) 824928
10.30-3, 5.30 (6 Sat)-11; 12-3.30,
7-10.30 Sun
**Adnams Bitter, seasonal beers;
guest beers** Ⓗ
Quiet two-bar local in a fishing
village with a friendly atmosphere, serving good home-
cooked food.
Q 🏵 ◑ ▶ 🍺 ⇌ P

ROSE & CROWN
The Quay (near B1028)
☎ (01206) 826371
11-2.30 (3 Sat), 6-11; 12-3,
7-10.30 Sun
**Adnams Bitter; Friary Meux BB;
Fuller's London Pride; guest
beers** Ⓗ
Snug little pub on the quay side
with seating outside to watch the
boats sailing out. Inside it has a
little library with books and maps
- ideal for a winter's night reading by the fire whilst you enjoy
your pint. Eve meals Mon, Tue,
Thu and Fri.
🏚 Q 🏵
◑ ▶ ♣

WOODHAM FERRERS

BELL
Main Road (B1418, N of town)
☎ (01245) 320443
11-3, 6-11; 12-3, 7-10.30 Sun
**Adnams Bitter; Ridleys IPA;
guest beers** Ⓗ
Traditional pub with two bars and
a restaurant; a 19th-century pub
with new extensions and large
gardens, giving good views of the
surrounding area. Quite a
favourite with hikers and bikers
in summer.
🏚 Q 🏵 ◑ ▶ 🍺 ♣ P

WOODHAM MORTIMER

HURDLEMAKERS ARMS
Post Office Road (off A414)
☎ (01245) 225169
11.30-2, 6.30-11; 12-2, 6.30-
10.30 Sun
**Greene King IPA, Abbot;
Shepherd Neame Spitfire** Ⓗ
Cosy, two-bar village pub with a
large garden and children's play
area. A wood fire and flagstone
floor feature in the saloon bar.
🏚 Q 🏵 ◑ ▶ ♿ ♣ P

WORMINGFORD

CROWN INN
Main Road (B1508)
☎ (01787) 227405
11.30-3, 6-11; 12-3, 7-10.30 Sun
Greene King IPA, Ⓗ **Abbot** Ⓖ
Old coaching inn of character:
two bars, public and a lounge,
offer something for everyone,
plus a no-smoking dining area. A
fine Greene King house, worth
seeking out. Q 🏵 🚗 ◑ ▶
🍺 ♣ P

WRITTLE

INN ON THE GREEN
57 The Green
☎ (01245) 420266
11-3, 6-11; 11-11 Wed-Sat;
12-10.30 Sun
**Adnams Broadside; Courage
Directors; Mighty Oak
Burntwood; Nethergate IPA;
guest beer** Ⓗ
Large, one-bar pub next to the
village green, characterised by
its olde-worlde bric-à-brac.
Extensive bar menu and a restaurant upstairs (open Fri/Sat eves
and Sun lunch). Large garden.
🏚 🏵 ◑ ▶ ♣ P

WHEATSHEAF
70 The Green (near A1060)
☎ (01245) 420695
11-2.30, 5.30-11; 11-11 Sat;
12-10.30 Sun
**Greene King IPA, Abbot; guest
beers** Ⓗ
Popular village pub frequented by
locals. Two bars, one a traditional public bar, the other a cosy
lounge; its small size ensures an
intimate atmosphere. Limited
parking. Q 🏵 🍺 ♣ P

Ridley's Brewery: still family-owned and brewing in Essex, where it began in 1842.

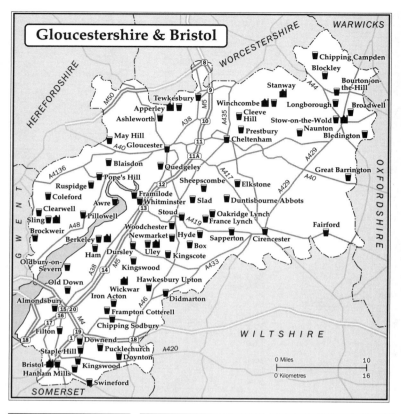

Gloucestershire & Bristol

ALMONDSBURY

BLACK SHEEP
Aztec West (off M5 jct 15, Aztec West Business Pk, behind Aztec Hotel)
☎ (01454) 201592
12-3 (not Sat); 5-11; 12-3, 7-10.30 Sun
Thwaites Bitter, seasonal beer Ⓗ
Split-level, farmhouse-style modern pub serving the business park and residents of nearby Bradley Stoke in the evenings. Substantial meals are available; there is a segregated, no-smoking dining area.
❀ ◑ ▶ ♿ P

APPERLEY

COAL HOUSE INN
Gabb Lane (off B4213)
☎ (01452) 780211
11-2.30 (3 Sat), 6 (7 winter)-11; 12-3, 7-10.30 Sun
Wickwar Coopers' WPA; Wadworth 6X; guest beer Ⓗ
Originally a coal wharf, now a welcoming, recently-refurbished pub on the banks of the River Severn, half a mile from the village centre. Moorings are provided.
🚲 Q 🐾 ❀ ◑ ▶ Å ♣ P ✂

ASHLEWORTH

BOAT INN
The Quay (on road to quay) OS819251
☎ (01452) 700272
11-2.30, 7-11; 12-3, 7-10.30 Sun
Brandy Cask Whistling Joe; Oakhill Yeoman; guest beers Ⓖ
Delightful old pub beside the River Severn. A small miracle of survival, which has been owned by the same family for 400 years. The interior has hardly changed for a century. Lunchtime snacks. CAMRA South-Western region *Pub of the Year* in 1996. Moorings available.
Q ❀ ♣ ⌣ P

AWRE

RED HART
Off A48, S of Newnham OS709080
☎ (01594) 510220
11-3, 5.30-11; 11-11 Sat; 12-10.30 Sun
Draught Bass; guest beers Ⓗ
Off the beaten track, this cosy pub features a well in the bar. Good food and atmosphere, with regular food and drink themes. Up to four guest ales.
❀ ⇔ ◑ ▶ ♣ P

BERKELEY

MARINERS ARMS
Salter Street (W end of village)
☎ (01453) 811822
11-11; 12-10.30 Sun
Berkeley Dicky Pearce; Courage Best Bitter Ⓗ
A friendly, two-bar pub built in 1490 as a nunnery; it became a pub during the Reformation. with a skittle alley. Live music Sat eves. 🚲 Q ❀ ◑ 🍴 ♣ ⌣ P

BLAISDON

RED HART INN
2 miles off A40/A48 OS702169
☎ (01452) 830477
12-3, 6-11; 12-3, 7-10.30 Sun
Hook Norton Best Bitter; Tetley Bitter; guest beers Ⓗ
Stone-flagged, one-bar pub with an adventurous guest beer policy – three guest beers served. Good home-cooked food. Children's certificate; large outdoor area.
🚲 ❀ ◑ ▶ Å ♣ P

BLEDINGTON

KINGS HEAD
Via B4450 OS243228
☎ (01608) 658365
11-3, 7-11; 12-3, 7-10.30 Sun

**Hook Norton Best Bitter;
Wadworth 6X; guest beers** H
Delightful, 16th-century inn over-
looking the village green.
Convivial atmosphere.
Specialises in food – booking
essential at weekends. Cider
summer only.
🏨 Q 🍽 🛏 🚪 ◑ ▶ ⊟ ♣ ▲ ♠
🖴 P ✄

BLOCKLEY

GREAT WESTERN ARMS
Station Road (B4479)
☎ (01386) 700362
11-2.30 (3 Sat), 6.30 (6 Fri &
Sat)-11; 12-3, 7-10.30 Sun
**Hook Norton Best Bitter,
Generation, Old Hooky; guest
beers** H
Simple, friendly local, formerly a
blacksmith's but originally built
for navvies on the nearby railway.
Q 🍽 ◑ ▶ ⊟ ♣ P

BOURTON-ON-THE-HILL

HORSE & GROOM
On A44
☎ (01386) 700413
11-3, 6.30-11; 12-3, 7-10.30 Sun
**Draught Bass; Hook Norton Best
Bitter; guest beer** H
Comfortable, small hotel with a
welcoming bar in an attractive
village. Changing guest beers. No
food Sun eve.
🏨 Q 🍽 🍽 🛏 ◑ ▶ ♣ P

BOX

HALFWAY HOUSE
OS856003
☎ (01453) 832631
11.30-3, 6 (5.30 Fri & Sat)-11;
12-3, 7-10.30 Sun
**Adnams Bitter; Marstons Bitter,
Pedigree; Taylor Landlord;
guest beer** H
Friendly and comfortable pub at
the road junction at the south
end of Minchinhampton Common.
Skittle alley and function room.
Interesting guest beers.
Q 🍽 ◑ ▶ ♣

BRISTOL

ANNEXE
Seymour Road, Bishopston (next
to Sportsman Hotel)
☎ (0117) 949 3931
11.30-2.30, 6-11; 11.30-11 Sat;
12-10.30 Sun
**Courage Georges BA, Best Bitter;
Marston's Pedigree; Smiles
Best; Theakston Best Bitter;
Wadworth 6X; guest beer** H
Near to the county cricket and
memorial grounds, this pub
serves a large beer range for the
area – in lined glasses – and
good value pub food. There is a
safe, large garden and disabled

access and toilet. Bar skittles.
Children are not allowed in the
main bar, but there is a special
children's room and garden.
🐕 🍽 ◑ ▶ ♿ ♣ ✄ ⊟

BAG O'NAILS
141 St George's Road
☎ (0117) 940 6776
12-2.30, 5.30-11; 12-11 Fri & Sat;
12-10.30 Sun
**Draught Bass; Fuller's London
Pride; guest beers** H
Small, traditional, gas-lit, single-
room pub dating from the mid-
19th century. Good selection of
bottle-conditioned ales and
European bottled beers. Up to
four guest ales available.
Lunchtime meals Mon-Fri.
Q ◑ ♣

BELL
21 Alfred Place, Kingsdown
☎ (0117) 907 7563
5.30-11; 12-11 Sat; 12-4, 7-10.30
Sun
**RCH Pitchfork; Wickwar BOB,
Olde Merryford** H
Friendly, small, back-street pub
which is candlelit at night; wood
panelling adds to the cosy atmosphere. (Don't be fooled by the
Usher's pub sign.) Q

BRIDGE INN
16 Passage Street
☎ (0117) 949 9967
11.30-11; 12-11 Sat; 12-2.30,
7.30-10.30 Sun
**Bath Gem, Barnstormer;
Courage Best Bitter; guest beers**
(occasional) H
Arguably Bristol's smallest pub.
Near Courage Brewery and fire
and ambulance HQs and a short
walk from Broadmead shops.
Cosy and comfortable, it brings
folk together. Correct beer tem-
peratures guaranteed ingenious-
ly. No food Sun.
◑ ⇌ (Temple Meads)

CADBURY HOUSE
60 Richmond Road, Montpelier
☎ (0117) 924 7874
11-11; 12-10.30 Sun
**Courage Best Bitter; Wickwar
BOB, Olde Merryford** H
Busy, cosmopolitan pub with a
large rear garden. Very popular
with students and others: old
one-armed bandits and space
invaders machines feature. Can
get very busy sometimes.
Wickwar's other beers are sold
occasionally. West Country cider.
Food served until 7pm.
🏨 🍽 ◑ ⇌ (Montpelier) ♣ 🖴

COMMERCIAL ROOMS
43-45 Corn Street
☎ (0117) 927 9681
11-11; 12-10.30 Sun
**Draught Bass; Butcombe Bitter;
Courage Directors; Theakston
Best Bitter; guest beers** H

Superb, Wetherspoons conversion of a former gentlemen's
club. Winner of the English
Heritage/CAMRA *Pub Design
Award* in 1996. Separate, no-
smoking room at the rear – note
the original gas lamps and high
bar counter. Disabled access via
side door. Weston's cider.
Q ◑ ▶ ♿ 🖴 ✄ ⊟

CORNUBIA
142 Temple Street (near Courage
Brewery)
☎ (0117) 925 4415
11.30-8.30;11.30-11 Fri; closed
Sat & Sun
**RCH Pitchfork; Tisbury Best
Bitter; Wickwar BOB; guest
beers** H
Small pub near the fire station.
Formerly the Courage Brewery
hospitality suite, the pub, specialising in beers from local microbreweries, is now open to the
public. The restaurant must be
booked. Opening hours may vary.
Q ◑ ▶ ⇌ (Temple Meads) P

HARE ON THE HILL
41 Thomas Street North,
Kingsdown
☎ (0117) 908 1982
12-2.30, 5-11; 12-11 Fri & Sat;
12-10.30 Sun
**Bath SPA, Gem, Barnstormer;
guest beer** H
Bath Ales' first pub, formerly the
Mason's Arms. Friendly and welcoming, it is located up a steep
hill close to Stokes Croft. The
guest ale is usually renowned,
strong, and not found locally.
There is a limited menu. Local
CAMRA *Pub of the Year* 1998.
◑ ▶ ♣

HIGHBURY VAULTS
164 St Michael's Hill, Kingsdown
☎ (0117) 973 3203
12-11; 12-10.30 Sun
**Smiles Golden Brew, Best,
Heritage, seasonal beers; Brains
SA; guest beers** H
Renowned, two-bar traditional
pub at the top of a steep hill. It
has a large, attractive, heated,
semi-covered patio area at the
rear. The wood-panelled interior
has low-level lighting and no
jukebox. Popular with students.
Good food (eve meals Mon-Fri till
8.30). 🍽 ◑ ▶ ♣

HOPE & ANCHOR
38 Jacobs Wells Road, Hotwells
☎ (0117) 929 2987
12-11; 12-10.30 Sun
Beer range varies H
Popular, genuine free house with
five regularly changing ales. The
secluded rear garden gets busy
in the summer. Interesting range
of bar meals, plus barbecues in
summer. Parking can be awk-
ward at busy times.
🍽 ◑ ▶

KELLAWAY ARMS
138-140 Kellaway Avenue,
Horfield ☎ (0117) 949 7548
11.30-2.30 (3 Fri), 6.30-11; 11-11
Sat; 12-3, 7.30-10.30 Sun
**Courage Georges BA, Best
Bitter; Marston's Pedigree;
Wells Bombardier** Ⓗ
Comfortable, friendly two-bar
local near Horfield Common.
Deceptively large public bar,
smaller lounge plus sizeable gar-
den. A regular entry in this Guide.
Q ❀ ◖ 🍴 ♣

KING'S HEAD ☆
60 Victoria Street
11-3, 5.30-11; 11-11 Wed-Fri;
7.30-11 Sat; 12-3, 7.30-10.30 Sun
**Draught Bass; Courage Georges
BA, Best Bitter,** Ⓗ
Small, unspoilt Victorian pub,
boasting a superb bar back. Good
lunchtime snacks (not Sun).
Decor features many old prints
and photographs of Bristol.
Closed Sat lunchtimes. Within
short walk of Temple Meads
station.
Q ◖ ≠

KNOWLE HOTEL
Leighton Road, Knowle
☎ (0117) 977 7019
12-3, 5.30-11; 11.30-11 Sat;
12-10.30 Sun
**Ind Coope Burton Ale; Tetley
Bitter; Smiles Best; guest beer** Ⓗ
Large, friendly, two-bar, locals'
community pub, with panoramic
views over Bristol. Popular with
many age groups. Guest beer
changes every two weeks. Quiz
night Tue. No food Sat.
❀ ◖ 🍴 ♣

PRINCE OF WALES
5 Gloucester Road, Bishopston
☎ (0117) 924 5552
11-11; 12-10.30 Sun
**Butcombe Bitter; Courage
Directors; guest beer** Ⓗ
Busy pub, popular with students.
Two bars and leaded glass provide a homely feel. There is a
small patio for outdoor drinking
in the summer.
Q ❀ ◖ ≠ (Montpelier)

PRINCE OF WALES
84 Stoke Lane, Westbury-on-
Trym
☎ (0117) 962 3715
11.30-3, 5.30-11; 11-11 Sat; 12-3,
7-10.30 Sun
**Draught Bass; Courage Georges
BA; Smiles Best; Theakston Best
Bitter; guest beer** Ⓗ
Friendly free house, displaying
decorative mirrors and sporting
cartoons. There is a well-
equipped conference room. Large
garden where boules is played.
Boys Bitter is Courage Georges
BA. Good wine list. No-smoking
area lunchtime.
❀ ◖ ♣ ✂

RAILWAY TAVERN
Station Road, Fishponds
☎ (0117) 965 8774
12-11; 12-3, 7-11 Mon; 12-11;
12-10.30 Sun
**Ind Coope Burton Ale; Marston's
Pedigree; Tetley Bitter; guest
beer** Ⓗ
Friendly local with skittle alley
and pool room close to Bristol-
Bath cycle track. Families welcome. The publican is a Burton
Ale Master Cellarman and the
guest beer is from the Tapster's
Choice list. Good value Sun lunches. ❀ ◖ ♣

RECKLESS ENGINEER
Temple Gate (opp Temple Meads
station) ☎ (0117) 929 0425
12-11; 12-3, 7.30-11 Sat; 12-
10.30 Sun
Tetley Best Bitter; guest beers Ⓗ
The former Isambard Brunel was
converted in 1996 to an excellent
alehouse. Features local and
other brews from micros;
reduced-priced ale Wed eves. Live
rocks bands at weekends (free
entry with CAMRA card). ◖ ▶ ≠

ROBERT FITZHARDING
24 Cannon Street, Bedminster
☎ (0117) 966 2794
11-11; 12-10.30 Sun
**Draught Bass; Butcombe Bitter;
Courage Directors; Theakston
Best Bitter; guest beers** Ⓗ
New Wetherspoons outlet, a former furniture store. One large
bar, with no-smoking and disabled facilities. Thatcher's cider.
Q ◖ ▶ 🚻 ⌂ 🖵 ✂

SEVEN WAYS
23 New Street, St Judes
☎ (0117) 955 6862
11.30-3, 6.30-11; 12-3, 7-10.30 Sun
**Courage Best Bitter; Ushers Best
Bitter, Founders, seasonal
beers** Ⓗ
Friendly, two-bar local in the Old
Market drinking area. Acclaimed
for its black pudding and bacon
rolls; Sun lunches must be
booked (no food Sat). Popular
venue for skittle functions. Quiet
in eves. Q ◖ 🖵 ♣

VICTORIA
20 Chock Lane, Westbury-on-
Trym ☎ (0117) 950 0441
12-3, 5.30-11; 12-4, 7-10.30 Sun
Adnams Broadside Ⓟ**; Badger
Tanglefoot** ⒼⒽ**; Draught Bass;
Smiles Best; Wadworth IPA, 6X**
Ⓗ**, seasonal beers** ⒼⒽ
Built in the 1700s, once a courthouse, this comfortably furnished
pub is hidden down a quiet lane.
Boules played. Only pizzas served
in the evening, with a take-away
facility. ❀ ◖ ▶ ♣ ✂

Try also: Post Office Tavern,
Westbury Hill, Westbury on Trym
(Free)

BROADWELL

FOX INN
Off A429 ☎ (01451) 870909
11-3, 6-11; 12-3, 7-10.30 Sun
Donnington BB, SBA Ⓗ
Attractive, one-bar, stone-built
pub overlooking the village
green. Original flagstone flooring
in the main bar area. Good food
and a very friendly atmosphere.
🏨 Q ❀ ◖ ▶ ▲ ♣ ⌂ P

BROCKWEIR

BROCKWEIR COUNTRY
INN
Off A466 OS540011
☎ (01291) 689548
12-2.30, 6-11; 12-11 Sat; 12-3,
7-10.30 Sun
**Hook Norton Bitter; Thwaites
Bitter; guest beers** Ⓗ
Unspoilt village pub near the
banks of the Wye. The beams
come from a ship built in
Brockweir many years ago.
Popular with walkers; Tintern
Abbey and Offa's Dyke are near-
by. Good B&B and food.
🏨 ❀ 🚗 ◖ ▶ 🍴 ▲ ♣ ⌂ P

CHELTENHAM

ADAM & EVE
8 Townsend St ☎ (01242) 690030
10.30-3, 5-11; 10.30-11 Sat; 12-3,
7-10.30 Sun
**Arkells Bitter, 3B, seasonal
beers** Ⓗ
No-frills, terraced local, 15 mins'
walk from the town centre. Public
bar and small comfortable
lounge. Strong community focus.
🍴 ♣

BAYSHILL INN
92 St George's Place (near bus
station) ☎ (01242) 524388
11-3, 5-11; 10.30-11 Sat; 12-3,
7-10.30 Sun
**Badger Tanglefoot; Wadworth
IPA, 6X, seasonal beers; guest
beer** Ⓗ
Friendly, town-centre local, refurbished and extended in 1997 to
include a comfortable lounge, but
retaining the 'public bar'-style
area. Good value food. Busy at
lunchtimes. No food Sun. Bulmers
cider. Q ❀ ◖ ⌂

HEWLETT ARMS
Harp Hill ☎ (01242) 228600
11-2.30 (3 Thu & Fri), 4-11; 11-5,
6-11 Sat; 12-5, 7-10.30 Sun
**Boddington's Bitter; Gales HSB;
Goff's Jouster; Wadworth 6X;
guest beers** Ⓗ
Comfortable, relaxed pub attracting a diverse clientele. Situated
on the outskirts of the town,
towards the racecourse, it is also
in walking distance of the football
ground. Large, neat, front garden. Good food range (no meals
Sun eve). ❀ ◖ ▶ P

KEMBLE BREWERY INN
27 Fairview Street (off ring road)
☎ (01242) 243446
11.30-2.30 (3 Fri), 5.30-11; 11.30-11 Sat; 12-4, 7-10.30 Sun
Archers Village, Best Bitter, Golden; guest beer ⊞
Deservedly popular, small back-street local. Hard to find, but worth the effort. Good atmos-phere. The only Archers tied house in the area. Good value, home-cooked food. Walled gar-den. Q ❀

ROYAL UNION
37 Hatherley Street, Tivoli (off A40, nr Westall Green round-about)
☎ (01242) 224686
11-11; 12-10.30 Sun
Tetley Bitter; guest beers ⊞
Gloucestershire CAMRA was born in this back-street local in 1975. It now has a strikingly dec-orated snug to contrast with the traditional public bar. Excellent value food (weekend lunchtimes only). Q ◖ ♣

TAILORS
Cambray Place
☎ (01242) 255453
11.30-11; 12-10.30 Sun
Badger Tanglefoot; Wadworth IPA, 6X, seasonal beers; guest beer ⊞
Large converted Victorian villa in town centre with an attractive exterior. Popular with younger drinkers, especially at weekends. No food Sun. ❀ ◖

Try also: Beaufort Arms, London Road (Wadworth)

CHIPPING CAMPDEN

VOLUNTEER
Lower High Street
☎ (01386) 840688
11.30-3, 5-11; 12-3, 7-10.30 Sun
Highgate Saddlers; Stanway Stanney Bitter; Theakston XB; guest beers ⊞
Stone-built pub with a courtyard and a pleasant garden, located to the west of the village centre. It has been a pub since 1709; the present name dates from the 1840s. Photographs of old village scenes are displayed in the bar. CAMRA County *Pub of the Year* 1998.
🏚 Q ❀ 🛏 ◖ ▶ ⅗ ♣

CHIPPING SODBURY

BEAUFORT HUNT
Broad Street ☎ (01454) 312871
10.30-3, 5 (6.30 Sat)-11; 11.30-3, 7-10.30 Sun
Draught Bass; Tetley Bitter; guest beers ⊞
In the main street of this market town, a snug, two-bar pub full of collections, jugs, pump clips and

so on. Often features unusual guest beers. Good pub food. Winner of a brewery award for the interesting toilets: the gents' must be visited!
Q ❀ ◖ 🍴

CIRENCESTER

CORINIUM COURT HOTEL
12 Gloucester Street (off A435 at north end of town)
☎ (01285) 659711
11-2.30, 6-11; 12-2.30, 7-10.30 Sun
Hook Norton Best Bitter ⊞, **Old Hooky, seasonal beers** 🄶; **Wadworth 6X** ⊞
Upmarket hotel in a 16th-century building with charming courtyard and garden entrances and a small flagstoned bar opening on to a comfortable lounge. Conversation prevails. Restaurant. There is an attractive walled garden.
🏚 Q ❀ 🛏 ◖ ▶ ⅗ ▲ P

DRILLMANS ARMS
Gloucester Road, Stratton (on old A417) ☎ (01285) 653892
11-3, 5.30-11; 11-11 Sat; 12-4, 7-10.30 Sun
Archers Village, Best Bitter; Fuller's London Pride; Wadworth 6X; guest beer ⊞
Very popular Georgian inn. A small, low-beamed lounge with a good log fire leads to a much-enlarged rear bar and skittle alley where families are wel-come. Mini-beer festival August Bank Holiday. Guest beer changes weekly. Real flowers in immaculate toilets.
🏚 ❀ ◖ ▶ 🍴 ⅗ ▲ ♣ P

GOLDEN CROSS
20 Blackjack St (near Corinium Museum)
☎ (01285) 652137
11-3, 6-11; 11-11 Sat; 12-3, 7-10.30 Sun
Arkells Bitter, 3B, seasonal beers ⊞
Gimmick-free pub relying on friendly and efficient service and good company, appealing to all ages. Full-sized snooker table. Families welcome in skittle alley when not in use.
🏚 ❀ 🛏 ◖ ⅗ ▲ ♣

TWELVE BELLS
12 Lewis Lane (off A435)
☎ (01285) 644549
11-11; 12-10.30 Sun
Beer range varies ⊞
A beer drinkers' haven. Lovingly resurrected by the owner/land-lord. Lively front bar and quieter, panelled rooms at the rear. Five guest beers on (300 a year) including a local session beer. Excellent food from a good value, wide-ranging menu.
🏚 🐕 ❀ ◖ ▶ ⅗ ▲ 🍴 P

CLEARWELL

LAMB
High Street (Redbrook road)
☎ (01594) 835441
6-11; 12-3, 6-11 Fri & Sat; 12-3, 7-10.30 Sun
Freeminer Bitter, guest beers 🄶
Featuring a small cosy bar with a larger lounge, this pub has a friendly landlord. Always at least one guest beer. Well-behaved children welcome. Bulmers cider.
🏚 Q ❀ ▲ ♣ 🍴 P

CLEEVE HILL

HIGH ROOST
On B4632
☎ (01242) 672010
11.30-2.30 (3.30 Sat), 7-11; 12-4, 7-10.30 Sun
Hook Norton Best Bitter, Old Hooky; guest beer ⊞
One-bar pub set on the highest hill in the county, reached up a flight of stone steps. Two large bay windows give good views. An area away from the bar is set aside for meals. Children allowed until 8pm. Facilities include a jukebox, dart board and bar skit-tles. ❀ 🛏 ◖ ▶ ♣ P

COLEFORD

ANGEL
Market Place (town centre)
☎ (01594) 833113
11-11; 12-10.30 Sun
Beer range varies ⊞
Comfortable, town-centre pub, dating from at least 1608. The Malt & Hops real ale bar serves a rolling range of five real ales. Well-behaved children welcome.
❀ 🛏 🚪 ♣ P

DIDMARTON

KINGS ARMS
The Street (A433) OS818875
☎ (01454) 238245
12-3, 6-11; 12-3, 7-10.30 Sun
Archers Golden; John Smith's Bitter; Theakston XB; Uley Hogshead ⊞
Low-key exterior belies the warm and welcoming interior of this tastefully refurbished 17th-centu-ry coaching inn leased from the Beaufort family in 1760 for 1,000 years at six pence a year — the perils of inflation! Good value bar food (no food Sun eve). Separate restaurant with an excellent innovative menu from the French chef. 🏚 Q ❀ 🛏 ◖ ▶ 🚪 ♣ P

DOWNEND

WHITE SWAN
70 North St ☎ (0117) 975 4154
11-11; 12-5, 7-10.30 Sun
Ushers Best Bitter, Founders, seasonal beers ⊞
Friendly, one-bar cider and ale

house with four draught ciders on tap. Can get smoky at times. Lunchtime snacks served. Garden at rear. Ciders: Taunton Trad, Bulmers Trad and West Country, Inch's Stonehouse Trad. 🏵 ♣ ⌷

DOYNTON

CROSS HOUSE
High Street (1 mile N of A420 at Wick) OS720741
☎ (01275) 822261
11-3.30, 6-11; 12-3.30; 7-10.30 Sun
Draught Bass; Courage Best Bitter Ⓗ
Hospitable local with an interesting collection of cigarette cards. No food Sun eves. 🏵 ◖ ▶ ▲ P

DUNTISBOURNE ABBOTS

FIVE MILE HOUSE ☆
Off A417 at Centurion services OS979089
☎ (01285) 821432
12-3, 6-11; 12-3, 7-10.30 Sun
Marston's Bitter; Taylor Landlord Ⓗ
Beautifully resurrected old pub. The tiny bar has a Grade II listed interior. To the left of the bar is a wonderful curved settle – a 1930s time warp. Separate smart restaurant. The no-smoking double cellar bar is available for functions. 🏰 Q ⛵ 🏵 ◖ ▶ ▲ P ⤧

DURSLEY

OLD SPOT INN
Hill Road (by bus station)
☎ (01453) 542870
11-3, 5-11; 11-11 Fri & Sat; 12-4, 7-10.30 (12-10.30 summer) Sun
Draught Bass; Uley Old Ric, Old Spot; guest beers Ⓗ
Excellent independent free house. Built in 1776 as a farmhouse, it has been a pub for 100 years. Lovingly refurbished by the owner. Real locals' pub and popular with walkers. Folk music Wed. Good value doorstep sandwiches and Old Ric beer sausages. Guest beers from Bath Ales, Hampshire and Otter. CAMRA regional *Pub of the Year* 1997 and national runner up 1997-98. 🏰 Q 🏵 ♣ ⤧ 🍺

ELKSTONE

HIGHWAYMAN
Beech Pike (A417) OS965107
☎ (01285) 821221
11-2.30, 6-11; 12-2.30, 7-10.30 Sun
Arkells Bitter, 3B, Kingsdown Ⓗ
Comfortable, 16th-century roadhouse on the Ermin Way, featuring a long bar with roaring fires, low ceilings and plenty of atmosphere. Good selection of food and sandwiches. Separate restaurant. Stage coach in car park. 🏰 Q ⛵ 🏵 ◖ ▶ ▲ P

FAIRFORD

BULL HOTEL
Market Place
☎ (01285) 712535
11-11; 12-10.30 Sun
Arkells Bitter, 3B, Kingsdown Ⓗ
Historic 15th-century Cotswold coaching inn, occupying an imposing position on the town square, and with a secret tunnel to the famous church opposite. Bustling and cheerful interior. Good value food and beer (eve meals until 9.15pm). Families welcome. Public car park adjacent.
🛏 ◖ ▶ & ⤧

FILTON

RATEPAYERS ARMS
Filton Recreation Centre, Elm Road (at mini roundabout turn off A38, left by police station)
☎ (0117) 908 2265
11-2 (2.30 Thu & Fri), 6.30 (4 winter)-11; 12-3 (2 summer), 7-10.30 Sun
Butcombe Bitter; Ind Coope Burton Ale; Smiles Best; Tetley Bitter; guest beer Ⓗ
Comfortable, well-laid-out bar in the recreation centre open to the public. Facilities include a skittle alley, snooker room and darts. Occasional live music Sun eve. Rare outlet for Burton Ale in the area.
Q & ⇌ (Filton Abbey Wood)
♣ P

FRAMILODE

SHIP INN
By B4071 from A38 and M5 jct 15 OS751103
☎ (01452) 740260
11-3, 7 (6 Fri & Sat)-11; 12-3, 7.10.30 Sun
Draught Bass; Wickwar BOB Ⓗ
Situated by the old Stroudwater canal, this has been a pub since 1779. Fine food in the bar and restaurant (eve meals until 9.30). Children's play area in the large gardens.
🏰 ⛵ 🏵 ◖ ▲ ♣ P ⤧

FRAMPTON COTTERELL

RISING SUN
43 Ryecroft Road (off Church Road, opp post office)
☎ (01454) 772330
11.30-3, 7-11; 12-3, 7-10.30 Sun
Draught Bass; Butcombe Bitter; Smiles Best; Wadworth 6X; Wickwar Cooper's WPA; guest beer Ⓗ
Popular, family-run genuine free house, supporting local brewers. Local CAMRA *Pub of the Year* in 1995. Skittle alley and an upper-level dining area. No food Sun lunchtimes. Q 🏵 ◖ ♣ P

FRANCE LYNCH

KINGS HEAD
OS 903035
☎ (01453) 882225
12-3 (4 Sat), 6-11; 12-4, 7-10.30 Sun
Archers Best Bitter; Hook Norton Best Bitter; guest beers Ⓗ
Friendly, single-bar pub in the middle of a compact village of narrow winding streets. The eating area is an extension of the bar. Children's play area outside. The village name originates from former Huguenot connections. No food Sun eve; creche Fri eve; camping facilities at Oakridge.
🏰 Q ⛵ 🏵 ◖ ▲ ♣ P

Try also: Old Neighbourhood Inn, Chalford Hill (Free)

GLOUCESTER

AVENUE
227 Bristol Road
☎ (01452) 423468
11-11; 12-10.30 Sun
Banks's Bitter; Ⓟ **Marston's Pedigree** Ⓗ
Tastefully refurbished Victorian hotel that is now a lively sporting pub. Wide range of facilities including children's play area. Eve food 6-9; no food Sun or Mon eves.
Q 🏵 ◖ ▶ & ♣ P ⤧ 🍺

ENGLAND'S GLORY
66-68 London Road
☎ (01452) 302948
11.30-2.30, 5-11; 12-3, 7-10.30 Sun
Badger Tanglefoot; Mayhem's Odda's Light; Wadworth IPA, 6X; guest beers Ⓗ
Largely rebuilt in 1992, the protected frontage was retained with part of the core and double skittle alley. Warm and welcoming. Children permitted. Quizzes and occasional live music.
🏰 🏵 ◖ ▶ & ⇌ ♣ P ⤧

REGAL
Kings Square ☎ (01452) 332344
11-11; 12-10.30 Sun
Archers Golden; Butcombe Bitter; Courage Directors; Theakston Best Bitter; guest beers Ⓗ
Wetherspoons superpub in former cinema of the same name. The major architectural features have been retained, with the screen replaced by a wall of glass looking on to a patio. Excellent guest beer policy. Food served all day. Occasional beer festivals. Weston's Old Rosie cider. Wheelchair WC.
Q 🏵 ◖ ▶ & ⇌ ⌷ ⤧ 🍺

WHITESMITHS ARMS
81 Southgate Street
☎ (01452) 414770
11-11; 12-3, 7-10.30

Arkells Bitter, 3B, Kingsdown, seasonal beers H
Fine old building, opposite the historic docks, with the ceiling opened up to expose the medieval timbers. The maritime theme in the pub's name is extended to much of the decor. Popular with office workers at lunchtime. Families welcome. Eve meals served 7-9.30.
🏠 Q ❀ ◗ ▶ 🚻 ♣

WINDMILL
83-83 Eastgate Street
☎ (01452) 500370
11-11; 12-10.30 Sun
Bateman Mild; Marston's Bitter, Pedigree, Owd Rodger, HBC H
Large and tastefully decorated city pub that was once a wine bar. Bottle-conditioned beers and imported lagers are available. Good value lunches. Inch's cider. Wheelchair WC.
🏠 ◗ 🚻 ⇌ ♣ ↻ ✂

GREAT BARRINGTON

FOX INN
1 mile N of A40 OS205131
☎ (01451) 844385
11-11; 12-10.30 Sun
Donnington BB, SBA H
Excellent, stone-built pub in a beautiful position by the River Windrush. Popular with walkers and locals. Huge garden.
🏠 ❀ ⇌ ◗ ▶ ♣ P

HAM

SALUTATION
OS680983
☎ (01453) 810284
11 (10 Sat)-3, 7 (4 Sat)-11; 12-3, 7-10.30 Sun
Draught Bass; Berkeley Old Friend, Dicky Pearce H
Smart and welcoming two-bar country pub with a skittle alley. Situated south of Berkeley Castle, it is popular with walkers. Features an attractive garden with children's play area. Lined glasses being phased in.
Q ⛱ ❀ ◗ ▶ ♣ ↻ P ⊟

HANHAM MILLS

OLD LOCK & WEIR
From Hanham go to foot of Abbots Rd, turn right
☎ (0117) 967 3793
11-11; 12-10.30 Sun
Draught Bass; Exmoor Gold, Stag; Marston's Pedigree; guest beer (occasional) H
Friendly, 300-year-old riverside pub mentioned in Conan Doyle's *Micah Clark*. A genuine free house. Local CAMRA *Pub of the Year* in 1996. Children welcome. Book for meals Fri and Sat eves and Sun lunchtimes. August Bank Holiday beer festival.
Q ❀ ◗ ▶ ♣ P

HAWKESBURY UPTON

BEAUFORT ARMS
High Street (1 mile from A46)
☎ (01454) 238217
12-3, 5.30-11; 12-11 Sat; 12-10.30 Sun
Wickwar BOB; guest beers H
Worth a detour, this friendly two-bar free house is close to the Cotswold Way and Westonbirt Arboretum. Good food and service at reasonable prices. Interesting collection of old enamel signs and pub memorabilia. Well deserves its popularity with locals.
Weston's Traditional Draught Scrumpy.
🏠 Q ❀ ◗ ▶ ⊟ ▲ ♣ ↻ P

HYDE

RAGGED COT
OS887012
☎ (01453) 884643
12-2.30, 6-11; 12-3, 7-10.30 Sun
Draught Bass; Theakston Best Bitter; Uley Old Spot; Wadworth 6X; guest beer H
Busy, comfortable, 16th-century free house in open countryside near Minchinhampton Common and Gatcombe Park. It stocks over 50 malt whiskies. Booking advisabe for meals.
🏠 Q ❀ ⇌ ◗ ▲ ♣ ↻ P

IRON ACTON

ROSE & CROWN
High Street (off B4058)
☎ (01454) 228423
5-11; 12-2.30, 6-11 Sat; 12-3, 7-10.30 Sun
Draught Bass; Flowers IPA; Marston's Pedigree; Uley Pig's Ear; Wickwar Olde Merryford H
Friendly local, in the centre of the village, dating from the 1680s. Free house with two separate bars; it prefers to concentrate on drink, so no food is sold. Rare local outlet for Uley beer.
🏠 Q ❀ ⇌ ⊟ ♣

KINGSCOTE

HUNTER'S HALL
On A4153 OS814960
☎ (01453) 860393
11-11; 12-10.30 Sun
Draught Bass; Theakston Best Bitter; Uley Hogshead; guest beer H
Rambling, 16th-century Cotswold coaching inn, with five rooms set around a central bar. The rustic wall, fireplaces, settles and sofas are evocative of a bygone era. Families are welcome. There is an extensive range of home-cooked bar meals; snacks at lunchtime only. Live music on Sun. No food winter Sun eve.
🏠 ⛱ ❀ ⇌ ◗ ▶ ⊟ ♣ P

KINGSWOOD

DINNEYWICKS INN
The Chippings (near Wotton-under-Edge)
☎ (01453) 843328
11.30-2.30, 6 (5 Fri)-11; 11.30-11 Sat; 12-3, 7-10.30 Sun
Adnams Broadside; Wadworth IPA, 6X; guest beers H
An imposing three-storey structure that blends with the surrounding buildings. A friendly, one-bar pub with a strong local trade. It is named after a nearby hill that was a horses' burial ground during the Civil War.
❀ ◗ ▶ ♣

KINGSWOOD (BRISTOL)

HIGHWAYMAN
Hill Street (on A420, 1/2 mile from Kingswood centre)
☎ (0117) 967 1613
11.30-2.30 (3 Sat), 5.30-11; 12-4, 7-10.30 Sun
Ind Coope Burton Ale; Smiles Best; Tetley Bitter H
Large, L-shaped bar with stone walls and wooden beams in a coachouse style. There is a TV for sports in the bar and a family room. The genial landlord has been at the pub five years. Good value lunchtime food available (12-2); no-smoking area lunchtimes only.
⛱ ❀ ◗ P ✂

LONGBOROUGH

COACH & HORSES
Off A424
☎ (01451) 830325
11-2.30, 7-11; 12-3, 7-10.30 Sun
Donnington XXX, BB, SBA (occasional) H
Friendly, one-bar pub in a quiet village which has morris dancing connections. Firefighting mementoes in the pub reflect the proximity of the fire services college. Parking can be difficult.
🏠 Q ❀ ♣

MAY HILL

GLASSHOUSE INN
Off A40, west of Huntley
OS710213
☎ (01452) 830529
11.30-3, 6.30-11; 12-3, 7-10.30 Sun
Butcombe Bitter; guest beers G
Unspoilt country pub which still has its original quarry-tiled floor. The outdoor drinking area has an old cider press and bench with a yew bridge canopy. Real cider is available sometimes.
🏠 Q ❀ ◗ ▲ ♣ P

NAUNTON

BLACK HORSE INN
OS119234
☎ (01451) 850565
11.30-3, 6-11; 12-3, 7-10.30
Sun
Donnington BB, SBA Ⓗ
Traditional Cotswold stone village inn, offering a friendly welcome. The interior features include flagstone flooring, a real fire and wooden settles. Single bar: the old snug is now a dining room.
♨ Q ❀ ⇌ ◖ ▶ ♣ P

NEWMARKET

GEORGE INN
OS839997
☎ (01453) 833228
11-3, 6-11; 11-11 Fri; 12-3, 7-10.30 Sun
Archers Village; Draught Bass; Uley Old Spot Ⓗ
Pleasant, stone-built pub with a friendly atmosphere, looking southwards over the valley above Nailsworth. Traditional food is cooked by an award-winning chef. Separate restaurant behind a glass panel (booking essential). Limited parking.
Q ❀ ◖ ▶ P

OAKRIDGE LYNCH

BUTCHERS ARMS
N end of village
OS915038
☎ (01285) 760371
11-3, 6-11; 12-4, 7-10.30 Sun
Archers Best Bitter; Goff's Jouster; Hook Norton Old Hooky; Tetley Bitter; Theakston Best Bitter Ⓗ
Stone-built former butcher's shop, now a popular two-bar local. Separate restaurant open Wed-Sat and Sun lunchtime (food available in the bar all times except Sun eve). Caravans are allowed in the campsite.
♨ Q ⛺ ❀ ◖ ▶ ⊞ ▲ ♣ P

OLDBURY-ON-SEVERN

ANCHOR
Church Road (4 miles off A38)
☎ (01454) 413331
11.30-2.30, 6.30-11; 11.30-11 Sat; 12-10.30 Sun
Draught Bass; Black Sheep Bitter; Butcombe Bitter; Theakston Best Bitter, Old Peculier; Worthington Bitter Ⓗ
Lovely, traditional, two-bar country pub with a no-smoking restaurant. Games in the pleasant garden include petanque; there is a footpath to the estuary opposite. Inch's cider is served..
♨ Q ❀ ◖ ▶ ⊞ ♣ ⌂ P ⌿

OLD DOWN

FOX INN
The Inner Down (1 mile off A38)
☎ (01454) 412507
12-3, 7-11; 12-4, 6-11 Sat; 12-4, 7-10.30 Sun
Draught Bass; Courage Best Bitter; Mole's Best Bitter; Theakston Best Bitter Ⓗ
Cosy, stone-built village pub. The picturesque terrace/garden has a children's play area and a boules pitch. Black Rat cider. Worth hunting out - though it can be hard to find.
♨ Q ❀ ◖ ▶ ♣ ⌂ P

PILLOWELL

SWAN
400 yds E of B4234
OS625065
☎ (01594) 562477
7-11; 12-3, 7-11 Sat; 12-3, 7-10.30 Sun
Ledbury Challenger; Thwaites Bitter; guest beer Ⓗ
Comfortable and friendly local with a knowledgeable landlord. Situated on a sharp bend near a disused railway line. Thatchers cider. Farmhouse cheeses a speciality. No children.
♨ Q ▲ ♣ ⌂ P ⊟

POPE'S HILL

GREYHOUND
On A4151, between Elton & Littledean OS686141
☎ (01452) 760344
11-3, 5.30-11; 12-3, 7-10.30 Sun
Freeminer Speculation, Stairway to Heaven; guest beer Ⓗ
Good value beer and food, a friendly welcome and brasses, beams and roaring fire make for a good country pub. Large garden, play area and family room, but children are not allowed in the bar. ♨ ⛺ ❀ ◖ ▶ ▲ ♣ P

PRESTBURY

ROYAL OAK
The Burgage
☎ (01242) 522344
11.30-2.30, 5-11; 12-3, 7-10.30 Sun
Archers Best Bitter; Boddingtons Bitter; Flowers IPA; Wadworth 6X Ⓗ
Attractive, two-bar, 16th-century inn, situated in what is reputedly known as the most haunted village in England. It retains a traditional atmosphere despite its proximity to Cheltenham. No food Fri and Sat eves or Sun lunch.
Q ❀ ◖ ▶ ⊞ ♣ P

PUCKLECHURCH

ROSE & CROWN
68 Parkfield Road
(¼ mile off Westerleigh road)
☎ (0117) 937 2351

12-2.30, 6.30-11; 12-2.30, 7-10.30 Sun
Draught Bass; Wadworth IPA, 6X; seasonal beers Ⓗ
Two-bar village local. Lounge has a formal area plus two additional rooms in the older part. Darts and cribbage played in the public bar. No-smoking restaurant (booking advised; no food Sun eve and all day Mon). Play area in garden. ♨ Q ❀ ◖ ▶ ⊞ ♣ P

QUEDGELEY

LITTLE THATCH HOTEL
141 Bristol Road (B4008)
☎ (01452) 720687
12-2.30 (not Sat), 6.45-11; 12-2.30, 6.45-11 Sun
Hook Norton Best Bitter; guest beers Ⓗ
Fine, 14th-century building with a modern hotel extension. Tradition has it that Anne Boleyn stayed here when Henry VIII visited, and the restaurant bears her name. Always tries to provide interesting beers. Note closed Sat lunchtime. ❀ ⇌ ◖ ▶ P

RUSPIDGE

NEW INN
On B4227 OS651119
☎ (01594) 824508
7-11; 12-11 Sat; 12-10.30 Sun
Wye Valley Bitter; guest beers Ⓗ
Comfortable village pub. Separate games area with an interesting selection of actitivies, including table skittles. No food, but friendly welcome.
♨ ❀ ▲ ♣ P

SAPPERTON

DANEWAY INN
West of village OS939034
☎ (01285) 760297
11-2.30, 6.30-11; 11-3 (5 summer), 6.30-11 Sat; 12-3 (5 summer), 7-10.30 Sun
Adnams Bitter; Wadworth IPA, 6X Ⓗ
Lovely old pub built in 1784 for canal workers near the now disused Sapperton Tunnel. The comfortable lounge is dominated by a magnificent fireplace with Dutch carving. Very friendly; popular with walkers. Large garden. No-smoking family room. Weston's Old Rosie cider.
♨ Q ⛺ ❀ ◖ ▶ ⊞ ▲ ♣ ⌂ P ⌿ ⊟

SHEEPSCOMBE

BUTCHERS ARMS
Signed off A46 and B4070
OS892104 ☎ (01452) 812113
11.30 (11 Sat & summer)-3.30, 6.30 (6 Sat & summer)-11; 12-4, 7 (6.30 summer)-10.30 Sun
Archers Best Bitter; Hook Norton Best Bitter; Uley Old Spot Ⓗ

Large, 17th-century pub whose carved sign of a pig tied to a butcher's leg is one of the most photographed in the country. Comfortable bar and restaurant and good menu. Children's certificate. Eve meals served till 9.30.

♨ Q ❀ ◖ ▶ ▲ ♣ ⌂ P ⌿

SLAD

WOOLPACK
On B4070
☎ (01452) 813429
12-3 (11-4 Sat), 6-11; 12-3.30, 7-10.30 Sun
Boddingtons Bitter; Fuller's London Pride; Uley Old Spot, Pig's Ear; Wadworth 6X Ⓗ
Three-bar, 16th-century Cotswold stone pub on the edge of the scenic Slad valley. A games room is on the lower level, with quoits and shove ha'penny. Wide range of food available. Made famous by the author the late Laurie Lee.
♨ Q ☙ ❀ ◖ ▶ ♣ ⌂ P ⌿

SLING

MINERS ARMS
On B4228 OS581079
☎ (01594) 836632
11.30 (11 Sat)-11; 12-3, 7-10.30 Sun
Freeminer Bitter, Speculation Ⓗ
Basic, no-frills pub which is the Freeminer Brewery tap. Large car park and camping area. Hot pies and Bulmers cider available.
♨ ❀ ▲ ♣ ⌂ P

STAPLE HILL

HUMPER'S OFF-LICENCE
26 Soundwell Road
☎ (0117) 956 5525
12-2, 5-10.30; 12-10.30 summer Sat; 12-2, 5-10.30; (12-10.30 summer) Sun
Ash Vine Hop & Glory; Draught Bass; Butcombe Bitter; Smiles Best; Wickwar BOB Ⓟ; **guest beers** Ⓖ
Five regular ales and ever-changing guests (three-four a week), all at attractive prices, make this off-licence a rare gem. Thatchers cider is served and there is an increasing range of bottled beers; large choice of polypins at Christmas.
⌂

STOW-ON-THE-WOLD

QUEENS HEAD
The Square
☎ (01451) 830563
11-2.30, 6-11; 12-3, 7-10.30 Sun
Donnington BB, SBA Ⓗ
Fine old Cotswold pub, deservedly popular with tourists and locals alike. No food Sun.
♨ Q ❀ ◖ ▶ ⊞

STROUD

GOLDEN FLEECE
Nelson Street ☎ (01453)764850
5.30 (11 Fri & Sat)-11; 12-3, 7-10.30 Sun
Draught Bass; Boddingtons Bitter; Greene King Abbot; Wadworth 6X Ⓗ
Stroud's jazz and blues pub; one main bar with two alcoves leading off. Customers may play records of their choice in the upper alcove. Musical instruments and jazz memorabilia line the walls. Live music Thu eve. Sun lunch served. ♨ ≕ ♣

SWINEFORD

SWAN INN
Bath Road (A431 between Bath and Bitton) ☎ (0117) 932 3101
11-2.30, 5-11; 12-2.30, 7-10.30 Sun
Draught Bass; Ⓖ **Butcombe Bitter; Courage Georges BA; guest beer** Ⓗ
Traditional village pub with main bar snug and no-smoking restaurant. Proud of ale quality, particularly their Bass on gravity behind the bar under cooling jackets. One cheap beer every Thu eve. Extensive menu (must book for Sun lunch; two sittings). No-smoking restaurant. ♨ ❀ ◖ ▶ P

INDEPENDENT BREWERIES

Berkeley:
Berkeley
Butcombe:
Bristol
Donnington:
Stow-on-the-Wold
Farmer's Arms:
Lower Apperley
Freeminer:
Coleford
Goff's:
Winchcombe
Uley:
Dursley
Wickwar:
Wickwar
Smiles:
Bristol
Ross:
Bristol
Stanway:
Cheltenham

TEWKESBURY

OLDE BEAR BEAR INNE
68 High Street ☎ (01684) 292202
11-11; 12-10.30 Sun
Greenalls Bitter, Ⓗ **Original; Smiles Best** Ⓖ; **Wadworth 6X** Ⓗ; **guest beers** Ⓖ
The oldest inn in the county, dating from 1308. Featuring rambling bar areas, one with leather work on the ceiling dated to 1600. Pleasant terrace patio overlooking the garden and the River Avon (moorings available). No food Sun eve. ❀ ◖ ▶ ▲ ♣

WHITE BEAR
Bredon Road (off north end of High St) ☎ (01684) 296614
11-11; 12-10.30 Sun
Wye Valley Hereford Bitter; guest beers Ⓗ
Lively, friendly, one-bar pub with convivial hosts and a very large dog. Cheapest pint in town.
❀ ▲ ♣ ⌂ P

ULEY

OLD CROWN
The Green ☎ (01453) 860502
11.30-2.30 (11-3 Sat), 7-11; 12-3, 7-10.30 Sun
Uley Bitter, Pig's Ear; guest beers Ⓗ
Single-bar Cotswold village pub built in 1638. It has recently been improved internally. It has an upstairs games room. Close to Uley Brewery and the Cotswold Way. Three guest beers. Reasonably priced, home-cooked food. En suite accommodation.
❀ ⇌ ◖ ▶ ♣ P

Try also: Kings Head, The Street (Wadworth)

WATERLEY BOTTOM

NEW INN
Signed from North Nibley (OS map recommended) OS758964
☎ (01453) 543659
12-2.30, 7-11; 12-3, 7-10.30 Sun
Cotleigh Tawny; Greene King Abbot; Smiles Best; Ⓗ **Theakston Old Peculier** Ⓖ
Large free house in a beautiful setting surrounded by steep hills. Large-scale map advised for first-time visitors. The house beer WB is a variation of Cotleigh Harrier SPA. CAMRA regional *Pub of the Year* 1993.
♨ ❀ ⇌ ◖ ▶ ⊞ ♣ ⌂ P

WHITMINSTER

OLD FORGE
Bristol Road (A38, near M5 jct 13) ☎ (01452) 741306
11-3, 5-11; 11-11 Sat; 12-4, 7-10.30 Sun
Exmoor Ale; Uley Bitter, Old Spot; guest beer Ⓗ

15th-century building known to have been a pub in the 18th century, but more recently a shop, garage and then a restaurant. the adjoining forge survived right until the 1930s. There are also book fairs and theme nights for charity. Occasional farmhouse cider. Q ✿ ◖ ▶ ▲ ♣ ⌣ P

WINCHCOMBE

BELL INN
Gretton Road (¹/₂ mile from centre) ☎ (01242) 602205

11-11; 12-10.30 Sun
**Donnington BB, SBA;
Eldridge Pope Royal Oak;
Greene King Abbot;
Shepherd Neame Spitfire;
guest beer** Ⓗ
Former Donnington pub, which is now a free house. A cosy local pub, it has darts and cribbage teams. Bar snacksare available lunchtimes.
♨ ✿ ⌂ ♣ ⌣ P

Try also: Olde White Lion, North Street (Free)

WOODCHESTER

RAM INN
Station Road (signed from A46)
☎ (01453) 873329
11-11; 12-10.30 Sun
**Archers Best Bitter;   John
Smith's Bitter; Uley Old Spot;
Woodforde's Wherry; guest
beers** Ⓗ
Stone-built, 17th-century pub. Four regular beers and two or three changing guests. One of the few outlets for Woodforde's in the area. ♨ Q ✿ ◖ ▶ ♣ P ⊔

Whitbread to close Cheltenham Brewery

Cheltenham Brewery, where Flower's is produced, is just one of those on the seemingly endless list of brewery closures.

The plans to close the brewery come ironically from a company which in 1991 held what it called a celebration of cask ales, a roadshow aimed at the licensed trade, which toured the company's sites, including Cheltenham. In his preamble to the brochure which accompanied the tour, Whitbread Beer Company MD Miles Templeman said, 'We at Whitbread are wholeheartedly committed to traditional cask ales, because they are the foundation stone on which we are built.'

Mr Miles went on to say, 'We believe in the regional nature of the market. We know that a great pint in Brighton isn't necessarily a great pint in Burnley. Secondly, we known that choice is very important and that today's consumers demand quality, variety and real, not spurious, product differentiation.'

Since then, rationalisation is exactly what destroys what Mr Miles's wise words salute.

CAMRA's local brewery liaison officer, Alan Stephens, accused Whitbread of abandoning the once popular Flower's brands in favour of Wadworth 6X, even though recent recipe changes had improved their quality immeasurably. He said Flower's had been deliberately neglected and that there were only three stockists left in the whole of Gloucestershire.

'Flower's has been starved of support all the way down the line,' he said. 'They're only interested in supporting Boddingtons and 6X.'

Seeing how lightly Cheltenham is being cast aside, it is hard to remember that 10 years ago it was seen as a brewery with a future, the strategic centre of the whole of the West and the South, a facility into which millions of pounds were being poured. Its capacity was repeatedly boosted throughout the mid and late 1980s until in 1988 it could produce 450,000 barrels a year, even on a single shift working.

Cheltenham Breweries began life in 1760. In 1958 it merged with Stroud Brewery to form West Country Breweries.

Flower's of Stratford was founded in 1831 and by the 1950s was an ambitious family firm with a new product - Flower's keg. It was Watney's which invented the keg version of bitter in 1930s, but Flower's ran out of financial road trying to build it up. That led to Flower's merging in 1954 with J.W. Green of Luton, on condition that brewing would continue at Stratford for at least 20 years. But a trading agreement with Whitbread was accompanied by a Whitbread shareholding, and in 1962 Flowers was bought out. West Country Breweries succumbed a year later, bringing over 1,200 pubs with it.

Cheltenham was chosen by Whitbread to be the main production, distribution, sales and administrative area for the region.

The Stratford brewery, which had wanted 20 years of life in 1954, didn't get it; it was closed in 1968. The evocation of Stratford, nevertheless, appeared on the pump clips right into the 1990s in the shape of a Tudor scribe with a distinct likeness to Mr Shakespeare. Those who thought they were buying a beer brewed by the banks of the Avon thought wrong. It was being brewed at Cheltenham in Whitbread's megaplant, which was largely used used to make ghost beers: beers with the names of breweries that had been closed years previously. This is the case with many brands sold nationally: they carry the name of once distinctive local breweries but they are about as genuine as a British flag made in Hong Kong – or a Chinese beer brewed in Burton.

It has to be said that many of the old breweries didn't exactly struggle; with antiquated plant and management practices they were starving for lack of investment and new ideas. Some owners were sitting on property portfolios which hadn't been revalued since before World War One. In most cases, mergers took place by invitation.

Once under the mega-brewer's banner plants are subject to closure depending on the corporate plan or the prevailing trend of the time.

Country Breweries of Cheltenham fell into the hands of Whitbread in 1962, and is one of the only two survivors of 21 regional breweries bought by Whitbread between 1961 and 1971. The other is Nimmo's of Castle Eden – which Whitbread also plans to close.

This article first appeared in What's Brewing, CAMRA's monthly newspaper. To read more about CAMRA's campaigns, join CAMRA and find out what's brewing every month.

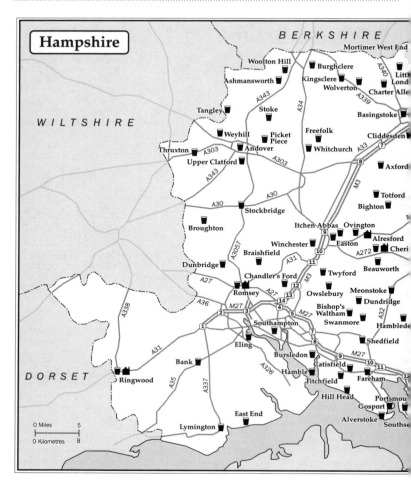

ALDERSHOT

DUKE OF YORK
248 Weybourne Road
☎ (01252) 321150
12-3, 5-11; 12-11 Fri & Sat; 12-4,
7-10.30 Sun
**Courage Best Bitter, Directors;
guest beers** Ⓗ
Large pub of five distinct drinking areas, including a pool room
and a restaurant where drinkers
can retreat to a no-smoking
atmosphere. Diners may also
eat in one of the smoking areas
away from the central bar. No
food Sun eve.
🛏 ℂ🄳 ⛫ ♿ P

RED LION
Ash Road
☎ (01252) 403503
12-11; 12-4, 7-10.30 Sun
Guest beers Ⓗ
Large, one-bar pub originally
used for prisoners en route to
prisons. Regular cask milds.
Local CAMRA *Pub of the Year*

1997 and '98. Lunch served Tue-
Fri. 🛏 ⊛ ℂ ⬱ P 🄳

Try Also: Garden Gate (Greene
King)

ALTON

FRENCH HORN
The Butts
☎ (01420) 83269
11-2.30, 5.30 (6 Sat)-11; 12-3,
7-10.30 Sun
**Ushers Best Bitter, Founders,
seasonal beers** Ⓗ
Some way out of the town but
worth the trip, a large pub with a
single bar. The chalkboard menu
is crammed with interesting
meals. Quiet pub despite its size,
with a refined yet friendly atmosphere. 🛏 Q ⛄ ⊛ ⛫ ℂ🄳 P 🄳

ALVERSTOKE

ALVERBANK
Stokes Bay Road
☎ (01705) 510005

11-11; 12-10.30 Sun
**Ringwood Best Bitter; guest
beers** Ⓗ
Country house hotel overlooking
Stokes Bay, once frequented by
Lily Langtry. Normally a quiet
relaxing atmosphere, but be prepared for wedding receptions
and other functions at weekends. Annual autumn beer
festivals.
🛏 ⊛ ⛫ ℂ🄳 🄰 P

ANDOVER

BLACKSMITHS ARMS
134 New Street
☎ (01264) 352881
11.30-2.30 (not Tue), 5-11; 12-3,
7-10.30 Sun
**Fuller's London Pride; Marston's
Bitter; Taylor Landlord; guest
beer** Ⓗ
Welcoming two-bar roadside
town pub with special enthusiasm for horse racing and cricket.
Live music Sat.
🛏 ⊛ ♣ P

stillage behind the bar. Limited parking. ♨ Q ❀ ◖ ▶ Å ♣ P

AXFORD

AXFORD ARMS
Farleigh Road
☎ (01256) 389492
12-2.30, 6-11; 12-3, 7-10.30 Sun
Greene King Abbot; Fuller's London Pride; guest beers Ⓗ
Pretty country hamlet pub; a real rural treasure. The garden looks out on to open farmland. See the *Last Supper* tapestry in the restaurant.
♨ Q ❀ ◖ ▶ ⌷ ♣ P

BANK (LYNDHURST)

OAK INN
Pinkney Lane (off A35, 1¼ miles SW of Lyndhurst) OS286072
☎ (01703) 282350
11.30-2.30 (3 Sat), 6-11; 12-3, 7-10.30 Sun
Ringwood Best Bitter; guest beers Ⓗ
Early 18th-century building in a New Forest hamlet, frequented by walkers. Its characterful, low-ceilinged, beamed bar is dimly lit and cosy, with much wood and many unusual artefacts. Most food is home made; there are at least three guest beers.
♨ ❀ ◖ ▶ ♣ P

BASINGSTOKE

BASINGSTOKE & NORTH HAMPSHIRE CRICKET CLUB
Mays Bounty, Fairfield Road
☎ (01256) 473646
12-3, 6-11; 12-3, 7-10.30 Sun
Fuller's London Pride, seasonal beers; guest beers Ⓗ
Members-only cricket and social club, situated on a green oasis donated by Basingstoke brewer John May in 1905. Card-carrying CAMRA members welcome (except in county cricket week in June); normal restrictions apply. CAMRA Wessex *Club of the Year* 1997.

QUEEN'S ARMS
Bunnian Place (near station)
☎ (01256) 465488
11-3, 5-11; 11-11 Fri & Sat; 12-3, 7-10.30 Sun
Courage Directors; Wadworth 6X; guest beers Ⓗ
Neat, Victorian pub spared from destruction by redevelopers. It enjoys trade from the adjoining tower block offices and its regulars too. Some call it The Glue Pot - hard to get out of.
❀ ◖ ⌷ ⇌

Try also: Bounty, County Rd (Ushers)

BEAUWORTH

MILBURYS
S of A272, 1 mile beyond Beauworth hamlet OS570246
☎ (01962) 771248
10.30-2.30, 6-11; 12-3.30, 7-10.30 Sun
Boddingtons Bitter; Cheriton Diggers Gold; Hampshire Pendragon; Itchen Valley Godfathers Ⓗ
Remote, 18th-century inn where flagstones and beams abound. A massive treadmill, 250-years-old, with a 300ft well features in one bar. The house beer is blended by Hampshire brewery. Extensive food range. Opens at 9.30 on Sundays for brunch.
♨ Q ⛟ ❀ ⇌ ◖ ▶ Å ♣ P

BENTWORTH

SUN INN
Off A339
☎ (01420) 562338
12-3, 6-11; 12-10.30 Sun
Bunces Pigswill; Cheriton Pots Ale; Courage Best Bitter; Ringwood Best Bitter; guest beers Ⓗ
Picturesque inn dating from the 17th century in a small village, serving from a good home-cooked menu. The local micros are well represented here. The house beer is by Hampshire Brewery.
♨ Q ⛟ ❀ ◖ ▶ P

BIGHTON

THREE HORSESHOES
Off A31/B3046) OS616344
☎ (01962) 732859
11-2.30 (not Mon), 6-11; 12-3, 7-10.30 Sun
Gale's Butser, Winter Brew, HSB Ⓗ
Delightful rural pub with two bars; a quiet, relaxing, lounge and a livelier bar displaying country crafts. A pub since 1615 but can cater for wheelchair users who should use rear entrance. Good portions of simple pub food (not served Mon). Handy for the Mid Hants Railway.
♨ Q ❀ ◖ ⌷ ♿ Å ♣ P

BISHOP'S WALTHAM

BUNCH OF GRAPES
St Peter's Street
☎ (01489) 892935
10-2, 6-11; 12-2, 7-10.30 Sun
Courage Best Bitter; Ushers Best Bitter, seasonal beers Ⓗ Ⓖ
This small, unspoilt village pub has been run by the same family for 85 years, but do not expect historic prices as this is a pub with no food income. Winner of the 1997 *Bishop's Waltham in Bloom* award. Q ❀ ♣

LAMB INN
21 Winchester Street (near police station)
☎ (01264) 323961
11-3, 6 (5 Fri, 7 Sat)-11; 12-3, 7-10.30 Sun
Wadworth IPA, 6X, seasonal beers; guest beers Ⓗ
Long, three-beer pub: the lounge is particularly small and cosy with cheaper beer. The garden and patio are popular in summer.
♨ Q ❀ ◖ ♣

ASHMANSWORTH

PLOUGH
☎ (01635) 253047
12-2.30 (not Tue, 12-3 Sat), 6-11 (closed Mon, except bank hols); 12-3, 7-10.30 Sun
Archers Village, Best Bitter, Golden; guest beers Ⓖ
Hampshire's highest pub (700 ft above sea level): a traditional, unspoilt village house, very welcoming and good walking country close to Highclere Castle. The casks are well-cooled and are on

BRAISHFIELD

Dog & Crook
Crook Hill
☎ (01794) 368530
11-3, 6-11; 12-3, 7-10.30 Sun
Draught Bass; Brakspear Bitter; Flowers Original; guest beer Ⓗ
There has been a pub here for 500 years but most of the present building now dates from 1955 after a fire gutted the old house. A comfortable pub with strong food emphasis (no-smoking dining area); the outside patio is heated for all-year use.
❀ ◑ ▶ ♣ P

Newport Inn
Newport Lane
☎ (01794) 368225
10-2.30, 6-11; 12-2.30, 7-10.30 Sun
Gales Butser, GB, Winter Brew, HSB Ⓗ
Little gem in a time-warp - worth seeking out. The doorstep sandwiches and ploughmans are famous countywide. Communal singing around the piano on Sat eve (be ready to join in). Large garden. ❀ Q ❀ ◑ ♣ P

BROUGHTON

Tally Ho!
High Street
☎ (01794) 301280
12-3, 6-11; 12-3, 7-10.30 Sun
Cheriton Pots Ale; Ringwood True Glory; guest beer Ⓗ
Fine Georgian building, once the village doctor's home; now a comfortable free house. A conversationalists' pub, offering a good range of food (no eve meals Tue). A worthwhile stop on the Clarendon Way long distance path. ❀ Q ❀ ◑ ▶ ⊞ ♣

BURGHCLERE

Queen
Harts Lane (1 mile E of A34)
☎ (01635) 278350
11-3, 6-11; 12-3, 7-10.30 Sun
Adnams Bitter, Broadside; Ansell's BB Ⓗ
Roomy, single-bar, village local, well worth the short diversion from the nearby A34 (south end of Newbury bypass). No food Sun. Q ❀ ◑ ♣ P

BURSLEDON

Linden tree
School Road (off A27/A3025)
☎ (01703) 402356
11-2.30 (3 Sat), 6-11; 11-11 Fri; 12-3, 7-10.30 Sun
Draught Bass; Wadworth IPA, 6X, Farmers Glory (summer)**, Old Timer** Ⓗ
Comfortable, friendly, one-bar pub with no obtrusive gaming machines. A pergola and children's play area make it ideal for summer, while a real log fire welcomes the winter visitor. High quality home-cooked lunches (not served Sun).
❀ Q ❀ ◑ ♣ P

CATISFIELD

Limes
34 Catisfield Lane (500 yds from A27) ☎ (01329) 842926
12-2.30, 5-11; 12-3, 7-11 Sat; 12-3, 7-10.30 Sun
Gales HSB; Gibbs Mew Salisbury, Ⓗ **Bishops Tipple;** Ⓖ **Ringwood Fortyniner, Old Thumper** Ⓗ
Large Victorian building converted to a pub: two bars and a function room staging occasional live music. Petanque area in the garden. Good value, home-cooked food. Q ❀ ◑ ▶ ⊞ ♣ P

CHALTON

Red Lion
OS731160
☎ (01705) 592246
11-3, 6-11; 12-3, 7-10.30 Sun
Gale's Butser, GB, HSB, seasonal beers; guest beer Ⓗ
Considered the oldest pub in Hampshire, beginning life as a workshop during the building of the local church, it became a pub in 1503. Its thatched roof, white daub and wood construction high up in the South Downs make it one of the most idyllic pubs in the area. ❀ Q ❀ ◑ ▶ ⊞ P

CHANDLERS FORD

Cleveland Bay
1 Pilgrims Close
☎ (01703) 269814
11-11; 12-10.30 Sun
Wadworth IPA, 6X, seasonal beers; Ⓗ **guest beers** Ⓗ
Typical 1980s pub with a large, L-shaped, marble-topped bar with various drinking areas branching off. The large garden has a children's play area. Good value, home-cooked daily specials. It has occasional beer festivals. ❀ ⌛ ❀ ◑ ▶ ♿ P ✄

CHARTER ALLEY

White Hart
White Hart Lane (1 mile W of A340)
☎ (01256) 850048
12-2.30 (3 Sat), 2-11; 12-3, 7-10.30 Sun
Greene King Abbot; Harveys BB; Morrells Mild, Bitter, Varsity; guest beer Ⓗ
Large village pub with a skittle alley and a restaurant; the front bar has a large wood-burning stove. The ever-changing beer range makes this a very popular choice. Cider in summer.
❀ Q ❀ ◑ ▶ ⊞ ♿ ♣ ⌂ P ⊟

CHERITON

Flower Pots Inn
W of B3046, at south of village
☎ (01962) 771318
12-2.30, 6-11; 12-3, 7-10.30 Sun
Cheriton Pots Ale, Best Bitter, Diggers Gold Ⓖ
Charming village local. Intimate bars, recently seamlessly extended and an attractive garden provide the ideal location for sampling the beers produced here. Good value food (no meals Sun eve).
❀ Q ❀ ⇔ ◑ ▶ ⊞ ⚑ ♣ ⌂ P

CLIDDESDEN

Jolly Farmer
Farleigh Road (B3046, 1 mile SW of A339) ☎ (01256) 473073
12-3, 5.30-11; 12-11 Sat; 12-10.30 Sun
Ushers Best Bitter, seasonal beers Ⓗ
Listed village local, originally three cottages, in a peaceful location. The large public bar features a circular pool table; note the cartoon dated 1907 picturing contemporary customers; also a small snug. Balloon rides take off from the large garden. No food Sun eve. Q ⌛ ❀ ◑ ▶ ⚑ ♣ P

COSHAM

Churchillian
Widley Walk, Portsdown Hill Road (B2150, near Fort Widley)
☎ (01705) 371803
11-11; 12-10.30 Sun
Draught Bass; Gibbs Mew Salisbury, Wiltshire, Bishop's Tiple Ⓗ
Large, single bar on top of Portsdown Hill with superb views of Portsmouth, Gosport, Hayling Island, the Isle of Wight and the New Forest. Children admitted for meals. ❀ ❀ ◑ ▶ P

COVE

Old Courthouse
80 Cove Road (off A325)
☎ (01252) 543031
11-11; 12-10.30 Sun
Draught Bass; Fuller's London Pride, ESB; Hancock's HB; Highgate Dark; Worthington Bitter; guest beer Ⓗ
Attractive, one-bar suburban pub offering a good lunch menu with daily specials (no food Sun).
❀ ◑ ♿ ⇌ (Farnborough) ♣ P

Plough & Horses
90 Fleet Rd ☎ (01252) 545199
11-11; 12-10.30 Sun
Ansells Mild; Friary Meux BB; Ind Coope Burton Ale; Marston's Pedigree; Tetley Bitter; guest beer Ⓗ
Traditional Victorian pub that caters for all tastes. The 'Big Steak' menu plus daily specials

represent good quality and value. Still maintains a village pub atmosphere. ❀ ◐ ◗ ♿ ♣ P

Thatched Cottage
122 Prospect Road
☎ (01252) 543118
11.30-11; 12-10.30 Sun
Courage Best Bitter; Greene King Abbot; Wadworth 6X; Webster's Green Label; guest beers H
Grade II listed thatched cottage with oak beams where a quiet lounge bar contrasts with a music bar which has quizzes, Sky TV and discos (Sat). Very big garden. Home-cooked specials feature on a good value menu.
Q ❀ ◐ ◗ ⇌ P

DUNBRIDGE

Mill Arms
Barley Hill (B3084, by station)
☎ (01794) 340401
11 (12 winter)-3, 6-11; 12-3, 7-10.30 Sun
Beer range varies H
18th-century ex-coaching inn with many rooms including a fine skittle alley. Popular with ramblers and anglers, it holds many summer events. House beers, by Hampshire and Itchen Valley complement the guest beers. Cider in summer.
♨ Q ♞ ❀ ⛟ ◐ ◗ ⛺ ⇌ ♣ ⌓ P

DUNDRIDGE

Hampshire Bowman
Dundridge Lane (1½ miles off B3035) OS578185
☎ (01489) 892940
11-2.30 (3 Sat, 12-2 Mon), 6-11; 12-3, 7-10.30 Sun
Archers Village, Golden; Ringwood Fortyniner; guest beers G
This brick-floored, cosy welcoming pub is home of the Portuguese Sardine Racing Club. Excellent menu (no food Sun eve or Mon). Dogs welcome and usually present. Worth the trip up the lane. ♨ Q ❀ ◐ ◗ ⛺ P

EAST END (LYMINGTON)

East End Arms
Main Road (3 miles E of IoW ferry) OS362968
☎ (01590) 626223
11.30-3, 6-11; 12-3, 7-10.30 Sun
Ringwood Best Bitter, H **Fortyniner; guest beers** G
Turn of the century pub in a New Forest village off the tourist trail: two welcoming bars. The home-made food features local produce (no meals Sun eve or Mon). Children's certificate until 8pm. Thatchers cider in summer. No no-smoking area but no-smoking eves Tue and Thu.
♨ ❀ ◐ ◗ ⊟ ♣ ⌓ P

EASTON

Cricketers Inn
Off B3047
☎ (01962) 779353
11.30-3, 6-11; 12-3, 7-10.30 Sun
Otter Ale; Ringwood Best Bitter; guest beers H
Traditional local in the country, but only two miles from Winchester. The L-shaped bar has a charming fireplace and a cricketing theme. The changing range of beers features small brewers; cider in summer. Good range of home-cooked food.
♨ Q ❀ ⛟ ◐ ◗ ♣ ⌓ P

ELING

King Rufus
Eling Hill OS368121
☎ (01703) 868899
11.30-2.30, 6.30-11; 12-3, 7-10.30 Sun
Gale's HSB; Ringwood Best Bitter; Theakston Old Peculier; guest beer H
Attractive 19th-century pub on the edge of the village, near the country's only working tide mill. One bar and a small restaurant, decorated in a welcoming cottage style with Victorian embellishments. No food Sun eve.
❀ ◐ ◗ P

EMSWORTH

Coal Exchange
21 South Street
☎ (01243) 375866
10.30-3, 5.30-11; 10.30-11 Sat; 12-10.30 Sun
Gales Butser, GB, HSB, seasonal beers; guest beers H
Built in the 1680s as a pork butchery and ale house, the name derives from its use for exchanging coal delivered by sea with local produce. Emsworth harbour, popular with sailors, is nearby.
♨ ❀ ◐

FAREHAM

White Horse
44 North Wallington (½ mile from Delme roundabout)
☎ (01329) 235197
11-3, 5-11; 11-11 Fri & Sat; 12-3, 7-10.30 Sun
Draught Bass; Hop Back Summer Lightning; guest beers G
Small, two-bar village local with a patio garden by the River Wallington, accessible by footbridge from the High Street. Home-cooked fish and chips available Fri and Sat eves.
♨ Q ❀ ◐ ⊟ ♣

Try also: Bird in Hand, Gosport Rd (Enterprise Inns)

FARNBOROUGH

Prince of Wales
184 Rectory Road
☎ (01252) 545578
11.30-2.30, 5.30-11; 12-3.30, 7-10.30 Sun
Badger Dorset Best, Tanglefoot; Fuller's London Pride; Hogs Back TEA; Ringwood True Glory; guest beers H
The best free house for miles, in which the good beer range, including unusual guests, is matched by the efficient and friendly service. Always one beer at £1.50. The decor and atmosphere is just right for enjoyable drinking. Good value lunches.
Q ❀ ◐ ⇌ (North) P

FREEFOLK

Watership Down
Off B3400
☎ (01256) 892254
11.30-3, 6-11; 12-3.30, 7-10.30 Sun
Archers Best Bitter; Brakspear Bitter; guest beers H
Early 19th-century one bar house, known as the 'Jerry', where serving good food doesn't detract from a friendly pub atmosphere. The large garden has children's amusements and rabbits; inside are some playable penny arcade machines. Always a mild as one of three guest beers.
♨ ❀ ◐ ◗ ♣ P ⛉

FROXFIELD

Trooper
Alton Road OS727273
☎ (01730) 827923
11.30-3 (3.30 Sat), 5.45-11; 12-4, 7-10.30 Sun
Draught Bass; Marston's Pedigree; Ringwood Best Bitter, Fortyniner; guest beers H
Remote, genuine free house, three miles from Petersfield affording a friendly atmosphere; well worth finding. An extensive food menu is available at all times. ♨ Q ❀ ◐ ◗ P

GOSPORT

Queens Hotel
143 Queens Road
☎ (01705) 525518
11.30-2.20, 7-11; 11.30-11 Sat; 12-3, 7-10.30 Sun
Archers Village; Black Sheep Special; Ringwood Fortyniner; guest beers H
Award-winning pub, hidden away in the back streets, but well worth seeking out. There are three drinking areas, the focal point being an old open fire with an elegant, carved wood surround. Local CAMRA *Pub of the Year* 1997. Real cider in summer.
♨ ♣ ⌓

HAMBLE

KING & QUEEN
High Street
☎ (01703) 454247
11-11; 12-10.30 Sun
Boddingtons Bitter; Fuller's London Pride; Wadworth 6X; guest beer H
Unpretentious pub used by locals and mariners, with a laundry for visiting yacht crews. Book for Sun lunch. The eve meals are served in the dining room (from 7pm Tue-Sat). Brakspear Bitter is sold under a house name: 'Totally Pissed'. ❀ ◖ ▶ P

HAMBLEDON

BAT & BALL
Hyden Farm Lane (2¹/₂ miles from village on Clanfield road)
OS677167
☎ (01705) 632692
11.30 (12 Sat)-3, 6-11 (12-11 summer Sat); 12-3.30, 7-10.30 (12-10.30 summer) Sun
Gale's Best Bitter, HSB; guest beer H
Old pub, high up on Broadhalfpenny Down, known as the cradle of cricket and now restored as a museum of the game. Open all day when there is a match on at the cricket ground.
❀ Q ❀ ◖ ▶ ✚ P

NEW INN
West Street
☎ (01705) 632466
12-2.30, 7-11; 12-2.30, 7-10.30 Sun
Ballard's Trotton; Ringwood True Glory, Fortyniner, Old Thumper H
Friendly village pub where the art of conversation has not been lost, a genuine free house, easy to miss, due to the lack of any pub signs. ❀ Q ❀ ⊞ ✚ P

HARTLEY WINTNEY

WAGGON & HORSES
High Street (A30)
☎ (01252) 842119
11-11; 12-3, 7-10.30 Sun
Courage Best Bitter; Gale's HSB; guest beer H
Friendly, village-centre pub, with a cosy saloon, a lively public bar and always an imaginative guest beer. ❀ ❀ ◖ ⊞ ✚

HAVANT

OLD HOUSE AT HOME
2 South St ☎ (01705) 483464
11-11; 12-10.30 Sun
Gale's Butser, GB, HSB, seasonal beers; guest beers H
Reputedly the oldest dwelling in Havant, one of two buildings to survive the fire in 1760. Its interesting features include two beams in the lounge which are

thought to have been recovered from the Spanish Armada. Live music Sat eve. ❀ ❀ ◖ ⊞ ≋

Try also: Parchment Makers, 1 Park Rd North (Wetherspoons)

HAWKLEY

HAWKLEY INN
Pococks Lane OS747292
☎ (01730) 827205
12-2.30 (3 Sat), 6-11; 12-3, 7-10.30 Sun
Beer range varies H
Popular free house in a village well off the beaten track, attracting walkers. Furnished in a very individual style (note the moose head), it offers six ales from independent breweries. The landlord's own cider is occasionally available. ❀ Q ❀ ◖ ▶ ✁

HILL HEAD

OSBORNE VIEW
67 Hill Head Road
☎ (01329) 664623
11-11; 12-10.30 Sun
Badger IPA, Dorset Best, Tanglefoot; Gribble Reg's Tipple, Blackadder II H
Large, open-plan bar with panoramic views of the Solent. Extended in May 1997 to be on three levels, with steps down to the garden and beach. Although the emphasis is on food, there is plenty of room for drinkers. ❀ ❀ ◖ ▶ ▲ P ✁

HORNDEAN

SHIP & BELL
6 London Road
☎ (01705) 592107
10.30-11; 12-10.30 Sun
Gale's Butser, GB, IPA, HSB, seasonal beers; guest beer H
Gale's brewery tap, it was the original brewery before the present one was built alongside. The well in the public bar was recently uncovered for viewing. Opens for breakfast 7.15 (8.15 weekends). No food Sun eve.
Q ❀ ◖ ▶ ⊞ P

ITCHEN ABBAS

TROUT INN
Main Road (B3047)
☎ (01962) 779537
11-3, 6-11; 12-3, 7-10.30 Sun
Marston's Bitter, Pedigree, Owd Rodger, HBC H
Smart country inn with two bars and a dining room, situated in the lovely Itchen Valley on a classic chalk river. The two bars are adorned with breweriana and local views, the bar having a jovial atmosphere. Quality accommodation and food. Children's play area in the garden. ❀ Q ❀ ❀ ◖ ▶ ⊞ ✚ P

KINGSCLERE

SWAN
Swan Street
☎ (01635) 298314
11-3, 5.30-11; 12-3, 7-10.30 Sun
Tetley Bitter; Theakston XB; guest beers H
Listed hotel in the village centre. A mile from the famed Watership Down where walkers and kite flyers are attracted by stunning views and fresh air. Limited parking. ❀ Q ❀ ◖ ▶ ✚

LANGSTONE

SHIP
Langstone Road
☎ (01705) 471719
11-11; 12-10.30 Sun
Gale's Butser, GB, HSB, seasonal beers; guest beers H
Large, one-bar pub on the shore of Langstone Harbour, a popular sailing venue. The now-closed Hayling Island branch line passed close by. Opposite the pub is the berth of the also long-gone Isle of Wight train ferry. The menu specialises in fish dishes. ❀ ❀ ❀ ◖ ▶ ❀ P ✁

LASHAM

ROYAL OAK
Off A339
☎ (01256) 381213
11-3, 6-11; 12-3, 7-10.30 Sun
Fuller's London Pride; Hogs Back TEA; Ringwood Best Bitter; guest beers H
Unspoilt pub next to the church in a pretty village. A premier gliding airfield is nearby. The house beer is brewed by Beckett's.
❀ Q ❀ ◖ ▶ ✚ P

Try also: Fox, Ellisfield (Free)

LISS

BLUEBELL
Farnham Road (A325)
☎ (01730) 892107
11.30-3.30, 5-11; 11.30-11 Sat; 12-10.30 Sun
Flowers IPA; Fuller's London Pride; Young's Special; guest beers H
Set in picturesque countryside, this house is run by a friendly landlord whose enthusiasm for his beers is unsurpassable and whose philosophy is affordable excellence. No food Sun eve.
❀ ❀ ◖ ▶ ❀ ≋ P ✁

LITTLE LONDON

PLOUGH INN
Silchester Road (1 mile E of A340)
☎ (01256) 850628
12-2.30, 6-11; 12-3, 6-10.30 Sun
Ringwood Best Bitter, True Glory; guest beers H

Small country pub, very friendly and stocking a good range of changing beers (some are served from false wooden casks). Runs its own Internet pages. Bar billiards is popular. No food Sun.
🏰 Q 🍴 ⊛ ◑ ♣ P

LYMINGTON (PENNINGTON)

MUSKETEER
26 North St
☎ (01590) 676527
11.30-2.30 (3.30 Sat), 5.30-11; 12-3, 7-10.30 Sun
Brakspear Bitter; Ringwood Best Bitter, Fortyniner; guest beer Ⓗ
Traditional, comfortable, one-bar local in the village centre. An excellent menu offers home-cooked specials (no food Sun). A converted Edwardian coach house is available on a weekly let. In this *Guide* for 21 years.
🐶 ⊛ ◑ ♣ P

MEDSTEAD

CASTLE OF COMFORT
Castle Street (2 miles N of A31 at Four Marks) OS655373
☎ (01420) 562112
11-2.30 (3 Sat), 6-11; 12-3, 7-10.30 Sun
Ushers Best Bitter, Founders, seasonal beers Ⓗ
Attractive, unspoilt, 17th-century village local, split into a comfortable lounge and a refurbished public bar. The regulars make you welcome. Steam trains run on the nearby Watercress Line. Lunchtime snacks available.
🏰 Q ⊛ ⊕ ♣ P ⊟

MEONSTOKE

BUCKS HEAD
Bucks Head Hill
☎ (01489) 877313
11-3, 6-11; 11-11 Sat; 12-10.30 Sun
Morland Tanners Jack, Old Speckled Hen; Ruddles Best Bitter; Wells Bombardier Ⓗ
17th-century, former coaching inn alongside the River Meon. Two traditional bars with log fires. The extensive menu features game as a speciality; no meals Mon eve.
🏰 Q ⊛ ← ◑ ▶ ⊕ ♣ P

MORTIMER WEST END

TURNERS ARMS
West End Road
☎ (0118) 933 2961
11.30-2.30 (3 Sat), 6-11; 12-3, 7-10.30 Sun
Brakspear Bitter, Special, seasonal beers Ⓗ
A good local, just outside the village: one bar and a restaurant. It has been extended to provide more bar space with a french window overlooking the garden.

A changing menu of interesting bar snacks is available; also regular speciality food eves.
🏰 Q ⊛ ◑ ▶ P

NORTH CAMP

OLD FORD
Lynchford Road
☎ (01252) 544840
11-11; 12-10.30 (12-4, 7-10.30 Jan-Mar) Sun
Courage Best Bitter; Hogs Back TEA; Theakston Best Bitter; guest beers Ⓗ
Impressive, 19th-century railway hostelry, untainted by fads or themes. The single long bar has a (family) dining room on one side (no food Sun eve) and a pool/skittles room at the rear. The large, safe, riverside garden with play area and pets corner is justly popular.
🐶 ⊛ ◑ ▶ ← ♣ P

NORTH WARNBOROUGH

LORD DERBY
Bartley Heath (A287, 1 mile off M3, jct 5)
☎ (01256) 702283
12-3, 6-11; 12-3, 7-10.30 Sun
Fuller's London Pride; guest beers Ⓗ
Large, traditional pub used for meetings by local classic car clubs. ⊛ ◑ ▶ ⊟ ♣ P

OAKHANGER

RED LION
Off B3004
☎ (01420) 472232
11-3, 6-11; 12-3, 7-10.30 Sun
Courage Best Bitter, Directors; FFF Moondance Ⓗ
The ideal country pub where the landlord has been supporting his local breweries for many years and serves their beers in tip-top condition. The Moondance sold here is probably the best outside the brewery. Do eat there, the experience is sublime.
🏰 Q ⊛ ◑ ▶ P

OVINGTON

BUSH INN
N of A31, 1 mile W of Alresford OS561319
☎ (01962) 732764
11-2.30 (3 Sat), 6-11; 12-3, 6-10.30 Sun
Wadworth IPA, 6X, Farmers Glory, Old Timer; guest beer Ⓗ
Ancient inn - lots of beams, flagstones, nooks and crannies, cluttered with bric-à-brac. The large garden runs by the Itchen. Extensive, fairly upmarket, home-made food. Scrabble and other board games on request.
🏰 Q 🐶 ⊛ ◑ ▶ P

OWSLEBURY

SHIP INN
Off B2177, 1½ miles N of Marwell Zoo
☎ (01962) 777358
11-3, 6-11 (11-11 summer Sat); 12-10.30 Sun
Bateman Mild; Marston's Bitter, Pedigree, HBC Ⓗ
Lively, busy, two-bar country inn: the comfortable main bar has nautical and cricketing memorabilia; a second bar has a dining area serving good, home-cooked food. A large garden boasts a pond, a children's play area, animals and a bowling green.
🏰 Q ⊛ ◑ ▶ ♣ P

PICKET PIECE

WYKE DOWN COUNTRY PUB
Wyke Down (from A303 follow brown campsite signs)
☎ (01264) 352048
12-3, 6-11; 12-3, 7-10.30 Sun
Ringwood True Glory; guest beer Ⓗ
Large, multi-roomed conversion of an early 18th-century barn. It forms part of a family-run leisure park, including a touring camping and caravan site and a golf driving range. Friendly, comfortable atmosphere. The pub name is pronounced 'wick'.
🏰 Q 🐶 ⊛ ◑ ▶ ⅍ ▲ ♣ P ⊟

PORTSMOUTH

CONNAUGHT ARMS
119 Guildford Road, Fratton
☎ (01705) 646455
11.30-2.30, 6-11; 11.30-11 Fri & Sat; 12-4, 7-10.30 Sun
Fuller's London Pride; Wadworth 6X; guest beers Ⓗ
Gem of a pub of attractive Brewer's Tudor design on a corner site, justly famed as Portsmouth's pastie pub. Portsmouth and South East Hampshire CAMRA *Pub of the Year*. ⊛ ◑ ← (Fratton) ♣ ⌣

DIAMOND
70 King Street, Southsea
☎ (01705) 822071
11.30-3, 7-11; 12-3, 7-10.30 Sun
Wadworth IPA, 6X, seasonal beers; guest beers Ⓗ
Friendly corner local favoured by regulars, with a warm welcome for visitors. There is a quiet area to one side of the bar which usually offers one beer at a special low price.
⊛ ◑ ← (Portsmouth and Southsea) ♣

ELDON ARMS
15-17 Eldon Street, Southsea
☎ (01705) 851778
11.30-2.30 (3 Sat), 5 (6 Sat)-11; 11.30-11 Fri; 12-3, 7-10.30 Sun

Draught Bass; Eldridge Pope
Hardy Country, Royal Oak; guest
beers Ⓗ
The tiled facade is unusual for an
Eldridge Pope pub, although the
old Portsmouth and Brighton
United Brewery's tiled frontages
are numerous in the city. The
multi-level single bar features
games and bric-à-brac.
⊛ ◖ ➤ ≠ (Portsmouth and
Southsea) ♣ ⌣

FIFTH HAMPSHIRE
VOLUNTEER ARMS
74 Albert Road, Southsea (near
Kings Theatre) ☎ (01705) 827161
12-11; 12-10.30 Sun
Gale's GB, IPA, HSB, seasonal
beers; guest beers Ⓗ
Two-bar local in an area of
Southsea with plenty of places to
eat. A lively public bar with darts,
TV and rock music. The quiet
lounge displays military memorabilia. It boasts probably the best
ladies loo in the city. Q ⊞ ♣

FLEET & FIRKIN
1 King Henry 1st Street (opp
Guildhall) ☎ (01705) 864242
11-11; 12-10.30 Sun
Firkin Admir Ale, Fleet, Jolly
Roger, Dogbolter, seasonal
beers Ⓗ
An outstanding conversion by
Firkin of a derelict, ex-fire station. This is a non-brewing Firkin;
however the beer quality is
excellent due to the hard work of
the staff who are invariably
cheerful. Always crowded as next
to the university.
⊛ ◖ ➤ ⊞ ♿ ≠ (Portsmouth
and Southsea) ♣ P

FLORIST
324 Fratton Road, Fratton
☎ (01705) 820289
11-2.30, 6-11; 11-11 Sat;
12-10.30 Sun
Wadworth IPA, 6X, seasonal
beers Ⓗ
Attractive corner local with a
Brewer's Tudor exterior and a
witch's hat tower. The rear
lounge, which has the original
stained glass window preserved,
is quiet, whilst the public bar has
darts, pool, jukebox and TV.
⊞ ≠ (Fratton) ♣

FUZZ & FIRKIN
2 Albert Road, Southsea
☎ (01705) 294353
11-11; 12-10.30 Sun
Firkin BBB, Fuzz Bitter,
Truncheon Stout, Dogbolter,
seasonal beers Ⓗ
Standard Firkin conversion of the
old Southsea police station. The
BBB and Truncheon Stout are
brewed here and are not from the
standard Firkin brew book. Caters
for a young market, but the service and beer are second-to-none,
however busy .⊛ ◖ ➤ ♿ ♣ ⌣

GRAHAM ARMS
51 George Street, Buckland
☎ (01705) 646886
12-3, 5-11; 12-11 Fri; 11-11 Sat;
12-4, 7-10.30 Sun
Badger Tanglefoot; Wadworth
6X Ⓗ
Attractive, street-corner house
with a large garden. Although a
single bar, the former lounge is
still a quiet nook whilst the public
side boasts wonderful antique
crystal spirit optics over the bar-
back. ⊛ ♣

OLD OYSTER HOUSE
291 Locksway Road, Milton,
Southsea (off A288, near university's Langstone site)
☎ (01705) 827456
12-11; 12-10.30 Sun
Fuller's London Pride; Brewery
on Sea Spinnaker; guest beers Ⓗ
Large, single bar based around a
nautical theme offering reduced
prices on selected beers during
the week: one scrumpy always
available. The pub is by the only
remaining section of the Portsea
Canal. ⊛ ♣ ⌣

RED WHITE & BLUE
150 Fawcett Road, Southsea
☎ (01705) 780013
11-11; 12-10.30 Sun
Gale's Butser, GB, IPA, HSB,
seasonal beers Ⓗ
Compact local which can get
crowded on darts, dominoes, and
occasional live music eves. The
large range of games includes
Uckers. Canada Day is celebrated
on the nearest Saturday to 1 July
with Canadian breakfasts and
moose milk.
≠ (Fratton) ♣

RMA TAVERN
58 Cromwell Road, Eastney,
Southsea (opp old Royal Marine
barracks entrance)
☎ (01705) 820896
10.30-11; 12-10.30 Sun
Gale's Butser, HSB, seasonal
beers; guest beers Ⓗ
Surprisingly spacious corner pub
with two main bars, a patio and a
skittle alley. An extensive range
of malt whisky is available in the
lounge. Numerous games played;
live blues music Thu eve.
Children's certificate.
Q ⊛ ◖ ➤ ⊞ ▲ ♣ ⌣

SIR LOYNE OF BEEFE
152 Highland Road, Eastney,
Southsea
☎ (01705) 820115
11-11; 12-6, 7.30-10.30 Sun
Draught Bass; Hop Back
Summer Lightning; Ringwood
Old Thumper; guest beers Ⓗ
The first in a growing chain of
'SLOBS', extending from
Portsmouth to Brighton. A small
lounge bar and larger public bar
are complemented by a newly

opened bistro and wine bar at
the rear. Up to five guest beers
available at any one time.
Q ◖ ⊞ ▲ ♣

SIR ROBERT PEEL
Astley Street, Southsea
☎ (01705) 345708
11.45-3.30 (4.30 Sat), 7-11;
12-4.30, 7-10.30 Sun
Bateman XB; Cheriton Pots Ale;
Ringwood Best Bitter, Old
Thumper; guest beers Ⓗ
1960s estate pub, a friendly, genuine free house - don't be
deterred by its location.
Inexpensive, wholesome bar
meals (not served Sun) and six
ales available. A haven for
golfers, line dancing, darts players and malt whisky fanatics.
◖ ⊞ ♿ ≠ (Portsmouth and
Southsea) ♣ ⌣ P

WETHERSPOONS
2 Guildhall Walk (opp Guildhall)
☎ (01705) 295112
11-11; 12-10.30 Sun
Courage Directors; Hop Back
Summer Lightning; Ringwood
Fortyniner; Theakston Best
Bitter, XB; guest beers Ⓗ
One bar, excellently converted
from the old Portsmouth and
Gosport gas company offices;
now a friendly, pleasant venue to
eat and drink (good selection of
wines of the world available).
The staff are always pleasant,
even when the pub is crowded.
Q ◖ ➤ ♿ ≠ (Portsmouth and
Southsea) ⌣ ⊁ ⊟

PRIORS DEAN

WHITE HORSE (PUB WITH
NO NAME)
400 yds off main road, signed E
Tisted OS714290
☎ (01420) 588387
11-2.30 (3 Sat), 6-11; 12-3,
7-10.30 Sun
Ballard's Best Bitter; Draught
Bass; Fuller's London Pride;
Gale's HSB; Ringwood
Fortyniner; guest beers Ⓗ
Famous old pub hidden down a
gravel track in a field (second
track from main road). The pub
sign fell down years ago, hence
the nickname. There are up to
ten beers on offer, two of which
are house beers (the stronger is
from Ringwood, the other is from
Gales). ⌸ Q ⊛ ⊞ ♿ ▲ P

RINGWOOD

INN ON THE FURLONG
Meeting House Lane
☎ (01425) 475139
11-3, 5-11; 11-11 Wed, Fri & Sat;
12-3.30, 7-10.30 Sun
Ringwood Best Bitter, True
Glory, Fortyniner, XXXX Porter,
Old Thumper; guest beers Ⓗ
Superb, thriving local in the

centre of town. A central bar serves a multi-roomed pub with flagstones and traditional furnishings, plus a pleasant rear conservatory/dining area with a patio. Daily newspapers always available. Large car park opposite. Live music Tue.
🏚 🍺 🕯 ◐ ♿

LONDON TAVERN
Linford Road, Poulner (¹/₂ mile N of Poulner jct on A31)
☎ (01425) 473819
11.30-2.30 (3 Sat), 5.30-11; 11.30-11 Fri; 12-3, 7-10.30 Sun
Fuller's London Pride; Ringwood Best Bitter; guest beers H
19th-century local at the edge of town, named after the first landlord whose nickname was 'Londoner'. A regular prize winner in the *Ringwood in Bloom* competition. The family room is occasionally used for meetings. No food Sun. 🏚 🍺 🕯 ◐ ♣ P

ROMSEY

TUDOR ROSE
3 Cornmarket
☎ (01794) 512126
10-11; 12-4, 7-10.30 Sun
Courage Best Bitter, Directors H
Friendly, one-bar, no-frills pub in the town centre. The courtyard is very attractive in summer, with flower baskets and tubs. It hosts regular 'folk music with attitude'. Eve meals in summer; no food winter Sun.
🏚 Q 🕯 ◐ ▶ ≈ ♣

ROTHERWICK

FALCON
The Street
☎ (01256) 762586
11-11; 12-10.30 Sun
Brakspear Bitter; Flowers Original; Morrells Varsity; guest beers H
Friendly, popular village local, now extended to provide a well-appointed restaurant at the rear. Normally offers a local micro's beer as a guest.
🏚 Q 🕯 ◐ ▶ ♣ P

SELBORNE

SELBORNE ARMS
High Street ☎ (01420) 511247
11-3, 5.30-11; 11-11 Sat & summer; 12-10.30 Sun
Courage Best Bitter; Wadworth 6X; guest beers H
Three distinct drinking areas are provided in this delightful rural idyll: a long saloon area for eating is separate from a small open bar with a log fire. The large garden is popular with families in summer. This is a good area for walking, and handy for the Gilbert White Museum.
🏚 Q 🕯 ◐ ▶ ♣ P 🍴

SHEDFIELD

WHEATSHEAF INN
Botley Road (A334)
☎ (01329) 833024
12-11; 12-10.30 Sun
Beer Seller Hampshire Hog; H **Cheriton Pots Ale;** G **Hop Back Summer Lightning;** H **guest beers** (weekends) G
Traditional roadside inn with two comfortable bars. A former Marston's house, now an excellent free house without gimmicks, serving home-made food. The house beer is brewed by Hampshire Brewery. Cider in summer. Q 🕯 ◐ 🍴 ♣ ⌂ P

SHEET

QUEENS HEAD
Sheet Green ☎ (01730) 264204
11-2.30, 5.30-11; 12-3, 7-10.30 Sun
Boddingtons Bitter; Brakspear Bitter; Fuller's London Pride; Wadworth 6X; guest beer H
Typical local next to the village green and church. The public bar, nearly 400 years old, generates local trade of all ages. Eve meals Thu-Sat; no food Sat lunch.
🏚 Q 🕯 ◐ 🍴 ♣ P

SOUTHAMPTON

ALEXANDRA
6 Belle Vue Road (off London Road) ☎ (01703) 335071
11-11; 12-10.30 Sun
Boddingtons Bitter; Flowers Original; Fuller's London Pride; Wadworth 6X; guest beers H
Traditional, town-centre alehouse with a mixed clientele. Office workers and students are attracted by the pleasant atmosphere, interesting guest beers, quiz nights, Belgian beers and good value food (eve meals Mon-Thu). The sheltered rear patio is a haven from the city bustle.
🕯 ◐ ♣

BEVOIS CASTLE
63 Onslow Road, Bevois Valley
☎ (01703) 330350
11-3, 6.30-11; 11-11 Sat; 12-10.30 Sun
Beer range varies H
Pleasing, one-bar local in a popular drinking area, serving good value Sunday roasts and home-cooked fare (no eve meals Mon, other eves until 7.30pm). Small courtyard for summer drinking and barbecues. Four draught ales; foreign bottled beers; good selection of cognacs. Limited parking.
🕯 ◐ ▶ ♣ P

BITTER VIRTUE (OFF-LICENCE)
70 Cambridge Road, Portswood (off The Avenue)
☎ (01703) 554881

10.30-8 (closed Mon & Tue); 10.30-2 Sun
Brakspear Bitter, seasonal beers; guest beer (occasional) G
Opened in 1997, a welcome real ale off-licence with more than 200 bottle-conditioned beers from UK and abroad. Mail order available for bottled beers.

BOSUN'S LOCKER
Castle Square, Upper Bugle Street ☎ (01703) 333364
11-3, 5-11; 11-11 Fri & Sat; 12-10.30 Sun
Draught Bass; Fuller's London Pride; guest beers H
Large mock-Tudor pub, close to the old city walls, overlooking the city centre leisure development area. The bar is complemented by a no-smoking restaurant and games areas. Cider in summer.
🏚 🛋 🕯 ◐ ▶ ♣ ⌂

CROWN INN
9 Highcrown Street, Highfield (off Highfield Lane, road access from Hawthorn Rd)
☎ (01703) 315033
11-11; 12-10.30 Sun
Archers Best Bitter; Brakspear Special; Flowers Original; Fuller's London Pride; Wadworth 6X H
Large, one-bar pub with a bit of a rustic feel. Close to the university and the common, it is popular with students and locals alike. Good value food features interesting specialities. Covered patio area outside.
🕯 ◐ ▶ P

DUKE OF WELLINGTON
36 Bugle Street
☎ (01703) 339222
11-11; 12-10.30 Sun
Draught Bass; Boddingtons Bitter; Courage Best Bitter; Theakston Best Bitter; Wadworth 6X; H **guest beers** H G
Partly dating back to the 13th century, this pub is situated in the old town close to the Tudor House Museum and city walls. Meeting room available. Some of the guest beers are served straight from the casks in the cellar (check the blackboard).
🏚 🕯 ◐ ▶ ⌂

EAGLE
1 Palmerston Road
☎ (01703) 333825
11-11; 12-10.30 Sun
Boddingtons Bitter; Flowers Original; Wadworth 6X; guest beers H
Corner pub, just away from the city centre. Recently refurbished, it now stocks a reduced beer range following its release from the Hogshead chain, but still offers at least four guest beers. 🕯

FREEMANTLE ARMS
31 Albany Road, Freemantle
☎ (01703) 320759
10.30-3, 6-11; 10.30-11 Fri 6 Sat;
12-10.30 Sun
Banks's Mild; Marston's Bitter, Pedigree, HBC H
Welcoming, two bar local in a quiet cul-de-sac.
❀ ◫ ⇌ (Hillbrook) ♣ ⊟

GROVE TAVERN
68-70 Swift Road, Woolston
☎ (01703) 322918
12-3, 7-11; 12-11 Fri, 6 Sat;
12-10.30 Sun
Flowers IPA; guest beers H
A rare survivor, this large, former Brickwood pub, near Southampton Water and Woolston's shipyard, retains three bars. The garden has alcoves and is home to ducks, chickens, rabbits and owls. The IPA is sold as 'El Jeffe's', alongside two guest beers.
❀ ◫ ♣ P

JUNCTION INN
Priory Road, St Denys
☎ (01703) 584486
11.30-3.30, 5-11; 11.30-4, 5.30-11 Sat; 12-5, 7-10.30 Sun
Banks's Mild; Marston's Bitter, Pedigree, HBC H
Splendid Victorian corner pub with an award-winning restored interior and an attractive garden. Good value lunches.
Q ☜ ❀ ◫ ⇌ (St Denys) ♣ P ⌦

NEW INN
16 Bevois Valley Road
☎ (01703) 228437
11-11; 12-10.30 Sun
Gale's Butser, Best Bitter, IPA, Winter Brew, HSB, seasonal beers; guest beers H
Comfortable, one-bar corner pub once owned by Scrase's Star Brewery, and by Strong's from the 1920s, whose etched windows remain. Now a Gale's pub, selling their full range plus foreign bottled beers and over 100 malt whiskies. ❀ ◖ ♣

PARK INN
37 Carlisle Road, Shirley
☎ (01703) 486948
11.30-3, 5-11; 11-4, 7-11 Sat;
12-3, 7-10.30 Sun
Badger Tanglefoot; Wadworth IPA, 6X, seasonal beers; guest beers H
Community local near the High Street, where a good mix of customers use the lounge and public areas in its single bar. Note the large collection of mirrors.
❀ ◖ ♣

PLATFORM TAVERN
Town Quay ☎ (01703) 337232
12-3, 5-11; 11-11 Fri, Sat & summer; 12-10.30 Sun

Marston's Bitter, Pedigree H
Convenient for the Isle of Wight ferry and old town, this small, comfortably furnished pub incorporates part of the old town hall in its single bar.
◖ ▶

RICHMOND INN
108 Portswood Road
☎ (01703) 554523
11-11; 12-10.30 Sun
Banks's Mild; Marston's Bitter, Pedigree, Owd Rodger (occasional)**; HBC** H
Traditional Victorian, two-bar suburban pub. The basic public bar (with Sky TV) hosts live Irish music Thu; the cosy lounge has a splendid old £sd cash register. Good whisky selection.
❀ ◫ ♣

SALISBURY ARMS
126 Shirley High Street, Shirley
☎ (01703) 774624
10-11; 12-3, 7-10.30 (12-10.30 summer) Sun
Banks's Mild; Marston's Bitter, Pedigree, HBC H
Comfortable pub in a shopping district. The island bar serves the main drinking area whilst the back room is used for dining or skittles. Sparklers are not used but are available. Live music Tue (jazz) and Sat eves.
◖ ♣ ⌦

STANDING ORDER
30 High Street
☎ (01703) 222121
11-11; 12-10.30 Sun
Courage Directors; Hop Back Summer Lightning; Ringwood Fortyniner; Theakston Best Bitter; guest beers H
Formerly a bank, a more relaxed atmosphere now prevails in this typical Wetherspoons conversion, where food is served all day.
Q ❀ ◖ ▶ ♿ ⇗ ⌦ ⊟

WATERLOO ARMS
101 Waterloo Road, Freemantle
☎ (01703) 220022
12-11; 12-10.30 Sun
Hop Back GFB, Crop Circle, Entire Stout, Thunderstorm, Summer Lightning; guest beer H
Popular one-bar local whose walls are festooned with awards for Hop Back beers. An annual beer festival is held in Sept. Food available daily until 9.30 pm, unusual speciality sausages feature. Only ten minutes walk from the central station.
❀ ◖ ▶ ⇌ (Millbrook) ♣ ⌣

WELLINGTON ARMS
56 Park Road, Freemantle
☎ (01703) 227356
11.30-2.30, 5.30 (7 Sat)-11;
12-3.30, 7-10.30 Sun

Courage Directors; Fuller's London Pride; Ringwood Best Bitter, Fortyniner, XXXX Porter, Old Thumper; Wadworth 6X; guest beers H
Busy, comfortable, friendly back-street free house - try the excellent real ale sausages and mash (weekdays only). No machines but quiet piped music and a wealth of Wellington memorabilia.
Q ◖ ⇌ (Central/Millbrook)

STOCKBRIDGE

THREE CUPS INN
High Street
☎ (01264) 810527
11-2, 5-11; 11-2, 7-10.30 Sun
Draught Bass; Fuller's London Pride; guest beer H
Small, cosy bar with pleasant character and an interesting history. The restaurant is closed Sun eve. Enjoy walks on the nearby Test Way. ㎃ ❀ ⇌ ◖ ▶ P

STOKE

WHITE HART
Off B3048, 1 mile N of St Mary Bourne ☎ (01264) 738355
12-2 (3 Sat), 6.30-11; 12-3, 7-10.30 Sun
Fuller's London Pride; Hampshire King Alfred's; guest beers H
Vital amenity in a pretty village in the Bourne Valley. The large, open-plan pub has a games room with a full-size snooker table. Interesting home cooked menu. No food Sun eve or Mon.
㎃ Q ☜ ❀ ◖ ◫ ♣ P ⊟

SWANMORE

NEW INN
Chapel Road
☎ (01489) 893588
11-2.30, 5-11; 12-3, 7-10.30 Sun
Bateman Mild; Marston's Bitter, Pedigree, HBC H
Welcoming village local; one bar to suit all tastes. Good, home-made food with pies and curries a speciality (no meals Sun eve or Tue). Q ❀ ◖ ▶ ▲ ♣ P

TANGLEY

CRICKETERS ARMS
Tangley Bottom (signed at cross-roads in Tangley) OS3227528
☎ (01264) 730283
11-3, 7-11; 12-3, 7-10.30 Sun
Draught Bass; Cheriton Pots Ale; guest beer (occasional) G
Remote 18th-century drovers inn. A large dining room at the rear serves good quality home cooking including pizzas (book weekends). Look out for the old rack which holds the barrels (the beer is served from them). CC field for campers behind the pub.
㎃ Q ❀ ◖ ▶ ♿ ♣ P

THRUXTON

WHITE HORSE
Off A303
☎ (01264) 772401
11-3, 6-11; 12-3, 7-10.30 Sun
Fuller's London Pride; Greene King IPA; guest beer Ⓗ
Thatched country pub almost under the A303. Retreat inside for a friendly welcome and forget about the traffic. Live folk music alternate Tue; eve meals Tue-Sat. ⚬ ⚘ ◑ ▶ ⌂ P

TITCHFIELD

WHEATSHEAF
East Street
☎ (01329) 842965
12-2.30, 6-11; 11-11 Fri; 12-3, 7-10.30 Sun
Fuller's London Pride; Woodforde's Wherry; guest beers Ⓗ
Cosy village pub in a conservation area. A single bar with three distinct seating areas and a nice log fire in winter. No food served Tue. ⚬ Q ⚘ ◑ ▶

Try also: Queens Head, High St (Free)

TOTFORD

WOOLPACK
On B3046, between Candovers and Alresford
☎ (01962) 732101
11.30-3, 6-11; 12-3, 7-10.30 Sun
Eldridge Pope Hardy Country; Palmers IPA; guest beers Ⓗ
16th-century flint and stone inn set in a tiny rural hamlet, featuring an unspoilt interior and a pretty garden, looking out on to open farmland. Recommended B&B. ⚬ Q ⚘ ⇔ ◑ ▶ P

TWYFORD

PHOENIX
High Street (B3335, 1 mile S of M3 jct 11)
☎ (01962) 713322
11.30-3, 6-11; 12-3, 7-10.30 Sun
Banks's Mild; Marston's Bitter, Pedigree, HBC Ⓗ
Busy, friendly village inn serving a wide range of good value food. The skittle alley can be booked for functions.
⚬ ⚬ ⚘ ◑ ▶ ♣ P

UPPER CLATFORD

CROOK & SHEARS
Off A343, S of Andover
☎ (01264) 361543
11-3, 6-11; 11-11 Sat; 12-3, 7-10.30 Sun
Flowers Original; Fuller's London Pride; Greene King Abbot; guest beers Ⓗ
Cosy, 17th-century, two roomed village pub where low ceilings and open fires make for an attractive interior. The small restaurant features a speciality sausage menu. Skittle alley. Children welcome.
⚬ Q ⚘ ◑ ▶ ⌂ ♣

WEYHILL

WEYHILL FAIR
Weyhill Road (A342)
☎ (01264) 773631
11-3, 6 (5 Fri, 6.30 Sat)-11; 12-3, 7-10.30 Sun
Morrells Bitter, Varsity, Graduate; guest beers Ⓗ
Popular, genuine free house, usually serving three guest beers, rapidly changing, and an inviting menu of home-cooked food (not served Sun eve). A large field for camping for the regular beer-themed weekends and cycling events. An excellent pub for conversation.
⚬ Q ⚬ ⚘ ◑ ▶ ⅙ ▲ ♣ P
⚹ ⏚

WHITCHURCH

PRINCE REGENT
London Road
☎ (01256) 892179
11-11; 12-10.30 Sun
Archers Best Bitter; Hop Back GSB; guest beer (occasional) Ⓗ
Friendly, one-bar pub, overlooking the Test Valley. Try the rare nine-ball American pool in the cellar room. A real 'local' atmosphere with meat draws etc. Good value snacks. ⚘ ♣ ⌂ P

RED HOUSE
London Street
☎ (01256) 895558
11.30-3.30, 6-11; 12-3, 7-10.30 Sun
Itchen Valley Godfathers, seasonal beers Ⓗ
Two-bar, welcoming pub with an emphasis on tradition: good value food in the restaurant area, an unspoilt public bar and an excellent garden with family area. Children welcome.
⚬ Q ⚘ ◑ ▶ ⅙ ⇌ ♣ P

WINCHESTER

ALBION
2 Stockbridge Road
☎ (01962) 853429
11-11; 12-10.30 Sun
Draught Bass; Hook Norton Best Bitter; Worthington Bitter; guest beer (occasional) Ⓗ
Prominent street-corner, no-nonsense boozer; lively and sometimes boisterous, but a friendly atmosphere prevails. Small cosy interior with only standing room at busy times. Good range of lunches; many table games. An ideal stop for rail users (station 250 yds).
Q ◑ ⇌ ♣

HYDE TAVERN
57 Hyde St ☎ (01962) 862592
11.30-2.30, 5-11; 11.30-3, 6-11 Sat; 12-3, 7-10.30 Sun
Marston's Bitter, Pedigree Ⓗ
Interesting double gable-fronted, two-bar pub below street level; the oldest pub in town (15th century). The homely comfortable interior has low ceilings, sloping floors and painful door frames for tall people. Q ⅙ ⇌

OLD GAOL HOUSE
11 Jewry Street
☎ (01962) 850095
11-11; 12-10.30 Sun
Courage Directors; Ringwood Fortyniner; Theakston Best Bitter; guest beers Ⓗ
Georgian building, originally built as the city gaol, later becoming the library and then a furniture store. Wetherspoons have done a good conversion into an excellent pub, with all their normal features - good prices, extensive no-smoking area, food at all times etc.
Q ◑ ▶ ⅙ ⇌ ⌂ ⚹ ⏚

WILLOW TREE
14 Durngate Terrace
☎ (01962) 877255
12-3, 6-11; 12-11 Sat; 12-10.30 Sun
Marston's Bitter, Pedigree, HBC Ⓗ

One of the last multi-bar Marston's pubs; on the banks of the Itchen with a lovely garden surrounded by water. It offers a wide range of food, much home-made; the restaurant overlooks the garden.
❀ ◖▶ ⌗ ⅋ ♣

WYKEHAM ARMS
75 Kingsgate Street
☎ (01962) 853834
11-11; 12-10.30 Sun
Draught Bass; Gale's Butser, Best Bitter, HSB Ⓗ
Large, busy and attractive, cor-ner back-street pub, tucked away near the cathedral and college (limited parking). Striving to pro-vide old-fashioned qualities in its drinking and eating areas; cosy rooms and old school desks are features. Extensive menu and wine list. ♨ Q ❀ ⇌ ◖▶

WOOLTON HILL

RAMPANT CAT
Broad Layings (off A343)
☎ (01635) 253474
11.30-2.30 (not Mon, 12-3 Sat), 6.30-11; 12-3, 7-10.30 Sun
Archers Best Bitter; Arkell's 3B; guest beers Ⓗ
Pleasant, slate-clad pub in a

quiet country village: an L-shaped bar with a restaurant off. The patio and garden are popular in summer. No food Sun eve or Mon. ♨ Q ❀ ◖▶ ♣ P

WOLVERTON

GEORGE & DRAGON
1 mile from A339
☎ (01635) 298292
12-3, 5.30-11; 12-3, 7-10.30 Sun
Brakspear Special; Fuller's London Pride; Hampshire King Alfreds; Wadworth IPA, 6X Ⓗ
Large country pub with a feature fireplace and oak beams, offering a good selection of food. The skittle alley doubles as a function room. Large garden.
♨ ❀ ◖▶ P

INDEPENDENT BREWERIES

Ballard's:
Petersfield
Beckett's:
Basingstoke
Cheriton:
Alresford
Gales:
Horndean
Hampshire:
Romsey
Itchen Valley:
Alresford
Ringwood:
Ringwood
Spikes:
Southsea
Triple fff: Alton
Winfields:
Portsmouth

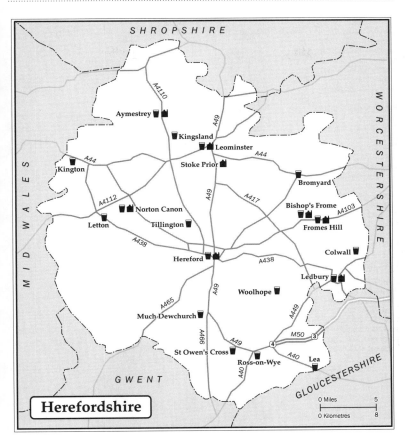

Herefordshire

AYMESTREY

RIVERSIDE INN
On A4110
☎ (01568) 708440
12-3, 6.30-11; 12-3, 7-10.30 Sun
Woodhampton Old Rooster, Kingfisher, Wagtail, seasonal beers Ⓗ
Beautifully-situated 16th-century free house which serves as the tap for the nearby Woodhampton brewery. An adventurous menu is available both in the attractive bar and in the restaurant.
🏚 ❀ ⇔ ◖ ▶ Ⓐ ♣ P

BISHOPS FROME

CHASE INN
On B4214
☎ (01885) 490234
12-2.30, 6-11; 12-3, 7-10.30 Sun
Marches Priory Ale; Marston's Bitter; Wye Valley Bitter Ⓗ
At the heart of a thriving village, this pub caters for all tastes - two bars with neither drinking area or dining area dominating; a good balance. The good value menu includes popular Sunday roasts. Ideal for a B & B stopover.
🏚 Q ❀ ⇔ ◖ ▶ ⊞ ♣ P

BROMYARD

ROSE & LION
5 New Road
☎ (01885) 482381
11-3, 6-11; 11-11 Sat; 12-3, 7-10.30 Sun
Wye Valley Bitter, HPA, Supreme; guest beer Ⓗ
Friendly, traditional side-street pub. This multi-room pub is part of the Wye Valley's estate whose top-notch landlady ensures the pub grows in popularity. Pool room at the rear. Q ❀ ⊞ ♣ P

COLWALL

CHASE INN
Chase Road (off B4218, Walwyn Road at hairpin bend)
☎ (01684) 540276
12-2.30 (not Tue), 7-11; 12-2.30, 7-10.30 Sun
Donnington BB, SBA; Hobsons Best Bitter; Wye Valley seasonal beers Ⓗ
Two-bar pub with a small cosy lounge on one side and a larger L-shaped public bar with a pool table. The garden affords superb views of the countryside and Black Mountains. No food Tue or Sun. Well worth the 25-minute walk from Colwall station. Q ❀ ◖ ♣ P

FROMES HILL

WHEATSHEAF
On A4103 ☎ (01531) 640888
12-11; 12-10.30 Sun
Fromes Hill Buckswood, Dingle, Overture; M&B Brew XI Ⓗ
Large, open-plan roadside pub with exposed stonework in its single bar (TV). The brewery tap for Fromes Hill brewery. Children's play area outside.
🏚 ❀ ◖ ▶ Ⓐ ♣ P

HEREFORD

BARRELS
69 St Owen Street
☎ (01432) 274968
11-11; 12-10.30 Sun
Wye Valley Bitter, HPA, Supreme, Brew 69, seasonal beers; guest beer Ⓗ

CAMRA award-winning home of the Wye Valley Brewery. A multi-room pub, it has all that an independent brewers' tap should have - character, choice and quality; no frills, no food. It draws a good mix of locals, students and visitors; very welcoming.
❀ ⌸ ⇌ ♣ ⌣

LICHFIELD VAULTS
11 Church Street
☎ (01432) 267994
11-11; 12-10.30 Sun
Ansells Mild; Marston's Pedigree; Tetley Bitter; guest beers Ⓗ
Festival Ale House with the best selection of guest ales in the city. Sympathetically refurbished, the wood-panelled bar divides into two pleasant drinking areas; very popular at weekends. 'Twixt cathedral and shopping area, so parking is not easy. Small patio.
❀ ◖ ♣

SPREAD EAGLE
King Street ☎ (01432) 272205
11-3, 6-11; 11-11 Fri, Sat & summer; 12-10.30 Sun
Boddingtons Bitter; Marston's Pedigree; Morland Old Speckled Hen; guest beer Ⓗ
Refurbished, centrally located pub with a knocked-through bar stretching back from the main street. More modern at the front, the quieter back area maintains much character with bench seats and beams. Popular with the young, with a slightly metropolitan air. ◖ ▶

THREE ELMS INN
1 Cannon Pyon Road
☎ (01432) 273338
11-11; 12-10.30 Sun
Boddingtons Bitter; Flowers Original; Marston's Pedigree; guest beers Ⓗ
This managed Whitbread house benefits from a very dedicated landlord. One large L-shaped refurbished bar accommodates drinkers and diners alike. Good for families, with indoor and outdoor play areas. Herefordshire CAMRA *Pub of the Year* 1998. Wheelchair WC.
⛺ ❀ ◖ ▶ ৬ P

TREACLE MINE
83-85 St Martins Street (S of river)
☎ (01432) 266022
12-3, 6-11 11-11 Fri & Sat; 12-10.30 Sun
Banks's Mild, Bitter; guest beers Ⓗ
Well patronised by locals, sports fans and city weekend drinkers. Old and new mix in an unusual refurbishment - bare beams and bricks contrast with modern decor. Satellite TV for sport;

always lively in the small single bar with alcoves. ♣ ⊟

VICTORY
88 St Owen Street
☎ (01432) 274998
11-11; 12-10.30 Sun
Wye Valley Bitter, HPA, Supreme, seasonal beers; guest beer Ⓗ
Popular Wye Valley house: live music and a lively crowd in the long narrow bar, but quieter at the rear. Decked out in a galleon theme, this pub always features on city pub crawl circuits. Parking tricky.
❀ ৬ ♣

VOLUNTEER
Harold Street
☎ (01432) 276189
11-11; 12-10.30 Sun
Brains Bitter; Draught Bass; Greene King Abbot; Worthington Bitter; guest beers Ⓗ
Hereford's premier cider outlet, a back-street local with stripped floors and functional seating: always a warm welcome. Many of its regular are local artists and musicians who organise events at the pub. Cider festival around apple day (Oct). Children welcome. Sunday vegetarian Brunch is essential eating. Meals served 10-5 daily. Braille menu.
🚌 Q ❀ ◖ ৬ ♣ ⌣

KINGSLAND

CORNERS INN
On B4360, village crossroads
☎ (01568) 708385
9.30-2.30, 5.30-11; 12-3, 7-10.30 Sun
Ruddles Best Bitter; guest beer Ⓗ
Much-improved since a new landlord took over two years ago. He has built up a reputation for good home-made food in the restaurant (booking advisable). Quoits played. 🚌 ◖ ▶ ⌸ ♣ P

KINGTON

OLDE TAVERN ☆
22 Victoria Road
☎ (01544) 231384
11.30-3 (not Mon-Fri), 7.30-11; 12-2.30, 7.30-10.30 Sun
Ansells Bitter Ⓗ
Herefordshire CAMRA runner-up *Pub of the Year* 1997. The bar is packed with curios and boasts a superb beer engine - no swan-necks here. On CAMRA's register of pubs with outstanding interiors. Enjoy! Q ▲ ♣

OLD FOGEY
37 High Street
☎ (01544) 230685
5.30 (10.30 Sat)-11; 12-10.30 Sun
Hobsons Best Bitter; Wood Special; guest beer Ⓗ

Welcoming one-bar pub with friendly locals who enjoy watching sport on TV. A patio at the rear provides an outdoor drinking area.
❀ ♣

Try also: Queens Head, Bridge St (Three Tuns)

LEDBURY

BREWERY INN
Bye Street
☎ (01531) 634272
11-3.30, 7-11; 12-3.30, 7-10.30 Sun
Banks's Mild; Marston's Bitter Ⓗ
Back-street pub near the fire station. Two bars include a superb snug with the smallest bar in the county. The other bar is larger and modernised but keeps a traditional atmosphere. The locals are very much into pub games. Limited parking nearby.
Q ❀ ⌸ ♣ ⌣

HORSESHOE INN
The Homend
☎ (01531) 632770
12-11; 12-10.30 Sun
Boddingtons Bitter; Flowers IPA; Hobsons Best Bitter; Wood Shropshire Lad; guest beers Ⓗ
One-bar pub up a short flight of steps from the street. Inside is a long, narrow bar with exposed beams; the fittings are modern but it has some character and cosy alcoves by the front bay windows. Best pub in Ledbury for guest beers.
🚌 ❀ ◖ ⇌

PRINCE OF WALES
Church Lane
☎ (01531) 632250
11-3, 7-11; 12-3; 7-10.30 Sun
Banks's Bitter; Hanson's Mild Ⓗ
This 16th-century black and white inn in the cobbled church lane appears on many a chocolate box. Inside, the two-bar pub is a little more contemporary but with alcoves and beams giving a good mix of comfort and character. Live folk sessions (Wed). Cider in summer. Eve meals summer weekends.
Q ❀ ◖ ▶ ♣ ⌣

ROYAL OAK HOTEL
The Southend
☎ (01531) 632110
11-11; 12-10.30 Sun
Ledbury Challenger SB, seasonal beers Ⓗ
The downstairs public bar is popular with a wide range of people, following its refurbishment. Upstairs, redecoration has enhanced the lounge bar with original beams uncovered. Ledbury brewery is located at the rear of the hotel.
🚌 ⇋ ◖ ▶ ♣ P ⊟

LEOMINSTER

BLACK HORSE
74 South Street
☎ (01568) 611946
11-2.30, 6-11; 11-11 Sat; 12-3, 7-10.30 Sun
Hobsons Town Crier; guest beers Ⓗ
Popular free house offering an excellent selection of guest beers. Lively public bar and a quieter lounge with a restaurant area. An interesting menu includes vegetarian options (no food Sun eve). The house beer is from Marches brewery, which started in the pub's old bottle store.
🍴 Q ◑ ▶ ⌂ ♣ P

GRAPE VAULTS
4 Broad Street
☎ (01568) 611404
11-3, 5-11; 12-4, 6.30-10.30 Sun
Banks's Mild; Marston's Bitter, Pedigree; guest beer Ⓗ
Cosy, town-centre pub with a fine wood-panelled interior behind a fairly plain facade. Its features include fireplaces, much etched glass and a wonderful snug. The bar menu offers very good value choice.
🍴 Q ◑ ▶

LETTON

SWAN INN
On A438
☎ (01544) 327304
11-3, 6-11; 11-11 Wed-Sat; 12-3, 7-10.30 Sun
Beer range varies
Roadside pub with a small public bar at the front and a much larger lounge and restaurant at the back. The house beer is brewed by Wye Valley. Food is served whenever the pub is open. Fishing in the River Wye is available. An ideal base for Wye Valley walks and Offa's Dyke.
🍴 🌸 ⌂ ◑ ▶ ⌂ ⚲ ♣ P

MUCH DEWCHURCH

BLACK SWAN INN
On B4348 ☎ (01981) 540295
12-3, 6-11; 12-3, 7-10.30 Sun
Adnams Bitter; Draught Bass; Courage Directors; Taylor Landlord; guest beers Ⓗ
Country pub with two bars, it claims to be the county's oldest. Four areas including a bar, lounge and a games room. No jukebox. Good food.
🍴 Q 🌸 ⌂ ◑ ▶ ♣ ⌂ P

NORTON CANNON

THREE HORSESHOES INN
On A480 between Yazor and Eccles Green ☎ (01544) 318375

1 (12 summer, 11 Sat)-3, 7 (6 summer)-11; 12-3, 7-10.30 Sun
Shoes Norton Ale; Cannon Bitter Ⓗ
Rural local selling beers from its own brewery. Comfortable and friendly, it has its own shooting gallery and orchard. Two bars - one complete with sofas, piano and table lamps, the other more straightforward. Very traditional - no gimmicks. Children welcome. Cider in summer.
🍴 Q 🌸 ◑ ⚲ ♣ ⌂ P

ROSS-ON-WYE

CROWN & SCEPTRE
Market Place
☎ (01989) 562765
11-11; 12-10.30 Sun
Archers Best Bitter; Draught Bass; Greene King Abbot; guest beers Ⓗ
The real ale pub in Ross. This single-bar, town-centre pub is always popular. It caters for all but is popular with the younger set at weekends. Parking is a problem. 🍴 🌸 ◑ ♣ ⌂

ST OWENS CROSS

NEW INN
At A4173/B4521 jct
☎ (01989) 730274
12-2.30, 6-11; 12-3, 7-10.30 Sun
Draught Bass; Fuller's London Pride; Smiles Best Bitter; Tetley Bitter; guest beer Ⓗ
Two-bar, 16th-century roadside pub with much character and beauty - its hanging baskets win prizes. One bar acts as a restaurant, the other as a plush locals' bar with some informal dining at weekends. The accommodation includes four-posters. Good food, using local seasonal ingredients.
🍴 🌸 ⌂ ◑ ⚲ ♣ P

TILLINGTON

BELL INN
Tillington Road (village cross-roads) ☎ (01432) 760395

11-3, 6-11; 11-11 Sat; 12-5, 6-10.30 Sun
Draught Bass; Fuller's London Pride; guest beers Ⓗ
Pleasant, modernised inn with a restaurant that does not dominate a good village local. A lively public bar contrasts with a plush lounge and patio area. Families are welcome. Good garden. No food Sun eves.
🍴 🌸 ◑ ▶ ⌂ ⚲ ♣ ⌂ P

WOOLHOPE

CROWN INN
☎ (01432) 860465
11-2.30, 6.30-11; 12-3, 7-10.30 Sun
Hook Norton Best Bitter; Smiles Best Bitter; guest beers (summer) Ⓗ
Open-plan pub with dining and lounge areas surrounding a small central bar area. Popular with diners from Hereford, it enjoys a good reputation for its food. (booking advised).
Q 🌸 ◑ ▶ ♿ ⌂ P

INDEPENDENT BREWERIES

Fromes Hill:
ledbury

Frome Valley:
Bishop's Frome

Ledbury:
Ledbury

Marches:
Leominster

Shoes:
Norton Canon

SP Sporting Ales:
Stoke Prior

Woodhampton:
Aymestrey

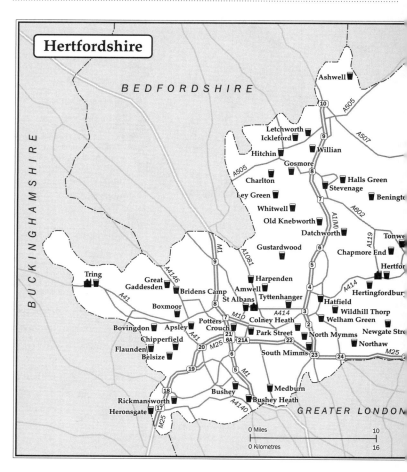

ALBURY

CATHERINE WHEEL
Gravesend (at traffic lights in Little Hadham)
OS440258
☎ (01279) 771277
11.30-3, 6-11 (11.30-11 summer Sat); 12-3.30, 7-10.30 (12-10.30 summer) Sun
Greene King IPA; Flowers Original; guest beer Ⓗ
Thatched, weatherboarded pub: two bars and a children's room, the smaller bar has a log fire. Good food. The pub is at the north end of the village in a hamlet near Patmore Heath Nature Reserve.
🏚 ⏲ ❀ ◖❱ P

AMWELL

ELEPHANT & CASTLE
Amwell Lane (left fork at top of Brewhouse Hill, Wheathampstead) OS167133
☎ (01582) 832175
12-3, 5.30-11; 12-11 Sat; 12-10.30 Sun
Marston's Bitter, Pedigree, HBC; guest beers Ⓗ
Early 18th-century pub, which was formerly three cottages, with two large gardens. Glass covers a 200-ft deep well in the main bar. No eve meals Sun or Mon. Sparklers removed on request.
🏚 Q ❀ ◖❱ P

APSLEY

WHITE LION
44 London Road
☎ (01442) 268948
11-11; 12-10.30 Sun
Fuller's Chiswick, London Pride, ESB, seasonal beers Ⓗ
A very friendly landlord runs this street-corner local on the busy London Road. Excellent food. Limited parking.
❀ ◖ P

ASHWELL

BUSHEL & STRIKE
Mill Street, (opp church)
☎ (01462) 742394
11-3, 6 (5.30 Fri)-11; 11-11 Sat; 12-10.30 Sun
Wells Eagle, Bombardier Ⓗ; **guest beers** ⒽⒼ
With 17th century origins, the pub has been much extended and includes a restaurant and sizeable garden. The tallest church steeple in Hertfordshire overshadows the pub which is set in a charming old village.
❀ 🛏 ◖❱ ⅃ ▲ ♣ ⌂ P ⚥ 🍴

BELSIZE

PLOUGH
Dunny Lane (Sarratt-Chipperfield road) OS034008
☎ (01923) 262800
11-3, 5.30-11; 12-3, 7-10.30 Sun
ABC Best Bitter; Greene King IPA Ⓗ

142

CAMBRIDGESHIRE

M11

Nuthampstead

hipping

Buntingford

Albury

A120

Green Tye

eside   Sawbridgeworth

Widford

are   High Wych

Pye Corner

A414

altham Cross

Isolated pub with a children's certificate and a pleasant garden. Try the unusual pub game, invented by one of the locals which is a cross between table football and tiddly winks. No food Sun eve. 🏨 ❀ ◖ ▶ ♣ P ⅙

BENINGTON

LORDSHIP ARMS
42 Whempstead Road (3 miles E of Stevenage via B1037)
OS308227
☎ (01438) 869665
12-3, 6-11; 12-3, 7-10.30 Sun
McMullen AK; Fuller's London Pride; Young's Special; guest beers Ⓗ
Excellent country local serving guest beers from small breweries far and wide. Telephone memorabilia adorns the pub. Bar snacks weekday lunchtimes and home-cooked Sunday roasts. Local CAMRA *Pub of the Year* 1997. 🏨 ❀ ♣ ⌂ P ⟊

BOVINGDON

WHEATSHEAF
High Street
☎ (01442) 832196
11-2.30 (3 Sat), 6-11; 12-3, 7-10.30 Sun
Boddingtons Bitter; guest beer Ⓗ
Fine example of a traditional village pub - friendly, cosy and unspoilt. Dating back to the 15th century, it features lots of brass, old photos of the village, unusual board games and sewing machine tables. Fresh food.
Q ❀ ◖ ♣ P

BOXMOOR

BOXMOOR VINTNERS (OFF LICENCE)
25-27 St Johns Rd
☎ (01442) 252171
9.30-1, 4.30-9.30; 12-2, 7-9 (Sun & Bank Hols)
Beer range varies Ⓗ
Independent off-licence, the only one in the area with draught ales. Low prices and an unusual range of ales, plus a good selection of British bottled beers. Four handpumps.

BRIDENS CAMP

CROWN & SCEPTRE
Red Lion Lane, Water End (off A4146, Leighton Buzzard-Hemel Hempstead Rd)
☎ (01442) 253250
12-3, 6-11 (12-11 summer); 12-10.30 Sun
Greene King IPA, Abbot Ⓗ
Smart country pub in a small village. The darts area doubles as a family room. Guest beers may be dispensed by cask breather. Extensive menu, changed weekly.
🏨 ⛱ ❀ ◖ ▶ ⊟ ♿ ♣ P

BUNTINGFORD

CROWN
17 High Street
☎ (01763) 271422
12-3, 5.30-11; 12-11 Sat; 12-3.30, 7-10.30 Sun
Courage Best Bitter; Mauldons Mole Trap; Wadworth 6X; guest beer Ⓗ
Town pub with two drinking areas, a covered patio (children welcome) and a meeting room. Regular theme nights with speciality food are staged — booking essential. Secluded garden.
⛱ ❀ ◖ ▶

BUSHEY

SWAN
25 Park Road (off High St)
☎ (0181) 950 2256
11-11; 12-10.30 Sun
Benskins BB; Ind Coope Burton Ale; Young's Bitter Ⓗ

Traditional, no-frills pub in a side street. A single public bar appeals to a wide cross-section of the public.
🏨 ♣

BUSHEY HEATH

BLACK BOY
19 Windmill Street
☎ (0181) 950 2230
11.30-3, 5.30-11; 11.30-11 Fri; 12-4, 6-11 Sat; 12-4, 7-10.30 Sun
Adnams Bitter; Benskins BB; guest beers Ⓗ
Friendly back-street pub, well worth finding, with usually five beers available. Very popular for food at lunchtimes; no eve meals Sun.
❀ ◖ ▶ P

CHAPMORE END

WOODMAN
30 Chapmore End (off B158, near A602 jct) OS328164
☎ (01920) 463143
12-3, 6-11; 12-3 (4 summer), 7-10.30 Sun
Greene King IPA, Abbot, seasonal beers Ⓖ
Unspoilt village pub, local CAMRA *Pub of the Year* 1996. Bar food menu ranges from sandwiches to balti (not served Sun). Regular live music and other events are staged. The large garden boasts a mini zoo.
🏨 Q ❀ ◖ ⊟ P

CHARLTON

WINDMILL
Charlton Road
(off A602 from Hitchin)
OS178281
☎ (01462) 432096
11-2.30, 5.30-11; 11-11 Sat; 12-3, 7-10.30 Sun
Wells Eagle, Bombardier; guest beer Ⓗ
Village pub whose large garden runs down to the River Hiz. One of Charles Wells's best outlets and twice local CAMRA *Pub of the Year*. Good home-cooked food (not served Tue or Sun eve).
❀ ◖ ▶ P

CHIPPERFIELD

ROYAL OAK
1 The Street
☎ (01923) 266537
12-3, 6-11; 12-3, 7-10.30 Sun
Draught Bass; Young's Bitter, Special Ⓗ**; guest beer** Ⓖ
Immaculate pub, very friendly; 18 years in the *Guide*. Highly polished wood and brass abound. Good food (eve meals by arrangement; sandwiches only Sun). 🏨 Q ❀ ◖ ▶ ♣ P

Try also: Boot, Tower Hill (Free)

CHIPPING
COUNTRYMAN INN
Ermine Street (A10)
☎ (01763) 272721
12-11; 12-10.30 Sun
Draught Bass; Greene King IPA; guest beer 🅷
17th-century roadside pub boasting a superb carved wooden bar showing the farming seasons. Food is served all day.
🏚 🏵 ◑ ▶ P

COLNEY HEATH
CROOKED BILLET
88 High Street ☎ (01727) 822128
11-3, 5.30-11; 11-11 Sat;
12-10.30 Sun
Greene King Abbot; Fuller's London Pride; Worthington Bitter; guest beers 🅷
Cottage-style pub, over 200 years old, but refurbished in keeping with its origins. Large garden area for children; popular with walkers. Eve meals served on Wed, Fri and Sat.
🏚 Q 🍺 🏵 ◑ ▶ 🌢 P

DATCHWORTH
TILBURY
1 Watton Road (1 mile from B197 at Woolmer Green)
OS270183
☎ (01438) 812496
11-3, 5-11; 11-11 Thu-Sat;
12-10.30 Sun
Draught Bass; guest beers 🅷
This friendly, two-bar pub, with a no-smoking dining room, has an unusual ale bar which displays a graveyard of keg memorabilia. The guest beers are complemented by two house ales brewed by the landlord at the Museum Brewing Co.
Q 🏵 ◑ ▶ 🍴 🎍 ♣ P

FLAUNDEN
BRICKLAYERS ARMS
Hogpits Bottom
☎ (01442) 833322
11.30-2.30 (3 Sat), 6-11; 12-3, 7-10.30 (12-10.30 summer) Sun
Brakspear Bitter; Fuller's London Pride; guest beers 🅷
Smart, food oriented, country pub which is still drinker-friendly, offering a varied range of ales. Pleasant garden.
🏚 Q 🏵 ◑ ▶ P

Try also: Green Dragon (Free)

GOSMORE
BIRD IN HAND
High Street (Hitchin turn from A1(M), second left at first roundabout) OS187272
☎ (01462) 432079
12-3, 5.30-11; 12-11 Sat;
12-10.30 Sun

Greene King XX Mild, IPA, Abbot 🅷
Popular, two-bar village local, a rare outlet for XX Mild. No meals Sun eve.
Q 🏵 ◑ ▶ ♣ P

GREAT GADDESDEN
COCK & BOTTLE
Off A4146
☎ (01442) 255381
11.30-3, 5.30-11; 12-3, 7-10.30 Sun
Fuller's ESB; Greene King Abbot; Hop Back Summer Lightning; Taylor Landlord; guest beers 🅷
Set in the Gade Valley, close to Hemel Hempstead, this ever-improving pub welcomes drinkers, diners and families. Very reasonable prices for ale and food (booking advised). Cider in summer; regular beer festivals.
🏚 🍺 🏵 ◑ ▶ ♣ 🌢 P 🍴

GREEN TYE
PRINCE OF WALES
Off B1004
OS443184
☎ (01279) 842517
11.30-3, 5.30-11; 11-11 Sat;
11.30-3, 7-10.30 Sun
Flowers IPA; McMullen AK; guest beers 🅷
Small country pub. A marquee in the garden used for beer festivals is available for special events. Popular with ramblers.
🏚 🏵 ◑ ♣ P

GUSTARD WOOD
CROSS KEYS
Ballslough Hill
(off B651, 1 mile N of Wheathampstead)
OS174165
☎ (01582) 832165
11-3, 5.30-11; 12-5, 7-10.30 Sun
Fuller's London Pride; Greene King IPA; guest beers 🅷
17th-century pub with a single bar and an inglenook. Abbots of Westminster Abbey were formerly lords of the manor and had crossed keys on their coat of arms. Eve meals Sat only. Large garden. The family room is not always open.
🏚 Q 🍺 🏵 🛏 ◑ ▶ ♣ P 🍴

HALLS GREEN
RISING SUN
Weston Road (minor road to Cromer) OS275287
☎ (01462) 790487
11-2.30, 6-11; 12-3, 7-10.30 Sun
Draught Bass; Courage Directors; McMullen AK, Country, Gladstone, seasonal beers 🅷
Lovely single-bar pub in the countryside east of Stevenage. An

enormous garden has a children's play area, petanque pitch and a marquee which hosts functions. The conservatory acts as a restaurant (families welcome). Local CAMRA 1998 *Pub of the Year.*
🏚 🏵 ◑ ▶ ♣ P 🍴

HARPENDEN
CARPENTERS ARMS
Cravells Road, Southdown (off A1081)
☎ (01582) 460311
11-3, 5.30-11; 12-3, 7-10.30 Sun
Courage Best Bitter; Ruddles County; Webster's Yorkshire Bitter; guest beer 🅷
Homely, welcoming 200-year old pub featuring much motoring memorabilia. Guest beers are often from local small independent breweries. No food Sun. Dog friendly.
🏚 Q 🏵 ◑ ♣ P

CROSS KEYS
39 High Street (A1081)
☎ (01582) 763989
11.30-2.30, 5-11; 12-3, 7-10.30 Sun
Boddingtons Bitter; Brakspear Bitter; Fuller's London Pride; Taylor Landlord 🅷
This 300-year-old pub is a gem of yesteryear with its flagstoned floor and pewter bar top. Totally unspoiled. A real fire adds a perfect background to the oak beams hung with pewter jugs. Pictures of old Harpenden adorn the walls.
🏚 Q 🏵 ◑ 🚆 ♣

OAK TREE
15 Leyton Green (off High St)
☎ (01582) 763850
11-3, 5.30-11; 11-11 Fri & Sat;
12-4, 7-10.30 Sun
Fuller's London Pride; McMullen AK; Tetley Bitter; guest beers 🅷
Comfortable, one-bar free house with a friendly atmosphere, popular with locals. Good range of guest ales (usually four); ask for your pint in a lined glass. Good food.
Q 🏵 ◑ 🚆 ♣ P

HATFIELD
EIGHT BELLS
2 Park Street (old town, 400 yds from station) ☎ (01707) 266059
11-3, 5.30-11; 11.30-11 Sat;
11.30-10.30 Sun
Adnams Bitter; Tetley Bitter, seasonal beers; guest beers 🅷
This 600-year-old Festival Alehouse stands in the picturesque old town. A wide-ranging clientele includes students from the nearby university. It boasts literary connections with Dickens's *Oliver Twist* as the pub Bill Sykes fled to.
🏚 🏵 ◑ ▶ 🚆 ♣ 🌢

HERONSGATE

Land of Liberty, Peace & Plenty
Long Lane (800 yds from M25 jct 17) OS023949
☎ (01923) 282226
12-11; 12-3, 7-10.30 (12-10.30 summer) Sun
Brakspear Special; Courage Best Bitter; Young's Special; guest beers [H]
Country free house serving up to three guest beers from micro-breweries and a range of draught Belgian beers. Occasional beer festivals. Local CAMRA *Pub of the Year* 1997. Book for eve meals.
❀ ◐ ◗ P

HERTFORD

White Horse
33 Castle St ☎ (01992) 501950
12-2.30 (3 Fri), 5.30 (5 Fri)-11; 12-11 Sat; 12-10.30 Sun
Dark Horse Ale, Sunrunner, seasonal beers; Fuller's London Pride; Hook Norton Best Bitter [H]; **guest beers** [H][G]
Traditional, unspoilt country town pub. The Dark Horse Brewery tap but still a free house. It has guest beers from many small microbreweries and a range of fruit wines. Two downstairs bars; the upstairs no-smoking area is open to children. Lunchtime food 12-2 Mon-Sat.
Q ◐ (North/East)

HERTINGFORDBURY

Prince of Wales
244 Hertingfordbury Rd (400 yds from A414) ☎ (01992) 581149
11-2.30, 5.30 (6 Sat)-11; 12-3, 7-10.30 Sun
Dark Horse Sunrunner; Fuller's London Pride; McMullen AK; Wadworth 6X; guest beers [H]
One-bar village local where strangers are always made to feel welcome. Make way at the bar when Buster the dog is thirsty! Sky TV. ❀ ◐ ◗ ♣ P

HIGH WYCH

Rising Sun
☎ (01279) 724099
12-3, 5.30 (5 Fri & Sat)- 11; 12-3, 7-10.30 Sun
Courage Best Bitter; guest beers [G]
Guide regular for over 20 years, known locally as Sid's or Granny Prior's. Catch it before it's too late. Q ❀ ♣ P

HITCHIN

Hitchin Rugby Football Club
King George V playing field, Old Hale Way (½ mile from A600)
☎ (01462) 432679
7-11 Tue & Thu; 12-11 Sat; 12-6 Sun
Brains Bitter; Bateman XB; guest beers [H]
Well-run club in Hitchin; see its collection of rugby programmes. Families welcome (playground for children). East Anglia CAMRA *Club of the Year* 1997-'98.
P

Sunrunner
24 Bancroft
☎ (01462) 440717
12-3, 5.30-11; 12-11 Fri & Sat; 1-5, 8-10.30 Sun
Dark Horse Ale, Sunrunner; Fuller's London Pride, seasonal beers; guest beers [H]
Timber-framed, 16th-century building with wooden floors, the second tied house of the Dark Horse Brewery stable, offering guest beers from micros. A wide choice of fruit wines and occasional cider. Live music Wed, folk music Sun lunch and twice yearly beer festivals. No food Sun. ◐

ICKLEFORD

Plume of Feathers
Upper Green (400 yds from A600, down Turnpike Lane)
☎ (01462) 432729
11-3 (4 Sat), 6-11; 12-5, 7-10.30 Sun
Boddingtons Bitter; Fuller's London Pride; King & Barnes Sussex; Wadworth 6X; guest beers [H]
Friendly village local run by two sisters; changed over the years but not spoilt. Good quality, home-cooked food. Lively but not noisy. Q ❀ ◐ ◗ ♣ P

LETCHWORTH

Hogshead
The Colonnade, Station Place
☎ (01462) 486807
11-11; 12-10.30 Sun
Boddingtons Bitter; Castle Eden Ale; Marston's Pedigree; Morland Old Speckled Hen; Wadsworth 6X [H]; **guest beers** [G]
Recently converted to one large bar with several distinct drinking areas in a spacious, semi-open-plan layout. Some bottle conditioned beers available. Tables outside in summer.
❀ ◐ ◗

LEY GREEN

Plough
Plough Lane OS162243
☎ (01438) 871394
11-11; 12-4.30, 7-10.30 Sun
Greene King IPA, Abbot [H]
Country local overlooking farmland and woods. The enormous garden has children's play equipment. ❀ ◐ ♣ P

MEDBURN

Waggon & Horses
Watling Street (A5183)
☎ (0181) 953 1406
11.30-3, 5.30 (6.30 Sat)-11; 12-3, 7-10.30 Sun
Greenalls Original; Shipstone's Bitter; guest beer [H]
Historic roadside pub, circa 1471 with an inglenook and a sunken dartboard in the games area. A large garden overlooks the countryside. ❀ ◐ ♣ P

Try also: Cat & Fiddle, Radlett (Free)

NEWGATE STREET

Coach & Horses
61 Newgate Street Village
☎ (01707) 872326
11-11; 12-10.30 Sun
Draught Bass; Greene King IPA; Marston's Pedigree; M&B Brew XI; Tetley Bitter [H]
Genuine, old, ivy-covered pub next to the church. A popular venue for many different clubs, like horse-riding and classic motorcycles. ❀ ◗ P

NORTH MYMMS

Old Maypole
43 Warrengate Road, Water End (turn off B197 at bus depot) OS229041
☎ (01707) 642119
11-2.30, 5.30-11; 12-3, 7-10.30 Sun
Greene King IPA, Abbot; seasonal beers; [H]
16th century split-level pub near the Royal Veterinary College. No food Sun; eve meals Mon, Wed and Fri (fish & chips). No-smoking family room; the lower bar boasts an inglenook.
Q ❀ ◐ ◗ P

NORTHAW

Two Brewers
1 Northaw Road
☎ (01707) 652420
11-3, 6-11; 12-3, 7-10.30 Sun
Adnams Bitter; Benskins BB; Ind Coope Burton Ale; Marston's Pedigree; Tetley Bitter [H]
One-bar village pub divided into several areas, so maintaining an intimate atmosphere. The landlord is the winner of *London in Bloom* 1997. ❀ ◐ ♣ P

NUTHAMPSTEAD

Woodman Inn
Follow signs to village off A10 (near Royston) OS413346
☎ (01763) 848328
11-3.30, 5.30-11; 11-11 Sat; 12-4, 7-10.30 Sun
Adnams Bitter; Greene King IPA, Abbot; guest beer [H]
Traditional, comfortable country

pub with a real fire in both bars. Note the memorabilia of USAF WWII 398th bomber group and the monument at the car park entrance. Good food and accommodation.
🏚 Q 🕸 🛏 ◖🌙 P 🖽

OLD KNEBWORTH

LYTTON ARMS
Park Lane
OS229202
☎ (01438) 812312
11-3, 5-11; 11-11 Fri & Sat; 12-10.30 Sun
Draught Bass; Fuller's London Pride; Theakston Best Bitter Woodforde's Wherry; guest beers Ⓗ
Celebrating ten years in the *Guide,* this 19th-century Lutyens pub sits on the edge of Knebworth Park. The regular beers are complemented by house beers from the Millennium Brewing Co, plus a large range of foreign beers and malt whiskies.
🏚 Q 🕸 ◖🌙 ♿ ♣ 👐 P ✗

PARK STREET

OVERDRAUGHT
86 Park Street (main road S of station)
☎ (01727) 874280
11-11; 12-3, 7-10.30 Sun
Marston's Bitter, Pedigree; guest beers Ⓗ
Friendly, two-bar village local. The lounge bar has a homely atmosphere enhanced by old photographs and a piano. Two guest beers come from micro-breweries. Good value meals. Children's certificate.
🏚 Q 🕸 ◖🍽 ⇌ P

POTTERS CROUCH

HOLLYBUSH
Bedmond Lane (off A4147)
OS116053
☎ (01727) 851792
11.30 (12 Sat)-2.30, 6 (7 Sat)-11; 12-2.30, 7-10.30 Sun
Fuller's Chiswick, London Pride, ESB Ⓗ
Early 18th-century, oak-beamed pub in rural surroundings, boasting large oak tables from the Isle of Man and period chairs.
🏚 Q 🕸 ◖P

PYE CORNER

PLUME OF FEATHERS
On High Wych road, between Harlow and Sawbridgeworth
☎ (01279) 424154
11.30-3, 5.30 (7 Sat)-11; 12-4, 7-10.30 Sun
Courage Best Bitter; Marston's Pedigree; guest beers Ⓗ
Former court house and coaching inn with a resident ghost, offer-ing three regularly changing guest beers and occasional live music. Family oriented, it has a small public bar and an enclosed rear patio and is popular on summer eves.
🏚 🕸 ◖🌙 🍽 ♣ P

RICKMANSWORTH

FOX & HOUNDS
183 High Street
☎ (01923) 441119
11-11; 12-10.30 Sun
Courage Best Bitter, Directors; guest beer Ⓗ
Traditional town pub retaining two separate bars: a friendly, comfortable public bar, and a pleasant lounge at the rear. The good lunchtime specials are home cooked.
🏚 Q 🕸 ◖🍽 ⇌ ⊖ ♣ P

SAWBRIDGEWORTH

GATE INN
81 London Road (Harlow side of mini-roundabouts)
☎ (01279) 722313
11.30-2.30, 5-30 (5 Fri & Sat)-11; 12-3, 7-10.30 Sun
Adnams Bitter; Brakspear Special; Castle Eden Ale; King & Barnes Sussex; guest beers Ⓗ
18th-century pub on the site of the town's Parsonage Gate, very popular with all ages. Regularly changing guest beers (over 1,200). Mini-fest held every bank holiday. No food Sun.
◖♿ ⇌ ♣ 👐 P 🖽

SOUTH MIMMS

BLACK HORSE
65 Blackhorse Lane (200 yds from B556) ☎ (01707) 642174
11-3, 5.30-11; 11-11 Fri & Sat; 12-3, 7-10.30 Sun
Greene King IPA, Abbot, season-al beers Ⓗ
Lively local with a friendly wel-come; darts in the public bar, cosy lounge. Meals served Mon-Sat lunch and Tue eve.
🏚 🕸 ◖🐕 P

ST ALBANS

BLACKSMITHS ARMS
56 St Peters Street (on round-about, N end) ☎ (01727) 855761
11-11; 12-10.30 Sun
Boddingtons Bitter; Flowers IPA; Marston's Pedigree; Whitbread Abroad Cooper; Wadworth 6X; guest beers Ⓗ Ⓖ
Hogshead chain, large city-centre ale house with open-plan, split-level bar. Old photographs of St Albans mingle with breweriana. Up to six guest beers plus cider on gravity. Food all day but not after 4 Fri & Sat. Patio tables and a car park at the rear.
🕸 ◖🌙 ⇌ (City) 👐 P

FARMERS BOY
134 London Road
☎ (01727) 766702
11-11; 12-10.30 Sun
Adnams Bitter; Verulam Special, IPA, Farmers Joy; guest beer Ⓗ
One-bar pub, the home of Verulam Brewery. Food is served all day including Sun.
🏚 🕸 ◖🌙 ⇌ (City)

LOWER RED LION
34-36 Fishpool Street
☎ (01727) 855669
12-2.30, 5.30-11; 12-11 Sat; 12-3, 7-10.30 Sun
Adnams Bitter; Fuller's London Pride; guest beers Ⓗ
This 17th-century coaching inn is a genuine free house serving five guest beers from microbreweries and a house beer from Tring. Annual beer festivals in May and August. No food Sun. Occasional cider. Good B&B.
🏚 Q 🕸 🛏 ◖👐 P

MERMAID
98 Hatfield Rd ☎ (01727) 854487
11-3, 5-11; 12-5 Sun
Adnams Bitter; Everards Bitter, Tiger, Original; guest beers (occasional) Ⓗ
Friendly, one-bar pub whose licensee is a winner of Everards top Cellarmanship award. Backgammon and Go played Mon and Wed. Weekday lunches.
🕸 ◖♣ P

WHITE LION
21 Sopwell Lane
☎ (01727) 850540
12-3, 5-11; 12-11 Sat; 12-3, 7-10.30 Sun
Adnams Bitter; Draught Bass; Tetley Bitter; guest beer Ⓗ
Two-bar, 16th-century pub. The large garden has a boules pitch and children's play area. Children admitted if supervised.
🕸 ◖🌙 ♿

STEVENAGE

FISHERMAN
Fishers Green (off Clovelly Way)
☎ (01438) 725778
11-11; 12-10.30 Sun
Benskins BB; Marston's Pedigree; Morland Old Speckled Hen; Tetley Bitter Ⓗ
Large, one-bar pub with two din-ing areas (steaks a speciality). Fishing equipment features in the decor. Wheelchair WC.
Q 🐕 🕸 ◖🌙 ♿ ♣ P

TONWELL

ROBIN HOOD & LITTLE JOHN
14 Ware Road ☎ (01920) 463352
12-2.30 (3 Sat), 5.30-11; 12-3, 5.30-11 Sun
Dark Horse Ale; guest beers Ⓗ
Well refurbished pub; one bar on

split levels with a no-smoking restaurant annexe.This free house offers an excellent choice of changing guest beers, and a range of food at reasonable prices, but it remains a pleasant village local. 🏚 🕸 �'🍺 ◖ 🇩 P

TRING

KINGS ARMS
King Street (near Natural History Museum) ☎ (01442) 823318
12 (11.30 Sat)-2.30 (3 Fri & Sat), 7-11; 12-4, 7-10.30 Sun
Adnams Bitter; Brakspear Special; Wadworth 6X; guest beers Ⓗ
Back-street local, always busy even though hard to find. A constantly changing range of ales and ciders draws a mixed clientele. A good drinking pub serving healthy, wholesome food. Covered, unusual, heated beer garden. No-smoking area lunchtime only.
🏚 Q 🕸 ◖ 🇩 ♣ ⏷ 🍴 🗒

ROBIN HOOD INN
1 Brook Street (by cattle market) ☎ (01442) 824912
11.30-2.30, 5.30-11; 11-3, 6.30-11 Sat; 12-3, 7-10.30 Sun
Fuller's Chiswick, London Pride, ESB, seasonal beers Ⓗ
Superb olde-worlde pub, always gleaming. The excellent menu specialises in seafood (all fresh). The licensee has many Fuller's awards including *Country Pub of the Year*. A friendly and lively place. 🏚 🕸 ◖ 🇩 ♣

TYTTENHANGER GREEN

PLOUGH
Off A414, St Albans-Hatfield road ☎ (01727) 857777
11-2.30 (3 Sat), 6-11; 12-3, 7-10.30 Sun
Fuller's London Pride, ESB; Greene King Abbot; guest beers Ⓗ
Popular free house serving good value lunches. A large collection of bottled beers; the house ale is brewed by Mansfield. The garden is popular in summer (good play equipment). 🏚 🕸 ◖ ♣ P

WALTHAM CROSS

VAULT
160 High Street (opp McDonald's) ☎ (01992) 631600
11-11; 12-3.30, 7-10.30 Sun
Beer range varies Ⓗ
One bar pub, an independent free house, hosting live music Thu and quiz nights Sun. Children allowed until 7pm. Traditional home-cooked food, with children's meals available. The piped music can be rather loud. Popular with all ages. Good range of fruit country wines. 🕸 ◖ ≈

WARE

ALBION
12 Crib Street (behind St Mary's church) ☎ (01920) 463599
11-11; 12-4, 7-10.30 Sun
Adnams Bitter; Boddingtons Bitter; Flowers IPA; Fuller's London Pride Ⓗ
Oak-beamed bar in a 16/17th-century half-timbered building adorned with wonderful floral displays outside in summer. No food Sun. 🏚 ◖ ≈

CROOKED BILLET
140 Musley Hill ☎ (01920) 462516
12-2.30 (not Wed or Thu), 6-11; 12-11 Sat; 12-10.30 Sun
Greene King XX Mild or **IPA, Abbot, seasonal beer** Ⓗ
Friendly local, well worth finding. 🏚 🕸 ◖ 🇩 ♣

WORPPELL
35 Watton Rd ☎ (01920) 462572
11.30-2.30, 5-11; 11-11 Fri & Sat; 12-5, 7-10.30 Sun
Greene King IPA, Abbot, seasonal beers Ⓗ
Well deserving *Guide* regular with a loyal following. Pictures of the town adorn the walls.
◖ ≈ ♣

WARESIDE

CHEQUERS INN
On B1004 (Much Hadham-Ware road) ☎ (01920) 467010
12-3, 6-11; 12-11 Sat; 12-10.30 Sun
Adnams Bitter; Greene King Abbot; guest beer Ⓗ
Friendly village pub, with a restaurant room to the rear. A popular stop for ramblers. The house ale is brewed by the Dark Horse Brewery. Book for Sun lunch (no meals Sun eve). Good B & B. 🏚 Q �'🍺 ◖ 🇩 🍺 ♣ P

WELHAM GREEN

HOPE & ANCHOR
2 Station Road ☎ (01707) 262935
11-2.30, 5-11; 11-11 Sat; 12-10.30 Sun
Courage Best Bitter, Directors; John Smith's Bitter Ⓗ
Early 19th-century pub, originally in the hands of the church organist who paid the bell ringers in ale. Two contrasting bars featuring brass in the saloon. Prize-winning gardens. No food Sun. Q 🕸 ◖ 🍺 ♿ ≈ ♣ P

WHITWELL

MAIDENS HEAD
67 High Street ☎ (01438) 871392
11.30-3, 5-11; 11.30-4, 6-11 Sat; 12-3, 7-10.30 Sun

Draught Bass; McMullen AK, Country, seasonal beers Ⓗ
Timbered village pub of character, populated by friendly locals and staff. Good home-cooked food (not served Mon eve). One of McMullen's best outlets and 1996 CAMRA East Anglian *Pub of the Year*. 🏚 🕸 ◖ 🇩 🍺 ♣ P

WIDFORD

GREEN MAN
High Street (B180) ☎ (01279) 842454
12-11; 12-10.30 Sun
Courage Directors; McMullen AK, Gladstone, seasonal beers Ⓗ
One-bar village pub with a large garden to the rear. Out of the way, but worth finding, it attracts a mixture of local and passing trade. Live jazz every Sun eve. Meals always available. ◖ 🇩 ♣ P

WILDHILL THORP

WOODMAN
45 Wildhill Lane (between A100 and B158) OS265068 ☎ (01707) 642618
11.30-2.30, 5.30-11; 12-2.30, 7-10.30 Sun
Greene King IPA, Abbot, seasonal beers; McMullen AK; guest beers Ⓗ
Welcoming local which supports micro-breweries with its guest beer policy. Local CAMRA *Pub of the Year* 1997. A pub worth finding. Q 🕸 ◖ ♣ P 🗒

WILLIAN

THREE HORSESHOES
Baldock Lane (tiny lane opp the church, 1 mile off A1(M) jct 9) OS225308 ☎ (01462) 685713
11-11; 12-10.30 Sun
Greene King IPA, Abbot, seasonal beers; guest beers Ⓗ
Comfortable, single-bar pub, offering a friendly welcome; popular with locals. Darts and bridge tournaments (held in the function room) and regular music eves help make this a real community pub. 🏚 🕸 ◖ 🇩 ♣

INDEPENDENT BREWERIES

Dark Horse:
Hertford

McMullen:
Hertford

Tring:
Tring

Verulam:
St Albans

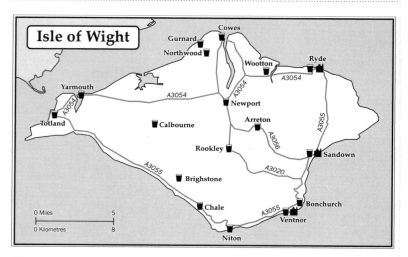

Isle of Wight

ARRETON

WHITE LION
Main Road ☎ (01983) 528479
11-3, 6-11 (11-11 summer); 12-3, 6-10.30 (12-10.30 summer) Sun
Badger Dorset Best; Draught Bass; Fuller's London Pride Ⓖ Ⓗ
Excellent refurbishment of a traditional country pub, with a collection of genuine old pub signs and an aviary at the back. Near many places of interest to visitors. Good food.
🏚 Q ⛵ ❀ ◖ ▶ ♣ P ⅃

BONCHURCH

BONCHURCH INN
The Shute (off Sandown Road)
☎ (01983) 852611
11-4 (3 winter), 6.30-11; 12-3, 7-10.30 Sun
Courage Best Bitter, Directors Ⓖ
Superbly preserved stone pub tucked away in a courtyard, formerly the stables of the adjacent manor house. The floors are from a ship's deck, the chairs from a liner. Authentic Italian food served. Q ❀ ⛵ ❀ ◖ ▶ ♿ ♿ ♣

BRIGHSTONE

COUNTRYMAN
Limerstone Rd ☎ (01983) 740616
11-3, 7-11 (11-11 summer); 12-3, 7-10.30 Sun
Badger Dorset Best, Tanglefoot; Goddards Special Ⓗ
Spacious, friendly, country roadhouse with a large lounge bar and extensive function room. A good family pub with a reputation for good food.
🏚 Q ⛵ ❀ ◖ ▶ Å ♣ P ⅃

CALBOURNE

BLACKSMITHS ARMS
Park Cross
☎ (01983) 529265
11-3, 6-11 (11-11 summer); 12-10.30 Sun
Beer range varies Ⓗ
National CAMRA runner-up *Pub of the Year* 1997, serving a diverse range of British and imported beers including examples of rare brewing styles. Popular for its German food, it has panoramic views of Parkhurst Forest and the NW of the island.
🏚 Q ⛵ ❀ ◖ ▶ Å ♣ P ⅃

Try also: Sportsmans Rest, Porchfield (Ushers)

CHALE

WIGHT MOUSE
Church Place, Newport Road
☎ (01983) 230431
11-11; 12-10.30 Sun
Boddingtons Bitter; Gale's HSB; Marston's Pedigree; Morland Old Speckled Hen; Wadworth 6X; Whitbread Fuggles Imperial Ⓗ
Very busy, old stone pub with an adjoining hotel, near Blackgang Chine theme park. This award-winning family and whisky pub has a garden with a play area. Three family rooms and 'Mouseworld' indoor play area for children. Food served all day (late supper licence); live music nightly.
🏚 Q ⛵ ❀ ⇖ ◖ ▶ ♿ Å P ⅃

COWES

ANCHOR INN
High Street ☎ (01983) 292823
11-11; 12-10.30 Sun
Boddingtons Bitter; Flowers Original; Fuller's London Pride; Greene King Abbot; Wadworth 6X; guest beers Ⓗ
Extended town pub, very popular with locals and yachtsmen. Live music, good food (interesting and varied menu, with barbecues in summer) and a good variety of ales are features.🏚 ❀ ◖ ▶

KINGSTON ARMS
Newport Road
☎ (01983) 293393
11-3, 6-11; 11-11 Mon, Fri & Sat; 12-4, 7-10.30 Sun
Gale's HSB; Ind Coope Burton Ale; Tetley Bitter Ⓗ
Large, friendly, local out of the town centre, offering home cooking. ⛵ ❀ ◖ ▶ ⊟ ♣ ☍ P

GURNARD

WOODVALE HOTEL
Princes Esplanade
☎ (01983) 292037
11-11; 12-10.30 Sun
Draught Bass; Fuller's London Pride; Goddards Fuggle-Dee-Dum; Wadworth 6X; guest beers Ⓗ
Superbly located, seafront pub with a large garden giving sunset views over the Solent. Live music Sat.🏚 ⛵ ❀ ◖ ▶ ♣

NEWPORT

CASK & CRISPIN
8-10 Carisbrooke Road
☎ (01983) 520666
11-3, 6-11; 12-3, 7-10.30 Sun
Burts Nipper, VPA, Newport Nobbler, seasonal beers; Goddards Special, Fuggle-Dee-Dum Ⓗ
Well refurbished, old town pub with a public car park at the rear; very much a beer drinker's establishment. It boasts stained wood, tiled floors and several intimate drinking areas. One of the five Burts' pubs on the island.
🏚 ❀ ♣ ☍

CASTLE
91 High Street
☎ (01983) 522528
11-11; 12-10.30 Sun
Draught Bass; Boddingtons Bitter; Fuller's London Pride; guest beer (summer) Ⓗ

Characterful, 17th-century stone, single-bar pub, replete with flag-stones and beams. It has served as a venue for cockfighting, a marriage parlour and a thieves' sanctuary. Eve meals in summer. ❀ ◖ ▶

PRINCE OF WALES
36 South Street (opp bus station)
☎ (01983) 525026
11-11; 12-10.30 Sun
Ushers Best Bitter, Founders, seasonal beers H
Lovely old-fashioned town local; this mock-Tudor building has so far resisted being themed.
Q ◖ ♣ ⌂ ☗

PRINCESS ROYAL
25 Cross Lane (off Staplers-Wootton road)
☎ (01983) 522056
11-4, 6-11; 11-11 Fri & Sat; 12-10.30 Sun
Ushers Best Bitter H
Delightful side-street local out of the town centre. ❀ ♣ P ☗

RAILWAY MEDINA
1 Sea Street
☎ (01983) 528303
11-3, 6-11 (11-11 summer); 12-4, 7-10.30 Sun
Gale's HSB; Marston's Pedigree; Webster's Green Label; guest beers H
Back-street corner local, full of character. Its name is derived from the now demolished railway station; railway memorabilia adorns the walls. Q ❀ ♣ ☗

NITON

WHITE LION
High Street
☎ (01983) 730293
11-3.30, 7-11; 12-3, 7-10.30 Sun
Boddingtons Bitter; Brakspear Special; guest beer H
Beautiful, historic village inn, serving good home-cooked food in a large (no-smoking) family dining room.
♨ Q ☎ ❀ ◖ ▶ ⌿ ▲ P ⨡

NORTHWOOD

TRAVELLERS JOY
85 Pallance Road (A3020 Yarmouth road out of Cowes)
☎ (01983) 298024
11-2.30, 5-11; 11-11 Fri & Sat; 12-3, 7-10.30 Sun
Goddards Special; Badger Best Bitter; Courage Directors; Ruddles County; Theakston Old Peculier; guest beers H
Well-supported beer exhibition house and regular local CAMRA award-winner. Eight handpumps give a good selection of beers all year round. Large car park and garden with children's play area and pets corner.
☎ ❀ ◖ ▶ ▲ ♣ ⌂ P ⨡

ROOKLEY

CHEQUERS
Niton Road (off A3020)
☎ (01983) 840314
11-11; 12-10.30 Sun
Courage Best Bitter, Directors; John Smith's Bitter; Marston's Pedigree H
Country pub at the heart of the island: a lounge bar, a large restaurant, a flagstoned public bar and spacious children's play area inside and out. An extensive menu of home-cooked food always includes fresh fish.
♨ ☎ ❀ ◖ ▶ ⌿ ▲ ♣ P ⨡

RYDE

FALCON INN
17 Swanmore Road
☎ (01983) 563900
11-3, 6-11; 11-11 Fri & Sat; 12-3, 7-10.30 Sun
Gale's Best Bitter, HSB H
Stone-built town local in a residential area, close to the town centre. ⌿ ≈ (St Johns Rd) ♣

HOLE IN THE WALL
68 St Johns Road (by station)
☎ (01983) 615405
11-3, 6-11; 11-11 Sat; 12-3, 7-10.30 Sun
Burts Nipper, Newport Nobbler; guest beers H
One of five Burts' pubs on the island, stocking several guests in addition to the Burts' range. A nicely extended and refurbished street-corner local, it hosts live music and periodic beer festivals.
♨ ☎ ❀ ≈ (St Johns Rd)

SIMEON ARMS
Simeon Street
☎ (01983) 614954
11-3, 6-11; 11-11 Sat; 12-10.30 Sun
Courage Best Bitter, Directors; Gale's HSB; guest beer H
Locals' pub, tucked away in a back street near the seafront. Eve meals in summer.
☎ ❀ ◖ ▶ ≈ ♣

Try also: Partlands, Swanmore Rd (Ushers)

SANDOWN

SANDOWN BREWERY & STILLROOM
15 St Johns Road (off High St)
☎ (01983) 403848
11-11; 12-10.30 Sun
Burts Nipper, VPA, Newport Nobbler; Fuller's London Pride; Theakston Old Peculier; guest beers H
Old commercial hotel which has undergone a complete refurbishment in both bars, with flagstones, wood floors, benches, settles and pub memorabilia. Behind the pub in a converted coach house is Burts brewery.

Outside, a large garden has a children's play area and petanque piste.
☎ ❀ ⌿ ◖ ▶ ⌂ ≈ ♣ P ⨡

TOTLAND

HIGHDOWN INN
Highdown Lane 1½ miles E of Alum Bay on old road) OS324858
☎ (01983) 752450
11-3, 7-11; (11-11 summer); 12-10.30 Sun
Ushers Best Bitter, Founders H
Country pub near some fine walks. Once a notorious smuggling den, it is now an excellent stopping off point during a bracing visit to Tennyson Down. Good food. ♨ Q ❀ ◖ ▶ ⌿ ▲ ♣ P ⨡

VENTNOR

VOLUNTEER
Victoria Street
☎ (01983) 852537
11-11; 12-10.30 Sun
Badger Best Bitter, Tanglefoot; Bateman Mild; Tetley Bitter; Ventnor Golden Bitter H
Traditional, friendly town local renovated to preserve its original character and displaying interesting memorabilia. ♨ Q ♣

WOOTTON

WOODMANS ARMS
119 Station Road
☎ (01983) 882785
11.30-3, 6-11; 12-3, 7-10.30 Sun
Flowers Original; Ventnor Golden Bitter; Wadworth 6X H
Pleasant country pub and restaurant on the outskirts of the village. Q ☎ ❀ ◖ ▶ ▲ ≈ ♣ P ☗

YARMOUTH

WHEATSHEAF
Bridge Road
☎ (01983) 760456
11-3, 6-11; 11-11 Sat & summer; 12-3, 7-10.30 Sun
Flowers Original; Goddards Fuggle-Dee-Dum; Morland Old Speckled Hen H
Old coaching house, now with additional rooms; spacious and comfortable for families, with good value food and beer.
♨ Q ☎ ❀ ◖ ▶ ⌿ ♣

INDEPENDENT BREWERIES

Burts:
Sandown
Goddards:
Ryde
Ventnor:
Ventnor

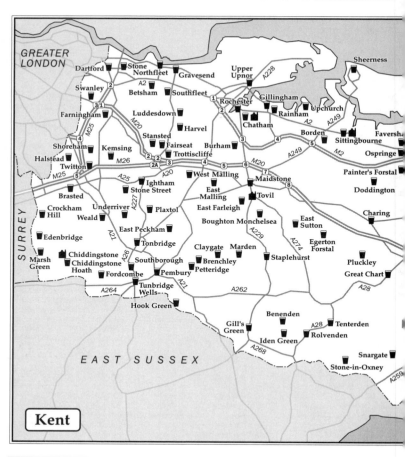

Kent

ACOL

CROWN & SCEPTRE
The Street
☎ (01843) 842079
11-11; 12-10.30 Sun
Shepherd Neame Master Brew Bitter, Best Bitter, Spitfire, seasonal beers H
Popular, two-bar pub, the focal point of the village, with a cosy lounge and lively public bar. Good value food.🕰 ❀ ◖ ▶ ♣ P

ASHFORD

SOUTH EASTERN TAVERN
79 Torrington Road
☎ (01233) 621344
11-11; 12-10.30 Sun
Shepherd Neame Master Brew Bitter H
Friendly, back-street town local with an L-shaped bar and hop-decorated high ceilings.
❀ 🚪 ⇌ ♣ P

BADLESMERE

RED LION
Ashford Road ☎ (01233) 740320

150

11.30-3, 6-11 (11.30-11 Fri & Sat); 12-10.30 Sun
Fuller's London Pride; Greene King XX Mild, Abbot; Shepherd Neame Master Brew Bitter; guest beers H
Popular free house offering a wide range of beers, and a rare local outlet for Theobolds cider. Beer festivals are held throughout the year, normally during bank holiday weekends. Live music Tue and Fri eves; happy hour Thu 7.30-8.30; no food Sun eve.
🕰 ❀ ◖ ▶ ▲ ♣ ⌂ P

BENENDEN

KING WILLIAM IV
The Street
☎ (01580) 240636
11-3, 6-11; 12-3, 7-10.30 Sun
Shepherd Neame Master Brew Bitter, Spitfire, seasonal beers H
Excellent, two-bar village local with a friendly, relaxed atmosphere and good food. Families welcome in the public bar.
🕰 Q ❀ ◖ ▶ 🍺 ♣ P

BETSHAM

COLYER ARMS
Station Road (B262, 1 mile S of A2) ☎ (01474) 832392
11-11; 12-10.30 Sun
Courage Best Bitter, Directors; Greene King Abbot; Shepherd Neame Master Brew Bitter; guest beers H
Village pub named after a local WWI VC hero. Hosts quiz nights and bat and trap and petanque teams. Good food in the restaurant, especially the Greek menus Tue-Sat eves (no food Sun eve). The large garden has a children's play area. The public bar has darts and pool. ❀ ◖ ▶ ♣ P

BISHOPSBOURNE

MERMAID
The Street (off A2, S of Canterbury) ☎ (01227) 830581
11.30-3, 6.10-11; 12-3, 7-10.30 Sun
Shepherd Neame Master Brew Bitter, seasonal beers H
Attractive, unpretentious pub (no fruit machines) in a typical Kentish village, worth a short

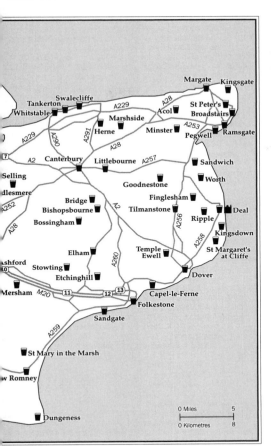

campsite are handy for the May beer festival.

BRASTED

BULL INN
High Street (A25)
☎ (01959) 562551
10.30-2.30, 5.30-11 (10.30-11 Sat & Bank Hols); 12-3, 7-10.30 Sun
Shepherd Neame Master Brew Bitter, Spitfire, Bishops Finger H
At the western end of a village noted for its antique shops. Popular for food but maintains its role as a focus for community life. Q ❀ ◑ 🍴 ⅃ ♣ P

BRENCHLEY

BULL
High Street
☎ (01892) 722701
11.30-3, 5-11; 11-3, 6-11 Sat; 12-4, 7-10.30 Sun
Greene King IPA, Abbot; Harveys BB; guest beer H
Victorian inn set at the heart of a picturesque village. The single bar with three drinking areas offers a warm welcome for strangers. The rear courtyard gives access to the gardens and function hall where a beer festival is held. ♨ ❀ ⇌ ◑ 🍴 ♣

BRIDGE

PLOUGH & HARROW
86 High Street OS183543
☎ (01227) 830455
11-3, 6-11; 11-11 Sat; 12-3, 7-10.30 Sun
Shepherd Neame Master Brew Bitter H
Traditional village local decorated with hop bines. It often wins Shepherd Neame's *Cellar of the Year* award. Good for games; friendly welcome. ♨ Q ♣

BROADSTAIRS

LANTHORNE
20 Callis Court Road
☎ (01843) 861952
11-3, 6-11; 11-11 Sat; 12-10.30 Sun
Courage Directors; Shepherd Neame Master Brew Bitter; Webster's Yorkshire Bitter; guest beers H
Busy, one-bar pub popular with drinkers of all ages. Close to St Peters recreation ground. Home of Thanet Wanderers rugby team. Sky TV. ❀ ♣ P

LORD NELSON
11 Nelson Place (opp parish church)
☎ (01843) 861210
11-4.30, 7-11; 11-11 Fri, Sat & summer; 12-10.30 Sun
Beards Best Bitter; Bateman Mild, XXXB; guest beer H
Welcoming, unspoilt, friendly

detour off the A2. In this *Guide* for 17 years. The electronic device by the dartboard takes all the hard work out of tossing a coin. Simple menu; eve meals most weekdays.
♨ Q ❀ ◑ 🍴 ♣

BORDEN

MAYPOLE
The Street OS883629
☎ (01795) 424253
12-2.30, 5.30-11; 12-11 Sat; 12-6 (10.30 summer) Sun
Shepherd Neame Master Brew Bitter; guest beers H
Popular, two-bar village local with an excellent restaurant, a large garden and a children's play area. Quiz Wed eve; discounted lunchtime meals Mon and Tue for senior citizens; eve meals Wed-Sat.
Q ⇌ ❀ ◑ 🍴 ⅃ P

BOSSINGHAM

HOP POCKET
The Street ☎ (01227) 709866
12-3.30, 7-11; 12-3.30, 7-10.30 Sun

Shepherd Neame Master Brew Bitter, Spitfire; Harveys BB; guest beers H
19th-century, candlelit pub, its ceiling hung with hops; popular for food (conservatory dining area). Selection of fruit wines. Huge garden.
♨ Q ⇌ ❀ ◑ 🍴 ▲ ♣ ⌂ P

BOUGHTON MONCHELSEA

RED HOUSE
Hermitage Lane (S off B2163, down Wierton Lane and East Hall Hill) OS783488
☎ (01622) 743986
12-3 (not Tue), 7-11; 12-11 Sat; 12-10.30 Sun
Burton Bridge Porter; Cotleigh Barn Owl; Greene King Abbot; Hop Back Summer Lightning; Otter Bitter; guest beers H
Ten consecutive years in this *Guide*, a welcoming country free house with an enterprising landlord, offering a good selection of guest beers, an extensive range of imported bottled beers and fruit wines. The large garden and

local, a short walk up from the harbour and beach. The building began life as a tailor's and draper's, becoming a pub in 1815. Watch out for the enormous (but never angry) Boss - the host's Great Dane.
🏠 ❀ ♣ P

PRINCE ALBERT
38 High Street
☎ (01843) 861937
10.30-11; 12-10.30 Sun
Courage Directors; Marston's Pedigree; Morland Old Speckled Hen; John Smith's Bitter; guest beers H
Small, cosy, one-bar pub, 100 yards from the main beach with a warm atmosphere. Excellent home-cooked food includes Sunday bar nibbles of locally caught seafood. Live music Mon and Fri eve; regular charity nights held. ◖ ▶ ≢

TARTAR FRIGATE
37 Harbour Street
☎ (01843) 862013
11-11; 12-10.30 Sun
Flowers IPA; Webster's Yorkshire Bitter; guest beers H
Classic, 17th-century flint-clad pub opposite the harbour and the beach. Read about local history here. Seafood restaurant. Children's certificate.
🏠 Q ◖ ♣

Try also: Bradstow Mill, High St (Whitbread)

BURHAM

TOASTMASTERS
65-67 Church Street
☎ (01634) 865299
12-11; 12-10.30 Sun
Greene King IPA; Young's Special; guest beers H
This tucked-away local features two different parts: the front bar has the real ale on seven handpumps; at the rear is an Asian restaurant. Well worth finding.
◖ ▶ ♣ P

CANTERBURY

CANTERBURY TALES
12 The Friars (opp Marlowe Theatre) ☎ (01227) 768594
11-11; 12-10.30 Sun
Shepherd Neame Master Brew Bitter; guest beers H
City-centre pub and bistro serving regular Kentish beers and an ever-changing variety of guests, including mini festivals. Live music Mon eve, jazz some Sun afternoons plus theme nights. Cider in summer (varies).
◖ ▶ ≢ (West) ♣ ⌂

JOLLY SAILOR
75 Northgate (near Cathedral and King's School)

☎ (01227) 463828
11-11; 12-10.30 Sun
Boddingtons Bitter; Flowers Original; Whitbread Abroad Cooper; guest beers H
Popular Hogshead pub celebrating its centenary this year. ◖

NEW INN
19 Havelock Street
☎ (01227) 464584
11.30-3, 6 (may vary)-11; 12-10.30 Sun
Greene King IPA; guest beers H
Mid-terrace Victorian traditional pub with a modern conservatory, used by locals and students alike.
🏠 ❀ ◖ 🕭 (East)

OLDE BEVERLIE
St Stephen's Green
☎ (01227) 463974
11.30-3, 6-11; 12-3, 6-10.30 Sun
Shepherd Neame Master Brew Bitter, Spitfire H
Traditional, comfortable local in the heart of the St Stephen's conservation area. Hosts quiz nights and monthly special food nights. Bat and trap played in the attractive walled garden.
❀ ◖ ♣ P

CAPEL-LE-FERNE

ROYAL OAK
New Dover Road (B2011, E of village) ☎ (01303) 244787
11.30-3 (4 Sat), 6 (7 Sat)-11; 12-4, 8-10.30 Sun
Shepherd Neame Master Brew Bitter; guest beers H
Old, split-level free house near the western end of White Cliffs heritage country. Snug bar and a games room. No food Wed.
🏠 Q ❀ ▶ Å ♣ P

CHARING

BOWL INN
Egg Hill Road OS950514
☎ (01233) 712256
5 (12 Fri & Sat)-11; 12-10.30 Sun
Fuller's London Pride; guest beers H
Normally three guest beers in a remote 16th-century inn. With its warm, friendly welcome, it is well worth finding. Annual beer festival in June with camping in the pub grounds.
🏠 ❀ Å ♣ P

CHATHAM

ALEXANDRA
43 Railway Street
☎ (01634) 300084
11-11; 12-3, 7-10.30 Sun
Shepherd Neame Master Brew Bitter, Spitfire, seasonal beers H
Ideally situated for the rail and bus stations. Noted for the dog in the window.
❀ ≢ ♣

CHIDDINGSTONE HOATH

ROCK INN
From Chiddingstone turn S through Wellers Town OS497432
☎ (01892) 870296
11.30-3, 6-11 (closed Mon); 12-3, 7-10.30 Sun
Larkins Bitter; Shepherd Neame Master Brew Bitter; guest beer H
Old, timber-framed rural building with a brick floor. Note the unusual octagonal wooden pump handles. Larkins beer is brewed locally. Ringing the Bull played. No food Sun eves.
🏛 Q ❀ ◖ ▶ ♣ P

CLAYGATE

WHITE HART
On B2162, Yalding-Horsmonden road ☎ (01892) 730313
11-3, 6-11; 12-3, 7-10.30 Sun
Goacher's Light; Shepherd Neame Master Brew Bitter; Wadworth 6X H
Comfortable, Victorian country inn set in open countryside, amid orchards and hop gardens. Large restaurant serving excellent value food. Biddenden cider. Large garden.
🏛 Q ❀ ⇔ ◖ ▶ 🕭 Å ⌂ P ♣ 🕭

CROCKHAM HILL

ROYAL OAK
Main Road (B2026/B269 jct)
☎ (01732) 866335
11.30-2.30, 6-11; 12-3, 7-10.30 Sun
Shepherd Neame Master Brew Bitter, Spitfire; guest beers H
Attractive, small country pub at the centre of village life. Small car park and garden. Eve meals Tue-Sat. 🏛 ❀ ◖ ▶ ♣ P

DARTFORD

PAPER MOON
55 High Street
☎ (01322) 281127
10-11; 12-10.30 Sun
Courage Directors; Fuller's London Pride; Shepherd Neame Spitfire; Theakston Best Bitter; Younger Scotch; guest beers H
Town-centre Wetherspoons pub, formerly a bank. Three guest beers always available from a wide portfolio, plus regular competitively-priced beer festivals. Good value food served until one hour before closing time. Wheelchair WC.
Q ◖ ▶ 🕭 ≢ ⅏ 🕭

TIGER
28 St Albans Road (off A226, East Hill) ☎ (01322) 293688
11-11; 12-10.30 Sun
Courage Best Bitter; Shepherd Neame Master Brew Bitter; guest beers H

Side-street, corner local with darts, pool and football teams creating a bustling atmosphere. No meals at weekends.
🏠 ◖ ⇌ ♣

WAT TYLER
80 High Street
☎ (01322) 272546
10-11; 12-10.30 Sun
Courage Best Bitter; Greene King Abbot; Young's Special; guest beers Ⓗ
Historic, town-centre free house, named after the 14th-century leader of the Peasants' Revolt. Good value ales and food with constantly changing guest beers. Occasional live music Fri and Sat eves but no juke box or piped music.
Q ◖ ⇌

DEAL

ADMIRAL PENN
79 Beach Street
☎ (01304) 374279
11-3, 6-11; closed Sun
Draught Bass; Fuller's London Pride; Wells Bombardier Ⓗ
Smart seafront bar with much nautical memorabilia and a notable selection of continental spirits and liqueurs.
🏠 ◖ ⇌ ♣

ALMA
126 West Street
☎ (01304) 360244
10-3, 6-11; 12-3, 6-10.30 Sun
Shepherd Neame Master Brew Bitter; guest beers Ⓗ
Single bar local, close to the station, stocking an interesting range of guest beers.
⇌ ♣

ANTWERP
45 Beach Street
☎ (01304) 374843
10.30-5, 7-11 (not Tue eve); 12-4, 7-10.30 Sun
Beer range varies Ⓗ
Inventive free house selling beers from Swale and Kent breweries. An interesting range of non-alcoholic beverages includes nettle ale and elderflower water. Lunches Thu-Sat.
◖ ⇌

SARACENS HEAD
1 Alfred Square
☎ (01304) 381650
10.30-11; 12-6 Sun
Shepherd Neame Master Brew Bitter, Spitfire, Bishops Finger Ⓗ
Large single bar pub towards the northern end of the historic part of town.
🏠 🍴 ◖ ⇌ ♣

Try also: Deal Hoy, Duke St (Shepherd Neame)

DODDINGTON

CHEQUERS
The Street
OS935573
11-3.45, 7-11; 11-11 Fri & Sat; 12-3, 7-10.30 Sun
Shepherd Neame Master Brew Bitter, Bishops Finger, seasonal beer Ⓗ
Excellent and popular two-bar village pub with a warm and friendly welcome. South East CAMRA Pub of the Year 1995 and a regular entry in this Guide. Always well worth a visit.
🏠 Q ⛺ 🏠 ◖ 🍴 ♣ P

DOVER

BLAKES
52 Castle Street (100 yds from Market Sq)
☎ (01304) 202194
12-3 (not winter Sat), 6-11; 6-10.30 (closed winter) Sun
Fuller's London Pride; Hancock's HB; guest beers Ⓗ
Small basement bar/restaurant in a mid-19th-century terrace. The ground-floor bar is available for overflow/functions. Popular with the business community and cross-channel travellers, but also retains a local following. Wide selection of Scottish and Irish whiskies.
🏠 ◖ 🍴 ⇌ (Priory)

CASTLE INN
Russell Street (off A20, next to bus garage)
☎ (01304) 202108
11-11; 12-10.30 Sun
Beer range varies Ⓗ
Enterprising, rejuvenated managed house. Two differing strength ales from micros or regional breweries change weekly.
◖ ⇌ (Priory)

FLOTILLA & FIRKIN
1 Bench Street (off A20, York St. roundabout)
☎ (01304) 204488
11-11; 12-10.30 Sun
Firkin Brewery Cast-Ale, Flotilla, Chann-ale, Dogbolter, seasonal beers Ⓗ
Formerly the Dover Tavern alehouse now refurbished in Firkin style. Next to the White Cliffs Experience.
◖ ⇌ (Priory)

MOGUL
Chapel Place (50 yds off York St. roundabout)
11-11; 12-10.30 Sun
Beer range varies Ⓗ
Turn of the century, one-bar pub, boasting views over the town centre and harbour. Emphasis on local brews. Keen sports/games interest.
🏠 ⇌ ♣

DUNGENESS

BRITANNIA
Dungeness Road
☎ (01797) 321959
11-11; 11-10.30 Sun
Fuller's London Pride; John Smith's Bitter; Morland Old Speckled Hen; guest beers Ⓗ
This beach-side pub started life as an army blockhouse. A warm welcome is assured. Popular with locals for both beer and food.
🏠 🏠 ◖ 🍴 P

EAST FARLEIGH

FARLEIGH BULL
Lower Road
☎ (01622) 726282
11-11; 12-10.30 Sun
Adnams Bitter; Boddingtons Bitter; Fuller's London Pride; King & Barnes Sussex; Wadworth 6X Ⓗ
Comfortable Victorian pub with a warm welcome. Large gardens house various animals including Winston, the pot-bellied pig. The petanque piste is used for major tournaments. Pig roast in summer (not Winston). A focus for the village community. Children's certificate. Cider varies.
🏠 🏠 ◖ 🍴 ⛺ ⇌ ♣ 🍷 P 🍴

VICTORY
Farleigh Bridge (by station)
☎ (01622) 726591
11-11; 12-10.30 Sun
Goacher's Dark; Tetley Bitter; guest beer Ⓗ
Friendly, mid-Victorian local close to the River Medway and ancient Farleigh bridge. The large garden boasts picturesque views and a children's play area. Popular for Sun lunch (booking advised), with a no-smoking dining area. Use station car park.
🏠 ◖ 🍴 ⛺ ⇌ ♣

WHITE LION
Dean Street
☎ (01622) 727395
11.30-3, 6.30 (7 Sat)-11 (closed Mon); 12-3, (closed eve) Sun
Fuller's London Pride; Harveys BB; Larkins Traditional Ale; guest beer Ⓗ
Charming 16th-century free house, dating from 1565 with an interesting history. Business clientele at lunchtime, a cosy, intimate atmosphere eves.
🏠 Q 🏠 ◖ 🍴 P 🍴

EAST MALLING

RISING SUN
125 Mill Street ☎ (01732) 843284
12-11; 12-10.30 Sun
Goacher's Light; Shepherd Neame Master Brew Bitter; guest beers Ⓗ
Good village local with interesting guest beers. Games area at

the back; sport on TV. Very keen beer prices for the area. No food weekends. 🐓 🍺 ≈ ♣

EAST PECKHAM

HARP
218 Hale Street (A228/B2015 jct) ☎ (01622) 872334
11-11; 12-10.30 Sun
Fuller's London Pride; Harveys BB; Ruddles Best Bitter; guest beer 🅷
Pub with two bar areas featuring old beams and brasses. A good atmosphere is enhanced by events, games and excellent food. ⚔ 🐓 🍺 ♿ ♣ ⌂ P

Try also: Bush, Blackbird & Thrush (Shepherd Neame)

EAST SUTTON

SHANT & PRINCE OF WALES HOTEL
East Sutton Road (A274, left at Weald Golf Club, pub 1¼ miles) ☎ (01622) 842235
11-11; 12-3, 7-10.30 Sun
Beer range varies 🅷
Deriving its name from hop picking slang, the pub is surrounded by hop fields and orchards. A flagstone floor leads to a comfortable dining area. Low beams aplenty and a vast log fire in winter. Six beers usually available. (three guests). Cask breather is used on John Smith's.
⚔ Q 🐓 🛏 🍺 ⚓ P ✄

EDENBRIDGE

CROWN
High Street
☎ (01732) 867896
11-11; 12-3, 7-10.30 (12-10.30 summer) Sun
King & Barnes Sussex; Larkins Traditional Ale; Shepherd Neame Master Brew Bitter; guest beers 🅷
15th-century coaching house whose sign spans the street. Friendly welcome with a good atmosphere.
⚔ 🚌 🐓 🛏 🍺 ≈ P

EGERTON FORSTAL

QUEEN'S ARMS
OS893464
☎ (01233) 756386
11.30 (11 summer)-2, 6.30-11; 12-3, 7-10.30 Sun
Harveys BB; Rother Valley Level Best; Swale Kentish Pride; Wells Bombardier; guest beers 🅶
Quiet village local with beamed ceilings; hard to find but well worth it. Wells Bombardier was named after the landlady's father - Bombardier Billy Wells. Good home-cooked food (not served Tue); steaks cooked to order.
⚔ Q 🐓 🍺 ♣ ⌂ P

ELHAM

ROSE & CROWN
High Street
☎ (01303) 840226
11-3, 6-11; 12-3, 7-10.30 Sun
Bateman XB; guest beers 🅷
Traditional pub serving three guest beers with an occasional mild. Good range of home-cooked food (children allowed in eating areas). Accommodation is in a converted stable
⚔ Q 🐓 🛏 🍺 ♣ P ✄

ETCHINGHILL

ETCHINGHILL GOLF CLUB
☎ (01303) 862929
11-11; 12-7 Sun
Shepherd Neame Master Brew Bitter; guest beer 🅷
Comfortable club house bar offering good views of the course and surrounding countryside. Wheelchair WC.
⚔ 🐓 🍺 ♿ ♣ P ✄

FAIRSEAT

VIGO INN
Gravesend Road (A227, 1 mile N of A20/M20)
☎ (01732) 822547
12-3 (not Mon, 12-4 Sat), 6-11; 12-4, 7-10.30 Sun
Flagship Ensign Ale; Harveys XX Mild, BB; Young's Bitter, Special; guest beer 🅷
Traditional ale drinkers' haven with at least one mild available and local brewers supported (no real cider). Ancient drovers' inn named in honour of local resident who fought in the famous battle. Features the rare Dadlums table (Kentish skittles). Not to be missed. ⚔ Q 🐓 ♣ P ✄ 🎲

FARNINGHAM

CHEQUERS
High Street ☎ (01322) 865222
11-11; 12-10.30 Sun
Fuller's London Pride, ESB; Taylor Landlord; guest beers 🅷
Excellent corner local in a picturesque riverside village. Up to six guest beers usually available. Good reputation for home-made lunches (not served Sun). 🍺 ♣

FAVERSHAM

ANCHOR
52 Abbey Street
☎ (01795) 536471
11-3.30, 7-11; 12-3, 7-10.30 Sun
Shepherd Neame Master Brew Bitter, Spitfire, seasonal beers 🅷
Ancient, two-bar pub across the end of one of the town's most historic streets. Just a few steps from Standard Quay with its many sailing barges. Enjoy the ambience of real fires and good company. ⚔ 🐓 🍺 🎲

CROWN & ANCHOR
41 The Mall
☎ (01795) 532812
10.30-3, 5.30-11; 10.30-4, 6.30-11 Sat; 12-3, 7-10.30 Sun
Shepherd Neame Master Brew Bitter 🅷
A warm welcome awaits those who enter this likeable pub. The beer is the pint to judge others upon. The goulash is recommended as it is authentic - the landlord is Hungarian. Weekday lunches.
🍺 ≈ ♣

SHIPWRIGHTS ARMS
Hollowshore (at Davington right at pub's sign into Ham Rd, then left, then right)
OS017636
☎ (01795) 590088
11-11; 12-10.30 Sun
Goacher's Mild; Shepherd Neame Master Brew Bitter; guest beer (occasional) 🅶
A lonely outpost in the empire of real ale, enjoying superb views across creek and marsh. Generates its own electricity. Probably the only pub outlet for the local Pawley Farm cider. Dadlums, bagatelle and other games played.
⚔ 🚌 🐓 🍺 ⚓ ⌂ P ✄

SWAN & HARLEQUIN
Quay Lane
☎ (01795) 532341
11-11; 12-10.30 Sun
Adnams Bitter; Boddingtons Bitter; Marston's Pedigree; Shepherd Neame Master Brew Bitter; Wadworth 6X 🅷
Two-bar pub close to the brewery and creekside industries. Note the fine collection of pub signs and other memorabilia.
⚔ 🚌 🐓 🛏 🍺 ⚓ ≈ ♣ P

FINGLESHAM

CROWN
The Street
☎ (01304) 612555
11-3, 6-11; 12-3, 7-10.30 Sun
Courage Best Bitter, Directors; Shepherd Neame Master Brew Bitter; guest beers 🅷
Award-winning, popular local with a dining area (booking advisable).
🐓 🍺 ⚓ P

FOLKESTONE

CLIFTON HOTEL
The Lees (opp Lees Cliff Hall)
☎ (01303) 851231
11-3, 5.45-midnight; 11.30-3, 7-10.30 Sun
Draught Bass; Courage Directors 🅷
Popular with Bass drinkers, the plush bar of this three-star hotel overlooks the English Cannel.
Q 🚌 🐓 🍺 ≈ (Central) ♣

LIFEBOAT INN
42 North Street (near yacht club)
☎ (01303) 243958
11.30-11; 12-10.30 Sun
Draught Bass; Fuller's London Pride; M&B Brew XI; guest beer Ⓗ
Classic, back-street pub serving up to four beers, with guest ales often from independent microbreweries. Eve meals served 5-7.
🏮 ◖ ▶ ♣

SPORTSMANS BAR
Folkestone Sports Centre,
Radnor Park Avenue
12-3, 6-11; 12-3, 7-10.30 Sun
Boddingtons Bitter; guest beers Ⓖ
Sports club bar with a comfortable lounge, stocking three guest beers. ◖ ▶ ♿ ⇌ P

FORDCOMBE

CHAFFORD ARMS
Springhill (B2188)
11-2.30 (3 Sat), 6-11; 12-3, 7-10.30 Sun
Beer range varies Ⓗ
Typical country inn with ivy-clad exterior: a lounge and public bar with original open fires plus a restaurant.
🏮 🏮 ◖ ▶ 🍴 ♣ P

GILLINGHAM

BARGE
63 Layfield Rd ☎ (01634) 850485
12-3, 7-11; 12-11 Sat; 12-10.30 Sun
Wadworth 6X; guest beers Ⓗ
Thriving end-of-terrace single-bar town house. The house beer Joshua Ale is brewed by Flagship and is named after the publican's son, born early in 1998. Free folk club Mon eve. Good views of River Medway from the garden. Candlelit in eves. 🏮 ◖ ♣

DOG & BONE
21 Jeffrey Street
☎ (01634) 576829
11-11; 12-10.30 Sun
Beer range varies Ⓗ
Transformed into a single-bar town pub since the back bar was changed into a restaurant. Still retains its friendly atmosphere. Food is good value. Welcomes away supporters going to football matches at local professional club's ground.🏮 🏮 ◖ ▶ ⇌ ♣

FALCON
95 Marlborough Road
☎ (01634) 850614
12-3, 5.30-11; 12-11 Sat;
12-10.30 Sun
Ruddles Best Bitter; John Smith's Bitter; guest beers Ⓗ
Busy but compact single-bar local. Two guest beers usually available. Look for the painted mural on the garden wall.
◖ ▶ ⇌ ♣

FROG & TOAD
38 Burnt Oak Terrace
☎ (01634) 852231
12.30-3.30 (not Tue), 7-11; 12-3.30, 7-10.30 Sun
Fuller's London Pride; guest beers Ⓗ
A homely, one-bar town house that has no juke box or fruit machines, ideal for quiet conversation. Sunday barbecues in summer. Lucy's Ale when on is Flagship's Ensign rebadged (named after the pub dog).
Q 🏮 ⇌ ♣

PRINCE OF GUINEA
49 Medway Road
☎ (01634) 851534
11-11; 12-4, 7-10.30 Sun
Harveys Pale Ale BB, Armada, seasonal beers Ⓗ
Excellent policy of not selling keg bitters. This one-bar detached property offers a friendly welcome to a varied clientele, including long distance lorry drivers arriving at the docks nearby.
◖ ▶ ♣

ROSENEATH
79 Arden Street
☎ (01634) 852553
11.30-11; 12-10.30 Sun
Beer range varies Ⓗ
Popular, busy single-bar town house which offers six ales, generally from microbreweries. The ceiling is covered with toy parrots collected by the landlady.
🏮 ⇌ ♣

WILL ADAMS
73 Saxton Street
☎ (01634) 575902
12-3, 7-11; 12-3, 7-10.30 Sun
Fuller's London Pride; guest beers Ⓗ
Stays open all day Sat when the 'Gills' are playing home matches. Sells Imperial Russian Stout (bottle-conditioned ale); Good value food. Friendly welcome.
🏮 ◖ ⇌ ♣ ⌂

GILL'S GREEN

WELLINGTON ARMS
Off A229, N of Hawkhurst
☎ (01580) 753119
12-11; 12-10.30 sun
Bateman XXXB; Harveys BB; guest beers Ⓗ
Hidden away pub, popular with ramblers and those seeking wholesome food in pleasant, friendly surroundings (meals all day). Dates back to Elizabethan times. 🏮 🏮 ◖ ▶ P

GOODNESTONE

FITZWALTER ARMS
The Street
☎ (01304) 840303
11.30-3, 6 (7 winter)-11; 12-3, 7-10.30 Sun

Shepherd Neame Master Brew Bitter Ⓗ
Originally a gate lodge for the local landowner, hence the distinctive design. A good and very English village local. No food Sun eves. 🏮 🛏 ◖ ▶ ♣

GRAVESEND

JOLLY DRAYMAN
1 Love Lane, Wellington Street
☎ (01474) 352355
11.30 (12 Sat)-3, 6 (7 Sat)-11;
12-3, 7-10.30 Sun
Draught Bass; Fuller's London Pride; guest beers Ⓗ
Comfortable lounge-style, town-centre pub with low beams, the only pub in Kent to appear in every edition of this *Guide*. Part of the former Wellington Brewery, it is known locally as the Coke Oven. Lunches Tue-Fri; barbecues summer weekends.
🏮 ◖ ⇌ ♣

SOMERSET ARMS
10 Darnley Road (near station)
☎ (01474) 533837
11-11 (midnight Thu-Sat); 12-10.30 Sun
Beer range varies Ⓗ
Six continually rotating ales from all over Britain, not available elsewhere in town, in this country-style, town-centre pub, featuring wooden church pews and lots of brass. Disco Thu-Sun eves. ◖ ⇌

GREAT CHART

HOODEN HORSE
The Street OS982421
☎ (01233) 625583
11.30-2.30, 6 (5 Fri)-11; 11.30-11 Sat; 12-10.30 Sun
Goacher's Light; Hook Norton Old Hooky; Hop Back Summer Lightning; Rother Valley Level Best; Theakston Old Peculier; guest beers Ⓗ
Hop-strewn ceilings and candlelit tables feature in this tiled, timber-floored pub, the original in the Hooden Horse chain. Good food is served up to 15 minutes before closing time. 🏮 ◖ ▶ ⌂

HALSTEAD

ROSE & CROWN
Otford Lane (1/2 mile W of A224) OS489611
☎ (01959) 533120
11.30-11; 12-10.30 Sun
Courage Best Bitter; Harveys XX Mild (summer)**, Old; Larkins Traditional Ale; guest beers** Ⓗ
200-year-old flint-faced two-bar pub in a small village serving three interesting and oft-changing guest beers. Children welcome in the games room. Bat and trap played. Weekday lunches.
🏮 Q ⛱ 🏮 ◖ 🍴 ♿ ♣ P

HARVEL

AMAZON & TIGER
David Street ☎ (01474) 814705
12-3, 6-11; 12-10.30 Sun
Beer range varies Ⓗ
Comfortable, two-bar pub backing on to the village cricket green. Three handpumps serve constantly changing guest beers. Quiz Mon eve, live entertainment Fri eve. Eve meals Thu-Sat.
🏰 ❀ ◖ ▶ Å ♣ P

HERNE

HERNE VILLAGE FLORIST AND BEER CELLAR
Colonial Shop, Herne Street
☎ (01227) 371000
9-7 (midday Wed, 5 Sat); closed Sun and Bank Hols
Adnams Broadside; Fuller's London Pride, ESB; guest beers Ⓗ
The only licensed florist shop in the *Guide*, the owner moved his beer shop out from Canterbury in 1997. Well situated for locals and commuters for a good selection of English and Belgian bottled beers.

SMUGGLERS
1 School Lane ☎ (01227) 741395
11-3, 6-11; 11-11 Sat; 12-4, 7-10.30 Sun
Shepherd Neame Master Brew Bitter, Spitfire, seasonal beers Ⓗ
Popular local, swathed in hops, with two bars and a meeting room. The licensee takes full advantage of his brewery's seasonal beers. Only a slight detour from the A299 - well worth it! Meals Mon-Sat. ❀ ◖ ▶ ♣

HOOK GREEN

ELEPHANT'S HEAD
Furnace Lane (B2169)
☎ (01892) 890279
11 (12 Sat)-3, 6-11 (11-11 summer Sat); 12-3, 7-10.30 Sun
Harveys Pale Ale, BB, Old, Armada, seasonal beers Ⓗ
Stone-built, 15th-century pub in an isolated position, with a large garden and patio. Good selection of home-made meals, Sun carvery and barbecues in summer. Caravan sites at rear. A popular venue.
🏰 Q ❀ ◖ ▶ Å ♣ P

IDEN GREEN (BENENDEN)

WOODCOCK INN
Woodcock Lane (take lane to Standen St at crossroads, then left) OS807313
☎ (01580) 240009
11-11; 12-10.30 Sun
Draught Bass; Beards Best Bitter; Fuller's London Pride; Harveys BB; Rother Valley Level Best; guest beers Ⓗ

Isolated weatherboarded inn set amongst woodland, worth finding. The low-beamed main bar has cosy armchairs by the fire. Large garden. Families welcome in the dining area. Has a late licence until midnight.
🏰 Q ❀ ◖ ▶ P

IGHTHAM

OLD HOUSE ☆
Redwell lane (between A25 and A227, ½ mile SE of village) OS590559
☎ (01732) 882383
12-3 (not Mon-Fri), 7-11(9 Sat); 12-3, 7-10.30 Sun
Flowers IPA; Ⓗ **Otter Bitter; guest beer** Ⓖ
Hard-to-find hostelry with no pub sign: two unspoilt bars with a large open fireplace. A rare outlet for gravity dispensed ales: the range is liable to change but always interesting. 🏰 Q Å P

KEMSING

RISING SUN
Cotmans Ash Lane OS563599
☎ (01959) 522683
11-3, 6-11; 12-3, 6-10.30 Sun
Flowers Original; guest beers Ⓗ
Isolated hilltop country pub in pleasant countryside, attracting hikers all year and families in summer to the garden. Excellent quality home-cooked food. Two rotating guest beers, often from Kentish breweries, frequently including a mild; occasional cider.
🏰 Q ➤ ❀ ◖ ▶ Å ♣ P

KINGSDOWN

KINGS HEAD
Upper Street ☎ (01304) 373915
5-11; 12-3, 7-11 Sat; 12-3, 7-10.30 Sun
Draught Bass; Hancock's HB; guest beer Ⓗ
Smart village local in a narrow street leading to the beach. Opening hours subject to change. Eve meals Wed-Sat (booking advisable). ❀ ▶ Å ♣

Try also: Rising Sun, Cliffe Rd (Free)

KINGSGATE

FAYRENESS HOTEL
Marine Drive (½ mile off B2052 by Botany Bay) OS393710
☎ (01843) 861103
11-11; 12-10.30 Sun
Draught Bass; Courage Directors; Webster's Yorkshire Bitter; Young's Special; guest beers Ⓗ
Large, two-bar clifftop hotel with good views over the North Sea. Good value food in the restaurant. Children's certificate.
❀ ⇔ ◖ ▶ ♣ P

LITTLEBOURNE

KING WILLIAM IV
High Street (A257)
☎ (01227) 721244
11-11; 12-10.30 Sun
Draught Bass; Boddingtons Bitter; Shepherd Neame Master Brew Bitter; guest beers Ⓗ
Well maintained village inn with separate public bar and restaurant areas. Popular with ramblers. League darts and quiz nights held. 🏰 ❀ ⇔ ◖ ▶ ♣ P

LUDDESDOWN

COCK INN
Henley Street OS664672
☎ (01474) 814208
12-11; 12-10.30 Sun
Adnams Bitter, Broadside; Goacher's Mild; Young's Special; Ⓗ **guest beers** ⒽⒼ
Highly recommended, two-bar, genuine free house with a new conservatory, serving a wide range of beers and traditional ciders. No music or children; quiz Tue eve. Accessible by footpath from Sole Street station. Popular with ramblers.
🏰 Q ❀ ◖ ▶ Å ♣ ⌣ P

MAIDSTONE

HARE & HOUNDS
45-47 Lower Boxley Road (opp Prison) ☎ (01622) 678388
11-3.30 (12-5 Sat), 5.30-11; 12-3, 7-10.30 Sun
Flowers IPA; Fuller's London Pride; Taylor Landlord Ⓗ
Always a friendly welcome at this community award-winning, one-bar pub. Eve meals (Mon-Fri) end at 7pm; no lunch Sun.
❀ ◖ ▶ ⇌ (East) ♣

HOGSHEAD
24 Earl Street (off Week St)
☎ (01622) 758516
11-11; 12-10 Sun
Boddingtons Bitter; Flowers Original; Ⓗ **Harveys BB;** Ⓖ **King & Barnes Sussex; Marston's Pedigree;** Ⓗ **guest beers** ⒽⒼ
Traditional-style, town-centre pub drawing a varied clientele. A heated canopy warms the courtyard. Regular beer festivals. Live music Sun.
🏰 ❀ ◖ ⇌ (East) ⌣

PILOT
25-27 Upper Stone Street (A229)
☎ (01622) 691162
11-3, 6 (7 Sat)-11; 12-3, 7-10.30 Sun
Harveys XX Mild, BB, Old, Armada, seasonal beers Ⓗ
Grade II listed building, a regular *Guide* entry, with three distinct drinking areas, featuring water jug and hat collections. No food Sun. Petanque played.
🏰 Q ❀ ◖ ▶ ♣

RIFLE VOLUNTEERS
28 Wyatt Street
☎ (01622) 758891
11-3.30, 6-11; 11-4.30, 7-11 Sat;
12-3.30, 7-10.30 Sun
Goacher's Mild, Light, Dark Ⓗ
Original unspoilt, back-street pub
where beer and conversation
rule. Novel miniature soldiers are
used as tokens for 'beer in the
wood'. Excellent value, home-
cooked food (eve meals must be
booked). A Goacher's tied house.
Q ❀ ◖ ▶ ≠ (East) ♣

SWAN INN
2 County Road (follow signs to
County Hall)
☎ (01622) 751264
11-11; 12-10.30 Sun
**Shepherd Neame Master Brew
Bitter, Spitfire** Ⓗ
Friendly local community pub:
one bar with traditional games.
Lunchtime sandwiches and soup
available plus barbecues summer
weekends. ❀ ≠ (East) ♣ ☐

MARDEN

STILEBRIDGE INN
Staplehurst Road (A229 to
Linton) ☎ (01622) 831236
11.30-3, 6-11; 12-10.30 Sun
Beer range varies Ⓗ
A warm welcome is extended to
all at this spacious comfortable
inn with several bar areas and
impressive wood panelling. The
bias is towards rare micros, the
1,000th different ale being
served during 1998; up to seven
beers normally on. The beamed
restaurant serves excellent food
(all day Sun).
Q ➢ ❀ ◖ ▶ ♣ P ⅍

MARGATE

SPREAD EAGLE
25 Victoria Road (off B2055)
☎ (01843) 293396
11.30-3, 5.30-11; 11.30-11 Fri &
Sat; 12-10.30 Sun
**Fuller's London Pride; Greene
King IPA; Kent Swifty, Delight,
Crafty One; guest beers**
Cosy, award-winning back-street
local with a friendly welcome,
well worth seeking out. Good
value food (pizzas a speciality);
must book Sun. Thanet CAMRA
Pub of the Year for the last three
years. Children's certificate.
❀ ◖ ▶ ≠ ♣

MARSH GREEN

WHEATSHEAF
On B2028, Dormansland-
Edenbridge Road
☎ (01732) 864091
11-3, 5.30-11; 11-11 Sat;
12-10.30 Sun
**Adnams Bitter; Harveys BB;
Larkins Traditional Ale; Taylor
Landlord; guest beers** Ⓗ

Popular, friendly local with a conservatory dining area, specialising
in home-cooked food. Excellent
value. Guest beers usually include
a mild. Well worth a visit.
♨ Q ➢ ❀ ◖ ▶ ♿ ♣ ➾ P ⅍

MARSHSIDE

GATE INN
Take Chislet turning off A28 at
Upstreet ☎ (01227) 860498
11-2.30 (3 Sat), 6-11; 12-3, 7-11 Sun
**Shepherd Neame Master Brew
Bitter, Spitfire, seasonal beers** Ⓖ
Splendid country pub, now 22
years in this *Guide*. It features
apple trees, ducks, rugby and
themed food eves.
♨ Q ➢ ❀ ◖ ▶ Å ♣ P

MERSHAM

FARRIERS ARMS
Flood Street (approx 1 mile off
A20) ☎ (01233) 720444
11-2.30, 6.30-11; 12-3, 7-10.30 Sun
**Friary Meux BB; Morland Old
Speckled Hen; Young's Special** Ⓗ
Comfortable, two-bar pub next to
a mill stream, serving a wide
ranging menu.
♨ ❀ ⇋ ◖ ▶ Å ♣ P

MINSTER (THANET)

NEW INN
2 Tothill Street
☎ (01843) 821294
11.30-3, 6-11; 11-11 Fri & Sat;
12-10.30 Sun
**Greene King IPA; Wadworth 6X;
guest beers** Ⓗ
Attractive, one-bar village local,
displaying a collection of rustic
brass. Food comes in generous
portions (eve meals Tue-Sat).
♨ ❀ ◖ ▶ ♿ ≠ ♣ P

NEW ROMNEY

PRINCE OF WALES
Fairfield Road
☎ (01797) 562012
12-3, 6 (5 Thu)-11; 11-11 Fri &
Sat; 12-5, 7-10.30 Sun
**Ind Coope Burton Ale; Shepherd
Neame Master Brew Bitter;
guest beer** Ⓗ
Friendly community local away
from the town centre. Many
social activities and pub games,
including chess. Rolls available.
Handy for the Romney, Hythe and
Dymchurch light railway.
♨ Q ❀ ⊕ Å ♣

NORTHFLEET

EARL GREY
177 Vale Road (off Perry St, near
Cygnet Centre)
☎ (01474) 365240
11-2.30, 4.30-11; 11-11 Thu-Sat;
12-10.30 Sun
**Shepherd Neame Master Brew
Bitter, Spitfire, seasonal beers** Ⓗ

A fine Kentish flint exterior houses this strong community pub.
The oldest part of the building
dates from 1610 and it has been
a hostelry since 1780. A warm
atmosphere prevails. Pleasant
garden.
❀ ♣ P

OSPRINGE

ANCHOR
33 Ospringe Street
☎ (01795) 532085
12-3, 6-11; 12-11 Sat; 12-10.30
Sun
**Shepherd Neame Master Brew
Bitter** Ⓗ
Classic, three-bar pub on the
busy A2, a mile from Faversham
centre. A lively and active local.
Children welcome in the 'library'.
♨ ➢ ❀ ♣

PAINTERS FORSTAL

ALMA
OS992589
☎ (01795) 533835
10.30-3, 6-11; 12-3, 7-10.30 Sun
**Shepherd Neame Master Brew
Bitter, Spitfire, seasonal
beers** Ⓗ
Delightful village pub at the heart
of hop country. It has an extended saloon bar and a classic public
bar. Once known as 'the
Candlehouse' as window candles
showed the way to hop workers
from the surrounding fields. Eve
meals Tue-Sat.
❀ ◖ ▶ ⊕ Å ♣ P

PEGWELL

BELLE VUE
Pegwell Road
☎ (01843) 593991
11-11; 12-10.30 Sun
**Shepherd Neame Master Brew
Bitter, Best Bitter, Spitfire, seasonal beers** Ⓗ
Single-bar pub and restaurant
recently refurbished, enjoying
good views over Pegwell Bay and
the English Channel. A large
Tomson and Wotton mirror
adorns one wall. Children's certificate. Sky TV.
♨ ❀ ◖ ▶ Å P

PEMBURY

BLACK HORSE
12 High Street
☎ (01892) 822141
11-11; 12-3, 7-10.30 Sun
**Courage Directors; Morland
Old Speckled Hen; Theakston
Best Bitter, XB; Young's
Special** Ⓗ
Old village pub with a central bar
which divides the room into two
areas. A house beer is also available. Popular seafood restaurant
in the grounds.
♨ ❀ ◖ ▶

PETTERIDGE

HOPBINE
Petteridge Lane (2 miles N of A21) OS668413
☎ (01892) 722561
12 (11 Sat)-2.30, 6-11; 12-3, 7-10.30 Sun
King & Barnes Mild, Sussex, Broadwood, Festive, seasonal beers Ⓗ
Attractive, friendly brick and weatherboard pub on a hilly corner site. The only King & Barnes house in Kent; worth seeking out. No food Wed. ᐈ ❀ ◖❱ ⟲ P

PLAXTOL

GOLDING HOP
Sheet Hill (follow lane north from Church) OS600547
☎ (01732) 882150
11-3, 6-11; 11-11 Sat; 12-4, 7-10.30 Sun
Adnams Bitter, Broadside; Young's Special; guest beers Ⓖ
A gem of 15th-century origin, tucked away in a valley north of the village. The beers, direct from the barrel, can be enjoyed in a group of four whitewashed and beamed rooms, two with fires. Bar billiards available. The garden boasts a stream, ducks and a playground.
ᐈ Q ❀ ◖ ♣ ⟲ P

PLUCKLEY

DERING ARMS
Station Road
☎ (01233) 840371
12-2 (may extend), 6-11; 12-2, 7-10.30 Sun
Goacher's Dark, Ⓗ **Maidstone Porter** Ⓖ
Originally built as a hunting lodge for the Dering family, it features Dutch gables and 'Dering' windows. Excellent fresh food. The house beer is also from Goachers.
ᐈ Q ❦ ⇄ ◖❱ ⇌

RAINHAM

MACKLAND ARMS
213 Station Road
☎ (01634) 232178
10-11; 12-10.30 Sun
Shepherd Neame Master Brew Bitter, Best Bitter, Spitfire, seasonal beers Ⓗ
The single, L-shaped bar in this terraced pub makes visitors feel part of the crowd. Try the hard to find Best Bitter. ⇌ ♣

ROSE INN
249 High St ☎ (01634) 231047
11-11; 12-10.30 Sun
Shepherd Neame Master Brew Bitter Ⓗ
Two-bar friendly local. Home-cooked food available Mon-Sat.
◖❱ ⊟ ⇌ ♣ P

RAMSGATE

ADDINGTON ARMS
45 Ashburnham Road (off A253)
☎ (01843) 591489
11-11; 12-10.30 Sun
Courage Best Bitter; Fuller's London Pride; Morland Old Speckled Hen; guest beers Ⓗ
Popular, comfortable back-street local appealing to all. It had the distinction, as the Australian Arms, of being the last beer house in Thanet (gaining a full licence in the 1960s). The name changed after a major refurbishment. Good value food. Children's certificate. ⇄ ❀ ◖ ⅄ ♣

ARTILLERY ARMS
36 Westcliff Road (next to hospital) ☎ (01843) 853282
12-11; 12-10.30 Sun
Draught Bass; guest beers Ⓗ
Superb, small, corner local well worth seeking out for its adventurous and ever-changing roster of beers. The landlord promotes real ale to all his customers. Real cider sold occasionally. ♣ ⟲

CHURCHILL TAVERN
19-22 The Paragon (opp Motor Museum) ☎ (01843) 587862
11.30-11; 12-10.30 Sun
Courage Directors; Fuller's London Pride; Ringwood Old Thumper; Theakston Old Peculier; Taylor Landlord; guest beers Ⓖ
Excellent 'country pub' in the town, popular with locals and visitors alike. Good sea views. Outstanding food in the bar and restaurant. Regular live music eves: jazz (Wed), folk/blues (Sun), downstairs in Churchill's. Children's certificate.
ᐈ ◖ ⅄ ♣

RIPPLE

PLOUGH INN
Church Lane
☎ (01304) 360209
11-3, 6-11; 11-11 Sat; 12-10.30 Sun
Fuller's London Pride, ESB; Shepherd Neame Master Brew Bitter, Spitfire Ⓗ
Attractive, one-bar, beamed, 18th century village inn, serving a large selection of home-made dishes. A typical country inn, popular with locals. Children welcome in the restaurant area. Very friendly and cosy.
ᐈ ❀ ◖❱ P

ROCHESTER

MAN OF KENT ALE HOUSE
6-8 John St ☎ (01634) 818771
12-11; 12-10.30 Sun
Goacher's Gold Star; guest beers Ⓗ
Specialising in Kentish produce, selling local ales, wines and cider

as well as a range of up to 12 German bottled beers, this pub is a must! Live music Sun eve.
ᐈ ⇌ ♣ ⟲

STAR
Star Hill ☎ (01634) 826811
12-11; 12-3 Sun
Beer range varies Ⓗ
Cosy, single-bar pub with little nooks and seven changing beers. Busy Fri & Sat eves. Eve meals Mon-Thu, 7-9. ᐈ ⇌

Try also: Greyhound, Rochester Ave (Shepherd Neame); White Horse, Borstal (Greene King)

ROLVENDEN

STAR
30 High Street ☎ (01580) 241369
11-11; 12-10.30 Sun
Bateman Mild; Beards Best Bitter; Shepherd Neame Master Brew Bitter; guest beers Ⓗ
Traditional, one-roomed village local on three levels. Hops decorate the ceiling. Near the Kent and East Sussex steam railway.
ᐈ ❀ ◖❱

ST MARGARET'S AT CLIFFE

HOPE INN
High Street ☎ (01304) 852444
11-11; 12-3, 7-10.30 Sun
Shepherd Neame Master Brew Bitter, Spitfire Ⓗ
Attractive village local in a popular holiday area. Skittle alley available. ᐈ ❀ ◖❱ ⅄ ♣ P

Try also: Cliffe, High St (Free)

ST MARY IN THE MARSH

STAR INN
Opp church OS065279
☎ (01797) 362139
11-3, 7-11; 12-3, 7-10.30 Sun
Shepherd Neame Master Brew Bitter; Wadworth 6X; guest beers Ⓗ
15th-century free house in the middle of Romney Marsh near Romney Hythe & Dymchurch Light Railway. Popular in summer with families, and locals in winter. Interesting guest beers.
ᐈ Q ❀ ⊟ ◖❱ ♣ P

ST PETER'S

RED LION
2 High Street ☎ (01843) 861402
11.30-3, 7-11; 11.30-11 Sat; 12-10.30 Sun
Boddingtons Bitter; Flowers Original; Kent Delight Ⓗ
Friendly, one-bar local opposite a Norman church. Built in the early 1800s, its large open bar maintains the style of a traditional village local. ⇄ ◖❱ ⅃ ♣ P

SANDGATE

CLARENDON
Brewers Hill
☎ (01303) 248684
11.45-3, 6 (7 Sat)-11; 12-3,
7-10.30 Sun
**Shepherd Neame Master Brew
Bitter, Spitfire, Bishops Finger,
seasonal beers** Ⓗ
Small, two-bar pub clinging to the
hillside above the coast road.
Meals prepared using real ales.
🏚 Q 🍽 🕸 ◖ ▶ ♣ 🍺

SANDWICH

ADMIRAL OWEN
8 High Street
☎ (01304) 620869
11-11; 12-10.30 Sun
Greene King IPA, Abbot Ⓖ
Recently renovated old inn next
to the Barbican (Tollgate). It has
wooden bench seating and few
frills. Guest beers planned.
◖ ▶ ≈ ⌣

MARKET INN
7 Cattle Market
☎ (01304) 611133
10-11; 12-10.30 Sun
**Shepherd Neame Master Brew
Bitter, Spitfire, seasonal beer** Ⓗ
Friendly meeting place at the
heart of this historic Cinque Port.
Much to see of interest within
walking distance. ◖

Try also: Kings Arms, Strand St
(Pubmaster)

SELLING

ROSE & CROWN
Perry Wood (1 mile S of village)
OS042552
☎ (01227) 752214
11-2.30 (3 Sat), 6.30-11; 12-3,
7-10.30 Sun
**Adnams Bitter; Goacher's Dark;
Harveys BB; guest beer** Ⓗ
Historic pub in the middle of
Perry Wood, popular with walkers and other visitors. Noted for
its good food and Christmas dec-
orations! The large award-winning garden has a play area and
aviary. Eve meals Tue-Sat.
🏚 🕸 ◖ ▶ ♣ P

SONDES ARMS
Selling Road ☎ (01227) 752246
12-3 (4 Sat), 7-11; (11-11 summer Sat); 12-4, 7-11 (12-10.30
summer) Sun
**Shepherd Neame Master Brew
Bitter;** Ⓖ **seasonal beers** Ⓗ
Attractive village pub, well away
from main roads, but outside
Selling station. It was originally
built by a local landowner for his
farmworkers. A large aviary and
a children's play area in the back
garden (bat and trap played).
Live music Mon eve.
🏚 Q 🕸 ◖ ≈ ♣ P ✂

SHEERNESS

RED LION
High Street, Blue Town
☎ (01795) 663165
12-3, 6 (8 Sat)-11; 12-3, 8-10.30
Sun
Beer range varies Ⓗ
A regular entry in this *Guide*.
Three ever-changing beers are
always available, mostly from
independent breweries. Don't be
fooled by the clock. Weekday
lunches.Q ◖ ⊞ ≈ ♣

SHOREHAM

ROYAL OAK
2 High Street
☎ (01959) 522319
10.30-3, 6.30-11; 12-3, 7-10.30
Sun
**Adnams Bitter, Broadside;
Brakspear Bitter; Fuller's
London Pride; guest beers** Ⓗ
Highly recommended hostelry in
the heart of an attractive Darent
Valley village. The hub of local
life, welcoming to strangers and
a good stopping point for ramblers. Excellent value home cooking, especially Sun lunch. A rare
outlet for mild (varies) and
draught cider.
🏚 🕸 ◖ ▶ ≈ ⌣

Try also: Old George Inn,
Church St (Free)

SITTINGBOURNE

FOUNTAIN
Station Street
☎ (01795) 472015
11-3, 5.30-11; 11-11 Fri & Sat;
12-10.30 Sun
**Shepherd Neame Master Brew
Bitter** Ⓗ
Large, busy pub, near the station.
🏚 🕸 ◖ ≈ ♣ P

OLD OAK
East Street
☎ (01795) 472685
10.30-2.30, 7-11; 12-2.30,
7-10.30 Sun
Flowers IPA; guest beer Ⓗ
Timeless pub amongst the hustle
and bustle of busy East Street; a
very welcome oasis, it always
has a different guest beer.
🕸 ◖ ▶ ≈ ♣

RED LION
58 High Street
☎ (01795) 472706
11-3, 6-11; 11-11 Fri & Sat; 12-3,
7-10.30 Sun
**Fuller's London Pride; guest
beers** Ⓗ
Considerably altered over the
years, this former coaching inn
stocks a fine range of ales. Six
are normally on offer, including
one from the local Swale
Brewery. Limited parking.
🕸 ◖ ▶ ≈ P

SNARGATE

RED LION ☆
2 miles from Brenzett on B2080
☎ (01797) 344648
11-3, 7-11; 12-3, 7-10.30 Sun
**Bateman XB; Goacher's Light;
Rother Valley Level Best; guest
beers** Ⓖ
Built in 1540, this unspoilt pub
has been owned by the same
family since 1911. No carpets,
outside loos and a marble top
counter are features. Run with
love and devotion, not by accoun-
tants. Annual beer festival in
June. A *Guide* regular.
🏚 Q 🕸 ♣ ⌣ P

SOUTHBOROUGH

BAT & BALL
141 London Road (E side of A26)
☎ (01892) 518085
2 (12 Sat)-11; 12-10.30 Sun
Beer range varies Ⓗ
Small, two-bar free house on the
main road, with a small patio.
Garden at the rear. Many of the
beers are rare for the area.
Chess played. 🏚 🕸 ♣

SOUTHFLEET

BLACK LION
Red Street ☎ (01474) 832386
11-11; 12-10.30 Sun
Courage Best Bitter; guest beers Ⓗ
Attractive thatched pub in a
pleasant village setting. An abundance of exposed beams and a
lively atmosphere await the visitor. Frequently changing range of
guest beers. 🏚 🕸 ◖ ▶ P

STANSTED

BLACK HORSE
Tumblefield Road (1 mile N of
A20) ☎ (01732) 822355
11-11; 12-10.30 Sun
**Greene King Abbot; Larkins
Traditional Ale; Young's Special;
guest beers** Ⓗ
The focus of village community life
and a popular point of call for ramblers. Good food served until
10pm with Thai cuisine a speciality, Tue-Fri; traditional roasts Sun.
Supports Kentish ales, ciders and
wines. Strictly no music. Garden
popular in summer.
🏚 Q 🕸 ⇌ ◖ ▶ ▲ ♣ ⌣ P

STAPLEHURST

LORD RAGLAN
Chart Hill Road (½ mile N of
A229 at Cross-at-Hand garage)
OS786472
☎ (01622) 843747
12-3, 6-11; 12-4 (closed eve) Sun
**Goacher's Light; Harveys BB;
guest beers** Ⓗ
Popular, unspoilt country pub
with a large garden set amongst
orchards. The hop-adorned bar

has no distractions other than lively conversation and excellent quality food. Children welcome.
🏚 Q 🕸 🕘 🚪 P

STONE (DARTFORD)

BRICKLAYERS ARMS
62 London Road (A226)
☎ (01322) 284552
11-11; 12-10.30 Sun
Courage Best Bitter; guest beers Ⓗ
Small, welcoming family oriented terraced pub serving two regularly changing beers from independent microbreweries, plus Biddenden cider in summer. Live music most Fri or Sat eves.
🕸 ♣ ⌣

STONE-IN-OXNEY

CROWN
Follow signs from Appledore on B2080 OS939277
☎ (01233) 758789
12-3, 6.30-11; 12-3, 7-10.30 Sun
Otter Bitter; Shepherd Neame Master Brew Bitter; guest beers Ⓗ
Cosy village pub with hops around the bar and an inglenook. Two bars (one for food) and a pool room. No food Sun eve or Mon. Next to public footpaths and the Saxon Shore Way.
🏚 🕸 🕘 🚪 ♣ P

STONE STREET

PADWELL ARMS
Stone Street (1 mile S of A25, between Seal and Ightham)
OS569551
☎ (01732) 761532
12-3, 6-11; 12-3, 7-10.30 Sun
Badger Dorset Best; Harveys BB; Hook Norton Old Hooky; guest beers Ⓗ
Kent CAMRA *Pub of the Year* 1994 and '97, joint winner in 1995. This old, dimly-lit pub stands opposite an apple orchard. Barbecues every Sat and Sun June to Sept. Convenient for Ightam Mote.
🏚 🕸 🕘 ♣ ⌣ P

STOWTING

TIGER
Off B2068, 6 miles E of Ashford
OS121414 ☎ (01303) 862130
12-3 (not Mon), 7-11; 12-3.30, 7-10.30 Sun
Everards Tiger; Fuller's London Pride; Theakston Best Bitter, Old Peculier; guest beers Ⓗ
Recently saved from extinction by the local villagers. This unspoilt inn serves home-cooked foods with a regularly changing menu, using locally reared trout, venison and beef. Bookings advisable Sat eve and Sun lunch. Jazz Mon eves. 🏚 ☎ 🕸 🕘 🚪 ♣ P

SWALECLIFFE

EDDERY'S
St Johns Road (B2205 to Herne Bay)
☎ (01227) 792428
11-11; 12-10.30 Sun
Draught Bass; Shepherd Neame Master Brew Bitter; Webster's Yorkshire Bitter; guest beers Ⓗ
Formerly known as 'The Plough', this superb pub became a Thorley Tavern in 1990. Guest beers are wide ranging in both style and origin. Popular with locals and workers from the surrounding industrial estates. Apparently named after a renowned equestrian. Eve meals Wed-Sun.
🏚 🕸 🕘 🚪 ➥ P

WHEATSHEAF
74 Herne Bay Road (B2205)
☎ (01227) 792310
11-11; 12-10.30 Sun
Beards Best Bitter; Fuller's London Pride; Thwaites Mild; guest beers Ⓗ
Attractive 1930s roadhouse boasting original oak panels and period fittings. Friendly atmosphere, and good value food in the bar and restaurant, the garden has a petanque piste and children's play area. Wheelchair WC.
🏚 🕸 🕘 ♿ ⚡ ➥ (Chestfield) ♣ P

SWANLEY

LAMB INN
Swanley Village Road (off B258, Hextable Road)
☎ (01322) 669921
12-3, 5.30-11; 12-4.30, 7.30-10.30 Sun
Shepherd Neame Master Brew Bitter, Spitfire, Bishops Finger, Ⓗ **seasonal beers** ⒽⒼ
Convivial, one-bar village local decorated with brass ornaments. Shepherd Neame *Master Cellarman* award-winner.
🏚 🕸 🕘 ♣ ⌣ P

TANKERTON

TANKERTON ARMS
Tower Hill (off B2205, on seafront road near castle)
☎ (01227) 272024
12-11; 12-10.30 Sun
Fuller's London Pride; Shepherd Neame Master Brew Bitter; guest beers Ⓗ
Comfortable pub with a traditional wood and mirror bar back. Enjoy sea views and an imaginative menu with excellent vegetarian choices in a relaxed atmosphere. Benches outside overlooking the sea. Live jazz Tue; other music events summer Fri and Sat.
🏚 ☎ 🕸 🕘 🚪 ♣

TEMPLE EWELL

FOX
High Street (off B2060)
☎ (01304) 823598
11-3, 6.30-11; 12-3, 7-10.30 Sun
Marston's Pedigree Ⓗ
Traditional social serving the village and suburban community. Close to Kearsney Abbey and gardens. Skittle alley.
🏚 ☎ 🕸 ➥ (Kearsney) ♣ P🕀

TENTERDEN

WHITE LION HOTEL
High Street (B1580) 765077
11-11; 12-10.30 Sun
Draught Bass; Harveys BB; seasonal beers; Rother Valley Level Best; guest beers Ⓗ
Lively locals' bar in a pleasant hotel, opposite the Kent and East Sussex light railway. Regular live jazz Thu eve.
🏚 🕸 🛏 🕘 🚪 ⚡ ♣ P

WILLIAM CAXTON
West Cross
☎ (01580) 763142
11-11; 12-10.30 Sun
Shepherd Neame Master Brew Bitter, Best Bitter, Spitfire, Bishops Finger, seasonal beers Ⓗ
Locals' pub in an attractive town: two bars with a friendly atmosphere and home-cooked food; a great little pub. Once the Black Horse it was renamed in honour of the famous son of the Weald.
🏚 🕸 🛏 🕘 🚪 🍴 ⚡

TILMANSTONE

RAVENS
Upper Street (off A256)
☎ (01304) 617337
11-2.30, 7-11; 12-3, 7-10.30 Sun
King & Barnes Sussex; Young's Special; guest beers Ⓗ
Refurbished village local, popular with the farming community. Booking is advisable for meals.
🏚 🕸 🕘 ♣ P

TONBRIDGE

HOODEN HORSE
59 Pembury Roadd
☎ (01732) 366080
12-2.30, 6-11; 12-10.30 Sun
Goacher's Light; Hook Norton Old Hooky; Hop Back Summer Lightning; guest beer Ⓗ
Although rather food-oriented (Mexican/Oriental), it offers a good choice of ales from small breweries. The tables are candlelit.🕸 🕘 🚪 ➥ ⌣ P

NEW DRUM
54 Lavender Hill (off A26)
☎ (01732) 365044
11-11; 12-5, 7-10.30 Sun
Fuller's London Pride; Harveys BB; guest beers Ⓗ
Recently refurbished, family-run

free house offering a friendly welcome. Guest beers constantly vary. No food Sun. 🐕 🍺 ⇌ ♣

Try also: Primrose, Pembury Rd (Free); Priory Wine Cellars (off-licence), 64 Priory St (Free)

TROTTISCLIFFE

PLOUGH
Taylors Lane ☎ (01732) 822223
11.30-2.30, 6-11; 12-4, 7-10.30 Sun
Flowers IPA; Theakston XB; Wadworth 6X; guest beer H
15th-century village pub close to Pilgrims Way, Trosley Country Park and Coldrum Long Barrow. Meals are available in both bars which display photos of bygone village scenes. Occasional live music eves. No food Sun eve.
🏨 Q 🐕 🍺 🍴 ♣ P

TUNBRIDGE WELLS

BEDFORD
2 High Street
☎ (01892) 526580
11-11; 12-10.30 Sun
Greene King XX Mild, IPA, Abbot, seasonal beers; guest beers H
Single-bar pub, opposite the station and near the Pantiles. Popular with office workers and shoppers during the day; commuters and regulars eves. Regularly changing guest beers. No food Sun.
🍺 ⇌ ♣

TWITTON

RISING SUN
Twitton Lane (1 mile W of Otford along Pilgrims Way)
☎ (01959) 525489
4 (12 Fri & Sat)-11; 12-10.30 Sun
Courage Best Bitter; Greene King IPA, seasonal beers; guest beer H
Small, very friendly single bar, near Danes Hollow battleground. Pub games include bat & trap and shut the box. Lunches Sat and Sun, steak night Fri eve. The garden affords splendid views of the Darent Valley.
🏨 🐕 🍺 🍴 ♣

UNDERRIVER

WHITE ROCK
Carters Hill (2½ miles SE of Sevenoaks but route is indirect)
OS556521
☎ (01732) 833112
11-3, 6-11; 12-3, 7-10.30 Sun
Harveys BB; King & Barnes Sussex; guest beer H
Friendly, attractive country pub: one large bar with pool, darts and machines, plus a small quiet bar with a real fire. Excellent restaurant. Large garden.
🏨 Q 🐕 🍺 🍴 ♣ P

UPCHURCH

BROWN JUG
76 Horsham Lane OS842675
☎ (01634) 235287
11-2.30 (3 Sat), 6-11; 12-3, 7-10.30 Sun
Shepherd Neame Master Brew Bitter H
Nothing has altered at this two-bar pub for a number of years, including the landlord who has been there more than 30 years. In keeping with its name, it boasts a fine collection of jugs.
🏨 🚲 🐕 ♣ P

UPPER UPNOR

TUDOR ROSE
29 High St ☎ (01634) 715305
11.30-3.30, 7-11; 12-3.30, 7-10.30 Sun
Young's Bitter, Special; guest beers H
Friendly, multi-roomed pub next to Upnor Castle and overlooking the River Medway and the former dockyard. Good value food (not served Sun or Mon eve).
🏨 🚲 🐕 🍺 ♣

Try also: Kings Arms, High St (Free)

WEALD

WINDMILL
Windmill Road (W of A21 jct for Tonbridge N) ☎ (01732) 463330
11-11; 12-10.30 Sun
Greene King IPA, Abbot; seasonal beers H
A village local retaining public and saloon bars known for its October beer festival. Lunches Wed-Mon, eve meals Thu-Sat. Nominated for *Community Pub of the Year* finals.
🏨 Q 🐕 🍺 🍴 🛏 🚻 ⛺

WEST MALLING

LOBSTER POT
47 Swan St ☎ (01732) 843265
12-2.30; 6-11 Mon-Sat; 12-4, 7-10.30 Sun
King & Barnes Sussex; Morland Old Speckled Hen; guest beers H
Revitalised under new ownership: six ales always available, usually featuring Kent or Sussex independents. Hosts occasional live music. No food Sun eve.
🍺 🍴 ⇌

Try also: Wheatsheaf, on A20 (Free)

WHITSTABLE

ALBERRES
Sea Street ☎ (01227) 273400
11.30-4, 7-11; 11.30-11 Fri & Sat; 12-10.30 Sun
Ind Coope Burton Ale; Tetley Bitter; guest beer H

Small, friendly, one-bar local close to the beach, historical Horsebridge and oyster stores (now a cinema) ♣

COACH & HORSES
37 Oxford St ☎ (01227) 264732
10-11; 12-10.30 Sun
Shepherd Neame Master Brew Bitter, Spitfire, Porter H
Quiet, friendly 19th-century pub. The dining area serves home-cooked good value food. Small and sunny patio area at the rear.
Q 🐕 🍺 🍴

NOAHS ARK
83 Canterbury Road
☎ (01227) 272332
11-3, 6-11; 12-3, 7-10.30 Sun
Shepherd Neame Master Brew Bitter H
Good, old-fashioned local run by the area's longest serving publican. Small garden. 🐕 🍺 🛏 P

SHIP CENTURION
111 High St ☎ (01227) 264740
11-11; 12-10.30 Sun
Adnams Bitter; Hop Back Summer Lightning; guest beers H
Centrally located, busy, one-bar pub. Genuine home-cooked bar food is served all day using local and organic produce whenever possible. Live jazz first Wed in month. Conservatory with Sky TV.
🍺 🍴 🚻 ⇌

WORTH

ST CRISPIN
The Street ☎ (01304) 612081
11-2.30, 6-11; 12-10.30 Sun
Boddingtons Mild, Gale's HSB; Marston's Pedigree; Shepherd Neame Master Brew Bitter; guest beers H
Well established local with a popular restaurant. The large garden is always busy in summer (bat and trap played), two ever-changing guest beers, often from Kent brewers.
🏨 🐕 🛏 🍺 🍴 P

INDEPENDENT BREWERIES

Flagship: Chatham
Goacher's: Maidstone
Kent: Deal
Larkins: Chiddingstone
Shepherd Neame: Faversham
Swale: Sittingbourne

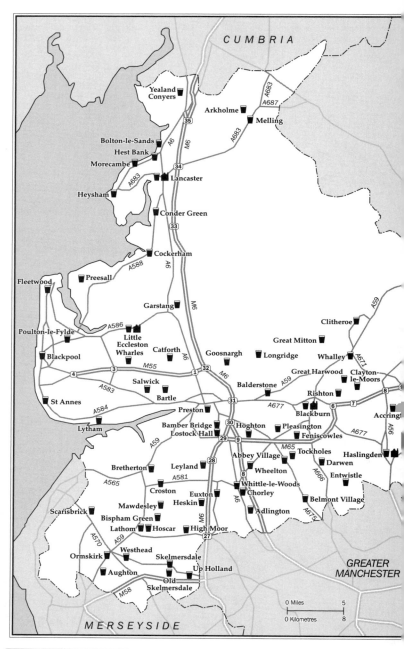

Map of Lancashire showing: Yealand Conyers, Arkholme, Melling, Bolton-le-Sands, Hest Bank, Morecambe, Lancaster, Heysham, Conder Green, Cockerham, Preesall, Fleetwood, Garstang, Poulton-le-Fylde, Little Eccleston Wharles, Catforth, Goosnargh, Longridge, Clitheroe, Great Mitton, Whalley, Blackpool, Salwick, Bartle, Balderstone, Great Harwood, Clayton-le-Moors, St Annes, Preston, Rishton, Blackburn, Accrington, Lytham, Bamber Bridge, Lostock Hall, Hoghton, Pleasington, Feniscowles, Abbey Village, Tockholes, Haslingden, Bretherton, Leyland, Wheelton, Darwen, Entwistle, Croston, Euxton, Whittle-le-Woods, Chorley, Scarisbrick, Mawdesley, Heskin, Adlington, Belmont Village, Bispham Green, Lathom, Hoscar, High Moor, Ormskirk, Westhead, Skelmersdale, Up Holland, Aughton, Old Skelmersdale. Bordered by CUMBRIA, GREATER MANCHESTER, MERSEYSIDE.

0 Miles 5 / 0 Kilometres 8

ABBEY VILLAGE

HARE & HOUNDS
129 Bolton Road (A675/Dole Lane jct) ☎ (01254) 830534
12-2.30, 5-11; 12-11 Sat; 12-10.30 Sun
Boddingtons Bitter; Taylor Landlord Ⓗ
Popular country inn; one large main room with a central bar and a games room at the back; a good local, handy for walks. Food is served all day Sat and Sun until 8.30. ♨ ☆ 🏵 ◖ ▶ ♣ P

ACCRINGTON

ARDEN INN
85 Abbey Street (A680)
☎ (01254) 385971
12-11; 12-10.30 Sun
Boddingtons Bitter; Lees Bitter; guest beers Ⓗ
Very friendly, family-run town centre pub: open plan with a games room. ⇌ ♣

BROOKS CLUB
Infant Street (A680)
☎ (01254) 234039
12-5, 7-11; 12-3, 7-10.30 Sun
Boddingtons Bitter; guest beer Ⓗ

162

N O R T H
Y O R K S H I R E

Salterforth

Black Lane
Ends

cko

rowford   Colne   Laneshaw Bridge
13
12   Brierfield

Burnley

Cliviger   *WEST*
YORKSHIRE

Modern, purpose-built club with a lounge, games area and a concert room. Show this *Guide* or CAMRA membership card to be signed in. One of the few local outlets for real cider. ⇌ ♣ ⌂

CROWN INN
Whalley Road, (A680)
☎ (01254) 383272
12-3, 6-11; 12-11 Sat; 12-10.30 Sun

Courage Directors; Theakston Best Bitter; guest beers Ⓗ
Open-plan, U-shaped room with a games area. Lunches served Tue, Fri and Sun. ◖

PEEL PARK HOTEL
Turkey Street ☎ (01254) 235830
12-11; 12-10.30 Sun
Mitchell's Mild, Original, Lancaster Bomber or seasonal beers Ⓗ
Open-plan pub with a games room. ❀ ♣ P

VICTORIA
Manchester Road (A680)
☎ (01254) 237727
11-11; 12-10.30 Sun
Thwaites Best Mild, Bitter, seasonal beers Ⓗ
Open-plan, U-shaped room with a pool table. ♣ P

ADLINGTON

WHITE BEAR
5a Market Street (A6)
☎ (01257) 482357
11-11; 12-10.30 Sun
Courage Directors; Theakston Mild, Best Bitter, Old Peculier; guest beers Ⓗ
Old, stone, town pub with a low beamed ceiling. Handy for the Leeds-Liverpool canal. No food Mon eve.🏨 ❀ 🛏 ◖ ▶ ⇌ ♣ P

ARKHOLME

BAY HORSE
On B6254 ☎ (015242) 21425
11.30-3, 6-11; 12-3, 7-10 Sun
Mitchell's Original, seasonal beers Ⓗ
Small, old-fashioned, country inn in a tourist-free village. Three rooms: one is used by families, one for games (no muddy boots). Own bowling green. Up to four draught beers at a time.
❀ ◖ ♣ P

AUGHTON

DOG & GUN
223 Long Lane (off A59)
☎ (01695) 423303
5-11; 12-2, 7-10.30 Sun
Burtonwood Mild, Bitter, Forshaw's Ⓗ
Excellent village local, a short walk from the station, where good conversation and a quiet pint can be enjoyed. A central bar serves two lounges. Bowling green at the rear.
🏨 Q ❀ ⇌ (Aughton Pk) ♣ P

BALDERSTONE

MYERSCOUGH
Whalley Road (A59)
☎ (01254) 812222
11.30-3, 6-11; 12-3, 7-10.30 Sun
Robinson's Hatters Mild, Best Bitter Ⓗ

Pleasant country inn, close to the main entrance of Salmesbury Aerodrome, with a cosy wood-panelled lounge and a small no-smoking room with a coal fire. Quality meals (finish 8.30). A third Robinson's beer is also sold. Three en-suite bedrooms are a recent addition.
🏨 Q ❀ ⇌ ◖ ▶ P ⊁

BAMBER BRIDGE

OLDE ORIGINAL WITHY TREES
157 Station Road (A6)
☎ (01772) 330396
11-11; 12-10.30 Sun
Burtonwood Bitter, Buccaneer Ⓗ
Spacious former farmhouse, a short walk from the station, with a strong darts following and a large-screen TV for main sporting events. Children's play area to the rear. ❀ ◖ ⇌ ♣ P

BARROWFORD

WHITE BEAR
Gisburn Road (A682)
☎ (01282) 440931
11.30-3, 5.30-11; 11.30-11 Thu-Sat & summer;12-10.30 Sun
Draught Bass; Worthington Bitter; guest beer Ⓗ
One-bar serves two rooms and a no-smoking dining room in this 17th-century village inn, steeped in local history. An extensive menu is served lunch and eves (12-8 Sun). ❀ ◖ ▶ P

BARTLE

SADDLE INN
Sidgreaves Lane, Lea Town
OS487326 ☎ (01772) 726982
12-3, 5-11; 12-11 Sat; 12-10.30 Sun
Thwaites Best Mild, Bitter, Chairman's, Daniels Hammer, seasonal beers Ⓗ
Recently refurbished and knocked into one room, this well-known country pub, close to the BNFL factory, sells the full Thwaites range. Children's playground. ❀ ⇌ ◖ ▶ Å ♣ P

BELMONT VILLAGE

BLACK DOG INN
2 Church Street (A675)
☎ (01204) 811218
12-4 (3 Mon-Wed), 7-11; 12-4, 6.30-10.30 Sun
Holt Mild, Bitter Ⓗ
Popular, homely, traditional village pub, multi-roomed and decorated with antiques. Eve meals for residents only Mon-Tue.
🏨 Q ⛱ ❀ ⇌ ◖ ▶ P

BISPHAM GREEN

EAGLE & CHILD
Malt Kiln Lane (off B5246)
☎ (01257) 462297

12-3, 5.30-11; 12-10.30 Sun
**Coach House Gunpowder Mild;
Theakston Best Bitter; Thwaites
Bitter; guest beers** Ⓗ
Outstanding, 16th-century village
local with antique furniture and
stone-flagged floors. It is
renowned for its food. The cider
varies. The pub also has its own
bowling green.
🏔 Q ⌂ 🐾 ◑ ▶ ♣ ⌂ P ⌖

BLACKBURN

ADELPHI BEER EMPORIUM
Railway Road (by bus station)
11-11; 12-10.30 Sun
**Boddingtons Mild, Bitter;
Marston's Pedigree; Whitbread
Trophy; guest beers** Ⓗ
Large, town-centre pub offering a
changing guest beer in a comfortable atmosphere, refurbished
with a mix of rich dark wood and
mirrors. ☎ ◑ ♿ ⇌

GLOBE INN
2 Higher Eanam (near Thwaites
Brewery) ☎ (01254) 671789
12-11; 12-10.30 Sun
**Mitchell's Mild, Original,
Lancaster Bomber, seasonal
beers** Ⓗ
A friendly welcome awaits at this
corner local, with its cosy snug,
large lounge, games room and
vault. Weekly entertainment is
staged in the lounge.
Q ☎ 🏠 ⇌ ♣

MALT & HOPS
1 Barton Street
☎ (01254) 699453
10.30-1am; 12-10.30 Sun
**Boddingtons Mild, Bitter;
Flowers Original; Marston's
Pedigree; guest beers** Ⓗ
A student clientele weekday
lunchtimes gives way to a mixed
aged group of drinkers at eves
and weekends, taking advantage
of its late licence. A good town-
centre pub offering wholesome
meals. 🐾 ◑ ▶ ♿ ⇌

NAVIGATION INN
Canal Street, Mill Hill
☎ (01254) 53230
11-11; 12-10.30 Sun
Thwaites Best Mild, Bitter Ⓗ
Popular, traditional boozer next
to Leeds-Liverpool Canal, run by
one of Blackburn's longest-serving landladies. A true community
pub with a warm welcome for all.
Handy for Blackburn Rovers FC.
Plenty of room to moor canal
craft. 🐾 🏠 ⇌ (Mill Hill) ♣

POSTAL ORDER
15 Darwen Street
☎ (01254) 676400
11-11; 12-10.30 Sun
**Courage Directors; Theakston
Best Bitter; Thwaites Best Mild;
guest beers** Ⓗ

Former post office, converted in
the grand Wetherspoons way,
offering a wide range of beers in
spacious surroundings.
Q ◑ ▶ ♿ 🏠 ⌂ ⌖ 🍴

Try also: Cellar Bar, 39 King St
(Blackburn)

BLACK LANE ENDS

HARE & HOUNDS
☎ (01282) 863070
12-3, 7-11 (closed Tue); 12-3,
7-10.30 Sun
**Taylor Mild, Best Bitter,
Landlord** Ⓗ
Small, friendly pub on the old
road between Colne and Skipton.
A welcome stop for walkers on
the Pendle Way.
🏔 🐾 ◑ ▶ ⛺ ♣ P ⌖

BLACKO

CROSS GAITS INN
Beverley Rd ☎ (01282) 616312
5.30-11; 12-3, 6-11 Fri & Sat;
12-4, 7-10.30 Sun
**Burtonwood Bitter, Top Hat;
guest beers** Ⓗ
Comfortable country pub serving
excellent food Fri-Sun lunch and
every eve except Tue. A welcome
outlet for Burtonwood in the
area. 🏔 🐾 ◑ ▶ ♣ P

BLACKPOOL

BISPHAM
Red Bank Road (next to
Sainsbury's) ☎ (01253) 351752
11-11; 12-10.30 Sun
Samuel Smith OBB Ⓗ
Popular with tourists and
resident, this busy pub has a
large lounge, with music on
some evenings, and a small
vault/games room. Meals are
available Tue-Sat. Gents'
wheelchair WC.
Q ◑ ▶ 🏠 ♿ ⊖ (Bispham)

EMPRESS HOTEL
59 Exchange Street, (behind
North station) ☎ (01253) 751121
11-11; (12.30am Fri & Sat); 12-
10.30 Sun
Thwaites Best Mild, Bitter Ⓗ
Spacious, Victorian, old fashioned
basic hotel with a large games
room, a dance floor boasting a
Wurlitzer organ, and a big-screen
TV. Lancashire's only ever-pre-
sent *Guide* entry. Special B&B
rates for CAMRA members.
🛏 🏠 ⇌ (North) ⊖ (Pleasant
St) ♣

RAMSDEN ARMS HOTEL
204 Talbot Road (near bus and
rail stations) ☎ (01253) 623215
10.30-11; 12-10.30 Sun
**Boddingtons Bitter; Ind Coope
Burton Ale; Marston's Pedigree;
Tetley Mild, Bitter; Ushers
Rascals Bitter; guest beers** Ⓗ

Rare, unspoilt, classic, multi-
award winning inn. This imposing
Tudor-style building features an
oak-panelled interior displaying
bric-à-brac and memorabilia.
A choice of over 100 whiskies.
Children welcome until 8pm in
the games room.
🛏 🏠 ⇌ (North) ♣ P

SADDLE INN
286 Whitegate Drive (A583)
☎ (01253) 798900
11.30-11; 12-10.30 Sun
**Bass Mild, Draught Bass; guest
beers** Ⓗ
This pub has served ale since
1776, now complemented by
excellent food. Recently refurbished to include a no-smoking
room, a new car park layout and
outside tables. It now has a
licence to conduct weddings.
🏔 Q 🐾 ◑ ▶ P ⌖ 🍴

SHOVELS
260 Commonedge Road, Marton
(B5261) ☎ (01253) 762702
11.30-11; 12-10.30 Sun
**Courage Directors; Theakston
Best Bitter; guest beers** Ⓗ
Large, traditionally, refurbished
open-plan pub on the edge of
town, near the airport and M55.
It has an interesting line in guest
beers and hosts an annual beer
festival. Good food includes kangaroo, crocodile, camel and
ostrich steaks. 🐾 ◑ ▶ 🍴 ♣ P

WHEATSHEAF
194-196 Talbot Road, (A586, opp
station) ☎ (01253) 25062
10.30-11; 12-10.30 Sun
**Theakston Mild, Best Bitter, XB,
Old Peculier; guest beers** Ⓗ
Friendly, down-to-earth local
where the somewhat weird decor
includes sharks, scarecrows and
a chandelier. 🏔 ◑ ⇌ (North) ♣

BOLTON-LE-SANDS

BLUE ANCHOR
68 Main Road (A6)
☎ (01524) 823241
11-11; 12-10.30 Sun
**Mitchell's Mild, Original,
seasonal beers** Ⓗ
18th-century coaching inn, now a
local in the old attractive part of
an overgrown village; one cosy
bar and two contrasting rooms
off (children admitted). Aviary
and pets in the garden.
🏔 🐾 🛏 ◑ ▶ ♣

BRETHERTON

BLUE ANCHOR
South Road (B5247)
☎ (01772) 600270
11.30-3, 5-11; 11.30-11 Fri & Sat;
12-10.30 Sun
**Boddingtons Bitter; Flowers IPA;
guest beers** Ⓗ
Well-kept inn with a large gar-

den, serving excellent value meals (served all day Sat and Sun) and interesting guest beers. Q ❀ ◖▶ ♣ P

BRIERFIELD

POULTRY FANCIERS WMC
39 Railway View
☎ (01282) 612404
7.30-11; 8.30-10.30 Sun
Moorhouse's Premier; Thwaites Bitter; guest beers (occasional) Ⓗ
Friendly, relaxed workingmen's club, serving the best selection of real ale in the area. Show this *Guide* or CAMRA membership card to be signed in. All guest beers are from Thwaites.
点 ≈ ♣ P 🗄

BURNLEY

COAL CLOUGH
41 Coal Clough Lane (200 yds E of M65 jct 10) ☎ (01282) 423226
11-11; 12-10.30 Sun
Draught Bass; Boddingtons Bitter; Worthington Bitter Ⓗ
This busy, friendly, end-of-ter-race community local has won the Bass national award for beer quality for the past two years. All keg beers have been replaced by beers brewed specially for the pub by Bass Museum. ♣
🍺 ≈ (Barracks) ♣

DUGDALE ARMS
Dugdale Road ☎ (01282) 423909
11-11; 12-10.30 Sun
Thwaites Bitter, seasonal beers Ⓗ
Large, post-war, multi-roomed pub with a central bar area, set in its own grounds with a large car park.
Q 🍺 ❀ 点 Å ≈ (Barracks) ♣ P

BURNLEY

GARDEN BAR
131-133 St James Street
☎ (01282) 414895
11-11; 12-10.30 Sun
Lees Bitter Ⓗ
Large, open-plan pub where the decor reflects the pub's name. Discos at weekends.
点 ≈ (Central) P

SPARROW HAWK HOTEL
Church Street
☎ (01282) 421551
11-3, 6-11; 11-11 Sat; 12-3, 7-10.30 Sun
Moorhouse's Premier, Pendle Witches Brew; Theakston Best Bitter; guest beers Ⓗ
Hotel with excellent accommodation and superb bar meals, handy for the town centre. There is always a constantly changing range of three guest beers; entertainment at weekends.
🛏 ◖▶ 点 ≈ (Central) P ⌗ 🗄

TIM BOBBIN HOTEL
319 Padiham Road, Padiham (A678) ☎ (01282) 424165
11-11; 12-10.30 Sun
Samuel Smith OBB Ⓗ
Busy main road pub with a large, comfortable lounge and a games room, selling low-priced beer. The pub is named after a local dialect poet. ❀ 🍺 ♣ P

CATFORTH

BAY HORSE
Catforth Road (off B5269)
☎ (01772) 690389
11-11; 12-10.30 Sun
Draught Bass; Boddingtons Bitter; Theakston Best Bitter Ⓗ
Good, homely village local with a friendly atmosphere, offering good food, good drink, good humour! Children welcome in a designated area until 9pm.
🛏 Q 🍺 ❀ ◖▶ 🍺 点 Å ♣ P

CHORLEY

DUKE OF YORK
124 Bolton St (A6, S of centre)
☎ (01257) 275001
12-11; 12-10.30 Sun
Holt Mild, Bitter Ⓗ
Large, mock-Tudor pub with a split-level lounge and a large public bar. Note the windows from the long closed Sumners Brewery. ◖ 🍺 ♣ ♣

MALT 'N' HOPS
50-52 Friday Street (near station) ☎ (01257) 260967
12-11; 12-10.30 Sun
Boddingtons Bitter; Cains Mild; Taylor Landlord; guest beers Ⓗ
Single-bar pub of character, furnished with Victoriana. An excellent vantage point for trainspotters. Fine guest beers ≈

POTTERS ARMS
42 Brooke Street (next to Morrisons superstore)
☎ (01257) 267954
12-11; 12-3.30, 7-11 Sat; 12-4, 7-10.30 Sun
Boddingtons Bitter; Tetley Bitter; guest beer Ⓗ
Recently extended, traditional local. The central bar serves games areas and comfortable lounges. Formerly known as the Oddfellows. ≈ ♣ P

RAILWAY
20-22 Steeley Lane (behind station) ☎ (01257) 411449
12-11; 12-10.30 Sun
Draught Bass; John Smith's Bitter; Theakston Mild, Best Bitter; guest beers Ⓗ
Lively local, decorated in Edwardian style, with a single bar, large alcoves and an unusual display of model vehicles.
🛏 ≈ ♣

TUT 'N' SHIVE
Market Street (opp Town Hall)
☎ (01257) 262858
11-11; 12-10.30 Sun
Castle Eden Ale; Flowers Original; guest beer Ⓗ
Split-level bar upstairs with single cellar bar downstairs. Popular with the young at weekends, it is a must for TV sports fans with no fewer than 12 screens! Eve meals served 5-7.
◖▶ ≈ ⌣

CLAYTON-LE-MOORS

ALBION
243 Whalley Road (A680)
☎ (01254) 238585
12 (5 Mon & Tue)-11; 12-10.30 Sun
Porter Mild, Bitter, Rossendale, Porter, Sunshine, seasonal beers Ⓗ
Open-plan pub close to the mid-point of the Leeds-Liverpool Canal with a canalside patio. Microbrewer Dave Porter's second pub serving excellent value beers. Cider varies.
Q ❀ 点 ♣ ⌣ P

CLITHEROE

NEW INN
Parson Lane
☎ (01200) 423312
11-11; 12-10.30 Sun
Moorhouse's Premier; guest beers Ⓗ
Friendly local, opposite the castle, with four rooms. Folk music Fri eve. Limited parking.
🛏 Q 🍺 ❀ ◖▶ Å ≈ ♣ P

CLIVIGER

QUEENS HEAD
412 Burnley Road (A646)
☎ (01282) 436712
11-11; 12-10.30 Sun
John Smith's Bitter; guest beers Ⓗ
Welcoming, two-roomed roadside local: no gimmicks, no noise, just friendly regulars and good beer from microbreweries, with up to four guests on tap.
🛏 Q Å ♣

Try also: Ram, Burnley Rd (Bass)

COCKERHAM

MANOR
Main Street (B5272)
☎ (01524) 791252
12-3, 6-11; 11-11 Sat; 12-10.30 Sun
Mitchell's Original, Lancaster Bomber Ⓗ
Modernised village local with two bars, a no-smoking restaurant, and a garden play area. No food Tue, nor Mon-Thu in winter.
❀ ◖▶ ♣ P

COLNE

ADMIRAL LORD RODNEY
Mill Green, Waterside
☎ (01282) 864079
12-3 Thu-Sat summer only,
7-midnight; 12-11 Sun
**Theakston Black Bull, XB, Old
Peculier; guest beers** 🅷
Multi-roomed authentic pub,
hosting theme nights. (Late
licence.) 🌣 ⬛ ⬤ ◗ ⭥ ⇌ P 🚪

CONDER GREEN

STORK
On A588 ☎ (01524) 32606
11-11; 12-10.30 Sun
**Boddingtons Bitter; Tetley
Bitter; guest beers** 🅷
Long, panelled, beamed building
with several small rooms (chil-
dren welcome) and down a level,
the main bar area and restau-
rant. Handy for Lune Estuary
Path. Two guest beers.
🏚 🌣 ⬛ ⬤◗ ▲ ♣ P

Try also: Plough, Galgate
(Boddingtons)

CROSTON

BLACK HORSE
Westhead Rd ☎ (01772) 600338
11-11; 12-10.30 Sun
**Theakston Mild, Best Bitter;
guest beers** 🅷
Excellent village local much
extended by a recent refurbishment. Six guest beers always
available and well known for its
good value food. It has a bowling
green, and, with Crostons
Twinning with Azay-le-Rideau, it
has become the centre of a thriving boules league. 🌣 ◗ ⭥ ♣ P

DARWEN

BOWLING GREEN HOTEL
386 Bolton Road (A666)
☎ (01254) 702148
11.30-4, 7-11; 11.30-11 Fri & Sat;
12-10.30 Sun
**Matthew Brown Bitter;
Theakston Mild, Best Bitter;
guest beers** 🅷
Community local with a good
games following. Weekend barbecues in summer.🏚🌣⭐♣P

GREENFIELD
Lower Barn Street (off Watery
Lane) ☎ (01254) 703945
12-3, 5.30-11; 12-11 Fri & Sat;
12-10.30 Sun
**Boddingtons Bitter; Taylor
Landlord; Thwaites Best Mild,
Bitter; guest beers** 🅷
Open-plan pub, next to the Sough
Tunnel, Darwen's prime beer
house, it serves good value,
home-cooked food (all day Sun
until 7, no eve meals Tue). Four
guest beers usually include a
porter. Q 🌣 ⬛ ◗ ▶

GEORGE HOTEL
169 Blackburn Road (A666,
1 mile from centre)
☎ (01254) 771847
11.30-11; 12-3, 7-10.30 Sun
Thwaites Best Mild, Bitter 🅷
Large, open-plan, yet multi-
roomed local with a very friendly
atmosphere. Good value food on
offer; children welcome. ◗ ⭐ ♣

PUNCH HOTEL
Chapels (¹/₂ mile from centre)
☎ (01254) 702510
12-11; 12-10.30 Sun
Whitbread Trophy; guest beers 🅷
Large, multi-roomed, friendly
games pub. The only outlet for
cider and perry in town.
🌣 ⬛ ◗ ⭐ ♣ ⬠ P

Try also: Punch Bowl Inn,
Roman Road (Thwaites)

ENTWISTLE

STRAWBURY DUCK
Overshores Road (signed on the
Edgworth-Darwen old road)
☎ (01204) 852013
12-3 (not Mon), 7-11; 12-11 Sat;
12-10.30 Sun
**Boddingtons Bitter; Moorhouse's
Pendle Witches Brew; Taylor
Landlord; guest beers** 🅷
Old, isolated but busy, country pub
by the station. Good base for
walks in hill country. Children wel-
come till 8.30; no motorcyclists.
🏚 Q 🐕 🌣 ⬛ ◗ ⇌ ♣ P ⤢

EUXTON

EUXTON MILLS
Wigan Road (A49/A581 jct)
☎ (01257) 264002
11.30-3, 5.30-11; 11.30-11 Sat;
12-10.30 Sun
**Burtonwood Mild, Bitter,
Forshaw's, Buccaneer** 🅷
Comfortable, split-level pub
where there is always a friendly
welcome. Well known for good
value, home-cooked food. Handy
for the recently opened Euxton
station. Q 🌣 ◗ ▶ ⬛ ⇌ ♣ P

FENISCOWLES

FEILDENS ARMS
673 Preston Old Road
☎ (01254) 200988
12-11; 12-10.30 Sun
**Boddingtons Bitter; Flowers IPA;
Marston's Pedigree; guest
beers** 🅷
Local community pub which
caters for all ages and retains a
small vault. Most times a mild is
available. Meals 12-2 Tue-Sat.
🏚 🌣 ⬛ ◗ ⇌ (Pleasington) P

FLEETWOOD

NORTH EUSTON HOTEL
The Esplanade (near bus and
tram termini)

☎ (01253) 876525
11-11; 12-10.30 Sun
**Boddingtons Bitter; Ruddles
County; Theakston Best Bitter;
Webster's Yorkshire Bitter;
Wilson's Mild, Bitter; guest
beer** 🅷
Large, stone-fronted Victorian
building overlooking the River
Wyre and Morecambe Bay with
spacious rooms. The family room
closes at 7pm and the no-smoking area 7.30. The house beer
comes from Moorhouse's.
🌣 ⬛ ◗ ⭐ ⬠ (Ferry) P ⤢

QUEENS HOTEL
Poulton Road ☎ (01253) 876740
12-11; 12-10.30 Sun
Thwaites Bitter, seasonal beers 🅷
Busy, friendly pub, where a central bar serves several alcoves.
Games room for pool, snooker
and darts with Sky TV. Can get
busy Fri and Sat eves. 🌣 P

SHIP
24-26 Warren Street (near council offices) ☎ (01253) 872610
11-11; 12-10.30 Sun
**Boddingtons Bitter; Gray's
Bitter** 🅷
Busy, friendly pub, recently refurbished with a central bar and a
comfortable lounge with pool and
darts room. Occasional live music.
🏚 🌣 ◗ ⭐ ⬠ (Church St)

STEAMER
1-2 Queens Terrace (opp market) ☎ (01253) 771756
11-11; 12-10.30 Sun
Theakston Mild, Best Bitter 🅷
Victorian riverside pub next to
the traditional market. One bar
serves two lounges and a room
for games. Lunches in summer.
🏚 🌣 ◗ ⬠ (Ferry)

WYRE LOUNGE BAR
Marine Hall, The Esplanade (next
to swimming baths)
☎ (01253) 771141
12-4, 7-11; 12-4, 7-10.30 Sun
**Courage Directors; Moorhouse's
Premier, Pendle Witches Brew;
Phoenix Oak Bitter; guest
beers** 🅷
Part of the attractive Marine Hall
and gardens complex, famous for
its guest beers and the venue for
Fleetwood Beer Festival.
Q 🌣 ⭐ ⬠ (Ferry) P

GARSTANG

ROYAL OAK
Market Place (B6430)
☎ (01995) 603318
11-3 (4 Thu), 7-11; 11-11 Fri &
Sat; 12-10.30 Sun
**Robinson's Hatters Mild,
Hartleys XB, Best Bitter,
Frederics** 🅷
Partly a 15th-century farmhouse,
but this is mostly a 1670 coach-
ing inn, thoughtfully renovated

with intimate drinking areas.
🦮 🍺 ◑ ▶ ♣ P

TH'OWD TITHEBARN
Church Street (off B6430, by
Lancaster Canal)
☎ (01995) 604486
11-3, 6-11 (11-11 summer); 12-
10.30 Sun
**Mitchell's Original, Lancaster
Bomber, seasonal beers** Ⓗ
Real old tithe barn in an attractive canalside setting. Most of
the space is a restaurant in cod-
medieval style, but one end is
more pubby. Upstairs is a small
canal museum. 🦮 Q 🦮 ◑ ▶ P

GOOSNARGH
GRAPES
Church Lane (off B5269)
☎ (01772) 865234
11-3, 7-11; 11-11 Thu-Sat & summer; 12-10.30 Sun
**Boddingtons Bitter; Tetley Dark
Mild, Bitter; Theakston Best
Bitter; guest beers** Ⓗ
Attractive village pub with a
bowling green, next to the church
and near the village green. The
lounge has a double-sided fire in
the centre. Reputedly since
Oliver Cromwell, there has been
a pub on this site since the
Domesday Book. Eve meals Tue-
Sun, 6-8. 🦮 🦮 🦮 ◑ ▶ ♣ P

GREAT HARWOOD
DOG & OTTER
Cliffe Lane (opp Cricket Ground)
☎ (01254) 885760
11.30-3, 5.30-11; 12-10.30 Sun
**Jennings Bitter, Cumberland
Ale; guest beers** Ⓗ
Comfortable, open-plan pub and
restaurant serving a good range
of beer and food. Families welcome. 🦮 ◑ ▶ Å P

ROYAL HOTEL
Station Road (by Lomax Sq)
☎ (01254) 883541
12-1.30 (not Mon & Tue), 7-11;
12-3, 7-10.30 Sun
**Black Sheep Best Bitter; guest
beers** Ⓗ
Victorian, open-plan pub, with
four changing guest beers, also a
wide range of bottled beers and
home-cooked meals. Winner of
several CAMRA awards. Parking
for residents.
Q 🦮 🍺 ◑ ▶ ♣ 🍺

GREAT MITTON
OWD NED'S RIVER VIEW TAVERN
Mitton Hall, Mitton Road (B6246)
☎ (01254) 826544
11-11; 12-10.30 Sun
**Boddingtons Mild, Bitter;
Flowers Original; Jennings
Cumberland Ale; Marston's
Pedigree** Ⓗ

Overlooking the River Ribble in
picturesque country, this pub
places an emphasis on food and
good facilities for children. Opens
7.30 for breakfast.
🦮 🦮 🦮 🍺 ◑ ▶ ♿ ❤ P

HASLINGDEN
GRIFFIN INN
86 Hud Rake (off A680)
☎ (01706) 214021
12-11; 12-10.30 Sun
**Porter Mild, Bitter, Rossendale,
Porter, Sunshine, seasonal
beers** Ⓗ
Open-plan brewpub on a hillside,
enjoying a view over the valley.
Great for conversation. 🦮 Q ♣

HESKIN
FARMERS ARMS
85 Wood Lane (B5250, 1 mile S
of Eccleston) ☎ (01257) 451276
12-11; 12-10.30 Sun
**Boddingtons Bitter, OB, Mild;
Castle Eden Ale; Flowers IPA;
guest beers** Ⓗ
Country pub with an emphasis on
food (served 12-9.30): comfortable split-level lounge and dining
area, plus a public bar. Families
are welcome (large play area);
near Camelot Theme Park.
🦮 ◑ ▶ 🍺 ♿ Å ♣ P

HEST BANK
HEST BANK
Hest Bank Lane (off A5105
coastal road) ☎ (0154) 824339
11.30-11; 12-10.30 Sun
**Boddingtons Bitter; Marston's
Pedigree; guest beers** Ⓗ
The pub's colourful history may
be discovered within. Greatly
extended in the 1980s leaving
intact two older rooms (one a
lounge, the other for games) and
lantern window. A popular local
and an eating house. Canalside
garden. 🦮 🦮 ◑ ▶ ♣ P

HEYSHAM
ROYAL
7 Main Street (off A589)
☎ (01524) 859298
11-11; 12-10.30 Sun
**Mitchell's Mild, Original,
Lancaster Bomber** Ⓗ
Old, four-roomed, low-ceilinged
pub near St Patrick's chapel and
rock-hewn graves. It enjoys a
busy local trade, also plenty of
holidaymakers in season. Children
admitted to the games room until
7.30pm.
🦮 🦮 🍺 ♣ P

HIGH MOOR
RIGBYE ARMS
2 Whittle Lane
☎ (01257) 462154
12-3, 5.30-11; 12-10.30 Sun

**Ind Coope Burton Ale; Marston's
Pedigree; Tetley Dark Mild,
Mild, Bitter** Ⓗ
Remote award-winning rural pub,
popular with ramblers – can be
busy in summer – with a
deserved reputation for food.
Own bowling green. 🦮 Q 🦮 ◑ ▶ ♣ P

HOGHTON
BLACK HORSE
Gregson Lane (off A675, at
Higher Walton)
☎ (01254) 852541
11.30-11; 12-10.30 Sun
**Matthew Brown Bitter; Ruddles
County; Theakston Best Bitter;
guest beers** Ⓗ
Large, friendly open-plan village
pub where children are allowed
in for food. 🦮 ◑ ♿ ♣ P

ROYAL OAK
Blackburn Old Road, Riley Green
(A675/A6061 jct)
☎ (01254) 201445
11.30-3, 5.30-11; 11.30-11 Sat;
12-10.30 Sun
**Thwaites Best Mild, Bitter, sea-
sonal beers** Ⓗ
Traditional, low-ceilinged country
pub, formed from a row of cottages, with several cosy drinking
areas and a dining area.
🦮 Q 🦮 🦮 ◑ ▶ P ✂

HOSCAR
RAILWAY TAVERN
Hoscar Moss Road (by station)
☎ (01704) 892369
12-3 (not Mon), 5-11; 12-11 Sat;
12-10.30 Sun
**Jennings Bitter; Tetley Mild,
Bitter; guest beers** Ⓗ
Rural local, popular with cyclists,
serving excellent, home-cooked
food. It holds an annual beer festival. Recently refurbished without loss of character.
🦮 Q 🦮 🦮 ◑ ▶ 🍺 ♿
Å 🚉 (Hoscar Moss) ♣ P

LANCASTER
BOBBIN
36 Cable Street (next to bus station) ☎ (01524) 32606
11-11 (may vary); 12-10.30 Sun
**Mitchell's Original, Lancaster
Bomber, seasonal beers** Ⓗ
Formerly the priory, totally
revamped in 1997 with a cotton
industry theme, including a var-
nished floor, big curtains and
strange things on the walls. Rock
music Thu eve; a big band first
Sun in the month. 🚉 ♣

BOWERHAM
Bowerham Road (off A6)
☎ (01524) 65050
11-5, 6-11; 12-10.30 Sun
**Mitchell's Original, Lancaster
Bomber, seasonal beers** Ⓗ

Large, turn-of-the-century suburban pub with several rooms, drawing a lively local trade. Bowling green. 🏡 🍺 ♣

GEORGE & DRAGON
24 St George's Quay (off A6)
☎ (01524) 844739
11.30-11; 12-10.30 Sun
Ward's Thorne BB, Best Bitter; guest beers Ⓗ
Narrow, single-bar pub, decorated in plain, modern style, close to the Maritime Museum. All beers are served through a tight sparkler. 🏡 🍺 ▶ ⇌ P

GOLDEN LION
Moor Lane (near brewery)
☎ (01524) 63198
12-3, 7-11; 7-10.30 Sun
Theakston Best Bitter, Black Bull, XB, Old Peculier; guest beer Ⓗ
A pub since at least 1612: An L-shaped bar and an adjoining games room, plus a no-smoking 'Heritage' room. 🏡 ♣ ⚥

JOHN O'GAUNT
35 Market Street (off A6)
☎ (01524) 65356
11-3 (5 Sat), 6 (7 Sat)-11; 11-11 Thu & Fri; 12-3, 7-10.30 Sun
Boddingtons Bitter; Ind Coope Burton Ale; Jennings Bitter; Tetley Bitter; guest beers Ⓗ
Small pub, often packed, with a handsome original frontage. Frequent live music - the landlord is a jazz enthusiast. Just snacks for Sun lunch. 🏡 🍺 ⇌

Try also: Friary & Firkin, Rosemary Lane (Firkin)

LANESHAWBRIDGE

EMMOT ARMS
Keighley Road (A6068, Colne Road) ☎ (01282) 863366
12-3, 5.30-11; 12-11 Sat; 12-10.30 Sun
Boddingtons Bitter; Chester's Best Mild; guest beers Ⓗ
Popular village pub near Wycoller Country Park with excellent home cooking (no food Mon). 🏚 🏡 🚲 🍺 ⚹ ♣ P

LATHOM

SHIP INN
Wheat Lane (off A5209, by canal) ☎ (01704) 893117
11.30-3, 5.30-11; 11.30-11 Fri & Sat; 12-10.30 Sun
Beer range varies Ⓗ
Free house situated in a conservation area at a junction of the Leeds-Liverpool Canal. 🍺 P

LEYLAND

EAGLE & CHILD
30 Church Road (B5248)
☎ (01772) 433531

11.45-11; 12-10.30 Sun
Burtonwood Bitter, Forshaw's, Top Hat, Buccaneer; guest beer Ⓗ
Ancient inn near the historic cross. One long bar is divided into several drinking areas. Attracts all age groups. 🏡 🍺 ♣ P

GEORGE IV
63 Towngate
☎ (01772) 464051
11.30-11; 12-10.30 Sun
Boddingtons Bitter; Flowers Original; Greenalls Bitter; Tetley Bitter; guest beer Ⓗ
Attractive town pub, hosting live bands some eves; popular with young people at weekends. The guest beer is now only changed about once every six months and supplied by Whitbread. 🍺 ♣ P

LITTLE ECCLESTON

CARTFORD HOTEL
Cartford Lane (½ mile off A586 by toll bridge) ☎ (01995) 670166
12-3, 6.30 (7 winter)-11; 12-4, 6-10.30 Sun
Beer range varies Ⓗ
Delightfully situated free house by the River Wyre. An extensive bar menu includes a children's menu. Six changing guest beers always include two from Hart, whose award-winning brewery is at the rear. Local CAMRA award-winning pub.
🏚 🏡 🚲 🍺 ▶ ⚹ ♣ ⌂ P

LONGRIDGE

ALSTON ARMS
Inglewhite Road
☎ (01772) 783331
11.30 (5 winter Tue)-11; 12-10.30 Sun
Matthew Brown Lion Bitter; Theakston Mild, Best Bitter; guest beer Ⓗ
Comfortable pub, well within reach of the town centre. A newly-built conservatory offers good views of the Ribble Valley. The garden is home to various animals. Very accommodating for families. The floral decoration in summer is often impressive.
🏚 Q 🐕 🏡 🍺 ▶ ⚹ ♣ P

FORREST ARMS
2 Derby Road ☎ (01772) 782610
12-2 (not Tue & Wed), 5 (7 Tue & Wed)-11; 12-11 Fri & Sat; 12-10.30 Sun
Boddingtons Bitter; guest beers Ⓗ
Enterprising, terraced stone pub at the bottom of the town's main road. Home to a well-known soccer team and has its own real ale society. CAMRA award winner. The new garden contains a boules pitch. Guest beer may be unusual for the area. Hours may be extended in summer.
🏡 🍺 ⚹ ♣

TOWNLEY ARMS
41 Berry Lane
☎ (01772) 782219
11-11; 12-10.30 Sun
Tetley Dark Mild, Bitter Ⓗ
Multi-room, town-centre, drinkers' pub, a former railway station. Sells seafood over the bar and is handy for the shops. A pub for the more mature clientele: no juke box, but tapes or local radio played.
🏚 Q 🍺 ⚹ ♣ P

LOSTOCK HALL

VICTORIA
Watkin Lane
☎ (01772) 335338
11-11; 12-10.30 Sun
John Smith's Bitter; guest beers Ⓗ
Large pub, set back from the main road. A true community local, it is the meeting place for several clubs and societies. The two guest beers tend to be stronger ales. No food Mon.
🏡 🍺 🍺 ⇌ (Lockstock) ♣ P

LYTHAM

HOLE IN ONE
Forest Drive (off B5261)
☎ (01253) 730598
11.30-3, 5.30-11; 11.30-11 Fri & Sat; 12-10.30 Sun
Thwaites Bitter Ⓗ
Busy, friendly, modern local near Fairhaven golf course and displaying golfing memorabilia. A large games room; good home-made food (new restaurant extension). Children are most welcome. Wheelchair WC.
Q 🐕 🏡 🍺 ▶ Å 🍺 ♣ P

TAPS
12 Henry Street
(off Clifton Sq)
☎ (01253) 736226
11-11; 12-10.30 Sun
Beer range varies Ⓗ
Busy, friendly, basic alehouse, serving a wide choice of changing guest beers. Recently refurbished with new air conditioning. Award-winning licensee. Difficult parking. Wheelchair WC.
🏚 Q 🏡 🍺 🍺 ⇌ ⌂

MAWDESLEY

BLACK BULL
Hall Lane
(off B5246) OS499151
☎ (01704) 822202
12-11; 12-10.30 Sun
Greenalls Mild, Bitter, Original, guest beers Ⓗ
Welcoming, 400-year-old, stone built country pub with a prize-winning display of hanging baskets in summer. Noted locally for its food (no eve meals winter Mon). Boules pitch in the garden.
🏚 🏡 🍺 ▶ ⚹ ♣ P

ROBIN HOOD
Bluestone Lane
OS506163
☎ (01704) 822275
11.30-3, 6-11; 11-11 Sat;
12-10.30 Sun
Boddingtons Bitter; Castle Eden Ale; Flowers IPA; Robinson's Hartley's XB; Taylor Landlord; guest beers Ⓗ
Food oriented, isolated country pub located at a crossroads between Croston, Eccleston and Mawdesley. Seven ales and a warm welcome are always on offer.
🛏 ❀ ◖ 🍴 P ✂

MELLING

MELLING HALL
On A587
☎ (0152 42) 22022
12-3, 6-11; 11-11 Sat; 12-10.30 Sun
Boddingtons Bitter; Taylor Golden Best (occasional)**, Landlord; Theakston Best Bitter** Ⓗ
17th-century manor house which became a hotel in the 1940s, with two contrasting bars. Garden play area.
🛏 ❀ ◖ 🍴 🌳 ♣ P

MORECAMBE

DAVY JONES' LOCKER
26 Marine Road West (promenade)
☎ (01524) 410180
11-11; 12-10.30 Sun
Mitchell's Original, Lancaster Bomber Ⓗ
Independent cellar bar beneath the Clarendon Hotel, with nautical decor. Other Mitchell's beers are stocked.
🛏 ❀ ⇌ ♣ P

OWL'S NEST
Elms Hotel, Elms road (B5275)
☎ (01524) 411501
11-11; 12-10.30 Sun
Mitchell's Mild, Original Ⓗ
When the Elms Hotel was a private house, this was the lodge. Now a separately-run small bar for locals.
❀ ⇌ (Bare Lane) ♣ P

SMUGGLERS' DEN
Poulton Road (near police station)
☎ (01524) 421684
11-3, 7-11; 12-10.30 Sun
Boddingtons Bitter; Jennings Bitter; Tetley Bitter; guest beer Ⓗ
The smugglers are long gone, but stained glass and nautical knick-knacks remind customers of this low-beamed, stone-floored pub's past. Busy in summer. The patio houses caged cockatiels.
🛏 ❀ ♣ P

OLD SKELMERSDALE

HORSE SHOE INN
137 Liverpool Road (B5312, 1 mile from M58 jct)
☎ (01695) 731676
11-11; 12-10.30 Sun
Cains Bitter; Walker Mild; guest beers Ⓗ
Victorian community pub, originally built to serve the local mining community. Excellent value food includes breakfasts served from 7.30 (9.30 weekends). Building a reputation for its guest beers.
🛏 Q 🛏 ❀ ◖ 🍴 ▲ ♣ P

ORMSKIRK

GOLDEN LION
39 Moor Street (edge of pedestrian zone)
☎ (01695) 572354
11-11; 12-10.30 Sun
Tetley Mild, Bitter; guest beer Ⓗ
Popular, town-centre pub with a central bar serving two rooms and a split-level lounge. Regular quiz and entertainment. The house beer is brewed at Carlsberg-Tetley's Burton brewery. Good food always available.
🛏 ◖ 🍴 🌳 ⇌

MAYFIELD
22 County Road (A59 Liverpool road)
☎ (01695) 571157
12-11, 12-10.30 Sun
Courage Directors; John Smith's Bitter; Theakston Best Bitter; guest beers Ⓗ
Extremely popular and friendly free house on the edge of town, where small micros' beers feature predominantly. Winner of many CAMRA awards and Courage *Cellarman of the Year* award. Excellent meals (eves finish 8.30). Good wheelchair access. Worth the walk from town.
❀ ◖ 🍴 ♿ ⇌ P 🚃

QUEENS HEAD
30 Moor Street
☎ (01695) 574380
12-11; 12-10.30 Sun
Tetley Bitter; guest beers Ⓗ
Corner local, popular with students, gaining an excellent reputation for its guest beers at reasonable prices. Recently branded a Festival Alehouse, staging regular beer festivals.
🛏 ◖ ⇌

Try also: Yew Tree, Yew Tree Rd (Greenalls)

PLEASINGTON

RAILWAY HOTEL
Pleasington Lane
☎ (01254) 201520
12-11; 12-10.30 Sun

Boddingtons Bitter; Tetley Bitter; Wilson's Mild, Bitter; guest beers Ⓗ
Old farmhouse converted at the coming of the railway around 1850. No meals Mon and Sun eves. Intimate local catering for all ages. Own bowling green.
🛏 Q 🛏 ❀ ◖ 🍴 ⇌ ♣ P 🚃

POULTON-LE-FYLDE

THATCHED HOUSE
12 Ball Street (in St Chads church grounds)
11-11; 12-10.30 Sun
Boddingtons Bitter; Greenalls Original; Wells Bombardier; guest beer Ⓗ
Recently renovated, extremely popular, picturesque Greenalls pub. No music, children or food but a lively, warm and friendly atmosphere; a local institution. Wheelchair WC.
🛏 Q ♿ ▲ ⇌

Try also: Golden Ball, Ball St (Carlsberg-Tetley)

PRESSALL

BLACK BULL
192 Park Lane
☎ (01253) 810294
12-3 (not Mon), 6-11; 12-3, 7-10.30 Sun
Tetley Mild, Bitter; guest beers Ⓗ
Old-fashioned, low-beamed, friendly rural village pub. The mainly mature local clientele enjoy high quality food (not served Mon). The host was a national finalist in 1997 Tetley's *Cellarmanship* competition. Children welcome. The house beer is Theakston's Black Bull.
Q ◖ ▲ ♣ P

PRESTON

ASHTON INSTITUTE & SOCIAL CLUB
10-12 Wellington Road, Ashton (off A5085)☎ (01772) 726582
7 (4 Fri & Sat)-11; 12-10.30 Sun
Boddingtons Bitter; Jennings Cumberland Ale; guest beers Ⓗ
Lively social club in a residential area. Guest beers always include a mild. Annual beer festival (Oct). Loyal golfing society. Show CAMRA membership card or this *Guide* to be signed in. ❀ ♣

BLACKAMOOR
92 Lancaster Road (near market)
☎ (01772) 251590
10.30-11; 12-6 Sun
Barnsley Bitter; John Smith's Bitter; Vaux Samson Ⓗ
Market pub, recently refurbished with bare wood to the fore. Busy right through the day. Now free of tie and hoping to introduce guest beers. No food Sun.
🛏 ❀ ◖ ♣ ✂

GREYFRIARS
144 Friargate (off Ringway)
☎ (01772) 558542
11-11; 12-10.30 Sun
Courage Directors; Mitchell's Original; Morland Old Speckled Hen; Theakston Best Bitter; Thwaites Best Mild; guest beers H
Modern town-centre pub in an old carpet showroom. It has all the usual Wetherspoons features: cheap beer, comfortable surroundings, regular beer festivals. At least two guest beers. Gets very busy Fri and Sat eves.
Q ◖ ◗ ♿ ⇌ ⅟ ▯

HOGSHEAD (MOSS COTTAGE)
99 Fylde Road (A583)
☎ (01772) 252870
11-11; 12-10.30 Sun
Boddingtons Bitter; Whitbread Abroad Cooper H; **guest beers** H G
Former doctor's surgery, restored as a cask ale house. Its good, friendly atmosphere attracts a wide range of customers. Up to 12 beers, including two stillaged behind the bar. Local CAMRA *Pub of the Year* 1998. Food served all day until 7 (Sun 12-3).
Q ❀ ◖ ♿ ⌓

LANE ENDS
442 Blackpool Road, Lane Ends (A5085/B5411 jct)
☎ (01772) 733362
11-11; 12-10.30 Sun
Boddingtons Bitter; guest beers H
Lively, former coaching house, which is a popular meeting place. A large screen TV shows many sporting events. Guest beers normally include a mild. Accessible by many bus routes. It fields a golf society and successful soccer team. Eve meals weekdays.
❀ ◖ ◗ ♣ P

LIMEKILN
288 Aqueduct Street, Ashton (off A583) ☎ (01772) 493247
11-11; 12-10.30 Sun
Banks's Mild, Bitter H
One-roomed local, recently acquired by Banks'. Runs its own fishing club and a newly founded football team. Situated between the Blackpool and the West Coast rail lines.
❀ ♣ P

MITRE TAVERN
90-91 Moor Lane (A6)
☎ (01772) 251918
12-3, 5.30-11; 12-11 Sat; 12-10.30 Sun
Vaux Samson; Ward's Best Bitter; guest beers H
Welcoming pub: a comfortable lounge and a basic vault with pool and darts. Two guest beers from Vaux tenants' scheme change every 12 weeks.
No food Sat.
◖ ⊞ ♣ P

MOORBROOK INN
370 North Road (A6)
☎ (01772) 201127
4 (12 Sat)-11; 12-3, 7-10.30 Sun
Thwaites Best Mild, Bitter, seasonal beers H
Small, homely, wood-panelled local with two small rooms off the main bar area which seems to be supported by two lamp posts. Impromptu folk eves.
Q ❀ ♣

NEW BRITANNIA
6 Heatley Street (off Friargate)
☎ (01772) 253424
11-3 (4 Sat), 6-11; 7-10.30 (closed lunch) Sun
Boddingtons Bitter; Flowers Original; Castle Eden Ale; Marston's Pedigree; guest beers H
Small, cosy, single-bar town-centre pub, close to the university. Note the Britannia windows. Weekday food.
❀ ◖ ⇌ ♣ ⌓

OLD BLACK BULL
35 Friargate (Ringway jct)
☎ (01772) 823397)
10.30-11; 12-10.30 Sun
Boddingtons Bitter; Cains Bitter H; **guest beers** H G
Tudor-fronted pub with a snug, a games area and a lounge off the main bar, plus a tiny vault at the front. A homely alehouse with six changing guest beers (two stillaged behind the bar). No food Sun. Cider changes. Wheelchair WC.
❀ ◖ ⊞ ♿ ⇌ ♣ ⌓

OLDE BLUE BELL
114 Church street (off A6)
☎ (01772) 251280
11-3 (3.30 Fri & Sat), 5.30 (6 Fri & Sat)-11; 12-4, 7-10.30 Sun
Samuel Smith OBB H
This is the oldest pub in Preston, which is similar to a country cottage, with two small rooms off the bar area. Good for conversation but busy Fri and Sat eves. Good value food (eve meals Mon-Thu until 8).
♨ ◖ ◗

OLDE DOG & PARTRIDGE
44 Friargate
☎ (01772) 252217
11-2.30, 6-11; 12-3, 7-10.30 Sun
Draught Bass; Highgate Dark; Worthington Bitter; guest beers H
Well known bikers' pub but also popular with students and a wide clientele. Excellent value lunches (Mon-Sat) and a rare cask mild outlet for the town centre. Often has guests from micros. There is a DJ on Sun eve.
◖ ⇌ ♣

PLUNGINGTON TAVERN
85 Plungington Road
☎ (01772) 252339
12-11; 12-3, 7-10.30 Sun
Bass Mild; Stones Bitter; Whitbread Toby; Worthington Bitter H
Street-corner local boasting an impressive tiled frontage in a shopping area. A plain, simple interior offers a friendly welcome. Supports local community activities.
⊞ ♣

REAL ALE SHOP
47 Lovat Road (off A6, N of town)
☎ (01772) 201591
11-2, 5-10; 12-2, 6-10 Sun
Beer range varies H
Superb off-licence which, apart from up to four beers and a cider on draught, offers an excellent choice of specialist beers, fruit wines and spirits. Parties catered for. Fancy dress hire above. Video hire. ⌓

SUMNERS
Watling St Road, Fulwood (B6242)
☎ (01772) 705626
11.30 (11 Sat)-11; 12-10.30 Sun
Boddingtons Bitter; Marston's Pedigree H
Large, busy modern pub, handy for the football ground: a wood-panelled lounge, no-smoking conservatory, a spacious games room and a large patio. Large screen TV for football matches. Meals served all day until 7pm.
❀ ◖ ◗ ⊞ ♿ ♣ P ⅟

RISHTON

RISHTON ARMS
Station Road
☎ (01254) 886396
7 (11 Sat)-11; 12-10.30 Sun
Thwaites Best Mild, Bitter, seasonal beers H
Large, comfortable two-roomed community local, featuring a grandfather clock in the lounge.
⇌ ♣ P

ST ANNES

VICTORIA HOTEL
Church Road (off B5233)
☎ (01253) 721041
11-11; 12-10.30 Sun
Boddingtons Bitter; Flowers Original, OB Mild; guest beer H
Large pub with a 100-year-old public bar. Live music most eves.
♘ ❀ ◖ ◗ ⊞ ♣ P ⅟

SALTERFORTH

ANCHOR INN
Salterforth Lane
☎ (01282) 813186

12-11; 12-10.30 Sun
Bass Mild, Draught Bass; John Smith's Bitter; Theakston Best Bitter; Worthington Bitter H
Welcome stop on the Leeds-Liverpool canal, dating from 1655. It boasts an impressive array of stalactites in the cellar.
🏚 🕸 ⓓ ▶ Å ♣ P

SALWICK

HAND & DAGGER
Treales Road (off A583, past BNFL) OS463330
☎ (01772) 690306
12-3, 5-11; 12-11 Sat; 12-10.30 Sun
Boddingtons Bitter; Greenalls Bitter, Original H
Attractive, 200-year-old pub in a rural setting at the bridge over the Lancaster canal. Good value bar meals, plus a restaurant area. Children welcome until 7pm.
🏚 🕸 ⓓ ▶ �¬ P

SCARISBRICK

HEATONS BRIDGE INN
2 Heatons Bridge Road (B5242, by Leeds-Liverpool Canal)
☎ (01704) 840549
11-11; 12-10.30 Sun
Tetley Mild, Bitter; guest beers H
This popular canalside inn, dating from 1837, has been extended and refurbished but without loss of character. The small rooms off the bar are ideal for conversation. Excellent value food (all day Sun); children welcome in the dining area. Camping by prior arrangement.
🏚 Q ⇥ ⓓ ▶ ♿ Å ♣ P ⅛

SKELMERSDALE

TAWD VALE INN
Berry Street (behind Crow Orchard School)
☎ (01695) 733294
1-5, 7-11; 12-5, 7-10.30 Sun
John Smith's Bitter; guest beer H
Friendly local, popular with a wide age range. The name and pub sign commemorate a former colliery. 🕸 ♣ P

TOCKHOLES

ROYAL ARMS
Tockholes Road
☎ (01254) 705373
12-3, 7-11; 12-11 Fri, Sat & summer; 12-10.30 Sun
Thwaites Best Mild, Bitter, Chairman's, seasonal beers H
Very cosy, attractive moorland pub with a fire in each of its four rooms. Handy for walks. The food is recommended. This is the only Thwaites outlet in the area and it has the full range on offer.
🏚 Q ⇥ 🕸 ⓓ ▶ ♣ P ⅛

UPHOLLAND

OLD DOG
6 Alma Hill ☎ (01695) 623487
8-11; 8-10.30 Sun
Draught Bass; Boddingtons Bitter; Weetwood Old Dog; Worthington Bitter H
Traditional, multi-roomed pub with a small bar, stocking an incredible range of liqueurs. Difficult to park nearby. Q ⇥ ♣

WHITE LION
10 Church St ☎ (01695) 622727
12-3, 7.30 (7 Fri & Sat)-11; 12-3, 7-10.30 Sun
Thwaites Bitter; guest beers H
Genuine local with an L-shaped lounge, reputedly haunted. No food Sat. Limited parking. 🏚 🕸 ⓓ P

WESTHEAD

PRINCE ALBERT
109 Wigan Road (A577)
☎ (01695) 573656
12-3, 5-11; 12-11 Fri & Sat; 12-10.30 Sun
Tetley Mild, Bitter; guest beers H
Comfortable village local, renowned for its excellent value meals and guest beers. Accommodation recently opened.
🏚 Q ⇥ ⓓ ▶ Å ♣ P

WHALLEY

SWAN AT WHALLEY
62 King Street (A59)
☎ (01254) 822195
11-11; 12-10.30 Sun
Boddingtons Bitter; Thwaites Bitter; guest beers H
Excellent pub in the centre of a historic village serving good value food. A consortium within the pub runs race horses; the 2-1 house beer is from Moorhouse's.
⇥ ⓓ ▶ ➞ ♣ P

Try also: Dog Inn, 55 King St (S&N)

WHARLES

EAGLE & CHILD
1 Church Road (3 miles NE of Kirkham, between Treales and Inskip) OS448356
☎ (01772) 690312
12-3 (not winter Mon-Fri), 7-11; 12-4, 7-10.30 Sun
Beer range varies H
Remote, but very pleasant old-fashioned free house. No entry for children and no food. But there is antique furniture and beamed ceilings plus an ever-changing range of beers.
🏚 Q ♣ P

WHEELTON

RED LION
196 Blackburn Road (off A674)
☎ (01254) 830378

INDEPENDENT BREWERIES

Bank Top:
Bolton

Blackburn:
Blackburn

Hart:
Eccleston

Mitchell's:
Lancaster

Moorhouses:
Burnley

Porter:
Haslingden

Red Lion:
Accrington

Thwaites:
Blackburn

12-11; 12-10.30 Sun
Boddingtons Bitter; Theakston Best Bitter; guest beers H
Popular, village-centre pub with a split-level interior: a comfortable bar and a games room. A short walk from the Leeds-Liverpool Canal at Johnsons Hillock. Lunches Sat-Sun (daily in summer), eve meals Fri-Sun, 4.30-8.
🏚 ⓓ ▶ ♣ P

WHITTLE-LE-WOODS

ROYAL OAK
216 Chorley Old Road
☎ (01257) 276485
2.30-11; 12-10.30 Sun
Hanby Black Magic; Ruddles County; Theakston Black Bull; Webster's Yorkshire Bitter; Wells Bombardier H
Splendid, small, one-bar terraced village pub, a meeting place for mature motorcylce enthusiasts. Note the Nuttalls windows.
🏚 Q 🕸 ♣

YEALAND CONYERS

NEW INN
40 Yealand Road (off A6)
☎ (01524) 732938
11-3, 5.30-11; 11-11 Sat and summer; 12-10.30 Sun
Robinson's Hatters Mild, Hartleys XB, Best Bitter, Frederics, Old Tom H
Old village inn, an attractive bar and restaurant, popular for food. The opening of another pub nearby under the same management has returned the bar to drinkers.
🏚 🕸 ⓓ ▶ ♣ P

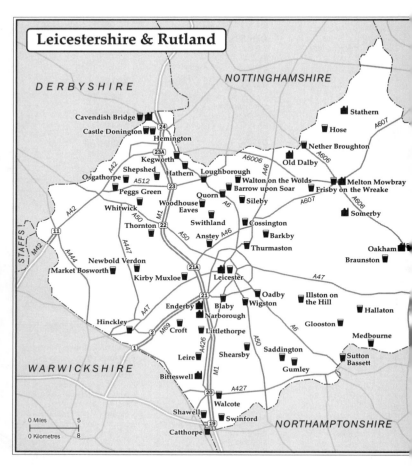

Leicestershire & Rutland

Rutland entries can be found on page 177

ANSTEY

OLD HARE & HOUNDS
34 Bradgate Road
☎ (0116) 236 2496
11-3.30, 6.30-11; 11-11 Fri & Sat;
12-3, 7-10.30 Sun
Marston's Bitter, Pedigree, HBC Ⓗ
Split-level pub with three rooms and a central bar; a popular local.
Q ❀ ♣ P

BARKBY

MALT SHOVEL
27 Main Street
☎ (0116) 269 2558
11.30-2.30, 6-11; 12-3, 7-10.30 Sun
Banks's Mild; Marston's Bitter, Pedigree; Theakston XB, Old Peculier guest beer
(occasional) Ⓗ
Cosy village pub; one U-shaped room, large car park and garden

and patio with good children's play area.
❀ ◖ ▶ P

BARROW ON SOAR

NAVIGATION INN
Mill Lane
☎ (01509) 412842
11-3, 5.30-11; 11-11 Sat; 12-3, 7-10.30 Sun
Marston's Pedigree; Shipstone's Mild, Bitter; guest beers Ⓗ
Busy village canalside pub with limited street parking. No lunches Sat or Sun but weekend barbecues in summer months. Guest beers favour microbreweries. Worth a visit.
🏨 Q ⏱ ❀ ◖ ♣

BLABY

BULL'S HEAD
22 Lutterworth Road (on old main road)
☎ (0116) 277 1860
11-2, 5.30-11; 12-2.30, 7-10.30 Sun
Ansells Bitter; Ind Coope Burton Ale; Tetley Bitter Ⓗ

Comfortable local in the centre of the village with one large lounge.
❀ P

CASTLE DONINGTON

CROSS KEYS
90 Bondgate ☎ (01332) 812214
11-3, 5.30-11; 11-11 Sat; 12-3, 7-10.30 Sun
Draught Bass; Courage Directors; Marston's Pedigree; Theakston Best Bitter, XB; guest beer Ⓗ

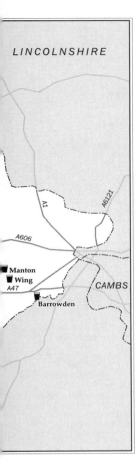

LINCOLNSHIRE

A1

A6121

A606

■ Manton
▼ Wing
A47

CAMBS

■ Barrowden

11-3, 5-11; 12-3.30, 7-10.30 Sun
**Draught Bass; Marston's
Pedigree; guest beers** Ⓗ
Friendly, atmospheric village pub
with a collection of breweriana,
including several hundred water
jugs. Three guest beers, cider in
summer, and home-cooked
lunches on offer. A gem.
🏵 ◖ ♣ ⌣ P

COSSINGTON

ROYAL OAK
105 Main Street
☎ (01509) 813937
12-3 (2.30 Sat; closed Mon);
6-11; 12-3, 7-10.30 Sun
**Everards Beacon, Tiger; guest
beer** Ⓗ
Small, wood-panelled village
local featuring one L-shaped
room with plain wooden tables,
and a conservatory. Popular with
diners (no food Mon, Sat lunch or
Sun eve). The guest beer is from
Everards Old English Ale Club.
Q 🏵 ◖ ◗ ♣ P 🗄

CROFT

HEATHCOTE ARMS
Hill Street
☎ (01455) 282439
12-2 (2.30 Fri), 5.30-11; 12-11
Sat; 12-3, 7-10.30 Sun
**Everards Beacon, Tiger, Old
Original; guest beer** Ⓗ
Unspoilt, friendly village pub on a
hilltop overlooking the river.
Comprising three rooms, it has a
relaxed atmosphere. Table and
long-alley skittles played. Guest
beer is from Old English Ale Club.
🏚 Q 🏵 ◖ 🍴 ♣ P

FRISBY ON THE WREAKE

BELL INN
2 Main Street ☎ (01664) 434237
12-2.30, 6-11; 12-2.30, 7-10.30 Sun
**Bateman XB; Greene King
Abbot; Marston's Pedigree;
Tetley Bitter; guest beers** Ⓗ
Large, friendly village local dating
from 1759, now free of Allied
Breweries tie and serving at
least two guest beers. Popular
with diners. Q 🚲 🏵 ◖ ◗ P

GLOOSTON

OLD BARN INN
Main Street ☎ (01858) 545215
12-2.30 (not Mon-Fri), 7-11; 12-3
(closed eve) Sun
**Theakston Best Bitter; guest
beers** Ⓗ
16th-century rural inn with an
open fire, situated in a small village on a Roman road with no
through traffic. Award-winning
food is served in the no-smoking
restaurant where the menu
changes monthly. No Sun eve
meals. 🏚 Q 🏵 🍴 ◖ ◗ P

GUMLEY

BELL INN
2 Main Street ☎ (0116) 279 2476
11-3, 5.30-11; 12-3, 7-10.30 Sun
**Draught Bass; Boddingtons
Bitter; Ridleys IPA; Wadworth
6X; guest beer** Ⓗ
Welcoming, beamed village local
with an L-shaped drinking area
and a separate no-smoking
restaurant. No eve meals Sun or
Mon. No children under five.
🏚 Q 🏵 ◖ ◗ ♣ ⌣ P

HALLATON

BEWICKE ARMS
1 Eastgate ☎ (01858) 555217
12-3, 7-11; 12-3, 7-10.30 Sun
**Marston's Pedigree; Ruddles
Best Bitter, County; guest
beers** Ⓗ
400-year-old thatched country
inn situated on the green of a village famous for its Easter
Monday bottle-kicking contest
with neighbouring village,
Medbourne. Recommended for
its food.
🏚 🏵 🍴 ◖ ◗ ♣ P

HINCKLEY

RAILWAY HOTEL
Station Road
☎ (01455) 615285
11-3.30, 6.30-11; 11-11 Sat;
12-3.30, 7-10.30 Sun
**Banks's Mild; Marston's Bitter,
Pedigree** Ⓗ
Spacious local with a basic bar, a
recently refurbished comfortable
lounge and a conservatory housing a pool table. Live sing-along
music Wed and Fri eves.
Q 🚲 🏵 🍴 ◖ ⇌ ♣ P

HATHERN

THREE CROWNS
Wide Lane (1st right after traffic
lights on A6 from Loughborough)
☎ (01509) 842233
12-2.30, 5.30-11; 12-11 Sat; 12-3,
7-10.30 Sun
**Draught Bass; Highgate Dark;
M&B Mild; Worthington Bitter;
guest beer** Ⓗ
Popular village local with three
rooms, a skittle alley and a large
garden.
🏚 Q 🏵 🍴 ▲ ♣ P ✗ 🗄

HEMINGTON

JOLLY SAILOR
21 Main Street (off A6, near M1
jct 24)
☎ (01332) 810448
11-11; 12-10.30 Sun
**Draught Bass; Greene King
Abbot; M&B Mild; Mansfield
Bitter; Marston's Pedigree;
guest beers** Ⓗ
Small, two-roomed village local,
heavily timbered. Artefacts adorn

Traditional two-roomed drinkers'
pub. Home to two local rugby
teams at weekends. Note the
original Offilers Brewery etched
windows. 🏚 🏵 ◖ ♣ P

CATTHORPE

CHERRY TREE
Mound Street (off A5, opp Rugby
turn, M6/A14 jct)
☎ (01788) 860430
12-2.30 (not Mon-Wed), 5-11; 12-
4, 7-11 Sat; 12-10.30 Sun
**Ansells Bitter; Draught Bass;
Hook Norton Best Bitter; guest
beers** Ⓗ
Cosy country inn with a friendly
welcome and a local following.
Happy hour is from 5-7pm Mon-
Fri. Private buffet parties for up
to 28 people can be arranged in
the restaurant. Book for Sun
lunch. Q 🚲 🏵 ◖ ♣ P

CAVENDISH BRIDGE

OLD CROWN
400 yds off A6 at Trent Bridge
☎ (01332) 792392

the walls and ceilings. Four guest beers on offer plus cider in summer. ᴍ Q ⅏ ⊛ ♣ ⟜ P

HOSE

BLACK HORSE
21 Bolton Lane ☎ (01949) 860336
12-2.30, 6.30-11; 12-4, 7-10.30 Sun
Brains Dark; Castle Eden Ale; Home Bitter; guest beers Ⓗ
Three-roomed village pub with an unspoilt bar, traditional lounge and a wood-panelled restaurant. It often offers guest beers from local microbreweries. Eve meals served Wed-Sun.
ᴍ Q ⊛ ⊅ ▮ ⊟ ♨ ▲ ♣ P

ROSE & CROWN
43 Bolton Lane
☎ (01949) 860424
12-3, 7-11; 12-3, 7-10.30 Sun
beer range varies Ⓗ
Traditional free house with up to eight guest beers, including a mild, normally from independents and microbreweries. This single-room pub has two distinct drinking areas plus a separate function and dining room.
ᴍ ⊛ ⊅ ♿ ▲ ♣ P ⅟ ⊟

ILLSTON ON THE HILL

FOX & GOOSE
Main Street ☎ (0116) 259 6340
12-2.30 (not Mon-Tue or Wed-Thu winter), 5.30 (7 Mon)-11; 12-2.30, 7-10.30 Sun
Everards Beacon, Tiger, Old Original; guest beer Ⓗ
A gem: cosy, unchanged ex-Ruddles village pub with a timeless feel, displaying a collection of local mementos and hunting memorabilia. Tucked away but well worth seeking out. Accommodation in a self-catering flat. ᴍ Q ⊛ ⇆ ⊟ ♣

KEGWORTH

CAP & STOCKING
20 Borough Street
☎ (01509) 674818
11.30-3 (2.30 winter), 6.30-11; 12-3, 7-10.30 Sun
Draught Bass; Ⓖ Hancock's HB; M&B Mild; guest beer Ⓗ
Three-roomed pub in old part of village, close to the M1, East Midlands Airport and Donington Park. Barbecues in summer in the lovely garden where petanque may be played. Bass is served from a jug.
ᴍ Q ⊛ ⊅ ▮ ♣ P

RED LION
24 High Street
☎ (01509) 672466
11-11; 12-10.30 Sun
Bateman Mild, XB; Castle Rock Hemlock; Marston's Pedigree; guest beers Ⓗ
A character pub with four individual rooms of simple decor, HQ for the Tynemill Pub Group. The large garden has a children's play area. Regularly changing cider usually available. Good food served.
ᴍ Q ⅏ ⊛ ⊅ ▮ ⊟ ♿ ♣ ⟜ P ⅟

KIRBY MUXLOE

CASTLE HOTEL
Main Street
☎ (0116) 239 5337
11-11; 12-3, 7-10.30 Sun
Marston's Bitter, Pedigree Ⓗ
Close to Kirby Castle, this 350-year-old former farmhouse became a restaurant in 1974 and later developed into a hotel. The comfortable bar was refurbished in 1996, making it more open-plan but retaining a well defined drinking area.
⊛ ⇆ ⊅ ▮ P

ROYAL OAK
35 Main Street
☎ (0116) 239 3166
11-2.30, 6-11; 11-3, 6-11 Sat; 12-3, 7-10.30 Sun
Adnams Bitter; Everards Beacon, Tiger, Old Original; guest beer Ⓗ
A modern exterior conceals a comfortable, traditionally-styled lounge bar with a restaurant, popular with business folk and locals. The guest beer is from Everards Old English Ale Club.
⊛ ⊅ ▮ P

LEICESTER

BLACK BOY
35 Albion Street
☎ (0116) 254 0222
11-11; 12-10.30 Sun
Draught Bass; Highgate Dark; Tolly Cobbold Original; Worthington Bitter; guest beers Ⓗ
Classic city-centre local with a charming, Victorian feel and a cosmopolitan clientele, popular with theatregoers. A cosy lounge with wood panelling, oval bar and ornate decorative ceiling, plus a basic bar. Traditional lunches served (not Sun).
Q ⊛ ⊅ ⇌ ♣

BLACK HORSE
1 Foxon Street (on Braunstone Gate) ☎ (0116) 254 0030
12-2.30 (not Tue-Thu), 5.30-11; 12-11 Fri & Sat; 12-10.30 Sun
Everards Beacon, Tiger; guest beers Ⓗ
Established for 12 years, this is a beer-drinker's pub close to the city centre, popular with students. Two separate rooms with a central bar, untouched by refurbishment. Guest beers (usually two) are from Everards Old English Ale Club. ⊛

BOWLTURNERS ARMS
156 Belgrave Gate
☎ (0116) 253 2081
12-2, 5.30-11; 11-11 Fri & Sat; 12-10.30 Sun
Shipstone's Mild, Bitter Ⓗ
Recently refurbished, now one large room, this pub still retains a tiled floor and all the atmosphere of a basic town-centre beer-drinkers' bar.
⊛ ⊅ ♣ P

CLARENDON
7-9 West Avenue (near London Road, A6)
☎ (0116) 244 9901
11.30-11; 12-10.30 Sun
Draught Bass; M&B Mild; Fuller's London Pride; guest beer (occasional) Ⓗ
Friendly, two-roomed corner pub in a terraced residential area. Popular in evenings with locals and students, it offers a no-smoking area and covered yard.
⊛ ⊅ ⊟ ♣

FUZZOCK & FIRKIN
203 Welford Road (A50)
☎ (0116) 270 8141
12-11; 12-10.30 Sun
Firkin Titleys Fuzzock, ASS Dogbolter; guest beer (occasional) Ⓗ
Formerly the Storks Head, the first of six Firkin pubs in Leicestershire with beer supplied by the Phantom & Firkin in Loughborough. With basic wooden floor and furniture, it is popular with students and young clientele in evenings and all in the day. Food served 12-6pm.
⊛ ⊅ P

HAT & BEAVER
60 Highcross Street
☎ (0116) 262 1157
11-3 (4 Sat), 6-11; 12-3, 7-10.30 Sun
Hardys & Hansons Best Mild, Best Bitter, Classic Ⓗ
Basic two-roomed former Bass local with a relaxed atmosphere, one of Leicester's few remaining traditional pubs. TV in the bar, handy for the Shires Shopping Centre. Well-filled cobs usually available. ⊛ ⊟ ♣

THREE CRANES
82 Humberstone Gate
☎ (0116) 251 7164
11-11; 12-10.30 Sun
Draught Bass; M&B Mild; Worthington Bitter; guest beers Ⓗ
City-centre free house, popular with beer drinkers. The large U-shaped bar offers at least four guest beers from small independent breweries. Known as the Boulevard in the 1980s, the old outside wall mouldings survive. B & B discounts for CAMRA members. ⊛ ⇆ ⊅ ▮ ♣

VAULTS
1 Wellington Street
☎ (0116) 255 5506
5-11; 12-11 Fri & Sat; 12-3, 7-11 Sun
Steamin' Billy Mild, Bitter; guest beers Ⓗ
Cellar bar with bohemian atmosphere. Over 500 guest beers per year, mainly from microbreweries; a mecca for real ale lovers. Live R&B music Sun eves (entrance fee usually charged). Steamin' Billy beers are supplied by Leatherbritches.⌂ ✁

VICTORIA JUBILEE
112 Leire St (200 yds from A46 Melton Rd) ☎ (0116) 266 3599
11-2.30 (3.30 Sat), 6-11; 12-4, 7-10.30 Sun
Marston's Bitter, Pedigree Ⓗ
Friendly, two-roomed street corner locals' pub with a basic bar and a comfortable lounge, situated in a terraced residential area. Known as The Full Moon until Queen Victoria's jubilee in 1897.
※ 🍴 ♣

WILKIE'S CONTINENTAL BAR
29 Market St ☎ (0116) 255 6877
12-11; closed Sun
Adnams Extra; Bateman XB; Woodforde's Great Eastern; guest beers ※
Established; friendly free house in the pedestrian city-centre. Up to six guest beers, cider, Belgian and German beers and over 100 bottled continental beers on offer. German food served 12-6.30 daily. ※ ◖ ⇌ ⌂

LEIRE

QUEEN'S ARMS
Main Street ☎ (01455) 209227
12-3, 5.30-11; 11-11 Sat; 12-10.30 Sun
Marston's Bitter, Pedigree, HBC Ⓗ
Warm, traditional, rural village local comprising one open bar with a beamed lounge. It offers good facilities for customers with disabilities. Barbecues in summer. ⌂ ※ 🐕 ◖ ▶ ♣ ♣ P

LITTLETHORPE

PLOUGH
7 Station Road ☎ (0116) 286 2383
11-2.30 (3 Sat), 6-11; 12-3, 7-10.30 Sun
Everards Beacon, Tiger; guest beers Ⓗ
Thatched village local with a cosy lounge, a bar and a dining area. With no juke box or machines its food and hospitality attract a wide range of customers. Long alley skittles available by arrangement. No food Sun eves.
Q ※ ◖ ▶ ⚅ ⇌ (Narborough) ♣ P

LOUGHBOROUGH

ALBION
Canal Bank (400 yds off Bridge St, up canal bank)
☎ (01509) 213952
11-3 (4 Sat), 6-11; 12-3, 7-10.30 Sun
Mansfield Riding Mild, Bitter; Samuel Smith OBB; guest beer Ⓗ
Tranquil canalside pub with a bar, darts room and quiet lounge serving good value beer and home-cooked food. Outside drinking is on the canal bank or the patio which has an aviary and a rabbit. Hosts Sunday beer cruises in summer. Convenient moorings.
Q ※ ◖ ▶ ⚅ ⇌ ♣ P

BOAT INN
Meadow Lane
☎ (01509) 214578
11-3, 5-11; 11-11 Fri & Sat; 12-10.30 Sun
Banks's Mild; Marston's Bitter, Pedigree, HBC Ⓗ
Cosmopolitan canalside pub on the edge of town where a friendly welcome is assured. Popular with boaters in summer months (moorings available).
※ ◖ ⚅ ⇌ ♣ P

SWAN IN THE RUSHES
21 The Rushes
☎ (01509) 217014
11-11; 12-10.30 Sun
Archers Golden; Castle Rock Hemlock, Elsie Mo; Marston's Pedigree; Tetley Bitter; guest beers Ⓗ
Traditional two-roomed free house with a separate dining room. Guest beers always include a mild and one beer from Batemans. Good food is complemented by a range of real coffees. Regular live music in an upstairs function room. No eve meals weekends.
⌂ Q ※ ⚅ ◖ ▶ ⚅ ⚅ ⇌ ♣ ⌂ P

TAP & MALLET
36 Nottingham Road
☎ (01509) 210028
11.30-2.30, 11-11 Sat; 11.30-11 Sat; 12-10 .30 Sun
Courage Best Bitter; Ruddles County; Theakston Mild; guest beers Ⓗ
Genuine free house between the town-centre and station. Up to six guest beers available, mostly from an interesting range of microbreweries, with discounts for CAMRA members. The Theakston may be replaced by a guest mild. The large patio/garden has a children's play area/pets corner.
⌂ ※ ⇌ ♣ ⌂

Try also: Tap & Spile, Bedford St (Century Inns)

MARKET BOSWORTH

RED LION
1 Park Street ☎ (01455) 291713
11-2.30, 7-11; 11-11 Sat; 12-3, 7-10.30 Sun
Banks's Mild, Bitter; Camerons Bitter; Marston's Pedigree; Theakston XB, Old Peculier; guest beers Ⓗ
This large, split-level L-shaped village pub was once Hoskins' sole tied house. It is popular with locals and tourists from the nearby Bosworth Railway and battle site. ⌂ ※ ⚅ ◖ ▲ ♣ P

MEDBOURNE

HORSE & TRUMPET ☆
12 The Old Green
7-11; 12-2.30, 7-10.30 Sun
Bateman XB; Greene King IPA Ⓗ
Classic, basic, unspoilt pub; a free house since the early 1970s, it is a former Watneys house and still has an illuminated red barrel pub sign. In the same family since 1939, this unique beer-drinkers' pub is well worth a visit. ⌂ Q ※ ※ ♣

NEVILL ARMS
12 Waterfall Way
☎ (01858) 565288
12-2.30, 6-11; 12-3, 7-10.30 Sun
Adnams Bitter; Ruddles Best Bitter, County; guest beers Ⓗ
Built in 1876 as a coaching inn on the village green, next to a stream with tame ducks, this is a popular weekend venue for families. Unusual pub games played by arrangement. Excellent food.
⌂ ※ ⚅ ◖ ▶ ♣ P

MELTON MOWBRAY

BRICKLAYERS ARMS
16 Timber Hill (200 yds behind Safeway towards Norman Way)
☎ (01664) 565178
12-11; 12-10.30 Sun
Ansells Bitter; Marston's Pedigree; guest beer Ⓗ
Basic, open-plan local with two pool tables and a raised darts area. Tattooing session on Thu and live music nights. Guest beers are usually from local microbreweries. Note the fluffy-toy handpump warmers.
⌂ ⇌ ♣

CROWN
10 Burton St ☎ (01664) 564682
11-3.30, 7-11; 11-11 Sat; 12-3, 7-10.30 Sun
Everards Beacon, Tiger, Old Original, seasonal beers; guest beer Ⓗ
Friendly two-roomed town pub with a long-serving landlord. Popular with office workers and shoppers at lunchtime and diverse age groups at night.
⌂ 🐕 ◖ ⚅ ⇌ ♣

MASH TUB
58 Nottingham Street
☎ (01664) 410051
11-3 (4 Fri), 6-11; 11-11 Sat;
12-4, 7-10.30 Sun
Banks's Mild, Bitter Ⓗ
Single bar, split-level town pub
with good value lunches (not
served Sun)
◖ ≠ ♣ 🍺

Try also: Boat, Burton St
(Burtonwood); White Hart,
Sherrard St (Marston's)

NETHER BROUGHTON

RED LION HOTEL
23 Main Road
☎ (01664) 822429
11-2.30, 6-11; 11-11 Sat;
12-10.30 Sun
**Draught Bass; Highgate Dark;
Worthington Bitter; guest
beers** Ⓗ
Spacious family-run hotel with a
friendly atmosphere. Traditional
bar and lounge and excellent
restaurant which features occasional theme night menus. No
food Sun eve or Mon. It offers a
pets corner outside, also a
petanque pitch and skittle alley.
🚶 Q 🛏 🍺 ◖ ⌖ ♣ ♣ ⚐ ♣
▲ ♣ P

NEWBOLD VERDON

JUBILEE INN
80 Main Street
☎ (01455) 822698
11-2.30, 7 (6 Wed)-11; 12.30-11
Fri; 11-11 Sat; 12-10.30 Sun
Marston's Bitter, Pedigree Ⓗ
Friendly two-roomed village
local, cosy and unspoilt.
🚶 ♣ ♣ P

OADBY

COW & PLOUGH
Stoughton Farm Park, Gartree
Road (follow Farmworld signs off
A6) ☎ (0116) 2720852
5-9; 7-9 Sun
**Fuller's London Pride; Hoskins &
Oldfield HOB Bitter, Steamin'
Billy Mild, Bitter; guest beers** Ⓗ
Part of a leisure park during the
day, its atmospheric vaults are
adorned with breweriana. It
offers ever-changing guest
beers. Q 🛏 ♣ ♣ ♣ ⌂ P ⌿

OSGATHORPE

ROYAL OAK
20 Main Street
☎ (01530) 222443
7-11; 12-3, 7-10.30 Sun
**Marston's Pedigree; Offilers
Mild** Ⓗ
Quiet village local with assorted
brasses and other memorabilia
adorning the bar. Closed
lunchtimes except Sun.
🚶 Q 🍺 ♣ 🛏 ⌖ ▲ P

PEGGS GREEN

NEW INN
Clay Lane (B587, 200 yds from
A512 at Griffydam roundabout)
☎ (01530) 222293
12-2 (3 Sat), 5.30 (7 Sat)-11;
12-3, 7-10.30 Sun
**Draught Bass; M&B Mild;
Marston's Pedigree** Ⓗ
Traditionally village local with
several rooms and a good Irish
welcome. Occasional folk nights.
🚶 Q 🛏 🍺 ⚐ ♣ P

QUORN

BLACKSMITHS ARMS
29 Meeting Street
☎ (01509) 412751
12-2 (11-2.30 Sat), 5.30-11; 12-3,
7-10.30 Sun
Marston's Bitter, Pedigree Ⓗ
Busy village local with low-
beamed bar and cosy snug.
🚶 Q ⚐ ♣

Try also: White Hart, High St
(Pubmaster)

SADDINGTON

QUEEN'S HEAD
Main Street
☎ (0116) 240 2536
11-3, 5.30-11; 12-3, 7-10.30 Sun
**Adnams Bitter; Everards Beacon,
Tiger; guest beers** Ⓗ
Discover lovely views of the
Laughton Valley and Saddington
Reservoir from the garden or
conservatory-style restaurant,
hiding behind the standard
facade of this village local. No
eve meals Sun.
🚶 Q 🍺 ◖ ▶ P ⌿

SHAWELL

WHITE SWAN
Main Street (signed on A5 island
from M1 jct 19 towards Rugby)
☎ (01788) 860357
7-11; 12.30-2.30, 7-10.30 Sun
**Adnams Bitter; Marston's Bitter,
Pedigree; guest beers** Ⓗ
Olde worlde village inn with bags
of character, boasting wood panelling, real fires and sumptuous
armchairs plus a quality restaurant. Closed lunchtime except
Sat. 🚶 Q 🍺 ◖ ▶ ♣ P 🍺

SHEARSBY

CHANDLER'S ARMS
Fenney Lane
☎ (0116) 247 8384
12-2.30, 7-11; 12-3, 7-10.30 Sun
**Marston's Bitter, Pedigree;
Fuller's London Pride; guest
beer** Ⓗ
Pleasant country pub in a picturesque village with a homely
atmosphere and award-winning
garden. Excellent food served.
🍺 ◖ ▶ ⌿

SHEPSHED

BLACK SWAN
21 Loughborough Road
☎ (01509) 506783
12-3, 5.30-11; 12-4, 7-10.30 Sun
**Ansells Mild; Draught Bass;
Tetley Bitter; guest beer** Ⓗ
Smart, multi-roomed pub with an
emphasis on good food (booking
required Sun/Mon eves).
Children welcome in the restaurant. ◖ ▶ P

BULL & BUSH
61 Sullington Road
☎ (01509) 506783
12-3, 5.30-11; 12-4, 7-10.30 Sun
**Banks's Mild; Marston's
Pedigree, HBC** (occasional) Ⓗ
Traditional, unspoilt local with a
fine carved wood bar in its one
room. 🍺 ♣ P

CROWN
Market Place
☎ (01509) 502665
11-3 (not Mon-Tue), 6 (5 Mon-
Tue)-11; 11-11 Fri & Sat; 12-
10.30 Sun
**Everards Beacon, Tiger, Old
Original** Ⓗ
Busy locals' pub. 🚶 🍺 ♣ ⌂

Try also: Britannia, Britannia St
(Hardys & Hansons)

SILEBY

FREE TRADE
11 Cossington Road (100 yds off
High St opp library)
☎ (01509) 814494
11.30-3, 5.30-11; 11.30-3, 6.30-
11 Sat; 12-3, 7-10.30 Sun
**Everards Beacon, Tiger, Old
Original, seasonal beers** Ⓗ
Popular local with thatched roof,
catering for all age groups.
Petanque court to the rear.
Booking advisable for Sun lunch.
🍺 ◖ ≠ ♣ P

SUTTON BASSETT

QUEEN'S HEAD
Main Street
☎ (01858) 463530
11.45-3, 6.30-11; 12-3, 7-10.30 Sun
**Adnams Bitter; Ruddles Best
Bitter, County; guest beers** Ⓗ
Rural village pub and restaurant,
which offers a minimum of five
guest beers and tries to maintain
variety. Hosts regular beer festivals and sells a personalised
guest beer brewed by
Grainstore. 🚶 Q 🍺 ◖ ▶ P

SWINFORD

CHEQUERS
High Street (½ mile from
A14/M6 jct, opp church)
☎ (01788) 860318
12-2 (not Mon), 6-11; 12-3,
7-10.30 Sun

Ansells Mild, Bitter; Marston's Pedigree; guest beers (occasional) H
Village local with a friendly, cosy atmosphere. Offers traditional pub games, dining area, and a large garden with a play area.
🏚 Q ❀ ◑ ▶ ♣ P

SWITHLAND

GRIFFIN INN
174 Main Street
☎ (01509) 891096
12-2.30 (3 Sat), 6-11; 12-3, 7-10.30 Sun
Adnams Bitter; Everards Beacon, Tiger, Old Original; guest beer H
Friendly village local whose landlord is an ex-footballer. It comprises three comfortable rooms, a small games/family room and long alley skittles. Don't miss the photos in the passageway. No meals Sun eve or Mon-Tue eves in winter.
🏚 Q ⌂ ❀ ◑ ▶ ♣ P

THORNTON

BRICKLAYERS ARMS
Main Street
☎ (01530) 230808
12 (11 summer)-3, 6 (5 summer)-11; 12 (11 summer)-11 Sat; 12-10.30 Sun
Everards Tiger, Old Original; guest beer H
Unspoilt, traditional village local, partly dating from the 16th-century, with a basic, quarry-tiled bar and comfortable lounge. It overlooks the Thornton Trout Fisheries. Guest beers are from Everards Old English Ale Club. No food Mon.
🏚 Q ❀ ◑ ▶ P

THURMASTON

UNICORN & STAR
796 Melton Road
☎ (0116) 269 2849
11-3, 6-11 (varies bank hols); 12-3, 7-10.30 Sun
Shipstone's Mild, Bitter H
A basic beer drinkers' bar with no frills and a comfortable lounge, known to locals as the Top House.
❀ ♣ P

WALCOTE

BLACK HORSE
Main Street
☎ (01455) 552684
12-2 (not Mon-Tue), 7 (5.30 Fri, 6.30 Sat)-11; 12-3, 7-10.30 Sun
Hook Norton Best Bitter; Hoskins & Oldfield HOB Bitter; Litchfield Steeplejack; guest beers H
Single-bar free house close to M1 jct 20, well worth the detour.

Excellent home-cooked Thai food to order. Banquets catered for. Guest beers are from independent breweries.
❀ ◑ ♣ ⌂ P ✂

WALTON ON THE WOLDS

ANCHOR
2 Loughborough Road
☎ (01509) 880018
12-3, 5.30-11; 12-3, 7-10.30 Sun
Marston's Bitter, Pedigree; Taylor Landlord; guest beers H
Single-roomed village locals' pub, featuring a garden at the front, with large patio and grass area at the rear. Excellent food is available, with occasional themed nights (no food served Sun eve).
Q ❀ ◑ ▶ ♣ ⌂ P

WHITWICK

THREE HORSHOES
11 Leicester Road
☎ (01530) 837311
11-3, 6.30-11; 12-2, 7-10.30 Sun
Draught Bass; M&B Mild; guest beer (occasional) H
Unspoilt traditional alehouse known locally as 'Polly's', with a basic bar and tiny smoke room containing wood-backed pews.
🏚 Q ❀ ⌒ ♣ P

WIGSTON

STAR & GARTER
114 Leicester Road
☎ (0116) 288 2450
11-2.30, 5-11; 11-11 Sat; 12-3, 7-10.30 Sun
Bateman Mild; Everards Beacon, Tiger; guest beer H
Friendly two-roomed pub catering for all ages with a wood-panelled bar and a cosy, beamed lounge. Long alley skittles by arrangement. The guest beer is from Everards Old English Ale Club.
❀ ◑ ⌒ ♣ P

WOODHOUSE EAVES

WHEATSHEAF
Brand Hill (½ mile from village towards Swithland)
☎ (01509) 890320
12-2.30, 7 (6.30 Fri 7 Sat)-11; 12-3, 7-10.30 Sun
Boddingtons Bitter; Draught Bass; Marston's Pedigree; Ruddles County; Taylor Landlord; guest beers H
Comfortable pub and restaurant near Swithland Woods and Bradgate Park. Guest beers are usually of the stronger variety. No food Sun eve.
🏚 Q ❀ ◑ ▶ ⌂ P

Rutland

BARROWDEN

EXETER ARMS
28 Main Street (off A47)
☎ (01572) 747247
12-2.30, 6-11; 12-3, 7-10.30 Sun
Marston's Bitter, Pedigree; guest beers H
Stone pub in an idyllic setting on the village green opposite the duck pond. One long room with bare walls and oak beams. Cider in summer. 🏚 ❀ ◑ ▶ ⌒ P ✂

BELMESTHORPE

BLUE BELL
Sherherd Walk
☎ (01780) 763859
11-2.30, 6-11; 11-11 Sat; 12-10.30 Sun
Draught Bass; Hook Norton Old Hooky; guest beer H
Three cottages of lcoal limestone, one originally a mortuary and one a butcher's, make up this attractive pub. It features a central bar with a games room at one end and a restaurant at the other. Excellent food served.
🏚 Q ❀ ◑ ▶ ♣ P

BRAUNSTON

OLD PLOUGH INN
High Street
☎ (01572) 722714
11-3, 6-11; 12-3, 6-10.30 Sun
Grainstore Cooking (summer), **Triple B, Ten Fifty** (winter); **Ruddles Best Bitter, County; guest beers** H
Country pub with cosy low-beamed lounge and pleasant gardens, where families are welcome. The conservatory restaurant has a false ceiling made from parasols. It sometimes sells all three Rutland breweries' beers at the same time.
🏚 ❀ ◑ ▶ ⌒ ▲ ♣ P ✂

MANTON

HORSE & JOCKEY
2 St Mary's Road (off A6003)
☎ (01572) 737335
11-2.30, 7-11; 12-3, 7-10.30 Sun
Mansfield Riding Bitter, Old Baily H
A rarity near Rutland Water, this unspoilt 250-year-old village local offers cyclists puncture repair outfits for sale. 🛏 ◑ ⌒ ▲ ♣ 🍺

OAKHAM

GRAINSTORE BREWERY TAP
Station Approach
☎ (01572) 770065
11-2.30, 6-11; 11-2.30, 5-11 Fri &
Sat; 12-2.30, 7-10.30 Sun
**Grainstore Cooking, Triple B,
Ten Fifty, seasonal beers; guest
beers** Ⓗ
Refurbished grain warehouse;
the beer cellar used to be a rail-
way siding. Beer on traditional
dispense at south end of bar,
swan necks at the north end.
Sparklers may be used.
Occasional live bands. Tours of
the brewery by arrangement.
Limited parking.
Q ❀ ఈ ☛ ♣ P ⊟

WING

CUCKOO
3 Top Street
☎ (01572) 787340
11.30-3 (not Tue), 6.30-11; 12-4,
7-10.30 Sun
**Marston's Pedigree; Grainstore
Triple B; guest beers** Ⓗ
Whitewashed, unspoilt village
local. Hosts a steam rally and
beer festival in summer. Curries
a speciality.
🏨 ❀ ◖ ▶ Å ♣ P

INDEPENDENT BREWERIES
Belvoir: Old Dalby
Brewsters: Stathern
Everards: Narborough
Featherstone: Enderby
Grainstore: Oakham
Hoskins: Leicester
Hoskins & Oldfield: Leicester
Man in the Moon: Ashby Magna
O'Gaunt: Burrough onthe Hill
Parish: Somerby
Ruddles: Langham
Shardlow: Cavendish Bridge

When any brewery is bought by another, the threat of closure raises its ugly head. So it was when Morland bought Ruddles in late 1997. Morland owed CAMRA a debt of gratitude: it had escaped Greene King's hostile bid by the skin of its teeth in 1992, cheerfully admitting that CAMRA's vigorous support had helped vastly.

But by 1997 it wanted Ruddles' brands to supplement Old Speckled Hen, which had wide-spread distribution but wasn't delivering what Morland wanted in terms of actual cash-money sales. Ruddles had been one of the few companies which flew the flag for cask ales when CAMRA was formed over 25 years ago. Ruddles was sold to GrandMet; then it became part of a pubs for breweries swap and found itself under the aegis of Courage – who then sold it to Grolsch. And when a residual supply deal with Scottish Courage ran out last year, Morland's picked up Ruddles and its brands for a song.

The brewery would stay open, said Morland.

The brewery will close, Morland then announced.

That's confusing, because Ruddles's 420,000 barrel capacity brewery at Langham is bigger than Morland's, despite recent expansion at the Oxfordshire company's Abingdon plant. Langham is also better placed logistically for trans-port distribution. And Langham also has room for a bottling hall; the group's bottling is presently contracted out, and this market will be of growing importance over the next decade.

But the clincher comes from the 4,000 strong Grand Pub Company. Many of its pubs are old GrandMet tenancies, which over the years built up a taste for Ruddles, only to find the beers hard to get after the Courage contract ran out.

Now, under GPC's new SupplyLine deal, Morland has unfettered access to 4,000 pubs, many of them willing customers. Already, according to a GPC spokesman, sales of Ruddles' beers throughout the estate have picked up measurably.

'We are providing an avenue to the market for Ruddles,' he said. 'We have the potential to save a brewery because we are offering a distribution route to 4,000 pubs.'

The potential of sales through GPC may or may not have influenced the Morland board in its decision to close Langham. But from CAMRA's point of view, it makes Langham salvageable.

It's up to Morland to re-evaluate the situation, but maybe its share-holders should be asking whether closing Langham is not only writing off the past, but writing off the future as well?

This article by Ted Bruning first appeared in What's Brewing

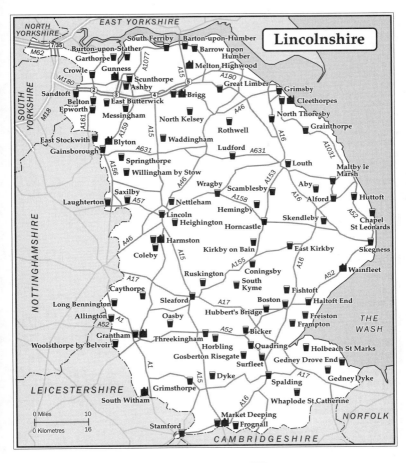

Lincolnshire

ABY

RAILWAY TAVERN
Main Road
☎ (01507) 480676
12-3, 7-11 (midnight Sat); closed
Tue; 12-3, 7-10.30 Sun
Beer range varies Ⓗ
Very friendly pub with an open-
plan bar and a games room.
Train photos and rural memorabilia displayed. Popular with
cyclists. ♨ ❀ ◑ ▶ ♣ P

ALFORD

HALF MOON
West Street
☎ (01507) 463477
10-11 (1am Fri & Sat); 12-10.30 Sun
**Draught Bass; Everard's Tiger;
Worthington Bitter; guest beers** Ⓗ
Welcoming, ever-expanding, lively pub with a large garden, situated in a market town famed for
its craft fairs. It boasts a popular
restaurant serving excellent
food. An ideal base for visiting
the Wolds and Tennyson country.
🛏 ❀ ◑ ▶ ⊟ ♣ P

ALLINGTON

WELBY ARMS
The Green ☎ (01400) 281361
12-2.30 (3 Sat), 6-11; 12-4,
7-10.30 Sun
**Draught Bass; John Smith's
Bitter; Taylor Landlord; guest
beers** Ⓗ
Set in a lovely rural location and
a regular *Guide* entry, this pub
provides a traditional atmosphere in the bar, away from the
extensive dining area. Superb
home-cooked food served. Over
100 guest beers were stocked
last year. Well worth seeking out.
♨ Q ❀ ◑ ▶ & P

ASHBY

MALT SHOVEL
219 Ashby High Street
☎ (01724) 843318
11-11; 12-10.30 Sun
**Barnsley Bitter; John Smith's
Bitter; Theakston Old Peculier;
guest beers** Ⓗ
Single-roomed, welcoming pub,
decorated in rural style with floral
furnishings and timber beams.
Popular, good value meals served.
♨ ◑ ▶

QUEEN BESS
Derwent Road ☎ (01724) 840827
11.30-3.30 (4 Sat), 6-11; 12-3,
7-10.30 Sun
Samuel Smith OBB Ⓗ
1960s estate pub with a loyal
local following; public bar, a well
appointed lounge with a real fire
and a large function room to the
rear. ♨ ❀ ⊟ ♣ P

BARROW-ON-HUMBER

SQUASH CLUB
Manor Farmhouse, Thorngarth
Lane (behind church)
☎ (01469) 530686
6.30-11; 7-10.30 Sun
**Ward's, Best Bitter; Thorne BB;
guest beer** Ⓗ
A members-only club but card-
carrying CAMRA members are
admitted. Guest beers are from
the Vaux Classic Cask Collection.
♨ ♣ P

179

BARTON-ON-HUMBER

WHEATSHEAF HOTEL
3 Holydyke OS032218
☎ (01652) 633175
11-3 (4.30 Sat), 6-11; 12-10.30 Sun
**Vaux Mild, Waggle Dance;
Ward's Thorne BB, Best Bitter** H
Friendly, quiet, three-roomed pub
in the town centre with a multi-
levelled garden. No longer a
hotel but serving excellent pub
food (not lunchtime Sat or Sun).
Q 🏠 ❀ ◖ ▶ 🍴 ⚒ ≽ P

BELTON

CROWN INN
Stockshill, Churchtown
☎ (01427) 872834
4-11; 12-11 Sat; 12-10.30 Sun
**Courage Directors; John Smith's
Bitter; Theakston Best Bitter;
guest beers** (occasional) H
Quaint, family-run local hidden
away behind the church with a
friendly and relaxed atmosphere.
Inexpensive bar snacks available
(5-10.30pm). The pub organises
the annual Belton Barrow Race.
🏠 ❀ ▶ ♣ P 🍴

WHEATSHEAF INN
152 Westgate Rd
☎ (01427) 872504
12-3 (not Mon-Thu), 5-11; 11-11
Sat; 11-10.30 Sun
**Vaux Samson; Ward's Thorne
BB; guest beers** H
Welcoming, unspoilt, cosy village
local close to the transport centre (for trolley bus preservation).
It features a garden and barbecue to the rear and piano singa-
longs Sun eves. Eve meals served
Thu-Sat; lunches Sun only.
🏠 ❀ ▶ ♣ P

BICKER

RED LION
Donington Road (100 yds off
A52) ☎ (01775) 821950
11-3, 6-11; 12-10.30 Sun
Draught Bass; Bateman XB H
Renovated 17th-century pub
serving a variety of quality home-
cooked food at reasonable
prices. 🏠 ❀ ◖ ▶ P

BOSTON

CARPENTER'S ARMS
20 Witham St ☎ (01205) 362840
11-3, 7-11; 11-11 Fri & Sat;
12-10.30 Sun
Bateman XB; guest beers H
Multi-roomed, low-ceilinged, traditional local, situated in the
maze of side streets off the
medieval Wormgate. Two guest
ales available. Music can be very
loud. 🏠 ❀ ≽ ♣

COACH & HORSES
Main Ridge East
☎ (01205) 362301

5 (6 Fri)-11; 11-3, 7-11 Sat; 12-3,
7-10.30 Sun
Bateman Mild, XB, XXXB H
Small, friendly, one-roomed local.
Home of numerous darts, pool
and domino teams. 🏠 ≽ ♣

EAGLE
144 West Street (near station)
☎ (01205) 361116
11-2.30, 6(5 Thu-Fri)-11; 11-11
Sat; 12-3, 7-10.30 Sun
**Adnams Broadside; Everards
Beacon; Fuller's London Pride;
Taylor Landlord; guest beers** H
Basic town pub with an interesting range of ever-changing guest
beers. The function room hosts a
number of societies, including
Boston Folk Club. Several speciality beer festivals held each
year.
⚒ ≽ ♣ ○

NAPOLEON
17 Fishtoft Road
☎ (01205) 361713
11-4, 7-11; 11-11 Thu-Sat;
12-10.30 Sun
**Draught Bass; Bateman XB,
XXXB** H
Clean, friendly and comfortable
community pub with parking on
street outside.
🏠 ❀ ♣

OLDE MAGNET TAVERN
South Square
☎ (01205) 369186
11.30 (11 Thu-Sat)-11, 12-4,
7-10.30 Sun
**Draught Bass; Bateman XB; M&B
Mild; Stones Bitter; Taylor
Landlord** H
Friendly, popular town pub by the
river, standing amongst converted warehouses housing an arts
centre and residential accommodation. The lounge has a flagstone floor.
🏠 ❀ ❀ ◖ ▶ ⚒ ≽

RAILWAY HOTEL
84 London Road
☎ (01205) 362399
11-11; 12-10.30 Sun
**Vaux Samson; Ward's Best
Bitter; guest beer** H
Part-owned by one of a family of
local butchers, this pub has a
monthly-changing guest beer.
The railway in the title refers to
the former Boston to Spalding
line, now the A16 road.
🏠 ❀ ◖ ▶ ⚒ ♣ P

STILL
23 Market Place
☎ (01205) 369009
10.30-4 (5 Fri & Sat), 7.30 (7 Fri
& Sat)-11; 12-3, 7-10.30 Sun
**Shipstone's Mild, Bitter; Tetley
Bitter** H
Traditional town-centre pub built
in an interesting Dutch style, with
quiet drinking and noisy games at
opposite ends. ≽ ♣

BRIGG

QUEENS ARMS HOTEL
Wraby Street ☎ (01652) 653174
12-2, 5-11; 11-11 Sat; 12-3,
7-10.30 Sun
**Draught Bass; Briggs Own Bitter
(BOB), Grannys; Worthington
Bitter** H
Popular town pub catering for all
ages. Open plan with three drink-
ing areas. The fine two-barrel
brew plant can be viewed from
the bar. Good accommodation.
Brigg station only open Sat.
Q 🛏 ◖ ≽ ♣

BURTON-UPON-STATHER

FERRY HOUSE
Stather Road (follow campsite
signs through village)
☎ (01724) 721299
7-11; 12-4.30, 7-11 Sat; 12-4.30,
7-10.30 Sun (weekend hours may
extend summer)
Worthington Bitter; guest beer H
Friendly village pub next to the
River Trent with a large room with
distinct drinking areas. Outdoor
entertainments held throughout
the summer on Sat eves, weather
permitting, plus barbecues. Guest
beers from independent brewers.
❀ ▲ ♣ P

CAYTHORPE

RED LION
62 High Street ☎ (01400) 272632
11-2.30, 6-11; 12-2.30, 6-11 Sun
**Draught Bass; Bateman XB;
guest beers** H G
Welcoming 17th-century inn with
two bars and a restaurant, serving an excellent range of ale and
food. Its beer and curry festivals
are a must. Cider varies.
🏠 Q 🏠 ❀ ◖ ▲ ♣ ○ P

CHAPEL ST LEONARDS

SHIP
109 Sea Road ☎ (01754) 872640
12-3.30, 7-11; 12-3, 7-10.30 Sun
**Bateman Mild, XB, XXXB, sea-
sonal beers** H
Cosy, welcoming local, away
from the bustle of this popular
seaside resort. The full Bateman
range is often available in summer. 🏠 ❀ ▲ ♣ P

CLEETHORPES

CROW'S NEST HOTEL
Balmoral Road
☎ (01472) 698867
11-3, 6.30-11; 12-3, 7-10.30 Sun
Samuel Smith OBB H
Large 1950s estate pub with a
quiet, comfortable lounge and
basic, occasionally lively, bar.
The only Sam Smith's outlet in
the locality and one of its cheapest pints. Q 🏠 ❀ 🛏 ⚒ P

THE KINGSWAY CLUB
3 Kingsway
☎ (01472) 699145
12-5, 7.30-11; 12-11 Sat; 12-5,
7.30-10.30 Sun
**Highwood Tom Wood Best
Bitter; Ind Coope Burton Ale;
Tetley Mild, Bitter; guest beer** Ⓗ
Friendly, first-floor club on the
seafront with panoramic views of
the River Humber. Show this
Guide or CAMRA membership
card to gain entry.
⇌ ♣ P

NOTTINGHAM HOUSE
5-7 Sea View Street (½ mile from
station on main sea front)
☎ (01472) 694386
12 (11 Sat)-11; 12-10.30 Sun
Tetley Mild, Bitter; guest beer Ⓗ
Comfortable, basic three-
roomed pub with a snug,
popular with more mature
drinkers. Free bread and drip-
ping on offer; Sun lunch and
quiz Sun eve. The guest beer
rotates weekly.
🏚 Q 🍺 ⇌ ♣

No. 2 REFRESHMENT ROOM
Station Approach
☎ (01472) 697951
12-11; 12-10.30 Sun
**Mansfield Riding Mild; John
Smith's Magnet; guest beers** Ⓗ
Basic locals' bar. Watch out for
the ferries passing down the
Humber as they interfere with
the TV picture!
⇌

WILLYS PUB AND BREWERY
17 High Cliff Road
☎ (01472) 602145
11-11; 12-10.30 Sun
**Bateman XB; Willy's Original;
guest beers** Ⓗ
A regular in the *Guide* since
opening in 1986. Good food and
sea views make this a popular
venue at lunchtime. The brewery
can be viewed from the bar and
visits may be arranged at short
notice.
◖ ⇌

COLEBY

TEMPEST ARMS
Hill Rise (off A607, 7 miles S of
Lincoln)
☎ (01522) 810287
11.30-2.30, 6.30-11; 12-3,
7-10.30 Sun
**Bateman XB; Theakston Old
Peculier; guest beer** Ⓗ
Friendly free house hosting
fundraising events, the centre of
village life. Situated on the Viking
Way, it boasts views over the
Trent Valley and features a new
restaurant and regular guest
beer.
🍺 ◖ ▶ ♣ P

CONINGSBY

LEAGATE INN
Leagate Road (on B1192, E of village, off A153)
☎ (01526) 342370
11-3, 6.30 (7 winter)-11; 12-10.30
(12-3, 7-10.30 winter) Sun
**Bateman XB; Boddingtons
Bitter; Marston's Pedigree;
guest beer** Ⓗ
Dating from the 16th-century,
this pub stands close to the site
of a former gibbet and comes
complete with a priest hole and
antique furniture. A superb
atmosphere; a good place to
break the journey to or from the
coast. The garden is popular with
children. 🏚 🍺 ◖ ▶ ◖ 🛌 P

CROWLE

LOCK STOCK & BARREL
6-8 Cross Street
☎ (01724) 711192
12-3 (not winter), 5-11; 12-4,
5-11 Sat; 12-4, 7-10.30 (12-10.30
summer) Sun
**Marston's Bitter, HBC; A Dark
Tribe beer is usually available;
guest beer** Ⓗ
Converted from the former
Hunters Inn, this pub re-opened
as a traditional alehouse in 1996,
winning both local and regional
CAMRA *Pub of the Year* awards in
1997. It hosts a folk night (Wed),
live artiste (Sat) and a quiz and
disco (Sun). The restaurant (which
serves as a family room when
closed) has a supper licence.
🏚 Q 🍺 🍴 ◖ ▶ ◖ ♣ 🛢

DYKE

WISHING WELL INN
Main Street ☎ (01778) 422970
11-3, 6-11; 11-3, 7-10.30 Sun
**Everards Tiger; Greene King
Abbot; guest beer** Ⓗ
Bustling village pub with a reputation for good food but not at the
expense of its beer trade. Over
1,000 guest beers have been
available in the last 4½ years. The
wishing well can be seen in the restaurant. Booking advisable for meals.
🏚 🍴 🛌 ◖ ▶ ◖ 🛌 Δ ♣ P

EAST BUTTERWICK

DOG & GUN
High Street OS838057
☎ (01724) 783419
7 (5 Thu & Fri)-11; 12-11 Sat;
12-10.30 Sun
John Smith's Bitter; Ⓗ
No-frills, three-roomed village
pub located beside the River
Trent with a friendly welcome. A
roaring fire in the main bar in
winter. Main outlet for the local
Dark Tribe brewery – the beer
alternates. Good beer prices.
🏚 Q 🍴 🍺 ♣ P

EAST KIRKBY

RED LION
Main Road ☎ (01790) 763406
12-2.30, 7-11; 12-3, 7-10.30 Sun
**Bateman XB; John Smith's
Bitter; guest beers** Ⓗ
Popular pub, adorned with clocks,
old tools and breweriana, close to
a wartime airfield and Air
Museum. The pool room was once
a butcher's shop. Guest beers
usually from Highwood Brewery.
🏚 🛌 🍴 ◖ ▶ 🛌 Δ ♣ P

EAST STOCKWITH

FERRY HOUSE INN
24 Front St ☎ (01427) 615276
11.30-3, 7-11; 12-4, 7-10.30 Sun
**Bigfoot Genesis; John Smith's
Bitter; Webster's Yorkshire
Bitter; guest beers** Ⓗ
Quality free house with a good
mix of clientele, catering for all
ages. A 250-year-old listed building, associated with the former
Trent Ferry. Local outlet for the
nearby Bigfoot Brewery. Good
value food and accommodation.
No food Mon eve.
🏚 🍴 🛌 ◖ ▶ ♣ P

EPWORTH

RED LION HOTEL
Market Place
☎ (01427) 872208
11-11; 12-10.30 Sun
**Ind Coope Burton Ale; Tetley
Bitter; guest beers** Ⓗ
Residential, olde-worlde coaching
inn, serving good food in the bar
or delightful restaurant from an
extensive menu (sizzling steaks a
speciality). 🏚 🍴 🛌 ◖▶ P ✂

Try also: Olde School Inn,
Battle Green (Free)

FISHTOFT

BALL HOUSE
Wainfleet Road (on A52, 1 mile N
of Boston town centre)
☎ (01205) 364478
11-3, 6.30-11; 12-3, 7-10.30 Sun
Draught Bass; Bateman Mild, XB Ⓗ
Mock-Tudor pub with award-winning summer floral displays and
a well-kept garden. Excellent
home-cooked food is popular
(booking advisable weekend
eves). Sited on a former cannon
ball store for nearby Rochford
Tower - hence the unusual name.
🏚 🍴 🛌 ◖ ▶ 🛌 ♣ P

FRAMPTON

MOORES ARMS
Church End ☎ (01205) 722408
11.30-3, 6-11, 11.30-11 Sat;
12-10.30 Sun
**Draught Bass; Bateman XB;
guest beer** Ⓗ
Attractive friendly village pub

dating back to 1690, near the marshes and popular with bird-watchers and walkers. Extensive menu available in the bar and restaurant.🏛 ◑ ▶ ⊞ P ⌣

FREISTON

KING'S HEAD
Church Road
☎ (01205) 760368
11-3, 7-11; 11-11 Sat; 12-3, 7-10.30 Sun
Draught Bass; Bateman Mild, XB Ⓗ
15th-century, traditional village pub with a homely atmosphere. The Lancaster Restaurant (open Tue-Sat eves) serves quality home-cooked food.
🏛 Q 🏛 ◑ ♣ P

FROGNALL

GOAT
155 Spalding Road (old A16, 1½ miles E of Market Deeping)
☎ (01778) 347629
11-2.30 (3 Sat), 6-11; 12-3, 6.30-10.30 Sun
Adnams Bitter; Bateman XB; guest beers Ⓗ
A much-changed, spacious 1640s ale house with a large garden featuring an under-fives play area. A good range of beers always available from micro-breweries throughout Britain, whilst still being a food-oriented pub. 🏛 Q 🏛 🏛 ◑ ♿ ♣ Å P

GAINSBOROUGH

EIGHT JOLLY BREWERS
Ship Court, Silver Street (off Market Place)
☎ (01427) 677128
11-3, 7-11; 11-11 Fri & Sat; 12-10.30 Sun
Taylor Landlord; guest beers Ⓗ
Deservedly popular real ale haven featuring a constantly changing range of nine beers, mainly from northern micro-breweries. The house beer is brewed by Highwood. Folk club meets here alternate Fri eve. CAMRA *Pub of the Year* finalist 1996. No food Sun.
Q 🏛 ◑ P ⌗ 🍺

PEACOCK HOTEL
Corringham Road
☎ (01427) 615859
11.30-3, 5-11; 11.30-11 Fri & Sat; 12-10.30 Sun
Marston's Bitter, Pedigree, HBC Ⓗ
With its large, comfortable lounge, public bar, and attractive garden featuring a well-equipped children's play area, this pub is popular with families. The good quality bar meals offer a wide choice.
🏛 ◑ ▶ ⊞ ♿ ⇌ (central)♣ P ⌗

GARTHORPE

BAY HORSE
Shore Road ☎ (01724) 798306
12-2 (3 Sat), (not Mon & Tue), 7-11; 12-3, 7.30-10.30 Sun
Mansfield Riding Bitter, Old Baily Ⓗ
Comfortable, traditional pub with a small entrance bar, a public bar, a small family room and a lounge bar. Live entertainment Sat. Good value, home-cooked food (Wed-Sun). The garden has an aviary. 🏛 🏛 🏛 ◑ ▶ ⊞ ♣ P

GEDNEY DROVE END

NEW INN
Main Road (end of B1359)
☎ (01406) 550389
7-11; 12-4, 7-11 Sat; 12-4, 7-10.30 Sun
Elgood's Cambridge Bitter Ⓗ
A rural gem, well worth seeking out. The landlady has built up an extensive display of pig-related artefacts during her 20-plus years here. A stall in the car park sells produce from the pub's smallholding. 🏛 🏛 ◑ ▶ Å ♣ P

GEDNEY DYKE

CHEQUERS
Main Street ☎ (01406) 362666
12-2, 7-11; 12-3, 7-10.30 Sun
Adnams Bitter; Draught Bass; Elgood's Pageant; Greene King Abbot (summer)**; Morland Old Speckled Hen** Ⓗ
Comfortable country pub and restaurant which is popular with both diners and drinkers. Situated in a quiet village, it dates from 1795 and has a deserved reputation for imaginative, quality meals.🏛 🏛 ◑ ▶ P

GOSBERTON RISEGATE

DUKE OF YORK
106 Risegate Road (B1397, 1½ miles from Gosberton)
☎ (01775) 840193
12-11; 12-4, 7-10.30 Sun
Bateman XB; John Smith's Bitter; guest beers Ⓗ
Friendly village local with a widespread and growing reputation for good value beer and food. A large outside play area features goats, chickens and ducks. Multi-roomed inside with a no-smoking dining room. At least two guest beers normally available. No food Mon lunch. 🏛 🏛 ◑ ▶ Å ♣ P 🍺

GRAINTHORPE

BLACK HORSE
Mill Lane (off A1031)
☎ (01472) 388229
12-3 (summer only), 7-11; 12-3, 7-10.30 Sun
Bateman XB; guest beers Ⓗ

Comfortable, friendly village pub with separate bar and lounge. The lounge displays a collection of old film posters and breweriana. The house beer, Old Blackie is brewed for the pub by Highwood. Lunches served summer, and winter weekends.
🏛 Q 🏛 ◑ ▶ ⊞ ♣ P

GRANTHAM

ANGEL & ROYAL HOTEL
High Street ☎ (01476) 565816
12-2 Mon-Wed; 5-11 Thu; 11-11 Fri; 11-11 Sat; 12-3, 7-10.30 Sun
Banks's Bitter; Camerons Bitter; Morells Graduate; guest beer Ⓗ
Attractive, 13th-century bar with timbered ceilings, tapestries and a large fire in winter.
🏛 Q 🏛 🏛 ◑ ▶ ⊞ ♿ P

BEEHIVE
10-11 Castlegate
☎ (01476) 567794
11-11; 11-5, 7-11 Sat; 7-10.30 Sun
Beer range varies Ⓗ
Busy, town-centre local, popular with students. It is renowned as the pub with a living sign. Bateman and Oldershaw beers alternate as regulars; two guest beers are stocked. 🏛 ◑ ⇌ 🍺

BLUE BULL
64 Westgate ☎ (01476) 570929
11-3 (4 Sat), 7-11; 12-3, 7-10.30 Sun
Beer range varies Ⓗ
Welcoming, two-bar pub with a restaurant serving excellent value home-cooked meals, including daily specials. A good selection of beers always available, plus occasional cider on gravity dispense (varies). Local CAMRA *Town Pub of the Year* 1998. Q ◑ ▶ ⇌ ♣ ⌣ P

BLUE PIG
9 Vine Street ☎ (01476) 563704
11 (10.30 Sat)-11; 12-10.30 Sun
Boddingtons Bitter; Castle Eden Ale; Flower's Original; John Smith's Bitter; Taylor Landlord; guest beers (occasional) Ⓗ
One of only three Tudor buildings left in Grantham, and part of the town pub scene since 1826. This is a busy town-centre pub with a friendly atmosphere serving five real ales and excellent value food. 🏛 ◑

TOLLEMACHE INN
17 St Peters Hill ☎ (01476) 594696
11-11; 12-10.30 Sun
Bateman Mild, Valiant; Courage Directors; Theakston Best Bitter; guest beers Ⓗ
Bustling town-centre pub, popular with all ages. No music, a separate no-smoking area and an excellent range of food available all day with daily specials. No children allowed.
Q 🏛 ◑ ▶ ♿ ⇌ ⌣ ⌗ 🍺

GREAT LIMBER

NEW INN

High Street ☎ (01469) 560257
11-3.30, 6-11; 11-11 Sat; 11-10.30 Sun
Boddingtons Bitter; Samuel Smith OBB; Worthington Bitter; guest beer Ⓗ
Friendly, two-roomed village pub, deservedly popular for its good food, served in the lounge, whilst the traditional bar offers a relaxed atmosphere and is popular with locals, especially on games nights.
♨ ❀ ▬ ◐ ◗ ⊟ ♣ P

GRIMSBY

SWIGS

21 Osborne St ☎ (01472) 354773
11-11; 7-10.30 (closed lunch) Sun
Bateman XB; Willy's Original; guest beers Ⓗ
The second outlet for Willy's beers. Popular with a young clientele in the evening, but quieter during the day. A regular *Guide* entry since opening. Excellent lunches available (not served Sun). ◐ ≠ (Town)

TAP & SPILE

Haven Mill, Garth Lane (cross Frederick Ward Way from Freshney Place)
☎ (01472) 357493
12-4, 7-11; 12-11 Fri & Sat; 12-4, 7-10.30 Sun
Beer range varies Ⓗ
Large, one-roomed, open-plan former flour mill, retaining old stone, brick and woodwork. Popular eves; up to 8 real ales including 'Grimberian', specially brewed by Tomlinsons. Twice monthly folk nights and African drums last Tue of the month.
❀ ◐ ♿ ≠ (Town) ♣ ⌓

YARBOROUGH HOTEL

29 Bethlehem Street (next to Grimsby Town station)
☎ (01472) 268283
11-11; 12-10.30 Sun
Bateman Mild; Courage Directors; Theakston Best Bitter; guest beers Ⓗ
Spacious ground floor of a Victorian hotel, beautifully refurbished by Wetherspoons. Well patronised and popular with all age groups. No music: food served all day.
Q ❀ ◐ ◗ ♿ ≠ (Town) ⌓ ⊘ ▯

GRIMSTHORPE

BLACK HORSE INN

☎ (01778) 591247
11.30-2.30, 6.30-11; 12-3, 7-10.30 Sun
Bateman XXXB Ⓗ
Built in 1717, the original stone walls, dark beams and open fires add to the atmosphere of this welcoming village inn, holder of Lincs *Best Dining Pub* award 1997. House beers are brewed to the landlord's recipe by Batemans. ♨ Q ❀ ▬ ◐ ◗ P

HALTOFT END

CASTLE

Wainfleet Road (A52, 2 miles NE of Boston) ☎ (01205) 760393
11-11; 12-10.30 Sun
Bateman Mild, XB; guest beer Ⓗ
Friendly, roadside local which serves superb value meals. Excellent adventure playground for children. ♨ ❀ ▬ ◐ ◗ ♣ P

HARMSTON

THOROLD ARMS

High Street (off A607)
☎ (01522) 720358
11-3 (4 Sat), 6-11; 12-4, 7-10.30 Sun
Beer range varies Ⓗ
18th-century, one-bar, traditional, friendly village inn, reputedly haunted. Stone-built with an in-house brewery and a large feature fireplace. A wide range of traditional pub games played. Wholesome bar food available using fresh local produce (not served Mon or Sun eves).
♨ Q ❀ ◐ ◗ ♿ ♣ ⌓ P ▯

HEIGHINGTON

BUTCHER & BEAST

High Street ☎ (01522) 790386
11-3.30 (5 Sat), 7-11; 12-5, 7-10.30 Sun
Draught Bass; Bateman Mild, XB, XXXB; guest beer Ⓗ
Friendly village pub with a warm welcome. Note the original handpumps fitted on the wall. No food Sun or Mon eves.
♨ ♘ ❀ ◐ ◗ ♣ P ▯

HEMINGBY

COACH & HORSES

Horncastle (between A158/A153, 2 miles W of Horncastle) ☎ (01507) 578280
12-3 (not Mon-Tue), 7 (8 Wed-Fri)-11; 11-11 Sat; 12-10.30 (may close eves in winter) Sun
Bateman XB; Tom Wood Harvest Bitter; guest beer Ⓗ
Pleasant welcoming pub next to the village church with a pleasant outside drinking area. Watch out for low beams! Excellent bar meals served (not Sun-Tue eves). Booking advisable for Sun lunch.
♨ ❀ ◐ ◗ ▲ ♣ ⊘

HOLBEACH ST MARKS

NEW INN

Main Road ☎ (01406) 701231
12-2.30 (not Mon-Tue), 7-11; 12-11 Sat; 12-10.30 Sun
Bateman Mild; Tetley Bitter; guest beer Ⓗ
A former slaughterhouse and butchers, this popular village local has recently been refurbished. Live music Sat eve.
♨ Q ❀ ◐ ◗ ▲ ♣ P

HORBLING

PLOUGH INN

4 Spring Lane ☎ (01529) 240263
11-3, 7-11; 12-3, 7-10.30 Sun
Bateman XB; guest beer Ⓗ
Owned, somewhat unusually, by the local Parish Council, this late 17th-century pub is reputedly home to a ghost who walks late at night. The landlord is a keen supporter of the Sail Training Association. The restaurant hosts regular speciality nights (booking advisable). ♨ ◐ ◗ ⊟ ♿ ♣ P

HORNCASTLE

ADMIRAL RODNEY HOTEL

North Street ☎ (01507) 523131
11-2.30, 5.30-11; 11-11 Sat; 12-3, 7-10.30 Sun
John Smith's Bitter; Ruddles County; guest beer Ⓗ
Bar of a town-centre hotel; the monthly changing guest beer is often from a small independent brewery. ♘ ❀ ▬ ◐ ◗ ⊟ ♿ P ▯

FIGHTING COCKS

West Street ☎ (01507) 527307
11-4, 7-11; 12-3, 7-10.30 Sun
Draught Bass; Bateman XB; Courage Directors; Fuller's London Pride; Marstons Pedigree; John Smith's Bitter Ⓗ
Modernised, 200-year-old pub with a cheerful and bustling atmosphere. Reputedly haunted by a cat and a cavalier. The restaurant is closed Sun.
Q ❀ ▬ ◐ ◗ ♿ ▲ ♣ P

HUBBERT'S BRIDGE

WHEATSHEAF

Station Road ☎ (01205) 290347
11-3, 5-11; 11-11 Sat; 12-3, 7-10.30 Sun
Vaux Samson, Double Maxim; Ward's Thorne BB; guest beer (occasional) Ⓗ
Friendly, family-run bankside pub near to golf and fishing facilities. Excellent food served, including vegetarian dishes and cheap lunch specials.
♨ ❀ ▬ ◐ ◗ ▲ ≠ ♣ P

HUTTOFT

AXE & CLEAVER

Sutton Road (A52)
☎ (01507) 490205
11-3, 6-11; 12-3, 7-10.30 Sun
John Smith's Magnet; Theakston Mild, Best Bitter; guest beer (occasional) Ⓗ
Friendly rural pub on the coastal route. A collection of plates and photographs decorate the walls.

Auctions held Thu eves. Eve meals in summer only.
Q ⇌ ✿ ◖ ▶ & ♣ P

KIRKBY ON BAIN

EBRINGTON ARMS
Main Street
☎ (01526) 354560
12-3, 7-11 (11-11 summer); 12-4, 7-10.30 (12-10.30 summer) Sun
Beer range varies Ⓗ
16th-century village inn with a constantly changing choice of guest beers and ciders, usually from small breweries. The house beer comes from Batemans. Beer festivals held Easter and August bank holidays. The Bainside Restaurant has a good reputation.
🏚 ✿ ◖ ▶ & ▲ ♣ ⌂ P ⊟

LAUGHTERTON

FRIENDSHIP INN
Main Road
☎ (01427) 718681
11.30-2.30 (3 Sat), 6-11; 12-3, 7-10.30 Sun
Bateman XXXB; Marston's Pedigree; Ward's Best Bitter; guest beer Ⓗ
Comfortable village pub with games, lounge and dining areas. Good home-cooked food (try 'Mum's Pie'). Live music Sun eve. The campsite is Caravan Club only. 🏚 ✿ ◖ ▶ ▲ ♣ P

LINCOLN

DOG & BONE
10 John Street (off Monks Rd past college)
☎ (01522) 522403
12-3, 7(5 summer Fri)-11; 11-11 Sat; 12-10.30 Sun
Draught Bass; Bateman XB, Valiant, Salem Porter, XXXB; guest beers Ⓗ
Friendly, one-roomed pub, popular with students. It stages fun nights during term and boasts an array of antiques and old relics with a touch of humour. Big screen TV for sport. Annual beer festival held in June. Wheelchair access is at the rear.
🏚 ✿ ◖ & ⇌ (Central) ♣ P ⊟

GOLDEN EAGLE
21 High Street ☎ (01522) 521058
11-3, 5-11; 11-11 Fri-Sat; 12-10.30 Sun
Bateman XB; Brains Dark; Everards Beacon; Fuller's London Pride; Taylor Landlord; guest beers Ⓗ
Welcoming two-bar pub, near the football ground; the lively back bar has a TV for sport, the quieter lounge displays football memorabilia and photos of old Lincoln. Guest beers are constantly changing; annual cider festival held.
Q ✿ ⊞ ♣ ⌂ P

JOLLY BREWER
26 Broadgate
☎ (01522) 528583
11-11; 12-10.30 Sun
Draught Bass; Shepherd Neame Spitfire; Theakston XB; Youngers Scotch, No 3; guest beers Ⓗ
Well-known city-centre pub, a regular *Guide* entry, decorated in Art Deco style, catering for a wide range of the community. A large variety of guest beers complement the regular range.
🏚 ✿ ◖ & ⇌ ♣ ⌂ P

MORNING STAR
11 Greetwell Gate (200 yds from Cathedral)
☎ (01522) 527079
11-11; 12-10.30 Sun
Draught Bass; Ruddles Best Bitter; Theakston XB; Wells Bombardier; guest beers Ⓗ
Small, pleasant pub, within sight of the cathedral with a cosy lounge and appropriately named hosts - Mr & Mrs Beers. Regular pub pianist plays Fri and Sat eves. 🏚 ✿ ◖ P ⊟

PEACOCK HOTEL
23 Wragby Road (400 yds from cathedral) ☎ (01522) 524703
11-11; 12-10.30 Sun
Hardys & Hansons Mild, Best Bitter, Classic, seasonal beers Ⓗ
Traditional, friendly pub (now a *Guide* regular) within sight of the cathedral, which offers a restaurant serving excellent home-cooked food. The various games played generate a good following. 🏚 ✿ ◖ ▶ ♣ P

PORTLAND ARMS
50 Portland Street
☎ (01522) 513912
11-11; 12-10.30 Sun
Draught Bass; Courage Directors; John Smith's Bitter; Wilson's Mild; guest beers Ⓗ
Friendly town pub with a buzzing public bar/games area and a quieter lounge serving up to six continually changing guest beers plus a cider. A genuinely free house where the focus is on quality beer. Q ⊞ ⇌ ♣ ⌂ P

QUEEN IN THE WEST
12 Moor Street (just off main A57 road) ☎ (01522) 880123
12-3 (5 Sat), 5.30 (7 Sat)-11; 11.30-11 Fri; 12-5, 7-10.30 Sun
Courage Directors; John Smith's Bitter; Morland Old Speckled Hen; Ruddles Best Bitter; Shepherd Neame Spitfire; Theakston XB Ⓗ
Pleasant street-corner local which serves both the community and local factory workers at lunchtime. A recent refurbishment has not removed any of the bar's character.
◖ ⊞ ♣

SIPPERS
26 Melville Street
☎ (01522) 527612
11-2, 5 (4 Fri, 7 Sat)-11; 7-10.30 (closed lunch) Sun
Courage Directors; Marston's Pedigree; Morland Old Speckled Hen; John Smith's Bitter; Theakston Mild; guest beers Ⓗ
Handy for both rail and bus stations, this pub is popular with local workers at lunchtime and quieter eves. Usually three guest beers from small breweries sold. Excellent food (not served Sat eve or Sun). ◖ ▶ & ⇌ ♣

VICTORIA
6 Union Road (by West Gate of Castle) ☎ (01522) 536048
11-11; 12-10.30 Sun
Bateman XB; Everards Old Original; Taylor Landlord; guest beers Ⓗ
A good mix of clientele in this two roomed pub in the shadow of the castle walls. Up to seven guest beers, always including a mild. Summer and winter beer festivals and regular brewery events are a feature. Good value chip and microwave-free home-cooked lunches. Q ✿ ◖ ⊞ ⌂

LONG BENNINGTON

WHEATSHEAF
96 Main Road ☎ (01400) 281486
12-2.30 (4 Sat), 7-11; 12-4, 7-10.30 Sun
Boddingtons Mild, Bitter; Castle Eden Ale; Marston's Pedigree; guest beer Ⓗ
Attractive two-bar village pub with a restaurant operating throughout the week.
🏚 ✿ ◖ ▶ ⊞ ⌂ P

LOUTH

NEWMARKET INN
Newmarket ☎ (01507) 605146
6-11 (closed lunch); 12-3, 7.30-11 Sun
Castle Eden Ale; Flowers Original; guest beers Ⓗ
A popular inn, nicely decorated with a pleasant atmosphere. The restaurant serves eve meals Fri and Sat. Limited parking. Guest beers are from Highwood.
🏚 Q ✿ ▶ P

Try also: Boars Head, Newmarket (Bateman)

WHEATSHEAF
62 Westgate
☎ (01507) 603159
11-3, 5-11; 11-11 Sat; 12-4, 7-10.30 (12-10.30 summer) Sun
Draught Bass; Boddingtons Bitter; Flowers Original; Tipsy Toad Ale; guest beers Ⓗ
Standing in the shadow of Louth spire and set in a Georgian terrace, this very popular pub dates

from 1612. It has a stone-floored passageway and is adorned with magnificent hanging baskets in summer. ㎶ Q ❀ ◖ P

WOODMAN INN
134 Eastgate (150 yds from bus station)
☎ (01507) 602100
11-3 (4 Wed & Fri); 7-11; 11-11 Sat; 12-3.30, 7-10.30 Sun
John Smith's Bitter; guest beers Ⓗ
Popular, town-centre pub serving a constantly changing selection of guest beers. An impressive collection of film posters and Gary Larson cartoons adorn the walls. Real ales also available in the function room. Folk night Tue. No lunches Sun. ❀ ◖ ㊅ P

WOOLPACK
Riverhead (off Eastgate)
☎ (01507) 606568
11-3, 5-11; 11-11 Sat; 12-4, 7-10.30 Sun
Bateman Mild, XB, XXXB; Marston's Pedigree; guest beers Ⓗ
Opened in 1770, this historic pub stands at the head of what was once the busiest canal in the country. Local CAMRA *Pub of the Year* 1997 and '98. The home-cooked, hearty food uses local produce (not served Mon).
㎶ Q ❀ ◖ 🍴 ♣ P

Try also: Lincolnshire Poacher, Eastgate (Hardys & Hansons)

LUDFORD

WHITE HART INN
Magna Mile
☎ (01507) 313489
12-2 (4 Sat), 7-midnight; 12-4, 7-11 Sun
Mansfield Bitter, Old Baily; Wells Bombardier; guest beers Ⓗ
First used as an inn in 1742, this pub features two bars, a restaurant, beamed ceilings and wood panelling plus a real fire in both bars. Well decorated with a pleasant, welcoming atmosphere, it offers excellent food (lunches served from Easter-Nov plus Christmas).
㎶ Q ⛺ ❀ ⚓ ◖ ▶ ♣ P

MALTBY LE MARSH

CROWN INN
School Lane (A157/A1104 jct)
☎ (01507) 450349
12 (11 Sat)-3, 7-11; 12-3, 7-10.30 Sun
Bateman XB, XXXB Ⓗ
Oak-beamed, olde-worlde inn with a welcoming atmosphere, established in 1761. Its three rooms are tastefully furnished and decorated and an extensive collection of crockery is displayed in the main bar. Good value food served. ◖ ▶ ㊅ ♣ P

VINE
19 Church Street (A15 towards Bourne)
☎ (01778) 342387
11.30-2 (3 Sat), 5.30 (6 Sat)-11; 12-3, 7-10.30 Sun
Badger Tanglefoot; Wells Bombardier, Eagle; guest beer Ⓗ
Traditional, friendly village local, converted from a school, with a large beer garden. Ask to see the model train set. Regular charity events held. Q ❀ ㊅ ▲ ◖ 🍴 ⌂ P

Try also: Bull, Market Place (Everards)

MESSINGHAM

HORN INN
High Street ☎ (01724) 762426
11-11; 12-10.30 Sun
Highwood Tom Wood Shepherd's Delight or seasonal beer; John Smith's Bitter; guest beer Ⓗ
Friendly, roadside village pub with a good reputation for lunches, particularly on Sun. The single, well-appointed room with several discrete drinking areas is enhanced by dark wood fittings. Live music midweek. Guest beer is from Scottish Courage.
㎶ ❀ ◖ ㊅ ♣ P

Try also: Bird in the Barley, Northfield Rd (Marston's)

NETTLEHAM

BLACK HORSE
Chapel Lane ☎ (01522) 750702
11.30-3(4.30 Sat), 7 (5.30 Fri)-11; 12-5.30, 7-10.30 Sun
Boddingtons Bitter; Tetley Bitter; Theakston Best Bitter, XB; Wilson's Mild; guest beers Ⓗ
Friendly 18th-century stone pub, serving ever-changing guest beers. It features a recently reinstalled real fire and a variety of music from live groups. Sunday roast served 12-2pm.
㎶ Q ◖ 🍴 ♣

NORTH KELSEY

BUTCHERS ARMS
Middle Street ☎ (01652) 678002
12-11; 12-10.30 Sun
Highwood Tom Wood Best Bitter, Lincolnshire Legend or Shepherd's Delight, Harvest Bitter, Lincolnshire Longwood, seasonal beers Ⓗ
Friendly, basic old village pub, refurbished and reopened after several years' closure. It now offers a range of Highwood beers and serves cold weekday lunches. The superb wood-burning fire is very tempting on cold winter nights. ㎶ Q ❀ ◖ ♣ P

Try also: Queens Head, North Kelsey Moor (Free)

NORTH THORESBY

NEW INN
Station Road
☎ (01472) 840270
12-3, 6-11; 12-11 Sat; 12-4, 7-10.30 (12-10.30 summer) Sun
Bateman Mild; Marston's Bitter, Pedigree; guest beers (weekends) Ⓗ
Popular village local, newly enlarged to add a restaurant, but retaining character. Beer festivals Whit weekend; Sun eve quiz.
㎶ ❀ ㊅ ♣ P

OASBY

HOUBLON ARMS
Main Street
☎ (01529) 455215
12-2.30 (not Mon), 7 (6 Fri & Sat)-11; 12-3, 7-10.30 Sun
Draught Bass; Bateman XB; guest beers Ⓗ
Built of local stone, this popular old village pub is a rural gem. It features a beamed interior, real fires, abundant ornaments and a friendly atmosphere.
㎶ Q ❀ ⚓ ◖ ▶ ㊅ ♣ P

QUADRING

RED COW
128 Main Road
☎ (01775) 821143
11-11 (6.30-11 Tue-Thu); 11-10.30 Sun
Vaux Samson; Ward's Best Bitter Ⓗ
A good example of a village local with a friendly welcome. Unusual tiled canopy to the bar.
㎶ ❀ ♣ P

ROTHWELL

NICKERSON ARMS
Hill Rise
☎ (01472) 371300
12-3, 7-11; 12-4, 7-10.30 Sun
Bateman XB, XXXB; Courage Directors; Fuller's London Pride; Marston's Pedigree; guest beers Ⓗ
Cosy pub serving excellent beer and food. Very popular with walkers. ㎶ Q ❀ ◖ ▶ P

RUSKINGTON

BLACK BULL
10 Rectory Road
☎ (01526) 832270
11.30-2.30 (3 Fri & Sat), 6.30-11; 12-3, 7-10.30 Sun
Draught Bass; Bateman XB; guest beers (occasional) Ⓗ
Friendly, comfortable and lively local, playing its part in a thriving village. Popular quiz nights each Wed. Note the interesting local sculptures above the entrance. Booking advised for Sun lunch and eve meals (no food Sun eve).
❀ ⚓ ◖ ▶ 🍴 ㊅ ⇌ ♣ P

SANDTOFT

REINDEER INN
☎ (01724) 710774
12-4 (not Mon-Thu), 7 (6 Mon-Thu)-11; 12-4, 7-10.30 Sun
**John Smith's Bitter;
Worthington Bitter** H
Cosy, inviting country pub with a private function room. Traditional home-cooked food is always available. Very popular at weekends. 🏚 🍽 ❀ ◖ ▶ ♣ P 🍺

SAXILBY

ANGLERS
65 High Street
☎ (01522) 702200
11-2.30, 6 (7 Fri &Sat) -11;
12-3, 7-10.30 Sun
**Mansfield Home Bitter;
Theakston Best Bitter; guest
beer** H
Lively two-bar village local; can be boisterous when crib, dominoes or darts teams are playing. Quieter weekday lunchtimes when table skittles may be played.
🍴 ❀ ♣ P

SCAMBLESBY

GREEN MAN
Old Main Road (off A153 Louth-Horncastle road)
☎ (01507) 343282
12-2 (3 Sat), 7-11 (closed winter Tue & Wed); 12-3, 7-10.30 Sun
Beer range varies H
Country pub in the Lincolnshire Wolds on the Viking Way, close to Cadwell Park Motor Racing Circuit and busy when meetings are on. A friendly welcome, good food, real fire and bar billiards feature in this ex-Bateman's pub once known as 'Win's Place'.
🏚 ❀ ◖ ▶ 🍺 ♣ P

SCUNTHORPE

HONEST LAWYER
70 Oswald Road
☎ (01724) 849906
11-11; 7-10.30 Sun
Beer range varies H
Small but popular single-bar, town-centre pub with upstairs drinking area. Crowded at weekends and closed Sun lunchtime. Beer range varies and prices are above average. Occasional cider.
◖ ❀ ⌀

THE TAVERN
143 High Street
☎ (01724) 281272
11-11; 12-3, 7-10.30 Sun
Ward's Best Bitter; guest beer H
Recently refurbished town-centre pub attracting shoppers with good value meals (not served winter eves), comprising a single large room with several alcoves and raised seating in one corner.

A relaxed atmosphere with framed prints and dark wood fittings. Guest beer from Ward's or Vaux. ◖ ▶ ❀

Try also: Crosby, Normanby Rd (Marston's)

SKEGNESS

LUMLEY HOTEL
Lumley Square (opp station)
☎ (01754) 763536
11-11; 12-10.30 Sun
Hardys & Hansons Best Bitter, P
Classic, seasonal beers H
Town-centre pub with a large family room. Often very crowded in summer.
🏚 ❀ ◖ ❀ 🍺

VINE
Vine Road (1 mile S of town centre, off Drummond Rd)
☎ (01754) 763018
11-11; 12-10.30 Sun
**Bateman Mild, XB, Valiant,
XXXB, seasonal beers** H
An oasis of peace and calm in a secluded woodland setting, away from the hurlyburly of the resort. Leafy gardens in summer, roaring fires in winter!
🏚 Q ❀ 🚪 ◖ ▶ ⌂ ♣ P

SKENDLEBY

BLACKSMITH'S ARMS
Main Road
☎ (01754) 890662
11.30-3, 6.30-11; 12-3, 7-10.30 Sun
Bateman XB, G H **XXXB** H
Very food-oriented with a tiny bar and two restaurant areas for which booking is advised. Claims to be the only pub in Lincs to offer XB straight from the cask.
🏚 ❀ ◖ ▶ P

SLEAFORD

CARRE ARMS
Mareham Lane
☎ (01529) 303156
11-3, 5.30-11; 12-3, 7-10.30 Sun
Draught Bass; M& B Brew XI H
Town hotel with a comfortable bar, restaurant and extensive lounge
❀ 🚪 ◖ ▶ 🍺 ❀ P

NAGS HEAD
64 Southgate
☎ (01529) 413916
11-11 (12.30am Thu-Sat); 12-10.30 Sun
**Bateman XB, XXXB, Valiant;
guest beers** H
Recently refurbished pub with a nostalgic atmosphere.
🏚 ❀ ◖ ❀ P

Try also: Rose & Crown, Watergate (Mansfield); Whichcote Arms, Osbournby (Free)

SOUTH FERRIBY

HOPE & ANCHOR
Sluice Road
☎ (01652) 635242
12-3, 6-11 (11-11 summer Sat);
12-3, 7-10.30 (12-10.30 summer) Sun
**Adnams Bitter; Bateman XXXB;
Mansfield Riding Mild, Riding
Bitter; Morland Old Speckled
Hen** H
On the banks of the River Humber, at the confluence of the River Ancholme and next to the lock gates, this pub boasts superb views over the river and the Humber Bridge. It features three rooms and a children's outdoor play area. Eve meals served Sat. 🏚 ❀ ◖ ▶ ⌂ ♣ P

SOUTH KYME

HUME ARMS
High Street ☎ (01526) 861004
7-11, 12-4, 7-11 Sat; 12-4, 7-10.30 Sun
**Bateman XB; Tetley Bitter; guest
beer** H
This imposing village inn features two bars and has its own fishing lake. Guest beer is usually from a small independent or microbrewery.
🏚 ❀ 🚪 ◖ ▶ 🍺 ⌂ Å ♣ P 🍺

SPALDING

LINCOLN ARMS
4 Bridge Street (close to Market Place, by river)
☎ (01775) 722691
11-3 (4 Sat), 7-11; 12-3, 7-10.30 Sun
**Mansfield Riding Bitter, Bitter,
Old Baily** H
Comfortable 18th-century riverside pub that attracts a wide range of customers. A meeting place for numerous clubs.
🚪 ❀ ♣

LINCOLNSHIRE POACHER
11 Double Street
☎ (01775) 766490
11-3, 5-11; 11-11 Sat; 12-3, 7-10.30 Sun
**Hoskins Bitter, Churchills Pride,
Old Nigel; guest beers** H
Pleasant, busy riverside pub with a lively atmosphere. Although now owned by Hoskins, it still regularly offers up to three guest beers. ❀ 🚪 ◖ ▶ ⌂ ❀

SHIP ALBION
37 Albion Street
☎ (01775) 769644
11.30-3, 7-11; 11-11 Fri & Sat;
12-3, 7-10.30 Sun
**Draught Bass; Bateman XB;
Boddingtons Bitter; guest beer** H
Friendly, comfortable pub offering reasonably priced food. Home of Spalding Folk Club.
🏚 ❀ 🚪 ◖ ▶ ♣ P

SPRINGTHORPE

NEW INN
Hill Road ☎ (01427) 838254
7-11 (closed Mon); 12-2, 7-10.30
Sun

**Bateman XXXB; Marston's
Pedigree; guest beers** Ⓗ
A real gem, just like visiting
someone's home. Excellent beer
and fantastic home-cooked food
served by the infamous singing
landlord. Lunches served Sun
only. ♨ Q ❀ ◖ ▶ ⊟ P ▤

STAMFORD

DANIEL LAMBERT
20 St Leonard's Street (just outside town centre)
☎ (01780) 755991
11.30-2.30 (3 Sat), 6-11; 11.30-11
Fri; 12-3, 6-10.30 Sun
**Adnams Bitter; Courage
Directors; John Smith's Bitter;
Taylor Landlord; guest beer** Ⓗ
Named after one of Britain's
heaviest men, whose picture
adorns the chimney breast, this
is a pleasant 200-year-old stone-
built local. Occasional piano sing-
alongs and fortnightly quiz (Sun)
are features. The Cloister
Restaurant is downstairs (no eve
meals Mon). ♨ Q ◖ ▶ ≋ ♣

GREEN MAN
29 Scotgate (on Oakham-Melton
road) ☎ (01780) 753598
11-11; 12-10.30 Sun
**Theakston Best Bitter; guest
beers** Ⓗ
One of the guest beers (which
are frequently from micros and
independent breweries) is
always on special offer in this
thriving ex-Ward's pub, 300 yds
from the town centre. Beer festivals held Easter and late summer. Occasional cider; no food
Sun. ♨ ◄ ◖ ≋ ♣ ◔ ▤

PERIWIG
Red Lion Square
☎ (01780) 762169
11-11; 12-10.30 Sun
**Courage Directors; Hop Back
Summer Lightning; Oakham
JHB; John Smith's Bitter; Taylor
Landlord; guest beers** Ⓗ
Formerly the 'Marsh Harrier',
this one-room ale house features
seating on three levels. Popular
with the young. No food Sun.
◖ ≋

ST PETER'S INN
11 St Peter's Street (up hill from
town centre and Leicester Rd bus
depot) ☎ (01780) 763298
12-2.30 (not Mon), 5.30-11; 12-11
Fri & Sat; 12-10.30 Sun
**Marston's Bitter, Pedigree;
guest beers** Ⓗ
Well furnished friendly local,
comprising a front bar with a
restaurant to the rear, and a cel-

lar bar opening mainly at weekends. Eve meals (served Wed-
Sun), include a wide vegetarian
menu. Limited parking.
Q ❀ ◖ ▶ ⊟ ≋ P

SURFLEET

MERMAID
2 Goberton Road
☎ (01775) 680275
11.30-3, 6.30-11; 12-3, 7-10.30 Sun
**Adnams Broadside; John Smith's
Bitter; guest beers** Ⓗ
Former brewery beside the River
Glen, offering a warm welcome
and generous meals in the bar
and restaurant. The large garden
is ideal for children.
♨ Q ❀ ⇔ ◖ ▶ P

THREEKINGHAM

THREE KINGS
Salters Way (100 yds S of A52)
☎ (01529) 240249
11-3, 7-11; 12-3, 7-10.30 Sun
**Draught Bass; M&B Brew XI;
guest beer** Ⓗ
Notice the effigies above the
entrance of this welcoming village pub; a reminder of the 9th-
century battle of nearby Stow
Green when the Danish army
was routed and three of their
chieftains, or kings, were killed -
hence the pub's name.
♨ ❀ ◖ ▶ ⊟ ♿ ▲ ♣ P

WADDINGHAM

MARQUIS OF GRANBY
High Street (signed 1½ miles E
from A15)
☎ (01673) 818387
12-3, 7-11; 12-3, 7-10.30 Sun
Ward's Best Bitter; guest beer
(occasional) Ⓗ
Very smart village pub, popular
for meals, comprising a single
room with contrasting drinking
areas. Holder of brewery, cellar
and many other awards. The
guest beer is from Ward's.
Evening meals served Thu-Sat.
Wheelchair WC.
♨ Q ❀ ◖ ▶ ♿ ♣ P

WHAPLODE ST CATHERINE

BLUEBELL
Cranesgate (B1168, 3 miles from
Holbech, right turn at bridge and
second left)
☎ (01406) 540300
7-11; 12-3, 7-11 Sat; 12-3,
7-10.30 Sun
**Everards Tiger; Vaux Samson;
guest beer** Ⓗ
Friendly fenland local, whose
landlord has been in place 30
years. A variety of mugs and
brasses are displayed and the
pub hosts summer barbecues
and occasional live music.
♨ ❀ ◖ ▶ ▲ ♣ P

WILLINGHAM BY STOW

HALF MOON INN
23 High St ☎ (01427) 788340
12-2 (3 Sat, closed Mon), 7
(6 Fri)-11; 12-3, 7-10.30 Sun
Castle Eden Ale; guest beers Ⓗ
Lively village local with traditional values and a warm welcome.
Excellent bar meals (no food
Mon). ♨ ❀ ◖ ▶ ⊟ ♣ ▤

WOOLSTHORPE BY BELVOIR

RUTLAND ARMS
Woolsthorpe Wharf (on
Sedgebrooke road, 1 mile E of
Belvoir Castle) ☎ (01476) 870360
11-3, 6.30-11 (may extend summer); 11-11 Sat; 12-10.30 Sun
**Castle Eden Ale; Flowers
Original; guest beers** Ⓗ
Typical country pub with plenty of
olde-worlde charm, displaying
lots of brass and copper. Situated
on the Grantham-Nottingham
Canal and involved with country
pursuits, this pub is suitable for
families, campers and caravanners. The home-cooked food features local produce.
Q ⛟ ❀ ◖ ▶ ⊟ ♿ ▲ ♣ P

WRAGBY

TURNOR ARMS
Market Place
☎ (01673) 858205
11-11; 12-5, 7-10.30 Sun
**Highwood Tom Wood Best
Bitter, Harvest Bitter,
Lincolnshire Legend, seasonal
beers; Theakston Mild** Ⓗ
This imposing old pub, dominating the market place, has two
bars, a games room and a
restaurant serving interesting
food. ♨ ❀ ◖ ♣ P

INDEPENDENT BREWERIES

Bateman: Wainfleet

Bigfoot: Blyton Carr

**Blue Cow: South
Witham**

Brigg: Brigg

DarkTribe: Gunness

**Deeping: Market
Deeping**

Duffield: Harmston

**Highwood: Melton
Highwood**

Oldershaw: Grantham

Willy's: Cleethorpes

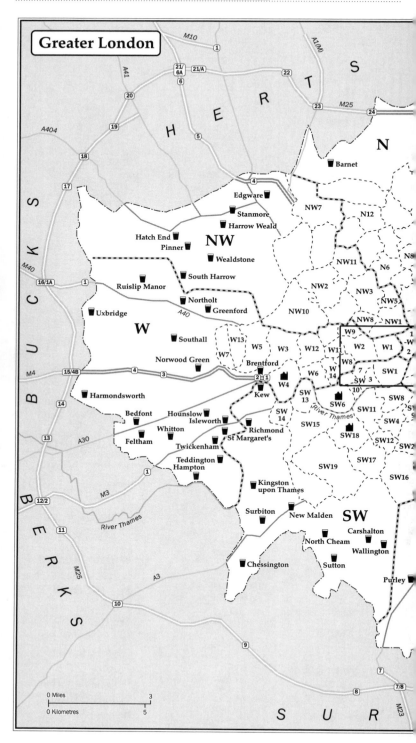

Greater London

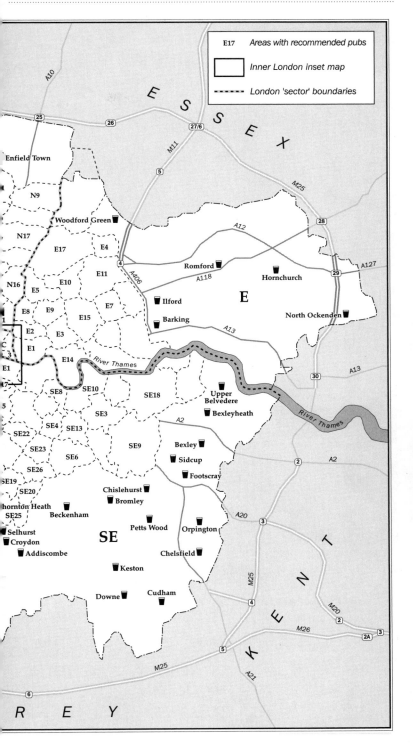

E17   Areas with recommended pubs

Inner London inset map

London 'sector' boundaries

ESSEX

A10

25

26

27/6

M11

5

M25

Enfield Town

N9

Woodford Green

28

A12

N17

E17

E4

Romford

N16

E10

E11

A118

Hornchurch

29

A127

E5

A406

E

E8

E9

E7

Ilford

North Ockenden

30

E2

E15

Barking

A13

E3

E1

A13

E1

E14   River Thames

SE8

SE10

SE18

Upper Belvedere

River Thames

SE3

Bexleyheath

SE4

SE13

A2

SE22

SE9

Bexley

SE23

SE6

Sidcup

2

A2

SE26

Footscray

SE19

A2

SE20

Chislehurst

Thornton Heath

Bromley

A20

SE25

Beckenham

3

Selhurst

SE

Petts Wood

Orpington

Croydon

Addiscombe

Chelsfield

Keston

M25

K

Downe

Cudham

4

E

M20

2

N

M26

2A

3

5

T

M25

A21

6

S   U   R   R   E   Y

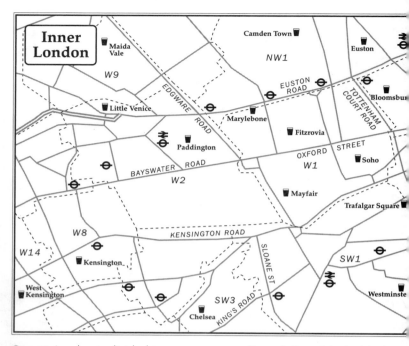

Greater London is divided into seven areas: Central, East, North, North-West, South-East, South West and West, reflecting the London postal boundaries. Central London includes EC1 to EC4 and WC1 and WC2. The other six areas have their pubs listed in numerical order (E1, E4, etc) followed in alphabetical order by the outlying areas which do not have postal numbers (Barking, Hornchurch, and so on). The Inner London map, above, shows the area roughly covered by the Circle Line. Note that some regions straddle more than one postal district.

Central London

EC1: CLERKENWELL

ARTILLERY ARMS
102 Bunhill Row
☎ (0171) 253 4683
11-11; 11-3, 7-11 Sat; 12-3, 7-10.30 Sun
Fuller's Chiswick, London Pride, HSB, seasonal beers Ⓗ
Long-standing *Guide* entry. A Fuller's house near the historic Bunhill Fields cemetery, catering for city and local residential clientele. Weekday lunches.
◖ ▶ ≉ ⊖ (Old St/Moorgate)

JERUSALEM TAVERN
55 Britton Street
☎ (0171) 490 4281
11-11; closed Sat & Sun
St Peter's Fruit Beer, Best Bitter, Wheat Beer, Extra, Strong, seasonal beers Ⓟ
Small, busy pub, recently con-

verted from a coffee house in a building dating from 1720. The only regular London outlet for St Peter's Brewery.
♨ Q ◖ ≉ ⊖ (Farringdon)

LEOPARD
33 Seward Street
☎ (0171) 253 3587
11-11; closed Sat & Sun
Gibbs Mew Salisbury; Greene King Abbot; guest beers Ⓗ
Busy pub off Goswell Road with an imaginative interior. Full menu available all day. Regular beer festivals, often with a beer theme. ♨ ❀ ◖ ▶ ⊖ (Barbican)

MASQUE HAUNT
168-172 Old Street
☎ (0171) 251 4195
11-11; 12-10.30 Sun
Courage Directors; Fuller's London Pride; Theakston Best Bitter; guest beers Ⓗ
Long, one-bar pub with a raised

drinking area at the rear.
Q ◖ ▶ ≉ ⊖ (Old St) ⌿ ⊟

O'HANLON'S
8 Tysoe Street
☎ (0171) 837 4112
12-11; closed Sun
O'Hanlon's Dry Stout, seasonal beers Ⓗ
Small, busy, traditional Irish pub selling a wide range of beers from John O'Hanlon's own brewery. An extensive menu is reasonably priced. Extremely busy Fri eves. Local CAMRA *Pub of the Year 1998*.
Q ◖ ▶ ≉ (Farringdon)
⊖ (Angel)

SEKFORDE ARMS
34 Sekforde Street
☎ (0171) 253 3231
11-11; 12-3 (closed eve) Sun
Young's Bitter, Special, Winter Warmer, seasonal beers Ⓗ
Small, one-bar corner pub with a

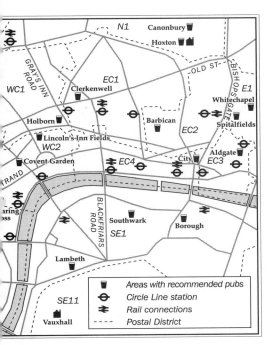

WC1: BLOOMSBURY

CALTHORPE ARMS
252 Gray's Inn Road
☎ (0171) 278 4732
11-3, 5-11; 11-11 Wed-Sat; 12-10.30 Sun
Young's Bitter, Special, seasonal beers H
Friendly corner pub, popular with locals and office workers. An upstairs dining room is open lunchtimes; eve meals on request. Benches outside for summer drinking.
◖ ▶ ≅ (Kings Cross)
⊖ (Russell Sq) ❀

KINGS ARMS
11a Northington Street
☎ (0171) 405 9107
11.30-11; closed Sat & Sun
Draught Bass; Fuller's London Pride; Greene King IPA; guest beers H
A hidden gem. Always a friendly welcome in this popular side-street pub off Gray's Inn Road, frequented by the local legal community and office workers alike.
◖ ≅ (Farringdon) ⊖ (Chancery Lane)

LAMB
94 Lamb's Conduit Street
☎ (0171) 405 0713
11-11; 12-4, 7-10.30 Sun
Young's Bitter, Special, seasonal beers H
Dark green upholstery and etched glass snob screens create a resplendent interior in this Grade II listed Victorian local. Music hall memorabilia, a working polyphon and a comfortable no-smoking snug add to the atmosphere. Eve meals finish early.
Q ❀ ◖ ▶ ⊖ (Russell Sq)
♣ ✦

WC1: HOLBORN

CITTIE OF YORKE ☆
22 High Holborn
☎ (0171) 242 7670
11.30-11; closed Sun
Samuel Smith OBB H
This 15th-century inn and coffee house was rebuilt in 1923 using some of the original materials. The main bar boasts huge vats, screened compartments and an unusual triangular stove. Also a more intimate front bar and a cellar bar. Very busy early eves.
♨ Q ◖ ▶ ≅ (Farringdon)

THREE CUPS
21-22 Sandland Street
☎ (0171) 831 4302
11-11; closed Sat & Sun
Young's Bitter, Special, seasonal beers H
Corner pub with a changing clientele, depending on the time of

---

pavement drinking area.
❀ ◖ ▶ ≅ ⊖ (Farringdon)

EC2: BARBICAN

CROWDERS WELL
Andrews House (off Fore St/Wood St jct)
☎ (0171) 628 8574
11-11: closed Sat & Sun
Boddingtons Bitter; Greene King IPA, Abbot; Marston's Pedigree; Wadworth 6X H**; guest beers** G
Edge of City alehouse with up to eight guest beers on gravity dispense. Hidden away in the heart of the Barbican, with views of the arts centre.
◖ ▶ ≅ (Moorgate) ⊖

EC3: ALDGATE

HOOP & GRAPES
47 Aldgate High Street
☎ (0171) 265 5171
11-10 (11 Thu & Fri); closed Sat & Sun
Fuller's London Pride; guest beers H
Historic alehouse on edge of the City with interesting guest beers. Occasional beer festivals.
◖ ▶ ≅ (Liverpool St)
⊖ (Aldgate)

EC3: CITY

COCK & WOOLPACK
6 Finch Lane
11-9; closed Sat & Sun
Beer range varies G
A rare example of an ordinary,

---

un-themed pub in the City. The beer range varies, but all are served direct from the cask. Light lunchtime snacks available.
≅ (Liverpool St) ⊖ (Bank)

ELEPHANT
119 Fenchurch Street
☎ (0171) 623 8970
11-10; closed Sat & Sun
Young's Bitter, Special, Winter Warmer, seasonal beers H
Two-bar pub with a busy early eve City trade. May close early if quiet.
◖ ≅ (Fenchurch St) ⊖ (Aldgate)

EC4: CITY

OLD BANK OF ENGLAND
192 Fleet Street
☎ (0171) 430 2255
11-11; closed Sat & Sun
Fuller's Chiswick, London Pride, ESB, seasonal beers H
Flagship Fuller's Ale & Pie House.
Q ◖ ≅ (City Thameslink)
⊖ (Temple)

VINTRY
30 Queen Street
☎ (0171) 329 8985
11-11 (may close earlier); closed Sat & Sun
Fuller's Chiswick, London Pride, ESB, seasonal beers H
Small City pub with mock Victorian decor and a convivial atmosphere. Sky TV. Lunches served 12-4.
◖ ≅ (Cannon St) ⊖ (Mansion House)

day. Seating around the edge gives good views of the knick-knacks displayed. Close to a large range of restaurants in Red Lion Street. Eve meals on request.
🍴 🍺 ≠ (Farringdon)
➌ (Holborn ♣

MARQUIS OF GRANBY
51 Chandos Place
☎ (0171) 836 7657
11-11; 12-10.30 Sun
Adnams Bitter; Marston's Pedigree; Tetley Bitter; guest beer Ⓗ
Friendly wedge-shaped pub, featuring chapel-type partitions and unusual ceiling heaters. Monthly malt whisky feature. Lunches served until 5pm.
🍺 Q ≠ ➌

WC2: COVENT GARDEN

CROSS KEYS
21 Endell Street
☎ (0171) 836 5185
11-11; 12-10.30 Sun
Courage Best Bitter, Directors; Marston's Pedigree Ⓗ
Small, intimate pub with much greenery outside and filled with bric-à-brac, including Beatles memorabilia. Note the Isleworth Brewery sign above the clock.
🍺 ➌

HOGSHEAD
21 Drury Lane
☎ (0171) 240 2489
11-11; 12-10.30 Sun
Boddingtons Bitter; Flowers IPA, Original Ⓗ**; guest beers** ⒽⒼ
Small, friendly pub, opposite the New London Theatre. Hot baguettes available. ➌

HOGSHEAD IN COVENT GARDEN
23 Wellington street
☎ (0171) 836 6930
11-11; 12-10.30 Sun
Boddingtons Bitter; Flowers IPA, Original Ⓗ**; guest beers** ⒽⒼ
Corner pub, opposite the Lyceum Theatre with a constantly varying selection of guest beers. No food Sun.
🍺 ▶ ➌

LAMB & FLAG ☆
33 Rose Street
☎ (0171) 497 9504
11-11 (10.45 Fri & Sat); 12-10.30 Sun
Courage Best Bitter, Directors; Marston's Pedigree ; John Smith's Bitter Ⓗ
Reputedly the oldest pub in Covent Garden, this historic pub has connections with Samuel Butler and the poet, John Dryden who was mugged in the side alley. It was also known in earlier times as the 'Bucket of Blood'

because of prize fighting connections. No food Sun.
🍺 ≠ (Charing Cross)
➌ (Leicester Sq)

NEWTON ARMS
33 Newton Street
☎ (0171) 242 8797
11-11; 11.30-3.30, 5.30-11 Sat; closed Sun
Adnams Bitter; Ind Coope Burton Ale; Tetley Bitter Ⓗ
Welcoming, modern pub near Kingsway. Board games available on request. A house beer is also sold.
🍺 ➌ (Holborn) ♣

PRINCE OF WALES
150 Drury Lane
☎ (0171) 836 5183
11-11; 12-10.30 Sun
Courage Best Bitter, Directors; Theakston Best Bitter, XB; guest beers Ⓗ
Large corner pub in typical T & J Bernard style.
🍺 ▶ ➌

WC2: LINCOLN'S INN FIELDS

SEVEN STARS
53 Carey Street
☎ (0171) 242 8521
11-11 (9.30 Mon-Wed); closed Sat & Sun
Courage Best Bitter, Directors Ⓗ
Genuinely old pub, handy for the Royal Courts of Justice and used by the legal profession.
Q 🍺 ▶ ➌ (Chancery Lane)

East London

SPITALFIELDS

ALMA
41 Spelman Street
☎ (0171) 247 5604
11-11; 12-10.30 Sun
Fuller's London Pride; Young's Bitter; guest beers Ⓗ
Fine, back-street pub, home of Edward Tilney and Co's Alma Brewery until 1927. Local CAMRA *Pub of the Year* 1997.
🍺 ≠ (Liverpool St) ➌ (Aldgate East) 🏚

PRIDE OF SPITALFIELDS
3 Heneage Street (off Brick Lane)
☎ (0171) 247 8933
11-11; 12-10.30 Sun
Crouch Vale Woodham IPA; Fuller's London Pride, ESB; guest beers Ⓗ
Busy little back-street pub with regularly changing guests. The decor shows scenes of the old East End, photos of the area and a fascinating collection of beer bottles. Pavement drinking area.
🏚 🍺 🍺 ≠ (Liverpool St)
➌ (Aldgate East)

E1: WHITECHAPEL

LORD RODNEY'S HEAD
☎ (0171) 247 9795
11-11; 12-10.30 Sun
B&T Shefford Bitter, SOS, SOD, Black Bat Ⓗ
Long, narrow, one-bar pub with over 50 clocks on display but only one that works. Stocks a selection of foreign bottled beers. Popular live music venue.
🍺 ➌ ♣ ♣ ⌣

E2: BETHNAL GREEN

APPROACH TAVERN
47 Approach Road
☎ (0181) 980 2321
12-11; 11-11 Sat; 12-10.30 Sun
Adnams Bitter; Fuller's London Pride; Marston's Pedigree; Wadworth 6X; guest beer Ⓗ
Large, friendly, one-bar pub which has a patio area in front with benches. Art gallery upstairs. 🏚 🍺 🍺 ➌ ♣

E2: HACKNEY

MARKSMAN
254 Hackney Road
☎ (0171) 739 7393
11-11; 12-10.30 Sun
Courage Directors; guest beers Ⓗ
Small, one-bar pub displaying old local framed posters on the walls, also a military theme. A haven for locals.
≠ (Cambridge Heath)

E3: BOW

COBORN ARMS
8 Coborn Road
☎ (0181) 980 3793
11-11; 12-10.30 Sun
Young's Bitter, Special, seasonal beers Ⓗ
Large, comfortable local, just off the Mile End Road.
🍺 🍺 ▶ ⚤ ➌ (Bow Rd) ♣

E4: CHINGFORD

BULL & CROWN
The Green, Kings Head Hill
11-11; 12-10.30 Sun
Ridleys IPA; Tetley Bitter Ⓗ
Large, two-bar pub with plenty going on: quiz nights, discos, line dancing etc. Well known for its good, cheap beer.
🍺 🛏 🍺 🍺 ⚤ ≠ P

KINGS FORD
250 Chingford Mount Road
☎ (0181) 523 9365
11-11; 12-10.30 Sun
Courage Directors; Fuller's London Pride; Theakston Best Bitter; Younger Scotch; guest beers H
One of the best Wetherspoon houses you could find.
Q ◖ ▶ ⅏ ⅏ ⊟

KINGS HEAD
2B Kings Head Hill
☎ (0181) 529 1655
12 (11 Sat)-11; 12-10.30 Sun
Marston's Pedigree; Morland Old Speckled Hen; Tetley Bitter; guest beers H
Small, due for renovation, offering a constantly changing range of guest beers. Chess played.
⍟ ◖ ▶ ⊞ ⇌ ♣ ⌣ P

E5: CLAPTON

ANCHOR & HOPE
15 High Hill Ferry
☎ (0181) 806 1730
11-3, 5.30-11; 12-3, 7-10.30 Sun
Fuller's London Pride, ESB H
Small, riverside, one-bar pub, popular with locals and just about anyone passing on the Lee towpath. An East London institution. There is some seating by the river.⍟ ⇌ ♣

PRINCESS OF WALES
146 Lea Bridge Road
☎ (0181) 533 3463
11-11; 11-10.30 Sun
Young's Bitter, Special, seasonal beers H
Large riverside pub known until January 1998 as the Prince of Wales.Q ◖ ▶ ⊞ ⇌ ♣ P

E7: FOREST GATE

OLD SPOTTED DOG
212 Upton Lane
☎ (0181) 472 1794
11-3, 5.30 (7 Sat)-11; 12-4, 7-10.30 Sun
Courage Directors; Marston's Pedigree; guest beers H
Large pub of 16th-century origin. It has an extension which houses the family room and restaurant (vegans catered for). There is a superb beer range (with three regularly changing guest beers); plus cider and perry. Dogs welcome.
⌂ ⍨ ⍟ ◖ ▶ ⊞ ♣ ⌣ P

E8: DALSTON

PRINCE ARTHUR
95 Forest Road
☎ (0171) 254 3439
11.30-11; 11.30-4, 7-11 Sat; 12-4, 7-10.30 Sun
Adnams Bitter; Greene King Abbot; Fuller's London Pride H
Friendly one-bar, side-street pub. An oasis for locals. Paved outside area for drinkers. Its 16th-consecutive year in this *Guide*. (formerly Lady Diana).
⍟ ◖ ▶ ⇌ (Hackney Central) ♣

E9: HACKNEY

ROYAL INN ON THE PARK
111 Lauriston Road
☎ (0181) 985 3321
12-11; 12-10.30 Sun
Flowers Original; Fuller's London Pride, ESB; Wadworth 6X H
Large pub on the edge of Victoria Park: one bar and a restaurant.
⍟ ◖ ▶ ♣

E10: LEYTON

WILLIAM IV
816 High Road, Leyton
☎ (0181) 556 2460
11-11; 12-10.30 Sun
Fuller's London Pride, ESB; guest beers H
Vastly improved High Street pub which employs a successful guest beer policy. Chess and backgammon are played in the rear bar. No food is available Sun eve.
⍟ ◖ ▶ ⇌ (Leyton Midland Rd) ♣

E11: LEYTONSTONE

BIRKBECK TAVERN
45 Langthorne Rd
☎ (0181) 539 2584
11-11; 12-10.30 Sun
Courage Best Bitter; guest beers H
Welcoming community pub with a pleasant garden and a wide ranging selection of guest beers. A recent local CAMRA *Pub of the Year*.
⍟ ⊞ ⊖ (Leyton) ♣

E11: WANSTEAD

DUKE OF EDINBURGH
Nightingale Lane
☎ (0181) 989 0014
12-11; 12-10.30 Sun
Adnams Bitter; Young's Bitter; guest beers H
Excellent local, fielding two darts teams. Large screen satellite TV for sporting events. There is a house beer available, plus guest beers from the Tapster's Choice range.
⍟ ◖ ⊖ (Snaresbrook) ♣

East London's Pig's Ear Beer Festival at Stratford Town Hall is opened by Tony Banks MP. This terrific, busy, December festival is organised by the East London and City branch of CAMRA. Left to right: John Cryne, CAMRA's then National Chairman, festival press officer Robyn Boorman, Tony Banks, and festival organiser Bernard Boorman.

George
High Street ☎ (0181) 989 2921
11-11; 12-10.30 Sun
Courage Directors; Fuller's London Pride; Theakston Best Bitter; guest beers Ⓗ
Vast Wetherspoons house directly opposite the tube station. Extremely busy weekend eves.
Q ◑ ◗ ⊖ P ⊬ ⊡

E14: ISLE OF DOGS

Cat & Canary
Fisherman's Walk, Canary Wharf
☎ (0171) 512 9187
11-9; 12-3 Sat; closed Sun
Fuller's Chiswick, London Pride, ESB, seasonal beers Ⓗ
Modern, single bar pub in a dockside location.
◑ ◗ ⊖ (Canary Wharf DLR) ♣

E14: LIMEHOUSE

Oporto Tavern
43 West India Dock Road
11-11; 12-10.30 Sun
Everards Tiger; Fuller's London Pride; guest beer Ⓗ
Revived local's bar with a lively atmosphere. See the many old photos of this historic area on show.
◑ ≠ ⊖ (West Ferry DLR)

Queens Head
8 Flamborough Street
☎ (0171) 790 6481
11-2.30, 5.30-11; 12-3, 7.30-11 Sat; 12-3, 7-10.30 Sun
Young's Bitter, Special, seasonal beers Ⓗ
You've seen the pictures of the Queen Mother pulling a pint – well, this is where it happened. This small pub in a conservation area features a London Fives dartboard.
◑ ⊡ ≠ ⊖ ♣

E15: STRATFORD

Goldengrove
146 The Grove
☎ (0181) 519 0750
11-11; 12-10.30 Sun
Courage Directors; Fuller's London Pride; Theakston Best Bitter; guest beers Ⓗ
Reliable Wetherspoons pub on the edge of Stratford town centre, deservedly popular.
Q ❀ ◑ ◗ ≠ ⊖ ⌓ P ⊬ ⊡

E17: WALTHAMSTOW

Flowerpot
128 Wood Street
☎ (0181) 223 9941
12 (11 Sat)-11; 12-10.30 Sun
Draught Bass; Fuller's London Pride Ⓗ
Roomy, comfortable local with TV and music, boasting a notable mirror.
❀ ≠ (Wood St)

Village
31 Orford Road
☎ (0181) 521 9982
11-11; 12-10.30 Sun
Otter Bitter; Vaux Waggle Dance; Ward's Best Bitter; guest beers Ⓗ
Busy, popular pub at the heart of Walthamstow village with a cosy, quiet snug at the rear.
♘ ≠ (Central) ⊖ ❀

BARKING

Britannia
1 Church Road (near A123, Ilford Lane)
☎ (0181) 594 1305
11-3, 5-11; 11-11 Sat; 12-10.30 Sun
Young's Bitter, Special, Winter Warmer, seasonal beers Ⓗ
Young's most easterly pub north of the Thames: comfortable saloon bar and a more basic public. Note the caryatids outside - a now rare example in East London. Local CAMRA *Pub of the Year* 1997.
❀ ◑ ◗ ⊡ ≠ ⊖ ♣ P

HORNCHURCH

Chequers
North Street (Billet Lane jct, near A124)
☎ (01708) 442094
11-11; 12-3, 5.30-11 Fri; 11-4, 6-11 Sat; 12-4, 7-10.30 Sun
Friary Meux BB; Young's Bitter; guest beer Ⓗ
Victorian pub with a friendly atmosphere in a residential area. Refurbished recently but not spoilt. The guest beer is from the Tapster's Choice range and the house beer is Ind Coope. The beer prices are very competitive.
Q ≠ (Emerson Pk) ♣ P

Pit Bar (Queens Theatre)
Billet Lane (near A124)
☎ (01708) 456118
12-3, 6-11; 12-3, 7-10.30 Sun
Greene King IPA, Abbot, seasonal beers Ⓗ**; guest beers** Ⓖ
Modern theatre bar, open to the public, recently modernised as the Green Room. Usually three guest beers, representing good value. Closed Sun eve if no performance; jazz Sun lunch. Eve meals finish early.
Q ♘ ◑ ◗ ≠ (Emerson Pk) ⊖ P

ILFORD

Rose & Crown
16 Ilford Hill (A118, near A406 flyover) ☎ (0181) 478 7104
12-11; 12-10.30 Sun
Marston's Pedigree; Tetley Bitter; guest beers Ⓗ
Pleasant, wood-panelled Tetley Festival Alehouse with various drinking areas around a central bar. The best selection of guest beers in the area – up to five usually available from independent breweries. The house beer is from Carlsberg-Tetley. Eve meals weekdays 5-7
❀ ◑ ◗ ≠ ♣

Try also Great Spoon of Ilford, 114 Cranbrook Rd (Wetherspoons)

NORTH OCKENDON

Old White Horse
Ockendon Road (B186)
☎ (01708) 853111
11-3, 6-11; 12-3, 7-10.30 Sun
Beer range varies Ⓗ
Excellent old two-bar local invigorated by a fine new landlord. Handpumps in the lounge serve three real ales, usually from the Ind Coope range. An escape from the modern world. Strongly recommended.
❀ ◑ ◗ ⊡ ⛺ ♣ P

ROMFORD

Moon & Stars
99-103 South Street (near station)
☎ (01708) 730117
10-11; 12-10.30 Sun
Courage Best Bitter, Directors; Fuller's London Pride; Greene King IPA; guest beers Ⓗ
The first and still the best of Romford's new generation of pubs. The selection of beers keeps changing, but not the quality. Food available all day.
Q ◑ ◗ ♿ ≠ ⊬ ⊡

WOODFORD GREEN

Cricketers
299-301 High Road (A11)
☎ (0181) 504 2734
11-3, 5.30-11; 11-11 Sat; 12-10.30 Sun
McMullen AK, Country, Gladstone, seasonal beers Ⓗ
Pleasant, comfortable, suburban local with a wood-panelled lounge and a more basic public bar. Good value pensioners' lunches weekdays (no food Sun). CAMRA London *Pub of the Year* 1991. Petanque played.
Q ❀ ◑ ⊡ ♣ P ⊡

Rose & Crown
31 Mill Lane (near A104)
☎ (0181) 504 0420
11-11; 12-10.30 Sun
Boddingtons Bitter; Flowers Original; Fuller's London Pride; Marston's Pedigree; Wells Bombardier; Whitbread seasonal beers Ⓗ
Lively pub with a mixture of young and older customers. Dark wood panelling, framed cartoons, TV, video games, a restaurant

area and live music are its attractions. Limited parking.
❀ ◖ ▶ ⊞ P

TRAVELLERS FRIEND
496-498 High Road (A104)
☎ (0181) 504 2435
11-11; 12-3.30, 7-10.30 Sun
Courage Best Bitter, Directors; Ridleys IPA; guest beers Ⓗ
Still a real gem of a pub hosted by a friendly landlord. Although it has had a facelift, all the original features have been retained, including the snob screens and wood panelling. A good place to stop for a pint or two. Limited parking.Q ❀ ◖ P

North London

N1: CANONBURY

COMPTON ARMS
4 Compton Avenue
☎ (0171) 359 6883
11-11; 12-10.30 Sun
Greene King IPA, Abbot Ⓗ
Small, friendly cottage-style pub, a country local in London. Can get very busy at weekends. No food Tue eve.
❀ ◖ ▶ ≆ (Highbury & Islington) ⊖

EARL OF RADNOR
106 Mildmay Grove South
☎ (0171) 241 0318
11-11; 12-10.30 Sun
Fuller's London Pride, ESB Ⓗ
Cosy local with wrought iron fittings and Art Deco glass. Pavement tables for outside drinking.
❀ ≆ (Dalston Kingsland) ♣

MARQUESS TAVERN
32 Canonbury Street
☎ (0171) 354 2975
11-11; 12-10.30 Sun
Young's Bitter, Special, seasonal beers Ⓗ
Magnificent 19th-century local serving home-cooked food. Pavement tables.Local CAMRA *Pub of the Year* 1998.
🏨 Q ❀ ◖ ▶ ≆ (Essex Rd) ⊖ (Highbury & Islington)

N1: HOXTON

WENLOCK ARMS
26 Wenlock Road
☎ (0171) 608 3406
12-11; 12-10.30 Sun
Adnams Best Bitter; Nethergate Golden Gate; Tetley Bitter; guest beers Ⓗ
North London's premier real ale free house offers an ever-changing range of ales with a mild usually available. Live jazz Sun lunch. Local CAMRA *Pub of the Year* 1995 and '96. Real cider or perry usually available.
🏨 ≆ (Old St) ⊖ ♣ ⌢ ⊟

N6: HIGHGATE

FLASK ☆
77 Highgate West Hill
☎ (0181) 340 7260
11-11; 12-10.30 Sun
Adnams Bitter; Ind Coope Burton Ale; Greene King Abbot Ale; Morland Old Speckled Hen; Tetley Bitter; Young's Bitter Ⓗ
17th-century pub with small rooms on different levels. The large outside drinking area is heated. A very popular local.
🏨 ❀ ◖ ▶ ⊖ ♣

GATEHOUSE
1 North Road
☎ (0181) 340 8054
11-11; 12-10.30 Sun
Courage Directors; Greene King Abbot; Theakston Best Bitter; guest beers Ⓗ
Popular, cosmopolitan Wetherspoons, opened in 1994 after being closed for many years. Reputedly haunted – some staff refuse to visit the cellar alone. Independent theatre upstairs. Q ❀ ◖ ▶ ⅄ ⊖ ⅍ ⊟

RED LION & SUN
25 North Road
☎ (0181) 340 1780
11-11; 12-10.30 Sun
Greene King IPA, Abbot Ⓗ
Wood-panelled 1920s mock-Tudor local, set back behind a pleasant, tree-lined courtyard. It hosts quiz nights Thu and Sun; jazz Wed and Sat eves. No eve meals Sun. 🏨 ❀ ◖ ▶ ⅄ ♣ P

N8: CROUCH END

HOGSHEAD
33-35 Crouch End Hill
☎ (0181) 342 8465
11-11; 12-10.30 Sun
Beer range varies Ⓗ
Converted funeral parlour opened May 1997, offering up to 14 real ales, including customers' choices. Food served until 9pm Mon-Thu, 7pm Fri-Sat, 5pm Sun. Wheelchair lift and WC.
🏨 ◖ ▶ ⅄ ♣ ⌢

N9: LOWER EDMONTON

LAMB
52-54 Church Street
☎ (0181) 887 0128
11-11; 12-10.30 Sun
Courage Directors; Fuller's London Pride; Theakston Best Bitter; guest beers Ⓗ
This Wetherspoons conversion of a former restaurant is a welcome oasis in an area full of pubs with over-loud jukeboxes and out of tune karaoke singers. Named after Charles Lamb, the 19th-century essayist, who lived locally. Wheelchair WC.
Q ❀ ◖ ▶ ⅄ ≆ ⅍ ⊟

N12: NORTH FINCHLEY

ELEPHANT INN
283 Ballards Lane
☎ (0181) 445 0356
11-11; 12-10.30 Sun
Fuller's Chiswick, London Pride, ESB, seasonal beers Ⓗ
Formerly Moss Hall Tavern, this far-flung Fuller's outpost recently lost its public bar for conversion to a Thai restaurant. No food Sun eve. ❀ ◖ ▶ ♣

TALLY HO
749 High Rd ☎ (0181) 445 4390
11-11; 12-10.30 Sun
Courage Directors; Fuller's London Pride; Greene King IPA; Theakston Best Bitter; guest beers Ⓗ
Large pub in a commanding location rescued from years of Bass neglect by Wetherspoons. The island bar serves three distinct drinking areas. The upstairs bar/restaurant is no-smoking.
Q ♣ ◖ ▶ ⌢ ⅄ ⊟

N16: STOKE NEWINGTON

ROCHESTER CASTLE
145 Stoke Newington High Street (near BR station)
☎ (0171) 249 6016
11-11; 12-10.30 Sun
Courage Directors; Fuller's London Pride; Greene King Abbot; Hop Back Summer Lightning; Theakston Best Bitter; guest beers Ⓗ
Recently refurbished, this very large Wetherspoons has a friendly atmosphere. Two full walls feature original listed tiling. Conservatory plus a small outdoor area. Formerly the Tanners Hall. Q ❀ ◖ ▶ ⅄ ≆ ♣ ⅍ ⊟

N17: TOTTENHAM

NEW MOON
413 Lordship Lane
☎ (0181) 801 3496
11-11; 12-3, 7-10.30 Sun
Courage Directors; Greene King IPA; Marston's Pedigree; Younger Scotch; guest beers Ⓗ
Standard Wetherspoons shop conversion, but expect a very warm welcome from staff in this busy pub. Popular with local real ale enthusiasts, it is an absolute oasis in a real beer desert.
Q ◖ ▶ ⊖ (Wood Green) ⅍ ⊟

N21: WINCHMORE HILL

ORANGE TREE
18 Highfield Rd
☎ (0181) 360 4853
12-11; 12-10.30 Sun
Adnams Bitter; Greene King IPA; guest beers Ⓗ

Friendly, down-to-earth local with a strong community focus; off the beaten track, but worth a detour. Live music Sat eve; big screen TV for sport. Large garden with a play area and barbecue. Good lunches (eve meals finish at 7pm).
❀ ⓓ ⍑ ♣ P

BARNET

KING WILLIAM IV
18 Hadley Highstone
☎ (0181) 449 6728
11-3, 5.30-11; 12-4, 7-10.30 Sun
Benskins BB; Hook Norton Best Bitter; Ind Coope Burton Ale; Marston's Pedigree Ⓗ
Unspoilt, 17th-century pub in an upmarket community on the very edge of London. Mercifully free of fruit machines.
🐾 Q ❀ ⓓ P

MOON UNDER WATER
148 High Street
☎ (0181) 441 9476
11-11; 12-10.30 Sun
Courage Directors; Greene King IPA; Marston's Pedigree; Theakston XB; guest beer Ⓗ
Unusual, early Wetherspoons conversion. Follow the long narrow bar and then browse through the library at the end.
Q ❀ ⓓ ⍑ 🗗

WHITE LION
50 St Albans Road
☎ (0181) 449 4560
11-2.30, 5-11;11-3, 6-11 Sat; 12-4, 7-10.30 Sun
ABC Bitter; Greene King IPA, Abbot; guest beers Ⓗ
Comfortable free house on the edge of town, rescued by an award-winning licensee from terminal decline. Fish and chip eves on Mon. Extensive range of malt whiskies. Local CAMRA *Pub of the Year* 1996. No food Sun. Wheelchair access is via rear door.
❀ ⓓ 🍴 ⚹ ♣ P

ENFIELD TOWN

OLD WHEATSHEAF
3 Windmill Hill
☎ (0181) 363 0516
11-11; 12-3, 7-10.30 Sun
Adnams Bitter; Benskins BB; Tetley Bitter; guest beers Ⓗ
Attractive, two-bar Edwardian pub, famed for its floral displays and bodybuilding gym. Popular with dog lovers. Stocks the Tapster's Choice guest beer range. Some pavement tables. No food Sun.
❀ ⓓ ⍑ (Enfield Chase) P

STAG
1 Little Park Gardens
☎ (0181) 363 1836
11-11; 12-10.30 Sun

Draught Bass; Fuller's London Pride; Greene King IPA; Tetley Bitter Ⓗ
Traditional town-centre pub by the bus terminal. TV for major sports events. Excellent upstairs restaurant and function room.
❀ ⓓ ⍑ (Enfield Chase) ♣

NEW BARNET

RAILWAY BELL
13 East Barnet Road
☎ (0181) 449 1369
11-11; 12-10.30 Sun
Courage Directors; Fuller's London Pride; Theakston Best Bitter; guest beers Ⓗ
Large, one-bar, split-level pub displaying railway memorabilia. Popular with office workers at lunchtime; evenings it welcomes a younger crowd.
Q ❀ ⓓ ⍑ P ⚹ 🗗

North-West London

NW1: CAMDEN TOWN

SPREAD EAGLE
141 Albert Street
☎ (0171) 267 1410
11-11; 12-10.30 Sun
Young's Bitter, Special, seasonal beers Ⓗ
Busy pub, altered to give separate areas in a single bar. Built in 1838 and expanded into adjoining buildings in 1930s and 1963, it is handy for Camden Lock market.
❀ ⓓ ⍑ (Camden Rd) ⊖

NW1: EUSTON

HEAD OF STEAM
1 Eversholt Street (by BR and bus stations)
☎ (0171) 388 2221
12-11; 12-10 Sun
Highgate Mild; Shepherd Neame Master Brew Bitter; guest beers Ⓗ
Pub on the first floor of a modern office block, full of railway memorabilia, with a raised no-smoking area and a family area. Holds regular themed beer festivals. The beer range always includes a brew from Hop Back and B&T plus four guests.
👶 ⓓ ⍑ ⊖ ♣ 🍴 ⚹

NW1: MARYLEBONE

PERSEVERANCE
11 Shroton Street
☎ (0171) 723 7469
11-11; 12-3.30, 7-10.30 Sun
Draught Bass; Fuller's London Pride, seasonal beer
(Christmas) Ⓗ
Friendly 19th-century former coaching inn with one horseshoe bar. It has endured two major floods in the last couple of years

but has been put back together well. ❀ ⓓ ⍑ ⊖ ♣

NW2: CRICKLEWOOD

BEATEN DOCKET
50-56 Cricklewood Broadway
☎ (0181) 450 2972
11-11; 12-10.30 Sun
Courage Directors; Greene King Abbot; Marston's Pedigree; Theakston Best Bitter; guest beers Ⓗ
Large Wetherspoons pub, which has become more of a local than many others. In an area not known for decent beer, it can get busy at weekends.
❀ ⓓ ⍑ ⚹ ⍑ 🗗

NW3: BELSIZE PARK

WASHINGTON
50 Englands Lane
☎ (0171) 722 6118
11-11; 12-10.30 Sun
Ind Coope Burton Ale; Marston's Pedigree; Morland Old Speckled Hen; Tetley Bitter; Young's Bitter; guest beers Ⓗ
Magnificent Victorian pub (1865) with original tiling, etched glass and mirrors. Home to several sports teams and the Hampstead Comedy Club. Opens 10am for breakfast.
ⓓ ⍑ ⊖ ♣

NW3: HAMPSTEAD

DUKE OF HAMILTON
23-25 New End
☎ (0171) 794 0258
11-11; 12-10.30 Sun
Fuller's London Pride, ESB; guest beers Ⓗ
Friendly bolt-hole just off busy Heath Street, popular with locals, sports fans and patrons of the New End Theatre next door. Local CAMRA *Pub of the Year* 1997.
❀ ⊖ ⍀

FLASK
14 Flask Walk
☎ (0171) 435 4580
11-11; 12-10.30 Sun
Young's Bitter, Special, seasonal beers Ⓗ
Famous watering-hole in a picturesque location. Four drinking areas, including a genuine public bar. No food sun or Mon eves. Wheelchair WC.
Q ❀ ⓓ 🍴 ⍑ ⊖

Try also: Holly Bush, Holly Mount (Allied Domecq)

NW5: KENTISH TOWN

PINEAPPLE
51 Leverton St ☎ (0171) 209 4961
12.30-11; 12-10.30 Sun
Greene King IPA; Marston's Pedigree; Theakston Best Bitter Ⓗ

Cosy, Victorian back-street local with a loyal following. Occasional quiz nights and banjo music. Note the magnificent Bass brewery mirror above the fireplace.
≠ ⊖ ♣

NW7: MILL HILL

Rising Sun
137 Marsh Lane
☎ (0181) 959 3755
12-3, 5.30-11; 12-3, 7-10.30 Sun
Ind Coope Burton Ale; Young's Bitter; guest beer H
Historic country pub of character, which was once owned by colonial administrator and London Zoo founder Sir Stamford Raffles. Unusual raised snug, a small bar area and a saloon with an additional lounge open at busy times. Outside toilets.
Q ❀ ◑ ♣ P

NW8: ST JOHN'S WOOD

Clifton
96 Clifton Hill
☎ (0171) 624 5233
11-11; 12-10.30 Sun
Adnams Bitter; Greene King Abbot; Marston's Pedigree; Tetley Bitter; guest beers H
Exquisite alcoved pub hidden in an opulent Abbey Road side-street. However, this is a cosmopolitan establishment serving a changing range of fine guest beers. It has an almost rural atmosphere and a fine range of food (meals finish 6pm on Sun).
Q ♨ ❀ ◑ ◗

NW10: HARLESDEN

Grand Junction Arms
Acton Lane
☎ (0181) 965 5670
11-11 (midnight Tue-Thu); 12-1am Fri & Sat; 12-10.30 Sun
Young's Bitter, Special H
Spacious, three-bar pub with moorings on the Grand Union canal. Late opening only in the canalside bar, with no entry after 10.30. Live music Fri.
❀ ◑ ◗ ⊟ ♣ P

NW11: GOLDERS GREEN

White Swan
243 Golders Green Road
☎ (0181) 458 2036
11-11; 12-10.30 Sun
Ind Coope Burton Ale; Marston's Pedigree; Tetley Bitter; guest beers H
Friendly, largely unspoilt local in a sparsely pubbed area. The secluded garden houses ducks and hens. Home-cooked food. Pool room/function room.
❀ ◑ ◗ ⊖ (Brent Cross) ♣

EDGWARE

Change of Hart
21 High Street
☎ (0181) 952 0039
11-11; 12-10.30 Sun
Marston's Pedigree; Tetley Bitter; guest beers H
Formerly known as the White Hart, this pub sits adjacent to the Dean's Brook. There is parking and a garden at the back. Inside, there is an island-type bar with three areas to drink and eat in. Food available until 9pm (weekdays), 12-5 Sat.
Q ❀ ◑ ◗ ♿ ⊖ P

Try also: Blacking Bottle, High St (Wetherspoons)

HARROW WEALD

Seven Balls
749 Kenton Lane
☎ (0181) 954 0261
11-11; 12-10.30 Sun
Benskins BB; Morland Old Speckled Hen; Tetley Bitter; guest beer H
Recently rebadged as a 'Feasting Fox', thankfully this characterful old coaching inn has lost none of its charm. The guest beer is usually from the Tapster's Choice range.
❀ ◑ ◗ ⊟ ♣ P

HATCH END

Moon & Sixpence
250 Uxbridge Road
☎ (0181) 420 1074
11-11; 12-10.30 Sun
Courage Directors; Fuller's London Pride; Theakston Best Bitter; Younger Scotch; guest beers H
Wetherspoonsconversion of a former bank that enjoys a real pub atmosphere. Outside there is a pleasant garden.
Q ❀ ◑ ◗ ≠ ⚟ ⊓

PINNER

Queens Head
31 High Street
☎ (0181) 866 4607
11-3.30, 5-11; 12-3.30, 7-10.30 Sun
Benskins BB; Ind Coope Burton Ale; Tetley Bitter; Young's Special; guest beer H
This is Grade II listed building and Pinner's oldest inn, dating from 1540, although an alehouse is believed to have offered refreshment on this site to patrons of the first Pinner Fair in 1336. Inside it proves to be a lovely, wood-beamed pub. Well worth a visit.
♛ Q ❀ ◑ ◗ P ⚟

Try also: Oddfellows, 2 Waxwell Lane (Carlsberg-Tetley)

SOUTH HARROW

Fornax & Firkin
South Hill Avenue
☎ (0181) 422 0505
11-11; 12-10.30 Sun
Firkin Starbright, Fornax, Golden Glory, Dogbolter; guest beer H
Large one-bar pub previously known as the Constellation (Fornax means a constellation of seven stars). Popular with students; live rock music Tue, Thu and Sat. Disco Fri (late licence Thu-Sat).
❀ ◑ ♿ ⊖ ♣ ⌓ P ⚟

STANMORE

Malthouse
7 Stanmore Hill
☎ (0181) 420 7265
11-11; 12-10.30 Sun
Boddingtons Bitter; guest beers H
Easily the area's most enterprising pub; community oriented, there's always something happening. An entertainment licence means the pub is regularly open late Fri and Sat but arrive before 10. ❀ ◑ ⊖ ♣

WEALDSTONE

Royal Oak
60 Peel Road
☎ (0181) 427 3122
11-11; 12-10.30 Sun
Ind Coope Burton Ale; Tetley Bitter; guest beers H
Now cut off from the town by the new road system, this airy and comfortable 1930s pub has a pleasant conservatory. Guest beers are often from Adnams. Limited parking.
❀ ◑ ⊟ ≠ (Harrow & Wealdstone) ⊖ ♣ P

Sarsen Stone
32 High Street
☎ (0181) 863 8533
11-11; 12-10.30 Sun
Courage Directors; Fuller's London Pride; Theakston Best Bitter; Younger Scotch; guest beer H
Long, narrow, Wetherspoons pub. A haven from the town's much maligned road system. Occasional beer festivals.
Q ◑ ◗ ≠ (Harrow & Wealdstone) ⊖ ⚟ ⊓

South-East London

SE1: BANKSIDE

FOUNDERS ARMS
52 Hopton Street
☎(0171) 928 1899
11-11; 12-10.30 Sun
Young's Bitter, Special, seasonal beers Ⓗ
Purpose-built, city pub with impressive views over the River Thames to St Paul's and the City. The pub is on the Thames Walk close to Blackfriars Bridge and the Globe Theatre.
❀ ◖ ▶ ≉ (Blackfriars)

SE1: BOROUGH

GEORGE INN
77 Borough High Street
☎(0171) 407 2056
11-11; 11-10.30 Sun
Boddingtons Bitter; Flowers Original; Fuller's London Pride; Greene King Abbot; Morland Old Speckled Hen; Wadworth 6X; guest beers Ⓗ
Impressive 17th-century coaching inn owned by the National Trust, popular with tourists and the local business community. Restaurant open Mon-Fri lunch, Wed-Fri eve. Beer is expensive; monthly beer festivals.
Q ❀ ◖ ▶ ≉ (London Bridge) ⊖

GLOBE
8 Bedale Street
☎(0171) 407 0043
11-11; closed Sat & Sun
Ward's Best Bitter; guest beers Ⓗ
Revitalised pub in the middle of Borough market, popular with surrounding office workers, offering a selection of real ales. Often used as a film set because of its atmosphere and Victorian-looking interior.Q ♣

ROYAL OAK
44 Tabard Street
☎(0171) 357 7173
11-11; closed Sat & Sun
Harveys Mild, Pale Ale, BB, Armada, seasonal beers Ⓗ
Harvey's first London pub opened in August 1997 following a major refurbishment. Excellent home-cooked food available throughout the day, starting with breakfast from 8am.
Q ◖ ▶ ≉ (London Bridge) ⊖

SHIPWRIGHTS ARMS
88 Tooley Street
☎(0171) 378 1486
11-11; 12-10.30 Sun
Beer range varies Ⓗ
This pub has been given a new lease of life by its current tenants; a true free house with regularly changing ales. The function

room offers fantastic views of Tower Bridge. Note the tiled mural by the bar.
◖ ≉ (London Bridge) ⊖

WHEATSHEAF
6 Stoney Street
☎ (0171) 407 1514
11-11; 12-3 Sun
Courage Best Bitter, seasonal beers; guest beers Ⓗ
Excellent two-bar pub on Borough market, currently under threat of closure due to railway track widening. A dark beer is usually available and real cider is sold occasionally.
◖ ≉ (London Bridge) ⊖ ⌂

SE1: SOUTHWARK

SHIP
68 Borough Road
☎ (0171) 403 7059
11-11; 12-3, 8-10.30 Sun
Fuller's Chiswick, London Pride, ESB, seasonal beers Ⓗ
This long, narrow pub has a distinctly nautical flavour. It is frequented by office workers and local residents. No food Sun eve.
❀ ◖ ▶ ≉ (London Bridge) ⊖

SE3: BLACKHEATH

BITTER EXPERIENCE
129 Lee Road
☎ (0181) 852 8819
11-9.30 (10 Fri); 10-10 Sat; 12-3, 7-9 Sun
Beer range varies Ⓖ
Well-established, very friendly independent off-licence, which always has a choice of at least five real ales, plus an extensive range of British and imported bottled beers. Very helpful staff.
≉ (Lee)

HARE & BILLET
Hare & Billet Road
☎ (0181) 852 2352
11-11; 12-10.30 Sun
Adnams Bitter; Boddingtons Bitter; Flowers Original; Whitbread Abroad Cooper, Fuggles IPA Ⓗ **; guest beers** ⒽⒼ
Busy, long-standing theme pub; an original Hogshead Ale House that has retained its charm. Reasonably priced food; draught Belgian beers. Well worth a visit.
Q ◖ ≉

SE4: CROFTON PARK

BROCKLEY JACK
410 Brockley Road
☎ (0181) 699 3966
12-11; 12-10.30 Sun
Greene King Abbot, IPA; guest beers Ⓗ
Former Courage pub adorned with bric-à-brac around the windows; wall and ceiling mirrors give the pub an open look. A

fringe theatre is situated at the side and it can be very busy at show times. ◖ ▶ ≉ ♣

SE5: CAMBERWELL

FOX ON THE HILL
149 Denmark Hill
☎ (0171) 738 4756
11-11; 12-10.30 Sun
Courage Directors; Shepherd Neame Bishops Finger; Theakston Best Bitter; Younger Scotch; guest beers Ⓗ
Large converted manor house, opposite Kings College Hospital. Food available all day until an hour before closing.
Q ❀ ♿ ▲ ≉ (Denmark Hill) ⌂ P ⚲ 🖙

SE6: CATFORD

RUTLAND ARMS
55 Perry Hill
☎ (0181) 291 9426
11-11; 12-10.30 Sun
Adnams Broadside; Draught Bass; Fuller's London Pride; Young's Bitter, Special, Winter Warmer Ⓗ
Unpretentious pub with a plain but spacious interior. Live jazz or R & B most nights. ◖ ♣

SE8: DEPTFORD

CRYSTAL PALACE TAVERN
105-107 Tanners Hill
☎ (0181) 692 0682
4-11; 1pm-2am Fri; 12-2am Sat; 12-10.30 Sun
Beer range varies Ⓗ
Lively pub, a treat for those seeking new and rare beers (nine handpumps). Live music Fri and Sat eves make this a popular choice for locals too. Belgian Beer Club meets monthly. Barbecues in the garden. Eve meals weekends.
🛏 ❀ ▶ ≉ (New Cross) ⊖ ♣ ⌂ 🖙

DOG & BELL
116 Prince Street
☎ (0181) 692 5664
11.30-11; 12-10.30 Sun
Fuller's London Pride, ESB, seasonal beers; guest beers Ⓗ
A warm welcome is assured at this excellent, small, back-street local, SE London CAMRA *Pub of the Year* 1993 and '96. Good food (weekdays) and a selection of malt whiskies. Occasional live music and regular quiz Sun eve.
🛏 ❀ ◖ ≉ ♣

OLD MANOR HOUSE
58 Bush Rd ☎ (0171) 394 0841
12-11; 11-11 Sat; 12-10.30 Sun
Young's Bitter, guest beers Ⓗ
A small, wedge-shaped bar makes this pub an excellent local serving the modern Surrey Quays area. ◖ ⊖ (Surrey Quays) ♣

SE9: ELTHAM

HOWERD CLUB
447 Rochester Way
☎ (0181) 856 7212
12-3 (not Mon-Fri), 7.30-11; 12-2.30, 7.30-10.30 Sun
Fuller's London Pride; Shepherd Neame Master Brew Bitter; guest beers H
Good community centre attached to St Barnabas Church Hall, named after Frankie Howerd who grew up locally. CAMRA National *Club of the Year* 1996. A warm welcome for all visitors; well worth finding.
Q ☆ ও ≠

SE10: GREENWICH

ASHBURNHAM ARMS
25 Ashburnham Grove
☎ (0181) 692 2007
11-3, 6-11; 12-3, 7-10.30 Sun
Shepherd Neame Best Bitter, Master Brew Bitter, Spitfire, seasonal beers H
Outstanding Shep's pub, London CAMRA *Pub of the Year* 1996. Excellent food (a recent winner of Shepherd Neame's *Community Food Pub of the Year*). Eve meals Tue & Fri.
☆ ◖ ≠

TRAFALGAR TAVERN
Park Row
☎ (0181) 858 2437
11-11; 12-10.30 sun
Courage Best Bitter, Directors; guest beer H
Large, multi-roomed pub on the riverside. Close to the Naval College. *Evening Standard Pub of the Year* 1996. Good quality food; live jazz Fri, Sat and Mon.
☆ ◖ ▶

SE13: LEWISHAM

HOGSHEAD
354 Lewisham High Street
☎ (0181) 690 2054
11-11; 12-10.30 Sun
Boddingtons Bitter; Whitbread Fuggles IPA; guest beers H
Small, busy pub close to Lewisham Hospital. Popular with locals. No food Sun.
☆ ◖ ≠ (Ladywell) ♣ ▭

WATCH HOUSE
198-204 Lewisham High Street
☎ (0181) 318 3136
11-11; 12-10.30 Sun
Courage Best Bitter, Directors; Fuller's London Pride; Theakston Best Bitter; guest beers H
Large, new Wetherspoons pub in former shop premises. Named after Watch House Green which used to be nearby. Wheelchair WC.
☆ ◖ ▶ ও ≠ (Ladywell/Lewisham) ✂ ▤

SE17: WALWORTH

BEEHIVE
60-62 Carter Street
☎ (0171) 703 4992
11-11; 12-10.30 Sun
Courage Best Bitter, Directors; Fuller's London Pride; Wadworth 6X; guest beers (summer) H
Very welcoming, back-street gem, just off the Walworth Road. This pub has everything for the drinker: over 50 whiskies, plus an extensive range of spirits and wines, and guest ales in summer. Don't miss the chamber pots on the ceiling. Food is available 12-10.
☆ ◖ ▶

SE18: WOOLWICH

PRINCE ALBERT (ROSE'S)
49 Hare Street
☎ (0181) 854 1538
Beer range varies H
Located in the town centre, this popular pub has a good range of real ales, and is a favourite with the locals.
◖ ≠ (Arsenal/Dockyard)

SE19: CRYSTAL PALACE

RAILWAY BELL
14 Cawnpore Street
☎ (0181) 670 2844
12-11; 12-10.30 Sun
Young's Bitter, Special, seasonal beers H
A delightful, cosy, friendly pub. An award-winning garden increases its popularity for locals.
☆ ◖ ≠ (Gypsy Hill) ♣

SE20: PENGE

MAPLE TREE
52-54 Maple Road
☎ (0181) 778 8701
11-11; 12-10.30 Sun
Fuller's London Pride; Shepherd Neame Master Brew Bitter; Young's Bitter, Special H
In a road once famed for its pub crawl, the Maple Tree has stylish decor and a large, pull-down screen for TV sports fans. No food Sun.
☆ ◖ ⊞ ≠ (Penge W/Anerley)

MOON & STARS
164-166 High Street
☎ (0181) 776 5680
11-11; 12-10.30 Sun
Courage Directors; Fuller's London Pride; Theakston Best Bitter; guest beers H
Large, busy Wetherspoons pub, popular with locals.
Q ☆ ◖ ▶ ও ≠ (Kent House/Penge E) ▭ P ✂ ▤

SE22: EAST DULWICH

CRYSTAL PALACE TAVERN
193 Crystal Palace Road
☎ (0181) 693 4968
11-11; 12-10.30 Sun
Marston's Pedigree; Ind Coope Burton Ale; Tetley Bitter; guest beer H
Friendly, two-bar local which uses the Tapster's Choice guest list extensively. Retains many of its original Victorian architectural features. ⚒ Q ⊞ ও ♣ P

SE23: FOREST HILL

BIRD IN HAND
35 Dartmouth Road
☎ (0181) 699 7417
11-11; 12-10.30 Sun
Courage Directors; Hop Back Summer Lightning; Theakston Best Bitter; Younger Scotch; guest beers H
Medium-sized Wetherspoons pub in former Charrington premises. Regular beer festivals. Good value food and beer. Pavement drinking area.
☆ ◖ ▶ ≠ ✂ ▤

SE24: HERNE HILL

LORD STANLEY
31 Hinton Road
12-11; 12-3, 7-10.30 Sun
Courage Best Bitter; Fuller's London Pride; guest beers H
Good value, friendly free house in an area not noted for real ale. Licence plates from almost every US state are displayed; also large collection of teapots. Good value meals at all times.
Q ☆ ◖ ▶ ⊞ ≠ (Loughborough Jct) ♣

SE25: SOUTH NORWOOD

ALLIANCE
91 High Street (A213)
☎ (0181) 653 3604
11-11; 12-10.30 Sun
Courage Best Bitter, Directors; guest beers H
Small, street-corner pub facing the clock tower, with brass and copper artefacts hanging from the ceiling, and pictures around the walls.
◖ ≠ (Norwood Jct) ♣

CLIFTON ARMS
21 Clifton Road
☎ (0181) 771 2443
12 (11 Sat)-11; 12-10.30 Sun
Adnams Bitter; Fuller's London Pride; Ind Coope Burton Ale; guest beers H
Small, popular, real ale pub close to Selhurst Park, hence gets busy before a match. Barbecues in summer; annual beer festival. Weekday meals.
☆ ◖ ≠ (Selhurst/Norwood Jct)

GOAT HOUSE
2 Penge Road
11-11; 12-10.30 Sun
Fuller's Chiswick, London Pride, ESB, seasonal beers; guest beers H
Friendly, spacious, Fuller's pub which has been renovated in Victorian style. The focus tends to be on entertainment (such as karaoke, live bands, quiz league), but has suitable seating for privacy. The food is excellent value (most meals are priced under £5). There is also a pool/darts area.
🏚 🕸 ◖ 🌓 ⇌ (Norwood Jct) ♣ P

PORTMANOR
1 Portland Road (A215)
☎ (0181) 655 1308
11-11; 12-10.30 Sun
Fuller's London Pride; Greene King Abbot; guest beers H
One-bar pub, which has been recently refurbished, and which also includes an upstairs restaurant and balcony. The guest beers come from small breweries and are served at a good price. Note the stained glass windows of Adam and Eve. No food Sun eve.
🕸 ◖ 🌓 ⇌ (Norwood Jct)

SE26: SYDENHAM

DULWICH WOOD HOUSE
39 Sydenham Hill
☎ (0181) 693 5666
11-11; 12-10.30 Sun
Young's Bitter, Special, seasonal beers H
Large single-bar pub with a garden bar in summer (children welcome).
🏚 Q ◖ 🌓 ⇌ (Sydenham Hill) P

SE27: WEST NORWOOD

HOPE TAVERN
49 Norwood High Street (off A215)
☎ (0181) 670 2035
11-11; 12-10.30 Sun
Young's Bitter, Special, seasonal beers H
Small, friendly, back-street local with a loyal following.
🕸 ◖ ⇌ ♣

SE27: DULWICH VILLAGE

CROWN & GREYHOUND
Dulwich Village Road
☎ (0181) 693 2466
11-11; 12-30-11 Sun
Ind Coope Burton Ale; Tetley Bitter; Young's Bitter H
Grand building in upper Dulwich Village: a circular bar and a quaint restaurant.
🏚 ◖ 🌓 & ⇌ P ✂

ADDISCOMBE

BUILDERS ARMS
65 Leslie Park Road (off A222)
☎ (0181) 654 1803
12-11; 12-10.30 Sun
Fuller's Chiswick, London Pride, ESB, seasonal beers H
Within easy walking distance of East Croydon station, this comfortably furnished, friendly local serves excellent ale. Home-cooked food (eves until 8.30 not Sat or Sun). CAMRA Croydon *Pub of the Year* 1996 and '97.
🏚 Q 🕸 ◖ 🌓 ⇌ (E Croydon) ♣

CLARET FREE HOUSE
5a Bingham Corner, Lower Addiscombe Road (A222)
☎ (0181) 656 7452
11.30-11; 12-10.30 Sun
Palmers IPA; Shepherd Neame Best Bitter; guest beers H
Small paned windows and a timbered interior combine to give this former shop an effective pub feel. The name relates to a period as a wine bar, but malt and hops matter now. Normally three guest beers from small and independent brewers.

BECKENHAM

JOLLY WOODMAN
9 Chancery Lane (off A222)
☎ (0181) 650 3664
11-11; 12-10.30 Sun
Draught Bass; Fuller's London Pride; guest beers H
A popular country-style pub, just outside the centre of Beckenham.
Q 🕸 ◖ ⇌ (Beckenham Jct) ♣

BEXLEY

CORK & CASK (OFF-LICENCE)
3 Bourne Parade, Bourne Road
☎ (01322) 528884
11-2, 4-10; 10-10 Sat; 12-3, 7-10 Sun
Beer range varies G
Off-licence which usually has five real ales and two real ciders available, plus an excellent range of British and foreign bottled beers. Over 400 different real ales sold in three years. Containers sold.
⇌ ◇

KINGS HEAD
65 Bexley High Street
☎ (01322) 526112
11-11; 11-4, 6-11 Sat; 12-4, 7-10.30 Sun
Courage Best Bitter; Greene King IPA, Abbot H
Historic, 16th-century timber framed building with genuine oak beams, in the heart of old Bexley village. A very popular, welcoming pub. Forecourt tables.
🕸 ◖ 🌓 ⇌ P

BEXLEYHEATH

ROBIN HOOD & LITTLE JOHN
78 Lion Road
☎ (0181) 303 1128
11-11; 12-10.30 Sun
Burtonwood Bitter; Courage Best Bitter; Flagship Friggin in the Riggin; Fuller's London Pride; Shepherd Neame Spitfire; guest beers H
Popular, two-bar, back-street local; the tables are made from old Singer sewing machines. Over 21s only. No food Sun.
🏖 🕸 ◖

ROYAL OAK (POLLY CLEAN STAIRS)
Mount Road
☎ (0181) 303 4454
11-3, 6-11; 11-11 Sat; 12-3, 7-10.30 Sun
Courage Best Bitter; guest beers H
Historic building, once the Upton Village store, converted to a pub in the 1850s. Now a village-style local in a suburban residential area: a real gem. Q 🕸 P

WRONG 'UN
234-236 Broadway
☎ (0181) 298 0439
11-11; 12-10.30 Sun
Courage Directors; Fuller's London Pride; Theakston Best Bitter; guest beers H
Wetherspoons, formerly a carpet shop, named after a cricketing term (googly) complete with a life-size model of WG Grace and old local photos. Bi-annual beer festivals and a changing range of guest beers, priced very competitively by their ABV%. Wheelchair WC. Q ◖ 🌓 & ⇌ ✂ 🚻

BROMLEY

BITTER END (OFF-LICENCE)
139 Masons Hill
☎ (0181) 466 6083
12-3 (not Mon), 5-10 (9 Mon); 11-10. Sat; 12-2, 7-9 Sun
Beer range varies G
Small off-licence, offering a wide range of bottle-conditioned beers. Three cask beers and up to three farmhouse ciders usually available. ⇌ (South) ◇

BROMLEY LABOUR CLUB
HG Wells Centre, St Marks Road
☎ (0181) 460 7409
11-11; 12-10.30 Sun
Shepherd Neame Master Brew Bitter, seasonal beers; guest beers H
Popular club committed to real ale and the Labour Party; card carrying CAMRA members welcome. Guest beers alternate with seasonal beers.
🏚 ⇌ (South) ♣

RED LION
10 North Road
☎ (0181) 460 2691
11-11; 12-10.30 Sun
Adnams Broadside; Beards Best Bitter; Harveys BB; guest beers [H]
Very friendly local which retains many original features after a sympathetic refurbishment. CAMRA SE London *Pub of the Year* 1997. Meals served 11-7.
♔ ❀ ◑ ◗ ⇌ (North) ♣

BROMLEY COMMON

TWO DOVES
37 Oakley Road (off A21, Biggin Hill/Keston turn)
☎ (0181) 462 1627
12-3, 5.30-11; 12-3, 7-10.30 Sun
Courage Best Bitter; Young's Bitter; guest beers [H]
Homely pub on the edge of Keston Common and woods; a friendly welcome in comfortable surroundings. Saturday platters are very popular (booking essential), but no other meals. Bus 320 stops outside. No machines.
Q ❀ ▯

Try also: Bird in Hand, 28 Gravel Rd (Courage)

CHELSFIELD

FIVE BELLS
Church Road (1 mile from M25 jct 4)
☎ (01689) 821044
11-3, 6-11; 12-4, 7-10.30 Sun
Courage Best Bitter; guest beers [H]
Unspoilt village local with a loyal following, operating an adventurous guest ale policy. The pub has been in the same family for 65 years. Q ❀ ◑ ◗ P

CHISLEHURST

SYDNEY ARMS
Old Perry Street
☎ (0181) 467 3025
11-3, 5.30-11; 11-11 Fri & Sat; 12-10.30 Sun
Courage Best Bitter, Directors; Morland Old Speckled Hen; Wells Bombardier [H]
Welcoming family house in the popular pub area of Chislehurst. Family garden and conservatory.
Q 🐴 ❀ ◑ ◗ ♿ ♣ P 🚭

CROYDON

CRICKETERS ARMS
21 Southbridge Place
☎ (0181) 239 7059
11-11; 12-10.30 Sun
Bass Toby Cask; Fuller's London Pride; Harveys BB; guest beers [H]
Comfortable, two-bar local in the Old Town area. Popular with office workers lunchtimes, and residents eves. Stages regular community events, quizzes and fund-raising activities. The interior is rather dimly lit.
◑ ⇌ (Waddon) ♣ P

GEORGE
17-21 George Street
☎ (0181) 649 9077
11-11; 12-10.30 Sun
Courage Directors; Fuller's London Pride; Theakston Best Bitter; guest beers [H]
Wetherspoons conversion of a furniture shop with two bar areas (no smoking at the rear). Usually crowded with drinkers of all ages, it is convenient for the main shopping areas.
Q ◑ ◗ ♿ ⇌ (East/West) 🍎 🚭 ▯

PRINCESS ROYAL
22 Longley Road (off Sumner Road, A213)
☎ (0181) 240 0046
11-3, 5.30-11; 12-3, 7.30-11 Sat; 12-3, 8-10.30 Sun
Greene King XX Mild, IPA, Abbot, seasonal beers [H]
Well-refurbished back-street local which, with its small cosy bar, roaring log fire in winter and warm welcome at all times, has more of a country pub feel. Known to the locals as the 'Glue Pot'. No food Sun.
♔ Q ❀ ◑ ◗ ♣

ROYAL STANDARD
1 Sheldon Street (off High St)
☎ (0181) 688 9749
11.30-11; 12-10.30 Sun
Fuller's Chiswick, London Pride, ESB, seasonal beers [H]
Street-corner local with fine etched glass windows and a tiled exterior. Three interconnected areas - public, saloon and snug, the latter has a stone-flagged floor and serving hatch to the bar. CAMRA London *Pub of the Year* 1996.
Q ❀ ◑ ◗ ⇌ (East) ♣

CUDHAM

BLACKSMITHS ARMS
Cudham Lane
☎ (01959) 572678
11-2.30 (3 Sat), 6-11; 12-3.30, 7-10.30 Sun
Courage Best Bitter, Directors; guest beers [H]
Warm, friendly village pub whose large garden attracts families in summer (bat and trap played).
♔ ❀ ♣ P

DOWNE

GEORGE & DRAGON
26 High Street
☎ (01889) 859682
11-3, 5.30 (6 Sat)-11; 12-10.30 Sun
Draught Bass; Fuller's London Pride; Hancock's HB; guest beers (summer) [H]
Very friendly village local serving guest beers with a northern bias and a house beer brewed by Bass. Although it doesn't have a children's room there are very good facilities. The recently reopened Down House (Charles Darwin's home) is nearby.
♔ ❀ ◑ ◗ ⊟ ♣

QUEENS HEAD
25 High Street
☎ (01689) 682145
11-3, 5.30-11; 11-11 Sat; 12-10.30 Sun
Ind Coope Burton Ale; Marston's Pedigree; Tetley Bitter [H]
Two-bar village local with parts dating from 1347. It supports the village cricket team. Charles Darwin lived at nearby Down House and reputedly drank here. Board games played regularly. Excellent views of Biggin Hill airshow from the garden. Expensive.
♔ Q 🐴 ❀ ◑ ◗ ⊟ ♣ P 🚭

FOOTSCRAY

SEVEN STARS
High Street
☎ (0181) 300 2057
11-11; 12-3, 7-10.30 Sun
Bass Toby Cask, Draught Bass; guest beer [H]
16th-century pub retaining many original features.
❀ ◑

KESTON

KINGS ARMS
Leaves Green Road
☎ (01959) 572514
11-11; 12-10.30 Sun
Courage Best Bitter; Harveys BB; Theakston Best Bitter [H]
This quaint old building incorporates two cosy, adjoining bars. There is a huge garden, and meals are available 12-9 (5 on Sun).
♔ ❀ ◑ ◗ ⊟ ♿ ♣ P

CROWN
Leaves Green Road
11-11; 12-4 Sun
Shepherd Neame Master Brew Bitter, Best Bitter, Spitfire, Bishops Finger [H]
Pleasant country pub with a circular bar and a restaurant area.
🐴 ❀ ◑ ◗ ♿ P 🚭

ORPINGTON

CRICKETERS
93 Chislehurst Road
☎ (01689) 812648
11-11; 12-10.30 Sun
Adnams Broadside; guest beers [H]
Friendly urban pub with a large TV screen. A large family room takes up the rear bar area.
🐴 ❀ P

PETTS WOOD

SOVEREIGN OF THE SEAS
109-111 Queensway
(01689) 891606
11-11; 12-10.30 Sun
Courage Directors; Theakston Best Bitter; guest beers Ⓗ
Large, one-bar pub now a popular local. Friendly welcome with all the usual Wetherspoons trademarks. Wheelchair WC.
Q ⊛ ◖ ▮ ⅍ ▲ ⌒ ⅟ 🛢

PURLEY

FOXLEY HATCH
8-9 Russell Hill Parade, Russell Hill Road (A23, one-way system)
☎ (0181) 963 9307
11-11; 12-10.30 Sun
Courage Directors; Fuller's London Pride; Greene King Abbot; Theakston Best Bitter; Younger Scotch; guest beers Ⓗ
Typical Wetherspoons shop conversion: one L-shaped bar, whose walls are decorated with photos of bygone Purley and numerous paintings of foxes in the rear 'modesty snugs'. Meals served until one hour before closing. Q ◖ ▮ ⅍ ⇌ ⌒ ⅟ 🛢

SELHURST

TWO BREWERS
221 Gloucester Road (off A213)
☎ (0181) 684 3544
11-11; 12-10.30 Sun
Shepherd Neame Master Brew Bitter, Best Bitter Ⓗ
Small, low-ceilinged, welcoming, award-winning community pub. A hop bine hanging from the ceiling symbolises current Kentish ownership. Weekday lunches.
⊛ ◖ ⇌ ♣

SIDCUP

ALMA
Alma Road ☎ (0181) 300 3208
11-2.30, 5.30 (6 Sat)-11; 11-11 Fri; 12-3, 7-10.30 Sun
Courage Best Bitter; Young's Bitter, Special Ⓗ
Popular back-street local, retaining some of its Victorian-style interior. Popular early eves with commuters. Weekday meals.
Q ◖ 🍺 ⇌

THORNTON HEATH

FOUNTAIN HEAD
114 Parchmore Road (B273)
☎ (0181) 653 4025
11-11; 12-10.30 Sun
Young's Bitter, Special, seasonal beers Ⓗ
Recently modernised one-bar local catering for all. Good food (weekdays); weekly quiz; large playground for children in the garden. Games include braille playing cards. ⊛ ◖ ⇌ ♣ P

RAILWAY TELEGRAPH
19 Brigstock Road
☎ (0181) 684 5809
11-11; 12-10.30 Sun
Young's Bitter, Special, Winter Warmer Ⓗ
Street-corner pub, two minutes' from the station. Large saloon bar whose walls are covered with pictures, many from the steam era; small public bar, both with real fires. No food Sun.
♨ ◖ 🍺 ⇌ ♣

UPPER BELVEDERE

ROYAL STANDARD
39 Nuxley road
☎ (01322) 432774
11-11; 12-10.30 Sun
Draught Bass; Caledonian 80/- or Deuchars IPA; Fuller's London Pride; Harveys BB; guest beers Ⓗ
Comfortable, popular, community pub catering for all tastes. Interesting guest beers and weekday meals are served in a friendly atmosphere. Bexley CAMRA Pub of the Year 1996 and 1997.
⇥ ⊛ ◖ P

South-West London

SW1: BELGRAVIA

FOX & HOUNDS
29 Passmore Street
☎ (0171) 730 6367
11-3, 5.30-11; 12-2, 7-10.30 Sun
Young's Bitter, Special Ⓗ
Tiny, unchanging gem, recently taken over by Young's who have promised to change nothing.
Q ⊖ (Sloane Sq)

STAR TAVERN
6 Belgrave Mews West
☎ (0171) 235 3019
11.30-11; 11.30-3, 6.30-11 Sat; 12-3, 7-10.30 Sun
Fuller's Chiswick, London Pride, ESB, seasonal beers Ⓗ
Famous mews pub in Belgravia, 25 years in this Guide. Difficult to find but well worth the effort. Excellent food.
♨ Q ◖ ▮ ⊖ (Knightsbridge/ Hyde Pk Cnr)

SW1: TRAFALGAR SQUARE

LORD MOON OF THE MALL
16-18 Whitehall
☎ (0171) 839 7701
11-11; 12-10.30 Sun
Courage Directors; Fuller's London Pride; Theakston Best Bitter; guest beers Ⓗ
Large, Wetherspoons pub in old bank premises next to Whitehall Theatre. Can be very crowded at times.
Q ◖ ▮ ⅍ ⇌ (Charing Cross)
⊖ ⌒ 🛢

SW1: VICTORIA

JUGGED HARE
172 Vauxhall Bridge Road
☎ (0171) 828 1543
11-11; 12-10.30 Sun
Fuller's Chiswick, London Pride, ESB, seasonal beers; guest beers Ⓗ
Fuller's Ale and Pie House, an impressive conversion of a former bank. Two downstairs seating areas, plus an upstairs gallery decorated with old prints and paintings; a chandelier hangs from the high ceiling. Mainly business clientele.
Q ◖ ▮ ⇌ ⊖ ⅟

SW1: WESTMINSTER

BUCKINGHAM ARMS
62 Petty France
☎ (0171) 222 3386
11-11; 12-3, Sun
Young's Bitter, Special, seasonal beers Ⓗ
Large, popular pub with a corridor drinking area at the rear where children may be allowed. Has featured in all editions of this Guide. ⊖ (St James's Pk)

WESTMINSTER ARMS
9 Storeys Gate
☎ (0171) 222 8520
11-11 (8 Sat); 12-8 Sun
Draught Bass; Brakspear Bitter; Greene King Abbot; Worthington Bitter; guest beers Ⓗ
Small pub with a downstairs wine bar and an upstairs restaurant, just off Parliament Square, handy for Westminster Abbey and the Houses of Parliament. ◖ ▮ ⇌

SW2: BRIXTON

CROWN & SCEPTRE
2 Streatham Hill
☎ (0181) 671 0843
11-11; 12-10.30 Sun
Courage Directors; Fuller's London Pride; Hop Back Summer Lightning; guest beers Ⓗ
Boasting one of the largest cask beer sales in the Wetherspoons chain, this pub has more character than most, being split into different areas. Q ⊛ ◖ ▮ ⌒ ⅟ 🛢

SW3: CHELSEA

BLENHEIM
27 Cale Street
☎ (0171) 349 0056
11-11; 12-10.30 Sun
Badger IPA, Dorset Best, Tanglefoot Ⓗ
Large, roomy, one-bar pub, open plan with pine fittings and many prints. Big screen TV for sports events.
◑ ▶ ♣

CROWN
153 Dovehouse Street
☎ (0171) 352 9505
11-11; 12-10.30 Sun
Beer range varies Ⓗ
Popular community pub frequented by staff from the local hospitals. It holds weekly quizzes and raffles to support them.
◑ ⊖ (S Kensington) ⛨

QUEENS'S HEAD
25-27 Tryon Street
☎ (0171) 589 0262
11-11; 12-10.30 Sun
Courage Best Bitter, Directors Ⓗ
One of London's longest established gay pubs: a quieter snug bar to the front attracts a more mixed straight/gay local clientele. This traditional three-bar pub serves good value bar meals and snacks. Busy Sun. Pavement tables.
🚠 ❀ ◑ ▶ 🍴 ⅙ ⊖ (Sloane Sq)

SW4: CLAPHAM

BREAD & ROSES
68 Clapham Manor Street
☎ (0171) 498 1779
11-11; 12-10.30 Sun
Adnams Bitter; guest beers Ⓗ
This modern, open-plan pub has shown the way for others to follow: a clutter-free environment which has now a joint CAMRA/English Heritage award for *Best Pub Design*. The Workers Ale house beer is brewed by Smiles. (See the article in the front of this *Guide*.)
🚠 ❀ ◑ ▶ ⇌ (High St)
⊖ (North)

SW6: PARSONS GREEN

DUKE OF CUMBERLAND
235 New Kings Road
☎ (0171) 736 2777
11-11; 12-10.30 Sun
Young's Bitter, Special, seasonal beers Ⓗ
Large, airy pub with attractive wood and tilework. ◑ ▶ ⊖

WHITE HORSE
1 Parsons Green
☎ (0171 736 2115
11-11; 12-10.30 Sun
Draught Bass; Highgate Dark; guest beers Ⓗ
Large, upmarket pub facing the green with an outside terrace. It hosts many beer festivals and tastings and stocks all available Trappist bottled beers.
🚠 ◑ ▶ ⊖

SW7: SOUTH KENSINGTON

ANGLESEA ARMS
15 Selwood Terrace
☎ (0171) 373 7960
11-11; 12-10.30 Sun
Adnams Broadside; Brakspear Bitter, Special; Fuller's London Pride; Wadworth 6X; Young's Special Ⓗ
Two-level, upmarket pub just off Fulham Road, in this *Guide* for many years. Charles Dickens and DH Lawrence lived nearby.
◑ ▶ ⊖

SW8: BATTERSEA

BRITISH LION
137 Thessaly Road
☎ (0171) 498 3648
11.30 (11 Sat)-11; 12-10.30 Sun
Courage Best Bitter Ⓗ
Listed original Victorian frontage and an ornate bar back add dignity and charm to this established haven for locals. Attentive staff are happy to adjust or remove sparklers.
❀ ⇌ (Wandsworth Rd) ♣ ⅙

SW8: SOUTH LAMBETH

MAWBEY ARMS
7 Mawbey Street
☎ (0171) 622 1936
11-11; 12-10.30 Sun
Shepherd Neame Master Brew Bitter, Spitfire Ⓗ
Handsomely refurbished, listed pub in a quiet cul-de-sac. All are welcome in the single, spacious bar, partitioned into three drinking areas. Good food is especially popular Sun lunch; booking advisable eves.
❀ ◑ ▶ ⊖ (Stockwell) ♣

PRIORY ARMS
83 Lansdowne Way
☎ (0171) 622 1884
11-11; 12-10.30 Sun
Harveys BB; Young's Bitter, Special; guest beers Ⓗ
Grade II listed building with a classic South London pub exterior and refurbished interior. Two guest beers change frequently (there have been over 1,000 to date); and German and other bottled beers are stocked. Sky TV for sport. Three times SW London CAMRA *Pub of the Year*.
❀ ◑ ⊖ (Stockwell) ♣ ⌣

The Buckingham Arms receives a plaque for being one of the select band of pubs which have been in the Good Guide for 25 years (this edition marks its 26th appearance). The award was presented by Sarah Porter, CAMRA regional director for Greater London.

SURPRISE
16 Southville
☎ (0171) 622 4623
11-11; 12-10.30 sun
Young's Bitter, Special, Winter Warmer H
Small gem, tucked away next to Larkhall Park with a large outdoor patio. A surprise indeed to find such a haven so near the bustle of the Wandsworth Road.
🏨 Q 🕮 🕭 ▶ ⊖ (Stockwell) ♣

SW9: BRIXTON

BEEHIVE
407 Brixton Road
☎ (0171) 738 3643
11-11; 12-10.30 Sun
Adnams Extra; Courage Directors; Hop Back Summer Lightning; Theakston Best Bitter; guest beers H
Lively Wetherspoons pub, a former shoe shop, in the centre of Brixton and handy for public transport. A beacon for real ale in the area.
Q 🕭 ▶ ⇌ ⊖ ⌣ ✂ 🖿

SW10: WEST CHELSEA

FINCH'S
190 Fulham Road
☎ (0171) 351 5043
11-11; 12-10.30 Sun
Young's Bitter, Special, seasonal beers H
Busy pub with much original wood and tilework; note the circular window declaring stout, Burton and bitter at 2d a glass. Originally the Kings Arms, but was known as Finch's and this name stuck. 🕭

SW11: BATTERSEA

EAGLE (ALE HOUSE)
104 Chatham Road
☎ (0171) 228 2328
11-11; 11-10.30 Sun
Boddingtons Bitter; Flowers Original; guest beers H
Local which often runs beer festivals and promotions. Well worth a visit. 🕮 ⇌

FOX & HOUNDS
66 Latchmere Road
11-11; 12-10.30 Sun
Draught Bass; Fuller's London Pride; Highgate Saddlers P H
Recently remodernised to one bar, to make more room, also redecorated to make it a more updated family pub. Good atmosphere.
🕮 ⇌ (Clapham Jct) ♣

SW11: CLAPHAM JUNCTION

BEEHIVE
197 St Johns Hill
☎ (0171) 207 1267
11-11; 12-10.30 Sun

Fuller's Chiswick, London Pride, ESB, seasonal beers H
Small, one-bar local, twice SW London CAMRA *Pub of the Year*.
🕭 ⇌

SW12: BALHAM

GROVE
39 Oldridge Road
☎ (0181) 673 6531
11-11; 12-10.30 Sun
Young's Bitter, Special H
Large, Victorian, two-bar pub which is not as well used as it deserves to be. Vast saloon bar. Pavement tables.
Q 🕮 🕮 ⇌ ⊖ (Clapham S) ♣

MOON UNDER WATER
194 Balham High Road
☎ (0181) 673 0535
11-11; 12-10.30 Sun
Courage Directors; Greene King IPA; Hop Back Summer Lightning; Theakston Best Bitter; guest beers H
Good, down-to-earth Balham boozer with friendly service and a quieter section towards the rear (no-smoking).
Q 🕭 ▶ ⇌ ⊖ ⌣ ✂ 🖿

SW13: BARNES

COACH & HORSES
27 Barnes High Street
☎ (0181) 876 2695
11-11; 12-10.30 Sun
Young's Bitter, Special, Winter Warmer H
Cosy, welcoming, conversational local with interesting etched glass. The large garden includes a children's play area.
🏨 Q 🕮 🕭 ⇌ (Barnes Bridge) ♣

SW14: MORTLAKE

HARE & HOUNDS
216 Upper Richmond Road
☎ (0181) 876 4304
11-11; 12-10.30 Sun
Young's Bitter, Special, Winter Warmer H
Comfortable, roomy pub: the oak-panelled lounge has a pleasant atmosphere; part of the bar is set aside for snooker. A large walled garden provides a children's play area and hosts barbecues. Wide choice of good value food. 🏨 Q 🕮 🕭 ▶ ⇌

SW15: PUTNEY

SPOTTED HORSE
120-122 Putney High Street
☎ (0181) 288 0246
11-11; 12-10.30 Sun
Young's Bitter, Special, seasonal beers H
Large, busy pub located at the heart of Putney's shopping area. Often an oasis of calm behind its listed frontage. Pictures of old

Putney adorn the walls. No meals Sun eve.
🕭 ▶ ⇌ ⊖ (Putney Bridge) ♣

SW16: STREATHAM COMMON

PIED BULL
498 Streatham High Road
☎ (0181) 764 4003
11-11; 12-10.30 Sun
Young's Bitter, Special, seasonal beers H
An ideal resting place for weary shoppers from the vast nearby superstore. Still the best bet in the area, despite an increase of rival pub chain outlets.
Q 🕮 🕭 ▶ 🕮 ⇌ (Common)

SW17: TOOTING

CASTLE
38 Tooting High Street
☎ (0181) 672 7018
11-11; 12-10.30 Sun
Young's Bitter, Special, Winter Warmer H
Large, single-bar pub; a calm oasis by a busy crossroads.
🏨 Q 🕮 🕭 ♿ ⊖ (Broadway) P

JJ MOONS
56a Tooting High Street
☎ (0181) 672 4726
11-11; 12-10.30 Sun
Courage Directors; Fuller's London Pride; Hop Back Summer Lightning; Theakston Best Bitter; guest beer H
One-bar pub which is deceptively long. Very busy at all times: move to the rear for a quieter drink.
Q 🕭 ▶ ⊖ (Broadway) ⌣ ✂ 🖿

PRINCE OF WALES
646 Garratt Lane
☎ (0181) 946 2628
11-11; 12-4, 7-10.30 Sun
Young's Bitter, Special H
Large, tiled-front, corner pub on a busy roundabout; spacious and comfortable, built in 1898 on the site of the Surrey Iron Railway. At weekends it is very much a busy local. Seafood stall outside.
🏨 🚲 🕮 🕭 🕮 ♣ P

SW18: WANDSWORTH

GRAPES
39 Fairfield Street
☎ (0181) 877 0756
11-11; 12-4.30, 7-10.30 Sun
Young's Bitter, Special H
Curtains and carpets make this a comfortable, homely little pub.
🕮 🕭 ⇌ (Town) ♣

OLD SERGEANT
104 Garratt Lane
☎ (0181) 874 4099
11-11; 12-10.30 Sun
Young's Bitter, Special H
Comfortable, cosy, two-bar pub, bought from Earl Spencer in 1857. Weekday lunches. 🕭 🕮 ♣

QUEEN ADELAIDE
35 Putney Bridge Road
☎ (0181) 874 1695
11-11; 12-10.30 Sun
Young's Bitter, Special, seasonal beers ⓗ
Quiet local on the main road, close to Young's Wandsworth HQ and is often used by the company to try out new cask brews. Mementos of Queen Adelaide adorn the walls; always worth a visit for the lovely interior and garden.
 Q ❀ ♣ ♣

SPOTTED DOG
72 Garratt Lane
☎ (0181) 875 9531
11-11; 12-10.30 Sun
Courage Directors; Hop Back Summer Lightning; Theakston Best, XB; guest beers ⓗ
Wetherspoons refurbishment of a locals' favourite. An enterprising guest beer policy means there is always something interesting to try. Guests are often themed according to the time of year – Christmas is especially eccentric! Occasional cider.
❀ ◑ ▶ ⌂ ⍾

SW19: MERTON

PRINCESS OF WALES
98 Morden Road, Wimbledon
☎ (0181) 542 0573
11-3, 5-11; 11-11 Fri & Sat; 12-10.30 Sun
Young's Bitter, Special, seasonal beers ⓗ
Mid-19th-century building with an unspoilt frontage. Renamed after it was saved from demolition in 1997 following a campaign by locals and CAMRA. Sky TV for sports. Twinned with the Horse Brass pub, Portland, Oregon.
🚶 ❀ ◑ ▶ ⊞ ⊖ (S Wimbledon) ♣ P

PRINCESS ROYAL
25 Abbey Road
☎ (0181) 542 3273
11-3, 5.30-11; 11-11 Fri & Sat; 12-4, 7-10.30 Sun
Courage Best Bitter, Directors; Fuller's London Pride; guest beer ⓗ
Gem of an early 19th-century corner local: two attractively decorated bars with a large secluded patio extending behind. Televised football is popular with the friendly local clientele.
Q ❀ ◑ ▶ ⊞ ⊖ (S Wimbledon) ♣

SW19: SOUTH WIMBLEDON

SULTAN
78 Norman Road
☎ (0181) 542 4532
12-11; 12-4, 7-10.30 (12-10.30 summer) Sun

Hop Back GFB, Crop Circle, Entire Stout, Summer Lightning, Thunderstorm ⓗ
A Hop Back pub since 1994; a well-preserved 1950s building on the site of a bombed original, named after a racehorse. An attractive patio adjoins the wood-panelled main bar; the Ted Higgins Bar is normally quiet. Occasional beer festivals.
Q ❀ ♿ ⍾ ⊖ ♣ P

SW19: WIMBLEDON

HAND IN HAND
6 Crooked Billet
☎ (0181) 946 5720
11-11; 12-10.30 Sun
Young's Bitter, Special, seasonal beers ⓗ
Popular pub on the edge of the common: SW London CAMRA's *Pub of the Year* 1997. Comfortable alcove seating to the rear of the bar, with another room (suitable for families) at the front. Much outdoor drinking in summer. No-smoking area only until early eve.
🚶 Q ➴ ❀ ◑ ▶ ♣ ⌿

SW19: WIMBLEDON VILLAGE

ROSE & CROWN
55 High Street
☎ (0181) 947 4713
11-11; 12-10.30 Sun
Young's Bitter, Special, Winter Warmer ⓗ
Splendid building, a pub since the mid-17th century and one of the first Young's houses. Ample, yet intimate, drinking areas around one bar include a no-smoking snug. No music or fruit machines. No eve meals Fri or Sun. Over 21s only.
Q ❀ ◑ ▶ P ⌿

CARSHALTON

FOX & HOUNDS
41 High Street
☎ (0181) 773 3468
11-11; 12-4, 7-10.30 Sun
Benskins BB; Friary Meux BB; Ind Coope Burton Ale; Morland Old Speckled Hen; Wadworth 6X; guest beers ⓗ
Large roadside pub transformed into an Allied Domecq Festival Alehouse, retaining many original features. Famous for its live jazz sessions Wed eves. Fits in well in the old town area.
❀ ◑ ▶ ⍾ ♣ P

GREYHOUND HOTEL
2 High Street (A232)
☎ (0181) 647 4914
10.30-11; 12-10.30 Sun
Young's Bitter, Special, seasonal beers ⓗ
Cheerful, atmospheric 18th-century hotel overlooking

picturesque wildfowl ponds. The authentic low-ceilinged interior boasts oak carvings; large screen TV for sports and a darts room. Good selection of quality meals (no food Sun eve). No heavy workgear or boots.
Q ❀ ⋈ ◑ ▶ ⍾ ♣ P

RACEHORSE
17 West Street (off A232 near station)
☎ (0181) 647 6818
11-11; 12-4, 7-10.30 Sun
Courage Best Bitter, Directors; Gale's HSB; King & Barnes Sussex; guest beers ⓗ
Popular local offering something for everyone: the public bar for games, the saloon for food and occasional live music. The landlord also runs the nearby Windsor Castle.
Q ❀ ◑ ▶ ⍾ ♣ P

WINDSOR CASTLE
378 Carshalton Road (A232)
☎ (0181) 669 1191
11-11; 12-10.30 Sun
Draught Bass; Fuller's London Pride; Hancock's HB; Worthington Bitter; guest beers ⓗ
One-bar crossroads pub with a restaurant end. The roof beams are adorned with beer mats and pump clips showing the range of microbrewery beers that have been sold. Four-pint jugs for the price of three. CAMRA London *Pub of the Year* 1997. Annual spring beer festival. No food Sun eve when live music is staged.
❀ ◑ ▶ ♿ ⍾ (Carshalton Beeches) ♣ P

CHESSINGTON

WHITE HART
378 Hook Road (A243)
☎ (0181) 397 3257
11-3, 5-11; 11-11 Fri & Sat; 12-10.30 Sun
Courage Best Bitter, Directors; Theakston XB ⓗ
Two-bar family oriented pub. The background music in the saloon bar is unobtrusive, whilst darts and pool are played in the public bar. The large garden includes a recreation area for children. Weekday meals.
Q ❀ ◑ ⊞ ⍾ (North) P

KEW

COACH & HORSES
8 Kew Green
☎ (0181) 940 1208
11-11; 12-10.30 Sun
Young's Bitter, Special, seasonal beers ⓗ
Large, traditional pub, known locally for its food. Handy for Kew Gardens.
🚶 Q ❀ ⋈ ◑ ▶ ⍾ (Bridge) ⊖ (Gardens) P

GREYHOUND
82 Kew Green
☎ (0181) 940 0071
11.30-11; 12-10.30 Sun
Adnams Broadside; Brakspear Bitter; Courage Best Bitter; Marston's Pedigree H
Very smart, well modernised pub enjoying attractive views across Kew Green. An excellent restaurant serves a modern à la carte menu; bar snacks available.
❀ ◖ ▶ ⇌ (Bridge)

BOATERS INN
Canbury Gardens, Lower Ham Road (off A307)
☎ (0181) 541 4672
11-3, 5.30-11; 11-11 Fri, Sat & summer; 12-10.30 Sun
Draught Bass; Brakspear Bitter; Greene King IPA; guest beers H
Split-level pub with a verandah overlooking an attractive stretch of the Thames, downstream from Kingston Bridge. Dining area to the rear and an outside drinking area; it can get very busy in summer. Jazz Sun eve (free). Annual beer festival (March).
❀ ◖ ▶

BRICKLAYER ARMS
53 Hawks Road (off A2043)
☎ (0181) 546 0393
12-11; 12-10.30 Sun
Greene King Abbot; Morland Original; Ruddles Best Bitter, County H
Ex-Hodgsons pub dating back to the 1800s. Originally a farmhouse, it has a U-shaped bar: one side used for dining, the other a lounge area. Nice green garden.
❀ ◖ ▶ ⇌ (Norbiton) ♣ ⊟

CANBURY ARMS
49 Canbury Park Road
☎ (0181) 288 1882
11-11; 12-10.30 Sun
Courage Best Bitter, Directors; guest beers H
Has the feel of a rural pub in an urban setting, offering a broad mix of activities from MENSA branch quizzes to TV football; live music Fri and Sat. No food Sun (or after 8pm Sat).
❀ ◖ ⇌ ♣ ⌂ P ⊟

COCOANUT
16 Mill Street
☎ (0181) 546 3978
11-3, 5.30-11; 11-11 Sat; 12-3, 7-10.30 Sun
Fuller's Chiswick, London Pride, ESB, seasonal beers H
Large community local fielding darts and pool teams: quiz night Mon. Named after long-gone local industry. No food Sun. Limited parking. Q ❀ ◖ ♣ P

PARK TAVERN
19 New Road (close to Kingston Gate of Richmond Park)
10.30-11; 12-10.30 Sun

Brakspear Special; Young's Bitter; guest beers H
Attractive comfortable friendly local situated in a narrow residential road near Richmond Park. Local CAMRA *Pub of the Year* 1997.
♨ Q ❀ ♣

WILLOUGHBY ARMS
47 Willoughby Road
☎ (0181) 546 4236
10.30-11; 12-10.30 Sun
Flowers Original; Fuller's London Pride; Shepherd Neame Master Brew Bitter; Wadworth 6X H
Much-improved, Victorian backstreet local: two bar areas and a room for pool. A guest beer is sold at a competitive price Sun lunchtime.
❀ ♣

WYCH ELM
93 Elm Road
☎ (0181) 546 3271
11-3, 5-11; 11-11 Sat; 12-3, 7-10.30 Sun
Fuller's Chiswick, London Pride, ESB, seasonal beers H
Highly regarded pub: the saloon bar has been refurbished in keeping with its turn of the century origins; there is also a plain, neat public bar. In summer the pub front is hidden by a riot of colourful flowers; it enjoys a prize-winning garden. No food Sun.
❀ ◖ ⊡ ♣

NEW MALDEN

ROYAL OAK
Coombe Road (B283)
☎ (0181) 942 0837
11-11; 12-10.30 Sun
Adnams Bitter; Benskins BB; Ind Coope Burton Ale; Tetley Bitter; Young's Bitter; guest beer H
Large old coaching house dating back to 1867. Popular with visiting noblemen and gentry in the early 1900s. The garden was an early bowling green. It has a small public bar and large lounge divided into three areas. Recently refurbished in traditional pub style.
♨ Q ⛴ ❀ ◖ ⊡ ⇌ ♣ P ⅍

WOODIES
Thetford Road
☎ (0181) 949 5824
11-11; 12-10.30 Sun
Flowers Original; Fuller's London Pride; Young's Bitter, Special; guest beers H
Former cricket pavilion with plenty of sporting and entertainment memorabilia. Children welcome if eating (in raised area). Home to a golf society, sea angling club and a ladies dart team. Popular quiz Tue eve.
♨ Q ❀ ◖ ⅙ ♣ P

NORTH CHEAM

WETHERSPOONS
552-556 London Road
☎ (0181) 644 1808
11-11; 12-10.30 Sun
Courage Directors; Fuller's London Pride; Theakston Best Bitter; guest beers H
Small Wetherspoons with a friendly staff and a good atmosphere. Note the statue of Henry VIII whose hunting lodge stood at nearby Nonsuch Park. Guest beers come from microbreweries.
Q ◖ ▶ ⅙ ⅍ ⊟

RICHMOND

OLD SHIP
3 King Street
☎ (0181) 940 5014
11-11; 12-10.30 Sun
Young's Bitter, Special, Winter Warmer H
Attractive, cosy wood-panelled, town-centre pub with a nautical theme (two welcoming real fires on the lower deck). Wholesome food is available most hours. Look-out bar on the pleasant, spacious upper deck.
♨ ◖ ▶ ⇌ ⊖ ⅍

ORANGE TREE
45 Kew Road
☎ (0181) 940 0944
11-11; 12-10.30 Sun
Young's Bitter, Special, Winter Warmer H
Fine, popular pub in a large Victorian building with a fringe theatre upstairs and a restaurant downstairs. Good variety of excellent bar food in the lounge; No food Sun eve. Pavement drinking area.
♨ Q ❀ ◖ ▶ ⇌ ⊖

WATERMANS ARMS
12 Water Lane
☎ (0181) 940 2893
11-3, 5.30-11; 11-11 Sat; 12-3, 7-10.30 Sun
Young's Bitter, Special, seasonal beers H
Small, Victorian pub in a cobbled stone lane leading to the river, with an attractive bar in its cosy, two-room layout. Food comprises soup and sandwiches plus Sunday roasts. Try the games – Horsey-Horsey and Shut the Box.
♨ Q ❀ ⇌ ⊖ ♣

WHITE CROSS
Water Lane
☎ (0181) 940 6844
11-11; 12-10.30 Sun
Young's Bitter, Special, seasonal beers H
Extremely popular, prominent Thames-side pub in an unrivalled setting, offering excellent bar food and service. The riverside terrace bar is open in summer

and sunny winter weekends, river level permitting.

🏔 Q ☸ ◖ ⇌ ⊖ ♣

SURBITON

BLACK LION
58 Brighton Road (A243)
☎ (0181) 399 1666
11-11; 12-10.30 Sun
Young's Bitter, Special, seasonal beers H
Smart, comfortable corner pub, run by friendly staff: one bar on two levels and a raised room, formerly the public bar. Soup and snacks served.
☸ ⇌ ♣

CORONATION HALL
St Marks Hill (B3370)
☎ (0181) 390 6164
11-11; 12-10.30 Sun
Courage Directors; Fuller's London Pride; Hogs Back TEA; Theakston Best Bitter; guest beers H
Wetherspoons pub opened in September 1997, reverting to its original name (the building opened as a lecture hall on the coronation of George V). It has since been a cinema, bingo hall and health club. Food all day. Wheelchair WC.
Q ◖ ▶ ♿ ⇌ ⌂ ⅟ 🖵

WAGGON & HORSES
1 Surbiton Hill Road (A240)
11-2.30 (3 Fri), 5-11; 11-11 Sat; 12-10.30 Sun
Young's Bitter, Special, seasonal beer H
Comfortable, multi-roomed local appreciated for its traditional atmosphere and friendly welcome. 1997 British Licensed Retailers Association *Community Pub of the Year*. Good food (not served Sat). The family room is open Sun.
Q ☸ ◖ ⌑ ⇌ ♣

SUTTON

MOON ON THE HILL
5-9 Hill Road
☎ (0181) 643 1202
11-11; 12-10.30 Sun
Courage Directors; Fuller's London Pride; Greene King Abbot; Theakston Best Bitter; Younger Scotch; guest beers H
Large Wetherspoons conversion of a former shop premises, off the pedestrianised High Street.
Q ☸ ◖ ▶ ♿ ⇌ ⌂ ⅟ 🖵

NEW TOWN
7 Lind Road (off A232)
☎ (0181) 770 2072
12-3, 5-11; 11-11 Sat; 12-4, 7-10.30 Sun
Young's Bitter, Special, seasonal beers H
Named after this part of Sutton which was 'new' in about 1870, a large corner-site local east of the town centre. Expansion into an adjoining lower house has created an unusual split-level saloon. Meals include a good vegetarian choice.
☸ ◖ ▶ ⌑ ⇌ ♣

WALLINGTON

DUKE'S HEAD
6 Manor Road, The Green (off A232)
☎ (0181) 647 1595
11-11; 12-4, 7-10.30 Sun
Young's Bitter, Special, seasonal beers H
Traditional, Grade II listed pub built about 1830. It commands a fine position on Wallington Green. The small, traditional public bar has lower prices. The low-ceilinged, wood-panelled lounge has a restaurant area with waitress service (no food Sat eve or Sun).
Q ☸ ◖ ▶ ⌑ ♣ P

WHISPERING MOON
25 Ross Parade, Woodcote Road
☎ (0181) 647 7020
11-11; 12-10.30 Sun
Courage Directors; Fuller's London Pride; Theakston Best Bitter; Younger Scotch; guest beers H
Wetherspoons conversion of a former cinema. Popular with all ages and can get busy. Photographs of local historical interest decorate the bar.
Q ◖ ▶ ♿ ⇌ ⅟ 🖵

West London

W1: FITZROVIA

DUKE OF YORK
47 Rathbone Street
☎ (0171) 636 7065
11-11 (5 Sat); closed Sun
Greene King IPA; Abbot; seasonal beers H
Friendly, corner pub at the end of a pedestrianised street, near Middlesex Hospital.
◖ ⊖ (Goodge St)

GEORGE & DRAGON
151 Cleveland Street
☎ (0171) 387 1492
11-11 (6 Sat); 12-3, 7-10.30 Sun
Greene King IPA, Abbot H
Narrow corner pub.
◖ ▶ ⊖ (Gt Portland St)

JACK HORNER
236 Tottenham Court Road
☎ (0171) 636 2868
11-11; closed Sun
Fuller's Chiswick, London Pride, ESB, seasonal beers H
Fuller's Ale & Pie House; always busy and handy for the Oxford Street shops.
◖ ▶ ⊖ (Tottenham Crt Rd)

W1: MARYLEBONE

BEEHIVE
7 Homer Street
☎ (0171) 262 6851
11-3, 5.30-11; 11-11 Fri & Sat; 12-10.30 Sun
Boddingtons Bitter; Fuller's London Pride H
Small, friendly back-street pub, recently refurbished, which has featured in may editions of the this *Guide*. Licensed until 1953 as a beer house, it is one of the smallest pubs in W1.
◖ ⊖ (Edgware Rd)

CARPENTERS ARMS
12 Seymour Place
☎ (0171) 723 1050
11-11; 12-10.30 Sun
Draught Bass; Fuller's London Pride; Marston's Pedigree; Webster's Yorkshire Bitter; guest beers H
The Carpenters is reputed to have tunnels connecting to other pubs in the area. Food is served 12-5 Mon-Sat. ◖ ⊖

HARCOURT ARMS
32 Harcourt Street
☎ (0171) 723 6634
11.30-11; 12-3, 5.30-10.30 (12-10.30 summer) Sun
Adnams Bitter; Tetley Bitter; guest beer H
Friendly, wood-panelled pub with a garden – unusual for this area.
☸ ◖ ▶ ⇌ ⊖

TURNERS ARMS
26 Crawford Street
☎ (0171) 724 4504
11-11; 12-3, 7-11 Sat; 12-3, 7-10.30 Sun
Shepherd Neame Master BrewBitter, Best Bitter, Spitfire, seasonal beers H
Smallish, narrow, one-bar pub. Sky TV for sport.
◖ ▶ ⇌ ⊖ (Baker St) ♣

WARGRAVE ARMS
42 Brendon Street
☎ (0171) 723 0559
11 (12 Sat)-11; 12-10.30 Sun
Young's Bitter, Special, seasonal beers H
Long, narrow, corner pub built in 1866, an ex-Finche's house.
◖ ▶ ⇌ ⊖ (Edgware Rd)

W1: MAYFAIR

WINDMILL
6-8 Mill Street ☎ (0171) 491 8050
11-11; 12-5 Sat; closed Sun
Young's Bitter, Special, seasonal beers H
Spacious, comfortable bar with two restaurants, renowned for its steak and kidney pies.
Q ◖ ▶ ⊖ (Oxford Circus)

Try also: Guinea, Bruton Place (Young's)

W1: SOHO

BLUE POSTS
28 Rupert Street
☎ (0171) 437 1415
11.30-11; 4.30-10.30 Sun
Beer range varies Ⓗ
A wide range of interesting beers (including bottle-conditioned) is on offer at this small Hogshead pub in the heart of the West End. The upstairs bar is available at weekends.
◖ ≉ (Charing Cross)
⊖ (Piccadilly Circus)

CLACHAN
34 Kingly Street
☎ (0171) 734 2659
11-11; 11.30-11 Sat; 12-10.30 Sun
Adnams Bitter; Fuller's London Pride; Greene King IPA; Taylor Landlord; Tetley Bitter; guest beers Ⓗ
Impressive side-street pub behind Liberty's store. Its ornate Victorian decor with an island bar draws a wide range of customers. ◖ ▶ ⊖ (Oxford Circus)

DOG & DUCK
18 Bateman Street
☎ (0171) 437 4447
12-11; 6-11 Sat; 7-10.30 Sun
Taylor Landlord; Tetley Bitter; guest beers Ⓗ
Small, attractive, well-kept Nicholson's pub with Heritage Inn status. Often crowded, the upstairs bar opens eves. Note the wall tiles.
⊖ (Tottenham Ct Rd)

KINGS ARMS
23 Poland Street
☎ (0171) 734 5907
11-11; 12-10.30 Sun
Courage Directors; Theakston Best Bitter Ⓗ
Friendly, gay pub attracting mainly men. Just off Oxford Street, it is handy for good value bar meals after the shops. Quieter upstairs bar with a pool table.
◖ ▶ ⊖ (Oxford Circus)

THREE GREYHOUNDS
25 Greek Street
☎ (0171) 287 0754
11-11; 4-10.30 Sun
Adnams Bitter, seasonal beers; Marston's Pedigree; Tetley Bitter; guest beers Ⓗ
Small pub on a very busy corner. The medieval style is overlaid by a theatrical theme and it is frequented by locals as well as tourists. Q ◖ ⊖ (Leicester Sq)

W2: LITTLE VENICE

BRIDGE HOUSE
13 Westbourne Terrace Road
☎ (0171) 286 7925
11-11; 12-10.30 Sun
Draught Bass; Worthington Bitter Ⓗ

Friendly, canalside pub with a theatre upstairs.
◖ ▶ ⊖ (Warwick Ave)

W2: PADDINGTON

ARCHERY TAVERN
4 Bathurst Street
☎ (0171) 402 4916
11-11; 12-10.30 Sun
Badger IPA, Dorset Best, Tanglefoot Ⓗ
Wood-panelled pub next to a mews with working stables, the name derives from a long-gone archery ground; many prints with an archery theme adorn the walls. Large selection of board games. Gribble beers from Sussex are also stocked.
◖ ▶ ≉ ⊖ ♣

VICTORIA
10a Strathearn Place
☎ (0171) 724 1191
11 (12 Sat)-11; 12-10.30 Sun
Fuller's Chiswick, London Pride, ESB, seasonal beers Ⓗ
Ornate pub, well refurbished by Fuller's, boasting a set of magnificent etched coloured mirrors. Restaurant downstairs and a piano bar upstairs (open Fri and Sat eves). No food Sun.
◖ ▶ ≉ ⊖

W3: ACTON

DUKE OF YORK
86 Steyne Rd
☎ (0181) 992 0463
11-11; 12-10.30 Sun
Brakspear Bitter; Courage Best Bitter; Fuller's London Pride; guest beers Ⓗ
One-bar pub with a dining area. A welcoming pub to one and all, with usually two guest beers.
➤ ❀ ◖ ▶ ≉ (Central)
⊖ (Town)

W4: CHISWICK

BELL & CROWN
11-13 Thames Street, Strand on the Green
☎ (0181) 994 4164
11-11; 12-10.30 Sun
Fuller's Chiswick, London Pride, ESB, seasonal beers Ⓗ
Riverside pub with two conservatories and a riverside terrace. No food Sun eve.
Q ❀ ◖ ≉ (Kew Bridge)

GEORGE IV
185 Chiswick High Road
☎ (0181) 994 4624
11.30-11; 12-10.30 Sun
Fuller's Chiswick, London Pride, ESB, seasonal beers; guest beer Ⓗ
Former coaching inn, now an imposing Fuller's Ale & Pie House, set back from the High Road. No food Sun eve.
❀ ◖ ▶ ₠ ⊖ (Turnham Green)
♣ ⊁

OLD PACKHORSE
434 Chiswick High Road
☎ (0181) 995 0647
11-11; 12-10.30 Sun
Fuller's Chiswick, London Pride Ⓗ
Impressive corner pub featuring much ornate woodwork. There is also large garden. Thai food is served. (No food is available on Sun eve.)
❀ ◖ ▶ ⊖ (Chiswick Park)

W5: EALING

NORTH STAR
43 The Broadway
☎ (0181) 567 4848
11-11; 12-10.30 Sun
Ind Coope Burton Ale; Marston's Pedigree; Tetley Bitter; Young's Bitter; guest beers Ⓗ
Deceptively large, three-bar pub: an oasis of tranquillity in the midst of Ealing's shopping area. The pub reflects great continuity, under the present landlord 17 years.
🏚 Q ❀ ◖ ≉ (Broadway) ⊖

RED LION
13 St Mary's Road
☎ (0181) 567 2541
11-11; 12-10.30 Sun
Fuller's Chiswick, London Pride, ESB, seasonal beers Ⓗ
Single bar institution near Ealing Film Studio, from which its alternative name, Stage Six, is derived. The walls are lined with film memorabilia while the terrace-style garden at the rear has won many awards and is very pleasant in summer. Occasional live music.
Q ❀ ◖ ▶ ≉ (Broadway)
⊖ (South)

ROSE & CROWN
Church Place, St Mary's Road
☎ (0181) 567 28811
11-11; 12-10.30 Sun
Fuller's Chiswick, London Pride, ESB, seasonal beers Ⓗ
Two-bar local tucked away behind St Mary's church. Recent alterations have spared the public bar, much to the relief of the regulars.
❀ Q ◖ ▶ ₠ ♿ ⊖ (South) ♣

Try also: Kings Arms, The Grove (Courage)

W6: HAMMERSMITH

ANDOVER ARMS
57 Aldensley Road
☎ (0181) 741 9794
11-11; 12-10.30 Sun
Fuller's Chiswick, London Pride, ESB, seasonal beers Ⓗ
Pleasant, two-bar local in Brackenbury village, well hidden, but worth seeking out. Excellent Thai food eves.
Q ◖ ▶ ⊖ (Ravenscourt Pk)

BLACK LION
South Black Lion Lane
☎ (0181) 748 2639
11-11; 12-10.30 Sun
Courage Best Bitter, Directors; Theakston Best Bitter; guest beers Ⓗ
Nice, single, large bar serving good traditional food, literally five seconds' walk from the Thames towpath. Originally a piggery 200 years ago. Bar billiards played. No food Sun eve.
🏚 🕸 ◖ ▶ ⊖ (Stamford Brook) ♣ P

BROOK GREEN
170 Shepherd's Bush Road
☎ (0181) 602 2643
11-11; 12-10.30 Sun
Young's Bitter, Special, seasonal beers Ⓗ
Large Victorian pub opposite Brook Green, handy for the Tesco superstore. Home-cooked food is a speciality. 🏚 Q 🛏 ◖ ▶ ⅄ ⊖

CROSS KEYS
57 Black Lion Lane
☎ (0181) 748 3541
11-11; 12-10.30 Sun
Fuller's Chiswick, London Pride, ESB, seasonal beers Ⓗ
Popular pub between King St and the river; pleasant garden at the back. Sunday roasts at lunchtime; no food Sat and Sun eves.
🕸 ◖ ▶ ⅄ ⊖ (Stamford Brook) ♣

THATCHED HOUSE
115 Dalling Road
☎ (0181) 748 6174
11-11; 12-10.30 Sun
Young's Bitter, Special, guest beers Ⓗ
Large, one-bar pub with an open fire and traditional furnishings. A good selection of snacks and hot meals are available (except Sun eve). No music.
🏚 Q 🕸 ◖ ⊖ (Ravenscourt Pk)

W7: HANWELL

DOLPHIN
13 Lower Boston Road
☎ (0181) 840 0850
11-11; 12-10.30 Sun
Draught Bass ⒼⒽ**; Gibbs Mew Wiltshire, Salisbury, Bishops Tipple; guest beers** Ⓗ
Despite the loss of a separate public bar, this pub has been magnificently transformed from something of a backwater to a permanent ale exhibition with guest beers often from microbreweries and special food and drink promotions. There's no excuse to pass this one by.
Q 🕸 ◖ ▶ ≠ ♣ ⅄

FOX
Green Lane
☎ (0181) 567 3912
11-11; 12-10.30 Sun
Courage Best Bitter, Directors; Marston's Pedigree or **seasonal beers** Ⓗ
Run by the area's longest-serving landlord, this pub is especially popular with Brent Valley Park walkers and Grand Union Canal users. Notable Sunday roasts are offered in this ex-Royal Brewery hostelry. Limited parking.
🕸 ◖ ⅄ ▲ ♣ P

VIADUCT INN
221 Uxbridge Road
☎ (0181) 567 1362
11-11; 12-10.30 Sun
Fuller's Chiswick, London Pride, ESB, seasonal beers Ⓗ
Wharncliffe railway crossing of the River Brent gives the pub its name. A distinctive tiled exterior conceals a nice little pub, noted for its 'Ha! Bloody Ha!' Comedy Club (Fri) in an ancillary building. Food until 8pm (5 Sat and Sun).
🕸 ◖ 🍽 ≠ ♣ P

W8: KENSINGTON

BRITANNIA
11 Allen Street
☎ (0171) 937 1864
11-11; 12-10.30 Sun
Young's Bitter, Special, seasonal beers Ⓗ
Two-bar local, just off Kensington High Street. A large conservatory at the rear doubles as a no-smoking area lunchtimes. Has been in all editions of this *Guide*. No food Sun eve.
◖ ▶ ⊖ (High St)

CHURCHILL ARMS
119 Kensington Church Street
☎ (0171) 727 4242
11-11; 12-10.30 Sun
Fuller's Chiswick, London Pride, ESB, seasonal beers Ⓗ
Extremely busy pub with a collection of Churchillian memorabilia and a plethora of photos, bric-à-brac and awards. It specialises in Thai food, also Sun roast lunches.
Q ◖ ▶ ⊖ (Notting Hill Gate)

SCARSDALE
23a Edwardes Square
☎ (0171) 937 1811
12-11; 12-10.30 Sun
Courage Directors; Theakston Best Bitter, XB; guest beers Ⓗ
Attractive corner pub with excellent floral displays.
Q 🕸 ◖ ▶ ≠ (Olympia) ⊖ (High St)

W9: LITTLE VENICE

WARWICK CASTLE
6 Warwick Place
☎ (0171) 286 6868
11-11; 12-10.30 Sun
Draught Bass; Worthington Bitter Ⓗ
Friendly, canalside pub boasting nice glass and an impressive print of Paddington station in the last century, also small intimate drinking areas.
◖ ▶ ⊖ (Warwick Ave)

W9: MAIDA VALE

TRUSCOTT ARMS
55 Shirland Rd ☎ (0171) 236 0310
11-11; 12-10.30 Sun
Draught Bass; Courage Directors; Greene King IPA; Abbot Ⓗ
Large pub: an oasis in this area. Note the impressive bank of ten handpulls.
◖ ▶ ⊖ (Warwick Ave) ♣

WARRINGTON HOTEL
93 Warrington Crescent
☎ (0171) 286 0310
11-11; 12-10.30 Sun
Brakspear Special; Fuller's London Pride, ESB; Young's Special; guest beer Ⓗ
Wonderful example of a 'gin palace': florid woodwork, tiles and mirrors. By contrast the old public bar is quite plain. Thai restaurant upstairs eves.
◖ ▶ ⊖ (Warwick Ave)

W11: BAYSWATER

COCK & BOTTLE
17 Needham Road
☎ (0171) 229 1550
12-11; 12-10.30 Sun
Brakspear Bitter, Special Ⓗ
Traditional, friendly back-street corner local with reasonable prices. Quiz night Tue.
🕸 ◖ ⊖ (Notting Hill Gate)

W12: SHEPHERDS BUSH

CROWN & SCEPTRE
57 Melina Road
☎ (0181) 743 6414
11-11; 12-10.30 Sun
Fuller's Chiswick, London Pride, ESB, seasonal beers Ⓗ
Two-bar pub, popular with QPR and Wasps (rugby) fans.
Q 🕸 ◖ ▶ ♣

MOON ON THE GREEN
172 Uxbridge Road
☎ (0181) 749 5709
11-11; 12-10.30 Sun
Courage Directors; Fuller's London Pride; Theakston Best Bitter Ⓗ
Glass-fronted, two-bar pub overlooking the green. The downstairs bar has wood panelling.
Q ◖ ▶ ⊖ ⅄ 🍺

W13: WEST EALING

DRAYTON COURT HOTEL
2 The Avenue ☎ (0181) 997 1019
11-11; 12-10.30 Sun
Fuller's Chiswick, London Pride, ESB, seasonal beers Ⓗ

Imposing Victorian edifice, built to serve the GWR station. The ebullient licensee presides over a large two-bar pub with its own theatre. Local CAMRA and Fuller's *Pub of the Year* 1997-98. Also a frequent *Cellarmanship* award winner.
🐕 🌳 🌜 🍺 🐾 🚻 ♿ ⇌ ♣

W14: WEST KENSINGTON

BRITANNIA TAP
150 Warwick Road
☎ (0171) 602 1649
11-11; 12-10.30 Sun
Young's Bitter, Special Ⓗ
Small, narrow, local pub on a busy road. Note the bank of willow pattern handpumps.
🏠 🌳 ⇌ (Olympia) ⊖ (Earls Court) ♣ 🗄

SEVEN STARS
253 Northend Road
11-11; 12-10.30 Sun
Fuller's London Pride, ESB Ⓗ
1930s Art Deco two-bar pub with a garden patio. Sunday roast lunchtime, no food Sun eve.
🌳 🌜 🍺 🐾 ⊖

BEDFONT

BEEHIVE
333 Staines Road
☎ (0181) 890 8086
12-11; 12-4, 7-10.30 Sun
Fuller's London Pride, ESB, seasonal beers Ⓗ
Pleasant pub with a friendly atmosphere. It features a Thai and a traditional menu (no food Sun eve); live music Fri eve.
🏠 🌳 🌜 🍺 P

BRENTFORD

BREWERY TAP
47 Catherine Wheel Road
☎ (0181) 560 5200
11-11; 12-10.30 Sun
Fuller's London Pride, ESB, seasonal beers Ⓗ
Cosy, lively Victorian local with three elevated bars, off the High Street, by the Grand Union Canal. Live music including trad jazz Tue and Thu. Good value, home-cooked food with man-sized portions of Sun roasts (booking advised). Eve meals until 8 weekdays. 🌳 🌜 🍺 ⇌ ♣

MAGPIE & CROWN
128 High Street
☎ (0181) 560 5658
11-11; 12-10.30 Sun
Beer range varies Ⓗ
Ever-changing range of up to four ales from micro and independent brewers, plus real cider (perry occasionally). Increasingly popular with locals and visiting ale enthusiasts.
🌳 🏠 🍺 ⇌ ♣ 🍶

WATERMANS ARMS
11 Ferry Lane
☎ (0181) 560 5665
11-11; 12-10.30 Sun
Morland Tanners Jack; Ruddles Best Bitter Ⓗ
Small, side-street pub with a friendly atmosphere. The large U-shaped bar is its central feature. 🌜

FELTHAM

MOON ON THE SQUARE
Unit 30, The Centre
☎ (0181) 893 1293
11-11; 12-10.30 Sun
Courage Directors; Fuller's London Pride; Greene King Abbot; Theakston Best Bitter; guest beers Ⓗ
Large, traditional corner pub, popular and friendly. For points of interest look through the lounge at the old prints and photographs of bygone Feltham. Good range of guest ales.
Q 🌜 🍺 ♿ ⇌ 🍴 🗄

GREENFORD

BRIDGE HOTEL
Western Avenue (A40/A4127 jct)
☎ (0181) 566 6246
11-11; 12-10.30 Sun
Young's Bitter, Special, seasonal beers Ⓗ
This pub began life completely misnamed, but in recent years has acquired a flyover at the front and extensive accommodation to the rear. Still a quiet pub though, serving excellent beers.
Q 🌳 🏨 ♿ ⇌ ⊖ ♣ P

Try also: Hare & Hounds, Ruislip (Courage)

HAMPTON

WHITE HART
70 High St ☎ (0181) 979 5353
11-3, 5.30-11; 11-11 Sat; 12-10.30 Sun
Greene King Abbot; Tetley Bitter; guest beers Ⓗ
Tudor-style, genuine free house with a friendly relaxed atmosphere enhanced by a large log fire. Eight handpumps serve a veritable cornucopia of real ale. Local CAMRA *Pub of the Year* 1996.🏨 Q 🌳 🌜

HARMONDSWORTH

CROWN
High Street ☎ (0181) 759 1007
11-11; 12-10.30 Sun
Brakspear Bitter; Courage Best Bitter; Fuller's London Pride; Morland Old Speckled Hen Ⓗ
True village local: bustling and lively, a welcoming retreat from Heathrow Airport. Good, wholesome home cooking on offer.
🏨 Q 🌳 🌜 🍺 ♣ 🍶

HOUNSLOW

CROSS LANCES
236 Hanworth Road (A314)
☎ (0181) 570 4174
11-11; 12-10.30 Sun
Fuller's London Pride, ESB Ⓗ
Early Victorian, traditional tiled local, with a popular public bar. The saloon has a large welcoming fire. Wholesome meals are served at all hours on request (book Sun lunch).
🏠 🌳 🍺 🐾 ⇌ ⊖ (Central) ♣ P

MOON UNDER WATER
84-88 Staines Road (A315)
☎ (0181) 572 7506
11-11; 12-10.30 Sun
Courage Best Bitter; Fuller's London Pride; Greene King Abbot; Hop Back Summer Lightning; Theakston Best Bitter; guest beers Ⓗ
Early Wetherspoons shop conversion, since extended but very welcoming, with up to six guest beers plus guest ciders in summer. Near Safeway's supermarket at the western end of Hounslow's High Street.
Q 🌳 🌜 🍺 ♿ ⊖ (Central) 🍶 P 🍴 🗄

ISLEWORTH

CASTLE
18 Upper Square, Old Isleworth
☎ (0181) 560 3615
11-11; 12-10.30 Sun
Young's Bitter, Special, seasonal beers Ⓗ
Prominent pub, a long-standing *Guide* entry, housing a large comfortable bar, plus a games area. Families are welcome in the conservatory. The substantial Sun roasts are recommended. The building replaces an earlier pub that served the nearby Thames docks.
🏠 Q 🐕 🌳 🌜 ♣ P

RED LION
92-94 Linkfield Road (near BR station) ☎ (0181) 560 1457
11-11; 12-10.30 Sun
Brakspear seasonal beers; Flowers IPA; guest beers Ⓗ
Tardis-like, this pub appears to be larger inside than out. Located in a quiet terrace, it plays host to regular blues-based live music every Sat, and is also a highly regarded venue for darts teams. Secluded but well worth the search. 🌳 🌜 🍺 🐾 ⇌ ♣

RISING SUN
407 London Rd ☎ (0181) 560 5868
11-11; 12-10.30 Sun
Fuller's Chiswick, London Pride, ESB, seasonal beers; guest beers Ⓗ
The turn-of-the-century, mock-Tudor exterior opens into a sin-

gle wood-panelled bar frequented by a lively blend of locals and students from the nearby college. 🍺 ◖▶ ≈ ♣ P

NORTHOLT

PLOUGH
Mandeville Road
☎ (0181) 845 1450
11-11; 12-10.30 Sun
Fuller's London Pride, ESB Ⓗ
Set at the end of Northolt village, the thatched roof is a landmark that is a welcome sight as you come out of the tube station. Thai restaurant downstairs.
🍺 ◖▶ ⊟ ⊖ ♣ P

Try also: Crown, Ealing Rd (Whitbread)

NORWOOD GREEN

PLOUGH
Tentelow Lane (A4127)
☎ (0181) 574 1945
11-11; 12-10.30 Sun
Fuller's Chiswick, London Pride, ESB Ⓗ
Oldest pub in the area, it has various sporting associations, including the adjacent bowls club. Archetypal village pub where nothing is too much trouble. No food Sun.
Q 🍺 ◖ ♣ P

RUISLIP MANOR

J J MOONS
12 Victoria Road
☎ (01895) 622373
11-11; 12-10.30 Sun
Courage Directors; Fuller's London Pride; Theakston Best Bitter; guest beers Ⓗ
Traditional-style mock-Victorian alehouse, converted from an old Woolworth's store. Very popular with all ages.
Q 🍺 ◖▶ & ⊖ ⊬ ⊟

SOUTHALL

BEACONSFIELD ARMS
63-67 West End Road
☎ (0181) 574 8135
11-11; 12-10.30 Sun
Greene King Abbot; Scanlon's Spike; guest beers Ⓗ
Despite its rather forbidding exterior, enjoy the atmosphere created by the genuine Irish hosts. With a mild ale invariably on offer and other beers from a growing range of breweries, don't miss this campaigning pub. Try the Black Country pork scratchings. 🍺 ≈ ♣ P ⊟

THREE HORSESHOES
2 High Street
☎ (0181) 574 2001
11-11; 12-10.30 Sun
Courage Best Bitter; Theakston XB Ⓗ

A former Royal Brewery gem, recently refurbished by new landlords. Still featuring three bars, it retains all the characteristics its architect, Nowell Parr, endowed. Narrowly saved from demolition in 1992, it gained listed status, revoked on a technicality. No food Sun. Q 🍺 ◖ ⊟ ≈ ♣ P

ST MARGARET'S

TURKS HEAD
28 Winchester Road
☎ (0181) 892 1972
11-11; 12-10.30 Sun
Fuller's London Pride, ESB Ⓗ
Traditional Edwardian local with a spacious public bar. The large function room features a comedy club Mon and Fri. No food Sun.
🏨 🍺 ◖ ⊟ ≈ ♣

TEDDINGTON

QUEEN DOWAGER
49 North Lane
☎ (0181) 977 2583
11-11; 12-10.30 Sun
Young's Bitter, Special, Winter Warmer Ⓗ
Quiet, relaxing pub with a nice garden in a side range near the High Street. A former local CAMRA *Pub of the Year*.
Q 🍺 ◖ ⊟ ≈

TWICKENHAM

EEL PIE
11 Church Street
☎ (0181) 891 1717
11-11; 12-10.30 Sun
Badger Dorset Best, Tanglefoot; Gribble Oving Bitter, Black Adder II; guest beers Ⓗ
In an historic street, just yards from the town centre and river, this pub enjoys a reputation for high quality lunches (not served Sun). A single-bar pub, it is roomy and comfortable.
◖ ≈ ♣ ⌂

HOGSHEAD
33-35 York Street
☎ (0181) 891 3940
11-11; 12-10.30 Sun
Boddingtons Bitter; Flowers IPA, Abroad Cooper; Fuller's London Pride; Marston's Pedigree; Wadworths 6X Ⓗ**; guest beers** ⒽⒼ
New building (1996) which conforms to the street's architectural style. Rugby-related bric-à-brac features in the upper bar. Food is served until 8pm (5 Fri-Sun). Up to six guest beers, including four on gravity.
◖▶ & ≈ ⌂

POPES GROTTO
Cross Deep (A310)
☎ (0181) 892 3050
11-3; 5.30-11; 11-11 Sat; 12-10.30 Sun

Young's Bitter, Special, Winter Warmer, seasonal beers Ⓗ
Large, post-war, three-bar pub overlooking a pretty riverside park. It enjoys a reputation for good food (carvery lunch Sun). The roomy, comfortable lounge is on two levels.
🏨 Q 🍺 ◖▶ ⊟
≈ (Strawberry Hill) ♣ P

UXBRIDGE

CROWN
Colham Green Road
☎ (01895) 442303
11-11; 12-10.30 Sun
Fuller's London Pride, ESB Ⓗ
Comfortable local with a lively public bar. Handy for Hillingdon Hospital. A new extension will see the introduction of live music Fri and Sat eves. Well cared for patio garden.
🍺 🍺 ◖▶ ⊟ ♣ P

LOAD OF HAY
Villiers Street
☎ (01895) 234676
11-3, 5.30 (7 Sat)-11; 12-3, 7-10.30 Sun
Beer range varies Ⓗ
Very welcoming country pub in the town: the smaller front bar is well worth a visit (open only at weekends). Local CAMRA *Pub of the Year* 1995 and '96. No food Sun eve.
Q 🍺 ◖▶ P ⊬

WHITTON

DUKE OF CAMBRIDGE
Kneller Road
☎ (0181) 898 5393
11-11; 12-10.30 Sun
Webster's Yorkshire Bitter; Young's Special Ⓗ
This small, cosy Georgian tavern, opposite the historic Kneller Hall Royal Military School of Music, is the nearest pub to Twickenham rugby stadium. The genial landlord hosts summer barbecues. No food Sun; eve meals by arrangement.
🍺 ◖ ≈ P

INDEPENDENT BREWERIES

O'Hanlon's:
Vauxhall, SE11
Pitfield:
Hoxton N1
Freedom:
Fulham SW6
Young's:
Wandsworth SW18
Fuller's: Chiswick W4

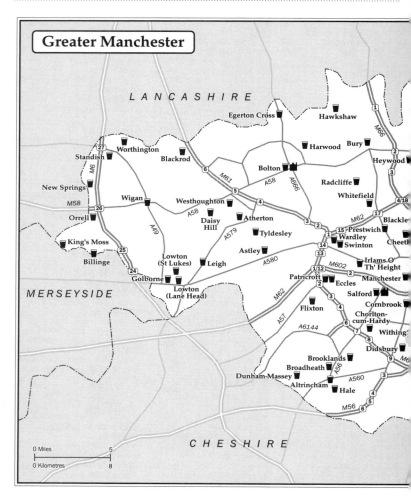

Greater Manchester

ALTRINCHAM

MALT SHOVELS
68 Stamford Street
☎ (0161) 928 2053
11.30-11; 12-4, 7-10.30 Sun
Samuel Smith OBB Ⓗ
Friendly, cosmopolitan town-centre pub, popular with the local business community at lunchtimes; good value meals (not served sun). Games room upstairs.
◑ ≈ ⊖ ♣

ORANGE TREE
13-15 Market Place
☎ (0161) 928 2600
11.45-11; 12-10.30 Sun
Marston's Pedigree; Theakston XB; Wilson's Bitter; guest beers Ⓗ
Friendly, family-run local, very accommodating to all. Note the old photos of Altrincham and neighbouring pubs, long since gone. Extensive range of good meals available until 9pm.
➷ ❀ ◑ ▶ ≈ ⊖ ♣ ✄

ASHTON-UNDER-LYNE

DOG & PHEASANT
528 Oldham Road
☎ (0161) 330 4894
12-11; 12-10.30 Sun
Banks's Mild; Marston's Bitter, Pedigree, HBC Ⓗ
Popular, friendly local, close to Oldham border and Medlock Valley Country Park. Good value food (not served Tue and Sun eves). ⚏ ❀ ◑ ▶ P

JUNCTION
Mossley Road (A670)
☎ (0161) 343 1611
12-3 (not Mon), 5.30-11; 12-11 Fri & Sat; 12-4, 7-10.30 Sun
Robinson's Hatters Mild, Best Bitter, Frederics Ⓗ
Stone terraced inn with numerous cosy rooms, adjacent to a golf links and open country. No food Sat. Q ◑ ♣ P

ODDFELLOWS
Kings Road, Hurst
☎ (0161) 330 3656
12-11; 12-10.30 Sun
Robinson's Hatters Mild, Best Bitter, Old Tom Ⓗ
Popular, multi-roomed local which boasts many traditional features, not least the splendid bar. Other beers from the Robinson's range appear occasionally. A welcoming and sociable local. ❀ ✄

STATION
2 Warrington Street
☎ (0161) 330 6776
11.30-11; 11-3 (4 summer), 7-11 Sat; 7-10.30 Sun
Boddingtons Bitter; Marston's Pedigree Ⓗ
This free house has established a reputation for serving well-kept

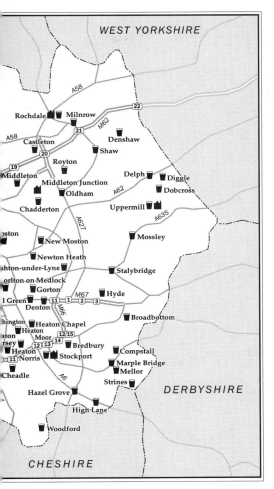

lounges and an upstairs function room, the meeting place for various societies. Popular shoppers' lunches. Note the George Shaw etched windows. ◖ ◗

BILLINGE

HOLTS ARMS (FOOT)
Crank Road (opp hospital)
☎ (01695) 622705
12-11; 12-10.30 Sun
Burtonwood Bitter, Top Hat; guest beer H
Listed building recently refurbished, retaining plenty of warmth and character with low ceilings and wooden beams. Local legend has it that it was once the local hospital mortuary.
🏚 ❀ ◖ ▶ Å ♣ P

BLACKLEY

PLEASANT INN
370 Chapel Lane (off A6104)
☎ (0161) 740 3391
1 (12 Sat)-11; 12-10.30 Sun
Robinson's Hatter's Mild, Best Bitter H
Small, three-roomed community pub in an ancient urban village. The lively vault, golf society room (known as the Pigsty) and the lounge attract a loyal local clientele in this somewhat remote location. Children welcome until 8pm. 🏧 ❀ 🍺 ♣

BLACKROD

GALLAGHERS
Little Scotland
☎ (01942) 833101
11.30-11; 12-10.30 Sun
Boddingtons Bitter; Tetley Bitter; Walker Bitter; Whitbread Trophy; guest beer H
Large but friendly old-style pub offering three guest beers a week. Reasonably-priced bar snacks, plus an excellent restaurant. ❀ ◖ & Å P

BOLTON

ARKWRIGHTS ALE HOUSE
Vallets Lane ☎ (01204) 845941
2 (12 Sat)-11; 12-10.30 Sun
Tetley Mild, Bitter H
Large, impressive, multi-roomed pub with an accent on sports.
♣ P

BOB'S SMITHY
1441 Chorley Old Road (B6226, ½ mile from A58 jct)
☎ (01204) 842622
12-3, 5-11; 12-11 Sat; 12-10.30 Sun
Boddingtons Bitter; Taylor Best Bitter; Walker Mild, Bitter; guest beers H
Popular pub on the moors just outside Bolton affording panoramic views of the area. Named after the local blacksmith who was a regular. 🏧 ❀ ♣ P

---

beers from all around Britain, with an emphasis on new and smaller breweries. Seven handpumps serve quickly changing guest beers, always including a mild. A Guide regular. Limited parking. ❀ ◖ ⇌ ⌂ P

ASTLEY

CART & HORSES
221 Manchester Road
☎ (01942) 870751
12-11; 12-10.30 Sun
Holt Mild, Bitter H
Popular roadside local with a busy tap room, large lounge (once two rooms) and a no-smoking lounge away from the bar.
❀ 🍺 ♣ P

ATHERTON

ATHERTON ARMS
6 Tyldesley Road
☎ (01942) 882885
11.30-11; 12-10.30 Sun
Holt Mild, Bitter H
Large, open lounge, a tap room with snooker and pool tables, a function room with a stage and bar, plus a corridor bar at the main entrance. 🍺 & ⇌ ♣ P

ROYAL
67-69 Wigan Road
☎ (01942) 994938
4.30 (7 winter)-11; 12-11 Sat; 12-10.30 Sun
Hydes' Anvil Mild, Bitter, seasonal beers H
Large, friendly roadside inn where a long bar serves a comfortable lounge. Popular tap room. It hosts occasional music nights. 🏧 ❀ ♣

WHEATSHEAF
48 Market Street
☎ (01942) 883020
11.30-3, 7-11; 12-3, 7-10.30 Sun
Lees GB Mild, Bitter H
Popular, town-centre local. A large lounge bar, two more

213

CLIFTON ARMS
94 Newport Street
☎ (01204) 392738
11-11; 11-3, 7-11 Sat; 12-2,
7-10.30 Sun
**Jennings Bitter; Moorhouse's
Black Cat, Premier; Tetley
Bitter; guest beers** Ⓗ
Friendly, town-centre pub near
the bus/rail interchange. Regular
folk and quiz nights are a feature;
also holds regular mini-beer festivals. ◖ ≈ ♣

HEN & CHICKENS
143 Deansgate
☎ (01204) 389836
11.30-11; 7.30-10.30 Sun
**Bass Toby Cask; Greenalls Mild,
Bitter; Stones Bitter; guest
beers** Ⓗ
Friendly local in the town centre,
handy for bus station, serving
excellent value home-cooked
lunches and a good range of
guest ales. ◖ ❺ ≈ ♣

HOWCROFT INN ☆
36 Pool Street
☎ (01204) 526814
12-11; 12-10.30 Sun
**Taylor Landlord; Walker Mild,
Bitter; guest beers** Ⓗ
Large, multi-roomed pub just outside the town centre. Has its own
bowling green which hosts the
pub's annual beer festival (over
180 beers). Close to Bank Top
Brewery, whose beers are
stocked regularly. ⌂ ❀ ◖ ♣ P

LODGE BANK TAVERN
260 Bridgeman Street
☎ (01204) 531946
12.30-4.30, 7.30-11; 12-11 Fri &
Sat; 12-10.30 Sun
Lees GB Mild, Bitter Ⓗ
Welcoming local, just outside the
town centre. One of the last pubs
in Bolton to be granted a spirits
licence. ❀ ≈ ♣ P

OLDE MAN & SCYTHE
Churchgate
☎ (01204) 527267
11-11; 12-10.30 Sun
**Boddingtons Bitter; Flowers
Original; Holt Bitter; guest
beers** Ⓗ
Reputedly Britain's fourth oldest
pub where the Earl of Derby had
his last drink before being exe-
cuted. Recently renovated expos-
ing original beams and many
other features. Known locally as
the Cider Owse. ❀ ◖ ≈ ♣ ⌂

SWEET GREEN TAVERN
127 Crook Street
☎ (01204) 392258
11.30-3, 6.30-11; 11.30-11 Thu &
Fri; 11.30-3.30, 7-11 Sat; 12-3,
7-11 Sun
Tetley Bitter; guest beers Ⓗ
Large community pub at the edge
of the town centre which has lost
none of its character. Ideally

positioned opposite the bus/rail
interchange. The house beer is
brewed by Moorhouse's.
⌂ ❀ ◖ ≈ ♣ P

YORK
114 Newport Street (opp station)
☎ (01204) 383892
11-11; closed Sun
**Burtonwood Forshaw's, Top Hat;
guest beer** Ⓗ
Comfortable, town-centre pub
with a central bar and a friendly,
warm atmosphere. Live entertainment Sat eve and karaoke
Wed and Fri. ⌂ ◖ ≈ ♣

BREDBURY

HORSFIELD ARMS
Ashton Road ☎ (0161) 430 6930
11.45-11; 12-3, 7-11 Sat; 12-3,
7-10.30 Sun
**Robinson's Hatters Mild, Best
Bitter** Ⓟ
Lively pub with a well-appointed
lounge and pool room. Next to
Robinson's bottling plant.
❀ ◖ ⊟ P ⊟

Try also: Arden Arms, Ashton
Rd (Robinson's)

BROADHEATH

RAILWAY INN
153 Manchester Road (A56)
☎ (0161) 941 3383
11-11; 12-10.30 Sun
**Boddingtons Bitter; Holt Mild,
Bitter** Ⓗ
Former street-corner local, now
an oasis on the edge of a new
retail park. Multi-roomed with a
railway (long-gone) theme and
plenty of period adverts.
Excellent value food virtually all
day from 7am breakfast to 7pm.
⌂ ❀ ⊨ ◖ ▶ ⊟
⊖ (Navigation Rd) ♣ P

BROADBOTTOM

CHESHIRE CHEESE
65 Lower Market Street
☎ (01457) 762339
6 (12 summer Sat)-11; 12-10.30
Sun
**Chester's Mild; Thwaites Best
Mild, Bitter; guest beers** Ⓗ
Friendly village pub, popular with
locals, surrounded by walking
country. The beers are served
without sparklers on request.
⌂ ❀ ⚠ ≈ ♣ ⌂ ⊟

BROOKLANDS

BROOK
Brooklands Station Approach
☎ (0161) 973 7773
12-11; 12-10.30 Sun
Lees Bitter Ⓗ
Converted station master's
house retaining a railway theme.
Lunchtime bar snacks, restaurant
open for Sun lunch. ❀ ⊖ P

BURY

BLUE BELL
840 Manchester Road (A56 near
Blackford Bridge)
☎ (0161) 766 2496
12-11; 12-10.30 Sun
Holt Mild, Bitter Ⓗ
Large, thriving, three-roomed
pub with a traditional vault. Run
by an amiable host and popular
with mature Man Utd fans. The
large, comfortable lounge is
mostly frequented by friendly
locals. Q ❀ ♣ P

OLD BLUE BELL
2 Bell Lane (B6221/B622 jct)
☎ (0161) 761 3674
12-11; 12-10.30 Sun
Holt Mild, Bitter Ⓗ
Extensive, multi-roomed pub,
where full use is made of all
available space; a busy vault and
quieter side rooms. Live music
Sat afternoons and discos Thu
and Sun eves. In the lounge the
pub serves as a genuine local.
Children welcome until 6pm.
Q ⊟ ⊖ ♣

ROBERT PEEL
Market Place (next to Peel
Monument) ☎ (0161) 764 7287
11-11; 12-10.30 Sun
**Boddingtons Bitter; Courage
Directors; Theakston Best Bitter;
Thwaites Bitter; guest beers** Ⓗ
Modern, attractive and inviting
town-centre pub; a large room
with quiet and cosy areas, and a
no-smoking area. Good friendly
service. Food all day until 10pm.
Q ❀ ◖ ❺ ⊖ ≈ ♣ ⌂ ⊁ ⊟

ROSE & CROWN
36 Manchester Old Road (off
A56) ☎ (0161) 764 6461
12-3, 5-11; 12-11 Fri & Sat; 12-3,
7-10.30 Sun
Beer range varies Ⓗ
Traditional local, liberated from
the Tap & Spile chain, with a
friendly atmosphere. A range of
good value bar snacks weekdays.
Occasional mini beer festivals;
the house beers are from Four
Rivers and Hull. ⊖

Try also: Two Tubs, The Fylde,
(Thwaites)

CASTLETON

BLUE PITS INN
842 Manchester Road (A664)
☎ (01706) 632151
12-4 (5 Fri & Sat), 7.30-11; 12-4,
7-10.30 Sun
Lees GB Mild, Bitter Ⓗ
Welcoming, friendly local in a former railway building, the three distinct
drinking areas now offer a much
warmer atmosphere. Recent winner of the JW Lees *Best Kept
Cellar* award. ≈ ♣ P

MIDLAND BEER COMPANY
826 Manchester Road (A664)
☎ (01706) 750873
11.30-11; 12-10.30 Sun
Thwaites Bitter; Ushers Best Bitter; guest beers H
Converted bank, housing a modern open-plan continental-style bar in an area not known for its choice of real ale. The prices are very competitive. ❀ ◑ ⇌ ♣

CHADDERTON

HORTON ARMS
19 Streetbridge (B6195)
☎ (0161) 624 7793
11-11; 12-10.30 Sun
Lees GB Mild, Bitter, Moonraker (winter) H
Comfortable pub with a rural feel. One quiet room and a large lounge, divided neatly into areas which lend atmosphere and a cosy feel. Weekday meals.
❀ ◑ P

HUNT LANE TAVERN
754 Middleton Road West (A669, $\frac{1}{2}$ mile from centre)
☎ (0161) 627 2969
11.30-11 (11.30-3, 5-11 winter); 12-10.30 Sun
Lees GB Mild, Bitter, seasonal beers H
Friendly, country-style pub in a suburban setting offering excellent value home cooking (eve meals Mon-Sat until 7.30). Quiz night Mon. Q ❀ ◑ ▶ ⊞ ♣ P

Try also: Railway & Linnet, Foxdenton Lane (Lees)

CHEADLE

QUEENS ARMS
177 Stockport Road (A560, 100 yds W of M63, jct 11)
☎ (0161) 428 3081
12-11 (12-3, 5.30-11 Mon); 12-10.30 Sun
Robinson's Hatters Mild, Old Stockport, Best Bitter H
Deceptively large pub which is close to the new AA centre. Children are welcome in the rear lounge adjoining the former bowling green (which is now a safe play area). These facilities ensure the pub is very busy in summer.
🚲 🐛 ❀ ♣ P ⊬ ⊟

CHEADLE HULME

CHURCH
90 Ravenoak Road (A5149)
☎ (0161) 485 1897
11-11; 12-10.30 Sun
Robinson's Hatters Mild, Best Bitter; guest beers H
Busy, welcoming local with a reputation for efficient service. The outward appearance is of a country cottage; inside are two comfortable, wood-panelled lounge

areas and a small vault. No food Sun eve. The guest beer is from Robinson's.
🚲 ❀ ◑ ▶ ⊞ ⇌ ♣ P

CHEETHAM

QUEENS ARMS
4-6 Honey Street (S of A665/A6010 jct)
☎ (0161) 834 4239
12-11; 12-10.30 Sun
Phoenix Bantam; Taylor Landlord; guest beers H
Warm and welcoming two-roomed free house with original Empress Brewery tiling on half the frontage. Watch the trains and trams and survey the Mancunian cityscape from the large rear garden. Guest beers usually include a mild; also Belgian bottled beers. Meals served 12-8.
🚲 ❀ ◑ ▶ ⇌ (Victoria) ⊖ ♣ ⌂

CHORLTON-CUM-HARDY

BEECH INN
72 Beech Road
☎ (0161) 881 1180
11-11; 12-10.30 Sun
Boddingtons Bitter; Flowers Original; Morland Old Speckled Hen; Taylor Best Bitter, Landlord; Whitbread Trophy; guest beers H
Thriving, three-roomed pub just off the village green. No food, no music, no gimmicks, popular with all ages. Q ❀ ⊞ ♣

CHORLTON-ON-MEDLOCK

DUCIE ARMS
52 Devas Street (behind university)
☎ (0161) 273 2279
11-11; 12-10.30 Sun
Burtonwood Bitter H
A real Irish pub without all the frills - small with just a stand up bar and back room, it is used by students. See the pictures dating back to the 1960s of celebrity fund-raising events and the cartoon character mural on the doorstep. Limited parking.
Q P

COMPSTALL

ANDREW ARMS
George Street
☎ (0161) 427 2281
11-11; 12-10.30 Sun
Robinson's Hatters Mild, Best Bitter H
Ideally placed for Etherow Country Park, a perennial and deserved *Guide* entry with a relaxing atmosphere.
🚲 Q ❀ ◑ ♣ P

CORNBROOK

HOPE INN
297 Chester Road, Hulme (A56)
☎ (0161) 848 0038
11-5, 7-11; 12-5, 7-10.30 Sun
Hydes' Anvil Light, Bitter, seasonal beers P
A rare example of a surviving Manchester stand up bar - telly (satellite), chat and a crossword library. A pool room at the rear has been converted into a lounge. Children welcome until 5pm. ♣ ⊟

DAISY HILL

ROSE HILL TAVERN
321 Leigh Road, Westhoughton (B5235) ☎ (01942) 815776
12-11; 12-10.30 Sun
Holt Mild, Bitter H
Large, busy roadside pub next to the station, with a warm friendly welcome. ❀ ⇌ ♣ P

DELPH

ROYAL OAK (TH'HEIGHTS)
Broad Lane (1 mile above Denshaw Road) OS982090
☎ (01457) 874460
7-11; 12-3.30, 7-10.30 Sun
Boddingtons Bitter; Coach House Gunpowder Mild; guest beers H
Isolated, 250-year-old stone pub on an historic pack-horse route overlooking the Tame Valley. A cosy bar and three rooms. Good, home-cooked food Fri-Sun eve (home-bred beef is often on the menu). The house beer is brewed by Moorhouse's. 🚲 Q ❀ ▶ P

DENSHAW

BLACK HORSE INN
2 The Culvert, Oldham Road (A672, 2 miles from M62 jct 22)
☎ (01457) 874375
12-4, 6-11; 12-11 Sat; 12-10.30 Sun
Banks's Hanson's Bitter, Mild, Bitter; guest beer H
Attractive 17th-century, stone pub in a row of terraced cottages; a cosy L-shaped bar area and two rooms (one is available for functions and parties). There is a wide range of home-cooked food available (meals served all day Sat).🚲 Q 🐛 ❀ ◑ ▶ P ⊬

Try also: Junction, Rochdale Rd (Lees)

DENTON

CHAPEL HOUSE
145 Stockport Road
11-11; 12-4, 7-10.30 Sun
Holt Mild, Bitter H
Imposing redbrick building with a large, comfortable lounge and a traditional vault. ❀ ⊞ ♣ P

DIDSBURY

STATION HOTEL
682 Wilmslow Road
☎ (0161) 445 9761
11-11; 12-10.30 Sun
Bateman Mild; Marston's Bitter, Pedigree, HBC H
Small, quiet three-roomed pub, converted from a bakery around 1890. One of the few remaining locals in a trendy village, it displays pictures of old Didsbury and is bedecked with flowering plants in summer. Lunchtime snacks served.
Q ✿ ≈ (East) ♣

DIGGLE

DIGGLE HOTEL
Station Houses (1/2 mile off A670)
OS011081
☎ (01457) 872741
12-3, 5-11; 12-11 Sat; 12-3, 5-10.30 Sun
Boddingtons Bitter; Flowers Original; OB Bitter; Taylor Golden Best, Landlord H
Popular and busy, especially in summer, 18th-century stone pub in a pleasant hamlet with a well kept bar and two rooms. Accent on home-cooked food (served all day Sat).
✿ ⊨ ◖ ▶ P

DOBCROSS

NAVIGATION INN
Wool Road (A670)
☎ (0161) 872418
11.30-3, 5-11; 11.30-11 Sat; 12-10.30 Sun
Banks's Mild, Bitter; Camerons Bitter; Marston's Pedigree; guest beer H
Next to the Huddersfield Narrow Canal, this stone pub was built in 1806 to slake the thirsts of the navvies cutting the Standedge tunnel under the Pennines. The open-plan lounge is a shrine to brass bands. No food Sun eve.
✿ ◖ ▶ ♣ P

SWAN INN
The Square ☎ (01457) 873451
12-3, 5-11; 12-3, 7-10.30 Sun
Moorhouse's Pendle Witches Brew; Phoenix Best Bitter, Wobbly Bob, seasonal beers; Theakston Mild, Best Bitter; guest beers H
Stone-built village local with an interesting history, dating from 1765: a renovated bar area with a flagged floor, plus three distinct drinking areas. Good value, home-cooked food includes Indian dishes. ♨ Q ✿ ◖ ▶ ⊁

DUNHAM MASSEY

ROPE & ANCHOR
Paddock Lane (B5160)
☎ (0161) 927 7901

12-3, 5.30-11; 12-10.30 Sun
Boddingtons Bitter; Greenalls Original; guest beer H
Food-based country pub, with drinking areas and upstairs restaurant. The garden has a burger stand in summer and is heated by hot air blowers. Playground outdoors for children who are allowed in for meals.
✿ ◖ ▶ ♣ P ⊁

ECCLES

CROWN & VOLUNTEER
171 Church Street (A57)
☎ (0161) 789 3866
11-11; 12-10.30 Sun
Holt Mild, Bitter H
Built in 1939: a tidy two-roomer where much of the original Art Deco wood and glass features remain. It attracts a mature clientele who like a chat and a singalong. A new bar fixture in the vault has enhanced a functional room. ⊞ ≈ ♣

LAMB HOTEL ☆
33 Regent Street (A57, opp bus station)
☎ (0161) 789 3882
11.30-11; 12-10.30 Sun
Holt Mild, Bitter H
Unspoilt Edwardian gem: a listed building where Art Nouveau tiling lines the walls and staircase. A now rare full-sized billiards table stands in the games room. Can get very busy at weekends.
◖ ⊞ ≈ ♣ P

Try also: White Lion, Liverpool Rd (Holt)

EGERTON

CROSS GUNS INN
Blackburn Road (A666)
☎ (01204) 303341
12-11; 12-10.30 Sun
Boddingtons Bitter; OB Bitter; Taylor Landlord; guest beers H
Good-sized locals' roadside pub at the north end of the village with a friendly reception. Chargrilled fillings on hot muffins are a speciality; the restaurant is run by an award-winning chef making modern English food with a continental flavour at reasonable prices. ♨ ✿ ◖ ▶ ▲ P

FLIXTON

BIRD IN T'HAND
Flixton Road
☎ (0161) 748 2014
11.30-11; 12-10.30 Sun
Boddingtons Bitter; Greenalls Bitter; Tetley Bitter; guest beer H
Suburban pub with a food-based lounge and a traditional vault. A children's play area is outside. Meals include a vegetarian option and are available all day

at the weekend. The guest beer is usually from an independent; can be very expensive.
✿ ◖ ▶ ≈ (Chassen Rd) ♣ P

CHURCH INN
34 Church Road (B5123, near station) ☎ (0161) 748 2158
11-11; 12-10.30 Sun
Greenalls Mild, Bitter, Original; guest beer H
Former schoolhouse and courtroom, licensed for over 120 years, comfortably furnished with various seating areas. Well-behaved children welcome until 7.30pm (small outside play area). No food Sun (eve meals 5-7).
♨ ✿ ◖ ▶ ≈ ♣ P

GOLBORNE

RAILWAY
131 High St ☎ (01942) 728202
12 (11 Sat)-11; 12-10.30 Sun
Theakston Mild, Bitter; guest beers H
At press time this pub will be brewing its own beers. A good community local, it hosts occasional festivals and live bands. The lounge and tap room are served from a central bar.
⊨ ♣ ⌂ P ⊟

GORTON

COACH & HORSES
227 Belle Vue Street
☎ (0161) 223 0440
5.30 (12 Sat)-11; 12-10.30 Sun
Robinson's Hatters Mild, Best Bitter H
Great family welcome in this warm-hearted, two-roomed community local where the ales are now even better value. Fans of Belle Vue Aces Speedway gather here, as do cinema goers and a friendly crowd of locals.
⊞ ≈ (Belle Vue) ♣ P

WAGGON & HORSES
736 Hyde Road (A57)
☎ (0161) 231 6262
11-11; 12-3.30, 7-10.30 Sun
Holt Mild, Bitter H
A highlight of the famous Hyde Road pub crawl and not just for Holt's usual low prices. A comfortable main lounge with a linked vault-style area. A games corner and a 'back room'. A serious drinkers' house and a friendly local. Live acts Sat eve.
≈ (Ryder Brow) ♣

HALE

RAILWAY
128-130 Ashley Road (opp station) ☎ (0161) 941 5367
11-11; 12-10.30 Sun
Robinson's Hatters Mild, Old Stockport, Hartleys XB, Best Bitter, Old Tom (winter) H
Reputedly haunted but friendly

and unspoilt, a 1930s multi-roomed local retaining much wood panelling. Families welcome until 8.30pm. No food Sun.
Q ❀ ◖ ⌑ ᗉ ⇌ (Altrincham)
⊖ ♣

HARWOOD

HOUSE WITHOUT A NAME
77 Lea Gate, Bradshaw (B6196)
☎ (01204) 300063
12-11; 12-10.30 Sun
Boddingtons Bitter; Holt Bitter Ⓗ
Small, friendly pub in a row of stone cottages dating from 1332. This roadside local (with pool table) was given its unusual name by an impatient magistrate.
❀ ♣

HAWKSHAW

RED LION
81 Ramsbottom Road (A676)
☎ (01204) 852539
12-3, 6-11; 12-10.30 Sun
Jennings Mild, Bitter, Cumberland Ale; guest beer Ⓗ
Set in a picturesque area, the pub was completely rebuilt in 1990 to give a single comfortable bar and a restaurant. ⇔ ◖ ▶ P

HAZEL GROVE

THREE BEARS
Jacksons Lane (A5143)
☎ (0161) 439 0611
11-11; 12-10.30 Sun
Robinson's Hatters Mild, Old Stockport, Best Bitter, Frederics Ⓗ
Compact modern pub facing open fields at the southern edge of the village. The attractive, cosy interior is divided into three distinct sections. Welcoming and often busy; eve meals end at 7.30 (food served all day Sun). Children welcome if dining. ❀ ◖ ▶ ᗉ ♣ P ⊟

HEATON CHAPEL

HINDS HEAD
Manchester Rd ☎ (0161) 431 9301
11.30-11; 12-10.30 Sun
Castle Eden Ale; Fuller's London Pride; Higsons Bitter; Marston's Pedigree; Taylor Landlord; guest beer Ⓗ
Cottage-style pub with a divided lounge and conservatory restaurant. Smart and attractive, it boasts a large front garden. Enjoyed by a mix of locals and business people. The restaurant is popular and busy. Children welcome if eating (no food Sun eve). ❀ ◖ ▶ ⌑ P

HEATON MERSEY

GRIFFIN
552 Didsbury Road (A5145)
☎ (0161) 443 2077
12-11; 12-10.30 Sun

Holt Mild, Bitter Ⓗ
Often very busy, this multi-roomed main road local is dominated by its superb mahogany and etched glass bar. CAMRA regional *Pub of the Year* 1997.
❀ ◖ ⇌ (Didsbury) P ✄

HEATON MOOR

CROWN
98 Heaton Moor Road, Stockport (B5169) ☎ (0161) 431 0221
11-11; 12-10.30 Sun
Boddingtons Bitter; Greenalls Bitter; Cains Mild; guest beer Ⓗ
Fine multi-roomed local in a busy shopping area, a favourite with a range of customers. A thriving vault supports darts teams (entrance at side).Character enhanced by recent refurbishment.
Q ❀ ᗉ ⇌ (Heaton Chapel) ♣

HEATON NORRIS

MOSS ROSE
63 Didsbury Road (A5145)
☎ (0161) 432 5168
11.30-3 (4 Sat), 5.30 (7 Sat)-11; 11.30-11 Mon & Fri; 12-5, 7.30-10.30 Sun
Hydes' Anvil Light, Bitter, Ⓟ **seasonal beers** Ⓗ
Don't judge this book by its cover - an unpromising exterior conceals a good community local with a contrasting large lounge and a smaller rear vault. Stronger seasonal beers are a recent addition. No food Thu or Sun. ◖ ᗉ ♣ P ⊟

NURSERY ☆
Green Lane (off A6)
☎ (0161) 432 2044
11.30-3, 5.30-11; 11.30-11 Sat & Bank Hols; 12-10.30 Sun
Hydes' Anvil Mild, Bitter, Ⓟ **seasonal beers** Ⓗ
Winner of a design award when built in 1939, this fine pub is little changed today. Tucked away in pleasant suburban area, it has its own bowling green. Excellent food (set lunches only Sun); children welcome if dining.
Q ❀ ◖ ᗉ ♣ P ⊟

HEYWOOD

WISHING WELL
89 York Street (A58)
☎ (01706) 620923
12-11; 12-10.30 Sun
Jennings Cumberland Ale; Moorhouse's Premier, Pendle Witches Brew; Phoenix Hopwood; Taylor Landlord; guest beers Ⓗ
Friendly free house serving a wide range of keenly priced ales; the house beers are from Phoenix and Moorhouse's. ◖ P ⊟

Try also: Browns No. 1, Bridge St (Free)

HIGH LANE

ROYAL OAK
Buxton Road (A6)
☎ (01663) 762380
12-2.30, 5.30-11; 12-11 Sat & summer; 2-10.30 Sun
Burtonwood Bitter, Buccaneer Ⓗ
Always plenty of attractions: quizzes, live music, a children's play area with a bouncy castle. Eve meals finish at 7 (8 summer). ⚅ ❀ ◖ ▶ ⇌ (Middlewood) ♣ P

HYDE

GODLEY HALL INN
Godley Hall, Godley (off Station Rd) ☎ (0161) 368 4415
12-11; 12-3, 7-10.30 Sun
Vaux Mild, Samson; guest beers Ⓗ
Hidden amidst a large factory, this cosy low-ceilinged pub retains a surprisingly rural feel. The old building stands on the site of a manorial hall. It is comfortably furnished and split into distinct areas. No food Sun eve.
⚅ ◖ ▶ ⇌ (Godley) P

SPORTSMAN INN
57 Mottram Road
☎ (0161) 368 5000
12-11; 12-10.30 Sun
Whim Magic Mushroom Mild; Hartington Bitter; Plassey Bitter; Taylor Landlord; guest beers Ⓗ
Outstanding free house, turned around in two years from a dismal, uneconomical ex-Whitbread house into a model community pub. At least one guest beer from an independent or micro brewery is available and competitively priced. Eve meals by arrangement.
❀ ◖ ᗉ ⇌ (Newton/Hyde Central) ♣ ⌣ P ⊟

WHITE LION
7 Market Place
☎ (0161) 368 2948
11-11; 12-3, 7-10.30 Sun
Robinson's Hatters Mild, Best Bitter, Old Tom Ⓟ
Bustling town-centre pub, especially busy on market days. Though the lounge has been 'Robinsonised', the tap room has retained its fittings and its charm and this narrow, finely tiled vault gives the best view of the impressive long bar.
◖ ᗉ ⇌ (Central) ♣

Try also: White Hart, Old Rd (Robinson's)

IRLAMS O' TH' HEIGHT

RED LION
279 Bolton Road (former A6)
☎ (0161) 736 9680
11-11; 12-3, 7-10.30 Sun
Holt Mild, Bitter Ⓗ
Pre-war, three-roomed pub,

catering for the older drinker. An organist accompanies local talent on several days each week.
🔥 ♣ P

KINGS MOSS

COLLIERS ARMS
Pimbo Road ☎ (01744) 892894
12-11; 12-10.30 Sun
Greenalls Mild, Bitter, Original; guest beers Ⓗ
Good home cooking in an out-of-the-way, family-run village pub, which retains a stone-flagged floor and two open fires. Enjoy the well kept beer garden. No food Mon eve, except bank hols.
🏨 Q 🕮 ◖ ▶ 🔥 ♣ P ⌿

LEIGH

MUSKETEER
15 Lord Street ☎ (01942) 701143
11-11; 12-10.30 Sun
Boddingtons Mild, Bitter; guest beer Ⓗ
Comfortable lounge with three distinct parts. Note the display of Lancashire pit plates and local rugby team photographs in the tap room. A popular local. No food Sun. Eve meals weekdays 5-7.30. Limited parking.◖ ▶ 🔥 ♣ P

RAILWAY
160 Twist Lane (A572/A579 jct)
☎ (01942) 203853
12-11; 12-10.30 Sun
Tetley Mild, Bitter; guest beers Ⓗ
Single-roomed local: a large lounge with a raised screened pool area and a small children's play area away from the bar. Ten minute walk from Leigh RLFC along Atherleigh Way. ♣ P

LITTLE LEVER

HORSESHOE INN
21 Lever St ☎ (01204) 572081
12-4, 7-11; 11-11 Sat; 12-4, 7-10.30 Sun
Hydes' Anvil Billy Westwood's Bitter, Mild, Bitter Ⓟ
Busy, friendly, two-roomed ale house. 🔥 ♣ 🍺

LOWTON (LANE HEAD)

RED LION
324 Newton Rd ☎ (01942) 671429
12-3.30, 5.30-11; 12-11 Fri & Sat; 12-10.30 Sun
Davenports Bitter; Greenalls Mild, Bitter, Original; Tetley Bitter; guest beer Ⓗ
Large roadside inn catering for all: a main lounge bar with a raised seating area, a dining room, and a small lounge leading to a bowling green/beer garden. Other games include pool, and a war games centre. The mild pump is in the tap room.
🚌 ◖ ▶ 🔥 ♣ P

LOWTON (ST LUKES)

HARE & HOUNDS
1 Golborne Rd ☎ (01942) 728387
12-11; 12-10.30 Sun
Tetley Mild, Bitter; guest beers Ⓗ
Large, open pub, catering for all ages. A horseshoe bar serves a tap room, low-beamed lounge and a dining area on a lower level. Garden and a children's playground (fenced). This Tetley Big Steak House hosts occasional festivals. 🕮 ◖ ▶ 🔥 ♣ P

MANCHESTER CITY CENTRE

BAR FRINGE
8 Swan Street (A62/A665 jct)
☎ (0161) 835 3815
12-11; 12-10.30 Sun
Flowers IPA; guest beer Ⓗ
This one-roomed bar boasts an unusual sawdust-covered floor, with cartoons and banknotes decorating its walls.
The guest beer is from Bank Top; also an extensive range of bottled Belgian and German beers. Food promotions/specials Fri.
🕮 ◖ ▶ ≈ (Victoria) ⊖ (High St/Market St) ⌂

BEER HOUSE
6 Angel Street (off A664, near A665 jct) ☎ (0161) 839 7019
11.30-11; 12-10.30 Sun
Courage Directors; Moorhouse's Pendle Witches Brew; Ushers Best Bitter; guest beers Ⓗ
Hugely popular, basic free house with an enormous blackboard listing a wide range of guest ales and forthcoming features. A guest mild always available; beer and cider festivals are a regular feature, as are food promotions (eve meals 5-7).
🕮 ◖ ▶ ≈ (Victoria) ⊖ ⌂ P

BULL'S HEAD
84 London Rd ☎ (0161) 236 1724
11.30 (12 Sat)-11; 12-10.30 Sun
Burtonwood Mild, Bitter, Forshaw's, Top Hat, Buccaneer, seasonal beers Ⓗ
Popular, open-plan city-centre local, rejuvenated by a recent refurbishment, drawing a varied clientele. Relaxed and inviting, a stone's throw from Piccadilly station. Eve meals end at 7pm.
◖ ▶ ≈ (Piccadilly) ⊖

CASTLE
66 Oldham Street (near A62/A665 jct) ☎ (0161) 236 2945
11.30-11; 12-10.30 Sun
Robinson's Dark Mild, Hatters Mild, Old Stockport, Hartleys XB, Best Bitter, Frederics, Old Tom Ⓗ
Robbie's only city-centre pub: a tiled facade and mosaic floor lead to friendly front bar with a cosy snug and a games room (pool, pinball and darts) to the

rear. The Manchester Draught Society meets Wed; live music Thu; occasional piano music. Family room closes at 7pm.
Q 🕮 ≈ (Piccadilly/Victoria) ⊖ (High St/Piccadilly Gdns) ♣

CIRCUS TAVERN ☆
86 Portland Street
☎ (0161) 236 5818
12-11 (may close 3.30-5); 12-4 (closed eve) Sun
Tetley Bitter Ⓗ
No lager, no juke box, and only Tetleys beer in Manchester's smallest pub. A true unspoilt gem with a tiny, one-man bar serving a lobby and two characterful rooms. A capacity of about 40 means it may close its doors at weekends, but the Dubliners folk group fitted a gig in!
🏨 Q ≈ (Piccadilly) ⊖ (Piccadilly Gdns)

CITY ARMS
48 Kennedy Street
11.30-11; 11.30-3, 7-11 Sat; closed Sun
Tetley Bitter; guest beers Ⓗ
Very popular Festival Ale House frequented by the business community. Good value food. A listed building with a noteworthy frontage.
◖ ♿ ≈ (Oxford Rd) ⊖ (St Peters Sq)

CROWN INN
321 Deansgate
☎ (0161) 834 1930
12-11; 12-10.30 Sun
Vaux Mild, Samson, guest beer Ⓗ
Former Wilson's pub in the Castlefield area - the only mild outlet around here. Its one bar manages to combine the atmosphere of both a lounge and a vault. Good value food and accommodation.Tram
🚃 ◖ ≈ (Deansgate) ⊖ (G.Mex) ♣

GREY HORSE
80 Portland St ☎ (0161) 236 1874
11-11; 12-10.30 Sun
Hydes' Anvil Mild, Bitter, seasonal beers Ⓗ
Much-loved, city-centre pub, now back to its best in the hands of a skilful licensee. The single room is ideal for a drink and a chat with just quiet radio or tapes. No kitchen but you may bring your own snacks. Local CAMRA *Pub of the Year* 1997.
≈ (Piccadilly) ⊖ (Piccadilly Gdns)

HARE & HOUNDS ☆
46 Shudehill (behind Arndale)
☎ (0161) 832 4737
11-11; 12-10.30 Sun
Holt Bitter; Tetley Dark Mild, Bitter Ⓗ
Three rooms with a central bar,

shining tiled walls, wood panels and stained glass transport one back to the 19th century. A jovial atmosphere and friendly service.
⊡ ⇌ (Victoria) ⊖ (High St) ♣

Marble Arch
73 Rochdale Road, Collyhurst (A664) ☎ (0161) 832 5914
11.30 (12 Sat)-11; 12-4 Sun
Marble Bitter, Totally Marbled, Dobber Strong; Marston's Pedigree; Phoenix Hopwood, Wobbly Bob [H]
19th-century drinkers' gem of an alehouse, with ornate tiling, a decorative wall frieze and a vaulted ceiling. Recently started its own micro brewing operation, with more beers promised (up to six regular ales, plus guests).
⛫ ❀ ☾ ◗ ♿ ⇌ (Victoria) ⊖ ♣ ⌓ ▯

Peveril on the Peak ☆
27 Great Bridgewater Street
☎ (0161) 236 6364
12-3 (not Sat), 5.30 (7 Sat)-11; 7-10.30 (closed lunch) Sun
Theakston Best Bitter; Wilson's Bitter; guest beers [H]
Welcome return for a long-standing entry in this *Guide* and Nancy (the longest serving landlady in the city centre). Note the newly revealed evidence of a superbly tiled exterior. Opens Sat lunch when MUFC are at home.
⛫ ❀ ☾ ⊡ ⇌ (Oxford Rd) ⊖ (St Peters Sq) ♣

Pot of Beer
36 New Mount Street (off A664)
☎ (0161) 834 8579
12-11; closed Sun
Boddingtons Bitter; Robinson's Dark Mild [H]**; guest beers** [H][G]
Rescued from demolition, now a popular pub with a half-panelled interior. Ever-changing micro-guests, some on gravity (cooled) dispense. Authentic Polish food available. A worthy addition to Manchester's Real Ale quarter.
⛫ ☾ ⇌ (Victoria) ⊖ (Market St) ⌓

Sand Bar
120 Grosvenor Street (off Oxford Rd) ☎ (0161) 273 3141
11 (12 Sat)-11; 5-11 (closed lunch) Sun
Phoenix Bantam; Wells Bombardier; guest beers [H]
Enterprising, independently-run cafe-bar displays local artists' work. Four ever-changing guest beers from micros are complemented by continental beers on draught and in bottle. Good juke box and a jazz DJ some eves. Weekday lunches. ☾ ⇌ (Oxford Rd)

Smithfield Hotel & Bar
37 Swan Street (A665)
☎ (0161) 839 4424
12-11; 7-10.30 Sun
Highgate Dark; Matthew Clark Twelvebore Bitter; guest beers [H]
Now an established fixture on the northern quarter drinking scene: chatty, convivial and keenly priced. Beer festivals are set to become a feature. Almost cafe-bar in style, a narrow bar leads to a back dining area.
🛏 ☾ ⇌ (Victoria) ⊖ (High St)

White House
122 Great Ancoats Street
☎ (0161) 228 3231
12-4 (4.30 Sat), 8-11; 12-11 Fri; 12-3, 8-10.30 Sun
Holt Bitter; Yates 1884 [H]
Friendly, two-roomed boozer, near the Rochdale-Ashton Canal: a large L-shaped lounge around a bar plus a vault.
❀ ☾ ⊡ ♿ ⇌ (Piccadilly) ⊖ ♣

White Lion
43 Liverpool Road, Castlefield
☎ (0161) 832 7373
11.30-11; 12-10.30 Sun
Boddingtons Bitter; Taylor Landlord; guest beers [H]
Pub at the heart of the Castlefield area, close to the canal basin and museums. Good value food is all made on the premises; the curries are highly recommended (no food Fri eve; Sun meals until 6pm).
❀ ☾ ◗ ♿ ⇌ (Deansgate) ⊖ (G.Mex)

Try also: Oxnoble, Liverpool Rd (Whitbread)

MARPLE BRIDGE

Travellers Call
134 Glossop Road
☎ (0161) 427 4169
12-11; 12-10.30 Sun
Robinson's Dark Mild, Hatters Mild, Best Bitter, Hartleys XB [H]
At the top of a long hill, it is worth the climb for the warmest of welcomes and Robinson's at its best.
Q ❀ ☾ ♿ P

Try also: Pineapple, Market St, Marple (Robinson's)

MELLOR

Oddfellows Arms
73 Moor End Road (3 miles from Marple Bridge on back New Mills road)
☎ (0161) 449 7826
11-3, 5.30-11 (closed Mon); 12-3, 7-10.30 Sun
Adnams Bitter; Marston's Bitter, Pedigree; guest beer [H]
Elegant, three-storey building, sympathetically altered internally in a picture postcard setting. Strong accent on quality food and an excellent choice of beers.
⛫ Q ❀ ☾ ◗ ♿ ▲ P ▯

MIDDLETON

Britannia
6 Middleton Gardens
☎ (0161) 643 3248
11-11; 12-10.30 Sun
Lees GB Mild, Bitter [H]
Attractive, town-centre pub, recently sympathetically renovated. A horseshoe-shaped bar serves two distinct drinking areas and a comfortable lounge. Popular with all, and handy for public transport. ☾ ♣

Crown Inn
52 Rochdale Road (A664)
☎ (0161) 654 9174
11-11; 12-10.30 Sun
Lees GB Mild, Bitter [H]
End-of-terrace pub with a small snug bar and a larger lounge area decorated with brass bric-à-brac. Very popular and busy - standing is often the only option.
⊡ ♣ P

Tandle Hill Tavern
Thornham Fold, Thornham Lane (1 mile off A671 or A664, along unmetalled road) OS898091
☎ (01706) 345297
7 (5 summer)-11; 12-11 Sat; 12-10.30 Sun
Lees GB Mild, Bitter, Moonraker (winter)**, seasonal beers** [H]
A gem, well hidden in an open rural setting. It attracts a varied and discerning clientele, the atmosphere is always warm and welcoming. Soup and sandwiches usually available lunchtime.
⛫ Q 🐎 ❀

Try also: Carters Arms, Manchester Old Road (Lees)

MILNROW

Crown & Shuttle
170 Rochdale Road, Firgrove (A640)
☎ (01706) 648259
12-11; 12-10.30 Sun
Lees GB Mild, Bitter [H]
Traditional pub, popular with locals and homeward-bound workers. Usually busy, with a friendly atmosphere, the three rooms provide a homely feel. Day trips and sports events are regularly organised. ⛫ ⊡ ♣ P

Try also: Wagon Inn, Butterworth Hall (Burtonwood)

MOSSLEY

Church Inn
82 Stockport Road
☎ (01457) 832021
11-11; 12-10.30 Sun
Ruddles Best Bitter; John Smith's Bitter; guest beers [H]
Friendly, cosy local, comprising a lounge, snug and a tap room. Usually two guest beers; the

landlord is phasing in oversized lined glasses. ♣ P

Try also: Tollemache, Manchester Rd (Robinson's)

MOSTON

BLUEBELL
493 Moston Lane (1 mile from A664 Rochdale Road)
☎ (0161) 683 4096
11-11; 11-4, 7-11 Sat; 12-4, 7-10.30 Sun
Holt Mild, Bitter Ⓗ
A monumental Edwardian pub, altered to create a semi-open-plan layout, but retaining distinct drinking areas. Children welcome until 7.30pm. ☜ ❀ ♣ P

NEW MOSTON

NEW MOSTON
52-54 Belgrave Road (near Failsworth station)
☎ (0161) 682 8265
12-4, 7-11; 11-11 Fri & Sat; 12-10.30 Sun
Banks's Mild; Marston's Bitter, HBC Ⓗ
Comfortable, thriving, two-roomed community local where activities include a sea angling club and a Wed quiz.
❀ ⊞ ⇌ (Failsworth) ♣

NEW SPRINGS

COLLIERS ARMS
192 Wigan Road, Aspull
☎ (01942) 831171
12.30-5.30 (not Thu), 7.30-11; 12-5, 7-10.30 Sun
Burtonwood Mild, Bitter, seasonal beers Ⓗ
Unspoilt, 18th-century pub near Leeds-Liverpool canal. A classic. Outdoor drinking is in the tiny car park. ⚓ ❀ ⊞ ♣ P

NEWTON HEATH

GROSVENOR ARMS
2 Eldridge Drive (near A62/B6293 jct)
☎ (0161) 205 2721
12-11; 12-10.30 Sun
Lees GB Mild, Bitter Ⓗ
Popular, friendly, two-roomer, catering for the local community. The larger vault, also known as the Gluepot, is very much sports-based (especially darts). The comfortable lounge hosts karaoke (Fri), a live performance or disco (Sat) and a quiz (Sun). Weekday lunches.
❀ ⊂ ⊞ ⇌ (Dean Lane) ♣ P

OLDHAM

DOG & PARTRIDGE
376 Roundthorn Road (off B6194) ☎ (0161) 624 3335
7 (4 Fri, 11 Sat)-11; 12-2, 7-11 Tue; 12-10.30 Sun

Lees GB Mild, Bitter Ⓗ
Popular, comfortably furnished, detached pub in a semi-rural setting with low-beamed ceilings. Busy Sunday lunch with local football teams.
❀ ♣ P

HARK TO TOPPER
5 Bow Street (off Yorkshire St)
☎ (0161) 624 7950
12-11; 12-4, 7.30-11 Tue & Wed; 7.30-10.30 Sun
Samuel Smith OBB Ⓗ
Town-centre pub (a former Rochdale and Manor house) with an impressive brick exterior, dating from 1835. Just off the main street, its pleasant open-plan interior has a central bar and etched glass windows. Close to the Coliseum Theatre. No food Sun. ⊂ ⇌ (Mumps)

Try also: Falconers Arms, Hollins Rd (Lees)

ORRELL

BIRD I' TH' HAND
Gathurst Road (by John Rigby College)
☎ (01942) 212006
11.45-11; 12-10.30 Sun
Theakston Mild, Best Bitter, Old Peculier; Webster's Green Label; guest beers Ⓗ
Welcoming, warm and friendly country local, popular with all ales. Excellent food.
❀ ⊂ ▶ ♿ ⇌ (Gathurst) P

PATRICROFT

QUEENS ARMS
Green Lane (by station)
☎ (0161) 789 2019
7-11; 12-3, 5-11 Fri; 12-11 Sat; 12.45-10.30 Sun
Boddingtons Mild, Bitter; Greenalls Bitter Ⓗ
Britain's first railway pub. Its pleasantly defined drinking areas are homely and welcoming; recent alterations have not diminished its character, in an area currently undergoing regeneration. Children welcome until 8pm.
☜ ❀ ⊞ ⇌ ♣ P

PEEL GREEN

GRAPES HOTEL
439 Liverpool Road (A57, near M63 jct 2)
☎ (0161) 789 6971
11-11; 12-10.30 Sun
Holt Mild, Bitter Ⓗ
Extravagantly lavish, high Edwardian style: four well-presented rooms surround a beautiful mahogany bar. Etched glass, fine tiling and polished wood together with a billiard room produce a splendid effect.
⊞ ⇌ (Patricroft) ♣ P

PRESTWICH

WOODTHORPE
Bury Old Road (near A665/A6044 jct)
☎ (0161) 795 0032
11-11; 12-10.30 sun
Holt Mild, Bitter Ⓗ
The original home of one of the Holt brewing family. A lovely old restored building set in its own grounds. One of the guest rooms has a four-poster bed. Home-cooked food (eve meals finish at 7pm).
Q ❀ ⇌ ⊂ ▶ ♿ ⊖ (Heaton Park) P

Try also: Red Lion, Bury New Rd (Holt)

RADCLIFFE

BRIDGE TAVERN
8 Blackburn Street (by shopping centre)
☎ (0161) 280 1572
11-11; 12-10.30 Sun
Burtonwood Bitter, seasonal beers Ⓗ
Friendly, town-centre pub recently renovated and extended. Overlooking the bandstand, this pub has an unusual 'happy hour': beers are discounted between 11-7 weekdays. ⊞ ⊖ ♣

ROCHDALE

ALBION
600 Whitworth Road (A671, 2 miles from centre)
☎ (01706) 648540
5-11; 12-11 Sat; 12-10.30 Sun
Lees Bitter; Taylor Mild, Best Bitter, Landlord; Theakston Best Bitter; guest beers Ⓗ
Traditional, three-roomed local attracting increasing custom following recent refurbishment. An interesting choice of food is served at weekends. ⚓ ❀ ⊂ ▶

BRITANNIA INN
4 Lomax Street (off Yorkshire St, A58) ☎ (01706) 646391
12-11; 12-3, 5-11 Tue-Thu; 12-10.30 Sun
Lees GB Mild, Bitter, seasonal beers Ⓗ
Friendly local just out of the centre. Voted Lees most popular pub in the 1997 Brewery Passport Trail. Long serving landlord. Happy hour 5-7 daily. The 1881 carved fireplace in the lounge is noteworthy. ❀ ⇌ ⊞ ♣

CASK & FEATHER
1 Oldham Road (Drake St jct)
☎ (01706) 711476
11-11; 12-10.30 Sun
McGuinness Feather Plucker Mild, Best Bitter, Junction Bitter, Tommy Todd Porter, seasonal beers Ⓗ
Distinctive stone-fronted pub

near the town centre. Customers are drawn by the McGuinness beers (the brewery can be viewed from the back of the pub) and good value lunches. ◖ ⇌

CEMETERY INN ☆
470 Bury Road (B6222/B6452 jct 1 mile from centre)
☎ (01706) 713932
12-11; 12-10.30 Sun
Lees Bitter; Taylor Mild, Best Bitter, Landlord; Theakston Best Bitter; guest beers Ⓗ
Famed free house returned to its former glory under new ownership. It retains four distinct drinking areas, each with its own character. Attractive original tiling is also a feature. Guest beers are usually from Phoenix or Moorhouse's. Good value, freshly-prepared food. ⚒ ◖ ▶ P

EAGLE
59 Oldham Road (A671/Wood St jct) ☎ (01706) 647222
12-3 (4 Sat), 5 (7 Sat)-11; 12-11 Fri; 12-10.30 Sun
Samuel Smith OBB Ⓗ
Popular stone pub, away from the town centre, boasting various interesting artefacts, furniture and period features. ⇌ ♣

SUCCESS TO THE PLOUGH
179 Bolton Road, Marland (A58, 1 mile from centre)
☎ (01706) 633270
12-11; 12-5, 7-10.30 Sun
Lees GB Mild, Bitter, seasonal beers Ⓗ
Imposing, detached redbrick pub with a deceptively spacious interior divided into different areas. A splendid bowling green to the rear is host to several crown green competitions. Weekday lunches. ⚙ ◖ P

ROYTON

DOG & PARTRIDGE
148 Middleton Road (B6195)
☎ (0161) 628 4198
11-11; 12-10.30 Sun
Lees GB Mild, Bitter Ⓗ
Traditional three-roomed pub close to the town centre where a warm welcome is guaranteed. Pencil sketches of old Royton adorn the walls of the beamed main bar. Excellent selection of malt whiskies. ⊞ ♣

RAILWAY HOTEL
1 Oldham Road
☎ (0161) 624 2793
11-11; 12-10.30 Sun
Lees GB Mild, Bitter Ⓗ
Large pub dominating the town's main junction. Three distinct drinking areas: a large, busy vault, a larger central lounge and a smaller snug. Quiz Sun eve. Weekday meals. ⚙ ◖ ⊞ ♣

SALFORD

CRESCENT
18-29 Crescent (A6, near university) ☎ (0161) 736 5600
12 (7.30 Sat)-11; 1-4, 7.30-10.30 Sun
John Smith's Bitter; guest beers Ⓗ
Rambling pub, benefiting from recent improvements and popular with students, lecturers and cats. Always an interesting selection of guest ales (the house beer is from Titanic). Good value food. ⚒ Q ◖ ▶ Ġ ⇌ (Crescent) ♣ ⌂ P ⊟

DOCK & PULPIT
1 Encombe Place (off A6, near Cathedral)
☎ (0161) 834 0121
12-3, 5-11; 12-11 Sat; 12-3, 7.30-10.30 Sun
Beer range varies Ⓗ
Hard-to-find gaslit gem, a one room free house full of character. The name derives from the former law courts and the church. The house beer is from John Smith's. ⚒ ⇌ (Central) ♣ ⌂

EAGLE INN
19 Collier Street (off A6041, near A6042 jct)
☎ (0161) 832 4919
11-11; 12-10.30 Sun
Holt Mild, Bitter Ⓗ
Back-street, old-fashioned gem. Although it is more exposed since the new trunk road opened, it can still be tricky to find. ⊞ ⇌ ♣

OLDE NELSON
285 Chapel Street (A6 opp Cathedral)
☎ (0161) 281 9607
12-3; 6.30-11; 11-5.30, 7-11 Sat; 12-5, 7-10.30 Sun
Chester's Mild; Boddingtons Bitter; Lees Bitter; Whitbread Trophy Ⓗ
Imposing, multi-roomed Victorian gem which has a large front vault accessible via a neat sliding door. A stand up drinking corridor lined with brewery and whisky mirrors leads to a plush lounge. More mirrors, brass hangings and etched windows complete the scene. Q ⊞ ⇌ (Central) ♣

UNION TAVERN
105 Liverpool Street (between A5063 and A5066)
☎ (0161) 736 2885
11-11; 12-10.30 Sun
Holt Mild, Bitter Ⓗ
Popular Holt's outlet in the old heart of Salford, now mainly light industrial area. A good, honest basic boozer; the mecca for local darts players, fielding five teams. ⊞ Ġ ⇌ (Crescent) ♣ P

WELCOME
Robert Hall Street (off A5066, near B5461 jct)
☎ (0161) 872 6040
11.45-4, 7.30-11; 12-3, 7-10.30 Sun
Lees GB Mild, Bitter Ⓟ
Community local, where the long-standing landlady always offers a friendly welcome in an area that has lost many pubs. The 'hand-pumps' activate electric motors.
Q ⊞ P

SHAW

BLACK HORSE HOTEL
203a Rochdale Road (B6194, ½ mile from centre)
☎ (01706) 847173
3.30 (12 Sat)-11; 12-10.30 Sun
Lees GB Mild, Bitter, seasonal beers Ⓗ
Traditional, friendly stone-built pub, a short walk from the centre with a comfortable lounge and a vault. ⊞ ♣ P

Try also: Morning Star, Grains Rd (Lees)

STALYBRIDGE

Q
3 Market Street
☎ (0161) 303 9157
11-11; 12-10.30 Sun
Marston's Bitter, Pedigree; guest beers Ⓗ
Converted from a shop and recently extended, the Q resurrects a previous pub name from the town, officially the shortest pub name in the UK. A pleasant open-plan interior is complemented by an upstairs bar. ⚙ ◖ ⇌ P

ROSE & CROWN
7 Market Street
☎ (0161) 303 7098
11-11; 12-5, 7-10.30 Sun
Vaux Mild, Bitter, Samson; guest beer Ⓗ
Traditional urban local, refurbished sympathetically to a high standard. A hub of community life with a loyal band of regulars. ⚒ ⇌ ♣ P

STATION BUFFET BAR ☆
Platform 1, Stalybridge Station, Market Street
☎ (0161) 303 0007
11.30 (11 Sat)-11; 11-10.30 Sun
Boddingtons Bitter; Flowers IPA; Wadworth 6X; guest beers Ⓗ
Historical and much-loved buffet bar, recently saved from ruin and restored to a high standard. A changing range of guest beers from independents; regular beer festivals and foreign bottled beers available. Occasional cider. ⚒ Q ⚙ ◖ ▶ ⇌ ⌂ P

WHITE HOUSE
1 Water St ☎ (0161) 303 2288
11-11; 12-10.30 Sun
**Exmoor Gold; Marston's Bitter,
Pedigree, seasonal beers;
Thwaites Bitter; guest beers** Ⓗ
Archetypal, true free house with
an ever-changing range of guest
beers, mainly from independent
and micro breweries. The eclectic mix of rooms has something
for most visitors; always lively
and welcoming. Foreign bottled
beers and malt whiskies on sale;
occasional cider. ◖ ≈ ⌂ P

STANDISH

BOARS HEAD
Wigan Road (A49)
☎ (01942) 749747
11-3, 5.30-11; 11-11 Sat; 12-3,
7-10.30 Sun
**Burtonwood Mild, Bitter,
Forshaw's, Top Hat, Buccaneer,
seasonal beers** Ⓗ
Old, characterful coaching house,
refurbished at the rear to accen-
tuate the patio which overlooks
the bowling green. Sport is
always on TV.
🏨 🏵 ◖ 🍴 P

DOG & PARTRIDGE
33 School Lane
☎ (01257) 401218
11-11; 12-10.30 Sun
**Boddingtons Bitter; Tetley Dark
Mild, Mild, Bitter** Ⓗ
Lively, male-oriented, open-plan
local with sport permanently on
TV. The weekend's Wigan RLFC
video is shown during the following week. Limited parking.
🏵 ♣ P

BISHOP BLAIZE
63 Lower Hillgate
☎ (0161) 429 9981
12-3, 5-11 (not Tue); 12-11 Sat;
1-10.30 Sun
**Burtonwood Bitter,
Buccaneer** Ⓗ
Three-roomed pub whose 1920s
interior boasts some attractive
original features. Formerly
called the Gladstone, it has
reverted to its original 19th-cen-
tury name.
🍴 ≈ ♣

CROWN
154 Heaton Lane (under viaduct,
200 yds from A6, at Debenhams)
☎ (0161) 429 0549
12-11; 12-3, 7-10.30 Sun
**Boddingtons Bitter; guest
beers** Ⓗ
Stockport's number one for real
ale choice, with a constantly
changing range of guest beers
usually from micros - up to nine
at any time. Currently for sale so
changes may occur during the
currency of this *Guide* - enjoy it
while you can.
🏵 ◖ 🍴 ≈ ♣ ✄

CROWN (CORNER CUPBOARD)
14 Higher Hillgate
☎ (0161) 480 7701
11-11; 12-10.30 Sun
**Vaux Mild, Samson, Waggle
Dance** Ⓗ
Two-roomed, street-corner local
with impressive high windows; it
has been revived after a period
of decline by the combination of
the licensee's enthusiasm and a
fine (long overdue) refurbishment.
🏵 ♣

FLORIST
100 Shaw Heath
☎ (0161) 666 0405
11-11; 12-3, 7-10.30 Sun
**Robinson's Hatters Mild, Best
Bitter** Ⓗ
Victorian, multi-roomed traditional pub, popular with locals.
Despite its busy main road location, there is a free public car
park at the rear. 🏵 ♿ ≈ ♣

GREYHOUND
27 Bowden Street, Edgeley
☎ (0161) 480 5699
11.30-11; 12-10.30 Sun
**Boddingtons Mild, Bitter; guest
beers** Ⓗ
A plain exterior hides a warm,
friendly, community local. Choose
either the comfortable L-shaped
lounge or the plainer but well-
used vault. Two guest beers usually available in this rare outlet
for cask Boddington's mild.
🏵 🍴 ≈ ♣

OLDE WOOLPACK
70 Brinksway (A560, near M63 jct
12)
☎ (0161) 429 6621
11.30-3 (4 Sat), 5 (7 Sat)-11; 11-
11 Fri; 12-10.30 Sun
**Marston's Pedigree;
Moorhouse's Black Cat Mild;
Tetley Bitter; Theakston Best
Bitter; guest beer** Ⓗ
Comfortable, three-roomed pub
overlooked by a giant blue pyramid. The guest beer (usually a
bitter) changes frequently. Take
the pleasant riverside walk (10
minutes from the town centre).
Good value food.
◖ 🍴 ♣ P

QUEEN'S HEAD ☆
12 Little Underbank
☎ (0161) 480 1545
11.30-11; 12-3, 7-10.30 Sun
Samuel Smith OBB Ⓗ
The key features of this small,
three-roomed pub are the spirit
taps on the bar and the world's
smallest gents. The pub was
originally the tasting rooms for
the wine vaults (Turners Vaults).
The CAMRA *Joe Goodwin* award
winner 1990 for the high standard of its restoration.
Q ◖ ≈ ✄

RAILWAY
1 Avenue Street (opp Peel
Centre)
☎ (0161) 429 6062
12-11; 12-4, 7-10.30 Sun
**Porters Mild, Bitter, Rossendale
Ale, Porter, Sunshine, seasonal
beers** Ⓗ
Single lounge corner pub, rescued from terminal decline by
Porter's brewery. A good range
of home-made food and keen
beer prices (with mild the biggest
seller) ensure its popularity. No
fruit machines, pool or juke box.
🏵 ◖ ♣ ⌂

UNITY
41 Wellington Road South (A6)
11.30-11; 11.30-4, 7-11 Sat;
7-10.30 (closed lunch) Sun
**Robinson's Hatters Mild, Best
Bitter** Ⓗ
Busy town-centre pub, by the station. A lively atmosphere flourish-
es in the plush single room which
plays host to darts teams eves.
Many popular promotions attract
a pleasingly mixed local clientele.
◖ ≈ ♣

STRINES

SPORTSMANS ARMS
105 Strines Road (1 mile from
Marple on New Mills road)
☎ (0161) 427 2888
11.30-3, 5.30-11; 12-3, 7-10.30
Sun
**Draught Bass; Boddingtons
Bitter; Cains Mild, Bitter** Ⓗ
Welcoming country pub with two
rooms - a vault and a lounge/din-
ing room. Enjoy the impressive
views over to Mellor. A winter ale
is sometimes stocked.
🏨 Q 🛏 ◖ ▶ ♿ Å ≈ P 🍴

SWINTON

WHITE LION
242 Manchester Road (A572/A6
jct)
☎ (0161) 288 0434
12-4, 7-11; 12-4, 7-10 Sun
**Robinson's Hatters Mild, Old
Stockport, Best Bitter, Old
Tom** Ⓗ
Comfortable, though much
changed late 18th-century local,
it comprises a spacious vault and
two lounges on separate levels,
the rear housing the Swinton
RLFC 'Hall of Fame'. A long-
established folk club meets Mon
eve. 🏵 🍴 ♣ P

WHITE SWAN
186 Worsley Road (200 yds off
A572/A580 jct)
☎ (0161) 794 1504
12-11; 12-10.30 Sun
Holt Mild, Bitter Ⓗ
Smart, four-roomed late 1920s
pub, the vault has its own
entrance and gents; the main
room is wood panelled; a rear

room is used as a family room Sun (until 7pm). The no-smoking dining room is for meals week-days and for meetings and func-tions at other times.
Q 🎍 🌺 ◖ 🍴 ♣ P

TYLDESLEY

HALF MOON
115-117 Elliot Street
☎ (01942) 873206
11-11; 12-10.30 Sun
Boddingtons Bitter; Holt Mild, Bitter; guest beers Ⓗ
Two-roomed, town-centre local: a low-beamed lounge and a pool room attracting all ages. Busy at weekends. Local CAMRA *Pub of the Year* 1998. 🌺 ♣

UPPERMILL

CHURCH INN
Church Lane (next to Saddleworth church)
☎ (01457) 820902
12-11; 12-10.30 Sun
Saddleworth More, Bert Corner Bitter, Hop Smacker, Shaftbender; John Smith's Bitter; Webster's Yorkshire Bitter Ⓗ
Well renovated old stone pub at the head of the valley overlooking Uppermill village; a semi-open-plan bar and a dining area. Cheap beers come from Saddleworth Brewery, located in an original stone brew house next to the pub. Food available all day Sat and Sun.
🎍 🌺 ◖ P ⏧

CROSS KEYS
Off Running Hill Gate (off A670, up Church Rd)
☎ (01457) 874626
11-11; 12-10.30 Sun
Lees GB Mild, Bitter, Moonraker, seasonal beers Ⓗ
Attractive, 18th-century stone building overlooking the Saddleworth church. The public bar has a stone-flagged floor and a Yorkshire range. The hub of many activities, including moun-tain rescue and clay pigeon shooting. Folk night Wed. Children's certificate.
🎍 Q 🎍 🌺 ◖ 🍴 🔔 A ♣ P

WARDLEY

MORNING STAR
520 Manchester Road (A6, near overhead M62; no access)
☎ (0161) 794 4927
12-11; 12-10.30 Sun
Holt Mild, Bitter Ⓗ
Friendly neighbourhood pub, handy for country walks and very popular for weekday lunches. The front bar parlour leads into an extended lounge and also has a vault.
🌺 ◖ 🍴 ≠ (Moorside) P

WESTHOUGHTON

CROSS GUNS
25 Bolton Road (B5235, ¹/₂ mile from A61)
☎ (01942) 811124
11.30-3, 7-11; 11.30-11 Sat; 12-10.30 Sun
Tetley Mild; Walker Best Bitter; guest beer (occasional) Ⓗ
Large, open-plan pub which has been extended to incorporate a pool table. A warm welcome is assured.
🎍 🌺 ≠ ♣ P

WHITEFIELD

COACH & HORSES
71 Bury Old Road (A665)
☎ (0161) 798 8897
12-11; 12-10.30 Sun
Holt Mild, Bitter Ⓗ
Traditional, unspoilt three-roomer: a snug, a lounge and a large tap. Hoping to open a fourth room due to its popularity. The regulars have their own golf society. Visitors are welcome to join them.
Q 🌺 ⊖ (Besses o' th' Barn) ♣

EAGLE & CHILD
Higher Lane (near A665/A56 jct)
☎ (0161) 766 3024
12-11; 12-10.30 Sun
Holt Mild, Bitter Ⓗ
Large, black and white pub set back from the road with limited car parking in front. It has a large L-shaped main bar with a cosy side room. The extensive large, well-kept bowling green at the rear makes it very popular in summer. Eve meals in summer.
🎍 🌺 ◖ 🍴 🔔 ⊖ (Besses o' th' Barn) P

NEW GROVE INN
183 Bury New Road (A56)
☎ (0161) 766 2190
11-11; 12-10.30 Sun
Holt Mild, Bitter Ⓗ
Spacious modernised two-roomer where the interior belies its 1920s brick exterior. Strong social and sporting support ensures that both bars are well frequented. ⊖ ♣

Try also: Wheatsheaf, Bury New Road (Robinson's)

WIGAN

BEER ENGINE
69 Poolstock Lane
☎ (01942) 321820
11-11; 12-10.30 Sun
Draught Bass; Exmoor Gold; Moorhouse's Pendle Witches Brew; John Smith's Bitter; Vaux Mild, Waggle Dance; guest beers Ⓗ
Former labour club with a com-fortable lounge and a large con-cert room. The recent pavilion

extension overlooks the bowling green. Hosts an annual Beer, Pie and Music festival.
🌺 ◖ 🍴 ♣ P

BIRD I' THE' HAND (TH' EN 'OLE)
102 Gidlow Lane
☎ (01942) 241004
12-11; 12-10.30 Sun
Lees Bitter; Tetley Mild, Bitter; Theakston Best Bitter; guest beer Ⓗ
Impressive mosaic work above the door fronts a great example of a back-street boozer, with a comfortable lounge and a lively tap room. Local CAMRA *Pub of the Year* 1997.
🌺 ◖ 🍴 🔔 🎍 ♣ P

BOLD HOTEL
161 Poolstock Lane
☎ (01942) 241095
12-4.30, 7-11; 12-3, 7-10.30 Sun
Burtonwood Mild, Bitter Ⓗ
Small, unchanged local on the edge of town. The tap room is full of rugby memorabilia. Q 🔔 ♣

BOWLING GREEN
106 Wigan Lane (A49)
☎ (01942) 516004
12-11; 12-10.30 Sun
Caledonian Deuchars IPA; Courage Directors; John Smith's Bitter; Theakston Black Bull; guest beers Ⓗ
Large, former Peter Walker out-let. The buzzing vault has sport on TV; waitress service in the busy lounge. The garden (with barbecue facilities) is a new addi-tion. 🎍 🌺 🚌 ♣ P

CHARLES DICKENS HOTEL
14 Upper Dicconson Street
☎ (01942) 323263
11-11; 12-10.30 Sun
Lees Bitter; Tetley Mild, Bitter Ⓗ
Hotel bar with flowers and mir-rors in abundance.
🚌 ◖ 🍴 P

DOUGLAS BANK
Woodhouse Lane
11-11; 12-10.30 Sun
Holts Mild, Bitter Ⓗ
This former bistro/fun pub is now a typical Holt's outlet: a comfortable lounge fronts a lively vault/tap room. Can be busy when Wigan Athletic are at home. ◖ 🔔 ♣ P

MILLSTONE HOTEL
67-68 Wigan lane
☎ (01942) 245999
3.30 (12 Fri & Sat)-11; 12-10.30 Sun
Thwaites Best Mild, Bitter Ⓗ
Quiet, relaxing local, a popular watering hole for the more mature sector of society, although all are made welcome. Semi-open plan layout.
🌺 ◖ 🎍 ♣

J.W. LEES & CO.
(BREWERS) LIMITED
ALE, STOUT & LAGER
BREWERS & BOTTLERS
WINE & SPIRIT MERCHANTS

MOON UNDER WATER
5-7a Market Place
☎ (01942) 323437
11-11; 12-10.30 Sun
Courage Directors; Tetley Bitter; Theakston Best Bitter; guest beers Ⓗ
Large pub, a former Halifax Building society office, right in the centre of town. Busy at weekends. The no-smoking area is to the rear. Local CAMRA *Best New Cask Outlet* winner 1997.
Q ⛄ Ⓓ ▶ ⇌ (North Western/Wallgate) ⚞ 🗑

ORWELL
4 Wigan Pier
☎ (01942) 323034
11-11 (11-3, 7-11 winter); 12-3, 7-10.30 Sun
Samuel Smith OBB ⒽⒼ**; Tetley Bitter** Ⓗ**; guest beers** ⒽⒼ
Former open-plan pub, now carefully partitioned, at the heart of the Wigan Pier complex, right next to the canal. Can be busy in summer.
Ⓓ 🍴 ♿ ⇌ (North Western/Wallgate)

SPRINGFIELD HOTEL ☆
47 Springfield Road
☎ (01942) 242072
12-2, 5-11; 12-11 Sat; 12-10.30 Sun
Tetley Mild, Bitter Ⓗ
Large, friendly pub opposite Wigan Athletic FC's Springfield Park (can be busy on match days). Note the classic Peter Walker decor and impressive woodwork. Tetley 'Feasting Fox' pub fare available.
Ⓓ ▶ ♣ P

SWAN & RAILWAY HOTEL
80 Wallgate
☎ (01942) 495032
11-11; 12-4, 7-10.30 Sun
Banks's Mild, Bitter; Marston's Pedigree Ⓗ
Listed, and saved from becoming a theme pub by the local CAMRA branch. Recently refurbished, it is as good an old-fashioned boozer as you'll get these days. Opposite North Western station.
Q ⛄ 🍴 Ⓓ ▶ ⇌ (North Western/Wallgate) 🗑

Try also: Gems, Upper Dicconson St (Free)

WITHINGTON
RED LION
532 Wilmslow Road (B5093 near Christie Hospital)
☎ (0161) 434 2441
11-11; 12-10.30 Sun
Bateman Mild; Marston's Bitter, Pedigree, Owd Rodger, seasonal beers Ⓗ
Extremely busy main road pub, popular with both locals and students and famous for its bowling green. An attractive country-style exterior gives way to waves of extensions, a vault and a large conservatory (family access until 8pm). ⛄ 🍴 Ⓓ ▶ 🍴 ♿ ♣ P

WOODFORD
DAVENPORT ARMS (THIEF'S NECK)
550 Chester Road (A5102)
☎ (0161) 439 2435
11-3.30, 5.15-11; 11-11 Sat; 12-3, 7-10.30 Sun
Robinson's Hatters Mild, Best Bitter, Old Tom ; Ⓟ **guest beers** Ⓗ

Superb, unspoilt multi-roomed farmhouse pub on the edge of suburbia. Children welcome at lunchtimes in the no-smoking snug and large, attractive garden. A year-round outlet for the increasingly rare Old Tom. The menu includes a good cheese list. Food served all day Sat (until 7pm). 🏚 Q ⛄ 🍴 Ⓓ 🍴 ♣ P 🗑

WORTHINGTON
CROWN HOTEL
Platt Lane OS576114
☎ (01257) 421354
11-11; 12-10.30 Sun
Boddingtons Bitter; Taylor Landlord; Tetley Bitter; guest beers Ⓗ
Rural pub featuring an attractive mahogany-panelled bar area. It actively promotes mild and guest beers. It has recently been converted to an hotel by extending along the terraced block.
🏚 🛏 Ⓓ ♣ P

INDEPENDENT BREWERIES

Bank Top:
Bolton
Holt:
Cheetham
Lees:
Middleton Junction
Marble:
Manchester
Mash & Air:
Manchester
McGuinness:
Rochdale
Old Pint Pot:
Salford
Phoenix:
Heywood
Robinson's:
Stockport
Saddleworth:
Uppermill

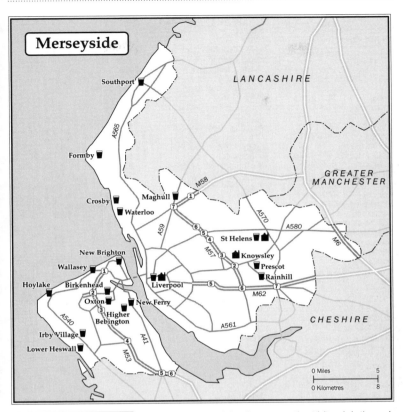

Merseyside

LANCASHIRE

Southport

Formby

GREATER MANCHESTER

Crosby
Maghull
Waterloo
St Helens
Knowsley
Prescot
New Brighton
Wallasey
Rainhill
Hoylake
Birkenhead
Liverpool
Oxton
New Ferry
Higher Bebington
Irby Village
Lower Heswall

CHESHIRE

0 Miles 5
0 Kilometres 8

BIRKENHEAD

CROWN ALE HOUSE
128 Conway Street (by Europa
Centre) ☎ (0151) 650 1095
11.30-11; 12-3, 7-10.30 Sun
**Cains Bitter; Greenalls Mild,
Bitter; Jennings Snecklifter;
guest beers** Ⓗ
Multi-roomed, listed building
offering five guest beers. A local
CAMRA award-winner, including
Pub of the Year 1997. Fittings in
bar are not to be missed. No
jukebox. Children welcome until
5pm. No food Sun. Cider varies.
Q ☎ Ⓓ ⧓ (Conway Park) ♣ ⏢

OLD COLONIAL
167 Bridge St (near Hamilton Sq
station) ☎ (0151) 666 1258
11-11; 12-10.30 Sun
**Cains Mild, Brewery Bitter,
Bitter, FA, seasonal beers; guest
beers** Ⓗ
Robert Cain Alehouse which has
undergone a recent extensive
refurbishment in Victorian style.
Eve meals 5-7 weekdays.
Ⓓ⧓ (Hamilton Sq) Ⓟ

STORK HOTEL
41-43 Price St
☎ (0151) 647 7506
11.30-11; 12-3, 7-10.30 Sun
Cains Bitter; guest beer Ⓗ

Splendid, four-roomed Victorian
pub built in 1840. It features an
island bar with a tiled frontage,
windows depicting Threfalls
Salford Ales and interesting photographs of old dock and ferry
scenes.
☎ ❀ Ⓓ ⧓ ⧓ (Hamilton
Sq/Conway Pk) ♣

CROSBY

CROSBY
75 Liverpool Road (S of
village)
☎ (0151) 924 2574
11-11; 12-10.30 Sun
Beer range varies Ⓗ
Whitbread Hogshead pub with an
ever-changing range of beers
from regional and microbreweries. The cellar, with beers on
stillage, is on view to the rear of
the bar.
❀ Ⓓ ⧓ ⧓ (Blundellsands/
Crosby)

CROW'S NEST
63 Victoria Road
☎ (0151) 931 3081
11.30-11; 12-10.30 Sun
Cains Bitter; guest beer Ⓗ
Friendly and very popular local,
with a public bar, lounge and a
tiny snug. No machines, no noise,
no pool – just good beer and con-

versation. Visit early in the week
to sample the guest beer – it
sells out quickly.
Q ❀ ⧓ ⧓ (Blundellsands/
Crosby) Ⓟ

FORMBY

FRESHFIELD HOTEL
1 Massams Lane (½ mile from
B5424) ☎ (01704) 874871
12-11; 12-10.30 Sun
Beer range varies Ⓗ
Popular local, part of
Whitbread's Hogshead chain. The
large bar serves 12 real ales and
a real cider. No children.
Weekday lunches.
♨ Q ❀ Ⓓ ⊖ ⏢ ⧓ (Freshfield)
Ⓟ

HIGHER BEBINGTON

TRAVELLERS REST
169 Mount Road
☎ (0151) 608 2988
12-11; 12-10.30 Sun
**Boddingtons Bitter; Cains
Bitter; Flowers IPA; Greene
King Abbot; Taylor Landlord;
guest beers** Ⓗ
Pleasant village inn dating from
1720, popular with locals and
walkers. One bar serves an open-
plan lounge with cosy partitioned
areas. Wheelchair WC. This pub

is also the Wirral CAMRA *Pub of the Year* 1998.
🏨 🍴 🍺 ♣ ✂

HOYLAKE

GREEN LODGE HOTEL
2 Stanley Rd ☎ (0151) 632 2321
11-11; 12-10.30 Sun
Burtonwood Bitter, Forshaw's Ⓗ
Large, friendly pub with a split-level lounge displaying photos of old Hoylake, a short walk from the promenade. Meals are served in the bar and restaurant.
🚲 🎵 🛏 🍴 🍺 ➤ P

IRBY VILLAGE

SHIPPONS INN
Thingwall Rd
☎ (0151) 648 0449
11-11; 12-10.30 Sun
Banks's Mild, Bitter; Camerons Strongarm; Marston's Pedigree; guest beer Ⓗ
Traditional village pub, converted in 1994 from an 18th-century farm building. It features an inglenook and attractions include Mon folk music, a lively Wed quiz and imaginative theme nights.
Q 🎵 🍴 🍺 P

LIVERPOOL: *CENTRE*

BALTIC FLEET
33a Wapping
☎ (0151) 709 3116
11-11; 12-10.30 Sun
Cains Mild; Ind Coope Burton Ale; Tetley Mild, Bitter; guest beers Ⓗ
Well-known landmark on the dock road just across from the Albert Dock. Resembling the prow of a steamship, it has three rooms, two of which share a double-sided open fire. Good food (served 12-9 Sun). Get there by Smart bus no. 3 (day), no. 5 (eve) to Gower St.
🚲 Q 🎵 🍴 🍺 ➤ (James St)
🍺 P ✂

BLACKBURNE ARMS
24 Catharine Street
☎ (0151) 708 0252
12-11; 12-10.30 Sun
Cains Bitter Ⓗ
Quiet pub on the edge of the city centre, popular with students and locals.
Q ➤ (Lime St) ➤ (Central)

BONAPARTES
21a Clarence Street
☎ (0151) 709 0737
12 (7 Sat) 12.30am; 7-10.30 Sun
Vaux Waggledance; Ward's Best Bitter; guest beer Ⓗ
Popular with students and locals for its late licence. Bare boards and candlelight create atmosphere.
🍴 ➤ (Lime St) ➤ (Central) ♣

CAMBRIDGE
51 Mulberry Street (near Liverpool University)
11.30 (12 Sat)-11; 12-10.30 Sun
Burtonwood Bitter, Forshaw's Top Hat, Buccaneer; guest beer Ⓗ
Recently refurbished, lively pub which still has a traditional feel. Popular with students and lecturers. Sunday breakfast available.
🚲 🍴 ➤ (Lime St) ➤ (Central) ♣

CARNARVON CASTLE
5 Tarleton St
☎ (0151) 709 3153
11-11; closed Sun
Draught Bass; Cains Mild, Bitter Ⓗ
City-centre pub, popular with shoppers. Note the impressive collection of model cars displayed in cases around the pub.
🚲 ➤ (Central) ➤ (Lime St)

CRACKE
13 Rice St
☎ (0151) 709 4171
11.30-11; 12-10.30 Sun
Cains Bitter; Marston's Pedigree; Phoenix Oak Bitter, Wobbly Bob; guest beers Ⓗ
Friendly, unusual free house comprising many rooms off a larger main bar. Lively atmosphere, but some side rooms are quiet. No lunch Sun but breakfast served 12-2.30. Two guest ciders.
Q 🍴 ➤ (Central) ➤ (Lime St) 🍺

DISPENSARY
87 Renshaw St
☎ (0151) 709 2160
11-11; 12-10.30 Sun
Cains Mild, Brewery Bitter, Bitter, FA, seasonal beers; guest beer Ⓗ
Formerly 'The Grapes', this magnificently refurbished pub is now a Cains tied house. Two original Robert Cain etched glass windows show this pub has now returned to its historic owner. Opened in 1998, it is already a popular, friendly watering-hole. Meals served 12-7.
Q 🍴 ➤ (Central) ➤ (Lime St)

EVERYMAN
9 Hope St ☎ (0151) 708 9545
12-12; closed Sun
Beer range varies Ⓗ
Usually four guest beers in this bistro/bar beneath the Everyman Theatre. Popular with theatregoers for meals early eve and lunchtime, and with drinkers later on. An interesting menu offers many vegetarian options; an entry in CAMRA's *Good Pub Food*. Q 🍴 🍺 🍺 ✂

FLORIN & FIRKIN
43 Lime Street (opp station)
☎ (0151) 709 4719
11.30-11; 12-10.30 Sun
Firkin Dog Bolter, Florin Bitter, Skinflint, Sovereign; guest beer Ⓗ

Listed building with its original character maintained; note the spectacular ceiling. Very popular with students. Large screen TV. Meals served 11-7. The guest beer is a Firkin Brew.
🍴 🍺 ➤ (Merseyrail) ➤ (Lime St) ♣

GLOBE
17 Cases Street (opp Central Station)
☎ (0151) 709 5060
11-11; 12-10.30 Sun
Cains Mild, Brewery Bitter, Bitter Ⓗ
Greenalls pub signed as a Robert Cain house. Often lively, with music from the 60s making it popular with young and old alike. The sloping floor tests customers' sense of balance.
➤ (Central) ➤ (Lime St)

PETER KAVANAGH'S
2-6 Egerton Street (off Catharine Street)
☎ (0151) 709 8443
12-11; 12-10.30 Sun
Cains Bitter; Greene King Abbot; Ind Coope Burton Ale; Tetley Bitter; guest beer Ⓗ
Friendly, quaint Victorian back-street pub. Can be lively, especially eves, but quiet, unspoilt snug rooms are available off the bar. Sun breakfast served 12-2.30. Q 🎵 🍴 ✂

PIG & WHISTLE
12 Covent Garden
☎ (0151) 236 4760
11.30-11; 12-10.30 Sun
Marston's Pedigree; Walker Mild, Bitter; Tetley Bitter Ⓗ
Comfortable, traditional pub in the business area with a convivial atmosphere. The upstairs bar opens lunchtime. Informal folk music session Thu. Weekday lunches.
🍴 ➤ (Moorfields/James St)

POST OFFICE
2 Great Newton Street
☎ (0151) 707 1005
12-11; 12-10.30 Sun
Cains Bitter; guest beer Ⓗ
Friendly pub with a quiet lounge; the bar has a juke box and a pool table. Popular with locals, hospital staff, lecturers and students, it is busiest at lunchtime and early in the evenings. It is also close to the Metropolitan Cathedral.
Q 🎵 🍴 🍺 ➤ ➤ (Lime St) ♣

ROSCOE HEAD
26 Roscoe Street (opp bombed-out church)
☎ (0151) 709 4490
11-11; 12-10.30 Sun
Ind Coope Burton Ale; Jennings Bitter; Marston's Pedigree; Tetley Mild, Bitter Ⓗ
Liverpool's premier pub, ever

present in this *Guide.* No gimmicks, just an excellent place for a drink where three snugs create a friendly atmosphere and conversation thrives. Snacks only Sat lunch.
Q ⊄ ⊖ (Central) ⇌ (Lime St)

SHIP & MITRE
133 Dale Street
☎ (0151) 236 0859
11 (12.30 Sat)-11; 12.30-10.30 Sun
Cains Mild; Matthew Clark Chadwick's Finest; guest beers Ⓗ
The city's premier real ale pub, four times local CAMRA *Pub of the Year.* It serves up to 10 unusual guest beers. A gaslit interior and a collection of vintage typewriters are features of this friendly pub. Excellent value food (weekdays), popular with students at lunchtime.
⊄ ⊖ (Moorfields) ⇌ (Lime St) ⌂ 🖵

SWAN INN
86 Wood Street
☎ (0151) 263 5281
11.30-11; 12-10.30 Sun
Cains Mild, Bitter; Marston's Pedigree; Phoenix Wobbly Bob; guest beers Ⓗ
Friendly, traditional pub, busy eves with a mixed clientele, it is popular with bikers. Extensive rock juke box. Friday is curry night; Sunday breakfasts served.
⊄ ⊖ (Central) ⇌ (Lime St) ⌂

UNITED POWERS
66-68 Tithebarn Street
☎ (0151) 474 4201
11-11; 12-10.30 Sun
Beer range varies Ⓗ
Recently refurbished in 1940s style with some genuine articles. A warm friendly atmosphere pervades this two-roomed pub. Sky TV. Always a mild on tap.
⊄ 🍴 ⊞ ⊖ (Moorfields) ♣

VERNON ARMS
69 Dale Street (opp Municipal Building)
☎ (0151) 236 4525
11.30-8 (11 Thu-Sat); closed Sun
Coachmans Gunpowder Mild; guest beers Ⓗ
Recent renovation has totally transformed this previously run-down city-centre pub. Friendly staff serve a relaxed atmosphere and serve an excellent range of food (12-7 Mon-Sat). Liverpool Brewery beers are also stocked.
⊄ 🍴 ⊖ (Moorfields) ⇌ (Lime St)

WHITE STAR (QUINNS)
2-4 Rainford Gardens
☎ (0151) 236 8520
11-11; 12-3, 7-10.30 Sun
Draught Bass; Cains Bitter; guest beers Ⓗ
Traditional pub surrounded by modern bars in the popular

Matthew Street area. See the impressive Bass mirror in the rear lounge. Occasional beer festivals. ⇌ (Lime St) ⊖ (Central))

LIVERPOOL: *EAST*

ALBANY
40-42 Albany Road
☎ (0151) 228 8597
11-11.30; 12-10.30 Sun
Cains Mild, Bitter Ⓗ
Lively, friendly back-street local, which is noted for the quality of its mild. No food at weekends. There are pavement benches for outdoor drinkers.⊛ ⊄ ♣

CLUBMOOR
119 Townsend Lane, Anfield
☎ (0151) 260 8170
12-11; 12-10.30 Sun
Cains Mild, Bitter Ⓗ
Handsome, detached pub on a main road with a large lounge and a public bar (darts and Sky TV), not far Everton and Liverpool FC grounds. Quiz night on Wednesdays.
⊛ 🍴 ♣

EDINBURGH
4 Sandown Lane, Wavertree
☎ (0151) 475 2648
12-11; 12-10.30 Sun
Cains Mild, Brewery Bitter, Bitter; guest beer Ⓗ
Tiny, popular local, now in Cains' ownership. A small lounge and an even smaller bar. Q 🍴

WILLOW BANK
329 Smithdown Road, Wavertree
☎ (0151) 733 5782
12-11; 12-10.30 Sun
Ind Coope Burton Ale; Marston's Pedigree; Tetley Mild, Bitter; guest beers Ⓗ
Deservedly thriving and popular with both students and locals, hosting four beer festivals a year. Floor service available if not too crowded. Rotation of interesting bottled beers, and at least four guest beers. No food Sat, or Sun eve.
⊄ 🍴 🍴 ⅋ P

LIVERPOOL: *NORTH*

CLOCK
167 Walton Road
☎ (0151) 207 3597
11-11; 12-10.30 Sun
Cains Mild Ⓗ
Pleasant and friendly street-corner local, handy for Everton FC. 🍴

QUEENS ARMS
202 Walton Road (A59)
☎ (0151) 207 1596
11-11; 12-10.30 Sun
Cains Bitter; Ⓗ
Three-roomed pub, close to

Everton Football Club (no food on match days or Sun eve). Children welcome if dining. Wheelchair WC in Ladies; Gents' access is difficult. ⊄ 🍴 🍴 🍴 ♣

LIVERPOOL: *SOUTH*

BREWERY TAP
35 Stanhope Street, Toxteth (by Cains Brewery)
☎ (0151) 709 2129
11-11; 12-10.30 Sun
Cains Mild, Bitter, FA, seasonal beers; guest beers Ⓗ
Winner of CAMRA's *Best Refurbishment* award. Deservedly popular, it gets busy when used as the base for brewery tours. See the interesting collection of breweriana. Meals served 12-7 (not Sun).
⊛ ⊄ P

ROYAL GEORGE
99 Park Road, Toxteth
☎ (0151) 708 9277
11-11; 12-10.30 Sun
Bass Mild, Toby; guest beer Ⓗ
Friendly pub, recently acquired by Bass, locally known as Black George's. there is live music a couple of nights a week, and cable TV. It offers a competitively priced beer.
🍴 ♣

LOWER HESWALL

DEE VIEW INN
Dee View Road
☎ (0151) 342 2320
12-11; 12-10.30 Sun
Boddingtons Bitter; Cains Bitter; Thwaites Bitter; guest beer Ⓗ
Popular, traditional pub dating from the 19th century, with views over the River Dee and Welsh hills. It stands opposite the war memorial on a hairpin bend. No food Sun.
⊄ ♣ P

MAGHULL

RED HOUSE
31 Foxhouse Lane
☎ (0151) 526 1376
11-11; 12-10.30 Sun
Marston's Pedigree; Tetley Bitter; Walker Mild; guest beers Ⓗ
Friendly, suburban local, possibly the last real pub in Maghull, an oasis for those not part of 'yoof' culture. Liverpool bus stop outside.
⊛ ⊄ 🍴 ⇌ P

NEW BRIGHTON

CLARENCE HOTEL
89 Albion St ☎ (0151) 639 3860
11-11; 12-10.30 Sun
Boddingtons Bitter; Cains Bitter; guest beers Ⓗ
Warm, welcoming corner local,

drawing a good mix of clientele to its split-level lounge. A Whitbread pub whose licensee likes to try new beers, mainly from micros. The house beer is brewed by Hart.
🏮 🍺 🍽 🍴 ≥ ♣

TELEGRAPH INN
25-27 Mount Pleasant Road
☎ (0151) 639 1508
11.30-11; 12-10.30 Sun
Boddingtons Bitter; Cains Bitter; Castle Eden Ale; guest beer Ⓗ
Historic pub with Mersey maritime connections. A recent extension complements the three small drinking areas. A very popular pub in a good drinking area. Good value food.
🏮 🍺 ♣ P

NEW FERRY
CLEVELAND ARMS
31 Bebington Road
☎ (0151) 645 2847
11.30-11; 12-10.30 Sun
Thwaites Best Mild, Bitter Ⓗ
Popular, friendly, open-plan local in a pedestrianised area, built 1859. Limited parking.
≥ (Bebington) ♣ P

OXTON
SHREWSBURY ARMS
38 Claughton Firs
☎ (0151) 652 1775
11-11; 12-10.30 Sun
Boddingtons Bitter; Cains Mild, Bitter, FA; Theakston Best Bitter; guest beer Ⓗ
Traditional, very popular pub with beamed ceilings attracting a cosmopolitan clientele. Enjoy a relaxing drink in the rose garden. No food Sun.
🏮 🍺 P ⌿

PRESCOT
CLOCK FACE
54 Derby Street (A57)
☎ (0151) 292 4121
11-11; 12-3, 7-10.30 Sun
Thwaites Bitter, Daniels Hammer Ⓗ
Attractive pub on the edge of the town, a private house converted in the 1980s with a relaxed friendly atmosphere. Eve meals end at 8pm.
Q 🏮 🍺 🍽 ≥ P

HARE & HOUNDS
10 Warrington Road (A57)
11-11; 12-10.30 Sun
Cains Mild, Bitter; guest beer Ⓗ
Known as Tommy Hall's and due to be officially named as such, this ex-Joseph Jones house enjoys a friendly atmosphere. Now L-shaped, it retains the two-room effect with two bars.
≥ ♣

SUN INN
11 Derby Street (A57)
12-11; 12-10.30 Sun
Greenalls Bitter, Original; guest beers Ⓗ
At over 200 years, this is the oldest pub in town. A traditional friendly pub with a real fire in the Mayor's Parlour.
🏚 Q 🍺 ≥ ♣

RAINHILL
COMMERCIAL
12 Station Road (off A57)
☎ (0151) 426 6446
12-11; 12-10.30 Sun
Cains Bitter Ⓗ
Marvellous Joseph Jones pub windows not being looked after by new owners, Greenalls, but the pub continues to prosper despite high prices and loud music in the best side.
🏮 🍺 ≥ ♣ P

MANOR FARM
Mill Lane (off M62, jct 7)
☎ (0151) 430 0335
11-11; 12-10.30 Sun
Burtonwood Bitter, Forshaw's; guest beers Ⓗ
Attractive, 15th-century manor farm house, popular with families, with a characterful, spacious interior and an extensive play area outside. Excellent meals are served all day in the upstairs restaurant.
🏚 🏮 🍺 🍽 P

ST HELENS
ABBEY HOTEL
Hard Lane, Denton's Green
☎ (01744) 28609
11-11; 12-10.30 Sun
Holt Mild, Bitter Ⓗ
Large, multi-roomed ex-Greenalls pub, a mile from the centre. ♣ P

BEECHAMS BAR & BREWERY
Water Street (A58, near clock tower) ☎ (01744) 623420
11-11; closed Sat & Sun
Beechams Bitter, Stout, seasonal beers; Thwaites Bitter, seasonal beers Ⓗ
Bar and brewery in the ex-Beecham's Powders offices, now part of St Helens College. The students learn brewing and bar management. The bar has a good atmosphere, attracting students and visitors.
Q ♿ ≥ (Shaw St) ⌿

TURKS HEAD
40-51 Morley Street
☎ (01744) 604426
11-11; 12-4, 7-10.30 Sun
Cains Bitter, Mild; Holt Bitter; guest beer Ⓗ
True, traditional pub which owns its own race horse (Crabbies Pride). Food recommended.
🏚 🏮 🍺 ≥ (Central) ♣

WHEATSHEAF
36 Westfield Street
☎ (01744) 601090
11-11; 12-10.30 Sun
Tetley Dark Mild, Bitter; guest beers Ⓗ
This traditional alehouse, a one-bar operation, attracts sporting enthusiasts (mainly rugby league and union, horse racing and cricket). A doubles bar, superb pork pies and black puddings are attractions; its pleasant atmosphere is not marred by loud music.
≥ (Central)

SOUTHPORT
BARON'S BAR
Scarisbrick Hotel, 239 Lord Street (opp Town Hall)
☎ (01704) 543000
11-11; 12-10.30 Sun
Boddingtons Bitter; Morland Old Speckled Hen; Tetley Bitter; guest beers Ⓗ
Opulently furnished, friendly lounge bar within a town-centre hotel, busy at weekends. The house beer, Flag and Turret, is brewed by Carlsberg-Tetley's Burton brewery. The annual beer festival starts at 6am May 1st. Food is available in the adjacent bars.
🛏 🏨 ≥ (Chapel St)

BLAKES HOTEL & PIZZA PUB
19 Queens Road
☎ (01704) 500811
4 (12 Sat)-11; 12-10.30 Sun
Adnams Bitter; Marston's Bitter; Fuller's London Pride; Moorhouse's Black Cat, Premier; Taylor Landlord Ⓗ
Hotel bar specialising in pizzas, but other dishes (especially pasta) are also available; also a children's menu. Comfortable family room at the back of the hotel. Always 10 ales available.
🛏 🏮 🍽 ≥ 🏨 P ⌿

GUEST HOUSE
16 Union Street (off Lord St near fire station)
☎ (01704) 537660
12-11; 12-10.30 Sun
Draught Bass; Boddingtons Bitter; Cains Mild; Taylor Landlord; guest beers Ⓗ
Traditional gem in the town centre: several rooms with a courtyard at the rear where skittles are played.
Q 🏮 ≥ ♣ ⌿

HESKETH ARMS HOTEL
Botanic Road, Churchtown
☎ (01704) 227084
11.30-11; 12-10.30 Sun
Greene King Abbot; Ind Coope Burton Ale; Marston's Pedigree; Tetley Mild, Dark Mild, Bitter Ⓗ
Old coaching house situated by

Cains contributes to Liverpool's lively arts scene as sponsor of the play *Two*. Steve Holt, managing director of Cains, was pictured with Dean Sullivan and Michael Starke, actors from the TV series *Brookside*. The Everyman Theatre bar is listed on page 226.

the village green and Botanical Gardens, three miles from the centre. Memorabilia adorns the walls in the central serving area. Happy hour Mon-Fri, 5-7. No juke box, but there is live jazz on Wednesday evening.
🏚 🏵 🕭 P

UP STEPS
20 Upper Aughton Road, Birkdale
☎ (01704) 569245
11.30-11; 12-10.30 Sun
Courage Directors; Theakston Mild, Best Bitter; guest beers Ⓗ
Friendly, traditional pub, supporting darts, dominoes and quiz teams. The guest beers change weekly.
Q 🏵 🕭 ≒ (Birkdale) ♣

WETHERSPOONS
93-97 Lord Street (200 yds S of A565/A570 jct)
☎ (01704) 530217
11-11; 12-10.30 Sun
Cains Mild; Courage Directors; Mitchell's Original; Theakston Best Bitter; guest beers Ⓗ
On Southport's famous Victorian main street, this pub opened in 1995 on the site of a former theme pub. A large, bustling place, it offers a varied food menu throughout the day, and follows Wetherspoon policies

which are supported by CAMRA. Not licensed for children.
Q 🕭 🛈 🕭 ≒ ⌂ ✄ 🕭

WALLASEY

FARMERS ARMS
225 Wallasey Village
☎ (0151) 638 2110
11.30-11; 12-10.30 Sun
Cains Bitter; Tetley Bitter; Theakston Best Bitter; guest beer Ⓗ
Former local CAMRA *Pub of the Year* which used to be two stone cottages. A front bar, side snug and a back lounge cater for all; no jukebox. The guest beer pump is in the bar. Weekday lunches, chinese stir-fry is a speciality.
🕭 🕭 ≒ (Grove Rd)

WATERLOO

MARINE
3-5 South Road (towards sea front from station)
12-11; 12-10.30 Sun
Cains Bitter; Ⓗ
Friendly, unspoilt and unchanged pub retaining its original layout with a bar/lounge and a large public bar with its own entrance. Reasonably priced meals. Handy for coastal walks.
Q 🏵 🕭 🕭 ≒

INDEPENDENT BREWERIES

Beecham's:
Merseyside
Cains:
Liverpool
Cambrinus:
Knowsley
Liverpool:
Liverpool
Passageway:
Liverpool

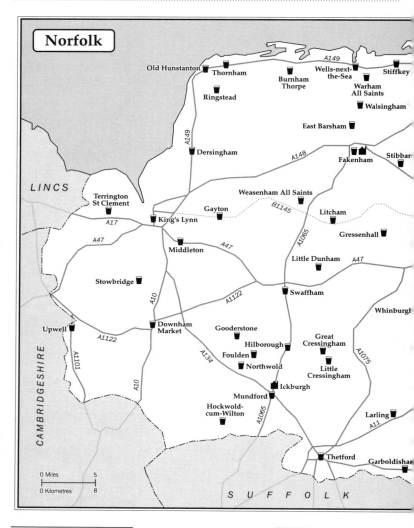

Norfolk

Map locations: Old Hunstanton, Thornham, Burnham Thorpe, Wells-next-the-Sea, Stiffkey, Ringstead, Warham All Saints, Walsingham, East Barsham, Dersingham, Fakenham, Stibbar, Terrington St Clement, Weasenham All Saints, Litcham, Gayton, King's Lynn, Gressenhall, Middleton, Little Dunham, Stowbridge, Swaffham, Whinburgh, Downham Market, Gooderstone, Hilborough, Great Cressingham, Upwell, Foulden, Northwold, Little Cressingham, Larling, Ickburgh, Mundford, Hockwold-cum-Wilton, Thetford, Garboldisha

LINCS

CAMBRIDGESHIRE

SUFFOLK

0 Miles 5
0 Kilometres 8

ATTLEBOROUGH

GRIFFIN HOTEL
Church Street
☎ (01953) 452149
10.30-3, 5.30-11; 12-3, 7-10.30
Sun
Greene King Abbot; Wadworth 6X; Wolf Best Bitter, Granny Wouldn't Like It; guest beer Ⓗ
Welcoming old coaching inn retaining much charm, serving strong guest beers from all over the country and a wide ranging menu.
Q ⇔ ◑ ▶ ▲ ⇌ P

AYLSHAM

FEATHERS
54 Cawston Road
☎ (01263) 732314
11-3 (5 Sat), 7-11; 12-5, 7-10.30
Sun

Adnams Mild, Bitter; Wells Eagle Ⓗ
Traditional pub attracting mainly a local trade. The games room displays trophies for the two pool teams and the darts team.
⇔ ❀ ♣ P

BANNINGHAM

CROWN INN
Colby Road (¼ mile from A140, Norwich-Cromer road)
☎ (01263) 733534
12-2.30, 7-11 Mon-Sat; 12-3, 7-10.30 Sun
Boddingtons Bitter; Greene King IPA, Abbot; Tetley Bitter Ⓗ
Comfortable village pub with a log fire. The bar is divided into several sections and features bar billiards. Good food; the restaurant area has a wheelchair ramp.
⇔ Q ❀ ◑ ▶ ▲ ♣ P

BLAKENEY

MANOR HOTEL
The Quay
☎ (01263) 740376
11-2.30, 6-11; 12-3, 6-10.30 Sun
Adnams Bitter, Broadside Ⓗ
Pleasant hotel bar overlooking the salt marshes, offering reasonably priced beer and good food.
Q ❀ ⇔ ◑ ▶ P

BLICKLING

BUCKINGHAMSHIRE ARMS
☎ (01263) 732137
11-3, 6-11; 12-3, 7-10.30 Sun
Adnams Bitter; Reepham Granary Ⓗ
Unspoilt pub next to Blickling Hall with its lovely walking and cycling routes. A delightful snug and a bar with a real fire. No food Sun

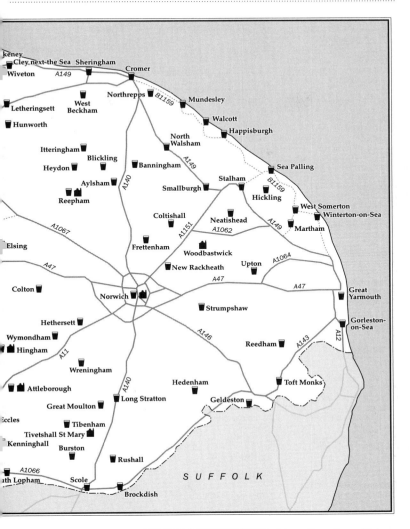

eve. The house beer is brewed by Woodforde's.
🏚 Q ✿ 🚍 ◑ ▶ P

BROCKDISH

GREYHOUND
The Street
☎ (01379) 668755
12-2 (not Mon-Wed); 12-2, 7-10.30 Sun
Buffy's Bitter, Polly's Folly, Mild; Old Chimneys Military Mild, Swallowtail IPA; Woodforde's Wherry G
Award-winning home-cooked food is served in this 16th-century coaching inn which is quirky, but welcoming. Jigsaw puzzles available. Up to 10 beers aee normally stocked, including the full Buffy's range.
🏚 Q ✿ ◑ ▶ ♣ P ⅍ 🍺

BURNHAM THORPE

LORD NELSON
Walsingham Road (off A149)
☎ (01328) 738241
11-3, 6-11; 12-3, 7-10.30 Sun
Greene King XX Mild, IPA, Abbot; Woodforde's Wherry, Nelson's Revenge (summer) G
Popular pub, displaying Nelson memorabilia. All beer is brought from the tap room; there is also a snug, a restaurant and a barn for live music. Very large garden.
🏚 Q ☎ ✿ ◑ ▶ ᚷ P ⅍

BURSTON

CROWN INN
Crown Green
☎ (01379) 741257
11.30-2.30 (3 Fri & Sat); 5.30-11; 12-3, 6.30-10.30 Sun

Adnams Bitter; Greene King Abbot; guest beers G
Delightful 17th-century pub which features oak beams and also has an intimate restaurant area.
🏚 Q ✿ ◑ ▶ 🍺 ᚷ Å ♣ P

CLEY-NEXT-THE-SEA

GEORGE & DRAGON HOTEL
High Street
☎ (01263) 740652
11-3 , 6 (7 winter)-11; 12-2.30, 7-10.30 Sun
Greene King IPA, Abbot, seasonal beers H
Birdwatchers' pub with two bars, plus a room for diners and families, bearing George and Dragon memorabilia. No eve meals winter Mon & Tue.
🏚 ✿ 🚍 ◑ ▶ ᚷ P

231

THREE SWALLOWS
Newgate Green
☎ (01263) 740526
11-2.30, 6-11; 12-3, 6-10.30 Sun
Greene King IPA; guest beers
(summer) ℍ
Two-bar pub with a TV room featuring Sky sports. The large garden has goats, an aviary and a children's play area. Reasonably priced accommodation.
🛏 Q ✿ 🛏 ◖ ▶ Å P

COLTISHALL

RED LION
Church Street
☎ (01603) 737402
11-3, 5-11; 12-3, 7-11 Sun
Adnams Bitter; Boddingtons Bitter; Greene King Abbot; Morland Old Speckled Hen; guest beers ℍ
Large pub with rooms on split levels. Note the windows etched with the pub lions. A local steam railway passes close by between Aylsham and Wroxham. The house beer is from Woodforde's.
✿ ◖ ▶ ᵫ ≑ ♣ ○ P

COLTON

UGLY BUG INN
High House Farm Lane
☎ (01603) 880794
12-3, 5.30-11.30; 12-3, 7-10.30 Sun
Hancock's HB; Morland Old Speckled Hen; guest beers ℍ
Single-bar pub converted from a barn, featuring a brick and beam interior and large gardens with ponds. The house beer is brewed by Iceni. No food Sun eve.
🛏 ✿ 🛏 ◖ ▶ ᵫ ♣ P

CROMER

ANGLIA COURT HOTEL
5 Runton Road (A149)
☎ (01263) 512443
10.30-11; 12-10.30 Sun
Woodforde's Wherry; Shepherd Neame Spitfire ℍ
Hotel situated on the clifftop facing out to sea. The smugglers bar at the front is decked with fishing nets etc. Cromer Smugglers Sea Shanty group are based here.
✿ 🛏 ◖ ▶ Å P

DERSINGHAM

FEATHERS
Manor Road ☎ (01485) 540207
11-2.30 (may extend summer), 5.30-11; 12-3, 7-10.30 Sun
Adnams Bitter; Draught Bass; guest beer ℍ
Close to Sandringham House, this pub offers something for everyone: a large safe garden with playthings, a separate bar for games and live music, a restaurant and two comfortable wood-panelled bars for a quiet drink.
🛏 Q ✿ 🛏 ◖ ▶ P

DOWNHAM MARKET

CROWN
Bridge Street
☎ (01366) 382322
11-2.30, 5-11; 11-11 Fri & Sat; 12-3, 7-10.30 Sun
Bateman XB; Courage Directors; Theakston Best Bitter; guest beer ℍ
This large, 17th-century coaching inn features a comfortable bar with a roaring fire. 🛏 Q 🛏 ◖ ▶ P

EAST BARSHAM

WHITE HORSE INN
Fakenham Road
☎ (01328) 820645
11-3, 7-11; 12-3, 7-10.30 (12-10.30 summer) Sun
Boddingtons Bitter; Greene King IPA, Abbot; guest beers ℍ
Comfortable, friendly 17th-century inn with a large inglenook and two restaurants (one for non-smokers). This lovely pub in an unspoilt village offers good accommodation and food.
🛏 ✿ 🛏 ◖ ▶ ♣ P

ECCLES

OLD RAILWAY TAVERN (ECCLES TAP)
Station Road OS018899
12-2.30, 5.30-11; 12-3, 7-10.30 Sun
Adnams Bitter Ⓖ**; Greene King IPA** ℍ**; guest beers** (occasional) Ⓖ
Quiet, unchanging drinkers' local. Relax and chat over a pint and give yourself time to appreciate this gem.
🛏 Q ✿ ≑ (Eccles Rd - limited service) ♣ P 🛢

ELSING

MERMAID INN
Church Street
☎ (01362) 637640
12-3, 7-11; 12-3, 7-10.30 Sun
Adnams Bitter, Broadside; Woodforde's Wherry; guest beers ℍ
Old, single-bar pub with a restaurant and games area. Note the mermaid handpumps and mirror. The church is famous for its brasses. 🛏 ✿ ◖ ▶ Å P 🛢

FAKENHAM

BULL
Bridge Street
☎ (01328) 862560
11-3, 7-11; 10.30-11 Thu; 11-11 Fri & Sat; 12-3, 7-10.30 Sun
Blanchfields Black Bull Mild, Bull Best Bitter, Raging Bull ℍ
Home brew pub in the town centre: a lounge bar, a public bar with pool and a no-smoking room. Full flavoured beers at a price you can afford. Lunches served Thu. Q 🛏 Å ♣ 🥄

STAR
Oak Street
☎ (01328) 862895
11-3, 7-11; 12-3, 7-10.30 Sun
Tolly Cobbold Original; guest beer ℍ
16th-century building; a traditional town pub with a strong local following.
✿ ♿ Å ♣ P

FOULDEN

WHITE HART INN
White Hart Street
☎ (01366) 328638
12-3, 6-11; 12-3, 7-10.30 Sun
Greene King XX Mild, IPA, Abbot; guest beers ℍ
Friendly, comfortable village pub, serving excellent home-cooked food. The addition of a no-smoking conservatory enhances this excellent pub. This is also a good place to try locally brewed Iceni and Wolf beers.
🛏 Q ✿ 🛏 ◖ ▶ ᵫ ♣ P 🥄

FRETTENHAM

ROSE & CROWN
Buxton Road
☎ (01603) 898341
12-3 (not Mon-Fri), 7-11; 12-3, 7-10.30 Sun
Ansells Mild; Ind Coope Burton Ale; Tetley Bitter; guest beer ℍ
Large, single-bar, sporting local with wood panelling throughout. See the rose and crown insignia in brick on the exterior wall.
🛏 ✿ ♣ P

GARBOLDISHAM

FOX
The Street
☎ (01953) 688151
11.30-3, 5-11; 11.30-11 Sat; 12-10.30 Sun
Adnams Bitter, Old, Extra, Broadside; Greene King IPA; guest beer ℍ
17th-century pub with a lovely old beamed interior, featuring inglenooks. The games room has a pool table. Small restaurant. Children welcome.
🛏 ✿ ◖ ▶ ♣ P 🥄

GAYTON

CROWN
Lynn Road
☎ (01553) 636252
11-2.30, 6 (5.30 Fri)-11; 12-3, 7-10.30 Sun
Greene King XX Mild, IPA, Abbot, seasonal beers ℍ
Although there is a restaurant and a small family room, this pub is well used by locals and is very much the centre of village life.
🛏 🛏 ✿ ◖ ▶ ♣ P

GELDESTON

WHERRY
7 The Street
☎ (01508) 518371
11-3, 7 (6 summer)-11; 12-3,
7-10.30 Sun
**Adnams Bitter, Broadside,
seasonal beers** Ⓗ
Friendly pub/restaurant which
retains the charm of a small village inn, with its original old bar
and a sympathetic modern extension. Family room open in
summer.
🏔 Q ⛄ 🐾 🍴 🍺 🛏 🅰 ♣ P

GOODERSTONE

SWAN
☎ (01366) 328365
12-3 (not winter), 7-11; 12-3,
7-10.30 Sun
**Elgood's Black Dog Mild;
Flowers IPA; Ruddles County;
guest beers** Ⓗ
Friendly, welcoming village local
with a conservatory and large
garden. It doubles as the village
post office. 🏔 ⛄ 🐾 🍴 🍺 ♣ P

GORLESTON

DOCK TAVERN
Dock Tavern Lane
☎ (01493) 442255
11-11; 12-10.30 Sun
**Adnams Broadside; Draught
Bass; Greene King IPA;
Woodforde's Norfolk Nog; guest
beers** Ⓗ
Attractive, comfortable, open-
plan local featuring china water
jugs, brass and seafaring
objects. Six guest beers.
🐾 ♣ P

GREAT CRESSINGHAM

WINDMILL INN
Water End
☎ (01760) 756232
11-3, 6-11; 12-3, 6.30-10.30 Sun
**Adnams Bitter, Broadside;
Draught Bass; Greene King IPA;
guest beers** Ⓗ
Built as a village local in the
1650s, since much extended, it
now features three bars, three
family rooms and a conservatory.
Regular Irish folk and jazz music.
🏔 Q ⛄ 🐾 🍴 🍺 ♣ P

GREAT MOULTON

FOX & HOUNDS
Frith Way OS169902
☎ (01379) 677506
12-3, 7-11; 12-3, 7-10.30 Sun
Adnams Bitter; guest beer Ⓗ
Good example of a timber-framed
rural Norfolk pub. The single bar
has comfortable sofas; separate
dining area. The outdoor area
houses animals. The house ale is
Hancock's HB rebadged.
🏔 Q 🍴 🍺 🅰 ♣ P 🍴

GREAT YARMOUTH

MARINERS TAVERN
69 Howard Street South
☎ (01493) 332294
11-3, 8-11 (closed Mon-Wed
eves); closed Sun
**Draught Bass; Woodforde's
Mardler's Mild, Wherry; guest
beers** Ⓗ
First-class, friendly free house
staging regular beer festivals. A
true real ale pub. No keg beers
but four guest ales from
independents.
🏔 Q 🐾 🍴 🅰 🚃 ♣ P

RED HERRING
24-25 Havelock Road (off St
Peters Rd)
☎ (01493) 853384
11-3, 6-11; 12-3, 7-10.30 Sun
**Adnams Bitter; Woodforde's
Mardler's Mild; guest beers** Ⓗ
Corner Victorian pub displaying
pictures of old Yarmouth. Difficult
to find.
Q ⛄ 🐾 🍴 🍺 ♣ 🍴

GRESSENHALL

SWAN
The Green
☎ (01362) 860340
11.30-2.30, 6-11; 12-3, 7-10.30
Sun
**Greene King IPA; Tetley Bitter;
Wadworth 6X; guest beer** Ⓗ
Friendly, welcoming local with
three areas for games, drinking
and food. A notice board lists
local events and beers (with
descriptions). No food available
Sun eve.
🐾 🍴 🍺 ♿ ♣ P

HAPPISBURGH

HILL HOUSE
Off B1159
☎ (01692) 650004
12-2.30, 7-11; 12-11 Sat & sum-
mer; 12-10.30 Sun
**Adnams Bitter; Scott's Blues &
Bloater; Shepherd Neame
Spitfire; guest beers** Ⓗ
16th-century village pub with
exposed beams originally called
the windmill, but changed to Hill
House in the 1700s. Sir Arthur
Conan Doyle wrote *The Dancing
Men* here.
🏔 ⛄ 🐾 ♿ 🍴 🅰 ♣ P

HEDENHAM

MERMAID
Norwich Road (B1332)
☎ (01508) 482480
12-3, 7-11; 12-3, 7-10.30 Sun
**Adnams Bitter; Greene King
IPA** Ⓗ
Comfortable, welcoming, 17th-
century country pub, popular with
locals and for food. It has a
beamed bar and a games area.
🏔 🐾 🍴 🅰 ♣ P

HETHERSETT

KINGS HEAD
36 Old Norwich Road
☎ (01603) 810206
11-2.30, 5.30 (5 Fri, 6 Sat)-11;
12-3, 7-10.30 Sun
**Courage Directors; Marston's
Pedigree; Morland Old Speckled
Hen; John Smith's Bitter;
Woodforde's Wherry** Ⓗ
Good example of a rural hostelry
which maintains a pub feel whilst
also serving food (not Sun eve).
The bar separates the cosy snug
from the larger lounge bar with
its wood burning stove. A warm
welcome awaits.
🏔 Q 🐾 🍴 🍺 🛏 ♣ P

HEYDON

EARLE ARMS
The Street
☎ (01263) 587376
12-3, 7-11; closed Mon; 12-3,
7-10.30 Sun
**Morland Old Speckled Hen;
Woodforde's Wherry, Gt Eastern**
(summer), **Norfolk Nog** Ⓗ
Early 17th-century pub in a picturesque village in good walking
country, built by Erasmus Earle
(Sergeant-at-Law to Charles I).
No juke box or fruit machines;
cider in summer. No food Sun
eves. 🏔 Q 🐾 🛏 🍴 ♣ P

HICKLING

GREYHOUND INN
The Green
☎ (01692) 598306
12-3, 6.30-11 (11-11 summer);
12-3, 7-10.30 Sun
Flowers IPA; guest beers Ⓗ
Single-bar pub with a games
area, a restaurant and a huge
garden. Friendly, welcoming
atmosphere; children welcome if
bolted down!
🏔 Q 🐾 🍴 🍺 ♿ 🅰 ♣ 🍴 P

HILBOROUGH

SWAN
Brandon Road (on A1065 to
Swaffham)
☎ (01760) 756380
11 (12 winter)-3, 6-11; 12-3,
7-10.30 Sun
**Adnams Bitter; Bateman Mild;
Greene King IPA, Abbot; guest
beers** Ⓗ
Fine pub with an excellent atmosphere; it doubles as the village
post office. 🏔 Q 🐾 🛏 🍴 ♣ P

HINGHAM

WHITE HART HOTEL
3 Market Place
☎ (01953) 850214
11-3, 6.30-11; 12-3, 7-10.30 Sun
**Adnams Bitter; Marston's
Pedigree** Ⓗ
An imposing facade opens to a

welcoming public bar, a no-smoking dining area and comfortable lounge. 🚶 Q 🍽 🛏 🌜 🍴 P

HOCKWOLD–CUM–WILTON

RED LION
114 Main St ☎ (01842) 828875
12-2.30, 11-11 Sat; 12-4, 7-10.30 Sun

Greene King IPA; guest beers H
Roomy, two-bar village local next to a small green. Pub teams are involved in local pool and darts leagues. Interesting choice of ales, particularly in summer.
🍴 🌜 🍴 🚪 ♣ P

HUNWORTH

HUNNY BELL
The Green ☎ (01553) 712300
11-3, 5.30-11; 12-3, 7-10.30 Sun

Adnams Bitter; Greene King Abbot; guest beer H
Comfortable bar with a log fire and a warm atmosphere, offering a good, varied bar menu, reasonably priced, and a restaurant.
🚶 🍽 🌜 🍴 ♣ P

ITTERINGHAM

WALPOLE ARMS
The Common
☎ (01263) 587258
12-3, 6-11; 12-3, 7-10.30 Sun

Adnams Bitter, Broadside;
Draught Bass; Woodforde's
Nelson's Revenge, seasonal
beers H
18th-century beamed building with a large bar and inglenook. A small theatre stages popular local productions. No meals Sun/Mon eves in winter.
🚶 🍽 🌜 🍴 🛢 👥 P ✗

KENNINGHALL

RED LION
East Church Street
☎ (01953) 887849
12-3 (not Mon-Tue), 6.30-11;
12-4, 5.30-10.30 Sun

Greene King XX Mild, IPA,
Abbot; Marston's Pedigree;
Morland Old Speckled Hen H
Reopened in Feb 1997, after a 10-year closure, this former beer house has been traced back to 1722 but is possibly older. Consisting of bar, snug (now listed) and a dining area, it has been restored to a high standard.
🚶 Q 🍽 🌜 🍴 🛢 👥 P

KING'S LYNN

DUKE'S HEAD (LYNN BAR)
Tuesday Market Place
☎ (01553) 774996
11-2.30, 5-11; 12-2.30, 6.30-10.30 Sun

Banks's Bitter; Draught Bass;

Marston's Pedigree; Woodforde's
Nelson's Revenge H
Small bar within a large hotel, a peaceful room with comfortable armchairs. Q 🛏 🌜 🍴 P

FENMAN
Blackfriars Road (opp station)
☎ (01553) 761889
11-11; 12-4, 7-10.30 Sun

Greene King IPA, Abbot;
Marston's Pedigree; guest beer (occasional) H
Popular local with a railway theme. 🍴 ⇌ ♣

LONDON PORTERHOUSE
78 London Road
☎ (01553) 766842
12-3, 6-11; 12-11 Fri & Sat;
12-10.30 Sun

Greene King IPA, Abbot G
Small, lively pub near the historic South Gates. Casks are racked behind the bar (except in hot weather). Q 🍴 ♣

OUSE AMATEUR SAILING CLUB
Ferry Lane (opp King St)
☎ (01553) 772239
12-2.30, 7-11; closed Sun

Bateman XB, XXB; guest beers G
Comfortable, one-roomer with a verandah overlooking the river, with usually six beers available. Show CAMRA membership or this *Guide* for entry. 🚶 🍴 🌜

STUART HOUSE HOTEL
35 Goodwins Road
☎ (01553) 772169
7-11; 12-3, 7-10.30 Sun

Adnams Bitter, Broadside;
Greene King IPA H
Head up the gravel drive off Goodwins Road to find a small hotel bar with a strong local following. Frequent special events and regular live music.
🚶 🍴 🛏 🍴 P

WHITE HORSE
9 Wootton Road, Gaywood
☎ (01553) 763258
11-3, 5.30-11; 11-11 Fri & Sat;
12-3, 7-10.30 Sun

Courage Directors; Greene King
IPA; Wells Bombardier; guest
beers H
Popular, two-bar local near the Gaywood clock. Pleasant and comfortable, this drinker's pub is at the heart of the community.
🚪 ♣ P

Try also: Admiral's Tap, St James St (Free); Hogshead, High St (Whitbread)

LARLING

ANGEL INN
On A11, 1 mile from Snetterton Racetrack) ☎ (01953) 717963
10.30-11; 11-10.30 Sun

Adnams Bitter; guest beers H

Popular country pub, the site for West Norfolk CAMRA beer festivals. Always three guest beers.
🚶 Q 🍴 🛏 🌜 🍴 🛢 ⇌ (E Harling) ♣ P

LETHERINGSETT

KINGS HEAD
Holt Road ☎ (01263) 712691
11-11; 12-10.30 Sun

Adnams Bitter; Greene King IPA,
Abbot H
Two-bar pub, specialising in local beers. The restaurant serves an imaginative home-cooked menu, based on fresh produce, with a very special children's menu. The garden has a play area and adventure castle. Games room.
🚶 🍽 🍴 🌜 🍴 ♣ P

LICHAM

BULL HOTEL
Church Street (B1145)
☎ (01328) 701340
11-11; 12-10.30 Sun

Marston's Pedigree; Morland Old
Speckled Hen; guest beers H
Fine old building in a lovely country town: a bar with a pool table, plus a restaurant/lounge bar with inglenook. No meals Sun eve. 🚶 🌜 🍴 ♣ P

LITTLE CRESSINGHAM

WHITE HORSE
Watton Road (off B1108, 3 miles W of Watton)
☎ (01953) 883434
12-3, 7-11; 12-3, 7-10.30 Sun

Flowers Original; guest beers H
17th-century inn, popular with walkers on the Peddars Way. A log fire, bar billiards, a fun quiz (Mon) and live music (Fri) are attractions. Home-cooked food includes Balti dishes.
🚶 🍴 🌜 🍴 🛢 ♣ P

LITTLE DUNHAM

BLACK SWAN
The Street
☎ (01760) 722200
12-3, 7-11; 12-3, 7-10.30 Sun

Beer range varies H
Lovely old village pub - comfortable and friendly. The large bar has areas for dining, drinking and pool. No food Tue.
🚶 🍽 🍴 🌜 🍴 🛢 ♣ P

LONG STRATTON

QUEENS HEAD
The Street
☎ (01508) 530164
11-2.30, 6.30-11; 12-3, 7-10.30 Sun

Adnams Bitter, Broadside; guest
beer H
Large, single-bar pub with drinking areas on different levels.
🍴 🍴 ♣ P

MARTHAM

KINGS ARMS
15 The Green ☎ (01493) 740204
11-11; 12-10.30 Sun
Adnams Bitter, Broadside, seasonal beers; guest beer H
Friendly two-bar local, opposite the village pond with its thriving bird life. It boasts the oldest pub bowling green in Norfolk. Quoits also played ♨ ⏳ ❀ ◖
⛏ ♣ P

MIDDLETON

GATE
Hill Road, Fair Green (N of A47)
☎ (01553) 840518
12-2.30, 7 (6 Fri)-11; 12-2.30,
7-10.30 Sun
Boddingtons Bitter; Greene King IPA; guest beers H
Pleasant, comfortable village local with good food and award-winning floral displays.
♨ Q ❀ ◖ ▶ ♣ P

MUNDESLEY

ROYAL HOTEL
Paston Road (A1159, coast road)
☎ (01263) 720416
11-3, 6-11; 12-3, 7-10.30 Sun
Adnams Bitter; Greene King IPA, Abbot; guest beer H
Hotel whose Nelson Bar has comfortable olde-worlde charm with an inglenook, leather chairs and Lord Nelson memorabilia.
♨ ⏳ ❀ ⛵ ◖ ▶ P

MUNDFORD

CROWN
Crown Street (signed from A1065) ☎ (01842) 878233
11-11; 12-10.30 Sun
Courage Directors; Iceni Fine Soft Day; guest beers H
Attractive, 17th-century hotel with an interesting interior, known for its good quality food. Can be very busy at weekends. Limited parking.
❀ ⛵ ◖ ▶ ⏏ Å P

LYNFORD HALL
Lynford (signed off A1065 Swaffham road)
☎ (01842) 878351
11-3, 7-11; 12-3, 7.30-11 Sun
Beer range varies H
Part of a country house hotel, dating from the 1850s surrounded by Thetford Forest next to the Arboretum. A well-known bird-spotting site. The beers are supplied by Iceni.
♨ Q ❀ ⛵ ◖ ▶ ⛏ ♣ P ✂

NEATISHEAD

BARTON ANGLER COUNTRY INN
Irstead Road
☎ (01692) 630740

11-2.30, 7-11 (11.30-11 summer);
12-3, 7-10.30 (12-11 summer)
Sun
Greene King IPA, Abbot H
The earliest part of this pub is 500 years old. A pleasant bar opens on to the patio and large garden. An extensive menu is served in the restaurant or bar. Rowing boats for hire.
❀ ⛵ ◖ ▶ P

Try also: White Horse, The Street (Pubmaster)

NEW RACKHEATH

SOLE & HEEL
2 Salhouse Road
☎ (01603) 720146
11.30-3, 6.30-11; 11-11 Sat; 12-4,
7-10.30 Sun
Beer range varies H
Unpretentious, friendly village local with distinctive 1930s architecture. Up to five beers from independent breweries. No food Sun eve. ♨ ❀ ◖ ▶ ♣ P

NORTH WALSHAM

ORCHARD GARDENS
Mundesley Rd ☎ (01692) 405152
11-11; 12-10.30 Sun
Courage Directors; guest beers H
Town pub combining local beers with friendly service. A games area and conservatory are features in this Victorian building; large garden. ❀ ♣ ♣ P

NORTHREPPS

PARSON'S PLEASURE
Church Barn, Church Street
☎ (01263) 579691
11-11; 12-10.30 Sun
Greene King IPA, Abbot H
Old flint and brick barn, serving 'divine' food.
♨ Q ⏳ ❀ ⛵ ◖ ▶ P

NORTHWOLD

CROWN
30 High Street ☎ (01366) 727317
12-2.30, 6-11; 11.30-11 Sat; 12-3,
7-10.30 Sun
Greene King IPA, Abbot; guest beers H
Lively 'chalk lump' local, dating from the 18th century, serving good food and at least two guest beers. Live music at weekends.
♨ Q ❀ ◖ ♣ P

NORWICH

ALEXANDRA
16 Stafford Street
☎ (01603) 627772
11-11; 12-10.30 Sun
Adnams Bitter; Chalk Hill CHB, Flintknapper's Mild, Old Tackle; Marston's Pedigree H
Classic example of a back-street, corner local; a rare outlet for

Chalk Hill beers. Two bars: a noisy public and a warm lounge. Note the vinyl jukebox. Banham's cider available. Ask for oversized glasses. ♨ Q ❀ ⏏ ◖ ⏳ ⛃

BILLY BLUELIGHT
27 Hall Road
☎ (01603) 623768
12-3, 7-11; 12-11 Fri & Sat;
12-10.30 Sun
Woodforde's Mardler's Mild, H
Gt Eastern, Nelson's Revenge, G
Wherry, seasonal beers; guest beers H
Woodforde's prettier pub in Norwich, a nitro-keg-free zone. It hosts live traditional music and a regular board games eve. Sunday breakfast served. ♨ ❀ ◖ ⛃

COACH & HORSES
Thorpe Road (near station)
☎ (01603) 477078
11-11; 12-10.30 Sun
Chalk Hill Tap Bitter, CHB, Dreadnought, Flinknapper's Mild, Old Tackle; Taylor Landlord; guest beers H
Deceptively large pub with bare boards throughout. The home of Chalk Hill brewery which can be seen from the back of the pub. Banham's cider sold. Sky TV.
❀ ◖ ▶ ⇌ ⛃ P

DYERS ARMS
24 Lawson Road
☎ (01603) 787237
10.30-3, 6.30-11; 12-3.30,
7-10.30 Sun
Adnams Bitter; Draught Bass; guest beers H
Small, traditional, welcoming local offering convivial conversation. The guest beers come from Woodforde's and the house beer from Bass.❀ ♣

EATON COTTAGE
75 Mount Pleasant
☎ (01603) 453048
11-11; 12-10.30 Sun
Adnams Bitter; Marston's Pedigree; Theakston Best Bitter; guest beers H
Friendly street-corner local retaining its original layout and 1960s door signs. Five guest beers, often featuring Scott's of Lowestoft. Live music weekly.
❀ ⏏ ⛏ ♣

FAT CAT
49 West End Street (off Dereham Rd)
☎ (01603) 624364
12 (11 Sat)-11; 12-10.30 Sun
Adnams Bitter; Greene King Abbot; Woodforde's Nelson's Revenge; H **guest beers** H G
Beer drinkers' paradise with many beers on gravity from an excellent tap room which can be viewed from the bar. Up to 20 beers at a time.
❀ ♣ ⛃

235

HORSE & DRAY
137 Ber Street
☎ (01603) 624741
11-2.30, 4.30-11; 11-11 Sat; 12-3,
7-10.30 Sun
**Adnams Bitter, Broadside, sea-
sonal beers; guest beer** Ⓗ
Comfortable public house; sympathetically renovated rear room
and improved garden facilities -
great for barbecues and children
in summer. Popular with local
office workers at lunchtimes. Ask
for oversized glasses.
🏠 ♿ ◖ ➤ ♣ 🍺

JUBILEE
26 St Leonards Road
☎ (01603) 618734
11-11; 12-10.30 Sun
**Draught Bass; Boddingtons
Bitter; Flowers Original; Fuller's
London Pride; Scott's Strong
Mild; guest beers** Ⓗ
Back-street pub which caters for
all tastes. Friendly staff create a
good atmosphere. The house
beer is brewed by Bass. One of
the few pubs with a mild always
available; also up to six guests.
Q 🏠 ➤ ◖

RIBS OF BEEF
24 Wensum St ☎ (01603) 619517
10.30-11; 12-10.30 Sun
**Adnams Bitter; Boddingtons
Bitter; Fuller's London Pride;
Marston's Pedigree; Theakston
Mild; Woodforde's Wherry;
guest beers** Ⓗ
Well-known pub serving a wide
range of real ales. Try the waterside cellar bar (moorings available. ◖ ✂

ROSE
235 Queens Rd
☎ (01603) 490290
11-11; 12-10.30 Sun
**Adnams Bitter, Broadside;
seasonal beers** Ⓗ
Friendly street-corner, L-shaped
pub, within reach of the city centre. A community and family-
based alehouse. Q 🐢 ◖ ♣ ✂

STEAM PACKET
39 Crown Road (behind Anglia
TV) ☎ (01603) 441545
11-11; 12-10.30 Sun
**Adnams Bitter, Broadside, sea-
sonal beer; guest beer** Ⓗ
Unusual layout in this Adnams-
owned traditional pub. Not far
from the waterfront and Castle
Hall shops. Norwich's alternative
music venue. No-smoking area at
lunchtime. 🐢 🏠 ◖ ➤ ♣ ✂ 🍺

TRAFFORD ARMS
61 Grove Road (near Sainsbury's)
☎ (01603) 628466
11-11; 12-10.30 Sun
**Adnams Bitter; Boddingtons
Bitter; Tetley Bitter;
Woodforde's Mardler's Mild;
guest beers** Ⓗ

Voted no. 1 public house by readers of the *Eastern Evening News*,
a regular Valentine's beer festival is held in a marquee. The two
house brews are brewed by
Woodforde's. 🏠 ▶ ♣ 🍺

WIG & PEN
6 St Martin at Palace Plain (near
Cathedral) ☎ (01603) 625891
11 (12 Sat)-11; 12-4 Sun
**Boddingtons Bitter; Buffy's
Bitter; Woodforde's Wherry;
guest beers** Ⓗ
Small, friendly one-bar pub near
the law courts. 🏠 🏠 ◖ ▶ ➤ ♣

OLD HUNSTANTON

ANCIENT MARINER
Golf Course Rd ☎ (01485) 534411
6.30-11; 11-11 Sat & summer;
12.30-10.30 Sun
**Adnams Bitter, Broadside;
Draught Bass; guest beer** Ⓗ
Large and very busy traditional
pub attached to the Le Strange
Arms Hotel. It bears a seafaring
theme. The large conservatory
and garden are suitable for families. 🐢 🏠 ⛵ ◖ ▶ P

REEDHAM

RAILWAY TAVERN
17 The Havaker (B1140)
☎ (01493) 700340
11-3, 6-11; 11-11 Fri & Sat; 12-
10.30 Sun
Beer range varies
A warm welcome awaits in this
Grade II listed Victorian pub
where beers from micro-breweries are often available. Also a
large choice of whiskies; cider in
summer. Holds regular beer festivals. Well worth finding.
🏠 Q 🏠 ⛵ ◖ ▶ Å ♣ 🍺 P

Try also: Ferry Inn, Ferry Rd
(Free)

REEPHAM

KINGS ARMS
Market Place ☎ (01603) 870345
11.30-3, 5.30-11; 11-11 Sat; 12-3,
7-10.30 Sun
**Adnams Bitter; Draught Bass;
Greene King Abbot; Woodforde's
Wherry** Ⓗ
Attractive, early 18th-century
coaching inn: two bars with three
real fires; good meals, live jazz in
the courtyard in summer and bar
billiards feature. Children welcome. 🏠 ◖ ▶ 🎱 ♣ P

RINGSTEAD

GIN TRAP
High Street ☎ (01485) 525264
11-2.30, 7 (6.30 summer)-11;
12-2.30, 7-10.30 Sun
**Adnams Bitter; Greene King
Abbot; Woodforde's Norfolk
Nog** Ⓗ

This gem of a village pub has a
split-level bar, a roaring fire, a
small dining room and a fearsome
collection of gin traps. Add great
food and a good landlord and you
have a cracking pub. Petanque
played. 🏠 🏠 ◖ ▶ ♣ P

RUSHALL

HALF MOON
The Street ☎ (01379) 740793
12-2.30, 6 (5 Sat)-11; 12-10.30 Sun
Adnams Bitter; guest beer Ⓗ
16th-century pub with beams and
inglenook, largely food oriented.
The house beer is by
Woodforde's.
🏠 🐢 🏠 ◖ ▶ Å P

SCOLE

SCOLE INN
☎ (01379) 740481
11-11; 12-3, 7-10.30 sun
**Adnams Bitter, Broadside;
Draught Bass; Greene King IPA** Ⓗ
Historic, 17th-century coaching
inn with an impressive, unspoilt
exterior. 🏠 Q ⛵ ◖ ▶ ♿ P

SEA PALLING

HALL INN
Waxham Road (B1159)
☎ (01692) 598323
11-11; 12-10.30 Sun
**Adnams Bitter, Broadside; guest
beer** Ⓗ
Dating from the early 18th century and formerly a farmhouse, it
has been a pub for 30 years. The
low-beamed ceiling and log fire
in the inglenook, a games room
and a restaurant all add to its
attraction.
🏠 🏠 ⛵ ◖ ▶ ♿ Å ♣ P

SHERINGHAM

WINDHAM ARMS
15-17 Wyndham Street
☎ (01263) 822609
11-11; 12-10.30 Sun
**Draught Bass; Greene King IPA,
Abbot; Woodforde's Mardler's
Mild, Wherry; guest beers** (summer) Ⓗ
Town-centre pub with two bars.
In keeping with the area, the pub
is of flint construction. A rare
local outlet for mild. No smoking
dining area.
🏠 Q 🏠 ◖ ▶ 🎱 Å ➤ ♣ P

SMALLBURGH

CROWN
North Walsham Road
☎ (01692) 536314
12-3, 5.30 (7 Sat)-11; 12-3
(closed eve) Sun
**Greene King IPA, Abbot;
Marston's Pedigree; Tetley
Bitter** Ⓗ
Comfortable, two-bar village pub
and restaurant in a 15th-century

thatched and beamed building. The games room opens on to a lovely garden. No food Sun eve. ♨ ❀ 🛏 ◐ ◗ ⛺ ♣ P

SOUTH LOPHAM

WHITE HORSE
The Street ☎ (01379) 687252
11-3, 6-11; 12-4, 6.30-10.30 Sun
Adnams Bitter; Greene King IPA, Abbot; guest beer [H]
Lovely, 300-year-old beamed local with inglenooks and a dining area at one end. A large outdoor green has play apparatus, well away from the bar - but in view. Children's certificate.
♨ ❀ ◐ ◗ ♿ ♣ P

STALHAM

KINGFISHER HOTEL
High Street ☎ (01692) 581974
11-2.30, 6-11; 12-2.30, 7-10.30 Sun
Adnams Bitter; Draught Bass; Woodforde's Wherry [H]
Modern building with a comfortable lounge and a dining room, serving excellent quality food and wines. ❀ 🛏 ◐ ◗ ♿ P

STIBBARD

ORDNANCE ARMS
Guist Bottom (A1067)
☎ (01328) 829471
11-2.30 (3 Sat), 5.30-11; 12-3, 5.30-10.30 Sun
Draught Bass; Greene King IPA [H]
Comfortable, unspoilt, three-bar pub with a pool table in one room. A sociable drinkers' pub with a Thai restaurant (open Tue-Sat eves) at the rear. Reasonably priced beers. ♨ Q ❀ ♣ P

STIFFKEY

RED LION
44 Wells Road (A149)
☎ (01328) 830522
11-2.30, 7 (6 summer)-11; 12-3, 7-10.30 Sun
Greene King Abbot [H]; **Woodforde's Wherry** [G]; **guest beers** [H]
Beamed building circa 1670, with several drinking areas of character. A friendly local with a commitment to local ales.
♨ Q ♞ ❀ 🛏 ◐ ◗ ⛺ ♣ P

STOWBRIDGE

HERON
Station Road ☎ (01366) 384147
11-3, 6-11; 12-3, 7-10.30 Sun
Adnams Bitter; Draught Bass; City of Cambridge Jet Black; Greene King IPA, Abbot; Woodforde's Wherry [H]
Friendly and welcoming pub, between the Great Ouse and the relief channel, crammed full of interesting artefacts.
♨ Q ♞ ❀ 🛏 ◐ ◗ ⛺ ♣ P

STRUMPSHAW

SHOULDER OF MUTTON
Norwich Road (Brundall-Lingwood road)
☎ (01603) 712274
11-11; 12-10.30 Sun
Adnams Bitter, Extra or **Broadside; guest beers** [H]
Large, friendly, single-bar pub, set back from the road: a thriving local displaying a number of games trophies. No food Sun eve winter. Very large, pleasant garden. ♨ ❀ ◐ ◗ ♣ P

SWAFFHAM

GEORGE
Station St ☎ (01760) 721238
11-2.30, 6.30-11; 11-2, 7-10.30 Sun
Greene King IPA, Abbot [H]
Calm, pleasant, split-level bar in the town centre. A comfortable meeting place for locals, hotel residents and visitors. Interesting bar meals. Q 🛏 ◐ ◗ P

Try also: Ostrich, Castle Acre (Greene King)

TERRINGTON ST CLEMENT

COUNTY ARMS
29 Marshland Street
☎ (01553) 828511
12-3, 7-11; 12-3, 7-10.30 Sun
Greene King XX Mild, IPA, Abbot; guest beers (occasional) [H]
Large local used by the people of this thriving village which boasts a beautiful church. ♨ ❀ ⊟ P

THETFORD

ALBION
93-95 Castle Street (opp Castle Park and Hill) ☎ (01842) 752796
11-2.30 (3 Fri), 6-11 (5 Fri); 12.30-2.30, 7-10.30 Sun
Greene King IPA, Abbot, seasonal beers; guest beers [H]
Competitively priced ales in a traditional setting, in a quieter part of the town, enjoying an excellent outlook. Facing the park - ideal for children. Outside tables and benches. ♨ Q ❀ ◐ ♿ ≋ ♣ P

ANCHOR HOTEL
Bridge Street (near bus station)
☎ (01842) 763925
11-3, 6-11; 12-3, 6-10.30 Sun
Greene King IPA, seasonal beers; guest beers [H]
Low-ceilinged areas on various levels in a pub with a well-stocked bar.
Q ❀ 🛏 ◐ ◗ ♿ ≋ P 🍺

DOLPHIN INN
Old Market St ☎ (01842) 752271
11-3, 6.30-11; 12-3, 7-10.30 Sun
Greene King IPA; guest beers [H]
Popular, multi-roomed pub near to the castle mound. Reputed to be the oldest pub in Thetford.
♨ ❀ ◐ ◗ ♣ P

THORNHAM

LIFEBOAT
Ship Lane ☎ (01485) 512236
11-11; 12-10.30 Sun
Adnams Bitter; Greene King IPA, Abbot; Woodforde's Wherry [H]
The Lamp Bar, lit by oil lamps, is a reminder of the humble origins of this large and busy pub which features accommodation, a restaurant and regular live music. Popular on long summer days and magical on a cold winter's eve. Q ♞ ❀ 🛏 ◐ ◗ P

TIBENHAM

GREYHOUND
The Street ☎ (01379) 677676
12-4, 6.30-11; 11-11 Fri & Sat; 12-10.30 Sun
Adnams Bitter; Wadworth 6X; guest beer (weekend) [H]
Local drinkers' pub with two adjoining bars in an old beamed building with a quarry tiled floor. Well worth finding.
♨ Q ❀ ⛺ ♣ P

TOFT MONKS

TOFT LION
Beccles Road (A143)
☎ (01502) 677702
11.30-2.30, 5-11; 12-3.30, 7-10.30 Sun
Adnams Bitter, Broadside; Woodforde's Wherry; guest beers [H]
Traditional village local dating from 1650: A single welcoming bar, a pool and darts room, plus an intimate dining area. Ensuite B&B accommodation.
♨ ❀ 🛏 ◐ ◗ ⛺ ♣ P

UPTON

WHITE HORSE
17 Chapel Rd ☎ (01493) 750696
11-11; 12-10.30 Sun
Adnams Bitter; Draught Bass; guest beers [H]
Traditional, old beamed pub with an iron stove in the inglenook. A cosy village local with a dining area and large garden, offering four real ales in a friendly atmosphere. ♨ ❀ ◐ ◗ ⛺ ♣ P

UPWELL

FIVE BELLS
1 New Road ☎ (01945) 772222
12-3 (not Mon), 6-11; 11-11 Fri & Sat; 12-3, 7-10.30 Sun
Draught Bass; Greene King IPA; Worthington Bitter; guest beers (summer) [H]
Friendly village inn by the river and church, catering for all the family. Eat in the bar or the smart restaurant. ❀ 🛏 ◐ ◗ ♣ P

WALCOTT

LIGHTHOUSE INN
On coast road (B1159)
☎ (01692) 650371
11-3, 6-11; 11-11 Sat & summer;
12-10.30 Sun
**Adnams Bitter; Tetley Bitter;
guest beers** Ⓗ
Friendly pub, popular with visitors and locals; good value food.
🏨 🛏 🍽 ◖ 🄳 ⚓ ♣ P

WALSINGHAM

BULL INN
Shirehall Plain ☎ (01328) 820333
11-3, 6-11; 11-11 Sat; 12-3,
7-10.30 Sun
**Marston's Pedigree; Tolly
Cobbold Original** Ⓗ
Old, two-bar inn catering for pilgrims and locals alike. Parking may be difficult in season as located close to the shrine and museum in historic Walsingham. Opens all day during pilgrimage season. 🏨 Q 🍽 ◖ 🄳 ⚓
🛬 ♣ P

WARHAM ALL SAINTS

THREE HORSESHOES
The Street
☎ (01328) 710547
11.30-2.30; 6-11; 12-3, 6-10.30 Sun
**Greene King IPA, Abbot;
Woodforde's Wherry**Ⓖ; **guest
beer** Ⓗ
The oldest part of the building dates from 1720, now enlarged and modernised with a 1920s style interior and gaslit bar. It specialises in local traditional beers and food.
🏨 Q 🛏 🍽 ◖ 🄳 ⚓
⚓ ♣ P

WEASENHAM ALL SAINTS

OSTRICH INN
Main Road (A1065)
☎ (01328) 838221
11.30-2.30 (not Mon), 6-11;
12-2.30, 7-10.30 Sun
Adnams Bitter Ⓗ
Genuine old-fashioned local where visitors are made welcome. Despite its appearance, the pub has not closed. Local produce on sale outside.
🏨 Q 🍽 ◖ 🄳 ⊟ ♣ P

WELLS-NEXT-THE-SEA

CROWN HOTEL
The Buttlands ☎ (01328) 710209
11-2.30, 6-11; 12-2.30, 7-10.30 Sun
**Adnams Bitter; Draught Bass;
Marston's Pedigree** Ⓗ
Attractive old coaching inn with a Georgian facade and a comfortable bar, featuring good beers, but also has a top-notch restaurant. 🏨 🛏 🍽 🍽 ◖ 🄳 ⚓ P

EDINBURGH HOTEL
Station Road ☎ (01328) 710120
11-2.30, 7 (6.30 Sat)-11; 12-3,
7-10.30 Sun
**Draught Bass; Hancock's HB;
guest beer** Ⓗ
19th-century pub named after a ship which sank early this century with eight Wells men on board. A long comfortable bar and a friendly welcome. No meals Thu in winter.
🏨 🍽 ◖ 🄳 ⚓ ♣ P ⊟

WEST BECKHAM

WHEATSHEAF
Church Road ☎ (01263) 822110
12-3, 7 (6 summer)-11; 12-3,
6-10.30 Sun
**Draught Bass; Woodforde's
Wherry, Nelson's Revenge; guest
beer** Ⓗ
Old brick and flint buildings, popular with tourists and locals, especially families, as children are well catered for in summer. 🏨 Q 🛏 🍽 🍽
◖ 🄳 ♣ ⌂ P ⚥

WEST SOMERTON

LION
At B1159/B1152 jct
☎ (01493) 393289
11-4 (3 winter), 6-11; 12-4, 6
(7 winter)-10.30 Sun
Greene King IPA, Abbot, seasonal beers; guest beers Ⓗ
Comfortable two-bar village pub which re-opened 25 years ago after being de-licensed for several years. Just a short walk from the Staithe, it stocks an excellent range of beers, including brews from Elgood's and Mauldons.
Q 🛏 ◖ 🄳 ♣ P

Try also: Nelson Head, Horsey (Free)

WHINBURGH

MUSTARD POT
Dereham Road (B1135)
☎ (01362) 692179
11-3, 6.30-11; 12-3, 7-10.30 Sun
**Woodforde's Wherry; guest
beers** Ⓗ
One-bar village local converted from a row of old cottages. The guest beers are local brews.
🏨 Q 🍽 ◖ 🄳 ⚓ ♣ P

WINTERTON-ON-SEA

FISHERMAN'S RETURN
The Lane (off B1159)
☎ (01493) 393305
11-2.30, 6 (7 winter)-11; 11-11
Sat; 12-10.30 Sun
Beer range varies Ⓗ
Popular, two-bar local, handy for the beach, offering a varying selection of beers, original home-cooked food and over 30 whiskies.
🏨 🛏 🍽 🍽 ◖ 🄳 ♣ ⌂ P ⚥

WIVETON GREEN

BELL
Blakeney Road
☎ (01263) 740101
11-3, 6-11; 12-3, 7-10.30 Sun
Guest beers Ⓗ
One large L-shaped bar, a large conservatory (where families are welcome) and a large enclosed garden. The landlord is a classic car enthusiast and has a jaguar engine in the fireplace. The beers are brewed specially for the pub by City of Cambridge brewery.
🏨 🛏 🍽 🍽 ◖ 🄳 ♿ ⚓ P

WRENINGHAM

BIRD IN HAND
Church Road (B1113)
☎ (01508) 489438
11.30-3, 5.30-11; 12-3, 6-10.30
Sun
**Adnams Bitter; Fuller's London
Pride; Woodforde's Wherry;
guest beers** Ⓗ
Large roadside pub re-opened and extended in the 1980s. The bar area has brick pillars and stone floors with a comfortable alcove. Complete with a wood burning fire. Emphasis on food with two no-smoking restaurants.
🏨 🍽 ◖ 🄳 ♿ P

WYMONDHAM

FEATHERS
13 Town Green (400 yds W of centre)
☎ (01953) 605675
11-2.30, 7 (6 Fri)-11; 12-3,
7-10.30 Sun
**Adnams Bitter; Greene King
Abbot; Marston's Pedigree;
guest beers** Ⓗ
Popular local stocking the best range of ale in town. Farm implements adorn the walls of this *Guide* regular. The house beer is brewed by Bass.
🍽 ◖ 🄳 ♣ ⌂

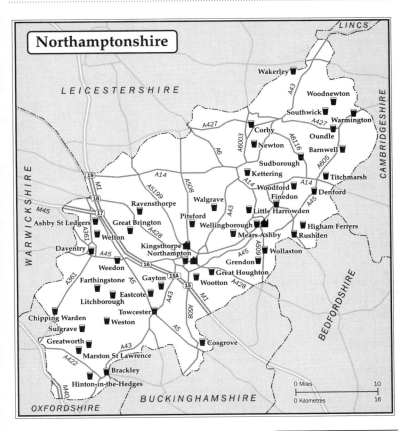

ASHBY ST LEDGERS

OLDE COACH HOUSE INN
100 yards off A361, N of
Daventry
☎ (01788) 890349
12-2.30, 6-11.30; 12-11 Sat; 12-4,
7-10.30 Sun
**Boddingtons Bitter; Everards Old
Original; Flowers Original; guest
beers** Ⓗ
The finest country pub in the
area, boasting old beams and
stone floors throughout: a public
bar with a large lounge leading to
the restaurant. Warm yourself by
the large wood fire in winter.
Eight real ales, including a house
beer from Chiltern.
🏠 ❀ 🚕 ◑ ▶ 🍺 ♣ P

BARNWELL

MONTAGU ARMS
Off A605, by Oundle turn
11-3, 6-11; 11-11 Fri & Sat; 12-
10.30 Sun
**Adnams Broadside; Flowers IPA,
Original; Hopback Summer
Lightning; guest beer** Ⓗ
Historic village pub of 16th-cen-
tury origin, built in stone. It comprises a large bar with exposed
timbers, a no-smoking restau-

rant, a games room and en-suite
accommodation. Outside is a
large garden and play area with
crazy golf and camp site.
Reputedly haunted.
🏠 Q ☎ ❀ ◑ ▶ 🚕 Å P

BRACKLEY

GREYHOUND
131 High Street
☎ (01280) 703331
11-3, 7-11; 12-4, 7-10.30 Sun
Beer range varies Ⓗ
Traditional, town-centre pub
offering five guest beers plus a
house beer, 'Skinny Mutt',
brewed by Vale. Over 40 malt
whiskies to try, plus cider in summer. The upstairs pool room has
two tables. 🏠 ◑ ▶ ♣ ⌣ P

RED LION
11 Market Place
☎ (01280) 702228
11-11; 12-10.30 Sun
**Wells Eagle, Bombardier; guest
beer** Ⓗ
Stone-built, 16th-century pub
with a TV, pool table and a
lounge bar. Eve meals Mon-Thu –
Texmex is a speciality; no food
Sun.
🏠 ❀ 🚕 ◑ ▶ ♣

CORBY

KNIGHTS LODGE
Tower Hill Road (off A6003)
☎ (01536) 742602
12-3 (4 Thu-Sat), 6-11; 12-3.30,
6-10.30 Sun
**Everards Beacon, Tiger, Old
Original; guest beer** Ⓗ
Old farmhouse with a low-
beamed ceiling, a welcome
retreat in this ex-steelworks
town. The long bar contains
brasses and farm implements. If
you are lucky, you may see one of
the eight ghosts.
🏠 ❀ ◑ ▶ ♣ P

CROSSGROVE

NAVIGATION INN
Thrupp Wharf, Castlethorpe Road
(signed from A508)
☎ (01908) 543156
11-3 (4 Sat), 6-11; 12-4, 7-10.30
Sun
**Fuller's London Pride; Hook
Norton Best Bitter; Morland Old
Speckled Hen; Wadworth 6X;
guest beers** Ⓗ
Stone pub set in rural countryside with the garden alongside
the Grand Union Canal. A balcony
offers fine views of boats and

summer sunsets. The restaurant serves excellent food and boasts two pianos.
🏨 ❀ ◖ ▶ P

DAVENTRY

COACH & HORSES
Warwick Street
☎ (01327) 876692
11-2.30, 5 (4.30 Fri)-11; 12-3, 7-11 Sat; 12-3, 7-10.30 Sun
Ind Coope Burton Ale; Marston's Pedigree; Tetley Bitter; guest beers Ⓗ
An open fire, flagstone and wood floors and stone walls give a warm welcoming feel to this large town-centre pub. Changing guest beers; weekday lunches.
🏨 Q ❀ ◖ & ♣

DUN COW
Brook Street
☎ (01327) 871545
11-3, 5-11; 10.30-11 Fri; 10.30-4.30, 7-11 Sat; 12-4, 7-10.30 Sun
Draught Bass; Davenports Bitter; guest beer Ⓗ
Early 17th-century coaching inn with an unspoilt snug bar. No food Sun. 🏨 Q ❀ ◖ ⌸ ♣ P

DENFORD

COCK
High Street
☎ (01832) 732565
12-3 (not Mon), 5.30-11; 12-3, 5.30-10.30 Sun
Boddingtons Bitter; Cains seasonal beers; Flowers IPA Ⓗ
The Cock is the second oldest pub in Denford with many other uses in the past including a blacksmith's, baker's and stables. One main lounge bar with Northants skittles, plus a restaurant (no food Sun eve).
🏨 ❀ ◖ ▶ ♣

EASTCOTE

EASTCOTE ARMS
6 Gayton Road ☎ (01327) 830731
12-2.30 (not Mon), 6-11; 12-3, 7-10.30 Sun
Draught Bass; Fuller's London Pride; Jennings Bitter; guest beer Ⓗ
Local CAMRA *Pub of the Year* runner-up 1995 and '96, an unspoilt, friendly village local upholding high standards. A small, no-smoking dining room through the snug serves excellent home-cooked food (Tue-Sun lunch, Thu-Sat eve; book lunches Thu and Sun). Q ❀ ◖ ▶ P

FARTHINGSTONE

KINGS ARMS
Main Street
☎ (01327) 361604
12-2.30 (not Mon), 6.30-11; 12-3, 7-10.30 Sun

Hook Norton Best Bitter; Tetley Bitter; guest beers Ⓗ
An inglenook in this seemingly small bar gives a very homely feel. Try the comfortable armchairs next to the stairs leading to an upper eating area. Northants skittles played.
🏨 Q ❀ ◖ ▶ ♣ P

FINEDON

BELL
Bell Hill
☎ (01933) 680332
11.30-3, 5.30-11; 12-3, 7-10.30 Sun
Hop Back Summer Lightning; Ruddles Best Bitter; Vaux Samson; Ward's Best Bitter Ⓗ
One of the oldest pubs in England, dating from 1042. The main bar has an inglenook with a wood burner; the back bar leads to a restaurant. Shove ha'penny played.
🏨 Q ❀ ◖ ▶ & ♣ P

GAYTON

EYKYN ARMS
20 High Street
☎ (01604) 858361
12-2 (not Mon), 7-11; 12-3, 7-10.30 Sun
Mansfield Bitter, Old Baily; Wells Eagle; guest beer Ⓗ
Named after Captain Eykyn, this excellent village free house has recently had a conservatory added. Northants skittles, darts and pool are played in the bar at the rear; pleasant lounge at the front. A good village local.
Q ❀ ◖ ⌸ ▲ ♣ P

GREAT BRINGTON

FOX & HOUNDS
High Street (2 miles from A428)
☎ (01604) 770651
11.30-3, 5.30-11; 11.30-11 Sat; 12-10.30 Sun
Theakston Best Bitter, XB, Old Peculier; guest beer Ⓗ
350-year-old coaching inn with flagstoned floors, original beams and some wood panelling. The olde-worlde interior is split into three characterful areas; log fires create a welcoming atmosphere. The games room affords a view of casks in the cellar. Eight guest beers. 🏨 ❀ ◖ ♣ P

GREAT HOUGHTON

OLD CHERRY TREE
Cherry Tree Lane
☎ (01604) 761399
12-3, 5.30 (6 Sat)-11; 12-3.30, 7-10.30 Sun
Wells Eagle, Bombardier; guest beers Ⓗ
Listed pub hidden down a dead-end lane, featuring exposed stonework, low ceilings, cosy inglenooks and a real fire in the

bar. Popular for lunch with local business people; dining room open Fri and Sat eves and special occasions - booking advised.
🏨 Q ❀ ⌸ ▶ P

Try also: White Hart, High St (S & N)

GREATWORTH

INN
Chapel Road (1 mile off B4525)
☎ (01295) 710976
11.30-2.30 (not Mon), 6-11; 12-4.30, 7-10.30 Sun
Hook Norton Best Bitter, Generation Ⓗ
Welcoming village local serving home-made organic food in a smoke-free room which doubles as a family room. Aunt Sally pitch in the garden.
🏨 ⛟ ❀ ◖ ▶ P ⌀

GRENDON

HALF MOON
42 Main Road
☎ (01933) 663263
12-3 (4 Sat), 6 (6.30 Sat)-11; 12-3, 7-10.30 Sun
Morland Old Speckled Hen; Shepherd Neame Spitfire; Wells Eagle Ⓗ
Traditional, oak-beamed pub in a pretty village, hosting regular themed food eves, including Thai food (no food Sun eve).
🏨 ❀ ◖ & ♣ P

HIGHAM FERRERS

GRIFFIN
7a High Street
☎ (01933) 312612
11.30 (12 Sat)-2.30, 6.30-11; 12-3, 7-10.30 Sun
Caledonian 80/-; Fuller's London Pride; Greene King IPA; Marston's Pedigree; Wells Eagle Ⓗ
Very pleasant pub, renowned for its good food and at least five real ales. Comfortable leather seats give a relaxed atmosphere. The building dates back to the 15th century but has only been a pub for 200 years. Watch out for the female ghost in Roundhead uniform. 🏨 ❀ ◖ ▶ P ⌷

HINTON-IN-THE-HEDGES

CREWE ARMS
☎ (01280) 703314
12-2.30, 7-11; 12-2.30, 7-10.30 Sun
Hook Norton Best Bitter; Marston's Pedigree; guest beer (occasional) Ⓗ
Cosy, stone-built local, tucked away in a tiny hamlet. One bar has a well-used real fire; the games room has a pool table and darts. Restaurant open daily.
🏨 Q ❀ ◖ ▶ ♣ P

KETTERING

PIPER
Windmill Avenue (off old A6)
☎ (01536) 513870
11-3, 5-11; 11-4, 6-11 Sat;
12-10.30 Sun
Ansells Mild; Theakston Best Bitter, XB, Old Peculier; guest beers Ⓗ
1950s pub, close to Wicksteed Park, featuring a comfortable lounge bar and a games room that is always popular. Bar food available at all times.
🏶 ◖▮ ⬱ ♣ P

PARK HOUSE
Holdenbury Road
☎ (01536) 523377
11-11; 12-10.30 Sun
Banks's Bitter; Marston's Pedigree Ⓗ
Large new pub near the cinema and Tesco's, providing a comfortable post-shopping refuge. The large ground-floor bar is divided into smaller drinking areas, the restaurant is upstairs (stair lift available). Pine and prints feature.🏶 ◖▮ & P 🗇

Try also: Old Market, Inn Sheep St (Free)

LITCHBOROUGH

RED LION
4 Banbury Rd ☎ (01327) 830250
11-3, 6.30-11; 12-3, 6.30-10.30 Sun
Banks's Bitter; Ⓟ **Marston's Pedigree; Morrells Varsity** Ⓗ
Attractive stone pub in a picturesque village, featuring an inglenook, flagstone floor and oak beams. A genuine pub with a landlord to match. A room for Northants skittles and pool. Food in good proportions Tue-Sat.
🏚 Q 🏶 ◖▮ ♣ P

LITTLE HARROWDEN

LAMB
Orlingbury Rd ☎ (01933) 673300
11-2.30, 5-11; 12-3, 7-10.30 Sun
Adnams Broadside; Badger Dorset Best, Tanglefoot; Morland Old Speckled Hen; Wells Eagle, Bombardier; Ⓗ
Popular village pub with a good range of regular beers and a good beer reputation. The public bar has Northants skittles; the lounge area is split into a small snug with a no-smoking restaurant on a raised level.
🏶 ◖▮ ♣ P

MARSTON ST LAWRENCE

MARSTON INN
1½ miles off B4525
☎ (01295) 711906
12-3 (not Mon), 7(6 Sat)-11; 12-3, 7-10.30 Sun

Hook Norton Best Bitter, Generation, Double Stout, seasonal beer or **guest beer** Ⓗ
Homely, rural pub offering a no-smoking dining room and a cocktail lounge-cum-restaurant with an extensive, well-priced menu (no food Sun eve/Mon lunch). Pub facilities are not extended to children, though campers can use the large garden, which contains an Aunt Sally pitch.
🏚 Q 🏶 ◖▮ Å ♣ 🗇 P ✼

MEARS ASHBY

GRIFFIN'S HEAD
Wilby Road (off A4500)
☎ (01604) 812945
11.30-3, 5.30-11; 11.30-11 Sat;
12-10.30 Sun
Marston's Bitter, Pedigree; Everards Beacon; guest beers Ⓗ
Classic, 19th-century brick-built pub with a traditional bar plus a lounge and restaurant (no food Sun eve or Mon). One guest beer is usually from Frog Island.
🏚 🏶 ◖▮ ⬱ ♣ P

NEWTON BROMSWOLD

SWAN
6 Church Lane
☎ (01933) 413506
11.30-2.30 (11-4 Sat); 5.30-11;
12-3, 7-10.30 Sun
Greene King IPA, Abbot Ⓖ
Idyllic, quiet country pub, set on the rural Beds border, an ideal stopover for walkers and cyclists. With its traditional interior it offers a friendly welcome and good food.
🏚 Q 🏶 ◖▮ ♣ P

NORTHAMPTON

DUKE OF EDINBURGH
Adelaide Street NW3 6BG
☎ (01604) 637903
12-3 (not Mon), 5-11; 11-11 Sat;
12-3, 7-10.30 Sun
Wells Eagle, Bombardier; guest beer Ⓗ
L-shaped bar with friendly staff; a finalist in the *Bar Person Award* of 1997.
Q 🏶 & ⬱ ♣ P

MALT SHOVEL TAVERN
121 Bridge Street (opp Carlsberg brewery)
☎ (01604) 234212
11.30-3, 5-11; 12-3, 7-10.30 Sun
Banks's Bitter; Boddingtons Mild; Castle Eden Ale; Frog Island Natterjack; guest beers Ⓗ
Superb free house, only recently refurbished and full of local breweriana. Local CAMRA *Pub of the Year* 1997. An excellent range of foreign draught and bottled beers and malt whiskies add to its appeal.
Q 🏶 ◖▮ & ⬱ ♣ 🗇

MOON ON THE SQUARE
The Parade
☎ (01604) 634062
11-11; 12-10.30 Sun
Courage Directors; Everards Tiger; Theakston Best Bitter, XB; guest beers Ⓗ
Typical Wetherspoons pub on the market square. Good value beer for the locality; food available all day. Spacious conservatory-style, no-smoking area.
Q ◖▮ & ⬱ ✼ 🗇

VICTORIA INN
2 Poole Street
☎ (01604) 633660
4 (12 Fri & Sat)-11; 12-10.30 Sun
Fuller's London Pride; Wadworth 6X; guest beers Ⓗ
Popular, single room, with a wood-panelled snug. Check out the cocktails, but drink the beer. Quiz Tue and Wed eves. ♣

OUNDLE

ROSE & CROWN
11 Market Place
☎ (01832) 273284
11 (8am Thu)-11; 12-10.30 Sun
Mansfield Riding Bitter, Bitter, Old Baily; guest beer Ⓗ
Historic market town pub, serving award-winning ales and superb food. A large lounge bar with dedicated dining area (children welcome); smartly dressed, polite bar staff. Opens 8am for breakfast on market day (Thu). No eve meals Tue or Fri.
🏚 Q 🏶 ◖▮ ⬱ &

PITSFORD

GRIFFIN
25 High Street (A508)
☎ (01604) 880346
12-2.30 (not Mon), 5.30-11; 12-3, 7-10.30 Sun
Fuller's London Pride; Theakston Best Bitter, Old Peculier; Wadworth 6X Ⓗ
16th-century Grade II listed pub: two friendly bars. Stocks over 20 single malt whiskies. Pitsford Reservoir is nearby (trout fishing).🏶 ◖ ♣ P

RAVENSTHORPE

CHEQUERS
Church Lane (off A428)
☎ (01604) 770379
12-3, 6-11; 12-11 Sat; 12-3, 7-10.30 Sun
Fuller's London Pride; Greene King Abbot; Mansfield Bitter; Shepherd Neame Spitfire; Thwaites Bitter Ⓗ
Popular old pub; a free house with good, reasonably priced food seven days a week. Children welcome. Northants skittles played.
🏶 ◖▮ ♣ P

RUSHDEN

Rushden Historical Transport Society
Rushden Station, Station Approach (A6)
☎ (01933) 318988
11-3 (not Mon-Fri), 7.30-11; 12-2.30, 7.30-10.30 Sun
Fuller's London Pride; Hop Back Summer Lightning; guest beers Ⓗ
Midland railway station saved by the Society. A private gaslit bar and a museum house transport memorabilia; a carriage by the platform is used as a no-smoking area. Four independents' guest beers with the accent on micro-breweries. Daily membership costs 50p. \♨ Q ❀ ♣ P ⚟ ▯

SOUTHWICK

Shuckburgh Arms
Main Street
☎ (01832) 274007
12-2 (3 Sat; not Mon), 6-11; 7-10.30 Sun
Fuller's London Pride; Marston's Pedigree; guest beer (summer) Ⓗ
Cosy, village local, dating from the 16th century: a through-bar with games and eating areas at one end and a large fireplace at the other. Set by the cricket pitch and close to Southwick Hall, it is popular with all sections of the community.
♨ ❀ ▲ ♣ P

SUDBOROUGH

Vane Arms
High Street (off A6116)
☎ (01832) 733223
11.30-2.30 (not Mon), 5.30 (6 Sat)-11; 12-3, 7-10.30 Sun
Beer range varies Ⓗ
Superb stone and thatched village pub offering an ever-changing range of unusual guest beers, in addition to draught Belgian beers and country fruit wines. Regular local CAMRA award-winner. No food is available Sun eve or Mon.
♨ ❀ 🛏 ◐ ◑ ⊟ ♣ ⌓

SULGRAVE

Star Inn
Manor Road
☎ (01295) 760389
11-2.30, 6-11; 12-5, closed eve (12-3, 7-10.30 summer) Sun
Hook Norton Best Bitter, Old Hooky, Generation; guest beer Ⓗ
Stone-built pub boasting flagged floors, beams and an inglenook, with a restaurant and four letting rooms. Handy for visitors to George Washington's birthplace. Note that children unwelcome in the bar.
♨ ❀ 🛏 ◐ ◑ P

TITCHMARSH

Dog & Partridge
6 High Street (off A605)
☎ (01832) 732546
12-2, 6-11; 12-4, 7-10.30 Sun
Wells Eagle, Bombardier; guest beers Ⓗ
18th-century local: one large bar with public bar, games and quiet areas. popular with ramblers.
♨ ❀ ⊟ ♣ P

TOWCESTER

Plough
Market Square, Watling Street (A5)
☎ (01327) 350738
11-11; 12-3, 7-10.30 Sun
Adnams Broadside; Wells Eagle; guest beer Ⓗ
Facing the market square, this basic pub has a small front bar leading to a larger seating area at the rear.
♨ ◐ ◑ P

WAKERLEY

Exeter Arms
Main Street
☎ (01572) 747817
12-20.30, 6-11; 12-3, 7-10.30 Sun
Adnams Broadside; Marston's Pedigree; guest beers Ⓗ
17th-century pub with a wood-burning stove in the lounge. Wheelchair access at the side door. No food Mon.
♨ 🛏 ◐ ◑ ♿ P

WALGROVE

Royal Oak
Zion Hill (off A43)
☎ (01604) 781248
12-2.30, 6-11; 12-4, 6.30-10.30 Sun
Adnams Bitter; Boddingtons Bitter; Flowers Original; Webster's Yorkshire Bitter; guest beers Ⓗ
Popular, comfortable village pub that specialises in good value food. Five car clubs and a motor-bike club meet here. Ask for the sparkler to be removed.
❀ ◐ ◑ P ⚟

WARMINGTON

Red Lion
Peterborough Road (off A605, follow signs through village)
☎ (01832) 280362
12-4, 7-11; 12-4, 7-10.30 Sun
Draught Bass; Bateman XXXB; guest beers Ⓗ
Traditional, 19th-century stone-built village free house, popular with locals and walkers. Two small bars, one adjoining a restaurant area; lots of dark wood and an inglenook. Ringing the bull and petanque played. No food Mon.
Q ❀ ◐ ◑ ♣ P

WEEDON

Globe Hotel
High Street (A5/A45 jct)
☎ (01327) 340336
11-11; 12-3, 7-10.30 Sun
Marston's Bitter, Pedigree; guest beers Ⓗ
Very professionally-run country inn, with a pub-like feel in the bar. It serves home-cooked food in the bar and higher quality food in the restaurant. Ideal for a weekend break (excellent B&B).
♨ Q 🛏 ◐ ◑ ♿ P

WELLINGBOROUGH

Red Well
16-17a Silver Street
☎ (01933) 440845
11-11; 12-10.30 Sun
Courage Directors; Theakston Best Bitter; guest beers Ⓗ
Typical Wetherspoons conversion of a row of shops. On the town centre one-way system, convenient for shops and offices. A busy pub, especially at week-ends. Q ❀ ◐ ◑ ♿ ⌓ P ⚟ ▯

Vivian Arms
153 Knox Road
☎ (01933) 223660
11-2.30, 6-11; 11-11 Sat; 12-10.30 Sun
Badger Dorset Best; Wells Eagle Ⓗ
Traditional, street-corner local with a wood-panelled bar, a cosy lounge and a large games room. Peace reigns in two of the three bars and there's not a diner in sight (unless you count the pies and toasties).
♨ Q ❀ ⊟ ♿ ≠ ♣ P

WELTON

White Horse
High Street ☎ (01327) 702820
12-2, 7-11; 12-2, 8-10.30 Sun
Courage Directors; Webster's Yorkshire Bitter; guest beers Ⓗ
Thatched pub and restaurant in the village centre, dating back to the early 1800s. Popular with business people at lunchtime, a friendly local eves. Some original features remain.
❀ ◐ ◑ ⊟ ♣ P

WESTON

Crown
2 Helmdon Road
☎ (01295) 760310
12-2.30 (not Mon), 6-11; 12-2.30 (not Jan-Mar), 6-10.30 Sun
Fuller's London Pride; Matthew Clark 12 Bore; guest beers Ⓗ
Dark, beamed 15th-century pub with an inglenook, a side area for darts and a pool room. With a varied menu, this family-run pub caters for all.
♨ Q 🛏 ◐ ◑ ♣ P

The opening of CAMRA's new HQ at St Albans. John Cryne, CAMRA National Chairman for nine years, attends to important business as the mayor cuts the ribbon!

WESTON FAVELL

BOLD DRAGOON
48 High Street
☎ (01604) 401221
11-3, 6(5 Fri)-11; 11-11 Sat; 12-3, 7-10.30 Sun
Banks's Bitter; Boddingtons Bitter; Flowers IPA; Fuller's London Pride; guest beers Ⓗ
Deservedly popular pub on the edge of Northampton which retains its village atmosphere. Recently refurbished and extended to include a conservatory restaurant. The front bar has games, the comfortable rear lounge has a central fire. Two constantly changing guest ales.
❀ ⊞ & ♣ P

WOLLASTON

CRISPIN ARMS
14 Winwick Road
☎ (01933) 664303
12-11; 12-10.30 Sun
Fuller's London Pride; Greene King Abbot; Theakston Best Bitter; Woodforde's Wherry; guest beers Ⓗ
A well patronised, two-roomed local serving six real ales at any one time. It has an Irish feel with

old Guinness posters and many pictures on the walls.
ᴁ Q ❀ P

WOODFORD

DUKES ARMS
83 High Street
☎ (01832) 732224
12-2, 7-11; 12-3, 7-10.30 Sun
Banks's Bitter; Flowers Original; Marston's Pedigree; Morrells Varsity; Wadworth 6X Ⓗ
On the green in a pretty village, this pub stocks a good selection of country wines and whiskies. Two main bars with a skittles room at the back, and a dining room upstairs (book for food Sat). ❀ ⊲ ▶ ♣ P

WOODNEWTON

WHITE SWAN
Main Street (3 miles N of Oundle)
☎ (01780) 470381
12-3, 6.30-11; 12-3.30, 7-10.30 Sun
Badger Tanglefoot; Fuller's London Pride; Oakham JHB; guest beer Ⓗ
Welcoming, 200-year-old village free house consisting of a single long room and a restaurant serving excellent food from an extensive menu (no meals Sun eve). A

rare outlet for Rockingham Ales.
❀ ⊲ ▶ & P

WOOTTON

WOOTTON WMC
23 High Street
☎ (01604) 761863
12-2.30, 7-11; 12-3, 7-10.30 Sun
Greene King IPA; Wells Bombardier; guest beers Ⓗ
Excellent workingman's club with a steward who ensures an ever-changing range of interesting guest ales. It has a concert room and a games room. CIU restrictions apply. ♣ P

INDEPENDENT BREWERIES

Cannon:
Wellingborough

Cock:
Kingsthorpe

Frog Island:
Northampton

Leyland:
Wellingborough

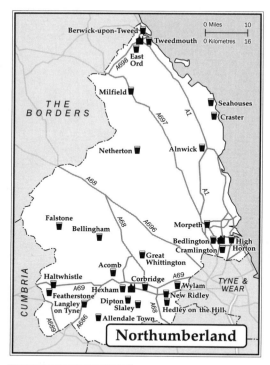

Northumberland

ACOMB

MINERS ARMS
Main Street
☎ (01434) 603909
12 (5 winter)-11 (may vary);
12-10.30 Sun
Big Lamp Bitter; Federation Buchanan's Original; guest beers H
Traditional village pub built in 1745, where locals and visitors are made welcome. The house beer is brewed by Big Lamp.
🍺 Q ⊟

ALLENDALE

GOLDEN LION
Market Place
☎ (01434) 863225
4 (11 Sat)-11; 12-10.30 Sun
Boddingtons Bitter; John Smith's Bitter; guest beers H
Quiet, basic and somewhat oddly furnished pub overlooking the market place. A warm friendly welcome awaits in comfortable surroundings. 🍺 Q ⛵ ♣

KING'S HEAD HOTEL
Market Place
☎ (01434) 683681
11-11; 12-10.30 Sun
Greene King Abbot; Jennings Cumberland Ale; Marston's Pedigree; Theakston Best Bitter; guest beers H
Busy, but comfortable hotel bar situated in an area of outstand-ing natural beauty. Serving excel-lent food, the bar boasts a selec-tion of 75 malt whiskies. Popular with locals and ramblers; an ideal base for a walking holiday. Good range of guest beers.
🍺 Q ⛵ 🛏 ◖ ▶ ♣

ALNWICK

JOHN BULL
Howick Street
☎ (01665) 602055
11-3, 7-11; 12-2, 7-10.30 Sun
Tetley Bitter; guest beers H
Quiet, basic pub built in the 1820s in the middle of a terrace of houses. At one time it had its own brewery and maltings. The unusual pub game Triominoes (three-sided dominoes) is played here. Q ♣

MARKET TAVERN
7 Fenkle Street
☎ (01665) 602759
11-11; 12-10.30 Sun
Vaux Samson; guest beers H
Popular, comfortable pub in the town centre, offering a good range of guest beers.
🍺 Q 🛏 ◖ ▶ ♣

OLD CROSS
Narrowgate
☎ (01665) 602735
11-11; 12-10.30 Sun
Theakston Best Bitter; guest beers H
Welcoming, listed building, over 200 years old, known locally as the 'Dirty Bottles' which refers to a sealed window of dirty bottles believed to be cursed (a full explanation can be found in the pub). 🍺 ◖ ▶ ♣ ⊟

BEDLINGTON

NORTHUMBERLAND ARMS
East End Front Street
☎ (01670) 822754
4 (12 Fri & Sat)-11; 12-10.30 Sun
Beer range varies H
Warm and welcoming, well-run pub, offering a good range of constantly changing guest beers. Food Fri-Sat. 🍺 ◖

BELLINGHAM

RIVERDALE HALL HOTEL
On C200, off B6320, near A69.
☎ (01434) 220254
11-11; 12-10.30 Sun
Ind Coope Burton Ale; Tetley Bitter H
Award-winning hotel with all amenities including a swimming pool/sauna. Hot-air ballooning is possible nearby. Very popular with anglers. Real ales available in the inviting bar-lounge which offers superb views of the North Tyne and the picturesque cricket field. 🍺 Q ⛵ ❀ 🛏 ◖ ▶ P

BERWICK UPON TWEED

BARRELS
59 Bridge Street
☎ (01289) 308013
11-3, 6-11; 7-10.30 Sun
Beer range varies H
Arguably the best pub in Berwick in terms of beer range and quali-ty, combined with a pleasant atmosphere and excellent food. It stands beside the Jacobean bridge linking Berwick and Tweedmouth and attracts a var-ied clientele.
Q ◖ ▶ ⇌

FREE TRADE ☆
Castlegate
☎ (01289) 306498
11-2, 8-11 (may vary); 7-10.30 Sun
Vaux Lorimer's Best Scotch H
Free Trade's historic, well-pre-served Victorian interior includes a screen between the entrance and the public bar. This two-roomed pub provides one real ale, which is superbly kept, and absolutely no frills. A must on any visit to Berwick.
Q 🚪 ⇌

CORBRIDGE

DYVELS
Station Road
☎ (01434) 633633
4 (12 Sat)-11; 12-4, 7-10.30 Sun

Draught Bass; Black Sheep Bitter; guest beers H

A warm welcome from the locals at this popular hotel bar makes this pub worth seeking out. An ideal base for exploring Hadrian's Wall.

Q ✧ ⇔ ≈ ♣ P ⊟

CRAMLINGTON

PLOUGH

Middle Farm Building
☎ (01670) 737633
11-3, 6-11; 11-11 Fri & Sat; 12-10.30 Sun

Boddingtons Bitter; Courage Directors; Marston's Pedigree; Theakston Best Bitter; guest beers H

Stone-built, former farm buildings converted into a pub with care and imagination. Facing the village church, the unusual gin-gan offers comfortable sitting areas off the main lounge. The bar has darts, and french windows leading to the garden.

✧ ◖⊞ ≈ P

CRASTER

JOLLY FISHERMAN

Haven Hill (head for the harbour)
☎ (01665) 576218
11-3, 6-11; 11-11 Sat & summer; 12-10.30 Sun

Ward's Thorne BB; Ushers Founders H

Friendly pub affording extensive sea views. It offers an adventurous seafood menu; Craster is famous for its kippers. ✉ Q ◖ P

DIPTON

DIPTON MILL INN

Dipton Mill Road
☎ (01434) 606577
12-2.30, 6-11; 12-4, 7-10.30 Sun

Hexhamshire Shire Bitter, Devil's Water, Whapweasel; Theakston Best Bitter; guest beers H

An excellent advertisement for Hexhamshire Brewery, this inn is set in beautiful countryside; the garden has its own burn. Bar billiards is played in the back room. CAMRA Northumberland *Pub of the Year.* Excellent range of home-cooked food.

✉ Q ☺ ✧ ◖ ▶ Å ♣ P ⊟

EAST ORD

SALMON INN

☎ (01289) 305227
12-11; 12-10.30 Sun

Vaux Lorimer's Best Scotch; guest beers H

A warm welcome is assured in this two-roomed local with a bar and a pool room. Hill fort remains and fishing on the River Tweed are nearby. Eve meals Thu-Sun.

✉ Q ✧ ◖ ▶ ⊞ Å ♣ P

FALSTONE

BLACK COCK INN

☎ (01434) 240200
11-3, 6-11; 11-11 Fri & Sat (may vary); 12-10.30 Sun

Boddingtons Bitter; Castle Eden Ale; Federation Buchanan's Best Bitter; guest beers H

The heart of village life and popular with water sports enthusiasts from nearby Kielder Water. The pub has a pool area, a dining room, piano and award-winning food. Peacocks and the other aviary birds are housed in the garden. The house beer is supplied by Whitbread.

✉ Q ✧ ⇔ ◖ ▶ ⌂ ⊟

FEATHERSTONE

WALLACE ARMS

Bowfoot ☎ (01434) 231872
12-2.30 (not Mon-Thu), 4-11; 11.30-11 Sat; 12-4, 7-10.30 Sun

Beer range varies H

Friendly pub in beautiful countryside, not far from Featherstone Castle. It hosts enjoyable music nights.

✉ ✧ ◖ ▶ Å ♣ P

GREAT WHITTINGTON

QUEENS HEAD INN

☎ (01434) 672267
12-2.30 (not Mon), 6-11; 12-3, 7-10.30 Sun

Courage Directors; Hambleton Bitter; guest beers H

This inn, set in beautiful countryside, close to Hadrian's Wall, dates from the 15th century and is reputed to be the oldest in the county. Four handpumps serve a variety of guest beers; the house beer is brewed by Hambleton. Good quality food is based on local produce. ✉ Q ◖ P

HALTWHISTLE

BLACK BULL

Market Place
☎ (01434) 320463
11-11 (may vary winter); 12-4, 7-10.30 Sun

Beer range varies H

Very cosy, unspoilt, stone pub with low ceilings, beams, a tiny snug and a warm welcome. Eve meals Mon-Fri.

✉ ⛵ ✧ ⇔ ◖ ▶ Å ≈

GREY BULL

Wapping
☎ (01434) 321991
11-11; 12-10.30 Sun

Federation Buchanan's Original; Stones Bitter; guest beers H

Busy town pub, popular with locals who make visitors more than welcome. The front bar is lively; the panelled back bar is quieter. Quoits played.

Q ⛵ ✧ ⇔ ◖ ▶ ⬥ ≈ ♣ P

HEDLEY ON THE HILL

FEATHERS INN

☎ (01661) 843607
6 (12 Fri & Sat)-11; 12-3, 7-10.30 Sun

Boddingtons Bitter; guest beers H

Friendly, country pub with an attractive bar and lounge. Both rooms have real fires, giving a cosy atmosphere. Excellent range of beers and food; the interesting menu changes weekly.

✉ Q ✧ ◖ ▶ P

HEXHAM

TAP & SPILE

Battle Hill
☎ (01434) 602039
11-11; 12-10.30 Sun

Theakston Best Bitter; guest beers H

Busy, town-centre pub with a changing range of real ales. It hosts regular live music, with Northumberland traditional music a favourite. ✉ ◖ ≈

HIGH HORTON

THREE HORSE SHOES

Hatherley Lane
☎ (01670) 822410
12-11; 12-10.30 Sun

Ind Coope Burton Ale; Marston's Pedigree; guest beers H

Large, friendly 18th-century coaching inn serving a wide variety of guest ales. Children welcome in the large conservatory and garden which has a play area. ✧ ◖ ▶ P

LANGLEY ON TYNE

CARTS BOG INN

On A686
☎ (01434) 684338
12-3, 7-11; 12-3, 7-10.30 Sun

Marston's Pedigree; Theakston Best Bitter; guest beers (summer) H

Historic pub built in 1730 on the site of an ancient brewery (1521). Very friendly, it is well worth a visit. There is a games room and a quoits pitch. Wheelchair WC.

✉ Q ⬥ ♣ P

MILFIELD

RED LION

Main Road (A697)
☎ (01668) 216224
11-11; 12-10.30 Sun

Theakston Best Bitter; guest beers H

Oldest building in the village, a former coaching inn dating back to 1740. A varied range of activities includes golf, fishing, horse riding and guided walks. Tourists are welcome to join in.

✉ Q ✧ ⇔ ◖ ▶ P

MORPETH

CHAMBERS
57 Bridge Street
☎ (01670) 518282
11.30-3, 5-11; 11.30-11 Fri & Sat;
12-10.30 Sun
**Courage Directors; guest
beers** H
Stone-flagged free house with a
glass-roofed inner chamber.
Framed old legal documents are
displayed on the walls and a collection of chamber pots hangs
from the rafters.
♣

JOINERS ARMS
3 Wansbeck Street
☎ (01670) 513540
11-11; 12-10.30 Sun
**Draught Bass; Tetley Bitter;
Theakston XB; guest beers** H
Friendly, comfortable two-
roomer, one of the Fitzgerald
chain.
🍺 ≠

TAP & SPILE
Manchester Street
☎ (01670) 513894
12-2.30, 6-11; 11-11 Fri & Sat;
12-10.30 Sun
Beer range varies H
A warm welcome awaits at this
award-winning, comfortable pub
offering up to eight guest ales.
Traditional pipe and fiddle sessions are held.
◗ 🍺 ♣ ⌂ ≠

NETHERTON

STAR INN ☆
On B634
☎ (01669) 630238
12-1.30, 7-11 (may vary winter);
12-1.30, 7-10.30 Sun
Castle Eden Ale G
The only pub in Northumberland
to have been in every edition of
this *Guide*. The beer is served on
gravity direct from the cellar in
this unspoilt gem. A warm welcome is assured and a visit is a
must if you are in the area.
Q ❀ P

NEW RIDLEY

DOCTOR SYNTAX
☎ (01661) 842383
12-3.30, 6-11; 12-11 Fri & Sat;
12-10.30 Sun
**Courage Directors; Jennings
Cumberland Ale; Theakston Best
Bitter; guest beer** H
Comfortable bars afford extensive views over the Tyne Valley
and reflects the exploits of a
famous early 19th-century racehorse.
Q ◗ ▶ P

SEAHOUSES

OLDE SHIP HOTEL
7 Main Street
☎ (01665) 720200
11-3, 6-11; 12-3, 7-10.30 Sun
**Boddingtons Bitter; McEwan
80/-; Marston's Pedigree;
Morland Old Speckled Hen;
Theakston Best Bitter; guest
beers** H
Built in 1745, this family-owned
ETB four-crown hotel has a small
bar, splendidly furnished with a
treasure house of genuine nautical artefacts. It stocks a good
range of beers, plus a changing
guest ale.
🏨 Q 🛏 🍴 ◗ ▶ 🍺 P ✂

SLALEY

ROSE & CROWN
Main Street
☎ (01434) 673263
11.45-3, 6-11; 12-3, 7-10.30 Sun
**Theakston Best Bitter; guest
beers** H
200-year-old pub; a cosy lounge
and a bar, serving excellent
home-cooked food.
🏨 Q 🛏 ❀ 🍴 ◗ ▶ ♣ P

INDEPENDENT
BREWERIES

Border:
Tweedmouth
Hexhamshire:
Hexham
Northumberland:
Ashington

TWEEDMOUTH

ANGEL
Brewery Bank
☎ (01289) 306273
11-3, 7-11; 11-11 Sat (may vary);
12-3, 7-10.30 (may vary) Sun
Beer range varies H
After a period of closure, this
pub was reopened by Border
Brewery and has since been
sold to new owners. It remains
the Border Brewery tap and is
an essential place to visit. Two
rooms, one with a pool table; a
well-presented pub with a good
range of ales.
≠ (Berwick)

WYLAM

BOATHOUSE
Station Road
☎ (01661) 853431
12-3, 6-11; 12-11 Fri & Sat;
12-10.30 Sun
**Marston's Pedigree; Morland
Old Speckled Hen; Taylor
Landlord; Theakston Best Bitter;
guest beers** H
Warm, friendly pub on the south
bank of the Tyne, it offers a
choice of guest ales and a guest
cider, also a good range of food.
🏨 Q 🛏 ❀ ◗ ▶ 🍺 ≠ ♣ ⌂ P

Although a number of breweries have been closed and clubland is still largely a cask
ale desert, in the last decade four independent breweries have set up. Life has not
been easy, but they have all found pubs to take their beer.
Unfortunately Belford's Longstone brewery collapsed in the mid-90s as a result of a
dependence on rural pubs, which themselves were feeling the effects of the recession, the ever-increasing price of a pint and the crackdown on drivers who drink
and move between rural outlets.
The Star at Netherton is one of the few pubs in the UK to have been included in
every *Good Beer Guide*. To sample some of the local beers: Border Brewery is a
stone's throw from the Angel in Tweedmouth; Hexhamshire
beers are available at the Dipton Mill Inn, currently
Northumberland *Pub of the Year* and which also featured in an
episode of *The Likely Lads*.
Northumberland beers can be drunk at a number of locations in
the North-East or at most of the North-East beer festivals.

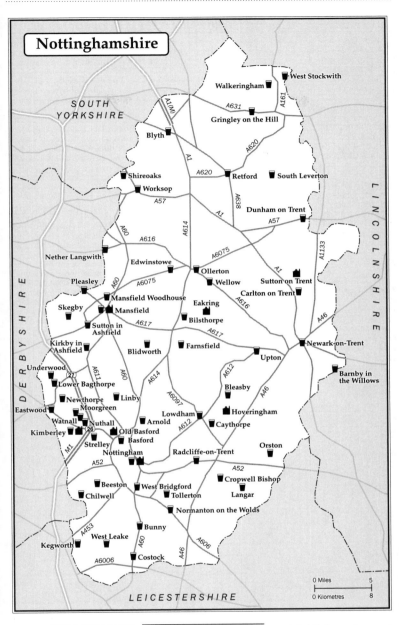

Nottinghamshire

(Map of Nottinghamshire showing towns including West Stockwith, Walkeringham, Gringley on the Hill, Blyth, Shireoaks, Worksop, Retford, South Leverton, Dunham on Trent, Nether Langwith, Edwinstowe, Ollerton, Wellow, Sutton on Trent, Carlton on Trent, Pleasley, Mansfield Woodhouse, Skegby, Mansfield, Eakring, Bilsthorpe, Newark-on-Trent, Sutton in Ashfield, Kirkby in Ashfield, Blidworth, Farnsfield, Upton, Barnby in the Willows, Underwood, Lower Bagthorpe, Bleasby, Newthorpe, Linby, Moorgreen, Eastwood, Lowdham, Hoveringham, Watnall, Nuthall, Arnold, Caythorpe, Kimberley, Old Basford, Basford, Strelley, Nottingham, Radcliffe-on-Trent, Orston, Beeston, West Bridgford, Cropwell Bishop, Chilwell, Tollerton, Langar, Normanton on the Wolds, Bunny, West Leake, Kegworth, Costock. Bordered by South Yorkshire, Lincolnshire, Derbyshire and Leicestershire.)

0 Miles 5
0 Kilometres 8

ARNOLD

DRUIDS TAVERN
109 High Street
☎ (0115) 926 5512
12-2.30 (3 Sat), 7-11; 12-3,
7-10.30 Sun
**Hardy & Hansons Best Mild, Best
Bitter, P Classic, seasonal
beers** H
Basic, popular, no-frills pub with
a pool room and an outside skittle alley.
🌼 ♣ P

BARNBY-IN-THE-WILLOWS

WILLOW TREE
Front Street (off A17)
☎ (01636) 626613
12-3 (not Mon), 7-11; 12-3,
7-10.30 Sun
**Marston's Pedigree; Rudgate
Viking; guest beers** H
17th-century coaching inn, in a
quiet village; a free house serving freshly cooked lunches from
an extensive menu, plus eve

meals Sat. Each room has a real
log fire in winter. Families welcome. The house beer is brewed
by Bateman. 🏨 Q 🌼 ⇌ ◖ P 🍺

BASFORD

FOX & CROWN
Church Street ☎ (0115) 942 2002
10.30-11; 12-10.30 Sun
**Fiddlers Mild, Best Bitter, Finest,
seasonal beers; guest beers** H
Very fine single-bar pub with
three distinct areas drawing a

247

varied clientele. The pub's brewery has a glass side so it can be viewed from outside. Beer festivals at two monthly intervals. Children's certificate.
❀ ◖ ▶ ₺ P

BEESTON

COMMERCIAL INN
19 Wollaton Road
☎ (0115) 925 4480
11-2.30, 5-11; 11-11 Fri & Sat; 12-10.30 Sun
Hardys & Hansons Best Mild, Best Bitter, Ⓟ **Classic, seasonal beers** Ⓗ
Established, friendly local. Despite appearances, the font-like electric pumps dispense real ale. ❀ ◖ ≈ ♣ P

VICTORIA HOTEL
Dovecoat Lane (by station)
☎ (0115) 925 4049
11-11; 12-10.30 Sun
Bateman XB; Castle Rock Hemlock; Courage Directors; Everards Tiger; Marston's Pedigree; guest beers Ⓗ
Busy, friendly pub, a Victorian architectural gem with four rooms. Over 100 whiskies and good food served. Watch the trains go by from the garden.
🏚 Q ❀ ◖ ▶ 🍴 ₺ ≈ ♣ ↻ P

BILSTHORPE

STANTON ARMS
Mickeldale Lane
☎ (01623) 870234
11-4, 7-11; 11-11 Fri & Sat; 12-10.30 Sun
Barnsley Bitter Ⓗ
Large estate pub in a former pit village with a lounge, public bar and a large function room.
🏚 ◖ ▶ ♣ P ✂

BLEASEY

WAGGON & HORSES
Gypsy Lane (1 mile S of station)
☎ (01636) 830283
12-3 (not winter Mon or Tue), 6.30-11; 12-3, 7-10.30 Sun
Banks's Bitter; Marston's Pedigree; guest beer (summer) Ⓗ
Originally a farmhouse, this

attractive, whitewashed village local enjoys a quiet setting overlooking the church. Fish (or chicken), chips and peas are served Fri eves.
🏚 Q 🍴 ❀ ◖ 🍴 ▲ ♣ P

BLIDWORTH

FOX & HOUNDS
Calverton Road, Blidworth Bottoms (1 mile off A614; 1 mile S of Blidworth) OS590547
☎ (01623) 792383
12-3.30, 6-11; 12-3, 7-10.30 Sun
Hardys & Hansons Best Mild, Best Bitter, seasonal beers Ⓗ
Traditional, welcoming three-roomed village pub serving excellent home-cooked food at reasonable prices. Sherwood Forest walks nearby. Thursday is folk night.
🏚 Q 🍴 ❀ 🍴 ▲ ♣ P

BLYTH

ANGEL INN
Bawtry Road (1 mile from A1)
☎ (01909) 591213
11.30-2.30, 6-11; 11.30-2.30, 6-11 Sat; 12-3, 7-10.30 Sun
Hardys & Hansons Best Mild, Best Bitter Ⓗ
Traditionally decorated pub with a warm, friendly atmosphere, serving good value, home-cooked food. Families very welcome.
🍴 ❀ 🍴 ◖ ▶ ₺ ▲ ♣ P ✂ 🍴

BUNNY

RANCLIFFE ARMS
139 Loughborough Road
☎ (0115) 984 4727
12-2.30, 6-11; 12-3, 7-10.30 Sun
Mansfield Riding Mild, Riding Bitter, Bitter, Old Baily Ⓗ
Former 17th-century coaching inn with two bars and a restaurant. Brass and copper adorn the wood-panelled walls. The extensive menu includes daily specials. The car park is on a sharp bend.
🏚 Q ❀ 🍴 ◖ ▶ ♣ P

CARLTON ON TRENT

GREAT NORTHERN INN
Ossington Road (300 yds from A1)
☎ (01636) 821348
12-2.30, 5.30-11; 12-3, 6-10.30 Sun
Mansfield Riding Bitter; guest beers Ⓗ
Set beside the main East Coast railway line, it is popular with families, who have their own large, comfortable room. The friendly locals' bar has an impressive array of pump clips and beer bottles; visitors are always made welcome. Children's play area outdoors.
🏚 🍴 ❀ ◖ ▶ ₺ ▲ ♣ P 🍴

CAYTHORPE

BLACK HORSE
29 Main Street (1 mile S of Lowdham station)
☎ (0115) 966 3520
12-2.30 (not Mon), 5.30 (6 Sat)-11; 12-3, 7-10.30 Sun
Dover Beck Bitter; Mansfield Bitter; guest beers Ⓗ
Delightfully traditional village inn dating back over 300 years and reputedly once a haunt of Dick Turpin. Excellent home cooking makes good use of fresh ingredients, especially fish; lunches Tue-Sat; must book eves. Dover Beck beers are brewed at the rear. 🏚 Q ❀ ◖ ▶ 🍴 ♣ P

CHILWELL

CADLAND
High Road
☎ (0115) 951 8911
11-11; 12-10.30 Sun
Draught Bass; guest beer Ⓗ
Friendly, multi-roomed pub with satellite TV in the bar; popular with all ages. Eve meals finish at 8pm.
❀ ◖ ▶ 🍴 ≈ (Attenborough) ♣ P

CHEQUERS INN
High Road
☎ (0115) 925 4312
11-11; 12-10.30 Sun
Marston's Pedigree; Shipstone's Bitter; Worthington Bitter Ⓗ
Recently refurbished one-room pub with old-style decor; popular with youngsters. Eve meals finish at 6pm.
❀ ◖ ▶ ≈ (Beeston) ♣ P

COSTOCK

GENEROUS BRITON
14 Main Street
☎ (01509) 852347
11.30-2.30, 6.30 (8 Wed)-11; 12-2.30, 7-10.30 Sun
Mansfield Riding Bitter, Bitter, Old Baily Ⓗ
A quiet and convivial atmosphere exists in this excellent village local - a centre for the local community. A comfortable lounge and a fine traditional bar - the sort that is increasingly rare and well worth visiting. 🏚 ❀ ◖ 🍴 ♣ P

CROPWELL BISHOP

WHEATSHEAF
11 Nottingham Road
☎ (0115) 989 2247
11-11; 12-10.30 Sun
Mansfield Riding Mild, Riding Bitter, Bitter, Old Baily Ⓗ
Two-roomed village local, dating back 500 years and reputedly haunted. Chinese banquets are provided for booked parties in an upstairs room.
🏚 ❀ ◖ ▶ 🍴 ♣ P

DUNHAM ON TRENT

BRIDGE INN
Main Street
☎ (01777) 228385
12-3, 5-11; 12-10.30 Sun
Springhead Bitter; guest beers H
Roadside pub, close to Dunham
toll bridge. One beer is keenly
priced; three changing guest
beers.🚶 🏵 🛏 🕼 🍴 🕭 P ⚡ 🖨

EASTWOOD

GREASLEY CASTLE
1 Castle Street, Hilltop, (off
B6010) ☎ (01773) 761080
10.30-3, 6 (5 Fri & Sat)-11 (may
open all day in summer); 12-4, 7-
10.30 Sun
**Hardys & Hansons Best Mild,
Best Bitter** P
Distinctive, comfortable,
Victorian corner local on a one-
way terraced street. Busy, with
live performers Fri & Sun eves.
🏵 🍺 ♣

EDWINSTOWE

FOREST LODGE HOTEL
2-4 Church Street
☎ (01623) 824443
12-3, 6.30-11 (12-11 summer);
12-4, 6.30-10.30 Sun
**Ruddles Best Bitter; Theakston
Best Bitter; guest beers** H
Sympathetically refurbished historic pub at the heart of
Sherwood Forest. A wide range
of food available (not Sun eve),
also accommodation (one room
boasts a four-poster bed).
🚶 Q 🛏 🕼 🍴 🕭 P ⚡

FARNSFIELD

RED LION
Main Street ☎ (01623) 882304
11-3, 6.30-11; 12-3, 7-10.30 Sun
**Mansfield Riding Mild, Riding
Bitter, Bitter, Old Baily** H
Friendly, family-run local on the
main road through the village.
Excellent, recently extended
restaurant (eve meals Tue-Sat).
🚶 Q 🐾 🏵 🕼 🍴 🕭 ♣ P 🖨

GRINGLEY ON THE HILL

BLUE BELL
High Street ☎ (01777) 817406
6-11; 12-10.30 Sun
**Marston's Pedigree; Tetley
Bitter; guest beers** H
Quiet pub, attracting mostly vil-
lage trade. 🚶 Q 🏵 🍴 ♣

KEGWORTH

STATION HOTEL
Station Rd (1½ miles from
Leicestershire village)
☎ (01509) 672252
11.30-2.30 (may extend summer),
6-11; 12-3, 7-10.30 Sun

Draught Bass; guest beers H
Built in 1847 as an hotel for the
now-closed station;it contains
three characterful rooms as well
as an upstairs restaurant
serving excellent home-cooked
food. The large garden affords
fine views.
🚶 Q 🏵 🛏 🕼 🍴 🕭 ♣ P

KIMBERLEY

NELSON & RAILWAY
Station Road
☎ (0115) 938 2177
11-3, 5-11; 11-11 Thu-Sat; 12-
10.30 Sun
Hardys & Hansons Best Mild, P
Best Bitter, H P **Classic, seasonal beers** H
Excellent village local, 100 yards
from the brewery: a wood-panelled bar, plus a restored
beamed lounge and a dining
area. Good value food on a wide
ranging menu; Sun meals served
12-6. Believed to have
Kimberley's only tap dancing
landlord!
🏵 🛏 🕼 🍴 🕭 ♣ P

QUEENS HEAD
Main Street (B6010)
☎ (0115) 938 2117
11-11; 12-10.30 Sun
**Hardys & Hansons Best Mild,
Best Bitter** H
Prominent corner pub: a busy bar
and a snug; the upstairs lounge
features live local artists and
singers Mon 4.30-7.30, and Wed,
Fri and Sat eves. Serves early
morning breakfasts and teas.
🕭 ♣

KIRKBY-IN-ASHFIELD

COUNTRYMAN
Park Lane (B6018, S of town)
☎ (01623) 752314
12-3 (4 Fri & Sat), 7-11; 12-3, 7-
10.30 Sun
**Draught Bass; Theakston Mild,
Best Bitter, XB; Townes
Sunshine, GMT; guest beers** H
Friendly, 18th-century roadside
inn with a cosy lounge bar and
beamed alcoves. Live music Fri
eve; No food sun eve. Occasional
ciders (mainly in summer).
🚶 🏵 🕼 🍴 ♣ ⌂ P

LANGAR

UNICORNS HEAD
Main Street
☎ (01949) 860460
11-3, 6-11; 11-11 Sat; 12-10.30
Sun
**Home Mild, Bitter; Mansfield
Riding Bitter; guest beers** H
Comfortable, two-roomed,
beamed village local in the Vale
of Belvoir. This no-frills pub has a
large garden. Live jazz Fri night;
other entertainment Sat.
🚶 🐾 🏵 🕼 🍴 🕭 🅰 P

LINBY

HORSE & GROOM
Main Street
☎ (0115) 963 2219
12-11; 12-10.30 Sun
**Home Mild, Bitter; Marston's
Pedigree; guest beers** H
Popular, four-roomed village pub
with a restaurant. Each room has
its own fire in winter. Extensive
children's play area in the garden. Linby won the *Best Kept
Village* award for 1998.
🚶 Q 🏵 🕼 🕭 🅰 ♣ P

LOWDHAM

WORLD'S END
Plough Lane (off Ton Lane, off
A6097) ☎ (0115) 966 3857
12-3, 5.30 (6 Sat)-11; 12-3.30, 7-
10.30 Sun
**Banks's Mild; Marston's Bitter,
Pedigree** H
Cosy, one-roomed village local.
The white-painted exterior is
bedecked with flower baskets in
summer. Good value home cook-
ing (not served Sun eve).
🚶 Q 🏵 🕼 🅰 ⇌ P

LOWER BAGTHORPE

DIXIES ARMS
School Road (off B600 at
Underwood)
☎ (01773) 810505
2 (12 Sat)-11; 12-10.30 Sun
Home Mild, Bitter; guest beers H
250-year-old, beamed country inn
with a tap room, a snug, and a
lounge, plus a large children's
play area. It supports its own
football team, pigeon club, gun
society and Morris dancing club;
a true village local. Live bands
(trad) Sat eves.
🚶 🏵 🅰 🅰 ♣ P

MANSFIELD

PLOUGH
180 Nottingham Road (A60
½ mile S of centre)
☎ (01623) 623031
11-11; 12-10.30 Sun
**Boddingtons Bitter; Flowers
Original; Marston's Pedigree;
Whitbread Fuggles IPA; guest
beers** H
Large, friendly one-roomer, with
eight real ales always on tap.
Good value food (not served Thu
eves). 🏵 🕼 🍴 ⇌ P

RAM INN
Littleworth
☎ (01623) 656071
11.30-11; 12-10.30 Sun
Mansfield Bitter, Old Baily H
Large, popular pub on the edge
of the town centre. The public
bar offers pub games and TV
sport; also a cosy lounge. 100
yards from the town's familiar
brewery site. 🕼 🍴 ♣ P

MANSFIELD WOODHOUSE

GREYHOUND INN
82 High Street
☎ (01623) 643005
12-11; 12-3, 7-10.30 Sun
**Home Mild, Bitter; Theakston
Best Bitter, XB; guest beers** H
Friendly village local in a central
location comprising a lounge and
a tap room with a pool table and
darts. Close to the Robin Hood
Railway Line.
Q ❀ ⊞ ≠ ♣ P

STAR
Warsop Road
☎ (01623) 624145
12-3, 6-11; 12-10.30 Sun
**Vaux Waggle Dance; Ward's
Best Bitter; guest beers** H
Old, low-beamed, three-roomed
pub, affording excellent garden
play facilities for children (who are
welcome inside for meals). Good
food (evening meals on weekdays).
Q ❀ ◖ ▶ ♣ P

MOORGREEN

HORSE & GROOM
Church Road (B600)
☎ (01773) 713417
11-11; 12-10.30 Sun
**Hardys & Hansons Best Mild, Best
Bitter, Classic, seasonal beers** H
17th-century pub, originally a
farmhouse, on the Greasley
Castle estate. Now one large,
L-shaped room with a restaurant
upstairs and a large well-
equipped garden.
🏾 ❀ ◖ ▶ P

NETHER LANGWITH

JUG & GLASS
Queens Walk (A632)
☎ (01623) 742283
11.30-4, 7-11; 12-4, 7-10.30 Sun
**Hardys & Hansons Best Bitter,
Classic, seasonal beer** H
Unpretentious stone pub, dating
from the 15th century. It stands
by the village stream, a popular
outdoor drinking venue.
🏾 ⇋ ◖ ▶ ⊞ ৬ ♣ P

NEWARK ON TRENT

FOX & CROWN
4-6 Appletongate
☎ (01636) 605820
11-11; 12-10.30 Sun
**Castle Rock Elsie Mo, Hemlock;
Everards Tiger; Hook Norton
Best Bitter; Marston's Pedigree;
guest beers** H
Closed since 1974 and reopened
summer '97, this is a beer
drinker's paradise: a comfortable, no-nonsense environment
in a good central location. Cider
varies.
Q ⇋ ◖ ▶ ৬ ≠ (Castle/North
gate) ○ ✂

HORSE & GEARS
21 Portland Street (200 yds from
Beamond Cross)
☎ (01636) 703208
11-3.30, 7-11; 11-11 Fri & Sat;
12-3, 7-10.30 Sun
**Mansfield Riding Bitter, Bitter,
Old Baily** H
Good value community pub with
something going on every night.
Local CAMRA *Pub of the Season*
spring 1998. ≠ (Castle) ♣ 🍺

MAILCOACH
13 London Rd ☎ (01636) 605164
11.30-2.30 (3 Wed & Fri), 5.30-11;
11-4, 7-11 Sat; 12-3, 7-10.30 Sun
**Boddingtons Bitter; Flowers IPA;
Marston's Pedigree; Wadworth
6X; guest beers** H
Welcoming, cosy, Georgian town
pub serving varied home-cooked
food. Live music Thu eve
(jazz/blues/folk).
🏾 ❀ ◖ ◖ ≠ (Northgate)
♣ ○ P

NEWCASTLE ARMS
34 George Street (100 yds from
Northgate Stn)
12-2.30 (not Tue; 12-3 Fri & Sat),
7-11; 12-3, 7-10.30 Sun
**Home Mild, Bitter; Wells
Bombardier; guest beers** H
Traditional Victorian local with a
basic public bar and a comfortable lounge.
Q ❀ ⊞ ৬ ≠ (Northgate) ♣

OLD MALT SHOVEL
25 Northgate ☎ (01636) 702036
11.30-3, 7(6 Fri & Sat)-11; 12-4,
7-10.30 Sun
**Taylor Landlord; Theakston XB;
guest beers** H
One room winds around the bar
in what was originally a 16th-
century bakery. A pub for all ages
with a continental-style restaurant, it has been in this *Guide*
since 1988. Eve meals Wed-Sun.
The house beer is from Rudgate.
🏾 ⛺ ❀ ◖ ৬ ≠ (Castle/
Northgate) ♣ P

NEWTHORPE

RAM INN
Beauvale (B6010)
☎ (01773) 713312
11-4, 5.30-11; 11-11 Sat; 12-3.45,
7-10.30 Sun
**Hardys & Hansons Best Mild,
Best Bitter, ℗ seasonal beers** H
1960s roadside community pub,
popular for darts, skittles and
quizzes. Excellent food.
🏾 Q ❀ ◖ ▶ ⊞ ♣ P

NORMANTON ON THE WOLDS

PLOUGH
Old Melton Road (off A606)
☎ (0115) 937 2401
11-3, 5.30-11; 11-11 Fri & Sat;
12-4, 7-10.30 Sun

**Draught Bass; Greenalls
Original; Shipstone's Bitter** H
Two-roomed village pub with a
large, attractive garden
(petanque played). Eve meals
available Thu 7-8.45.
🏾 ❀ ◖ ♣

NOTTINGHAM

BUNKERS HILL INN
36-38 Hockley (near ice stadium)
☎ (0115) 910 0114
11-11; 12-4, 7-10.30 Sun
Beer range varies H
Once a small bank, this one-
roomer with exposed brickwork
and wood panelling painted in
many shades of green, has a
warm, friendly atmosphere. Ever-
changing beers, eight in all,
mainly from micros, and good
value food (eve meals finish 7;
10pm Sun).
◖ ▶ ৬ ≠ ♣ ○

FOREST TAVERN
257 Mansfield Road
☎ (0115) 947 5650
4 (12 Wed-Sat)-11; closed Sun
**Castle Rock Hemlock; Greene
King Abbot; Marston's Pedigree;
Woodford's Wherry; guest
beers** H
A real café-bar atmosphere prevails, with a friendly bar staff
serving a good selection of
European bottled beers. Bar
snacks and food until late. The
night club attached is open late,
serving real ale.
Q ◖ ▶ ○

HOLE IN THE WALL
63 North Sherwood Street
☎ (0115) 947 2833
12-11; 12-10.30 Sun
**Mansfield Riding Mild, Riding
Bitter, Bitter, Deakins Golden
Drop, Old Baily; guest beers** H
Comfortable one-roomer.
Popular with students and real
ale aficionados. Good value
food and three guest beers are
served, accompanied by the
landlord's choice of soft rock
music. Evening meals (not Sun)
finish at 7pm.
❀ ◖ ▶ ৬

LIMELIGHT BAR
Wellington Circus (Nottingham
Playhouse Complex)
☎ (0115) 941 8467
11-11; 12-10.30 Sun
**Adnams Bitter; Bateman Mild,
XB; Castle Rock Hemlock;
Marston's Pedigree; Theakston
XB; guest beers** H
Traditionally-styled bar in a
1960s theatre complex, extended
to create two rooms. Six changing guest beers; music most Wed
and Thu eves. The delightful outside area is used for perfor-
mances in summer.
Q ❀ ◖ ▶ ○ ✂

LINCOLNSHIRE POACHER
161-163 Mansfield Road (A60, near Victoria Centre)
☎ (0115) 941 1584
11-11; 12-10.30 Sun
Draught Bass; Bateman Mild, XB, XXXB; Castle Rock Hemlock; Marston's Pedigree; guest beers Ⓗ
The city's leading alehouse with at least 10 beers, plus cider and over 80 whiskies. A no-smoking area is provided for diners (no food Sun eve), two other rooms, plus a conservatory. Regular brewery nights held.
Q ❀ ◖ ▶ ⌣

LION INN
44 Mosley Street, Basford
☎ (0115) 970 3506
11-11; 12-10.30 Sun
Beer range varies Ⓗ
Very popular, back-street pub, near the site of the old Shipstone's brewery. Bare brick walls and wooden floors belie the warm welcome. It hosts regular live music eves with folk, blues and jazz all showcased. Has 10 to 12 regularly changing guest beers. ♨ ❀ ◖ ▶ ♣ P

LORD NELSON
Thurgarton Street, Sneinton
☎ (0115) 911 0069
11-3 (4 Sat), 5.30-11; 12-4, 7-10.30 Sun
Hardys & Hansons Best Bitter, Classic, seasonal beers Ⓗ
Small, lively local, popular with young people, offering a large selection of board games. Originally two farm cottages converted into a pub around 1800, it is now surrounded by Victorian housing. Worth the effort to find. Has its own web site! Eve meals weekdays. Q ❀ ◖ ▶

MARCH HARE
248 Carlton Road, Sneinton
☎ (0115) 950 4328
11.30-2.30, 6-11; 12-2.30, 7-10.30 Sun
Courage Directors; John Smith's Bitter Ⓗ
Kept by the same hosts since opening in 1958, this friendly local has a comfortable lounge, a bar with pool and darts, and the cheapest lunches in town (not served Sun). ◖ ⌺ ⅍ ♣ P

O'ROURKES
10 Raleigh Street (300 yds from E side of Alfreton Rd)
☎ (0115) 970 1092
11-11; 12-10.30 Sun
Ward's Best Bitter; guest beers Ⓗ
A true Irish-themed street-corner local hosting Irish music sessions Thu eves, and other live music Fri & Sat eves. The decor features bare floorboards and distressed-effect walls. A pool table, but no juke box. ❀ P

RED LION
21 Alfreton Road (A610)
☎ (0115) 952 0309
11-11; 12-10.30 Sun
Boddingtons Bitter; Flowers Original; Greene King Abbot; Marston's Pedigree; Wadworth 6X; guest beers Ⓗ
Single-roomed pub just north of Nottingham's centre, boasting an unusual roof garden. Opens 11am Sun for brunch. ❀ ◖ ▶ ♣

OLDE TRIP TO JERUSALEM ☆
1 Brewhouse Yard, Castle Road
☎ (0115) 947 3171
11-11; 12-10.30 Sun
Hardys & Hansons Best Mild, Best Bitter, Classic, seasonal beers; Marston's Pedigree Ⓗ
Reputedly England's oldest pub, dating back to 1189. The back rooms are cut out of a cliff below Nottingham Castle. Restoration has revealed further caves and a cosy snug. Food is served 11-6.
♨ Q ⌺ ◖ ⇌ ♣

VAT & FIDDLE
12-14 Queensbridge Road (near station) ☎ (0115) 985 0611
11-11; 12-10.30 Sun
Archers Golden; Castle Rock Hemlock; Elsie Mo; Everards Tiger; Hook Norton Best Bitter; guest beers Ⓗ
The Castle Rock brewery tap; a traditional one-roomer, stocking five guest beers, including a mild, plus varied cider. Limited menu; eve meals 5-8. ❀ ◖ ▶ ⇌ ⌣

Try also: Coopers Arms, Porchester Road; Magpies, Meadows Lane (both Home)

NUTHALL

THREE PONDS
Nottingham Road (B6010)
☎ (0115) 938 3170
11-11; 12-10.30 Sun
Hardys & Hansons Best Mild, Best Bitter, Classic, seasonal beers Ⓗ
Busy roadside hostelry close to the M1 (jct 26). Three spacious, open-plan rooms, a skittle alley and a large garden with children's play facilities. Eve meals 6-8 Mon-Fri. ❀ ◖ ▶ ⌣ P

OLLERTON VILLAGE

SNOOTY FOX
Main Street (off A614)
☎ (01623) 823073
12-2 (3 Sat), 6-11; 12-3, 7-10.30 Sun
Barnsley Bitter; Theakston Mild, Best Bitter, XB; guest beers Ⓗ
Welcoming, traditional old pub, in a Grade II listed building, with a riverside garden. Varied home-cooked menu (no food Sun eve). Children welcome.
♨ ❀ ◖ ▶ ⌺ ♠ ♣ P

ORSTON

DURHAM OX
Church Street ☎ (01969) 850059
12 (11 Sat)-3, 6-11; 12-3, 7-10.30 Sun
Home Bitter; Marston's Pedigree; John Smith's Bitter; Theakston Best Bitter; guest beers Ⓗ
Pleasant, split-room, country pub with a large garden and pavement café areas. Table and long alley skittles played.
♨ Q ⌀ ❀ ♣ P ⌿

PLEASLEY

OLDE PLOUGH
Chesterfield Road North
☎ (01623) 810386
11.30-3, 5.30-11; 11-11 Sat; 12-3, 7-10.30 Sun
Marston's Bitter, Pedigree, Owd Rodger, seasonal beers Ⓗ
Old, beamed, stone pub, well renovated to give a large, open-plan area with alcoves. Wide range of home-produced food (no meals Sun eve). Music quiz Tue.
❀ ◖ ▶ ♣ P

RADCLIFFE-ON-TRENT

ROYAL OAK
Main Road ☎ (0115) 933 3798
11-11; 12-3.30; 7-10.30 Sun
Boddingtons Bitter; Castle Eden Ale; Marston's Pedigree; Morland Old Speckled Hen; Taylor Landlord; guest beers Ⓗ
Convivial village local with a comfortable lounge and boisterous bar; up to nine cask ales available. Eve meals Wed-Sun.
♨ ❀ ◖ ▶ ⌺ ⇌ P

RETFORD

CLINTON ARMS
24 Albert Rd ☎ (01777) 702703
11-11; 12-10.30 Sun
Courage Directors; John Smith's Bitter; Wells Bombardier; guest beers Ⓗ
Three-rooms, each with its own atmosphere; quiet during the day and lively at night. Regular live music (rock/blues) and large screen Sky TV. Home-cooked food served 11-7. At least one independent guest beer; occasional cider in summer.
Q ⌀ ❀ ◖ ⌺ ⅍ ⇌ ♣ ⌣ P ⊟

MARKET HOTEL
West Carr Rd ☎ (01777) 703278
11-3, 6-11; 11-11 Sat; 12-4, 7-10.30 Sun
Theakston Black Bull, Best Bitter, XB; guest beers Ⓗ
Busy, comfortable pub, locally renowned for the variety of its beers. A restaurant and large function room complete a fine facility. Q ❀ ◖ ▶ ⇌ P

TURKS HEAD
39 Grove Street (400 yds off market place)
☎ (01777) 702742
11-3 (3.30 Sat), 7-11; 12-3, 7-10.30 Sun
Vaux Samson; Ward's Best Bitter; guest beers H
Superbly attractive, cosy, oak-panelled pub off the town centre. A warm welcome is assured at this real ale supporting pub. Guest beers are from Ward's list. Good value food (not served Sun). Ringing the Bull played.
🏴 🍴 ◖ ♣ P

SHIREOAKS

HEWITT ARMS
Shireoaks Park, Thorpe Lane
☎ (01909) 500979
12-3, 6.30-11; 12-3, 7-10.30 Sun
Marston's Bitter, Pedigree; Morland Old Speckled Hen; guest beer H
Sympathetically converted, 18th-century coach house in the grounds of Shireoaks Hall, boasting a pleasant lakeside drinking area. Traditional home-cooked food (not served Sun eve).
🏴 Q ❀ ◖ ♿ ⅄ 🚲 P

SKEGBY

FOX & CROWN
116 Dalestorth Road
☎ (01623) 552436
11-11; 12-10.30 Sun
Home Bitter; Theakston Mild, XB; guest beers H
Recently refurbished, modern pub. A popular eating place attracting a friendly clientele. Children allowed in the restaurant and garden play area.
🛏 ❀ ◖ ▶ ♿ P ⅄

SOUTH LEVERTON

PLOUGH INN
Town Street ☎ (01427) 880323
2 (12 Sat)-11; 12-4, 7-10.30 Sun
Ruddles Best Bitter; guest beers H
True little gem, one of the smallest pubs in Nottinghamshire, which doubles as the village post office, hence the opening hours. No frills, just old wooden trestle tables and benches.
🏴 Q ❀ ♣ P 🍴

STRELLEY

BROAD OAK
Main St ☎ (0115) 929 3340
11-11; 12-10.30 Sun
Hardys & Hansons Best Mild, Best Bitter, Classic, seasonal beers H
Pleasant country pub in a small village on the outskirts of Nottingham. Catering for a large

food trade, it boasts a varied menu and offers a substantial discount on meals before 6pm.
❀ ◖ ▶ ♿ P

SUTTON-IN-ASHFIELD

KING & MILLER
King Mill Road (A38)
☎ (01623) 553312
11-11; 12-10.30 Sun
Hardys & Hansons Best Mild, Best Bitter, Classic, seasonal beers H
Roomy, pleasant atmosphere; its first 12 months have been a great success due to the beer, all day food and friendly welcome to all, especially families, with play areas inside and out.
❀ ◖ ▶ 🍴 ♿ P

TOLLERTON

AIR HOSTESS
Stanstead Avenue
☎ (0115) 937 2485
11.30-2.30, 5.30 (6.30 Sat)-11; 12-2.30, 7-10.30 Sun
Home Mild, Bitter; Marston's Pedigree; Theakston XB; guest beer H
Comfortable modern village pub with a lounge and bar, with sensible prices. Swings for children in the garden.
❀ ◖ 🍴 ♣ P 🍴

UNDERWOOD

RED LION
Church Lane (off B600)
☎ (01773) 810482
12-3, 5.30-11; 11.30-11 Fri & Sat; 12-10.30 Sun
Boddingtons Bitter; Flowers Original; Marston's Pedigree; guest beers H
300-year-old, beamed, friendly village pub with an eating area where children are welcome, plus a large garden and play area. Barbecues in summer.
❀ ◖ ▶ P

UPTON

CROSS KEYS
Main Street ☎ (01636) 813269
11.30-2.30; 11.30-11 Fri & Sat; 12-10.30 Sun
Boddingtons Bitter; Marston's Pedigree; Springhead Bitter; guest beers H
A *Guide* stalwart: a split-level bar in a pub of character, hosting two beer festivals a year (April and Oct). Good food.
🏴 Q ❀ ◖ ▶ ♣ P

WALKERINGHAM

THREE HORSESHOES
High Street
☎ (01427) 890959
11.30-3, 7-11; 12-4, 7-10.30 Sun

Draught Bass; Stones Bitter; Worthington Bitter; guest beers H
Comfortable village pub and restaurant noted for its beer and home-cooked food (book for Fri and Sat eves; no food Mon). The garden floral displays have won national awards.
Q ❀ ◖ ▶ ♿ ♣ ⅄ P 🍴

WATNALL

QUEENS HEAD
Main Road (B600)
☎ (0115) 938 3148
11-11; 12-10.30 Sun
Home Mild, Bitter; Theakston XB, Old Peculier; guest beers H
Old pub, sensitively renovated, keeping the small intimate snug with its low beams and coal fire. Spacious back garden and play area; good value food (eve meals 6-8; no food Sat eve or Sun).
🏴 Q ❀ ◖ ▶ ♣ P

WELLOW

RED LION
Eakring Road (opp Maypole)
☎ (01623) 861000
11.30-3, 5.30-11; 12-4, 5.30-11 Sun
Ruddles Best Bitter; Wells Bombardier H
Cosy, old pub, popular for meals. No music. The house beer is brewed by Maypole.
Q ❀ ◖ ▶ P ⅄

WEST BRIDGFORD

MEADOW COVERT
Alford Road (near Edwalton Golf Club) ☎ (0115) 923 2074
11-11; 12-4, 6-10.30 Sun
Hardys & Hansons Best Mild, Best Bitter, Classic, seasonal beers H
Very comfortable and well refurbished pub, located at the boundary with Edwalton. The bar/games room has a TV and two pool tables. No food Sun eve.
Q ❀ ◖ ▶ 🍴 ♣ P

WILLOW TREE
Rufford Way, (off Stamford Rd)
☎ (0115) 923 0011
11-11; 12-10.30 Sun
Draught Bass; Fuller's London Pride; M & B Mild, Brew XI; Worthington Bitter; guest beers H
Friendly community pub catering for all ages. A live band performs in the bar once a month. Visitors are always made to feel welcome. Q ❀ ◖ ▶ ♿ P

WEST LEAKE

STAR INN (PIT HOUSE)
Melton Lane ☎ (01509) 852233
11-2.30, 6-11; 12-3, 7-10.30 Sun
Draught Bass; Marston's Pedigree; Theakston XB; guest beers H

Traditional old alehouse dating from the 1700s; no juke box or one-armed bandits. Large terraced garden.
🏚 Q 🍺 🕷 ◖◗ ⊟ ♣ P

WEST STOCKWITH

WATERFRONT INN
The Marina, Canal Lane (off A161 at Misterton)
☎ (01427) 891223
12-3, 5-11; 12-11 Sat; 12-10.30 Sun
Marston's Pedigree; John Smith's Bitter; guest beers Ⓗ
Village pub, overlooking the marina on the Trent, popular in summer with boaters. Good food - vegetarian meals a speciality.
Q 🕷 ◖◗ Ă ♣ P ⊟

WORKSOP

GREENDALE OAK
Norfolk Street ☎ (01909) 489680
12-11; 12-4.30; 7-11 Sat; 12-3, 7-10.30 Sun
Stones Bitter; Tetley Bitter; guest beer Ⓗ
Cosy, gaslit mid-terrace pub built in 1790, fielding darts and dominoes teams. Excellent value home-made food. The back yard is safe for children.
Q 🕷 ◖◗ Ă ♣ P ⊟

MALLARD
Station Approach, Carlton Road (on station platform)

INDEPENDENT BREWERIES

Castle Rock:
Nottingham
Caythorpe:
Hoveringham
Fiddlers:
Old Basford
Hardys & Hansons:
Nottingham
Mallard:
Nottingham
Maypole:
Newark
Red Shed:
Nottingham
Springhead:
Newark

☎ (01909) 530757
12 (11 Sat)-11; 12-3, 7-10.30 Sun
Beer range varies Ⓗ
Genuine free house with constantly changing beers from small breweries and a wide range of foreign bottled beer.
Q 🕷 ♿ ⇌ ♣ P ⊟

SHIREOAKS INN
Westgate
☎ (01909) 472118
11.30-4, 6-11; 11.30-11 Sat; 12-4.30, 7-10.30 Sun
Barnsley Bitter; guest beer Ⓗ
Warm, friendly, family-run pub in converted cottages, serving good-value, home-cooked food.
Q 🕷 ◖◗ Ă ⇌ ♣ P ⌿ ⊟

Oxfordshire

NORTHAMPTONSHIRE

WARWICKSHIRE

Shutford
Banbury
Bloxham Bodicote
Hook Norton Adderbury
Wigginton
Deddington Souldern
Great Tew Fritwell
Steeple Aston Stoke Lyne
Chipping Norton Fewcott
Chadlington Bicester
Charlbury Tackley
Fifield
Stonesfield
Woodstock
Fulbrook Ramsden Murcott
North Leigh
Burford Kidlington
Witney
Eynsham
Botley Thame
Oxford Sydenham
Bampton Crowell
Sandford-on-Thames
West Hanney Chalgrove
Abingdon Lewknor
Faringdon Culham Watlington Christmas
Long Wittenham Common
Grove Dorchester-on-Thames
East Hendred Wallingford
Sparsholt South Moreton
Wantage
Childrey Blewbury
Goring Stoke Row
Henley-on-Thames
Rotherfield Peppard
Binfield Heath
Sonning Eye

BUCKINGHAMSHIRE

GLOUCESTERSHIRE

WILTSHIRE

BERKSHIRE

0 Miles 5
0 Kilometres 8

ABINGDON

BROAD FACE
30 Bridge Street
☎ (01235) 524516
11-3, 6-11; 12-3, 7-10.30 Sun
**Morland Original, Old Speckled
Hen; Ruddles County** or **guest
beer** (summer) Ⓗ
Large single-bar pub near the
historic abbey and the Thames,
built pre-1694. Its name refers to
the bloated face of a man hanged
at the old gaol opposite. Home-
cooked food, including Sunday
roasts. Use the public car parks
over the bridges. Q ⊛ ◖ ▶ ♣

OLD ANCHOR
1 St Helens Wharf
☎ (01235) 521726
11-2.30, 5-11; 11-11 Fri, Sat &
summer; 12-3, 7-10.30 Sun
**Morland Original, Old Speckled
Hen; Ruddles County, seasonal
beers** (occasional) Ⓗ

Famous old pub overlooking the
Thames, which was featured in
Jerome K Jerome's *Three Men
in a Boat*. There are several
cosy drinking areas in one rambling bar, plus a dining room.
Children are welcome on the
small patio in summer. Live
music Sun.
⊛ ⇌ ◖ ▶ ♣

ADDERBURY

COACH & HORSES
The Green (off A4260)
☎ (01295) 810422
12-3, 7-11; 12-4.30, 7-10.30
Sun
Wadworth IPA, 6X Ⓗ
Traditional welcoming inn overlooking the village green with
comfortable beamed bars and a
no-smoking dining area serving
good value food. Good local
support.
Q ◖ ▶ ♣ P

BAMPTON

MORRIS CLOWN
High Street
☎ (01993) 850217
12-2, 6-11; 12-11 Sat; 12-4,
7-10.30 Sun
**Courage Best Bitter; Theakston
Best Bitter; guest beer** Ⓗ
800-year-old pub with a welcoming atmosphere. The name
relates to the village history of
morris dancing.
⚐ ⊛ P

BANBURY

BELL
12 Middleton Road, Grimsbury
(400 yds from station)
☎ (01295) 253169
12-3, 7-11; 12-11 Sat; 12-4,
8-10.30 Sun
**Highgate Dark; Worthington
Bitter; guest beers** Ⓗ
Friendly, two-bar pub in a suburb

of Banbury. A rare outlet for the beer from the Banbury micro-brewery. Weekday lunches. Aunt Sally played in summer.
🏚 🌣 ⊄ ⊞ ≈ ♣ P

OLDE REINDEER
47 Parsons Street (near Market Sq) ☎ (01295) 264031
11-11; closed Sun
Hook Norton Mild, Best Bitter, Generation, Old Hooky 🄷
Gem of a 15th-century former coaching inn with a relaxed atmosphere (tidy dress - no under 21s). See the famous Jacobean globe room at the back. Excellent home-made lunches. Quiet background music.
🏚 Q 🌣 ⊄ ≈ ♣ P

BICESTER

SWAN
13 Church Street
☎ (01869) 369035
11.30-3, 7-11; 11.30-11 Fri & Sat; 12-10.30 Sun
Greene King IPA, Abbot, guest beers 🄷
Refurbished two-level town pub run by a friendly landlord. Interesting menu.
🏚 Q ⊄ ▶ ⊞ ≈ ♣

BINFIELD HEATH

BOTTLE & GLASS
Harpsden Road (off A4155, ½ mile NE of centre)
☎ (01491) 575755
11-4, 6-11; 12-4, 7-10.30 Sun
Brakspear Bitter, Old, Special 🄷🄿
Chocolate box, thatched, beamed, 17th-century, country pub with a flagstoned floor in its larger bar. Home-cooked food, including vegetarian options (no meals Sun eve). Large garden.
Q 🌣 ⊄ ▶ P

BLEWBURY

RED LION
Nottingham Fee (300 yds N of A417)
☎ (01235) 850403
11-2.30, 6-11; 12-3, 7-10.30 Sun
Brakspear Bitter, Special, seasonal beers 🄷
Unspoilt, picturesque pub, dating from 1785. Cosy and comfortable with beams, brasses, two old clocks and a large inglenook. An emphasis on food with daily specials and vegetarian choices, also a restaurant with a no-smoking area, plus a wine bar.
🏚 Q 🌣 ⇔ ⊄ ▶ ⅙ ♣ P

BLOXHAM

RED LION INN
High Street (A361)
☎ (01295) 720352
11.30-2.30, 7-11; 12-3, 7-10.30 Sun

Adnams Bitter; Wadworth 6X; guest beers 🄷
Friendly, two-bar pub attracting a good mix of ages, drinkers and diners. Large beer garden. It features a different special event/offer on meals each week.
🏚 Q 🌣 ⊄ ▶ ⊞ Å ♣ P

BODICOTE

PLOUGH
9 High Street
☎ (01295) 262327
11-2.30, 6-11; 12-3, 7-10.30 Sun
Bodicote Bitter, Three Goslings, No. 9, Porter, Triple X 🄷
Friendly, welcoming 14th-century, two-roomed village pub with its own brewery. Good home-cooked food is served in the lounge/dining room (meals cooked to order Sun). Beer festivals are held in Feb and Aug. Families welcome.
🏚 🌣 ⊄ ▶ ⊞ ♣

Try also: Horse & Jockey, High St (Courage)

BOTLEY

FAIR ROSAMUND
Chestnut Road
☎ (01865) 243376
12-2.30, 7-11; 12-3, 7-10.30 Sun
Marston's Bitter 🄷
1950s pub on the pleasant Elms Rise Estate. A large, L-shaped bar and a very comfortable lounge, with very reasonable beer prices for the area. Aunt Sally played. Q 🌣 ⊞ ♣ P

Try also: Wine Shop (off-licence), 8 The Square

BURFORD

LAMB
Sheep Street
☎ (01993) 823155
11-2.30, 6-11; 12-3, 7-10.30 Sun
Adnams Bitter; Hook Norton Best Bitter; Wadworth 6X 🄷
Cosy, flagstone-floored locals' bar in a very smart hotel. Comfortable and homely.
🏚 Q 🌣 ⇔ ⊄ ⊞ P

CHADLINGTON

TITE INN
Mill End (off A361)
☎ (01608) 676475
12-2.30, 6.30-11 (not Mon except Bank Hols); 12-3, 7-10.30 Sun
Archers Village; guest beers 🄷
Cotswold stone free house on the edge of the village, boasting fine open views and an extensive garden. A no-smoking garden room is open in summer. Children welcome. All food is freshly prepared and cooked for the restaurant. Guest cider.
🏚 Q 🌣 ⊄ ▶ Å ♣ ⌣ P ⅍

CHALGROVE

RED LION
High Street (off B480)
☎ (01865) 890625
12-3, 5.30 (6 Fri & Sat)-11; 12-3, 7-10.30 Sun
Brakspear Bitter; Fuller's London Pride; guest beer 🄷
Popular, 360-year-old, attractive village pub, Grade II listed, owned by the parish church. Several drinking areas; families welcome. A wide range of good value, home-cooked food includes vegetarian choices (no eve meals Sun); no smoking dining room. Wheelchair WC.
🏚 🌣 ⊄ ▶ ⅙ ♣ P

CHARLBURY

ROSE & CROWN
Market Street
☎ (01608) 810103
12 (11 Sat)-11; 12-10.30 Sun
Archers Village; guest beers 🄷
Popular, town-centre pub appealing to all ages, with a patio-courtyard. Excellent rotation of guest beers. Walkers very welcome. Live music Sun eve.
🏚 🌣 Å ≈

CHILDREY

HATCHET
High Street
☎ (01235) 751213
12-2.30 (3 Sat), 7-11; 12-4, 7-10.30 Sun
Flowers Original; Morland Original; guest beers 🄷
Very friendly, family-run village local. The ever-changing range of guest beers always includes a mild. 🌣 ⊄ ▶ Å ♣ P

CHIPPING NORTON

CHEQUERS
Goddards Lane (next to theatre)
☎ (01608) 644717
11-2.30, 5.30-11; 11-11 Sat; 12-3, 7-10.30 Sun
Fuller's Chiswick, London Pride, ESB, seasonal beers 🄷
Fuller's award-winning, friendly, traditional pub draws a good mix of clientele and age groups. Four comfortable drinking areas for good conversation. Good food menu, including Thai specials.
🏚 Q ⊄ ▶ ♣

CHRISTMAS COMMON

FOX & HOUNDS ☆
Off B480/B481 and B4009
OS715932
☎ (01491) 612599
11.30-2.30, 6-11; 12-2.30, 7-10.30 Sun
Brakspear Bitter, Special 🄶
Delightful, unspoilt, traditional Chilterns pub at the top of Watlington Hill, popular with hik-

ers and cyclists. Note the tiled floor in the small public bar which features a large inglenook. The family room is through the public bar.
♨ Q ⚘ ❀ ⊟ Å ♣ P

CROWELL

SHEPHERDS CROOK
The Green (off B4009 between Chinnor and M40 jct 6)
☎ (01844) 351431
11.30-3, 5-11; 11-11 Sat; 12-3, 7-10.30 Sun
Bateman XB; Batham Best Bitter; Hook Norton Best Bitter; guest beers [H]
Well refurbished pub situated under the Chiltern Ridge and off the main road, near a point-to-point course. Interesting choice of beers and occasional cider in summer. A good value, home-cooked food menu offers several fish dishes and a vegetarian choice.
♨ Q ❀ ◖ ◗ ♣ ⌓ P

CULHAM

RAILWAY INN
Station Approach
☎ (01235) 528046
11-3, 7-11; 11-11 Sat; 11-3 7-10.30 Sun
John Smith's Bitter; Marston's Pedigree; guest beer [H]
Original 1842 Brunel station building restored to its original purpose. Excellent cellar and thriving food and accommodation trade. A large bar plus a public bar. Occasional entertainment in the garden marquee. No meals Sun eve.
Q ❀ ⛟ ◖ ◗ ⊟ ⇌ ♣ P

DEDDINGTON

CROWN & TUNS
New Street (A4260 Oxford-Banbury road)
☎ (01869) 337371
11-3, 6-11; 12-3, 7-10.30 Sun
Hook Norton Mild, Best Bitter, Old Hooky, seasonal beers [H]
Pleasant, friendly, 16th-century redesigned inn catering for all ages. In every issue of this *Guide*. Families welcome. May extend afternoon opening.
♨ ❀ ◖ ♣

DORCHESTER-ON-THAMES

CHEQUERS
20 Bridge End (off High St, off A4074)
☎ (01865) 340015
12-2 (not Mon, 12-3 Sat), 7-11; 12-3, 7-10.30 Sun
Courage Best Bitter; Hook Norton Best Bitter; Wadworth IPA; guest beer (occasional) [G]
Genuine, 17th-century local in an attractive village which has an historic abbey. Lots of games, including Aunt Sally on summer Fri. Handy for walkers and the rivers Thames and Thame.
♨ Q ⚘ ❀ ⛟ ♣ P ⚟

EAST HENDRED

EYSTON ARMS
High Street
☎ (01235) 833320
12-3 (not winter Mon, Wed & Thu), 5 (6 winter)-11; 12-4, 7-11 Sat; 12-11 Sun
Courage Best Bitter; Wadworth 6X; guest beers [H]
Cosy, traditional, village local boasting original beams. The landlord is a real ale enthusiast, offering 140 real ales in 18 months. A small, quaint pool room is separate from the bar area. ♨ ❀ ♣ P

EYNSHAM

QUEENS HEAD
17 Queen Street
☎ (01865) 881229
12-2.30, 6-11; 12-2.30, 7-10.30 Sun
Morland IPA, Original; guest beers [H]
Friendly, 18th-century local comprising two bars: a quiet public bar and a more vibrant lounge. Railway memorabilia adorns both.
♨ Q ❀ ⛟ ◖ ⊟ ♣

FARINGDON

FOLLY
54 London Street
☎ (01367) 240620
5-11; 12-11 Sat; 12-10.30 Sun
Morrells Bitter, Varsity [H]
Charming and friendly basic boozer at the top of the town. A small public bar, a cosy lounge and a larger, recently opened, well decorated room with a pool table and TV.
♨ Q ❀ ♣

FEWCOTT

WHITE LION
Fritwell Road (off A43 at Ardley)
☎ (01869) 346639
7-11; 12-11 Sat; 12-4, 7-10.30 Sun
Beer range varies [H]
Friendly, 18th-century one-bar village local serving an excellent varied range of guest beers. A sporting pub - darts, pool, dominoes and Aunt Sally all played.
♨ ❀ ♿ ♣ P

FIFIELD

MERRYMOUTH INN
Stow Road (A424 Burford Road)
☎ (01993) 831652
11-3, 6-11; 12-3, 7-10.30 Sun
Banks's Bitter; Donnington BB, SBA; guest beers [H]
13th-century inn with a beamed bar and a stone floor. Good home cooking and accommodation.
♨ Q ⚘ ❀ ⛟ ◖ ◗ Å ♣ P

FRITWELL

KINGS HEAD
92 East Street
☎ (01869) 346738
12-3, 7-11; 12-3, 7-10.30 Sun
Draught Bass; Hook Norton Best Bitter; guest beers [H]
17th-century, Cotswold stone one-roomed pub. Warm and friendly, it is noted for traditional home-cooked food. Families are welcome.
♨ ❀ ◖ ◗ ♣ P

FULBROOK

MASONS ARMS
Shipton Road (A361, Burford Road)
☎ (01993) 822354
12-2 (not Mon or winter week-days), 6.30 (7 winter)-11; 12-3, 7-10.30 Sun
Hook Norton Best Bitter; Wadworth 6X [H]
Welcoming, 200-year-old village pub featuring bars with original beams and good value food. A 15-minute walk from Burford.
♨ Q ❀ ◖ ◗ Å ♣ ⚟

GORING

CATHERINE WHEEL
Station Road (off B4009, High St)
☎ (01491) 872379
11.30-2.30 (3 Sat), 6-11; 12-3, 7-10.30 Sun
Brakspear Mild, Bitter, Old, Special, seasonal beers [H]
The oldest pub in this popular riverside village. Extended into the old blacksmith's shop, it has low beams and an inglenook. Children are welcome in the 'Forge Bar' and large, safe garden. Good value, home-cooked food with daily specials (no meals Sun eve).
♨ Q ❀ ⛟ ◖ ◗ Å ⇌ ♣

GREAT TEW

FALKLAND ARMS
☎ (01608) 683653
11.30-2.30, 6 (5 summer)-11 (11 - 11 summer Sat); 12-3, 7-10.30 (12-10.30 summer) Sun
Hook Norton Best Bitter; Wadworth IPA, 6X; guest beers [H]
Traditional, one-bar rural gem in a picturesque village, featuring a flagstoned, beamed bar and award-winning food. Popular with tourists and locals; walkers are welcome but no children under 14. Recently refurbished accommodation. Small, no-smok-

ing dining room opens 7-8 eves.
🏰 Q ❀ ⇔ ◖ ▶ ⚘ ♣ ⌂

GROVE

VOLUNTEER
Station Road
☎ (01235) 769557
11-11; 12-10.30 Sun
Hook Norton Mild, Best Bitter, Generation, Old Hooky; guest beer Ⓗ
One of Hook Norton's most remote outposts, it was originally built to serve the former station. Although situated a mile north east of Grove, it has its own following who enjoy the variety of entertainment it offers, from regular live music to Aunt Sally. No food Sun eve or Mon.
❀ ⇔ ◖ ▶ ♣ ⌂ P ⊟

HENLEY-ON-THAMES

BIRD IN HAND
61 Greys Road (off A4155)
☎ (01491) 575775
11.30-3, 5-11; 11.30-11 Sat (may close winter afternoon); 12-10.30 Sun
Brakspear Mild, Bitter; Fuller's London Pride; guest beers Ⓗ
Comfortable, welcoming, one-bar, town local: the only real ale free house in Henley. Surprisingly large garden with a pond and pets, safe for children. No meals Sun. Two guest beers. No rail service in Jan and Feb.
Q ❀ ◖ ▲ ⇌ ♣

HOOK NORTON

SUN INN
High Street
☎ (01608) 737570
11.30-2.30, 6-11; 12-3, 7-10.30 Sun
Hook Norton Mild, Best Bitter, Generation, Old Hooky; guest beers Ⓗ
Welcoming village pub near the brewery. Spacious beamed bars with flagstone floors offer ample seating. Good mix of clientele of all ages. Separate restaurant.
🏰 Q ❀ ⇔ ◖ ▶ ⚘ ▲ ♣ P

Try also: Pear Tree Inn (Hook Norton)

KIDLINGTON

KINGS ARMS
4 The Moors
☎ (01865) 373004
11-2.30, 6-11; 11-11 Sat; 12-10.30 Sun
ABC Best Bitter; Marston's Pedigree; guest beer Ⓗ
Popular and attractive village pub with two small bars and a covered outdoor drinking area (Aunt Sally played).
❀ ◖ ▶ ♣ P

LEWKNOR

OLDE LEATHERN BOTTEL
1 High Street (off B4009, near M40 jct 6)
☎ (01844) 351482
11-2.30, 6-11; 12-3, 7-10.30 Sun
Brakspear Bitter, Special, seasonal beers Ⓗ
Comfortable, inviting, family-run village pub with a large inglenook, low beams and a large, well-kept garden. Excellent and extensive range of home-cooked food, reasonably priced, catering for all tastes (vegetarian options).
🏰 ⚊ ❀ ◖ ▶ ⚘ ⚘ ♣ P ✂

LONG WITTENHAM

MACHINE MAN INN
Fieldside (1 mile off A415 at Clifton Hampden, follow signs)
☎ (01865) 407835
11-3, 6-11; 12-4, 6-10.30 Sun
Adnams Bitter; Hop Back Summer Lightning; West Berkshire Skiff, Good Old Boy; guest beers Ⓗ
Welcoming, unpretentious village pub with a good mix of clientele, serving good value, home-made food (including vegetarian); book Sun eve. ETB approved accommodation. Families welcome. Three changing guest beers. A brisk walk from the annual (March) 'World Pooh Sticks' championship at Little Wittenham.
🏰 ❀ ⇔ ◖ ▶ ⚘ ♣ P

MURCOTT

NUT TREE INN
Main Street
☎ (01865) 331253
11-3, 6.30-11; 12-3, 7-10.30 Sun
Morrells Bitter, Varsity; guest beers Ⓗ Ⓖ
Attractive and welcoming village pub, offering up to three ever-changing guest ales and a superb menu. Although food plays an important role, the drinker is not overlooked. No meals Sun.
🏰 Q ❀ ◖ ▶ P

NORTH LEIGH

WOODMAN
New Yatt Road
☎ (01993) 881790
12-2.30, 6-11; 12-10.30 Sun
Hampshire King Alfred's; Hook Norton Best Bitter; Wadworth 6X; guest beers Ⓗ
Small, friendly, village pub serving freshly cooked home-made food (no eve meals Mon). The large terrace and garden host beer festivals Easter and Aug Bank Hols.
🏰 ❀ ⇔ ◖ ▶ ♣ P

OXFORD

ANGEL & GREYHOUND
30 St Clements Street
☎ (01865) 242660
11-11; 12-10.30 Sun
Young's Bitter, Special, seasonal beers Ⓗ
Popular, relaxed and friendly pub with a public car park conveniently placed behind. Small patios to the front and rear. No food Sun eve.
🏰 Q ◖ ▶ ♣

BUTCHERS ARMS
5 Wilberforce Street, Headington (off New High St)
☎ (01865) 761252
11.30-2.30 (3 Sat), 5.30 (4.30 Fri, 6 Sat)-11; 12-3, 7-10.30 Sun
Fuller's Chiswick, London Pride, ESB, seasonal beers Ⓗ
Friendly, back-street local with a single bar displaying collections of beer bottles, tankards and football match tickets. Weekday lunches.
🏰 ❀ ◖ ⚘ ♣

FIR TREE TAVERN
163 Iffley Road
☎ (01865) 247373
12-3, 5.30-11; 12-11 Sat; 12-10.30 Sun
Morrells Bitter, Mild, Varsity, Graduate, seasonal beers; guest beer Ⓗ
Small, split-level Victorian pub hosting live music most eves, including a very popular folk session on Tue. Food available all day at weekends - freshly made pizza a speciality. Real perry sometimes available in summer.
❀ ◖ ▶ ♣ ⌂

FOLLY BRIDGE INN
38 Abingdon Road
☎ (01865) 790106
11-11; 12-3, 7-10.30 Sun
Badger Tanglefoot; Wadworth IPA, 6X, Farmers Glory, Old Timer; guest beers Ⓗ
Open-plan, single-bar pub with a very good range of beers, hosting a monthly mini beer festival.
❀ ◖ ▶ ♣ P

FUGGLE & FIRKIN
14 Gloucester Street
☎ (01865) 727265
11-11; 12-10.30 Sun
Firkin Hophead, Fuggle, Be-Fuggled, Dogbolter; guest beer Ⓗ
Vibrant, city-centre pub in a pedestrianised area. A better-than-average Firkin redevelopment, avoiding a barn-like atmosphere. An excellent live music venue attracting big name jazz and blues acts.
❀ ◖ ▶ ⚘ ⇌

JUDE THE OBSCURE
54 Walton Street
☎ (01865) 557309
12-3, 5-11; 12-11 Sat; 12-10.30 Sun
Morrells Bitter, Mild, Varsity, Graduate; guest beer Ⓗ
Popular pub with a warm atmosphere. It features live Irish folk music Sun, regular poetry readings and the work of local artists is often on display. Can get busy.
🍴 ◖ ▶ ⌂ ⭤

MARLBOROUGH HOUSE
60 Western Road
☎ (01865) 243617
11-2.30, 6-11; 11.30-11 Sat; 12-10.30 Sun
ABC Best Bitter; Tetley Bitter Ⓗ
Small, friendly back-street local, popular with students and locals alike. Pool room upstairs; live music Wed eve.
◖ ♣

PHILOSOPHER & FIRKIN
286 Cowley Road
☎ (01865) 244386
12-11; 12-10.30 Sun
Firkin Thesis, Philosopher, Stout, Nostradamus, Dogbolter Ⓗ
Lively, popular Firkin with a large open-plan bar and a brewery on site (tours on request). The ale is competitively priced for Oxford and food is available all day. Wheelchair WC.
🍴 ◖ ▶ ♿

PRINCE OF WALES
73 Church Way, Iffley
☎ (01865) 778543
11-2.30, 6-11; 12-3, 7-10.30 Sun
Badger Dorset Best, Tanglefoot, Wadworth IPA, 6X; guest beers Ⓗ
Attractively furnished pub in a pleasant riverside village, two miles from the city centre and a short walk from Iffley Lock on the Thames. Excellent menu and range of ales.
🍴 ◖ ▶ ♣ P

ROSE & CROWN
14 North Parade Avenue
☎ (01865) 510551
10-3, 5 (6 Sat)-11; 12-3, 6-10.30 Sun
ABC Best Bitter; Ind Coope Burton Ale Ⓗ
Popular, unspoilt pub, purpose-built in the 1870s, with an unusual corridor drinking area and small bars front and rear. The courtyard drinking area at the rear is covered and heated in winter.
Q 🍴 ◖ ▶ ♣

TURF TAVERN
4 Bath Place (off Holywell St)
☎ (01865) 243235
11-11; 12-10.30 Sun
Adnams Broadside; Archers Golden; Flowers Original; Morland Old Speckled Hen; Whitbread Abroad Cooper; guest beers Ⓗ
17th-century tavern with low-beamed bars and an extensive outdoor drinking area in the form of courtyards (heated by flaming braziers on winter eves). Five or six imaginative and varied guest beers available at any one time.
Q 🍴 ◖ ▶

WHARF HOUSE
14 Butterwyke Place, St Ebbes
☎ (01865) 246752
11-3, 5.30-11; 11-11 Sat; 12-4, 7-10.30 Sun
Brakspear Special; Hook Norton Best Bitter; guest beers Ⓗ
Oxford's only true free house, offering two constantly changing guest beers, a superb range of Belgian beers, guest ciders and perry. A down-to-earth boozer with a mixed clientele.
🍴 ⭤ ⌂ P

WHITE HORSE
Broad Street
11-11; 12-10.30 Sun
Benskins BB; Ind Coope Burton Ale; Tetley Bitter; Wadworth 6X; guest beer Ⓗ
Small, 16th-century, city-centre pub next to Blackwells book shop and the Bodleian Library. Can get very crowded. ◖ ▶ ⭤

RAMSDEN

ROYAL OAK
High Street (off B4022, Witney-Charlbury road)
☎ (01993) 868213
11.30-2.30, 6.30-11; 12-3, 7-10.30 Sun
Archers Golden; Goff's White Knight; Hook Norton Best Bitter; guest beers Ⓗ
17th-century, former coaching inn. High quality local produce is served in the restaurant and bar. Friendly atmosphere; noted accommodation.
🏨 Q 🛏 🍴 🚪 ◖ ▶ P

ROTHERFIELD PEPPARD

RED LION
Peppard Common (B481)
☎ (01491) 628329
11-3, 5.30-11; 11-11 Sat & summer; 12-10.30 Sun
Brakspear Mild, Bitter, Old, Special, seasonal beers Ⓗ
Traditional, 18th-century village pub in a nice situation, overlooking a large common. A cosy and friendly atmosphere. One of the few Brakspear's pubs to take the whole of the brewery's range, including all six seasonal beers. Popular for food.
🏨 🛏 🍴 ◖ ▶ ⚓ P

SANDFORD-ON-THAMES

FOX
25 Henley Road
☎ (01865) 777803
12-2.30, 7-11; 12-2.30, 7-10.30 Sun
Morrells Bitter; guest beer Ⓗ
Locals' pub serving the best and cheapest Morrells in the area. A compact bar and cosy lounge.
🏨 Q 🍴 ⊞ ♣ P

SHUTFORD

GEORGE & DRAGON
Church Lane (1 mile off B4220, Banbury-Stratford road)
☎ (01295) 780320
7-11; 11-11 Sat; 12-3, 7-10.30 Sun
Fuller's London Pride; Hook Norton Best Bitter; guest beers Ⓗ
Traditional village pub partly dating back to the 11th century. An interesting mix of clientele includes locals, the farming community and tourists. Lunches at weekends only.
🏨 Q 🍴 🚪 ◖ ▶ ⊞ ♣

SONNING EYE

FLOWING SPRING
Henley Road (A4155, 2 miles E of Caversham)
☎ (0118) 969 3207
11.30 (11 Sat)-11; 12-10.30 Sun
Fuller's Chiswick, London Pride, ESB, seasonal beers Ⓗ
Traditional alehouse with a piano. It fields friendly sports teams and stages events in the huge garden. Varied menu of good quality food at reasonable prices (no food Sun or Mon eves).
🏨 Q 🍴 ◖ ▶ ⚓ ♣ P 🍴

SOULDERN

FOX
Fox Lane (near B4100, 400 yds off High St)
☎ (01869) 345284
11-3, 5-11; 12-3, 7-10.30 Sun
Draught Bass; Fuller's London Pride; Hancock's HB; Worthington Bitter; guest beers Ⓗ
Cotswold stone pub in the village centre. Award-winning food is served in the bar and restaurant.
🏨 Q 🍴 🚪 ◖ ▶ ♣ P

SOUTH MORETON

CROWN
High Street (off A4130, 1 mile E of Didcot)
☎ (01235) 812262
11-3, 5.30-11; 12-3, 7-10.30 Sun
Adnams Bitter; Badger Tanglefoot; Wadworth IPA, 6X; Ⓗ **guest beer** Ⓖ
This village local is deservedly popular for meals (including vegetarian choices). Water coolers are used on the casks behind the

bar. Families welcome. The best pub near Didcot.

🏠 🍺 ⊛ ◑ ▶ ♣ P

SPARSHOLT

STAR
Watery Lane
☎ (01235) 751539
12-3, 6-11; 12-11 Sat; 12-10.30 Sun
Butts Barbus Barbus; Morland Original; Worthington Bitter; guest beer Ⓗ
Friendly, thriving, oak-beamed village local with a strong horse-racing following. Good value food (no meals Mon lunch). Ask to camp in the pub's orchard.
Q 🍺 ⊛ 🛏 ◑ ▶ ♣ P ✄

STEEPLE ASTON

RED LION
South Side (off A4260)
☎ (01869) 340225
11-3, 6-11; 12-3, 7-10.30 Sun
Hook Norton Best Bitter; guest beers Ⓗ
Friendly, adult retreat with a collection of reference books to settle arguments. A classic. No food Sun. 🏠 Q ⊛ ◑ ▶ P

STOKE LYNE

PEYTON ARMS ☆
½ mile off B4100, near Bicester
☎ (01869) 345285
11.30-3 (not Mon), 6-11; 12-10.30 Sun
Hook Norton Mild, Best Bitter, Old Hooky, seasonal beers; guest beer (occasional) Ⓖ
Small, basic, two-bar village pub, unchanged by time. A rural gem! Aunt Sally played. Cold lunches.
🏠 Q ⊛ ♣ P

STOKE ROW

CHERRY TREE
Off B481 at Highmoor
☎ (01491) 680430
11-3, 6-11; 11-11 Sat; 12-3, 7-10.30 Sun
Brakspear Mild, Bitter, Special, seasonal beers Ⓖ
Low-beamed, attractive, popular, traditional village local close to the famous 'Maharajah's Well'. Families are welcome in the lounge and the games room; the garden has swings and a slide. Snacks available.
🏠 Q 🍺 ⊛ ♣ P

STONESFIELD

BLACK HEAD
Church Street
☎ (01993) 891616
10.30-2.30, 5.30-11; 12-3, 7-10.30 Sun
Courage Best Bitter; guest beers Ⓗ
Pleasant, welcoming, two-

roomed village pub. Usually two guest beers on tap.
🏠 ⊛ 🍺 ♣ P

SYDENHAM

CROWN
Sydenham Road (off B4445, between Thame and Chinnor) OS729018
☎ (01844) 351634
12-2, 6-11; 12-2, 7-10.30 Sun
Morrells Bitter, Varsity; guest beer Ⓗ
Pub dating from 1680, located in a quiet farming village off the beaten track. The cosy low-beamed single large bar offers good food from bar snacks to full a la carte menu (eve meals Tue-Sat). Home of Towersey Morris Men. Aunt Sally in the garden. Limited parking.
🏠 ⊛ ◑ ▶ P

TACKLEY

GARDINERS ARMS
95 Medcroft Road
☎ (01869) 331266
11-3, 6.30-11; 12-4, 6.30-10.30 (12-10.30 summer) Sun
Morrells Bitter, Varsity, Graduate; guest beers Ⓗ
Welcoming and pleasantly furnished 17th-century Cotswold stone pub which has a skittle alley/function room in a separate building.
🏠 ⊛ ◑ ▶ 🍺 ⇌ ♣ P

THAME

SWAN HOTEL
9 Upper High Street
☎ (01844) 261211
11-11; 12-10.30 Sun
Brakspear Bitter; Hook Norton Best Bitter; guest beers Ⓗ
Town-centre inn overlooking the market place. Note the unusual furniture and fittings, especially the boar's head! Constantly changing selection of wide-ranging guest beers. Excellent restaurant and bar meals, with vegetarian and children's choices. 🏠 🍺 🛏 ◑ ▶ ⓖ ♣

WALLINGFORD

COACH & HORSES
12 Kinecroft (off High St, 400 yds W of A329/A4130 jct)
☎ (01491) 825054
11.30-3, 6-11; 11-11 Fri, Sat & summer; 12-10.30 Sun
Fuller's Chiswick, London Pride, ESB, seasonal beers Ⓗ
300-year-old, two-bar pub adjoining the Kinecroft common (which acts as its garden). Formerly an alehouse, it is decorated with a collection of antiques, old family effects and photographs. No eve meals Mon-Thu in winter. Occasional cider. ⊛ ◑ ▶ ♣ ⌣

KINGS HEAD
2 St Martin's Street (A329, near A4130 jct)
☎ (01491) 838309
11-11; 12-10.30 Sun
Brakspear Bitter Ⓗ
Popular, one-bar, modern, town-centre pub which has recently been refurbished. Families welcome until 4pm.
ⓖ ♣ P

WANTAGE

ROYAL OAK
Newbury Street
☎ (01235) 763129
12-2.30 (not Mon-Thu), 5.30 (7 Sat)-11; 12-2, 7-10.30 Sun
Badger Tanglefoot; Draught Bass; Wadworth 6X; West Berkshire Dr Hexters, Wedding Ale; guest beers Ⓗ Ⓖ
A veritable cornucopia of convivial delights awaits the discerning drinker, a few hundred yards south of the market place. Both bars offer a warm welcome. Lunches served Fri and Sat.
🛏 ◑ ♣

WATLINGTON

FOX & HOUNDS
Shirburn Street (B4009)
☎ (01491) 612142
11-2.30 (3 Sat), 6 (5 Fri & Sat)-11; 12-3, 7-10.30 Sun
Brakspear Bitter, Old (winter), **Special, seasonal beers** Ⓗ
15th/16th-century, locals' inn. Extended to incorporate the butcher's shop next door, giving three drinking areas. Families welcome; the dining room is no-smoking. Large selection (40-45) of chilli dips, and an extensive menu of home-made food.
🏠 ⊛ 🛏 ◑ ▶ ⓖ Ⓐ ♣ P

WEST HANNEY

LAMB INN
School Road (off A338)
☎ (01235) 868917
11.30-3, 6-11; 12-3, 7-10.30 Sun
Draught Bass; Morland Original; Shepherd Neame Spitfire; Young's Special; guest beers Ⓗ
Friendly, free house near the village green. Renowned for the excellence of both its beer and its food. Annual beer festival held over the August bank holiday weekend.
⊛ ◑ ▶ P

Try Also: Plough, Church St (Free)

WIGGINTON

WHITE SWAN INN
Pretty Bush Lane (off A361, follow signs for waterfowl sanctuary) ☎ (01608) 737669
12-11; 12-3, 7-10.30 Sun

Brakspear, the 300-year-old brewery of Henley-on-Thames, gets its recipe for the future. The firm is planning a flotation and an expansion of its estate and it has brought in outside help to push these projects forward. Roger Budd (left) is a former director of Ladbroke and Whitbread, and will head the company's licensed estate; David Gyle-Thompson (centre) is also chairman of tea retailer Whittard of Chelsea. Jim Burrows (right) is Brakspear's chief executive. An imaginative approach to management really does make a difference.

In other parts of Oxfordshire, things were not so happy. Morland took over Ruddles and then announced it was to close the plant (see the feature in the Leicestershire county pub listing). In summer 1998 Morrells announced it was up for sale, with the prospect that the brewery could be closed and the site redeveloped.

Sadly, bereavement could mean that independent brewery Merivales will close.

Hook Norton Mild, Bitter, Generation, Old Hooky, seasonal beers; Ⓗ guest beers Ⓗ Ⓖ
Early 17th-century, stone pub with a quarry-tiled bar area and elm-beamed inglenook. O'Hagan sausage menus feature, plus game stews at weekends. Friendly locals; pets and muddy boots welcome.
⚐ Q ❀ ◖ ▶ ♣ ⌣ P

WITNEY

HOUSE OF WINDSOR
31 West End
☎ (01993) 704277
12-3 (not Mon-Fri), 6-11 Sat; 12-10.30 Sun
Hook Norton Best Bitter; Marston's Pedigree; Wadworth 6X; guest beers Ⓗ
Popular free house serving a varied and well chosen beer list. A comfortable and homely feel is enhanced by a roaring open fire. Small eating area at the rear.
⚐ Q ❀ ▶ ♣

THREE HORSESHOES
78 Corn Street
☎ (01993) 703086
11.30-2.30 (3 Sat), 6.30-11; 12-3, 7-10.30 Sun
Draught Bass; Morland Original; Wells Bombardier Ⓗ
16th-century inn, five minutes' walk from the town centre. A flagstone floor and antique furniture combine to give the pub a comfortable feel. Good food.
⚐ Q ➷ ❀ ◖ ▶

WOODSTOCK

BLACK PRINCE
2 Manor Road
☎ (01993) 811530
12-3, 6-11; 12-3, 6-10.30 Sun
Archers Village; Theakston XB, Old Peculier; guest beer (summer) Ⓗ
16th-century coaching inn on the banks of the River Glyme, which featured in an *Inspector Morse* story. ⚐ ❀ ◖ ▶ P

INDEPENDENT BREWERIES

Banbury:
Banbury

Brakspear:
Henley-on-Thames

Hook Norton:
Hook Norton

Merivales:
Chipping Warden

Morland:
Abingdon

Morrells:
Oxford

Plough Inn:
Bodicote

Wychwood:
Witney

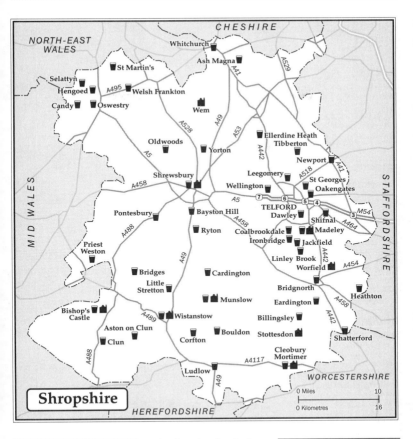

ASH MAGNA

WHITE LION
☎ (01948) 663153
12-2 (3 Sat; not Mon), 6-11; 12-3, 7-10.30 Sun

Draught Bass; Highgate Dark; Worthington Bitter; Ⓟ **guest beer** Ⓗ Ⓟ

Distinct lounge and public bar, the latter being full of real ale memorabilia. The lounge has an extensive collection of hicory-handled golf clubs. Bar billiards played and a bowling green adjacent. Popular barbecues summer weekends.
🏠 Q ❀ ◑ ▶ ⊞ ♣ ▯

ASTON ON CLUN

KANGAROO
☎ (01588) 660263
12-3, 7-11 (hours vary weekends and summer)

Draught Bass; Highgate Dark; guest beer (occasional) Ⓗ

Large public bar and a smaller, no-smoking lounge. The Australian connection is clear in mementos and decoration. Large garden plus camping in own grounds. A replaced rare black

poplar allows tree dressing to continue.
🏠 ◑ ▶ ▲ ⇌ (Broom) ♣ ✂

BAYSTON HILL

COMPASSES
Hereford Road ☎ (01743) 872921
5 (12 Fri & Sat)-11; 12-10.30 Sun

Draught Bass; M&B Mild, Brew XI; guest beer (weekend) Ⓗ

A snug and a large bar which contains many shipping mementos as well as an eye-catching display of carved elephants. Wheelchair access at the rear.
Q ◑ ▶ ♿ ♣

BILLINGSLEY

CAPE OF GOOD HOPE
On B4363, 7 miles S of Bridgnorth ☎ (01746) 861565
7-11; 12-3, 6-11 Sat; 12-3, 7-10.30 Sun

Banks's Mild, Bitter; guest beers Ⓗ

15th-century pub, set amongst the rolling countryside of south Shropshire. Its good value food attracts visitors from far and wide. Five rooms set around a central bar.
🏠 ❀ ◑ ▶ ⊞ ♿ ▲ ♣ P ✂ ▯

BISHOPS CASTLE

CASTLE HOTEL
Market Square ☎ (01588) 638403
12-2.30, 5.30-11; 7-10.30 Sun

Hobsons Best Bitter; Worthington Bitter; guest beer Ⓗ

Fine country town hotel. The front entrance leads to a snug bar with much original woodwork in evidence. There is a larger room off and a public bar at the rear. Excellent food and a good games selection; popular with locals. Large garden.
🏠 Q ❀ ⇌ ◑ ▶ ♣ P

SIX BELLS
Church Street ☎ (01588) 630144
12-2.30 (not Mon or winter Tue & Wed), 5-11; 12-3, 7-10.30 Sun

Six Bells Big Nev's, Cloud Nine, Spring Forward (summer) **Old Recumbent** (winter) Ⓗ

This pub is now run by the Six Bells Brewery's brewer and his partner. It is owned by the Six Bells Trust, formed to save it from redevelopment. The brewery is located at the rear of the pub. Friendly public bar and an attractive lounge.
🏠 Q ❀ ⊞ ♿ P

BOULDON

TALLY HO
2 miles off B4368 OS544815
☎ (01584) 841362
12-3, 6-11 (12-11 summer Sat); 12-3, 7-10.30 (12-10.30 summer) Sun
Church End What the Fox's Hat ⊞
Small country pub frequented mainly by locals and ramblers. Now serving real ales after a gap of 20 years. Other Church End beers available.
⚲ Q ⊛ ◖ ▶ ⊟ ♣ P

BRIDGES

HORSESHOE INN
OS394964
☎ (01588) 650260
12-3, 6-11 (not Mon, or winter Tue-Thu); 12-3, 7-10.30 Sun
Adnams Bitter, Broadside; Shepherd Neame Spitfire; guest beers ⊞
Attractively situated in a quiet valley between the River Onny and Stiperstones. An excellent local.
⚲ Q ⇆ ⊛ ◖ ⟲ ▲ ♣ ⌂ P ⚹

BRIDGNORTH

BEAR
Northgate ☎ (01746) 763250
11-2.30 (10.30 -3 Fri & Sat), 5.15 (6 Sat)-11; 12-3.0-2.30, 7.30-10.30 Sun
Batham Mild, Best Bitter; Holden's Bitter; Wood Shropshire Lad ⊞
Comfortable, friendly, two-roomed former brewpub off the High Street of this historic Market Town. This local offers a daily changing guest beer, exceptional food (book for the gourmet eve Thu) and above-average accommodation.
Q ⊛ ⇆ ◖ ⟲ ▲ ⇌ (SVR) ♣ P

BELL & TALBOT
Salop Street ☎ (01746) 763233
12-3 (not Mon-Wed), 7-11; 12-3, 7-10.30 Sun
Banks's Mild, Bitter; Marston's Pedigree; Morrells Varsity; guest beer ⊞
250-year-old coaching inn with three attractive bars, two with log fires. The old brewhouse is visible from the rear patio. Live Irish music Thu, Sat and Sun. Good food (no meals Sun).
⚲ Q ⊛ ⇆ ◖ ⟲ ▲ (SVR)⇌ ♣

BLACK HORSE (BENTLEY'S)
4 Bridge Street, Lowtown
☎ (01746) 762415
12-3, 6-11; 12-11 Sat; 12-10.30 Sun
Banks's Mild, Bitter; guest beers ⊞
Classic old English pub, run by a CAMRA ward-winning landlord and management team. Two bars and restaurant with a welcoming atmosphere, stocking a large selection of malts; Schnapps is also a special feature. Black Horse Best Bitter is Morrells Varsity rebadged. No meals Sun eve.
⊛ ⇆ ◖ ▶ ⟲ ⊟ ▲ ⇌ (SVR) ♣ P ⊟

RAILWAYMANS ARMS
Platform 1, Severn Valley Railway Station (off Holyhead Rd)
☎ (01746) 764361
11-3.30 (12-2 Nov-March), 7-11; 11-11 Sat; 12-10.30 Sun
Batham Mild, Best Bitter; Hobsons Best Bitter; Holden's Special; Worfield JLK; guest beers ⊞
Gem of a bar in a former waiting room on this steam railway platform. Adorned with much railway memorabilia, it is a regular haunt of rail buffs. A good selection of mainly independents' beers is usually available.
⚲ ⊛ ⟲ ▲ ⇌ (SVR) ♣ ⌂ P

CANDY

OLD MILL INN
W of Oswestry OSSJ2528
☎ (01691) 657058
11-3, 6-11; 12-3, 7-10.30 Sun
Beer range varies ⊞
Approached down hilly roads to the west of Oswestry, in a picturesque valley setting. The original stone building has been extended to provide a large L-shaped room.
⚲ Q ⊛ ⇆ ◖ ▶ ⟲ ▲ ♣ P

CARDINGTON

ROYAL OAK
OS506953 ☎ (01694) 771266
12-2.30, 7-11 (closed Mon); 12-2.30, 7-10.30 Sun
Hobsons Best Bitter, Town Crier; Marston's Pedigree; Woods Shropshire Lad ⊞
On the edge of the village, enjoying views across rolling country, this claims to be the oldest licensed pub in the county. An attractive, low-beamed interior, a huge open fireplace and wooden settles are features.
⚲ Q ⊛ ◖ ▶ P

CLEOBURY MORTIMER

KINGS ARMS HOTEL
Church Street
☎ (01299) 270252
11.30-11; 12-10.30 Sun
Hobsons Best Bitter, Town Crier; guest beers ⊞
Comfortable, 16th-century inn with three distinctive areas: one for eating, two for drinking. Classical music is played during the day, country/folk/jazz in eves. Only fresh ingredients are used in meals (not served Sun eve). Occasional cider.
⚲ ⇆ ◖ ▶ ▲

CLUN

WHITE HORSE
The Square
☎ (01588) 640305
11.30-3 (11-4 Sat), 6.30-11; 12-4, 7-10.30 Sun
Hook Norton Best Bitter; Ruddles Best Bitter; guest beer ⊞
Friendly, comfortable local in the centre of this timeless village. It attracts customers of all ages to its one L-shaped bar. Good range of board games provided to welcome families. One of the two guest beers is a local brew. Meals end at 8.30.
⚲ ⊛ ◖ ▶ ♣

CORFTON

SUN INN
On B4368
☎ (01584) 861239
11-2.30, 6-11; 12-3, 7 (6 summer)-10.30 Sun
Boddingtons Bitter; Flowers IPA; guest beers ⊞
Family-run, 17th-century inn, serving good food. Award-winning facilities for the disabled and children most welcome. Very popular with walkers. Good views of the Clee Hills from the garden. Note the interesting pub sign and the well in the restaurant.
⚲ Q ⊛ ◖ ▶ ⟲ ⊟ ⟲ ▲ ♣ ⌂ P ⚹ ⊟

EARDINGTON

SWAN INN
Knowle Sands
☎ (01746) 763424
5-11; 12-3, 6-11 Sat; 12-3, 7-10.30 Sun
Theakston Best Bitter; guest beers ⊞
18th-century inn with four rooms off a central bar area, plus a dining room serving good quality food; families welcome, Camping next door, and the Severn Valley Railway runs behind the pub.
⚲ ⇆ ⊛ ⇆ ◖ ⟲ ⊟ ▲ ⇌ (SVR) P

ELLERDINE HEATH

ROYAL OAK
Midway between A53 and A442
☎ (01939) 250300
11-3, 5-11; 11-11 Sat; 12-3, 7-10.30 Sun
Hanby Black Magic Mild, Drawell; Hobsons Best Bitter; Wood Shropshire Lad; guest beers ⊞
Lovely rural pub, known locally as the Tiddley Wink: it has a small bar with an adjoining games room and a large outside area. Good food (not served Tue) and low pried beer from Shropshire and beyond. Children's certificate.
⚲ Q ⊛ ◖ ▶ ▲ ♣ ⌂ P

HEATHTON

OLD GATE
From Claverley Village follow
signs to Bobbington OS813924
☎ (01746) 710431
12-2.30, 6.30-11; 12-3, 6.30-
10.30 Sun
**Draught Bass; Enville Ale; Tetley
Bitter; guest beers** Ⓗ
Bustling country pub off the beat-
en track: the lounge and old stable snug feature exposed beams
and log fires. Exceptional food.
Families welcome; the well maintained gardens have children's
play equipment.
🏚 🛏 Ⓒ ▶ ▲ ⌂ P

HENGOED

LAST INN
Off B4579, 3 miles N of Oswestry
OS283342 ☎ (01691) 659747
7-11; 12-3, 7-10.30 Sun
**Boddingtons Bitter; Wadworth
6X; guest beers** Ⓗ
Welcoming rural pub in attractive
Welsh borderland, offering a var-
ied selection of guest beers.
Families are well provided for.
Good food (not served Tue). A
long-standing *Guide* entry.
🏚 Q 🛏 Ⓒ ▶ ♣ ⌂ P

LINLEY BROOK

PHEASANT INN
Britons Lane (400 yds W of
B4373) ☎ (01746) 762260
12-2.30, 7 (6.30 summer)-11;
12-3, 7 (6.30 summer)-10.30 Sun
Beer range varies Ⓗ
Ever-changing guest beers, mainly local micros, are served from
three handpulls. A local authority
tourist sign on the Broseley-
Bridgnorth road guides you to
this two-roomed pub, set in a picturesque valley. One of
Shropshire's treasures.
🏚 Q 🛏 Ⓒ ▶ ♣ P

LITTLE STRETTON

RAGLETH
Ludlow Road ☎ (01964) 722711
12-2.30, 6-11; 12-10.30 Sun
**Hobsons Best Bitter; Morland
Old Speckled Hen; Theakston
Best Bitter; guest beers** Ⓗ
At the foot of Long Mynd, this
17th-century inn provides a convenient calling point on a number
of walks in the area. The public
bar boasts an inglenook, dark
woodwork and a brick and tiled
floor and is complemented by a
lounge and restaurant.
🏚 🛏 🛏 Ⓒ ▶ 🛏 ♣ P

LUDLOW

OLD BULL RING TAVERN
44 Bull Ring
☎ (01584) 872311
11-11; 12-10.30 Sun

Ansells Mild, Bitter; Tetley
Bitter; guest beer Ⓗ
Once plaster-covered, the timber
frame was revealed in the 1930s
and remains today. This cosy
pub, on one of Ludlow's most
ancient sites, comprises a
lounge, bar and upstairs restaurant. Very popular with all ages.
🏚 Ⓒ ▶ ≈ ♣

MUNSLOW

CROWN INN
On B4368, near Craven Arms
☎ (01584) 841205
12-2.30, 7-11; 12-3, 7-10.30 Sun
**Banks's Mild; Crown Boy's Pale
Ale, Munslow Ale; Marston's
Pedigree** Ⓗ
Roadside inn in a village setting
which brews its own beers - the
brew house is visible from the
bar. A varied menu offers continental and ethnic specialities.
🏚 Q 🛏 Ⓒ ▶ ⌂ P

NEWPORT

NEW INN
Stafford Road ☎ (01952) 814729
11.30-3.30, 7-11; 12-4, 7-10.30 Sun
**Banks's Mild, Bitter; Draught
Bass; Highgate Dark** Ⓗ
Three-roomed local with a friendly atmosphere. A cosy little snug
with a real fire, a good basic bar
and a large family room. Two
milds on at all times. Public car
park 50 yards away.
🏚 Q 🛏 🛏 🛏 ♣

OLDWOODS

ROMPING CAT
Near Bomere Heath
☎ (01939) 290273
12-3, 7-11; 12-2.30, 7-10.30 Sun
**Boddingtons Bitter; Castle Eden
ale; Fuller's London Pride; guest
beers** Ⓗ
No-frills country pub where the
beers are top priority; over
150 different beers in a year,
often featuring local breweries.
The locals are enthusiastic
charity supporters through cycle
rides, auctions etc.
🏚 Q 🛏 ♣ 🛢

OSWESTRY

BELL
61 Church Street
☎ (01691) 657068
11-11; 12-10.30 Sun
**Draught Bass; Highgate Dark;
M&B Brew XI; guest beers** Ⓗ
Active pub, opposite the ancient
parish church and one of the oldest pubs in town; reputedly 16th-
century but much altered.
Q 🛏 ♣ P

Try also: Oak Cross, Church St
(M&B); Foxes, Gobwen
(Marston's)

PONTESBURY

HORSESHOES INN
Minsterley Road (A488)
☎ (01743) 790278
12-3, 5-11; 12-4, 7-10.30 Sun
**Castle Eden Ale or Flowers
Original; guest beer** Ⓗ
Busy local in a large village, convenient for walks in the south
Shropshire hills. The service is
friendly and teams from the pub
participate in several local games
leagues. Up to three guest beers.
🛏 🛏 Ⓒ ▶ ♣ P

PRIEST WESTON

MINERS ARMS
OS293973 ☎ (01938) 561352
11-4, 7-11; 7-10.30 Sun
**Fuller's London Pride;
Worthington Bitter; guest beer** Ⓗ
Remote country pub, still largely
unspoilt. Although very much a
community pub, it also draws
walkers within the nearby stone
circle. Don't miss the indoor well.
Folk singing monthly; folk festival
Easter and Sept.
🏚 🛏 Ⓒ ▶ 🛏 ▲ ♣ P

RYTON

FOX
E of A49 at Dorrington
☎ (01743) 718499
12-3, 7-11; 12-3, 7-10.30 Sun
**Draught Bass; Taylor Landlord;
guest beer** (occasional) Ⓗ
On the edge of a small village,
with views across open countryside to the south Shropshire hills,
this L-shaped bar and restaurant
provides a very good range of
home-cooked food. Boules
played. 🛏 Ⓒ ▶ ♣ P

ST MARTINS

GREYHOUND INN
Overton Road (1 mile from St
Martins) ☎ (01691) 774307
12-11; 12-10.30 Sun
**Banks's Mild; Webster's
Yorkshire Bitter; guest beers** Ⓗ
Refurbished country pub. The bar
has a comprehensive display of
artefacts from the closed Ifton
Colliery. Steak and kidney pie is a
speciality (all food is home
made). An extensive outdoor
area has play facilities.
🏚 Q 🛏 🛏 Ⓒ ▶ ▲ ♣ P

SELLATTYN

CROSS KEYS ☆
On B4579, about 3 miles N of
Oswestry ☎ (01691) 850247
6-11; 12-3 (may vary), 7-10.30 Sun
Banks's Mild, Bitter Ⓗ
Prime example of a village pub.
Of 17th-century origin, it is on
CAMRA's National Inventory of
heritage pubs. Various rooms,
including a skittle alley. Close to

Offa's Dyke walk and the Welsh Hills, it has a holiday flat to let. Popular with pony trekkers.
🏨 Q 🐂 🍴 🚃 ♣ P

SHATTERFORD

RED LION
Bridgnorth Road
☎ (01299) 861221
11.30-2.30, 6.30-11; 12-3, 7.30-10.30 Sun
Banks's Mild, Bitter; ℗ Batham Best Bitter; guest beers Ⓗ
Family-owned roadside free house with smoking and no-smoking bars and a barn-style restaurant. Exceptional food includes fresh fish and daily chef's specials. Guest beers change frequently.
🏨 🍴 ◑ ▶ ♿ P ✂ 🍺

SHIFNAL

WHEATSHEAF TAP HOUSE
61 Broadway ☎ (01952) 460938
11-11; 12-10.30 Sun
Banks's Mild, Bitter; Camerons Strongarm; Marston's Pedigree Ⓗ
Pleasant Banks's Ale House operation. Three drinking areas boast much limed woodwork bearing jolly inscriptions. Very busy at weekends.
🏨 🍴 ◑ ▶ 🚃 🚉 ♣ P 🍺

WHITE HART
High Street (B4379)
☎ (01952) 461161
12-3.30, 6-11; 12-11 Fri & Sat; 12-4, 7-10.30 Sun
Ansells Bitter; Enville Mild, Simpkiss Bitter; Ind Coope Burton Ale; guest beers Ⓗ
Friendly, two-bar, ancient wood-framed local at the north end of town. No food Sun.
🍴 ◑ 🚃 🚉 ♣ P

SHREWSBURY

ALBERT HOTEL
Smithfield Road (near station)
☎ (01743) 358198
11-11; 12-3, 7-10.30 Sun
Banks's Mild, Bitter; Camerons Strongarm; Marston's Pedigree; guest beer Ⓗ
A welcome return for this pub, sympathetically refurbished by Banks's since its last appearance in the Guide; a recent winner of a Community Pub award (1998), the guest beer is often from a local brewery. Eve meals in summer.
◑ ▶ 🚉 ♣ 🍺

BOAT HOUSE
New Street, Port Hill (A488)
☎ (01743) 362965
11-11; 12-10.30 Sun
Boddingtons Bitter; Flowers IPA; Fuller's London Pride; Whitbread Abroad Cooper, Fuggles IPA; guest beers Ⓗ
Hogshead Ale House overlooking

Quarry Park. Tables in the terraced garden overlook the river. The pub can be approached from the park by a footbridge. Skittle Alley. Three guest beers, sometimes from local breweries.
🏨 Q 🍴 ◑ ▶ 🚃 ♣ ☕ P

CASTLE VAULTS
16 Castle Gates
☎ (01743) 358807
11.30-3, 6-11; 7-11 (closed lunch) Sun
Hobsons Best Bitter; Marston's Pedigree Ⓗ
Free house, one minute's walk from the station. Specialist Mexican food is served in a no-smoking area. Four ever-changing guest beers include a regular selection from Shropshire breweries. An unusual roof garden is overlooked by the castle.
🏨 Q 🍴 🚃 ◑ ▶ 🚉 ✂ 🍺

COACH & HORSES
Swan Hill
☎ (01743) 365661
11-11; 12-10.30 Sun
Draught Bass; guest beers Ⓗ
Victorian pub extended sympathetically by the present owner: the wood-panelled bar with a partitioned area off; the large extended lounge acts as a lunchtime restaurant. Q ◑ ▶

DOLPHIN
48 St Michaels Street
☎ (01743) 350419
5 (3 Fri & Sat)-11; 12-3, 7-10.30 Sun
Beer range varies Ⓗ
Early Victorian, gas-lit, drinking house with a porticoed entrance and its original layout. Up to six ales but no lager- not even bottled. Q 🚃 🚉 ▶

LOGGERHEADS (TAPHOUSE) ☆
Church Street
☎ (01743) 355457
10.30-11; 12-3, 7-10.30 Sun
Draught Bass; Banks's Mild, Bitter; Camerons Strongarm; guest beers Ⓗ
Top marks to Banks's for retaining the unique atmosphere of this town-centre pub. Do not miss the room left of entrance with its scrubbed-top tables and high-back settles.
Q ◑ ▶ 🚉 ♣ 🍺

PEACOCK
42 Wenlock Road (A458, 300 yds from Shire Hall)
☎ (01743) 355215
11-3, 6-11; 12-3, 7-10.30 Sun
Bateman Mild; Marston's Bitter, Pedigree, Owd Rodger, HBC Ⓗ
Spacious, comfortable, suburban, single-bar pub, which welcomes customers of all ages. An ornate peacock adorns the outside wall by the lounge entrance. No meals Sun eve. 🍴 ◑ ▶ ♣ P

TELFORD: COALBROOKDALE

COALBROOKDALE INN
12 Wellington Road
☎ (01952) 433953
12-3, 6-11; 12-3, 7-10.30 Sun
Courage Directors; guest beers Ⓗ
Welcoming pub, CAMRA national Pub of the Year 1995, its sells mainly premium beers, although lower gravity ales are available in the summer; 30 beers per week on seven handpumps. A clean air pub. Near the Museum of Iron. No food Sun.
🏨 Q 🍴 ◑ ▶ 🚉 ☕ P ✂

DAWLEY

THREE CROWNS INN
Hinksay Road (off B4373, at Finger Road garage)
☎ (01952) 590868
11.30-3 (11-4 Sat), 6.30-11; 12-3.30, 7-10.30 Sun
Marston's Bitter, Pedigree, HBC Ⓗ
Smart town pub with one bar, part of which is given over to darts and pool.
🍴 ◑ ♣ P

IRONBRIDGE

IRONBRIDGE BRASSERIE & WINE BAR
29 High Street
☎ (01952) 432716
12-3 (not Mon, nor Tue-Thu winter), 6.30-11; 1.30-4, 7-10.30 Sun
Brains SA; Hobsons Town Crier; guest beer Ⓗ
Formerly the Old Vaults, the new owners provide a warm welcome to complement the food and beer on offer in an intimate atmosphere. The popular 'lazy late Sunday lunch' is available from 1.30-4. The guest beer comes from established independents.
🏨 🍴 🚉 ◑ ▶

GOLDEN BALL
1 Newbridge Road (off B4373 at Jockey Bank)
☎ (01952) 432179
12-3, 6-11; 12-3, 7-10.30 Sun
Courage Directors; Marston's Pedigree; Ruddles Best Bitter; guest beer Ⓗ
18th-century inn, popular with locals and visitors. Excellent food at very reasonable prices can be enjoyed in a no-smoking dining room. Features in CAMRA's Room at the Inn. The house beer, Ironmaster is from the Crown Inn brewpub at Munslow.
🏨 Q 🍴 🚉 ◑ ▶ ♣ P 🍺

JACKFIELD

BOAT
Ferry Road (across river footbridge near incline)
☎ (01952) 882178
11 (5.30 Mon-Fri winter)-11; 11-11 Sun

Banks's Mild; Marston's Pedigree; Morrells Varsity; guest beer Ⓗ
A warm welcome is assured for locals and visitors to the Ironbridge Gorge Museum sites at this delightfully situated 18th-century riverside inn. Children welcome until 8.30 in a no-smoking family room. Note the Coalbrookdale range and flood level markers on the door.
🏚 Q ☺ ⊛ ◑ ▶ & ♣ ⌂ ✄ 🍺

LEEGOMERY

MALT SHOVEL
Hadley Park Road
☎ (01952) 242963
12-2.30 (3 Sat), 5-11; 12-3, 5-10.30 Sun
Banks's Mild; Marston's Bitter, Pedigree Ⓗ
Friendly, welcoming, two-roomer where horse brasses and rugby memorabilia decorate the walls. Weekday lunches.
🏚 ⊛ ◑ & ♣ P

MADELEY

ALL NATIONS
20 Coalport Rd
☎ (01952) 585747
12-3 (4 Sat), 7-11; 12-3.30, 7-10.30 Sun
All Nations Pale Ale Ⓗ
Famed home brewpub near Blists Hill Museum. In the same family for over 60 years, it has appeared in every edition of this *Guide*. One of only four home brewpubs still operating in 1971.
⊛ ▲ ♣ P 🍺

ROYAL OAK
High Street
☎ (01952) 585598
12-3, 5-11; 12-5, 7-10.30 Sun
Draught Bass; Burtonwood Mild, Bitter; Castle Eden Ale; guest beers Ⓗ
Licensed from 1831, once a coaching inn, but now a traditional beer drinkers' pub with a basic bar and cosy lounge. Six take-away restaurants are within easy walking distance. Try the Guess the Mystery Ale competition. An average of 100 beers a year.
🏚 Q ⊛ 🍺 ▲ ♣ P

OAKENGATES

CROWN INN
Market Street (near bus station)
☎ (01952) 610888
12-3, 7 (5 Thu)-11; 12-11 Fri; 12-3.30, 7-10.30 Sun
Hanby Black Magic Mild; Hobsons Best Bitter; Hook Norton Old Hooky; guest beers Ⓗ
Eleven handpumps are not all used continuously, but it hosts a new beers festival twice annually with an additional 18 handpumps. No frills: three distinct drinking

areas in this local CAMRA award-winning house. Eve meals can be booked. 🏚 ☺ ◑ ≈ ♣ ⌂

PEAR TREE BRIDGE
Holyhead Rd
☎ (01952) 414526
5-11; 12-5, 7-11 Sat; 12-5, 7-10.30 Sun
Boddingtons Bitter; Worthington Bitter; guest beers Ⓗ
Small, friendly, local on the old A5 offering changing guest beers. 🏚 ⊛ ≈ ♣ P

ST GEORGES

ALBION INN
Station Hill
☎ (01952) 614193
12-2.30 (4 Sat), 5 (7 Sat); 12-4, 7-10.30 Sun
Banks's Mild; Marston's Bitter, Pedigree, HBC Ⓗ
Pleasant, one-bar local with three drinking areas and a large award-winning garden looking out over the Shropshire plain. Good home-cooked food at reasonable prices.
⊛ ⊨ ◑ ▶ ≈ ♣ P 🍺

WELLINGTON

COCK HOTEL
Holyhead Rd ☎ (01952) 244954
4 (12 Thu-Sat)-11; 12-3, 7-10.30 Sun
Flowers IPA; guest beers Ⓗ
Popular, convivial, 18th-century coaching inn which dominates the crossroads. Up to six real ales available in the Old Wrekin tap bar which links via a wood-panelled reception area to a no-smoking lounge. Local CAMRA 1998 *Pub of the Year*. Eve meals finish at 8.
☺ ⊛ ⊨ ▶ ≈ ♣ P ✄ 🍺

TIBBERTON

SUTHERLAND ARMS
☎ (01952) 550533
12-2.30, 6 (5 Fri)-11; 12-11 Sat; 12-10.30 Sun
Banks's Mild; Marston's Bitter, Pedigree, Owd Rodger (winter), HBC Ⓗ
Everything a village pub should be: a selection of over 80 whiskies, several drinking areas and pub games. Popular with students. Eve meals Tue-Sat (6.30-8.30). 🏚 Q ⊛ ◑ ▶ 🍺 ♣ P

WELSH FRANKTON

NARROW BOAT INN
Ellesmere Road, Whittington (A495) ☎ (01691) 661051
11-3, 7-11; 12-3, 7-10.30 Sun
Tetley Bitter; guest beers Ⓗ
Ex-canal house, alongside the Shropshire Union (Llangollen) Canal, appropriately themed inside. It attracts a good mix of

clientele. Boat hire yard on site.
🏚 Q ☺ ⊛ ◑ ▶ ▲ P ✄

WHITCHURCH

RED COW
Pepper Street ☎ (01948) 664681
10-11; 12-10.30 Sun
Vaux Samson; guest beers Ⓗ
Busy town local: an L-shaped bar with another separate room to one side. The pub is tucked away, just off one of the main streets.
🏚 ⊛ ♣ ♣

WISTANSTOW

PLOUGH
Take A489 off A49, 1 mile N of Craven Arms, first right, ¼ mile
☎ (01588) 673251
12-3, 7-11; 12-3, 7-11 Sun
Wood Parish, Special, Shropshire Lad, seasonal beers; guest beers Ⓗ
The Wood Brewery tap: a village local with a good food reputation. Two bars: the public is split into a snug and games area; ramblers and cyclists are welcome. Newly refurbished lounge and toilets (including a wheelchair WC).
🏚 Q ⊛ ◑ ▶ 🍺 & ▲ ≈ (Craven Arms) ♣ P

YORTON

RAILWAY INN
Near station
☎ (01939) 220240
11.30-3.30, 6-11; 12-3.30, 7-10.30 Sun
Wadworth 6X; Wood Parish, Special, Shropshire Lad; Ⓗ guest beers Ⓗ Ⓖ
Friendly pub in the same family for over 60 years, now run by mother and daughter. A simple bar contrasts with a well-appointed lounge adorned with fishing trophies. A nearby request stop provides many visitors. 🏚 Q ⊛ ≈ ♣ P

INDEPENDENT BREWERIES

All Nations: Madeley
Crown Inn: Munslow
Davenport Arms: Worfield
Hanby: Wem
Hobsons: Cleobury Mortimer
Salopian: Shrewsbury
Six Bells: Bishop's Castle
Wood: Wistanstow
Woody Woodward's: Stottesdon
Worfield: Shropshire

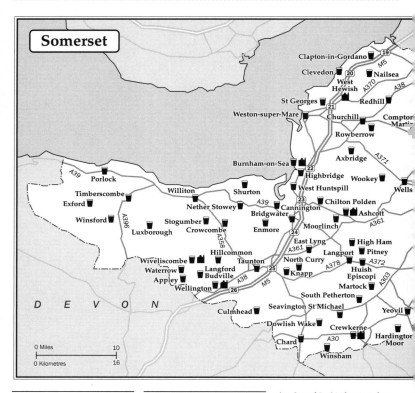

APPLEY

GLOBE INN ☆
2½ miles N of A38 at White Ball Hill OS071215
☎ (01823) 672327
11-3(not Mon), 6.30-11; 12-3, 7-10.30 Sun

Cotleigh Tawny; guest beer Ⓗ
Five-hundred-year-old village inn, tucked away deep in the countryside on the Devon border. The bar is basically a hatchway in the rough brick-floored corridor, with several cosy rooms leading off. Excellent range of high quality, home-cooked food. A real gem, well worth searching out. Cider in summer. Children's play equipment in the garden. No-smoking dining room.
🛏 Q ❀ ◖ ▶ Å ♣ ➪ P

ASHCOTT

RING O'BELLS
High Street (off A39, nr church)
☎ (01458) 210232
12-2.30, 7-11; 12-2.30, 7-10.30 Sun
Moor Withy Cutter; guest beers Ⓗ
Popular, multi-level village pub with a cosy bar area. Superb, award-winning, home-cooked food and separate restaurant. Guest beers often feature West Country microbreweries. CAMRA Somerset Pub of the Year 1998.
🛏 ❀ ◖ ▶ Å ♣ ➪ P

AXBRIDGE

LAMB INN
The Square ☎ (01934) 732253
12-2.30 (11.30-3 Sat), 6.30-11; 12-3, 7-10.30 Sun
Butcombe Bitter, Wilmot's; Wadworth 6X; guest beer (occasional) Ⓗ
Rambling old pub, now owned by Butcombe, opposite King John's hunting lodge, with a large terraced garden. The unusual bar is made of bottles. No meals Sun eve. Q ❀ ⇌ ◖ ▶ ♣

BATH

BELL INN
103 Walcot Street
☎ (01225) 460426
11.30-11; 12-3, 7-10.30 Sun
Bath Barnstormer; Courage Best Bitter, Directors; Fuller's London Pride; John Smith's Bitter; Smiles Best Ⓗ
Open-plan bar renowned for its music at least three times a week. Bohemian atmosphere.
❀ ⇌ ♣

BLADUD ARMS
Gloucester Road, Lower Swainswick ☎ (01225) 420152
12-3, 5.30-11; 12-3, 7-10.30 Sun
Draught Bass; Butcombe Bitter; Wickwar Brand Oak; guest beer Ⓗ
Friendly local on the edge of the city. One of Bath's few true free houses. Unusual colour scheme inside. Eve meals until 8pm.
❀ ◖ ▶ ♣ ➪ P

CROSS KEYS INN
Midford Road, Combe Down (B3110)
☎ (01225) 832002
11-2.30 (3 Sat), 6-11; 12-3, 7-10.30 Sun
Courage Best Bitter; Ushers Best Bitter, Founders, seasonal beers Ⓗ
Attractive Bathstone 'roadhouse'-type pub on the southern edge of the city. Two traditional bars, one with an annexe for private parties, meetings and so on. Aviary is a feature of the large, walled garden. Good value food.
🛏 ❀ ◖ ▶ ⊞ P ⊬ ☗

FORESTERS ARMS
Bradford Road, Combe Down
☎ (01225) 837671
11.30-3.30, 5-11; 11.30-11 Sat; 12-3.30, 7.30-10.30 Sun
Draught Bass; Courage Best Bitter; Otter Bitter, Head; guest beer Ⓗ
Comfortable, friendly main bar with adjacent skittle alley. One wall of the public bar is dominated by a vast, mirror-like mural, depicting many of the regulars. No meals Sat.
◖ ⊞ ♣ ➪ P

GLOUCESTERSHIRE & BRISTOL

Keynsham
Saltford
Chew Magna
Dunkerton
Timsbury
allatrow
Wellow
Norton St Philip
Shoscombe
nton Blewitt
Oakhill
Faulkland
Rudge
gh upon Mendip
Nettlebridge
helynch
Frome
A361
Doulting
Trudoxhill
Witham Friary
ercreech
North Brewham
Lovington
arkford
Wincanton
A303
Corton Denham
South Cheriton
Henstridge
Milborne Port

DORSET

Bath
WILTSHIRE

GOLDEN FLEECE
1-3 Avon Buildings, Lower Bristol
Road ☎ (01225) 429572
11-2.30, 5.30 (4.30 Fri)-11; 11-11
Sat; 12-10.30 Sun
**Courage Georges BA, Best
Bitter; guest beer** H
Popular, street-corner local, con-
venient for Twerton Park football
ground. The two guest beers
change daily. No meals Sat or Sun.
Q ◖ ≉ (Oldfield Park) ♣ P

HOBGOBLIN
47 St James' Parade
☎ (01225) 460785
11-11; 12-10.30 Sun
**Wychwood Special, DB,
Hobgoblin, Black Wych Stout,
guest beer** H
Large, noisy, busy, city-centre
pub, very popular with students.
Daily student discount (20%) 4-7.
Eve meals 4-7. ◖ ≉ ⌂

OLD FARMHOUSE
1 Lansdown Road
☎ (01225) 316162
12-11; 12-3, 7-10.30 Sun
**Abbey Bellringer; Badger
Tanglefoot; Draught Bass;
Butcombe Bitter; Wadworth IPA,
6X** H
Lively local of great character.
Unusual pub sign is a caricature
of its landlord. Live music four
nights a week. No meals Sun.
♨ ❀ ◖ ▮ ⌁ ♣ P

OLD GREEN TREE ☆
12 Green Street (behind GPO)
☎ (01225) 462357
11-11; 7-10.30 (closed lunch) Sun
**Oakhill Black Magic; RCH
Pitchfork; Wickwar BOB; guest
beer** H
Small, popular and traditional
pub, with three panelled rooms
with parquet flooring and no gimmicks. Specialises in local beers
(the range varies). Dress restriction may apply. No meals Sun.
Q ◖ ✁

RAM
20 Claverton Bldgs, Widcombe
☎ (01225) 421938
11-2.30, 5-11; 11-11 Fri & Sat;
12-7 Sun
**Draught Bass; Courage Best
Bitter; Smiles Best** H
Justly popular, wood-panelled
single-bar pub, over the bridge
from Bath station. Closed Sun
eves.
◖ ≉ ⌂

RICHMOND ARMS
7 Richmond Place, Lansdown
☎ (01225) 316725
12-3, 6-11; 12-3, 7-10.30 Sun
**Ushers Best Bitter, Founders,
seasonal beers** H
Small pub, recently renovated, in
a quiet row of terraced houses.
Q ❀ ◖ ▮ ♣

RING OF BELLS
10 Widcombe Parade
☎ (01225) 335454
11-3, 5-11; 11-11 Fri & Sat;
12-10.30 Sun
**Draught Bass; Fuller's London
Pride; Smiles Best** H
Bright, lively pub with a warm,
friendly welcome. There is a big
screen for sports fans upstairs,
well away from the main drinking
area.
◖ ≉ ♣

STAR ☆
23 The Vineyards
☎ (01225) 227843
6-11 Mon-Thu; 12-2.30, 5.30-11
Fri; 11-11 Sat; 12-3, 7-10.30 Sun
Draught Bass; G **Wickwar
BOB** H
Pub with a classic interior, with
many wood-panelled rooms.
Garden due to open in summer
1998. Cider in summer.
♨ Q ⌛ ❀ ♣ ⌂

BRIDGWATER

FOUNTAIN INN
1 West Quay (near town bridge)
☎ (01278) 424115
11.30 (11 Fri & Sat)-3, 6.30-11;
12-3, 7-10.30 Sun
**Badger Tanglefoot; Butcombe
Bitter; Wadworth IPA, 6X; guest
beer** H
One-room, riverside pub, a
friendly town-centre local. Guest

beers from Wadworth's list.
Lunchtime snacks available.
Q ⅋ ≉ ♣

Try also: Cross Rifles, Bath Rd
(Free); Horse & Jockey, West St
(Free)

BURNHAM-ON-SEA

ROSEWOOD
Love Lane (edge of town, on main
road from jct 22 of M5)
☎ (01278) 780246
11-3, 6-11 and summer, 11-11
Sat; 12-10.30 Sun
**Marston's Bitter, Pedigree,
seasonal beers** H
Large pub with one long bar.
Eating area at one end, TV, pool
table and darts board at the
other. Wheelchair WC.
❀ ◖ ▮ ⅋ ▲ ♣ P

VICTORIA HOTEL
25 Victoria Street
☎ (01278) 783085
4-11; 11-11 Sat; 12-10-30 Sun
**Banks's Mild; Draught Bass;
Castle Eden Ale; Flowers IPA;
Young's Special; guest beer** H
A quiet lounge and a public bar
with a pool table, juke box and
TV. Darts in both bars.
♨ Q ❀ ⇋ ⌁ ▲ ♣

CANNINGTON

MALT SHOVEL INN
Blackmoor Lane, Bradley Green
(off A39, E of Cannington)
☎ (01278) 653432
11.30-3, 6.30 (7 winter)-11; 12-3,
7-10.30 Sun
**Butcombe Bitter; Morland Old
Speckled Hen; John Smith's
Bitter; guest beer** H
Family-run free house overlook-
ing the Quantocks, boasting a
large garden and a skittle alley.
No meals winter Sun eves.
♨ Q ⌛ ❀ ⇋ ◖ ▮ ⅋ ⌂ P

CHARD

BELL & CROWN INN
Combe Street, Crimchard
☎ (01460) 62470
11-2.30 (not Mon), 7-11; 12-3,
7-10.30 Sun
**Shepherd Neame Best Bitter;
guest beers** H
Popular local, which still has gas
lighting. Ten mins walk from the
town centre. Good value food
(not available Sun and Mon eves).
Occasional beer festivals.
Q ❀ ◖ ▮ ♣ P

Try also: Ship Inn (Free)

CHELYNCH

POACHERS POCKET
1/2 mile N of A361 at Doulting
OS648438
☎ (01749) 880220

11.30 (12 Mon)-2.30, 6-11; 12-3, 7-10.30 Sun

Butcombe Bitter; Oakhill Best Bitter; Wadworth 6X; guest beer H

Set in a small village, part of this pub dates back to the 14th century. Mostly given over to food, but remains popular with locals. The large garden is well used in summer. ♨ Q ❀ ◁ ▶ ♣ ⇔ P

CHEW MAGNA

PONY & TRAP
Newtown (½ mile from village on Bath road) ☎ (01275) 332627
12-3, 7-11; 12-3, 7-10.30 Sun

Ushers Best Bitter, Founders, seasonal beers H

Cosy, multi-roomed converted cottage displaying the pub's original sign and old adverts. Good food at reasonable prices.
Q ☎ ❀ ◁ ▶ ⇔ P

CHILTON POLDEN

TOBY JUG INN
Chilton Polden Hill (A39, 6 miles E of Bridgwater) ☎ (01278) 722202
12-3 (not Mon), 6.30-11; 12-3, 7-10.30 Sun

Beer range varies H

Small, welcoming wayside pub with a single, split-level bar/restaurant. Features include inglenook, beams and stone. The large function room hosts monthly jazz sessions. Good value home-cooked food. Beer range includes regional and micros, and usually beers from Otter.
Q ❀ ♿ ▲ P

CHURCHILL

CROWN INN
The Batch, Skinners Lane (small lane just S of crossroads on A38) OS446596 ☎ (01934) 852995
11-3.30, 5.30-11; 12-10.30 Sun

Draught Bass; Palmers IPA; RCH PG Steam; Smiles Golden; guest beers G

Characterful, stone-built free house which supports local breweries. Outdoor areas, front and rear, can get busy in summer. Lunches use fresh local produce.
♨ Q ❀ ◁ ▲ P

CLAPTON-IN-GORDANO

BLACK HORSE
Clevedon Lane OS472739
☎ (01275) 842105
11-3, 6-11; 11-11 Fri & Sat; 12-3, 7-10.30 Sun

Courage Best Bitter; Smiles Best; G **guest beer** H

Delightful, flagstone-floored, 14th-century pub built at the same time as the local church. It was once used as the village lock-up. ♨ Q ☎ ❀ ◁ ⇔ P

CLEVEDON

LITTLE HARP
Elton Road
☎ (01275) 343739
11-11; 12-10.30 Sun

Marston's Bitter, Pedigree, HBC H

Large, open-plan pub with a central bar and good views over the Severn to Wales. Food available all day. ☎ ❀ ◁ ▶ ♣ P

COMPTON MARTIN

RING O' BELLS
Bath Road (A368)
☎ (01761) 221284
11.30-3, 6.30-11; 12-3, 7-10.30 Sun

Butcombe Bitter, Wilmot's; Wadworth 6X; guest beer H

Traditional village pub with excellent food. Voted local CAMRA *Pub of the Year* in 1997. With a fully-equipped family room and large garden, this pub has something for everyone.
♨ Q ☎ ❀ ▶ ◁ ⊟ ▲ ♣ P ⅍

CORTON DENHAM

QUEENS ARMS INN
3 miles S of A303
☎ (01968) 220317
12-2.30, 6.30-11; 11.30-2.30, 6-11 Fri, Sat & Summer; 12-2.30, 7-10.30 Sun

Archers Best Bitter; Cotleigh Tawny; Smiles Golden; guest beers H

Superb country inn, set in a valley with excellent hillside walks. Guest ales of the month are featured, and a wide choice of freshly prepared food is served in both bars.
♨ Q ❀ ⇔ ◁ ▶ ⊟ ♿ ⇔ P

CREWKERNE

CROWN INN
34 South Street
☎ (01460) 72464
6.30-11; 12-3, 6.30-11 Sat; 12-3, 7-11 Sun

Crewkerne Crookhorn, Monmouth's Revenge; guest beers H

Friendly brewpub with two bars, a former coaching inn dating back to 1635. At present, only snacks are available. Good value B&B. Look out for the ghost!
♨ ⇔ ⊟ ♣

Try also: Sparkling Choice Wine Bar, 13-15 Market St (Free)

CROWCOMBE

CAREW ARMS ☆
Off A358
☎ (01984) 618631
11-3, 6-11; 12-3, 7-10.30 Sun

Butcombe Wilmot's; H **Exmoor Ale** G

On CAMRA's National Inventory of heritage pubs, this unspoilt village inn is a real gem, situated at the base of the Quantocks. Features good quality food and accomodation and Lanes cider.
♨ Q ☎ ❀ ⇔ ◁ ▶ ♿ ▲ ♣ ⇔ P

CULMHEAD

HOLMAN CLAVEL
Off B3170 OS221161
☎ (01823) 421432
12-3, 5-11 (12-11 summer); 12-3, 7-10.30

Butcombe Bitter; Cotleigh Barn Owl; guest beers H

Fourteenth-century inn on top of the Blackdown Hills. Charlie, the local ghost, was a defrocked monk. There are plenty of exposed beams, and a roaring log fire in winter. Interesting and varied food (not served Sun eve).
♨ Q ❀ ⇔ ◁ ▶ ▲ ♣ P

Try also: Merry Harriers, Forches Corner (Free)

DOULTING

ABBEY BARN INN
On A361, 1 mile E of Shepton Mallet
☎ (01749) 880321
12-2.30, 6-11; 12-11 Sat; 12-2.30, 7-10.30 Sun

Draught Bass; Oakhill Best Bitter; Otter Bitter H

Friendly pub with two comfortable bars and separate skittles alley. Named after the nearby medieval tithe barn.
♨ ❀ ⇔ ◁ ▶ ⊟ ♣

DOWLISH WAKE

NEW INN
2 miles SE of Ilminster
☎ (01460) 52413
11-3, 6-11; 12-3, 7-10.30 Sun

Butcombe Bitter; Theakston Old Peculier; Wadworth 6X H

Charming, 350-year-old village pub with a warm atmosphere and decorated with hops hung from the beams. The bar menu features Swiss specialities. There are two wood-burning stoves. The 'Perry's' cider is made in the village and there is an excellent range of malt whisky.
♨ Q ☎ ❀ ◁ ▶ ⊟ ♿ ♣ ⇔ P

DUNKERTON

TITFIELD THUNDERBOLT
Bath Road
☎ (01225) 832347
12-2, 5-11; 12-2, 7-10.30 Sun

Draught Bass; Oakhill Best Bitter H

Simple, roadside pub near the old Somerset coal mines and full of mining memorabilia.
♨ ⇔ ♿ ♣ P

EAST LYNG

ROSE & CROWN
On A361
☎ (01823) 698235
11-2.30, 6.30-11; 12-3, 7-10.30
Sun
**Butcombe Bitter, Wilmot's;
Eldridge Pope Royal Oak** H
Quiet, comfortable village local
with a timeless, civilised feel.
There are exposed beams,
antique furniture and a large
stone fireplace. Good value food;
Book for the restaurant. There is
an attractive garden.
🏨 Q ❀ 🛏 ◑ ▶ ♣ P

ENMORE

ENMORE INN
Enmore Road (main road from
Bridgwater)
☎ (01278) 422052
11-3, 5.30-11 (11-11 summer);
12-3, 7-10.30 Sun
Butcombe Bitter; guest beers H
Large, welcoming roadside inn in
a rural setting, yet close to
Bridgwater, with a play area in
one of the two large gardens. Bar
billiards in the lounge. Guest
beers include a Cotleigh brew.
Excellent for families.
Q 🐂 ❀ ◑ ▶ ⊞ & ♣ ○ P
⊁

EVERCREECH

BELL INN
Bruton Road (B3081)
☎ (01749) 830287
11.30-3, 6.30-11; 11.30-11 Sat;
12-3, 7-10.30 Sun
Butcombe Bitter; guest beer
Large, rambling, 17th-century inn
with a single bar, restaurant and
games areas. Cottage supplies
the guest ale and the house beer
is from Courage.
🏨 Q ◑ ▶ ♣ P

EXFORD

CROWN HOTEL
Park Street
☎ (01643) 831554
11-3, 6-11; 12-3, 7-11 Sun
**Brakspear Bitter; Exmoor Ale;
Wadworth 6X** H
Cosy, half-timbered hotel bar,
decorated with sporting prints,
stuffed animals and hunting
memorabilia. The excellent bar
food is from an imaginative
menu. Lane's cider in simmer.
🏨 Q 🐂 ❀ 🛏 ◑ ▶ ▲ ○ P

WHITE HORSE INN
☎ (01643) 831229
11-11; 12-10.30 Sun
**Dartmoor Best Bitter; Eldridge
Pope Royal Oak; Tetley Bitter;
guest beers** (summer) H
Traditional country hotel with a
welcoming public bar, flagstones
and benches. Well placed for

country sports, including fishing
in the adjacent Exe River. Cider in
summer.
🏨 Q ❀ 🛏 ◑ ▶ & ▲ ♣ ○
P ⊁

FAULKLAND

TUCKERS GRAVE INN ☆
On A366, 1 mile E of village
☎ (01373) 834230
12-3, 6-11; 12-3, 7-10.30 Sun
Draught Bass; Butcombe Bitter
The burial site of Edward
Tucker, who committed suicide
in 1747: his story can be found
above the parlour. For 200 years
the cottage doubled as an inn,
which is why the three-roomed,
old-fashioned pub has no bar –
the stillage is set in a small bay
window.
🏨 Q ❀ ⊞ ▲ ♣ ○ P

FROME

HORSE & GROOM
1 mile SE of A361/B3092 jct
OS792445
☎ (01373) 462802
11.30 (12 Mon)-2.30, 6.30-11;
12-3, 7-10.30 Sun
**Butcombe Bitter; Shepherd
Neame Best Bitter; Wadworth
6X; guest beer** H
This 17th-century inn on the
western edge of the Longleat
estate features a cosy bar with
an open fireplace and flagstone
floor, plus a small dining room.
Seafood a speciality (no meals
Mon or Sun eve).
🏨 Q 🐂 ❀ ▶ ◑ ♣ P

PACK HORSE
13-14 Christchurch Street West
☎ (01373) 67161
11-3, 6-11; 12-3, 7-10.30 Sun
**Ushers Best Bitter, Founders,
seasonal beers** H
Friendly pub with a good range of
malt whiskies.
🏨 Q ◑ ▶ ⊞ P

HALLATROW

OLD STATION INN
Wells Road (A39, 400 yds from
A37 jct)
☎ (01761) 452228
11-3, 5 (6 Sat)-11; 12-3, 7-10.30
Sun
**Draught Bass; Mole's Best
Bitter; Oakhill Best Bitter; Otter
Ale; Wadworth 6X; guest
beer** H
Friendly village free house, full
of bric-à-brac on every wall and
ceiling. All beers are sold at the
same price. It has recently
become very food oriented,
and there is a full-size railway
carriage dining car in the garden
for more secluded meals.
Good, motel-type accom-
modation.
🏨 Q ❀ 🛏 ◑ ▶ ▲ ♣ P

HARDINGTON MOOR

ROYAL OAK
Moor Lane (off A30)
☎ (01935) 862354
12-3 (not Mon), 7-11; 12-3,
7-10.30 Sun
**Brakspear Bitter; Butcombe
Bitter; Hook Norton Old Hooky;
guest beers** H
Former farmhouse offering a
warm, friendly atmosphere.
There is a good choice of snacks
and meals (not served Mon),
three ciders usually available,
and a skittles alley for functions.
Beer festival in May. And say
hello to Oscar (a parrot).
🏨 Q ❀ ◑ ▶ ▲ ♣ ○ P

HIGH HAM

KINGS HEAD INN
Main Street
☎ (01458) 250268
12.30-3 (not Mon, Wed or Fri),
6.30-11; 12-3, 7-10.30 Sun
**Badger Tanglefoot; Cottage
Golden Arrow; Moor Merlin's
Magic; Oakhill Mendip Gold;
Otter Bright** H
Friendly village pub with some-
thing for everyone and all ales at
the same price. Basic bar snacks
served.
🏨 🐂 ❀ ◑ ▶ ⊞ & ♣ ○ P ⊟

HIGHBRIDGE

COOPERS ARMS
Market Street ☎ (01278) 783562
11-3, 5-11; 11-11 Fri & Sat; 12-3,
7-10.30 Sun
**Adnams Broadside; Fuller's
London Pride; guest beers** H
Large pub with six ales usually
available, including two house
beers supplied by big brewers.
There are two lounges and a bar
with a skittles alley.
Q ❀ ⊞ & ▲ ≈ ♣ P

Try also: Royal Artillery, West
Huntspill (Ushers)

HILLCOMMON

ROYAL OAK INN
On B3227
☎ (01823) 400295
11-3, 6.30-11; 12-3, 6.30-10.30 Sun
**Cotleigh Tawny; Exmoor Ale;
guest beer** H
Situated on the old Barnstaple
road, this freehouse caters for
both local and passing trade. It
has a large garden and serves
good food.
Q ❀ ◑ ▶ ⊞ & P

HINTON BLEWITT

RING OF BELLS
☎ (01761) 452239
11-3.30, 5 (6 Sat)-11; 12-3.30,
7-10.30 Sun
Wadworth 6X; guest beers H

Small, friendly village local, situated behind the church. Good food and up to three guest beers available. ♨ Q ❀ ◖ ◗ ♣ P

HUISH EPISCOPI

Rose & Crown (Eli's) ☆
Wincanton Road (A372, 1 mile from Langport) ☎ (01458) 250494
11.30-2.30, 5.30-11; 11.30-11 Fri & Sat; 12-10.30 Sun
Beer range varies [H]
Pub of unusual character, with a bar with four small snugs and a pool room. Real ale festival in summer (September).
Q ♞ ❀ ◖ ♿ ⛺ ♣ ⌂ P

KEYNSHAM

Ship Inn
Temple Street (off High St, near Civic Centre) ☎ (0117) 986 9841
12-3, 6.30 (5.30 Fri)-11; 12-11 Sat; 12-10.30 Sun
Draught Bass; Courage George's BA; Worthington Bitter; guest beers [H]
Two-bar pub with up to eight beers available, including local brew. Separate dining area is open all lunchtimes and Tues-Sat eves; bookings only for Sunday lunch. Very limited car parking.
❀ ◖ ◗ ⊞ ≈ ♣ P ⚡

LANGFORD BUDVILLE

Martlett Inn
½ mile off B3187 between Wellington and Milverton
☎ (01823) 400262
12-2.30 (3 Sat), 7-11; 12-3, 7-10.30 Sun
Cotleigh Tawny, Barn Owl; Exmoor Ale; guest beer [H]
Early 17th-century inn with wood-burning stoves. A quiet atmosphere, without juke box, fruit machines, and so on. Bar meals daily; booking advisable Sun.
♨ Q ❀ ◖ ◗ ♣ P

LANGPORT

Black Swan
North Street ☎ (01458) 250355
11-2.30, 6-11; 12-4, 7-10.30 Sun
Badger Tanglefoot; Mole's Tap Bitter; Wadworth 6X [H]
Converted coaching inn with two bars, a restaurant and function room for skittle evenings etc. Home-cooked food includes worldwide dishes.
♞ ❀ ◖ ◗ ⊞ ♿ ♣ P

LEIGH UPON MENDIP

Bell
High Street
OS692473 ☎ (01373) 812316
12-3, 7-11; 12-3, 7-10.30 Sun
Draught Bass; Butcombe Bitter; Wadworth IPA, 6X [H]

Village inn, much altered and extended, and comfortably furnished. Food served throughout the pub and in the restaurant. The emphasis is on the food trade, but it retains its friendly, local atmosphere at the bar.
♨ ❀ ◖ ◗ ♣ P

LUXBOROUGH

Royal Oak
☎ (01984) 640319
11-3, 6-11; 12-2.30, 7-10.30 Sun
Cotleigh Tawny; Exmoor Gold; [H] **guest beers** [G]
Situated in the heart of the Brendon Hills (superb for walks), this rural pub features open fires, exposed beams and flagstone floors. Noted for its home-cooked food; a restaurant has been recently added. Rich's and Cheddar Valley cider.
♨ Q ♞ ❀ 🛏 ◖ ◗ ⊞ ♿ ⛺ ♣ ⌂

MARTOCK

Nags Head
East Street (off B3165 at Pinnacle)
☎ (01935) 823432
12-3 (not Mon-Wed), 7-11; 12-3, 7-10.30 Sun
Oakhill Best Bitter; Otter Bitter; guest beer [H]
Friendly, 200-year-old former cider house, with a comfortable lounge bar and games-oriented public bar. Good, home-cooked food (no eve meals Mon-Tue). A few bottle-conditioned beers are stocked. The garden has a children's play area.
❀ 🛏 ◖ ◗ ⊞ ⛺ ♣ P ⚡

MILBORNE PORT

Queens Head
High Street (A30)
☎ (01963) 250314
11-11; 12-10.30 Sun
Butcombe Bitter; Flowers IPA, Original; Marston's Pedigree; Ringwood Fortyniner; guest beers [H]
Busy, multi-room village pub with a restaurant and a skittle alley/function room. Features good food (especially the curries) and a pleasant all-weather courtyard drinking area. A mystery beer is featured each week.
♨ Q ♞ ❀ 🛏 ◗ ◖ ⊞ ♣ ⌂ P ⚡

MOORLINCH

Ring O'Bells
Pit Hill Lane ☎ (01458) 210358
12-3 (not Mon), 7-11; 12-3, 7-10.30 Sun
Draught Bass; guest beers [H]
Cosy, traditional village pub, with a selection of real ales from West Country micros, plus Wilkins cider. Occasional music nights. ♨ Q ❀ ◗ ⊞ ♣ ⌂ P

NAILSEA

Blue Flame
West End OS449690
☎ (01275) 856910
12-3 (4 Sat), 6-11; 12-4,7-10.30 Sun
Draught Bass; Fuller's London Pride; Oakhill Best Bitter; Smiles Best; guest beer [G]
Situated on the outskirts of Nailsea, this excellent, 19th-century pub is popular with both drinkers from Nailsea and the local farming community.
♨ Q ♞ ❀ ⛺ ♣ ⌂ P

NETHER STOWEY

Rose & Crown
35 Mary Street
☎ (01278) 732265
12-11; 12-5, 7-10.30 Sun
Cotleigh Barn Owl; Cottage Golden Arrow; Moor Withy Cutter; Oakhill Mendip Gold [H]
16th-century coaching inn in the village centre. The restaurant can be hired as a function room. Children are welcome and there is a large garden. Occasional live music. Lane's cider.
❀ 🛏 ◖ ◗ ⊞ ♣ ⌂

NETTLEBRIDGE

Nettlebridge Inn
On A367, 1 mile N of Oakhill
☎ (01749) 841360
11.30-2.30, 5-11; 12-11 Sat; 12-10.30 Sun
Oakhill Best Bitter, Mendip Gold, Yeoman, Mendip Tickler [H]
Big roadside pub in a pretty valley on the edge of the Mendips. Priority is given to food in the large main bar. Bar snacks only in the smaller Bridges Bar, which has a more sophisticated city pub decor. ❀ 🛏 ◖ ◗ ⊞ P

NORTH BREWHAM

Old Red Lion
3 miles NE of Bruton on Bruton-Maiden Bradley road OS723369
☎ (01749) 850287
11-3, 6-11; 12-3, 7-10.30 Sun
Butcombe Bitter; guest beers [H]
Isolated country pub, with the bar located in the former dairy with stone walls and flagged floor. The ceiling is decorated with notes, cash and keyrings. One or two guest beers available.
♨ Q ❀ 🛏 ◖ ◗ ⛺ ♣ ⌂ P

NORTH CURRY

Bird in Hand
1 Queen Square
☎ (01823) 490248
12-3 (4 Sat; closed Mon lunch), 7-11; 12-4, 7-10.30 Sun
Butcombe Bitter; Badger Tanglefoot; Otter Bitter; guest beers [H]

Superbly renovated village local with low beams and up to three ever-changing guest ales. Good, home-cooked traditional food using local produce, with a seasonal menu (no food Sun eve). There is a good wine selection and Rich's farmhouse cider. Regular live music. The opening hours may be extended in fine weather.
🏚 Q 🕸 ◖ ▶ ▲ ♣ ⌂ P

NORTON ST PHILIP

FLEUR DE LYS
High Street (B3110) OS775558
☎ (01373) 834333
11-3, 5-11; 11-11 Sat; 12-3, 7-10.30 Sun
Draught Bass; Oakhill Best Bitter; Wadworth 6X; Worthington Bitter Ⓗ
Partly dating from the 13th century, this ancient stone building has recently been extensively but sympathetically refurbished. Sadly, the resited bar now blocks the old passageway through which the pub ghost was reputed to pass on his way to the gallows.
🏚 Q 🐛 🕸 ◖ ▶ ♣ P

PITNEY

HALFWAY HOUSE
On B3153
☎ (01458) 252513
11.30-2.30, 5.30-11; 12-3.30, 7-10.30 Sun
Butcombe Bitter; Cotleigh Tawny; Hopback Summer Lightning; Otter Bright; Teignworthy Reel Ale; guest beers Ⓖ
An absolute gem: this old village pub was the CAMRA National *Pub of the Year* in 1996. It features flagstone floors, rudimentary wooden furniture, and six to nine ales, mainly from West Country microbreweries. The good, home-cooked food includes superb curries (no food Sun). Wilkins cider available Easter-October.
🏚 Q 🕸 ◖ ▶ ▲ ⌂ P

PORLOCK

SHIP INN
High Street (foot of Porlock Hill, A39)
☎ (01643) 862507
10.30-11; 12-10.30 (11 summer) Sun
Draught Bass; Cotleigh Barn Owl (summer), **Old Buzzard; Courage Best; guest beer** (summer) Ⓗ
This 13th century thatched inn, within walking distance of both sea and moor, was mentioned in *Lorna Doone*. There is a historic bar with a stone floor, plus a games room.
🏚 Q 🐛 🕸 🛏 ◖ ▶ ▲ ♣ ⌂ P 🍴

REDHILL

BUNGALOW INN
Winford Lane OS513640
☎ (01275) 472386
12-3, 6-11; 12-11 Sat; 12-10.30 Sun
Draught Bass; Ⓟ Wadworth IPA, 6X; guest beer Ⓗ
Pub with two cosy bars, a well equipped children's room and a good function room. Handy for Bristol Airport. 'Sing-alongs' Wed eves; entertainment Sat.
🏚 🐛 🕸 ◖ ▶ ▲ ♣ P

ROWBERROW

SWAN INN
Signed off A38, S of Churchill
☎ (01934) 852371
12-3, 6-11; 12-3, 7-10.30 Sun
Draught Bass; Butcombe Bitter, Wilmot's; Wadworth 6X Ⓗ
Butcombe-owned pub, converted from three stone cottages. There are two bars, one with a large fireplace. Good food trade (no meals Sun eve). 🏚 Q 🕸 ◖ ▶ P

RUDGE

FULL MOON
1 mile N of A36 bypass at Standerwick OS829518
☎ (01373) 830936
12-3,6-11; 12-3, 7-10.30 Sun
Draught Bass; Butcombe Bitter; Fuller's London Pride Ⓗ
Splendid, 300-year-old building, greatly extended in 1991, but retaining some original features, including stone floors. Emphasis on food trade, families and accommodation. Facilities include a skittle alley.
🏚 Q 🕸 🛏 ◖ ▶ 🍽 ♿ ▲ ♣ P

ST GEORGES

WOOLPACK INN
Shepherds Way (off M5 jct 21)
☎ (01934) 521670
12-2.30 (3 Sat), 6-11; 12-3, 7-10.30 Sun
Courage Best Bitter; guest beers Ⓗ
Seventeenth-century coaching inn and former wool-packing station. Warm and friendly, well used by locals. At least three guest beers on sale; the restaurant and two bars serve a wide range of meals at reasonable prices. Large skittle alley/function room.
🏚 Q 🕸 ◖ ▶ 🍽 ▲ ➔ (Worle Parkway) ♣ P

SALTFORD

BIRD IN HAND
58 High Street (off A4)
☎ (01225) 873335
11-3 (4 Sat), 6-11; 12-4, 7-10.30 Sun
Abbey Bellringer; Draught Bass; Courage Best Bitter; guest beer Ⓗ

Food-oriented pub with a long L-shaped bar. The no-smoking eating area in the conservatory overlooks the Avon Valley Bristol-Bath cycle path. Usually busy. There is a garden with a fishpond. 🐛 🕸 ◖ ▶ ♣ ⌂ P

SEAVINGTON ST MICHAEL

VOLUNTEER
On old A303
☎ (01460) 240126
5.30-11; 12-11 Sat; 12-3, 7-10.30 Sun
Badger Dorset Best; guest beers Ⓗ
Friendly, family-run, roadside pub with two bars. The lounge has low beams and a central fireplace. Good food includes Sun lunch and Fri eve curries (no food Sun or Mon eves).
🏚 Q ◖ ▶ 🍴 ♣ P 🍴

SHOSCOMBE

APPLE TREE
1 mile S of A367 at Peasedown OS712565 ☎ (01761) 432263
7-11; 12-3, 7-11 Sat; 12-3, 7-10.30 Sun
Draught Bass; Bath SPA; Otter Bitter, Ale; guest beer Ⓖ
Friendly village local nestling in a hidden valley, well worth seeking out for the warm welcome. Big parties welcome.
🏚 🕸 ◖ ▲ ♣ ⌂ P

SHURTON

SHURTON INN
☎ (01278) 732695
11-2.30, 6-11; 12-3, 7-10.30 Sun
Badger Tanglefoot; Exmoor Ale; Morland Old Speckled Hen; guest beer Ⓗ
Comfortable village pub close to Hinckley Point power station. Varied menu of home-cooked food from local produce. Live music. 🏚 🕸 ◖ ▶ ♿ ♣ ⌂ P 🍴

SOUTH CHERITON

WHITE HORSE
On A357
☎ (01963) 370394
11-2.30, 5.30-11; 12-3, 7-10.30 Sun
Butcombe Bitter; Henstridge Vickery's Brew; guest beer Ⓗ
Friendly village local with skittle alley off the lounge.
🏚 🕸 ◖ 🍴 ♣ P 🍴

SOUTH PETHERTON

BREWERS ARMS
18 St James Street
☎ (01460) 241887
11.30-2.30, 6-11; 12-3, 7-10.30 Sun
Oakhill Best Bitter; Worthington Bitter; guest beers Ⓗ
17th-century coaching inn run by two brothers and popular with a

wide range of people. There is a single bar, a pleasant rear court-yard, and a skittle alley. The pub holds an annual beer festival and offers an extensive range of good value, home-cooked food.
🏚 ❀ ◖ 🚪 🅰 ⌂

SPARKFORD

SPARKFORD INN
High Street (off A303 towards Sparkford village)
☎ (01963) 440218
11-2.30, 6-11; 12-3, 7-10.30 Sun
Draught Bass; Worthington Bitter; guest beers Ⓗ
15th-century coaching inn retain-ing many original features, including several rooms and cor-ridors. Catering for all the family, it has indoor and outdoor chil-dren's play areas. Inch's cider in summer. Regular music evenings.
🏚 ❀ 🛏 ◖ 🚪 🏳 ⅙ 🅰 ♣ P ✀

STOGUMBER

WHITE HORSE
The Square (2 miles off A358)
☎ (01984) 656277
11-2.30, 6-11; 12-2.30, 6-10.30 Sun
Cotleigh Tawny; Otter Ale; guest beers Ⓗ
Traditional local opposite the 12th-century church serving good, wholesome country cook-ing in the bar and restaurant. Lane's cider is sold in summer. Handy for the West Somerset railway. 🏚 Q 🛏 ◖ 🚪 🏳 ⌂ P

TAUNTON

EAGLE
46 South St ☎ (01823) 275713
11-3, 6-11; 12-4, 7-10.30 Sun
Juwards Bitter; Butcombe Wilmot's; guest beers Ⓗ
Friendly local near the town cen-tre. Log fire in winter and live music Fri eves. Guest beers change regularly; cider in sum-mer. Good, inexpensive pub food.
🏚 ❀ ◖ 🏳 ♣ ⌂ P

HANKRIDGE ARMS
Hankridge Way, Riverside (retail park off M5 jct 25)
☎ (01823) 444405
11-11; 12-10.30 Sun
Badger Dorset Best, Tanglefoot Ⓗ
Commended conservation of a 16th-century farmhouse. Large, open inglenook in the bar. Quiet atmosphere. Popular for meals in both bar and restaurant. The house beer, Hankridge Ale, is brewed by Badger.
🏚 Q ❀ ◖ 🚪 🏳 P

HARPOON LOUIES
Station Road (400 yds from sta-tion) ☎ (01823) 324404
Closed lunchtimes; 7-12; 7-11 Sun
Cotleigh Tawny; guest beers Ⓗ

Bar/restaurant, open eves only, serving good food. There is a separate bar area. Jazz and blues monthly on Sun. Late hours for diners only. 🚪 ≈

MASONS ARMS
Magdalene Street (from centre follow Hammett St for 500 yds)
☎ (01823) 288916
10.30-3, 5 (6 Sat)-11; 12-3, 7-10.30 Sun
Draught Bass; Exe Valley Bitter; Juwards Premium; guest beers Ⓗ
Comfortable one-bar pub with a relaxing atmosphere, away from main streets. Fresh food is always available, including grill-stone steaks. Self-catering flat to let. Q ❀ 🛏 ◖ 🚪 ♣

PERKIN WARBECK
22-23 East Street
☎ (01823) 335830
11-11; 12-10.30 Sun
Courage Directors; Exmoor Gold; Theakston Best Bitter; guest beers Ⓗ
Wetherspoons conversion of an old furniture store into a large, one-roomed pub with two no-smoking areas. Guest beers change regularly; reasonably priced food.
Q ❀ ◖ 🏳 🏳 ⌂ ✀ 🗑

TIMBERSCOMBE

LION INN
Church Street (off A396 from Dunster) ☎ (01643) 841243
12-2.30 (3 summer), 7-11; 12-3, 7-10.30 (11 summer) Sun
Draught Bass (summer)**; Exmoor Ale, Gold** (summer)**; guest beers** Ⓗ
Traditional country inn set in the beautiful Exmoor National Park. Reputedly the oldest coaching inn in Somerset. The decor reflects the area's hunting traditions. Monthly 'song and ale' nights. One real ale in winter; cider only in summer. May be open all day in summer if busy.
🏚 🛏 ❀ ◖ 🅰 ♣ ⌂

TIMSBURY

SEVEN STARS
North Road
☎ (01761) 470398
12-3, 6-11; 12-3, 7-10.30 Sun
Ushers Best Bitter, Founders, seasonal beer Ⓗ
Warm, friendly village local. A deceptively large pub which has been well refurbished inside and out. Large garden.
🏚 ❀ ◖ 🏳 ♣ P

TRUDOXHILL

WHITE HART
1 mile S of A361 at Nunney Catch
OS749438
☎ (01373) 836324
11.30-3, 6-11; 12-3, 6-10.30 Sun

Ash Vine Bitter, Challenger, Hop & Glory; guest beer Ⓗ
Comfortable, open-plan village pub with exposed beams and a large fireplace. The beer range includes Ash Vine's monthly spe-cial brews.
🏚 ❀ ◖ 🚪 ⌂ P

WATERROW

ROCK INN
On B3227
☎ (01984) 623293
11-3, 6-11; 12-3, 7-10.30 Sun
Cotleigh Tawny; Exmoor Gold Ⓗ
Old inn set in a rockface, which forms part of the bar (public style at one end, and lounge and restaurant at the other).
🏚 Q 🛏 ◖ 🏳 🅰 ♣ ⌂ P 🗑

WELLINGTON

COTTAGE INN
31 Champford Lane
☎ (01823) 664650
11-3, 6-11; 12-3, 7-10.30 Sun
Banks's Bitter; Fuller's London Pride; Juwards Bitter; guest beers Ⓗ
Excellent local, a couple of min-utes' walk from the town centre and near the cinema. Three guest ales usually, often from local breweries. Good value, basic bar meals lunchtime Mon-Sat. Always seems to be something going on in the evening.
❀ ◖ 🏳 ♣ P

WELLOW

FOX & BADGER
Railway Lane (2 miles W of B3110 at Hinton Charterhouse)
OS741583
☎ (01225) 832293)
11.30-2.30, 6-11; 11-11 Fri & Sat; 12-2.30, 6-10.30 Sun
Draught Bass; Boddington's Bitter; Butcombe Bitter; Wadworth 6X; guest beer Ⓗ
The only pub in the pretty village of Wellow, a two-bar local where, unusually, the public bar is carpeted and the lounge bar is flagstoned. Can be difficult to park.
🏚 Q ❀ ◖ 🏳 ♣ ⌂

WELLS

BRITANNIA INN
Bath Road (B3139)
☎ (01749) 672033
12-3, 5-11 (11-11 Sat); 12-3, 7-10.30 Sun
Butcombe Bitter; Courage Best Bitter; Theakston Best Bitter; Ushers Best Bitter Ⓗ
Very popular local, serving hous-ing estates at the north end of the city. Two bars and a function room. Eve meals Fri-Sun.
❀ ◖ 🚪 ♣ ⌂ P

WEST HUNTSPILL

CROSSWAYS
Withy Road (A38 exit M5 jcts 22-23)
☎ (01278) 783756
11-3, 5.30-11; 12-3, 7-10.30 Sun
Eldridge Pope Royal Oak; Flowers IPA, Original; guest beers Ⓗ
Comfortable, 17th-century coaching inn with frequently-changing guest ales, an extensive menu of home-cooked food, and a skittle alley. The large bar is made cosy by its dividing walls.
🏚 Q 🍴 ⊛ 🛏 ◖ ◗ ₰ Ａ ♣ ➚ Ｐ ⚹

WESTON-SUPER-MARE

DRAGON INN
15 Meadow Street
☎ (01934) 621304
11-11; 12-10.30 Sun
Butcombe Bitter; Courage Directors; Theakston Best Bitter Ⓗ
Opened in 1996, this Wetherspoons conversion is not as large as most, but is still spacious and has a big, no-smoking area, and adequate disabled facilities. It can get crowded. Several guest ales available.
Q ⊛ ◖ ◗ ₰ ⇌ ➚ ⚹ 🗍

Try also: Regency, Lower Church St (Free)

WILLITON

EGREMONT
1 Fore Street (A39/A358 jct)
☎ (01984) 632500
11-11; 12-10.30 Sun
Butcombe Bitter; Tolly Cobbold Bitter; guest beers Ⓖ
Historic coaching inn, ideal for exploring Exmoor, the coast and the Quantock Hills. Family run, offering a warm welcome, good food and a friendly ambience. Folk nights Wed.
🏚 🐎 ⊛ 🛏 ◖ ◗ 🍺 ₰ ⇌
(Williton, West Somerset Rlwy)
♣ ➚ Ｐ 🗍

FORESTERS ARMS
55 Long Street (A39, near station)
☎ (01984) 632508
11-11; 12-10.30 Sun
Cotleigh Harrier, Tawny; guest beers Ⓗ
17th-century coaching inn, close to West Somerset Railway, and an ideal base for exploring the Quantocks. Reputed to be haunted by the ghost of a girl from the nearby former workhouse. Up to six real ales available, Rich's cider, and a Mastermind winner in its quiz team!
🏚 🐎 ⊛ 🛏 ◖ ◗ ₰ ⇌ (West Somerset Rlwy) ♣ ➚ Ｐ 🗍

WINCANTON

BEAR INN
12 Market Place
☎ (01963) 32581
11-3, 5.30-11; 11-4, 7-10.30 Sun
Draught Bass; guest beers Ⓗ
Large, former coaching inn with one main bar, plus substantial games and function rooms. Always two or three guest beers, including at least one from a local micro. 🏚 Q 🛏 ◖ ◗ ♣ Ｐ

Try also: Miller's Inn, Silver St, Wincanton (Free)

WINSFORD

ROYAL OAK
Follow sign for Tarr steps
☎ (01643) 851455
11-3, 6-11; 12-3, 6-11 Sun
Exmoor Ale Ⓖ; **Flowers IPA, Original** Ⓗ; **guest beer** Ⓖ
Popular, cosy thatched inn, dating from the 12th century, in the centre of a pretty village. Ideal base for exploring Exmoor. Good food. 🏚 Q 🐎 ⊛ 🛏 ◖ ◗ ₰ Ａ Ｐ

WINSHAM

BELL INN
Church Street ☎ (01460) 30716
12-2.30 (3 Sat); 12-3, 7-10.30 Sun
Branscombe Vale Branoc; Fuller's London Pride; guest beers Ⓗ
Two-roomed village pub with a comfortable lounge and a games area. The patio hosts many village summer activities. Occasional beer festival.
⊛ ◖ ◗ ♣ Ｐ

WITHAM FRIARY

SEYMOUR ARMS ☆
On minor road off B3092, by old railway station OS745410
☎ (01749) 850742
11-3, 6-11 (12-3, 7-10.30 Sun)
Ushers Best Bitter; guest beer (occasional) Ⓗ
Old village local, unspoilt by progress, featuring a central serving hatch and fine garden. Rich's cider on gravity.
🏚 Q ⊛ 🍺 Ａ ♣ ➚

WIVELISCOMBE

BEAR INN
10 North Street (off main square)
☎ (01984) 623537
11-11; 11.30-10.30 Sun
Cotleigh Tawny; Exmoor Gold; guest beers Ⓗ
Former 17th-century coaching inn, with a friendly bar and a dining room serving good, home-cooked food. It organises beer-lover's weekends in conjunction with local breweries; local farm cider is served in summer. The house beer is brewed by

Cotleigh. Skittles and quizzes feature. 🏚 🐎 ⊛ 🛏 ◖ ◗ ➚ Ｐ

WOOKEY

BURCOTT INN
On B3139 out of Wells
☎ (01749) 673874
11-2.30 (3 Sat), 6-11; 12-3, 7-10.30 Sun
Cottage Southern Bitter; guest beers Ⓗ
Deservedly popular roadside pub with a friendly atmosphere. It offers over 40 different guest beers a year. The L-shaped bar has a copper serving top, and there is a small games room. Good quality bar food and separate restaurant. The garden has an old cider press. Eve meals Tue-Sat. 🏚 Q ⊛ ◖ ◗ ♣ Ｐ

YEOVIL

ARMOURY
1 The Park ☎ (01935) 471047
12-2.30 (11-3 Fri & Sat), 6.30-11; 12-3, 7-10.30 Sun
Adnams Broadside; Butcombe Bitter; Wadworth 6X; guest beers Ⓗ
Lively, simply-furnished, open-plan town pub, formerly an armoury. Snacks and salads are available lunchtime (not Sun).
⊛ ₰ ♣ Ｐ

Try also: Bell Inn, Preston Rd (Marston's)

INDEPENDENT BREWERIES

Ash Vine:
Trudoxhill

Bath:
Henstridge

Berrow:
Burnham-on-Sea

Butcombe:
Butcombe

Cotleigh:
Wiveliscombe

Cottage:
Lovington

Exmoor:
Wiveliscombe

Henstridge:
Henstridge

Juwards:
Wellington

Moor:
Ashcott

Oakhill:
Oakhill

RCH:
West Hewish

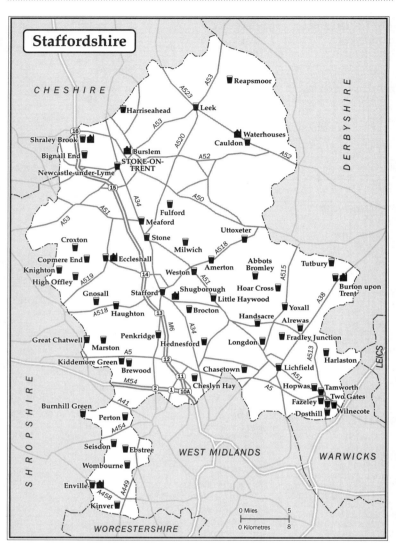

Staffordshire

ABBOTS BROMLEY

ROYAL OAK
Bagot St ☎ (01283) 840117
12-2.30, 6-11; 12-2.30, 7-10.30 Sun
Greene King Abbot; Marston's Pedigree, HBC Ⓗ
Attractive, beamed, 17th-century pub with an emphasis on the interesting and varied menu served in the restaurant. Children allowed in the lounge extension. ♨ Q ❀ ◖ ▶ Å P

ALREWAS

GEORGE & DRAGON
120 Main St ☎ (01283) 791476
11.30-2.30 (3 Sat), 5-11; 12-3, 7-10.30 Sun
Marston's Bitter, Pedigree Ⓗ

Traditional village local with a central bar and four drinking areas. The patio has a children's play area. It lies 300 yds from Trent & Mersey Canal. No food Sun. ❀ ◖ ▶ P

AMERTON

PLOUGH
On A518 ☎ (01889) 270308
11-11; 12-10.30 Sun
Marston's Bitter, Pedigree; Morland Old Speckled Hen; guest beer Ⓗ
Agreeable country inn opposite Amerton working farm, craft and garden centre. Meals are served in the dining room; the large garden has a children's play area.
♨ ☎ ❀ ⇔ ◖ ▶ ⊞ Å ♣ P

BIGNALL END

PLOUGH
2 Ravens lane (B5500, ½ mile E of Audley)
☎ (01782) 720469
12-3, 7-11; 11-11 Fri & Sat; 12-10.30 Sun
Banks's Bitter; Marston's Pedigree; guest beers Ⓗ
Popular roadside hostelry, catering for local and passing trade in a traditional bar and a split-level lounge. The beer enthusiast landlord ensures constantly changing guest beers. Excellent value meals (not served Sun eve). 1995 local CAMRA *Pub of the Year.*
❀ ◖ ▶ ⊞ ♣ P

BREWOOD

SWAN
15 Market Square
☎ (01902) 850330
12-2.30 (3 Sat), 7-11; 12-3,
7-10.30 Sun
**Mansfield Riding Bitter;
Marston's Pedigree; Theakston
XB; guest beer** Ⓗ
Comfortable village pub with low-beamed ceilings and two cosy snugs offering a good range of beers. Skittle alley at the rear. A recent local CAMRA *Pub of the Year.* ⚫ Ⓓ ♣ P

BROCTON

CHETWYND ARMS
Cannock Road (A34)
☎ (01785) 661089
11.30-3, 5.45-11; 11-11 Sat;
12-10.30 Sun
Banks's Mild, Bitter, Ⓟ **seasonal
beer; Marston's Pedigree** Ⓗ
Bustling main road pub at the north-west corner of Cannock Chase, boasting a genuine unspoilt bar. No meals Sat eve.
⊛ Ⓓ ▶ ⊡ ♣ P 🍺

BURNHILL GREEN

DARTMOUTH ARMS
Snowon Road OS787006
☎ (01746) 783268
12-3, 6-11; 12-3, 6-10.30 Sun
**Hobsons Best Bitter, Town
Crier** Ⓗ
Isolated, old pub on the Shropshire border (literally!). Its age is hidden beneath wisteria outside, oak beams and sympathetic renovation inside. A new outlet for Hobsons.
⊛ Ⓓ ▶ P

BURTON UPON TRENT

ALFRED
51 Derby Street
☎ (01283) 562178
11-3, 5-11; 11-11 Fri & Sat; 12-3,
7-10.30 Sun
**Burton Bridge XL, Bridge Bitter,
Porter, Festival Ale, seasonal
beers; guest beers** Ⓗ
Welcoming, friendly, two-bar, attractively decorated inn, offering games rooms and good food; families welcome. Budget-priced B&B. ⊭ Ⓓ ▶ ⇌ P

BASS MUSEUM – BURTON BAR
Horninglow Street
☎ (01283) 511000 (ext. 3504)
11-7 (5 Sat), 12-5 Sun
**Draught Bass; Museum No. 6
Mild, Offilers Bitter, P2** Ⓟ Ⓗ
Comfortable bar within Bass Museum of Brewing, selling an ever-changing range of beers from the museum's own micro-brewery (which uses old equipment from former breweries). It

stages regular displays of shire horses, steam engines etc. Free entry for card-carrying CAMRA members. ⛟ ⊛ Ⓓ ⚅ ⇌ P

BURTON BRIDGE INN
24 Bridge Street (Trent Bridge on A511) ☎ (01283) 536596
11.30-2.15, 5.30-11; 12-2,
7-10.30 Sun
**Burton Bridge XL, Bridge Bitter,
Porter, Festival Ale, Old
Expensive, seasonal beers; guest
beers** Ⓗ
Brewery tap for the Burton Bridge Brewery; a welcoming pub with distinctive wooden pews. There is an extensive range of whiskies and country wines. Function room and skittle alley. Q ⊛ Ⓓ ♣

COOPERS TAVERN
43 Cross Street
☎ (01283) 532551
12-3, 5 (7 Sat)-11; 12-3, 7-11 Sun
Draught Bass Ⓖ**; Hardys &
Hansons Best Bitter** Ⓗ**,
Classic** Ⓖ**; Marston's Pedigree** Ⓗ
Unspoilt, 19th-century, single-bar terraced pub with two rooms. Beers are stillaged in the bar. No meals Sun. ⚫ Q Ⓓ ⇌

DERBY INN
17 Derby Street ☎ (01283) 543674
11-3, 5.30-11; 11-11 Fri & Sat;
12-3, 7-10.30 Sun
Marston's Pedigree Ⓗ
Small, two-roomed local with a lively bar and a cosy wood-panelled lounge. Railway pictures and memorabilia feature in the public bar. Locally grown vegetables are sold at weekends.
Q ⊡ ♣

ROEBUCK
Station Street ☎ (01283) 568660
11-11; 10.30-3, 4-11 Sat; 12-3,
7-10.30 Sun
**Greene King Abbot; Ind Coope
Burton Ale; Marston's Pedigree;
Morland Old Speckled Hen;
Tetley Bitter; guest beers** Ⓗ
Popular pub close to the station and opposite the brewery, known locally as 'Ale House'. Normally eight beers on handpump. It has served over 700 guest beers. A very well-presented pub.
⊛ ⊭ Ⓓ ▶ ⚅ ⇌ ♣

THOMAS SYKES
Anglesey Road (off Evershed Way)
☎ (01283) 510246
11.30-3, 5 (7 Sat)-11; 11.30-11
Fri; 12-3, 7-10.30 Sun
**Draught Bass; Marston's
Pedigree,** Ⓗ **Owd Rodger;** Ⓖ
guest beers Ⓗ
Simple ale house, formerly a brewery stables where stone floors and breweriana complement the friendly atmosphere.
Q ⛟ ♣ P

CAULDON

YEW TREE
Off A52/A523
☎ (01538) 308348
11-3, 6-11; 12-3, 7-10.30 Sun
**Draught Bass; Burton Bridge
Bridge Bitter; M&B Mild** Ⓗ
One of the most characterful pubs in the country and winner of many awards. Objects from a bygone age feature in profusion: polyphons, pianolas, grandfather clocks; note the patent Acme dog carrier. A visit is a must. Snacks available most times. No expensive drinks sold.
Q ⛟ ⊛ ⚅ ⚊ ♣ P

CHASETOWN

UXBRIDGE ARMS
2 Church St ☎ (01543) 674853
12-3, 5.30-11; 12-11 Sat;
12-10.30 Sun
**Draught Bass; Highgate Dark;
Worthington Bitter; guest beers** Ⓗ
Comfortable and popular two-room local. The two guest beers change regularly and are usually from smaller breweries.
⊛ Ⓓ ▶ ⊡ ♣ P

Try also Junction, High St
(Free)

CHESLYN HAY

WOODMAN INN
Littlewood Lane (off B4156)
☎ (01922) 413686
12-3, 6.30-11; 11-11 Sat; 12-3.30,
7-10.30 Sun
**Marston's Pedigree; Theakston
Mild, Best Bitter, XB, Old
Peculier; guest beers** Ⓗ
Family-run with a welcoming atmosphere and a popular eating area, this former brewhouse had its own spring.
⛟ ⊛ Ⓓ ⊡ ⚊ ♣ P

COPMERE END

STAR
1½ miles W of Eccleshall
OS803294 ☎ (01785) 850279
12-3, 6-11; 12-11 Sat; 12-3,
7-10.30 Sun
Draught Bass; guest beers Ⓗ
Cosy, traditional country pub, popular with walkers, and a meeting place for a cycling club. Occasional auctions are held for summer produce. Situated opposite Cop Mere Pool.
⚫ Q ⛟ ⊛ Ⓓ ▶ ⊡ ⚊ ♣ P

CROXTON

VERNON YONGE ARMS
Blackwaters (B5026, 4 miles from Eccleshall)
☎ (01630) 620283
11.30-2.30 (not Mon & Tue, nor Wed & Thu in winter); 6.30-11;
12-3, 7-11 Sun

275

Marston's Pedigree; guest beers Ⓗ
Two-roomed roadside pub with a restaurant area. Family-friendly, its extensive children's play area features a junior football pitch. An occasional house beer is brewed by Titanic.
♨ ❀ ◖ ◗ ⊟ ▲ ♣ P ⚡

DOSTHILL

FOX
105 High Street
☎ (01827) 280847
12-3, 7-11; 12-3, 7-10.30 Sun
Ansells Mild; Tetley Bitter; guest beers Ⓗ
Welcoming local serving an excellent range of ever-changing guest beers - typically five available. A good selection of food both at the bar and the restaurant (booking essential at busy times, eg Sun lunch); no food Sun eve. Local CAMRA *Pub of the Year* 1997.
Q ❀ ◖ ◗ ⊟ ♣ P

EBSTREE

HOLLY BUSH INN
½ mile W of Staffs & Worcs Canal OS854959
☎ (01902) 895587
11.30-3, 6-11; 12-3, 7-10.30 Sun
Ind Coope Burton Ale; Morland Old Speckled Hen; Tetley Bitter Ⓗ
Pleasant country inn near the Staffs & Worcs Canal: large lounge area (children allowed), plus a more traditional public bar with games and a piano. No food Sun.
♨ ❀ ◖ ◗ ⊟ ♣ P

ECCLESHALL

GEORGE HOTEL
Castle Street
☎ (01785) 850300
11-11 (midnight supper licence), 12-10.30 Sun
Eccleshall Slaters Bitter, Original, Premium, Supreme, seasonal beers; guest beers Ⓗ
Originally a coaching inn, this town-centre hotel now has ten luxurious bedrooms and a bistro. Eccleshall's first brewery for over a century opened behind the hotel in 1995; eight cask beers are usually on sale. Local CAMRA *Pub of the Year* 1997.
♨ ♘ ❀ 🛏 ◖ ◗ ▲ ⌓ P

ENVILLE

CAT INN
Bridgnorth Road (A458)
☎ (01384) 827709
12-3 (maybe earlier); 7-11; closed Sun
Enville Ale, seasonal beers; guest beers Ⓗ
Four-roomed part 16th-century inn on the Staffordshire Way. 1997 CAMRA County *Pub of the Year*. ♨ ❀ ◖ ◗ ⊟ ♣ P

FAZELEY

THREE HORSESHOES
New Street (off A4091)
☎ (01827) 289754
12-3, 6.30-11; 12-11 Fri & Sat; 12-10.30 Sun
Draught Bass; M&B Mild, Ⓗ **Brew XI** Ⓟ**; Marston's Pedigree** Ⓗ
Cosy, traditional pub, popular with locals: two rooms (one for families) and an outside drinking area. Convenient for Drayton Manor Park and the junction of the Birmingham/Fazeley and Coventry canals. Cobs available Mon-Sat lunchtimes. ♘ ❀ ♣

FRADLEY JUNCTION

SWAN INN
1 mile W of Fradley village OS140140 ☎ (01283) 790330
11-3, 6-11; 12-2.30, 7-10.30 Sun
Ansells Bitter; Ind Coope Burton Ale; Marston's Pedigree Ⓗ
Very busy, two-roomed inn situated on the Trent & Mersey Canal; an ideal rural setting for walkers, cyclists and anglers.
❀ ◖ ◗ ⊟ ▲ P

FULFORD

SHOULDER OF MUTTON
Meadow Lane (1½ miles E of B5066) OS953380
☎ (01782) 388960
12-3, 7-11; 12-4, 7-10.30 Sun
ABC Bitter; Ind Coope Burton Ale; Ruddles Best Bitter; Theakston Best Bitter; guest beers Ⓗ
Previously a 17th-century farm with an alehouse, the pub still uses the natural cellar carved out of solid rock. The ghost of Mrs Kent, a former landlady is occasionally seen near the fireplace. The BSA owners club meets here.
♨ ❀ ◖ ◗ ⊟ ▲ ♣ P ⌑

GNOSALL

NAVIGATION
Newport Road (A518, by bridge 35 of Shropshire Union Canal)
☎ (01785) 822327
12-3, 6-11; 12-3, 7-10.30 Sun
Vaux Samson; Ward's Best Bitter Ⓗ
Large canalside pub with a restaurant. The garden has a children's play area. A third cask beer is available in summer. No lunches winter Mon or Tue. Tents welcome in the pub grounds.
❀ ◖ ◗ ⊟ ♿ ▲ ♣ P

ROYAL OAK
Newport Road (A518)
☎ (01785) 822362
12-3, 6-11; 12-3, 7-10.30 Sun
Greene King Abbot; Ind Coope Burton Ale; Tetley Bitter Ⓗ
This village local features bar skittles in its narrow public bar. The former lounge bar is now more of a restaurant area; also a carvery in the upstairs function room Sat eve and Sun lunch.
❀ ◖ ◗ ⊟ ♿ ♣ P

GREAT CHATWELL

RED LION
2 miles E of A41, near Newport OS792143
☎ (01952) 691366
6 (11 Sat)-11; 12-10.30 Sun
Draught Bass; Everards Beacon, Tiger; Worthington Bitter; guest beers Ⓗ
Friendly, family-run country pub offering a range of guest beers. Excellent play area in the garden for children, who are also welcome in the lounge. Good value food in the bar and restaurant.
♨ ♘ ❀ ◖ ◗ ⊟ ▲ ♣ P ⌑

HANDSACRE

CROWN INN
24 The Green (next to canal bridge)
☎ (01543) 490239
12-3.30, 5.45-11; 12-3.30, 7-10.30 Sun
Draught Bass; Worthington Bitter Ⓗ
Friendly, canalside local with a large lounge and a small bar, popular with dominoes and card players. ♨ ❀ ◖ ♣ P

HARLASTON

WHITE LION
Main Road
☎ (01827) 383691
12-3 (later if busy), 6-11; 12-3 (later if busy), 6-10.30 Sun
M&B Mild, Brew XI; Ⓟ **guest beers** Ⓗ
Friendly village local at a quiet road junction. Two guest beers are normally available and change weekly. The bar features a piano and bar billiard table; lively budgies adorn the oak-beamed lounge.
Q ❀ ◖ ◗ ⊟ ♣ P

HARRISEAHEAD

ROYAL OAK
42 High Street
☎ (01782) 513362
12-3 (not Mon-Fri), 7-11; 12-3, 7-10.30 Sun
Courage Directors; John Smith's Bitter; guest beers Ⓗ
Busy, genuine free house in a semi-rural location on the Kidsgrove side of Mow Cop Folly (NT). A smallish bar and a larger lounge cater for all ages; the lounge is notably free of muzak at most times. ❀ ⊟ ♣ P ⌑

HAUGHTON

BELL
Newport Road (A518)
☎ (01785) 780301
11.30-3, 6-11; 12-3, 7-10.30
Sun
Banks's Mild; Marston's Bitter, Pedigree; guest beer ℍ
Homely village free house with an L-shaped room, split into two distinct bar areas, displaying various collections.
🏨 ❀ ◐ ▶ ▲ ♣ P

HEDNESFORD

QUEENS ARMS
37 Hill Street (off A460)
☎ (01543) 878437
12-3, 6.30-11; 12-3, 7-10.30
Sun
Draught Bass; Highgate Dark; Worthington Bitter ℍ
Atmospheric, comfortable two-roomed pub serving good value lunches. Popular with locals.
Q ❀ ◐ ⊞ ♣ P

WEST CANNOCK INN
Mount Street (off A460)
☎ (01543) 422839
12-2.30, 7-11; 12-3.30, 6.30-11
Sat; 12-3, 7-10.30 Sun
Draught Bass; M&B Brew XI; guest beers ℍ
Well-maintained pub with comfortable lounge bars and a friendly atmosphere.
❀ ◐ ▶ ㅎ ⇌ ♣ P

HIGH OFFLEY

ANCHOR ☆
Peggs Lane, Old Lea (by bridge 42 of Shropshire Union Canal)
OS775256
☎ (01785) 284569
11-3, 6-11 summer only; 7-11
Fri; 11-3, 7-11 Sat winter;
12-3, 7-10.30 (not winter eve)
Sun
Marston's Pedigree (summer) Ⓖ;
Wadworth 6X ℍ
Once called the Sebastopol Inn, this classic, basic, two-bar canal-side pub is not easily found by road. Behind the pub is a canal ware gift shop. Note restricted winter hours.
🏨 Q ❀ ⊞ ▲ ♣ ⌣ P

HOAR CROSS

MEYNELL INGRAM ARMS
OS133234
☎ (01283) 575202
12-11; 12-10.30 Sun
Marston's Pedigree; guest beers ℍ
Unspoilt 16th-century former estate pub in a rural village setting; there are wo bars and also a recently built restaurant/function room. No food Sunday eve.
🏨 Q ❀ ◐ ▶ ♣ P

HOPWAS

RED LION
Lichfield Road (A51, 2 miles N of Tamworth) ☎ (01827) 62514
11-2.30 (3 Sat), 6-11; 12-3,
7-10.30 Sun
**Ansells Mild, Ⓟ Bitter;
Marston's Pedigree; guest beer** ℍ
Friendly pub with a large canal-side garden. Beware of the hump-back bridge.
❀ ◐ ▶ ⊞ ♣ P

KINVER

CROWN & ANCHOR
115a Enville Road (½ mile from village centre)
☎ (01384) 872567
12-4 (not winter Tue), 7-11;
12-11 Sat; 12-10.30 Sun
Banks's Mild; Marston's Pedigree; Thwaites Bitter; guest beer (occasional) ℍ
Lively, three-roomed pub, dating from 1853. Children's certificate. No food Mon or in winter.
❀ ◐ ▶ ♣ P

OLD WHITE HARTE HOTEL
111 High Street
☎ (01384) 872305
11.30-11; 12-10.30 Sun
**Banks's Hansons Mild, Bitter;
Camerons Strongarm** (summer)**;
Marston's Pedigree** ℍ
Large, old village-centre pub with a children's certificate.
❀ ◐ ▶ P ㅎ

PLOUGH & HARROW
High Street ☎ (01384) 872659
7 (12 Sat)-11; 12-10.30 Sun
Batham Mild, Best Bitter, XXX ℍ
Popular pub known as 'The Steps' as its rooms are on different levels. Food is available at weekends. Cider in summer.
❀ ◐ ▶ ⊞ ♣ ⌣ P

Try also Cross, Church Hill (Banks's)

KNIGHTON

HABERDASHERS ARMS
Between Adbaston and Knighton
OS753276
☎ (01785) 280650
12.30-11; 12-10.30 Sun
Banks's Mild, Bitter; guest beer ℍ
Welcoming, traditional, four-roomed early Victorian community pub, saved from closure in 1997. Sandwiches are often available.
🏨 Q ⬗ ❀ ⇌ ⊞ ▲ ♣ P ㅎ

LEEK

BLUE MUGGE
17 Osborn Street (off Buxton Road) ☎ (01538) 384450
11-2.30, 6-11; 11-11 Sat; 12-10.30 Sun
Draught Bass; Worthington Bitter; guest beers ℍ
Corner local with several rooms radiating off an island bar, much larger inside than it appears outside. It stocks ever-changing guest beers.
❀ ◐ ⊞ ♣

DEN ENGEL
St Edward Street
☎ (01538) 373751
10-4 (not Mon or Tue), 5
(7 Mon & Tue)-11; 11-4, 6-11 Sat;
12-4, 7-10.30 Sun
Beer range varies ℍ
Authentic, single-room Belgian-style bar, with waiter service, where the large range of draught and bottled beers are always served in the correct glass. Good range of Genevers. A Flemish restaurant upstairs offers beer-based specialities (Wed-Sun). Can be busy at weekends.
▶ ⌣ ㅎ

SWAN
2 St Edward Street
☎ (01538) 382081
11-3, 7-11; 12-3, 7-10.30 Sun
Draught Bass; Highgate Dark; Worthington Bitter; guest beer ℍ
Three-roomed former coaching inn; the lounge is given over to non-smoking diners at lunchtimes. The palatial function room hosts the Cuckoo's Nest Folk Club and mini-beer festivals. Diverse, ever-changing guest beers are stocked. Public car parks adjacent.
❀ ◐ ▶ ⊞ ♣

WILKES HEAD
16 St Edward Street
☎ (01538) 383616
11-3, 6-11; 11-11 Wed-Sat;
12-10.30 Sun
Whim Magic Mushroom Mild, Hartington Bitter; guest beers ℍ
Whim brewery's only tied house increases the choice in the best drinking town in North Staffs. A welcoming, basic, three-roomed real ale-led house where beer is king (two other Whim beers are also on tap). Small pub car park, but a larger public park to the rear.
❀ ♣ ⌣ P

LICHFIELD

EARL OF LICHFIELD ARMS
10 Conduit Street
☎ (01543) 251020
11-11, 11-4, 7-11 Sat; 12-3,
7-10.30 Sun
Banks's Mild; Marston's Bitter, Pedigree, HBC ℍ
Popular, city-centre bar in the corner of the market place. The outdoor drinking area provides a welcome retreat in summer. No food Sun. ❀ ◐ ⇌ (City)

GREYHOUND INN
121 Upper St Johns Street
☎ (01543) 262303
12-3, 5-11; 11-11 Fri & Sat; 12-4, 7-10.30 Sun
Ansells Bitter; Draught Bass; guest beers Ⓗ
The guest beers here are all premium bitters. A popular bar and extended lounge. Good for food.
☎ ❀ ◖ ▶ ≠ (City) ♣ P

QUEENS HEAD
14 Queens Street
☎ (01543) 410932
12-11; 12-3, 7-10.30 Sun
Adnams Bitter; Marston's Pedigree; Taylor Landlord; guest beers Ⓗ
Marston's alehouse near the city centre, very popular with locals and visitors alike. This one-roomed pub gets busy at weekends. Noted for its cheeseboard
◖ ≠ (City) ♣

SCALES
24 Market Street
☎ (01543) 441931
11-11; 12-10.30 Sun
Draught Bass; Lichfield Steeplejack; Worthington Bitter; guest beers Ⓗ
Very popular, city-centre shrine to Bass ale. The long bar serves drinkers of all ages; busy at weekends. Lunchtime snacks. ❀ ⓖ ≠ (City) ♣

Try also Kings Head, Bird St (Marston's)

LITTLE HAYWOOD

RED LION
Main Road ☎ (01889) 881314
12 (4 winter)-11; 12-4, 7-10.30 Sun
Marston's Bitter, Pedigree, HBC Ⓗ
Lively village pub, very much a community local. The garden won *Best Floral Display* for a commercial premises in the national *Best Kept Village* awards.
♨ ❀ ⊞ ▲ ♣ P

LONGDON

SWAN WITH TWO NECKS
40 Brook End (off A51)
☎ (01543) 490251
12-2.30 (3 Sat), 7-11; 12-3, 7-10.30 Sun
Ansells Bitter; Ind Coope Burton Ale; guest beers Ⓗ
400-year-old, beamed village pub with a stone-flagged bar, a comfortable lounge and a restaurant (open Fri and Sat eve) serving fine food. Also an extensive bar menu. ♨ Q ❀ ◖ ▶ P

MARSTON

FOX
1 mile NW of Wheaton Aston
OS835140 ☎ (01785) 840729
12-2.30 (not Mon-Fri winter; 12-3 Sat), 7-11; 12-3, 7-10.30 Sun
Draught Bass; Wells Eagle; guest beers Ⓗ
Remote, country free house with a relaxed, homely atmosphere with at least four guest beers always available; cider in summer.
♨ ☎ ❀ ◖ ▲ ♣ ⌂ P

MEAFORD

GEORGE & DRAGON
The Highway (100 yds S of A34/A51 jct)
☎ (01785) 818497
11-11; 12-10.30 Sun
Burtonwood Bitter, Forshaw's, Top Hat Ⓗ
Main road inn with a spacious, wood-panelled lounge bar. The first-floor restaurant is large enough to cater for parties.
❀ ◖ ▶ ⓖ ▲ ♣ P

MILWICH

GREEN MAN
Sandon Lane (B5027)
☎ (01889) 505310
12-2 (not Mon & Tue), 5-11; 12-11 Sat; 12-4, 7-10.30 Sun
Draught Bass; Worthington Bitter; guest beers Ⓗ
Welcoming village pub, well situated for hikers. A list of landlords since 1792 is displayed in the bar. ♨ ❀ ◖ ▲ ♣ P

NEWCASTLE-UNDER-LYME

ALBERT
1 Brindley Street (near Sainsbury's)
☎ (01889) 615525
11-3 (not Tue-Thu), 5-11; 12-11 Fri; 11-4, 7-11 Sat; 12-3, 7-10.30 Sun
Burtonwood Bitter, Top Hat, seasonal beers Ⓗ
Excellent corner local run by friendly tenants, attracting all ages; one small bar and a meeting room behind. Lunchtime snacks Fri and Sat. Q ♣ ✁

ALBION
99 High Street ☎ (01782) 719784
11-11; 12-10.30 Sun
Marston's Bitter, Pedigree, HBC, guest beers Ⓗ
This two-roomer is one of only two Marston's town-centre pubs. Opens 9am Mon-Sat for breakfast. ❀ ◖

CRICKETERS ARMS
Alexandra Road, May Bank
☎ (01782) 619169
11-3 (not Mon-Thu), 6-11; 11-11 Sat; 12-3, 6-10.30 Sun
Courage Directors; John Smith's Bitter; guest beers Ⓗ
Traditional local on the edge of Wolstanton Marsh. Comprising an entrance hall, bar, pool room and a comfortable lounge.

Understandably, it bears a darts theme as it is owned by world darts champion, Phil Taylor. Ever-changing guest beer. ⊞ ♣ P

CROSSWAYS
Nelson Place (top of Ironmarket)
☎ (01782) 616953
11-11; 11-5, 7-11 Sat; 12-5, 7-10.30 Sun
Ward's Best Bitter; guest beers Ⓗ
Busy, town-centre pub: one large bar with an adjoining pool/games room. The house beer, Bear Cross, is brewed by Coach House. Quiz night Tue. Sausages and chips available lunchtimes. ♣

IRONMARKET
21 Ironmarket
☎ (01782) 713131
11-11; 12-10.30 Sun
Boddingtons Bitter; Marston's Pedigree; Wadworth 6X; Whitbread Abroad Cooper, Fuggles IPA; Ⓗ **guest beers** ⒽⒼ
Well-run Hogshead Alehouse, offering the widest selection of beers in town and can get extremely busy Fri and Sat eves. Opens 10am for breakfast; meals served through until 7 (no food Sun). ◖ ⓖ ⌂

PENKRIDGE

STAR
Market Place
☎ (01785) 712513
11-11; 12-10.30 Sun
Banks's Mild, Bitter; P **Marston's Pedigree** Ⓗ
Village pub, reopened in 1981 after extensive refurbishment following a century's closure. No meals Sun.
❀ ◖ ≠ P 🕮

PERTON

WROTTESLEY ARMS
Severn Drive
☎ (01902) 755213
11-3, 6-11; 11-11 Fri & Sat; 12-10.30 Sun
Banks's Mild, Bitter; Ⓖ **Marston's Pedigree** Ⓗ
Large, modern estate pub with a lounge and smaller public bar. Popular with locals. No food Sun.
◖ ⊞ ❀ P 🕮

REAPSMOOR

BUTCHERS ARMS
Off B5053
OS082614 ☎ (01298) 84477
7-11; 12-3, 7-10.30 Sun
Beer range varies Ⓗ
Moorland gem with several drinking areas; characterful and atmospheric, this is no identikit pub. Superb value food; Sun lunches served. Camping for tents only (free to customers). It can be isolated during severe weather.

♨ Q ➳ 🐕 ▶ Å ♣ P

SEISDON

SEVEN STARS
Fox Road
☎ (01902) 896918
12-3.30, 5.30-11; 12-3.30,
7-10.30 Sun
**Ansells Mild, Bitter; Morland Old
Speckled Hen; Tetley Bitter;
guest beer** Ⓗ
1930s pub on the site of an 18th-
century inn. Note the fireplace
which forms part of the bar.
Good home-cooked food. A
Christmas visit is highly recommended. ♨ ❀ ◑ ▶ ♣ P

SHRALEY BROOK

RISING SUN
Knowle Bank Road (200 yds from
B5500)
☎ (01782) 720600
6.30 (11.30 Fri & Sat)-11; 11.30-
10.30 Sun
Beer range varies Ⓗ
Welcoming, traditional country
pub. It stocks a wide range of
malt whiskies, cider and foreign
bottled beers. Folk club meets
upstairs, also singarounds held.
Children welcome.
♨ Q ❀ ◑ ▶ ♿ ♣ Å ♣ ⌂ P ▯

STAFFORD

BIRD IN HAND
Mill Street (opp Crown Court)
☎ (01785) 252198
11-11; 12-10.30 Sun
**Courage Best Bitter, Directors;
John Smith's Bitter;
Worthington Bitter; guest
beer** Ⓗ
Justifiably popular and enterprising town-centre pub, a rarity in
having retained separate rooms.
The bar, snug, games room and
lounge satisfy clientele of all
ages. Occasional beer festivals.
No meals Sun.
♨ ❀ ◑ ▮ ≈ ♣

FORESTER & FIRKIN
3 Eastgate Street (opp Borough
Hall)
☎ (01785) 223742
12-11; 12-10.30 Sun
**Firkin Forester, Golden Glory,
Dogbolter, seasonal beers** Ⓗ
Furbished in a similar style to
other Firkin pubs, with basic
decor and student customers.
Snacks available all day. Behind
the pub is Stafford's first brewery since 1952. ❀ ◑ ♣ P

STAFFORD ARMS
Railway Street (opp station)
☎ (01785) 253313
12-11; 12-4, 7-10.30 Sun
**Titanic Best Bitter, Lifeboat,
Premium, Stout, Captain
Smith's, White Star,** Ⓗ
Wreckage; Ⓖ **guest beers** Ⓗ

Titanic Inns second pub sells the
full Titanic range and four guests
from independent brewers plus
cider in summer. Games include
bar billiards and corridor skittles.
Twice local CAMRA Pub of the
Year, it hosts two beer festivals a
year. No meals Sat eve or Sun.
❀ ◑ ▶ ≈ ♣ ⌂ P

TAP & SPILE
59 Peel Terrace (off B5066,
1 mile from centre)
☎ (01785) 223563
12-2.30, 6.30-11 (12-11 Fri &
Sat); 12-10.30 Sun
beer range varies Ⓗ
The 1994 sympathetic conversion
to a Tap & Spile has greatly
increased ale choice in northern
Stafford: eight continually changing guest beers, with 200 cask
ales sold each year. Regular
quizzes and free bar billiards.
♨ ❀ ◑ ▶ ♿ ♣ ⌂ ✗

Try also: Coach & Horses, Mill
Bank (Free)

STOKE ON TRENT:
BLYTHE BRIDGE

DUKE OF WELLINGTON
305 Uttoxeter Road (½ mile off
A50 Uttoxeter-Stoke road)
☎ (01782) 395129
12-3 (not Mon), 6.30-11; 12-3,
6.30-10.30 Sun
**Ansells Mild; Ind Coope Burton
Ale; Marston's Pedigree; Tetley
Bitter; guest beers** Ⓗ
Village pub built in 1851. Its
friendly atmosphere attracts all
ages. Lunches is served in both
the bar and lounge; crib, darts
and pool are played in the bar.
❀ ◑ ▯ ♿ ♣ P

Try also: Red Lion, Boundry (Free)

BURSLEM

VINE INN
Hamil Road ☎ (01782) 250294
12-4.30, 7-11; 11-11 Fri & Sat;
12-5, 7-10.30 Sun
**Coach House Posthorn Premium
Ale; Courage Best Bitter; guest
beers** Ⓗ
1930s pub converted from a few
small rooms to one medium-sized
lounge, but it retains a local pub
atmosphere. ♿ ♣

ETRURIA

PLOUGH
147 Etruria Road
☎ (01782) 269445
12-3, 6-11; 7-10.30 (closed lunch)
Sun
**Robinson's Dark Mild, Old
Stockport, Hartley's XB, Best
Bitter, Frederics, Old Tom** Ⓗ
A pleasant atmosphere, combining cask-conditioned ales and
home-cooked food from an exten-

sive blackboard menu.
Q ❀ ◑ ▶ ≈ (Etruria)

FENTON

SMITHY
Goldenhill Road
☎ (01782) 315522
7 (12 Fri & Sat)-11; 12-10.30 Sun
**Theakston Best Bitter; guest
beers** Ⓗ
Two-room pub; the lounge hosts
entertainment Thu, Fri and Sat
eves and the large garden hosts
summer barbecues. The beers
are mainly from Bass and S&N.
❀ ▣ ≈ ♣ P

Try also Malt & Hops, King St
(Free)

GOLDENHILL

CUSHION
230 Broadfield Road (off A50)
☎ (01782) 783388
5 (3 Fri)-11; 12-5, 7-11 Sat; 12-
10.30 Sun
**Greenalls Original; Marston's
Pedigree; Shipstones Bitter;
Titanic Premium; guest beers** Ⓗ
Small well refurbished pub which
reopened as a free house in
1997. One bar, but gives impression of two rooms, it has a
remarkably rural outlook for a
town pub. Experienced local owners involve this popular pub in
community affairs. ❀ ♣ P

HANLEY

HOGSHEAD
2-6 Perry Street
☎ (01782) 209585
11-11; 12-10.30 Sun
beer range varies Ⓗ Ⓖ
Large, city-centre house with 15
handpumped and four gravity dispensed ales, plus a large range
of Belgian bottled beers. Food is
served 11-7.30 Mon-Sat, 12-3
Sun. ◑ ♿ ⌂

TONTINE ALEHOUSE
20 Tontine street (near bus station)
☎ (01782) 263890
11-11; closed Sun
**Marston's Pedigree; Tetley
Bitter; guest beers** Ⓗ
Cosy, one-roomed, town inn,
serving home-made meals. At
least four guest beers and an
extensive range of malt whiskies
also available. Quarterly beer
festivals held. A friendly welcome
to all. ❀ ◑

HARTSHILL

OLD HOUSE AT HOME
544 Hartshill Road
☎ (01782) 610985
4.30 (12 Sat)-11; 12-5, 7-10.30 Sun
**Draught Bass; Ind Coope Burton
Ale; Marston's Pedigree; Tetley
Bitter** Ⓗ

Popular, two-roomed main road pub: a comfortable lounge and a basic public bar with an emphasis on games (including conkers!). Regular drinkers are also strong on quizzes. A locals' pub, but welcoming to all. 🕮 🍺 ♣

MIDDLEPORT

WHITE SWAN
107 Newport Lane, Burslem
☎ (01782) 813639
11-11; 11-4, 7-11 Sat; 11-3, 7-10.30 Sun
Vaux Mild, bitter, Samson, Double Maxim; Ward's Thorne BB; guest beers Ⓗ
Popular, friendly free house.
🚶 ⇌ (Longport) ♣

PENKHULL

CORKY'S
405 London Rd ☎ (01782) 413421
11-11 12-3, 7-10.30 Sun
Banks's Mild, Bitter; Marston's Pedigree; guest beers Ⓗ
Large but friendly pub, it boasts a snooker room with two full-size tables, plus a pool room. Excellent Thai food available (not served Tue). Children welcome.
🕮 ◐ ▶ ♣ 🛍

MARQUIS OF GRANBY
51 St Thomas's Place
☎ (01782) 847025
11.30-3 (4 Thu-Sat), 7-11; 12-2.30, 7-10.30 Sun
Banks's Mild; Marston's Bitter, Pedigree, HBC Ⓗ
Red-brick, corner pub opposite the church: a large, comfortable lounge and a busy public bar with fine etched windows. A well-appointed beer garden and outside drinking area complete the picture. Table skittles played.
🕮 ◐ 🍺 ♣ P

TUNSTALL

PARADISE INN
42 Paradise Street (off Tower Sq) ☎ (01782) 833266
12-11; 12-4, 7.30-11 Sat; 12-4, 7.30-10.30 Sun
Vaux Double Maxim; Ward's Thorne BB Ⓗ
Friendly, welcoming town-centre inn with a single U-shaped room, stocking rare brews for the area. Parking is easy in adjacent side streets; close to a main bus route. ⌂ 🛍

WHITE HART
43 Roundwell Street
☎ (01782) 835817
11.30-11; 12-5, 7.30-10.30 Sun
Marston's Bitter, Pedigree Ⓗ
Single (split) room pub just off the town centre. Friendly atmosphere, even when Port Vale has lost.
🕮 ♣ P

Try also White Horse, Brownhills Rd (Banks's)

STONE

PHEASANT
Old road ☎ (01785) 814603
11.30-11; 12-10.30 Sun
Banks's Mild, Bitter; Bateman Mild; Greene King Abbot; Marston's Bitter, Pedigree Ⓗ
Busy, friendly local where darts, dominoes, crib and football are well supported by the landlord. Good choice of home-cooked meals at sensible prices (eve meals Fri & Sat; no lunches Sun).
🕮 ◐ ▶ ⇌ ♣

STAR INN
21 Stafford Street (by Trent and Mersey canal)
☎ (01785) 813096
11-11; 12-10.30 Sun
Banks's Mild; Camerons Strongarm; Marston's Pedigree; guest beers Ⓗ
Dating from 1568, this canalside pub is located on 13 different floor levels. A new extension along the canalside has a bar and dining area; meals served 11.30-9.30 (12-9.30 Sun). It gets very busy in summer.
🚶 🕮 ◐ ▶ 🍺 ♣ P 🛍

TAMWORTH

ALBERT
32 Albert Road (opp station)
☎ (01827) 64694
12-2.30, 7-11; 12-2.30, 7-10.30 Sun
Banks's Mild, Bitter; Marston's Pedigree, HBC; Morrells Varsity Ⓗ
Popular, two-roomed, well-refurbished local on the edge of the town centre where a warm welcome is guaranteed. Local CAMRA *Pub of the Year* 1996.
Q 🚶 ◐ ▶ 🍺 ♣ P 🛍

JAILHOUSE ROCK BAR
97a Lichfield St ☎ (01827) 61280
11-11; 12-10.30 Sun
Boddingtons Bitter; Marston's Pedigree; guest beer Ⓗ
Lively pub on the edge of the town centre, attracting a varied clientele. Guest beers can be unusual; occasional beer festivals held. It gets busy at weekends. 🕮

Try also Moat House, Lichfield Street (Banks's); White Lion, Aldergate (Banks's)

TUTBURY

CROSS KEYS
Burton Street ☎ (01283) 813677
10.30-3, 5.30-11; 12-3, 7-10.30 Sun
Ind Coope Burton Ale; Tetley Bitter; guest beer Ⓗ
Village pub and restaurant with a friendly atmosphere. Home cook-

ing is a speciality.
Q 🕮 ◐ ▶ 🍺 ♿ ♣ P

TWO GATES

BULL'S HEAD
Watling Street
☎ (01827) 287820
12-2.30 (3 Sat), 6.30-11; 12-2.30, 7-10.30 Sun
Banks's Mild; Marston's Pedigree, HBC Ⓗ
Next to Two Gates traffic lights, this popular, friendly, comfortable local features a bar, lounge and an outdoor area. The pub notice board posts details of its golf society. Good value food served Mon-Sat.
Q 🕮 ◐ 🍺 ⇌ (Wilnecote) ♣ P

UTTOXETER

ROEBUCK
Dove Bank (A518)
☎ (01889) 565563
11-2, 5-11; 11-11 Fri & Sat; 12-3, 7-10.30 Sun
Theakston Best Bitter, XB; guest beers Ⓗ
Characterful, 17th-century building, once a beer retailing premises which only became a pub at the turn of this century. It comprises a bar area with pool table, two lounge areas and a room without a bar.
🕮 🏠 ◐ ▶ Å ⇌ ♣ P

SMITHFIELD HOTEL
Smithfield Road
☎ (01889) 562682
11-3, 7-11; 12-4, 7-10.30 Sun
Burtonwood Forshaw's, Top Hat, Buccaneer Ⓗ
Named the Plume of Feathers in 1627, and renamed circa 1900, it was run by the Jagger family for much of this century. The men-only bar was changed by an Act of Parliament but has been restored to its former architectural condition by the present landlord. Unusual roof garden. No eve meals Wed.
🕮 🏠 ◐ ▶ ♣

VAULTS
Market Place
☎ (01889) 562997
11-3, 5.30-11; 11-3.30, 5-11 Fri; 11-4, 7-11 Sat; 12-3.30, 7-10.30 Sun
Draught Bass; Worthington Bitter Ⓗ
Friendly, unspoilt three-roomer boasting a large bottle collection.
🍺 ⇌ ♣

WESTON

SARACENS HEAD
Stafford Road (A518)
☎ (01889) 270286
11.30-11; 12-3, 7-10.30 Sun
Draught Bass; Worthington Bitter; Ⓟ **guest beer** Ⓗ
Situated below Weston Bank, this

country pub has a conservatory for meals and a courtesy bus for regulars and parties of at least six diners.
🏚 ❀ ◑ ▯
▣ ♣ P 🖵

WOOLPACK
The Green
☎ (01889) 270238
11.30-3, 5.30-11; 11.30-11 Fri & Sat; 12-3, 7-10.30 Sun
Marston's Bitter, Pedigree; guest beer Ⓗ
This 17th-century Inn on the Green has been carefully extended, retaining separate drinking and dining areas. It offers a good selection of quality home-cooked meals at sensible prices. (no food Sun eve). 🏚 ❀ ◑ ▯ ♣ P

WILNECOTE

GLOBE

Watling Street ☎ (01827) 280885

1-3.30, 7-11; 12-3, 7-10.30 Sun
Banks's Mild; Marston's Pedigree, HBC Ⓗ
Basic one-roomed pub by the old A5 (now B5404)
❀ ⇌ ♣

PRINCE OF WALES
70 Hockley Road
☎ (01827) 280013
12-3, 7-11; 12-3, 7-10.30 Sun
Theakston Mild, Best Bitter, XB; guest beers Ⓗ
Five real ales (including two guest beers) and a range of single malts are available at this excellent, award-winning local. The lounge is quiet.
Q ❀ ▣ ♣ P

YOUR PUB AND CAMRA

There is nothing which has yet been contrived by man, by which so much happiness is produced as by a good tavern or inn.

•

SAMUEL JOHNSON

WOMBOURNE

NEW INN
1 Station Road (½ mile from A459/A463 jct)
☎ (01902) 892037
11-3, 5.30-11; 11-11 Thu-Sat; 12-3, 7-10.30 Sun
Banks's Mild, Bitter Ⓟ**; guest beer** Ⓗ
Large roadhouse-style pub near the village centre.
❀ ◑ ▣ ♣ P 🖵

YOXALL

CROWN INN
Main Street
☎ (01543) 472551
11.30-3, 5.30-11; 11.30-11 Sat; 12-10.30 (not winter) Sun
Marston's Pedigree, Owd Rodger (winter) Ⓗ
Pleasant village pub with a conservatory suitable for families.
🏚 ❀ ◑ ▯ ▣ ♿ ▲ ♣ P

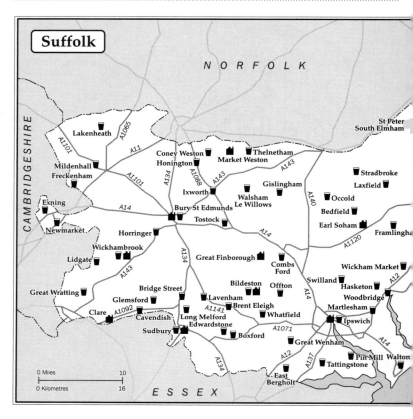

Suffolk

NORFOLK

Lakenheath

Mildenhall
Freckenham

Exning

Newmarket

Coney Weston
Honington

Market Weston
Thelnetham

St Peter
South Elmham

Stradbroke

Ixworth
Gislingham
Laxfield

Walsham
Le Willows
Occold

Bury St Edmunds
Bedfield

Tostock
Earl Soham

Horringer
Framlingha

Wickhambrook

Lidgate
Great Finborough

Combs
Ford
Wickham Market

Great Wratting
Bildeston
Offton
Swilland
Hasketon

Bridge Street
Lavenham
Whatfield
Woodbridge
Martlesham

Glemsford
Brent Eleigh

Clare
Cavendish
Long Melford
Edwardstone
Ipswich

Sudbury
Boxford

Great Wenham

Pin Mill Walton
Tattingstone

East
Bergholt

ESSEX

0 Miles 10
0 Kilometres 16

ALDEBURGH

MILL INN
Market Cross Place (opp Moot Hall) ☎ (01728) 452563
11-3, 5-11; 11-11 Fri , Sat & summer; 12-10.30 Sun
Adnams Bitter, Broadside, seasonal beers Ⓗ
Cosy seafront pub whose landlord is also a sea fisherman ensuring good fresh fish on the menu. 🚪 ◖ ▸ ▲ ♣

WHITE HART
222 High Street
☎ (01728) 453205
11.30-11; 12-10.30 Sun
Adnams Bitter, Extra, Broadside, seasonal beers Ⓗ
Popular local, next to the chip shop, a single bar with a nautical flavour. The small room can be very busy at weekends.
🚪 Q ❀ 🚪 ▲ ♣

BEDFIELD

CROWN
Church Lane (leave A1120 at Earl Soham)
☎ (01728) 628431
11.30-3, 6-11 (may vary afternoons); 12-10.30 Sun
Greene King IPA; guest beer Ⓗ

Friendly village local with many games, including bar billiards and shove ha'penny. No food Tue.
🚪 ❀ ◖ ▸ ▲ ♣ P ⊁

BILDESTON

KINGS HEAD
132 High St ☎ (01449) 741434
12-3, 5-11; 11-11 Sat; 12-10.30 Sun
Brettvale Bitter, First Gold; Old Chimneys Military Mild Ⓗ
Now brewing on the premises, this lively village centre pub continues to cater for all. It hosts live music at weekends when the full range of Brettvale beers is normally available, plus a beer festival Whit Bank Holiday. Cider in summer. 🍺 ❀ 🚪 ◖ ▸ ♣ ⌣ P

BOXFORD

WHITE HART
Broad St ☎ (01787) 211071
12-3, 6 (6.30 Mon-Fri winter)-11; 12-3, 7-10.30 Sun
Adnams Extra or **Broadside; Greene King IPA; guest beers** Ⓗ
Timber-framed free house in the village centre, offering an interesting range of guest beer and a good value house beer from Mansfield. Ask about Tornado Smith! 🚪 ❀ ◖ ▸ ♣ P

BRENT ELEIGH

COCK ☆
Lavenham Road
☎ (01787) 247371
12-3, 6-11; 12-3, 7-10.30 Sun
Adnams Bitter; Greene King XX Mild, IPA, Ⓗ **Abbot** Ⓖ
An absolute gem! Thatched, unspoilt and at peace with the world. 🚪 Q ❀ 🚪 ♣ ⌣ P

BRIDGE STREET

ROSE & CROWN
on A134 ☎ (01787) 247022
12-3, 6.30-11; 12-10.30 Sun
Greene King IPA, Abbot Ⓖ
Homely, village pub with an abundance of exposed beams and a friendly atmosphere. The ales are drawn straight from the cask and there is a wide selection of home-made food including blackboard specials. Near Long Melford and Kentwell Halls.
Q ❀ ◖ ▸ 🚪 ♣ P

BUNGAY

CHEQUERS INN
23 Bridge Street (near Market Place) ☎ (01986) 893579
12-3, 5-11; 12-11 Fri; 11-11 Sat; 12-10.30 Sun

Oulton
Oulton Broad
Lowestoft
Bungay
Carlton
Colville
Wangford
Venhaston
Southwold
Walberswick
...ton
Theberton
Snape
Chillesford
Aldeburgh
...utley

**Adnams Bitter; Draught Bass;
Fuller's London Pride; guest
beer** H
Popular, 17th-century inn with a
partially covered patio at the
rear. It stocks a minimum of six
guest beers. Weekday lunches.
♨ ❀ ◖ ▲ ♣ P

GREEN DRAGON
29 Broad St ☎ (01986) 892681
11-3, 5-11; 11-11 Fri & Sat; 12-4,
7-10.30 Sun
**Adnams Bitter; Green Dragon
Chaucer, Bridge Street, Dragon;
guest beer** H
Twin-bar inn with a dining
room/family area. Beer is
brewed at the rear of the premises. Good value food available,
including speciality nights (curry
Wed and fish and chips Fri).
♨ ⊃ ❀ ◖ ▶ ▲ P

BURY ST EDMUNDS

BUSHEL
28-29 St Johns Street
☎ (01284) 754333
11-2.30, 5-11; 11-11 Sat; 12-3,
6-10.30 Sun
**Greene King IPA, Abbot, season-
al beers** H
15th-century coaching inn that
retains much of its original char-

acter despite being fully
restored. Very good food (not
served Sun eve).
❀ ◖ ▶ ⇌ ♣ P

FALCON
58 Risbygate Street
☎ (01284) 754128
11-11; 12-10.30 Sun
Greene King IPA, Abbot H
Friendly, edge-of-town local
established in 1859, mostly
unmodernised but with a new
extension to the rear. No food
Sun eve when there's a free fun
quiz. ❀ ◖ ▶ ⊞ ♣ P

IPSWICH ARMS
1 Tayfen Road
☎ (01284) 703623
11-2 (2.30 Fri), 6.30-11; 11-11
Sat; 12-10.30 Sun
Greene King XX Mild (winter),
IPA, Abbot H
Unusual, semi-circular, 19th-cen-
tury light brick pub near the station, and named to celebrate the
rail link with Ipswich in 1864. An
early photograph of the area
taken from the top of St John's
church is displayed in the bar.
Good value food (eve meals
weekdays). ❀ ◖ ▶ ⇌ P

NUTSHELL ☆
The Traverse
☎ (01284) 705387
11-3, 6-11 (11-11 summer);
closed Sun
Greene King IPA, Abbot H
The smallest pub in Britain, full of
character. Look out for the mummified cat found during modernisation. Q

QUEENS HEAD
39 Churchgate Street
☎ (01284) 761554
11-11; 12-10.30 Sun
**Adnams Bitter, Broadside; Ind
Coope Burton Ale; Nethergate
IPA; Tetley Bitter; Wolf Hare of
the Dog** H
Lively free house close to Bury's
historic centre and the abbey.
Local beers feature, with
Nethergate IPA the great value
off-peak special (happy several
hours!). The range may vary.
Recently enlarged by a courtyard
conservatory linking to outbuildings. Regular beer festivals.
◖ ▶ ⇌

ROSE & CROWN
48 Whiting Street
☎ (01284) 755934
11.30-11; 11-3, 7-11 Sat; 12-2.30,
7-10.30 Sun
**Greene King XX Mild, IPA, Abbot,
seasonal beers** (winter) H
Highly recommended, this family-
run, unspoilt town local fronts on
to Westgate Street within sight
of the brewery and frequented by
all ranks of its staff. Good value
lunches prepared by the

landlady. A mild stronghold!
Q ⇙ ◖ ⊞ ♣

BUTLEY

OYSTER
☎ (01394) 450790
11.30-3, 6-11; 11-11 Sat; 12-3,
7-10.30 Sun
**Adnams Bitter, Broadside, sea-
sonal beers** H
A countryside jewel: good beer, a
good welcome, a good atmosphere and superb food. Music
Sun eves. ♨ Q ❀ ◖ ▶ ▲ ♣ P

CARLTON COLVILLE

BELL INN
The Street (off B1384)
☎ (01502) 582873
11-11; 12-10.30 Sun
**Green Jack Mild, Bitter,
Grasshopper, Golden Sickle,
seasonal beers; guest beer** H
Well renovated, open-plan public
house owned by Green Jack
brewery. The no-smoking area
doubles as a family room (children's certificate). Reasonably
priced, good quality home-cooked
food.
♨ Q ⌂ ❀ ◖ ▶ & ▲ P ⊁

CAVENDISH

BULL
High Street ☎ (01787) 780245
11-3, 6-11; 12-3, 7-10.30 Sun
Adnams Bitter, Broadside H
Friendly High Street pub with a
large garden and a wide selection of food. A rare Adnams tied
house this far west.
Q ❀ ◖ ▶ P

CHILLESFORD

FROIZE INN
Orford Road ☎ (01394) 450282
12-2, 6-11 (closed Mon); 12-11
Sat; 12-10.30 Sun
**Adnams Bitter; Woodforde's
Wherry; guest beers** H
Fine old country inn set in extensive grounds, with camping and
caravan sites. One large comfortable bar, now augmented by a
newly-built restaurant serving
fine food (especially the
seafood). The house beers
(Nuns) brewed by Mauldons.
♨ Q ❀ ⇙ ◖ ▶ & ▲ ♣ P

COMBS FORD

GLADSTONE ARMS
2 Combs Ford (1 mile from
Stowmarket centre on Needham
road) ☎ (01449) 612339
11-2.30, 5 (6 Sat)-11; 12-3,
7-10.30 Sun
Adnams Bitter, Old, Broadside H
Adnams tied house on the southern outskirts of Stowmarket.
Cross a bridge to the garden.
❀ ♣ P

CONEY WESTON

SWAN
Thetford Road
☎ (01359) 221295
12-3, 5 (6 Sat)-11; 12-3, 7-10.30 Sun
Greene King XX Mild, IPA, Abbot Ⓗ
Victorian local, run on most traditional lines – no food, no juke box, no noisy machines and proud of it. There is a good early evening trade from locals. The bowling green is popular in summer.
🏚 Q ❀ ⊟ ♣ P

EAST BERGHOLT

HARE & HOUNDS
Heath Road
☎ (01206) 298438
11.30-2.30, 5-11; 11-11 Sat; 12-2.30, 6-10.30 Sun
Adnams Bitter, Broadside; guest beers Ⓗ
Fine, 15th-century pub retaining a pargetted ceiling (deep plaster relief), dating from 1590, in the lounge. Much of the pub's character has only survived due to the efforts of the long-standing landlord and landlady. Guest beers come mainly from local breweries.
🏚 Q ☜ ❀ ◖▮ ⊟ ㅅ ▲ ♣ P

EDWARDSTONE

WHITE HORSE
Mill Green
OS951429
☎ (01787) 211211
12-3, 6.30-11; 12-3, 7-10.30 Sun
Greene King IPA; Morrells Mild; guest beers Ⓗ
Two-bar rural free house with a large car park and garden, a popular venue for pub games. Watch out for the fine collection of enamel signs in both bars. No food available Mon.
🏚 Q ❀ ◖▮ ⊟ ▲ ♣ P

EXNING

WHEATSHEAF
45 Chapel Street (loop road between church and PO)
☎ (01638) 577227
12-2.30 (not Sat), 7-11; 12-3, 7-10.30 Sun
Greene King XX Mild, IPA, Abbot Ⓗ
This handsome Victorian village pub is tucked away in small cul-de-sac. Surprisingly spacious inside, it has a large garden behind (where petanque is played). Mainly serves a traditional menu but there's always something unusual and adventurous (no meals available Wed eve). Parking difficult.
🏚 Q ❀ ◖▮ ♣ P ✁

FRAMLINGHAM

RAILWAY INN
9 Station Road
☎ (01728) 723693
12 (11 Sat)-3, 5.30-11; 12-3, 7-10.30 Sun
Adnams Bitter, Broadside, seasonal beers Ⓗ
Two-bar local catering for all tastes where a good welcome is assured by the affable landlord.
🏚 Q ❀ ♣ P

STATION INN
Station Road (B1119)
☎ (01728) 723455
12-3, 7-11; 12-3, 7-10.30 Sun
Earl Soham Gannet Mild, Victoria, Sir Roger's Porter, Albert Ale, Jolabrugg Ⓗ
Two-room Victorian pub with a spacious main bar boasting a fine Edwardian cabinet five pump set. An ideal venue for the dedicated real ale drinker. Freshly-cooked food is based on local produce.
🏚 Q ◖▮ ⊟ ㅅ ▲

FRECKENHAM

GOLDEN BOAR
The Street
☎ (01638) 723000
11-11; 12-4, 7-10.30 (12-10.30 summer) Sun
Adnams Bitter, Broadside; Nethergate Bitter, Old Growler Ⓗ
16th-century inn, formerly on the quay of the most inland port in Britain. Recent refurbishment has exposed interesting features. The garden has a petanque pitch.
🏚 ❀ ☜ ◖▮ ㅅ ♣ P

GISLINGHAM

SIX BELLS
High Street ☎ (01379) 783349
12-3, 7-11 (12-11 summer); 12-3, 7-10.30 Sun
Beer range varies Ⓗ
Spacious village centre pub which supports local microbreweries (Old Chimneys brews the two house beers). Large public bar and a restaurant serving excellent home-made food from an interesting menu (no food Mon). It hosts an annual Dwile Flonk for charity.
☜ ❀ ◖▮ ▲ ♣ P

GLEMSFORD

ANGEL
Egremont St ☎ (01787) 281671
12-2 (3 Sat), 5-11; 12-3, 7-10.30 Sun
Greene King IPA Ⓖ
Traditional pub at one end of a large village. Recently opened out, it is reputed to be the oldest house in the village, once home to Cardinal Wolsey's secretary, John Cavendish, whose ghost is said to appear. Q ❀ ♣ P

GREAT WENHAM

QUEENS HEAD
Capel St Mary Road (off B1070)
OSTM0738 ☎ (01473) 310590
12-2.30, 6.30-11; 12-2.30, 7-10.30 Sun
Adnams Bitter; Greene King IPA, Abbot; guest beers Ⓗ
Attractive, mid-19th-century country pub of character, popular with locals, walkers and cyclists in summer. Famous for its curry menu. No meals Mon lunch.
🏚 Q ❀ ◖▮ ㅅ ♣ P

GREAT WRATTING

RED LION
School Road ☎ (01440) 783237
11-3, 5-11; 12-3, 7-10.30 (11-10.30 summer) Sun
Adnams Mild (spring)**, Bitter, Extra, Broadside, seasonal beers** Ⓗ
Village local, known by its whalebone arch. A large back garden has children's games and pet animals. No food Sun eve or Tue.
🏚 Q ❀ ◖▮ ♣ P

HASKETON

TURKS HEAD
Low Road ☎ (01394) 382584
12-2.30 (not Mon), 6-11; 12-3, 7-10.30 Sun
Tolly Cobbold Mild, Original, IPA, Tollyshooter, seasonal beers; guest beer Ⓗ
Small, low-ceilinged, 16th-century village pub, now refurbished into a single room. A high-back settle, a large open fire and a wealth of antiques and memorabilia add charm and character. A lively conversation at the bar is assured. No food Sun eve or Mon. 🏚 ❀ ◖▮ ㅅ ▲ ♣ P

HORRINGER

SIX BELLS
The Street ☎ (01284) 735551
11.30-2.30, 6 (7 Sat)-11; 12-3, 7-10.30 Sun
Greene King XX Mild, IPA, Abbot, seasonal beers Ⓗ
Traditional local in a picturesque village near Ickworth Park (NT). Home-made meals include pies and blackboard specials.
🏚 Q ☜ ❀ ◖▮ ♣ P

Ale savers unite!
Join CAMRA and add your voice to support consumer choice!

IPSWICH

BREWERY TAP
Cliff Rd ☎ (01473) 281508
11-11; 12-10.30 (12-3, 7-10.30 winter) Sun
Tolly Cobbold Mild, Bitter, Original, IPA, Premium Ⓗ
Waterfront pub below the old Tolly Cobbold brewery, much of which is now a museum/visitor centre. Ask to have the sparkler removed if you wish, as all ales are served using swan necks. Eve meals must be booked.
🏨 Q ⛵ 🕸 ◑ Ⓓ & ♣ P ⅓ 🖤

CRICKETERS
51 Crown Street (opp bus station) ☎ (01473) 225910
11-11; 12-10.30 Sun
Adnams Broadside; Courage Directors; Theakston Best Bitter; guest beers Ⓗ
Large, town-centre pub where beer is served in lined glasses. Typical Wetherspoons decor.
Q 🕸 ◑ Ⓓ & ⌣ P ⅓ 🖤

FAT CAT (SPRING TAVERN)
288 Spring Rd ☎ (01473) 726524
12 (11 Sat)-11; 12-10.30 Sun
Adnams Bitter; Wells Bombardier Ⓗ**; Woodforde's Wherry** ⒽⒼ**, Norfolk Nog** Ⓗ**; guest beers** ⒽⒼ
An honest-to-goodness ale drinker's haunt serving the most extensive selection of ales in town, with up to 14 guest beers, many served on gravity.
Q 🕸 ≉ ⌣

GREYHOUND
9 Henley Rd ☎ (01473) 252105
11-2.30, 5-11; 11-11 Sat; 12-10.30 Sun
Adnams Mild, Bitter, Old, Extra, Broadside, seasonal beers Ⓖ
Attractive, busy, two-room pub, popular for food. 🕸 ◑ Ⓓ 🍴 ♣ P

LORD NELSON
81 Fore St ☎ (01473) 254072
11.45-3, 5-11; 11-11 Fri; 12-3, 7-10.30 Sun
Adnams Mild (occasional)**, Bitter, Broadside, Old, seasonal beers** Ⓖ
A recent, stylish refurbishment has transformed this pub close to the wet dock. Now more openplan, but with many beams and sympathetic furnishings. It uses an almost unique form of dispense with 'fake' wooden casks fronting a real stillage.
🕸 ◑ Ⓓ & ≉ P

Try also Lion's Head

IXWORTH

GREYHOUND
49 High Street ☎ (01359) 230887
11-3, 6-11; 12-3, 7-10.30 Sun

Greene King XX Mild, IPA, Abbot, seasonal beers Ⓗ
Three-bar local retaining a marvellous intimate, public snug. The lively public bar fields games teams; pool played.
◑ Ⓔ Ⓐ ♣ P

LAKEHEATH

PLOUGH
Mill Rd ☎ (01842) 860285
11-2.30, 6-11; 11-11 Sat; 12-4, 6-10.30 Sun
Greene King IPA, Abbot, seasonal beers Ⓗ
Very traditional village pub, which appeals to locals, as it has always done. The unspoilt flint exterior, typical of Breckland, conceals spacious bars hosting activities of all kinds. 🕸 Ⓔ ♣ P

LAVENHAM

ANGEL
Market Place
☎ (01787) 247388
11-11; 12-10.30 Sun
Adnams Bitter; Greene King IPA; Mauldons White Adder; Nethergate Bitter Ⓗ
Award-winning, 15th-century inn overlooking the old market place and Guildhall. The restaurant and bar have a refined, relaxing atmosphere, serving good food from local ingredients. High-standard accommodation.
🏨 Q ⛵ 🕸 🍴 ◑ Ⓓ ♣ P

COCK INN
Church St ☎ (01787) 247407
11-11; 12-10.30 Sun
Greene King IPA; Highgate Mild; Mauldon's seasonal beers Ⓗ
Traditional three-roomer opposite Lavenham's impressive church: a beamed bar with a stone floor, a lounge, and a nosmoking garden room is licensed for families. The large safe gardens have a play area. The house beer, O'Sullivans Strong Ale, comes from Mauldons.
🏨 Q ⛵ 🕸 🍴 ◑ Ⓓ Ⓔ ♣ ⌣ P ⅓

LAXFIELD

KINGS HEAD/ LOW HOUSE ☆
Gorams Mill Lane (off B1117, below churchyard)
☎ (01986) 798395
11-3, 6-11; 11-11 Tue; 12-3, 7-10.30 Sun
Adnams Bitter, Old, Extra, Broadside, seasonal beers; Greene King IPA Ⓖ
The finest pub in Suffolk? If not, then still a not-to-be-missed classic. A tap room with no bar, a warren of small rooms and outside drinking areas give plenty of ways to savour this timeless but still vibrant pub.
Q 🏨 ⛵ 🕸 ◑ Ⓓ Ⓔ Ⓐ ⌣ P

LIDGATE

STAR
The Street ☎ (01638) 500275
11-3, 5-11; 12-3, 6-10.30 Sun
Greene King IPA, Abbot, seasonal beers Ⓗ
Busy local with unusual belowbar level handpumps. The food is of a mostly Mediterranean flavour (no food Sun eve). Petanque played.
🏨 Q 🕸 ♣ P 🖤

LONG MELFORD

GEORGE & DRAGON
Hall Street
☎ (01787) 371285
11.30-11; 12-10.30 Sun
Greene King IPA, Abbot; Marston's Pedigree Ⓗ
Family-run, former coaching inn with a lounge-style, single bar and a restaurant serving an interesting menu. Still a good drinking pub hosting live music (folk and blues) Wed eve.
🏨 🕸 🍴 ◑ Ⓓ P

LOWESTOFT

FACTORY ARMS
214 Raglan St (off inner ring road) ☎ (01502) 574523
10.30-11; 12-10.30 Sun
Beer range varies Ⓗ
Basic, single room with a new bar counter, popular with young pool and darts players. Handy for Lowestoft Town FC. & ≉ ♣

TRIANGLE TAVERN
29 St Peter's Street (opp Triangle Market)
☎ (01502) 582711
11-11; 12-10.30 Sun
Green Jack Bitter, Canary, Grasshopper, Golden Sickle, Lurcher, seasonal beers; guest beer Ⓗ
Town-centre alehouse owned by Green Jack Brewery in a newly pedestrianised area. A cosy front bar with open fire and a rear pool room. 🏨 Ⓔ ♣ ≉

WELCOME
182 London Road North
☎ (01502) 585500
10.30-4, 7.30-11; 12-4, 7.30-10.30 Sun
Adnams Bitter, Old, Broadside; Greene King Abbot; guest beers Ⓗ
Popular, one-bar, town-centre pub: no frills, just good ales and company. ≉ ♣

MARTLESHAM

BLACK TILES
Main Road
☎ (01473) 610298
11-11; 12-10.30 Sun
Adnams Bitter, Broadside, seasonal beers Ⓗ

Excellent, out-of-town, two-bar pub with a large restaurant and a newly refurbished cocktail bar in Art Deco style. It hosts music nights Sun. ▨ Q ⬮ ⊛ ◖ ▮ P

MILDENHALL

MAID'S HEAD
9 Kingsway ☎ (01638) 713366
11-11; 12-10.30 Sun
Greene King IPA, Abbot Ⓗ
This well-established town pub has taken on a new lease of life after refurbishment and conversion to real ale. A spacious interior with a good atmosphere and a friendly welcome.
▨ ⊛ ◖ Ă ♣ P

NEWMARKET

BUSHEL
Market Street (Rookery Precinct)
☎ (01638) 663967
10.30 (10 Sat)-11; 12-3, 7-10.30 Sun
Greene King Martha Greene's, IPA, Abbot, seasonal beers Ⓗ
Town-centre pub reputed to be the oldest in Newmarket; the Rookery shopping arcade was built around it. Recently refurbished without loss of character. No food Sun eve. Q ◖ ▮ ♿ ♣

OFFTON

LIMEBURNERS
Willisham Road
☎ (01473) 658318
12-2.30 (not Mon), 5-11; 12-11 Sat; 12-3, 7-10.30 Sun
Adnams Bitter; Wells Eagle guest beer Ⓗ
Two-bar local with a large garden; named after a local limekiln. Sunday is buskers' night. No meals Thu eve. ⊛ ◖ ▮ P

OULTON

BLUE BOAR
28 Oulton Street
☎ (01502) 572160
11.30-3, 7(6 Fri)-11; 11-11 Sat; 12-3, 7.30-10.30 Sun
John Smith's Bitter; guest beers Ⓗ
Roomy local with a cosy saloon bar. The pool room doubles as a family room. The landlord supports microbreweries both near and afar. ⬮ ⊛ ◖ ⊞ ♿ ♣ P

PIN MILL

BUTT & OYSTER ☆
The Quay ☎ (01473) 780764
11-3, 7-11; 11-11 Sat & summer; 12-10.30 Sun
Tolly Cobbold Mild, Bitter Ⓖ**, Original, IPA, Tollyshooter, seasonal beers; guest beers** (occasional) Ⓗ
Classic riverside pub with plenty of history, serving local and

tourist trade equally. In every edition of the *Guide*
▨ Q ⬮ ⊛ ◖ ▮ ⊞ ♣ P

SIBTON

WHITE HORSE
Halesworth Road
☎ (01728) 660337
11.30-2.30, 7-11; 12-2.30, 7-10.30 Sun
Adnams Bitter, Broadside Ⓗ
Single bar local with a raised gallery area where well-behaved children are permitted. The large garden has a play area. It also has a restaurant (no meals Sun eve). ▨ ⊛ ⊠ ◖ ▮ ♿ ♣ P

SNAPE

GOLDEN KEY
Priory Road
☎ (01728) 688510
11-3, 6-11; 12-3, 7-10.30 Sun
Adnams Bitter, seasonal beers Ⓗ
Cosy bar area with a dining room serving fine food, well priced.
▨ Q ⊛ ⊠ ◖ ▮ Ă P

SOUTHWOLD

LORD NELSON
East Street
☎ (01502) 722079
10.30-11; 12-10.30 Sun
Adnams Bitter, Extra, Broadside, seasonal beers Ⓗ
Busy town local with much Nelson memorabilia and a collection of soda syphons around the back bar. Good value.
▨ Q ⊛ ◖ ▮ Ă ♣

SOLE BAY
7 East Green ☎ (01502) 723736
11-11; 12-10.30 Sun
Adnams Bitter, Broadside, seasonal beers Ⓗ
One-room bar next to the lighthouse and opposite the brewery. Note the collection of Adnams beer bottles above the bar.
⊠ ◖ ▮ Ă ♣

STRADBROKE

QUEENS HEAD
Queens Street (B1118)
☎ (01379) 384384
11.30-3, 6.30-11; 12-3.30, 7-10.30 Sun
Adnams Bitter, Broadside; John Smith's Bitter; guest beer Ⓗ
A castellated brick facade hides the 15th-century interior of this friendly local. The weekend guest beer and weekday lunches offer particularly good value.
▨ ⊛ ◖ ▮ P

SUDBURY

SPREAD EAGLE
Cross Street ☎ (01787) 377545
11-3, 7-11; 12-3, 7-10.30 Sun
Greene King IPA Ⓗ

Traditional two-bar local, in part dating from the 14th century, it retains distinctive etched windows. Petanque is played in summer.▨ Q ⊛ ◖ ⊞ Ă ⇌ ♣ P

WAGGON & HORSES
Acton Square ☎ (01787) 312147
11-3, 6.30 (5 Fri)-11; 12-3, 7.30-10.30 Sun
Greene King Mild, IPA, Abbot Ⓗ
Back-street local retaining an interesting layout: several different drinking areas, a games-cum-family area off the public bar, and a small restaurant area leading to a cosy snug. Next to the site of the old Phoenix Brewery.
▨ Q ⬮ ⊛ ⊠ ◖ ▮ ⇌ ♣

SWILLAND

MOON & MUSHROOM (HALF MOON)
High Road ☎ (01473) 785320
11-2.30 (not Mon), 6-11; 12-3, 7-10.30 Sun
Adnams Bitter; Nethergate Umbel Ale, Bitter; Scott's Blues & Bloater, Hopleaf; guest beers Ⓖ
Friendly local, formerly the Half Moon, now a single-bar free house with a low ceiling, exposed beams and a small eating area (meals Tue-Sat).
▨ Q ⊛ ◖ ▮ Ă ♣ P

TATTINGSTONE

ORANGE BOX
Church Road (opp School)
☎ (01473) 328330
12-3.30, 7.30-11; 12-3.30, 7.30-10.30 Sun
Adnams Bitter; guest beers (summer) Ⓗ
Tiny, one-roomer which gets its name from its exterior appearance. Can you tell who brews Box Bitter? Q ⊛ ♣ P

THEBERTON

LION
The Street ☎ (01728) 830185
11-2.30, 6-11; 12-3, 7-10.30 Sun
Adnams Bitter; guest beers Ⓗ
Lively village local with jazz every first Sun of the month. Excellent guest beers (three) usually come from East Anglia. Pool room.
▨ Q ⊛ ◖ ▮ ♿ Ă ♣ P

THELNETHAM

WHITE HORSE
Hopton Road (1 mile from Hopton Church, off B1111)
OS015784 ☎ (01379) 898298
11-2.30, 5-11; 11-11 Sat; 12-3, 7-10.30 Sun
Adnams Bitter; Greene King IPA Ⓗ**; Old Chimneys seasonal beers** Ⓖ**; Woodforde's Great Eastern; guest beers** Ⓗ
Popular, 17th-century free house serving an extensive menu and a

good beer range with occasional house specials brewed by Old Chimneys. Eve meals start at 7pm.

🏠 ❀ ◖ 🍺 ♣ P

TOSTOCK

GARDENERS ARMS
Church Road (off village green)
☎ (01359) 274060
11.30-2.30, 7-11; 12-3, 7-10.30 Sun
Greene King IPA, Abbot, seasonal beers Ⓗ
Fine old building with original beams; the public bar has a tiled stone floor (pool played), while the lounge has a large fireplace and an eating area to one side (good value home-made food). No meals Sun lunch or Mon/Tue eves. Large garden.

🏠 ❀ ◖ 🍺 ♣ P

WALBERSWICK

BELL
Ferry Road
☎ (01502) 723109
11-3, 6-11 (may extend summer); 12-3.30, 7-10.30 Sun
Adnams Bitter, Broadside, Extra, seasonal beers Ⓗ
This 600-year-old inn is always a favourite with locals and tourists. A recent extension and a larger bar give much more room to enjoy all the fine ales.

🏠 ⛺ ❀ 🛏 ◖ 🍺 ⚿ 🔥 ♣ P

WALSHAM LE WILLOWS

SIX BELLS
Summer Road
☎ (01359) 259726
11.30-2.30, 5.30 (6.30 Sat)-11; 12-2, 7-10.30 Sun
Greene King XX Mild, IPA, Abbot, seasonal beers Ⓗ
Fine, 16th-century village pub in tranquil surroundings. It boasts high-backed settles and a massive, curved oak bar. Now run (unchanged) by a local couple who used to be regulars of the pub. 🏠 Q ❀ 🛏 🍺 ♣ P

WALTON

TAP & SPILE (HALF MOON)
303 High St ☎ (01394) 282130
11-3, 5-11; 11-11 Thu-Sat; 12-4, 7-10.30 Sun
Adnams Mild, Bitter; guest beers Ⓗ
Two-bar pub furnished in traditional style, with bare floorboards, panelled walls and breweriana in classic T&S format; no juke box, restaurant or fruit machines. Popular with locals and visitors alike. Usually eight beers on tap.
🏠 Q ❀ 🍺 ⚿ ⇌ ♣ P

INDEPENDENT BREWERIES

Adnams:
Southwold
Brettvale:
Bildeston
Earl Soham:
Earl Soham
Green Dragon:
Bungay
Green Jack:
Lowestoft
Greene King:
Bury St Edmunds
Mauldons:
Sudbury
Nethergate:
Clare, Suffolk
St Peter's:
Bungay
Scott's:
Lowestoft
Tolly Cobbold:
Ipswich

WANGFORD

PLOUGH
London Road ☎ (01502) 578239
11-2.30 (3.30 Sat), 7-11; 12-3.30, 7-10.30 Sun
Adnams Bitter, Extra, seasonal beers Ⓖ
18th-century roadside inn with a cosy snug. Beer is served from cooling cabinets behind the bar. Gardens and camping at the rear.
🏠 Q ❀ ◖ 🍺 🔥 ♣ P

WENHASTON

STAR
Hall Road ☎ (01502) 478240
11-2, 6-11; 12-3, 7-10.30 Sun
Adnams Bitter, Extra, seasonal beers Ⓖ
Friendly pub at the village edge: three small rooms and a large garden. Beer is served from cooling cabinets behind the bar.
🏠 Q ⛺ ❀ ◖ 🍺 🔥 ♣ P

WHATFIELD

FOUR HORSESHOES
The Street ☎ (01473) 827971
11.30-3 (not Mon-Fri), 7-11; 12-3, 7-10.30 Sun
Adnams Bitter, Broadside; Greene King IPA; guest beer Ⓗ

Friendly, basic, two-bar pub of character. One room (also used as a family room) hosts war gaming on Mon eves and exhibits Napoleonic items. The main bar is L-shaped and cosy with a tiled floor, open log fire and simple furnishings. Sunday roast and other food at weekends.
🏠 ⛺ ❀ ◖ 🍺 🔥 ⚿ ♣ P

WICKHAMBROOK

GREYHOUND
Meetings Green
☎ (01440) 820548
11-3, 5.30-11; 11-11 Sat; 12-3, 7-10.30 Sun
Greene King XX Mild, IPA seasonal beers Ⓗ
Good village pub with a great atmosphere where it's very easy to get talking to people.
Q ❀ ◖ 🍺 🔥 ⚿ ♣ P 🍴

WICKHAM MARKET

GEORGE
95 High St
☎ (01728) 746306
11-3, 6-11; 12-3, 7-10.30 Sun
Tolly Cobbold Mild, Original, Old Strong, seasonal beers Ⓗ
Excellent community pub at the centre of this small town. Three drinking areas cater for all tastes: a lively area round the pool table, a quieter lounge area near the main bar and more food (lunchtime snacks) and family oriented seating in a recent extension.
🏠 ⛺ ❀ ⚿ 🔥 ⇌ ♣ P

WOODBRIDGE

KINGS HEAD
17 Market Hill ☎ (01394) 387750
11-3, 5 (6 Sat)-11; 12-3, 7-10.30 Sun
Adnams Bitter, Extra, Broadside, seasonal beers Ⓗ
One of the town's oldest buildings, dating in part back to the 13th century. Sympathetically renovated and extended by Adnams a few years ago, it is now very popular, especially eves. Good food at affordable prices. The patio overlooks the market.
🏠 Q ❀ ◖ 🍺 ⚿ ⇌ ♣ P

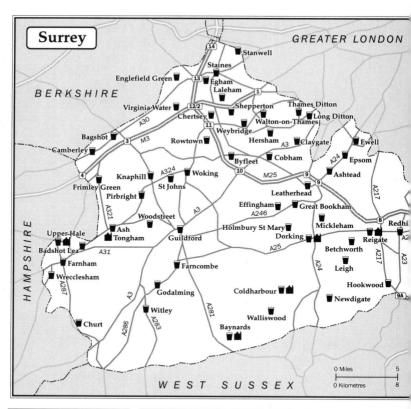

Surrey

GREATER LONDON

BERKSHIRE

HAMPSHIRE

WEST SUSSEX

Stanwell, Staines, Englefield Green, Egham, Laleham, Virginia Water, Chertsey, Shepperton, Thames Ditton, Long Ditton, Walton-on-Thames, Weybridge, Bagshot, Rowtown, Hersham, Claygate, Ewell, Camberley, Byfleet, Cobham, Epsom, Knaphill, Woking, Ashtead, Frimley Green, St Johns, Leatherhead, Pirbright, Effingham, Great Bookham, Woodstreet, Holmbury St Mary, Mickleham, Redhil, Upper-Hale, Ash, Guildford, Dorking, Reigate, Badshot Lea, Tongham, Betchworth, Farnham, Farncombe, Leigh, Wrecclesham, Godalming, Coldharbour, Hookwood, Churt, Witley, Newdigate, Walliswood, Baynards

0 Miles 5
0 Kilometres 8

ASH

DOVER ARMS
31 Guildford Road (A323)
OS901511
☎ (01252) 326025
11-3, 6-11; 12-4, 7-10.30 Sun
Beer range varies H
Roadside pub, over 200 years
old, offering a variety of real ales
with regulars from Ringwood,
Hampshire, Triple F, Sharp's and
Woodforde's. Families welcome.
Good food; extensive whisky
selection and occasional
whist eves.
🏠 ❀ ◖ ▶ ⊟ ⇌ P

ASHTEAD

BREWERY INN
15 The Street (A24)
☎ (01372) 272405
11-11; 12-10.30 Sun
**Friary Meux BB; Ind
Coope Burton Ale; King &
Barnes Sussex; Marston's
Pedigree; Tetley Bitter; guest
beer** H
Large Victorian pub on the site of
a former brewery. While the bar
area can get busy, the raised
lounge and dining area is more
sedate. Children welcome in the
dining area.
❀ ◖ ▶ ♣ P ⅟

BADSHOT LEA

CROWN INN
Pine View Close
☎ (01252) 320453
11-11; 12-3, 6.30-10.30 Sun
**Fuller's London Pride, ESB, sea-
sonal beers** H
Small village local; beware low
beams on entry. The juke box can
be a tad loud; very occasional
live music. Basic but good pub
fare (not served Mon eve).
Regular (free) Sun quiz.
❀ ◖ ▶ P

BAYNARDS

THURLOW ARMS
Off Baynards Lane OS076351
☎ (01403) 822459
11-3, 6-11; 12-10.30 Sun
**Badger Dorset Best,
Tanglefoot; Baynards Station
House Brew, Old Shunter,
Tunnel Vision; King & Barnes
Sussex; guest beer** H
Remote country brewpub next to
the long closed Baynards station.
The track is now a long distance
footpath. The interior is well dec-
orated with railway and agricul-
tural artefacts. Children welcome
in the games room. No food
Sun eve.
🏠 ⊱ ❀ ◖ ▶ ♣ P

BETCHWORTH

DOLPHIN INN
The Street (off A25)
☎ (01737) 842288
11-3, 5.30-11; 11-11 Sat;
12-10.30 Sun
**Young's Bitter, Special, Winter
Warmer, seasonal beers** H
Friendly, 16th-century village pub
with a flagstone floor and two
wood-burning inglenooks. In a
very attractive spot, it stands
opposite the village church and
the blacksmith's.
🏠 Q ❀ ◖ ▶ ♣ P

BLETCHINGLEY

WILLIAM IV
Little Common Lane (off A25)
☎ (01883) 743278
11-3, 6-11; 12-3, 7-10.30 Sun
**Adnams Bitter; Fuller's London
Pride; Harveys BB; Morland Old
Speckled Hen; Pilgrim Progress;
Young's Special** H
Fine country inn away from the
village centre. Built as two cottages in the 1850s, and unaltered
for decades, the pub consists of
two small bars which are alive
with chatter, and a rear dining
room. Outside is a secluded old
English garden.
Q ❀ ◖ ▶ ⊟ P

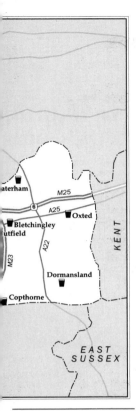

Courage Best Bitter; Marston's Pedigree; guest beer Ⓗ
Friendly local on the main road, popular with office workers at lunchtime and offering imaginative daily special dishes (no food Sun). The guest beer is usually from local micros.
🏚 ❀ 🛏 ◖ ▶ ⇌ (Blackwater) ♣ P

CATERHAM

CLIFTON ARMS
110 Chaldon Road (B2031)
☎ (01883) 343525
11-2.30, 5.30-11; 11-3, 6-11 Sat; 12-10.30 Sun
Draught Bass; Fuller's London Pride; Thwaites Daniels Hammer; guest beer Ⓗ
The main bar areas are absolutely covered with local photographs and myriad collections. The function room hosts live music Wed and Sat eve and Sun afternoon. Real cider is sold from polycasks kept in a cold cabinet. Eve meals Tue-Sat. ❀ ◖ ▶ ⌣ P

KING & QUEEN
34 High Street (B2030)
☎ (01883) 345438
11-11; 12-10.30 Sun
Fuller's Chiswick, London Pride, ESB, seasonal beers Ⓗ
400-year-old building with three distinct drinking areas and a small space at the back reserved for meals which include authentic oriental dishes. No food Sun eve.
🏚 ❀ ◖ ♣ P

CHERTSEY

COACH & HORSES
14 St Annes Road
☎ (01932) 563085
12-11; 12-3, 7-10.30 Sun
Fuller's Chiswick, London Pride, ESB, seasonal beers Ⓗ
A warm welcome awaits all who enter this tile-fronted pub. Regular quiz nights. Booking essential for accommodation. Mon lunch served, and eve meals Tue-Fri. ❀ 🛏 ▶ ♣ P

CHURT

CROSSWAYS
Churt Road (A287)
☎ (01428) 714323
11-3, 5-11; 11-11 Sat; 12-4, 7-10.30 Sun
Cheriton Best Bitter, Diggers Gold; Courage Best Bitter; Ⓗ Ringwood Fortyniner, Old Thumper; guest beers Ⓖ
Excellent, thriving village local set in good walking country. This real ale focussed free house holds an annual beer festival. The pub provides good food in a bright and comfortable environment. Not to be missed. No cider in winter.
Q ❀ ◖ 🗄 ▲ ♣ ⌣ P

CLAYGATE

GRIFFIN
58 Common Road
☎ (01372) 463799
11-11; 12-10.30 Sun
Badger Dorset Best; Fuller's London Pride; Pilgrim Surrey Bitter; guest beer Ⓗ
Traditional local with a lively public bar and an L-shaped lounge. Occasional mini-beer festivals held. Note the Mann, Crossman & Paulin windows. ❀ ◖ 🗄 P

COBHAM

PLOUGH
Plough Lane, Downside
OS107582 ☎ (01932) 862514
11-11; 12-10.30 Sun
Courage Best Bitter, Directors; guest beer Ⓗ
Parts of the pub are 450 years old. It has been a funeral parlour and a butcher's shop in its time. Some graffiti from the 1700s has been uncovered in the public bar. The French restaurant attached opens eves (not Sun). Children welcome in daytime.
🏚 ☎ ❀ ◖ ▶ 🗄 ♣ P

COLDHARBOUR

PLOUGH INN
Coldharbour Lane (Leith Hill-Dorking road) OS152441
☎ (01306) 711793
11.30-3, 6.30 (6 summer)-11; 11.30-11 Sat; 12-10.30 Sun
Adnams Broadside; Badger Dorset Best; Leith Hill Crooked Furrow, Tallywhacker; Ringwood Old Thumper; Wadworth 6X Ⓗ
Situated in good walking country near Leith Hill, this old pub can become very busy in the summer. Much of the bar area is given over to a restaurant. The tiny Leith Hill Brewery is sited in an old barn by the pub.
🏚 ❀ 🛏 ◖ ▶ ⌣ P

COPTHORNE

CHERRY TREE
Copthorne Bank
☎ (01342) 712427
11-11; 12-10.30 Sun
King & Barnes Sussex, Broadwood, Festive, seasonal beers Ⓗ
This 400-year-old pub was once a library. Extensive refurbishment in 1997 revealed an original inglenook. Eve meals Tue-Sat.
❀ ◖ ▶ P

DORKING

BUSH
10 Horsham Road (A2003, S of centre)
☎ (01306) 889830
12-2.30 (3 Sat), 6-11; 12-3, 7-10.30 Sun

BYFLEET

KINGS HEAD
59 Chertsey Rd ☎ (01932) 342671
11-11; 12-10.30 Sun
Eldridge Pope Royal Oak; Greene King IPA; Tetley Bitter; guest beer Ⓗ
Very friendly and comfortable family pub with a regularly changing guest beer. Strong darts following, and pool and large screen TV available. Weekday lunches.
☎ ❀ ◖ & ⇌ ♣ P

PLOUGH
104 High Road ☎ (01932) 353257
11-3, 5-11; 12-3, 7-10.30 Sun
Courage Best Bitter; Fuller's London Pride; guest beers Ⓗ
Superb beer enthusiasts' pub offering at least eight choices from a constantly changing array. The beer selection often includes unusual brews. The decor and atmosphere match the quality of the beer. Weekday lunches.
🏚 Q ❀ ◖ & ♣ P

CAMBERLEY

CROWN
494 London Road (A30)
☎ (01276) 684131
11-11; 12-4, 7-10.30 Sun

Brakspear Bitter; Fuller's London Pride; Thwaites Bitter; guest beer H
Good local, away from the town centre, which has house championships for marbles and conkers. There is a covered patio as well as a pleasant garden at the back. Eve meals Tue-Sat.
❀ ◖ ▶ ♣

CRICKETERS
81 South Street (A25, one-way system)
☎ (01306) 889938
12-11; 12-3, 7-10.30 Sun
Fuller's Chiswick, London Pride, ESB, seasonal beers H
Small, traditional local with bare brick walls, and a friendly atmosphere. The sheltered patio garden is extremely pleasant in summer. No food Sun.
❀ ◖

Try also: Queens Head, Horsham Rd (Fuller's)

DORMANSLAND
OLD HOUSE AT HOME
63-65 West Street
☎ (01342) 832117
12-3 (4 Sat), 6-11; 12-4, 7-10.30 Sun
Shepherd Neame Master Brew Bitter, H **Best Bitter, Spitfire, Bishop's Finger** G
On the western edge of the village, this cosy 500-year-old pub was originally a Quaker farmhouse. Good food is served both in the bar and restaurant (no eve meals winter Sun). Skittles and bagatelle played.
🚲 ❀ ◖ ▶ 🍺 ♣ P

EFFINGHAM
PLOUGH
Orestan Lane
☎ (01372) 458121
11-2.45 (3 Sat), 6-11; 12-3, 7-10.30 Sun
Young's Bitter, Special, seasonal beers H
Excellent food and beer at top Surrey prices. The single bar is always busy, especially early eve with diners. The nice, small garden has children's play equipment.
Q ❀ ◖ ▶ P ⚘

EGHAM
CROWN
38 High Street (off A30)
☎ (01784) 432608
11-3, 5.30 (6 Sat)-11; 12-3, 7-11 Sun
Adnams Bitter; Fuller's London Pride; Gale's HSB; Greene King Abbot; guest beers H
Welcoming, well-run 1930s pub with a pretty, secluded garden to the rear and benches at the

front. Interesting range of guest ales. No food Sun.
❀ ◖ 🍺 ≈ ♣ P

ENGLEFIELD GREEN
BEEHIVE
34 Middle Hill (outskirts of Egham, off A30)
☎ (01784) 431621
12-3, 5.30-11; 12-11 Sat; 12-10.30 Sun
Gale's Best Bitter, HSB; guest beers H
Friendly, popular village pub with one L-shaped bar, in a quiet residential road. Bar billiards table. Beer festivals are held over the spring and August bank holiday weekends. May stay open all day if busy.
🚲 ❀ ◖ ♣ P

EPSOM
OLDE KINGS HEAD
26 Church Street (B284)
☎ (01372) 729125
11-3; 5.30-11; 12-3.30, 7-10.30 Sun
Friary Meux BB; Fuller's London Pride; Marston's Pedigree; Young's Bitter; H
The oldest existing pub in Epsom. It has a loyal clientele. The two real fires provide a cosy atmosphere in winter, whilst summer brings a floral display. Home-cooked food with a daily special (no food Sun).
🚲 Q ❀ ◖

Try also: Rising Sun, Heathcote Rd (Charrington)

EWELL
EIGHT BELLS
78 Kingston Road (off A240)
☎ (0181) 393 9973
11-11; 12-10.30 Sun
Greene King IPA, Abbot, seasonal beers; guest beers H
Traditional Edwardian pub now converted to open-plan with a central bar area. Despite this, there is a quieter area that retains some of the snug character and includes the stone fireplace of the original neighbouring cottage. Appeals to old and young alike.
🚲 ❀ 🛏 ◖ ▶ ≈ (West) ♣ P

FARNCOMBE
CRICKETERS
37 Nightingale Road
☎ (01483) 420273
12-3, 6-11; 12-11 Sat; 12-10.30 Sun
Fuller's Chiswick, London Pride, ESB, seasonal beers H
Large, friendly pub drawing a good mix of all ages. Founded by former Surrey and England cricketer Julius Caesar. Runners-up in

Fuller's *Pub of the Year* 1997. One large room with a central bar, plus a no-smoking side room. ❀ ◖ ▶ 🚻 ≈ ♣ ⚘

Try also: Freeholders, St John St (Fuller's)

FARNHAM
DUKE OF CAMBRIDGE
East Street
☎ (01252) 716584
11-3, 5.15-11; 11-11 Fri & Sat; 12-10.30 Sun
Courage Best Bitter; Hogs Back TEA; Fuller's London Pride; guest beers H
Enterprising free house where seven handpumps have a high turnover of unusual beers. Re-opened in 1997 following substantial expansion and sympathetic renovation. Good, home-made food (not served Fri or Sun eve). Over 20 malt whiskies available; cider in summer.
🚲 ❀ 🛏 ◖ ▶ ♣ 🍺

LAMB
43 Abbey Street
☎ (01252) 714133
11-2.30, 5.30-11; 11-11 Fri & Sat; 12-10.30 Sun
Shepherd Neame Best Bitter, Spitfire, Bishops Finger, seasonal beers G
Good, friendly local between the station and the town centre which attracts a diverse clientele. A two-level garden is hidden at the back. Live music most weekends, karaoke alternate Thu (you have been warned!). Good value meals.
🚲 ❀ ◖ ▶ ♣ ⚘

QUEEN'S HEAD
9 The Borough
☎ (01252) 726524
11-11; 12-10.30 Sun
Gale's Buster, Best Bitter, HSB, seasonal beers; guest beers H
Comfortable, friendly inn dating from the 17th century. It boasts a temperature-controlled cellar and a Gale's *Cellarcraft* award. Music quiz on Thu; good mix of customers. No food Sun.
🚲 Q ❀ ◖ 🍺 ♣

WILLIAM CORBETT
4 Bridge Square, Abbey Street
☎ (01252) 726281
11-11; 12-10.30 Sun
Courage Best Bitter, Directors; Theakston Old Peculier; guest beer H
Birthplace to the eponymous social reformer and dating from the 16th century, this pub is an intriguing hotch-potch of olde-worlde, jokey kitsch and loud youth culture. Can be mobbed with younger customers at weekends, more congenial other times. ❀ ◖ ≈ ♣ P

FRIMLEY GREEN

OLD WHEATSHEAF
205 Frimley Green Road (A321)
☎ (01252) 835074
11-3, 5-11; 11-11 Fri & Sat; 12-4,
7-10.30 Sun
**Morland IPA, Original; Wells
Bombardier; guest beer** Ⓗ
100 year-old, meticulously cared
for, beamed, panelled and comfortably furnished one-bar pub.
The excellent home-cooked food,
skittle alley and covered patio
makes it attractive to all.
Q ⊛ ◖ ♣ P

GODALMING

ANCHOR
110 Ockford Road (A3100,
signed Milford from inner relief
road) ☎ (01483) 417085
12-2.30 (3 Sat), 5.30 (6 Sat)-11;
12-3, 7-10.30 Sun
**Brakspear Bitter; Flowers
Original; Gale's HSB; Badger
Tanglefoot; Hop Back Summer
Lightening; guest beers** Ⓗ
Large L-shaped bar with an array
of handpumps. Predominantly
youthful clientele in the eves.
Limited parking in street.
⊛ ◖ ≠ ♣

OLD WHARF
5 Wharf Street (High St jct)
☎ (01483) 419543
11-11; 12-10.30 Sun
**Boddingtons Bitter; Flowers IPA,
Original; Fuller's London Pride;
Marston's Pedigree; Wadworth
6X; guest beers** Ⓖ
Hogshead Alehouse: a long, single bar with a raised eating area
and food servery at the far end
(food served until 6pm).
Imaginative guest beer policy.
⚄ Q ◖ ≠ ♣ ☉

RED LION
1 Mill Lane
☎ (010483) 415207
11 (12 Sat)-3, 6.30-11; 12-3,
7-10.30 Sun
**Courage Best Bitter; Weltons
Best Bitter, Old Cocky; guest
beers** Ⓗ
Large pub comprising a quiet
lounge bar and a public bar-
come-games room in the town
centre next to the former grammar school. Imaginative guest
beer policy. Lined glasses on
request. Q ⊛ ◖ ⏛ ≠ 🛢

Try also: Sun, Bridge St
(Badge)r

GREAT BOOKHAM

ANCHOR
161 Lower Road (off A246, via
Eastwick Rd)
☎ (01372) 452429
11-3.30, 5.30-11; 12-3, 7-10.30
Sun

**Courage Best Bitter, Directors;
guest beers** Ⓗ
500-year-old local in contrast to
the surrounding suburbia.
Traditionally decorated with
exposed brickwork, oak beams
and a large inglenook. No food
Sun.
⚄ Q ⊛ ◖ ♣ P

GUILDFORD

KINGS HEAD
27 Kings Road, (A320)
☎ (01483) 568957
11-3, 5-11; 11-11 Fri & Sat;
12-10.30 Sun
**Fuller's Chiswick, London Pride,
ESB, seasonal beers** Ⓗ
Popular, multi-roomed pub featuring bare boards, an outdoor
patio and an illuminated well.
Quiz Wed eves; annual summer
beer festival. Good value food.
⚄ ⊛ ◖ ▶ ≠ (London Rd) ♣
P ⚲

SANFORD ARMS
58 Epsom Road
☎ (01483) 572551
11-2.40 (not Mon), 5.30-11;
11.30-3.10, 6-11 Sat; 12-3.40,
7-10.30 Sun
**Courage Best Bitter; guest
beer** Ⓗ
Quiet, friendly local: two wood-
panelled bars and a small conservatory. The pleasant garden
features an aviary and swings. It
has a cricket team, backgammon,
even jigsaws for the bored.
Breakfasts served on Sun from
11am.
Q ⊛ ◖ ⏛ ≠ (London Rd) ♣

HERSHAM

ROYAL GEORGE
130 Hersham Road (off A244)
☎ (01932) 220910
11-2.30, 5-11; 11-11 Sat;
12-10.30 Sun
**Young's Bitter, Special, seasonal
beers** Ⓗ
Popular, spacious, two-bar pub
with a nautical theme. The 1960s
building includes a friendly public
bar.
⚄ Q ⊛ ◖ ⏛ ♣ P

HOLMBURY ST MARY

KING'S HEAD
Pitland Street (50 yds from
B2126)
☎ (01306) 730282
11.30-3, 5.30-11; 11.30-11 Sat;
12-4, 7-10.30 Sun
**Ringwood Best Bitter,
Fortyniner, Old Thumper; guest
beers** Ⓗ
Lively local at the foot of the
wooded Holmbury Hill. The large
garden hosts summer barbecues.
Popular with ramblers, there is a
full menu (not served Sun eve).
⚄ ⊛ ◖ ▶ ♣

HOOKWOOD

BLACK HORSE
Reigate Road (A217)
☎ (01293) 773611
11-11; 12-10.30 Sun
**Badger Dorset Best, Tanglefoot
Wells Eagle, IPA** Ⓗ
Large and bright one-bar pub, a
convenient stopping off place for
Gatwick Airport.
⊛ ◖ ▶ ♣ P

KNAPHILL

GARIBALDI
136 High Street (off A322)
☎ (01483) 473374
11-11; 12-10.30 Sun
**Fuller's London Pride; Taylor
Landlord; guest beers** Ⓗ
At least two interesting guest
beers always attract the discerning drinker. Situated on crossroads at the edge of the village.
Serving excellent value lunchtime
meals, the two-bar compact interior is complemented by a quiet,
enclosed garden with children's
facilities. Q ⊛ ◖ ♣ P

ROBIN HOOD
Robin Hood Road
☎ (01483) 472173
11-11; 12-10.30 Sun
**Courage Best Bitter; guest
beers** Ⓗ
Imposing, elevated building with
a large sloping garden and children's play area overlooking
Goldworth Park. A modest yet
inviting interior divides into a
quiet drinking area contrasting
with the more lively main bar.
Two interesting guest beers generally available.
☎ ⊛ ◖ P

LALEHAM

FEATHERS
The Broadway (B377)
☎ (01784) 453561
11-11; 12-10.30 Sun
**Courage Best Bitter; Fuller's
London Pride; Morland Old
Speckled Hen; guest beers** Ⓗ
Friendly, cosy village local, five
minutes' walk from the Thames.
A 180-year-old pub, with two
adjoining drinking areas, it offers
two ever-changing guest beers
from independent breweries
(over 200 a year). Regular beer
festivals. Good food all day.
⚄ ⊛ ◖ ▶ ▲ ♣ P

LEATHERHEAD

PENNY BLACK
5 North Street
☎ (01372) 379612
11-11; 12-10.30 Sun
**Boddingtons Bitter; Brakspear
Bitter; Flowers Original; Morland
Old Speckled Hen; Wadworth
6X;** Ⓗ **guest beers** ⒽⒼ

Hogshead Alehouse which was until recently the main post office and features a postal theme, exposed brick walls and a nicotine-stained ceiling. Live music Wed eve.
🛏 Q ◖▮ ≉ ♣

RUNNING HORSE
38 Bridge Street (off B2122)
☎ (01372) 372081
11-11; 12-3, 7-10.30 Sun
Eldridge Pope Pope's Traditional; Friary Meux BB; Ind Coope Burton Ale; Marston's Pedigree; Morland Old speckled Hen; Young's Bitter H
Grade II listed Tudor two-bar pub recently saved from 'Firkinisation'. A genuine community local.
Q ❀ ◖▦ ≉ ♣ P

LEIGH
PLOUGH
Church Road
☎ (01306) 611348
11-11; 12-10.30 Sun
King & Barnes Sussex, Broadwood, Festive, seasonal beer H
Two-bar pub in an attractive village setting. The Victorian public bar houses the dart board and many unusual games; the 15th-century lounge has a separate restaurant to the rear and is popular with diners - the food is good. Q ❀ ◖▮ ♣ P

LONG DITTON
NEW INN
15 Rushett Road
☎ (0181) 224 2373
11-11; 12-11 Sun
Badger Dorset Best; Flower's Original; Marston's Pedigree; Young's Bitter; guest beers H
Friendly local in a quiet area: a large single room, a pleasant patio and garden at the rear. No food Sun or Mon. Sandwiches eves. ❀ ◖

MICKLEHAM
RUNNING HORSES
Old London Road (B2209)
☎ (01372) 372279
11.30-3, 5.30-11; 11.30-11 Sat; 12-3.30, 7-10.30 Sun
Friary Meux BB; Fuller's London Pride; King & Barnes Sussex; Morland Old Speckled Hen; Young's Bitter; guest beer H
Listed 16th-century coaching inn on the old route to London and just below Box Hill (NT). Two traditional bar areas, the main one is dominated by a large fireplace where a real fire blazes in winter. Extensive menu in the restaurant and bars. Popular with walkers.
🛏 ❀ 🛏 ◖▮ ♣ P

NEWDIGATE
SURREY OAKS
Parkgate Road, Parkgate
OS205436
☎ (01306) 631200
11.30-2.30, 5.30-11; 11.30-3, 6-11 Sat; 12-3, 7-10.30 Sun
Young's Bitter; guest beers H
Marvellous old country inn which has a justifiable reputation for the quality of its beer and food. The guest beer changes every cask and often features the esoteric. The food is home-made and usually includes Asian specials. No meals Sun eve. Lovely garden.
🛏 Q ❀ ◖▮ ▦ ♣ ⌓ P

NUTFIELD
CROWN INN
1 High Street (A25)
☎ (01737) 823240
12-3, 5-11; 12-11 Sat; 12-4, 7-10.30 Sun
Greene King IPA, Abbot H
Friendly, family-run pub, proud of its beer. Parts of the building are 400 years old. No food Sun.
🛏 ❀ ◖▮ ♣ P

OXTED
GEORGE INN
52 High Street, Old Oxted (off A25)
☎ (01883) 713453
11-11; 12-10.30 Sun
Badger IPA, Dorset Best, Tanglefoot; Boddingtons Bitter; Fuller's London Pride; Harveys BB H
500-year-old pub split into three areas, one of which is the restaurant. It enjoys a good reputation for food.
🛏 Q ❀ ◖▮ P

OXTED INN
Units 1-4, Station Road West
☎ (01883) 723440
11-11; 12-10.30 Sun
Courage Directors; Shepherd Neame Spitfire; Theakston Best Bitter; guest beers H
Wetherspoons pub built on a builder's merchants next to the station. Former resident, John Harrison, inventor of the chronometer, is remembered by various clocks. Food is served all day and there are two changing guest beers.
Q ◖▮ ♿ ≉ ⌓ ⌿ 🍴

PIRBRIGHT
ROYAL OAK
Aldershot Road (A324)
☎ (01483) 232466
11-11; 12-10.30 Sun
Boddingtons Bitter; Flowers Original; Marston's Pedigree; guest beers H
Delightful rural escape from the adjoining built-up areas; a

picturesque pub with a large garden and stream. The olde-worlde interior has low ceilings and three bar areas. Up to four interesting guest beers.
Q 🛏 🐕 ◖▮ P

REDHILL
GARLAND
5 Brighton Road (A23)
☎ (01737) 760377
11-11; 12-10.30 Sun
Harveys XX Mild, Sussex Pale Ale, BB, Armada, seasonal beer H
Local built in 1865; the decor features a large number of clowns. Darts is popular. No food Sun.
🛏 🐕 ❀ ◖≉ ♣ P

HOME COTTAGE
3 Redstone Hill (A25, behind station)
☎ (01737) 762771
10.30-11; 12-10.30 Sun
Young's Bitter, Special, seasonal beers H
Imposing Victorian pub: only one bar, but with distinct public and lounge areas, the former possessing a wonderful old set of handpumps. Note, too, the five etched glass windows. Children welcome in the conservatory. No food Sun eve.
🛏 🐕 ❀ ◖▮ ≉ ♣ P

Try also: White Lion, Linkfield St (Greene King)

REIGATE
NUTLEY HALL
8 Nutley Lane (behind car park on one-way road at W end of town)
☎ (01737) 241741
11-11; 12-10.30 Sun
King & Barnes Sussex, Broadwood, Old, Festive, seasonal beers H
Busy drinkers' pub with a quieter rear bar. Various teams make this a great social pub.
🛏 Q 🐕 ❀ ◖≉ ♣ P

PRINCE OF WALES
2 Holmesdale Road
☎ (01737) 243112
11-11; 12-10.30 Sun
Shepherd Neame Master Brew Bitter, Best Bitter, Spitfire; Bishops Finger H
Varied mix of customers in a friendly back-street local by the station. ❀ 🛏 ◖≉ ♣ P

ROWTOWN
CRICKETERS
32 Rowtown
☎ (01932) 842808
11-11; 12-10.30 Sun
Courage Best Bitter; Wadworth 6X; guest beer H
1860s pub where pictures of old

cricketers and old photos of nearby Addlestone adorn the walls. The bar area is capacious and open plan. A varied menu includes daily specials; food served 12-10. An inn sign is situated half a mile away on the village green.
❀ ◖▶ ㅤ ♣ P

ST JOHNS

ROWBARGE
St Johns Road
☎ (01483) 761618
11-11; 12-3, 7-10.30 Sun
Greene King Abbot; Tetley Bitter; guest beers Ⓗ
Small, attractive pub, set back from the main road and easily missed. A large enclosed garden backs on to the Basingstoke Canal. Two interesting guest beers generally available. No food Sun eve.
❀ ◖▶ P

SHEPPERTON

BARLEY MOW
67 Watersplash Road, Shepperton Green (off B376, at crossroads by the Bull)
OS073682
☎ (01932) 225580
11-11; 12-10.30 Sun
Adnams Broadside;Ⓖ **Courage Best Bitter, Directors; Theakston Best Bitter; Young's Special;** Ⓗ **guest beers** Ⓖ
Popular, single-bar pub with several drinking areas close to Shepperton Studios. Busy at weekends, and used regularly by members of the local football team. The food is highly recommended.
🏨 ❀ 🍴 ◖▶ ♣ P ✄

THREE HORSESHOES
131 High Street
☎ (01932) 225726
11-11 Fri & Sat; 12-10.30 Sun
Courage Best Bitter, Directors; guest beer Ⓗ
Friendly, one-bar pub near the town centre, a genuine local where the emphasis is on conversation.
🏨 Q ❀ 🍴 ⇌ ♣ P

STAINES

ANGEL HOTEL
24 High Street
☎ (01784) 452509
11-11; 12-10.30 Sun
Courage Best Bitter; guest beers Ⓗ
Welcoming town inn with its origins in the 14th century. Excellent range of guest beers from independent brewers; one is always offered as a bargain beer. Home-cooked food a speciality.
Q ❀ 🍴 ◖▶ ㅤ ⇌ P ✄

BELLS
124 Church Street
☎ (01784) 454240
11-11; 12-10.30 Sun
Young's Bitter, Special, seasonal beers Ⓗ
Popular, friendly 18th-century pub in a quiet part of town, a stone's throw from the river. Strong sporting ties - the pub supports football, golf and cricket teams. Always a good choice of tasty meals. Q ❀ 🍴 ▶ ㅤ ♣

GEORGE
2 High Street
☎ (01784) 462181
11-11; 12-10.30 Sun
Courage Directors; Fuller's London Pride; Theakston Best Bitter; Younger Scotch; guest beers Ⓗ
Sizeable Wetherspoons pub on two levels, with up to four guest beers on offer. The name is a reminder of a previous inn on the same site 200 years ago.
Q ◖▶ ㅤ ⇌ ⌓ ✄ 🗓

STANWELL

WHEATSHEAF
Town Lane
☎ (01784) 253372
11-11; 11-4, 7-11 Sat; 12-4, 7-10.30 Sun
Courage Best Bitter, Directors; Marston's Pedigree; Morland Old Speckled Hen Ⓗ
Village local, serving good food until 9pm on weekdays. Quiet background music played.
❀ ◖▶ ♣ P

THAMES DITTON

ANGEL
Angel Road (off A307)
☎ (0181) 224 4700
11-11; 12-10.30 Sun
Courage Best Bitter, Directors; Young's Bitter, Special Ⓗ
Friendly pub popular with locals. The no-smoking 'Alice in Wonderland' cocktail bar upstairs is open Fri and Sat eves; the 'Animal Farm' theme barn restaurant Thu-Sat eves. The beer range is expected to change.
🏨 Q ❀ ◖▶ ♣ P ✄

UPPER HALE

BALL & WICKET
104 Upper Hale Road
☎ (01252) 735278
4 (12 Sat)-11; 12-3, 7-10.30 Sun
B&T Dragon Slayer, Hale & Hearty, Upper Ale, Wicket Bitter, seasonal beers; Wadworth 6X Ⓗ
Cosy brewpub with abundant wood, brass and old beer bottles. Handy for the village cricket green opposite. Attracts drinkers from far and wide but retains local character. 🏨 ❀ P

BLACK PRINCE
147 Upper Hale Road
☎ (01252) 714530
12-11; 12-10.30 Sun
Fuller's Chiswick, London Pride Ⓗ
Pub has two contrasting bars - a quiet saloon bar for conversation and a larger public bar (with a pool room) where TV has to compete with a lively atmosphere. Meals served all day Tue-Sun. Lined glasses on request.
🏨 Q ❀ P 🗓

VIRGINIA WATER

ROSE & OLIVE BRANCH
Callow Hill (N of Hollow Lane)
OS993689
☎ (01344) 843713
11-3, 5.30-11; 12-3, 7-10.30 Sun
Morland Old Speckled Hen; Ruddles Best Bitter, County; Wells Bombardier Ⓗ
Cosy, slightly upmarket pub, out of the way but worth the effort, with outstanding food. Its name refers to a Civil War treaty - the Cavaliers gave a rose and the Roundheads an olive branch.
Q ❀ ◖▶ P

WALLISWOOD

SCARLETT ARMS
Walliswood Road OS119382
☎ (01306) 627243
11-2.30, 5.30-11; 12-3, 7-10.30 Sun
King & Barnes Mild, Sussex, Broadwood, Festive, seasonal beers Ⓗ
Charming old pub which dates from 1620, when it was built as two cottages. It became a pub in 1907. The main bar area includes a stone-flagged floor and a large inglenook. The food is good.
🏨 ❀ ◖▶ P

WALTON-ON-THAMES

REGENT
19 Church Street (A3050, opp Safeway) ☎ (01932) 243980
11-11; 12-10.30 Sun
Courage Directors; Fuller's London Pride; Theakston Best Bitter; guest beers Ⓗ
Refurbished former cinema, popular with all ages. No piped music; decor reflects local associations with the film industry. Food served 11-10 (12-9.30 Sun).
◖▶ ✄ 🗓

WEYBRIDGE

JOLLY FARMER
41 Princes Road (off A317)
☎ (01932) 856873
10.30-3, 5-11; 10.30-11 Sat; 12-3, 7-10.30 Sun
Courage Best Bitter; Fuller's London Pride; Hop Back Crop Circle, Entire Stout, Summer Lightning Ⓗ

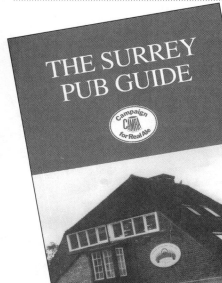

THE SURREY PUB GUIDE

The Surrey Pub Guide is available from CAMRA, price £4.95.

Comfortable, friendly back-street local with a low, beamed ceiling and an L-shaped bar surrounded by bench seats, with plastered walls and black beams.
❀ ◖ ♣ P

WITLEY

WHITE HART
Petworth Road (A283, opp church)
☎ (01428) 683695
11-2.30, 5.30-11; 11-11 Sat; 12-3, 7-10.30 (12-10.30 summer) Sun
Shepherd Neame Master Brew Bitter, Spitfire, seasonal beers Ⓗ
Picturesque black and white timber-beamed pub dating from the 14th-century and reputedly haunted. Friendly atmosphere, but mind your head on the low beams. The restaurant has wheelchair access.
🚗 ❀ ◖ ▶ ⌂ ♣ P

WOKING

WETHERSPOONS
51-57 Chertsey Road
☎ (01483) 722818
11-11; 12-10.30 Sun
Courage Directors; Hogs Back TEA; Theakston Best Bitter; Younger Scotch; guest beers Ⓗ
Deservedly popular, and often crowded pub, serving an excellent range of guest ales (especially during the regular beer festivals). Friendly and efficiently run, it attracts a range of clientele. Difficult to imagine the town centre without it now.
Q ◖ ▶ ♿ ≠ ⌂ ✗ ⊟

WOODSTREET VILLAGE

Hogs Back Brewery · Tongham · Surrey · Independent Brewery · Fine English Ales

ROYAL OAK
89 Oak Hill OS958510
☎ (01483) 235137
11.30 (3.30 Sat), 5-11; 12-3.30, 7-10.30 Sun
Courage Best Bitter; Hogs Back TEA; guest beers Ⓗ
Superb free house run by a landlord who is one in a million. Four

Try also:
Star, Wheeler St (Allied)

regularly changing guest beers, one always a mild. Excellent home-cooked lunches (not served Sun). Large, attractive garden; interesting mural in gent's toilet (outside). ❀ ◖ ♣ P

WRECCLESHAM

BAT & BALL
Bat & Ball Lane, Boundstone (off Upper Bourne Lane via Sandrock Hill) OS834444
☎ (01252) 794564
12-11; 12-10.30 Sun
Brakspear Bitter; Fuller's London Pride; Young's Special; guest beers Ⓗ
A family room at the front with TV showing sporting events leads to a traditional cosy bar, with unusual guest ales. The approach to the pub is along unsurfaced tracks or paths. Good baltis (no food Sun eve).
🚗 ❀ ◖ ▶ ♣ ⌂ P

SANDROCK
Sandrock Hill Road, Upper Bourne (off B3384, between Wrecclesham and Rowledge) OS830444
☎ (01252) 715865
11-11; 12-10.30 Sun
Batham Best Bitter; Brakspear Bitter; Enville Nailmaker Mild; guest beers Ⓗ
Long famous for the quality and range of its beers, this free house continues to impress. The pub is simple but comfortable, attracting a cross-section of locals and many beer-hunting visitors. Free minibus from Farnham by arrangement. No food Sun.
🚗 Q ❀ ◖ ♣ P

INDEPENDENT BREWERIES

Baynards:
Rudgwick
Hale & Hearty:
Farnham
Hogs Back:
Tongham
Leith Hill:
Dorking
Pilgrim:
Reigate
Weltons:
Dorking

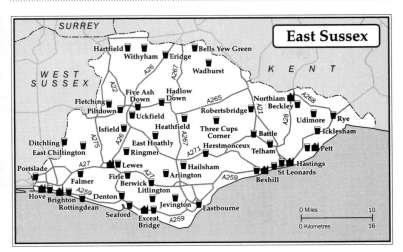

East Sussex

EAST SUSSEX

ARLINGTON

OLD OAK INN
Cane Heath (Hailsham Road)
OS558078
☎ (01323) 482072
11-3, 6-11; 12-3, 7-10.30 Sun
**Badger Dorset Best; Harveys BB;
guest beers** G
Cosy country pub, out in the
sticks by Abbots Wood nature
reserve which ensures a ready
supply of logs for the open fires.
All beers come straight from the
cask. Good food is served in the
restaurant or lounge bar.
🏚 Q ❀ ◖ ▶ ᵵ P

BATTLE

1066
High Street
☎ (01424) 773224
11-11; 12-3, 7-10.30 Sun
**Flowers Original; Fuller's
London Pride; Harveys BB; guest
beers** H
Large, lively town pub which is
friendly and welcoming. An added
attraction is Oscar the cockatoo.
🏚 ❀ ◖ ▶ ♣ P

Try also: King's Head, Mount St
(Courage)

BECKLEY

ROSE & CROWN
Northiam Road (B2188/B2165
jct)
☎ (01797) 252161
12-3, 5.30-11; 11-11 Fri & Sat;
11-10.30 Sun
**Black Sheep Best Bitter; Harveys
BB; guest beers** H
Spacious, welcoming, family pub,
affording fine views from the garden. Beers from distant breweries are always available; excellent food.🏚 Q ❀ ◖ ▶ ᵵ ♣ P

BELLS YEW GREEN

BRECKNOCK ARMS
300 yds from station
☎ (01892) 750237
11-3, 5.30-11; 12-3, 7-10.30 Sun
**Harveys Pale Ale, BB, seasonal
beers** H
Thriving village local in a small
hamlet. Eve meals Sun and Mon.
🏚 Q ⚲ ❀ ◖ ▶ ≢ ♣ P

BERWICK

CRICKETERS ARMS ☆
Off A27, W of Drusilla's roundabout
☎ (01323) 870469
11-3, 6-11 (11-11 summer Sat);
12-3, 6.30-10.30 Sun
**Harveys Pale Ale, BB, seasonal
beers** G
A long-standing entry in this
Guide and well deserved. Careful
modifications to this pub have
not spoilt its rare qualities of old
cottage charm. Peaceful, except
in high summer when it can get
very busy. Excellent gardens for
families.
🏚 Q ⚲ ❀ ◖ ▶ ♣ P

BEXHILL

ROSE & CROWN
158 Turkey Road
☎ (01424) 214625
11-3, 5.30-11; 12-3, 7-10.30 Sun
**Beards Best Bitter; Harveys BB;
guest beers** H
1930s Beards house, spacious
and comfortable, well worth finding. There are always four guest
ales on offer with an ever-changing range.
❀ ◖ ▶ ᵵ ▲ ♣ P ⌿

BRIGHTON

BASKETMAKERS ARMS
12 Gloucester Road
☎ (01273) 689006

Mon & Tues 11-3, 5.30 (5 Wed &
Thu)-11; 11-11 Fri & Sat; 12-
10.30 Sun
**Gale's Butser, Best Bitter, IPA,
HSB, Festival Mild, seasonal
beers; guest beers** H
Popular street-corner local displaying an interesting collection
of tins. Excellent menu; Sunday
roasts include a vegetarian
option. Eve meals Mon-Fri until
8.30. Winner of many Gale's *Best
Cellar* awards. One guest beer
comes from Gale's Beer Club.
◖ ▶ ≢

COBBLER'S THUMB
10 New England Road (near
A23/A270 jct, Preston Circus)
☎ (01273) 605636
11-11; 12-10.30 Sun
**Badger Tanglefoot; Harveys BB,
seasonal beers; Marston's
Pedigree; guest beers** H
Unspoilt, one-bar, two-roomed
corner local popular with all
ages. One room is used for pool.
Following a threat of closure,
there have been no internal
changes and the original fittings
remain. Note the recreation of
the original cobbler's workshop.
Good value food.
🏚 ❀ ◖ ≢ ♣

CONSTANT SERVICE
96 Islingword Road
☎ (01273) 607058
12-11; 12-10.30 Sun
**Harveys XX Mild, Pale Ale, BB,
Armada, seasonal beers** H
Unusually shaped pub, featuring
disused equipment from the adjacent reservoir which, being high
on a hillside, was able to offer a
'constant service' to the local
water supply. 🏚 ❀ ♣

DOVER CASTLE
43 Southover Street
☎ (01273) 889808
11-11; 11-3, 7-10.30 Sun

Shepherd Neame Master Brew Bitter, Best Bitter, Bishops Finger, seasonal beers ⓗ
Established corner local which offers a warm welcome to young and old. All sorts of pub games are to be found and the pub runs its own rambling society. ♣ 冚

EVENING STAR
55-56 Surrey Street (near station) ☎ (01273) 328931
12 (11 Sat)-11; 12-10.30 Sun
Dark Star Skinner's Pale Ale, Skinner's Golden Gate Bitter, Dark Star, seasonal beers; guest beers ⓗ
Home of the Dark Star Brewery, Brighton's permanent real ale festival, it features nine pumps dispensing an ever-changing range of in-house and rare guest beers; over 2,500 since March 1992. Occasional theme nights with live music. No food Sun.
❀ ◖ ⇌ ⌂ 冚

GREYS
105 Southover Street
☎ (01273) 680734
11-3, 5.30-11; 11-11 Sat;
12-10.30 Sun
Adnams Bitter; Flowers Original; guest beers ⓗ
Compact, popular corner pub offering a range of Belgian beers and an enterprising menu to complement them. Live music some eves. Eve meals Tue-Thu, no food Sun. ❀

HAND IN HAND
33 Upper St James's Street
☎ (01273) 602521
11-11; 12-10.30 Sun
Kemptown Brighton Bitter, Bitter, Olde Trout, SID, Old Grumpy; guest beers ⓗ
Compact home of Kemptown Brewery with unusual decor: the walls are covered with extracts from old newspapers and historic local pictures, whilst ties adorn the ceiling. ◖

PARK CRESCENT
39 Park Crescent Terrace
☎ (01273) 604993
3 (11 Sat)-11; 12-10.30 Sun
King & Barnes Sussex, Broadwood, seasonal beers ⓗ
Cosmopolitan atmosphere, popular with students. A wide ranging menu offers vegetarian options (no food Sun eve). Coffee and newspapers available. One of only three King & Barnes pubs in the area. ❀ ▶ ⌂

PRESTONVILLE
64 Hamilton Road
☎ (01273) 701007
5 (4 Fri, 11 Sat and summer)-11;
12-10.30 Sun
Gale's Butser, Best Bitter, IPA, HSB, seasonal beers; guest beers ⓗ

Unusual shaped pub hidden away in a residential area. Free from electronic games and pool, it offers good food (weekday eves, weekend lunches) in a comfortable atmosphere. Sister pub to the Basketmakers; worth the walk between the two. Guest ale comes from Gale's Beer Club.
❀ ◖ ▶

PRINCE ARTHUR
38 Dean Street
☎ (01273) 203472
12-11; 12-10.30 Sun
Draught Bass; Flowers Original; Fuller's London Pride; Gale's HSB; Harveys BB; guest beer ⓗ
Handy for the main shopping area, this unspoilt pub with no TV, darts or pool table, retains a warm welcome for visitors and locals alike. A single, wood-panelled bar with a small conservatory at the rear which accommodates children until 7pm. No food Sun.
Q ⇲ ❀ ◖

SIR CHARLES NAPIER
50 Southover Street
☎ (01273) 601413
4 (12 Fri & Sat)-11; 12-10.30 Sun
Gale's Butser, IPA, HSB; guest beer ⓗ
Now in its 17th year in this *Guide*, this Victorian-style pub is packed with local memorabilia. The small sheltered garden features a George V pillar-box. A yearly beer festival with up to 10 beers, is a recent innovation. Lunches Fri-Sun.
❀ ◖ ▶

SIR LOYNE OF BEEFE
63 Sussex Street
☎ (01273) 380580
12-11; 12-5, 7.30-10.30 Sun
Beer range varies ⓗ
Set high on a hill to the east of the town centre the 'SLOB' offers a panoramic view over the centre of Brighton. The SLOB Ale is usually John Smith's Bitter. Very competitive prices.
❀ ♣

SUSSEX YEOMAN
7 Guildford Road (near station)
☎ (01273) 327985
11-3, 5-11; 11-11 Sat; 12-10.30 Sun
Bateman XB; Harveys BB, seasonal beers; Hop Back Summer Lightning; guest beers ⓗ
Friendly, comfortable, popular single-bar corner pub. A selection of eight ales is served, plus 40 speciality sausages, including six vegetarian varieties; monthly curry nights. no food Sun eve. Occasional cider.
Q ◖ ▶ ⇌ ⌂

DENTON

FLYING FISH
42 Denton Road (off Avis Rd from Denton Corner/A26)
☎ (01273) 515440
11-3, 6 (5.30 Fri)-11; 12-3, 7-10.30 Sun
Shepherd Neame Best Bitter, Spitfire, Bishops Finger ⓗ
Converted a long time ago from a 16th-century barn, it retains its rural ambience. Very popular with walkers (and local schoolteachers Fri lunchtime). Beware! in bad weather it can be flooded. No food Sun, or Mon eve.
㋿ Q ❀ ◖ ▶ ⊞ ☗ ♣ P

DITCHLING

WHITE HORSE
16 West Street
☎ (01273) 842006
11-11; 12-10.30 Sun
Harveys BB; guest beers ⓗ
Friendly, single-bar pub near the foot of the South Downs. It stands opposite the village church, close to Anne of Cleves' house. The cellar is said to be haunted. ㋿ ❀ ◖ ▶

EAST CHILTINGTON

JOLLY SPORTSMAN
Chapel Lane (off B2116)
OS372153
☎ (01273) 890400
11-3 (not Mon), 6-11; 12-3, 7-10.30 Sun
Courage Best Bitter; King & Barnes Sussex; guest beer ⓗ
Isolated, small, friendly pub that is also a polling station and a general village community centre. Popular with ramblers. The garden offers good views of the Sussex Weald. Pub games and dining areas are separate from the bar area. Lunches Wed-Sun, eve meals Mon-Sat.
❀ ◖ ♣ P

EAST HOATHLY

KINGS HEAD
1-3 High Street (off A22)
☎ (01825) 840238
11-3, 6 (4.30 Sat)-11; 12-4, 7-10.30 Sun
Badger Dorset Best; Harveys BB; guest beers ⓗ
Although now bypassed, this big village pub still keeps busy for food and ale. Frequented by village football and rugby teams, although it is big enough for quiet corners to be found.
㋿ Q ❀ ◖ ▶ ⊞ ☗ ♣ P

EASTBOURNE

HURST ARMS
76 Willingdon Road (A22, 1½ miles N of centre)
☎ (01323) 721762

11-11; 12-10.30 Sun
Harveys BB, Armada, seasonal beers Ⓗ
In this *Guide* since 1978, a lively local. Music, TV and games in the large public bar: the lounge bar is quieter. ❀

LAMB INN
High Street, Old Town (A259, 1 mile W of centre)
☎ (01323) 720545
10.30-3, 5.30-11; 10.30-11 Fri & Sat; 12-4, 7-10.30 Sun
Harveys XX Mild, Pale Ale, BB, Armada, seasonal beers Ⓗ
Popular pub with parts dating back to 1290. Three rooms with two bars in an attractive, beamed building with a (now closed) passage from the cellar to the nearby church. Good food selection. Pavement drinking area.
Q ❀ ◖ ◗ ≠

TERMINUS
153 Terminus Road (½ mile from station)
☎ (01323) 733964
11-11; 12-10.30 Sun
Harveys BB, Armada, seasonal beers Ⓗ
Old-fashioned town pub, used by shoppers and students. Pavement drinking area.
❀ ◖ ◗ ≠

ERIDGE

HUNTSMAN
Eridge Road (by station, off A26)
☎ (01892) 864258
11.30-3, 6 (5.30 summer)-11; 12-3, 7-10.30 (12-4, 6-11 summer) Sun
King & Barnes Mild, Sussex, Broadwood, Festive, seasonal beers Ⓗ
Friendly, two-bar pub in a rural location, popular with walkers and climbers, offering traditional pub fare and American (New England-style) selections. Eve meals Tue-Sat. Riverside garden. King & Barnes bottle-conditioned beers available.
Q ❀ ◖ ◗ ▲ ≠ ♣ ⌓ P

EXCEAT BRIDGE

GOLDEN GALLEON
Off A259 (2 miles E of Seaford)
☎ (01323) 892247
11-11, 12-10.30 (5 winter) Sun
Cuckmere Haven Best Bitter, Saxon King, Guv'nor, Golden Peace; Greene King IPA; Harveys Armada; guest beers Ⓗ
Home of the Cuckmere Haven brewery. Enjoying fantastic views, it stands on the Round Britain Walk, South Downs Way and Vanguard Trail. Good selection of ciders; strong emphasis on food and up to ten beers.
⛫ Q ♘ ❀ ◖ ◗ ⌓ P ⊬

FALMER

SWAN
Middle Street, North Falmer
☎ (01273) 681842
11-2.30, 6-11; 12-3, 7-10.30 Sun
Gale's Best Bitter, HSB, Festival Mild; Gibbs Mew Bishop's Tipple; Palmers IPA, 200 Ⓗ
Three-bar village local (two no-smoking). Note the model train set in the middle bar and historic breweriana, in particular the sheep shearers' regulations from 1828. The pub has been in the same family since 1903.
⛫ Q ❀ ◖ ⊟ ≠ ⊬

FIRLE

RAM
Off A27 ☎ (01273) 858222
11.30-3, 7-11; 11.30-11 Sat; 12-10.30 Sun
Harveys BB; Otter Bitter; guest beers Ⓗ
Three-bar local nestled in the South Downs. Pictures of historic Firle adorn the walls. Good pub food and generally four beers on offer. Fine flint-walled garden; log fire in the snug. Handy for Charleston, country home of the Bloomsbury set. ⛫ Q ❀ ◖ ◗

FIVE ASH DOWN

FIREMANS ARMS
On A272, 1 mile E of Maresfield
☎ (01825) 732191
11.30-3, 6-11; 11-11 Sat; 11-3, 6.30-10.30 Sun
Greene King IPA; Harveys BB; guest beers Ⓗ
Family-run local with a wide range of bar food. Annual traction engine rally, Jan 1st. The landlord is a steam railway enthusiast. No food Tue eve.
⛫ ❀ 🛏 ◖ ◗ ⊟ ▲ ♣ ⌓ P ⊓

FLETCHING

GRIFFIN
High Street (N of A272, W of Maresfield) ☎ (01825) 722890
12-3, 6-11; 12-10.30 (may vary) Sun
Badger Tanglefoot; Ballard's Best Bitter; Harveys BB; guest beers Ⓗ
15th-century inn with bar food and a restaurant. Basic public bar. ⛫ ❀ 🛏 ◖ ◗ ♣ P

HADLOW DOWN

NEW INN
Main Road ☎ (01825) 830939
12-3 (not Thu), 7-11; 12-10.30 Sun
Harveys Pale Ale, seasonal beers Ⓗ
Classic, virtually unspoilt village local. Fairly basic, with usually three beers on tap.
⛫ Q ♘ ❀ ♣ P

Try also: Blackboys, Blackboys (Harvey's)

HAILSHAM

BRICKLAYERS ARMS
Ersham Road (South Rd jct)
☎ (01323) 841587
11-3, 5 (6 Sat)-11; 12-3, 7-10.30 Sun
Bateman XB; guest beer Ⓖ
Friendly local with an intimate saloon and a popular public bar, situated at a busy road junction. Varying guest beers from the local branch of the Beer Seller, always served direct from the cask. ❀ ◖ ⊟ ♣

GRENADIER
High Street ☎ (01323) 842152
11-11; 12-3, 7-10.30 Sun
Harveys XX Mild, BB, Old, Armada, seasonal beers Ⓗ
Popular, two-bar town pub, in the same family for over 40 years. An imposing building with a well renovated interior; spot the original gas lamp fittings. Close to the Cuckoo Trail foot and cycle path.
❀ ◖ ⊟ ♿ ♣

HARTFIELD

ANCHOR
Church Street ☎ (01892) 770424
11-11; 12-10.30 Sun
Flowers IPA; Original; Fuller's London Pride; Harveys BB; Wadworth 6X Ⓗ
Easily found at night but not so easy in daylight, this gem is hidden just behind the main village street. A good local with an unusual veranda overlooking a side street, Aussie-style.
⛫ Q ❀ 🛏 ◖ ◗ ♿ ♣ P ⊓

HASTINGS

CARLISLE
24 Pelham Place (seafront)
☎ (01424) 420193
11-11; 12-10.30 Sun
Old Forge Brothers Best, Pett Progress; guest beer (occasional) Ⓗ
Busy, loud, bikers'-type pub with three bars. Live music weekends. Handy for the town centre shops.
♘ ♿ ≠ ♣

FIRST IN LAST OUT
14 High Street, Old Town
☎ (01424) 425079
11-11. 12-11 Sun
FILO Crofters, Cardinal; guest beers Ⓗ
Brewpub, nestling in the picturesque old town, featuring alcove seating and a central fireplace. Busy weekends; mini beer festivals most bank hols.
⛫ Q ❀ ◖ ♿ ▲ P

QUEEN ADELAIDE
20 West Street, Old Town (opp boating lake) ☎ (01424) 430862
10-11; 12-10.30 Sun
Greene King Abbot; Rother Valley Lighterman; guest beer Ⓗ

Attractive, two-bar old town inn, popular with local fishermen, serving the town for over 100 years. Singalong with the piano Sun: live music Sat (seasonal). A real drinking pub. Old Forge brews the house beer. ♣

HEATHFIELD

PRINCE OF WALES
Station Road (B2203, E of centre)
☎ (01435) 862919
11-3, 5-11; 11-11 Sat; 12-10.30 Sun
Brewery on Sea Rain Dance; Greene King Abbot; Harveys BB; guest beer Ⓗ
Popular, busy local, featuring a good value carvery restaurant as well as a saloon and public bars. Close to the Cuckoo Trail foot and cycle path. ♨ ❀ ◐ ◑ 🏠 ♿ ♣ P

HERSTMONCEUX

BREWERS ARMS
Gardner Street (A271)
☎ (01323) 832226
11-2.30, 6-11; 12-3, 7-10.30 Sun
Harveys BB; guest beers Ⓗ Ⓖ
A local CAMRA *Pub of the Year* 1996. The choice of beers can be exceptional with up to seven on at any one time. The food's good too (not served Tue) with theme nights in winter.
♨ Q ❀ ◐ ◑ ♿ ♣ P

WELCOME STRANGER
Chapel Row (200 yds S of A271)
☎ (01323) 832119
12-2.30 (not Mon-Fri), 7-11; 12-3, 7-10.30 Sun
Harveys BB, Old; guest beer (occasional) Ⓗ
Small, unspoilt, country ale house, the last in Sussex to obtain a full licence: known locally as the 'Kicking Donkey' and in the same family for 90 years. Beer is served through a hatch into a simple bar room. Worth finding - but open eves only Mon-Fri. ♨ Q ❀ ♣ P ⬚

HOVE

ECLIPSE
33 Montgomery Street
☎ (01273) 272212
11-3, 6-11; 11-11 Sat; 12-4, 7-10.30 Sun
Harveys XX Mild, Pale Ale, BB, Old, seasonal beers Ⓗ
Formerly a Charrington house, this pub has been well restored into a comfortable local. Note the painted mouldings on the exterior - this pub has a connection with the turf. Eve meals Tue-Sat.
♨ ❀ ◐ ◑ 🏠 ♿ ⇌ ♣

FARM TAVERN
13 Farm Road (near Palmeira Square)
☎ (01273) 325902
11.30-11; 12-10.30 Sun

Bateman XB; Beards Best Bitter; Harveys BB; guest beers Ⓗ
True back-street local - small, cosy and well worth finding. Note the impressive coat of arms above the fireplace. Good food.
◐ ♣ ⬚

ICKLESHAM

QUEENS HEAD
Parsonage Lane (off A259)
☎ (01424) 814552
11-11; 12-5, 7-10.30 Sun
Beer range varies Ⓗ
Warm, friendly, tile-hung country pub boasting superb views and a grand mahogany bar. Up to six beers available. Sussex CAMRA *Pub of the Year* 1998. ♨ Q ❀ ◐ ▶ ♿ ⏝ P ⬚

ISFIELD

LAUGHING FISH
Station Road (¹/₂ mile W of A26, 2 miles S of Uckfield)
☎ (01825) 750349
11.30-3, 6-11; 11-11 Sat; 12-4, 7-10.30 (12-10.30 summer) Sun
Beards Best Bitter; Harveys Pale Ale, BB; Thwaites Best Mild; guest beer Ⓗ
Busy village local near Bentley Wildfowl Park and the Lavender Line. The cellar is cooled by a running stream. The front porch was once rebuilt by the Canadian army! Meals Tue-Sat. The no-smoking area is the family room.
♨ 🚲 ❀ ◐ ♣ P ✂

JEVINGTON

EIGHT BELLS
High Street ☎ (01323) 484442
11-3, 6-11; 12-3, 7-10.30 Sun
Adnams Bitter, Broadside; Courage Best Bitter; Harveys BB; Rother Valley Level Best; Shepherd Neame Best Bitter Ⓗ
Genuine village community centre run by the same landlord for over 30 years. Two bars with tiled or wooden floors. You can purchase fresh veg here, as well as bar snacks. A welcome return to the *Guide*. Q ❀ ♣ P

LEWES

BLACK HORSE
55 Western Rd ☎ (01273) 473653
11-2.30, 5.30 (6 Sat)-11; 12-2.30, 7-10.30 Sun
Beards Best Bitter; Brakspear Special; Harveys BB, seasonal beers; guest beers Ⓗ
This former coaching inn, now a Beards pub, features two contrasting bars: the public has a fascinating collection of old photographs and a CAMRA mirror, the smaller lounge is a quiet oasis of calm. Games include the Sussex game Toad in the Hole.
♨ Q ❀ 🚲 ◐ 🏠 ♣

BREWERS ARMS
91 High Street
☎ (01273) 479475
10.30-11; 12-10.30 Sun
Harveys BB, seasonal beers; guest beers Ⓗ
Comfortable local with a games bar frequented by young people. This site has been a pub since 1540; see the list of landlords since 1744. Children's certificate. Varied cider in summer.
Q 🚲 ◐ ⇌ ♣ ⏝

DORSET ARMS
22 Malling Street (near Harveys Brewery) ☎ (01273) 477110
11-3, 6-11; 12-4, 7-10.30 Sun
Harveys Pale Ale, BB, Armada, seasonal beers Ⓗ
Comfortable, two-bar pub with a restaurant and no-smoking family room. The Harveys' brewery tap. Eve meals Tue-Sat.
♨ Q 🚲 ❀ ◐ ⇌ P ✂

ELEPHANT & CASTLE
White Hill (A2029, near the police station)
☎ (01273) 473797
11.30-11; 12-10.30 Sun
Harvey's BB, seasonal beers; Morland Old Speckled Hen; guest beers Ⓗ
Boisterous and friendly, this is a two-bar pub with many other rooms including one for table football. This rugby-loving pub has its own team. A traditional bonfire society is also based here. ♨ 🚲 ◐ ⇌ ♣

GARDENERS ARMS
46 Cliffe High Street (near Harveys Brewery)
☎ (01273) 474808
11-11; 12-4, 7-10.30 Sun
Harveys BB, guest beers Ⓗ
Friendly, two-bar free house, sister pub of Brighton's Evening Star. Dark Star/Skinner's beers feature in a constantly changing selection. ⇌ ⏝ ⬚

ROYAL OAK
3 Station Street
☎ (01273) 474803
11-3, 5 (6.30 Sat)-11; 12-3, 7-10.30 Sun
Beards Best Bitter; Courage Directors; Harveys BB; guest beers Ⓗ
Dating from 1812; an early landlord was descended from the family that saved Charles II after the battle of Worcester, hence the name. A comfortable pub with an extensive menu.
♨ Q ❀ ◐ ▶ ⇌

LITLINGTON

PLOUGH & HARROW
Between Alfriston and Exceat
OS523018
☎ (01323) 870632
11-3, 6.30-11; 12-3, 7-10.30 Sun

Badger Dorset Best, Tanglefoot, Wells Bombardier; guest beers Ⓗ
Spacious country pub, popular with walkers and locals, close to River Cuckmere. A rare outlet for Badger beers in the area.
🏚 Q 🛏 🏮 ◖ 🍺 P

PETT

TWO SAWYERS
Pett Road ☎ (01424) 812255
11-3, 6-11; 11-11 Sat; 12-3.30, 6.30-10.30 Sun
Flowers Original; Old Forge Brothers Best; guest beers Ⓗ
Rural 17th-century inn serving good food. Guest beers come from the Old Forge Brewery opposite. Boules played in the large garden.
🏚 🏮 ◖ 🍺 Å ♣ ⇔

PILTDOWN

PEACOCK INN
Shortbridges (B2102, 1 mile S of A272) ☎ (01825) 762423
11-3, 6-11; 12-3, 7-10.30 Sun
Flowers IPA; Harveys BB; Morland Old Speckled Hen; Wadworth 6X; guest beer Ⓗ
Picturesque, oak-beamed pub with an inglenook, offering bar and restaurant menus. Two gardens. Near the site of the Piltdown Man hoax.
🏚 🏮 ◖ 🍺 P

PORTSLADE

STANLEY ARMS
47 Wolseley Road
☎ (01273) 701590
12-11; 12-10.30 Sun
Beer range varies Ⓗ
Lively, friendly local in what was once a real ale desert. The larger bar features live music. Imaginative, ever-changing ale range from small breweries often includes a mild or a stout. The house beer, HMS Bitter, is by Dark Star Brewery.
🏮 ⇌ ♣ (Fishersgate) ⇔ 🍺

RINGMER

CLOCK INN
Uckfield Road (off A26, 200 yds N of Ringmer turn)
☎ (01273) 812040
11-3, 6-11; 12-3, 7-10.30 Sun
Harveys XX Mild, BB, Old; guest beers Ⓗ
Over 400 years old, oak-beamed pub offering an extensive bar menu. 🏚 🛏 🏮 ◖ 🍺 P ✄

ROBERTSBRIDGE

OSTRICH
Station Road
☎ (01580) 881737
11-11; 12-10.30 Sun
Harveys BB; King & Barnes Sussex; guest beers Ⓗ

Former station hotel, now a good free house where Sussex beers predominate. Spacious, it has a games room.
🏚 🛏 🏮 🏮 ◖ 🍺 ⇌ ♣ P

ROTTINGDEAN

BLACK HORSE
65 High Street
☎ (01273) 302581
10.30-2.30, 6-11; 10.30-11 Sat; 12-4, 7-10.30 Sun
Beards Best Bitter; Harveys BB; Mansfield Old Baily; seasonal beers Ⓗ
16th-century local in the centre of an attractive village which has strong connections with Rudyard Kipling. The pub has two very different bars, plus a tiny snug. No-smoking area available at lunchtime. Q ◖ 🏮 ♣ ✄

RYE

INKERMAN ARMS
Rye Harbour (1½ miles from A259 jct, W of centre)
☎ (01797) 222464
12 (11 summer)-3, 7-11 (closed winter Mon); 11-3, 7-10.30 (closed winter) Sun
Greene King Abbot; Rother Valley Level Best; guest beers (summer) Ⓗ
Quiet, friendly, traditional pub with secluded dining areas, specialising in fish. Large garden with a boules piste; it stands next to Rye Harbour nature reserve.
🏚 Q 🏮 ◖ 🍺 Å ♣ P

YPRES CASTLE
Gun Garden (behind Ypres Tower)
☎ (01797) 223348
12-11; 12-10.30 Sun
Harveys XX Mild, BB; Old Forge Brothers Best, Pett Progress; guest beers Ⓗ
Not immediately obvious, this unspoilt pub is well worth seeking out. Access is on foot only. With a superb view of the harbour, it stands near Rye's most picturesque parts. Fresh fish, local game and poultry are specialities. Safe garden.
🏚 Q 🛏 🏮 ◖ 🍺 ⇌ ♣ ⇔

SEAFORD

WELLINGTON
Steyne Road
☎ (01323) 890032
11-11; 12-3, 7-10.30 Sun
Beards Best Bitter; Fuller's London Pride; Greene King IPA; Harveys BB; Wadworth 6X; guest beers Ⓗ
Local catering for a variety of clientele with generally a selection of eight ales. Note the daily motto on the blackboard list of beers. No food Sun.
🛏 ◖ ⇌

WHITE LION
74 Claremont Road
☎ (01323) 892473
11-2.30, 6-11; 11-11 Sat; 12-10.30 Sun
Fuller's London Pride; Harveys BB; guest beers Ⓗ
Recently refurbished, comfortable hotel bar with a conservatory; a pool table and Sky TV in a side area. ◖ 🍺 ⇌

ST LEONARDS

DRIPPING SPRING
34 Tower Road (off A2100, 1 mile N of Warrior Sq.)
☎ (01424) 434055
11-3, 5-11; 11-11 Fri & Sat; 12-3, 7-10.30 Sun
Fuller's London Pride; Tetley Bitter; Young's Special; guest beers Ⓗ
Small but friendly back-street local, well worth finding. Six beers available (600 guest beers to date), plus Biddenden cider.
🏮 ♣ (Warrior Sq) ♣ ⇔

NORTH STAR
Clarence Road (off A2100, top of Alexandra Park)
☎ (01424) 436576
11-3, 5.30-11; 11-11 Sat; 12-3, 7-10.30 Sun
Draught Bass; Fuller's London Pride; Harveys BB; guest beers Ⓗ
Town pub with reasonable prices, featuring an art gallery on the ceiling. Busy weekends (meals available Wed-Sat).
◖ 🍺 ♣ ⇔

TELHAM

BLACK HORSE
Hastings Road (A2100 to Battle)
☎ (01424) 773109
11-3, 5-11; 12-3, 7-10.30 Sun
Shepherd Neame Master Brew Bitter, Best Bitter, Spitfire, Bishops Finger Ⓗ
Splendid Shep's house, just outside Battle, boasting a games room on the first floor, a skittle alley in the attic and two boule pistes. An annual music festival is held in a marquee spring bank hol; occasional music in the bar.
🏚 Q 🏮 ◖ 🍺 ♣

THREE CUPS CORNER

THREE CUPS
On B2096 near Heathfield
☎ (01435) 830252
11-3, 6.30-11; 11-3, 6.30-10.30 Sun
Beards Best Bitter; Harveys BB; guest beer Ⓗ
Old country local with an inglenook in its cosy interior. Excellent food (no eve meals winter Sun); a no-smoking area for diners is available.
🏚 Q 🛏 🏮 ◖ 🍺 Å ♣ P

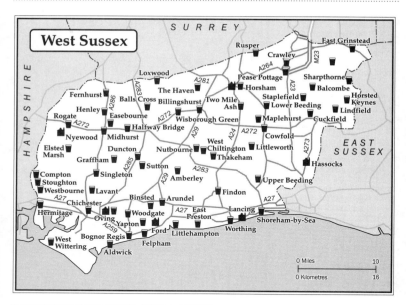

West Sussex

UCKFIELD

ALMA ARMS
Framfield Road (B2102, E of centre)
☎ (01825) 762232
11-2.30, 6-11; 12-2, 7-10.30 Sun
Harveys XX Mild, Pale Ale, BB, Old, Armada, seasonal beers Ⓗ
Traditional town pub, in the same family for generations, winner of 1998 Sussex *Community Pub* award. A rare chance to sample the full Harveys' range. Small garden. The no-smoking area is the family room. No food Sun.
Q ♿ ⊛ ◖ 🍴 & ⇌ ♣ P ⌖ 🗖

UDIMORE

KINGS HEAD
Udimore Road (B2089 W of village)
☎ (01424) 882349
11-4, 5.30-11; 12-4, 7-10.30 Sun
Harveys BB; guest beers Ⓗ
Built in 1535, this traditional village ale house boasts beams, open fires, wood floors, a skittle alley, a no-smoking dining room and home-cooked food. Scenic walks nearby.
🏚 Q ♿ ⊛ ◖ 🍴 & Å ♣ P

WADHURST

ROCK ROBIN
Station Hill (opp station)
☎ (01892) 783776
11-3, 5.45-11; 12-3, 7-10.30 Sun
Beer range varies Ⓗ
Recently re-opened after many years' closure: a cosy drinking area plus a restaurant. Six beers available.
🏚 Q ♿ ⊛ ◖ 🍴 ⇌ ♣ P 🗖

WITHYHAM

DORSET ARMS
On B2110 E of Hartfield
☎ (01892) 770278
11-3, 5 (6 Fri & Sat)-11; 12-3, 7-10.30 Sun
Harveys XX Mild, Pale Ale, BB, seasonal beers Ⓗ
An imposing house set in the heart of the Sussex Weald. The wooden floor in the bar is old Wealden timber from when this area was more wooded before the advent of iron-working. Quality restaurant.
🏚 Q ⊛ ◖ 🍴 ♣ P

WEST SUSSEX

ALDWICK

SHIP INN
Aldwick Street (1½ miles W of Bognor Regis)
☎ (01243) 865334
11-11; 12-10.30 Sun
Courage Best Bitter; Ⓗ
Harveys BB; Ⓖ **guest beer** Ⓗ
Late 18th-century village pub, now surrounded by housing. Although modernised, the structure is said to use timbers from a wrecked tea clipper, the mast supporting the bar floor. Once used by smugglers when the cellar was connected by a tunnel to the beach. No food Sun eve.
⊛ ◖ 🍴 ♣ P ⌖

AMBERLEY

SPORTSMANS ARMS
Rackham Road (½ mile E of village) OS039134

☎ (01798) 831787
11-2.30 (3 Sat), 6-11; 12-3, 6-10.30 Sun
Fuller's London Pride; Young's Bitter, Special; guest beer (occasional) Ⓗ
Friendly, 17th-century three-bar rural pub, popular with walkers and regulars. Excellent views of Amberley wild brooks. Good food, but the accent is on beer and a good pub atmosphere. Home of the Miserable Old Buggers Club; Spinnaker MOB is a house beer from Brewery on Sea.
🏚 Q ♿ ⊛ ♣ ⌣ P ⌖

ARUNDEL

KINGS ARMS
36 Tarrant Street
☎ (01903) 882312
11-3, 5.30-11; 11-11 Sat; 12-10.30 Sun
Fuller's London Pride; Hop Back Crop Circle; Young's Special; guest beer Ⓗ
Established circa 1625, this no-frills traditional local lies between the cathedral and the castle. Hosts Morrismen and other regular events throughout the summer. Small suntrap patio at the rear. ⊛ 🍴 Å ♣

SWAN HOTEL
27 High St ☎ (01903) 882314
11-11; 12-10.30 Sun
Arundel Best Bitter, Gold, ASB, Stronghold; guest beers Ⓗ
Brewery tap, attached to a respected hotel, selling the full range of Arundel Ales. Bar food as well as the à la carte restaurant. Parking for residents - public car park close by.
🛏 ◖ ⇌

BALCOMBE

COWDRAY ARMS
London Road (B2036/B2110 jct)
☎ (01444) 811280
11-3, 5.30-11; 12-3, 7-10.30 Sun
Adnams Extra; Beards Best Bitter; Harveys BB, seasonal beers; Ⓗ **guest beers** ⒽⒼ
Popular roadside pub with an extensive range of real ales; beer festivals in April. Very good and reasonably priced food in the large conservatory no-smoking eating area which has a children's certificate.
Q ☜ ⊛ ◑ ▶ ♣ P ⊟

BALLS CROSS

STAG
Kirdford Road (2 miles NE of Petworth off A283) OS987283
☎ (01403) 820241
11-3, 6-11; 12-3, 7-10.30 Sun
King & Barnes Mild, Sussex, Festive, seasonal beers Ⓗ
16th-century pub with an original stone floor and inglenook, on an old coaching route. A rare outlet in the country area for Mild Ale. No food Sun eve.
♨ Q ☜ ⊛ ⇔ ◑ ▶ ♣ P

Try also: Foresters Arms, Kirdford (King & Barnes)

BILLINGSHURST

LIMEBURNERS
Newbridge (visible from A272, 2 miles W of village)
☎ (01403) 782311
11-3, 6-11 (11-11 summer Sat); 12-3, 7-10.30 (12-10.30 summer) Sun
Gales's Best Bitter, IPA (summer), **Winter Brew, HSB** Ⓗ
Old country pub that has kept pace with the times without losing its charm. ♨ ◑ ▶ ▲ ⊂ P

BINSTED

BLACK HORSE INN
Binsted Lane (off A27/B2132)
OS980064
☎ (01243) 551213
11-3, 6-11; 12-3, 7-10.30 Sun
Courage Directors; Gale's HSB; Harveys BB; King & Barnes Broadwood; guest beers Ⓗ
Pub hidden off the beaten track amidst lovely countryside, offering excellent food in the bar or conservatory/restaurant. Note the 22 different sweets sold by the ounce or quarter alongside the more usual products.
♨ Q ⊛ ◑ ▶ ⅙ ♣ P

BOGNOR REGIS

HATTERS
2-10 Queensway
☎ (01243) 840406
11-11; 12-10.30 Sun
Courage Directors; Theakston Best Bitter; guest beers Ⓗ
Large, open-plan, one-bar pub. The no-smoking area is set aside for family dining until 9pm. The game and fruit machines are silent. Twice-yearly beer festival in this Wetherspoons pub, once a supermarket. Guest beers include a brew from Brewery on Sea.
Q ⊛ ◑ ▶ ⇔ ⊂ ⅙ ⊟

CHICHESTER

COACH & HORSES
125b St Pancras
☎ (01243) 782313
11-3, 6-11; 12-3, 7-10.30 Sun
King & Barnes Mild, Sussex, Broadwood or **seasonal beers, Festive** Ⓗ
Deceptively large, popular city pub. A true local with a friendly welcome, well worth the short walk from the centre. Toasted sandwiches until last orders, good value lunchtime meals and basic B&B. Pool played; large garden. ♨ ⊛ ⇔ ◑ ⇒ ♣

Try also: Chequers, Oving Rd (Whitbread)

COMPTON

COACH & HORSES
On B2146
☎ (01705) 631228
11-2.30, 6-11; 12-3, 7-10.30 Sun
Fuller's ESB; guest beers Ⓗ
16th-century pub in a charming downland village, surrounded by excellent walking country. The large front bar has two open fires. There is also a smaller rear bar, a restaurant (closed Sun eve and Mon) and a skittle alley
♨ ⊛ ◑ ▶ ♣

COWFOLD

HARE & HOUNDS
Henfield Road (A281)
☎ (01403) 865354
11.30-3, 6-11; 12-3, 7-10.30 Sun
Harveys BB; King & Barnes Sussex; Tetley Bitter; guest beers Ⓗ
Victorian village local refurbished in 1993, using timber from gale-damaged trees from nearby Leonardslee Gardens.
♨ ⊛ ◑ ▶ ♣ P

CRAWLEY

SNOOTY FOX
Haslett Avenue, Three Bridges
☎ (01293) 619759
11-11; 12-10.30 Sun
Friary Meux BB; Ind Coope Burton Ale; Tetley Bitter; guest beers Ⓗ
Modern, purpose-built pub, with a dining room where a wide range of food is available.
⊛ ◑ ▶ ⅙ ⇒ (Three Bridges) P ⅙

SWAN
1 Horsham Road, West Green (off Ifield Road)
☎ (01293) 527447
11-11; 12-10.30 Sun
Beer range varies ⒽⒼ
Comfortable, two-bar pub, hosting live music at weekends. Lunchtime snacks.
♨ ☜ ⊛ ♣

CUCKFIELD

WHITE HARTE
South Street
☎ (01444) 413454
11-3, 6-11; 12-3, 7-10.30 Sun
King & Barnes Sussex, Broadwood, Old, Festive, seasonal beers Ⓗ
This long-standing entry is situated on a double bend. The saloon has genuine beams and an inglenook; the contrasting public bar is more spartan. Family room opens in summer.
♨ Q ☜ ⊛ ◑ ⊞ ♣ P

Try also: The Ship, Whitemans Green (Free)

DUNCTON

CRICKETERS
Main Road (A285)
☎ (01798) 342473
11-2.30, 6-11; 12-3, 7-10.30 (not winter eve) Sun
Archers Golden; Ind Coope Burton Ale; Young's Special; guest beer (summer) Ⓗ
Cosy bar with a large welcoming inglenook and a split-level dining area. Attractive gardens and a skittles alley add to this historic hostelry. Advisable to book for Sun lunch. Barbecues and cider in summer.
♨ Q ⊛ ◑ ▶ ▲ ♣ ⊂ P

EASEBOURNE

WHITE HORSE
Easebourne Street (near A272 jct) ☎ (01730) 813521
11-11; 12-10.30 Sun
Greene King IPA, Abbot, seasonal beers Ⓗ
Friendly, two-bar village local. The varied restaurant menu features daily specials including vegetarian options. The large shady garden offers pleasant escapes from summer heat.
♨ Q ⊛ ◑ ▶ ⊞ ⅙ ♣ P

EAST GRINSTEAD

SHIP INN
Ship Street (off High St)
☎ (01342) 312089
10-4, 5.30-11; 10-11 Thu-Sat; 12-10.30 Sun
Fuller's London Pride; Harveys BB; Young's Bitter, Special; guest beers Ⓗ
Small, characterful local with a

ship theme. Public bar area and a restaurant/function room. Quiz Thu eve, plus live music nights. Note the framed Guinness posters and cigarette card displays. Weekday meals.
🏨 🐄 🚲 🍺 🍽 ♣ P

Try also: Dunnings Mill, Dunnings Rd (Harveys)

EAST PRESTON

FLETCHER ARMS
Station Road, Rustington (next to Angmering station)
☎ (01903) 784858
11-3, 5-11; 11-11 Fri & Sat; 12-4, 7-10.30 Sun
Gale's HSB; Greene King Abbot; Marston's Pedigree; Ringwood Best Bitter; guest beers H
Two-bar pub, handy for the station. The garden has a play area with a children's pets corner. Cider (varies) in summer.
🏨 Q 🌺 🍺 ► 🚲 (Angmering) ♣ 👜 P

ELSTED MARSH

ELSTED INN
Off A272, near old railway bridge OS834207
☎ (01730) 813662
11.30-3, 5.30 (6 Sat)-11; 12-3, 7-10.30 Sun
Ballard's Trotton, Best Bitter, Wassail, seasonal beers; Fuller's London Pride; guest beers H
Popular country pub, formerly serving the now-disused Elsted station but two miles from the village. Unchanged Victorian decor; note the unusual window shutters. Excellent home-cooked food in the cosy bars and restaurant. 🏨 Q 🌺 🚲 🍺 ► ♣ P

FELPHAM

OLD BARN
42 Felpham Rd ☎ (01243) 821564
11-11; 12-10.30 Sun
Arundel Best Bitter; Gale's Best Bitter; Hop Back Summer Lightning; Ringwood Best Bitter; guest beers H
Busy, one-bar pub with three distinct areas: a cosy front part; a main area with bare boards, two TVs and a dartboard; and a rear pool area. Handy for Butlins. The TV is always on for live football matches. Food served 11-7.
🌺 🍺 ♣ P

FERNHURST

KINGS ARMS
Midhurst Road (A286, 1 mile S of village)
☎ (01428) 652005
11-3, 5 (6 Sat)-11; 12-3, (closed eve) Sun
Gale's HSB; Otter Bright; guest beers H

Cosy, 17th-century free house, new to the *Guide*. A small bar and larger restaurant area - the extensive menu is popular. Camping in fields to the rear by arrangement. Kings Arms Ale is from Brewery-on-Sea; guest beers are from other small independents. 🏨 Q 🌺 🍺 ► ▲ ♣ P

Try also: Red Lion, Village Green (Free)

FINDON

GUN
High Street
☎ (01903) 873206
11-11; 12-10.30 Sun
Flowers Original; Fuller's London Pride; King & Barnes Sussex; guest beers H
Ancient village inn, threatened by opportunist property developers who view this Grade II listed building as residential units and its car park as granny flats. No food Mon.
Q 🌺 🍺 ♣ P

VILLAGE HOUSE HOTEL
The Square, Old Horsham Road
☎ (01903) 873350
10.30-11; 12-10.30 Sun
Courage Best Bitter; Harveys BB; King & Barnes Sussex; Morland Old Speckled Hen; Webster's Yorkshire Bitter H
Attractive, 16th-century village inn. Racing silks from local stables adorn the walls. Walkers welcome (minus boots). Extensive range of excellent food. Children's certificate.
🏨 Q 🌺 🚲 🍺 ► P

GRAFFHAM

FORESTER'S ARMS
☎ (01798) 867202
11-2.30, 5.30-11; 12-3, 7-10.30 Sun
Courage Directors; guest beers H
Traditional Sussex downland inn offering wholesome English fare. Popular with walkers along South Downs Way. Three constantly changing guest beers come from independent brewers. Note the welcoming inglenook.
🏨 Q 🌺 🍺 ► ▲ P

HALFWAY BRIDGE

HALFWAY BRIDGE INN
On A272, near Lodsworth
☎ (01798) 861281
11-3, 6-11; 12-3, 7-10.30 (closed winter eve) Sun
Cheriton Pots Ale; Fuller's London Pride; Gale's HSB; guest beer H
Rambling 18th-century former coaching inn, retaining much character in its several inter connecting rooms, all with real fires. Emphasis is on food which is of a high standard (book at

weekends). Gardens at front, sunny patio to the rear.
🏨 Q 🌺 🍺 ♣ 👜 P

Try also: Three Moles, Selham (Free)

THE HAVEN

BLUE SHIP ☆
500 yds down a lane W of A281 at Bucks Green OS084306
☎ (01403) 822709
11-3, 6-11; 12-3, 7-10.30 Sun
King & Barnes Sussex, Broadwood, seasonal beers G
Classic, four-roomed country pub of immense character. The gravity beers are served through a stable door. Mostly home-produced food and very good value (no food sun or Mon eves).
🏨 Q 🌺 🍺 ► P

HENLEY

DUKE OF CUMBERLAND
Off A286, 3 miles N of Midhurst OS894258 ☎ (01428) 652280
11-3, 5-11; 12-3, 7-10.30 Sun
Adnams Broadside; Brakspear Special; Flowers Original; Gale's Butser; Hop Back Summer Lightning; Theakston Old Peculier G
Pub well worth seeking out for its early 17th-century origins. A red tiled floor, scrubbed tables, gas lighting, back cellar, gravity served beer and trout pond in the lovely gardens are added attractions. No crisps, peanuts or snacks available, only full meals.
🏨 Q 🌺 🍺 ► 👜 P

HERMITAGE

SUSSEX BREWERY
On A259, ½ mile E of Emsworth
☎ (01243) 371533
11-11; 12-10.30 Sun
Badger Dorset Best, Tanglefoot; Shepherd Neame Spitfire; Taylor Dark Mild; Young's Bitter, Special H
Welcoming local in an attractive sailing village with a roaring log fire in winter and sawdust on the floor. Specialises in a sausage menu in the bar and restaurant (booking advisable eves). Hermitage Bitter is brewed by Hampshire Brewery.
🏨 Q 🌺 🍺 ► ▲ 🚲 (Emsworth) ♣ P 🍺

HORSHAM

DOG & BACON
North Parade ☎ (01403) 252176
11-3, 6-11; 12-3, 7-10.30 Sun
King & Barnes Sussex, Broadwood, Festive, seasonal beers H
Friendly pub on the edge of town with a no-smoking dining and family room at the front.

Occasional special themed food eves (no food Sun or Mon eves). Excellent floral hanging baskets in summer. Winner of *Pete King Memorial Shield*.
🏠 ⊛ ◖ ▶ ≒ ♣ P ⅟

MALT SHOVEL
15 Springfield Road
☎ (01403) 254543
11-11; 12-10.30 Sun
Boddingtons Bitter; Flowers Original; Marston's Pedigree; Young's Special; Ⓗ **guest beers** ⒽⒼ
Very popular town pub with a bare-boarded floor serving a wide selection of beers from six handpumps as well as three on gravity, plus foreign bottled beers. 🏠 ⊛ ◖ ▶ ≒ ♣ P

OLDE STOUT HOUSE
29 Carfax (opp bandstand)
☎ (01403) 267777
10-4, 7.30-11 (not Tue eve); 12-4, 7-10.30 Sun
King & Barnes Sussex, Festive, seasonal beers Ⓗ
Very popular town-centre pub which concentrates on beer. Food is limited to snacks. Recently refurbished in traditional style. ≒ ♣

TANNERS ARMS
78 Brighton Rd ☎ (01403) 250527
11-2, 6-11; 11-5.30, 7-11 Sat; 12-3.30, 7-10.30 Sun
King & Barnes Mild, Sussex, Festive Ⓗ
Friendly, serious drinkers' pub with a small, quiet lounge bar and a public bar. It fields many active teams including pool and darts. Q ⊛ ♣

Try also: Bedford, Station Rd (Free); Norfolk Arms, Crawley Rd (King & Barnes)

HORSTED KEYNES

GREEN MAN
1 mile from Bluebell Railway
☎ (01825) 790656
11-3, 5.30-11 (11-11 summer Sat); 12-3, 7-10.30 (12-10.30 summer) Sun
Adnams Bitter; Harveys BB; guest beer Ⓗ
Popular village pub with a locals' bar and a restaurant, facing on to the green. Children over five welcome in the restaurant.
🏠 Q ◖ ▶ ♣ P

LAVANT

EARL OF MARCH
Lavant Road (A286, 2 miles N of Chichester) ☎ (01243) 774751
10.30-3, 6-11; 12-3, 7-10.30 Sun
Badger Tanglefoot; Ballards Best Bitter; Cottage Southern Bitter; Ringwood Old Thumper; guest beers Ⓗ

Welcoming, spacious village pub affording a panoramic view of the downs from the garden. Close to the historic motor racing circuit at Goodwood. Good food features game (large, home-cooked portions). Children's certificate; regular live music, three guest beers. ⊛ ◖ ▶ ♣ ⌣ P

LINDFIELD

LINDEN TREE
47 High Street (B2028)
☎ (01444) 482995
11-3, 6-11; 12-3, 7-10.30 Sun
Arundel Best Bitter; Harveys Old; Marston's Pedigree; Ringwood Old Thumper; Wadworth 6X; guest beers Ⓗ
Friendly free house in a picturesque village. Look behind the pub to see remains of a long-defunct brewery. Usually two guest beers. No food Sun.
🏠 Q ⊛ ◖

LITTLEHAMPTON

LOCOMOTIVE
74 Lyminster Road, Wick
☎ (01903) 716658
11-2.30, 6-11 (11-11 summer Sat); 12-3, 7-10.30 (12-10.30 summer) Sun
Ansells Mild; King & Barnes Sussex; Ringwood Best Bitter; guest beers Ⓗ
Friendly, one-bar community inn with a thriving food trade. The large garden has a patio, boules pistes and a play area. Popular quiz Wed. 🏠 ⌂ ⊛ ◖ ▶ Å ♣ P

LITTLEWORTH

WINDMILL
Littleworth Lane (from A24 follow signs to Partridge Green, OS193205
☎ (01403) 710308
11.30-3, 5.30-11; 12-3, 7-10.30 Sun
King & Barnes Mild, Sussex, seasonal beers Ⓗ
Fine out-of-the-way local with a comfortable saloon and a public bar with a very rustic feel. No meals Sun eve.
🏠 Q ⊛ ◖ ▶ ⊟ ⅃ ♣ P

LOWER BEEDING

PLOUGH
Leech Pond Hill (A279 to Handcross, off A281, 4 miles S of Horsham) OS220274
☎ (01403) 891277
11-3, 6-11; 11-11 Fri & Sat; 12-10.30 Sun
King & Barnes Sussex, Festive, seasonal beers Ⓗ
Basic, two-bar pub with cheap beer for the area. Its position on the outside of a sweeping bend has meant a few lorries have dropped in over the years.
🏠 ⊟ ♣ P

LOXWOOD

SIR ROGER TITCHBOURNE
Billinghurst Road, Alfold Bars (B2133) ☎ (01403) 752377
12-2.30 (not Mon), 6-11 (not winter Mon); 12-3, 7-10.30 (not winter eve) Sun
King & Barnes Sussex, seasonal beers Ⓗ
Welcoming, traditional old low-beamed pub offering superb hospitality in a quiet saloon bar and a busier bar. Plenty of outdoor activities for children and adults. Eve meals Fri and Sat. 🏠 ⊛ ◖ ▶ ♣ P

MAPLEHURST

WHITE HORSE
Park Lane (between A281 and A272) ☎ (01403) 891208
12-2.30 (3 Sat), 6-11; 12-3, 6-10.30 Sun
Harveys BB; King & Barnes Sussex; guest beers Ⓗ
Friendly country pub with an ever-changing selection of ales (up to six at peak periods). The landlord is a classic car fanatic. Children's certificate and no-smoking area at lunchtime. Cider in summer. 🏠 Q ⌂ ⊛ ◖ ▶ ⊟ ♣ ⌣ P ⅟

MIDHURST

BRICKLAYERS ARMS
Wool Lane (50 yds from A286/A272 jct)
☎ (01730) 812084
11-3, 6-11; 12-10.30 Sun
Greene King IPA, Abbot, Ⓗ **seasonal beers** Ⓖ
Two-bar town pub, 400 years old, close to the shops and public car park. The public bar is wooden-floored with wall panels, while the main bar has bare brick walls. Polo is the theme of many photographs. Good value food. Limited parking. 🏠 ⊛ ◖ ▶ ⊟ ♣ P

CROWN
Edinburgh Square
☎ (01730) 813462
11-11; 12-10.30 Sun
Beer range varies ⒽⒼ
Popular town pub, close to the shops, with a large, ever changing beer range (gravity beer from a bar-level cellar). Justifiably busy at weekends. Lamb spit roast first Sun each month. Good B&B. Cider in summer.
🏠 ⊛ ⊨ ◖ ▶ ♣ ⌣

NUTBOURNE

RISING SUN
The Street ☎ (01798) 812191
11-3, 6-11; 12-3, 7-10.30 Sun
Fuller's London Pride; Greene King Abbot; King & Barnes Sussex; guest beers Ⓗ
Unspoilt village local, popular with walkers. Bare boards and an

open fire in the friendly village bar; a quieter, more restrained atmosphere in the saloon and adjacent dining area. Up to three guest beers. 🚲 Q 🍺 🐟 ◑ ▌

OVING

GRIBBLE INN
Gribble Lane ☎ (01243) 786893
11-3, 6-11 (11-11 summer); 12-3, 7-10.30 (12-10.30 summer) Sun
Badger Dorset Best; Gribble Ewe Brew, Ale, Reg's Tipple, Black Adder II, Pig's Ear Ⓗ
16th-century picture postcard thatched pub in a garden setting. A compact brewhouse (view the process) adjoins the skittle alley, producing a range of home-brewed ales that attract patrons from far and near. Deceptively spacious; mind the low beams. Interesting bar food. 🚲 Q 🍺 🐟 ◑ ▌ 🔥 ♣ ☕ P ✗

PEASE POTTAGE

JAMES KING
Brighton Road (off M23)
☎ (01293) 612261
11-2.30, 5.30-11; 11-3, 6-11 Sat; 12-3, 7-10.30 Sun
King & Barnes Sussex, Broadwood, Festive, seasonal beers Ⓗ
Large, nicely furnished pub with a relaxing atmosphere, displaying many old photographs of the pub and previous customers. Two restaurants, with a no-smoking area. Q 🐟 ◑ ▌ 🗄 🔥 P

ROGATE

WYNDHAM ARMS
North Street ☎ (01730) 821315
11.30-3, 6-11; 12-3, 7-10.30 Sun
Ballard's Wassail; Cheriton Pots Ale; Hop Back Summer Lightning; Ringwood Fortyniner; guest beers Ⓖ
Welcoming, 16th-century village inn, reputedly haunted. The beer stillages can be viewed via a glass panel from the bar. This former CAMRA Sussex *Pub of the Year* holds an annual midsummer beer festival and is recommended for good, imaginative food. 🚲 Q 🐟 🚪 ◑ ▌ 🔥 ▲ ♣ ☕ P

RUSPER

PLOUGH
High Street OS205374
☎ (01293) 871215
11-2.30, 6-11; 12-3, 7-10.30 Sun
Courage Best Bitter; Fuller's London Pride; King & Barnes Sussex; guest beers Ⓗ
Popular village pub with a re-instated stone floor in front of the bar and low beams. Parts date back to the 15th century. Good food; large garden. 🚲 Q 🐟 ◑ ▌ ♣ P

ROYAL OAK
Friday Street (1 mile W of village, left fork N of church)
OS186369 ☎ (01293) 871393
11-3, 6-11; 12-3, 7-10.30 Sun
King & Barnes Sussex, Festive, Broadwood, seasonal beers Ⓗ
15th-century rural local: the bar is long and narrow with two small rooms either side at each end, featuring split levels and low beams. No food Sun eve. 🚲 Q 🐟 ◑ ▌ ♣ P

Try also: Star, Horsham Rd (Free)

SHARPTHORNE

VINOLS CROSS
8 Top Road (2 miles E of B2028)
OS368325 ☎ (01342) 810644
12-3, 6-11; 12-11 Sat; 12-3, 6-10.30 Sun
Harveys BB; Wadworth 6X; guest beers Ⓗ
Welcoming country pub near the Bluebell Railway. Good food. 🚲 🐟 ◑ ▌ P

SHOREHAM

RED LION INN
Old Shoreham Road
☎ (01273) 423171
11.30-3, 5.30-11; 12-4, 7-10.30 Sun
Courage Best Bitter, Directors; guest beers Ⓗ
Former 16th-century coaching Inn, pleasantly situated by an old tollbridge. The Adur beer festival is held here at Easter. Rotating guest beers (at least five a week) include special monthly promotions from a micro. Good food. 🚲 Q 🐟 ◑ ▌ P ✗

ROYAL SOVEREIGN
6 Middle St ☎ (01273) 453518
11-11; 12-4.30, 7-10.30 Sun
Brains SA; Castle Eden Ale; Fuller's London Pride; Young's Special Ⓗ
The original green tiles and leaded windows of the United Brewery are still in place in this busy local. Hanging flower displays enhance its appeal. Public car park next door. Good food. 🚲 Q ◑ 🚃

SINGLETON

HORSE & GROOM
On A286 ☎ (01243) 811455
11-3, 6-11; 12-4, 6-10.30 (may vary) Sun
Ballard's Best Bitter; Cheriton Pots Ale; Gale's HSB; Hogs Back TEA; guest beer (occasional) Ⓗ
Friendly village free house near Goodwood and the Downland Museum. The large rear garden has swingboats and a trampoline. Good home-cooked food in the bar or restaurant (monthly theme food nights). Bar billiards

played. New en-suite accommodation. 🚲 🐟 🚪 ◑ ▌ ▲ ♣ P

Try also: Fox & Hounds, Singleton Lane (Gibbs Mew)

STAPLEFIELD

JOLLY TANNERS
Handcross Road (off B2114)
☎ (01444) 400335
11-3, 5.30-11; 11-11 Sat; 12-3, 7-10.30 Sun
Fuller's Chiswick, London Pride; Wadworth 6X; guest beer Ⓗ
Traditional two-bar pub on the green with a very large garden (barbecues in summer). Always well frequented and known locally for its good food. Children welcome in the restaurant. Always has a mild on tap. 🚲 🐟 ◑ ▌ ♣ P

STOUGHTON

HARE & HOUNDS
Off B2146, through Walderton
OS791107 ☎ (01705) 631433
11-3, 6-11; 12-10.30 Sun
Boddingtons Bitter; Gale's HSB; Gibbs Mew Bishops Tipple; Taylor Landlord; guest beers Ⓗ
Secluded 350-year-old classic Sussex flint building, in an area of outstanding natural beauty, with fine views from the gardens. Good value, home-made food includes fresh local seafood and game. Time stands still as you relax here. 24 years in this *Guide*. 🚲 Q 🐟 ◑ ▌ ♣ P

SUTTON

WHITE HORSE INN
The Street ☎ (01798) 869221
11-2.30, 6-11; 12-3, 7-10.30 Sun
Arundel Best Bitter; Courage Best Bitter; Gale's HSB; Young's Bitter; guest beers Ⓗ
Unspoilt downland inn close to Bignor Roman Villa. Its acclaimed restaurant does not detract from the uncompromisingly basic public bar, making this pub an attraction for locals, walkers and trenchermen alike. 🚲 Q 🍺 🐟 🚪 ◑ ▌ 🗄 ▲ ♣ P

THAKEHAM

WHITE LION
The Street ☎ (01798) 813141
11-3.30; 5.30-11 (may open 11-11 summer); 12-4, 6.30-10.30 (12-10.30 summer) Sun
Arundel ASB; Brewery on Sea Golden Lite; Flowers Original; Harveys BB, seasonal beers Ⓗ
500-year-old unspoilt, characterful village pub. Ask about the warren of tunnels beneath the pub and surrounding area. The main bar has an open log fire; also a small bar and a snug housing a pool table. 🚲 Q 🐟 ◑ ▌ ♣ P

TURNERS HILL

RED LION
Lion Lane OS342357
☎ (01342) 715416
11-3, 6-11; 12-10.30 Sun
Harveys XX Mild, BB, Old, seasonal beers Ⓗ
Simple, tile-hung building: a compact, cosy local with a raised saloon area and a thriving folk club in winter. No food Sun.
🏚 Q ❀ ◖ ♣ P

TWO MILE ASH

BAX CASTLE
On Christs Hospital-Southwater road OS148273
☎ (01403) 730369
11.30 (11 Fri & Sat)-2.30 (3 Sat), 6-11; 12-3, 7-10.30 Sun
Draught Bass; Brakspear Bitter; Fuller's London Pride; John Smith's Bitter; guest beers Ⓗ
Situated behind a former railway bridge, this pub is popular with walkers on the Downs Link. Large safe garden and a play area for children, also a good family room. 🏚 ⛺ ❀ ◖ ▶ ♣ P ✤

UPPER BEEDING

BRIDGE
High Street ☎ (01903) 812773
11-2.30, 4.45-11; 11-11 Sat; 12-10.30 Sun
King & Barnes Sussex, Broadwood, Festive, seasonal beers Ⓗ
Popular local where home cooking is a speciality (no meals Sun or Mon). Note the collection of hand tools on the ceiling.
🏚 ❀ ◖ 🍺 ♣

WESTBOURNE

GOOD INTENT
North Street ☎ (01243) 372656
10.30-2.30 (3 Sat), 5 (6 Sat)-11 (10.30-11 summer); 12-3, 7-10.30 Sun
Ansells Mild; Friary Meux BB; Ind Coope Burton Ale; John Smith's Bitter Ⓗ
16th-century, two-bar village local where open fires burn in winter and there's a warm welcome throughout the year. The lounge bar used to be a bakery; both bars are wood-panelled. No food Sun or Wed eve.
🏚 ❀ ◖ ▶ ⛭ ♣ P

WEST CHILTINGTON

FIVE BELLS
Smock Alley OS091172
☎ (01798) 812143
11-3, 5.30-11; 12-3, 7-10.30 Sun
King & Barnes Sussex; guest beers Ⓗ
Always an imaginative selection of guest ales, usually including a mild in this one-bar pub and

restaurant (meals Tue-Sat).
🏚 Q ❀ ◖ ♣ ⌂ P

WISBOROUGH GREEN

BAT & BALL
Newpound (B2133, 2 miles N of A272) ☎ (01403) 700313
11-2.30, 5-11; 11-3, 6-11 Sat; 12-3, 7-10.30 Sun
King & Barnes Sussex; Festive; seasonal beers Ⓗ
18th-century building with a former Victorian shop now incorporated into the bars. The large garden offers camping and caravan facilities. 🏚 ❀ ◖ ▶ ▲ P

WOODGATE

PRINCE OF WALES
Lidsey Road (A29, 3½ miles N of Bognor Regis)
☎ (01243) 543247
11-3, 5.30-11; 12-4, 7-10.30 Sun
Beards Best Bitter; Greene King IPA; Harveys BB; guest beer Ⓗ
1920s roadside pub recently restored to its original name after refurbishment. Three drinking areas at the front; a restaurant with a patio at the rear. Gardens on two sides and a field behind (camping by arrangement). A classic car club meets monthly.
🏚 ❀ ◖ ▶ ▲ ♣ P

WORTHING

ALEXANDRA
28 Lyndhurst Road
☎ (01903) 234833
11-11; 12-11 Sun
Draught Bass; Fuller's London Pride; Harveys BB, seasonal beers; guest beers Ⓗ
Deservedly popular local with two traditional bars and a games room. 🏚 ❀ 🍺 ♣

CRICKETERS
66 Broadwater Street (1 mile N of centre)
☎ (01903) 233369
11-3, 5.30-11; 11-11 Fri & Sat; 12-10.30 Sun
Draught Bass; Fuller's London Pride; Greene King IPA; Harveys BB; guest beers Ⓗ
Friendly one-bar pub, near Broadwater Green. The large saloon dining area includes a snug corner, whilst the bar area retains a traditional public bar atmosphere. Eve meals Tue-Sat.
Q ❀ ◖ ▶

RICHARD COBDEN
2 Cobden Road
☎ (01903) 236856
11-3, 5.30-11; 11-11 Fri & Sat; 12-3, 7-10.30 Sun
Beer range varies Ⓗ
Popular, street-corner local close to the town centre. No food Sun.
❀ ◖ ⇌ ♣

SWAN INN
79 High Street
☎ (01903) 232923
11-2.30 (3 Sat), 6-11; 12-4, 7-10.30 Sun
Courage Directors; Fuller's London Pride; Harveys BB; guest beers Ⓗ
Friendly pub close to the hospital. Popular at lunchtime and early eve. Children welcome for lunchtime meals. 🏚 ◖ ⇌

YAPTON

LAMB INN
Bilsham Road (B2132)
☎ (01243) 551232
11-3, 5.30 (5 Fri, 6 Sat)-11; 12-4.30, 6.30-10.30 Sun
Fuller's London Pride; Harveys BB; Young's Special; guest beers Ⓗ
Friendly roadside pub on the edge of the village. The large garden with play equipment and animal enclosure is fenced off from the road and has boules courts. A new restaurant room has just been added to this excellent community pub.
🏚 Q ⛺ ❀ ◖ 🍺 ⛭ ♣ P

Try also: Maypole, Maypole Lane (Free)

INDEPENDENT BREWERIES

(EAST SUSSEX)

Cuckmere Haven:
Exceat Bridge

Dark Star:
Brighton

First In Last Out:
Hastings

Harveys:
Lewes

Hedgehog and Hogshead:
Hove

Kemptown:
Brighton

Rother Valley:
Northiam

White:
Bexhill

(WEST SUSSEX)

Arundel:
Arundel

Ballard's:
Nyewood

Brewery on Sea:
Lancing

Gribble Inn:
Oving

King & Barnes:
Horsham

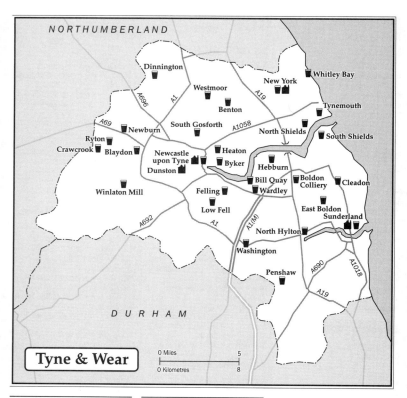

NORTHUMBERLAND

Dinnington
Westmoor
New York
Whitley Bay
Benton
Tynemouth
Newburn
South Gosforth
North Shields
South Shields
Ryton
Crawcrook
Blaydon
Heaton
Newcastle upon Tyne
Byker
Dunston
Hebburn
Bill Quay
Boldon Colliery
Cleadon
Wardley
Winlaton Mill
Felling
East Boldon
Sunderland
Low Fell
North Hylton
Washington
Penshaw

DURHAM

Tyne & Wear

0 Miles 5
0 Kilometres 8

BENTON

BENTON ALE HOUSE
Front Street, Longbenton
☎ (0191) 266 1512
11-11; 12-10.30 Sun
Banks's Bitter; Camerons Bitter, Strongarm; guest beers Ⓗ
Large, multi-area pub selling a good selection of guest beers. Popular at lunchtime with civil servants and with students eves. Just round the corner from the metro station.
Ⓓ ⊖ (Four Lane Ends) P ⊟

BILL QUAY

ALBION INN
Reay Street (foot of bank, by River Tyne)
☎ (0191) 469 2418
4-11; 11-11 Sat & summer (may vary); 12-10.30 Sun
Beer range varies Ⓗ
Free-standing, stone-built pub commanding excellent views across industrial Tyneside. It features a horseshoe-shaped bar decorated with nautical nicknacks; Hebburn Boat Club meets here. North-eastern microbreweries are usually represented in the beer range. Children are welcome in the conservatory until 7.30.
🏃 ❀ ⊖ (Pelan) P

BLAYDON

BLACK BULL
Bridge Street
☎ (0191) 414 2846
5-11; 12-3, 7-10.30 Sun
Camerons Bitter, Strongarm; Castle Eden Ale; guest beers Ⓗ
Well-run pub which holds live music eves. The bar has fine displays of photographs depicting the decline of Blaydon.
🏚 Q ❀ ⅌ ⇌ (limited service) ♣ P

BYKER

FIGHTING COCKS
127 Albion Row
☎ (0191) 276 1503
12-11; 12-3, 7-10.30 Sun
Four Rivers Moondance, Gladiator; guest beers Ⓗ
Four Rivers Brewing Co. pub where at least two of their beers are available at any one time. The view of the Tyne Bridge, the free juke box and real cider are added attractions. ⊖ ⌷ P ⊟

FREE TRADE INN
St Lawrence Road
☎ (0191) 265 5764
11.30-11; 12-10.30 Sun
Mordue Geordie Pride, Workie Ticket, Radgie Gadgie; Theakston Best Bitter, XB; guest beers Ⓗ
Wonderfully basic pub overlooking the River Tyne and the ever-changing quayside developments. A pleasant atmosphere makes this the ideal place to sample Mordue beers. Unusual tiered garden. 🏚 ❀ ⊖

TYNE
1 Maling St ☎ (0191) 265 2550
12-11; 12-10.30 Sun
Boddingtons Bitter; Castle Eden Ale; guest beers Ⓗ
Single-roomed pub under Glasshouse Bridge. It may be difficult to find the first time but is well worth seeking out as guest beers are from Mordue Brewery. An all-weather garden is sheltered by the brick arching of the bridge. ❀ ⊖

CLEADON

NEW SHIP INN
Sunderland Road (A1018, Harton road) ☎ (0191) 454 0183
11-3, 6-11; 12-3, 7-10.30 Sun
Vaux Samson; guest beer Ⓗ
Popular village pub situated between two large conurbations. With an overall homely atmosphere, families are welcome in the Wheel Room eves and weekends. Arrive early for weekend meals as it can get busy.
Q 🏃 ❀ Ⓓ ▶ P

CRAWCROOK

RISING SUN INN
Bank Top
☎ (0191) 413 3316
11.30-11; 12-10.30 Sun
Boddingtons Bitter; Castle Eden Ale; Mordue Workie Ticket; guest beers Ⓗ
Comfortable, spacious pub with a friendly atmosphere. There is an excellent combination of good food and ale, with consideration given for both diners and drinkers.
Q ✿ ◖▶ ♣ P

DINNINGTON

WHITE SWAN
Prestwick Road
☎ (01661) 820140
11-3, 6-11; 12-3, 6.30-10.30 Sun
Courage Directors; Ruddles Best Bitter, County; guest beers (summer) Ⓗ
Busy country pub offering a friendly welcome and an extensive food menu (theme night Mon).
✿ ◖▶ P

EAST BOLDON

BEAUMONT WINES (OFF-LICENCE)
6 Station Terrace
☎ (0191) 536 7152
10-10; 12-2, 6-10 Sun
Beer range varies Ⓗ
This off-licence sells from a stock of over 200 British bottle-conditioned and traditional ales. There are two handpumps which offer changing cask ales for home consumption. ≈

BLACK BULL
98 Front Street (A184)
☎ (0191) 536 3969
11-11; 12-10.30 Sun
Vaux Samson, Waggle Dance; guest beer Ⓗ
Very popular village pub, retaining its old farmhouse facade. Recently well renovated, the lack of a public bar detracts from the pub's otherwise pleasing ambience. A very busy venue for bar meals.
♨ ☎ ✿ ◖▶ ♿ ≈ P

GREY HORSE
14 Front Street (A184)
☎ (0191) 536 4186
11-11; 12-10.30 Sun
Vaux Samson, Waggle Dance; guest beers Ⓗ
Impressive village pub with helpful staff. It has a compact bar and a large lounge with small individual seating areas making it a comfortable, popular choice, especially weekend eves. Good value, basic meals (no food Sun eve).
Q ✿ ◖▶ ⊞ ♿ ≈ ♣ P

FELLING

OLD FOX
Carlisle Street
☎ (0191) 420 0357
12-11; 12-10.30 Sun
Bateman XB; Webster's Yorkshire Bitter; guest beers Ⓗ
Cosy, friendly pub with music and quiz eves. Fast turnover of guest ales; sparklers removed on request. ♨ ✿ ◖ ⊖ ♣ 🗗

WHEATSHEAF
26 Carlisle Street
☎ (0191) 420 0659
12-3, 6-11; 12-10.30 Sun
Big Lamp Bitter, Prince Bishop, Premium, Summerhill Stout; guest beer (occasional) Ⓗ
A loyal band of regulars gather in this traditional, cheerful, street-corner boozer. From the Felling Silver Band to Sky TV football followers, everyone is welcome.
♨ ⊖ ♣

HEATON

CHILLINGHAM
Chillingham Road
☎ (0191) 265 5915
11-11 (lounge closed 2.30-5 Mon-Thu); 12-10.30 Sun
Black Sheep Special; Courage Directors; Mordue Workie Ticket; Theakston Best Bitter; guest beers Ⓗ
Imposing roadside pub with a bar and lounge catering for both locals and the large student population. Popular quiz Wed eve. Eve meals (not Sun) finish at 7pm.
◖▶ ⊞ ⊖ (Chillingham Rd) ♣ P

HEBBURN

DOUGIES TAVERN
Blackett Street
☎ (0191) 428 4800
11.30-11; 12-10.30 Sun
Theakston XB; Stones Bitter; guest beer Ⓗ
Victorian-style free house with three public rooms and a warm atmosphere. The pub has a secure garden and play area which overlooks the banks of the River Tyne. Winner of the local council's *Catherine Cookson Hospitality Award* 1997. Children's certificate. Good value food.
☎ ✿ ◖▶ ♿ ⊖ ♣ P

NEW CLOCK TAVERN
Victoria Road West
☎ (0191) 424 1134
11-11; 12-10.30 Sun
Vaux Samson; guest beers Ⓗ
Refurbished community pub with a friendly atmosphere. Quiz nights and live music are very popular.
⊖ (Jarrow) ♣ P

LOW FELL

ALETASTER
706 Durham Road
☎ (0191) 487 0770
11-11; 12-10.30 Sun
Courage Directors; Marston's Pedigree; Mordue Workie Ticket, Radgie Gadgie; Theakston Best Bitter; Younger No. 3 Ⓗ
T & J Bernard's flagship pub has an L-shaped bar which is lively with a friendly atmosphere. Live music on Thu eve. Guest beers are always available. Regular beer festivals, with beers from independent brewers, make this a pub not to be missed.
✿ ☐ P

NEW YORK

SHIREMOOR FARM
Middle Engine Lane
☎ (0191) 257 6302
11-11; 12-10.30 Sun
Theakston Old Peculier; guest beers Ⓗ
Busy, Fitzgerald's pub based on a converted farm building. Well known for its excellent food, it stands close to the Steam Railway Museum and new industry. Meals served 12-9 daily.
Q ✿ ◖▶ ♿ P

NEWBURN

KEELMAN
Grange Road (next to Newburn Leisure Centre)
☎ (0191) 267 0772
11-11; 12-10.30 Sun
Big Lamp Bitter, Prince Bishop, Premium, Summerhill Stout Ⓗ
Big Lamp's showpiece pub and brewery now occupy this Grade II listed building. A former water pumping station, it is now a lively social centre with a strong local following. An attractive outdoor drinking area adjoins the Tyne Riverside Country Park.
✿ ⛺ ◖▶ ♿ P ⚥

NEWCASTLE UPON TYNE

BACCHUS
High Bridge
☎ (0191) 232 6451
11.30-11; 7-10.30 Sun
Draught Bass; Stones Bitter; Tetley Bitter; Theakston XB; guest beers Ⓗ
Excellent weekday food in a comfortable city-centre pub: two large rooms with a small, intimate snug leading off the back lounge.
◖ ≈ (Central) ⊖ (Monument)

BODEGA
125 Westgate Road
☎ (0191) 221 1552
11-11; 12-10.30 Sun

Butterknowle Conciliation Ale; Mordue Workie Ticket; Theakston Best Bitter; guest beers H
1997 Regional CAMRA *Pub of the Year*, this beautifully fitted pub offers a good choice of guest beers and food. Note the two original stained glass ceiling domes. Gets very busy if Newcastle United are at home or on TV. Mordue's Geordie Pride is sold here as No. 9.
◖ ≠ (Central) ⊖

BRIDGE HOTEL
Castle Square
☎ (0191) 232 6400
11-11; 12-10.30 Sun
Black Sheep Best Bitter; Draught Bass; Boddingtons Bitter; Theakston XB H
This pub guards the Newcastle end of the High Level Bridge and faces the old castle keep. Inside are a number of seating areas where the beers and food can be enjoyed in comfort. The outside drinking area to the rear allows views of the River Tyne and old town walls.
❀ ◖ ≠ (Central)
⊖ (Monument)

CROWN POSADA
33 Side
☎ (0191) 232 1269
11 (12 Sat)-11; 12-3, 7-10.30 Sun
Draught Bass; Boddingtons Bitter; Butterknowle Conciliation Ale; Jennings Cumberland Ale; Theakston Best Bitter; guest beers H
Beautiful, tiny pub with a fine ceiling and magnificent original stained glass windows. No TV, juke box or other distractions from the tasty beers and good conversation. A must on every visit to the city.
≠ (Central) ⊖ (Monument)

DUKE OF WELLINGTON
High Bridge
☎ (0191) 261 8852
11-11; 12-10.30 Sun
Ind Coope Burton Ale; Marston's Pedigree; Taylor Landlord; Tetley Bitter; guest beers H
Busy, city-centre pub with a friendly atmosphere. Two of the walls are packed with old photographs. The keen manager organises regular week-long mini beer festivals.
≠ (Central) ⊖ (Monument)

FITZGERALD'S
60 Grey Street
☎ (0191) 230 1350
11-11; 7-10.30 Sun
Boddingtons Bitter; Tetley Bitter; guest beers H
A deceptively large pub, very well fitted and furnished. The long entrance lounge leads to a serving area on various levels with a

choice of standing or seating. Alas, the garden is for viewing only.
◖ ≠ (Central) ⊖ (Monument)

HEAD OF STEAM
Neville Street
☎ (0191) 232 4379
11-11; 12-10.30 Sun
Black Sheep Best Bitter; Shepherd Neame Spitfire; guest beers H
Two bars, one on the first floor, one in the basement, serve a variety of beers to a mainly young clientele, accompanied by background music. The downstairs bar opens Thu-Sat.
◖ ≠ (Central) ⊖

TUT 'N' SHIVE
Clayton Street West
☎ (0191) 261 8778
11-11; 12-10.30 Sun
Boddingtons Bitter; Marston's Pedigree; guest beers H
Busy pub with an ever-changing range of guest beers – can be up to six at a time.
◖ ≠ (Central) ⊖

NORTH HYLTON

SHIPWRIGHTS HOTEL
Ferryboat Lane (signed from A1231)
☎ (0191) 549 5139
11-4, 5-11 (11-11 summer); 12-3, 7-10.30 Sun
Vaux Samson, Waggle Dance; Ward's Best Bitter; guest beer H
Listed, 350-year-old pub in a tranquil setting, next to the River Wear, yet close to the A19 road bridge. It has a small bar and three small adjoining rooms, full of brass fittings and wooden beams. Home-cooked food and good accommodation; 22 consecutive years in this *Guide*.
♨ ⇋ ◖ ▶ P

NORTH SHIELDS

CHAIN LOCKER
Duke Street, New Quay
☎ (0191) 258 0147
11-11; 12-10.30 Sun
Old Barn Sheepdog; Tetley Bitter; guest beers H
Opposite the Shields Ferry, this is the first port of call for those approaching from the south. A definite marine bias is reflected in the decor and menu. A provider of locally brewed beers, including re-badged house specials. Warm and friendly.
♨ ◖ ▶ ≠

COLONEL LINSKILL
Charlotte Street
☎ (0191) 257 5155
11-11; 12-10.30 Sun
Harviestoun Schiehallion; Theakston Best Bitter; guest beers H

Yet another in the new generation of fine pubs in the fertile, ale-rich town of North Shields. The manager's commitment to real ale ensures an ever-changing supply of guest beers. ⊖

GARRICKS HEAD
50 Saville Street
☎ (0191) 296 2040
11-11; 12-10.30 Sun
Draught Bass; Fuller's London Pride; guest beers H
Newly refurbished pub rescued from garish disco lighting by the current management who serve a selection of beers. Cheap specials available on the food menu.
◖ ⊖

MAGNESIA BANK
1 Camden Street
☎ (0191) 257 4831
11-11; 12-10.30 Sun
Black Sheep Best Bitter; Durham Magus; Mordue Geordie Pride, Workie Ticket; guest beers H
CAMRA award-winning pub, overlooking the River Tyne. The single room is divided into three distinct areas, providing the best in food and locally brewed beers at all times. Music sessions take place either in the bar or the upstairs function room.
♨ ❀ ◖ ▶ ⊖ ▯

TAP & SPILE
184 Tynemouth Road
☎ (0191) 257 2523
11-11; 12-10.30 Sun
Beer range varies H
Good choice of beers in a friendly atmosphere. ◖ ⊖ ⌂

PENSHAW

GREY HORSE
Village Green, Old Penshaw
☎ (0191) 584 4882
11-3.30 (4 Sat), 6-11; 12-4, 7-10.30 Sun
Tetley Bitter H
Entering its 18th year as a *Guide* regular, this friendly pub is easily located next to Penshaw Monument, a local tourist attraction and nationally listed site. Popular for its food, especially summer (no meals winter Sun). Limited parking.
❀ ◖ ⊞ ♣ P ▯

RYTON

OLDE CROSS
Barmoor Lane, Old Ryton Village
☎ (0191) 413 4689
11.30-11; 12-10.30 Sun
Ward's Best Bitter; guest beers H
Large, comfortable pub with an excellent Italian restaurant. Guest beers are usually from local microbrewers. Lunches served at weekends.
❀ ◖ ▶

SOUTH GOSFORTH

VICTORY
Killingworth Road
☎ (0191) 285 1254
12-11; 12-10.30 Sun
Courage Directors; McEwan 80/-; Morland Old Speckled Hen; Theakston Best Bitter, XB; guest beers Ⓗ
T & J Bernard's pub, small but well refurbished with a friendly atmosphere and some interesting guest beers.
❀ ⑴ ▶ ⊖ P

SOUTH SHIELDS

ALUM ALE HOUSE
River Drive (by ferry landing)
☎ (0191) 427 7245
11-11; 12-3, 7-10.30 Sun
Banks's Bitter; Camerons Strongarm; Marston's Pedigree; guest beers Ⓗ
Popular, traditional pub: the interior is decorated in natural wood, giving a warm, friendly atmosphere. With a long history as a public house, the copper-topped bar is a notable feature.
Q ⊖ 🍺

BAMBURGH
175 Bamburgh Ave, Horsley Hill Estate (coast road to Marsden)
☎ (0191) 454 1899
11-11; 12-10.30 Sun
Boddingtons Bitter; Castle Eden Ale; Flowers Original; Wadworth 6X; guest beers Ⓗ
Open-plan community inn which overlooks the leas with coastal views. It hosts quiz nights and an annual beer festival (November).
❀ ⑴ ▶ ₺ P

DOLLY PEEL
137 Commercial Road
☎ (0191) 427 1441
11-11; 12-3, 7-10.30 Sun
Courage Directors; Mordue Workie Ticket; Taylor Landlord; Younger No. 3; guest beers Ⓗ
Superb pub offering real ale, hospitality and a warm welcome. 1998 Sunderland and South Tyneside CAMRA *Pub of the Year*, a must for any visitors to the area.
Q ♣ P

RIVERSIDE
3 Commercial Road (near customs house/riverside area)
☎ (0191) 455 2328
11-11; 12-3, 7-10.30 Sun
Courage Directors; Taylor Landlord; Theakston Best Bitter; guest beers Ⓗ
Well-managed public house which has a respected policy of stocking beers from smaller independent breweries. A popular real ale venue (with three guests), this pub can get very busy. Q ❀ ⊖ ⌣

STEAMBOAT
51 Coronation Street
☎ (0191) 454 0134
12-11; 12-10.30 Sun
Vaux Samson, Waggle Dance; guest beers Ⓗ
Traditional pub, situated a short distance from the river ferry service. One of the town's oldest pubs – note the preserved wooden decor and maritime flags.
⊖ ♣

SUNDERLAND: *NORTH*

HARBOUR VIEW
Harbour View
☎ (0191) 567 1402
11-11; 12-10.30 Sun
Draught Bass; guest beers Ⓗ
A superb pub overlooking the harbour. A friendly and warm atmosphere welcomes the visitor. A supporter of local micros.
❀ ₺

NEW DERBY
Roker Baths Road
☎ (0191) 548 6263
11-11; 12-10.30 Sun
Castle Eden Ale; guest beers Ⓗ
A modern pub with a very pleasant atmosphere. Regular quiz nights and pool played. A warm welcome awaits locals and visitors alike. ⑴ ₺ P

SUNDERLAND: *SOUTH*

BREWERY TAP
9 Dunning Street (next to Vaux Brewery)
☎ (0191) 567 7472
11-11; 12-10.30 Sun
Vaux Samson Ⓗ
Small, cosy wood-panelled bar and lounge, bedecked with photographs of old Sunderland.
🚲 🍺 ⇌ ♣

CHESTER'S
Chester Road
☎ (0191) 565 9952
11-11; 12-10.30 Sun
Vaux Samson; Ward's Best Bitter; guest beer Ⓗ
Former vicarage set in its own grounds, just out of the city centre, with a large, open-plan interior carefully split up with partitions to add that cosy feel.
⑴ 🍺 ₺ P

FITZGERALD'S
10-12 Green Terrace
☎ (0191) 567 0852
11-11; 12-10.30 Sun
Boddingtons Bitter; Theakston Best Bitter, XB; guest beer Ⓗ
Popular with students and the younger crowd, this split-level pub near the university is always packed and noisy. It often features the local Darwin brews. Fine woodwork, brass fittings and stained glass predominate.
⑴ 🍺 ⇌

LANSDOWNE
32 Deptford Rd
☎ (0191) 567 1886
11-11; 12-10.30 Sun
Vaux Lorimer's Best Scotch, Samson; guest beer Ⓗ
Friendly pub, in a quiet side street; it has a medium-sized bar room with wooden alcoves. Also a partitioned pool area. ♣

SALTGRASS
36 Ayres Quay, Deptford
☎ (0191) 565 7229
11-11; 12-4, 7-10.30 Sun
Vaux Samson; Ward's Best Bitter; guest beers Ⓗ
Award-winning pub with a warm, friendly atmosphere. Free transport is provided to other local pubs at weekends. Note the original building – this pub was once the haunt of the North's greatest shipbuilders. Lunchtime snacks.
🚲 ❀ 🍺 ♣

WILLIAM JAMESON
30-32 Fawcett Street
☎ (0191) 514 5016
11-11; 12-10.30 Sun
Courage Directors; Theakston Best Bitter, XB; Vaux Samson; guest beer Ⓗ
Spacious, air-conditioned former department store in typical Wetherspoons style, offering a wide range of guest ales and good quality food (served all day). Children not allowed. Named after a local town planner. Q ⑴ ▶ ⇌ ⌣

TYNEMOUTH

FITZPATRICK'S
29 Front St ☎ (0191) 257 8956
11-11; 12-10.30 Sun
Theakston Best Bitter; guest beers Ⓗ
Beautifully furnished pub with a raised seating area and a small cosy snug. Good food means the pub is well used at lunchtime (eve meals in summer). Close to beach and Tynemouth Priory.
Q ⑴ ▶ ⊖

TYNEMOUTH LODGE
Tynemouth Rd ☎ (0191) 257 7565
11-11; 12-10.30 Sun
Draught Bass; Maclay 80/-; Village White Boar Ⓗ
18th-century free house with a friendly management, efficient staff and a warm welcome. In a historic area of Tyneside, it is always worth a visit. 🚲 Q ⊖ P

WARDLEY

GREEN
White Mare Pool
☎ (0191) 495 0171
11-11; 12-10.30 Sun
Boddingtons Bitter; Ruddles County; Theakston Best Bitter; guest beers Ⓗ

Large, roadside pub, part of the Sir John Fitzgerald's chain by Henworth golf course. A decent-sized, very pleasant lounge leads to a well-regarded restaurant. The comfortable bar stocks ever-changing guest beers, including some from local micros. Regular beer festivals. ❀ ◖ ▮ 🍴 ᵔ P

WASHINGTON

SANDPIPER
Easby Road, Biddick (follow signs for District 7)
☎ (0191) 416 0038
11-11; 12-10.30 Sun
Boddingtons Bitter; Castle Eden Ale; Flowers Original; Morland Old Speckled Hen; guest beers Ⓗ
Modern, single-storey pub with a lounge and bar. It hosts two beer festivals, in March and September and stocks up to six guest beers. ❀ ◖ ▮ ᵔ ♣ P

STEPPES
47-49a Spout Lane
☎ (0191) 415 1733
11-11; 12-10.30 Sun
Courage Directors; Boddingtons Bitter; guest beers Ⓗ
Comfortable, friendly, one-roomed village local, close to Washington Old Hall. ♣

THREE HORSE SHOES
Washington Road, Usworth (off A19, next to Nissan car plant)
☎ (0191) 536 4183
12-3 (4 Fri), 6.30-11; 12-11 Sat; 12-5 Sun
Vaux Samson, Waggle Dance, Double Maxim; Ward's Best Bitter; guest beers Ⓗ
Family-oriented country pub where food is available all day. It hosts an annual beer festival (early summer); normally offers up to 15 beers plus two ciders.
❀ ◖ ▮ 🍴 ᵔ ♣ P

WESTMOOR

GEORGE STEPHENSON
Great Lime Road
☎ (0191) 268 1073
12-3, 5-11; 12-11 Fri & Sat; 12-4, 7-10.30 Sun
Beer range varies Ⓗ
Two-roomed pub by the main East Coast railway line. Lunches Mon-Fri. The often changing range of three beers usually includes one from a local brewery. ❀ ◖ ♣ P ⌷

WHITLEY BAY

BRIAR DENE
The Links
☎ (0191) 252 0926
11-11; 12-10.30 Sun
Courage Directors; Theakston Best Bitter; Mordue Workie Ticket; guest beers Ⓗ

Large pub with several drinking areas and an indoor children's play area. Up to seven guest beers available and regular mini beer festivals held with unusual beers. Q ᵔ ◖ ▮ 🍴 ᵔ ♣ P

WHITLEY BAY

FITZGERALD'S
2 South Parade
☎ (0191) 251 1255
11-11; 12-10.30 Sun
Draught Bass; Boddingtons Bitter; Mordue Workie Ticket; Theakston Best Bitter; guest beer Ⓗ
Large lounge divided into a number of comfortable areas. A smaller, nautically-themed chart room offers a chance for a quiet chat. Very popular for food (eve meals finish at 8; 7 Fri-Sat).
◖ ▮ ⇌ P

WINLATON MILL

GOLDEN LION
Shotley Bridge Road (A694)
☎ (0191) 414 5840
12-3, 6-11; 12-10.30 Sun
Courage Directors; Theakston Best Bitter; guest beers Ⓗ
Lively, friendly pub, very popular with local residents. The downstairs restaurant has a deserved reputation. ❀ ◖ ▮ ♣ P ⌷

HUNTLEY WELL
Shotley Bridge Road (A694)
☎ (0191) 414 2731
12-4, 6-11; 12-11 Fri & Sat; 12-10.30 Sun
Ind Coope Burton Ale; Tetley Bitter; guest beers Ⓗ
Formerly a club, now a friendly pub that is a popular meeting place for locals. Visitors can expect a warm welcome. Rapid turnover of guest ales.
◖ ▮ ᵔ ♣ P

Tyne and Wear

Currently containing a number of independent breweries and the massive Scottish Courage Tyne brewery, only 20 years ago there was not a drop of real ale brewed in Tyne & Wear and precious little available in the pubs.

The last two decades have been a tale of almost continuous success for CAMRA. The Newcastle-based property company Sir John Fitzgerald's has always owned most of the architectural gems of the Newcastle pub world and, fortunately, have always been in favour of real ale. All Fitzgerald's needed was convincing that the public demand was there. On the coast, North and South Shields publicans have also proved that the public has a taste for cask-conditioned beer – and a wide variety is available.

In 1982 the Big Lamp brewery was set up in Newcastle, followed by Hadrian. Eventually even Scottish & Newcastle began to brew cask ale again, starting with Cask Exhibition and then concentrating on Theakstons. Mordue's Workie ticket was awarded Champion Beer of Britain in 1997.

Setbacks have included the loss of many historic pubs, either demolished or converted into one-room monstrosities with no quibbles from the planners; and the rash of theme pubs continues.

Times are still hard: as this book went to press Four Rivers temporarily ceased brewing owing to a series of trading difficulties, but it hopes to return.
Nick Whitaker, CAMRA regional director, North-East

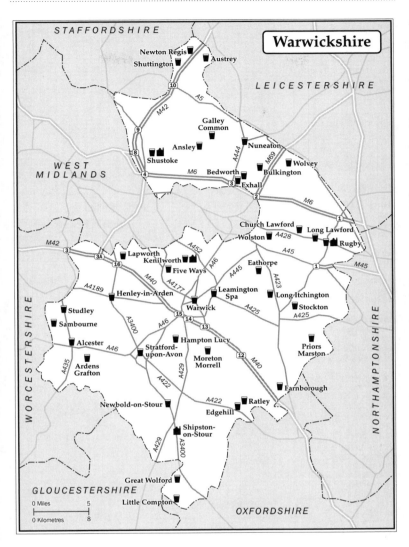

Warwickshire

STAFFORDSHIRE

Newton Regis
Shuttington
Austrey

LEICESTERSHIRE

Galley Common

Ansley
Shustoke

WEST MIDLANDS

Nuneaton
Bedworth
Bulkington
Wolvey
Exhall

Church Lawford
Long Lawford
Wolston
Rugby

Lapworth
Kenilworth
Five Ways
Eathorpe

Henley-in-Arden
Leamington Spa
Long Itchington
Warwick
Stockton

Studley
Hampton Lucy
Priors Marston

Sambourne
Stratford-upon-Avon
Moreton Morrell

Alcester
Ardens Grafton
Farnborough

WORCESTERSHIRE

Newbold-on-Stour
Ratley
Edgehill

Shipston-on-Stour

NORTHAMPTONSHIRE

Great Wolford

GLOUCESTERSHIRE
Little Compton

OXFORDSHIRE

0 Miles 5
0 Kilometres 8

ALCESTER

HOLLY BUSH HOTEL
Market Place
☎ (01789) 762482
12-2.30, 8-11; 8-10.30 Sun
Adnams Broadside; M&B Mild, Brew XI Ⓗ
Fine, unspoilt traditional local in an historic market town. Run by a long-serving landlord and landlady. Serious dominoes is played in the bar. Q ⊞ ♣

THREE TUNS
34 High Street ☎ (01789) 766550
12-11; 12-10.30 Sun
Goff's Jouster; Hobsons Best Bitter; guest beers Ⓗ
Welcoming, single bar with a stone-flagged floor and low beams. No music, no food, no

games: a drinker's paradise, serving up to eight ales, mainly from local independents. Q ▲

Try also: Holly Bush, Market Place (M&B)

ANSLEY

LORD NELSON INN
Birmingham Road (B4112)
☎ (01203) 392305
12-2.30, 5.30-11; 12-10.30 Sun
Draught Bass; M&B Brew XI; guest beers Ⓗ
Large roadside pub based on a naval theme. The public bar has a sloping floor and is adorned with hundreds of guest beer pumpclips. It promotes an excellent guest ale policy (up to four a week) and has an extensive,

quality menu; the restaurant opens eves (not Sun).
🏨 ⊛ ◑ ▶ ⊞ ♣ P

ARDENS GRAFTON

GOLDEN CROSS
Wixford Road OS114538
☎ (01789) 772420
11-2.30, 6-11; 12-2.30, 7-10.30 Sun
Goff's Jouster, HP&D Entire; guest beers Ⓗ
Old stone pub commanding views over the Vale of Evesham to the Cotswolds. Note the fine collection of dolls and teddies. Home to a plethora of societies and clubs. Always six ales, many from independent breweries, plus good and copious food – a trencherman's paradise.
⊛ ◑ ▶ ♣ P

AUSTREY

BIRD IN HAND
Church Lane
☎ (01827) 830260
12-4 (not Mon-Fri), 6.30-11; 12-4, 7-10.30 Sun
Banks's Mild; Marston's Pedigree, HBC Ⓗ
Popular village local, parts of which date back to the 11th century. A frequent local CAMRA *Pub of the Year* winner, it boasts a thatched roof and a restaurant (open Sun only).
🏘 Q 🕸 🕭 ▶ 🍺 P

BEDWORTH

PRINCE OF WALES
Bulkington Road
☎ (01203) 313202
12 (11 Sat)-4, 7-11, 12-4, 7-10.30 Sun
Banks's Mild; M&B Brew XI; Wells Eagle Ⓗ
The lively bar with a TV and pool table, dominates this small local. The lounge area is quieter.
🕸 🍺 ⇌ ♣ P

WHITE SWAN
All Saints Square
☎ (01203) 312164
11-11; 12-10.30 Sun
Banks's Mild; Wells Eagle, Bombardier Ⓗ
Town-centre pub, close to the Civic Hall. The large L-shaped lounge is popular with shoppers from the local market whilst the isolated snug provides an alternative to the pool-dominated bar.
🏘 🕭 🍺 ⇌ ♣

BULKINGTON

WEAVERS ARMS
12 Long Street, Ryton
☎ (01203) 314415
12-3.30, 6 (5.30 Fri)-11; 12-4, 7-10.30 Sun
Draught Bass; M&B Mild, Brew XI; guest beers Ⓗ
Built in 1841, this popular village two-roomed local free house has a traditional, friendly bar and a smaller, well-appointed lounge. No food Sun. 🏘 Q 🕸 🕭 🍺 ♣

CHURCH LAWFORD

OLD SMITHY
1 Green Lane (off A428)
☎ (01203) 542333
11-3, 5.30-11; 11-11 Sat; 12-10.30 Sun
Ansells Mild; Greene King IPA, Abbot; Marston's Pedigree; Judges Old Gavel Bender; Shipstone's Bitter; guest beers Ⓗ
Very friendly, improved village inn, a rare outlet for locally brewed Judges beers. A high quality restaurant is located in the conservatory.
🏘 🕸 🕭 ▶ ♣ P

EATHORPE

EATHORPE PARK HOTEL
The Fosse ☎ (01926) 632632
11-11; 12-10.30 Sun
Church End Cuthberts; Marston's Pedigree; guest beers Ⓗ
Warm, comfortable bar in a Victorian hotel in a country setting. It hosts a jazz night Wed and 'Murder-Mystery' weekend breaks. All food is freshly prepared. It stocks beers from Church End, including a house beer (Cuthberts).
Q 🕸 ⇌ 🕭 ▶ ♿ P 🍴

EDGEHILL

CASTLE
☎ (01295) 670255
11.15-2.30, 6.15-11; 12-3, 6.30-10.30 Sun
Hook Norton Best Bitter, Generation, Old Hooky; guest beer (summer) Ⓗ
A most unusual inn, well worth a visit. Built as a round tower in 1742 out of local stone, a wooden drawbridge links the 70ft tower with a smaller square tower. Views from the garden are some of the best in Warwickshire, looking over the Civil War battle site.
🏘 🕸 ⇌ 🕭 ▶ 🍺 🅰 ⌂ P

EXHALL

BOAT
188 Blackhorse Road, Longford
☎ (01203) 361438
12-3, 7-11; 12-3, 7-10.30 Sun
Ansells Mild, Bitter; Tetley Bitter; guest beers Ⓗ
In its 22nd year in the *Guide*, this pub has been run by the same family since 1840. Situated close to the canal (Sutton Stop), it has a friendly atmosphere and its distinct drinking areas add to the character. 🏘 Q 🕸 🍺 ♣ P

FARNBOROUGH

BUTCHER'S ARMS
Main Street ☎ (01295) 690615
12-2, 7-11; 12-10.30 Sun
Draught Bass; Boddingtons Bitter; Hook Norton Bitter; guest beer Ⓗ
Tucked away in the countryside, this pub is worth finding (look out for the pub sign). There is a warm welcoming bar through which is the high-quality restaurant. Popular with locals, it hosts live music some eves.
🏘 🕸 🕭 ▶ ♿ ♣ P

FIVE WAYS (HASELEY KNOB)

CASE IS ALTERED
Case Lane (off A4177/A414 roundabout) OS225701
☎ (01926) 484206
12-2.30, 6-11; 12-2, 7-10.30 Sun

Ansells Mild, Bitter; Flowers Original; Ⓖ **Greene King IPA;** Ⓗ **guest beer** (occasional) Ⓖ
Quintessential rural pub where time has almost stood still. The entrance room has a bar billiards table which takes old 6d coins. The bar is a perfect harmony of wood, brick and tile, making for a relaxed, happy atmosphere. The lounge has its own entrance and opens at weekends.
🏘 Q 🕸 ♣ P

GALLEY COMMON

PLOUGH INN
Plough Hill Road (½ mile off B4114) ☎ (01203) 392425
12-3 (4 Sat), 6-11; 12-3, 7-10.30 Sun
Home Mild, Bitter; Theakston Best Bitter, XB, Old Peculier Ⓗ
Popular roadside local; the tiled bar and side room are lively, with dogs in regular attendance. A cosy lounge at the rear provides a quieter atmosphere and access to the large garden and crown bowling green.
🕸 🍺 ♣ P

GREAT WOLFORD

FOX & HOUNDS
OS247345 ☎ (01608) 674220
12-3, 7-11 (closed Mon eve); 12-3 (closed eve) Sun
Hook Norton Best Bitter; guest beers Ⓗ
This pub stocks up to eight beers from a wide selection of independents, and 200 malt whiskies. An ancient stone-built farmhouse-type pub, it features original stone-flagged floors, inglenook and high-backed seating.
🏘 Q ⇌ 🕭 ▶ P

HAMPTON LUCY

BOARS HEAD
Church Street ☎ (01789) 840533
11.30-3, 6-11; 12-3, 7-10.30 Sun
Greene King IPA; Hook Norton Best Bitter; guest beers Ⓗ
Attractive 14th-century free house owned by the local church. Popular with visitors to nearby Charlecote Park (NT) this friendly, welcoming pub hosts regular music events and an annual beer festival. No eve meals Sun.
🏘 Q 🕸 🕭 ▶ 🍺 🅰 P

HENLEY-IN-ARDEN

WHITE SWAN
100 High Street ☎ (01564) 792623
11-11; 12-10.30 Sun
Ansells Mild, Bitter; Everards Beacon; Tetley Bitter; guest beers Ⓗ
Friendly, characterful coaching house, partly dating back to the 14th century, serving good value food in the lounge or restaurant.

It is reputedly haunted by a housemaid hanged at the gallows for murder. Live jazz Wed eve.
🏮 ⇦ ◖ ▮ ⇥ P

Try also: Nags Head, High St (Carlsberg-Tetley)

KENILWORTH

CLARENDON HOUSE HOTEL
6 High Street
☎ (01926) 857668
11.30 (11 Fri & Sat)-2.30 (3 Sat), 6-11; 12-3, 7-10.30 Sun
Boddingtons Bitter; Flowers IPA, Original; Hook Norton Best Bitter; Wadworth 6X Ⓗ
Welcoming bar situated in a plush hotel which also serves the local community well. Eve meals in the hotel's restaurant.
Q ⇦ ◖ ▮ P

VIRGINS & CASTLE
7 High Street (A429/A452 jct)
☎ (01926) 853737
12-11; 12-3, 7-10.30 Sun
Draught Bass; Davenports Bitter; Greenalls Original; Marston's Pedigree; guest beers Ⓗ
Extended medieval pub with low exposed beams and many rooms served by a central bar. It draws a cosmopolitan clientele and is especially popular with students.
🏰 Q ⌕ 🏮 ◖

WYANDOTTE INN
1 Park Road (off Manor Rd, off A429) ☎ (01926) 863219
5 (12 Sat)-11; 12-10.30 Sun
Bateman Mild; Marston's Bitter, Pedigree Ⓗ
Welcoming, street-corner local: a single room with a split-level bar and pleasant decor. The name is derived from a tribe of North American Indians. 🏮 ♣ P

LAPWORTH

NAVIGATION
Old Warwick Road (B4439)
☎ (01564) 783337
11-2.30, 5.30-11; 11-11 Sat; 12-10.30 Sun
Draught Bass; Highgate Dark; M&B Brew XI; guest beers Ⓗ
Excellent canalside pub with a pleasant atmosphere and traditional interior, sympathetically extended. A large canalside garden and constantly changing guest beers and ciders bring many visitors.
🏰 Q 🏮 ◖ ▮ 🅰 ⇥ ♣ ⌒ P

LEAMINGTON SPA

BENJAMIN SATCHWELL
112-114 The Parade
☎ (01926) 883733
11-11; 12-10.30 Sun
Courage Directors; Theakston Best Bitter; guest beers Ⓗ

One of only two pubs on the main shopping street, this huge new pub was once two shops. The long, split-level format works well. The policy of no music, reasonably priced food and beers makes it popular, especially at weekends. Occasional beer festivals. Q ◖ ▮ ♿ ✂ 🗇

HOPE & ANCHOR
41 Hill Street
☎ (01926) 423031
11-11; 12-10.30 Sun
Ansells Mild, Bitter; guest beer Ⓗ
Popular, thriving, corner local close to the town centre, busy with pub games and regular satellite TV sport. The guest beer is mainly from the Tapster's Choice range, although small independent brewers' beers are available occasionally. ♣

RED HOUSE
113 Radford Road
☎ (01926) 881725
12-2.30, 5-11; 11-11 Fri & Sat; 12-3, 7-10.30 Sun
Adnams Extra; Draught Bass; M&B Mild; Worthington Bitter Ⓗ
Popular pub at the hub of the local community. The real mild has returned by popular demand. Bring a rare cheese to be sampled and get it registered by the pub's Cheese Appreciation Society. The only regular Adnams outlet for miles. Q 🏮 ♣

SOMERVILLE ARMS
4 Campion Terrace (take Leicester St from centre)
☎ (01926) 426746
11-2.30 (3 Fri), 5.30-11; 11-11 Sat; 12-3, 7-10.30 Sun
Ansells Mild, Bitter; Ind Coope Burton Ale; Marston's Pedigree; Tetley Bitter; guest beer Ⓗ
Unchanging, popular back-street pub, well worth seeking out: a busy bar at the front, a cosy lounge tucked away at the back, displaying plenty of evidence of the landlord's humour. Relaxed and friendly atmosphere. Now in its 22nd year in this *Guide*.
Q 🍺 ♣ 🗇

WOODLAND TAVERN
3 Regent Street
☎ (01926) 425868
11-11; 12-10.30 Sun
Ansells Mild, Bitter; Marston's Pedigree; Morland Old Speckled Hen; guest beer Ⓗ
Traditional, 19th-century town pub with a comfortable lounge and bar which have separate entrances. Popular with students, professionals and mature drinkers alike, conversation often overpowers the juke box. The ceilings retain their original features.
🏮 🍺 ♿ ♣

LITTLE COMPTON

RED LION
Off A44
☎ (01608) 674397
12-3, 6-11.30; 12-3, 7-10.30 Sun
Donnington BB, SBA Ⓗ
Cotswold stone village local with a strong community involvement. Two French chefs ensure good food commendations. Donnington's only tied house in Warwickshire. Aunt Sally played.
🏰 🏮 ⇦ ◖ ▮ 🍺 ♣ P

LONG ITCHINGTON

HARVESTER
6 Church Road ☎ (01926) 812698
11-3, 6-11; 12-3, 7-10.30 Sun
Hook Norton Best bitter, Old Hooky; guest beer Ⓗ
Village local with a wide appeal: a small bar with a pool table, a comfortable lounge and a popular restaurant (booking advised). Originally two houses, it was a Hunt Edmunds pub until becoming a free house in 1976.
◖ ▮ 🍺 ♣ P

LONG LAWFORD

COUNTRY INN
29 Main Street ☎ (01788) 565188
12-2.30, 6-11; 12-11 Fri & Sat; 12-3.30, 7-10.30 Sun
Ansells Bitter; M&B Mild, Brew XI; guest beers Ⓗ
Friendly, single bar village free house, boasting genuine oak beams, a flagstone floor and a log fire. It has a games room and a good restaurant.
🏰 🍺 🏮 ◖ ▮ ♣ P

SHEAF & SICKLE
Coventry Road (A428, 1½ miles from Rugby)
☎ (01788) 544622
12-2.30, 6-11; 12-11 Sat; 12-10.30 Sun
Ansells Mild, Bitter; Tetley Bitter; guest beers Ⓗ
Friendly pub, stocking a good choice of guest beers. The quality restaurant is very popular, as are the well-priced bar snacks. A good local, with a quiet snug and a busy bar. Occasional beer festivals. 🏮 ◖ ▮ 🍺 ♿ 🅰 ♣ P

MORETON MORRELL

BLACK HORSE
☎ (01926) 651231
11.30-3, 7-11; 12-3, 7-10.30 Sun
Hook Norton Best Bitter; guest beer Ⓗ
Traditional village pub, popular with locals and students from the nearby agricultural college; games room at the back. A peaceful garden offers good views of rolling countryside. The filled rolls are good value.
Q 🏮 🅰

NEWBOLD-ON-STOUR

BIRD IN HAND
On A3400
☎ (01789) 450253
12-2.30, 6-11; 12-3, 7-10.30 Sun
Hook Norton Best Bitter, Generation, Old Hooky, seasonal beers; guest beer ⊞
Popular, friendly village local with a main bar and an adjacent games room. The food is highly recommended and often includes seasonal game dishes.
🚪 ✸ 🛏 ◐ ▶ ▲ ♣ ⌣ P

NEWTON REGIS

QUEENS HEAD
Main Road
☎ (01827) 830271
11-2.30 (3.30 Wed, 3 Sat), 6-11; 12-3, 7-10.30 Sun
Draught Bass; M&B Mild, Brew XI; guest beer ⊞
Two-roomed village local near the duck pond.
🚪 Q ✸ ◐ ▶ 🍺 ♣ P

NUNEATON

FELIX HOLT
3 Stratford Street
☎ (01203) 347785
11-11; 12-10.30 Sun
Draught Bass; Courage Directors; Marston's Pedigree; Theakston Best Bitter; guest beers ⊞
Wetherspoons town-centre pub, taking its name from the George Eliot novel. Popular with all ages, it usually stocks two guest beers. Occasional beer festivals held.
Q ◐ ▶ ❤ ⇌ ✂ 🖥

PRIORS MARSTON

HOLLY BUSH INN
Holly Bush Lane
☎ (01327) 260934
12-3, 5.30 (6 Sat)-11; 12-4, 7-10.30 Sun
Draught Bass; Flowers IPA; Hook Norton Best Bitter; Marston's Pedigree; guest beer ⊞
Lively, busy, village inn, tucked away in a quiet lane: a good traditional bar with a chatty atmosphere and a games room with TV. Features include a large central inglenook with a bakers oven and exposed beams. It has a large, thriving restaurant (no meals Sun eve).
🚪 Q ✸ 🛏 ◐ ▶ ♣ P

RATLEY

ROSE & CROWN
☎ (01295) 678148
12-2.30, 6-11; 12-3, 7-10.30 Sun
Badger Tanglefoot; Wells Eagle, Bombardier; guest beers ⊞
A superb country pub in a small secluded village. Stone built, with exposed beams, it dates back to

the 11th century. This friendly, family-run local is reputedly haunted by a Roundhead ghost from the nearby Battle of Edgehill. A cosy snug is a no-smoking area, popular with families. 🚪 Q 🛏 ✸ ◐ ▶ 🍺 ▲ ♣ ✂

RUGBY

ALEXANDRA ARMS
James Street (by multi-storey car park)
☎ (01788) 578660
11.30-3, 5-11; 11.30-11 Sat; 12-10.30 Sun
Ansells Bitter; Greene King Abbot; Marston's Pedigree; guest beers ⊞
Busy, friendly local just off the town centre with a comfortable, traditional lounge bar and a games room. It offers rapidly changing guest beers and good value bar food. Q ✸ ◐ ▶ ⇌ ♣

HALF MOON
28-30 Lawford Road
☎ (01788) 574420
4 (11 Fri & Sat)-11; 12-10.30 Sun
Ansells Mild, Bitter; Ind Coope Burton Ale; guest beers ⊞
Basic, no-frills, mid-terraced boozer, its character is enhanced by 19th-century pictures of Rugby and candlesticks on the tables. Popular with locals. 🚪 Q 🍺 ♣

RAGLAN ARMS
50 Dunchurch Road (opp Rugby School playing fields)
☎ (01788) 544441
12-3, 7-11; 12-11 Fri; 11-3, 5.30-11 Sat; 12-10.30 Sun
Fuller's London Pride; Greene King Abbot; Marston's Pedigree, HBC; Taylor Landlord; guest beers ⊞
Friendly local with a good atmosphere, a good selection of beers and no noisy machines. Rugby CAMRA *Pub of the Year* 1995 and '97. Q 🍺 ♣ P

STAG & PHEASANT
School Street, Hillmorton (take Watts Lane off A428)
☎ (01788) 544061
12-11; 12-10.30 Sun
Ansells Mild, Bitter; Ind Coope Burton Ale; guest beers ⊞
Old village local given a new lease of life under a caring management. The traditional bar, featuring bare floorboards and high-backed settles, is now complemented by a newly refurbished lounge. Guest beers from the Tapster's Choice range. ✸ 🍺 P

THREE HORSESHOES
22 Sheep Street
☎ (01788) 544585
11-3, 5.30-11; 12-3, 7-10.30 Sun
Greene King IPA, Abbot, seasonal beers; guest beer ⊞
Impressive, 18th-century hotel,

once a coaching inn, now an ideal retreat from the noisier pubs nearby. The cosy bar often features guests from local breweries. Dine in the Twickers Restaurant or stay in one of the 34 en-suite bedrooms. Limited parking. 🚪 🛏 🛏 ◐ ▶ P

VICTORIA
1 Lower Hillmorton Road
☎ (01788) 544374
12-2.30, 6-11; 12-3, 7-10.30 Sun
M&B Brew XI; guest beers ⊞
Fine example of a Victorian corner pub with much use of stained glass and etched windows. The excellent basic bar is complemented by a wonderfully refurbished lounge. Two guest beers from independent breweries always available. Weekday lunches. ◐ 🍺 ⇌ ♣

SAMBOURNE

GREEN DRAGON
The Village Green
☎ (01527) 892465
11-3, 6 (5.30)-11; 12-3, 7-10.30 Sun
Draught Bass; Hobsons Best Bitter; M&B Brew XI ⊞
Overlooking the village green, this attractive 17th-century inn offers two bars and a restaurant. Oak beams, brasses and pewter add to its character. It enjoys a good reputation for its food. Modern en-suite chalet accommodation available.
🚪 Q ✸ 🛏 ◐ ▶ P

SHUSTOKE

GRIFFIN INN
Coleshill Road, Church End (B4116, on a sharp bend)
☎ (01675) 481205
12-2.30, 7-11; 12-2.30, 7-10.30 Sun
Marston's Pedigree; guest beers ⊞
Old country village inn renowned for its wide-ranging guest beers. Low, beamed ceilings, log fires and Church End Brewery next door attract visitors. A must. No food Sun. 🚪 Q 🛏 ✸ ◐ 🍺 ▲ P

SHUTTINGTON

WOLFERSTAN ARMS
Main Road ☎ (01827) 892238
11-3, 6-11; 11-3, 6-10.30 Sun
Banks's Mild; Marston's Pedigree, HBC ⊞
Large hillside pub with a very popular restaurant (booking essential, especially at weekends). The extensive outside area offers panoramic country views. Q ✸ ◐ ▶ 🍺 P

STOCKTON

CROWN
High Street ☎ (01926) 812255
12-3, 7-11; 12-3, 7-11 Sun

Ansells Mild, Bitter; guest beers H

Village free house and restaurant, approaching 300 years old. It offers the usual pub games, plus petanque. No food Sun eve.
🏦 ◖ ▶ ♣ P

STRATFORD-ON-AVON

QUEEN'S HEAD
54 Ely Street
☎ (01789) 204914
11.30-11; 12-10.30 Sun
Draught Bass; Highgate Saddlers; M&B Brew XI; guest beer H
Lively 18th-century town-centre pub, featuring exposed beams, two real fires, a stone-flagged floor and an L shaped bar. Eve meals Fri and Sat.
🏦 ✿ ◖ ▶ ⇌

STUDLEY

LITTLE LARK
108 Alcester Road
☎ (01527) 853105
12-3, 6-11; 12-11 Sat; 12-4, 7-10.30 Sun
Ansells Mild; Little Lumphammer; Marston's Pedigree; Morrells Varsity; guest beers H
Friendly, Little Pub Co pub, bearing a newspaper theme, popular with local workers and residents. Meals from the varied and interesting menu are served in any of the three rooms around the central bar; roast lunch Sun.
🏦 ✿ ◖ ▶ ♣

RAILWAY INN
64 Station Road (B4092, ¹/₂ mile from centre)
☎ (01527) 857715
12-3, 5-11; 12-11 Fri & Sat; 12-4, 7-10.30 Sun
Ansells Mild, Bitter; Everards Tiger; Tetley Bitter H
Large single room with a small side room at the front. A large, well-organised garden at the rear. Live entertainment at weekends make this a busy and popular local which also boasts a friendly and chatty atmosphere.
🏦 ✿ ◖ ▶ ♣ P

WARWICK

OLD FOURPENNY SHOP
27-29 Crompton Street
☎ (01926) 491360
12-2.30, 5.30-11; 12-3, 5-11 Fri; 12-3, 6-11 Sat; 12-2.30, 6-10.30 Sun
M&B Brew XI; guest beers H
Once a run-down local, this pub has been transformed into a flourishing hotel. The comfortable lounge bar features five guest beers including a mild or

dark beer. The range has been known to change completely between lunch and evening, such is the enthusiasm of the customers!
🏦 ◖ ▶ ♣

ROSE & CROWN
30 Market Place
☎ (01926) 492876
11-11; 12-10.30 Sun
Draught Bass; Highgate Dark; M&B Brew XI; guest beer H
Town-centre pub with a popular front bar and a newly added no-smoking lounge. It has good access and newly installed wheelchair WC. Beers can be dispensed without sparklers if requested; cider varies. The rare, cosy little snug tucked in behind the bar is worth finding.
🏦 ◖ ♿ ⌂ ✄

WOLSTON

RED LION
23 Main Street (just off A428 Coventry-Rugby road) OS412755
☎ (01203) 542579
12-3, 5.30-11; 12-3, 7-10.30 Sun
Boddingtons Bitter; Flowers Original; Marston's Pedigree; Wadworth 6X; guest beers H
A village pub, well refurbished by Whitbread, very popular with villagers and visitors.
🏦 ✿ ◖ ▶ ♣ P

WOLVEY

AXE & COMPASS
Five Ways (1 mile S of A5/M69 jct)
☎ (01455) 220240
11-2.30, 5.30-11; 11.30-2.30, 6-11 Sat; 12-2, 7-10.30 Sun
Draught Bass; Highgate Dark; M&B Brew XI; Marston's Pedigree; guest beers H
Built in 1933 and well-known locally for its excellence of decor, service and cuisine. Note the many awards displayed in the large beamed and panelled lounge bar. It also has a small restaurant which opens eves.
🏦 ✿ ◖ ▶ P

BULLS HEAD
Church Hill
☎ (01455) 220383
11-3, 6-11; 12-3, 6-10.30 Sun
Marston's Bitter, Pedigree, HBC H
In the heart of the village, a large, two-roomed pub with a well-appointed bar and a deceptively large, well-decorated lounge, popular with locals.
✿ 🏦 ◖ ▶ ⊞ Å ♣ P

YOUR PUB AND CAMRA

There is nothing which has yet been contrived by man, by which so much happiness is produced as by a good tavern or inn.

SAMUEL JOHNSON

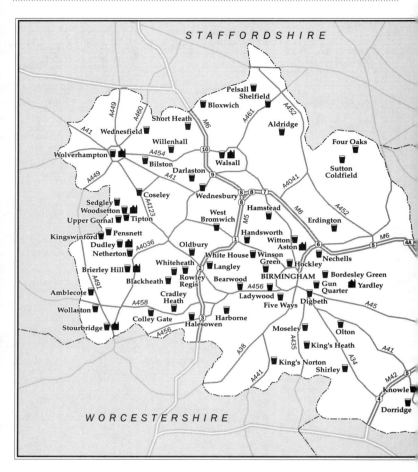

ALDRIDGE

LAZY HILL
196 Walsall Wood Road (1 mile from centre)
☎ (01922) 452040
12-2.30, 6-11; 12-2.30, 7-10.30 Sun
Ansells Mild, Bitter; Greene King Abbot; Ind Coope Burton Ale; Marston's Pedigree; Tetley Bitter Ⓗ
Comfortable, spacious 16th-century pub. Friendly and welcoming, it can get busy at weekends. The guest beer is from the Tapster's Choice range. ⚲ P

AMBLECOTE

MAVERICK
Brettell Lane (A491 jct)
☎ (01384) 824099
12-3, 4.30-11; 11-11 Fri & Sat; 12-10.30 Sun
Banks's Mild; Enville Ale; guest beer Ⓗ
Interesting, multi-area pub based on a Wild West theme. Regular live bands feature blues, rock and folk. Lunches served Fri; rolls usually available. Occasional cider.⚲ ♣ ⌂

STARVING RASCAL
Brettell Lane
☎ (01384) 834040
12-2.30 (not Mon or Tue), 7-11; 12-4, 7-10.30 Sun
Highgate Dark; Theakston Best Bitter; guest beers Ⓗ
Friendly, three-bar pub where guest beers are a regular feature. It has a cellar bar and restaurant and is a venue for folk music. No food Mon eve.
⚲ ⇆ ◖ ▶ ⊞ ♣ P

SWAN
10 Brettell Lane
☎ (01384) 76932
12-2.30 (not Tue or Wed), 7-11; 12-11 Sat; 12-3, 7-10.30 Sun
M&B Brew XI; guest beers Ⓗ
Welcoming, two-roomed local, including a public bar, offering a constant turnover of guest beers.
⚲ ⊞ ♣

BARSTON

BULLS HEAD
Barston Lane
☎ (01675) 442830
11-2.30, 5.30 (6 Sat)-11; 12-10.30 Sun
Draught Bass; M&B Brew XI; guest beers Ⓗ
Beamed country pub partly dating back to 1490. It is at the centre of village life and increasingly becoming known for its range of independent guest ales. No food Sun.
⚲ Q ⚲ ◖ ▶ P

BEARWOOD

BEAR TAVERN
500 Bearwood Road
(¼ mile from A456/A4030 jct)
☎ (0121) 429 1184
11-11; 12-10.30 Sun
Ansells Mild, Bitter; Marston's Pedigree; Morland Old Speckled Hen; Tetley Bitter; guest beers Ⓗ
Large pub, dominating a busy crossroads. The handpumps are

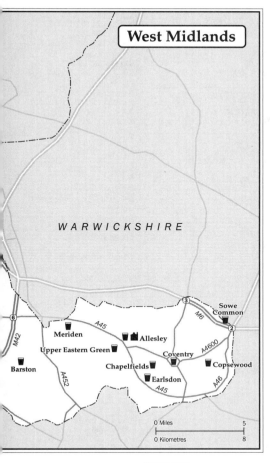

West Midlands

WARWICKSHIRE

Meriden
Upper Eastern Green
Barston
Allesley
Coventry
Chapelfields
Earlsdon
Sowe Common
Copsewood

0 Miles 5
0 Kilometres 8

in the lounge; there is also a traditional bar and 'Mr Q's Lounge'. It hosts jazz (Mon) and comedy (Tue) clubs, plus live music (weekends) in an upper room. Food available 11-10.30.

BILSTON

OLDE WHITE ROSE
20 Lichfield Street
☎ (01902) 493474
11-3, 5-11; 12-3, 7-10.30 Sun
Boddingtons Bitter; guest beers H
Recently refurbished with a plush lounge area and a long bar, plus a smaller snug off to one side.

SPREAD EAGLE
Lichfield Street
☎ (01902) 403801
11-3, 7-11; 12-3, 7-10.30 Sun
Beer range varies H
Three-roomed urban pub: a basic bar with wooden floorboards.

TRUMPET
58 High Street
☎ (01902) 493723
12-3.30 (not Mon-Fri), 8-11; 12-3.30, 8-10.30 Sun
Holden's Mild, Bitter, Special H
Popular, town-centre pub, known in the area for its jazz (eves and Sun). Local caricatures and celebrity photos on the walls.

BIRMINGHAM: BORDESLEY GREEN

TIPSY GENT
157 Cherrywood Road (off B4128) ☎ (0121) 772 1858
11-11; 12-10.30 Sun
Beer range varies H
Large front bar and a smaller, cosy lounge with sporting memorabilia make up this friendly local, which is busy lunchtimes and on soccer matchdays. The changing one or two guest beers often come from small independent and local breweries. Weekday lunches.
(Adderley Park)

CITY CENTRE

FIGURE OF EIGHT
236-239 Broad Street (near National Convention Centre)
☎ (0121) 633 0917
11-11; 12-10.30 Sun
Banks's Mild; Courage Directors; Theakston Best Bitter; Younger Scotch; guest beers H
Typically smart Wetherspoons pub offering reasonably priced beers in an area notorious for its high prices. Handy for the Sea Life Centre and canal basin.
Q (New St/Snow Hill)

OLD CONTEMPTIBLES
176 Edmund Street (right from Snow Hill station, then 1st right)
☎ (0121) 236 5264
12-11; closed Sun
Draught Bass; Highgate Dark; Hook Norton Old Hooky; M&B Brew XI H
Popular pub which attracts office workers and shoppers, built in the 1800s as a hotel but never opened as such. World War I memorabilia adorns the walls of this Grade II listed building. Lunches served Sat; eve meals weekdays until 8.
(Snow Hill/New St)

DIGBETH

ADAM & EVE
701 Bradford Street
☎ (0121) 693 1500
11-11; 7-10.30 (closed lunch) Sun
Draught Bass; M&B Mild; Marston's Pedigree H
A musical theme features in the cosy lounge area, which hosts live music nightly (except Tue). This two-roomed pub has a smaller room housing a pool table. A malt whisky of the month is promoted.

ANCHOR ☆
308 Bradford Street (behind coach station) ☎ (0121) 622 4516
11-11; 12-10.30 Sun
Ansells Mild; Tetley Bitter; guest beers H
Victorian corner pub boasting three rooms served from one bar with a friendly atmosphere. Regular beer festivals, a changing range of guest beers and bottled beers from around the world are features. Local CAMRA *Pub of the Year* 1996.
(New St/Moor St)

LAMP TAVERN
257 Barford Street
☎ (0121) 622 2599
12-11; 12-3, 7-10.30 Sun
Boddingtons Bitter; Church End Mild Quaker; Marston's Pedigree; Stanway Stanney Bitter; Wadworth 6X; guest beer (weekend) H

Popular pub with a wide-ranging clientele and an excellent choice of ales; still the only regular local outlet for Stanway beer. Regular live music in the back room.
◊ ⇌ (New St/Moor St)

WOODMAN ☆
106 Albert Street (opp Old Curzon St station)
☎ (0121) 643 1959
11-11; 12-4 (closed eve) Sun
Ansells Mild; HP&D Entire; Tetley Bitter ⊞
Victorian pub with a beautifully tiled interior unchanged since 1897, it has a public bar and a smoke room. Popular with local workers.
🏚 ◊ ▶ ⊕ ⇌ (Moor St) ♣

ERDINGTON

LAD IN THE LANE
22 Bromford lane (400 yds N of A38) ☎ (0121) 377 7471
11-11; 11-2.30, 5.30-11 Tue; 11-2.30, 5-11 Wed; 11-3, 6-11 Sat; 12-3, 7-10.30 Sun
Ansells Mild; Marston's Pedigree; Tetley Bitter ⊞
Excellent example of a 14th-century, cruck-framed building, well restored with a small basic bar and a large lounge on different levels. Friendly staff. Large garden. ❀ ◊ ▶ ⊕ P

FIVE WAYS

CITY TAVERN
38 Bishopgate Street (off Broad St) ☎ (0121) 643 4394
12-11; 12-10.30 Sun
Ansells Mild; Ind Coope Burton Ale; Marston's Pedigree; Tetley Bitter ⊞
Traditional two-roomed, back-street local which makes a change from most of the other pubs on Broad Street. Its prices are quite cheap for the area. Folk music bands play regularly.
⇌ (Five Ways)

WHITE SWAN
57 Grosvenor Street West (near Tesco's) ☎ (0121) 643 6064
11.30-2.30, 5-11; 12-3, 7-10.30 Sun
Ansells Mild, HP&D Entire; Marston's Pedigree; Tetley Bitter ⊞
Traditional, two-roomer with a large lounge and smaller front bar which has pool and darts. Popular with locals, residents and workers alike.
Q ◊ ▶ ⊕ ⇌ (Five Ways)

Try also: Vine, Hawlings St (Allied)

GUN QUARTER

GUNMAKER'S ARMS
92 Bath Street (near St Chads Cathedral) ☎ (0121) 236 1201

11-11; 11-3, 6-11 Sat; 12-3 (closed eve) Sun
Draught Bass; M&B Mild ⊞
Two-roomed pub with a display of gunmaking artefacts in the lounge.
❀ ◊ ▶ ⊕ ⇌ (Snow Hill) ♣

HAMSTEAD

BEAUFORT ARMS
42 Old Walsall Road (near station) ☎ (0121) 357 2355
11-11; 12-10.30 Sun
Theakston Mild; Courage Best Bitter; Morland Old Speckled Hen ⊞
Bustling, welcoming, large roadside pub catering for all tastes. It hosts regular live entertainment.
❀ ◊ ▶ ⇌ (Hamstead) P

HANDSWORTH

RED LION ☆
270 Soho Road
☎ (0121) 554 5159
11-11; 12-10.30 Sun
Ansells Mild ⊞
A lovely tiled interior is a feature of this two-roomed pub, which attracts mainly locals and is listed in the CAMRA inventory. A large TV dominates the end of the bar. Games.

WOODBINE TAVERN
45 Grove Lane (off Soho Rd)
☎ (0121) 241 1120
11-11; 12-10.30 Sun
Ansells Mild; Tetley Bitter; guest beers ⊞
Two-roomed back-street boozer. Thatchers dry cider is a rare find in an area not renowned for its traditional cider. ❀ ◊ ▶ ♣ ⌂

HARBORNE

BELL
Old Church Road
☎ (0121) 427 3477
12-11; 12-10.30 Sun
M&B Mild; ℗ **guest beer** ⊞
Classic, 300-year-old pub in a developing area. The bar is unusual as it is set within the hallway. Pleasant views of nearby St Peter's church can be enjoyed from the unusual L-shaped bowling green. The snug room is served from a small hatchway. ❀ ◊ ▶ ♣ P

JUNCTION
212 High Street
☎ (0121) 426 1838
11-11; 12-3, 7-10.30 Sun
Draught Bass; Highgate Dark; M&B Brew XI; guest beers ⊞
Single large room, served from an island bar, with up to seven ales. Some of the fixtures are originals from the Bass Museum. Guest beers are from the Cask Master range. No meals Sun eve.
❀ ◊ ▶ ⅋ ♣

NEW INN
74 Vivian Rd ☎ (0121) 427 5062
11-3.30, 5.30-11; 12-3, 7-10.30 Sun
Banks's Mild, Bitter; Camerons Strongarm ⊞
Two-roomed popular, friendly, village-style pub in a busy suburb, regularly used by shoppers, locals and students. The landlord is a Banks's *Cellarmanship* award-winner. No meals Sun eve. Wheelchair WC.
Q ❀ ◊ ⊕ ⅋ ♣ 🍴

WHITE HORSE
3 York Street (off High St)
☎ (0121) 427 6023
11-11; 12-10.30 Sun
Ansells Mild; Marston's Pedigree; Tetley Bitter; guest beers ⊞
Festival Ale House offering ever-changing guest beers, this friendly one-roomed pub has a large screen TV in one corner for sports events. ◊ ▶ ⊕ ♣

HOCKLEY

BLACK EAGLE
16 Factory Road (near Soho House Museum)
☎ (0121) 523 4008
11.30-3, 5.30-11; 11.30-11 Fri; 12-3, 7-11 Sat; 12-3, 7-10.30 Sun
Ansells Mild, Bitter; Marston's Pedigree; guest beers ⊞
Friendly pub, a frequent CAMRA award winner. Rebuilt in 1895 it retains most of the original features, including Minton tiles and period pieces. One of the few pubs in Birmingham selling Beowulf beers on a regular basis. Booking advisable for meals.
❀ ◊ ▶ ⊕ ⇌

CHURCH INN
22 Great Hampton Street
☎ (0121) 515 1851
11.30-11; 11.30-3, 6-11 Sat; 12-3 (closed eve) Sun
Ansells Mild; Batham Best Bitter; Morland Old Speckled Hen ⊞
Excellent out-of-town pub, famous for its food. Three rooms: the small back room displays old movie star pictures.
◊ ▶ ⊕ ⇌ (Jewellery Quarter)

RED LION
94-95 Warstone Lane (off A4540) ☎ (0121) 236 8371
12-11 (6.30 Sat, closed eve); 12-3 (closed eve) Sun
Banks's Mild, Bitter ℗
Cosy, two-roomed pub; an ornate mirrored wall in the lounge deceptively gives the room more depth. Convenient for the Jewellery Quarter.
❀ ◊ ⇌ (Jewellery Quarter) 🍴

WHITE HOUSE
Unett Street ☎ (0121) 523 0782
11-11; 12-4.30, 7.30-10.30 Sun

M&B Mild, Brew XI; guest beer H
Corner pub with a horseshoe bar, hosting live music Thu, Fri and Sat eves and Sun lunch.
🏮 ◖& ⇌ (Jewellery Quarter) ♣

KINGS HEATH

PAVILIONS
229 Alcester Road South
☎ (0121) 441 3286
12-3, 5-11; 12-3.30, 7-10.30 Sun
Banks's Mild, Bitter; Camerons Strongarm; Marston's Pedigree H
Modern, two-roomer inside an 1860 building. The interior has been designed with style and its traditional ambience does not feel contrived. Popular with a wide age range. Q ◖ ▶ ⊞ & P 🍺

KINGS NORTON

NAVIGATION INN
Wharf Road (off Redditch road)
☎ (0121) 458 1652
11-11; 12-3, 7-10.30 Sun
Banks's Mild: Draught Bass; Greenalls Original; Tetley Bitter; guest beer (occasional) H
This 19th-century pub took its name from the Irish who worked on the local canal. Very large lounge contrasts with a small bar. All food is home-made. Popular with students from the nearby college. 🏮 ◖ ▶ ⊞ & ⇌ ♣ P

LADYWOOD

FIDDLE & BONE
45 Sheepcote Street (off Broad St)
☎ (0121) 200 2223
11-11; 12-10.30 Sun
Adnams Bitter; Theakston Best Bitter, Old Peculier H
Large, canalside pub on the site of old stables for shire horses. Three levels include an eating area on the bottom level and a space for live music performed nightly on the middle level. Note the musical instruments around the pub. A house beer, Fiddlers Elbow, is brewed by Scottish-Courage.
Q ◖ ▶ & ⇌ (Five Ways) P

MOSELEY

BULLS HEAD
23 Saint Mary's Row
☎ (0121) 449 0586
11-11; 12-10.30 Sun
Courage Best Bitter, Directors; Morland Old Speckled Hen; Ruddles County; guest beer (occasional) H
Single room local on a major road junction, boasting a magnificent Victorian carved mahogany fireplace. Small but pleasant yard for outdoor drinking. 🏮 ♣

PRINCE OF WALES
118 Alcester Road
☎ (0121) 449 4198

11-3, 5.30-11; 11-3.30, 6-11 Sat; 12-3, 7-10.30 Sun
Ansells Mild; Ind Coope Burton Ale H
Traditional pub with two identities: for most of the week and lunchtimes it is a cosy relaxing pub, but on Fri and Sat eves the place is packed with mainly student drinkers. Do not miss the tiled corridor. 🏮 ⊞

NECHELLS

VILLA TAVERN ☆
307 Nechells Park Road
☎ (0121) 682 9862
11-2.30, 5.30-11; 11-11 Fri & Sat; 12-3, 7-10.30 Sun
Ansells Mild, Bitter; Greene King Abbot; Marston's Pedigree; Tetley Bitter H
Large, late Victorian corner house with a lively bar and a well-appointed lounge.
Q ⊞ ⇌ (Aston) ♣ P

WINSON GREEN

BELLEFIELD ☆
36 Winson St ☎ (0121) 558 0647
12-11; 12-10.30 Sun
Beer range varies H
Beautifully unspoilt pub with an ornate bar ceiling; the lounge has tile-framed pictures. It hosts regular mini-beer festivals; book for the recommended West Indian home-cooked lunches. Occasional cider. Q 🏮 ◖ ⌒ P

WITTON

SAFE HARBOUR
Moor Lane (between A4040 and A453) ☎
11-2.30 (3 Fri & Sat), 5 (6 Sat)-11; 12-3, 7-10.30 Sun
Ansells Mild; Tetley Bitter H
Popular, friendly pub next to the cemetery: a basic bar and a comfortable lounge. 🏮 ◖ ⊞ ♣

BLACKHEATH

HAWTHORNS
162 Ross, Rowley Regis (off A4100) ☎ (0121) 561 2276
12-2.30 (3 Fri-Sat), 7-11; 12-3, 7-10.30 Sun
Ansells Mild; Tetley Bitter; guest beer H
Friendly two-roomed local with a reputation for good food.
🍺 🏮 ◖ ▶ ⊞ ⇌ (Rowley Regis) ♣ P

WATERFALL
132 Waterfall Lane
☎ (0121) 561 3499
12-3, 5-11; 12-11 Fri & Sat; 12-10.30 Sun
Batham Best Bitter; Enville Ale; Freeminer Celestial Steam Gale; Holden's Special; Hook Norton Old Hooky; Marston's Pedigree; guest beers H

Busy, two-roomer on a steep hill, well worth the 10 minutes' walk down from the town. It offers regular music evenings and good food. Cider in summer.
🏮 ◖ ▶ ♣ ⌒ P

BLOXWICH

ROMPING CAT
97 Elmore Green Road
☎ (01922) 475041
12-11; 12-3, 7-10.30 Sun
Banks's Mild, Bitter P
Attractive corner pub with an intricate layout of three small, cosy rooms. A real local and a genuine Edwardian pub.
Q 🌄 ⊞ ⇌ ♣ 🍺

ROYAL EXCHANGE
24 Stafford Road
☎ (01922) 479618
12-3, 5-11; 12-11 Sun; 12-3, 7-10.30 Sun
Banks's Mild; Marston's Bitter, Pedigree H
Pleasant, 270-year-old local with a Grade II listed former brewery building at the rear. The small bar bears sporting memorabilia; the lounge has a quiet corner nook where children are welcome. Live music Wed and Sat eve. Weekday lunches.
🏮 ◖ ⊞ ⇌ ♣ P

BRIERLEY HILL

BLACK HORSE
52 Delph Road (B4122, near A4100 jct) ☎ (01384) 350633
12-11; 12-3, 7-10.30 Sun
Enville Ale, seasonal beers; Ruddles County H
Cosy, one-roomed pub on the famous Delph Run. Handy for Merry Hill Shopping Centre. No food Sun. 🏮 ◖ ♣ P

VINE (BULL & BLADDER)
10 Delph Road (B4172, near A4100 jct) ☎ (01902) 78293
12-11; 12-4, 7-10.30 Sun
Batham Mild, Best Bitter, XXX H
Famous, multi-roomed brewery tap at the top of the Delph Run. Note the award-winning extension into the old brewery offices. Weekday lunches served 12-2.
🍺 Q 🌄 🏮 ◖ ⊞ ♣ P

COLLEY GATE

WHY NOT
Why Not Street (½ mile from bottom of Windmill Hill - A458)
☎ (01384) 561019
12-3, 6-11; 12-11 Sat; 12-3, 7-10.30 Sun
Batham Best Bitter; guest beers H
Pub with mid-19th-century origins, on the edge of the countryside. Beyond the lounge, dining areas extend to the rear of the bar. The food is increasingly pop-

ular (booking advisable Fri and Sat eves and Sun lunch).
🏤 ❀ ◖ ▶ ♣ ◯ ☐

COSELEY

HURST HILL TAVERN
27 Caddick Street, Hurst Hill (off A463) ☎ (01902) 820280
1 (12 Sat)-5, 7-11; 12-4, 7-11 Sun
Banks's Hansons's Mild, Mild, Bitter; ℗ **Marston's Pedigree** ℍ
No-frills drinkers' local.
🏤 Q ❀ ♣ P ☐

PAINTER'S ARMS
Avenue Road (off A4123)
☎ (01902) 883095
12-11; 12-4, 7-10.30 Sun
Holden's Mild, Bitter ℗, **Special** ℍ
Very popular pub near Roseville which gets crowded, particularly at weekends. No food Sun.
🌣 ❀ ◖ ⇌ ♣ P ☐

WHITE HOUSE
1 Daisy Street (B4163)
☎ (01902) 402703
11-3, 6-11; 12-3, 7-10.30 Sun
Ansells Mild; Greene King Abbot; Tetley Bitter; guest beers ℍ
Cosy, two-roomed free house serving good value food and two guest beers, usually from independent brewers. Regular quizzes; no food Sun.
🏤 ❀ ◖ ▶ ⇌ ♣

COVENTRY: ALLESELY

RAINBOW INN
73 Birmingham Road (off A45)
☎ (01203) 402888
11-11; 12-3, 6-10.30 Sun
Courage Best Bitter, Directors; Rainbow Piddlebrook, Firecracker ℍ
Very old, village-centre pub on the outskirts of Coventry, at the heart of community life. Rainbow brewery is in the stables behind.
❀ ◖ ▶ P

CHAPELFIELDS

ALBANY
24 Albany Road, Earlsdon (near technical college)
☎ (01203) 715227
10-2.30 (3 Fri), 6-11; 10-11 Sat; 12-10.30 Sun
Marston's Bitter, Pedigree, Owd Rodger (seasonal)**, HBC** ℍ
Large, two-roomed Edwardian pub with a pool room upstairs. The busy lounge is popular with students, especially at weekends. Breakfast is served daily (opens 11 Sun). ❀ ◖ 🍺 ♣

CHESTNUT TREE
113 Craven Street
☎ (01203) 675830
12 (11 Sat)-11; 12-4, 7-10.30 Sun
Ansells Mild; Courage Directors; John Smith's Bitter; Webster's Yorkshire Bitter; guest beer ℍ

Popular, two-roomer in a traditional drinking area. Good value food includes Sunday roasts; eve meals end at 8.30 (not served Sun). It stocks an interesting range of whiskies and constantly changing guest beers. The outside drinking area is shaded by a large chestnut tree.
❀ ◖ ▶ 🍺 ♣ P

MALT SHOVEL
93 Spon End (B4101, ¹/₄ mile from inner ring road jct 7)
☎ (01203) 220204
12-3.30, 7-11; 12-11 Fri & Sat; 12-10.30 Sun
Donnington SBA; Tetley Bitter; guest beers ℍ
Characterful, popular pub with cosy, centrally served bar areas. A house beer may be available. The menu includes Sunday roasts and a vegetarian option; an upstairs room is open Sun for dining families.
🏤 ❀ ◖ P

NURSERY TAVERN
38-39 Lord Street
☎ (01203) 674530
11-11; 12-10.30 Sun
Courage Best Bitter; John Smith's Bitter; guest beers ℍ
Busy, three-roomed community pub which hosts regular beer festivals and organises social trips for its regulars. Four changing guest beers, always include one special value mild; the cider varies. Great value Sunday lunches. Q 🌣 ❀ ◖ 🍺 ♣ ◯

CITY CENTRE

GATEHOUSE TAVERN
42 Hill Street (by ring road jct 9)
☎ (01203) 256769
11-3, 5 (6 Sat)-11; 11-11 Fri; 12-3, 7-10.30 Sun
Draught Bass; M&B Brew XI; guest beers ℍ
Pub built by the current landlord from the remains of an old mill gatehouse. Popular with shoppers, office workers and rugby players. The long-awaited extension to the garden should be ready by summer 1998. No food Sat eve or Sun.
Q ❀ ◖ ▶ 🍺

OLD WINDMILL (MA BROWNS)
22 Spon Street
☎ (01203) 252183
11-11; 12-3, 7-10.30 Sun
Courage Directors; Marston's Pedigree; Morland Old Speckled Hen; guest beers ℍ
Medieval pub in a conservation area, divided into several small rooms. Regular guest beers come from microbreweries. Note the old brewhouse in the back room.
🏤 ◖

COPSEWOOD

BIGGIN HALL HOTEL
214 Binley Road (A428, 2¹/₂ miles E of centre)
☎ (01203) 451046
10.30-11; 10.30-3.30, 6-11 Sat; 12-10.30 Sun
Banks's Mild; Marston's Bitter, Pedigree, Owd Rodger, HBC ℍ
Prominent, convivial roadside pub built in distinctive mock-Tudor style. This regular *Guide* entry has been well refurbished. Sensibly priced, home-cooked lunches include Sunday roasts.
Q ❀ ◖ 🍺 ♣ P

EARLSDON

ROYAL OAK
28 Earlsdon Street
☎ (01203) 674140
5-11; (12-3, 7-10.30 Sun
ABC Best Bitter; Ansells Mild; Draught Bass; Tetley Bitter; guest beers ℍ
Busy, popular pub. The slate bar top and award-winning hanging baskets in summer are notable features.
🏤 Q ❀

SOWE COMMON

BOAT
31 Shilton lane, Walsgrave
☎ (01203) 613572
12-3.30, 7-11; 11-11 Sat; 12-10.30 Sun
Draught Bass; Worthington Bitter; guest beer ℍ
Old country pub now swallowed up by the city, but retaining its character. Weekday lunches. Look out for the pet pig (not part of the menu).
🏤 🌣 ❀ ◖ 🍺 ♣ P ✄

UPPER EASTERN GREEN

POACHERS RETREAT
Hockley Lane, Eastern Green
☎ (01203) 465127
12-3 (4 Fri), 6.30 (5.30 Fri)-11; 11-11 Sat; 12-4.30, 7-10.30 Sun
Draught Bass; M&B Mild, Brew XI; guest beers ℍ
Much improved, suburban pub which also serves the nearby rural community. A recently added restaurant area provides good value and quality food.
❀ ◖ ▶ 🍺 ♣ P

CRADLEY HEATH

RED HEN
78 St Anne's Road (off A4100)
☎ (01384) 635494
12-3, 6-11; 12-3, 7-10.30 Sun
Ushers Best Bitter, Founders ℍ
Formerly the Sausage & Porter, now chicken themed. American food is a speciality.
🏤 ◖ ▶ 🍺 ♣

DARLASTON

FALLINGS HEATH TAVERN
248 Walsall Road
☎ (0121) 526 3403
12-3, 7.30-11; 12-2.30, 7.30-
10.30 Sun
**Ansells Mild, Bitter; Tetley
Bitter; guest beer** (weekends) Ⓗ
Friendly, three-roomed roadside
pub on the Walsall side of town.
🐾 ❀ ⊕ ♣ P ☖

DORRIDGE

FOREST HOTEL
25 Station Approach (opp station)
☎ (01564) 772120
11-2.30, 5.30-11; 12-11 Sat; 12-3,
6-10.30 Sun
Draught Bass; guest beer Ⓗ
This 19th-century hotel with three
bars, a restaurant and a newly
refurbished function room is winner of the local CAMRA *Most
improved pub of the year* 1997
award. 🐾 ⇔ ◑ ▶ ⊕ ♿ ♣ P ✗

RAILWAY
Grange Road ☎ (01564) 773531
11-3, 4.30-11 (11-11 summer);
12-3, 7-10.30 Sun
**Draught Bass; Highgate Dark;
M&B Brew XI; guest beer** Ⓗ
Family-run pub, popular with
locals. 🏭 Q ❀ ◑ ▶ ⊕ ♿ ♣ P

DUDLEY

FULL MOON
58-60 High St ☎ (01384) 212294
11-11; 12-10.30 Sun
**Banks's Mild; Courage Directors;
Theakston Best Bitter; Younger
Scotch; guest beers** Ⓗ
Cavernous Wetherspoons conver-
sion in the town centre with at
least two guests usually on tap.
Q ◑ ▶ ♿ ⇔ ✗ ☖

LAMP TAVERN
116 High Street (A461/A459 jct)
☎ (01384) 254129
12-11; 12-10.30 Sun
Batham Mild, Best Bitter, XXX Ⓗ
Lively, welcoming, two-roomed
local. Note the former Queen's
Cross Brewery at the rear.
Weekday lunches.
🏭 ❀ ⇔ ◑ ⊕ ♿ ♣ P

LITTLE BARREL
68 High Street
☎ (01384) 256044
11-11; 12-3, 7-10.30 Sun
Beer range varies Ⓗ
Tiny one-roomed pub near the
top end of the High Street, with
limited parking. ◑ ♣ ⇔ P

FOUR OAKS

HALFWAY HOUSE
226 Lichfield Road (between
Mere Green and Four Oaks station) ☎ (0121) 308 1311
11-11; 12-10.30 Sun

Draught Bass; M&B Brew XI Ⓗ
Suburban pub which has undergone a typical 1990s refurbishment. Pleasant and comfortable
with local clientele. No food Sun.
❀ ◑ ▶ ⊕ ♿ ⇌ ♣ P ☖

HALESOWEN

HAWNE TAVERN
76 Attwood Street (200 yds from
A458) ☎ (0121) 602 2601
12-3, 7 (5.30 Sat)-11; 12-3,
7-10.30 Sun
Banks's Mild, Bitter; Ⓟ guest
beer Ⓗ
Traditional local, hidden in a side
street. The central bar serves a
comfortable lounge and a bar
that has been divided into several drinking areas, with a pool
table. ❀ ◑ ♣ P

KING EDWARD VII
88 Stourbridge Road, Hawne
(A458) ☎ (0121) 550 4493
12-3, 5.30-11; 12-11 Sat; 12-3,
7-10.30 Sun
**Enville Mild, Bitter, White; guest
beers** Ⓗ
Popular pub next to Halesowen
town football ground. A central
bar serves both a comfortable
lounge and a back bar. Good
value food. ◑ ▶ ⊕ ♣ P

WAGGON & HORSES
21 Stourbridge Road (A458)
☎ (0121) 550 4989
12-11; 12-10.30 Sun
**Batham Best Bitter; Enville Ale;
guest beers** Ⓗ
A friendly welcome awaits all at
this mecca for real ale drinkers -
14 ever-changing beers most
days, with microbreweries well
represented. A recent sympathetic refurbishment has been
completed keeping the pub's
character. ♣ ⇔

Try also: Fairfield, Fairfield Rd
(Banks's); Hare & Hounds,
Hagley Rd (Greenalls)

KINGSWINFORD

PARK TAVERN
182 Cot Lane (500 yds from
A4101) ☎ (01384) 287178
12-11; 12-3, 7-10.30 Sun
**Ansells Bitter; Batham Best Bitter;
Tetley Bitter; guest beers** Ⓗ
Popular, two-roomed pub near
Broadfield House Glass Museum.
❀ ⊕ ♣ P

UNION
Water Street (off A4101)
☎ (01384) 830668
12-2.30 (3 Fri), 6-11; 12-4, 7-11
Sat; 12-3, 7-10.30 Sun
Banks's Mild, Bitter Ⓟ
Small, friendly local, hidden in a
side street where the present
licensee has been in charge since
1962. ❀ ♣ P ☖

KNOWLE

VAULTS
St John's Close ☎ (01564) 773656
12-2.30, 5 (6 Sat)-11; 12-3,
7-10.30 Sun
**Ansells Mild; HP&D Bitter; Ind
Coope Burton Ale; Tetley Bitter;
guest beers** Ⓗ
Popular pub in a picturesque village; a former local CAMRA *Pub
of the Year*. No food Sun. ◑ ⇔

LANGLEY

FININGS & FIRKIN
91 Station Road (B4182, near M5
jct 2) ☎ (0121) 544 6467
12-11; 12-10.30 Sun
**Firkin Mild, Finings, Wort,
Dogbolter, seasonal beers** Ⓗ
Originally the HP&D brewery tap,
now supplying its Firkin ales to
the pub and other outlets (the
mild is not brewed here). Bright
and friendly atmosphere; unusual
pub games available. Brewery
tours by arrangement.
◑ ⇌ (Langley Green) P

MODEL INN
2 Titford Road (off A4127, near
M5 jct 2) ☎ (0121) 532 0090
11.30-11; 12-10.30 Sun
**Banks's Mild; Boddingtons
Bitter; M&B Brew XI; Ruddles
County; guest beer** Ⓗ
Though originally named after
the famous steam engine, the
pub's current sign employs a
more recent model. One U-
shaped room has a no-smoking
area at one end, with pool and a
large screen TV at the other.
◑ ▶ ⇌ (Langley Green) ♣ P

MERIDEN

QUEENS HEAD
Old Road
OS250820 ☎ (01676) 522256
12-11; 12-4, 7-10.30 Sun
**Draught Bass; M&B Brew XI;
guest beer** Ⓗ
Relatively unchanged, single-bar,
roadside pub off the Meriden
road from Coventry. No food Sun.
❀ ◑ ▲ P

NETHERTON

DRY DOCK
21 Windmill End (off A459)
☎ (01384) 235369
11-3, 6-11; 12-3, 6-10.30 Sun
Ushers Founders Ⓗ
Mad O'Rourke 'Little' pub at a
famous canal junction. The central bar is made from part of a
narrow boat. Frequent live music.
🏭 ❀ ◑ ▶ P

OLDBURY

FOUNTAIN
Albion Street (off A457)
☎ (0121) 544 6892

12-11; 12-5, 6.30-11 Sat; 12-4,
7-10.30 Sun
Banks's Mild, Bitter; guest beer
(occasional) H
Cosy, friendly local. ♨ ♣ ☐

WAGON & HORSES
Church Street (off A4034, opp
new council buildings)
☎ (0121) 552 5467
11.30-3.30, 5-11; 11.30-11 Sat;
12-3, 7-10.30 Sun
**Brains Mild, Bitter, SA; Everards
Tiger, Old Original; Marston's
Pedigree; Red Cross Nailer's
OBJ; guest beers** H
Two-roomed, listed, Victorian
pub near the town centre. It
hosts occasional snail racing! No
food Sun eve.
♨ ☜ ◖ ▶ ≈ (Sandwell &
Dudley) P ✂

Try also: Hardy, Park St
(Banks's)

OLTON

HARVESTER
Tanhouse Farm Road (off Old
Lode Lane, ½ mile from
A45/B425 jct) ☎ (0121) 742 0770
12-2.30 (3 Fri & Sat), 6-11; 12-3,
7-10.30 Sun
John Smith's Bitter; guest beers H
Estate pub which demonstrates
what a difference a landlord
makes. The refurbished bar and
cosy lounge give a warm welcome
while changing guest beers often
include rare examples. Good value
meals and snacks (no food Sun);
live music Wed. Children welcome
until 9. ❀ ◖ ▶ ⌸ ♣ P

PELSALL

SWAN INN
Wolverhampton Road
☎ (01922) 694696
12-3, 5.30 (6 Sat)-11; 12-3,
7- 10.30 Sun
Highgate Dark, Bitter, Saddlers H
Reputedly 400 years old; the
lounge with subdued lighting contrasts with a traditional, bright
saloon bar. Excellent food.
♨ ◖ ▶ ⌸ ≈ P ✂

PENSNETT

HOLLY BUSH INN
Bell Street (off A4101)
☎ (01384) 78711
1-4 (12-4.30 Sat), 7-11; 12-3,
7-10.30 Sun
Batham Mild, Best Bitter, XXX H
Popular, post-war pub where the
mild is the best seller. Q ❀ ♣ P

ROWLEY REGIS

SIR ROBERT PEEL
1 Rowley Village (B4171)
☎ (0121) 559 2835
12-4, 7-11; 12-3.30, 7-10.30 Sun
Ansells Mild, Bitter; guest beers H

Cosy local with three rooms and
a passage where beer is served.
This former police station is
extravagantly decorated at
Christmas. ♨ ❀ ≈ ♣

SEDGLEY

BEACON HOTEL ☆
129 Bilston Street (A463, 1½
miles from centre)
☎ (01902) 883380
12-2.30, 5.30-10.45 (11 Fri); 12-3,
6-11 Sat; 12-3, 7-10.30 Sun
**Hughes Pale Amber, Sedgley
Surprise, Ruby Mild; guest beer** H
Multi-roomed Victorian brewery
tap retaining many original features. Brewery trips available;
coach parties by prior arrangement only. Q ☜ ❀ ♠ ♣ P

SHELFIELD

FOUR CROSSES
1 Green Lane (off A461)
☎ (01922) 682518
11-11; 12-3, 7-10.30 Sun
**Banks's Mild; Marston's Bitter,
Pedigree; guest beers** H
Bright, traditional, saloon bar
hosting occasional live music,
and a small, comfortable lounge.
Try the gigantic hot pork sandwiches on crusty bread at
lunchtime. ❀ ⌸ ♣ P

SHIRLEY

BERNIE'S REAL ALE OFF-
LICENCE
266 Cranmore Boulevard (off
A34) ☎ (0121) 744 2827
12-2 (not Mon), 5.30-10; 12-2,
7-9.45 Sun
Beer range varies H P
Constantly changing range of
beers with an emphasis on the
small independents and micros.
Sampling glasses make the
choice even more difficult. ♿

RED LION
Stratford Rd ☎ (0121) 744 1030
11-2.30 (3 Sat), 5.30 (6.30 Sat)-
11; 12-3, 7-10.30 Sun
**ABC Best Bitter; Ansells Mild;
Marston's Pedigree; Morland
Old Speckled Hen; Tetley Bitter;
guest beer** H
Main road pub opposite the
Shirley Temple. Its plain precinct-
style exterior conceals a friendly,
comfortable interior. The back
bar is now a pool room. The front
has three seating areas: one is
popular for live sport on TV. No
food Sun. ◖ ✂

SHORT HEATH

DUKE OF CAMBRIDGE
82 Coltham Rd ☎ (01922) 408895
12-3, 7.30-11; 12-3, 7.30-10.30 Sun
Draught Bass H; **Highgate
Dark** P; **Saddlers; Worthington
Bitter; guest beer** H

17th-century farmhouse, converted in the 1820s to a cosy and
very friendly local.
♨ Q ❀ ⌸ ♣ P

STOURBRIDGE

HOGSHEAD
21-26 Foster Street
☎ (01384) 370140
11-11; 12-10.30 Sun
**Enville White; Marston's
Pedigree; Whitbread Abroad
Cooper, Fuggles IPA;** H **guest
beers** H G
Large, one-roomer: a long bar
where various seating areas on
two levels and wooden floors add
character. There is a TV but no
piped music. Regular quiz (Tue)
and live music (Thu). Meals
served 12-8.
❀ ◖ ♿ ≈ (Town) ⌁ ✂

NEW INN
2 Cherry Street (off B4186, via
Glebe Lane) ☎ (01384) 393323
12-2.30, 5-11; 12-3, 7-10.30 Sun
**Ansells Mild; Enville Ale; Greene
King Abbot; Marston's Pedigree;
Tetley Bitter** H
Popular, friendly local with two
rooms: a lively, games-oriented
bar with traditional decor and a
smart, comfortable lounge. Well
worth finding. ❀ ⌸ ♣ P

SEVEN STARS
21 Brook Road, Oldswinford
(B4186, opp Junction station)
☎ (01384) 394483
11-11; 12-10.30 Sun
**Batham Best Bitter; Courage
Directors; Theakston Best Bitter,
XB; guest beers** H
Bustling, friendly pub full of character. There are two large rooms
plus a restaurant with the same
excellent menu served throughout. Look out for the ornate tiling
and the beautifully carved wood
back bar fitting in the front room.
❀ ◖ ≈ (Junction) P

SHRUBBERY COTTAGE
28 Heath Lane, Oldswinford
(B4186) ☎ (01384) 377598
12 (11 Fri & Sat)-11; 12-10.30 Sun
**Holden's Mild, Bitter, Special;
guest beer** (occasional) H
Small, one-roomed local, a friendly, lively, drinkers' pub. The guest
beer is normally Holden's XB
served as Shrubbery Bitter. No
food Sun. ❀ ◖ ≈ (Junction) P

SUTTON COLDFIELD

DUKE INN
Duke Street (off Birmingham
road) ☎ (0121) 355 1767
11-3, 5.30-11; 12-3, 7-10.30 Sun
**Ansells Mild, Bitter; Ind Coope
Burton Ale; Tetley Bitter** H
Excellent, traditional pub, full of
character; the only unspoilt pub
in the area. The front bar fea-

tures ornate mahogany; the back lounge is quiet and cosy.
Q ❀ ❄ ♣ P

FALSTAFF & FIRKIN
19 High Street
☎ (0121) 355 2996
12-11; 12-10.30 Sun
Firkin Mild, Fal Ale, Golden Glory, Dogbolter; guest beer Ⓗ
Listed coaching inn, famous for its ghost. A cobbled passage with outside benches separates the two bars. Occasional beer festivals. Q ❀ ◖ & ≈ ♣ P

LAUREL WINES
63 Westwood Road (opp Sutton Park) ☎ (0121) 353 0399
12-2 (4 Sat), 5.30-10.30; 12-3, 7-10.30 Sun
Adnams Extra; Batham Best Bitter; Cottage Golden Arrow; Hook Norton Old Hooky; Morland Old Speckled Hen; guest beers Ⓖ
Friendly off-licence stocking a wide range of real ales and bottled beers. ⇌ P

WHITE HORSE
196 Whitehouse Common Road
☎ (0121) 378 0149
11-11; 12-10.30 Sun
Draught Bass; Davenports Bitter; Greenalls Mild, Original; guest beers Ⓗ
Large, food-oriented suburban pub. Meals are served all day. Families welcome when eating.
🐕 ❀ ◖ ▶ ⊞ & ♣ P ⊁

TIPTON

PORT 'N' ALE
178 Horsley Heath (A461)
☎ (0121) 557 7249
12-3, 5-11; 12-11 Fri & Sat; 12-5, 7-10.30 (may vary) Sun
Enville Ale; Highgate Dark; RCH Pitchfork; guest beers Ⓗ
Genuine free house on the main West Bromwich-Dudley road. Up to six guest beers come from independent brewers. Franklin's perry is usually available.
🐕 ❀ ≈ (Dudley Port) ♣ ⇌ P

RISING SUN
116 Horsley Road (off A461)
☎ (0121) 530 9780
12-2.30 (3 Sat), 5-11; 12-3, 7-10.30 Sun
Banks's Hanson's Mild, Mild, Bitter; Marston's Pedigree; guest beers Ⓗ
Friendly, two-roomed local offering three guest beers. No food Sun. 🏛 ▶ ⊞ ▲ ♣ ⇌ ⊟

UPPER GORNAL

BRITANNIA
109 Kent Street (A459)
☎ (01902) 883253
12-3.30, 7-11; 12-3.30, 7-10.30 Sun
Batham Mild, Best Bitter, XXX Ⓗ

Built in 1780 with a late 19th-century tap room where the beer is served from handpumps against the wall. A recent refurbishment has not detracted from its charm. Britannia Special is brewed by Batham or sometimes at the pub. 🏛 Q ❀ ♣ ⊁

JOLLY CRISPIN
25 Clarence Street (A459)
☎ (01902) 672220
7-11; 12-3, 7-10.30 Sun
Courage Directors; Ruddles County; guest beers Ⓗ
Oldest pub in Upper Gornal - a listed monument. Note the inglenook in the cosy front bar.
🏛 ❀ ⊞ ♣ P ⊟

WALSALL

BROWN LION
33 Wednesbury Road, Pleck
☎ (01922) 644423
12-11; 12-4, 7-10.30 Sun
Banks's Mild Ⓟ**, Bitter; Marston's Pedigree; guest beers** Ⓗ
Formerly a two-roomed local, now a single, split-level room with a central bar. Note the tiled exterior with the 'old' Highgate livery. 🏛 ♣ P

FOUNTAIN
49 Lower Forster Street (off ring road) ☎ (01922) 629741
12-11; 12-3, 7.30-10.30 Sun
Draught Bass; Highgate Dark; guest beer Ⓗ
Two-roomed pub with a loggia. Pleasant staff, warm rooms and a children's area add to its appeal. The guest beer is from the Tapster's Choice list.
Q 🐕 ◖ ⊞ ≈ ♣

KATZ
23 Lower Rushall Street
☎ (01922) 725848
12-2.30, 5.30 (7 Sat)-11; closed Sun
ABC Bitter; Greene King Abbot; Marston's Pedigree; guest beers Ⓗ
Two-roomed free house built in 1848, a very popular pub serving good value food. Originally the Albert and Victoria, the current name was coined by Irish navvies whose nickname for Queen Victoria was 'the Cat'. Eve meals served until 7, Mon-Thu. 🏛 ❀ ◖ ▶ ⊞ ≈

KING ARTHUR
Liskeard Road, Park Hall (next to Park Hall shopping precinct)
☎ (01922) 631400
12-3, 5.30-11; 11-11 Sat; 12-10.30 Sun
Courage Best Bitter, Directors; John Smith's Bitter Ⓗ
Estate pub with two large rooms and a friendly atmosphere. Good food includes an excellent range of curries (all home made); no food Sun eve or Mon. It hosts regular quizzes and other fund-

raising activities. The house bitter is brewed by Mansfield.
❀ ◖ ▶ ⊞ P

LANE ARMS
169 Wolverhampton Road West, Bentley (near M6 jct 10)
☎ (01922) 623490
12-3, 5-11; 12-11 Fri & Sat; 12-3, 7-10.30 Sun
Highgate Dark, Bitter, Saddlers, seasonal beers Ⓗ
Large pub with a comfortable lounge, a basic bar and small snug. Very reasonably priced food includes barbecues in summer (no food Sun eve). It hosts occasional beer festivals and regular live entertainment Fri and Sat eves. Large garden.
🏛 ❀ ◖ ▶ ⊞ ♣ P ⊁

LYNDON HOUSE HOTEL
Upper Rushall Street
☎ (01922) 612511
11-11; 12-10.30 Sun
Ansells Mild, Bitter; Boddingtons Bitter; Ind Coope Burton Ale; Morland Old Speckled Hen; guest beer Ⓗ
A Tardis experience: a small, comfortable, traditional local fronts a large, light and airy piano lounge. This opens on to a roof-level terrace with its own bar. Popular with business people, it operates dress restrictions. Eve meals in the restaurant. ◖ ▶ ≈

NEW BIRCHILLS
15 Birchills St ☎ (01922) 722599
11-3, 6 (6.30 Sat)-11; 12-3, 7-10.30 Sun
Banks's Mild, Bitter; Ⓟ **guest beers** Ⓗ
Small, modernised, one-roomed Victorian pub. Although a successful food pub it still manages to function as a great back-street local. No meals Sun eve.
❀ ◖ ▶ & ≈ ♣ P ⊟

OAK
336 Green Lane ☎ (01922) 645758
12-2.30 (3 Sat), 7-11; 8-10.30 (closed lunch) Sun
Flowers IPA; guest beers Ⓗ
Large, single-room pub with an island bar, just a short walk from the town centre. A busy pub, it is popular with office workers at lunchtime. Up to five regularly changing guest beers.
🏛 ❀ ◖ ≈ ♣ P ⊟

ROSE & CROWN
Old Birchills (off Green Lane)
☎ (01922) 720533
11-11; 12-10.30 Sun
Highgate Dark, Saddlers, seasonal beers Ⓗ
Fine late Victorian pub with a bar, lounge and a pool room.
🏛 🐕 ❀ ⊞ ♣

TAP & SPILE
John Street (off B4210)

☎ (01922) 627660
11-3, 5.30-11; 12-11 Fri & Sat;
12-3, 7-10.30 Sun
Highgate Dark; guest beers Ⓗ
Friendly, Victorian two-bar pub
known locally as the 'Pretty
Bricks', near the town centre. Up
to seven constantly changing
guest beers; no meals Sun or
Mon eve. ⚲ ❀ ◖ ▶ ≠ ♣

WHITE LION
150 Sandwell St (near Caldmore
Green)
☎ (01922) 628542
12-3.30, 6-11; 12-11 Sat; 12-3.30,
7-10.30 Sun
**Ansells Mild, Bitter; HP&D
Bitter, Entire; Ind Coope Burton
Ale; guest beer** Ⓗ
Outstanding community local, a
Victorian corner house with a
curiously sloping curved bar, a
smarter lounge and a games
room. Popular with all and can
get busy. The lunches are good
value. Q ❀ ◖ ▶ ⊞ ♣

Try also: Longhorn, Sutton Rd
(Carlsberg-Tetley); Parkbrook,
Wolverhampton Rd (Bass)

WEDNESBURY

OLD BLUE BALL
19 Hall End Road
☎ (0121) 556 0197
12-3, 5-11; 12-11 Fri; 12-3,
7-10.30 Sun
Draught Bass; Ⓗ **Highgate
Dark;** Ⓟ **guest beers** Ⓗ
Traditional warm and friendly
pub: a bar and a snug with a family room.
Ⓑ ❀ ♣ ⊟

WEDNESFIELD

VINE
35 Lichfield Road (A4124)
☎ (01902) 733529
11-3, 7-11; 12-3, 7-10.30 Sun
Flowers IPA; guest beers Ⓗ
Unspoilt inter-war pub of three
rooms, each with a coal fire; a
friendly local, but welcoming to
all visitors. Three guest beers -
one is always a mild.
⚲ ❀ ◖ ⊞ ♣ ⌣ P

WEST BROMWICH

CHURCHFIELD TAVERN
18 Little Lane (by Sandwell
General Hospital)
☎ (0121) 588 5468
11-11; 12-3, 7-10.30 Sun
**Banks's Hanson's Mild, Bitter;
Camerons Bitter,** Ⓟ**Strongarm** Ⓗ
Thriving community-conscious
pub with four rooms connected
by a central corridor. The bowling green and garden with children's play area are added
attractions. Eve meals served 6-8
(not Sun).
Ⓑ ❀ ◖ ▶ ⊞ P ⊟

OLD CROWN
56 Sandwell Road (near
A41/A4031 jct)
☎ (0121) 525 4600
12-4, 5 (6 Sat)-11; 12-4, 7-10.30 Sun
Beer range varies Ⓗ
One-roomed pub in a quiet side
street, popular for its three guest
beers and Indian menu. ◖ ▶ ⊟

ROYAL OAK
14 Newton Street (cul-de-sac off
A4031 one-way system, near
A4041) ☎ (0121) 588 2318
5 (11 Sat)-11; 12-10.30 Sun
M&B Mild, Brew XI; guest beers Ⓗ
Hidden from view, this friendly
two-roomed local continues to
grow in popularity. At least two
changing guest beers. ⊞ ♣

VINE
Roebuck Street (near M5 jct 1)
☎ (0121) 553 2866
11.30-2.30 (3 summer), 5-11; 11-
11 Fri & Sat; 12-10.30 Sun
Beer range varies Ⓗ
Extended corner house, famous
for its indoor Indian barbecue
where you can watch your food
being cooked. Guest beer comes
from an independent brewer.
❀ ◖ ▶ ≠ (Carlton Bridge) ⊟

WHITEHEATH

WHITEHEATH TAVERN
400 Birchfield Lane (A4034, near
M5 jct 2)
☎ (0121) 552 3603
12-3.30 (not Tue-Thu), 8-11; 12-
3.30, 8-10.30 Sun
Ansells Mild, Bitter; Ⓗ **Banks's
Mild** Ⓟ
Friendly local with two contrasting rooms, near head of Titford
branch canal.
⊞ ≠ ♣ (Rowley Regis) ⊟

WILLENHALL

FALCON
Gomer Street West (near Lock
Museum) ☎ (01902) 633378
12-11; 12-10.30 Sun
**Fuller's London Pride; Greene
King Abbot; Highgate Dark;
Hydes' Anvil Mild, Bitter; RCH
Pitchfork; guest beers** Ⓗ
No-frills pub serving a good
range of reasonably-priced
beers. Games are very much in
evidence in the bar; quieter
lounge. Q ❀ ⊞ ♣ ⅍ ⊟

ROBIN HOOD
54 The Crescent
☎ (01902) 608006
12-3, 5-11; 12-3, 7-11 Sat; 12-3,
7-10.30 Sun
**Ind Coope Burton Ale; Tetley
Bitter; guest beer** Ⓗ
Popular, friendly local with one
U-shaped room. Three times
local CAMRA *Pub of the Year*. The
family area is open 7-9pm.
❀ P

WOLLASTON

PLOUGH
154 Bridgnorth Road (A458)
☎ (01384) 393414
12-2.30 (3 Sat), 6-11; 12-3,
7-10.30 Sun
**Draught Bass; Enville Ale;
Stones Bitter** Ⓗ
Well-decorated old coaching
house with original windows. A
keen sporting pub, it has a
petanque piste at the rear. The
lounge is busy lunch and early
eve (until 7.30) for excellent quality and value meals (not served
Sun eve). Folk club Tue.
❀ ◖ ▶ ⅁ & ♣ P

PRINCESS
115 Bridgnorth Road (A458)
☎ (01384) 443687
11-11; 12-3, 7-10.30 Sun
**Banks's Mild; Draught Bass;
Gibbs Mew Salisbury, Deacon** Ⓗ
An old M&B house acquired by
Gibbs Mew prior to the takeover
by Enterprise Inns. Refurbished
in a traditional manner to appeal
to all ages. Another Gibbs Mew
beer is occasionally stocked.
❀ ◖ ▶ & P

UNICORN
145 Bridgnorth Road (A458)
☎ (01384) 394823
11-3, 6-11; 11-11 Fri & Sat; 12-4,
7-10.30 Sun
**Batham Mild, Bitter, seasonal
beers** Ⓗ
Former brewhouse (still standing
at the side of the pub) this basic
drinking house was recently
acquired by Bathams. Popular
with all ages and unspoilt by
progress. A large public car park
is behind the pub. Q ❀ ⊞ &

WOLVERHAMPTON

CHINDIT
113 Merridale Road
☎ (01902) 425582
12-3, 5-11; 11-11 Sat; 12-3,
7-10.30 Sun
Beer range varies Ⓗ
Basic, street-corner local with a
bar and lounge. Named after the
soldiers of 1st South Staffs
Regiment who fought in Burma in
1944. ⊞ ♣

CLARENDON HOTEL
38 Chapel Ash (next to Banks's
brewery) ☎ (01902) 420587
11-11; 12-10.30 Sun
Banks's Mild, Bitter; Ⓟ
**Camerons Strongarm; guest
beer** Ⓗ
Popular brewery tap with a large,
split-level lounge. The smaller
smoke room has its own bar and
can be quieter. Breakfast available from 8am. Eve meals end at
8pm (not Sat or Sun). No-
smoking restriction lifted at 8pm.
Ⓑ ◖ ▶ P ⅍ ⊟

EXCHANGE VAULTS
Cheapside (opp Civic Centre)
11-11; 12-10.30 Sun
Banks's Mild, Bitter; Camerons Bitter, Strongarm; guest beers H
Recently renovated into one room with a Camerons Tap House theme. Friendly bar staff give a good welcome to all.
🏠 ⬤ ▶ ⇌ ⏛

FEATHERS
Molineux Street (behind John Ireland stand of the Wolves football ground) ☎ (01902) 269424
11-11; 12-3, 7-10.30 Sun
Banks's Mild, Bitter P
Small, traditional two-bar pub near the football ground and university. 🌿 ⬤ ⇌ ♣ ⏛

FELINE & FIRKIN
9 Princess St ☎ (01902) 428806
12-11; 7-10.30 (closed lunch) Sun
Firkin Feline, Pussy Ale, Dogbolter H
Fairly small, split level pub in typical Firkin style with bare boards; popular with students. The beers are not brewed on the premises. No food Sun. 🌿 ⬤ ⇌ ♣

GREAT WESTERN
Sun Street (behind station - via underpass) ☎ (01902) 351090
11-11; 12-3, 7-10.30 Sun
Batham Best Bitter, Holden's Mild, Bitter, Special H
Characterful, award-winning town pub where a warm welcome awaits. Railway and Wolves FC memorabilia adorn the walls of the pub and conservatory. Excellent value meals and snacks (no food Sun). 🌿 ⬤ ⇌ ♣ P

HOMESTEAD
Lodge Road, Oxley (off A449 at Goodyear roundabout)
☎ (01902) 787357
12-3, 6-11; 12-3, 7-10.30 Sun
Ansells Bitter; Courage Directors; Tetley Bitter; guest beers H
Large, two-roomed suburban pub where children are welcome (large outdoor play area). Good home-cooked food.
🌿 ⇌ ⬤ ⊟ ♣ P

MITRE INN
Lower Green, Tettenhall Road (near A41/Lower St jct)
☎ (01902) 753487
12-2.30 (3 Sat), 6-11 (12-11 summer & Sat); 12-3, 7-10.30 (12-10.30 summer) Sun
Draught Bass; Stones Bitter; Worthington Bitter; guest beer H
Surprisingly spacious, two-roomed local in a pleasant location opposite the lower green.
🌿 ⬤ ▶ ⊟ ♣

MOON UNDER WATER
Lichfield Street (opp Grand Theatre) ☎ (01902) 422447

10-11; 12-10.30 Sun
Banks's Mild; Courage Directors; Marston's Pedigree; Theakston Best Bitter, XB; guest beers H
Large bar with some small panelled areas for a quieter pint. Very busy at weekends, otherwise it attracts all ages. Local memorabilia is displayed. Good food. Q ⬤ ▶ ♿ ⇌ ✗ ⏛

NEWHAMPTON
Riches Street, Whitmore Reans (off A41) ☎ (01902) 745773
11-11; 12-10.30 Sun
Courage Best Bitter, Directors; Marston's Pedigree; Ruddles County; John Smith's Bitter; guest beers H
Busy, corner local attracting a wide clientele to three distinctly different rooms. The large garden has a children's play area and a bowling green. The function room is used as a music venue. No-smoking area available at lunchtime.
🏠 🌿 ⬤ ▶ ♣ ⌂ ⏛

ROYAL OAK
70 Compton Road (A454)
☎ (01902) 422845
11-11; 12-3.30, 7-10.30 Sun
Banks's Mild, Bitter; Camerons Strongarm H
Pleasant extended local with a new, small outside drinking area. Can be noisy on nights when music is played. 🌿 ⬤ P ⏛

SHOULDER OF MUTTON
Wood Road, Tettenhall Wood
☎ (01902) 756672
11.30-3, 5.30-11; 11.30-11 Sat; 12-3, 7-10.30 Sun
Banks's Mild, Bitter; P
Marston's Pedigree H
Large, modern pub with a beamed interior: one long bar in the lounge with three smaller partitioned seating areas. Good food Mon-Sat.
🌿 ⬤ ♣ P ⏛

STAMFORD ARMS
Lime Street, Penn Fields (off Lea Rd) ☎ (01902) 424178
12-4, 7-11; 12-11 Sat; 12-10.30 Sun
Banks's Mild, Bitter P
Welcoming corner local with notable exterior tiling. The three unspoilt rooms are served by a single bar with a hatch. A hidden gem in an old residential area.
🌿 ⊟ ♣

STILE
23 Harrow Street (off Newhampton Rd E)
☎ (01902) 421595
12-3, 6-11; 11-11 Sat; 12-3, 7-10.30 Sun
Banks's Mild, Bitter P
Imposing, one-bar street-corner local featuring a wooden floor and bench seats in the bar, a small, quiet snug and a large

smoke room with a pool table. The outdoor drinking area includes a bowling green. Convenient for Wolves FC.
Q 🌿 ♣ ⏛

SWAN
Bridgnorth Road, Compton (A454/B4161 jct)
☎ (01902) 754736
11-3, 5-11; 12-4, 7-10.30 (12-10.30 summer) Sun
Banks's Mild, Bitter P
The refurbished lounge improves this listed Victorian pub with its small bar and snug.
🏠 Q ⊟ ♣ P ⏛

TAP & SPILE
35 Princess St ☎ (01902) 713319
11-11; 12-10.30 Sun
Highgate Dark; Tap & Spile Premium; guest beers H
Small, town-centre pub with a well thought-out traditional layout. Good food offers are a feature (eve meals end at 7.30).
⬤ ▶ ♿ ⇌ ♣ ⌂

WOODSETTON

PARK INN
George Street (off A457)
☎ (01902) 882843
11-11; 12-4, 7-10.30 Sun
Holden's Mild, Bitter, Lucy B, Special, seasonal beers H
Holden's brewery tap: a comfy lounge bar with a conservatory at the side. Happy hour 5-7 weekdays. 🏠 🐕 ⬤ ▶ ♣ P ✗

INDEPENDENT BREWERIES

Aston Manor:
Birmingham

Banks's:
Wolverhampton

Batham:
Brierley Hill

Beowulf:
Yardley

Enville:
Stourbridge

Highgate:
Walsall

Holden's:
Dudley

Hughes:
Dudley

Rainbow:
Coventry

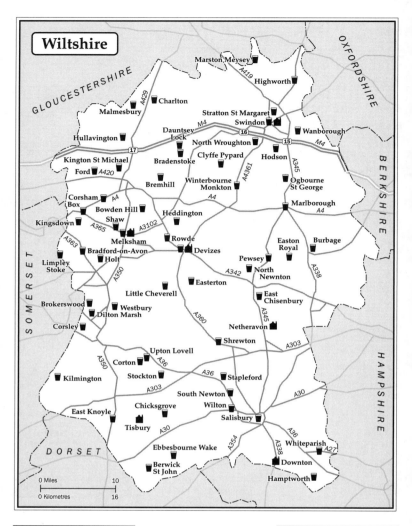

Wiltshire

(Map of Wiltshire showing locations including Marston Meysey, Highworth, Charlton, Malmesbury, Stratton St Margaret, Swindon, Wanborough, Hullavington, Dauntsey Lock, North Wroughton, Hodson, Kington St Michael, Bradenstoke, Clyffe Pypard, Ford, Bremhill, Winterbourne Monkton, Ogbourne St George, Corsham, Box, Bowden Hill, Heddington, Marlborough, Kingsdown, Shaw, Melksham, Rowde, Easton Royal, Burbage, Bradford-on-Avon, Holt, Devizes, Pewsey, Limpley Stoke, Easterton, North Newnton, Brokerswood, Little Cheverell, East Chisenbury, Westbury, Dilton Marsh, Netheravon, Corsley, Shrewton, Upton Lovell, Corton, Kilmington, Stockton, Stapleford, East Knoyle, South Newton, Chicksgrove, Wilton, Tisbury, Salisbury, Ebbesbourne Wake, Whiteparish, Berwick St John, Downton, Hamptworth)

0 Miles 10
0 Kilometres 16

BERWICK ST JOHN

TALBOT INN
The Cross ☎ (01747) 828222
12-2.30, 7-11; 12-2.30 (closed eve) Sun

Adnams Bitter, Broadside; Draught Bass; Wadworth 6X H **guest beer** (occasional) G
Historic pub with beams and inglenook, set in a remote valley - excellent walking country. Recently saved from closure, largely helped by Salisbury CAMRA. Meals served Tue-Sat.
♨ Q ⊛ ◑ ▶ & ▲ P

BOWDEN HILL

BELL
½ mile from Lacock toward Calne ☎ (01249) 730308
11-2.30 (7 Sat)-11; 12-3, 7-10.30 Sun

Beer range varies H
Pleasant pub with a large garden and pets corner. Good food.
🍴 ⊛ ⇔ ◑ ▶ ♣ P

BOX

QUARRYMANS ARMS
Box Hill (300 yds S of A4 at Box Hill) OS834693
☎ (01225) 743569
11-4, 6-11 (11-11 Thu-Sat); 12-10.30 Sun

Butcombe Bitter; Wadworth 6X; H **guest beer** G
Open-plan pub affording superb views over the valley, well hidden in a maze of lanes, yet only a short distance from the A4. The landlord advises phoning for directions, stating your location. Cider in summer. No-smoking family room.
♨ 🍴 ⊛ ⇔ ◑ ▶ ▣ ▲ ♣ ⇔ P ✂

BRADENSTOKE

CROSS KEYS
65 Bradenstoke (off B4069)
☎ (01249) 892200
12-3, 7 (6 Fri)-11; 12-3, 7-10.30 Sun

Archers Best Bitter; Marston's Pedigree; guest beers H
200-year-old local with a quiet lounge and busy public bar. Lunches served Fri-Sun.
♨ Q ⊛ ◑ ▶ ♣ P

BRADFORD ON AVON

BEEHIVE
263 Trowbridge Road
☎ (01225) 863620
12-2.30, 7-11; 12-3, 7-10.30 Sun
Butcombe Bitter; H **guest beer** H G
Canalside pub with an excellent and ever-changing range of real

ales, four being dispensed by gravity and three by handpump. A warm friendly atmosphere and a beer lover's dream. No food Sun eve. 🏠 Q ❀ ◖▶ ♣ P

DANDY LION
35 Market Street
☎ (01225) 863433
10.30-3, 6-11; 12-3, 7-10.30 Sun
Draught Bass; Wadworth IPA, 6X Ⓗ
Very popular, 18th-century town-centre pub.
◖▶ ⇌

MASONS ARMS
52 Newtown
☎ (01225) 863435
11-11; 12-10.30 Sun
Ushers Best Bitter, seasonal beer Ⓗ
Old-fashioned, unpretentious local set high above the main part of town.
❀ ♣ 🍺

BREMHILL

DUMB POST
Dumb Post Hill (off A4, W of Calne) OS975727
☎ (01249) 813192
11.30-2.30 (not Wed), 7-11; 12-3, 7-10.30 Sun
Archers Best Bitter; Wadworth 6X; seasonal or **guest beer** Ⓗ
Excellent country pub with fine views, outside the village. Its good value restaurant opens Wed eve to Sun lunch; bar food is always available. Occasional cider.
🏠 ❀ ◖▶ ⊟ ♣ 🍺 P

Try also: Soho Inn, on A4, Studley (Wadworth)

BROKERSWOOD

KICKING DONKEY
Follow signs to Woodland Park from A36 or A350 OS833520
☎ (01373) 823250
11.30-2.30, 6 (6.30 Sat)-11; 12-10.30 Sun
Smiles Best Bitter; Wadworth 6X; guest beer Ⓗ
17th-century country inn with exposed beams and horse brasses etc, divided into three drinking areas and a restaurant. The popular garden caters well, with seating for 200. The house beer is Bunces's Danish Dynamite rebadged. No eve meals Sun or Mon Jan-Feb.
🏠 ❀ ◖▶ Å 🍺 P

BURBAGE

THREE HORSESHOES
Stibb Green (off A346 Burbage bypass)
☎ (01672) 810324
12-2 (2.30 Sat), 6-11; 12-2.30, 7-10.30 Sun

Wadworth IPA, 6X, seasonal beers Ⓗ
Small, cosy, thatched pub on the edge of Savernake Forest, displaying railway artefacts and pictures. Good food (not served Sun eve).
🏠 Q ❀ ◖▶ ⊟ P ⊱

CHARLTON

HORSE & GROOM
The Street (B4040, Malmesbury-Cricklade road)
☎ (01666) 823904
12-3, 7-11 (12-11 summer Sat); 12-3, 7-10.30 (12-10.30 summer) Sun
Archers Village; Uley Old Spot; Wadworth 6X Ⓗ
Attractive Cotswold stone country inn, fronted by a lawn; a roomy public bar and a smaller bar which serves the restaurant (good food). Children are welcome.
Q ❀ ◖▶ ⊟ P

CHICKSGROVE (LOWER)

COMPASSES INN
Signed off A30
11-3, 6.30-11 (closed Mon except bank hols); 12-3, 7-10.30 Sun
Adnams Best Bitter; Draught Bass; Tisbury Old Wardour; Wadworth 6X Ⓗ
14th-century thatched free house with oak beams, flagstoned floor and inglenook. Single-room bar, with an adjoining room. Extensive and interesting menu of high-quality food, well kept beer.
🏠 Q ❀ ⇌ ◖▶ ♣ P

CORTON

DOVE INN
☎ (01985) 830109
12-3, 6-11; 12-11 Sat; 12-10.30 Sun
Beer range varies Ⓗ
Pleasant single room bar off the beaten track with separate dining and games areas. Friendly atmosphere and log fire - well worth searching out. Limited parking.
🏠 Q ❀ ◖▶ Å ♣ P

CLYFFE PYPARD

GODDARD ARMS
Wood Street OS074769
☎ (012793) 731386
12-2.30, 7-11; 12-3, 7-10.30 Sun
Flowers IPA; Greene King Abbot; Wadworth 6X; guest beer Ⓗ
Out-of-the-way village pub on split levels. Good value food: Thai cuisine is a house speciality. It displays many paintings and sculptures. The Manor Mouse cider is served direct from the barrel.
🏠 Q ⌣ ❀ ◖▶ ⊟ 🍺 P ⊱

CORSHAM

TWO PIGS
38 Pickwick (A4)
☎ (01249) 712515
7-11 (closed lunch); 7-10.30, 12-2.30 Sun
Bunces Pigswill; guest beers Ⓗ
Lovely drinkers' pub with a strong commitment to real ale (four guest beers). Regular local CAMRA *Pub of the Year*. Live blues performed on Mon. ❀

CORSLEY

CROSS KEYS
Lye's Green (1 mile N of A362 at Royal Oak jct) OS821462
☎ (01373) 832406
12.30-2.30 (not Mon, Tue, Thu or Fri, 12-3 Sat), 6.30 (7 Sat & Mon)-11; 12-3, 7-10.30 Sun
Draught Bass; Butcombe Bitter; Mole's Best Bitter; guest beer (occasional) Ⓗ
Welcoming free house of character, a popular, spacious pub with a splendid fireplace.
🏠 ❀ ◖▶ ♣ 🍺 P

DAUNTSEY LOCK

PETERBOROUGH ARMS
On B4069, Lyneham-Chippenham road
☎ (01249) 890409
11-2.30 (3 Sat), 6-11; 12-3.30, 7-10.30 Sun
Archers Best Bitter, Golden; Wadworth 6X; guest beers Ⓗ
Friendly free house with a cosy lounge and a log fire. Children welcome in skittle alley and the large garden which has a trampoline. Range of home-cooked food. Opening hours are extended in spring and summer.
🏠 Q ⌣ ❀ ◖▶ ⅙ Å ♣ P 🍺

DEVIZES

BRITISH LION
Estcourt Street
☎ (01380) 720665
11-11; 12-10.30 Sun
Beer range varies ⒽⒼ
Basic, reliable, town local whose range of beer has led to two *Certificates of Merit* from the local CAMRA branch. Don't let the rough and ready appearance put you off as it's well worth a visit. The house beer is by Ash Vine.
❀ ♣ 🍺 P 🍺

HARE & HOUNDS
Hare & Hounds Street
☎ (01380) 723231
11-3, 7-11; 12-3, 7-10.30 Sun
Wadworth IPA, 6X, seasonal beers Ⓗ
Popular, back-street local that has become a *Guide* fixture (the landlord has been in the *Guide* for 21 years). Good value, basic food (not served Sun). ❀ ◖♣ P

LAMB
20 St Johns Street
☎ (01380) 725426
11-11; 12-10.30 Sun
Wadworth IPA, 6X, guest beers Ⓗ
Tucked away behind the town hall, this pub was recently subjected to a sympathetic renovation featuring much bare wood. Its mixed clientele includes students, bikers and town councillors. ﹘ ﹠ ♣

WHITE BEAR
Monday Market Street
☎ (01380) 722583
11-2.30 (3 Sat), 7-11; 12-5, 7-10.30 Sun
Wadworth IPA, 6X Ⓗ
Cosy, town pub that has deservedly increased in popularity over the last couple of years.
﹘ Q ﹙ ◐ ▶

DILTON MARSH

PRINCE OF WALES
94 High Street (B3099)
☎ (01373) 865487
12-2.30, 7-11; 12-11 Sat; 12-3, 7-10.30 Sun
Federation Buchanan's Original; Fuller's London Pride; Hook Norton Best Bitter; Worthington Bitter; guest beer Ⓗ
Simple, well-run, open-plan local with a friendly atmosphere.
﹠ ◐ ▶ ⇌ ♣ P

EAST CHISENBURY

RED LION
Off A345
☎ (01980) 671124
12-2 (not Mon, 12-3 Sat), 7-11; 12-3, 7-10.30 Sun
Bunces Best Bitter; Flowers IPA; guest beer Ⓗ
200-year-old pub, formerly two cottages, on the edge of a plain, in a quiet setting. The landlord is an avid collector of wall plates; only the darts area escapes. A good local. Lunches served Tue-Sun.
﹘ Q ﹠ ◐ ▶ ♣ P ⊟

EAST KNOYLE

FOX & HOUNDS
The Green (1½ miles off A303 at Willoughby Hedge)
OS871314
☎ (01747) 830573
11-2.30 (3 Sat), 6-11; 12-3.30, 7-10.30 Sun
Fuller's London Pride; Smiles Golden; Wadworth 6X; guest beers Ⓗ
Remote, 15th-century, thatched inn in a hamlet at the top of a hill with panoramic views. Three bars and a skittle alley; good food served. Limited parking.
Q ﹠ ﹥ ◐ ▶ ♣ P

EASTERTON

ROYAL OAK
11 High Street
☎ (01380) 812343
11-3, 5.30 (6 Sat)-11; 12-3, 7-10.30 Sun
Wadworth IPA, 6X; guest beers Ⓗ
Comfortable, two-bar thatched village pub near a jam factory. The saloon bar is also the dining area; the public bar is for drinkers. The guest beers are supplied by Wadworth.
﹘ ﹠ ◐ ▶ ⊟ ♣ P

EASTON ROYAL

BRUCE ARMS ☆
On B3087
☎ (01672) 810216
11-2.30 (3 Sat), 6-11; 12-3, 7-10.30 Sun
Oakhill Best Bitter; Wadworth 6X Ⓗ
Fine basic bar with a brick floor and scrubbed pine tables. The recent games room/skittle alley extension does not spoil the rustic atmosphere.
﹘ Q ﹠ ⊟ ▲ ♣ ⌷ P

EBBESBOURNE WAKE

HORSESHOE
Handley Street
☎ (01722) 780474
12-3, 6.30-11; 12-4, 7-10.30 Sun
Adnams Broadside; Ringwood Best Bitter; Wadworth 6X; guest beer Ⓖ
Old village inn: two small bars displaying old working tools. No meals Sun or Mon eve.
Q ﹠ ﹥ ◐ ▶ ﹠ ⌷ P

FORD

WHITE HART
Off A420
☎ (01249) 782213
11-2.45, 5-11; 12-3, 7-10.30 Sun
Beer range varies Ⓗ Ⓖ
Superb 16th-century inn with a fabulous selection of ales (always ten available) and an award-winning restaurant. Situated beside a stream, it also offers high quality overnight accommodation. ﹘ Q ﹠ ﹥ ◐ ▶ ⌷ P

HAMPWORTH

CUCKOO INN
Hampworth Road (1 mile off A36 at Landford jct)
☎ (01794) 390302
11.30-2.30, 6-11; 11.30-11 Sat; 12-10.30 Sun
Badger Tanglefoot; Cheriton Pots Ale; Hop Back GFB, Summer Lightning; Wadworth 6X Ⓖ
Wonderful rustic cottage pub on the edge of a forest, with four

small public bars where conversation tops the agenda. A good garden for children plus an area for adults only - peace and quiet guaranteed.
﹘ Q ﹥ ﹠ ◐ ▶ ﹠ ▲ ♣ ⌷ P ⊬

HEDDINGTON

IVY
Stockley Road
☎ (01380) 850276
12-3, 6.30-11; 12-11 Sat; 12-10.30 Sun
Wadworth IPA, 6X Ⓖ
Picturesque 15th-century thatched village inn: a cosy single bar with a large log fire and excellent home-cooked food (eve meals Thu-Sat).
﹘ Q ﹠ ◐ ▶ ♣ P

HIGHWORTH

WINE CELLAR
High Street (opp Main Square)
☎ (01793) 763828
7 (11 Fri & Sat)-11; 12-10.30 Sun
Archers Village, Best Bitter, guest beer Ⓖ
A stairway between shop fronts leads down to a stone-walled cellar which serves a good choice of wines and whiskies, as well as the beers. Q ⌷

HODSON

CALLEY ARMS
Off B4005
☎ (01793) 740350
12-2.30 (11.30-3 Tue-Fri), 6.30-11; 12-3, 7-10.30 Sun
Wadworth IPA, 6X, seasonal beers; guest beer Ⓗ
Welcoming pub in a rural setting: an open-plan bar with a raised dining area. Large range of malt whiskies available. Above-average pub food (not served Sun eve or Mon). ﹘ ﹠ ◐ ▶ ⌷ P

HOLT

TOLLGATE INN
Ham Green (B3107, Bradford-Melksham road)
☎ (01225) 782326
11.30-2.30, 6-11; 12-3, 7-10.30 Sun
Flowers IPA, Original; Wadworth 6X; guest beer Ⓗ
18th-century inn in a picturesque village which hosts petanque eves in the summer. No meals Sun eve. ﹘ Q ﹠ ◐ ▶ ﹠ P

HULLAVINGTON

QUEEN'S HEAD
23 The Street
☎ (01666) 837221
12-2, 7-11; 12-2, 7-10.30 Sun
Archers Village; Mole's Tap Bitter; guest beers Ⓗ
Homely local with open fires and a skittle alley. No food Sun.
﹘ Q ﹠ ﹥ ⊟ ♣ ⌷

KILMINGTON

RED LION INN
On B3092, 2½ miles N of A303 at Mere
☎ (01985) 844263
11-3, 6.30-11; 12-3.30, 7-10.30 Sun
Butcombe Bitter; guest beers Ⓗ
Unspoilt, NT-owned pub near Stourhead Gardens and the South Wilts downs. A single bar with a separate no-smoking area. Popular with walkers, it serves good value food.
🏚 Q ❀ 🛏 ◖ ♣ ⌂ P ⊬

KINGSDOWN

SWAN
☎ (01225) 742269
12-3, 6-11; 11-11 Sat; 12-3, 7-10.30 Sun
Draught Bass; Gibbs Mew Salisbury; guest beer Ⓗ
Hillside pub showing interesting photographs of old workings at the nearby Swan mine. Enjoy fine views from the terraced gardens.
🏚 ❀ ◖ ▶ ♣ P

KINGTON ST MICHAEL

JOLLY HUNTSMAN
High Street
☎ (01249) 750305
11.30-3, 6.30 (5.30 Fri)-11; 12-3, 7-10.30 Sun
Badger Tanglefoot; Draught Bass; Fuller's London Pride; Wadworth 6X; guest beers Ⓗ
Friendly village local: a comfortable L-shaped lounge, plus a dining area, offering seven ales and excellent meals. Quiz Mon, live music Wed.
🏚 🛏 ◖ ▶ ♣ P

LIMPLEY STOKE

HOP POLE INN
Woods Hill (off A36) OS782612
☎ (01225) 723134
11-2.30 (3 Sat), 6-11; 12-3, 7-10.30 Sun
Draught Bass; Butcombe Bitter; Courage Best Bitter; guest beer Ⓗ
Comfortable, authentic village pub with a beautiful dark oak-panelled public bar. Large garden overlooks the Avon valley. A stone's throw from the Kennet and Avon canal.
❀ ◖ ▶ 🍺 P

LITTLE CHEVERELL

OWL
Lower Road
☎ (01380) 812263
12-2.30, 7-11, closed Mon; 12-2.30, 7-10.30 (9 winter) Sun
beer range varies Ⓗ
Popular, attractive village pub that features a stream at the bottom of the garden. Regular and interesting beer festivals are an extension of the normal guest beer policy.
🏚 Q ❀ ◖ ▶ ▲ ♣ P

MALMESBURY

RED BULL
Sherston Road (B4042, 1½ miles W of Malmesbury)
☎ (01666) 822108
11-2.30 (not Tue; 11.30-3 Sat); 6.30-11; 12-3, 7-10.30 Sun
Draught Bass; Flowers IPA; Fuller's London Pride; Wadworth 6X Ⓗ
Popular family pub with a garden play area and a children's room, plus a skittle alley and a boules piste.
🏚 Q 🍼 ❀ � ♣ P

SMOKING DOG
62 High Street
☎ (01666) 82583
11-11.30; 12-10.30 Sun
Archers Best Bitter; Marston's Bitter, Pedigree; Wadworth 6X Ⓗ; guest beers Ⓖ
Warm, friendly real ale pub.
🏚 Q ❀ ◖ ▶ � ♣

MARLBOROUGH

BEAR
1 High Street
☎ (01672) 515047
11-11; 12-10.30 Sun
Arkell's Bitter, 3B, Kingsdown, seasonal beers Ⓗ
There's plenty of atmosphere in this busy, bare-boarded bar, and good food.
Q ❀ 🛏 ◖ ▶

MARSTON MEYSEY

OLD SPOTTED COW
2½ miles from A419 OS129969
☎ (01285) 810264
11-3, 5.30-11; 11-11 Sat; 12-10.30 Sun
Draught Bass; Hook Norton Best Bitter; Wadworth 6X; guest beers Ⓗ
This Cotswold stone building, an old farmhouse, is now a lively local. 🏚 Q ❀ ◖ ▶ ▲ ♣ P

MELKSHAM

RED LION
3 The City
☎ (01225) 702960
11-3, 5 (6 Sat)-11; 11-11 Fri; 12-3, 7-10.30 Sun
Draught Bass; Church End Gravediggers; Oakhill Best Bitter; guest beer Ⓗ
13th-century stone pub of character; a rare outlet for mild ales plus frequently changing guest beers and a large selection of malt whiskies. Local CAMRA *Pub of the Year 1995.*
❀ ◖ ⇌ ♣ P

NORTH NEWTON

WOODBRIDGE INN
On A345
☎ (01980) 630266
11-11; 12-3, 7-10.30 Sun
Wadworth IPA, 6X, Farmers Glory Ⓗ
Smart, foody pub with an interesting collection of old signs and china. The riverside garden has angling rights.
🏚 ❀ 🛏 ◖ ▶ ▲ P

NORTH WROUGHTON

CHECK INN
Woodland View
☎ (01793) 845584
11-2.30, 6.30-11; 11-11 Fri & Sat; 12-10.30 Sun
Beer range varies Ⓗ
True free house with local and visiting clientele. A country pub in an urban area (a drop away from the M4), it has a single bar with a children's area, plus a garden bar in summer. Extensive range of Czech and German bottled beers; the cider varies.
🏚 ❀ ◖ ▶ & ▲ ♣ ⌂ P ⊬

OGBOURNE ST GEORGE

OLD CROWN
Marlborough Road (off A346)
☎ (01672) 841445
11.30-3, 7-10.30; 12-3, 7-10.30 Sun
Wadworth 6X; guest beer Ⓗ
Cosy, carpeted bar with a food emphasis; the restaurant features a well. Wheelchair ramp available on request. Cider in summer.
🏚 ❀ 🛏 ◖ ▶ ▲ ♣ ⌂ P

PEWSEY

COOPERS ARMS
Ball Road (off B3087) OS170595
☎ (01672) 562495
12-2, 7-11; 12-4, 7-10.30 Sun
Oakhill Mendip Gold; Wadworth 6X; guest beers Ⓗ
Bar of character in a thatched building hidden in a side road offering live bands, quiz nights and a games room. Can get rather smoky.
🏚 🍼 ❀ ▲ ⇌ ♣ ⌂ P

ROWDE

GEORGE & DRAGON
High Street
☎ (01380) 723053
12-3, 7-11; 12-3, 7-10.30 Sun
Butcombe Bitter; guest beers Ⓗ
High street village pub which has won national awards for the quality of its food. The beer is of an equally high standard; the guest beer policy favours small Wiltshire breweries.
Q ❀ ◖ ▶ ▲ ♣ P

SALISBURY

BLACKBIRD INN
30 Churchfields
☎ (01722) 502828
12-3, 5.30-11; 12-11 Fri & Sat;
12-6, 7-10.30 Sun
Courage Best Bitter; guest beers ℍ
Cosy, friendly one-roomer, serving a wide and constantly changing beer range and good value snacks at lunchtime.
Q ❀ ☙ ♣

DEACON ALMS
118 Fisherton Street
☎ (01722) 504723
5 (4 Fri, 12 Sat)-11; 12-10.30 Sun
Hop Back GFB; Wadworth 6X; guest beers ℍ
Unusual, split-level bar area in a pleasant town pub, with a friendly atmosphere. Guest beers often feature Bunces of Netheravon.
Q ⇔ ≒ ⏚

DEVIZES INN
53-55 Devizes Road (A360)
☎ (01722) 327842
4.30 (12 Fri, 11 Sat)-11; 12-10.30 Sun
Hop Back GFB, Summer Lightning; guest beer ℍ
Comfortable, friendly, two-bar local, a former fish shop and off-licence. Meals must be booked (not necessary for Sun lunch). Reduced accommodation rates for CAMRA members.
⛺ ⇔ ◖ ≒ ♣ P ⏚

STAR
69 Brown Street
☎ (01722) 327137
11-11; 12-10.30 Sun
Fuller's London Pride, ESB; Hop Back GFB; Wadworth 6X; guest beers ℍ
Lively city pub and very much a local, this unpretentious pub continues to grow in popularity. The good range of real ales are accompanied by loud rock music. Although very friendly, it is not for the faint-hearted.
🍺

VILLAGE FREEHOUSE
33 Wilton Road
☎ (01722) 329707
11-11; 12-10.30 Sun
Abbey Bellringer; Cottage Champflower; Oakhill Best Bitter, Mendip Gold; guest beers ℍ
Convivial corner pub near the station where a collection of railwayana includes working class 33 loco horns. Specialises in beers not usually found in the area. The Sun eve quiz is set by customers. The menu is sausage and mash with speciality bangers.
◖ ▶ ⛢ ≒ ♣

WIG & QUILL
1 New Street (behind BHS)
☎ (01722) 335665
11-11; 12-10.30 Sun
Badger Tanglefoot; Wadworth IPA, 6X; guest beers ℍ
Very old building: one large room divided by screen walls; the front room has an original stone flagged floor. A pleasant patio opens on to Cathedral Close. Extensive menu.
Q ❀ ◖ ▶

WYNDHAM ARMS
27 Estcourt Road (off inner ring road)
☎ (01722) 331026
4.30 (3 Fri, 12 Sat)-11; 12-10.30 Sun
Hop Back GFB, Crop Circle, Entire or Ginger Stout, Thunderstorm, Summer Lightning ℍ
No-frills, welcoming boozer, the first home of Hop Back Brewery, whose walls are all but hidden by brewery awards - not to be missed.
⛺ ♣ ✂

SHAW

GOLDEN FLEECE
Folly Lane (A365)
☎ (01225) 702050
11.30-2.30 (3 Sat), 6-11; 12-3, 7-10.30 Sun
Butcombe Bitter, Wilmot's; Marston's Pedigree; Wickwar BOB ℍ
Roadside pub with outdoor skittles in summer, and a cricket field adjacent. No meals Mon eve.
❀ ◖ ▶ ⏏ ♿ ♣ P

SHREWTON

GEORGE INN
On B3806
☎ (01980) 620341
11-3, 6-11; 12.30-7 Sun
Ushers Best Bitter; Wadworth 6X; guest beers ℍ
17th-century chalk and flint pub, once a brewery, with a large covered patio and garden. The pub is a hive of village activities, including skittles.
🍺 ❀ ◖ ▶ ⛺ ♣ P

SOUTH NEWTON

BELL INN
Warminster Road (A36)
☎ (01722) 743336
11-2.30, 7-11; 12-2.30, 7-10.30 Sun
Courage Best Bitter; John Smith's Bitter; guest beer ℍ
17th-century inn with oak beams, refurbished to offer comfort and a welcome to all. A local which invites passing trade. Good food.
🍺 Q ❀ ⇔ ◖ ▶ ♿ P

STAPLEFORD

PELICAN INN
Warminster Road (A36)
☎ (01722) 790241
11-2.30 (3 Sat), 6-11; 12-2.30, 7 (6 summer)-10.30 Sun
Otter Bitter; Ringwood Best Bitter, Fortyniner; guest beers ℍ
Extended, 18th-century coaching inn with a flagstone floor in the cosy restaurant (good value food). The large garden has swings and slides. It is named after a galleon.
🍺 Q ❀ ⇔ ◖ ▶ ♣ P

STOCKTON

CARRIERS ARMS
☎ (01722) 850653
12-2.30 (not Mon), 7-11; 12-2.30, 7-10.30 Sun
Ringwood Best Bitter; Wadworth 6X; guest beer ℍ
Welcoming pub with a log fire. The large bar has a dining area; the games room offers pool.
🍺 Q ❀ ◖ ▶

STRATTON ST MARGARET

WHEATSHEAF
167 Ermin Street
☎ (01793) 823149
11-3, 6-11; 12-3, 7-10.30 Sun
Arkell's Bitter, 3B, seasonal beers ℍ
Busy, popular community pub. No food Sun. ❀ ◖ ▶ ♣ P

SWINDON

CLIFTON
Clifton Street, Old Town
☎ (01793) 523162
11-2.30, 6-11; 12-3, 7-10.30 Sun
Arkell's Bitter, 3B, seasonal beer ℍ
Classic, back-street local, run by a popular landlord who serves Arkell's at its best. Opened in 1879, it has a resident ghost. P

GLUE POT
5 Emlyn Square
☎ (01793) 523935
11-11; 12-3, 7-10.30 Sun
Archers Village, Best Bitter, Golden; guest beers ℍ
Busy, one-bar, no-nonsense pub, built in the mid-19th-century as part of Brunel's railway village. Weekday lunches. Q ❀ ◖ ≒

KINGS ARMS
20 Wood Street, Old Town
☎ (01793) 522156
11-3, 6-11; 12-3, 7-10.30 Sun
Arkell's Bitter, 3B, Kingsdown, seasonal beer ℍ
Set in the busy Old Town area, a very popular, busy large single-bar hotel with seating on two levels. Wheelchair access is from the car park. ⇔ ◖ ▶ ♿ P

NINE ELMS
Old Shaw Lane, Nine Elms
(follow signs for Nine Elms,
to end of cul-de-sac)
☎ (01793) 770442
6 (12 Fri & Sat)-11; 12-
10.30 Sun
**Ushers Best Bitter,
Founders, seasonal beers**
H
Surrounded by a new hous-
ing estate, this old-style,
redbrick pub is worth seeking out. Frequented by
locals in winter but drawing many passing visitors
in summer to its comfort-
able and spacious bar.
Meals served Wed-Sun.
🏠 🍴 ◑ ▶ 🍺 ♿ ♣ P

RISING SUN
6 Albert Street, Old Town
☎ (01793) 529916
11-11; 11-10.30 Sun
**Courage Best Bitter; Ushers Best
Bitter, Founders, seasonal
beers** H
Friendly pub, hidden down a
back-street in Old Town. Known
to Swindonians as the Roaring
Donkey. Q 🍺

SAVOY
38-40 Regent Street
☎ (01793) 533970
11-11; 12-10.30 Sun
**Archers Best Bitter; Arkell's 3B;
Courage Directors; Theakston
Best Bitter; guest beers** H
Large, air-conditioned, popular
pub; a converted cinema with a
single bar. Built in 1937, it features cinema stills and old books.
The guest beers are constantly
changing.
Q ◑ ▶ ♿ ⬙ ⭢ ⌣ ✗ 🛢

WHEATSHEAF
32 Newport Street
☎ (01793) 523188
11-2.30, 5.30-11; 12-3, 7-10.30
Sun
**Adnams Bitter; Badger
Tanglefoot; Wadworth IPA, 6X,
Farmers Glory, seasonal beers;
guest beers** H
Popular, two-bar pub; the larger
back bar is busy Fri and Sat eves,
but there is a quieter front bar.
The small courtyard has seating.
No meals Sun eve or Sat.
🍴 ⭢ ◑ ▶ 🍺

Try also: Steam Railway,
Newport St (Greenalls)

WANBOROUGH

PLOUGH
High Street ☎ (01793) 790523
12-2.30, 5-11; 11-11 Fri & Sat;
12-2.30, 7-10.30 Sun
**Archers Village; Draught Bass;
Boddingtons Bitter; Fuller's
London Pride; Wadworth 6X;
guest beer** H

HOP BACK BREWERY SPECIAL
ABV ~ 4.0
THE HOP BACK BREWERY
THE WYNDHAM ARMS, SALISBURY.

Listed, thatched pub, featuring
beams, stone walls, log fires and
a cosy atmosphere. The Harrow
(100 yards away) under the same
management is also worth a visit
for its different beer range. Both
pubs have good food (meals
served Mon-Fri).
🏠 Q 🍴 ◑ ▶ ♣ P

UPTON LOVELL

PRINCE LEOPOLD
¹/₂ mile from A36, 4 miles from
Warminster
☎ (01985) 850460
12-3, 7-11; closed Mon; 12-3,
7-10.30 sun
Beer range varies H
Built in 1887 as a post office and
shop, the pub is named after
Queen Victoria's youngest son
who frequently visited. Smart
casual dress requested. Warm
and welcoming with excellent
food, specialising in curry and
fresh fish dishes. The riverside
gardens offer pleasant views.
🍴 ⭢ ◑ ▶ ♿ Å ♣ P

WESTBURY

CROWN INN
Market Place
☎ (01373) 822828
11-2.30, 5.30-11; 11-11 Fri; 11-3,
6-11 Sat; 12-3, 7-10.30 Sun
**Wadworth IPA, 6X; guest
beers** H
Welcoming, well-appointed local
next to the market square. Eve
meals Fri and Sat; no lunches
Sun.
🍴 ◑ ▶ 🍺 ♣ ⌣ P

WHITEPARISH

KINGS HEAD
The Street (A27)
☎ (01794) 884287
12-3.30, 6-11; 12-11 Sat; 12-3.30,
7-10.30 Sun
Brains SA; guest beers H

Traditional village local with
a restaurant, the hub of local
activities. Large play area in
a good-sized garden which is
home to ducks as well.
🏠 Q 🍴 ◑ ▶ Å ♣ P

Try also: Parish Lantern,
on A27 (Free)

WILTON

WHEATSHEAF
1 King Street (A36 next to
Wilton Shopping Village)
☎ (01722) 742267
11-2.30, 6.30-11 (11-11 summer); 12-3, 7-10.30 (11-
10.30 summer) Sun
**Badger Dorset Best, Tangle-
foot** H
A 'real' pub: two bars plus a
no-smoking restaurant and a
pleasant riverside garden.
The home cooked specials are
superb. Limited parking.
🏠 Q 🍴 ⭢ ◑ ▶ 🍺 ♿ ♣ P

Try also: Bell, West St (Bass)

WINTERBOURNE
MONKTON

NEW INN
Signed off A4369, N of Avebury
☎ (01672) 539240
11-3, 6-11; 12-3, 7-10.30 Sun
**Adnams Bitter; Wadworth 6X;
guest beer** H
Friendly local with a cosy, welcoming bar and a restaurant. The
gardens have a children's play
area. Cider in summer.
Recommended B&B.
🏠 Q 🍴 ⭢ ◑ ▶ Å ♣ ⌣ P

INDEPENDENT
BREWERIES

Archers:
Swindon

Arkell's:
Swindon

Bunces:
Netheravon

Hop Back:
Downton

Mole's:
Melksham

Tisbury:
Tisbury

Usher's:
Trowbridge

Wadworth:
Devizes

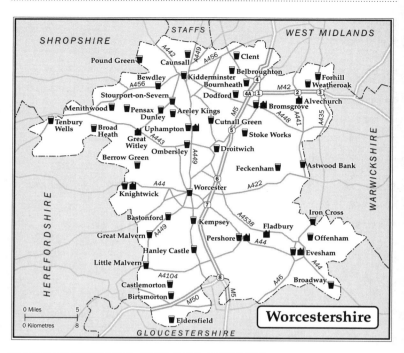

Worcestershire

ARELEY KINGS

KING'S ARMS
19 Redhouse Road (off B4196)
☎ (01299) 827132
12-3, 6-11; 11-11 Fri & Sat; 12-3,
7-10.30 Sun
Banks's Mild, H P Bitter; P
guest beer H
This local has a single bar in an
L-shaped room, plus a dining
room. Outside there is a garden
and bowling green. No food Sun
eve.
⌂ ❀ ◖ ▶ ♣ P ▯

ASTWOOD BANK

RED LION
31 Church Road
☎ (01527) 892848
11-3, 6-11; 12-3, 7-10.30 Sun
Banks's Mild, Bitter; guest
beer H
Unpretentious local: a traditional
bar and lounge, serving remarkably good value meals.
⌂ ⛵ ❀ ◖ ▶ ⊞ ♣ P ▯

ASTWOOD BANK

WHY NOT?
The Ridgeway (A441, 1 mile S of
village)
☎ (01527) 893566
11-2.30, 6-11; 12-3, 7-10.30 Sun
Boddingtons Mild, Bitter;
Wadworth 6X H
Friendly country pub: a small bar
and a larger lounge with a no-
smoking dining area.
⌂ ❀ ◖ ▶ ⊞ ♣ P

BASTONFORD

HALFWAY HOUSE
On A449
☎ (01905) 831098
12-2.30, 6-11; 12-2.30, 7-10.30 Sun
Marston's Bitter; Taylor
Landlord H
Food-oriented pub on the main
Worcester-Malvern road; howev-
er, drinkers are most welcome.
Relaxed bistro-style atmosphere
in two lounges. No eve meals
Tue. Q ❀ ◖ ▶ ⅙ ♣ P ▯

BELBROUGHTON

QUEENS
Queens Hill (B4188)
☎ (01562) 730276
11.30-3, 5.30 (6 Sat)-11; 12-3.30,
7-10.30 Sun
Marston's Bitter, Pedigree, HBC H
Popular, smart village inn where
three lounge areas are served by
one main bar. Good quality food
on a varied menu (no meals Sun
eve). ❀ ◖ ▶ ⅙ P

BERROW GREEN

ADMIRAL RODNEY
On B4197
☎ (01886) 821375
12-2.30 (not winter Mon-Thu),
6-11; 12-4, 7-10.30 Sun
Enville Gothic Ale; Hook Norton
Best Bitter; guest beer H
Large pub in extensive grounds,
set amidst rolling countryside.
The main bar has a side area
equipped with comfy armchairs;

an adjoining bar area has a pool
table and red plush seating. A
skittle alley and restaurant are in
a converted barn with lots of
beams. The house beer is
brewed by Enville. No lunches in
winter. ⌂ ❀ ◖ ▶ ▲ ♣ P

BEWDLEY

BLACK BOY
50 Wyre Hill (follow Sandy Bank
off B4194 at Welch Gate)
☎ (01299) 403523
12-3, 7-11; 12-3, 7-10.30 Sun
Banks's Mild, P Bitter; H P
Marston's Pedigree; guest
beer H
Welcoming 400-year-old pub situated high above the town (not to
be confused with the Black Boy
Hotel). Children may be allowed
in the games room when not in
use. It featured in Banks's *Best
Kept Cellar* awards and is a regular *Guide* entry.
⌂ Q ❀ ⊞ ♣ ▯

COCK & MAGPIE
Severnside North
☎ (01299) 403748
11-4, 6-11; 11-11 Sat & summer;
12-4, 7-10.30 (12-10.30 summer)
Sun
Banks's Mild, Bitter P
Well-established *Guide* entry by
the River Severn. Traffic is
restricted on the former quayside, and summer drinking often
spills out to the front of this traditional two-roomed pub.
⊞ ⇌ (SVR) ♣ ▯

GEORGE HOTEL
Load Street
☎ (01299) 402117
11-3, 5.30-11; 11-11 Sat; 12-4,
7-10.30 (12-10.30 summer) Sun
**Ind Coope Burton Ale; Tetley
Bitter; guest beer** Ⓗ
An impressive collection of
pump clips is displayed around
the bar, acquired from the regularly changing guest beer.
Access to the bar is via a side
passage; there is also a
large lounge.
🏨 Q ☎ ⛱ ⚓ ◖ ⍟ 🅰 ⇌
(SVR) Ⓟ

GREAT WESTERN
42 Kidderminster Road (E side of
river)
☎ (01299) 402320
11-11; 12-10.30 Sun
**Banks's Hanson's Mild, Mild,
Bitter;** Ⓗ⒫ **guest beer** Ⓗ
Friendly local close to the Severn
Valley steam railway, hosting live
music Sat eve. Eve meals must
be ordered in advance. Look out
for the pub's own news sheet.
Children's certificate.
☎ ⍟ ◖ ⊅ 🅰 ⇌ (SVR)
♣ ⛄ Ⓟ ⊁ 🍺

Try also: Black Boy Hotel,
Wribbenhall (Enterprise Inns);
Woodcolliers Arms, Welch Gate
(Free)

BIRTSMORTON

FARMERS ARMS
Birts Street (off B4208)
OS792363
☎ (01684) 833308
11-2.30, 6-11 (11-11 summer
Sat); 12-2.30, 7-10.30 Sun (12-
10.30 summer) Sun
**Hook Norton Best Bitter, Old
Hooky; guest beer** Ⓗ
Black and white country pub,
tucked away down a lane: a
small lounge with a very low
beamed ceiling, plus a larger,
more basic bar with darts and
games. The large garden has
swings and a fine view of the
Malverns. Guest beers come
from local breweries.
🏨 Q ⍟ ◖ ⊅ ♣ Ⓟ

BOURNHEATH

GATE
Dodford Road
☎ (01527) 878169
11-2.30, 6-10.30 (11 Fri & Sat);
12-3, 6-10.30 Sun
Smiles Best Bitter, Heritage Ⓗ
Food-oriented pub, specialising
in Cajun and Mexican dishes
with vegetarian options. A
rare outlet for Smiles ales.
Families are welcome (but facilities are minimal). Beer and food
is promoted at lower prices
6-7pm.
🏨 ⍟ ◖ ⊅ 🅰 Ⓟ

BROADHEATH
(TENBURY)

FOX INN
On B4204
☎ (01886) 853219
12-3, 6-11; 12-11 Sat; 12-3,
7-10.30 Sun
**Batham Best Bitter; Hobsons
Best Bitter** Ⓗ
Large country pub set amongst
rolling fields: a large lounge with
beams and a dining area; a
games bar with juke box, pool
table etc; a sunken snug and
family room. The main part of the
building dates back to the 16th
century. A request for sparklers
to be removed will be respected.
🏨 ⛱ ⍟ ⚓ ◖ ⊅ ⊞ 🅰 ♣
Ⓟ ⊁

BROADWAY

CROWN & TRUMPET
Church Street (Snowshill road)
☎ (01386) 853202
11-2.30 (3.30 summer), 4.45-11;
11-11 Sat; 12-3.30, 6-10.30 Sun
**Boddingtons Bitter; Flowers IPA;
Morland Old Speckled Hen;
Stanway Stanney Bitter;
Wadworth 6X** Ⓗ
Fine, 17th-century Cotswold
stone inn, complete with oak
beams and log fires in a comfortable interior. Deservedly popular
with locals, tourists and walkers,
it offers an unusual range of pub
games.
🏨 ⍟ ⚓ ◖ ⊅ 🅰 ♣ Ⓟ

BROMSGROVE

GOLDEN CROSS HOTEL
20 High Street
☎ (01527) 87005
11-11; 12-10.30 Sun
**Banks's Mild, Bitter; Theakston
Best Bitter; Courage Directors;
guest beer** Ⓗ
Large, modern open-plan
Wetherspoons town pub, popular
with the young after 9pm, especially at weekends. Food is available up to one hour before closing. No music or under 18s. Pay
and display parking to the rear.
⍟ ◖ ⊅ 🅰 Ⓟ ⊁ 🍺

HOP POLE
78 Birmingham Road
☎ (01527) 870100
12-2.30, 5.30-11; 12-3, 7-11 Sat;
12-3, 7-10.30 Sun
**Draught Bass; Red Cross OBJ,
OKJ** (occasional)**, Anniversary Ale**
(occasional) Ⓗ
Cosy, street-corner local near
the Rovers football ground. A
small bar serves two lounge
areas, one of which has a floor
made from gravestones. The
function room is used by various
societies. The main outlet for
Red Cross beers.
⍟ ◖ ♣

CASTLEMORTON

PLUME OF FEATHERS
Feathers Pitch (B4208)
☎ (01684) 833554
11-11; 12-10.30 Sun
**Brandy Cask Whistling Joe;
Hobsons Best Bitter; guest
beers** Ⓗ
Worcester CAMRA *Pub of the
Year* 1997, this country pub
enjoys fine views of the Malvern
Hills. A heavily-beamed lounge
with a dining room and a snug.
Good food: home-made dishes
and grills (no meals Sun eve).
Annual beer festival (Sept).
🏨 Q ⍟ ◖ 🅰 ♣ Ⓟ

CAUNSALL

ANCHOR
600 yds from A449
☎ (01562) 850254
12-4, 7-11; 12-3, 7-10.30 Sun
**Draught Bass; Highgate Dark;
Stones Bitter** Ⓗ
Just a short walk from the Staffs
& Worcs Canal, this pub has a
comfortable lounge and an
adjoining small room. It has been
owned by the current family for
70 years. Filled rolls available.
🏨 Q ⍟ 🅰 🅰 ♣ Ⓟ

CLENT

BELL & CROSS
Holy Cross (off A491, signed
Clent)
☎ (01562) 730319
12-3, 6-11; 12-4, 7-10.30 Sun
**Banks's Mild, Bitter; Marston's
Pedigree; guest beer** Ⓗ
Unspoilt gem based on traditional
values; four cosy rooms, most
with a real fire. Families welcome. Morris dancers perform in
summer. Eve meals Tue-Sat,
Drinks served from one bar. The
guest beer is supplied by
Banks's.🏨 Q ⛱ ⍟ ◖ 🅰 ♣

CUTNALL GREEN

NEW INN
Kidderminster Road (A442)
☎ (01299) 851202
12-3, 5.30 (6 Sat)-11; 12-3,
7-10.30 Sun
Marston's Pedigree, HBC Ⓗ
Welcoming village local serving
good, home-cooked food and a
full restaurant menu with an
international flavour.
🏨 ⍟ ◖ ⊅ ♣ Ⓟ

DODFORD

DODFORD INN
Whinfield Road (off A448, near
Bournheath) OS939726
☎ (01527) 832470
12-3, 7 (6 summer)-11; 12-3 (4
summer), 7-10.30 Sun
Greenalls Bitter; guest beers Ⓗ
Excellent, traditional, single-bar

country pub in beautiful surroundings, ideal for walkers and cyclists. it offers three changing guest beers and good value home-cooked food. Children's certificate. Local CAMRA *Pub of the Year* 1996. Folk and beer festival staged in summer.

🏚 ❀ ◖ ▮ ⚭ ♣ ⛺ P ✹

DROITWICH

RAILWAY INN
Kidderminster Road
☎ (01905) 770056
12-11; 12-4, 7-11; Sun
Banks's Mild; Marston's Bitter, Pedigree, HBC Ⓗ
Small, basic, two-roomed canalside pub with a good atmosphere. Rooms are adorned with steam railway memorabilia; the friendly landlord is a railway enthusiast. Good value bar snacks are all freshly prepared. A large rooftop patio overlooks the restored canal basin. No food Sun lunch.

❀ ◖ ▮ ⚭ ≈ ♣ P

DUNLEY

DOG INN
On A451, Sourport-Gt Whitley Road
☎ (01299) 822833
12-3, 5.30-11; 12-11 Sat; 12-4, 7-10.30 Sun
Hobsons Best Bitter; guest beers Ⓗ
Wisteria-clad, two-bar pub in a pleasant setting; outside the garden and safe play area overlook open countryside. Inside a small snug can be used by families.

🏚 ❀ ⚭ ◖ ▮ ⚭ ▲ ♣ P

ELDERSFIELD

GREYHOUND INN
Lime Street (off B4211)
OS815304
☎ (01452) 840381
11.30-3.30, 6-11; 12-3, 7-10.30 Sun
Butcombe Bitter; Wadworth 6X; guest beers Ⓖ
Very traditional, isolated country pub, comprising a lounge and adjoining bar, plus skittle alley-cum-function room. An archetypal rural pub with a warm welcome, featuring bentwood benches in the bar and a dovecote in the garden. Enjoy a game of quoits. Beer festival in June. No food Mon.

🏚 Q ❀ ◖ ▮ ▲ ♣ P

EVESHAM

GREEN DRAGON
17 Oat Street (near library)
☎ (01386) 446337
11-2.30, 7-11; 11-11 Fri & Sat;
12-2.30, 7-10.30 Sun
Evesham Asum Ale, Asum Gold; guest beers Ⓗ

Busy, town-centre pub which has its own brewery and skittle alley in a 16th-century building. A large bar/games area and a cosy lounge/dining area complete the picture. Late licence (midnight Thu-Sat); no food Sun eve.

❀ ◖ ▮ ≈ ♣ ♣

TRUMPET
13 Merstow Green
☎ (01386) 446227
11-11; 12-10.30 Sun
Banks's Bitter; guest beers Ⓗ
Popular, lively pub where the large lounge area is elegantly decorated with risqué 1950s prints.

🏚 ❀ ◖ ≈

FECKENHAM

LYGON ARMS
1 Droitwich Road (B4092)
☎ (01527) 893495
11-3 (3.30 May), 6.30-11; 12-3, 7-10.30 Sun
Marston's Pedigree; Theakston Best Bitter Ⓗ
Very pleasant village pub with a no-smoking restaurant that features home-cooked food (no meals Sun eve).

🏚 Q ❀ ◖ ▮ ♣ ⛺ P

FORHILL

PEACOCK INN
Icknield Street (2 miles from A441) OS054775
☎ (01564) 823232
12-11; 12-10.30 Sun
Banks's Mild, Bitter; Enville Bitter; Hobsons Best Bitter; Judges Old Gavel Bender; guest beers Ⓗ
Popular country pub with a pleasant rustic atmosphere on the side of an old Roman road. Usually about 10 real ales available and a full and interesting menu served in the bars and restaurant. Open fires and friendly staff make for a warm welcome. Games played in the bar.

🏚 ❀ ◖ ▮ ▤ ▲ ♣ P ✹

GREAT MALVERN

FOLEY ARMS HOTEL
14 Worcester Road
☎ (01684) 573397
12-3, 5.30-11; 12-11 Sat; 12-3.30, 7-10.30 Sun
Draught Bass; guest beers Ⓗ
Very popular bar in an enlarged 1810 coaching inn, boasting superb views across the Severn Valley from the main bar and terrace. Three imaginative guest beers offer a range of gravities. Busy at weekends. There is a quieter drinking area in an adjacent lounge.

❀ ⚭ ◖ ▮ ≈ ♣ P ✹

HANLEY CASTLE

THREE KINGS
Church End (off B4211)
OS838420
☎ (01684) 592686
12-3 (may vary), 7-11; 12-3, 7-10.30 Sun
Butcombe Bitter; Thwaites Bitter; guest beers Ⓗ
Marvellous, unspoilt village pub, over 85 years in the same family: a tiny bar with an inglenook plus the larger 'Nells Bar' next door. A great atmosphere and welcome at CAMRA's regional *Pub of the Year* 1997 (national winner 1993 and runner-up 1997). No eve meals Sun.

🏚 Q ⚭ ❀ ⚭ ◖ ▮ ▤ ♣ ⛺

IRON CROSS

QUEENS HEAD
On B4088 (old A435)
☎ (01386) 871012
11-11; 12-10.30 Sun
Fat God's Bitter, KFB, Thunder & Lightning, seasonal beers; guest beers Ⓗ
Lively pub with a strong commitment to the local community and good causes. Always four beers brewed on the premises, plus guests. A festival is held in June with 30 beers over a week. Try the beer bread made with yeast from the brewery. Wheelchair WC.

🏚 ❀ ◖ ▮ ♿ ▲ ♣ ⛺ P

KEMPSEY

WALTER DE CANTELUPE INN
Main Road (A38)
☎ (01905) 820572
12-2.30, 6-11 (closed Mon); 12-3, 7-10.30 Sun
Marston's Bitter; Taylor Landlord; guest beer Ⓗ
Cosy, relaxing village pub - no fruit machines or muzak. There is a bar area with a real fire. A bistro-style restaurant-cum-lounge and a pleasant patio. Eve meals Tue-Sat. One of the real ales is chosen by a 'beer election'.

🏚 Q ❀ ◖ ▮ ▲ ♣ P

KNIGHTWICK

TALBOT HOTEL
Off A44, Leominster road
☎ (01886) 821235
11-11; 12-10.30 Sun
Hobsons Best Bitter; Teme Valley T'Other, This, That, Wot? Ⓗ
This traditional coaching inn dates back to the 14th century. The pub is home to the Teme Valley Brewery, established here in 1997. Hops for the brewery are grown locally by the landlord's family. Produce for the

large restaurant is also sourced locally. 🏨 ❀ 🛏 ◖ ▶ 🍴 ♣ P

KIDDERMINSTER

BOAR'S HEAD (TAP HOUSE)
39 Worcester Street (next to Magistrates Court)
☎ (01562) 862450
11-11; 12-3, 7-10.30 Sun
Banks's Mild, Bitter; Camerons Strongarm; Marston's Pedigree; guest beers Ⓗ
Lively town-centre pub with two bars and a large, covered, heated yard with plenty of seats and tables. Bar billiards played; Quiz alternate Wed eves. No food Sun. 🏨 ❀ ◖ ⇌ (SVR) ♣ 🍴

KING & CASTLE
SVR Station, Comberton Hill (next to mainline station)
☎ (01562) 747505
11-3, 5-11; 11-11 Sat; 12-10.30 Sun
Ansells Mild; Batham Bitter; Marston's Pedigree; guest beers Ⓗ
Friendly, single room pub, part of the Severn Valley's southern terminus, built on the plan of a 1930s station bar and buffet. Quiet children allowed (away from the bar area) until 9pm. Shops and wheelchair WC are on the platform.
🏨 Q ❀ ◖ ▶ 🚹 ⇌ (& SVR) ♣ P

STATION INN
7 Farfield (off Comberton Hill)
☎ (01562) 822764
12-3, 6-11; 12-11 Fri & 7 Sat; 12-3, 7-10.30 Sun
Banks's Mild; Davenports Bitter; Greenalls Original; Tetley Bitter Ⓗ
Tucked away in a quiet street, you will find this welcoming pub comprising a public bar, comfortable lounge and an enclosed garden. Filled rolls available evenings and weekends.
Q ❀ ◖ 🍴 🚹 ⇌ (& SVR) ♣ P

Try also: Red Man, Blackwell St (Carlsberg-Tetley)

LITTLE MALVERN

MALVERN HILLS HOTEL
Wynds Point (A449/B4232 jct)
☎ (01684) 540237
11-11; 11-10.30 Sun
Hobsons Best Bitter; Morland Old Speckled Hen; Wood Shropshire Lad Ⓗ
Comfortable, upmarket weekend retreat, ideally placed on the ridge of the Malvern Hills; walkers warmly welcomed. The restaurant offers a full à la carte menu. Plainer bar food also served.
🏨 ❀ 🛏 ◖ ▶ P

MENITHWOOD

CROSS KEYS INN
1 mile off B4202 OS709690
☎ (01584) 881425
11-3, 6-11; 11-11 Thu-Sat; 12-3, 7-10.30 Sun
Marston's Bitter, Pedigree; guest beer Ⓗ
Friendly, country pub popular with locals and visitors. There are a number of drinking areas around the bar. Excellent sandwiches always available. Well worth the short detour.
🏨 Q ❀ 🚹 🌲 ♣ P

OFFENHAM

BRIDGE INN
Boat Lane
☎ (01386) 446565
11-11; 12-10.30 Sun
Caledonian Deuchars IPA, 80/-; Theakston XB; guest beers Ⓗ
Ancient riverside inn with its own moorings and newly-created garden/patio. Guest beers are usually from local independents. There is a free courtesy minibus which is available for parties and groups.
🏨 ❀ ◖ ▶ 🍴 🚹 ♣ P

OMBERSLEY

CROWN & SANDYS ARMS
Main Road (off A449)
☎ (01905) 620252
11-3, 5.30-11; 12-3, 6.30-10.30 Sun
Hobsons Best Bitter; Hook Norton Old Hooky; guest beers Ⓗ
Smart hotel in a pretty village. The low-beamed lounge has a wonderful open fireplace and mountaineering artefacts. An excellent range of food with vegetarian options is served in the grill room and restaurant.
🏨 Q ❀ 🛏 ◖ ▶ P ⊬

PENSAX

BELL
On B4202 ☎ (01299) 896677
12-2.30 (not Mon, 12-3 Sat), 5-11; 12-3, 5-10.30 Sun
Enville Bitter; Taylor Landlord; guest beers Ⓗ
Popular country pub with a single bar giving different drinking areas plus a separate dining room. The garden offers superb views of the surrounding countryside.
🏨 ❀ ◖ ▶ ♣ ⌂ P

Try also: Nags Head, Eardiston (Marston's)

PERSHORE

BRANDY CASK
25 Bridge Street
☎ (01386) 552602
11.30-2.30 (3 Sat), 7-11; 12-3, 7-10.30 Sun

Draught Bass; Brandy Cask Whistling Joe, Brandysnapper, John Baker's Original; M&B Brew XI Ⓗ
Popular, town-centre brew pub with an attractive riverside garden. The beer is brewed in a building at the rear. Annual beer festival - August bank holiday.
🏨 Q ❀ ◖ 🚹 ♣ 🌲

POUND GREEN

OLDE NEW INN
½ mile from B4194 at Button Oak, down no-through road
☎ (01299) 401271
12-3, 7 (6 Sat & summer)-11; 12-3, 6 (7 winter)-10.30 Sun
Draught Bass; Theakston Mild; guest beer Ⓗ
Country local and restaurant, a steep but rewarding walk uphill from the Severn Valley railway at Arley. Live music most Fri and Sat eves; open evenings are held for musicians. Children's certificate.
🏨 🚌 ❀ 🛏 ◖ ▶ 🚹 🌲 ⇌ (SVR, Arley) ♣ P

STOKE WORKS

BOAT & RAILWAY
Shaw Lane (1 mile from B4091 jct) OS943663
☎ (01527) 831065
11.30-3, 6-11; 12-3, 7-10.30 Sun
Banks's Hanson's Mild, Bitter; Morrell's Varsity Ⓗ
Busy, canalside village local: a small lounge and a tidy public bar plus a skittle alley. Popular with boat folk (moorings available); canalside patio. No food Sun eve.
🏨 ❀ ◖ ▶ 🚹 ♣ 🌲

STOURPORT-ON-SEVERN

RISING SUN
50 Lombard Street (opp fire station)
☎ (01299) 822536
10.30-11; 12-10.30 Sun
Banks's Hanson's Mild, Ⓟ Mild, Bitter Ⓗ Ⓟ; Marston's Pedigree; guest beers Ⓗ
Single, split-level room, popular with locals. Close to the town centre. The small garden backs on to the canal. Meals available Tue-Sat. 🏨 ❀ ◖ ▶ 🚹 ♣ 🌲

WHEATSHEAF
39 High Street
☎ (01299) 822613
10.30-11; 12-10.30 Sun
Banks's Hanson's Mild, Mild, Bitter; Ⓟ Marston's Pedigree Ⓗ
Town-centre pub close to the canal and riverside with a typical locals' bar and a comfortable lounge. ❀ ◖ ▶ 🚹 🌲 ♣ P 🌲

Try also: Bird in Hand, Holly Rd (Whitbread)

PROTECTING RURAL GEMS
The future of the National Trust-owned Fleece at Bretforton, Worcestershire, as a beer-drinkers' heaven looked to be in danger after its manager quit after eight years. He claimed that the licencees, European Leisure, had tried to force him to introduce pool and Sky TV and replace the pub's wide range of real ales with Worthington.

European Leisure refused to comment to *What's Brewing* in April, but a Wychavon council spokeswoman said that there was little chance of planning permission being granted for a satellite dish on the building.

The pub is on CAMRA's National Inventory of pubs of outstanding historic interest.

Matters have settled down under the new landlord, Graham Brown, from the Bird in Hand in Stafford.

TENBURY WELLS

SHIP INN
Teme Street
☎ (01584) 810269
11-2.30, 7-11; 12-3, 7-10.30 Sun
Hobsons Best Bitter; guest beer H
Well furnished market town pub of character, placing an emphasis on food. it features a no-smoking restaurant area and a large garden. A preference for quality rather than quantity results in two interesting ales being offered.
❀ ⇔ ◖ ▶ P

Try also: Pembroke House, at B4214/A4112 jct (Free)

UPHAMPTON

FRUITERER'S ARMS
Uphampton Lane (off A449, at Reindeer pub) OS839649
☎ (01905) 620305
12.30-3, 7-11; 12-3, 7-10.30 Sun
Cannon Royall Fruiterer's Mild, Arrowhead, Buckshot, Olde Merrie (winter)**; John Smith's Bitter** H
Country pub run by the same family for 150 years. A friendly

place to enjoy a very reasonably-priced pint. The cosy, wood-panelled lounge features a wood burning stove; the bar is larger. Home of the Cannon Royal Brewery and local CAMRA *Pub of the Year* 1998. No food Sun.
▥ Q ❀ ◖ ▤ ▴ ♣ ⌣ P

WEATHEROAK

COACH & HORSES
Weatheroak Hill (Alvechurch-Wythall road) ☎ (01564) 823386
11.30-2.30, 5.30-11; 12-10.30 Sun
Boddingtons Bitter; Flowers Original; Hook Norton Old Hooky; Weatheroak Ale; Wells Bombardier; Wood Special H
Attractive pub set in hilly countryside. Casks are racked at the back of the bar and food is served in all the rooms, as well as the restaurant (no meals Sun eve). Weatheroak Ale is brewed by Weatheroak Brewery in an outbuilding at the pub.
▥ ❀ ◖ ▶ ▤ ▴ ♣ ⌣ P

WORCESTER

DRAGON
51 The Tything
☎ (01905) 25845

11-11; 4-10.30 Sun
Marston's Bitter; Taylor Landlord; guest beers H
One-roomed bar drawing a good mix of customers. A *Guide* regular, it is advantageously situated near good curry houses. Regular live music. Parking can be tricky.
❀ ⇌ (Foregate St)

OLDE TALBOT HOTEL
Friar Street
☎ (01905) 23573
11-11; 12-10.30 Sun
Banks's Bitter; Greene King Abbot; guest beers H
Two-star hotel, convenient for the cathedral and city centre. Popular with diners and drinkers alike, the single bar has areas for watching Sky TV or sitting and relaxing. Creaking floorboards add to its character.
❀ ⇔ ◖ ▶ ⇌ (Foregate St)

POSTAL ORDER
18 Foregate Street (opp Odeon cinema)
☎ (01905) 22373
11-11; 12-10.30 Sun
Banks's Mild; Courage Directors; Theakston Best Bitter; guest beers H
Typical 'Wetherspoonisation' of a former telephone exchange with well laid out areas away from the bar. Popular with all, especially weekends, but never rowdy. Beer festivals and promotions are run throughout the year. Good quality food at sensible prices. Wheelchair WC.
Q ◖ ▶ ♿ ⇌ (Foregate St)
⌣ ✂ ▯

INDEPENDENT BREWERIES

Brandy Cask:
Pershore

Cannon Royall:
Uphampton

Evesham:
Evesham

Fat God's:
Iron Cross

Red Cross:
Bromsgrove

Teme Valley:
Knightwick

Woodbury:
Great Witley

Wyre Piddle:
Fladbury

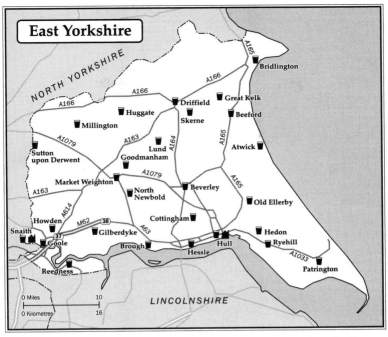

Yorkshire (East)

ATWICK

BLACK HORSE INN
The Green ☎ (01964) 532691
11-4, 7-11; 11-11 Sat; 12-10.30 Sun
John Smith's Bitter; guest beers Ⓗ
Super village local dating from
circa 1750 overlooking the green.
A comfortable interior offers
three drinking areas and food is
served in both the restaurant and
bar areas. Guest ales change
almost daily. ❀ Ⓓ ⅋ P

BEEFORD

TIGER INN
Main Street (A165/B1249 jct)
☎ (01262) 488733
11.30-3, 6-11; 11-11 Sat;
12-10.30 Sun
John Smith's Bitter; guest beers Ⓗ
Old coaching inn with its original
horse mounting steps outside. A
bar, restaurant and lounge with
real fire are complemented by
extensive gardens and a play
area (barbecues in summer).
♨ ❀ Ⓓ Ⓓ ⅋ ♣ P

BEVERLEY

GROVEHILL
183 Home Church Lane (1 mile E
of centre) ☎ (01482) 867409
11.30-2, 7-11; 11-11 Sat;
12-10.30 Sun
Marston's Bitter Ⓗ
1920s roadside pub (ex-Moors &
Robson) with a plain public bar

and well furnished lounge.
Popular with pigeon fanciers,
model enthusiasts and motor
cyclists. A rare local outlet for
Marston's. ⅋ ❀ ⅋ ♣ P

QUEEN'S HEAD
Wednesday Market
☎ (01482) 867363
11-11; 12-10.30 Sun
**Vaux Waggle Dance; Ward's
Thorne BB, Best Bitter; guest
beer** Ⓗ
A 'Brewer's Tudor' exterior on
the town's smaller market place.
Well refurbished in 1996 it was
opened out into a modern extension which forms a lounge and
games area. Meals finish at 5.30
weekends. Ⓓ Ⓓ ⇥

ROSE & CROWN
North Bar Without
☎ (01482) 862532
11-3, 5-11; 12-10.30 Sun
**Vaux Mild, Waggle Dance;
Ward's Thorne BB, Best Bitter;
guest beer** Ⓗ
Substantial 'Brewer's Tudor' pub
next to the historic North Bar
Westwood and racecourse.
Popular for home-made food in
the comfortable lounge and
smoke room (eve meals 5-9).
Q ❀ Ⓓ Ⓓ ⅋ ♣ P

ROYAL STANDARD INN
30 North Bar Within
☎ (01482) 882434
12-11; 12-10.30 Sun
**Vaux Double Maxim; Ward's
Thorne BB** Ⓗ

Two-roomed town local in a
white-painted terrace between
North Bar and St Mary's church.
The front bar features 1920s
bentwood seating and an etched
Darley's window; a well furnished lounge is set to the rear.
❀ ⅋

TAP & SPILE (SUN INN)
1 Flemingate
☎ (01482) 881547
12-11; 12-10.30 Sun
Beer range varies Ⓗ
Sympathetic restoration of a
medieval timber-framed building;
Beverley's oldest pub, set opposite the Minster. The large range
of guest beers has transformed
the local drinking scene.
❀ Ⓓ ⇥ ♣ ⌣ ⅋

WHITE HORSE INN
(NELLIES) ☆
22 Hengate (by bus station)
☎ (01482) 861973
11-11; 12-10.30 Sun
Samuel Smith OBB Ⓗ
One of Beverley's landmarks.
This historic inn offers a multi-
roomed interior with gas lighting,
stone-flagged floors, coal fires
and home cooking. Folk and jazz
eves upstairs. No food Mon.
♨ Q ❀ Ⓓ ⅋ ♣ P ⅋

WOOLPACK INN
37 Westwood Road (near
Westwood Hospital)
☎ (01482) 867095
12-3 (not Mon), 5(6.30 Mon)-11;
12-11 Fri & Sat; 12-10.30 Sun

Burtonwood Bitter, Top Hat,
Buccaneer ⊞
Superbly located pub in a residential street near the Westwood, built circa 1830. Formerly
a pair of cottages; read its history in the no-smoking snug.
Compact beer garden. Eve meals
5-7.30 Tue-Sun. ❀ ◖ ▶ ⅙

BRIDLINGTON

BULL & SUN INN
11 Baylegate ☎ (01262) 676105
11-11; 12-3.30, 7-10.30 Sun
Vaux Mild, Double Maxim;
Ward's Thorne BB; guest beer ⊞
Former hat shop near the historic
Baylegate and Priory: a large
one-roomer with two distinct
drinking areas. Sun lunches
served.

OLD SHIP INN
90 St John St ☎ (01262) 670466
11-11; 12-4, 7-10.30 Sun
Vaux Mild, Lorimer's Best
Scotch, Samson; Ward's Thorne
BB; guest beer ⊞
Thriving local by the old town
with a traditional atmosphere,
comfortable drinking areas and a
pool table in the large bar.
Outdoor play area for children.
Q ❀ ◖ ▶ ♣

PACK HORSE INN
7 Market Place
☎ (01262) 675701
11-3 (may extend summer), 7-11;
12-3, 7-10.30 Sun
Burtonwood Bitter, Forshaw's,
Top Hat ⊞
Listed building in the old town,
thought to be 300 years old. The
upper windows give the impression of three storeys but the pub
is in fact two (a relic from the
daylight tax days). Inside is an
open-plan lounge and pool room
with bar skittles. ♨ ❀ ◖ ♣

SEABIRDS
6 Fortyfoot (1 mile N of centre)
☎ (01262) 674174
11-11; 12-10.30 Sun
Camerons Bitter, Strongarm
Marston's Pedigree ⊞
Large, attractively extended pub:
a comfortable bar with a pool
table, and a well-furnished
lounge decorated with sailing
items. Children's play area outside. ❀ ◖ ▶ ♿ ♣ P 冖

INDEPENDENT BREWERIES

Hull:
Hull
Old Mill:
Goole

BROUGH

RED HAWK
Welton Road
☎ (01482) 666168
11.30-11; 12-10.30 Sun
Banks's Mild; Camerons Bitter,
Strongarm ⊞
Well designed pub built in 1995,
the bar includes various separated games areas. The other room
incorporates a stone-flagged
snug, a raised carpeted lounge
and a conservatory area (children's certificate). Outdoor play
area.❀ ◖ ▶ ⊡ ♿ ≠ ♣ P ⅙ 冖

COTTINGHAM

HALLGATE TAVERN
125-127a Hallgate
☎ (01482) 844448
11-11; 12-10.30 Sun
Camerons Bitter, Strongarm ⊞
This deceptively large pub has
four distinct drinking/eating
areas. The attractive green tiled
Hallgate frontage is a remnant
from its former use as a butchers. Popular with younger
drinkers at weekends when it can
be noisy. Eve meals 5.30-7.30.
❀ ◖ ▶ ♿ ≠ ♣ P ⅙ 冖

DRIFFIELD

BELL HOTEL
Market Place ☎ (01377) 256661
10-2.30, 6-11; 10-11 Thu; 12-3,
7-10.30 Sun
Beer range varies ⊞
Historic coaching inn and restaurant, with a wood-panelled bar
serving 250 whiskies. Leather
seating, substantial fireplaces
and antiques lend a quality feel.
Hotel accommodation.
Q ⇔ ◖ ▶ ⊡ ♿ P

MARINER'S ARMS
47 Eastgate South (near cattle
market)
☎ (01377) 253708
3-11 (11.45 Sat); 12-10.30 Sun
Burtonwood Mild, Bitter,
Buccaneer, seasonal beers ⊞
Traditional market town, street-
corner local that has retained its
two rooms and a friendly atmosphere. ❀ ⊡ ≠ ♣ P

GILBERDYKE

CROSS KEYS INN
Main Road (B1230, W edge of
village) ☎ (01430) 440310
12-11; 12-10.30 Sun
Boddingtons Bitter; John
Smith's Bitter; Tetley Bitter;
guest beers ⊞
Welcoming pub on the old A63,
enjoying a strong local following
of all ages who appreciate the
emphasis on traditional beer and
games. Three rotating guest
beers.
♨ ❀ ♣ ⌣ P

GOODMANHAM

GOODMANHAM ARMS
Main Street ☎ (01430) 873849
12-4 (not Mon-Fri), 7-11 Sat; 12-
4, 7-10.30 Sun
Black Sheep Best Bitter;
Theakston Best Bitter; guest
beer ⊞
Friendly village pub on the Wolds
Way and opposite the church.
The bar has a tiled floor and a
Victorian fireplace. The comfort-
able front parlour opens on to a
recently restored hallway with a
quarry-tiled floor, brick fireplace
and a wooden bar. Outside gents
WC. ♨ Q ❀ ⇔ ⊡ ▲ ♣ P

GOOLE

MACINTOSH ARMS
13 Aire Street
☎ (01405) 763850
11-11; 12-10.30 Sun
John Smith's Bitter; Tetley Dark
Mild, Bitter; guest beer ⊞
Former courthouse, built about
1830 alongside Goole docks, decorated with historic photos of the
docks and ships. Friendly and
welcoming, it gets very busy
weekend eves. Goole Motorbike
Club meets here twice a month.
❀ ≠ ♣ P

GREAT KELK

CHESTNUT HORSE
Main Street (between A165 and
A166, near Foston on the Wolds)
☎ (01262) 488263
12-2.30 (not Mon-Thu), 6.30-11;
12-3, 7-10.30 Sun
John Smith's Bitter; Tetley
Bitter; guest beers ⊞
Cosy, 18th-century local in a
small village off the beaten track.
One bar and a hatch into the corridor serve this two-roomed pub
and restaurant. Well worth a
detour. ♨ Q ❀ ◖ ▶ ♣ P

HEDON

SHAKESPEARE INN
9 Baxtergate
☎ (01482) 898371
12-11; 12-10.30 Sun
Vaux Mild, Samson; Ward's Best
Bitter; guest beers ⊞
Popular one-roomer noted for its
food and range of whiskies. Note
the brewery memorabilia and
interesting photos of old Hedon
with modern comparison shots.
Eve meals weekdays (end 7.30).
Two guest beers.♨ ❀ ◖ ▶ ♣ P

HESSLE

DARLEYS
Boothferry Road (A1105 near
Humber Bridge)
☎ (01482) 643121
11-3, 5.30-11; 11-11 Sat; 12-
10.30 Sun

Vaux Samson; Ward's Thorne BB, Best Bitter Ⓗ
Substantial 'Brewer's Tudor' roadhouse on the old western approach to Hull. Built in 1939 and named after the brewery closed in 1986 it retains its public bar, comfortable lounge, carvery restaurant (open eves & Sun lunch) plus a new function room. ❀ ◖ ▶ 🍴 ♣ P

HOWDEN

BARNES WALLIS
Station Road (B1228, 1 mile N of town) ☎ (01430) 430639
5 (7 Mon, 12 Sat)-11; 12-10.30 Sun
Flowers IPA; Taylor Golden Best; guest beers Ⓗ
Friendly open-plan pub next to the station, twice winner of York CAMRA *Pub of the Season*. It always has two guest beers from independent breweries. Weekend lunches. ₳ ❀ ◖ & ➡ P

HUGGATE

WOLDS INN
Driffield Rd ☎ (01377) 288217
12-3, 7-11 (closed Mon); 12-3, 7-10.30 Sun
John Smith's Bitter; Tetley Bitter; Theakston XB Ⓗ
The main part of this pub dates from the 16th century. Although Huggate village is mainly made up of a farming community, the inn is very popular with walkers, situated as it is between the Wolds Way and the Minster Way. Pool table in the bar. ❀ ➾ ◖ ▶ 🍴 ♣ P 🍺

HULL

ANLABY ALE HOUSE
283-285 Anlaby Road ☎ (01482) 328971
11-11; 12-10.30 Sun
Banks's Bitter; Camerons Bitter; Marston's Pedigree; guest beers Ⓗ
Refurbished Camerons Ale House: a split front room comprising a bar area with pool and darts, plus a basic lounge area; a more comfortable quieter separate lounge is to the rear. The house beer, Kingston Mild, is Hanson's Mild rebadged. Handy for Hull Sharks RLFC. Street tables outside. ❀ 🍴 ♣ 🍺

BAY HORSE
115-117 Wincolmlee (400 yds N of North Bridge on W bank of River Hull) ☎ (01482) 329227
11-11; 12-10.30 Sun
Bateman Mild, XB, XXXB, Victory (occasional), seasonal beers; Tetley Bitter Ⓗ
Cosy street-corner local, Bateman's only tied pub north of the Humber. The public bar contrasts with the spectacular, lofty,

stable lounge. Home-cooked food is a speciality. Note the rugby league and Bateman's memorabilia. ₳ ◖ ▶ 🍴 ♣ ♠ P

DUKE OF WELLINGTON
104 Peel Street (N of Spring Bank) ☎ (01482) 329603
12-3, 6-11; 12-11 Sat; 12-10.30 Sun
Taylor Landlord; Tetley Bitter; guest beers Ⓗ
Modernised Victorian back-street corner pub, popular with locals and students (big screen TV for sports). A central bar serves an L-shaped room plus a pool area. Eve meals weekdays (until 7.45); Sun meals 12-5. ❀ ◖ ▶ ♣ P

GARDENERS ARMS
35 Cottingham Road ☎ (01482) 342396
11-11; 12-10.30 Sun
Marston's Pedigree; Tetley Bitter; guest beers Ⓗ
Tetley Festival Ale House near the university. The front room is popular with locals and students with its dark wood, bare brick walls and original matchboard ceiling. Mr Q's games room is at the rear. Up to five guest beers. ❀ ◖ & ♣ P

KING WILLIAM HOTEL
41 Market Place, Old Town ☎ (01482) 227013
11-11; 12-10.30 Sun
Draught Bass; Courage Directors; Cropton King Billy; John Smith's Bitter; guest beer Ⓗ
Large, recently-built pub on the site of the old King William Hotel. It features a wood-panelled lounge and a local sporting heroes hall of fame. Regular live music during the week; very busy weekends. Eve meals weekdays 5-7. ❀ ◖ ▶ & ♣ P

KINGS ALE HOUSE
10 King Street, Market Place, Old Town ☎ (01482) 210446
11-11; 12-3, 7-10.30 Sun
Black Sheep Bitter, Special; Boddingtons Bitter; Stones Bitter; guest beers Ⓗ
Deceptively large one-roomer, situated in the open market place opposite Holy Trinity, the largest parish church in England, and near the old grammar school (now a museum). ◖ ♣

MISSION
11-13 Postergate, Old Town (by Princes Quay shopping centre) ☎ (01482) 221187
12-11; 12-3. 7-10.30 (12-10.30 summer) Sun
Old Mill Mild, Nellie Dene, Bitter, Old Curiosity, Bullion, seasonal beers Ⓗ
Old Mill's first Hull pub is a converted seaman's mission. Very large, somewhat like a baronial hall, it includes a minstrel's

gallery and a deconsecrated chapel. Very busy at weekends. Children's certificate. ◖ & ➡ (Paragon) ♣

NEW CLARENCE
77 Charles St ☎ (01482) 320327
11.30-11; 12-10.30 Sun
Marston's Pedigree; Tetley Dark Mild, Bitter; guest beers Ⓗ
Festival Ale House off Kingston Square, near the New Theatre. It caters for all in a relaxed atmosphere. Belgian bottled beers stocked. Eve meals until 7.30 (not Sun). ◖ ▶ ➡ (Paragon) ♣ ♡

OLD BLUE BELL
Market Place, Old Town (down alley next to covered market, opp Argos) ☎ (01482) 324382
11-11; 12-4, 7-10.30 Sun
Samuel Smith OBB Ⓗ
Dating from the 1600s this pub has retained a multi-roomed interior. A popular meeting place for local societies, it boasts a collection of bells. Children welcome in the snug. Pool upstairs. No food Sun. ❀ ◖ ♣

OLDE BLACK BOY
150 High Street, Old Town ☎ (01482) 326516
12-3, 5-11; 12-3, 7-10.30 Sun
Beer range varies Ⓗ
Pub situated in Hull's historic old town and sympathetically refurbished as an unbadged Tap & Spile. It retains a bar, a wood-panelled front room, displaying the pub's history, and two upstairs rooms. It stocks foreign bottled beers and draught Hoegaarden. ₳ ♣ ♡

OLDE WHITE HARTE ☆
25 Silver Street, Old Town ☎ (01482) 326363
11-11; 12-10.30 Sun
Courage Directors; McEwan 80/; Theakston XB, Old Peculier; guest beers (occasional) Ⓗ
16th-century courtyard pub, once the residence where the Governor of Hull resolved to deny Charles I entry to the city. Superb woodwork, sit-in fireplaces, and stained glass feature. Varied lunch menu in the bar and the upstairs dining room. Q ❀ ◖ ▶

RED LION
Clarence Street (400 yds E of Drypool Bridge) ☎ (01482) 324773
12-2.30 (3 Sat), 7-11; 12-11 Fri; 12-3.30; 7-10.30 Sun
Hull Mild, Bitter, seasonal beers; guest beer (occasional) Ⓗ
Built in 1939 for Moors & Robson, now the first tied house for Hull Brewery. It retains two rooms, staging entertainment in the rear wood-panelled lounge at weekends. 🍴 ♣ P

SPRING BANK TAVERN
29 Spring Bank
☎ (01482) 581879
11-11; 12-10.30 Sun
Mansfield Riding Mild, Riding Bitter, Deakins Golden Drop, Old Baily; guest beers Ⓗ
Mansfield's first cask ale house, sympathetically refurbished as a street-corner local after purchasing the next door shop. A collection of old Hull photos is displayed. Usually three guest beers. ◑ & ≠ (Paragon) ♣

ST JOHN'S HOTEL
10 Queens Road (off Beverley Road, 1 mile N of centre)
☎ (01482) 343669
12-11; 12-10.30 Sun
Mansfield Riding Mild, Riding Bitter, Old Baily Ⓗ
Victorian pub, the epitome of a street-corner local, well-loved by regulars and friendly to visitors; 'Johnnies' is an unpretentious multi-roomer. The front corner bar retains its original gaslight pipes across the windows. Family room until 8.30.
Q ⅏ ◑ ⊕ & ♣ P

TAP & SPILE (EAGLE)
169-171 Spring Bank
☎ (01482) 323518
12-11; 12-10.30 Sun
Beer range varies Ⓗ
Conversion of a street-corner local into a large, friendly ale house serving the city's largest range of constantly changing beers and ciders. It can be busy but the atmosphere is always welcoming. Local CAMRA *Pub of the Year* 1996 and '97. Sun lunch served. ❀ & ⌂ ⌁

VARSITY
10 Bowlalley Lane, Old Town
☎ (01482) 226543
11.30-11; 11-11 Sat; 12-10.30 Sun
Banks's Bitter; Camerons Strongarm; Marston's Pedigree; Morrells Varsity Ⓗ
Recent conversion of the Law Society's hall in the heart of the old town on the Land of Green Ginger. A loud circuit pub at weekends. No-smoking area until 6pm. ◑ ▶ & ⌁ ⎅

LUND

WELLINGTON INN
19 The Green ☎ (01377) 217294
12-3 (not Mon), 7-11; 12-10.30 Sun
Bateman Mild; Black Sheep Best Bitter; Taylor Landlord; guest beer (summer) Ⓗ
Attractive inn overlooking the village green and church. The building was renovated in 1995 with York flagstones and open fires. The high quality restaurant opens Tue-Sat eve and Sun lunch; lunchtime bar meals.
⅏ ❀ ◑ ▶ ⊕ & ♣ P

MARKET WEIGHTON

HALF MOON
39 High Street ☎ (01430) 872247
5 (11 Fri & Sat)-11; 12-10.30 Sun
Burtonwood Bitter, Buccaneer Ⓗ
Basic pub in the town centre. The building's shabby exterior belies its recently redecorated interior. A glazed entrance lobby divides the pub into a comfortable lounge and a bar/games area. Meals lunch and teatime.
❀ ◑ ♣ P

MILLINGTON

GATE INN
☎ (01759) 302045
12-3.30 (not Mon-Fri), 7-11; 12-5, 7-10.30 Sun
Old Mill Bitter; John Smith's Bitter; Tetley Bitter Ⓗ
Friendly village local in a beautiful Yorkshire Wolds setting. Note the Yorkshire map on the ceiling. Pool room. No eve meals Sun.
⅏ ❀ ◑ ▶ ♣ P

NORTH NEWBALD

TIGER INN
The Green ☎ (01430) 827759
12-3, 6-11; 12-11 Sat and summer; 12-10.30 Sun
Black Sheep Bitter; Boddingtons Bitter; guest beer Ⓗ
Former farmhouse overlooking the village green. The bar has a log fire and matchboarded ceiling with a pool room off; the lounge features a window seat. Eve meals to 8.30; no lunches Mon. good B & B.
⅏ ❀ ⇌ ◑ ▶ ⊕ ♣ P

OLD ELLERBY

BLUE BELL INN
Crabtree Lane (old Hull-Hornsea road) ☎ (01964) 562364
12-5 (not Mon-Fri), 7-11; 12-5, 7-10.30 (12-10.30 summer) Sun
Tetley Dark Mild, Bitter; guest beers Ⓗ
Unspoilt cosy village local. An L-shaped bar serves this one-roomer which has low beams, brasses and a superb real fire in winter. It also has a games room and a large outside area for families. Camping facilities available.
⅏ ❀ & ⋏ ♣ P

PATRINGTON

HILDYARD ARMS
1 Market Place
☎ (01964) 630234
12-11; 12-10.30 Sun
Tetley Dark Mild, Bitter; guest beers Ⓗ
Well refurbished former coaching inn which once served as a corn exchange for local farmers. A central bar serves a variety of rooms including a public bar, a

lounge bar, main lounge and a pool room. Two guest beers always available. No eve meals Sun. ⅏ Q ❀ ◑ ▶ ⊕ ♣ P

REEDNESS

HALF MOON
Main Street OS795232
☎ (01405) 704484
12-3 (not winter Mon-Fri), 7-11; 12-4, 7-10.30 (12-10.30 summer) Sun
Boddingtons Mild, Bitter; John Smith's Bitter; Theakston Black Bull; guest beer Ⓗ
Traditional, polished local with a caravan and campsite behind on the bank of the River Ouse, close to Blacktoft Sands RSPB Reserve. Excellent food (booking advised).
⅏ Q ⅏ ❀ ◑ ▶ ⊕ ⋏ ♣ P ⎅

RYEHILL

CROOKED BILLET
Pitt Lane (400 yds from A1033)
☎ (01964) 622303
11-11; 12-10.30 Sun
Burtonwood Bitter, Top Hat, seasonal beers Ⓗ
This 17th-century inn was reconstructed in 1939. It features an attractive beamed ceiling in the bar area; the lounge has a stone-floored lower level. Brass abounds.
⅏ ❀ ◑ ▶ ♣ P

SKERNE

EAGLE INN ☆
Wansford Rd ☎ (01377) 252178
12-2 (not Mon-Fri), 7-11; 12-3, 7-10.30 Sun
Camerons Bitter Ⓗ
Classic, unspoilt village local with a basic bar and a front parlour. Drinks are served to your table from a small cellar off the entrance corridor. Beer is dispensed from a Victorian cash register beer engine. Outside WCs. ⅏ Q ❀ ⊕ ♣ P

SNAITH

BLACK LION
9 Selby Road ☎ (01405) 860282
12-4.30, 7-11; 12-4, 7-10.30 Sun
Tetley Bitter Ⓗ
Central bar serving the lounge bar and the pool room. The cosy, comfortable atmosphere is enjoyed by a mature clientele.
❀ ◑ ▶ ♣ P

BREWERS ARMS
10 Pontefract Rd
☎ (01405) 862404
11.30-3, 6-11; 12-3, 7-10.30 Sun
Old Mill Mild, Nellie Dene, Bitter, Old Curiosity, Bullion, Black Jack Ⓗ
The flagship pub for Old Mill brewery carries the full portfolio of its beers. The decor is of old-

fashioned style in this fairly busy pub and restaurant. Organist and singalong Sun eves.
🏨 🚪 🌓 ▶ P

DOWNE ARMS
15 Market Place
☎ (01405) 860544
11.30-2.30, 5-11; 12-11 Sun
Mansfield Bitter, Deakins Golden Drop Ⓗ
A central bar area serves three rooms, two with fires. There is big screen TV in the bar and a pool room. Busy Sun eves (karaoke). Home-cooked food (not served Tue or Wed).
🏨 🏵 🌓 ♣ P

SUTTON UPON DERWENT

ST VINCENT ARMS
Main Street (turn on to B1228 from A1079)
☎ (01904) 608349
11.30-3, 6-11; 12-3, 7-10.30 Sun
Camerons Strongarm; Fuller's Chiswick, London Pride, ESB; John Smith's Bitter; Taylor Landlord; Wells Bombardier; guest beers Ⓗ
Welcoming, multi-roomer with an excellent reputation for food (no-smoking restaurant). No loud music or games machines.
🏨 Q 🏵 🌓 ▶ Å P 🍺

Yorkshire (North)

ACASTER MALBIS

SHIP INN
Moor End (W bank of River Ouse, 4 miles S of York)
☎ (01904) 705609
11.30-3, 6.30-11; 11.30-11 Fri & Sat; 12-10.30 Sun
Taylor Landlord; Tetley Mild, Bitter; Ⓗ
Riverside 17th-century coaching inn. Popular with boaters and campers. Barbecues on the terrace in summer.
🏨 🏵 🚪 🌓 Å ♣ P

APPLETREEWICK

NEW INN
Main Street ☎ (01756) 720252
12-3 (not Mon), 7-11; 12-3, 7-11 Sun
Daleside Nightjar; John Smith's Bitter; Theakston Best Bitter Ⓗ
Attractive, traditional country inn overlooking the River Wharfe and moors. Popular with locals, walkers, mountain bikers and cyclists. On the Dales Way. Large selection of foreign bottled beers. Good B&B. 🏨 Q 🏵 🚪 🌓 Å ♣ P

ASKRIGG

CROWN
Main Street ☎ (01969) 650298
11-3, 6-11; 11-11 Sat & summer; 12-11 Sun

Black Sheep Best Bitter, Special; John Smith's Bitter; Theakston Best Bitter, Old Peculier (summer) Ⓗ
Bustling village pub, popular with locals and visitors alike.
🏨 Q 🌓 & ♣ 🍺

KINGS ARMS
Main Street ☎ (01969) 650258
11-3, 6.30-11; 12-3, 7-10.30 Sun
Dent Bitter; John Smith's; Theakston XB; Younger No. 3; guest beer Ⓗ
18th-century coaching inn in a Dales village, boasting stone flags, massive fireplaces and much paraphernalia. Popular with walkers. The award-winning restaurant serves all tastes; also an extensive bar menu.
🏨 Q 🏵 🚪 🌓 ▶ ♣ P

BECK HOLE

BIRCH HALL INN ☆
1 mile N of Goathland OS822022
☎ (01947) 896245
11-3, 7.30-11 (closed winter Mon eve), (11-11 summer); 7.30 (12 summer)-10.30 Sun
Black Sheep Best Bitter; Theakston Mild (summer)**, Best Bitter; guest beer** Ⓗ
Do not miss this tiny, two-roomed pub in a charming village in *Heartbeat* country. It also has a small shop and offers afternoon teas. Popular with walkers, it is near the North York Moors Railway. Cleveland CAMRA *Pub of the Year* 1994. 🏨 Q 🏵 🕭 ♣

BIRSTWITH

STATION
Station Road ☎ (01423) 770254
11.30-2.30 (not Mon), 5.30-11; 11.30-5, 7-10.30 Sun
Tetley Bitter; guest beer Ⓗ
Traditional Victorian public house near to a disused station: very friendly, open plan with an attractive dining room. The house beer is Station Bitter from Rudgate. 🏨 🏵 🚪 🌓 ▶ ♣ P 🍺

BISHOP MONKTON

LAMB & FLAG
Boroughbridge Rd ☎ (01765) 677322
12-3, 5.30-11; 12-3, 7-10.30 Sun
Black Sheep Best Bitter; Tetley Bitter Ⓗ
Friendly, welcoming two-roomed village inn in a picturesque setting, enjoying a good local trade.
🏨 Q 🏵 🌓 ▶ ♣ P

BOROUGHBRIDGE

BLACK BULL
6 St James's Sq ☎ (01423) 322413
11-11; 12-10.30 Sun
Black Sheep Best Bitter; John Smith's Bitter; guest beer Ⓗ

Historic, 13th-century inn with a small snug and a larger bar area. Wood panels and low beams give the bars and corridors a cosy traditional feel; a large inglenook dominates the bar. Popular restaurant to the rear of the premises.
🏨 Q 🏵 🌓 ▶ Å

THREE HORSESHOES ☆
Bridge Street
☎ (01423) 322314
11-3, 5-11; 12-10.30 Sun
Black Sheep Best Bitter; Ⓗ
Vaux Samson Ⓟ
Superb gem of a 1930s hotel; the lounge and bar are both full of character; note the original bar fittings with leaded glass panels. Very friendly and sociable atmosphere; not to be missed - a true classic.
🏨 Q 🚪 🖭 Å ♣ P

BREARTON

MALT SHOVEL
Off B6165
☎ (01423) 862929
12-3, 6.30-11 (closed Mon); 12-3, 7-10.30 Sun
Black Sheep Best Bitter; Daleside Nightjar; Theakston Best Bitter; guest beers Ⓗ
Welcoming, unspoilt village pub dating from the 16th century with exposed stone and beams. Home-cooked food served (not Sun eve or Mon). Local CAMRA *Pub of the Year* 1997. Cider in summer.
🏨 Q 🌣 🏵 🌓 & ♣ 🖙 P

BROMPTON

CROWN INN
Station Road
☎ (01609) 772547
12-3 (not Tue), 7-11; 11-11 Fri & Sat; 12-10.30 Sun
Boddingtons Bitter; John Smith's Bitter, Magnet; guest beer Ⓗ
Straightforward, friendly village pub on the edge of the green, offering a good selection of guest beers. Children welcome.
🏨 Q 🏵 ♣ P

BROMPTON BY SAWDON

CAYLEY ARMS
On A170
☎ (01723) 859372
11.30-2.30 (not Mon), 5.30-11; 12-3, 7-10.30 Sun
Tetley Bitter; Theakston Best Bitter, XB; guest beer Ⓗ
Prominent roadside pub with a children's play area. The excellent food includes local specialities. The guest beer is usually from the Tapster's Choice range.
🏨 Q 🌣 🏵 🌓 ▶ Å ♣ P 🍺

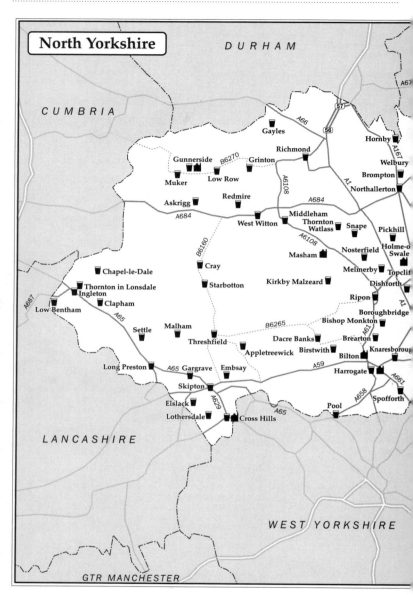

North Yorkshire

DURHAM

CUMBRIA

Gayles
Richmond
Hornby
Gunnerside Grinton Welbury
Muker Low Row Brompton
Askrigg Redmire Northallerton
Middleham
West Witton Thornton
Watlass Snape Pickhill
Nosterfield Holme-o
Swale
Masham Melmerby Topclif
Chapel-le-Dale Cray Dishforth
Thornton in Lonsdale Starbotton Kirkby Malzeard Ripon
Ingleton Clapham
Low Bentham Boroughbridge
Settle Malham Bishop Monkton
Threshfield B6265 Dacre Banks Brearton
Long Preston Appletreewick Birstwith Knaresborou
Gargrave Embsay Bilton
Skipton Harrogate
Elslack
Lothersdale Cross Hills Pool Spofforth

LANCASHIRE

WEST YORKSHIRE

GTR MANCHESTER

CARLTON IN CLEVELAND

BLACKWELL OX
Off A172, near Stokesley
☎ (01642) 712287
11.30-3, 6.30 (5.30 summer)-11;
11-11 Sat; 12-10.30 Sun
John Smith's Bitter; Theakston XB; guest beers [H]
Only pub in the village. The pleasant interior has a central bar with seating areas at different levels. Good food (Thai cooking a speciality). Popular with locals, campers/caravanners, walkers.
🏚 Q ☻ ⊛ 🚭 🌙 🛦 ♣ P ✠

CASTLETON

ESKDALE HOTEL
Next to station
☎ (01287) 660234
12-3, 7-11 (11-11 summer); 12-10.30 Sun
Camerons Strongarm; Tetley Bitter [H]
Purpose-built former station hotel in a valley bottom. Large and airy, it is popular with locals.
🏚 Q ☻ ⊛ 🌙 🚻 👤 🛦 ⇌ ♣ P 🍴

Try also: Downe Arms, 3 High St (Pubmaster)

CAWOOD

FERRY
King Street
☎ (01757) 268515
12-4 (not Mon-Fri), 6.30-11; 12-4, 7.30-10.30 Sun
Mansfield Riding Bitter, Bitter; Taylor Landlord; guest beers [H]
16th-century inn of great character: the main bar has a wood-burning stove, also numerous smaller rooms and a riverside terrace.
🏚 Q ☻ ⊛ 🚭 🌙 🛦 ♣ P

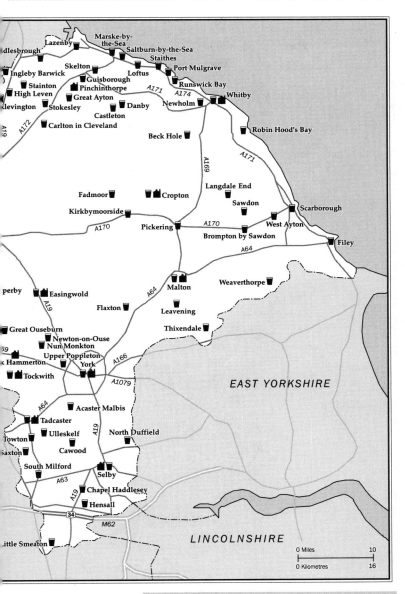

CHAPEL HADDLESEY

JUG INN
Main Street
☎ (01757) 270307
12-3, 6-11; 11-11 Sat; 12-10.30 Sun
Marston's Bitter; guest beers H
Small, 250-year-old village pub
which used to be a blacksmith's
shop, now two bars with a homely atmosphere. Fascinating collection of jugs hangs from the
low ceiling beams. Folk musicians visit weekly for impromptu
entertainment. The garden leads
to the north bank of the River
Aire. ♨ Q ✿ ◑ ▶ ⊞ ♿ ♣ P

INDEPENDENT BREWERIES

Black Dog: Whitby
Black Sheep: Masham
Cropton: Pickering
Daleside: Harrogate
Easingwold: Easingwold
Franklin's: Harrogate
Hambleton: Thirsk
Malton: Malton

Marston Moor: Hammerton
North Yorkshire: Pinchinthorpe
Old Bear: Cross Hills
Rooster's: Harrogate
Selby: Selby
Samuel Smith: Tadcaster
Swaled: Richmond

CHAPEL-LE-DALE

HILL INN
On B6255
☎ (015242) 41256
12-3 (may extend summer), 7-11;
11.30-11 Sat; 12-3, 7-10.30 Sun
**Black Sheep Best Bitter; Dent
Bitter; Tetley Bitter; Theakston
Best Bitter, XB, Old Peculier;
guest beers** H
Well-known, isolated pub on the
Three Peaks walk, with bare
floorboards, exposed stonework,
a pool room and food bar (children welcome). Live music Sat
eve; folk Sun lunch.
🏚 Q 🛏 🍴 ▶ Å ♣ P

CLAPHAM

NEW INN
☎ (015242) 51203
11.30-3, 7-11; 11.30-11 Sat; 12-
10.30 Sun
**Black Sheep Best Bitter; Dent
Bitter; Tetley Bitter; Theakston
XB; guest beer** H
Large coaching inn dated 1776:
two lounge bars with oak panelling (1990 vintage) and a display of cycling and caving pictures. No-smoking restaurant
(children welcome). The house
beer is rebadged Flying Firkin
Aviator.
🏚 🛏 🍴 ▶ Å ♣ P

CRAY

WHITE LION INN
On B6160, N of Buckden
☎ (01756) 760262
11-11; 12-10.30 Sun
**Moorhouse's Premier, Pendle
Witches Brew; Tetley Bitter;
guest beer** H
Traditional Dales pub, the highest
in Wharfedale, in an excellent
walking area, close to Buckden
Pike. Two rooms with original
beams and open fire. Ringing the
Bull played.
🏚 Q 🐴 🛏 🍴 ▶ 🕭
Å ♣ P ⚬

CROPTON

NEW INN
Follow signs to Cropton on A170
Pickering-Helmsley road
☎ (01751) 417310
12-3, 7-11 winter; 11-11 Sat &
summer; 12-3, 7-10.30 Sun
**Cropton King Billy, Two Pints,
Scoresby Stout, Backwoods
Bitter, Monkmans Slaughter,
seasonal beers; Tetley Bitter** H
Busy but friendly country pub at
the top of a steep hill, popular
with tourists and locals alike.
One of the best small breweries
is situated in the backyard so
beer supply in winter is never a
problem.
🏚 Q 🐴 🛏 🍴 ▶ 🕭
Å ♣ P ⚬

CROSS HILLS

OLD WHITE BEAR
6 Keighley Road
☎ (01535) 632115
11.30 (5 Mon)-11; 12-10.30 Sun
**Boddingtons Bitter; Old Bear
Bitter** H
Large, old, multi-roomed brew
pub at the heart of village life.
Original ship's beams form part
of the structure. The brewery,
next to Aunty Wainwright's
Eating 'Ole, utilises local well
water. No food Sun eve or Mon.
Brewery trips available.
🏚 🍴 ▶ 🕭 ♣ P

DACRE BANKS

ROYAL OAK
☎ (01423) 780200
12-2 (3 Sat), 7-11; 12-3, 7-10.30
Sun
**Black Sheep Best Bitter;
Daleside Old Legover; Theakston
Best Bitter** H
18th-century, traditional Dales
inn where the cosy, oak-panelled
bar is decorated with quotations
about food and drink. Garden and
boules piste in the summer.
Extensive menu of home-cooked
food (not Sun eve).
🏚 🚲 🍴 ▶ ♣ P

DANBY

DUKE OF WELLINGTON
2 West Lane ☎ (01287) 660351
11-3 (not Mon), 7-11; 12-3,
7-10.30 Sun
**Camerons Strongarm; Morland
Old Speckled Hen; John Smith's
Magnet; guest beer** H
Coaching inn, dating from 1732,
popular with locals, families and
walkers alike. It also has a
restaurant. Recommended B & B.
🏚 Q 🍴 🛏 ▶ Å ♣

DISHFORTH

CROWN
Main Street ☎ (01845) 577398
12-3, 6.30-11; 12-3, 7-10.30 Sun
**Hambleton Bitter; Robinson's
Bitter; Taylor Golden Best; guest
beer** H
Popular, friendly village local,
keen to promote guest beers.
Local CAMRA *Pub of the Year*
1996. Occasional outlet for Pipkin
cider. 🏚 🍴 ♣ ⌂ P

EASINGWOLD

STATION HOTEL
Knott Lane, Raskelf Road
☎ (01347) 822635
4 (12 Thu-Sat)-11; 12-3.30,
7-10.30 Sun
**Easingwold Steamcock, Full
Steam, Inspector's Special, seasonal beers; John Smith's Bitter;
guest beers** H
Former railway hotel with a lively

main bar and quieter room off.
Its award-winning beers are
brewed in outbuildings. York
CAMRA *Pub of the Year* 1998.
🏚 Q 🍴 🛏 🕭 ⚬ ♣ 🍺

ELSLACK

TEMPEST ARMS
On A56 ☎ (01282) 842450
11-11; 12-10.30 Sun
**Black Sheep Best Bitter, Special;
Jennings Mild, Bitter,
Cumberland Ale, Sneck Lifter** H
Large, rambling 18th-century inn,
very popular for its food.
Purchased by Jennings in 1996, it
offers a high standard of accommodation (ETB recommended).
🏚 Q 🍴 🛏 ▶ 🕭 P

EMBSAY

ELM TREE
5 Elm Tree Square
☎ (01756) 790717
11.30-3, 6.30-11; 12-3, 7-10.30 Sun
**Bateman XB; Cains Bitter;
Fuller's London Pride; Greene
King Abbot; Holt Bitter; guest
beers** H
Village pub on the edge of the
Yorkshire Dales National Park
near the Embsay-Bolton Abbey
steam railway station. Good food
and an ever-changing range of
guest beers; dining area for non-
smokers. Q 🍴 🛏 🕭 ▶ P

FADMOOR

PLOUGH
☎ (01751) 431515
12-2.30, 6.30-11; 12-2.30,
7-10.30 Sun
**Black Sheep Best Bitter; John
Smith's Bitter** H
Stylishly revitalised village inn,
retaining much internal character
with a separate snug.
🏚 Q 🍴 🕭 ▶ P 🍺

FILEY

IMPERIAL VAULTS
20-22 Hope Street
☎ (01723) 512185
12-11; 12-10.30 Sun
**Boddingtons Bitter; John
Smith's Bitter; Wadworth 6X;
guest beer** H
Refurbished, friendly, two-
roomed town-centre pub. Meals
available until early eve in summer. 🛏 🕭 ▶ Å ⚖ ♣

FLAXTON

BLACKSMITHS ARMS
(½ mile off A64, York-Malton
road) ☎ (01904) 468210
12-3 (not Mon-Fri), 7-11; 12-3,
7-10.30 Sun
**Black Sheep Special; John
Smith's Bitter; Theakston XB;
guest beers** H
Village pub enjoying considerable

patronage from a wide local area: an opened-up, large public bar, a lounge and a dining room. The cellar was the original mortuary for the village. Guest beers are from local breweries.
🏚 🕏 ◖ ▶ P 🗓

GARGRAVE

OLD SWAN INN
20 High Street
☎ (01756) 749232
11-3, 5.30-11; 11-11 Sat; 12-3, 7-10.30 Sun
Greene King Abbot; Morland Old Speckled Hen; Tetley Bitter; guest beers Ⓗ
Friendly, multi-roomed, former coaching inn on the main road near the village centre. A comfortable main bar adjoins the restaurant, and there is a smaller family dining room at the front, opposite the unspoilt traditional snug with dartboard and bar football. No eve meals winter Sun. 🏚 Q 🍺 🕏 ◖ ▶ Å ≈ ♣

GAYLES

BAY HORSE
☎ (01833) 621468
12-3 (not Mon-Fri, except Bank Hols), 6-11; 12-3, 7-10.30 Sun
Butterknowle Conciliation; Younger Scotch (occasional)**; guest beers** (summer) Ⓗ
Hillside village pub with fine views over lower Teesdale. Dating from the 17th-century it has been opened out into a beamed bar with a lounge/dining room to one side. Excellent meals. Q 🕏 ◖ ▶ Å ♣ P 🗓

GREAT AYTON

BUCK
1 West Terrace (A173 near bridge) ☎ (01642) 722242
11-11; 12-10.30 Sun
Boddingtons Bitter; Flowers Original; Whitbread Trophy; guest beers Ⓗ
Coaching inn dating from the 1700s by the river in Captain Cook's village. A friendly atmosphere with strong local patronage. Beer festivals held.
Q 🍺 🕏 ◖ ▶ ♣ P

Try also: Royal Oak, High Green (Courage)

GREAT OUSEBURN

CROWN
Main Street
☎ (01423) 330430
5-11; 11-11 Sat; 12-10.30 Sun
Black Sheep Best Bitter; John Smith's Bitter; Theakston Best Bitter; guest beers Ⓗ
Attractive village inn with many old features and a reputation for good food. 🏚 Q 🕏 ◖ ▶ P ✄

GRINTON

BRIDGE INN
☎ (01748) 884224
11-11; 12-10.30 Sun
Black Sheep Best Bitter, Special; John Smith's Bitter; Theakston Old Peculier; guest beers Ⓗ
Hospitable pub in a peaceful setting on the River Swale with views to the hills and moors. Excellent bar and restaurant meals and very good accommodation. Families are well catered for, with the restaurant doubling as a family room.
🏚 Q 🍺 🕏 🛏 ◖ ▶ 🍴 ♿ Å ♣ P ✄

GUISBOROUGH

ANCHOR INN
16 Belmongate
☎ (01287) 632715
11.30-11; 12-10.30 Sun
Samuel Smith OBB Ⓗ
18th-century cottage pub, well refurbished.
🏚 Q 🍺 🕏 ◖ ▶

GLOBE
Northgate
☎ (01287) 632778
5.30 (12 Sat)-11; 12-10.30 Sun
Banks's Bitter; Camerons Strongarm; guest beer Ⓗ
Friendly, busy street-corner pub with a bustling public bar and a large lounge. Live music Fri and Sun.
🍺 🕏 🛏 🍴 ♣ P 🗓

SHIP INN
145 Westgate
☎ (01287) 632233
11.30-11; 12-10.30 Sun
Draught Bass Ⓗ
Busy, town-centre pub, a former coaching inn with an authentic, unaltered interior and a large garden. Bar snacks are available.
🏚 🍺 ♣

TAP & SPILE
Westgate
☎ (01287) 632983
11-3, 5.30-11; 11-11 Thu-Sat; 12-3, 7-10.30 Sun
Beer range varies Ⓗ
Old-town-centre pub in traditional style with no-smoking room at the rear. The cider varies.
🍺 ◖ ♣ ⚱ ✄

GUNNERSIDE

KINGS HEAD
☎ (01748) 886261
12-2 (3 summer), 7-11; 12-3, 7-10.30 Sun
Beer range varies Ⓗ
Old pub at the heart of the village, opened out into a single drinking area but retaining character. A regular outlet for Swaled

Ale brewed in the village, stocked alongside a regularly changing beer range. 🏚 ◖ ▶ ♣ 🗓

HARROGATE

GARDENERS' ARMS ☆
Bilton Lane ☎ (01423) 506051
12-3, 6 (7 Sat)-11; 12-3, 7-10.30 Sun
Samuel Smith OBB Ⓗ
Ancient hostelry, popular with locals. Featuring a large stone fireplace, and thick stone walls, wood-panelled in places. Eve meals served Sept-April; no lunches Wed. 🏚 🕏 ◖ ▶ P

PRINCE OF WALES
49 High Street, Starbeck
☎ (01423) 884235
11-11; 12-10.30 Sun
John Smith's Bitter Ⓗ
Very strong community pub with a large children's play area.
🍼 🕏 ◖ 🍴 ♿ ≈ (Starbeck) ♣ P

PUMP ROOMS
51 Parliament Street
☎ (01423) 502759
11-11; 12-10.30 Sun
Tetley Bitter; guest beers Ⓗ
Recently refurbished as a Festival Ale House, this pub offers one of the widest ale choices in town (up to seven guests) and a good selection of food. The evening atmosphere is enlivened by the upstairs pool hall. ◖ ≈

SLIP INN
30 Cold Bath Road
☎ (01423) 560437
11-11; 12-10.30 Sun
John Smith's Bitter, Magnet; guest beers Ⓗ
Cheerful little gem; a traditional single-roomed local with a good year-round trade, handy for the town centre and conference area. Some entertainment Wed -Sat. Pipkin cider.
Q ♿ ♣ ⚱ P

TAP & SPILE
Tower Street (off West Park Stray) ☎ (01423) 526785
11-11; 12-10.30 Sun
Beer range varies Ⓗ
Town-centre pub with a brick interior and wooden furniture; Three rooms served by a central bar offering up to eight beers. No food Sun. 🕏 ◖ ≈ ♣ ⚱

Try also: Hales Bar, Crescent Rd (Bass)

HELPERBY

GOLDEN LION
Main Street (signed from A59 York-Thirsk Road)
☎ (01423) 360870
6 (11 Sat)-11; 12-3, 6-10.30 Sun

Taylor Bitter; guest beers Ⓗ
With a range of at least six real
ales available from the bar, a
finer example of a village pub you
will not find. It has good food,
real fires and york stone floors.
Note the bizarre painting in the
gents. ♨ ❀ ◖ ♦ ♣ ⛫

HENSALL

ANCHOR
Main Street ☎ (01977) 661634
6.30 (12 Sat)-11; 12-10.30 Sun
John Smith's Bitter; guest beer Ⓗ
Busy, one-roomed village pub
with a guest beer from a variety
of breweries. Very infrequent
service to local station.
♨ ❀ ♦ ⇌ ♣ P ⛫

HIGH LEVEN (YARM)

FOX COVERT
Low Lane (A1044)
☎ (01642) 760033
11.30-3, 5-11; 12-3, 7-10.30 Sun
Vaux Samson, Double Maxim Ⓗ
This whitewashed longhouse-
style pub dominates at its crossroads setting. Of farmhouse origin and believed uniquely named,
its open-plan interior welcomes
locals and visitors alike. Strong
emphasis on food and a regular
entry in this Guide.
♨ ❀ ◖ ♦ ♣ P

HORNBY

GRANGE ARMS
☎ (01609) 881249
12-3, 7-11; (closed Mon except
Bank Hols); 12-3, 7-10.30 Sun
Theakston XB, Old Peculier;
guest beer Ⓗ
Pleasant, whitewashed, red-pan-
tiled village local with a two-part
beamed bar and a dining room.
♨ Q ❀ ◖ ♦ ⊞ ♣ P ⛫

INGLEBY BARWICK

MYTON HOUSE FARM
Ingleby Way (access from A1044
roundabout)
☎ (01642) 751308
11-11; 12-10.30 Sun
Camerons Bitter, Strongarm Ⓗ
Newly built (1997) in farmhouse
style to serve a new village
between Yarm and Thornaby.
Several drinking areas around a
large island bar offer a warm,
friendly welcome. ❀ ◖ ♦ ⛫ P ⛫

INGLETON

BRIDGE
New Road ☎ (015242) 41183
11-11 (11-3, 6-11 winter); 12-3,
7-10.30 Sun
Black Sheep Best Bitter;
Theakston Best Bitter; guest
beers Ⓗ
Main road hotel with a spacious
pub/restaurant. Children's play

area outside. Other Black Sheep
beers are often on tap.
♨ ❀ ⇌ ◖ ♦ ᕕ ▲ ♣ P

WHEATSHEAF
22 High Street
☎ (0152 42) 41275
11 (12 winter)-11; 12-10.30 Sun
Black Sheep Best Bitter, Special
(summer), Riggwelter;
Moorhouse's Pendle Witches
Brew; Theakston Mild, Best
Bitter; guest beers Ⓗ
Pub with a single, long, cosy bar,
handy for finish of the Waterfalls
Walk. No-smoking dining room.
❀ ⇌ ◖ ♦ ▲ P

KIRKBY MALZEARD

HENRY JENKINS
Main Street
☎ (01765) 658557
12-3, 6-11 (11-11 summer)
12-10.30 Sun
Black Sheep Best Bitter; John
Smith's Bitter; Theakston Best
Bitter; guest beers Ⓗ
Popular community village local.
The spacious lounge doubles as a
restaurant area and there is a
small pool room to the rear. It
takes its name from Yorkshire's
reputedly oldest character who
died allegedly aged 169!
♨ ◖ ♦ ⊞ ♣ P ⛫

KIRKBYMOORSIDE

GEORGE & DRAGON
Market Place
☎ (01751) 433334
11-3, 6-11; 12-3, 7-10.30 Sun
Black Sheep Best Bitter; Taylor
Landlord; Theakston Best Bitter;
guest beer Ⓗ
17th-century coaching inn at the
town centre. The large, comfortable lounge is divided into distinct areas.
♨ ❀ ⇌ ◖ ♦ ᕕ P ⛫

WHITE SWAN
4 Church St ☎ (01751) 431041
12-11; 12-10.30 Sun
Black Sheep Best Bitter; Tetley
Bitter; guest beers Ⓗ
Fine, basic pub, opposite the
market place: a bar with an
adjoining pool room. ♨ ❀ ♣

KIRKLEVINGTON

CROWN
Thirsk Road (A67, near A19
Grathorn interchange)
☎ (01642) 780044
5 (12 Sat)-11; 12-10.30 Sun
Boddingtons Bitter; Castle Eden
Ale; John Smith's Magnet; Ⓗ
Medium-sized village pub with
two distinct drinking areas, both
with real fires, giving a homely
atmosphere and a warm welcome. Home-cooked food on an
imaginative menu is always available. ♨ ❀ ◖ ♦ ᕕ ♣ P

KNARESBOROUGH

BEER-RITZ (OFF
LICENCE)
17 Market Place
☎ (01423) 862850
10 (9 Sat)-10; 11-10 Sun
Beer range varies Ⓖ
Speciality off-licence selling over
300 beers as well as cask ales
and cider. The inexpensive house
beer is brewed by Daleside.
Discount on draught beers to
card-carrying CAMRA members.
⇌ ⏚

BLIND JACKS
19 Market Place
☎ (01423) 869148
5.30 (4 Tue & Wed, 12 Thu & Fri,
11.30 Sat)-11; 12-10.30 Sun
Village White Boar;
guest beers Ⓗ
Intimate gem recreated in a
Georgian building overlooking the
town's historic market place. The
upstairs rooms have recently
been opened up to allow extra
drinking space. CAMRA's Best
New Pub award winter 1992.
Well worth a visit.
Q ⇌ ⊱

HALF MOON
Abbey Road (off Briggate)
☎ (01423) 862663
5.30 (11 Sat)-11; 12-10.30 Sun
Mansfield Bitter Ⓗ
Small, comfortable one-roomed
pub overlooking the River Nidd,
well-known for its Boxing Day tug
of war over the river. Weekend
lunches. ◖

MARQUIS OF GRANBY
31 York Place (A59, towards
York) ☎ (01423) 862207
11.30-3, 5.30-11; 11.30-11 Wed,
Fri & Sat; 12-10.30 Sun
Samuel Smith OBB Ⓗ
Pleasant, friendly, two-roomed
town pub decorated in Victorian
style displaying prints of old
Knaresborough. Sam Smith's
Bitter is sold at a bargain price.
No food Sun.❀ ◖ ⊞ ▲ ♣ P

LANGDALE END

MOORCOCK INN
OS938913 ☎ (01723) 882268
7 (11 summer)-11 (closed winter
Mon-Tue); 11-3, 7-11 (11-11 sum-
mer) Sat; 12-3, 7-10.30 Sun
Daleside Old Legover, Monkey
Wrench; Malton Double Chance;
guest beers Ⓗ
Remote stone pub, sympatheti-
cally renovated, near a forest
drive. Busy in summer.
♨ Q ❀ ◖ ♦ ▲ ♣ P ⊱

LAZENBY

HALF MOON
High St ☎ (01642) 452752
11-11; 12-10.30 Sun

Boddingtons Bitter; Fuller's
London Pride; Greene King
Abbot; Marston's Pedigree;
guest beers Ⓗ
Large, Whitbread managed pub,
with a dining area at the rear,
and a semi-enclosed lounge and
bar; food is available all day
throughout the pub. Quiz Wed
eve. ❀ ◖ ▶ ᵫ ♣ P

LEAVENING

JOLLY FARMERS
Main Street ☎ (01653) 658276
12-3, 7-11; 12-3, 7-10.30 Sun
Hambleton Stallion; John
Smith's Bitter; Tetley Bitter;
guest beer Ⓗ
Friendly, award-winning 17th-
century village local, extended
but retaining cosiness. The dining
room serves locally caught game.
▨ ➴ ❀ ◖ ▶ ♣ P ▯

LITTLE SMEATON

FOX
Main Street ☎ (01977) 620254
12-3 (not Mon-Thu, 12-4 Sat),
7-11; 12-10.30 Sun
John Smith's Bitter; Stones
Bitter; guest beer Ⓗ
Cosy, comfortable free house
with a single L-shaped room. A
traditional village local in an
attractive setting near the River
Went. ❀ ♣ P

LOFTUS

WHITE HORSE
73 High St ☎ (01287) 640758
12-11; 12-10.30 Sun
Morland Old Speckled Hen;
John Smith's Bitter Ⓗ;
Recently refurbished local; one
large room with a central bar.
▨ ❀ ᵫ ᵫ ♣ P

LONG PRESTON

MAYPOLE INN
On A65
☎ (01729) 840219
11-3, 6-11; 11-11 Sat; 12-10.30 Sun
Boddingtons Bitter; Castle Eden
Ale; Taylor Landlord; Worth
Alesman Ⓗ
White-painted pub facing the village green and maypole. The
public bar is on one side and a
comfortable lounge on the other
with a real fire and adjoining
restaurant. Real cider in summer.
▨ Q ❀ ᵫ ◖ ▶ ➳ ♣ ◌ P

LOTHERSDALE

HARE & HOUNDS
Dale End
☎ (01535) 630977
12-3.30, 6-11; 12-4, 7-10.30 Sun
Tetley Bitter; Ward's Thorne BB;
guest beer Ⓗ
One of the oldest buildings in the
village. The car park opposite

used to be the sheep market.
Two rooms with a garden to the
rear, including an aviary. A welcome watering-hole on the
Pennine Way.
❀ ◖ ▶ ᵫ P

LOW BENTHAM

PUNCH BOWL
☎ (015242) 61344
12-3 (not Mon); 6.30-11; 12-10.30
Sun
Mitchell's Original Ⓗ
Small, country pub run by locals
for locals. A cosy bar, plus a
room down steps with games and
extra seating. The restaurant
(no-smoking) is open Fri & Sat
eves and Sun lunch.
▨ ❀ ᵫ ◖ ▶ ▲ ♣ P

LOW ROW

PUNCH BOWL INN
☎ (01748) 886233
11-11; 12-10.30 Sun;
Morland Old Speckled Hen;
John Smith's Bitter; Theakston
Best Bitter, XB, Old Peculier;
guest beer Ⓗ
Inn offering everything for lovers
of outdoor pursuits, including
cheap bunkhouse accommodation. Very lively at weekends.
Lead mining and potholing artefacts adorn the bar which stocks
over 130 malt whiskies. It also
has a general store and tea
room. Panoramic views of
Swaledale.
▨ Q ➴ ❀ ᵫ ◖ ▶ ▲ ♣
P ᵫ

MALHAM

LISTER ARMS
Gordale Scar Road
☎ (01729) 830330
12-3, 7-11; 12-3, 7-10.30 Sun
Theakston Best Bitter, XB;
Younger Scotch;
guest beers Ⓗ
Popular, three-roomed pub dating from 1702 boasting an original inglenook and a large sheltered garden. A wide range of
bottled Belgian beers, plus real
cider in summer.
▨ ❀ ᵫ ◖ ▶ ▲ ♣ ◌ P

MALTON

CROWN HOTEL
(SUDDABY'S)
12 Wheelgate
☎ (01653) 692038
11-11; 12-4, 7-10.30 Sun
Bateman XB; Malton Double
Chance, Crown Bitter, Owd Bob;
guest beers Ⓗ
Busy, town-centre pub with a
conservatory eating area. Malton
brewery is situated in the rear
courtyard and brewery tours are
welcome by appointment.
▨ Q ➴ ᵫ ◖ ▲ ➳ P

KINGS HEAD
5 Market Place
☎ (01653) 692289
10.30-2.30 (later in summer),
7-11; 12-3, 7-10.30 Sun
Caledonian Deuchars IPA;
Marston's Bitter, Pedigree;
guest beers Ⓗ
Ivy-clad pub, popular with locals
and visitors, and busy on market
days. Excellent, good value food.
Q ᵫ ◖ ▶ ▲ ➳ ♣ P ᵫ ᵫ

MARSKE

FRIGATE
Hummers Hill Lane (opp cricket
club)
☎ (01642) 484302
1 (12 Sat)-11; 12-5, 7-10.30 Sun
John Smith's Magnet Ⓗ
Well established estate pub with
a nicely decorated lounge, bar
and snug. Plenty of entertainment with live music Tue, three
quiz nights and pool and darts in
the bar (resident teams). Snacks
available all day.
Q ❀ ᵫ ➳ ♣ P ᵫ

ZETLAND HOTEL
9 High Street (near station)
☎ (01642) 483973
12-11; 12-4, 7-10.30 Sun
Vaux Samson Ⓗ
Old established hotel: a bar,
lounge and games room. The
upstairs function room hosts a
folk club (Thu) and American and
continental acts other eves.
Three house beers. Hot snacks
available all day.
ᵫ ➳ ♣ P

Try also: Marske Cricket Club,
Windy Hill Lane (Courage)

MELMERBY

GEORGE & DRAGON
Main Street
☎ (01765) 640303
12-2, 5-11; 11-11 Sat; 12-3,
7-10.30 Sun
Theakston Best Bitter; guest
beers Ⓗ
Pleasant, traditional village local
with three rooms. The guest
beers include Franklins when
available. Meals served at weekends.
▨ Q ◖ ▶ ♣ P

MIDDLEHAM

WHITE SWAN HOTEL
☎ (01969) 622093
11-11; 12-10.30 Sun
Black Sheep Best Bitter, Special;
Hambleton Bitter; John Smith's
Bitter Ⓗ
Comfortable drawing room-style
lounge bar overlooking the market place. The restaurant offers
noteworthy menus.
▨ Q ➴ ❀ ᵫ ◖ ▶ ᵫ ♣ ᵫ
ᵫ

MIDDLESBROUGH

ISAAC WILSON
61 Wilson Street
☎ (01642) 247708
11-11; 12-10.30 Sun
Courage Directors; Theakston Best Bitter, XB; Worthington Bitter; guest beers Ⓗ
Wetherspoons pub, a conversion of the former county court. Friendly and comfortably furnished, it has lots of cosy corners. Excellent range of micro-brewery beers; food all day.
Q ◐ ▶ ⇌ ♣ ⌣ ✂ 🗇

TAP 'N' BARREL
86 Newport Road (near bus station)
☎ (01642) 219995
11-11; 7-10.30 Sun
Beer range varies Ⓗ
Cosy pub with a Victorian-style bar and an upstairs function room. The six beers come from Century Inn's portfolio. No food Sun; eve meals 5-7 Mon-Fri.
◐ ▶ ⇌ ♣ ⌣

TAVERN
228 Linthorpe Road
☎ (01642) 242589
11-11; 12-10.30 Sun
Boddingtons Bitter; Castle Eden Ale; guest beers Ⓗ
Large pub with a continually changing list of beers from the Whitbread portfolio, and a games room. It is popular with students from the university nearby. Occasional cider.
❀ ◐ ♿ ♣ ⌣

MUKER

FARMERS ARMS
☎ (01748) 886297
11-3, 7-11; 12-3, 7-10.30 Sun
Butterknowle Banner Bitter; John Smith's Bitter; Theakston Best Bitter, XB, Old Peculier Ⓗ
Dales village local, opened out into a single room but retaining its old character, with massive stone flags and an open fire. Good value pub grub.
🏚 Q ⛴ ❀ ◐ ▲ ♣ P

NEWHOLM

OLDE BEEHIVE INNE
Off A171, 2 miles from Whitby
☎ (01947) 602703
11.30-3, 7-11; 12-3, 7-10.30 Sun
Theakston Best Bitter, Old Peculier; John Smith's Magnet; guest beers Ⓗ
Originally a drovers' inn, this authentic village pub is full of character, with oak beams. The pub sign is written in verse. Family-run, it offers good food and en-suite accommodation.
🏚 Q ❀ ♿ ◐ ▶ ▲ ♣ P 🗇

NEWTON-ON-OUSE

BLACKSMITH'S ARMS
Cherry Tree Avenue (off A19, York-Easingwold road)
☎ (01347) 848249
7 (12 Sat)-11; 12-10.30 Sun
Camerons Bitter, Strongarm; Marston's Pedigree Ⓗ
A blacksmith's forge once stood on the site of this genuine village local. An opened-up public bar/lounge and an adjacent room for pool; team sporting activities include fishing. Sun lunch served.
🏚 ❀ ♿ ▶ ♣ P 🗇

NORTH DUFFIELD

KINGS ARMS
Main Street (300 yds off A163)
☎ (01757) 288492
4 (11 Sat)-11; 12-10.30 Sun
Black Sheep Best Bitter; John Smith's Bitter; guest beers Ⓗ
Welcoming local next to an attractive village green and duck pond. It offers constantly changing guest beers, plus good value, home-cooked food served either in the bar or the no-smoking dining room. Cider available in summer.
🏚 ❀ ◐ ♣ ⌣ P

NORTHALLERTON

TANNER HOP
2A Friarage Street (off High St)
☎ (01609) 778482
7-11 (midnight Thu, 1am Fri); 12-1am Sat; 12-10.30 Sun
Courage Directors; Hambleton Bitter; John Smith's Bitter; guest beers Ⓗ
Very busy, town-centre conversion of one-time brewery. It hosts beer festivals and live music (late licence). Always a Hambleton ale and another local guest. Games include giant Jenga. ⛴ ▶ ♿ ⇌ ♣ ⌣

NOSTERFIELD

FREEMASONS ARMS
On B6267, between Masham and the A1 ☎ (01677) 470548
12-3, 6-11 (closed Mon); 12-3, 7-10.30 Sun
Black Sheep Best Bitter; Taylor Landlord; Tetley Bitter; Theakston Best Bitter Ⓗ
Welcoming, cottage-style inn with beams and a flagstoned bar area displaying fascinating wartime and vintage motorcycle sport memorabilia. High quality meals make it very busy at times. Occasional Pipkin cider.
🏚 Q ◐ ▶ ⌣ P 🗇

NUN MONKTON

ALICE HAWTHORN
Signed off the A59 York-Harrogate road at Skipbridge
☎ (01423) 330303

12-2, 6.30-11; 12-10.30 Sun
Boddingtons Bitter; Camerons Bitter; Tetley Bitter; guest beers Ⓗ
Off the beaten track in an idyllic setting near the village duck pond. A food-oriented pub with an excellent and varied menu. Well worth a visit; the landlord always makes you welcome.
🏚 Q ❀ ◐ ▶ ♿ ♣ ▲ P

PICKERING

WHITE SWAN HOTEL
Market Place
☎ (01751) 472288
11-3, 6-11; 11-11 Sat; 12-3, 7-10.30 Sun
Black Sheep Best Bitter, Special; guest beers Ⓗ
Former coaching inn, with a small cosy bar offering welcoming Yorkshire hospitality. The excellent bar menu is based on local produce. The guest beers all come from Yorkshire breweries.
🏚 Q ⛴ ❀ ♿ ◐ ▲ ⇌ (N York Moors Rlwy) P ✂ 🗇

PICKHILL

NAGS HEAD
☎ (01845) 567391
11-11; 12-10.30 Sun
Black Sheep Special; Hambleton Bitter; Theakston Black Bull; John Smith's Bitter; guest beers (occasional) Ⓗ
Comfortable village pub, renowned for its food: a small lounge and a cosy bar noted for its large tie collection and bar draughts game.
🏚 ❀ ♿ ◐ ▶ ♿ ▲ ♣ P

POOL

HUNTERS INN
Harrogate Road (½ mile N of Pool on A658, Harrogate road)
☎ (0113) 284 1090
11-11; 12-10.30 Sun
Tetley Bitter; Theakston Best Bitter; guest beers Ⓗ
A mixed clientele in a pub where children are welcome. Pool table, juke box and a real fire complement the range of nine beers.
🏚 ❀ ◐ P

PORT MULGRAVE

SHIP
20 Rosedale Lane (off A174 at Hinderwell)
☎ (01947) 840303
11-11; 12-10.30 Sun
Marston's Pedigree; Theakston Black Bull; Stones Bitter; guest beer Ⓗ
Local bearing a nautical theme near high cliffs and the Cleveland Way; well worth a visit. No-smoking area for diners.
🏚 Q ⛴ ♿ ◐ ▶ ▲ ♣ P

REDMIRE

KINGS ARMS
☎ (01969) 622316
11-3, 6-11; 11-3, 6-10.30 Sun
Black Sheep Special; John Smith's Bitter; Theakston Black Bull, Best Bitter, XB; guest beers H
Small, cosy village local sporting humorous murals. A good variety of home-cooked food includes fish and game dishes. Good views. ♨ Q ✿ ⇔ ◖ ▯ ⊞ Å ♣ P

RICHMOND

BLACK LION HOTEL
12 Finkle Street
☎ (01748) 823121
11-11; 12-10.30 Sun
Camerons Strongarm; Flowers Original; Tetley Bitter, Imperial; guest beer H
Residential coaching inn, a very popular local meeting place.
♨ Q ⇔ ◖ ▯ ⊞ ♣ P ⊟

RIPON

GOLDEN LION
69 Allhallowgate
☎ (01765) 602598
11-3 (maybe 4 summer), 7-11; 12-3, 7-10.30 Sun
Black Sheep Best Bitter; Hambleton Goldfield; John Smith's Bitter; Theakston Best Bitter; guest beer H
Spacious, L-shaped bar, sub-divided into smaller areas, one of which is a restaurant. Note the collection of naval memorabilia. No food Sun eve. ◖ ▯ ♣

ONE EYED RAT
51 Allhallowgate
☎ (01765) 607704
12-2 (not Mon-Wed, 12-3 Sat), 6 (5.30 Fri)-11; 12-3, 7-10.30 Sun
Black Sheep Best Bitter; Taylor Landlord; guest beers H
Popular, terraced pub close to the city centre offering excellent guest beers plus a range of specialist bottled German beers and guest ciders. ♨ Q ✿ ♣ ⊘

WHEATSHEAF
Harrogate Road (S outskirts of town, near bypass)
☎ (01765) 602410
12-3 (not Mon), 7-11; 12-3, 7-10.30 Sun
Vaux Samson; Ward's Best Bitter; guest beer H
Friendly old inn on the edge of the city, with a sunken garden at the rear. ♨ Q ✿ ✿ ♣ P

ROBIN HOODS BAY

VICTORIA HOTEL
Station Road ☎ (01947) 880205
11-3, 6.30-11; 11-11 Fri, Sat & summer); 12-3, 7-10.30 (12-10.30 summer) Sun

Camerons Bitter, Strongarm; guest beers H
Large hotel, built in 1897 on the clifftop overlooking the bay and village, where all pubs sell real ale.
♨ Q ✿ ✿ ⇔ ◖ ▯ ♣

Try also: Laurel Inn, New Rd (Free)

RUNSWICK BAY

RUNSWICK BAY HOTEL
Top of bank
☎ (01947) 841010
12-3, 7-11 (11-11 summer); 12-3, 7-10.30 (12-10.30 summer) Sun
Tetley Bitter; guest beers (summer) H
Central bar with two rooms off, plus a dining room.
♨ ✿ ✿ ⇔ ◖ ▯ ⊞ Å ♣ P

SALTBURN

SALTBURN CRICKET, BOWLS & TENNIS CLUB
Marske Mill Lane (by Saltburn Sports Centre)
☎ (01287) 622761
8 (6 summer Sat & Sun)-11 (open all day for cricket matches)
Tetley Bitter; guest beers H
Private sports club with its own cricket and bowls teams. The bar spans the lounge and games areas which can together be converted into a function room. Bar snacks available all day. Casual visitors welcome.
✿ Å ⇌ ♣ P

VICTORIA
Dundas Street (near station)
☎ (01287) 624637
11-3, 7-11; 11-11 Sat; 12-10.30 Sun
Tetley Bitter; Ind Coope Burton Ale; John Smith's Magnet H; **guest beers** H P
A relatively new pub, the only true pub in Saltburn, converted from a furniture warehouse and taxi office. The lounge bar and upstairs function room are decorated in Victorian style. Live music Thu and Sun. No food available on Mon.
◖ ⊞ Å ⇌ ♣ ⊟

SAWDON

ANVIL INN
Main Street (off A170)
☎ (01723) 859896
11-11; 12-10.30 Sun
Theakston Best Bitter; Younger Scotch; guest beers H
Friendly, restored blacksmith's shop with a recently extended dining area (excellent value meals). Scarborough CAMRA rural *Pub of the Year* 1997.
♨ Q ✿ ✿ ⇔ ◖ ▯ Å ♣ P ⊟

SAXTON

GREYHOUND ☆
Main Street (1 mile W of A162)
☎ (01937) 557202
11.30-3.30, 5.30-11; 11-11 Sat; 12-3, 7-10.30 Sun
Samuel Smith OBB H
Old village inn (Grade II listed) which retains wood partitioned rooms and a narrow entrance passage. Considered to be one of the few pubs in the area worthy of preservation.
♨ Q ✿ ✿ ⊞ ⅄ ♣ P

SCARBOROUGH

ALMA INN
1 Alma Parade
☎ (01723) 375587
11.30-2.30 (3 Thu); 11.30-11 Fri & Sat; 12-3, 7-10.30 Sun
Barnsley Black Heart Stout; Tetley Bitter; Theakston XB; Younger Scotch; guest beer H
Busy, three-roomer, just off the main shopping precinct. Good value meals (no food Sun).
✿ ◖ Å ⇌ ♣

ANGEL INN
46 North Street (near multi-storey car park)
☎ (01723) 365504
11-11; 12-10.30 Sun
Camerons Bitter; Tetley Bitter H
Friendly local with a horseshoe-shaped, one-roomed bar. Games oriented, it features photographs of the landlord's professional RL career, alongside paintings of Scarborough harbour. The garden is a recent addition.
✿ ⇌ ♣

CELLARS
35-37 Valley Road
☎ (01723) 367158
7 (11 summer)-11; 12-3, 7-10.30 Sun
Tetley Bitter; guest beers H
Local family pub in the cellars of an elegant Victorian building which has been converted to self-contained holiday apartments and a restaurant. Seating on a sunny patio. *Scarborough in Bloom* award winner.
✿ ⇔ ◖ ▯ ⅄ Å ⇌ P

HIGHLANDER
Esplanade
☎ (01723) 365627
11-11; 12-10.30 Sun
Tetley Bitter; Younger IPA; guest beers H
Busy, one-roomed pub with a patio at the front overlooking South Bay. It boasts an extensive range of malt whiskies, plus a showman's steam engine. The WM Clark Mild is contract brewed by Clarks of Wakefield.
♨ ✿ ⇔ ◖ ⅄ Å ⇌ ⊟

HOLE IN THE WALL
26-32 Vernon Road
☎ (01723) 373746
11.30-2.30 (3 Sat), 7-11; 12-3,
7-10.30 Sun
**Brakspear Bitter; Durham Magus;
Fuller's ESB; guest beers** H
Busy but friendly conversational
pub, near the town centre and
the Spa complex. Vegetarian
meals available. CAMRA *Town
Pub of the Year* 1997.
Q ◑ ▲ ⇌ ♣ ⌂

LORD ROSEBERY
85-87 Westborough
☎ (01723) 361191
11-11; 12-10.30 Sun
**Courage Directors; Tetley Bitter;
Theakston Best Bitter; guest
beers** H
Typical Wetherspoons outlet: a
prominent Victorian building
recently converted on two levels
in the town centre. Frequently
changing guest beers.
Q ◑ ▶ ⅏ ▲ ⇌ ⌂ ⚲ ⊟

OLD SCALBY MILLS HOTEL
Scalby Mills Road (by Sea Life
Centre) ☎ (01723) 500449
11-11; 12-10.30 Sun
**Daleside Monkey Wrench; guest
beers** H
Historic 500-year-old building
(formerly a watermill) on the
Cleveland Way boasting views
across the bay. Busy in summer;
Children's certificate.
Q ⚙ ◑ ⅏ ▲ ♣

SCARBOROUGH ARMS
1 North Terrace
☎ (01723) 373575
11-11; 12-10.30 Sun
**Camerons Bitter, Strongarm;
Marston's Pedigree; guest beer** H
Popular pub just off the town
centre, offering a welcoming
atmosphere and excellent value
food (eve meals until 8pm).
⚙ ◑ ▶ ⅏ ▲ ♣ P ⊟

TAP & SPILE
28 Falsgrave Road
☎ (01723) 363837
11-11; 12-10.30 Sun
**Big Lamp Bitter; Tap & Spile
Premium; Theakston Old
Peculier; guest beers** H
Sympathetically renovated busy
old coaching inn, displaying local
memorabilia: three rooms and a
large patio. Excellent value
home-cooked lunches.
Q ⚙ ◑ ▲ ⇌ ⌂ P ⚲

SELBY

ALBION VAULTS
Near swing bridge over River
Ouse ☎ (01757) 213817
12-11; 12-10.30 Sun
**Old Mill Mild, Nellie Dene,
Bitter, Black Jack, seasonal
beers** H
One of the oldest pubs in town,

refurbished with Edwardian-style
decor. The rear bar is used for
darts, pool and Sky sports TV.
Q ⚙ ◑ ⅏ ⅏ ⇌

CRICKETERS
Market Place
☎ (01757) 702120
11-11; 12-10.30 Sun
Samuel Smith OBB H
Timber-panelled alcoves for seat-
ed drinkers, a cricketing theme,
Sky sports TV and the cheapest
beer in town are the elements of
this pub. Wheelchair access is
from the rear. ⚙ ◑ ⅏ ⇌

ROYAL OAK
70 Ousegate (near swing bridge
over River Ouse)
☎ (01757) 291163
12 (6 Tue)-11; 12-10.30 Sun
**Boddingtons Mild; Marston's
Pedigree; Taylor Landlord; guest
beers** H
Large, one-room bar with seating
on varied levels and photos of
the nearby shipyard. Popular at
the weekends. The house beer,
from Brown Cow Brewery, is
named after the local nickname
of the pub.
Q ⚙ ⅏ ⇌ ♣

SETTLE

ROYAL OAK
Market Place
☎ (01729) 822561
11-11; 12-10.30 Sun
**Boddingtons Bitter; Flowers IPA;
Taylor Best Bitter, Landlord;
guest beer** H
Comfortable, civilised, early 19th-
century, town-centre inn with a
single bar and two main drinking
areas. The revolving door, wood
panelling and Art Nouveau lamps
date from a mid-1930s refurbishment.
⚙ ⇌ ◑ ▶ ⅏ ▲ ⇌ ♣ P ⚲

SKELTON

ROYAL GEORGE
North Terrace (A173, W end of
town)
☎ (01287) 650326
4 (2 Mon & Fri)-11; 12.30-11 Sat;
12-10.30 Sun
John Smith's Magnet H
Pub enjoying strong local patronage: a small front bar with a
large room at the rear. ⚙ ⅏ ♣

SKIPTON

RAILWAY
13-15 Carleton Street (opp
Tesco's)
☎ (01756) 793186
11-11; 12-10.30 Sun
Tetley Mild, Bitter; guest beer H
Welcoming old-fashioned two-
roomed, street-corner local, decorated with railway photos and
prints. Popular with sports enthu-

siasts in the afternoons and
domino players eves. The guest
beer is from the Tapster's Choice
range. ⅏ ⅏ ⇌ ♣

Try also: Royal Shepherd, Canal
St (Whitbread)

SNAPE

CASTLE ARMS INN
☎ (01677) 470270
12-3, 6-11; 12-3, 7-10.30 Sun
**Black Sheep Best Bitter;
Hambleton Bitter; John Smith's
Bitter** H
Busy, traditional pub in a pretty
village near an arboretum. Good
value substantial meals (restaurant is closed Mon). Quoits
played. ⚌ Q ◑ ▶ ▲ ♣ P

SOUTH MILFORD

QUEEN OF T'OWD THATCH
101 High Street
☎ (01977) 682367
11.30-3, 6-11; 12-3, 7-10.30 (12-
10.30 summer) Sun
**Vaux Bitter, Samson; guest
beers** H
Grade II listed village inn (the
name refers to the craft of roof
thatching). Its recently refurbished interior retains the atmosphere of separate rooms; the
rear bar and dining area were
once a tithe barn. Extensive
choice of bar meals.
⚌ Q ⚙ ◑ ▶ ⅏ ⅏ ⇌ ♣
P ⊟

SPOFFORTH

KING WILLIAM IV
Church Hill ☎ (01937) 590293
12-3 (not Mon), 5.30-11; 12-11
Sat; 12-10.30 Sun
**John Smith's Bitter; guest
beers** H
Small, friendly two-roomed village local, tucked away from the
main road. The unofficial club
house for the local golf course.
Above average food draws custom from a wide area.
⚌ Q ⚙ ◑ ▶ ♣ P

STAINTON MIDDLESBROUGH

STAINTON INN
2 Meldyke Lane
☎ (01642) 599902
11.30-3, 6-11; 12-3, 7-10.30 Sun
**Banks's Bitter; Camerons
Strongarm** H
Victorian red-brick pub in the village centre, extended in recent
years into adjacent cottages. The
rear car park is surrounded by
pleasant gardens. Food oriented
lounge and a less formal public
bar. ⚙ ◑ ▶ ⅏ ▲ ♣ P ⊟

Try also: Pathfinders, Maltby
(Whitbread)

STAITHES

BLACK LION
High Street OS781185
☎ (01947) 841132
6 (12 Fri, Sat & summer)-11; 12-10.30 Sun
Draught Bass; John Smith's Magnet; guest beer H
Georgian coaching inn where the cosy bar and lounge both boast real fires. Cottage and bunk accommodation available.
🏠 🏃 🛏 ◖ ▶ ⟁ ♣

STARBOTTON

FOX & HOUNDS
☎ (01756) 760269
11.30-3 (not winter Mon), 6.30-11; 12-3, 7-10.30 Sun
Black Sheep Best Bitter; Taylor Landlord; Theakston Best Bitter, Old Peculier H
Building dating back 400 years in the beautiful countryside of Upper Wharfedale, a renowned walking area including the Dales Way. The bar features a large stone fireplace, oak beams hung with jugs, flagstone floor and an old still. 🏠 Q 🛏 ◖ ▶ P

STOKESLEY

SPREAD EAGLE
39 High Street
☎ (01642) 710278
11-11; 12-10.30 Sun
Camerons Strongarm; Marston's Pedigree H
Small, unspoilt, town-centre local with a garden leading to the river. Excellent home-cooked food all day - good value and popular, so book at peak times. Local CAMRA *Pub of the Year* 1998. In the front room only the fire is permitted to smoke.
🏠 🏃 ❀ ◖ ▶ ⌿ 🍺

WHITE SWAN
1 West End (W end of High St)
☎ (01642) 710263
11.30-3, 5.30 (7 Sat)-11; 12-3, 7-10.30 Sun
Castle Eden Ale; Rudgate Ruby Mild; guest beers H
Traditional pub decorated with agricultural memorabilia. Local CAMRA *Pub of the Year* 1997 and national winner of the *Perfect Ploughman's* award 1997. No juke box or piped music. Just conversation and a range of unusual games. Rooster's Outlaw beer range is stocked as available. Q ◖ ♣ ⌿ 🍺

TADCASTER

BRITANNIA INN
2 Commercial Street (E bank of River Wharfe)
☎ (01937) 832168
11.30-2.30, 5-11; 11.30-3, 7-11 Sat; 12-3, 7-10.30 Sun

Samuel Smith OBB H
Town pub with two rooms, plus a dining room also used for families and functions. The garden overlooks the River Wharfe. Large TV in the public bar.
Q 🏃 ❀ ◖ ▶ ⟁ 🛏 ♿ ♣ P

THIXENDALE

CROSS KEYS
☎ (01377) 288272
12-3 (not winter Mon), 6-11; 12-3, 7-10.30 Sun
Jennings Bitter; Tetley Bitter; guest beer H
One-roomed village gem in a beautiful setting in the Yorkshire Wolds. Unspoilt and welcoming, it is popular with walkers and locals alike. Children welcome in garden. No meals between Christmas and New Year.
🏠 ❀ ◖ ▶ ⟁ ♣

THORNTON-IN-LONSDALE

MARTON ARMS
Off Waterfalls road, $\frac{1}{2}$ mile from Ingleton
☎ (0152 42) 41281
12-3, (not winter Mon-Fri), 6 (7 winter)-11; 11-11 Sat; 12-10.30 Sun
Black Sheep Best Bitter; Dent Bitter; Theakston Best Bitter; guest beers H
Pre-turnpike coaching inn, dated 1679: a large, comfortable oak-beamed lounge and a restaurant (food all day Sun). Up to 15 beers, one always from Taylor. A ten-minute walk from the start of the Waterfalls Walk.
🏠 ❀ 🛏 ◖ ▶ ♣ ⌾ P

THORNTON WATLASS

BUCK INN
☎ (01677) 422461
11-3, 6-11; 11-11 Sat; 12-3, 6.30-10.30 Sun
Black Sheep Best Bitter; John Smith's Bitter; Tetley Bitter; Theakston Best Bitter; guest beer H
Pub with strong cricket connections, on the village green. A focus for community activities, live music etc. Popular restaurant; bottle conditioned beers stocked.
🏠 Q 🏃 ❀ 🛏 ◖ ▶ ♣ P

THRESHFIELD

OLD HALL INN
On B6265
☎ (01756) 752 441
11.30-3 (not Mon), 6-11; 12-3, 7-10.30 Sun
Taylor Golden Best, Best Bitter, Landlord; guest beers (summer) H
Popular village pub with several distinct areas. A conservatory

---

extension at the side leads to the garden. A Yorkshire range and two open fires keep you warm. It is also renowned for its extensive, excellent food menu (no food Sun eve or Mon in winter).
🏠 Q 🏃 ❀ 🛏 ◖ ▶ ♿ ⟁ ♣ P

TOCKWITH

SPOTTED OX
Westfield Road (off B1224)
☎ (01423) 358387
11-3, 5.30-11; 11-11 Fri & Sat; 12-10.30 Sun
Tetley Bitter; guest beers H
Busy, community-focused village local; this multi-sectioned interior boasts some original beams. It has a good reputation for food: indoor and outdoor barbecues for special occasions. The widest range of beers for miles around.
🏠 ❀ ◖ ▶ ♿ ♣ P

TOPCLIFFE

SWAN
Front Street
☎ (01845) 577207
12-3, 7-11; 11-11 Sat; 12-10.30 Sun
John Smith's Bitter; Vaux Samson H
Traditional village local, recently carefully refurbished to form two rooms with a central servery, one room being no-smoking.
🏠 ♣ P ⌿

TOWTON

ROCKINGHAM ARMS
On A162, 3 miles S of Tadcaster
☎ (01937) 832811
11.30-3, 5-11; 11.30-11 Sat; 12-10.30 Sun
Vaux Bitter, Samson; guest beers H
Roadside village pub whose decor commemorates the battle of Towton Moor, fought in 1461 on the edge of the village. Great claims are made for the pub's fish and chips. Games include 'Merrils', said to be one of the oldest pub games, and a six-sided pool table.
🏠 Q ❀ ◖ ▶ ♣ P

ULLESKELF

ULLESKELF ARMS
Church Fenton Lane
☎ (01937) 832136
6-11; 12-3, 6.30-11 Sat; 12-3, 7-10.30 Sun
Black Sheep Best Bitter; John Smith's Bitter; guest beers H
Railway pub: the garden entrance leads to the station. Live country music Fri. Good value B & B.
Q ❀ 🛏 ◖ ▶ ⇌ ♣ P

UPPER POPPLETON

LORD COLLINGWOOD
The Green (off A59, signed to Poppleton)
☎ (01904) 794388
12-3, 5.30-11; 12-11 Sat; 12-4, 6.30-10.30 Sun
Mansfield Riding Bitter, Bitter, Old Baily Ⓗ
Olde-worlde style pub in a commuter village, it also serves as the village shop. See the amazing collection of clocks, cups, mugs and jugs. 🏘 🌸 🕒 🌙 ≈ ♣ P 🛢

WEAVERTHORPE

STAR INN
Off A64 ☎ (01944) 738273
12-4.30 (not Mon-Fri), 7-11; 12-4.30, 7-10.30 Sun
Banks's Bitter; Camerons Bitter, Strongarm; Hambleton Stallion; guest beer Ⓗ
Popular, family-owned Yorkshire Wolds village inn offering comfortable B & B accommodation, quality home-made bar and restaurant food and seasonal ale and food specialities.
🏘 Q 🌸 🛏 🕒 🍴 ♣ P ✂

WELBURY

DUKE OF WELLINGTON
☎ (01609) 882464
11-3.30 (not Mon, Tue), 7-11; 12-10.30 Sun
John Smith's Bitter, Magnet; guest beer Ⓗ
Long, ivy-clad, village pub with a linked lounge, restaurant and bar. Friendly atmosphere and a good menu. 🏘 🌸 🛏 🕒 🌙 ♣ P

WEST AYTON

OLDE FORGE VALLEY INN
5 Pickering Road (A170)
☎ (01723) 862146
11.30-11; 12-10.30 Sun
Camerons Bitter; Tetley Bitter; guest beer Ⓗ
300-year-old coaching inn, comprising a wood-panelled lounge bar, a locals' bar and a restaurant. Popular with visitors to the North York Moors National Park.
🏘 Q 🍴 🌸 🛏 🕒 🌙 ♣ P

WEST WITTON

FOX & HOUNDS
Main Street ☎ (01969) 623650
11-4, 7-11 (11-11 summer); 12-10.30 Sun
Black Sheep Best Bitter; John Smith's Bitter; Theakston Best Bitter; guest beer Ⓗ
15th-century village inn, originally a rest house for the monks of Jervaulx Abbey, enjoying beautiful views at the rear. Bottle-conditioned beers and Pipkin cider stocked. Quoits played.
🏘 🌸 🛏 🕒 🌙 ♣ 🥂 🛢

WHITBY

DUKE OF YORK
Church Street (foot of Abbey steps)
☎ (01947) 600324
11-11; 12-10.30 Sun
Black Dog Rhatas; Courage Directors; John Smith's Bitter, Magnet; guest beer Ⓗ
Very busy, unspoilt pub with traditional decor and fine views of Whitby harbour. Popular in Folk Week. Worth a visit before or after the 199 Abbey steps. The new Black Dog Brewery beers are sold here. 🛏 🕒 🌙 ≈ ♣

TAP & SPILE
New Quay Road (opp bus and rail stations)
☎ (01947) 603937
12 (11 summer)-11; 12-4, 7-10.30 (12-10.30 summer) Sun
Tap & Spile Premium; guest beers Ⓗ
Large, multi-roomed red brick pub. Various guest beers and three ciders are stocked. Meals served 12-7 (4 Sun).
Q 🥂 🕒 🌙 ≈ ♣ 🥂 ✂

YORK

ACKHORNE
St Martins Lane
☎ (01904) 629820
12-3, 6-11; 12-3, 7-10.30 Sun
Beer range varies Ⓗ
Welcome oasis, just off Micklegate, this pub specialises in beers from independent Yorkshire breweries - usually five on offer. 🕒 ≈ ♣

BLUE BELL ☆
Fossgate
☎ (01904) 654904
12-11; 12-10.30 Sun
Vaux Bitter, Samson, Waggle Dance; Ward's Best Bitter; guest beers Ⓗ
Excellent, small, city-centre pub with York's only surviving Edwardian interior. Sample the atmosphere of either of the two rooms or stand awhile in the corridor. 🍴 ≈ ♣

GOLDEN BALL
Bishophill ☎ (01904) 652211
11.30 (4 Mon-Wed)-11; 12-10.30 Sun
Marston's Pedigree; John Smith's Bitter, Magnet; Theakston XB; York Yorkshire Terrier Ⓗ
Unspoilt, traditional pub in a quiet residential area within the city walls; three rooms, plus a tiny snug. Full of character, plus an impressive facade. Friendly and welcoming to all, the beer is sensibly priced. Well worth a visit.
Q 🌸 🍴 ≈ ♣

MALTINGS
Tanners Moat (below Lendal Bridge) ☎ (01904) 655387
11-11; 12-10.30 Sun
Black Sheep Best Bitter; guest beers Ⓗ
A veritable cornucopia of microbreweries' ales always available in this idiosyncratic institution. Don't miss the regular beer festivals or splendid value food.
🕒 ≈ ♣ 🥂

The White Swan at Stokesley receives its Perfect Ploughman's Award from Sue Novak, author of The *Good Pub Food Guide*, published by CAMRA Books.

MINSTER
24 Marygate
☎ (01904) 624499
11.30-11; 12-10.30 Sun
Draught Bass; John Smith's Bitter; guest beers Ⓗ
Small, Edwardian inn opposite the ruins of St Mary's Abbey. A central corridor with a bar and three cosy rooms.
Q ❀ ⊈ ♣ ⊬

ROSE & CROWN
13 Lawrence Street
☎ (01904) 636947
12-11; 12-10.30 Sun
Tetley Bitter; guest beers Ⓗ
Multi-roomed Tetley Festival Ale House which was originally a row of cottages. The good atmosphere is enhanced by a sensible refurbishment which has retained the authentic tilework.
❀ ◖ ◗ ⊈ ሌ ♣ P

ROYAL OAK
Goodramgate
☎ (01904) 635850
11-11; 12-10.30 Sun
Ind Coope Burton Ale; Tetley Bitter; guest beers Ⓗ
Traditional pub, which comprises three rooms plus a central corridor. Give the coffee bars a miss next time and come here for some real food and real ale. A must. Evening meals finish at 8pm.
Q ⛴ ◖ ◗ ⇌ ⊬

SADDLE INN
Main Street, Fulford
☎ (01904) 633317
12-3, 6.30-11; 12-11 Sat; 12-10.30 Sun
Banks's Bitter; Camerons Bitter, Strongarm Ⓗ
Attractive comfortable main road pub: a large L-shaped bar with a dining room off.
ᨠ ⛴ ❀ ⇌ ◖ ◗ ሌ ♣ P 🏺

TAP & SPILE
29 Monkgate
☎ (01904) 656158
11.30-11; 12-10.30 Sun
Old Mill Bitter; Tap & Spile Premium; guest beers Ⓗ
Recently well refurbished, now divided into two rooms. Excellent food. Well worth a visit.
ᨠ ❀ ◖ ◗ P

WELLINGTON
47 Alma Terrace
☎ (01904) 654642
11-3 (not Mon), 6-11; 11-5, 7-11 Sat; 12-4, 7-10.30 Sun
Samuel Smith OBB Ⓗ
Classic, mid 19th-century terraced local: a convivial public bar, small lounge and a pool room off a central corridor. Well worth seeking out.
ᨠ Q ⛴ ❀ ⊈ ♣

YORK BEER SHOP (OFF-LICENCE)
Sandringham Street (off A19/Fishergate)
☎ (01904) 647136
11 (4.15 Mon, 10 Sat)-10; 6-10 Sun
Bateman XB; Taylor Landlord; guest beers Ⓗ
Off-licence with a great range of British bottle-conditioned beers and a selection of top quality foreign ones. Draught beer and cider to take out in any quantity. Treat yourself to some fine cheese too. ⌣

Yorkshire South

BARNBY DUN

GATEWAY INN
Station Road
☎ (01302) 882849
12-3 (not Mon), 6-11; 12-3, 7-10.30
Barnsley Bitter; John Smith's Bitter; guest beers Ⓗ
A grown-ups' pub and restaurant. The bar has a warm, friendly atmosphere and the restaurant is highly recommended.
⇌ ◖ ◗ P

BARNSLEY

DURTY O'DWYERS
22 Market Hill
☎ (01226) 786100
11-11; 12-10.30 Sun
Barnsley Bitter; Tetley Bitter; guest beer Ⓗ
A rarity on the town centre circuit, catering for all ages. Don't be put off by Irish theme. No food Sun. ◗ ሌ ⇌

FEALTY & FIRKIN
Church Street
☎ (01226) 203658
11-11; 12-10.30 Sun
Firkin Royalty Ale, Fealty Ale, Knight Ale, Dogbolter Ⓗ
Open-plan pub, split into three drinking areas, featuring large barrel drinking tables near bar. A large games playing area offers games such as Connect Four, Jenga and Kerplunk, popular with students. Meals finish at 7pm.
◖ ◗ ⇌ ♣

SHAW INN
Racecommon Road
☎ (01226) 294021
3.30-11, 12-11 Fri & Sat; 12-3, 7-10.30 Sun
Beer range varies Ⓗ
Just off the 'bunny run', thus avoiding the weekend excesses of the town centre, this pub is home to many clubs, including the Barnsley Longsword Dancers.
⛴ ❀ ⊈ ♣ P

Try also: Yates Wine Lodge, Market Hill (Free)

BAWTRY

TURNPIKE
High Street
☎ (01302) 711960
11-11; 12-10.30 Sun
Barnsley Bitter; John Smith's Bitter; Worthington Bitter; guest beers Ⓗ
Welcoming pub, opposite the market place, with lots of wood panelling and a flagstone floor around the bar. CAMRA awards adorn the walls. Eve meals Tue-Fri. ❀ ◖ ◗

BIRDWELL

COCK INN
Pilley Hill (off A61)
☎ (01226) 742155
12-3, 7-11; 12-3, 7-10.30 Sun
Draught Bass; John Smith's Bitter Ⓗ
Popular, 200-year-old village local in Yorkshire stone, with a slate floor, a superb fireplace and much brass. The extensive garden has a quality play area. No food Sun eve.
ᨠ Q ⛴ ❀ ◖ ◗ ♣ P

BLACKBURN

SPORTSMAN INN
Grange Mill Lane, Blackburn Road
☎ (01709) 551124
11-5, 7-11; 12-3, 7-10.30 Sun
Barnsley Bitter; Tetley Bitter; guest beer Ⓗ
Multi-roomed, friendly local near the Meadowhall Complex. Its beer prices are competitive.
Q ⊈ ♣ P

BRAMLEY

MASTER BREWER
Main Street
☎ (01709) 541103
11-11; 12-3, 7-10.30 Sun
Mansfield Riding Mild, Riding Bitter Ⓗ, **Bitter** Ⓟ, **Old Baily** Ⓗ
Modern, two-roomed, brick-built pub. The beamed lounge is quiet and softly lit with a friendly atmosphere; the bar caters mainly for the young. Good selection of home-made meals.
❀ ◖ ◗ ♣ P

BROOMHILL

OLD MOOR TAVERN
Everill Gate Lane
☎ (01226) 755455
11-11; 12-10.30 Sun
Marston's Pedigree; John Smith's Bitter; Theakston Best Bitter; guest beers Ⓗ
A popular secluded pub set between two nature reserves. Book meals. Ask for lined glasses.
Q ❀ ◖ ◗ ሌ ♣ P 🏺

353

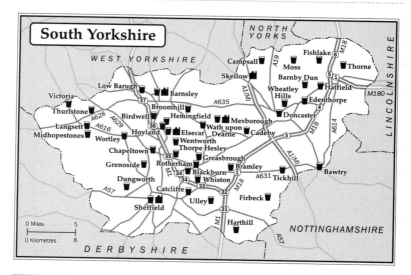

South Yorkshire

Map showing locations including Campsall, Fishlake, Moss, Barnby Dun, Thorne, Skellow, Wheatley Hills, Hatfield, Edenthorpe, Low Barugh, Barnsley, Doncaster, Victoria, Broomhill, Thurlstone, Birdwell, Hemingfield, Mexborough, Langsett, Hoyland, Wath upon Dearne, Cadeby, Midhopestones, Wortley, Elsecar, Wentworth, Chapeltown, Thorpe Hesley, Greasbrough, Grenoside, Rotherham, Bramley, Dungworth, Blackburn, Whiston, Bawtry, Catcliffe, Tickhill, Sheffield, Ulley, Firbeck, Harthill. Neighbouring counties: West Yorkshire, North Yorks, Lincolnshire, Nottinghamshire, Derbyshire.

CADEBY

CADEBY INN
Main Street
☎ (01709) 864009
11.30-2.30, 5-11; 11.30-11 Sat; 12-3, 7-10.30 Sun
Courage Directors; John Smith's Bitter, Magnet; Samuel Smith OBB; Tetley Bitter; guest beers Ⓗ
Smart, comfortable, converted farmhouse with a large lounge and a smaller bar. Strong emphasis on food at times. The large front garden is popular with families. Guest beers from Carlsberg-Tetley Tapster's Choice range.
♨ ❀ ◗ ▶ ⌂ P ⚲

CAMPSALL

OLD BELLS
High Street ☎ (01302) 700423
11-3, 5.30-11; 12-3, 7-10.30 Sun
Black Sheep Best Bitter; John Smith's Bitter; Tetley Bitter Ⓗ
At over 850 years old, this is the oldest pub in Doncaster Borough: a lounge, a small smoke room, a tiny snug and two restaurants. It is situated in the old part of the village. ❀ ◗ ▶ P

CATCLIFFE

WAVERLEY
Brinsworth Road (1 mile from M1 jct 33)
☎ (01709) 360906
12-4, 6-11; 11-11 Sat; 12-4, 7-10.30 Sun
Beer range varies Ⓗ
Modern three-roomed, genuine freehouse with four guest beers, featuring independent local breweries. It has a large comfortable family room, patio and a garden. Children's entertainment is provided on Fri and Sat eves.
☠ ❀ ◗ ♿ ♣ P

CHAPELTOWN

COMMERCIAL
107 Station Road
☎ (0114) 246 9066
12-3, 5.30-11; 12-11 Sat; 12-3, 7-10.30 Sun
Boddingtons Bitter; Ward's Best Bitter; guest beers Ⓗ
Built in 1889 by Stroutts brewery, the pub retains its lounge, tap-room and snug. It hosts quizzes Thu and Sun, plus occasional beer festivals. Good food.
Q ❀ ◗ ▲ ≠ ♣ ⌂ P ⚲

PRINCE OF WALES
80 Burncross Road (near swimming baths)
☎ (0114) 246 7725
11-3, 5.30-11; 11-11 Fri; 11-4, 6.30-11 Sat; 12-2.30, 7-10.30 Sun
Ward's Best Bitter Ⓗ Ⓟ
Traditional town pub with a tap room and a lounge. The long-serving landlord runs a fine community establishment with a welcome for all. No food Sun.
Q ❀ ◗ ▤ ≠ ♣ P

DONCASTER

CHESWOLD
Herten Way (in Doncaster leisure park)
☎ (01302) 533000
11-11; 12-10.30 Sun
Boddingtons Bitter; Morland Old Speckled Hen; Whitbread Trophy; guest beer Ⓗ
Modern pub aimed at families and including 'Charlie Chalk's Fun Factory'. Meals available all day but drinkers are also welcome. The open-plan layout around a central bar allows the childless to evade the exuberance of Mr Chalk.
☠ ❀ ◗ ▶ ♿ P

CORPORATION BREWERY TAPS
135 Cleveland Street (side of dual carriageway, by high rise flats) ☎ (01302) 363715
12-11; 12-3, 6-11 Wed & Thu; 12-10.30 Sun
Samuel Smith OBB Ⓗ
Near the town centre, this local has its own concert room, plus a snug and a public bar. One of the cheapest pints in town.
⌂ ≠ ♣

GREYFRIARS INN
Greyfriars Road
☎ (01302) 360096
12-3 (not Mon, Wed & Thu), 7.30-11; 12-4, 7.30-10.30 Sun
Barnsley Bitter; guest beer (occasional) Ⓗ
Characterful and welcoming oasis in the shadow of St George's church, just away from the town centre. Twice winner of Doncaster CAMRA *Pub of the Season* award.
Q ❀ ▤ ≠ ♣ P ⚲

MASONS ARMS
Market Place
☎ (01302) 364391
10.30 (11 Mon, Wed; 11.30 Thu)-4, 7.30 (8 Fri & Sat)-11; 12-4, 8-10.30 Sun
Tetley Bitter Ⓗ
A Tetley Heritage Inn, 200 years old. Its delightful beer garden is a refuge from the bustle of the market. ❀ ≠

PLOUGH
8 West Laith Gate
☎ (01302) 738310
11-11; 12-3, 7-10.30 Sun
Barnsley Bitter; Draught Bass Ⓗ
Warm, friendly and traditional: a bustling bar with an emphasis on dominoes and TV sport contrasts with the quiet, comfortable

lounge. The beer garden is possibly the world's smallest.
Q ❀ ⊞ ≠ ♣

Salutation
14 South Parade (near Odeon Cinema)
☎ (01302) 368464
11.30-3, 5-11; 11.30-11.30 Thu-Sat; 12-3, 7-10.30 Sun
Ind Coope Burton Ale; Marston's Pedigree; Tetley Bitter; guest beers [H]
Increasingly popular, town-centre pub, originally a coaching inn dating from 1764 and reputedly haunted by a white lady. It has been much altered in recent years to open-plan with friendly, intimate nooks. 1998 Local CAMRA *Pub of the Year*.
♛ ❀ ◖ ◗ ♿ ≠ ♣ P

Try also: White Swan, Frenchgate (Ward's)

DUNGWORTH

Royal
Main Road (B6076)
☎ (0114) 285 1213
12-3 (not Mon), 7-11; 12-4, 7-10.30 Sun
John Smith's Magnet; Stones Bitter; Tetley Bitter; guest beer [H]
Popular village local with spectacular views across South Yorkshire. This community pub hosts regular evening events, and a May Day beer festival. A haven for weary walkers! Excellent Sun lunches; eve meals Tue-Fri.
♛ Q ❀ ◖ ◗ ▲ ♣ P ⚡

EDENTHORPE

Beverley Inn
117 Thorne Road (off A18 near Tesco)
☎ (01302) 882724
11.45-3, 5 (6.30 Sat)-11; 12-3, 7-10.30 Sun
John Smith's Bitter; Theakston XB; guest beer [H]
Busy, friendly local serving a mature clientele and specialising in a choice of good quality food and drink. Background music played at most times. No eve meals Sun.
❀ 🛏 ◖ ◗ ♿ P ⚡ ⊓

FIRBECK

Black Lion
9 New Road
☎ (01709) 812575
12-3, 5.30 (7 Sat)-11; 12-3.30, 7-10.30 Sun
Barnsley Bitter; Ruddles County; John Smith's Bitter; Stones Bitter; guest beer [H]
17th-century pub, reputedly haunted. See the photographs of locals and celebrities.
♛ ❀ 🛏 ◖ ◗ ♣ P ⊓

FISHLAKE

Hare & Hounds
Church Street
☎ (01302) 841208
12-4, 7-11; 12-2.30, 7-10.30 Sun
Mansfield Riding Bitter, Old Baily [H]
Large, very comfortable lounge, decorated with much brass and old village photos, as well as a smaller, traditional bar where darts and dominoes are still played. A Deakins beer may be available.
❀ ♣ P

Try also: Old Anchor, Main St (Scottish Courage)

GREASBROUGH

Prince of Wales
9 Potter Hill
☎ (01709) 551358
11-4, 7-11; 12-3, 7-10.30 Sun
John Smith's Bitter [P]; **guest beer** [H]
Friendly, two-bar village local. A community pub with a traditional taproom and a comfortable lounge. The ever-changing guest beer from independent breweries is competitively priced.
❀ ⊞ ♣ ⊓

GRENOSIDE

Cow & Calf
88 Skew Hill Lane (½ mile of A61)
☎ (0114) 246 8191
11.30-3, 6-11; 11.30-11 Sat; 12-10.30 Sun
Samuel Smith OBB [H]
Converted from a working farmhouse in 1877 with three distinct drinking areas and a welcoming, rural atmosphere. Good value ale and food (no meals Sun eve).
Q ♞ ❀ ◖ ◗ ♣ P ⚡

HARTHILL

Beehive
16 Union Street
☎ (01909) 770205
12-3 (not Mon), 6 (7 Sat)-11 (10 Mon); 12-3, 7-10.30 Sun
Marston's Pedigree; Tetley Bitter; guest beer [H]
Typical three-roomed country pub in a picturesque village.
❀ ◖ ◗ ▲ ♣ P ⊓

HATFIELD WOODSIDE

Green Tree
Bearswood Green, Tudworth Road (A18, Thorne Road)
☎ (01302) 840305
11-11; 12-10.30 Sun
Vaux Samson; Ward's Thorne BB; guest beer [H]
Old coaching inn recently refurbished by Vaux: a large single bar sub-divided internally, with a no-smoking area and a children's area. There is a heavy emphasis on food; the guest beer changes regularly from a list provided by the brewery. Wheelchair WC.
♞ ❀ 🛏 ◖ ◗ ♿ P ⚡

HEMINGFIELD

Lundhill Tavern
Beechhouse Road
☎ (01226) 752283
11-11; 12-10.30 Sun
Barnsley Bitter; John Smith's Bitter; Samuel Smith OBB; guest beers [H]
Probably one of the reasons why fewer people leave Barnsley than any other town in England.
♞ ❀ ◗ ♣ P

HOYLAND

Beggar & Gentleman
7 Market Street
☎ (01226) 742364
11-11; 12-10.30 Sun
Barnsley Bitter; Boddingtons Bitter; Whitbread Trophy; guest beers [H]
Spacious, town-centre alehouse catering for all ages. Good value lunches (not served Sun), plus free pie and peas Tue eve.
❀ ◖ ♿ ≠ (Elsecar) ♣ P

Furnace Inn
163 Milton Road (B6097)
☎ (01226) 742000
12-3.30, 6.30-11; 12-3, 7-10.30 Sun
Vaux Samson; Ward's Thorne BB [P], **Best Bitter; guest beer** [H]
Award-winning, friendly village local alongside the old forge pond. National Pub Superloo champion.
Q ❀ ≠ (Elsecar) ♣ P ⊓

LANGSETT

Waggon & Horses
On A616
☎ (01226) 763259
12-2.30, 5.30-11; 11.30-11 Fri & Sat; 12-3, 7-10.30 Sun
Courage Directors; Theakston Best Bitter [H]
Cosy, friendly roadside pub with an excellent reputation for its food.
♛ Q ❀ 🛏 ◖ ◗ ▲ P

LOW BARUGH

Millers Inn
Dearne Hall Road (B6428)
11.30-2.30, 5.30-11; 11.30-11 Fri & Sat; 12-3, 7-10.30 Sun
Barnsley Bitter, Oakwell, Black Heart Stout; Taylor Landlord; guest beers [H]
Free house backing on to the River Dearne; a meeting place for various clubs.
Q ❀ ◖ ◗ ♿ ♣ P

MEXBOROUGH

CONCERTINA BAND CLUB
9a Dolcliffe Road
☎ (01709) 580841
12-4, 7-11; 12-2, 7-10.30 Sun
Concertina Best Bitter, Bengal Tiger; Mansfield Bitter; John Smith's Bitter; guest beers Ⓗ
Visitors are welcome at this small, friendly club which is steeped in local history. Other Concertina beers (brewed here) are often available. A frequent winner of CAMRA awards.
≉ ♣ ⑂

FALCON
12 Main St ☎ (01709) 513084
11.30-11 (may vary); 12-3, 7-10.30 Sun
Old Mill Bitter Ⓗ
Lively pub, featuring a smart lounge with raised seating areas and a games-oriented tap room. Other beers from the Old Mill range are occasionally available.
❀ ⑭ ≉ ♣

GEORGE & DRAGON
81 Church Street (off A6023, near river and canal)
☎ (01709) 584375
12-11; 12-10.30 Sun
Vaux Samson; Ward's Best Bitter; guest beers Ⓗ
Friendly, welcoming pub with a central bar. The pleasant garden is popular with families (children welcome inside until 8pm). Winner of many brewery awards, especially for its floral displays.
❀ ⅍ P ⑂

MIDHOPESTONES

MIDHOPESTONES ARMS
Mortimer Road (250 yds from A616, Stocksbridge bypass)
☎ (01226) 762305
11.30-3, 6 (7 in winter)-11; 12-10.30 Sun
Badger Tanglefoot; Barnsley Bitter; Courage Directors; Ruddles County; Taylor Landlord; Ward's Best Bitter; guest beer Ⓗ
Characterful 300-year-old pub (formerly the Club Inn) with four rooms featuring real fires, beamed ceilings, stone-flagged floors and high-back settles. Good food includes game dishes in season.
♨ Q ❀ ◑ ▶ ⚔ ♣ P

MOSS

STAR INN
Moss Road (between Askern and Moss)
☎ 01302) 700497
6 (7 Sat)-11; 12-3, 9 (7 summer)-10.30 Sun
Ward's Thorne BB; guest beer Ⓗ
White-walled country pub with an interesting layout and an aero-

nautical theme. The garden has a children's playground. Good value home-cooked food; folk music Thu eves.
♨ ⅋ ❀ ◑ ▶ ⅍ ⚔ P

ROTHERHAM

BRECKS
Bawtry Road ☎ (01709) 543216
11-11; 12-10.30 Sun
Boddingtons Bitter; Flowers Original; Marston's Pedigree; Wadworth 6X Ⓗ
Beefeater restaurant that is also the local community pub. On a busy road, it is frequented by travellers and locals alike. Very large public bar area; it attracts a mature clientele.
⇔ ◑ ▶ ⅍ P ⑂

CHARTER ARMS
Eastwood Lane (above the new central market)
☎ (01709) 373066
10.30 (11 Sat)-11; 12-3, 6-10.30 Sun
Mansfield Riding Bitter, Bitter, Old Baily; guest beer Ⓗ
Friendly, modern, well-appointed pub offering excellent food, a comfortable lounge and a games room. Very popular with shoppers. Tiny garden. ❀ ◑ ≉ ♣

EFFINGHAM ARMS
Effingham Street
☎ (01709) 539030
11-11; 12-3, 7-10.30 Sun
Draught Bass; Fuller's London Pride; Stones Bitter; guest beer Ⓗ
Friendly, multi-roomed, town-centre Victorian pub with 1930s stained glass windows depicting Captain Effingham's exploits.
≉ ♣

LIMES
38 Broom Lane
☎ (01709) 363431
11-11; 12-10.30 Sun
Banks's Bitter; Camerons Strongarm; Marston's Pedigree; guest beer (occasional) Ⓗ
Originally a large Victorian house, now sympathetically converted into a large Banks's pub/hotel. A very popular local venue for its comfortable, spacious bar with an exceptional food menu. ⇔ ◑ ▶ P

MOULDERS REST
110-112 Masbrough Street, Masbrough (near Rotherham FC at Millmoor)
☎ (01709) 560095
12-3, 6 (7.30 Sat)-11; 12-3, 7-10.30 Sun
Stones Bitter; guest beer Ⓗ
Large, main road corner pub with a busy taproom and a through lounge, popular for games. Good value beers (weekdays), and guest beers at competitive prices.
⇔ ◑ ⑭ ≉ ♣ P

WOODMAN
Midland Road, Masbrough (off A269, opp bus garage)
☎ (01709) 512128
12-3, 7-11; 12-2, 7-10.30 Sun
Stones Bitter; guest beer Ⓗ
Friendly, former Bentley's pub with a traditional taproom, a snug lounge and a garden/play area outside. An upstairs snooker room is for hire. Very much a local. The guest beer is constantly changed. ❀ ⑭ ♣

SHEFFIELD: *CENTRAL*

BANKERS'S DRAFT
11 Market Place
☎ (0114) 275 6609
11-11; 11-10.30 Sun
Courage Directors; Tetley Bitter; Theakston Best Bitter; guest beers Ⓗ
Wetherspoons bank conversion: split-level with a no-smoking areas on both floors. No children allowed. A tram stop is on the doorstep. Cheap meals and beer promotions are a regular feature.
Q ◑ ▶ ⅍ ≉ (Midland)
⊖ (Castle Sq) ⑂ ⑂

FAT CAT
23 Alma St ☎ (0114) 249 4801
12-3, 5.30-11; 12-3, 7.30-10.30 Sun
Kelham Island Bitter, Pale Rider, seasonal beers; Taylor Landlord; guest beers Ⓗ
Sheffield's first real ale free house, opened in 1981. Two comfortable rooms, a corridor drinking area and an upstairs function room, used for overspill and families. Kelham Island Brewery is situated in the grounds and three of its beers are always on sale.
♨ Q ⅋ ❀ ◑ ⊖ (Shalesmoor)
⊂ P ⑂

FOUNDRY & FIRKIN
240 West St ☎ (0114) 275 7805
12-11; 12-10.30 Sun
Firkin Stoked, Foundry, Premium, Dogbolter; guest beers Ⓗ
Large, lively town-centre 'Firkin' with its own brewery. One-off beers regularly appear, especially milds and stouts. Live music Sun. Food served 12-7.
❀ ◑ ▶ ⅍ ⊖ (West St/University)

HOGSHEAD
25 Orchard St ☎ (0114) 272 1980
11-11; 12-10.30 Sun
Boddingtons Bitter; Marston's Pedigree; Whitbread Abroad Cooper; guest beers Ⓗ
Small, lively, split-level, city-centre, bareboarded Whitbread Alehouse. The rear door opens on to Orchard Square shopping precinct (not eves), with outside tables. Breakfast from 9.30.
❀ ◑ ≉ (Midland)
⊖ (Cathedral) ⊂ ⑂

LORD NELSON
166 Arundel Street
☎ (0114) 272 2650
12-11; 12-10.30 Sun
Hardys & Hansons Best Bitter; Stones Bitter ⊞
Community street-corner local, affectionately known as Fanny's, situated in old industrial quarter next to Moor shopping centre.
≈ (Midland) ♣

MORRISSEY'S RIVERSIDE
1 Mowbray Street
☎ (0114) 275 7306
5-11; 12-3, 7-11 Sat;
Highwood Tom Wood Best Bitter; guest beers ⊞
Three-roomed, street-corner pub with an upstairs function room where entertainment includes comedy and poetry. A pleasant garden overlooks the River Don.
Q ✿ ♣ ⊁

RED HOUSE
168 Solly Street
☎ (0114) 272 7926
12-3, 5.30-11; 12-4, 7.30-11 Sat; 12-3, 7-10.30 Sun
Ward's Thorne BB, Best Bitter; guest beer ⊞
Comfortable, three-roomed local with an impressive view from the rear snug. Folk musicians often gather in the wood-panelled front room; the pool table is well used. Weekday lunches.
◖ ⊖ (Nethertorpe Rd) ♣

RED LION
109 Charles Street
☎ (0114) 272 4997
11-11; 12-3, 7-10.30 Sun
Ward's Best Bitter; guest beers ⊞
Surviving 19th-century pub sandwiched between Sheffield Hallam University and the new national centre for popular music. A long bar runs through the drinking area to a food servery at the rear; a taproom is tucked away. The conservatory has smoking restrictions. Weekday lunches.
✿ ◖ ≈ (Midland) ⊖ (Castle Sq)

RUTLAND ARMS
86 Brown St ☎ (0114) 272 9003
11.30-11; 11-4, 7-11 Sat; 12-3, 7-10.30 Sun
Barnsley Bitter; Greene King Abbot; Ind Coope Burton Ale; Marston's Pedigree; Tetley Bitter ⊞
Well-preserved Gilmour's frontage to a one-roomed, comfortable corner pub in the city's expanding cultural quarter. Popular early eve meals Mon-Fri.
✿ ⇔ ◖ ≈ (Midland)
⊖ (Hallam)

SHIP INN
312 Shalesmoor
☎ (0114) 281 2204
12-3 (not Sat), 7 (7.30 Sat)-11; 7.30-10.30 Sun

Hardys & Hansons Best Bitter ⊞
Small, friendly, family-run pub with an impressive Tomlinson's frontage: an L-shaped lounge with a pool room behind. Weekday lunches. Limited parking. ◖ ⊖ (Shalesmoor) ♣ P ⊟

SHEFFIELD: *(EAST)*

ALMA
76 South Street, Mosborough (behind Eckington Hall)
☎ (0114) 248 4781
11.30-3.30, 7-11; 12-4, 7-10.30 Sun
Ward's Best Bitter ℗**; guest beer** ⊞
Quiet, two-roomed local at the far end of the village. A traditional tap room with a dartboard and a cosy lounge with a low-beamed ceiling which caters for the older generation. Welcoming to visitors at all times. Rotating Vaux/Ward's guest beer.
Q ✿ ⊞ ♣ P

COCKED HAT
75 Worksop Road, Attercliffe
☎ (0114) 244 8332
11-11; 11-3, 7-11 Sat & Bank Hols; 12-3, 7-10.30 Sun
Marston's Bitter, Pedigree, HBC ⊞
One of Sheffield's smallest pubs, next to Don Valley Stadium. Behind a curved exterior lies a single room with bar billiards. A *Guide* regular since 1986.
⇔ ✿ ◖ ⊖ (Attercliffe) ♣

MILESTONE
12 Peaks Mount, Waterthorpe
☎ (0114) 247 1614
11.30-11; 12-3, 7-10.30 Sun
Banks's Bitter ℗**; Camerons Strongarm; Marston's Pedigree** ⊞
Modern pub on the bus station approach to Crystal Peaks shopping centre, a popular meeting place before the cinema. Large lounge with conservatory where children are welcome if dining. The public bar sells cheaper beer.
✿ ◖ ▸ ⊞ ও ⊖ (Crystal Peaks)
♣ P ⊁ ⊟

NEW CROWN INN
343 Handsworth Road, Handsworth (B6200)
☎ (0114) 269 2396
12-11; 12-3, 7-10.30 Sun
Boddingtons Bitter; guest beers ⊞
This friendly local serves a wide cross-section of the community, with clubs and sports teams meeting regularly. Two main rooms: one a traditional tap room with a dartboard and a large function room hosting weekly live music. Eve meals Mon-Fri, 5-7.
✿ ◖ ▸ ⊞ ও ♣ P

WENTWORTH HOUSE
26 Milford Street, Attercliffe (beside Forgemaster Steels)
☎ (0114) 244 1594
11.30-2.30, 6.30 (8.30 Sat)-11; 12-3, 7.30-10.30 (may close early) Sun
Ward's Best Bitter; guest beer (occasional) ⊞
Welcoming little local next to a steelworks. A major refurb has breathed new life into the 'Wenty'. Now a single U-shaped room with a flagged floor and high quality fixtures. Full breakfast is served from 8am Sun. Handy for Sheffield Arena. ◖ ⊟

Try also: Carlton, Attercliffe Rd (Free)

SHEFFIELD: *(NORTH)*

CASK & CUTLER
1 Henry Street, Shalesmoor
☎ (0114) 249 2295
12-2 (not Mon), 5.30-11; 12-11 Fri & Sat; 12-3, 7-10.30 Sun
Beer range varies ⊞
Shrine to real ale, serving an ever-changing range of six beers from independent breweries at probably the lowest prices in the city. Eve meals finish at 6.30, not served Sun eve or Sat lunch.
⇔ Q ✿ ◖ ▸ ⊖ (Shalesmoor)
⇧ ⊁ ⊟

MORRISSEY'S EAST HOUSE
18 Spital Hill ☎ (0114) 272 6916
5 (6 Sat)-11; 6-10.30 Sun
Flowers IPA; John Smith's Magnet; Taylor Landlord; guest beers ⊞
Long, narrow, community pub: a single bar with a real Irish ambience serving a good range of Irish whiskeys. Draught beer sold to take away to the excellent curry houses opposite. Q ♣ P

NEW BARRACK TAVERN
601 Penistone Road
☎ (0114) 234 9148
12-11; 12-10.30 Sun
Barnsley Bitter, IPA; John Smith's Magnet; Stones Bitter; guest beers ⊞
Lively, three roomed local close to Hillsborough Barracks, serving up to five guest beers, plus imported Czech and Belgian draught lagers. Regular live music and special events Wed eves. Eve meals 5.30-7.30.
Q ✿ ◖ ▸ ⊞ ⊖ (Bamforth St)
♣ ⇧ ⊁

ROCK HOUSE
168-172 Rock St
☎ (0114) 272 4682
1 (12 Sat)-5, 8-11; 12-5, 8-10.30 Sun
John Smith's Bitter, Magnet; Theakston Best Bitter ⊞
Friendly, open-plan community pub with an L-shaped lounge and smaller snug on the lower level.

Stocks over 50 scotch whiskies.
Q ❀ ♣

SHEFFIELD: *(SOUTH)*

ARCHER ROAD BEER STOP (OFF-LICENCE)
57 Archer Road
☎ (0114) 255 1356
11 (10.30 Sat)-10; 12-2, 6-10 Sun
Taylor Landlord; guest beers H
Very popular, small, corner
shop/off-licence stocking a wide
range of British bottle-conditioned and foreign beers, plus
Biddenden cider. ➝

BROADFIELD
452 Abbeydale Road
☎ (0114) 255 0200
11-11; 12-10.30 Sun
**Boddingtons Bitter; Castle Eden
Ale; Taylor Landlord; guest
beers** H
Large, lively tavern, an integral
part of the local social scene with
its traditional bar and games
room. Good food is available until
8 on weekdays (6 Sat and Sun);
breakfast from 11 at weekends.
Children welcome for meals. Up
to nine beers at any time.
❀ ◖ ▶ ♣

CREMORNE
185 London Road
☎ (0114) 255 0126
12-11; 12-3, 7-30-11 Sat; 12-3,
7-10.30 Sun
**Marston's Pedigree; Tetley
Bitter; guest beers** H
Tetley Festival Ale House in the
stone and bare boards tradition:
a large L-shaped drinking area,
plus a lower level games area
with pool. One of the better
places to drink in an area awash
with pubs. A minimum of four
guest beers change weekly. ♣

OLD MOTHER REDCAP
Prospect Road, Bradway
☎ (0114) 236 0179
11.30-3, 5.30-11; 11.30-11 Sat;
12-10.30 Sun
Samuel Smith OBB H
Modern farmhouse-style building
at Bradway bus terminus, with a
single L-shaped lounge, popular
with all ages. Eve meals Thu and
Fri. ❀ ◖ ▶ ≈ ⊖ (Dore) ♣ P ⊟

SHAKESPEARE
106 Well Road
☎ (0114) 255 3995
12-3.30 (5 Sat), 5.30 (7 Sat)-11;
12-3, 7-10.30 Sun
**Marston's Pedigree; Stones
Bitter; Tetley Bitter, Imperial;
guest beer** H
Attractive, welcoming, community pub close to Heeley City Farm.
One bar serves three drinking
areas. Run by the same landlord
for 37 years. The guest beer is
from the Tapster's Choice range.
❀ ♣ P

WHITE LION
615 London Road
☎ (0114) 255 1500
12-11; 12-4, 7-10.30 Sun
**Ind Coope Burton Ale; Marston's
Pedigree; Taylor Landlord;
Tetley Bitter; guest beers** H
Multi-roomed Tetley Heritage
pub with a Festival Ale House with
its original character maintained
following refurbishment in 1994.
Features include an original tiled
corridor, two snugs and a no-
smoking lounge. Very popular
with all ages; busy at weekends.
❀ ♣ ⌷

SHEFFIELD: *(WEST)*

COBDEN VIEW
40 Cobden View Road
☎ (0114) 266 3714
4 (1 Sat)-11; 12-10.30 Sun
**Barnsley Bitter; Boddingtons
Bitter; Castle Eden Ale; guest
beers** (occasional) H
Comfortable local with two bars
and rooms off, including a games
area with pool. Live folk music
Thu. ❀ ♿ ♣

DEVONSHIRE ARMS
118 Ecclesall Road
☎ (0114) 272 2202
11-11; 12-10.30 Sun
Ward's Best Bitter; H P **guest
beers** H
Extensively renovated local with
several partitioned seating areas
and a conservatory. The Ward's
brewery tap.
❀ ◖ P

NOAH'S ARK
94 Crookes
☎ (0114) 266 3300
12 (11 Sat)-11; 12-10.30 Sun
**Boddingtons Bitter, Castle Eden
Ale; Flowers IPA; Fuller's
London Pride; Ward's Best
Bitter; guest beers** H
Busy community pub with several
distinct seating areas around a
central bar. Early eve meals.
❀ ◖ ▶ ♣

OLD GRINDSTONE
3 Crookes
☎ (0114) 266 0322
11-11; 12-10.30 Sun
**Taylor Landlord; Vaux Samson;
Ward's Best Bitter** H
Substantially extended local in a
student area which caters for all
ages. A single bar serves several
seating areas and a raised
games section with snooker. Eve
meals finish at 7.30.
◖ ▶ ♿ ♣

OLD HEAVYGATE
114 Matlock Road
☎ (0114) 234 0003
2-4 (12-5 Sat), 7-11 (12-11 winter
Sat); 12-4, 7-10.30 Sun
**Hardys & Hansons Best Bitter,
seasonal beers** H

Two-roomed community pub dating from 1696, formerly a toll
house and adjoining cottage. Quiz
night Wed.
❀ ♣ P ⌷

PORTER BROOK
565 Ecclesall Road
☎ (0114) 266 5765
11-11; 12-10.30 Sun
**Black Sheep Best Bitter;
Boddingtons Bitter; Whitbread
Abroad Cooper;** H **guest
beers** H G
Recently opened Whitbread
Hogshead in a converted house
on the banks of the River Porter.
A welcome addition to beer
choice on the Ecclesall Road
scene and consequently always
lively. Meals served all day (until
8.30).
🏴 Q ◖ ▶

THORNE

CANAL TAVERN
South Parade (next to canal flyover bridge)
☎ (01405) 813688
11.30-3, 5.30-11; 11.30-11 Sat;
12-4, 7-10.30 Sun
**Boddingtons Bitter; John
Smith's Bitter; Tetley Bitter
guest beers** H
Canalside hostelry, popular with
boaters, offering a wide range of
beers and a large menu (roasts a
speciality). Hosts regular events.
🏴 ❀ ◖ ▶ ≈ (South/North)
♣ P

Try also: Green Dragon, Silver
St (Wards)

THORPE HESLEY

MASONS ARMS
Thorpe Street (2 mins from M1
jct 35)
☎ (0114) 246 8079
12-3, 6-11; 12-3, 7.10.30 Sun
**Courage Directors; John Smith's
Bitter; Theakston Best Bitter,
Old Peculier** H
Traditional village pub with excellent home-cooked food and a
very friendly, welcoming atmosphere.
Q ❀ ◖ ▶ ♣ P

THURLSTONE

HUNTSMAN
136 Manchester Road (A628)
☎ (01226) 764892
12-4 (not Mon-Thu), 6-11; 12-4,
7-10.30 Sun
**Clark's Bitter, Black Cap; John
Smith's Bitter; Stones Bitter;
guest beers** H
Charming old terraced pub,
boasting a working Yorkshire
range, as well as a large open
log fire. Tue and Thu are quiz and
supper nights; live music Fri.
🏴 Q ❀ ▶

TICKHILL

SCARBROUGH ARMS
Sunderland Street
☎ (01302) 742977
11-3, 6-11; 12-3, 7-10.30 Sun
Courage Directors; Ruddles County; John Smith's Bitter, Magnet; guest beers Ⓗ
Popular local with three rooms of differing character. Home-made lunches (Tue-Sat) include imaginative vegetarian dishes. Twice winner of local CAMRA *Pub of the Season* award.
♨ Q ❀ ◑ ⊞ ♣ P ⬚

ULLEY

ROYAL OAK
Turnshaw Road
☎ (0114) 287 2464
11-3, 6-11; 12-3, 6-10.30 Sun
Samuel Smith OBB Ⓗ
Large country pub over 300 years old, very comfortable with, brasses and beams. An excellent dining room, large gardens and a children's room add to its attraction. ⛺ ❀ ◑ ▶ P

VICTORIA

VICTORIA INN
Hepworth (A616, near pipe works) ☎ (01484) 682785
12-2 (not Mon-Thu), 7-11; 12-2, 7-10.30 Sun
Tetley Bitter Ⓗ
Barnsley area's longest standing *Guide* entry, with possibly the longest serving licensees (since 1956) offering a good welcome.
♨ ⊞ P

WATH UPON DEARNE

STAITHES
Doncaster Road
☎ (01709) 873546
12-11; 12-10.30 Sun
John Smith's Bitter; Stones Bitter; guest beer Ⓗ
Spacious, comfortable, well-appointed free house; multi-roomed with nooks and crannies crammed with artefacts. Extensive home-cooked menu; a family atmosphere is encouraged by an outside children's play area.
♨ ❀ ◑ ▶ P ⚹

WENTWORTH

GEORGE & DRAGON
Main Street
☎ (01226) 742440
11-11; 12-10.30 Sun
Stones Bitter; Taylor Landlord; guest beers Ⓗ
Quiet country pub in picturesque Wentworth. A special 'walkers' breakfast' served from 10-12. The garden has a children's playground.
♨ ❀ ◑ ▶ P

ROCKINGHAM ARMS
Main Street
☎ (01226) 742075
11-11; 12-10.30 Sun
Theakston Mild, Best Bitter, XB, Old Peculier Ⓗ
This pub boasts several snugs, and a large garden. Entertainment is staged in the barn.
♨ Q ⛺ ❀ ⇔ ◑ ▶ ⊞ P

WHEATLEY HILLS

CUMBERLAND
Thorne Road (near Doncaster Royal Infirmary)
☎ (01302) 360000
11-11, 12-10.30 Sun
Boddingtons Bitter; Jennings Cumberland Ale; guest beer Ⓗ
Large old pub with a friendly atmosphere, refurbished in 1997: a large L-shaped room with side alcoves. Music and quizzes hosted Tue; good food; not a family pub.
❀ ◑ ▶ ♣ P

WHEATLEY HOTEL
Thorne Road
☎ (01302) 364092
11-11; 12-5.30, 7-10.30 Sun
John Smith's Bitter, Magnet; guest beers (occasional) Ⓗ

Large, friendly hotel with a comfortable lounge divided by impressive wood/leaded glass sliding doors. Well equipped children's play area.
⛺ ❀ ⇔ ◑ ▶ P

WHISTON

GOLDEN BALL
7 Turner Lane (off High St)
☎ (01709) 378200
11.45-11; 12-10.30 Sun
Greene King Abbot; Ind Coope Burton Ale; Taylor Landlord; Tetley Bitter; guest beer Ⓗ
Picture postcard pub offering a pleasant outside drinking area. Full of olde-worlde charm, it boasts an extensive menu.
♨ ❀ ◑ ▶ ♣ P ⚹

WORTLEY VILLAGE

WORTLEY ARMS HOTEL
On A629 (off A616)
☎ (0114) 288 2245
12-3, 5-11; 11-11 Sat; 12-10.30 Sun
John Smith's Bitter; Taylor Golden Best, Best Bitter, Landlord, Ram Tam, seasonal beers; Tetley Bitter; guest beers Ⓗ
Attractive 16th-century coaching inn featuring stone walls and bare floorboards in the tap room; a large fireplace and wooden beams in the lounge. Ideally placed in a picturesque village, it is popular with walkers and cyclists.
♨ Q ⛺ ❀ ⇔ ◑ ▶ ⊞ ♿ ⚘ ♣ ◔ P ⚹

INDEPENDENT BREWERIES

Barnsley:
Barnsley

Concertina Band Club:
Mexborough

Glentworth:
Doncaster

Kelham Island:
Sheffield

Oakwell:
Barnsley

Ward's:
Sheffield

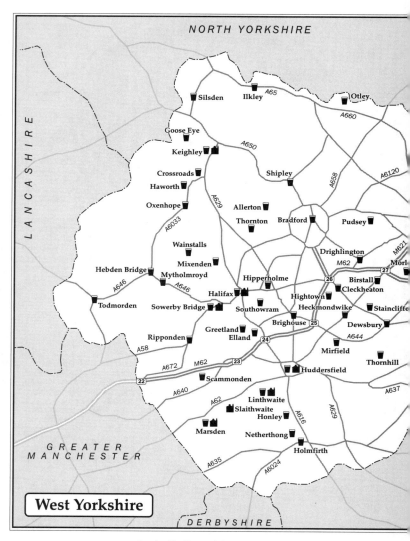

NORTH YORKSHIRE

Silsden · Ilkley · Otley

Goose Eye

Keighley

Crossroads

Shipley

Haworth

Oxenhope · Allerton · Bradford · Pudsey

Thornton

Drighlington

Wainstalls

Mixenden

Hebden Bridge · Mytholmroyd · Hipperholme · Birstall · Cleckheaton · Morl

Halifax · Hightown · Heckmondwike · Staincliffe

Todmorden · Sowerby Bridge · Southowram · Brighouse · Dewsbury

Ripponden · Greetland · Elland · Mirfield · Thornhill

Scammonden · Huddersfield

Linthwaite · Slaithwaite · Honley

Marsden · Netherthong · Holmfirth

L A N C A S H I R E

G R E A T E R
M A N C H E S T E R

West Yorkshire

D E R B Y S H I R E

Yorkshire (West)

ALLERTON BYWATER

BOAT INN
Boat Lane, Main Street
☎ (01977) 552216
11.30-3, 6-11; 11.30-3, 7-10.30 Sun
Tetley Bitter; guest beers Ⓗ
Traditional riverside pub with an
outside drinking area and a
walled garden. No meals Sun eve
or Mon.Q ❀ ◑ ▶ ⊞ ₺ P

BARWICK IN ELMET

NEW INN
17 Main Street
☎ (0113) 281 2289
11.30-11; 12-3, 7-10.30 Sun
John Smith's Bitter; guest beersⒽ

Lovely old cottage pub in a country village outside Leeds. A
friendly welcome and the best
value for miles around for guest
beers. Eve meals Tue-Thu.
Q ◑ ▶ ₺ ♣

BIRSTALL

WHITE BEAR
108 High street (B6125)
☎ (01924) 476212
12-3, 5.30-11; 12-11 Fri & Sat;
12-10.30 Sun
Tetley Mild, Bitter; guest beer Ⓗ
Compact corner pub with a comfortable lounge and a traditional
tap room offering good value B &
B. Usually live entertainment at
weekends. Eve meals Mon-Fri
until 8pm.
❀ ⇔ ◑ ▶ ⊞ ♣ P

BRADFORD

BLACK HORSE
2 Lockwood Street, Low Moor
(A638, by railway bridge, 2 miles
from centre).
☎ (01274) 671357
11.30-3, 5.30-11; 11.30-11, Fri &
Sat; 12-10.30 Sun
Samuel Smith OBB Ⓗ
Traditional English local with an
open fire and stone floors: a
lounge area, plus an old-fashioned tap room offering games.
Friendly atmosphere; popular at
lunchtimes with simple home-
cooked food.🏔 ◑ ⊞ P

BLUE PIG
Fagley Road, Lower Fagley (200
yds down lane at end of Fagley
Rd) ☎ (0113) 256 2738

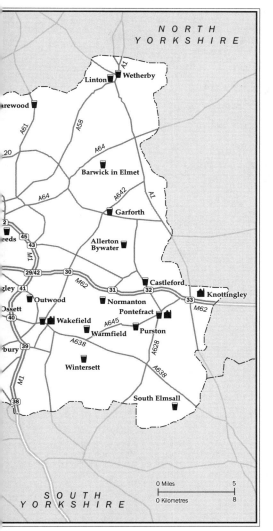

Imaginative conversion of part of a Lloyds Bank building, using fine Art Deco-style glass features and wrought ironwork. Very busy at weekends when a smart/casual dress code applies (from 8pm Fri and Sat).
◖ & ⇌ (Forster Sq/ Interchange)

FIGHTING COCK
21-23 Preston Street (400 yds from B6145, ½ mile from the centre)
☎ (01274) 726907
11.30-11; 12-10.30 Sun
Black Sheep Special; Greene King Abbot; Old Mill Bitter; Taylor Golden Best, Landlord; Theakston Old Peculier; guest beers Ⓗ
Down-to-earth drinkers' haven in an industrial area stocking at least 12 beers at all times plus traditional cider. The menu (not served Sun), includes the famous 'dockers wedge' sandwiches and chilli.
♨ ❀ ◖ ⌂

GAPING GOOSE
5-6 Slack Bottom Road, Wibsey (off Buttershaw Lane)
☎ (01274) 601701
2-5, 7-11; 2-5, 7-10.30 Sun
Black Sheep Best Bitter; Taylor Landlord; Tetley Bitter Ⓗ
Intimate, two-roomed village local, well worth seeking out. A comfortable lounge with much brassware and pottery. A second room is more games oriented.
❀ & ♣ P

HAIGY'S BAR
31 Lumb Lane (300 yds from B6144) ☎ (01274) 731 1644
5 (12 Fri & Sat)-1am; closed Sun
Black Sheep Best Bitter; Fuller's London Pride; Greene King Abbot; Tetley Bitter; guest beers Ⓗ
City Gent Ale, brewed by Clark's is available on City match days. in this excellent pub, made famous by its appearances in *Band of Gold* (ITV) and, more recently, since redecoration in the colours of the nearby Bradford City club. Late bar and very good value food. Limited parking. ❀ ▶ P

IDLE WORKING MEN'S CLUB
23 High Street, Idle
☎ (01274) 613602
12-3 (4 Fri & Sat), 7.30 (7 Fri & Sat)-11; 12-3, 7.30-10.30 Sun
Tetley Mild, Bitter; guest beers Ⓗ
Friendly social club with live entertainment Sat and Sun eves. A different guest beer is available in the downstairs games room. Show this *Guide* or CAMRA membership to be signed in. No children allowed in the concert room Sat eve. ♣

3 (12 Fri & Sat)-11; 12-10.30 Sun
Tetley Bitter; guest beers Ⓗ
Split-level pub on the Leeds Country Way with a good atmosphere and an excellent family room. Regular quiz nights.
☃ ❀ ♣ P

CASTLE
20 Grattan Road (off Westgate)
☎ (01274) 393166
11.30-11; closed Sun
Mansfield Riding Mild, Riding Bitter, Bitter; guest beers Ⓗ
Popular city-centre house, built in 1898. The single room has been partitioned to provide a drinking area away from the main bar. Free food Fri lunchtime. Car park open eves and weekends.
Q ⇌ (Interchange/Forster Sq)

CORN DOLLY
110 Bolton Road
☎ (01274) 720719
11.30-11; 12-10.30 Sun
Black Sheep Best Bitter; Moorhouse's Premier; Theakston Best Bitter; guest beers Ⓗ
Busy, city-centre pub drawing a varied clientele. Formerly known as the Wharf because of its proximity to the canal basin. No meals Sat or Sun.
♨ ❀ ◖ ⇌ (Forster Sq/Interchange) ♣ P

CITY VAULTS
33 Hustlergate
☎ (01274) 739697
10.30-11; 11-11 Sat; 12-3, 5-10.30 Sun
Mansfield Riding Bitter, Bitter, Old Baily Ⓗ

MACRORY'S BAR
4 Easby Road
☎ (01274) 728165
11.30 (12 Sat)-11; 12-10.30
Sun
Courage Directors; John Smith's Bitter, Magnet; guest beer Ⓗ
Busy one-roomed cellar bar under the Beechfield Hotel near the University and colleges. A genuine local, with a wide mix of customers and a rare outlet for Magnet, it features live music Sun and Wed eves and a curry night on Tue (no food Sat). Limited Parking.
🕸 ⇔ Ⓓ ▶ ⇌ (Interchange) P

MELBORN HOTEL
104 White Abbey Road (B6144, ¹/₂ mile from centre)
☎ (01274) 726867
12-11; 12-10.30 Sun
Tetley Bitter; Moorhouse's Premier; guest beers Ⓗ
A friendly, welcoming atmosphere is the keynote at this large three-roomed local. It has Irish connections - real, not themed, and is dubbed the 'People's Music House': it hosts the Topic Folk Club Thu eve and features traditional and blues music Fri-Mon eves.
🕸 ⇔ 🍺 ⇌ (Forster Sq) ♣ P

BEEHIVE INN ☆
171 Westgate (¹/₄ mile from centre on B6144)
☎ (01274) 721784
12-11; 11.30-1am Fri & Sat; 7-10.30 Sun
Goose Eye Bitter; Lloyds Derby Bitter; Taylor Golden Best, Landlord; Worth Alesman; guest beers Ⓗ
Well-preserved and atmospheric Edwardian gaslit, multi-roomed inn, stocking an extensive range of over 70 malt whiskies. Entertainment includes live jazz on Fri, a skittle alley and barbecues in summer. No food available Sun.-
🕸 🛏 🕸 ⇔ Ⓓ 🍺 ⇌ (Forster Sq/Interchange) ♣ ⌂ P

OAKLEIGH HOTEL
4 Oak Avenue, Manningham (off A650, Keighley Road, 1 mile from centre)
☎ (01274) 544307
12-11; 12-10.30 Sun
Greene King Abbot; Mansfield Riding Bitter, Bitter, Old Baily; guest beer (occasional) Ⓗ
Free house which has been renovated and seems more spacious than ever, with a large garden and patio. Near Lister Park. No food Sat.
🕸 Ⓓ P

OLD BANK
69 Market Street
☎ (01274) 743680
11-11; 12-10.30 Sun
Boddingtons Bitter; Castle Eden Ale; Flowers Original; Wadworth 6X; Whitbread Abroad Cooper; guest beers ⒽⒼ
Large, two-level pub, sympathetically converted from a former Barclays Bank. Gas lit, it is decked out with old banking memorabilia along with historic Bradford items. The upper floor has its own bar and a wonderful ornate ceiling. Wheelchair WC. Eve meals finish at 7 Fri & Sat (no food Sun eve).
🛏 Ⓓ ▶ ♿

QUEEN ALE HOUSE
863 Thornton Road, Fairweather Green (B6145, 2 miles from centre) ☎ (01274) 542898
5 (11 Fri & Sat)-11; 12-10.30 Sun
Greene King Abbot; Boddingtons Bitter; Flowers Original; Wadworth 6X; guest beers Ⓗ
Busy, two-roomed free house with an ever-changing guest beer range. Local stone and slate flooring add to the character. Bradford CAMRA *Pub of the Year* 1997. 🛏 ♣ 🍺 ⌂ P

RED LION
589 Thornton Road, Girlington (B6145, 1¹/₂ miles from centre)
☎ (01274) 496684
11-11; 12-10.30 Sun
Samuel Smith OBB Ⓗ
Small, friendly local with a large lounge and a small tap room offering many social activities. No meals Sun. Ⓓ 🍺 ♣ P

ROYAL OAK
32 Sticker Lane
☎ (01274) 665265
John Smith's Bitter; Theakston Best Bitter; Younger Scotch Ⓗ
Friendly local with wood-panelled walls and games area. Weekday lunches. 🕸 Ⓓ P

ROYAL OAK
39 Stony Lane, Eccleshill
☎ (01274) 639182
11-11; 12-10.30 Sun
Tetley Mild, Bitter; Ⓗ
Two-roomed, friendly local with a tap room (no access from the lounge except through the gents).
🕸 🍺 ♣ P

SHEARBRIDGE
111 Great Horton Road (by university)
☎ (01274) 732136
12-11; 12-10.30 Sun
Black Sheep Best Bitter, Special; Marston's Pedigree; Morland Old Speckled Hen; Tetley Bitter; guest beers Ⓗ
Festival Ale House with bare boards, stone floors and lots of stained wood panelling. An interesting menu includes the legendary Yorkshire pudding loaf and a 1lb pastie. Busy with students during termtime. 🕸 Ⓓ P

STEVE BIKO BAR
D Floor, Richmond Building, Bradford University, Richmond Road.
☎ (01274) 233257
11 (7 Sat)-11; 7-10.30 Sun
Courage Directors; Ruddles County; John Smith's Bitter; Theakston Bitter, XB; guest beers Ⓗ
Thriving, open-plan bar run by the Students Union. However, it can get very busy, especially during their regular cheap beer promotions. Eve meals weekdays. Car park available eves only.
Ⓓ ▶ ♣ ⌂ P

Try also: Goldsborough, Bolton Road (Free)

BRIGHOUSE

GLOBE
66-68 Rastrick Common, Rastrick (off A643)
☎ (01484) 713169
12-3.30 (not Mon), 7-11; 12-3.30, 7-10.30 Sun
Tetley Bitter; Wards Thorne BB; guest beer Ⓗ
Comfortable, well-decorated pub with a restaurant and a conservatory eating area (eve meals Tue-Sat). The guest beer is from the Vaux list.
🛏 🕸 Ⓓ ♣ P

RED ROOSTER
123 Elland Road, Brookfoot
☎ (01484) 713737
12-1 (not Mon-Wed), 5 (4.30 Fri)-11; 12-11 Sat; 12-3, 7-10.30 Sun
Black Sheep Best Bitter; Moorhouse's Pendle Witches Brew; Old Mill Bitter; Rooster's Yankee; Theakston XB; guest beers Ⓗ
Stone-built, compact, friendly, roadside free house where everyone is made welcome. Country fruit wines and varying cider supplement the five guest beers.
🛏 🕸 ♣ ⌂ P

CASTLEFORD

GARDEN HOUSE
Wheldon Road (near River Aire bridge)
☎ (01977) 552934
11.30-4, 5-11; 12-3.30, 7-10.30 Sun
Ward's Thorne BB; Vaux Samson, Boxing Hare; guest beers Ⓗ
Traditional, two-roomer: the lounge and bar are full of local rugby team memorabilia. Small garden with a play area and children are also welcome in the lounge. Sun eve singalong; quiz Thu eve.
Ⓠ 🕸 Ⓓ ▶ 🍺 ⇌ ♣ P

CLECKHEATON

MARSH
28 Bradford Road (A638, near bus station)
☎ (01274) 872104
11.45-3 (not Wed), 7-11; 12-4, 7-10.30 Sun
Old Mill Mild, Bitter, Bullion, seasonal beers Ⓗ
Decorated in Old Mill 'house' style with a quiet dais and crinkly brick walls, this pub has gently mellowed into a fine local with a strong regular following.♣ P

CROSSROADS

QUARRY HOUSE INN
Bingley Road, Lees Moor (¹/₂ mile from A629/A6033 jct) OS054380
☎ (01535) 642239
12-3, 7-11 (11.30 for diners); 12-3, 7-10.30 (11 for diners) Sun
Taylor Golden Best, Landlord; Tetley Bitter; guest beer (summer) Ⓗ
Family-run, converted farmhouse, set in open countryside with extensive views. The bar is a former church pulpit set in a small cosy area. Excellent food. Twice local CAMRA *Pub of the Season*; families are very welcome at all times.
♨ Q ☎ ❀ ◖ ▶ ᴖ ▲ P

DEWSBURY

JOHN F KENNEDY
2 Webster Hill ¹/₄ mile from station, westbound on ring road)
☎ (01924) 455828
8 (7 Fri & Sat)-11; 7.30-10.30 Sun
Taylor Landlord; guest beers Ⓗ
Multi-roomed pub drawing a mixed clientele. It has a pool room and supports local football teams. Same licensee for 30 years. Note the limited opening hours. ᴖ ⇌ ♣ P

'SIR' GEOFFREY BOYCOTT
125 High Street, Westtown
☎ (01924) 457610
11-3, 5.30-11; 9.30am-11 Sat; 9.30am-10.30pm Sun
Bass Mild, Draught Bass, seasonal beers; guest beers Ⓗ
Designed with the physically less able in mind the pub uses a lot of wooden and natural material finishes inside. Breakfast served Sat and Sun (no eve meals Sun). Often hosts cider events and occasional live bands.
♨ ❀ ◖ ▶ ᴖ ♣ ᴖ P

WEST RIDING LICENSED REFRESHMENT ROOMS
Dewsbury Railway Station, Wellington Road (inner ring road) ☎ (01924) 459193
11-11; 12-10.30 Sun
Bateman Mild, XB, XXXB; Linfit English Guineas (winter)**; guest beers** Ⓗ

Created out of part of the Grade II listed station building, the rooms have a policy of focusing on microbrewery beers for its guest ales. It runs an established music festival and charity events. Eve meals Tue and Wed. No-smoking area available until 6pm.
♨ ❀ ◖ ▶ ᴖ ⇌ ᴖ P ⊬

DRIGHLINGTON

PAINTERS ARMS
35 Bradford Road
☎ (0113) 285 2557
11-11; 12-10.30 Sun
Boddingtons Bitter; Tetley Bitter Ⓗ
Single central bar serving two contrasting areas: at the front a juke box, pool table, bare boards, karaoke etc. for the younger drinker; at the rear, carpet, comfort and conversation for the more mature. ❀ ◖ ⊡ P

SPOTTED COW
122 Whitehall Road
☎ (0113) 285 2558
11-3, 5-11; 11-11 Sat; 12-10.30 Sun
John Smith's Bitter; Theakston XB Ⓗ
Popular, single-bar, village main street local with a restaurant. A good mix of clientele of all ages enjoy the various drinking areas tucked away around the central bar. ◖ ▶ ᴖ P

ELLAND

GOLDEN FLEECE
Lindley Road, Blackley (1 mile S of Elland, near M62 jct 24)
☎ (01422) 372704
12-2.30 (not Sat), 7-11; 12-3, 7-10.30 Sun
Vaux Samson; Ward's Thorne BB; guest beer Ⓗ
Pictures and brassware create a warm atmosphere in this hilltop village local. Business lunches are a speciality. ❀ ◖ ♣ P

GARFORTH

GAPING GOOSE
41 Selby Road
☎ (0113) 286 2127
11.30-11; 12-10.30 Sun
Tetley Mild, Bitter Ⓗ
Busy roadside local, famous for its beer quality; Garforth RU team exclusively drinks here. Big screen TV for major sporting events. It hosts the marvellous annual Goose Fair in July.
Q ❀ ♣ P

MINERS ARMS
4 Aberford Road
☎ (0113) 286 2105
12 (11.30 Sat)-11; 12-10.30 Sun
Tetley Bitter; guest beers Ⓗ
Low-ceilinged, Tetley Festival Ale House within a stone's throw of Garforth station, bringing a much

welcomed diversity for local ale drinkers. Weekday lunches.
❀ ◖ ⇌ ♣ P ⊬

GOOSE EYE

TURKEY INN
1 mile from B6143, Keighley-Oakworth Road near Laycock
☎ (01535) 681339
12-3, 5.30-11; 12-5, 7-11 Sat; 12-3, 7-10.30 Sun
Tetley Bitter Ⓗ
Recently refurbished country pub with leaded windows from Kings Brewery and low-beamed ceilings (one formed from barrel staithes). Three rooms, two boast open fires and one is a games room, plus a restaurant (no food Mon). The house beer is supplied by Tetley.
♨ Q ❀ ◖ ▶ ♣ P

GREETLAND

STAR
1 Lindwell (off B6113)
☎ (01422) 373164
12-4 (not Tue), 7-11; 12-3, 7-10.30 Sun
Ward's Thorne BB, Best Bitter; guest beer Ⓗ
Friendly village local with a busy tap room and a cosy lounge. One end of the Calderdale Way is nearby. ❀ ♣

HALIFAX

BIG SIX INN
10 Horsfall Street, King Cross
☎ (01422) 350169
7 (1 Fri, 12 Sat)-11; 12-4, 7-10.30 Sun
Flowers IPA; Higsons Bitter; Ind Coope Burton Ale; Tetley Bitter; Wadworth 6X; guest beers Ⓗ
A must for all those who are interested in the heritage of Halifax: the details of the pub's history are displayed on the walls. Bar billiards played.
♨ Q ❀ ♣

BROWN COW
569 Gibbet Street, Highroad Well
(1¹/₂ miles W of centre)
☎ (01422) 361640
11.30-11; 12-10.30 Sun
Castle Eden Ale; Taylor Landlord; Whitbread Trophy; guest beer Ⓗ
Unpretentious and deservedly popular pub with strong sporting connections. Quiz Tue eve. Weekday lunches (food served Sun 4-7). ❀ ◖ ♣

SHEARS INN
Paris Gates, Boys Lane
☎ (01422) 362936
11.45-11; 12-10.30 Sun
Taylor Golden Best, Best Bitter, Landlord; Younger Scotch, No. 3; guest beer (occasional) Ⓗ
Cosy, low-roofed pub with bay

window seating, nestling in the valley bottom, overlooked by a large mill complex. Lunches Mon-Sat. ♛ ❀ ◖ ⇌ ♣ P

Tap & Spile
1 Clare Road, Wards End
☎ (01422) 362692
11-11; 12-10.30 Sun
Old Mill Bitter; guest beers [H]
Opened by Ramsdens Brewery in 1931, this elaborate mock Tudor building is now listed for its architectural interest. Many original features survive in its two drinking areas. Popular with all ages and a meeting place for many local groups. ◖ ⇌ ♣ ⌓

Three Pigeons Ale House
1 Sun Fold, South Parade (between station and the Shay)
☎ (01422) 347001
12-3, 5-11; 12-11 Sat; 12-3, 7-10.30 Sun
Beer range varies [H]
Popular free house with three separate rooms often used by groups for meetings. Note overhead mural in the octagonal central area, and the 3D pub sign. The house beer is by Coach House; the six other beers include one or more from Black Sheep and Timothy Taylor. Weekday lunches.
♛ Q ❀ ◖ ⇌ ♣ P

West End Hotel
216 Parkinson Lane (1 mile W of centre)
☎ (01422) 250559
11-11; 12-10.30 Sun
Boddingtons Bitter; Old Mill Bitter; guest beer [H]
Spacious, former hotel now converted into a pub with a large upstairs function room. See the collection of football shirts on display. Quiz Sun eve.
♛ ❀ ♣ P

Yew Tree
20 The Green, Northowram (3 miles NE of centre)
☎ (01422) 202316
11.30-3, 6-11; 11.30-11 Fri & Sat; 12-10.30 Sun
Black Sheep Best Bitter; guest beers [H]
Friendly village pub which does a lot to support local charities. The management (and pets) promote local brewers' products, with two guests from regional micros. Note the old car memorabilia. Eve meals Fri-Sun.
♛ ◖ ◗ P

HAREWOOD

Harewood Arms
Harrogate Road (A61)
☎ (0113) 288 6566
11-11; 12-10.30 Sun
Samuel Smith OBB [H]
Prominent roadside inn; comfortable surroundings, including a dining area with friendly, efficient staff. Close to Harewood House.
Q ⛟ ◖ ◗ P

HAWORTH

Fleece Inn
67 Main Street
☎ (01535) 642172
12-11; 12-10.30 Sun
Taylor Golden Best, Mild, Best Bitter, Porter, Landlord, Ram Tam [H]
Popular, well-known, ex-coaching inn on the main tourist route. Three distinct areas downstairs include a family room; two upstairs rooms (one for functions). Always a cheap beer option, plus happy hours Mon-Fri teatimes.
♞ ⇌ (KWVLR) ♣

Kings Arms
1 Church Street
☎ (01535) 643146
12-2.30, 5-11 (11-11 Sat & summer), 12-10.30 Sun
Greene King Abbot; Ind Coope Burton Ale; Tetley Bitter [H]
Cosy, traditional pub: a mixture of stone and dark and light wood with wooden beams, offering a warm, hospitable welcome to visitors. This former manor toll house dates from 1600; the restaurant is in the Victorian part of the building.
Q ❀ ◖ ◗ ♿ ⛺ ⇌ (KWVLR)

Royal Oak Inn
2 Mill Hey (opp station)
☎ (01535) 643257
12-2.30, 7 (5.30 Fri)-11; 12-11 Sat; 12-10.30 Sun
Black Sheep Best Bitter; John Smith's Bitter; Webster's Yorkshire Bitter [H]
Comfortable open lounge area, decorated with brass and copper; a small family room displaying railway memorabilia (open till 8pm). Formerly the village mortuary during the Plague.
♛ ♞ ❀ ◖ ◗ ⛺ ⇌ (KWVLR) ♣ P

HEATH

Kings Arms ☆
Heath Common (off A655, Wakefield Road)
☎ (01924) 377527
11-3, 5.30-11; 12-10.30 Sun
Clark's Bitter, Black Cap; Taylor Landlord; Tetley Bitter [H]
17th-century pub: it has three oak panelled rooms with gas lighting; plus an à la carte restaurant and a family conservatory. There are extensive gardens to rear and a village green in front.
♛ Q ♞ ❀ ◖ ◗ ♿ P

HEBDEN BRIDGE

Fox & Goose
9 Heptonstall Road
☎ (01422) 842649
11.30-3, 7-11; 12-3, 7-10.30 Sun
Goose Eye Bitter; guest beers [H]
A haven for sociable people - a pub with no juke box or bandit. It also offers three changing guest beers from independent breweries.
Q ❀ ⇌ ♣ ⛉

Hare & Hounds
Billy Lane, Chiserley, Old Town (1 mile off A6033 at Peckett Well) OS005280
☎ (01422) 842671
12-3 (4 Sat, not Mon or Tue except Bank Hols), 7-11; 12-10.30 Sun
Taylor Golden Best, Best Bitter, Landlord, Ram Tam [H]
Hillside pub above Hebden Bridge, known locally as 'Lane Ends'. Families with well-behaved children welcome. No eve meals Mon.
♛ Q ❀ ⛟ ◖ ◗ P ♣

White Lion Hotel
Bridge Gate
☎ (01422) 842197
11-11; 12-3, 7-10.30 Sun
Boddingtons Bitter; Castle Eden Ale; Flowers Original; Taylor Landlord; guest beers [H]
Former coaching inn, pleasantly opened out, to offer a mix of styles to a wide-ranging clientele. Wheelchair WC. Good B & B.
♛ ♞ ❀ ⛟ ◖ ◗ ♿ ⇌ P ⚡

Old Hall
New North Road (½ mile NW of the 'Green')
☎ (01924) 404774
11.30-3, 6-11; 11.30-11 Sat; 12-10.30 Sun
Samuel Smith OBB [H]
Dating from the 1470s this Grade I listed building boasts a rare aisle construction and a Royal Acorn whitewashed ceiling. Once the home of the isolator of oxygen, Joseph Priestley, now home to a ghost and small collection of royal portraits.
❀ ◖ ◗ P

HIGHTOWN

Cross Keys
283 Halifax Road (A649 1 mile from A62 jct)
☎ (01274) 873294
12-2.30 (not Mon-Wed), 5.30-11; 12-11 Sat; 12-10.30 Sun
Bateman Mild; Marston's Bitter, Pedigree, HBC [H]
Opened-up pub with a conservatory dining area and views across the valley. No eve meals Mon.
❀ ◖ ◗ P

HIPPERHOLME

BROWN HORSE INN
Denholme Gate Road, Coley
☎ (01422) 202112
11-11; 12-3, 7-10.30 Sun
John Smith's Bitter; Taylor Landlord; Theakston Best Bitter; Webster's Yorkshire Bitter H
Yorkshire's only Brown Horse pub. The interior is comfortably spacious. Food is cooked to order (eve meals Mon-Fri). ❀ ◖ ▶ P

HOLMFIRTH

ROSE & CROWN (NOOK)
Victoria Square (off Hollowgate)
☎ (01484) 683960
11.30-11; 12-10.30 Sun
Samuel Smith OBB; Stones Bitter; Taylor Best Bitter, Landlord; Tetley Mild; Younger No. 3; guest beers H
With a long-serving landlord and over 20 years' standing in this *Guide*, this no-frills alehouse continues to attract loyal devotees. The pub is larger than it might appear at first with several rooms and passageways radiating from the small bar area.
❀ Q ⌂ ❀ ♣

HONLEY

JACOBS WELL
16 Woodhead Road (A6024)
☎ (01484) 666135
11-2.30, 5-11; 11-11 Sat; 12-4, 7-10.30 Sun
Black Sheep Special; Ind Coope Burton Ale; Tetley Mild, Bitter; guest beers H
Popular, comfortably furnished, roadside pub with an excellent reputation for good food (eve meals Mon and Wed). Open-plan design with full air conditioning throughout. ◖ ▶ ≈ ♣

HORBURY

BOONS
Queen Street (off High St)
☎ (01924) 274506
11-3, 5-11; 11-11 Sat; 12-3, 7-10.30 Sun

What's Brewing?
CAMRA's monthly newspaper has all the latest news on pubs, breweries, campaigns, as well as dates of all the beer festivals

Clark's Bitter; John Smith's Bitter; Taylor Landlord; Tetley Bitter; guest beer H
Situated in the town centre, a former keg-only pub until it was taken over by Clark's who have turned it into a successful outlet for real ale. ❀ ❀ ♣ P

CALDERVALE HOTEL
Millfield Road (400 yds from A642) ☎ (01924) 275351
12-4, 6.30-11; 12-3, 7-10.30 Sun
John Smith's Bitter; guest beers (occasional) H
Situated in Horbury Junction on the outskirts of town it can be difficult to find, but worth the effort. ⌂ ❀ ⇌ & ♣ P

KINGS ARMS
37 New Street ☎ (01924) 264269
12-3, 5.30-11; 11-11 Sat; 12-5, 7-10.30 Sun
Marston's Bitter, Pedigree, HBC H
Large, white pub close to the town centre. The family room doubles as a restaurant.
⌂ ❀ ◖ ▶ ♣ P

HUDDERSFIELD

HEAD OF STEAM
St George's Square
☎ (01484) 454533
11-12.30; 12-10.30 Sun
Beer range varies H
Conversion from rooms in one wing of the Grade I listed Huddersfield railway station. Four rooms with interconnecting doors, each with its own ambience and character. Popular with students; regular live music. Premium prices. ◖ ▶ ≈

MARSH LIBERAL CLUB
31 New Hey Road (A629, 1¹/₂ miles from centre)
☎ (01484) 420152
12-2, 7-11 (12-11 Sat); 12-10.30 Sun
Black Sheep Best Bitter; Taylor Best Bitter; Theakston Best Bitter; guest beers H
Lively club, usually stocking four guest beers, including a mild (over 150 guests in the last year). Two snooker tables, a bowling green and many other sporting connections. Show this *Guide* or a CAMRA membership card to be signed in at the bar.
❀ ♣ P

RAT & RATCHET
40 Chapel Hill (A616, near ring road) ☎ (01484) 516734
3.30 (12 Wed-Sat)-11; 12-10.30 Sun
Adnams Bitter; Bateman Mild; Greene King Abbot; Marston's Bitter; Taylor Best Bitter, Landlord; guest beers H
A haven for real ale drinkers on the edge of the town centre, with

the widest selection of beers offered by any pub locally - up to 14, often including one brewed on the premises. Occasional beer festivals. Lunches Wed-Sat, eve meals Tue (chilli) and Wed (curry). ❀ ◖ ▶ ≈ ♣ P

SHOULDER OF MUTTON
11 Neale Road, Lockwood (off B6108 near A616 jct, 1 mile S of centre)
☎ (01484) 424835
7 (3 Sat)-11; 12-3.30, 7-10.30 Sun
Boddingtons Bitter; Taylor Best Bitter, Landlord; Tetley Mild, Bitter; guest beers H
Endearing pub at the head of a short cobbled street; a genuine free house of high quality with a convivial atmosphere. It has been in this *Guide* for over 10 consecutive years; the same landlord for over 20 years.
❀ ≈ (Lockwood) ♣

SLUBBERS ARMS
1 Halifax Old Road, Hillhouse (off A641, ³/₄ mile from centre)
☎ (01484) 429032
11-3, 7-11; 12-3, 7-10.30 Sun
Marston's Pedigree; Taylor Golden Best, Best Bitter, Landlord; guest beers H
A glimpse into Huddersfield's history - a 150-year-old end of terrace pub with relics of slubbing and other skills unique to the textile industry. The only Taylor-owned pub in town. ❀ Q ◖ ♣

ZENECA RECREATION CLUB
509 Leeds Road (A62 1¹/₂ miles NE of town) ☎ (01484) 421784
11-11; hours vary Sun
Taylor Best Bitter; Tetley Mild, Bitter; guest beers H
Competitively-priced ales and extensive sports facilities combine to make this comfortable, spacious club very appealing. Twice winner of CAMRA's National *Club of the Year*. Show this *Guide* or CAMRA membership for entry. ❀ ◖ ♣ P ✂

Try also Wooldale Arms, Wooldale

ILKLEY

ILKLEY MOOR VAULTS
Stockeld Road (off Skipton Road towards Addingham)
☎ (01943) 607012
12-11; 12-10.30 Sun
Taylor Best Bitter, Landlord; Tetley Bitter; guest beers H
Tetley Festival Ale House near the river Wharfe. Its stone floors and wood attract a wide range of customers. The small snug-like room is warm and welcoming. All that remains of the once large Ilkley Moor Hotel. Hot snacks all day. ❀ ❀ ◖ ♣ P

MIDLAND HOTEL
Station Road (opp station)
☎ (01943) 607433
11-11; 12-10.30 Sun
John Smith's Bitter; Theakston XB; guest beers Ⓗ
Convenient for both bus and train stations, this pub makes a good starting point when visiting the town. There are two rooms, both with fine wooden barbacks and glasswork, lots of pictures of old Ilkley and railway history.
🏚 Q ◑ ⊞ ≉ ♣ P

Try also: Riverside Hotel, Riverside Gdns (Free)

KEIGHLEY

BOLTMAKERS ARMS
17 East Parade
☎ (01535) 661936
11.30-11; 11-4, 7-11 Sat; 12-4, 7-10.30 Sun
Taylor Golden Best, Best Bitter, Landlord; guest beers Ⓗ
This gem has been run by the same couple for more than 20 years. An extremely popular pub which should not be missed. The one-room split-level pub is due for a minor refurb during 1998.
≉ ♣

BREWERY ARMS
Longcroft/Sun Street
☎ (01535) 603102
11.30-11; 12-10.30 Sun
Worth Alesman, Best Bitter, seasonal beers; guest beers Ⓗ
Friendly real ale pub, just off the town centre, well worth the short walk. You are guaranteed a friendly welcome and a relaxed comfortable atmosphere. There are up to five guest beers usually available. The doorstep sandwiches are a must.
🏵 ◑ ▮ ≉ ♣ P

GLOBE
2 Parkwood Street
☎ (01535) 610802
11.30-11; 12-10.30 Sun
Taylor Golden Best, Best Bitter, Landlord; Tetley Bitter Ⓗ
Friendly, refurbished local. The Worth Valley railway passes the window. Weekday lunches; snacks at all times.
🏚 Q ☡ ◑ ≉ ♣ P

RED PIG
Church Street
☎ (01535) 605383
12-11; 12-10.30 Sun
Taylor Golden Best, Landlord; guest beers Ⓗ
Small, town-centre free house with much of the interior stripped back to the underlying brickwork. Busy weekend eves.
🏚 ≉ ♣

VOLUNTEER ARMS
Lawkholme Lane
☎ (01535) 600173
11-11; 12-10.30 Sun
Taylor Golden Best, Best Bitter Ⓗ
Compact, town-centre local with two rooms, the smaller used mainly for games. Handy for the bus station. Can get smoky.
≉ ♣

KEIGHLEY TO OXENHOPE AND BACK

KEIGHLEY & WORTH VALLEY RAILWAY BUFFET CAR
Stations at Keighley, Ingrow West, Oakworth, Haworth & Oxenhope
☎ (01535) 645214; talking timetable 647777
Sat, Sun & Bank Hols, March-Oct
Beer range varies Ⓗ
Volunteer-run railway buffet car giving changing views of the Worth valley.
Q ▲ ≉ (Keighley, Ingrow and Oxenhope) P ⊁ ⊟

LEEDS: *CITY*

DUCK & DRAKE
43 Kirkgate
☎ (0113) 246 5806
11-11; 12-10.30 Sun
Old Mill Bitter; Taylor Landlord; Theakston Best Bitter, XB, Old Peculier; Younger No 3; guest beers Ⓗ
One of the original, bare wood-floored pubs before they became fashionable is still going strong. Locals tend to use the right-hand (back) bar with its rare Yorkshire dartboard, the other bar serves a wide range of customers. Live music is a feature.
🏚 ◑ ≉ ♣

HORSE & TRUMPET
The Headrow
☎ (0113) 243 0338
11-11; 12-10.30 Sun
Marston's Pedigree; Tetley Bitter; guest beers Ⓗ
Town-centre local in Tetley Festival Ale House style. Up to five guest beers. Handy for Leeds Theatres. No food Sun. ◑ ≉

LONDONER
Lovell Park Road (back of Merrion Centre)
☎ (0113) 245 3666
11.30 (11 Fri & Sat)-11; 12-3, 7.30-10.30 Sun
Marston's Pedigree; Tetley Bitter; guest beers Ⓗ
Open-plan Festival Ale House, the first in central Leeds with a number of alcove seating areas. Serves six ever-changing guest ales and hosts regular beer festivals. Weekday lunches.
🏵 ◑ ♣ P ⊁

PALACE
Kirkgate
☎ (0113) 244 5882
11-11; 12-10.30 Sun
Ind Coope Burton Ale; Marston's Pedigree; Tetley Mild, Bitter, Imperial; guest beers Ⓗ
Tetley Festival Ale House, offering up to 12 beers: one hand-pump always dispensing a guest stout or porter; another always serves a beer from Rooster's Brewery. Quiz Wed eve.
🏵 ◑ ♣ ⊁

PRINCE OF WALES
Mill Hill
☎ (0113) 245 2434
11-11; 12-10.30 Sun
Black Sheep Best Bitter; John Smith's Bitter; guest beers Ⓗ
City-centre retreat from the explosion of themed bars in the area; busy but rarely packed. A basic pool/TV room with a larger lounge; very handy for the station. Three guest beers from independent breweries. ◑ ≉ ♣

SCARBROUGH
Bishopsgate Street
☎ (0113) 243 4590
11.30-11; 12-3, 7-10.30 Sun
Black Sheep Best Bitter; Marston's Pedigree; Tetley Bitter; guest beers Ⓗ
Open-plan, single-room Tetley Festival Ale House with its original Ind Coope tiled exterior. Occasional beer festivals held; the pub gets busy at weekends and eves. No food Sun. ◑ ≉ ⌂

VIADUCT
11 Lower Briggate
☎ (0113) 245 4863
11-11; 12-3, 7-10.30 Sun
Ansells Mild; Ind Coope Burton Ale; Marston's Pedigree; Tetley Dark Mild or **Mild, Bitter; guest beers** Ⓗ
Multi-award-winning, long, narrow pub, boasting three milds and a great staff. Customers with disabilities are actively catered for. Tapster's Choice guest beer. A shining beacon in the wake of city-centre circuit pub mania.
Q 🏵 ◑ ♿ ≉ ⊁

VICTORIA FAMILY & COMMERCIAL HOTEL
Great George Street (behind Town Hall)
☎ (0113) 245 1386
11.30-11 Mon-Sat; 12-4, 7-10.30 Sun
Black Sheep Best Bitter; Taylor Landlord; Tetley Mild, Bitter; guest beers Ⓗ
After an extensive £2.5 million refurbishment, this three-roomed pub comes complete with snug booths, wonderfully ornate decor and up to five (albeit pricey) guest beers. An enjoyable drinking experience. Q ◑ ≉ ♣ ⊁

WHIP INN
Bowers Yard (off Duncan St)
☎ (0113) 245 7571
11-11; 12-3, 8-10.30 Sun
Tetley Mild, Bitter H
Leeds' oldest traditional pub. The epitome of no-nonsense drinking, with a basic courtyard drinking area. Unfortunately now sells lager. One of the last of a vanishing breed of true city-centre locals. Q ❀ ⇌ ♣

WHITELOCKS ☆
Turks Head Yard (off Briggate)
☎ (0113) 245 3950
11-11; 12-10.30 Sun
Theakston Best Bitter, XB, Old Peculier; Younger Scotch, IPA; guest beers H
Wonderfully attractive old pub first licensed in 1715. A feast of brass and glass greet the wide range of drinkers, who spill out into the long, outside alleyway when things get too busy eves. The restaurant serves up hearty cuisine Mon-Sat eves.
🏚 Q ❀ ◖ ▶ ⇌

LEEDS: *NORTH*

CHEMIC TAVERN
9 Johnson Street, Woodhouse
☎ (0113) 295 0195
11 (11.30 Sat)-11; 12-3, 7-10.30 Sun
Taylor Landlord; Tetley Bitter; guest beer H
Two-roomed, detached pub with a comfy lounge but the back room retains its olde-worlde feel with low beams, stone floor and a lovely etched mirror. Outside drinking area in front of the pub.
Q ❀ ⊞ ♣ P

CITY OF MABGATE INN
45 Mabgate (near bus station, under York Rd flyover)
☎ (0113) 245 7789
11-11; 12-3, 7-10.30 Sun
Black Sheep Special; Boddingtons Bitter; Taylor Landlord; Whitbread Trophy; guest beers H
Friendly pub of great character: a basic public bar for TV or games, and a comfy lounge for lunchtime meals or evening chat. The beer range usually includes a Rooster's brew. 🏚 ❀ ◖ ⊞ ♣

FEAST & FIRKIN
229 Woodhouse Lane (by University Engineering Dept)
☎ (0113) 245 3669
11-11; 12-10.30 Sun
Firkin Fuzz Bitter, Feast Bitter, Dragon, Dogbolter H
Former library and police station, 'Firkinised' in 1994, catering largely to students. A spacious downstairs bar and a large upstairs room for functions, occasional live bands or for simply drinking. ◖ ♣ P

NEW ROSCOE
Bristol Street, Sheepscar
☎ (0113) 246 0778
11.30-11; 12-10.30 Sun
Tetley Bitter; guest beers H
Large, three-roomed pub adorned with images of the 'original' (now-demolished) Roscoe. Always a friendly welcome, whether the pub is quiet or busy. Regular live music and a weekly, high quality talent night.
❀ ◖ ⊞ ♣ P

PACK HORSE
203 Woodhouse Lane (opp University) ☎ (0113) 245 3980
11-11; 12-10.30 Sun
Taylor Landlord; Tetley Bitter; guest beers H
Multi-roomed local served by a central corridor. The pool and TV area at the back is popular with students. Tapster's Choice guest beer. ◖ ⊞

LEEDS: *SOUTH*

BLOOMING ROSE
19 Burton Row, Hunslet
☎ (0113) 270 0426
11-11; 12-10.30 Sun
Tetley Dark Mild or **Mild, Bitter; guest beers** H
Smashing, traditional local tucked away behind Hunslet Moor. Business people flock to the pub at lunchtime where the great value meals haven't risen in price for four years. A pool table can be found in the tap room extension. The best pub in South Leeds by far.
❀ ◖ ⊞ ♣ ✂

GROVE
Back Row, Holbeck
☎ (0113) 243 9254
12-11; 12-4, 7-11 Sat; 12-4, 7-10.30 Sun
Courage Directors; Ruddles County; John Smith's Bitter; Theakston XB; Younger No. 3; guest beer H
Extremely well-preserved 1930s pub - the original plan remains with four intact rooms and a West Riding drinking corridor. Live music most eves, attracting people from near and far. No food Sat. Q ❀ ◖ ⊞ ⇌ ♣

LEEDS: *WEST*

CARDIGAN ARMS ☆
364 Kirkstall Road, Burley
☎ (0113) 274 2000
12-11; 12-10.30 Sun
Marston's Pedigree; Morland Old Speckled Hen; Tetley Bitter; guest beers H
Multi-roomed local: a front public bar with a sports flavour and a large corridor drinking area: home of the Cardigan Folk Club. Tapster's Choice guest beers.
◖ ⊞ ♣ P

DAISY
168 Stanningley Road, Bramley
☎ (0113) 216 4300
11-11; 12-10.30 Sun
Tetley Bitter H
A three-roomed local. Two small rooms at the front: one a basic tap room with the hatch servery displaying photographs of old Bramley on the wall; the other is much more comfortably furnished. The main bar area is multi-levelled creating distinct areas. Weekday meals.
◖ ▶ ⊞ ⇌ (Bramley) ♣ P

FOX & NEWT
9 Burley Street, Burley
☎ (0113) 243 2612
11-11; 12-10.30 Sun
Boddingtons Bitter; guest beers H
Popular alehouse near Park Lane college. A warm welcome in this one-roomed pub with a cosier raised area at one end. Also stocks a good choice of bottle-conditioned beers and up to five guest beers.
◖

HIGHLAND
36 Cavendish Street, Burley (500 yds W of inner ring road, off Burley Road)
☎ (0113) 242 8592
11-11; 12-10.30 Sun
Tetley Mild, Bitter H
Victorian local where a good selection of sandwiches is always available. Difficult to find, but worth the effort.
❀ ◖ ♣

OLD VIC
17 Whitecote Hill, Bramley
☎ (0113) 256 1207
4 (2 Fri, 11 Sat)-11; 12-3, 7-10.30 Sun
Black Sheep Best Bitter; Taylor Landlord; Tetley Dark Mild, Bitter; guest beers H
Former vicarage in its own grounds, this popular free house has two lounges and a tap/games room.
🏚 Q ❀ ♿ ♣ P

LINTHWAITE

SAIR INN
139 Lane Top (top of Hoyle Ing off A62) OS100143
☎ (01484) 842370
7 (5 Fri, 12 Sat)-11; 12-10.30 Sun
Linfit Mild, Bitter, Swift, Special, Janet Street Porter, Autumn Gold, seasonal beers H
Near-legendary brewpub which has won widespread acclaim and numerous awards including CAMRA's 1997 national *Pub of the Year*. On a steep hillside overlooking the Colne Valley, it has several small rooms (one no-smoking). A popular meeting-place. 🏚 Q ☕ ♣ ⌂ ✂

LINTON

WINDMILL INN
Main Street (98 bus route from
Leeds or Wetherby)
☎ (01937) 582209
11.30-3, 5-11; 11-11 Sat; 12-
10.30 Sun
**John Smith's Bitter; Theakston
Best Bitter; guest beers** H
Attractive stone-built pub,
licensed since 1674 and reputedly
haunted by a jilted bride. Split-
level, beamed bars with a dining
and function room at the rear. The
inn sign acts as the bus stop. No
food Sun eve. ♨ Q ✿ ◖ ▮ P

MARSDEN

RIVERHEAD BREWERY TAP
2 Peel Street (off A62)
☎ (01484) 841270
5 (11 Sat)-11; 12-10.30 Sun
**Riverhead Sparth Mild, Butterley
Bitter, Deer Hill Porter, Cupwith
Light, Black Moss Stout, March
Haigh** H
Pennine village brewpub which
was once a Co-op store. Popular
with locals and visitors, it is situated in a noted rambling area
whose upland reservoirs are the
inspiration for the names of the
pub's regular beers.Q ᴅ ⇌ ⌂

TUNNEL END INN
Reddisher Road (near station)
☎ (01484) 844636
7.30-11 (12-3, 7-30-11 summer
Sat); 12-3, 7.30-10.30 Sun
**Tetley Mild, Bitter; guest
beers** H
Friendly local, tucked away from
the village by the Tunnel End
Countryside Centre. The large
main room features an open fire
and a piano, a room off this welcomes families. A further pool
room is hidden away at the back.
♨ ⍩ ⇌ ♣

MIRFIELD

RAILWAY
212 Huddersfield Road (western
edge of centre, A644)
☎ (01924) 480868
12-11; 12-3.30, 7-10.30 Sun
**Bass Toby, Draught Bass; Stones
Bitter; Worthington Best Bitter;
guest beer** H
Recently extended to meet
expanding catering demand, this
main road pub was situated
close to a long vanished railway
line. Always has two guest beers.
♨ ◖ ▮ & ⇌ ♣ P 🍺

MIXENDEN

HEBBLE BROOK
2 Mill Lane ⅔ mile of A629)
☎ (01422) 242059
12-3, 5.15-11; 12-11 Sat; 12-
10.30 Sun

**Taylor Golden Best; guest
beers** H
Friendly, unassuming but fiercely
independent pub attracting customers from far and wide.
Usually four guest beers, plus
regular 'guest brewery' weekends and occasional themed beer
festivals. Eve meals Mon
(steaks), and Wed (curry).
♨ Q ✿ ◖ ▮ ▲ ♣ ⌂ P

MORLEY

STUMP CROSS
Britannia Road
☎ (0113) 253 4655
11.30-11; 12-10.30 Sun
**Marston's Pedigree; Tetley Mild,
Bitter** H
Fab little local just on the edge of
Morley. Friendly staff dispense
fine ales from the central bar,
which is flanked by a real tap
room and a higgledy-piggledy
lounge. Named after the stump of
a cross, which acted as a nearby
boundary stone. Weekday lunches. ✿ ◖ ▯ P

MYTHOLMROYD

SHOULDER OF MUTTON
38 New Road (B6138)
☎ (01422) 883165
11.30-3, 7-11; 11.30-11 Sat; 12-
10.30 Sun
**Black Sheep Best Bitter;
Boddingtons Bitter; Castle Eden
Ale; Flowers IPA; Taylor
Landlord; guest beer** H
Popular roadside local with a fine
display of toby jugs and china.
Eve meals 7-8.30 (not Tue).
◖ ▮ ⇌ P ⌿

NORMANTON

HUNTSMAN
84 Dalefield Road (500 yds from
A655)
☎ (01924) 892212
11 (4 winter)-11; 12-10.30 Sun
Burtonwood Bitter, Forshaw's H
Thriving community local, with a
small lounge and a large tap
room, frequented by all ages. The
only Burtonwood tied house in
the Wakefield area.
✿ ▯ ⇌ ♣ P

OSSETT

BREWERS PRIDE
Low Mill Road ☎ (01924) 273865
12-3, 5.30-11; 12-11 Fri & Sat;
12-10.30 Sun
Taylor Landlord; guest beers H
Popular, true free house with a
ten-barrel brewery designed and
built by the landlord behind the
pub. A five min walk from the
Calder and Hebble canal, the pub
is decorated with old brewery
memorabilia. Five guest beers
include a mild. Good choice of
meals Fri & Sat. ♨ Q ✿ ⌂

RED LION
73 Dewsbury Road (A629, 1 mile
from M1 jct 40)
☎ (01924) 273487
12-11; 12-3, 7-10.30 Sun
**John Smith's Bitter; Tetley
Bitter; guest beers** H
18th-century inn with a low-oak
beamed ceiling and a small central bar. Popular for good value
home-cooked meals (no food Sun
or Mon eves) One guest beer,
usually from a Yorkshire brewery. ◖ ▮ P

OTLEY

BAY HORSE
20 Market Place
☎ (01943) 461122
11-11; 12-10.30 Sun
Tetley Bitter; guest beers H
Small, cosy, two-roomed pub
with a tap room to the front. One
guest beer, often from local independents. Outside toilets.
✿ ▯ ♣

JUNCTION
44 Bondgate
☎ (01943) 463233
11-11; 12-10.30 Sun
**Black Sheep Best Bitter; Taylor
Best Bitter, Landlord; Tetley
Bitter; Theakston Old Peculier;
guest beers** H
One-roomed friendly pub featuring exposed stonework and a
tiled floor. Unplugged music sessions Mon; live music alternate
Tue; quiz Sun and Wed. Biker
friendly. Not to be missed when
in town. ♨ ◖ ♣

OUTWOOD

KIRKLANDS HOTEL
605 Leeds Road
☎ (01924) 826666
11-11; 12-3, 7-10.30 Sun
**Old Mill Mild, Nellie Dene,
Bitter, seasonal beers** H
Hotel with three large rooms
around a central bar area. Tied
to Old Mill Brewery, it is always
busy with passing trade and
locals. Reasonably priced meals
(not served Sun eve). Children
welcome early eve.
Q ✿ 🛏 ◖ ▮ ⇌ P

OXENHOPE

LAMB INN
Denholme Road (B6141)
☎ (01535) 643061
12-3, 7-11; 12-11 (12.30-4.30,
6.30-11 winter) Sat; 12-10.30
Sun
**Ward's Thorne BB; guest
beers** Ⓗ
Comfortable, traditional, country
inn with two rooms: a warm cosy
lounge decorated with pictures
and a family room displaying railway memorabilia (children welcome until 8pm). Popular folk
band Thu eve. No food Mon.
🏚 Q ☎ ❀ ◗ ▲ ⇌ (KWVL
R) ♣ P

PONTEFRACT

COUNTING HOUSE
Swales Yard (opp war memorial)
☎ (01977) 600388
11-3, 7-11; 12-3 (not winter),
7-10.30 Sun
**Old Mill Old Curiosity;
Tomlinson's Sessions, De Lacy;
guest beers** Ⓗ
14th-century listed building converted to a pub after extensive
alterations. The open-plan bar
has a stone floor and old church
seats. A large upstairs room
opens at weekends.
◗ ⇌ (Tanshelf) ♣ ⚲

GREYHOUND
13 Front Street (opp
Courthouse)
☎ (01977) 791571
12.30-4.30 (not Tue) 7-11; 11-11
Sat; 12-4, 10.30 Sun
**John Smith's Bitter; Tomlinson's
Sessions** Ⓗ
Lively, town pub with a busy bar.
Live music Fri nights in the
lounge. Pool room.
🏚 ⊞ ⇌ (Tanshelf) ♣

ROBIN HOOD INN
4 Wakefield Road (off A645)
☎ (01977) 702231
11.30-3.30 (4.30 Fri & Sat), 7-11;
12-3.30, 7-10.30 Sun
**John Smith's Bitter; Tetley
Bitter; Theakston Old Peculier;
guest beer** Ⓗ
Busy public bar and three other
drinking areas in a pub at the
edge of town. Quiz Tue and
Sun nights.
🏚 ❀ ⊞ ⇌ (Tanshelf/Baghill)
♣

TAP & SPILE
28 Horsefair (opp bus station)
☎ (01977) 793468
12-11; 12-3, 7-10.30 Sun
Beer range varies Ⓗ
Chain alehouse with bare floorboards and brickwork, split into
three drinking areas. The changing beer range includes a house
beer.
⇌ ♣ ◌ P

PUDSEY

BUTCHERS ARMS
Church Lane
☎ (0113) 256 4313
11-11; 12-10.30 Sun
Samuel Smith OBB Ⓗ
Recently refurbished stone-built
pub on the main street. The forecourt is used as an outside drinking area. ❀ ◗ ♣

PURSTON

WHITE HOUSE
257 Pontefract Road (A645, near
Featherstone)
☎ (01977) 791878
11-4, 7-11; 12-3, 7-10.30 Sun
Samuel Smith OBB Ⓗ
Busy roadside local; the open-
plan central bar displays pictures
of local RL and soccer teams;
popular with Rover supporters.
No food Sun. ◗ ♣ P

RIPPONDEN

ALMA
Cottonstones, Mill Bank, Sowerby
Bridge (1¼ miles off A58 at
Triangle pub) OS028215
☎ (01422) 823334
6 (12 Sat)-11; 12-10.30 Sun
**Taylor Golden Best; Tetley
Bitter; guest beers** Ⓗ
Welcoming, stone-flagged village
inn, enjoying extensive views.
Over 80 bottled beers,s mostly
Belgian, promoted with annual
Belgian and German weekend
festivals. Lunches Sat and Sun.
🏚 ❀ ⇌ ◗ ▲ ♣ P

FLEECE
Ripponden Bank, Barkisland
(B6113)
☎ (01422) 822598
12-11; 12-10.30 Sun
**Black Sheep Special; Taylor
Landlord; Theakston Best Bitter;
guest beers** Ⓗ
Roadside inn on two levels, the
lower area once a barn or coach
house has the main bar, with a
dining area above forming a
gallery. Live music twice weekly
in the upstairs bar. Supper
licence. Meals served 12-6.30
Sun. 🏚 ❀ ◗ ▲ P

OLD BRIDGE INN
Priest Lane (off A58, near B6113
jct)
☎ (01422) 822595
11.30-3, 5.30-11; 12-11.30 Sat;
12-10.30 Sun
**Black Sheep Best Bitter, Special;
Taylor Golden Best, Best Bitter;
guest beer** Ⓗ
Possibly Yorkshire's oldest pub,
recorded as early as 1307, in a
picturesque setting by a pack-
horse bridge over the Ryburn.
Only the guest beer pumps are
labelled.
🏚 Q ❀ ◗ ▶ P

SCAMMONDEN

BROWN COW
Saddleworth Road, Deanhead
(B6114, 2½ miles S of
Barkisland) OS045165
☎ (01422) 822227
12-3 (not Mon-Thu), 7-11; 12-3,
7-10.30 Sun
**Mansfield Riding Bitter, Bitter;
guest beers** Ⓗ
In an elevated moorland setting
above Scammonden Water, this
old coaching inn still provides a
welcome to cross-pennine travellers. Note the collections of
firefighting equipment and walking sticks. Lunches Fri-Sun, eve
meals Tue-Sun.
🏚 Q ☎ ❀ ◗ ▲ ♣ P

SHIPLEY

FANNY'S ALE & CIDER HOUSE
63 Saltaire Rd ☎ (01274) 591419
11.30-3, 5.30-11; 11.30-11 Fri &
Sat; 12-10.30 Sun
**Old Mill Bitter; Taylor Landlord;
guest beers** Ⓗ
Cosy, nostalgic atmosphere with
old-fashioned furniture in a gaslit
lounge. Usually four guest beers
and three ciders on offer. Near
the historic village of Saltaire. No
lunches Sat.
🏚 Q ◗ ▶ ⇌ (Saltaire) ◌

SHIPLEY PRIDE
1 Saltaire Road (200 yds from
Fox Corner on A657 to Keighley)
☎ (01274) 585341
11.30 (11 Sat)-11; 12-3, 7-10.30
Sun
**Clark's Burglar Bill; Old Bear
Ursa Minor; Tetley Bitter; guest
beers** Ⓗ
Late 19th-century, two-roomed
friendly inn, popular with locals,
originally Hammonds Old
Beehive. Home-made lunches.-
❀ ◗ ⇌ (Shipley/Saltaire) ♣ P

VICTORIA HOTEL
192 Saltaire Road
☎ (01274) 585642
11.30-11; 12-10.30 Sun
**Boddingtons Bitter; Taylor
Landlord; Whitbread Trophy;
guest beers** Ⓗ
Friendly local with Victorian style
decor of stained glass and wood.
Near the historic village of
Saltaire. Eve meals end at 8 (no
food Sat or Sun). Bradford
CAMRA *Pub of the Year* 1998.
Q ◗ ▶ ⊞ ⇌ (Saltaire) P

Try also: Branch, Bradford Rd
(Tetley)

SILSDEN

BRIDGE INN
60 Keighley Road
☎ (01535) 653144
11-11; 12-10.30 Sun

Black Sheep Best Bitter; John Smith's Bitter; Tetley Bitter; Theakston XB Ⓗ
Canalside pub which predates the canal, being first recorded in 1660. The original drinking rooms are now the cellar and toilets; the outside drinking area was originally the main road. Parking for boats only. Meals served daily 12-7. Ringing the Bull played.
Q ☎ ❀ ⇔ ◑ ▶ ♣

SOUTH ELMSALL

BARNSLEY OAK
Mill Lane (800 yds from A628/B6428 roundabout)
☎ (01977) 643427
12-3.30 (5 Sat), 7-11; 12-3, 7-10.30 Sun
John Smith's Bitter Ⓗ
1960s estate pub on the outskirts of an ex-mining village. The conservatory offers scenic views of the Elms Valley. Free sausages Sun eve. Quiz Tue eve.
☎ ❀ ◑ 🖥 ⬥ ⇌ (S Elmshall/Moorthorpe) ♣ P

SOUTHOWRAM

SHOULDER OF MUTTON
14 Cain Lane ☎ (01422) 361101
11 (3 Wed)-11; 12-10.30 Sun
Greene King Abbot; Ruddles County; John Smith's Bitter; guest beers Ⓗ
Expanding range of independent beers in this hilltop village local. Regular activities include charity quizzes and slide shows. ⚔ ♣ 🖥

SOWERBY BRIDGE

MOORINGS
No. 1 Warehouse, Canal Basin (off Wharf St, A58)
☎ (01422) 833940
12-11; 12-10.30 Sun
Black Sheep Special; Taylor Landlord; Theakston Best Bitter; guest beers Ⓗ
Successful conversion from a canal warehouse to a free house enjoying splendid views over the canal basin. Two guest beers, plus Moonshine Bootleggers Ale from Marston Moor, exclusive to the pub chain company. The dining room becomes a no-smoking area after 9pm when meals finish.
☎ ❀ ◑ ⇌ P ⌀

Try also: Puzzle Hall Inn, Hollins Mill Lane (Wards)

STAINCLIFFE

BELLE VUE
150 Staincliffe Road ³/₄ mile off A638, towards Dewsbury)
☎ (01924) 501155
12-4 (not Mon-Thu), 7-11; 12-4, 7-10.30 Sun
Boddingtons Bitter; Tetley Bitter; Whitbread Trophy; guest beers Ⓗ

Recently refurbished to open plan with a pool/games room. Sepia prints of old local public houses are displayed. Active social club.
❀ ♣ P

THORNHILL

SAVILE ARMS
Church Lane (B6117, 2¹/₂ miles S of Dewsbury)
☎ (01924) 463738
5-11; 12-3, 7.30-11 Sat; 12-3, 8-10.30 Sun
Black Sheep Best Bitter; Tetley Bitter; guest beers Ⓗ
Next to a fine 15th-century church (full of Savile family monuments), this 600-year-old pub known as the Church House, is built on consecrated ground. A convivial local, it has strong community affiliations, including local artists' paintings for sale. Lunches served Sat.
❀ ♣ P

THORNTON

THORNTON CRICKET CLUB
104a Hill Top Road
☎ (01274) 834585
8 (2 Sat)-11 (closed winter Sat); 8-10.30 Sun
Taylor Golden Best, Best Bitter, Landlord; guest beers (occasional) Ⓗ
Well run by volunteers, this comfy bar serves cricketers and visitors alike and provides relief from the often bracing weather. The views are spectacular. Worth finding. Show CAMRA membership card or this Guide to be signed in. ❀ ♣

TINGLEY

BRITISH OAK
407 Westerton Road
☎ (0113) 253 4792
12-3, 6 (7 Sat)-11; 12-3, 7-10.30 Sun
Boddingtons Bitter; Castle Eden Ale; Flowers Original; guest beers Ⓗ
Classic, friendly local staging live music and quiz nights. Leeds CAMRA Pub of the Year 1996. Guest beers are always from small independent breweries.
❀ ♣ P

TODMORDEN

CROSS KEYS
649 Rochdale Road, Walsden
☎ (01706) 815185
12-11; 12-10.30 Sun
Black Sheep Best Bitter; Highgate Dark; Tetley Bitter; guest beers Ⓗ
Busy, traditional pub with a conservatory overlooking the canal and a cosy tap room. Five guest beers change regularly.
❀ ⇔ ◑ ⬥ ⇌ (Walsden) ♣

ROSE & CROWN
355 Halifax Road (A646, 1 mile E of Todmorden)
☎ (01706) 812428
12-2.30 (5 Sat), 7-11; 12-5, 7-10.30 Sun
Boddingtons Bitter; Castle Eden Ale; Chester's Mild; Taylor Landlord; Whitbread Trophy; guest beer Ⓗ
Traditional main road pub, renovated but retaining its original character. A feature has been made of the former cellar area to the rear. The function room/restaurant upstairs has separate access. Q ◑ ▶ ⬥ ♣ P

TOP BRINK
Brink Top, Lumbutts ¹/₄ mile W of Mankinholes) OS957235
☎ (01706) 812696
12-3 (not Mon-Fri), 7-11; 12-10.30 Sun
Boddingtons Mild, Bitter; Castle Eden Ale; Flowers Original; Taylor Landlord; guest beer Ⓗ
Large pub on a valley terrace overlooked by moorland hills. The large bar faces three panelled areas displaying pictures and plates, hanging jugs and brassware. Popular with diners (order at the kitchen door). Supper licence. ❀ ◑ ▶ ▲ P

WHITE HART
White Hart Fold
☎ (01706) 812198
11.30-3.30, 7-11; 11-11 Fri & Sat; 12-10.30 Sun
Tetley Mild, Bitter; guest beers Ⓗ
Imposing, 'Brewer's Tudor' pub by the station; popular, especially at weekends. Two ever-changing guest beers. ❀ ◑ ▲ ⇌ ♣ P

WAINSTALLS

CAT I' TH' WELL INN
Wainstalls Lane, Lower Saltonstall (¹/₄ mile W of Wainstalls) OS042285
☎ (01422) 244841
7-11 (12-3, 6-11 summer); 12-3, 7 (6 summer)-11 Sat; 12-3, 7 (6 summer)-10.30 Sun
Castle Eden Ale; Taylor Golden Best, Best Bitter, Landlord Ⓗ
Comfortable, traditional country inn, set in a picturesque wooded valley. The interior is enhanced with oak panelling which came from a demolished Victorian castle. Popular with walkers. Lunches served Sat, sandwiches Sun. Q ❀ ♣ P

WAKEFIELD

HENRY BOON'S
130 Westgate (near station)
☎ (01924) 378126
11-11; 12-10.30 Sun
Clark's Bitter, Festival, Black Cap; Taylor Landlord; Tetley Bitter Ⓗ

The classic Leeds pub, Whitelocks,. has avoided havings its historic interior ripped out and rebuilt as a theme pub. There aren't many city pubs like this left.

Two-roomed pub, one room used mostly for live bands; the other, with bare floorboards and open fires, for games and drinking. Bar food weekday lunch. Clark's Brewery is in the yard behind the pub. 🚶 🏵 ◖ ≠ (Westgate) ♣

NAVIGATION
Broad Cut Road, Calder Grove (A636 3 miles from centre)
☎ (01924) 274361
12-11; 12-10.30 Sun
Taylor Landlord; Tetley Dark Mild or **Bitter** Ⓗ
Two-bar pub. The children's room has an indoor play area; the top bar is for over 18s only. Large garden looking out on to the canal. Pub food all week except Sun eve. 🚶 Q 🐸 🏵 ◖ ▮ P

REDOUBT ☆
28 Horbury Road (Westgate jct)
☎ (01924) 377485
11-11; 12-4, 7-10.30 Sun
Taylor Landlord; Tetley Mild, Bitter Ⓗ
Four-roomed Tetley Heritage pub with strong RL connections. Traditional pub games are played in this outstanding, unspoilt, cosy pub. 🏵 ♿ ≠ ♣ P

TALBOT & FALCON
56 Northgate (near bus station)
☎ (01924) 201693
11-11; 12-10.30 Sun
Marston's Pedigree; Taylor Landlord; Theakston Old Peculier; Tetley Bitter; guest beers Ⓗ
Long, narrow, Tetley Festival Ale House with bare floorboards and a single central bar serving five guest beers. Local CAMRA *Pub of the Year* 1996 and '97, it hosts four mini beer festivals a year. Occasional cider. ◖ ⌂

WAGON
45 Westgate End (near station)
☎ (01924) 372478
12-11; 12-10.30 Sun
Black Sheep Best Bitter; Hopback Summer Lightning; Tetley Bitter; guest beers Ⓗ
Popular, friendly local on the Westgate run, attracting a varied clientele. Reasonable prices. Outside benches for summer drinking. 🏵 ≠ (Westgate) ♣ P

WAKEFIELD LABOUR CLUB
18 Vicarage Street (near market)
☎ (01924) 215628
11-3 (not Mon-Thu), 7-11; 12-3, 7-10.30 Sun
Barnsley Bitter; guest beers Ⓗ
Welcoming club that offers beers from small breweries at reasonable prices, plus a large range of Belgian beers and occasional ciders. CAMRA's Yorkshire *Club of the Year* and national Club runner-up.
Q 🏵 ≠ (Westgate/Kirkgate) ♣ ⌂ P

WATERLOO INN
101 Westgate End
☎ (01924) 376717
11-11; 12-10.30 Sun
Hopback Summer Lightning; Tetley Bitter; guest beers Ⓗ
Open-plan main room with much bric-à-brac, plus a games room. It draws a wide cross-section of clientele during the week and good local support at weekends. Hosts four beer festivals a year. Weekday lunches.
🏵 ◖ ≠ (Westgate) ♣ P

PLOUGH
45 Warmfield Lane (400 yds from A655)
☎ (01924) 892007
12-2, 5 (6 Sat)-11; 12-2, 7-10.30 Sun
John Smith's Bitter; Theakston Best Bitter, XB, Old Peculier; guest beers (summer) Ⓗ
Unspoilt, 18th-century inn overlooking the lower Calder Valley, with low beamed ceilings and a small corner bar. Popular for its good value bar meals.
Q 🏵 🛏 ◖ ▮ P

WETHERBY

SWAN & TALBOT
34 North St ☎ (01937) 582040
11-3, 5.30 (6 Sat)-11; 12-3, 7-10.30 Sun
Draught Bass; Tetley Bitter; John Smith's Bitter; Worthington Bitter Ⓗ
Former coaching inn, recently refurbished to form a U-shaped bar with a comfortable, friendly atmosphere. Q 🏵 🛏 ◖ ▮ P

WINTERSETT

ANGLER'S RETREAT
Ferry Top Lane (between villages of Crofton and Ryhill)
OS382157 ☎ (01924) 862370
12-3, 7-11; 12-3, 7-10.30 Sun
Barnsley Bitter; Tetley Bitter; Theakston Best Bitter, XB; guest beer Ⓗ
Cosy, quiet, rural pub, handy for anglers and bird watchers visiting Wintersett Reservoir and Heronry. Information about the heronry is available in the pub. Biker friendly.
🚶 Q 🏵 ♿ ♣ P

INDEPENDENT BREWERIES

Black Horse:
Halifax

Clark's:
Wakefield

Fernandes:
Wakefield

Goose Eye
Keighley

Huddersfield:
Huddersfield

Kitchen:
Huddersfield

Linfit:
Huddersfield

Rat & Ratchet:
Huddersfield

Riverhead:
Huddersfield

Ryburn:
Halifax

Steam Packet:
Knottingley

Taylor:
Keighley

Tigertops:
Wakefield

Tomlinson's:
Pontefract

Worth:
Keighley

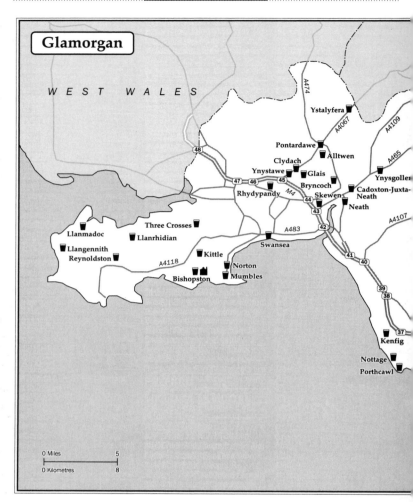

Authority areas covered: Bridgend UA, Caerphilly UA, Cardiff UA, Merthyr Tydfil UA, Neath & Port Talbot UA, Rhondda, Cynon, Taf UA, Swansea UA, Vale of Glamorgan UA

ABERAMAN

TEMPLE BAR
Cardiff Road ☎ (01685) 876137
12-4, 7-11; 12-4, 7-10.30 Sun
Beer range varies Ⓗ
Friendly, single bar, where time seems to have stopped; it has been in the same family for over 100 years. 🏵 ♣ P

ABERCYNON

ROYAL OAK
Incline Top (off A4059)
OS089956 ☎ (01443) 742229
12-2.30, 4.30-11; 12-11 Sat;
12-10.30 Sun
Hancock's HB; guest beer Ⓗ
Welcoming, pleasantly furbished village local at the top of the locks of the former

Glamorganshire canal. A bit difficult to find, but worth the effort.
🏵 ◖ ▶ ⊞ ♣ P

ABERTHIN

HARE & HOUNDS
On A4222 ☎ (01446) 774892
11.30-11; 12-10.30 Sun
Draught Bass Ⓖ**; Hancock's HB** Ⓗ**; Worthington Bitter** Ⓖ
An excellent example of a village local. A pub where we can gladly say the only change in years has been the extension to the family room. A good garden for children. Limited parking. 🚶Q ⛵ 🏵 ▲ P

ALLTWEN

BUTCHERS ARMS
Alltwen Hill ☎ (01792) 863100

12-3, 6.30-11; 12-3, 6.30-10.30 Sun
Courage Directors; Everards Old Original; John Smith's Bitter Wadworth 6X; guest beer Ⓗ
Hillside local where the atmosphere is ideal for talking, drinking and eating (meals are generous). No food Sun eve. 🚶 🏵 ◖ ▶ P

BEDWELLTY

NEW INN
Near church ☎ (01443) 831625
12-3.30, 7-11; 12-3 (shut eve) Sun
Buckley's Rev James; Hancock's HB; Morland Old Speckled Hen; guest beer Ⓗ
Welcoming, pleasantly furnished free house with a plush drinking area and restaurant (eve meals Tue-Sat). A rare outlet for Hoegaarden. 🚶 🏵 ◖ ▶ P

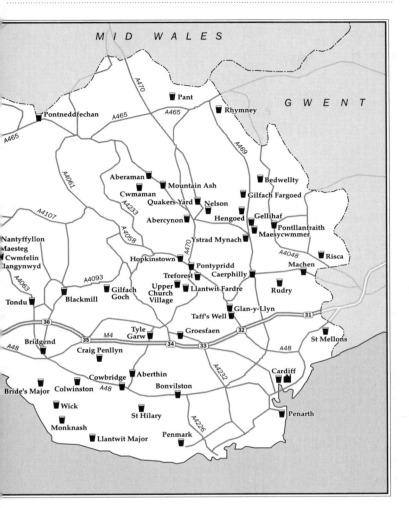

BISHOPSTON

JOINERS ARMS
50 Bishopston Road
☎ (01792) 232658
11-11; 12-10.30 Sun
Courage Best Bitter; Felinfoel Double Dragon; John Smith's Bitter; Swansea Bishops Wood Bitter, Three Cliffs Gold; guest beers Ⓗ
Comfortable village local, a free house with with good value food and a wide variety of ales. Home of Swansea Brewery, it stages occasional beer festivals.
🏚 Q 🕸 🅑 🍺 ♣ P

BLACKMILL

OGMORE JUNCTION HOTEL
On A4061 ☎ (01656) 840371
11.30-11; 12-10.30 Sun
Draught Bass; Worthington Bitter; guest beers Ⓗ

Attractive, old, friendly, well-run pub, stocking an exceptional variety of beer for the area. No food Sun eve. Q 🕸 🅑 🍺 ♣ P

BONVILSTON

RED LION
On A48 ☎ (01446) 781208
11.30-3, 5-11; 11-11 Sat; 12-3, 7-10.30 Sun
Brains Dark, Bitter, SA Ⓗ
Award-winning, roadside village pub. Reputation for good food. Eve meals Tue-Sat. 🕸 🅑 ♣ P

BRIDGEND

COACH
37 Cowbridge Road
☎ (01656) 649321
11-11; 12-10.30 Sun
Draught Bass; Worthington Bitter Ⓗ
Friendly, quiet pub near the college. No food Sun.
🏚 Q 🕸 🅑 🍺 ♿ ⇌

FAMOUS PENYBONT INN
Derwen Road ☎ (01656) 652266
11.30-11; 12-10.30 Sun
Brains SA; Marston's Pedigree; Wadworth 6X; Worthington Bitter; guest beers Ⓗ
Popular, town-centre pub with a cosy, friendly atmosphere and much railway memorabilia. Reasonably priced meals (not served Sun eve) and up to six cask-conditioned beers. Handy for the railway and bus stations and the shops. Q 🅑 🍺 ♿ ⇌

FIVE BELLS INN
Ewenny Road
(A4063/B4265/A4061 jct)
☎ (01656) 664941
11.30-4, 6-11; 11.30-11 Wed-Sat; 12-10.30 Sun
Draught Bass; Worthington Bitter Ⓗ
Cosy pub on a busy junction: a spacious comfortable bar with an adjoining games area, plus a

373

quiet lounge on an upper level. No food Sun. ◖ ⊕ & ≉ P

HAYWAIN
Coychurch Road, Brackla
☎ (01656) 669945
11.30-11; 12-10.30 Sun
Wadworth 6X; Worthington Bitter; guest beer Ⓗ
Large, busy estate pub, popular for lunches (no food Sun eve). Up to three guest beers. ❀ ◖ ▶ & P

PRINCESS OF WALES
17 Market St ☎ (01656) 654107
11-11; 12-10.30 Sun
John Smith's Bitter; Theakston XB; Worthington Bitter Ⓗ
Very basic pub near the bus station where beer prices are notably low for the area. & ≉

RED DRAGON
Litchard Hill (A4061)
☎ (01656) 654753
11-11; 12-10.30 Sun
Courage Best Bitter, Directors; guest beer Ⓗ
Large, popular pub on the outskirts of Bridgend near the M4.
❀ ◖ ⊕ ♣ P

BRYNCOCH

DYFFRYN ARMS
Neath Road ☎ (01639) 636184
12-3, 7-11; 12-3, 7-10.30 Sun
Boddingtons Bitter; Wadworth 6X; Worthington Bitter Ⓗ
The Dyffryn is a very popular local, it has a large comfortable lounge and restaurant. On display are over 200 water jugs and a collection of local pictures. Quiz Sun eve; children's playground.
❀ ◖ P

CADOXTON JUXTA NEATH

GREEN DRAGON
Church Road ☎ (01639) 635782
11-11; 12-4, 7-10.30 Sun
Boddingtons Bitter; Greene King Abbot; Worthington Bitter; guest beer Ⓗ
Homely pub with a popular locals' bar. ◖ ♣ P

CAERPHILLY

COURTHOUSE
Cardiff Road ☎ (01222) 888120
11-11; 12-10.30 Sun
Courage Best Bitter; Greene King Abbot; Wye Valley Classic; guest beer Ⓗ
Traditional, 14th-century longhouse with some original features. The conservatory boasts panoramic views over the moat to the castle, the second largest in the UK. Q ❀ ◖ ▶ ≉

GREEN LADY
Pontygwyndy Road
☎ (01222) 851510

11-11; 12-3, 7-10.30 Sun
Banks's Bitter; Cameron Strongarm Ⓗ
Newly-built, traditionally furnished pub with a good atmosphere and a warm welcome. Good facilities for visitors with disabilities. No eve meals Fri or Sun. ◖ ▶ & P ✕ ☐

CARDIFF

BLACK LION
Cardiff Road, Llandaff
(A4119/High St jct)
☎ (01222) 567312
11-11; 12-3, 7-10.30 Sun
Brains Dark, Bitter, SA; guest beer Ⓗ
Quiet, friendly, traditional Brains house, a regular entry in this *Guide*, near Llandaff Cathedral. A Brains Cellarmanship award winner. Q ◖ ⊕ ≉ (Fairwater) ♣

BUTCHERS ARMS
29 Llandaff Road, Canton
(B4267) ☎ (01222) 227927
11-11; 12-3, 7-10.30 Sun
Brains Dark, Bitter, SA Ⓗ
Smallish local on a street corner, in the vicinity of Chapter Arts Centre, comprising a public bar plus a lounge. Well behaved children welcome. ⊕ ♣

CITY ARMS
Quay Street (off High St, near Millennium Stadium entrance)
☎ (01222) 225258
11-11; 12-10.30 Sun
Brains Dark, Bitter, SA Ⓗ
Popular, traditional pub attracting all ages. Recently and sympathetically refurbished – sit on one of the old pews. Late licence Fri and Sat. ⊕ & ≉ (Central)

CONWAY
Conway Road, Pontcanna (off A4119) ☎ (01222) 232797
12-11; 12-10.30 Sun
Boddingtons Bitter; Flowers IPA, Original; Wadworth 6X; guest beers Ⓗ
Large corner pub whose bar and lounge appeal to a wide clientele. No meals Sun. Q ❀ ◖ ⊕

FFYNON WEN
Thornhill Road, Llanishen (A469)
☎ (01222) 522535
11.30-11; 12-10.30 Sun
Banks's Bitter; Camerons Strongarm; Marston's Pedigree Ⓗ
Modern pub built around what was once a farmhouse. A bar, lounge and restaurant make up three distinct areas.
❀ ◖ ▶ & P ☐

FOX & HOUNDS
Old Church Road, Whitchurch
☎ (01222) 693377
12 (11 Sat)-11; 12-10.30 Sun
Brains Dark, Bitter, SA; guest beer Ⓗ

Quiet, friendly local, near Whitchurch village, with a skittle alley. Q ❀ ⊕ ≉ (Llandaff) ♣ P

FULL MOON (OFF-LICENCE)
88 Ty'n y Parc Road, Rhiwbina (near Monico Cinema)
☎ (01222) 623303
12-9.15; 5-9 Sun
Beer range varies Ⓖ
Enterprising off-licence, specialising in interesting cask ales, invariably from independents, and often new breweries. Stocks a wide range of bottle-conditioned and other bottled beers both British and imported. Occasional cider and perry.
& ≉ (Rhiwbina) ▭

HOGSHEAD AT THE OWAIN GLYNDWR
St Johns Square
☎ (01222) 221980
11-11; 12-10.30 Sun
Beer range varies Ⓗ
Typical Hogshead theme pub: a split-level drinking area with wheelchair access to the lower level. Good variety of guest beers. Occasional live music Tue/Wed; hear the bellringing Thu and Sun eves.
❀ ◖ ▶ & ≉ (Central) ▭

ROATH COTTAGE
Rose Street (off City Rd via Cyfarthfa St) ☎ (01222) 481128
11-11; 12-10.30 Sun
Brains Dark, Bitter, SA Ⓗ
Refurbished, but unspoilt, back-street pub with a friendly atmosphere. ⊕ ♣

ROYAL OAK
Merthyr Road, Whitchurch
☎ (01222) 695061
11-11; 12-10.30 Sun
Hancock's HB Ⓗ
Popular local for young and old, situated on the main road through Whitchurch village; recently renovated. Q ❀ ⊕

THREE ARCHES
Heathwood Road, Llanishen
☎ (01222) 753831
11-11; 12-10.30 Sun
Brains Dark, Bitter, SA; Buckley's Rev James Ⓗ
One of Brains's largest pubs with three bars catering to a varied clientele. Warm, friendly and comfortable, it has a good skittle alley, a wide-screen TV for sport and darts, cards and pool in the public bar. No food Sun eve.
Q ◖ ▶ ⊕ & ≉ (Heath High/Low Levels) P

THREE HORSE SHOES
Merthyr Road, Gabalfa (400 yds N of Gabalfa interchange, A48/A470 jct) ☎ (01222) 625703
11-11; 12-10.30 Sun
Brains Dark, Bitter, SA Ⓗ

Modern replacement of the original pub, demolished by a road improvement. A friendly welcome in the bar and lounge. No food Sat. Q ☸ ◖ ⊞ ♣ P

VULCAN
10 Adam Street (A4160, near prison) ☎ (01222) 461580
11-8 (11 Fri, 6 Sat, may vary); 12-5 Sun
Brains Dark, Bitter Ⓗ
Traditional, down-to-earth pub, just outside the city centre. Good value lunches in the lounge Mon-Sat. A great example of a real pub, with a classic tiled frontage. Q ◖ ⊞ ⇌ (Queen St) ♣

WHITE HART
James Street, Cardiff Bay (A4119) ☎ (01222) 472561
11-11; 12-5 Sun
Brains Dark, Bitter Ⓗ
Mainly locals' pub in the vicinity of Cardiff Bay redevelopment area and the Techniquest Science Exploratory Centre. Bar meals are not advertised but are available on request.☸ ⇌ (Bay) ♣

Try also: Horse & Groom, Womanby St (Welsh Brewers)

CLYDACH

NEW INN
Lone Road (off High St, take Vadre Road, past park) ☎ (01792) 842839
11-4, 6-11; 11-11 Fri & Sat; 12-3, 7-10.30 Sun
Fuller's London Pride; Greene King Abbot; Morland Old Speckled Hen; Taylor Landlord; Worthington Dark Ⓗ
Friendly local: three bars, plus a pool room. Popular with walkers; children's certificate; very good food. ♨ ⌂ ☸ ◖ ▶ ⊞ ⅙ ♣ P

COLWINSTON

SYCAMORE TREE
Off A48 ☎ (01656) 652827
12-3 (not Mon or Tue winter), 6 (6.30 winter)-11; 12-3, 7-10.30 Sun
Draught Bass; Hancock's HB; guest beer (occasional) Ⓗ
This marvellous pub has been a regular in this *Guide* and the *Good Pub Food Guide* for some years now, deservedly so. No-smoking dining area; children welcome if eating. No meals Mon, or Tue lunch.
♨ Q ☸ ◖ ▶ ⊞ Ⓐ ♣ P

COWBRIDGE

EDMONDES ARMS
High Street ☎ (01446) 773192
3 (12 Sat)-11; 12-10.30 Sun
Hancock's HB Ⓗ
Classic, street-corner boozer, the last working-class pub in town. A good local following includes pool

teams, etc. It can get noisy and smoky eves, just like a proper pub. ♨ ⊞ ♣

CRAIG PENLLYN

BARLEY MOW
1½ miles N of A48 OS978773 ☎ (01446) 772558
12-3 (not Mon), 6-11; 12-3, 7-10.30 Sun
Hancock's HB; guest beer Ⓗ
Friendly, welcoming pub popular with locals and visitors for its good beer and food. The car park is across the road. Any background music tends to be drowned out by conversation and laughter. ♨ ☸ ◖ ▶ ⊞ ♣ P

CWMAMAN

FALCON INN
1 Incline Row (off B4275) OS008998 ☎ (01685) 873758
11-11; 12-10.30 Sun
Beer range varies Ⓗ
Small, friendly pub offering at least three beers at any one time. Currently being extended, it is hard to find, but well worth the effort. ☸ ◖ ▶ P

GELLIHAF

COAL HOLE
Bryn Road ☎ (01443) 830280
12-3, 6.30-11; 12-4, 7-10.30 Sun
Hancock's HB; guest beer Ⓗ
Popular, one-bar pub with a dining area, offering good value food (no eve meals Sun). Large play area outside for children.
☸ ⌂ ◖ ▶ P

GILFACH FARGOED

CAPEL
Park Place ☎ (01443) 830272
12-4 (5 Wed), 7-11; 12-11 Fri & Sat; 12-10.30 Sun
Brains SA; Courage Best Bitter; John Smith's; guest beer Ⓗ
Large, friendly traditional valleys pub with lots of original features. Lunches served Sat and Sun.
⌂ ◖ ▶ ⊞ ⅙ ⇌ ✄

GILFACH GOCH

GRIFFIN INN
Hendreforgan (½ mile off A4093) OS988875 ☎ (01443) 672247
7 (12 Sat)-11; 12-3, 7-10.30 Sun
Brains SA; guest beer (summer) Ⓗ
Traditional local nestled at the bottom of the valley. Bric-à-brac and hunting trophies abound.
☸ ⊞ ♣ P

GLAIS

OLD GLAIS INN
625 Birchgrove Road (400 yds from A4067) ☎ (01792) 843316
12-3, 6-11; 12-3, 7-11 Sun

John Smith's Bitter; Watkin Bitter; Wells Bombardier; Worthington Bitter; guest beers Ⓗ
Attractive pub with a bar, lounge and restaurant; pool and darts. Families welcome. Occasional live music (juke box in lounge and bar).
☸ ◖ ▶ ⊞ ⅙ ♣ P

GLAN-Y-LLYN

FAGIN'S ALE & CHOP HOUSE
Cardiff Road (1 mile N of Taffs Well station) ☎ (01222) 811800
12-11; 12-10.30 Sun
Brains SA; Caledonian Deuchars IPA, 80/-; Courage Directors; Hancock's HB; Morland Old Speckled Hen Ⓗ**; guest beers** Ⓖ
Pub and restaurant converted from an old terraced cottage, offering a terrific range of ales from independents (up to eight guests and occasional beer festivals). Regional CAMRA *Pub of the Year* 1994. Occasional cider. Eve meals Tue-Sat. ☸ ◖ ▶

GROESFAEN

DYNEVOR ARMS
Llantrisant Road (A4119) ☎ (01222) 890530
11-11; 12-3, 7-10.30 Sun
Draught Bass; Hancock's HB; guest beer Ⓗ
Large, open-plan, recently refurbished roadside pub with a dining area. Guest beer changes weekly. Eve meals Tue-Sat.☸ ◖ ▶ ⌂ P

HENGOED

JUNCTION
9 Kings Hill (near station) ☎ (01443) 812192
12-4 (4.30 Fri & Sat), 7-11; 12-3, 7-10.30 Sun
Hancock's HB; Worthington Bitter; guest beer (occasional) Ⓗ
Immaculately appointed local featuring railway memorabilia, on the western side of the Hengoed viaduct. ◖ ▶ ⇌ ♣

HOPKINSTOWN

HOLLYBUSH
Ty Mawr Road (main Pontypridd-Rhondda Rd) ☎ (01443) 402325
11-11; 12-10.30 Sun
Hancock's HB; Worthington Bitter; guest beer Ⓗ
Popular roadside inn with a sporting bar, complemented by a comfortable lounge where meals are served (not Sun eve). The guest beer is always keenly priced. CAMRA regional *Pub of the Year* 1997. ◖ ▶ ⊞ ⅙ ♣ P ⊟

KENFIG

PRINCE OF WALES
Maudlam OS804818 ☎ (01656) 740356

11.30-4, 6-11; 12-10.30 (may vary) Sun
Draught Bass G; **Worthington Bitter** H G; **guest beer** (occasional) G
Historic pub with exposed stone walls and large open fireplace; the former town hall of the lost city of Kenfig. Renowned for its Bass on gravity. The garden adjoins a nature reserve. ⚒ Q ❀ P

KITTLE

BEAUFORT ARMS
18 Pennard Rd ☎ (01792) 234521
11.30-11; 12-10.30 Sun
Brains SA; Buckley's Best Bitter, Rev James, seasonal beers H
Village pub with an adjoining restaurant and large outside play area; the centre of the local community. Q ❀ ◑ ▶ ⊞ ♣ P ⊬

LLANGENNITH

KINGS HEAD
☎ (01792) 386212
11-11; 12-10.30 Sun
Buckley's Best Bitter; guest beer (weekends/summer) H
Intimate, stone-walled pub on the village green. Good view of Rhossili Bay, which is within walking distance (for the energetic). Games room. Food served all day. Q ❀ ◑ ▶ ⊞ ♠ ♣ P

LLANGYNWYD

OLD HOUSE (YR HEN DY)
West of A4063 OS858889
☎ (01656) 733310
11-11; 12-10.30 Sun
Flowers IPA, Original; guest beers H
One of Wales' oldest pubs (1147), a thatched house full of atmosphere and extremely popular, with a renowned restaurant (booking advised eves and Sun). Traditional Mari Lwyd is performed at New Year. It was the favoured local of Wil Hopcyn who courted the Maid of Cefn Ydfa. ⚒ Q ⛵ ❀ ◑ ▶ ♠ P

LLANMADOC

BRITANNIA INN
☎ (01792) 386624
11.30-3.30 (not Tue-Wed winter); 7-11 (11-11 summer); 12-10.30 Sun
Marston's Pedigree H
17th-century pub, home to a small menagerie. Good views to the coast from the rear garden, in a good walking area. More beers are available in summer. ⚒ Q ⛵ ⇥ ◑ ▶ ⊞ ♠ ♣ P ⊬

LLANRHIDIAN

GREYHOUND INN
Oldwalls
☎ (01792) 391027
11-11; 12-10.30 Sun

Draught Bass; Boddingtons Bitter; Marston's Pedigree; guest beers H
Excellent free house at the heart of Gower, stocking up to three guest ales. Renowned for its cuisine, especially local fish. The games room doubles for families. ⚒ Q ⛵ ⇥ ❀ ◑ ▶ ⊞ ♠ P

LLANTWIT FARDRE

BUSH INN
Main Road ☎ (01443) 203958
4 (12 Sat)-11; 12-4, 6.30-10.30 Sun
Hancock's HB; guest beer H
Small, welcoming village local. Limited parking. ❀ ♣ P

LLANTWIT MAJOR

LLANTWIT MAJOR SOCIAL CLUB
The Hayes, Colhugh Street (beach road) ☎ (01446) 792266
11.30-3.30 (not Wed), 6.30-11; 12-2, 7-10.30 Sun
Hancock's HB; Worthington Bitter; guest beer H
Imposing stone-built, three-storey building, set in its own grounds. Members range from teens to nineties. Snooker and darts room, pool room, bar and function room (functions nearly every night). Take this *Guide* to be signed in. Q ⛵ ♠ ♣ P

MACHEN

WHITE HART INN
Nant y Ceisiad (100 yds N of A468 under railway bridge) OS203892 ☎ (01633) 441005
11.30-4, 6.30-11; 11-11 Sat & summer; 12-10.30 Sun
Hancock's HB; guest beers H
Rambling pub with extensive wood panelling, some salvaged from a luxury liner. Enterprising range of beers (three guests); one or two mini beer festivals held yearly. Good range of food. ⚒ Q ❀ ⇥ ◑ ▶ P

MAESTEG

SAWYER'S ARMS
4 Commercial Street
☎ (01656) 734500
11-11; 12-3, 7-10.30 Sun
Brains Bitter, SA H
An oasis: a popular traditional public bar and a smart lounge offering quizzes and live music at times. No food Sun. ◑ ♿ ⇌

MAESYCWMMER

MAESYCWMMER INN
Main Road ☎ (01443) 814385
11-11; 12-3, 7-10.30 Sun
Hancock's HB; Wadworth 6X H
Small bar and a comfortable lounge in a pub by the eastern side of the Hengoed viaduct. ❀ ⊞ ⇌ (Hengoed) ♣ P

MONKNASH

PLOUGH & HARROW
Off B4265, between Llantwit Major and Wick OS920706
☎ (01656) 890209
12-11; 12-10.30 Sun
Draught Bass; Hancock's HB; Shepherd Neame Spitfire; Worthington Bitter H; **guest beers** G
In a 12th-century monastic grange, only a short walk from the coast, this popular local has two distinct bars. A pub of great character; local CAMRA *Pub of the Year* for the past three years. Book for eve meals. ⚒ ❀ ◑ ▶ ⊞ ♣ ⌣

MOUNTAIN ASH

JEFFREYS ARMS
Jeffrey St ☎ (01443) 472976
7 (12 Fri & Sat)-11; 12-10.30 Sun
Worthington Bitter; guest beer H
Large village pub with a basic bar and a plush lounge, a good atmosphere and interesting guest ales. ⊞ P

MUMBLES

PARK INN
23 Park Street ☎ (01792) 367712
12-3 (not Mon), 5.30-11; 12-11 Sat; 12-10.30 Sun
Marston's Pedigree; Ruddles County; Worthington Bitter; guest beers H
Popular, 19th-century local in a back street, away from the busy 'Mumbles Mile'. A free house, offering a wide range of guest beers and home of MADRAS (Mumbles and District Real Ale Society). Mini beer festival Nov. Cider in summer. TV switched on only for sport. ⚒ Q ♣ ⌣

VICTORIA INN
21 Westbourne Place
☎ (01792) 365111
11.30-11; 12-10.30 Sun
Draught Bass; Worthington Dark, Bitter H
Refurbished old back-street local featuring lots of wood and an interesting well. Local CAMRA award-winner. ♣

VINCENT'S
580 Mumbles Road (seafront)
☎ (01792) 368308
3 (11.30 Sat)-11; 1-4, 7-10.30 Sun
Draught Bass G; **Hancock's HB; Worthington Bitter; guest beer** (occasional) H
Seafront pub with a Spanish theme and an extensive Tapas menu until 8. Popular with students and business people. ◑ ▶

NANTYFFYLLON

GENERAL PICTON
3 Picton Place ☎ (01656) 732474

11-11; 12-11.30 (supper licence) Sun

Brains Bitter; John Smith's Bitter; guest beer (occasional) H
A delightful surprise in an area where possible *Guide* qualifiers are sparse. Very highly regarded over a wide area for its catering, good company and a courtesy bus to get you home after. Children welcome in skittle alley and restaurant. ❀ ◑ ▶ ⊟ & ♣ P ⅟

NEATH

HIGHLANDER
2 Lewis Road ☎ (01639) 633586
12-2.30, 6-11; 12-11 Sat; 12-3, 7-10.30 Sun
Draught Bass; Worthington Bitter; guest beers H
Always two ever-changing guest beers at this very popular local, catering for a wide age range. One large, split-level room downstairs; the restaurant upstairs enjoys a well-deserved reputation for good value food (no meals Sun eve). ◑ ▶ ⇌

STAR INN
83 Penydre ☎ (01639) 637745
12.30-5, 6-11; 12.30-11 Fri & Sat; 12-2.30, 7-10.30 Sun
Draught Bass; Hancock's HB; Hook Norton Best Bitter; guest beer H
Refurbished pub and restaurant close to Neath RFC and busy on match days. The beer engines date from the 1950s. No food Sun. ❀ ◑ ⇌ P

NELSON

DYNEVOR ARMS
Commercial Street, The Square
☎ (01443) 450295
11-11; 12-10.30 Sun
Brains Bitter; Hancock's HB; Worthington Bitter H
Former brewpub (and mortuary), over 200 years old, with a busy public bar. Live music Sat eve.
⊟ ♣ P

NORTON

BEAUFORT ARMS
1 Castle Road (turn by Norton House Hotel, off Mumbles Road)
☎ (01792) 407001
11.30-11; 12-10.30 Sun
Draught Bass; Worthington Dark, Bitter H
Popular village local with a cosy lounge and a bar. It has a strong involvement in the local annual Mumbles raft race. Quiz night Tue. Snacks available.
🚌 Q ❀ ⊟ ♣

NOTTAGE

FARMER'S ARMS
Lougher Row ☎ (01656) 784595
11.30-11; 12-10.30 Sun

Draught Bass; Worthington Bitter; guest beers H
Rambling village pub by the green. Two guest beers – one changes daily. 🚌 ❀ ◑ ▶ ⊟ & ♣ P

ROSE & CROWN
Heol-y-Capel ☎ (01656) 784850
11.30-11; 12-10.30 Sun
Courage Directors; Ruddles Best Bitter; guest beers H
A smart old pub with a rustic ambience, Dickensian in the best sense of the word, and pleasantly modernised. The beer range may vary within the Scottish Courage list. ❀ 🚌 ◑ ▶ 🅰 P

SEAGULL
Sandpiper Road (shopping precinct off West Park Drive)
☎ (01656) 785420
11.30-11; 12-5, 7-10.30 Sun
Brains SA; Buckley's Best Bitter, Rev James H
Pleasant estate pub, popular for meals, a rare Buckley's outlet for this area. No food Sun eve.
Q ❀ ◑ ▶ & P

SWAN
West Road ☎ (01656) 782568
11.30-11; 12-10.30 Sun
Draught Bass; Courage Best Bitter, Directors; John Smith's Bitter; guest beer H
A very popular pub frequented especially by locals and rugby notables; interesting collection of rugby memorabilia. No food Sun.
❀ ◑ 🅰 P

PANT

PANT CAD IFOR
By mountain railway
☎ (01685) 723688
11-11; 11-10.30 Sun
Draught Bass; Hancock's HB Worthington Bitter; guest beers H
Bustling, welcoming pub with a good range of beers. Quiz Tue eve. No food Sun eve. 🚌 ❀ ◑ ♣ P

PENARTH

GOLDEN LION
69 Glebe Street (N of A4160)
☎ (01222) 701574
12.30-11; 12-10.30 Sun
Cains Bitter; Hancock's HB H
Welcoming, comfortable, characterful local. ◑ ▶ ⊟ ⇌ (Dingle Rd)

PILOT
67 Queens Road (N of A4160)
☎ (01222) 702340
12-11; 12-10.30 Sun
Brains Dark, Bitter, SA H
Locals' pub with a bar and lounge overlooking Cardiff Bay. Weekday lunches. 🚌 ❀ ◑ ⊟ ⇌ (Dingle Rd)

ROYAL HOTEL
1 Queens Road (N of A4160)
☎ (01222) 708048
11-11; 12-10.30 Sun

Bullmastiff Cardiff Dark, Gold Brew, Son of a Bitch; Hancock's HB; guest beers H
Lively, cliff-top local, sadly the only regular outlet for Bullmastiff ales. A welcome change from the Brains/Welsh Brewers stranglehold in the area. Excellent pricing policy. ❀ 🚫 ⊟ ⇌ (Dingle Rd) ♣

PENMARK

SIX BELLS
☎ (01446) 710229
12-11; 12-10.30 Sun
Hancock's HB H
The contrasting bar and lounge/restaurant offer something for everyone. Close to Cardiff Airport. No eve meals Sun. Q ❀ ◑ ▶ & 🅰 ♣ P

PONTARDAWE

PONTARDAWE INN
Herbert St ☎ (01792) 830791
12-11; 12-10.30 Sun
Buckley's Best Bitter, Rev James; Camerons Strongarm; guest beer H
This 16th-century coaching house, locally known as the Gwachel is home to Pontardawe International Music Festival.
❀ ◑ ▶ & ♣ P

Try also: Dillwyn Arms, The Cross (guest beers)

PONTLLANFRAITH

CROWN
The Bryn ☎ (01495) 223404
12-3, 5-11; 12-11 Fri & Sat; 12-3, 7-10.30 Sun
Courage Best Bitter; John Smith's Bitter; Morland Old Speckled Hen; guest beer H
Two-roomed pub with a basic public bar and a spacious lounge; a haven for golfers and locals alike. Children's play equipment in garden. ❀ ◑ ▶ ⊟ ♣ P ⅟

PONTNEDDFECHAN

ANGEL INN
Pontneathvaughan Road
☎ (01639) 722013
11.30-4, 6.30-11 (11.30-11 summer) 12-3, 7-10.30 Sun
Draught Bass; Boddingtons Bitter; Wadworth 6X H
Attractive 16th-century farmhouse, recently renovated, at the gateway to the South Wales waterfall country on River Neath. Ideal for walkers, climbers, cavers; muddy boots welcome in the hikers bar. Children's certificate. Reasonably priced meals.
❀ ◑ ▶ & 🅰 P

PONTYPRIDD

LLANOVER ARMS
Bridge Street ☎ (01443) 403215

11-11; 12-3.30, 7-10.30 Sun
Brains Dark, Bitter, SA; Worthington Bitter; guest beer Ⓗ
Bustling town pub, attracting a diverse group of drinkers to three drinking areas. Restaurant at the rear. ❀ ⊟ ⇌ ♣ P

PORTHCAWL

Royal Oak
1 South Road ☎ (01656) 782684
11.30-11; 12-10.30 Sun
Draught Bass; Worthington Bitter; guest beer (occasional) Ⓗ
Comfortable, characterful pub on the fringe of the shopping area. No meals Sun eve.
Q ❀ ◖ ◗ ♿ ▲ P

QUAKERS YARD

Glantaff Inn
Cardiff Road ☎ (01443) 410822
12-4, 7-11; 12-4, 7-10.30 Sun
Brains SA; Courage Best Bitter, Directors; John Smith's Bitter; guest beer Ⓗ
Comfortable inn boasting a large collection of water jugs and a warm friendly atmosphere. Good food in the upstairs restaurant (no eve meals Sun). Q ❀ ◖ ◗ P

REYNOLDSTON

King Arthur Hotel
Higher Green ☎ (01792) 391099
11-11; 12-10.30 Sun
Draught Bass; Brains SA; Worthington Bitter; guest beer (summer) Ⓗ
Large village pub and restaurant; the bar features open wood fires and there is a games room where children are welcome. Various entertainments are staged throughout the year.
♛ Q ♞ ❀ ⊨ ◖ ◗ ⊟ ▲ ♣ P

RHYDYPANDY

Masons Arms
Rhydypandy Road (follow signs for Morriston Hospital nearby)
☎ (01792) 842535
12-11; 12-10.30 Sun
Courage Best Bitter; Marston's Pedigree; Theakston XB; guest beers Ⓗ
Two-roomed, 17th-century inn with a friendly atmosphere, on a country lane. ♛ ❀ ⊟ ♣ P

RHYMNEY

Farmers Arms
Brewery Row ☎ (01685) 840257
12-11; 12-3, 7-10.30 Sun
Boddingtons Bitter; Brains Bitter; Morland Old Speckled Hen; guest beer Ⓗ
Friendly, spacious, comfortable pub and restaurant; traditionally furnished. Bric-à-brac includes Rhymney Brewery memorabilia. No eve meals Sun. ◖ ◗ ♣ ⇌

RISCA

Railway Tavern
Danygraig Rd ☎ (01633) 612770
11-4.30, 7-11; 11-11 Fri & Sat; 12-3, 7-10.30 Sun
Draught Bass; Hancock's HB Ⓗ
Small, comfortable, two-roomed pub. Friendly atmosphere. ◖ P

RUDRY

Maenllwyd Inn
☎ (01222) 888505
11-11; 12-10.30 Sun
Courage Best Bitter, Directors; Theakston XB; guest beer Ⓗ
Characterful old country inn with stone walls and low beamed ceilings which has been well extended to provide discrete eating and drinking areas. Good food. Forestry walks nearby.
♛ Q ♞ ❀ ◖ ◗ P

SKEWEN

Crown
216 New Road ☎ (01792) 813309
12 (11 Sat)-11; 12-10.30 Sun
Brains Dark, MA, SA Ⓗ
Friendly local, having an upstairs snooker room with a bar and a very comfortable lounge downstairs. The only known regular outlet for Brains MA. Live music Fri eve. ❀ ◖ ⊟ ⇌ ♣

ST BRIDES MAJOR

Farmers Arms
Wick Road ☎ (01656) 880224
12-3, 6-11; 12-10.30 Sun
John Smith's Bitter; Ushers Best Bitter, Founders, seasonal beers Ⓗ
This bustling roadside inn, known as the Pub on the Pond, sports a friendly public bar and a comfortable restaurant. Good ale, good food, good service. ♛ Q ❀ ◖ ◗ P

Try also: Fox & Hounds, Ewenny Rd (Free)

ST HILARY

Bush Inn
¾ mile S of A48
☎ (01446) 772745
11-11; 12-10.30 Sun
Draught Bass Ⓖ**; Hancock's HB** Ⓗ**; Morland Old Speckled Hen** Ⓖ
Wonderful old, stone-built, thatched hostelry. Attracts visitors of all kinds with an appreciation of great pubs. The food is excellent (no meals Sun eve); families welcome. Westons Old Rosie cider.
♛ Q ❀ ◖ ◗ ⊟ ▲ ♣ ⌓ P

ST MELLONS

Fox & Hounds
Chapel Row (off B4487 Newport road) ☎ (01222) 777046
11-11; 12-3.30, 7-10.30 Sun
Brains Dark, Bitter, SA Ⓗ
A lounge and restaurant area make up this pub; children's play area to the rear. ❀ ◖ ◗ P

SWANSEA

Eli Jenkins Alehouse
24 Oxford Street (near bus station) ☎ (01792) 465289
11-11; 7-10.30 (closed lunch) Sun
Draught Bass; Worthington Bitter; guest beers Ⓗ
Pub enlarged and renamed in 1995 after the *Under Milk Wood* character. Wooden alcoves and nooks feature. ◖ ◗ ♿ ⊬

Glamorgan Hotel
88 Argyle Street (opp County Hall) ☎ (01792) 455120
12-11; 12-10.30 Sun
Banks's Bitter; Marston's Bitter, Pedigree; guest beers Ⓗ
Recently refurbished, one-bar pub serving the local community; darts well supported and a fun quiz Sun eve. ❀ ◖ ◗ ♣

O'Brien's Exchange
10 The Strand (off Wind St)
☎ (01792) 645345
11-11; 12-10.30 Sun
Brains Dark, SA Ⓗ
Worth visiting for the collection of jazz photographs and unusual wooden fittings, a welcome break from the theme experiences in the locality. ◖ ◗ ⇌

Potters Wheel
86-88 The Kingsway
☎ (01792) 465113
11-11; 12-10.30 Sun
Courage Directors; Theakston Best Bitter, XB; guest beers Ⓗ
Large, popular, city-centre Wetherspoons pub. The no-smoking area offers good food. Selection of good bottled beers and regular beer festivals.
Q ◖ ◗ ♿ ⇌ ⊬ ⊟

Queens Hotel
Gloucester Place
☎ (01792) 643460
11-11; 12-10.30 Sun
Buckley's Dark Mild, Best Bitter; Theakston Best Bitter, Old Peculier; guest beers Ⓗ
One-roomed lounge bar on the edge of the marina with pavement tables. Numerous pictures reveal the maritime history of the area. Excellent lunches. Quiz nights Wed and Sun. ❀ ◖ ♿ ⇌

Ryddings
Brynmill Ave, Brynmill (1 mile W of Swansea) ☎ (01792) 648885
11-11; 12-10.30 Sun
Smiles Best Bitter; Tetley Bitter Ⓗ**; guest beer** Ⓖ
Large pub in the centre of a residential area, frequented largely by students. ❀ ◖ ⊟ ♣

SINGLETON
1-2 Dillwyn Street (near Grand Theatre) ☎ (01792) 655987
11-11; 12-10.30 Sun
Brains SA; Courage Best Bitter; Swansea Three Cliffs Gold Ⓗ
A fine, late Victorian building: a single bar with a split-level two-room set-up. Live music most nights. Occasionally other beers from Swansea Brewery are sold.
🛏 ◖ ▮

ST GEORGE
30 Walter Rd ☎ (01792) 469317
11.30-11; 12-10.30 Sun
Felinfoel Double Dragon; Hancock's HB; Worthington Bitter Ⓗ
Friendly, one-roomed pub on the main road near the city centre. Live music Sun eve, quiz Tue; sporting events shown on big screen. The Felinfoel is unavailable in high summer.◖ &

VIVIAN ARMS
Gower Road, Sketty
☎ (01792) 203015
12-11; 12-10.30 Sun
Brains Bitter, SA, seasonal beers Ⓗ
Public bar and a comfortable lounge. Excellent food menu. Well worth a visit. ❀ ◖ ▮ ♣

WESTBOURNE HOTEL
11 Bryn-y-mor Road
☎ (01792) 459054
11-11; 12-10.30 Sun
Draught Bass; Hancock's HB; Worthington Dark; guest beers Ⓗ
Traditional, two-bar town corner pub. The outside drinking area is an elevated patio on to the street. Mind the step in the public bar. Eve meals end 8pm; no smoking in the lounge till 9pm.
❀ ◖ ▮ ⊞ ♣ ✁

Try also: Safe Deposit Pub, Wind St (Wetherspoons)

TAFF'S WELL

ANCHOR HOTEL
Cardiff Road ☎ (01222) 810104
11-11; 12-3, 7-10.30 Sun
Brains Bitter; Marston's Pedigree; Wadworth 6X Ⓗ
Comfortable pub with a nautical theme; the restaurant offers Mongolian cuisine. ◖ ▮ ⇌ P

THREE CROSSES

POUNDFFALD INN
☎ (01792) 873428
12-11; 12-10.30 Sun
Greene King Abbot; Marston's Pedigree; Morland Old Speckled Hen; Worthington Bitter Ⓗ
Welcoming village local with a collection of horse bridles in the bar; also note the curved pound wall incorporated into the building. 🛏 ❀ ◖ ▮ ⊞ ♣ P

TONDU

LLYNFI ARMS
Maesteg Road ☎ (01656) 720010
1 (12 Fri & Sat)-4, 6.30-11; 12-4, 6.30-10.30 Sun
Worthington Bitter Ⓗ**; guest beers** ⒽⒼ
Roadside pub with a lively bar and a comfortable lounge, offering an adventurous range of guest beers selected by the landlord's careful research. Lunches Fri-Sun; eve meals Wed-Sun.
◖ ▮ ⊞ & ⇌

TREFOREST

OTLEY ARMS
Forest Road (near station)
☎ (01443) 402033
11-11; 12-10.30 Sun
Brains SA; Bullmastiff Gold Brew; Crown Buckley SBB; Worthington Bitter; guest beer Ⓗ
Popular with students from the nearby university; quieter outside term-time when the beer range may be reduced. Limited parking. ◖ ⇌ ♣ P

TYLE GARW

BOARS HEAD
Coed Cae Lane ☎ (01443) 225400
12-4, 7-11; 12-3, 7-10.30 Sun
Beer range varies Ⓗ
Unspoilt, simply furnished, traditional local. Forest walks opposite. Q ❀ ⊞

UPPER CHURCH VILLAGE

FARMERS ARMS
St Illtyds Road ☎ (01443) 205766
11-11; 12-10.30 Sun
Draught Bass; Hancock's HB; guest beers (occasional) Ⓗ
Busy village pub with a varied clientele and a strong local atmosphere offering a warm welcome. No food Sun. ❀ ◖ P

WICK

LAMB & FLAG
St Brides Road (B4265)
☎ (01656) 890278
11.30-5, 7-11; 11.30-11 Sat; 12-4, 7-10.30 Sun
Draught Bass; Hancock's HB; Worthington Bitter; guest beer Ⓗ
Unspoilt village inn with welcoming staff and locals.
🛏 Q ⌂ ❀ ◖ ▮ ⊞ ♣ P

STAR INN
Ewenny Road (B4265)
☎ (01656) 890519
12-3, 5-11 (11-11 summer); 12-5.30, 7-10.30 Sun
Hancock's HB; Worthington Bitter; guest beer Ⓗ
Welcoming village inn, catering for local and passing trade; an ideal base to explore the coast.

The guest ale is usually from the Bass list.
🛏 Q ❀ ◖ ▮ & ♣ P ⊟

YNYSGOLLEN

ROCK & FOUNTAIN INN
Glyn-Neath Road, Aberdulais (A465)
☎ (01639) 642681
12-3, 6.30-11; 12-3, 7-10.30 Sun
Felinfoel Double Dragon; guest beers Ⓗ
One of the few regular local outlets for Double Dragon; the guest ales are usually from local independent brewers.
◖ ▮ P

YNYSTAWE

MILLERS ARMS
Clydach Road (next to Ynystawe School)
☎ (01792) 842614
11-11; 12-10.30 Sun
Flowers Original; Wadworth 6X; guest beers Ⓗ
Popular pub serving good food in the restaurant at the rear.
Q ❀ ⊞ ♣ P ✁

YSTALYFERA

WERN FAWR INN
47 Wern Road
☎ (01639) 843625
7-11; 11-3, 7-10.30 Sun
Beer range varies Ⓗ
A friendly, cosy, village local; a lounge and a bar with a stove fire. The bar boasts a large collection of old curios both domestic and industrial, also over 2000 matchboxes. 1960s music played. Well worth finding.
🛏 Q ⊞ ♣ ✁

YSTRAD MYNACH

ROYAL OAK
Commercial Street
☎ (01443) 814196
12-3, 5.30-11; 12-11 Sat; 12-3, 7-10.30 Sun
Draught Bass; Hancock's HB Ⓗ
Unmistakable 'Brewer's Tudor' pub with interesting acid etched windows. Busy public bar area where renovations have managed to retain separate areas. Good food.
❀ ◖ ▮ ⊞ ⇌ ♣ P

INDEPENDENT BREWERIES

Brains:
Cardiff
Bullmastiff:
Cardiff

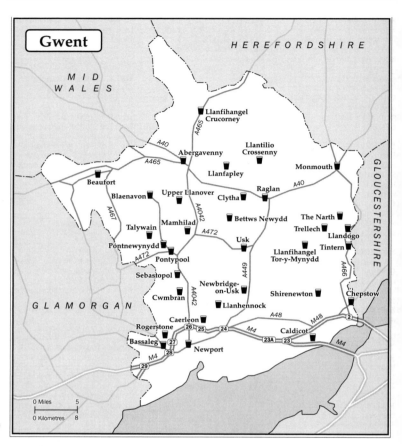

Gwent

HEREFORDSHIRE

MID WALES

GLOUCESTERSHIRE

GLAMORGAN

Llanfihangel Crucorney

Llantilio Crossenny

Abergavenny

Monmouth

Llanfapley

Beaufort

Raglan

Blaenavon · Upper Llanover · Clytha

The Narth

Trellech

Talywain · Mamhilad · Bettws Newydd

Llandogo

Tintern

Pontnewynydd · Usk

Sebastopol · Pontypool

Llanfihangel Tor-y-Mynydd

Cwmbran · Newbridge-on-Usk

Shirenewton

Chepstow

Llanhennock

Caerleon

Rogerstone · 26 · 25 · 24

Caldicot

Bassaleg · 27 · 23A · 23

28 · Newport

29

M4

0 Miles 5
0 Kilometres 8

Authority areas covered: Blaenau Gwent UA, Monmouthshire UA, Newport UA, Torfaen UA

ABERGAVENNY

COACH & HORSES
41 Cross Street
11-11; 12-3, 7-10.30 Sun
Draught Bass; Brains SA; Flowers IPA; Wadworth 6X ⒣
Old pub standing by the site of a former town gate. A popular open-plan bar with a pool room leading from it. Wooden beams above the bar have old Whitbread tankards hanging on them. Near the bus station.
🏵 ♣

STATION
37 Brecon Road
☎ (01873) 854759
12-11; 12-3, 7-10.30 Sun
Draught Bass; Freeminer Bitter; Tetley Bitter; guest beer ⒣
Very popular, vibrant free house with a traditional no-frills interior which attracts a wide cross-section of people. Freeminer Bitter is now a firmly established resident which is joined by adventurous guest beers

from other small breweries.
🏚 ⌕ ♣ P

Try also: Kings Arms, Neville Street (Free); Somerset Arms, Victoria St (Free)

BASSALEG

TREDEGAR ARMS
4 Caerphilly Road (off M4 jct 28)
☎ (01633) 893247
11-11; 12-10.30 Sun
Badger Tanglefoot; Brains Bitter ⒣; **Greene King Abbot** ⒢; **guest beers** ⒣⒢
South Wales CAMRA *Pub of the Year* 1997, offering the most extensive range of beers (up to 13) in the area. Extensive dining areas, including one for families, lead from the main bar. Comprehensive menu with many standard favourites and some appetising variations. The lounge offers cosy surroundings around a log fire. Children's play area. Bulmer's cider in summer.
🏚 ⌕ 🏵 ◑ ▶ ⌕ ⌂ P ⌽

BEAUFORT

RHYD Y BLEW
Rassau Road, Carmeltown
☎ (01495) 308935
12-3 (11.30-3.30 Sat), 6 (6.30 Mon, Tue & Thu)-11; 12-3, 7-10.30 Sun
Brains SA; Flowers IPA, Original; guest beer ⒣
An oasis for local real ale enthusiasts. The multi-level interior has several linked but discrete areas. The name means 'Ford of the Hairs' which locals take pleasure in explaining – the distinctive pub sign provides a clue. No lunches Sat & Sun. 🏵 ◑ ♣ P

BETTWS NEWYDD

BLACK BEAR
Village signed off B4598
OS361062
☎ (01873) 880701
11-3 (not Mon), 5-12.30; 12-10.30 Sun
Beer range varies ⒢
Good, old-fashioned pub with

flagstone floors. Very popular with ramblers. Good reputation for home-cooked food built on its speciality fish dishes. No lunches Mon. ♨ Q ❀ ◑ ▸ ⌐ P

BLAENAVON

CAMBRIAN INN
80-81 Llanover Road
☎ (01495) 790327
6 (11 Fri, 12 Sat)-11; 12-3,
7-10.30 Sun
Brains Bitter, SA; guest beers Ⓗ
Friendly corner local decorated with old photographs of the area. Separate games room and a cosy lounge lead off the bar. Q ⊞ ♣

CASTLE HOTEL
94 Broad Street
☎ (01495) 792477
11-11; 12-3, 7-10.30 Sun
Tetley Bitter; guest beer Ⓗ
Welcoming, open-plan pub with a dining area and a games room. Good value accommodation (the only accommodation in the town centre) makes this a useful base for exploring local history sites. Bookings only for evening meals.
🛏 ◑ ▸ ♣ ⌐

CAERLEON

KINGS ARMS
Belmont Hill
☎ (01633) 420329
11-3, 6-11; 11-11 Fri & Sat;
12-10.30 Sun
Brains Dark, SA; Hancock's HB, seasonal beer Ⓗ
Tucked away near the bottom of one of the steepest hills for miles around. Several distinct drinking areas and a restaurant. A rare outlet for a mild beer in Gwent. Wonderful coal fire complements the relaxed atmosphere.
♨ ❀ ◑ ▸ P

CALDICOT

CROSS INN
1 Newport Road
☎ (01291) 420692
11-4, 7-11; 11-11 Fri & Sat; 12-3,
7-10.30 Sun
Brains Dark, SA; Courage Best Bitter; John Smith's Bitter; Theakston Old Peculier; guest beer Ⓗ
Busy, white-washed two-bar pub in centre of village. Two-three guest beers per week. Bulmer's cider.❀ ⊞ ♣ ⌐ P

CHEPSTOW

FIVE ALLS
Hocker Hill Street
☎ (01291) 622528
11.30-5, 7.30-11; 12-4.30,
7-10.30 Sun
John Smith's Bitter; Ushers Best Bitter, Founders, seasonal beers Ⓗ

Traditional pub with a single, L-shaped room decorated with various memorabilia. The superb pub sign depicts the 'Five Alls'. Close to castle and about 10 mins walk from bus and rail stations.
♣

CLYTHA

CLYTHA ARMS
Nr Abergavenny on old Raglan Road
☎ (01873) 840206
12-3, 7-11; 12-3, 7-10.30 Sun
Banks's Mild; Draught Bass; Hook Norton Best Bitter; guest beers Ⓗ
Former dower house with outside play area for children. You can while away the hours studying the landlady's various teapots and the impressive collection of pumpclips. Excellent, innovative bar food and an award-winning restaurant (closed Sun eve and Mon).
♨ Q ❀ 🛏 ◑ ▸ ♣ ⌐ P ⌐

CWMBRAN

COMMODORE HOTEL
Mill Lane, Llanyrafon (off A4042 and Llanfrechfa Way)
☎ (01633) 484091
11-11; 12-10.30 Sun
Brains Bitter; Buckley's Best Bitter; guest beer Ⓗ
Friendly, very comfortable family-run hotel where real ale is served in the relaxing surroundings of the Pilliners Lounge. Good value bar meals plus à la carte dining in the Willows Restaurant. Popular base for visitors to the area.
❀ 🛏 ◑ ▸ P

MOUNT PLEASANT INN
Wesley Street
☎ (01633) 484289
12-3, 7-11; 12-2.30, 7-10.30 Sun
Ushers Best Bitter, Founders Ⓗ
Homely pub set in a terrace in the heart of Cwmbran village. The bar and split-level lounge are comfortably furnished and tastefully decorated. Just the place for a quiet drink and a meal.
❀ ◑ ▸ ⊞ ♣ P

LLANDOGO

SLOOP INN
On A466 near Tintern
☎ (01594) 530291
12-2.30 (11-30-3.30 summer), 6-11; 11.30-11 Sat; 12-4, 7-10.30 Sun
Buckley's Best Bitter; Freeminer Bitter; guest beer Ⓗ
Only two miles from Tintern Abbey, the main attraction in the Wye Valley. The large bar contains several enormous beams. The rear lounge boasts fine views over the valley and an

extensive menu. High standard of accommodation. One guest beer in winter, two in summer.
♨ ❀ 🛏 ◑ ▸ ⊞ ♣ P

LLANFAPLEY

RED HART INN
On B4233 nr Abergavenny
☎ (01600) 780227
12-3 (not Tue), 6-11; 12-3,
7-10.30 Sun
Draught Bass; guest beers Ⓗ
Fine example of a country inn. Quiet and relaxing even when busy. Extensive garden looks out on rolling countryside. Home-cooked meals (not served Sun eve or Tue).
♨ ❀ ◑ ▸ ♣ P

LLANFIHANGEL CRUCORNEY

SKIRRID INN
Hereford Road (off A465, 4 miles N of Abergavenny)
☎ (01873) 890258
11-3, 6-11; 11-11 Sat & summer;
12-10.30 Sun
Ushers Best Bitter, Founders, seasonal beers Ⓗ
Heavily beamed ceilings and stone-flagged floors give huge character to what claims to be Wales' oldest pub. Award-winning food and garden and highly praised accommodation add to the delight for locals, walkers and visitors alike, supporting the full range of Ushers' beers.
♨ Q ❀ 🛏 ◑ ▸ ⊞ ♣ P

LLANFIHANGEL TOR-Y-MYNYDD

STAR INN
Near Llansoy OS459023
☎ (01291) 650256
11.30-3, 6.30-11; 12-3, 7-10.30 Sun
Ind Coope Burton Ale; Marston's Pedigree; Tetley Bitter; Ⓗ
Large, friendly family-run pub with three separate drinking areas and a huge, welcoming log fire. Wide selection of food available, including vegetarian. John Wesley stayed here in 1798. Caravans are allowed in the camping area.
♨ Q ❀ ◑ ▸ ⊞ ♣ P

LLANHENNOCK

WHEATSHEAF INN
Near Caerleon OS 353929
☎ (01633) 420468
11-3, 5-11 (may open all day summer); 12-3, 7-10.30 Sun
Draught Bass; Worthington Bitter; guest beer Ⓗ
Charming countryside pub set on a hill overlooking southern Gwent. Very busy in summer when boules is played in the garden. Interesting range of

lunchtime food. The bar area is full of pictures and plaques of local interest. Watch out for the parrots! 🏠 Q ⊛ ◖ ⊞ ♣ P

LLANTILIO CROSSENNY

HOSTRY INN
On B4233
☎ (01600) 780278
12-3 (not winter Mon-Fri), 6-30-11; 12-3, 7-10.30 Sun
Freeminer Bitter, Speculation Ale; guest beer Ⓗ
Friendly, 15th-century rural pub near Offa's Dyke footpath. Good range of food including vegetarian meals and Sunday lunch. A hall and vintage Rolls Royce are available for functions. Dogs on leads welcome. Skittles played.
⊛ ◖ ▶ Å ♣ P ⌦

MAMHILAD

STAR INN
Signed off A4042
☎ (01495) 785319
11-3, 6-11; 12-4, 7-10.30 Sun
Draught Bass; Hancock's HB; guest beers Ⓗ
Quiet country pub opposite a churchyard with reputedly the oldest yew trees in the county. Children's area in the garden. Welcoming fire awaits you on which chestnuts roast in winter months on Sun eves. No meals Mon. 🏠 Q ⊛ ◖ ▶ P

MONMOUTH

GREEN DRAGON
St Thomas Square
☎ (01600) 712561
11-11; 12-10.30 Sun
Draught Bass; Hancock's HB; Marston's Bitter, HBC; guest beers Ⓗ
Two-bar, comfortably furnished pub featuring a cartoon gallery in the gents toilet. Extensive home-cooked menu. Live jazz bands Wed eve. Q ⊛ ◖ ▶ Å P

OLD NAG'S HEAD
Granville Street, St James Square ☎ (01600) 713782
12-2, 6-11; 11-11 Sat; 12-4, 7-10.30 Sun
Buckley's Rev James; Fuller's London Pride; guest beers Ⓗ
Two-bar corner pub with separate rooms, including one in a medieval tower and a pool room. Busy weekends. A few minutes' stroll north of the main shopping area. ⊛ ◖ ⊞ Å ♣

THE NARTH

TREKKERS
Near Trellech OS525064
☎ (01600) 860367
11-3.30, 6-11; 11-11 Sat; 12-10.30 Sun

Boddingtons Bitter; Felinfoel Bitter; Freeminer Bitter; guest beer Ⓗ
Found in the beautiful Wye Valley, this log-cabin-styled country pub is a must to visit. A central open fire divides bar/dining area; the skittle alley doubles as a family room. Landlady serves excellent home-cooked food (booking advised for Sun lunch) Extensive garden with bandstand. Good base for country walks.
🏠 ⭤ ⊛ ◖ ▶ ♿ Å ♣ P

NEWBRIDGE-ON-USK

NEWBRIDGE INN
OS384948
☎ (01633) 450227
11.30-3, 6.30-11 (may vary); 12-3.30, 7-10.30 Sun
Draught Bass; Fuller's London Pride; guest beers Ⓗ
Large country pub situated beside one of the few bridges across the river Usk affording superb views from the large bay windows. Good reputation for food. Skittles played.
🏠 ⊛ ◖ ▶ ♣ P

NEWPORT

GEORGE HOTEL
157 Chepstow Road, Maindee
☎ (01633) 255528
11-11; 12-10.30 Sun
Everards Beacon, Tiger; John Smith's Bitter; guest beer (occasional) Ⓗ
Very large pub which can be busy and noisy, situated on a large road junction in a busy shopping area. Very competitive prices in an area with many pubs. Occasional music, etc. Sporting events shown on a large screen.
⊛ ♣

HANDPOST
Bassaleg Road and Risca Road jct
☎ (01633) 264502
11-3, 5.30-11; 11-11 Wed, Fri & Sat; 12-10.30 Sun
Ansells Bitter; Ind Coope Burton Ale; Tetley Bitter, Burton Ale; guest beers Ⓗ
Attractive, large open-plan single-bar pub. Popular watering hole with local residents. Log fire during winter months. Weekday lunches. 🏠 ◖ ♣

RED LION
47 Stow Hill
☎ (01633) 264398
11-11; 12-10.30 Sun
John Smith's Bitter; Ushers Best Bitter, seasonal beers; Ⓗ
Friendly corner local offering a few surprises, including homemade pickled eggs and pickles. Home-cooked, good value food, for carnivores only, with daily specialities. No food Sun. Patio

garden. Live music Fri. Gwent CAMRA *Pub of the Year* 1997. Shove Ha'penny played.
🏠 ⊛ ◖ ▶ ⭤ ♣ ⌣

ST JULIAN INN
Caerleon Road
☎ (01633) 258663
11.30-11; 12-10.30 Sun
Courage Best Bitter; John Smith's Bitter; guest beers Ⓗ
Comfortable riverside pub that caters for all age groups. Wonderful in summer when the balcony offers superb views across the River Usk. Guest beers change regularly and are often interesting. Handy for the village of Caerleon and its historic attractions. No meals Sun. Occasional cider.
⊛ ◖ ▶ ♣ ⌣ P

WETHERSPOONS
Units 10-12 Cambrian Centre, Cambrian Road
☎ (01633) 251752
11-11; 12-10.30 Sun
Courage Directors; Felinfoel Double Dragon; Theakston Best Bitter, XB; guest beers Ⓗ
Large, open-plan pub in Newport's superpub ghetto. Photos and local history articles decorate the walls. Keenly priced beers and a handy place for refreshment after a long train journey.
Q ◖ ▶ ♿ ⭤ ⌣ ⌦ ⊟

PONTNEWYNYDD

HORSESHOE INN
Hill Street
☎ (01495) 762188
12-11; 12-10.30 Sun
John Smith's Bitter; Ushers Best Bitter; guest beer Ⓗ
Pleasant former coaching inn with a small public bar and cosy lounge downstairs, and a popular games room and Hayloft Restaurant upstairs. Children's certificate applies to the lounge (12-3, 7-9) and there is play equipment in the enclosed garden. Booking advised for Sun lunch. The guest beer is from Ushers. ⭤ ⊛ ◖ ⊞ ♣ P

PONTYPOOL

LABOUR IN VAIN
39 High Street
☎ (01495) 762863
6.30 (12 Sat)-11; 12-3, 7-10.30 Sun
Hancock's HB; guest beers Ⓗ
Friendly traditional pub with a strong community focus. The bar has a photo of the old, politically incorrect pub sign which had to be removed and which vanished years ago. Local interest in real ale has been stimulated by the enthusiastic licensee. Limited parking. 🏠 ⊛ ⭤ ⊞ ♣ P

RAGLAN

SHIP INN
High Street
☎ (01291) 690635
11-11 Mon-Sat; 12-10.30 Sun
Draught Bass; Hancock's HB; guest beers Ⓗ
Friendly, 16th-century coaching inn with an attractive cobbled forecourt and water pump. The large stone fireplace reputedly came from Raglan Castle. Two bars and a dining room.
ᗰ ⊛ ⬧ ▶ ⊞ ♣

ROGERSTONE

TREDEGAR ARMS
Cefn Road
☎ (01633) 664999
12-3, 5.30-11; 12-11 Fri & Sat; 12-3, 7-10.30 Sun
Courage Best Bitter; Ruddles County; guest beer Ⓗ
Popular roadside pub with a small public bar and a spacious lounge where tasty lunches and tempting evening meals can be enjoyed. Interesting guest ales from small independent breweries.
⊛ ⬧ ▶ ⊞ ♣ P

SEBASTOPOL

OPEN HEARTH
Wern Road (off South St)
☎ (01495) 763752
11.30-3, 6-11; 11-11 Sat; 12-4, 7-10.30 Sun
Archers Golden; Boddingtons Bitter; Buckley's Rev James; Greene King Abbot; Hancock's HB; guest beers Ⓗ
Cosy, CAMRA award-winning canalside pub where blackboards list the beers dotted around its three rooms. Daily specials supplement a wide, appetising menu. The canal towpath outside is popular in find weather. There is also a children's play area in the garden.
⊛ ⬧ ▶ ⊞ ♣ P

SHIRENEWTON

CARPENTERS ARMS
Usk Road (B4235)
☎ (01291) 641231
12-2.30; 6-11; 12-3, 7-10.30 Sun
Boddingtons Bitter; Flowers IPA; Fuller's London Pride; Marston's Pedigree, Owd Rodger; Wadworth 6X; guest beer Ⓗ
Rambling, 400-year-old country pub with many linked rooms containing old pictures and items of local history. A good atmosphere, comprehensive menu (not available Sun), over 50 malt whiskies plus its wide real ale selection ensure its continuing popularity.
ᗰ ⏩ ⊛ ⬧ ▶ ⊞ ♣ P

TREDEGAR ARMS
The Square
☎ (01291) 641274
12-3 (may vary), 6-11; 12-11 Sat; 12-4, 7-10.30 Sun
Draught Bass; Hancock's HB; Hook Norton Best Bitter; guest beers Ⓗ
Situated in the centre of the village, this pub has a large bar and games area and a smaller lounge which is mainly used by diners. Recommended restaurant.
ᗰ Q ⊛ ⇔ ⬧ ▶ ⊞ ♣ ⌂ P

TALYWAIN

GLOBE INN
Commercial Road (B4246)
☎ (01495) 772053
6.30 (11 Sat)-11; 12-4, 7-10.30 Sun
Brains Dark (winter)**, Bitter; Hancock's HB; guest beer** Ⓗ
Traditional local with a distinctive 'globe' sign. The small public bar has a real fire in winter. A pool room leads off a narrow comfortable lounge, which hosts live entertainment at weekends. Cider in summer.
ᗰ ⊞ ♣ ⌂

TINTERN

CHERRY TREE
Devauden Road (off A466)
OS 526001
☎ (01291) 689292
11.30-2.30 (not Mon winter), 6 (6.30 winter)-11; 12-3, 7-10.30 Sun
Hancock's HB Ⓖ
The only Welsh pub to feature in every edition of this *Guide*. A single-roomed pub offering beer brought up from the cellar. Rare Hancock's 'toastmaster' sign outside. Bulmers cider is sold. Often described as a 'time warp', the pub has a 70-year-old bar-billiards table. Limited parking.
ᗰ Q ⊛ ♣ ⌂ P

TRELLECH

LION INN
☎ (01600) 860322
12-3, 7 (6 Thu-Sat)-11; 12-3 (closed eve) Sun
Beer range varies Ⓗ
Welcoming, 16th-century inn situated in what was once the largest town in Wales! A split-level pub with two real fires and a collection (or pride?) of lions. No eve meals Sun.
ᗰ ⏩ ⊛ ⇔ ⬧ ▶ ⊞ Å ♣ P

UPPER LLANOVER

GOOSE & CUCKOO
2 miles up lane off A4042 near Llanover OS 292073
☎ (01873) 880277
11.30-3 (not Mon), 7-11; 12-3, 7-10.30 Sun
Beer range varies Ⓗ
Out of the way but not hard to find, on the edge of the Brecon Beacons. With fine views and surrounding woods it is very popular with walkers. All the food is home produced, even the bread and ice cream. No meals Mon lunch and Thu eve. Beers come from Bullmastiff, plus guests. Large malt whisky selection. A pub you will want to go back to.
ᗰ Q ⏩ ⊛ ⬧ ▶ ♣ P

USK

GREYHOUND INN
Old Chepstow Road
☎ (01291) 672074
12-3, 6-11; 12-3, 7-10.30 Sun
Hancock's HB; guest beers Ⓗ
Single-roomed pub which attracts both visitors and locals keen to try the good range of guest beers, three of which are normally on sale. Home-cooked food uses local produce. The various types of pie are a popular choice.
⊛ ⬧ ▶ P

KINGS HEAD HOTEL
18 Old Market Street
☎ (01291) 672963
11-11; 12-10.30 Sun
Badger Tanglefoot; Flowers Original; Fuller's London Pride; Marston's Pedigree Ⓗ
Fishing mementos form part of the decoration in the lounge which also boasts a large log fire. The landlord is very proud of the quality of his real ale and refuses to sell nitrokeg products.
ᗰ ⇔ ⬧ ▶ ♣ P

Try also: Nag's Head, Twyn Square (Free)

The Gwent branch of the Campaign for Real Ale raised its voice in protest when Brains applied for planning permission to wreck the interior of the Hen and Chickens, in Abergavenny.

The pub dates back to the 17th century and the brewery wanted to knock out internal walls and move the bar, which has been in the same place since the 1850s. Monmouthshire council rejected the application in April 1998, but Brains said it would appeal.

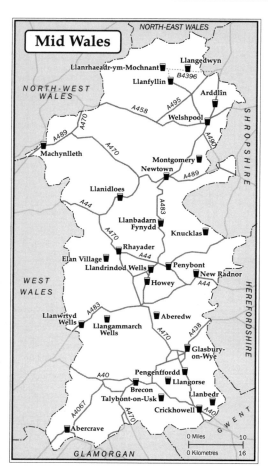

Mid Wales

NORTH-EAST WALES

Llangedwyn
Llanrhaeadr-ym-Mochnant
B4396
Llanfyllin
Arddlin
NORTH-WEST WALES
A458
A495
Welshpool
A470
A489
Machynlleth
A470
Montgomery
Newtown
A489
Llanidloes
A44
A483
Llanbadarn Fynydd
Knucklas
A470
Rhayader
A44
Elan Village
Llandrindod Wells
Penybont
New Radnor
WEST WALES
Howey
A44
Llanwrtyd Wells
A483
Aberedw
A438
Llangammarch Wells
A470
Glasbury-on-Wye
Pengenffordd
Llangorse
Brecon
Talybont-on-Usk
Llanbedr
Crickhowell
A40
A4067
Abercrave
GLAMORGAN

SHROPSHIRE
HEREFORDSHIRE
GWENT

0 Miles 10
0 Kilometres 16

ABERCRAVE

COPPER BEECH
133 Heol Tawe ☎ (01639) 730269
12-11 Mon-Sat; 12-10.30 Sun
Brains SA; Courage Best Bitter; Worthington Best Bitter; Yates Bitter; guest beer H
Close to Brecon Beacons National Park, this pub has a long-standing tradition for real ale. Very relaxed atmosphere.
🏨 ❀ 🛏 ◖ ▮ P

Try also: Abercrave Inn, Heol Tawe (Free)

ABEREDW

SEVEN STARS INN
On minor road off B4567
☎ (01982) 560494
11.30-2.30, 6.30-11 (closed winter Tue); 12-2.30, 7-10.30 Sun
Robinson's Best Bitter; Wood Shropshire Lad; guest beer (occasional) H
Warm, friendly village pub, recently restored, set amid

splendid countryside in the Wye Valley. Good food and well-kept ales. Winner of South and Mid Wales CAMRA *Pub of the Year.*
🏨 Q ◖ ▮ ♣ 🍺

ARDDLIN

HORSESHOE
On A483 ☎ (01938) 590318
12-3, 5.30-11; 12-4, 6-10.30 Sun
Banks's Bitter; Marston's Pedigree H
Welcoming village pub with a public bar and a lounge/restaurant serving a wide range of well priced food. Children's play area in the garden. Weston ciders served. ❀ ◖ ▮ 🔲 ♣ ⌂ P

BRECON

GEORGE HOTEL
George Street (off The Struet)
☎ (01874) 623421/2
11-11; 12-10.30 Sun
Greene King Abbot; Ind Coope Burton Ale; Morland Old Speckled Hen; Tetley Bitter H

Historic 17th-century inn with warm, comfortable bars offering a good range of beers and bar meals. Popular with the local business community.
🛏 ◖ ▮ P

OLD BOAR'S HEAD
14 Ship Street
☎ (01874) 622856
11 (11.30 Mon)-2.30, 5.30-11; 11-11 Fri & Sat; 12-4.30, 7-10.30 Sun (may extend summer)
Everards Beacon, Tiger; Fuller's ESB; Thwaites Bitter; guest beers H
Ancient riverside pub offering six real ales in a smart, modern public bar or a spacious rear lounge, popular with a young clientele.
🏨 ❀ ◖ 🔲 P

Try also: Old Cognac, High St (Bass)

CRICKHOWELL

BEAR HOTEL
On A40 in town centre
☎ (01873) 810408
11-3, 6-11; 12-3, 7-10.30 Sun
Draught Bass; Ruddles Best Bitter; John Smith's Bitter; , County; guest beers (occasional) H
Historic coaching inn dating back to the 15th century. Now a renowned award-winning hotel. Very popular and busy at all times. Parking difficult.
🏨 Q 🛏 ❀ 🛏 ◖ ▮ P

WHITE HART INN
Brecon Road (A40, to W of town)
☎ (01873) 810473
12-3, 6-11; 12-11 Sat; 12-3, 7-10.30 Sun (may extend summer)
Draught Bass; Brains Bitter; Hancock's HB; guest beer H
Small, friendly old inn, formerly a toll house where the tolls are still displayed on the outside wall. Interesting collection of old photos in the dining room. Good range of food including Welsh dishes. Quiz night Mon.
Q ❀ ◖ 🅰 ♣ P

Try also: Bridge End Inn, Bridge St (Free)

ELAN VILLAGE

ELAN VALLEY HOTEL
On B4518, approx 3 miles W of Rhayader OS937659
☎ (01597) 810448
11.30-3 (not winter) 6-11; 11-10.30 Sun
Hancock's HB; guest beers H
Built as a Victorian fishing lodge, this family-run hotel is near the magnificent Elan Valley, Wales' lakeland. Comprising two bars, a restaurant and a tea room, it provides comfort and good value in an easy-going atmosphere.
🏨 Q 🛏 ❀ 🛏 ◖ ▮ 🔲 ♣ P

GLASBURY-ON- WYE

HARP INN
On B4350, near A438 jct
☎ (01497) 847373
11-3, 6 (6.30 winter)-11; 12-3,
7-10.30 Sun
**Boddingtons Bitter; Brains SA;
Robinson's Best Bitter; guest
beer** Ⓗ
Friendly village inn, formerly an
18th-century cider house. A good
base from which to sample the
wide range of outdoor activities
available in the area.
Accommodation, food and ales
are keenly priced and good value.
🏚 Q ❀ 🛏 ◑ ▮ ♣ P

HOWEY

DROVERS ARMS
Off A483, 1½ miles S of
Llandrindod Wells
☎ (01597) 822508
12-2.30 (not Tue), 7-11; 12-3,
7-10.30 Sun
Beer range varies Ⓗ
Pleasant, two-bar village inn on
the original drover's route with a
13th-century cellar. The varied
home-cooked menu includes local
produce. The beer includes locally-brewed Drovers Ale and
guests from Welsh breweries.
🏚 Q ❀ 🛏 ◑ ▮ 🞿 ▲ ♣ P

KNUCKLAS

CASTLE INN
Off B4355 in village centre
☎ (01547) 528150
11-11 (may close afternoons);
12-10.30 Sun
**Draught Bass; Worthington
Bitter; guest beer** Ⓗ
Solidly built hotel with wood-panelled and stone walls. Two large
rooms furnished with settles plus
a function room where lectures
may be held. Walkers on Offa's
Dyke Path catered for. Opens
8am for breakfast. If closed at
lunchtime, try ringing the bell.
🏚 Q 🛏 ◑ ▮ 🞿 ▲ ≈ ♣ P

LLANBADARN FYNYDD

NEW INN
On A483
☎ (01597) 840378
12 (11 summer)-3, (closed winter
Tue & Wed), 7 (6 summer)-11;
12-4, 6.30-10.30 Sun
**Wood Shropshire Lad; guest
beer** Ⓗ
Comfortable inn with a public bar
and games room, a superbly furnished lounge-cum-restaurant
and a stylish conservatory overlooking the large garden. Opens
10.30 in summer for coffee and
has midnight supper licence.
Open Tue & Wed lunchtimes in
winter by arrangement only.
🏚 ➹ ❀ 🛏 ◑ ▮ 🞿 ♿
▲ ♣ P

LLANBEDR

RED LION
☎ (01873) 810754
12-2.30 (not winter Mon & Tue),
7-11; 12-11 Sat (may extend in
school holidays); 12-3, 7-10.30
Sun
Worthington Bitter; guest beers Ⓗ
Cosy old pub in a small village set
in glorious surroundings beneath
the Black Mountains. Renowned
for the quality of its ales, serving
good food including vegetarian
dishes, it is popular with hill-
walkers. Limited parking.
🏚 Q ➹ ❀ ◑ ▮ ▲ ♣ P

LLANDRINDOD WELLS

CONSERVATIVE CLUB
South Crescent
(01597) 822126
11-2, 5.30 (4.30 Fri)-11; 11-11
Sat; 11.30-2.30, 7-10.30 Sun
Worthington Bitter; guest beers Ⓗ
A comfortable and quiet club, not
as political as its name implies.
Two snooker tables and occa-
sional entertainment on offer.
Cooked lunches except Mon and
Tue. Non-members must be
signed in. Q ◑ ♿ ≈ ♣

ROYAL BRITISH LEGION
CLUB
Tremont Road (A483 between
hospital and fire station)
☎ (01597) 822558
7.30-11; 12-11 Sat; 12-10.30 Sun
**Brains SA; Worthington Bitter;
guest beers** Ⓗ
This friendly club offers a comfortable lounge, a games room
with juke box, snooker table,
pool, darts, quoits and dominoes
and a large function room. Home-
cooked food is available during
most sessions. Non-members
must be signed in.
➹ ▮ ♿ ≈ ♣ ⌣ P

Try also: Llanerch Inn, Llanerch
Lane (Free)

LLANFYLLIN

CAIN VALLEY HOTEL
High Street (A490)
☎ (01691) 648366
11-11; 12-10.30 Sun
**Ansells Bitter; Brains Bitter;
Worthington Bitter** Ⓗ
Long-running entry in this *Guide*
with a public bar, a large back
bar and a plush wood-panelled
lounge and dining area.
Q ❀ 🛏 ◑ ▮ 🞿 ♣ P

LLANGAMMARCH
WELLS

ABERCEIROS INN
SW end of village
☎ (01591) 620227
12-3 (not Mon-Wed), 6.30-11;
12-3, 7-10.30 Sun

**Hancock's HB; Worthington
Bitter; guest beer** Ⓗ
This pub has remained in the
same family for over 150 years
and although recently modernised, it remains quiet and
traditional in its attractive rural
setting.
🏚 Q ❀ 🛏 ◑ ▮ ▲ ≈ ♣ P ⊟

LLANGEDWYN

GREEN INN
On B4396
☎ (01691) 828234
11-3, 6-11 (12-3, 7-10.30 winter);
12-3.30-6-10.30 Sun
Boddingtons Bitter; guest beers Ⓗ
Fine 17th-century free house in a
picturesque valley. The three distinct drinking areas feature hop-
bines, inglenooks and slate
floors. Good home-cooked food
complements four changing
guest ales. Large garden and
fishing rights on River Tanat.
Cider in summer.
🏚 ❀ ◑ ▮ 🞿 ♣ ⌣ P

LLANGORSE

CASTLE INN
☎ (01874) 658225
12-2.30, 6-11 (extended summer); 12-3, 7-10.30 Sun
**Brains Bitter, SA; Watkin OSB;
guest beers** Ⓗ
Friendly old village pub in the
heart of Brecon Beacons National
Park, close to Llangorse Lake
(popular for water sports and
other activities). Offers a good
range of reasonably priced food
and gets very busy in summer.
🏚 Q ❀ ◑ ▮ 🞿 ♣ P

LLANIDLOES

COACH & HORSES
Smithfield Street (A470)
☎ (01686) 412266
12-11; 12-10.30 Sun
**Brains SA; Tetley Bitter; guest
beers** Ⓗ
Very friendly pub with an outstanding range of beer for the
area. Upstairs pool room with a
downstairs pool room for youngsters. The house beer is James
Williams IPA, brewed by Brains.
❀ 🛏 ◑ ▮ ♣

MOUNT INN
China Street
☎ (01686) 412247
11-11; 12-10.30 Sun
**Draught Bass; Worthington
Dark, Bitter** Ⓗ
Excellent many-roomed inn,
including two basic bars, a plush
lounge and a games and TV
room. One bar has a stove and
settles. The listed original stone
floor was once part of a castle.
May close on weekday afternoons if quiet.
🏚 ❀ 🛏 ◑ ▮ 🞿 ♣ P

LLANRHAEDR-YM-MOCHNANT

HAND INN
On B4580 ☎ (01691) 780413
11-11; 12-10.30 Sun
Banks's Mild; Buckley's Rev
James; guest beers Ⓗ
Many-roomed pub with a number
of large stone fireplaces and a
tiled public bar. 🏚 🍴 ◖ ▶ 🍺 ♣

THREE TUNS
On B4580 ☎ (01691) 780263
11-11; 12-10.30 Sun
Banks's Mild; Marston's Bitter Ⓗ
Unspoilt village pub with a basic
public bar complete with tiled
floor and inglenook plus a second
room. 🏚 ◖ ▶ 🍺 ♣

LLANWRTYD WELLS

NEUADD ARMS HOTEL
The Square (A483)
☎ (01591) 610236
11.30-11 (may close afternoons);
12-3, 7-10.30 Sun
Draught Bass; Felinfoel Double
Dragon; Hancock's HB; guest
beers Ⓗ
Georgian hotel, extended in the
1860s; an excellent activities
centre in the surrounding mountains and forests. The venue for
the Mid Wales Beer Festival
(Nov) and Saturnalia Beer
Festival (Jan), plus a host of
other wonderfully eccentric
events. 🏚 Q 🌸 🍴 ◖ ▶
🍺 🅰 🍺 ♣ P 🚫

STONECROFT INN
Dolecoed Road (off A483)
☎ (01591) 610332
12-11 (5-11 weekdays winter);
12-10.30 Sun
Brains SA; Ruddles County;
guest beers Ⓗ
Friendly Victorian pub catering
for locals and visitors alike, a
good base for visiting the area.
Attractive patio garden with barbecue area. Children welcome. A
Mid-Wales Beer Festival venue.
🏚 🌸 🍴 ◖ ▶ 🅰 🍺 ♣ P

MACHYNLLETH

SKINNERS ARMS
Main St (A487) ☎ (01654) 702354
11-11; 12-10.30 Sun
Burtonwood Forshaw's; guest
beer Ⓗ
Friendly, timbered town pub with
a lively public bar and games
area and a comfortable
lounge/dining area which has a
superb stove fire in a large stone
inglenook. No children under 16
allowed in bar. No food Mon.
🏚 🌸 ◖ ▶ 🍺 🍺 ♣

WYNNSTAY ARMS HOTEL
Maengwyn St ☎ (01654) 702941
11-11; 12-10.30 Sun
Beer range varies Ⓗ
Small bar in town centre hotel,
serving guest beers from a wide
range of breweries. Two beers
available on handpump. Good
selection of malt whiskies.
🏚 🍴 ◖ ▶ 🍺 P

MONTGOMERY

DRAGON HOTEL
Off B4385 ☎ (01686) 668359
11-3, 6-11; 12-3, 7-10.30 Sun
Beer range varies Ⓗ
Excellent plush bar in a 17th-
century coaching inn. Guest
beers are from independent
breweries, always including one
from Wood's brewery. Jazz Wed
eves. Q 🍴 ◖ ▶ ♣ P

NEW RADNOR

EAGLE HOTEL
Broad Street ☎ (01544) 350208
12-11 (opens at 8am for breakfast; supper licence till 12); 12-
10.30 (opens at 8am for breakfast; supper licence till 11.30) Sun
Draught Bass; Hook Norton Best
Bitter; guest beer Ⓗ
Old coaching inn, now somewhat
altered, with two bars, restaurant, coffee shop and terrace.
Handy for outdoor activities.
🏚 🌸 🍴 ◖ ▶ 🍺 🅰 ♣ ⌂ P 🚫

NEWTOWN

BELL HOTEL
Commercial Street (B4568)
☎ (01686) 625540
12-2, 5-11; 12-10.30 Sun
Six Bells Big Nev's, Spring
Forward; Tetley Bitter Ⓗ
Edge of town hotel with live music
at weekends. Popular with a wide
range of clientele. Six Bells beers
are supplied to the hotel without
using fish finings, making them
vegetarian! 🍴 ◖ ▶ P

RAILWAY TAVERN
Old Kerry Road (off A483)
☎ (01686) 626151
12-2.30, 6.30-11; 11-11 Tue, Fri &
Sat; 12-4, 7-10.30 Sun
Draught Bass; Worthington
Bitter; guest beers Ⓗ
Small, friendly stone-walled locals'
pub, handy for the station. 🍺 ♣

SPORTSMAN
Severn Street (off A483)
☎ (01686) 625885
11-2.30, 5.30-11; 11-11 Fri & Sat;
12-3, 7-10.30 Sun
Ind Coope Burton Ale; Tetley
Bitter; guest beers Ⓗ
Friendly, town-centre local, popular with a wide range of customers. Celtic music nights every
Tue. Q 🌸 ◖ 🍺 ♣

INDEPENDENT BREWERIES

Red Lion:
Llanidloes

PENGENFFORDD

CASTLE INN
On A479, 3 miles S of Talgarth
☎ (01874) 711353
11-3, 7-11 (11-11 Sat, summer &
bank hols); 12-3, 7-10.30 Sun
Wadworth 6X; guest beers
(summer) Ⓗ
Isolated roadside inn, formerly a
drovers' inn situated in the heart
of the Black Mountains. Popular
with hill-walkers and pony
trekkers. 🏚 🌸 🍴 ◖ ▶ 🍺 🅰 ♣ P

PENYBONT

SEVERN ARMS HOTEL
At A44/A488 jct
☎ (01597) 851224
11-2.30, 6-11; 12-3, 7-10.30 Sun
Draught Bass; Worthington
Bitter; guest beers Ⓗ
Roadside inn with an extensive
garden sloping to the River Ithon,
with fishing rights. A large public
bar, games room, quiet , secluded lounge bar and restaurant.
🏚 Q 🌸 🍴 ◖ ▶ 🍺 ♿ 🅰 ♣ P

RHAYADER

TRIANGLE
Off Bridge Street (B4518)
☎ (01597) 810537
12-3, 6.30-11; 11-11 Fri & Sat;
12-3, 7-10.30 Sun
Draught Bass; Hancock's HB Ⓗ
Beautiful little weatherboarded
pub overlooking the River Wye.
The ceilings are so low that customers have to stand in a hole to
play darts. Eve meals end at 8.30
(Sat). Q 🌸 ◖ ▶ 🅰 ♣ P

TALYBONT-ON-USK

STAR INN
On B4558, in centre of village
☎ (01874) 676635
11-3, 6-11; 11-11 Sat; 12-10.30 Sun
Beer range varies Ⓗ
Old canalside pub renovated in
1995 but retaining its traditional
atmosphere. Splendid open fireplace in main bar. Good food
available. Popular with hill walkers, it serves a wide choice of
beers, up to 15 in summer.
🏚 🌸 🍴 ◖ ▶ 🅰 ⌂

Try also: White Hart (Free)

WELSHPOOL

ROYAL OAK HOTEL
Severn Street (off A483)
☎ (01938) 552217
11-3, 5.30-11; 11-11 Mon; 12-3,
7-10.30 Sun
Worthington Bitter; guest beers Ⓗ
Plush, 350-year-old coaching inn,
formerly the manor house of the
Earls of Powis, now a hotel which
has been in the same family for
over 60 years.
🏚 Q 🍴 ◖ ▶ 🍺 P

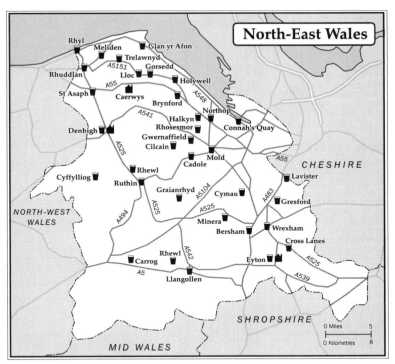

North-East Wales

Authority areas covered: Denbighshire UA, Flintshire UA, Wrexham UA

Denbighshire

CARROG

GROUSE INN
On B5436/7, off A5
☎ (01490) 430272
12-11; 12-10.30 Sun
Lees Bitter H
Lively, comfortable village local, near the Llangollen Railway. Its superb location attracts many summer visitors. Food all day.
🏨 ❀ ◐ ▶ ▲ ⇌ (Llangollen Rlwy)♣ P

CYFFYLLIOG

RED LION
3 miles W of Ruthin off B5105 at Llanfwrog OS060577
☎ (01824) 710664
7-11; 11-11 Sat & July-Aug; 7-10.30 (11-10.30 summer) Sun
Lees Bitter, seasonal beers H
Fine village pub with an unspoilt interior, former coaching inn. Near Clocaenog Forest. No meals Tue; lunches Sat and Sun. The family room is the no-smoking area.🏨 Q ☎ ❀ ⇌ ◐▶♣P⚲▤

DENBIGH

EAGLE INN
Back Row ☎ (01745) 813203
12-11 (12-4, 7-11 Jan-Mar, Mon-Thu); 12-10.30 Sun

Banks's Mild (occasional) **Bitter; Camerons Bitter, Strongarm; Marston's Pedigree** H
Listed inn, dating from 1647; the largest pub in Denbigh, with a large fireplace and a full-size snooker room. 🏨 ❀ ◐ ▲ ♣ P

MASONS ARMS
Rhyl Road (A525)
☎ (01745) 812463
11-11; 12-10.30 Sun
Vaux Samson, Double Maxim; guest beer H
Open-style pub with single bar, and large-screen TV. Guest beers change fortnightly. 🏨 ◐ ▶ ▲ P

GRAIANRHYD

ROSE & CROWN
Llanarmon Road (B5430)
☎ (01824) 780727
12-11; 12-10.30 Sun
Boddingtons Bitter; Flowers IPA; guest beer H
Two-roomed pub with a dining area where children are welcome, serving good value food. Popular with locals and visitors alike. 🏨 ❀ ◐ ▶ ⊟ ♣ P

LLANGOLLEN

SUN
49 Regent St ☎ (01978) 860233
12-11; 12-10.30 Sun
Plassey Bitter; Cains Mild;

Weetwood Best Bitter; guest beers H
Boisterous boozer offering convivial company and a wealth of local independents' ales. The landlord offers discounts to CAMRA members. Regular folk nights. The cider varies.
Q ❀ ⇌ ◐ ♿ ▲ ◔

WYNNSTAY ARMS
Bridge St ☎ (01978) 860710
12-3, 7-11 (11-11 summer); 12-3.30, 7-10.30 Sun
Greene King Abbot; Ind Coope Burton Ale; Morland Old Speckled Hen H
Friendly, family-run hotel with a cosy bar and open fire. The restaurant serves home-cooked food. Garden overlooks the Dee.
🏨 Q ❀ ⇌ ▶ ⊟ ▲ ♣ P

MELIDEN

MELYD ARMS
Ffordd Talargoch (1 mile S of Prestatyn, off A547)
☎ (01745) 852005
11.30-11; 12-10.30 Sun
Banks's Mild; Marston's Bitter H
Early 19th-century inn, once known as the Miners Arms as it served the lead-mining community in the last century, now a popular four-roomed pub for locals and holidaymakers. Good value food.
☎ ❀ ⇌ ◐ ▶ ⊟ ♿ ♣ P

RHEWL (LLANGOLLEN)

SUN
Off B5103 OS178448
☎ (01978) 861043
12-3, 6-11; 12-3, 7-10.30 Sun
Worthington Bitter; guest beers Ⓗ
Historic, 14th-century drover's inn with stone floors; a drop-off place for walkers and fell runners. 🚶 Q ❀ ◖ 🍴 ⏍ ▲ ♣ P

RHEWL (RUTHIN)

DROVERS ARMS
On A525, 2 miles NW of Ruthin
☎ (01824) 703163
12-3 (not Mon), 6-11; 12-10.30 Sun
Dyffryn Clwyd Dr Johnson's, Drover's Special Ⓗ
The flagship for the Vale of Clwyd brewery and their only tied house with three Dyffryn Clwyd beers regularly on sale, plus seasonal brews. Restaurant serves meals Wed-Sun. ❀ ◖ 🍴 ▲ P

RHUDDLAN

NEW INN
High Street (off A525)
☎ (01745) 591305
12-3, 5-11; 12-11 Fri & Sat;
12-10.30 Sun
Theakston Best Bitter, XB; guest beer Ⓗ
Central bar with multiple drinking areas plus a dining area. Guest beers at premium prices for the area. ❀ 🛏 ◖ 🍴 ▲ P

RHYL

SPLASH POINT
Hilton Drive ☎ (01745) 353783
11.30-3, 6.30-11; 12-3, 7-10.30 Sun
Draught Bass; Plassey Bitter; guest beer Ⓗ
Seaside bistro at the end of the promenade;a regular outlet for Welsh ales. Beware the fake handpump and cask breather on M&B Mild. ❀ ◖ 🍴 ▲ P

SWAN
13 Russell Rd ☎ (01745) 336694
11-11; 12-10.30 Sun
Banks's Mild; Marston's Bitter, Pedigree, HBC Ⓗ
Two-bar local close to the town centre.❀ ≥ ♣ ♣

Try also: Prince of Wales, Vale Rd (Marston's)

RUTHIN

WINE VAULTS
St Peters Sq ☎ (01824) 702067
11-11; 12-10.30 Sun
Robinson's Best Bitter Ⓗ
Basic, two room busy local,off the town square. ❀ ▲ ♣ P

Try also: Eagles Hotel, Clwyd St (Marston's)

ST ASAPH

KENTIGERN ARMS
High St (A525) ☎ (01745) 584157
12-3, 7-11; 12-3, 7-10.30 Sun
Bateman Mild; Marston's Bitter, Pedigree; guest beer Ⓗ
Welcoming, traditional local, downhill from Britain's smallest cathedral. A central bar serves a lounge with a large fire.
🚶 🛏 🍴 ◖ ▲ P

Flintshire

BRYNFORD

LLYN Y MAWN
Brynford Hill (1 mile S of Holywell on B5121) ☎ (01352) 714367
5.30-11; 12-3, 6-11 Sat; 12-3, 7-10.30 Sun
Buckley's Best Bitter; guest beers Ⓗ
CAMRA regional *Pub of the Year* 1997, a family-run, former coaching house, much restored and enlarged. It stages the Ales of Wales beer festival in February or March each year. Quiz night Wed, live music Fri eve, no food Mon. 🚶 Q ❀ ◖ ▲ ♣ ⏝ P ⏍

CADOLE

COLOMENDY ARMS
Ruthin Road (100 yds off A494)
☎ (01352) 810217
7 (12 Fri & Sat)-11; 12-10.30 Sun
Marston's Bitter; guest beers Ⓗ
Friendly, two-roomed pub, popular with walkers; near Loggerheads Country Park. Weekly changing range of three guest beers. 🚶 Q ❀ ⏍ ▲ ♣ P

CILCAIN

WHITE HORSE
The Square (B5122)
☎ (01352) 740142
12-3, 5.30 (7 Sat)-11; 12-3, 7-10.30 Sun
Thwaites Bitter; guest beers Ⓗ
Attractive village inn, near Moel Fammau Country Park. Meals served in the split-level lounge.
🚶 Q ◖ 🍴 ⏍ ▲ ♣ P

CONNAHS QUAY

SIR GAWAIN & THE GREEN KNIGHT
Golftyn Lane ☎ (01244) 812623
12-3, 5.30-11; 12-11 Sat;
12-10.30 Sun
Samuel Smith OBB Ⓗ
Comfortable pub, with lunches served Thu-Tue, no eve meals Mon-Fri. The garden houses an aviary. ❀ ◖ ▲ ♣ P

CYMAU

TALBOT
Cymau Road (off A541)
☎ (01978) 761410

12-5 (not Mon-Fri), 7-11; 12-4, 7-10.30 Sun
Hydes' Anvil Mild, Bitter Ⓟ
Hilltop pub with two rooms: a locals' bar with Sky TV and games and a more convivial lounge. Near Hope Mountain Country Park.
Q 🛏 ❀ ◖ ▲ ♣ P ⏍

GLAN-YR-AFON

WHITE LION
West of A548 at Ffynnongrow, 1 mile past Pen-y-Ffordd OS815119
☎ (01745) 560280
12-2 (not winter or summer Mon & Tue); 6-11; 12-3, 7-10.30 Sun
Webster's Yorkshire Bitter; guest beer Ⓗ
Pub of real character with a bar, dining room, no-smoking snug and a conservatory, the former home of the distinguished actor/writer, Emlyn Williams. Spacious outdoor area, where wildlife is encouraged. Lunches served Sat and Sun. 🚶 ❀ ◖ 🍴 ♣ P ⏝

GORSEDD

DRUID INN
☎ (01352) 710944
7-11; 12-3, 7-10.30 Sun
Boddingtons Bitter; Taylor Landlord; guest beers (summer) Ⓗ
400-year-old pub with many rooms. Conservatory restaurant. No meals Sun or Mon eves; Sun lunch served. One of only three Welsh longhouse pubs.
🚶 Q ❀ ◖ ⏍ ▲ ♣ P

GWERNAFFIELD

MINERS ARMS
Church Lane ☎ (01352) 740803
11-11; 12-10.30 Sun
Marston's Bitter, Pedigree, HBC; Thwaites Bitter Ⓗ
Quiet, friendly village pub that gets busy eves, with two drinking areas. Q ❀ ⏍ ▲ ♣ P

HALKYN

BRITANNIA
Pentre Road (off A55)
☎ (01352) 780272
11-11; 12-10.30 Sun
Lees GB Mild, Bitter, Moonraker, seasonal beers Ⓗ
500-year-old stone pub with wonderful views over the Dee. Conservatory restaurant. The garden is home to various animals: shout 'Piggy' and out he comes.
🚶 Q 🛏 ❀ ◖ 🚻 ▲ ♣ P

HOLYWELL

GLAN YR AFON
Milwr Road (signed from A5026)
☎ (01352) 710052
12-3, 7-11; 12-3, 7-10.30 Sun
Courage Directors; Ruddles Best Bitter; Webster's Yorkshire Bitter Ⓗ

Traditional Welsh longhouse with many small rooms; well known for food. ᵐ Q ⊛ ◖ ▮ ♣ P

RED LION
28 High St ☎ (01352) 710097
11-4, 7-11; 12-3, 7-10.30 Sun
Tetley Bitter Ⓗ
Friendly, one-bar, town-centre local. The house beer is brewed by Carlsberg-Tetley. Q ♣

LLOC

ROCK INN
Off A55, 1 mile from W end of A5026 OS766144
☎ (01352) 710049
12-11; 12-10.30 Sun
Burtonwood Bitter, Top Hat Ⓗ
Two-roomed pub and restaurant. The lounge boasts a collection of teapots. Food always available (except Tue eve). Games include boules. ᵐ ⊛ ◖ ▮ ♣ P

MOLD

Y PENTAN
New St ☎ (01352) 758884
11.30-3, 6.30-11; 11-11 Fri & Sat;
12-10.30 Sun
Bateman Dark Mild; Marston's Bitter, Pedigree, HBC Ⓗ
Town-centre pub with an L-shaped lounge, plus a sports TV/games bar. The Daniel Owen theme honours the 19th-century Welsh-language novelist. Public car park adjacent. ⊛ ◖ ⌼ ♣

NORTHOP

STABLES AT SOUGHTON HALL
Soughton Hall (signed off A5119)
☎ (01352) 840577
12-3, 6-11; 12-10.30 Sun
Plassey Bitter; guest beers Ⓗ
Interesting conversion of a stable block of a country hotel, rustic yet cosy. Stables Bitter is brewed by Plassey. Bar snacks until 9.30. Upstairs is an à la carte restaurant. Accommodation in the hotel is at the luxury end of the market. ᵐ ⊛ ⌂ ◖ ▮ ♣ P

RHOSESMOR

RED LION
Rhosesmor Road (B5123, 1 mile from A541) ☎ (01352) 780570
12-2 (not Mon & Wed), 7-11;
12-6, 7-10.30 Sun
Burtonwood Bitter Ⓗ
Unspoilt pub with two rooms plus a pool room in a hilltop location. ᵐ ⊛ ▮

TRELAWNYD

CROWN
London Road (A5151)
☎ (01745) 571580
12-3, 6-11 (12-11 summer);
12-10.30 Sun

Greenalls Mild, Bitter; Tetley Bitter; guest beer Ⓗ
Cheerful, comfortable single-bar village inn with adjoining rooms and a restaurant. Beware, some guest beers may use cask breathers. ᵐ ⌷ ⊛ ◖ ▮ ♣ P

Wrexham

BERSHAM

BLACK LION INN
Y Ddol (off B5097)
☎ (01978) 365588
12-4 (5 Fri), 7-11; 12-11 Sat & summer; 12-10.30 Sun
Hydes' Anvil Billy Westwood's, Mild, Bitter Ⓟ; **guest beers** Ⓗ
Parlour-style bar with rooms offset. Cosy and convivial; recently refurbished to include a garden by the banks of the Clywedog. Next to Bersham Heritage Centre on the Clywedog Industrial Trail. ᵐ ⊛ ⌷ ♣ P

CROSS LANES

KILN INN
On B5130, off A525 at crossroads, signed Cock Bank
☎ (01978) 780429
5.30 (7 Mon)-11; 12-3, 7-11 Sat;
12-3, 7-10.30 Sun
Plassey Bitter; guest beers Ⓗ
Convivial and friendly; three small rooms surround a central servery. Open Sun lunch and eves, except Mon, the little restaurant at the rear (booking advised) does not interfere with the intrinsic 'pubbiness' of this fine village local. A second real ale (often from Hanby) is stocked. ᵐ ⊛ ♣ P

EYTON

PLASSEY LEISURE PARK
Signed from A483, off B5426
☎ (01978) 780905
11-11 (Tree tops Bar closed Nov-March); 12-10.30 Sun
Plassey Bitter, Cwrw Tudno, Stout, Dragons Breath Ⓗ
Treetops Inn is on the caravan park and the Hay Bank Inn is the golf clubhouse. Plassey beer is also sold in the bistro. See the unusual farm crafts on site. Q ⌷ ◖ ▮ P

GRESFORD

GRIFFIN
Church Green
☎ (01978) 852231
1 (12.15 Sat)-4.30, 7-11; 1-4,
7-10.30 Sun
Greenalls Mild, Bitter Ⓗ
Conversation rules in this oasis of calm. The long-serving licensee has overseen few changes during the pub's long tenure in this *Guide*. No food, no juke box, just convivial company. ⊛ ♣ P

GRESFORD

PANT-YR-OCHAIN
Old Wrexham Rd (800 yds from A483/A543) ☎ (01978) 853525
12-3, 5.30-11; 12-11 Sat;
12-10.30 Sun
Boddingtons Bitter; Flowers Original; Plassey Bitter; Taylor Landlord; guest beer Ⓗ
Attractively converted, 16th-century country house in its own grounds with a small lake. Popular with diners and slightly upmarket; no children after 6pm. ᵐ Q ⊛ ◖ ▮ ⌷ & P ⌿

LAVISTER

NAGS HEAD
Old Chester Road (B5445)
☎ (01244) 570486
11.30-3 (not Mon-Tue), 5.30-11;
11.30-11 Sat; 12-10.30 Sun
Boddingtons Bitter; Plassey Bitter; Thwaites Bitter; guest beers Ⓗ
A lively, comfortable village local. Plush, well-appointed lounge; the dining area is a recent addition. ᵐ ⊛ ◖ ▮ ♣ P

MINERA

TYN-Y-CAPEL
Church Road (off A525)
☎ (01978) 757502
7-11; 12-4, 7-11 Sat; 12-4,
7-10.30 Sun
Tetley Bitter; Thwaites Bitter; guest beer Ⓗ
Three-roomed pub, an unspoilt rural free house. The garden has fine views; the Industrial Heritage Trail is close by. ᵐ Q ⊛ ⌷ ♣ P

WREXHAM

ALBION HOTEL
1 Pen-y-Bryn ☎ (01978) 364969
12.30-4, 7-11; 12-3, 7-10.30 Sun
Lees Bitter Ⓗ
Victorian hotel with many original features, which has avoided the improvements thrust on other central pubs. The only local Lees outlet. Q ⌷ ⇌ (Central) ♣

RAILWAY
Railway Road, Stansty (between Plas Coch Retail Park and Rhosddhu) ☎ (01978) 311172
11-3, 7-11; 12-3, 7-10.30 Sun
Banks's Mild; Marston's Bitter Ⓗ
Quiet back-street local, near the football ground. Very good value food. Q ◖ ⇌ (Central) P

INDEPENDENT BREWERIES

Dyffryn Clwyd: **Denbigh**
Plassey: **Eyton**
Travellers Inn: **Caerwys**

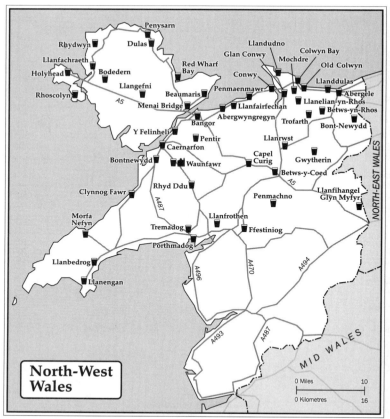

North-West Wales

Authority areas covered: Anglesey UA, Conwy UA, Gwynedd UA

Anglesey/Ynys Môn

BEAUMARIS

OLDE BULLS HEAD
Castle Street
☎ (01248) 810329
11-11; 12-10.30 Sun
Draught Bass; Worthington Bitter; guest beers H
Historic, early 17th-century coaching inn where Dr Johnson and Dickens both stayed. Oak beams, weapons, armour and china are features. It enjoys a reputation for good food.
🏚 Q 🏵 🕸 🛏 🕽 ◗ P

Try also: Liverpool Arms, Main St (Free)

BODEDERN

CROWN HOTEL
Church Street ☎ (01407) 740734
12-3, 6-11; (11-11 summer); 12-3, 7-10.30 Sun
Burtonwood Bitter H
Popular village pub: a basic public bar and a comfortable lounge with a pool/children's room adjacent. 🏚 🏖 🛏 🕽 ◗ ⊞ P

DULAS

PILOT BOAT
On A5025 ☎ (01248) 410205
11-11; 12-10.30 Sun
Robinson's Dark Mild (summer)**, Old Stockport** (summer)**, Best Bitter** H
Rural family pub with a pleasant atmosphere: a games room, dining room with its own bar and a boat-shaped lounge bar. Ideal for coastal walks. Meals all day.
🏚 Q 🏵 🕽 🛆 ♣ P

HOLYHEAD

79
79 Market St ☎ (01407) 763939
11-4, 6.30-11; 12-3, 7-10.30 Sun
Brains SA; guest beer H
Town pub, busy at weekends. The dining area overlooks the ferry port. 🕽 ⇌

Try also: Boston, London Rd (Burtonwood)

LLANFACHRAETH

HOLLAND HOTEL
On A5025 (Cemaes road)
☎ (01407) 740252

11-3.30, 7-11 (11-11 summer); 12-3, 7-10.30 Sun
Lees GB Mild, Bitter, Moonraker (summer) H
Pleasant little village pub with various rooms, including a restaurant, served from a central bar. Ideal for touring and coastal walks, with access to the Irish ferries. Q 🏖 🏵 🛏 🕽 ◗ ♣ P

LLANGEFNI

RAILWAY INN
High Street (opp ex-rail station)
☎ (01248) 722166
12-3.30, 6.30-11; 11-11 Sat; 12-4, 7-10.30 Sun
Lees Bitter H
Friendly pub which recreates the atmosphere of the old railway station. The lounge bar is cut into the rockface. ♣

Try also: Market Hotel (Greenalls)

MENAI BRIDGE

LIVERPOOL ARMS
St Georges Pier ☎ (01248) 713335
11.30-3, 5.30-11; 12-3, 7-10.30 Sun

Greenalls Bitter, Original, seasonal beers; guest beers [H]
Nautically themed, 150-year-old pub, popular with students and the sailing fraternity. Two bars boast several nooks and crannies, plus a conservatory. Very good food and accommodation.
Q ✿ ❀ ⚓ ◖ ▶

VICTORIA HOTEL
Telford Road ☎ (01248) 712309
11-11; 12-10.30 Sun
Draught Bass; guest beers [H]
Popular, comfortable residential hotel; the conservatory and gardens offer excellent views of the Straits. Ideal for island exploration (and licensed for weddings).▲ ✿ ❀ ⚓ ◖▶ ♿ ▲ P ✄

PENYSARN

Y BEDOL
Off A5025 ☎ (01407) 832590
12-11; 12-3, 7-10.30 Sun
Marston's Bitter, Pedigree; guest beers (summer)
Welcoming, family-run pub in a small village. Lounge and a pool/games room. Guest beers are from Marston's list and change regularly. ▲ Q ❀ ▲ ♣ P ⬛

RED WHARF BAY

SHIP INN
1½ miles off A5025, Amlwch road OS525813
☎ (01248) 852568
12-3.30, 7-11 (11-11 summer); 12-10.30 Sun
Benskins BB; Friary Meux BB; Ind Coope Burton Ale; Tetley Dark Mild, Bitter; guest beers [H]
Nautically-themed old pub on the beach, enjoying wonderful views and serving award-winning food. Log fires in winter, stone walls and wooden beams. Busy summer and at weekends.
▲ Q ✿ ❀ ◖ ▶ ▲ ♣ P ✄

RHOSCOLYN

WHITE EAGLE
OS270756 ☎ (01407) 860267
11-3.30, 6.30-11; 12-3, 7-10.30 Sun
Marston's Bitter, Pedigree; guest beers [H]
Modern country pub giving views of Lleyn Peninsula. Holds an annual fireworks display in Nov.
✿ ❀ ◖ ▶ ♿ P

RHYDWYN

CHURCH BAY INN
Off A5025, Valley Rhydwyn/Church Bay turn
☎ (01407) 730867
6 (12 Sat & summer)-11; 12-10.30 Sun
Marston's Bitter; guest beers [H]
Converted rectory with fabulous views of Holyhead Bay; cliff top walks nearby. Excellent bar food, but not available winter weekdays. ▲ ✿ ❀ ◖ ▶ P

Conwy

ABERGELE

BULL HOTEL
Chapel Street ☎ (01745) 832115
11-3, 6-11; 12-3, 7-10.30 Sun
Lees GB Mild, Bitter, seasonal beers [H]
Two-roomed pub with a large, homely lounge and restaurant (children welcome), popular with locals. One of town's oldest buildings. ▲ Q ❀ ◖ ▶ ▲ ≈ ♣ P

GWYNDY
Bridge Street ☎ (01745) 833485
11-11; 12-10.30 Sun
Banks's Mild; Marston's Bitter, Pedigree [H]
Lounge and bar with no-smoking dining area. A friendly popular pub in the town centre.
❀ ◖ ▶ ⬛ ▲ ≈ ♣

BETWS-Y-COED

GLAN ABER HOTEL
Holyhead Road ☎ (01690) 710325
11-11; 12-10.30 Sun
Tetley Dark Mild, Bitter; Dyffryn Clwyd Pedwar Bawd; Morland Old Speckled Hen [H]
Very popular, family-run hotel, centrally located. Non-residents have the choice of three rooms which cater for all tastes, in which the highly recommended meals are served. Three-star en-suite accommodation.
Q ✿ ❀ ⚓ ◖ ▶ ▲ ≈ ♣ P

PONT-Y-PAIR
Holyhead Road ☎ (01690) 710407
11-11; 12-10.30 (11 summer extension) Sun
Dyffryn Clwyd Pedwar Bawd; Greene King Abbot; Tetley Bitter [H]
Comfortable, family-run hotel opposite the famous bridge over the Afon Llugwy. Good selection of freshly cooked meals in the bar and lounge. ▲ Q ⚓ ◖ ▶ ▲ ≈

BETWS-YN-RHOS

WHEATSHEAF INN
☎ (01492) 680218
12-3, 6.30-11; 12-3, 6.30-10.30 Sun
Banks's Mild; Marston's Bitter, Pedigree, HBC (summer); **Taylor Landlord** [H]
Original 17th-century village inn, extended to the rear, on split levels, but retaining a pleasant bar area at the front; oak beams and stone pillars. Good food available in both the lounge (children welcome) and bar. Wheelchair WC.
Q ❀ ⚓ ◖ ▶ ♿ ▲ ♣ P

BONT NEWYDD

DOLBEN ARMS
3 miles W of A525 OS013708
☎ (01745) 582207
7-11 (midnight supper licence); 12-10.30 Sun

Theakston XB; guest beer [H]
16th-century inn and restaurant, in a remote location beside the Afon Elwy at Cefn, near St Asaph. Narrow lanes lead to this charming inn where one bar separates into a restaurant, bar lounge and games/family areas. Popular for Sunday lunches. Q ❀ ▶ ♣ P

CAPEL CURIG

BRYN TYRCH HOTEL
Holyhead Road ☎ (01690) 720223
12-11; 12-10.30 Sun
Castle Eden Ale; Flowers IPA; Wadworth 6X; guest beer (occasional) [H]
Old pub with a quiet room and a TV room, situated in a walkers' paradise in Snowdonia. Extensive menu. ▲ Q ⚓ ◖ ▶ ⬛ ▲ P

COLWYN BAY

WINGS CLUB
Station Square ☎ (01492) 530682
12-3, 6.30-11; 11-11 Sat; 12-3, 7-10.30 Sun
Lees GB Mild, Bitter [H]
Ex-RAFA club, now a social club for visitors and families: CAMRA members especially welcome. It has a large lounge, billiards room, pool & darts room, and snug with TV. Great value. Q ≈ ♣

CONWY

OLDE MAIL COACH INN
High Street ☎ (01492) 593043
12-3; 6-11; 11-11 Sat & summer; 12-10.30 Sun
Theakston Best Best Bitter, Old Peculier (summer); **XB** (occasional) **guest beer** [H]
Former coach inn with a pleasant relaxing atmosphere, now a continental-style café bar which appeals to the over 25s. Entertainment most summer weekends. ▲ Q ❀ ◖ ▶ ≈

GLAN CONWY

CROSS KEYS INN
☎ (01492) 580292
7 (12 Sat)-11; 12-3, 7-10.30 Sun
Marston's Pedigree [H]
Small, traditional, terraced village local, 100 yards from the station, with a bar area. Pool room and a lounge at the rear; upstairs WCs. Socially important, the pub produces its own newspaper. Sandwiches available in summer. ▲ Q ❀ ≈ ♣

GWYTHERIN

LION INN
☎ (01745) 860244
12-2 (not Mon); 7-11 (12-11 summer); 12-3.30, 7-10.30 Sun
Marston's Bitter, Pedigree; guest beer (seasonal) [H]
Traditional village local reputed to be over 300 years old; well furnished, a mixture of old and

new. Offering three crown Welsh Tourist Board accommodation, it is well off the beaten track in a remote village near Abergele. ⚏ Q ✿ ⇔ ◖ ▶ ⊞ ▲ ♣ P

LLANDDULAS

VALENTINE INN
Mill Street ☎ (01494) 518189
12-3 (not winter Mon-Fri), 6.30
(5.30 Sat)-11; 12-3, 7-10.30 Sun
Draught Bass; M&B Mild; Ⓗ
Well renovated, retaining plenty of character, history and a warm welcome; the lounge has an inviting coal fire. The tiny public bar is cosy and warm.
⚏ Q ✿ ◖ ⊞ ▲ ♣

LLANDUDNO

FAT CAT
Mostyn Street ☎ (01492) 871844
11-11; 12-10.30 Sun
Boddingtons Bitter; Theakston XB; guest beers Ⓗ
Pub in the style of a traditional café bar, with wooden floors and furniture. Popular with drinkers and diners of all ages. ✿ ◖ ▶ ≈

OLDE VICTORIA
Church Walks ☎ (01492) 860949
11-11; 12-10.30 Sun
Banks's Mild, Bitter; Camerons Strongarm; Marston's Pedigree; guest beer Ⓗ
The 'Olde Vic' is a popular, traditional Victorian pub with a homely atmosphere. Good value homemade food is served in the lounge or restaurant. Quiz and folk evenings held. Children welcome. Q ⛴ ✿ ◖ ▶ ≈ ♣

PARADE HOTEL
Church Walks ☎ (01492) 876883
11-11; 12-10.30 Sun
Greene King Abbot; Theakston Best Bitter; guest beers Ⓗ
Near the pier, this typical seaside pub has a front lounge and a rear bar with a pool table. ✿ ⊞ ≈ ♣

LLANELIAN-YN-RHOS

WHITE LION INN
☎ (01492) 515807
11-3, 6-11; 11-3, 6-10.30 Sun
Marston's Bitter, Pedigree; guest beer Ⓗ
'Olde worlde' traditional Welsh village inn with an extension for diners, featuring a slate-floored bar, a tiny snug and a lounge; part dates to the 16th century. A true free house where the beers are selected by the landlord.
⚏ Q ✿ ⇔ ◖ ▶ ⊞ ▲ ♣ P

LLANFAIRFECHAN

VIRGINIA INN
Mill Road ☎ (01248) 680584
11-11; 12-2, 7-10.30 Sun
Boddingtons Mild Ⓗ
In the old village, this busy, basic terraced pub is next to the

smithy. The quarry tile floored hallway leads to a small bar and three rooms. A real gem; the landlady has been here for 25 years. The only outlet for the Mild in the county. Q ≈ ♣

LLANFIHANGEL GLYN MYFYR

CROWN INN
On B5105 ☎ (01490) 420209
7 (12 Sat)-11 (closed Mon); 12-10.30 Sun
Draught Bass; guest beer Ⓗ
Lovely old inn beside the Afon Alwen where a warm welcome awaits in the front bar with its open fire. Pool room and a room at the rear. Fishing rights owned by the pub; permits available. Children welcome.
⚏ Q ✿ ⇔ ▶ ▲ ♣ P

LLANRWST

NEW INN
Denbigh Street ☎ (01492) 640476
11-11; 12-10.30 (summer extension until 11); closed sun
Bateman Mild; Marston's Bitter, Pedigree, HBC Ⓗ
Popular, traditional town pub with a single bar, a snug, a general seating area and a rear games area. A hospitable landlord, friendly clientele and good conversation. ⚏ ✿ ▲ ≈ ♣

MOCHDRE

MOUNTAIN VIEW
7 Old Conwy Road
☎ (01492) 544724
11.30-3, 5-11; 11.30-11 Sat; 12-4, 7-10.30 (12-10.30 summer) Sun
Burtonwood Best Bitter, Top Hat, Buccaneer, seasonal beers Ⓗ
Village local: a large lounge with raised dining area and a bar with pool table and TV; good atmosphere. Q ✿ ◖ ▶ ⊞ ♣ P ⅄

OLD COLWYN

RED LION
385 Abergele Road
☎ (01492) 515042
5 (12 Sat)-11; 12-10.30 Sun
Boddingtons Bitter; Higsons Bitter; M&B Mild; guest beers Ⓗ
Popular, traditional town pub: a bar and two lounges; a proper meeting place for locals, where all are welcome. Local CAMRA *Pub of the Year* 1996 and '97. Seven cask ales on, including at least one mild. ⚏ Q ✿ ⊞ ♣

PENMACHNO

MACHNO INN
☎ (01690) 760317
12-3, 6-11; 12-11 Sat; 12-10.30 Sun
Tetley Bitter; Theakston Best Bitter; guest beer Ⓗ
Modern village pub in a remote valley, comfortably catering for all. Benches are set beside a

small stream. Extensive menu. The Theakston's beer range varies. ⚏ ✿ ⇔ ◖ ▶ ♣ P

PENMAENMAWR

ALEXANDRA
High Street ☎ (01492) 622484
11-11; 11-10.30 Sun
Marston's Pedigree; Tetley Dark Mild, Bitter; guest beer Ⓗ
Mid-terraced Victorian pub displaying caricatures of the locals. Fine views from the rear lounge towards Puffin Island. The seasonal guest beers come from Coach House. ⊞ ≈ ♣

LEGEND INN
☎ (01492) 623231
11-11; 11-10.30 Sun (hrs may vary)
Banks's Mild, Bitter; Camerons Bitter; Marston's Pedigree Ⓗ
Step into a legend: full of character, almost overflowing with artefacts, an old-style lounge with a no-smoking snug off. Also has a restaurant, carvery and a bar. Sea views and a children's certificate complete the picture.
Q ✿ ⇔ ◖ ▶ ▲ ≈ ♣ P ⅄ ⊟

TROFARTH

HOLLAND ARMS
Llanrwst Road (B5113, Colwyn Bay road) ☎ (01492) 650777
12-3, 7-11; 12-3, 7-10.30 Sun
Ansells Mild; Tetley Bitter; guest beer Ⓗ
18th-century coaching inn, offering a traditional warm Welsh welcome, set in a country landscape, within sight of Snowdonia. Families welcome until 9.30. Has a bar, lounge bar and a restaurant, popular for good value meals. ⚏ Q ✿ ◖ ▶ ⊞ ♣ P

Gwynedd

ABERGWYNGREGYN

ABER FALLS HOTEL
Off A55, between Llanfairfechan and Bangor ☎ (01248) 680579
11-11; 12-10.30 Sun
Banks's Bitter Ⓗ
Large pub and restaurant in a small village, near the impressive Aber waterfalls and mountains. Families welcome. Aber Original is brewed by Coach House.
⚏ Q ✿ ⇔ ◖ ▶ P

BANGOR

ALBION HOTEL
158 High St ☎ (01248) 370577
12-11; 12-10.30 (Sun)
Burtonwood Bitter, seasonal beers Ⓗ
Open-plan pub, popular with students; has a games room. ✿ ≈

CASTLE
Glanrafon ☎ (01248) 355866
11-11; 12-10.30 Sun
Beer range varies Ⓗ Ⓖ

Spacious, one-roomer offers the widest range of ales in the area, to a good mix of locals and students. The menu (served 12-7) includes specials. ⅃&≈♡⅍

BONTNEWYDD

NEWBOROUGH ARMS
On Porthmadog Road (A487), 2 miles S of Caernarfon
☎ (01286) 673126
11-11; 12-10.30 Sun
Courage Directors; Ind Coope Burton Ale; Marston's Pedigree; Tetley Dark Mild, Bitter; guest beers (summer) H
Busy, often crowded village pub and restaurant, very popular for food, with friendly staff. Families welcome. ▲ ➘ ❀ ⅃▶♣ P

CAERNARFON

ALEXANDRA
North Road (opp Safeway on Bangor road) ☎ (01286) 672871
11-11; 12-10.30 Sun
Draught Bass; Boddingtons Bitter; Chester's Best Mild; Flowers Original H
Pub of original style on the outskirts of town. This free house features two bars offering an excellent variety of beers; a friendly local. Q ❀ ⇔ Å ♣ P

BLACK BOY INN
Northgate St ☎ (01286) 673604
11-11; 12-10.30 Sun
Draught Bass; guest beers H
Old, original pub within the town walls near the castle: a public bar and small lounge, each with roaring fires, plus a restaurant; 25 years in this *Guide*. Limited parking. ▲ ⇔ ⅃▶& ♣ P

CLYNNOG FAWR

COACH INN
On A499, Caernarfon-Pwllheli road ☎ (01286) 660785
12-11; 12-10.30 Sun
Marston's Bitter, Pedigree; guest beers (summer) H
17th-century Grade I listed building overlooking the sea, with an open fire, beams and stone walls. Families welcome; busy in summer. ▲ ➘ ❀ ⇔ ⅃▶Å ♣ P

FELINHELI

GARDD FÔN
Beach Road
☎ (01248) 670359
11-11; 12-10.30 Sun
Burtonwood Bitter, Forshaw's, Top Hat, Buccaneer; guest beer H
18th-century, friendly, nautically themed pub on the quayside near the marina. Popular with locals and visitors, it gets busy in summer. Nice views over the Menai Straits and the sailing races in summer. The guest beer is from Burtonwood.
▲ ➘ ❀ ⅃▶♣ P

FFESTINIOG

PENGWERN ARMS HOTEL
Church Square ☎ (01766) 762210
12-3, 6-11; (12-11 summer); 12-3, 6-10.30 (12-10.30 summer) Sun
Draught Bass H
Three-bar, 14th-century village hotel, popular with walkers and anglers. Local attractions include the Ffestiniog Railway, slate mines and Portmerion. The dining room is open to non-residents.
➘ ❀ ⇔ ⅃▶⊞& P

LLANBEDROG

SHIP INN
Through village off A499 to Aberdaron OS321319
☎ (01758) 740270
11-3, 5.30-11; 11-11 Sat & July-Aug; 12-3, 6-10.30 (12-10.30 July-Aug) Sun
Burtonwood Mild, Bitter; guest beer (summer) H
Friendly local with an interesting layout: a two-tiered lounge, a family/no-smoking area and a public bar serving cheaper beer. Recommended for good value meals, it gets busy in summer.
▲ Q ➘ ❀ ⅃▶⊞Å ♣ P ⅍

LLANENGAN

SUN INN
Through Abersoch to village.
☎ (01758) 712660
12-3, 6-11 (12-11 summer); 12-3, 6-10.30 (12-10.30 summer) Sun
Ind Coope Burton Ale; Tetley Bitter; guest beer H
Five minutes from the beach, this 17th-century free house boasts nice wood panelling, excellent food and safe gardens. Try the award-winning Burton Ale.
▲ Q ➘ ❀ ⅃▶♣ P

LLANFROTHEN

BRONDANW ARMS
On A4085 ☎ (01766) 770555
12-3, 6 (5 Fri)-11; 12-11 Sat & summer; 12-3, 6-10.30 (12-10.30 summer) Sun
Hartleys XB; Robinson's Best Bitter; guest beer H
Hard-to-find local, worth finding: uninspiring exterior hides a large lounge, popular with locals and hill walkers. Live music Fri & Sat. Extensive garden has a children's play area. ▲ Q ➘ ❀ Å P

MORFA NEFYN

CLIFFS INN
Beach Road ☎ (01758) 720356
12-3, 6-11; 12-3, 6-10.30 (not winter eve) Sun
Brains SA; Morland Old Speckled Hen H
Large, friendly pub near the beach and NT coastline. Families welcome, it gets busy in summer. Self-catering flats available.
Q ➘ ❀ ⇔ ⅃▶& Å P

PENTIR

VAYNOL ARMS
Just off B4366, between A5 and Llanberis ☎ (01248) 362895
12-3, 6-11; 12-11 Sat; 12-3, 7-10.30 Sun
Dyffryn Clwyd Pedwar Bawd; Tetley Bitter; Theakston Old Peculier; guest beer H
Pleasant village inn with a locals' bar and a lounge. The restaurant enjoys a good reputation. One of the few outlets for locally-brewed beer. ▲ ❀ ⅃▶♣ P

PORTHMADOG

SHIP
Lombard St ☎ (01766) 512990
11-11; 12-10.30 Sun
Ind Coope Burton Ale; Morland Old Speckled Hen; Tetley Dark Mild, Bitter; guest beers H
Centrally located, characterful pub displaying interesting maritime memorabilia, near the Ffestiniog Railway. Cantonese restaurant upstairs; beer festival in October. ▲ Q ⅃▶& ≈ P ⅍

RHYD DDU

CWELLYN ARMS
On A4085, Caernarfon-Beddgelert Rd ☎ (01766) 890321
11-11; 12-10.30 Sun
Draught Bass; Highgate Dark; Worthington Bitter; guest beers H
Beamed, 200-year-old pub at the foot of Snowdon. Six guest beers and extensive menus mean it gets busy in summer. Children's playground. ▲ Q ❀ ⇔ ⅃▶Å P

TREMADOG

GOLDEN FLEECE
The Square (A487, 1 mile N of Porthmadog) ☎ (01766) 512421
11-3, 6-11; 12-3, 6-10.30 Sun
Draught Bass; Dyffryn Clwyd Pedwar Bawd H
Old coaching inn, now a friendly local with a bistro, serving excellent value meals. Children welcome. ▲ Q ❀ ⇔ ⅃▶& ⅍

WAUNFAWR

SNOWDONIA PARC
Beddgelert Rd (A4085 Caernarfon rd) ☎ (01286) 650218
12-2, 6-11 (12-3, 5-11 summer); 12-10.30 Sun
Marston's Bitter, Pedigree; guest beers H
Popular pub for walkers, climbers and campers in the heart of Snowdonia. ➘ ❀ ⅃▶Å ♣ P

INDEPENDENT BREWERIES

Waunfawr:
Snowdonia

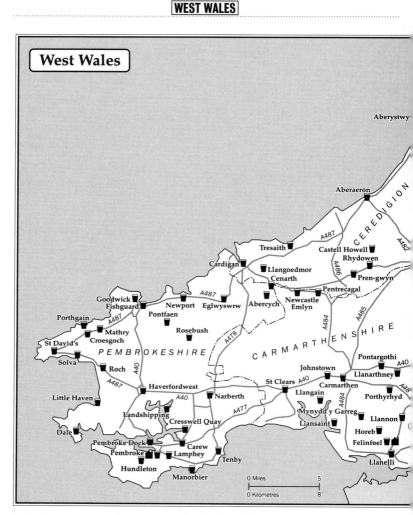

West Wales

Aberystwy

Aberaeron

Tresaith
Castell Howell
Rhydowen
Cardigan
Llangoedmor
Cenarth
Pren-gwyn
Pentrecagal
Goodwick
Fishguard
Newport
Eglwyswrw
Abercych
Newcastle
Emlyn
Porthgain
Pontfaen
Mathry
Croesgoch
Rosebush
St David's
Solva
Roch
Haverfordwest
Johnstown
Pontargothi
Llanarthney
St Clears
Carmarthen
Porthyrhyd
Little Haven
Narberth
Llangain
Landshipping
Cresswell Quay
Mynydd y Garreg
Llannon
Dale
Llansaint
Horeb
Pembroke Dock
Carew
Lamphey
Tenby
Felinfoel
Pembroke
Hundleton
Manorbier
Llanelli

0 Miles 5
0 Kilometres 8

Authority areas covered: Camarthenshire UA, Ceredigion UA, Pembrokeshire UA

bCarmarthenshire

AMMANFORD

WERNOLAU
31 Pontamman Road
☎ (01269) 592598
5-11; 12-3, 7-10 Sun
**Buckley's Best Bitter; guest
beers** Ⓗ
A welcome island of real ale in a
sea of keg. Look hard or you will
miss the entrance. Families welcome.
🏰 Q 🏵 🛏 ▶ 🅰

CAIO

BRUNANT ARMS
Church Street (1 mile NE of
A482)
☎ (01558) 650483
12-3, 6.30-11; 12-11 Sat; 12-3,
7-10.30 Sun
**Badger Tanglefoot; Boddingtons
Mild; Worthington Bitter; guest
beers** Ⓗ
Friendly, characterful pub, in the
centre of the UK's largest parish,
close to the Dolaucothi Gold
Mines. It boasts a vast number of
pub games. Families welcome;
good B&B.
🏰 Q 🏵 🛏 ◁ ▶ 🅰 ♣ ⌂ P

CARMARTHEN

MANSEL ARMS
1 Mansel Street (near produce
market)
☎ (01267) 236385
11 (9 Wed & Sat)-11; 12-10.30
Sun
**Draught Bass; Worthington
Dark, Bitter; guest beers** Ⓗ
A lively town pub, popular with
shoppers and locals.
🏵 ◁ 🅑 ⇌

QUEENS HOTEL
Queen Street
☎ (01267) 231800
11-11; 12-10.30 Sun
**Draught Bass; Worthington
Bitter; guest beers** Ⓗ
Convivial, town-centre pub, popular with all ages. Very busy at
weekends. Lunchtime snacks
are available
🏵 🕮 ⇌

Try also: Boar's Head, Lammas
St (Felinfoel)

CENARTH

THREE HORSESHOES
On A484
☎ (01239) 710119
11-11; 12-10.30 (closed winter
eves) Sun
Draught Bass Ⓖ**; Buckley's Best
Bitter** Ⓗ**, Rev. James** Ⓖ

FELINFOEL

ROYAL OAK
33 Farmers Row (opp brewery)
☎ (01554) 751140
11-11; 12-4, 7-10.30 Sun
Felinfoel Bitter, Double Dragon Ⓗ
Welcoming pub with good food (served Wed-Sat).
Ⓓ ▶ &

HOREB

WAUNWYLLT INN
Horeb Road (off B4309 at Fiveroads, 3 miles from Llanelli)
☎ (01269) 860209
12-3, 6.30-11; 12-3, 7-10.30 Sun
Felinfoel Double Dragon; guest beers Ⓗ
Popular pub with a good reputation for food; families welcome. It offers a house bitter brewed by Wye Valley in summer.
🏔 Q ✿ ⊨ Ⓓ ▶ Ⓓ Ａ P

JOHNSTOWN

FRIENDS ARMS
St Clears Road
☎ (01267) 234073
11-11; 12-10.30 Sun
Ansells Mild; Ind Coope Burton Ale; Tetley Bitter Ⓗ
Vibrant local pub; watch for the lights at Christmas. ✿

Try also: Poplars, Pond Side (Watkin)

LLANARTHNEY

GOLDEN GROVE
On B4300
☎ (01558) 668551
12-2.30, 6-11; 11-11 Sat;
12-10.30 Sun
Buckley's Best Bitter, Rev James; Worthington Bitter Ⓗ
Former coaching inn, at the heart of the Towy valley: excellent food, a warm friendly atmosphere. Families welcome. Reasonably priced B&B.
🏔 Q ✿ ⊨ Ⓓ ▶ ♣ P

LLANDEILO

CASTLE HOTEL
113 Rhosmaen Street
☎ (01558) 823446
12-11; 12-3, 7-10.30 Sun
Watkin BB, OSB, seasonal beers; guest beer Ⓗ
Restored pub with a brewery at the back. Very popular with all ages. The OSB won the *Beer of Wales* award in 1998.
🏔 ✿ Ⓓ ▶ ≈ ⅄

WHITE HORSE INN
125 Rhosmaen Street
☎ (01558) 822424
12-11; 12-10.30 Sun
Wells Bombardier; Worthington Bitter; guest beers Ⓗ

Friendly, old coaching inn hosting live music every Fri. Public car park behind the pub.
🏔 ⭐ ✿ Ⓓ ▶ ≈

LLANDOVERY

CASTLE HOTEL
Kings Road (A40)
☎ (01550) 720343
11-10; 12-3 Sun
Watkin OSB; Worthington Bitter; guest beer Ⓗ
Friendly, town-centre hotel bar.
Q ⊨ Ⓓ ▶ & Ａ ≈ P ⅄

WHITE SWAN
High Street (A40)
☎ (01550) 720816
12-3.30, 7-11; 12-3, 7-10.30 Sun
Wadworth 6X (summer); guest beers Ⓗ
Comfortable pub with a warm welcome for visitors.
🏔 ✿ Ａ ≈ ♣

LLANDYBIE

IVY BUSH
18 Church Street (near station)
☎ (01269) 850272
12-4 (not Mon), 6-11; 12-2 Sun
Buckley's Best Bitter; Ind Coope Burton Ale; Worthington Bitter; guest beers (summer) Ⓗ
Friendly pub with a gym and sauna at the rear. Ⓓ ≈ ♣ ⅄

LLANELLI

APPLE TREE
Station Road ☎ (01554) 774562
11-11; 12-10.30 Sun
Draught Bass; guest beers (occasional) Ⓗ
Basic pub, full of local character.
≈

LEMON TREE
2 Prospect Place (behind old Buckley's brewery)
☎ (01554) 775121
12-11; 12-10.30 Sun
Buckley's Best Bitter; guest beer Ⓗ
Popular local with a bowling green at the back. It holds a beer festival each Easter. ✿ ♣

UNION INN
Bryn Road, Seaside (off new bypass, by roundabout)
☎ (01554) 759514
11-11; 12-10.30 Sun
Crown Buckley CPA; Buckley's Best Bitter; guest beer Ⓗ
Due to start a meals service from summer 1998.
🏔 Q ✿ Ⓓ ▶ Ⓓ ≈ P

LLANGAIN

TAFARN PANTYDDERWEN
☎ (01267) 241560
12-3, 6-11; 12-3, 6-10.30 Sun
Flowers Original; guest beers Ⓗ
Village pub with a golf course

Cosy, traditional inn with a thatched former brewhouse at the rear. The garden overlooks Cenarth Falls.
🏔 Q ✿ Ⓓ ▶ Ａ ♣ P

Try also: White Hart (Free)

CWMANN

RAM INN
On A482, outskirts of village
☎ (01570) 422556
11-11; 12-10.30 Sun
Draught Bass; Fuller's London Pride; guest beers Ⓗ
Dating from the 16th century, this traditional pub also has a large garden. Interesting guest beers always available. CAMRA's *Best Pub in Wales* 1997.
🏔 Q ✿ Ⓓ ▶ Ⓓ & ♣ P

Try also: Cwmann Tavern, Carmarthen Road (Courage)

attached. The building was recently extended to provide a comfortable restaurant offering a wide range of food and wines at sensible prices. Good range of guest beers.
❀ ◖ ▶ ᕇ ♣ P

LLANNON

RED LION
3 Heol y Plas
☎ (01269) 841276
5 (12 Sat)-11; 12-3, 7-10.30 Sun
Felinfoel Dark, Bitter, Double Dragon Ⓗ
Pub with a long history, featuring a well and a secret tunnel. A full a la carte menu includes some unusual dishes.▲ Q ⌣ ▶ P

LLANSAINT

KINGS ARMS
13 Maes y Eglwys
☎ (01267) 267487
12-2, 6-11; 12-2 (not winter), 7-10.30 Sun
Beer range varies Ⓗ
Traditional pub with stone walls and a beamed ceiling, serving good food.
▲ Q ❀ ✉ ◖ ▶ ᕇ ᐱ ♣ P

LLANSAWEL

BLACK LION
10 miles N of Llandeilo on B4337
☎ (01558) 685263
5 (11 Sat)-11; 12-4, 7-10.30 Sun
Ansells Mild; Worthington Bitter; guest beers Ⓗ
Unspoiled village pub, doubling as the local rugby club HQ.
▲ ✉ ◖ ▶ ♣

MYNYDD Y GARREG

PRINCE OF WALES INN
Heol Meinciau
☎ (01554) 890522
5-11; 12-3, 7-10.30 Sun
Beer range varies Ⓗ
Cosy, atmospheric village inn displaying cinema memorabilia. Six ever changing beers; excellent food for every taste including vegetarian dishes and Sunday lunches in a no-smoking restaurant. No under-fourteens.
▲ Q ❀ ▶ ᐱ P

NEWCASTLE EMLYN

BUNCH OF GRAPES
Bridge Street (near Market Sq)
☎ (01239) 711185
12-11; 12-10.30 (closed winter eve) Sun
Courage Directors; Theakston Best Bitter; guest beer Ⓗ
Busy, listed town pub: one main bar with an exposed oak-beamed ceiling and wood floors. Popular with all ages. Live music Thu eve. Meals in summer.
▲ ❀ ◖ ▶ ᐱ

COOPERS ARMS
Station Road (A484, E of town centre)
☎ (01239) 710323
12-3.30, 5.30-11; 12-3, 7-10.30 Sun
Draught Bass; Worthington Bitter Ⓗ
Friendly pub offering excellent food and an extensive wine list. Noisy children are not welcome.
❀ ◖ ▶ ᐱ ♣ P ✄

Try also: Ivy Bush, Emlyn Sq. (Free)

PENTRECAGAL

PENSARNAU ARMS
On A484
☎ (01559) 370339
12-11; 12-10.30 Sun
Draught Bass; Ⓖ **Crown Buckley CPA; Worthington Bitter** Ⓗ
Friendly country pub with good quality food; families with children are welcome. Situated very near the Henllan tourist railway.
▲ Q ◖ ▶ ᐱ ♣ ⌣ P

PONTARGOTHI

CRESSELLY ARMS
On A40, midway between Carmarthen and Llandeilo
☎ (01267) 290221
12-3, 6.30-11; 12-3, 7-10.30 Sun
Flowers Original; Marston's Pedigree; guest beers Ⓗ
Good pub with good food, situated on the river bank. The garden has play equipment for younger children.
▲ Q ❀ ◖ ▶ P

Try also: Salutation, on A40 (Felinfoel)

PORTHYRHYD

MANSEL ARMS
Banc y Mansel (off A48)
☎ (01267) 275305
12-3 (not Mon-Fri), 6-11; 12-3, 7-10.30 Sun
Beer range varies Ⓗ
Comfortable pub, a couple of miles off the A48. One guest ale stocked. Eve meals Fri and Sat.
▲ ▶ ᐱ ♣ P

RHANDIRMWYN

ROYAL OAK INN
☎ (01550) 760201
11-11 (may vary winter); 12-2, 7-10.30 (may vary) Sun
Ind Coope Burton Ale; Tetley Bitter; guest beer (summer) Ⓗ
A gem of a pub with a good view. Nice to visit after going to the nearby bird reserve or reservoir.
▲ ❀ ✉ ◖ ▶ ᐱ ♣ P

ST CLEARS

CORVUS
Station Road (off dual carriageway, far end of village)
☎ (01994) 230965
11-11; 12-10.30 Sun
Courage Best Bitter; Worthington Bitter; guest beers Ⓗ
Pleasant pub where the guest beers vary according to the tastes of the locals.
◖ ▶ ▣ ♣

Ceredigion

ABERAERON

ROYAL OAK
North Road (A487)
☎ (01545) 570233
11-11 (may close afternoon); 12-10.30 (may close afternoons) Sun
Ind Coope Burton Ale; Tetley Bitter Ⓗ
A decorative lounge bar leads to a large public bar/games room behind.
▲ Q ⌣ ◖ ▶ ▣ ᕇ ᐱ ♣

ABERYSTWYTH

CAMBRIAN HOTEL
Alexandra Road
☎ (01970) 612446
11-11; 12-10.30 Sun
Hancock's HB; guest beer Ⓗ
Elegant, though slightly jaded, hotel opposite the railway and bus termini. A lounge bar and a cocktail lounge. Popular with locals, students and visitors.
✉ ◖ ▶ ᐱ ≈ ♣

COOPERS (Y CWPS)
Northgate Street
☎ (01970) 624050
11-11; 11-10.30 (may close afternoon) Sun
Felinfoel Bitter, Cambrian Bitter Double Dragon; Ⓗ
This is a strongly Welsh pub with a basic, long, narrow bar, bedecked with posters and 'maps Cymraeg' and a small snug. Self-catering accommodation available in summer.
✉ ◖ ᐱ ≈ ♣

FLANNERY'S BREWERY TAP
High Street
☎ (01970) 612334
12-11; 12-10.30 Sun
Flannery's Granny Flan's, Celtic Ale, Oatmeal Stout, Rheidol Reserve; guest beer Ⓗ
Authentic Irish pub (the landlady is from Kilkenny). The intimate bar is popular with students and locals alike. It serves Flannery's range of beers and a guest beer (usually from a microbrewery). Weekend lunches.
◖ ᐱ ≈ ♣

FOUNTAIN INN
Trefechan
☎ (01970) 612430
12-11; 12-10.30 Sun
Banks's Mild; Hancock's HB; guest beer H
Characterful, edge-of-town local with a warm welcome. The wide spectrum of clientele makes for a fascinating atmosphere.
※ ◁ ▶ ⛃ ⌂ ⚲ ≈ ♣

RUMMERS WINE BAR
Bridge Street
☎ (01970) 625177
7-11; 7-10.30 Sun
Ind Coope Burton Ale; Tetley Bitter; guest beer H
A spacious L-shaped, one-roomed bar with a slate floor, situated on the riverside. The bar stages live music Thu and Fri, ranging from blues and jazz to folk in a relaxed but busy atmosphere. Late licence most eves. Pizzas available to take away.
※ ▶ ⌂ ≈

BORTH

FRIENDSHIP INN
High Street
☎ (01970) 871213
12-3, 7-11 (may extend Aug & Sep); 12-4, 7-10.30 Sun
Ansells Bitter; Benskins BB; guest beer (occasional) H
Cottage-style pub in a seaside village, featuring an art gallery to the rear which also serves as a no-smoking family room. A free house, it has been run by the same family since 1921. Lunchtime snacks in summer.
🏠 ※ ⌂ ≈ ♣ ½

CARDIGAN

EAGLE INN
Castle Street
☎ (01239) 612046
11.30-3.30, 5.30-11; 11.30-11 Mon & Sat; closed Sun
Buckley's Best Bitter; Worthington Bitter; guest beer (occasional) H
Beautiful little pub with a tiled floor and impeccably polished furniture. The main bar leads into a quiet area and a lounge bar-cum-restaurant. Suntrap garden.
Q ⛴ ※ ◁ ▶ ⛃ ⛘ ♣

CASTELL HOWELL

CASTLE HOWELL INN/TAFARN BACH
On B4459
☎ (01545) 590269
11-11; 12-10.30 Sun
Buckley's Best Bitter; guest beer (summer) H
Friendly village pub run by the same landlord for over 20 years.
🏠 ※ ◁ ▶ ♣ P

CELLAN

FISHERS ARMS
On B4343, 1 mile NE of A482
☎ (01570) 422895
11-11; 12-10.30 Sun
Worthington Bitter; guest beer H
Roadside pub with a large bar, a pool room (children admitted) and a restaurant. Popular with anglers - the river Teifi is just across the road. Book Sun lunch.
🏠 ※ ◁ ▶ ♣ P

GOGINAN

DRUID INN
7 miles E of Aberystwyth
☎ (01970) 880650
6-11; closed Sun
Banks's Bitter; guest beers H
Free house on the hillside in a former lead mining village, offering two changing guest beers. Families welcome. 🏠 ※ ▶ ♣ P

LLANBADARN FAWR

BLACK LION
Off A44 ☎ (01970) 623448
11-11; 12-10.30 Sun
Banks's Mild, Bitter; Marston's Pedigree; guest beer H
Friendly pub, frequented by locals and students. Live music most Fri eves with a late licence.
※ ◁ ▲ ♣ P ⛿

LLANGOEDMOR

PENLLWYNDU
Penllwyndu Cross (on B4570, 4 miles E of Cardigan)
☎ (01239) 682533
12-11; 12 (1 winter)-10.30 Sun
Draught Bass; Brains SA; guest beer H
Traditional split-level bar, featuring a large inglenook and scrub-top tables in a friendly atmosphere. Occasional live music. The garden has a spacious play area for children. 🏠 ※ ◁ ▶ ▲ ♣ P

PREN-GWYN

GWARCEFEL ARMS
On A475
☎ (01559) 362720
11-11; 12-3 (closed eve) Sun;
Buckley's Best Bitter; guest beer H
Excellent pub, popular for meals where children are welcome.
🏠 ◁ ▶ ▲ ♣ P

RHYDOWEN

ALLT YR ODYN ARMS
(at A475/B4459 jct)
☎ (01545) 590319
12-11; 12-10.30 (4 winter) Sun
Badger Tanglefoot; Buckley's Best Bitter; guest beer H
Friendly village pub dating back to Queen Elizabeth I. Note the exceptional collection of mugs

and jugs. Good food. Play horseshoes. Large garden.
🏠 Q ※ ⛱ ◁ ▶ ▲ ♣ P
CAMRA Ceredigion Pub of the Year 1997.

TREGARON

TALBOT HOTEL
In Main Square
☎ (01974) 298208
11-11; 12-10.30 Sun
Boddingtons Bitter; Flannery's Celtic Ale; Marston's Pedigree H
The principal hotel in one of Wales' smallest and most remote towns - an excellent base for exploring the Cambrian mountains. Established in the 14th century, rebuilt in the 1870s and containing much period furniture, the Talbot oozes character and tradition.
🏠 Q ⛴ ※ ⛱ ◁ ▶ ⛃ ▲ ♣ P

Try also: Teifi Inn, Ffair-Rhos (Hancock's)

TRESAITH

SHIP INN
Next to beach ☎ (01239) 810380
12-2.30 (3 summer), 6-11; 12-4 Sun
Buckley's Best Bitter; guest beer H
Stylish lounge bar with a no-smoking conservatory looking out over the beach and the coast beyond. A games room and a large patio complete the picture. Imaginative menu. Wheelchair WC. 🏠 Q ⛱ ※ ⛘ P

Pembrokeshire

ABERCYCH

NAGS HEAD
☎ (01239) 841200
11-3, 5.30-11; 11-11 Sat; 12-10.30 Sun
Flowers Original; Nags Head Old Emrys; Worthington Bitter; guest beers H
Well-restored old smithy with a beamed bar, riverside garden and microbrewery. Phone to check on the availability of Old Emrys. 🏠 Q ⛴ ※ P

CAREW

CAREW INN
☎ (01646) 651267
12-2.30, 4.30-11; 11-11 (Sat & summer); 7-10.30 Sun
Buckley's Rev James; Worthington Bitter; guest beer H
Traditional pub opposite an historic castle. Live music Thu throughout the summer and sometimes in winter.
🏠 ※ ◁ ▶ ▲ P

Try also: Plough Inn, Sageston (Free)

CRESSWELL QUAY

CRESSELLY ARMS
☎ (01646) 651210
12-3, 5-11; 12-3, 7-10.30 Sun
Worthington Bitter; guest beer
(Monday) G
Waterside pub, unaltered since
1900, where the beer is served in
jugs. Popular with all ages.
🏠 Q P

CROESGOCH

ARTRAMONT ARMS
On A487
☎ (01348) 831309
7-11 (12-3, 6-11 summer); 12-3,
6-10.30 Fri & Sat; 12-3, 7-10.30
Sun
Brains SA; guest beers H
Friendly local with a large bar
and a dining room offering an
interesting menu.
🏠 ❀ ◑ ▶ ▲ P ⚞

DALE

GRIFFIN INN
☎ (01646) 636227
7 (11 summer)-11; 12-10.30 Sun
**Worthington Bitter; guest
beers** H
Harbour pub at the end of the
bay with outside seating on the
sea wall and benches. Table skittles played.
🏠 ◑ ▶ ♣

EGLWYSWRW

BUTCHERS ARMS
On A487, Newport-Cardigan Road
☎ (01239) 891630
11-3, 7-11; 11-11 Sat; 12-3,
7-10.30 Sun
**Buckley's Rev James; Tetley
Bitter; Worthington Bitter** H
Pub with a cosy bar offering
meals in summer (also weekends
in winter) in a no-smoking
restaurant.
🏠 Q ⊨ ◑ ▶

FISHGUARD

FISHGUARD ARMS
Main Street
☎ (01348) 872763
11-3, 6.30-11; 12-3, 7-10.30 Sun
**Worthington Bitter; guest
beer** G
Step back in time at this unspoilt,
friendly old pub.
🏠 Q ⊞ ▲

ROYAL OAK INN
Market Square
☎ (01348) 872514
11-11; 12-10.30 Sun
**Draught Bass; Hancock's HB;
guest beer** H
Charming, friendly, comfortable
pub with historic connections
(French forces surrendered here
following the last invasion of
mainland Britain in 1797). Home

cooking at good prices with a
varied menu.
❀ ◑ ▶ ⊞ ▲ ♣

Try also: Ship Inn, Lower Town
(Free)

GOODWICK

ROSE & CROWN
☎ (01348) 874449
11-11; 12-3, 7-10.30 Sun
**James Williams IPA; Worthington
Bitter; guest beer** H
Picturesque pub, close to the
ferry with harbour views. It has a
small but welcoming no-smoking
restaurant.
❀ ◑ ▲ ⇌ ♣ P

Try also: Harp, Letterston
(Whitbread)

HAVERFORDWEST

PEMBROKE YEOMAN
Hill Street (off St Thomas Green)
☎ (01437) 762500
11-11; 12-3, 7-10.30 Sun
**Flowers IPA; Worthington
Bitter;** H **guest beers** H G
Comfortable local attracting all
ages. Good food. ◑ ▶ ♣

HUNDLETON

SPECULATION INN
☎ (01646) 661306
12-3 (2 winter), 6-11; 12-3,
7-10.30 Sun
**Felinfoel Bitter, Double Dragon;
Worthington Bitter; guest beer**
(summer) H
Built in 1730 as a local for farm
workers, this unspoilt pub holds
a children's certificate. Very inexpensive, basic menu; snacks only
eves.
🏠 Q ⌂ ❀ ◑ ⊞ ▲ ♣ P

LAMPHEY

DIAL INN
☎ (01646) 672426
11-3 (possibly later summer), 6-
11; 11-11 Sat; 12-10.30 Sun
**Draught Bass; Hancock's HB;
Worthington Bitter; guest beer** H
Pub situated in the middle of a
quiet village of historical interest.
Excellent food; families welcome.
🏠 Q ⌂ ❀ ◑ ▶ ▲ ⇌ ♣
P ⚞

LANDSHIPPING

STANLEY ARMS
OS11118
☎ (01834) 891227
12-3, 6-11; 12-3, 7-10.30 Sun
**Draught Bass; Worthington
Bitter; guest beer** H
Attractive pub, near the estuary
in a quiet location offering an
excellent choice of beers and
food.
🏠 Q ❀ ◑ ▶ ⊞ ▲ ♣ P

LITTLE HAVEN

SWAN
☎ (01437) 781256
11.30-3, 6-11 (11.30-2.30, 7-11
winter); 12-3, 7 (6 summer)-10
Sun
**Draught Bass; Wadworth 6X;
Worthington Bitter** H
Waterside pub near the beach,
popular for food.
🏠 Q ◑ ▲

Try also: Dylans, Bistro St
Brides Way (Free)

MANORBIER

CASTLE INN
☎ (01834) 871268
11-11; 12-10.30 Sun
**Theakston Best Bitter; Old
Peculier; Wadworth 6X; guest
beer** (summer) H
Situated in a small, unspoilt, picturesque village, close to the
beach and castle, this pub and
restaurant serves good food.
Families welcome.
❀ ◑ ▶ ▲ ♣

MATHRY

FARMERS ARMS
Off A487
☎ (01348) 831284
11-11; 12-3, 7-10.30 Sun
**Draught Bass; Hancock's HB;
Worthington Bitter** H
Rural pub with a timbered
interior: a monk's brewhouse in
1291. Friendly welcome.
🏠 ❀ ⊨ ◑ ♿ ▲ ♣ P

NARBERTH

KIRKLAND ARMS
East Gate, St James Street
☎ (01834) 860423
11-11; 12-3, 7-10.30 Sun
**Felinfoel Bitter, Double Dragon;
guest beer** H
Pub with an unspoilt bar and
original fittings. ▲ ⇌ P

NEWPORT

CASTLE HOTEL
Bridge Street (A487)
☎ (01239) 820742
11-11; 12-10.30 Sun
**Wadworth 6X; Worthington
Bitter; guest beer** H
Friendly, popular local. The
attractive bar has a real fire;
extensive dining area.
🏠 ⌂ ❀ ⊨ ◑ ▶ ▲ P

PEMBROKE

CASTLE INN
Main Street
☎ (01646) 682883
11-11; 12-10.30 Sun
**Greene King Abbot; Wadworth
6X; Worthington Bitter; guest
beer** H

Very popular with young people especially at the weekend; an old pub in an historic town.
🏕 🅰 ⇌ ♣ P

OLD CROSS SAWS INN
Main Street
☎ (01646) 682475
11-11; 12-10.30 Sun
Buckley's Best Bitter, Rev James; guest beers Ⓗ
Friendly pub, popular with rugby followers, centrally located. The menu is good and well-priced. Live music Sat eve.
🏕 ⇋ ◖▮ 🅰 ⇌ ♣ P

PEMBROKE DOCK

FIRST & LAST
London Road
☎ (01646) 682687
11-11; 12-10.30 Sun
Worthington Bitter; guest beer Ⓗ
Popular, friendly, local offering a good variety of guest beers. Live music Sat eves. Cheap meals and snacks served.
🏕 ◖▮ 🅰 ⇌ ♣ P

STATION INN
Dimond Street
☎ (01646) 621255
7-11; 12-2, 7-10.30 Sun
Pembroke Darklin, Dimond Lager, Main Street Bitter, Old Nobbie, Off the Rails; guest beer Ⓗ
This redundant station building at the end of the line has been brought back to life as the tap for the Pembroke Brewery. A new beer every Tue plus a beer festival in June. Live music Sat.
🏕 Q 🅰 ⇌ P

Try also: Brewery Inn, Cosheston (Free)

PONTFAEN

DYFFRYN ARMS
Off B4313
☎ (01348) 881305
Hours vary
Draught Bass or Ind Coope Burton Ale Ⓖ
1920s front room where time has stood still; beer is still served by the jug and conversation is a

must. Set in the Gwain valley between the Preseli mountain and Fishguard. ♣
🏕 Q 🏕 🅰 ♣

PORTHGAIN

SLOOP INN
☎ (01348) 831449
11.30-3, 6-11 (11-11 summer); 12-4, 6-10.30 Sun
Brains SA; Felinfoel Double Dragon; Worthington Bitter Ⓗ
Old fishing pub featuring quarrying and shipping ephemera.
🏕 🏕 ◖▮ ♣ P

ROCH

VICTORIA INN
On A487
☎ (01437) 710426
12-3, 7-11; 12-6 Sun
Draught Bass; Worthington Bitter; guest beer Ⓗ
Small, family-run pub, popular with locals where families are welcome. Active in the local darts and pool leagues.
🏕 Q 🏕 🅰 ♣ P

ROSEBUSH

NEW INN
On B4329
☎ (01437) 532542
11-11; 12-3, 7-10.30 Sun
Buckley's Best Bitter, Rev James; guest beers Ⓗ
Pub close to the spa village of Rosebush, specialising in continental bottled beers. Two guest ales in summer, one in winter. Booking advised for meals at this popular eatery.
🏕 Q 🏕 ◖▮ 🅰 ⌣

SOLVA

HARBOUR INN
Main Street
☎ (01437) 720013
11.30-11; 12-10.30 Sun
Draught Bass; Worthington Bitter; Ⓗ **guest beers** Ⓖ
Popular harbourside inn, which is decorated with fishing and shipping paraphernalia.
🏕 ⇋ ◖▮ ⊞

SOLVA

SHIP INN
Main Street
☎ (01437) 721247
11-11; 12-3, 7-10.30 Sun
Draught Bass; Worthington Bitter; guest beers Ⓗ
Small, 300-year-old pub, popular with holidaymakers, in a pretty fishing village setting. Lunches in summer. 🏕 Q 🏕 🏕 ◖▮ ⅊ ♣

ST DAVIDS

FARMERS ARMS
12-14 Goat Street
☎ (01437) 720328
11-11; 12-10.30 Sun
Flowers Original; Worthington Bitter Ⓗ
19th-century, stone-built pub maintaining many old features. Popular with fishermen and farmers, it serves good, home-cooked meals. 🏕 Q 🏕 ◖▮ ⊞ 🅰

TENBY

CROWN INN
Lower Frog Street
☎ (01834) 842796
11 (12 winter)-11; 12-10.30 Sun
Banks's Bitter; Worthington Bitter; guest beer (summer) Ⓗ
Small pub, inside the walls of Tenby. No meals in winter.
🏕 ◖ ⊟

HOPE & ANCHOR
St Julian Street
☎ (01834) 842131
11-3, 7-11 (11-11 summer); 12-10.30 Sun
Buckley's Rev James; Worthington Bitter; guest beer Ⓗ
Friendly local, close to the harbour. Q 🅰 ⇌

INDEPENDENT BREWERIES

Felinfoel:
Felinfoel
Flannery's:
Aberystwyth
Nag's Head:
Abercych
Pembroke:
Pembroke
Watkin:
Llandeilo

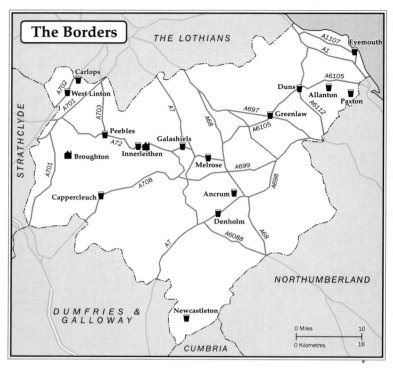

Authority areas covered: The Borders UA

ALLANTON

ALLANTON INN
On B6437 ☎ (01890) 818260
12-2.30, 6-11 (1am Fri); 12-1am
Sat; 12-midnight Sun
Beer range varies Ⓗ
Old village coaching inn with a
restaurant; the exterior still has
hitching rings for horses. The
comfortable, functional interior
features a stone-flagged floor in
the bar. Three-four real ales
available (cider in summer).
Children's certificate. CAMRA
members receive a 10% discount
on accommodation.
🛏 ❀ ⋈ ◖ ▶ ♣ ♙ P

ANCRUM

CROSS KEYS INN ☆
The Green, B6400, off A68
☎ (01835) 830344
12-2.30, 6-11 (midnight Thu, 5-
1am Fri); 12-midnight Sat; 12.30-
11 Sun
**Alloa Arrol's 80/-; Caledonian
Deuchars IPA; guest beer** Ⓗ
Friendly and wonderfully unspoilt
village pub, virtually unaltered
since refurbishment in 1908 by
the now-defunct Jedburgh
Brewery. The lounge retains the
overhead tramlines of the former
cellar. Children's certficate.
🛏 Q ⋈ ❀ ◖ ▶ ⊟ ♣ P

AUCHENCROW

CRAW INN
On B6438, off A1
☎ (01890) 761253
12-2, 6-11.30; 12-11.30 Sat; 12-
11.30 Sun
Beer range varies Ⓗ
Attractive village local, possibly
dating from 1680. The cosy,
wooden-beamed bar is decorated
with equestrian trophies and
warmed by a log fire. Two rooms,
one no-smoking, serve as a
restaurant, which is recommended. A small snug is used as a
family room.
🛏 Q ⋊ ❀ ⋈ ◖ ▶ ♿ ♣ P

CAPPERCLEUCH

TIBBIE SHIELS INN
St Mary's Loch (off A708 at S end
of St Mary's Loch)
☎ (01750) 42231
11-11 (midnight Fri & Sat); closed
Mon, Tue, & weekday winter
afternoons; 11-11 Sun
**Belhaven 80/-; Broughton
Greenmantle Ale** Ⓗ
Cosy, intimate historic inn idylli-
cally set between two lochs in the
remote Yarrow valley. A haven for
walkers, water-sports enthusiasts
and anyone seeking peace and
solitude. Children welcome.
🛏 Q ⋈ ◖ ▶ ⊟ ♿ ▲ ♣ P ⚥

CARLOPS

ALLAN RAMSAY HOTEL
Main Street (A702)
☎ (01968) 660258
11-midnight; 12-midnight
**Belhaven Sandy Hunter's Ale,
80/-, Caledonian Deuchars
IPA** Ⓗ
Pub in a small village by the
Pentland Hills. A former flax mill
dating from 1792, it has been
knocked through into a single
eating/drinking area, but
retains atmosphere by its dark
panelling and log fires. Meals
12-9 (9.30 Fri & Sat). Children's
certificate.
🛏 ❀ ⋈ ◖ ▶ ♣ P

DENHOLM

AULD CROSS KEYS INN
Main Street (A698)
☎ (01450) 870305
11-2.30 (not Mon), 5-11 (midnight
Thu, 1am Fri); 11-midnight Sat;
12.30-11 Sun
Beer range varies Ⓗ
Picturesque, 18th-century inn
overlooking the village green.
The low ceiling and blazing fire
add to the cosy conviviality of the
bar. The high teas are particularly recommended. Children's
certificate.
🛏 ❀ ◖ ▶ ⊟ ♣ P

400

DUNS

WHIP & SADDLE
Market Square
☎ (01361) 883215
11-11 (midnight Fri, 11.30 Sat);
12.30-11.30 Sun
**Caledonian Deuchars IPA;
Theakston XB; guest beer** Ⓗ
Dating from 1790, this town-
centre bar overlooks the square
and has a modern, airy interior
with wooden floors and leaded
windows. The upstairs dining
room is also a family room. River
Whiteadder angling permits are
available. No meals Sun.
Q ☎ Ⓓ ♣

EYEMOUTH

SHIP HOTEL
Harbour Road
☎ (01890) 750224
11-midnight (11.30 Sat); 12.30-
midnight Sun
Beer range varies Ⓗ
A real fisherman's haunt, with
more trawlers than cars parked
outside. Features a warm fire,
vast range of rums, and maritime
memorabilia. The restaurant has
a small menu which is extended
by fish pies and specials.
Children's certificate.
🏨 ❀ 🛏 Ⓓ ⊞ Ⓐ ♣ P ✂

GALASHIEL

LADHOPE INN
33 Buckholmside (A7, ½ mile N
of town centre)
☎ (01896) 752446
11-3, 5-11; 11-11 Wed; 11-mid-
night Thu-Sat; 12.30-midnight
Sun
**Caledonian Deuchars IPA; guest
beer** Ⓗ
Well-appointed, friendly locals'
bar built into the hillside and dating from 1792, though much
altered since. Vibrant Borders
atmosphere.
❀ ♣

SALMON INN
54 Bank Street (by fountain, opp
gardens)
☎ (01896) 752577
11-11 (midnight Thu, 1am Fri &
Sat); 12.30-11 Sun
**Ind Coope Burton Ale; Tetley
Bitter; guest beer** Ⓗ
Attractive, well-appointed large
pub with old photos of Galashiels
in the bar. Popular with locals
and offering a friendly welcome
to visitors. No meals Sun.
❀ Ⓓ ♿ ♣

GREENLAW

CROSS KEYS HOTEL
3 The Square
☎ (01361) 810247
11-midnight (11.30 Sat); 12.30-
11.30 Sun
Wadworth 6X; guest beer Ⓗ
Well-used, friendly local dating
from 1867 (though the bar and
lounge are due to be refurbished
in 1998). A collection of whisky
water jugs hangs above the
wooden-fronted counter.
🏨 🛏 Ⓓ Ⓐ ♣

INNERLEITHEN

TRAQUAIR ARMS HOTEL
Traquair Road (B709, off A72
close to centre)
☎ (01896) 830229
12-11; 11-midnight Fri & Sat; 12-
11 Sun
**Broughton Greenmantle Ale;
Traquair Bear Ale** Ⓗ
Elegant, family-run hotel. The
plush lounge has a log fire; both
it and the adjacent dining room
offer good, home-cooked food
made from local produce. The
only regular outlet in Scotland for
draught Traquair beers. No CO₂
on Addlestones cider.
🏨 ❀ 🛏 Ⓓ Ⓐ ♣ ⌂ P

MELROSE

BURT'S HOTEL
Market Square
☎ (01896) 822285
11-2, 5-11; 12-2, 6-11 Sun
**Belhaven 80/-; Draught Bass;
guest beer** Ⓗ
Well-appointed, elegant hotel
and restaurant. The plush lounge
bar decor reflects the hunting,
fishing and shooting interests of
many of the clientele. Near the
entrance is a comfortable, no-
smoking seating area. Children's
certificate.
🏨 Q 🛏 Ⓓ Ⓐ P ✂

NEWCASTLETON

GRAPES HOTEL
16 Douglas Square
☎ (01387) 375245
11-11 (1am Fri-Sat); 12-11 Sun
**Caledonian Deuchars IPA; guest
beer** (summer) Ⓗ
Friendly, family-run village local
with busy, basic public bar and
games area. Railway buffs will
appreciate the old photos on the
walls. Good selection of malt
whiskies and good value food.
🏨 ❀ 🛏 Ⓓ ♿ ♣

PAXTON

HOOLITS NEST
Off B6460
☎ (01289) 386267
11-2.30 (not Mon), 6.30-midnight;
12.30-2.30, 6.30-midnight Sun
**Orkney Dark Island; guest
beer** Ⓗ
Comfortable village bar and dining room with the theme of
'hoolits' (owls): stuffed, wooden,
brass, painted, porcelain, pottery, as bottles, as jugs, as
miniatures, they survey the pub
from every nook and cranny. A
stately home, Paxton House, is
nearby. Children's certificate in
dining room.
❀ Ⓓ ♣ ♿ P

PEEBLES

GREEN TREE HOTEL
41 Eastgate (A72, east end of
town)
☎ (01721) 720582
11-midnight; 12-midnight Sun
Caledonian 80/-; guest beers Ⓗ
Town-centre hotel which has a
friendly locals' bar at the front
with interesting leaded windows.
The comfortable lounge at the
rear, where children are welcome, is more relaxed. Two
guest ales. The restaurant has
recently been refurbished.
🏨 ❀ 🛏 Ⓓ ⊞ ♿ Ⓐ ♣ P

NEIDPATH INN
27-29 Old Town (A72, W of centre)
☎ (01721) 721721
11-2.30, 5-11 (midnight Thu);
11-midnight Fri & Sat; 12.30-
midnight Sun
**Caledonian Deuchars IPA; guest
beer** Ⓗ
An airy, functional public bar with
a real fire contrasts with a well-
appointed, comfortable lounge.
Note the wood and brasswork.
Peebles folk club meets here
fortnightly. (Meals and garden
were due to be available from
mid-1998.)
🏨 ❀ Ⓓ ⊞ Ⓐ ♣

WEST LINTON

GORDON ARMS HOTEL
Dolphinton Road (A702)
☎ (01968) 660208
11-midnight; 12-midnight Sun
**Alloa Arrol's 80/-; Orkney
Raven; guest beer** Ⓐ
The airy, functional public bar
has a blazing fire and settles. A
collection of local prints, imperial
memorabilia and other items provides conversation topics. An
attractive, wooden-floored
restaurant serves good food and
has a children's certificate.
🏨 Q ❀ 🛏 Ⓓ ⊞ ♣ P

INDEPENDENT BREWERIES

Broughton:
Broughton
Traquair:
Innerleithen

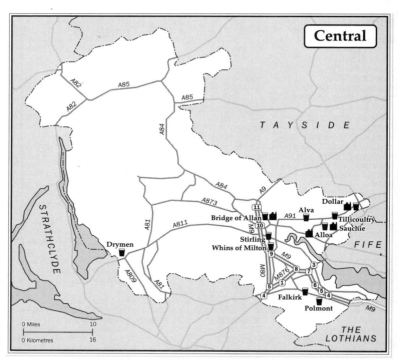

Central

UA areas covered: Clackmannan UA, Falkirk UA, Stirling UA

ALVA

CROSS KEYS
120 Stirling Street
☎ (01259) 760409
11-11 (midnight Thu, 1am Fri & Sat); 11-11 Sun
Maclays 80/-, Wallace, IPA; guest beer Ⓗ
Comfortable two-bar local with a spacious lounge.
♨ ◑ ▶ ⌑

BRIDGE OF ALLAN

QUEENS HOTEL
24 Henderson Street
☎ (01786) 833268
12-midnight (1am Fri & Sat); 12-midnight Sun
Alloa Arrol's 80/-; Bridge of Allan Stirling Brig; Tetley Bitter; guest beers Ⓗ
Comfortable bar within a hotel. It has its own microbrewery, open to the public; tours are available on request. Popular with families. The cask-only bar downstairs has viewing to the brewery and cellar.
❀ ⌂ ◑ ▶ ⌑ ⇌ P

DRYMEN

CLACHAN
2 Main Street
☎ (01360) 660824
11 (12 Sun)-midnight

Caledonian Deuchars IPA Ⓗ
Busy pub in a small village which caters for tourists. The lounge is now used as a restaurant where children are welcome. Very cosy bar, alive with conversation.
◑ ▶ ⌑

DOLLAR

CASTLE CAMPBELL
11 Bridge Street
☎ (01259) 742519
11-11.30 (1am Fri & Sat); 12.30-11 Sun
Fuller's London Pride; Harviestoun 80/-; guest beers Ⓗ
Coaching inn, dating back to 1822, with good facilities. It is named after the nearby NT property. Sloe gin competition every Feb. Good variety of fresh, wholesome food. No real ale in the public bar.
♨ ⇞ ❀ ⇔ ◑ ▶ ⌑ P

DOLLAR

KINGS SEAT
23 Bridge Street
☎ (01259) 742515
11-midnight (1am Fri & Sat); 12.30-midnight Sun
Harviestoun 80/-; guest beers Ⓗ
Comfortable pub on the main

street, with an ever-changing range of guest beers and a wide choice of home-cooked food.
◑ ▶

LORNE TAVERN
17 Argyll Street
☎ (01259) 743423
11-midnight (1am Fri & Sat); 12.30-midnight Sun
Harviestoun Schiehallion; guest beers Ⓗ
Pub with the oldest licence in Dollar (1850), handy for the Ochil Hills. Lunches at weekends.
♨ ⇞ ❀ ⇔ ◑ ▶ ⌑ ⅃ ♣ P

FALKIRK

EGLESBRECH AT BEHIND THE WALL
14 Melville Street
☎ (01324) 633338
12-11.30 (1am Thu-Sat); 12.30-midnight Sun
Belhaven 80/-; Courage Directors; Theakston Best Bitter; guest beers Ⓗ
Alehouse on the upper floor of a former Playtex bra factory. Food is served in all areas except the alehouse on Sat. Mexican food is a speciality. Local CAMRA *Pub of the Year* 1997. There is always a beer from both the Broughton and Harviestoun range.
❀ ⇌ (Grahamston)

POLMONT

BEANCROSS
☎ (01324) 718333
10-11 (midnight Thu-Sat);
12.30-11 Sun
**Caledonian 80/-;
Heather Fraoch Heather
Ale; guest beers**
(summer) H
Built from the remnants of a
former pig farm, the premises
have been imaginatively
designed; a pyramid roof covers
the bar area. There is a bistro, a
restaurant and a supervised children's play area both indoors and
out.
◖ ▶ ⅅ P

SAUCHIE

MANSFIELD ARMS
7 Main Street
☎ (01259) 722020
11 (12.30 Fri & Sat)-11; 11-11
Sun
**Devon Original, Thick Black,
Pride** A
Devon pub-brewery; a family-run
local with good, inexpensive
meals until 9pm.
❀ ◖ ▶ ⊟ P

STIRLING

BIRDS & BEES
Easter Cornton Road,
Causewayhead (off
Causewayhead Rd)
☎ (01786) 473663
11-3, 5-midnight; 11-1am Fri &
Sat; 12.30-midnight Sun
**Caledonian 80/-; Fuller's
London Pride; guest beers** H
Originally a farm, now a bar
retaining many of the original
features in a spacious and
charming layout; the sheep make
good seats. A tourist board

award-winner, it has a function
room and a restaurant. Petanque
played.
🏨 ⚞ ❀ ◖ ▶ ⊟ ♣ P

HOGSHEAD
2 Baker Street
☎ (01786) 448722
11-midnight (1am Fri & Sat);
12.30-midnight Sun
**Boddingtons Bitter; Caledonian
Deuchars IPA; Castle Eden Ale;
Flowers Original; Whitbread
Abroad Cooper** H
Friendly, town-centre local, a
popular stop for families and visitors. Meals until 7pm daily. Very
helpful staff; children's
certificate.
◖ ▶ ⅅ ⇌ ⌂

STIRLING MERCHANT
39 Broad Street (road from
castle)
☎ (01786) 473929
12-2.30, 5.30-midnight; 12-mid-
night Sat; 12.30-midnight Sun
**Maclay Wallace IPA; guest
beers** H
Small, but friendly bar with a
good selection of Belgian and
German bottled beer and regular
beer tastings (phone for details).
The guest beers are also from
Maclay.
◖ ▶ ⅅ

WEST END BAR
2 Lower Bridge Street
☎ (01786) 447147
11 (12.30 Sun)-midnight
Beer range varies H
Student-oriented pub with a
good evening atmosphere;
live music Wed eve and
entertainment most nights.
Mexican speciality meals
until 9pm daily, Sun special full
brunch until 4pm, open 7am for
breakfast Mon-Sat.
◖ ▶ ⇌ P

PORTCULLIS
Castle Wynd
☎ (01786) 472290
11.30 (12 Sun)-midnight
**Orkney Dark Island; guest
beer** H
Next to Stirling Castle, the
Portcullis was originally the
grammar school built in 1787. It
is now an hotel with excellent
accommodation and a homely
lounge bar with a real log fire.
🏨 ❀ ⊨ ◖ ▶ P

TILLICOULTRY

WOOLPACK
1 Glassford Square (W end of
town)
☎ (01259) 750332
11-midnight (1am Fri & Sat);
12.30-11 Sun
beer range varies H
Traditional old drovers' inn with
five ales on tap. A friendly pub
with a strong local trade and
occasional business from walkers on the Ochil Hills.
◖ ▶ ♣

WHINS OF MILTON

PIRNHALL INN
Glasgow Road
☎ (01786) 811256
11 (12.30 Sun)-10
Caledonian 80/-; guest beers H
'Brewers Fayre' pub with has
been converted from an original
pub. Friendly, food and family oriented. Hotel accommodation.
⊨ ❀ ⊨ ◖ ▶ ⅅ ♠ P ⅙

Your beer needs you as much as you need your beer!

Thousands of pubs are being closed or ruined
The Campaign for Real Ale campaigns
● locally to save individual pubs
● nationally on planning, licensing and tax laws
● with official bodies to extend 'listing' to historic pubs
● to encourage people to use their community local.

Join today!
You're welcome to get involved.
● CAMRA has been called 'Europe's most successful
consumer organisation' – but we still need your help.
CAMRA is run locally and nationally by elected,
unpaid volunteers. CAMRA is a not-for-profit body and
is completely independent of any commercial interest.
● CAMRA relies totally on people like you for funds
and support.
● Help us stand up for the rights and choice of ordinary
drinkers.

INDEPENDENT BREWERIES

Bridge of Allan:
Bridge of Allan
Devon:
Sauchie
Harviestoun:
Dollar
Maclay:
Alloa

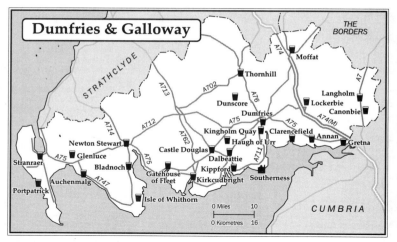

Dumfries & Galloway

THE BORDERS

Authority area covered: Dumfries & Galloway UA

ANNAN

BLUE BELL INN
10 High St ☎ (01461) 202385
11-11 (12.30am Thu-Sat); 12.30-11 Sun
Theakston Best Bitter; guest beers Ⓗ
Very popular and friendly pub by the river. Consistent winner of CAMRA awards. ⚬ 🅰 ≉ ♣

BLADNOCH

BLADNOCH INN
On A714, 6 miles S of Newton Stewart ☎ (01988) 402200
11-11 (midnight Fri & Sat); 12.30-11 Sun
Courage Director's; Sulwath Criffel; guest beers Ⓗ
A rare regular outlet for Galloway's only brewery, this local gem is next to the newly-reopened Bladnoch Distillery. There are bar snacks as well as a restaurant that offers vegetarian options. Children's certificate.
⚬ Q ☎ ⚬ ⚬ ⚬ Ⓓ P

CANONBIE

RIVERSIDE
☎ (0138 73) 71512
12-3, 6.30-11 (closed Sun eve and Sun all day in winter)
Caledonian Deuchars IPA; Yates Bitter Ⓗ
Situated by the River Esk, this comfortable, charming pub also serves superb food.
⚬ Q ⚬ ⚬ Ⓓ ⚬ P

CASTLE DOUGLAS

ROYAL HOTEL
17 King Street ☎ (01556) 502040
11 (12.30 Sun)-midnight
Tetley Bitter; guest beers Ⓐ
Situated on the edge of the town

centre, this hotel has a front bar with attached games room and a larger rear lounge. Food is available all day. Children's certificate. ⚬ ⚬ Ⓓ ♣

CLARENCEFIELD

FARMERS ARMS
Main Street ☎ (01387) 870675
11-2.30, 6-11.30 (12.30am Fri);
11-12.30am Sat; 12.30-11.30 Sun
Maclay 80/-; Theakston Best Bitter; guest beer Ⓗ
This welcoming, 18th-century inn was once a temperance hotel – but not so when used by Robert Burns, who reputedly drank here.
⚬ Q ☎ ⚬ ⚬ Ⓓ Ⓖ 🅰 ♣ P

DALBEATTIE

PHEASANT HOTEL
1 Maxwell Street (A711)
☎ (01556) 610345
10.30-midnight; 12.30-midnight Sun
Beer range varies Ⓗ
Lively and friendly open-plan bar with a juke box and large-screen TV, very popular with locals. There is a pool table to the rear. The restaurant (12-2.30, 6-9) offers a weekend carvery and buffet. Children's certificate.
☎ ⚬ Ⓓ ⚬ ♣

DUMFRIES

NEW BAZAAR
39 Whitesands ☎ (01387) 268776
11-11; 11-midnight (Thu-Sat); 11-11 Sun
Belhaven St Andrew's Ale; Broughton Greenmantle Ale; McEwan 80/-; Ⓐ **guest beers** Ⓗ
In the town centre with views across the river towards the camera obscura, this traditional pub features a superb Victorian bar. ⚬ Q ≉ ♣

SHIP INN
97 St Michael St ☎ (01387) 255189
11-2.30, 5-11; 12.30-2.30, 6.30-11 Sun
Courage Directors Ⓗ**; McEwan 80/-; Theakston XB;** Ⓐ **guest beers** Ⓗ
Welcoming, traditional bar with a large selection of real ales. Local CAMRA *Pub of the Year* 1997.
Q ≉ ♣

TAM O'SHANTER
113 Queensbury Street
☎ (01387) 254055
11-11 (midnight Wed-Sat); 12.30-11 Sun
Caledonian Deuchars IPA; Ⓐ **guest beers** Ⓗ
Traditional bar full of character. Good value snacks available lunchtime. Q ≉ ♣

DUNSCORE

GEORGE HOTEL
Main St ☎ (01387) 820250
12-11 (midnight Mon, Thu, Fri; 1am Sun); 12.30-11 Sun
Caledonian 80/-; guest beer Ⓗ
Traditional village local, with views over the open country. Cosy public bar and larger function room which stages monthly live entertainment. Bar meals and snacks served; a more extensive evening menu features local game. ⚬ Ⓓ P

GATEHOUSE OF FLEET

MASONIC ARMS
Ann Street ☎ (01557) 814335
11-2.30; 5-midnight; 12-3, 6.30-midnight Sun
Beer range varies Ⓗ
Exposed beams and timber screens are a feature of the comfortable lounge bar. A no-smoking eating area is in the conservatory,

with vegetarian options and children's specials. Children's certificate. ❄ ◖ ▶ ☖ ⚲

GLENLUCE

KELVIN HOUSE HOTEL
53 Main Street (off A75)
☎ (01581) 300303
11-11 (midnight Fri & Sat); 12-11.30 Sun
Orkney Red MacGregor; guest beers Ⓗ
This small, friendly hotel is near Luce Bay in a bypassed village. It features excellent home-cooked meals, using local game and produce. ➳ ❄ ⇔ ◖ ▶ ☖ ⚲

GRETNA

SOLWAY LODGE HOTEL
Annan Road ☎ (01461) 338266
12-11 (midnight Fri & Sat, 3 winter Mon)
Tetley Bitter; guest beer Ⓗ
Comfortable, welcoming hotel serving food value food. The guest beer is from Broughton and varies by the week.
➳ ❄ ⇔ ◖ ▶ ☖ ⇌ P

HAUGH OF URR

LAURIE ARMS HOTEL
On B794, 1 mile S of A75
☎ (01556) 660246
11.45-2.30, 5.30-midnight (11 Mon-Wed winter); 11.45-3.30; 6-midnight Sun
Beer range varies Ⓗ
With its wood-panelled bar and stone fireplace, this attractive country inn offers a welcome to all. Off the beaten track, it has up to three guest beers; wide range of bar meals (very popular - book at weekends). Local CAMRA *Pub of the Year* in 1996. Children's certificate. ⚏ ❄ ◖ ▶ P

ISLE OF WHITHORN

STEAMPACKET INN
Harbour Row (A750)
☎ (01988) 500334
11-11; 12.30-11 Sun
Theakston XB; guest beer Ⓗ
On the harbourside of a popular sailing centre, this quaint inn features an unusual, stone-clad bar with a large stone fireplace. Children's certificate.
⚏ Q ➳ ⇔ ◖ ▶ ☖ ⚲

KINGHOLM QUAY

SWAN HOTEL
On B726, 1½ miles S of Dumfries
☎ (01387) 253756
12-2.30; 5-11 (11.30 Thu, midnight Fri & Sat); 11.30-3, 5-11 Sun
Theakston Best Bitter Ⓗ
Riverside hotel on the edge of town, renowned locally for its food. Good bus service to central Dumfries. ⚏ ❄ ⇔ ◖ ▶ ☖ ⚲ P

KIPPREFORD

ANCHOR HOTEL
Main Street ☎ (01556) 620205
11-3; 6-11 (midnight Fri); 11-midnight Sat; summer: 11-11 (midnight Fri & Sat; 11-11 Sun
Boddingtons Bitter; Theakston Best Bitter; guest beers Ⓗ
Traditional village inn in a popular sailing centre. Wood-panelled bar, a larger lounge and a new family and pool room to the rear. The menu has very good local seafood. Children's certificate.
⚏ ⇔ ◖ ▶ ☖ ⚲ P

KIRKCUDBRIGHT

SELKIRK ARMS HOTEL
High Street
☎ (01557) 330402
11-midnight; 12-midnight Sun
Draught Bass; Sulwath Criffel; guest beers Ⓗ
This upmarket lounge bar is comfortable and plush, in the hotel where Burns reputedly wrote his *Selkirk Grace*. No real ale in the public bar, but it is brought through on request. Award-winning good. Children's certificate.
Q ⚏ ❄ ⇔ ◖ ▶ ☖ ⚲ ⚏

Try also: Masonic Arms, Castle St (free)

LANGHOLM

CROWN HOTEL
High Street ☎ (0138 73) 80247
11 (12 Sun) -11 (midnight Thu-Sun)
Beer range varies Ⓗ
Comfortable, 18th-century inn, with Langholm Common Riding connections. High teas served.
⚏ ➳ ⇔ ◖ ▶ ☖ ⚲

LOCKERBIE

SOMERTON HOUSE HOTEL
35 Carlisle Rd ☎ (01576) 202583
11-11 (midnight Thu-Sat); 11-11 Sun
Broughton Greenmantle Ale; Caledonian Deuchars IPA Ⓗ
Well appointed hotel, close to the M74; deservedly popular. Excellent meals and first-class service.
➳ ❄ ⇔ ◖ ▶ ☖ ⚲ ⇌ P

MOFFAT

BLACK BULL HOTEL
Church Gate ☎ (01683) 220206
11-11 (midnight Thu-Sat); 11-11 Sun
McEwan 80/-; Theakston Best Bitter; guest beers Ⓗ
Historic inn, dating from 1568, features Burns memorabilia in the comfortable lounge and railway mementos in the public bar. A separate restaurant serves good, well-priced food in a welcoming atmosphere.
❄ ⇔ ◖ ▶ ☖ ⚲

NEWTON STEWART

CREEBRIDGE HOUSE HOTEL
On old main road, E of river
☎ (01671) 402121
11-2.30; 6-11 (11.30 Sat); 12.30-2.30, 7-11 Sun
Orkney Dark Island; guest beers Ⓗ
Set in spacious grounds, this beautiful country house hotel has been tastefully refurbished. Excellent home-cooked meals with a Scottish flavour. Children's certificate. ➳ ❄ ⇔ ◖ ▶ ☖ ⚲ P

GLENCAIRN HOTEL
14 Arthur Street (A714)
☎ (01671) 402355
11-11.30 (midnight Fri & Sat); 12-11.30 Sun
Beer range varies Ⓗ
Hotel with a comfortable pine-clad public bar and a quiet lounge bar. Friendly service and a separate restaurant. Children welcome (certificate).
Q ➳ ⇔ ◖ ▶ ☖ ⚑ ⚲ ⚲ P

PORTPATRICK

HARBOUR HOUSE HOTEL
53 Main Street ☎ (01776) 810456
11-11.15 (11.45 Fri & Sat); 12-11.15 Sun
Black Sheep Best Bitter; guest beers Ⓗ
Harbour-front hotel, overlooking the picturesque port. Comfortable lounge bar, with a pool table. Separate restaurant. Food available in the bar March-Sept. Children's certificate.
⚏ ❄ ⇔ ◖ ▶ ☖ ⚲ P

STRANRAER

GEORGE HOTEL
49 George St ☎ (01776) 702487
12-3; 6-11 (12-11 summer); including Sun
Theakston Best Bitter; guest beer Ⓗ
Coaching inn dating from 1731. Two lounges share one bar.
➳ ⇔ ◖ ▶ ☖ ⚲ ⇌ (Stranraer Harbour) ⚲ P

THORNHILL

BUCCLEUGH AND QUEENSBURY HOTEL
112 Drumlanrig Street
☎ (01848) 330215
11-1am; 11-midnight Sun
Beer range varies Ⓗ
Hotel with a comfortable lounge meals served all day (breakfast as early as needed in the fishing season).⚏ Q ➳ ⇔ ◖ ▶ ☖ ⚑ ⚲ ⚲ P

INDEPENDENT BREWERIES

Sulwath:
Southerness

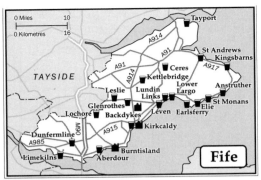

Authority area covered: Fife UA

ABERDOUR

ABERDOUR HOTEL
38 High Street
☎ (01383) 860325
4-11; 3-11.45 Fri; 11-11.45 Sat;
12-11 Sun
**Draught Bass; Marston's
Pedigree; Fuller's London Pride;
guest beer** H
Old coaching inn with a large bar.
Lunchtime bar meals Sat & Sun
only, but the restaurant is open
4-11 Mon-Thu.
🏚 🛏 🖢 🕻 🕽 ♿ ⇌ ♣ P

CEDAR INN
20 Shore Road
☎ (01383) 860310
11-2.30, 5-midnight; 11-midnight
Sat; 12-midnight Sun
Beer range varies H
Pleasant village local off the main
street. There is a lively main bar
and a cosy snug adjoining. Handy
for beaches and golf course.
Good pub food; there is also a
restaurant (no food Mon eve).
Children's certificate.
🛏 🏵 🖢 🕻 🕽 & ⇌ ♣ P

ANSTRUTHER

DREEL TAVERN
16 High Street
☎ (01333) 310727
11-midnight; 12.30-11 Sun
Orkney Dark island; guest beers H
Traditional, stone-built pub,
linked with James IV. At least
three reals are on offer, with the
emphasis on microbreweries.
Excellent food served in the
adjoining dining area. Can be
busy in summer (and smoky).
🏚 Q 🏵 🕻 🕽 ♣

CERES

CERES INN
The Cross (B939)
☎ (01334) 828305
11-2.30, 5 (6 Tue)-midnight (1am
Thu & Fri); 12.30-2.30, 6.30-11 Sun
Beer range varies H
Popular local in an attractive conservation village with a restaurant. Two different ales available.
Pool, dominoes and board games
are played. High tea served at
weekends (eve meals in winter
only at weekends).
Q 🏵 🕻 🕽 P

DUNFERMLINE

COADYS
16 Pilmuir Street (200 yds from
bus station)
☎ (01383) 723865
11-11.30; 12.30-11.30 Sun
Theakston Best Bitter H
Busy, street-corner bar with bare
wooden floorboards, a sitting
room at the rear and pool room
upstairs. ⇌ ♣

COMMERCIAL
Douglas Street (western
entrance to shopping centre)
☎ (01383) 733876
11-11 (midnight Fri & Sat); 12.30-
11 Sun
**Theakston Best Bitter; Thwaites
Bitter; Tomintoul Bard; guest
beers** H
Busy, town-centre pub with bare
floorboards and friendly staff.
Food served all day. Pictures of
breweries and brewing line the
walls. 🕻 🕽 ⇌

HALBEATH PARK
Halbeath Retail Park (on A92 off
M90 jct 3)
☎ (01383) 620737
11-11
**Boddingtons Bitter; Flowers
Original; Morland Old Speckled
Hen; Wadworth 6X** H
Comfortable, attractive restau-
rant and bar. Children's certifi-
cate. 🏵 🕻 🕽 & P

EARLSFERRY

GOLF TAVERN, 19TH HOLE
Links Road (by Alie Golf Course)
☎ (01333) 330610
11-midnight (1am Fri); 12.30-11
(11-2.30, 5-midnight Oct-Apr) Sun

**Caledonian Deuchars IPA;
Maclay 80/-; guest beers**
(summer) H
Traditional, friendly bar, with
views over the golf course, which
attracts locals and visitors alike.
Friendly staff and good quality,
well-priced food. Children welcome until 8.
🏚 Q 🛏 🕻 🕽 ♿ ⇌ ♣

ELIE

SHIP INN
The Toft (by Elie Harbour)
☎ (01333) 330246
11-midnight; 12.30-11 Sun
Belhaven 80/- H
Inn dating back to 1838, with
stone-flagged floors and original
beams. Three dining areas with
views over the harbour. Lively
summer programme includes
cricket on the sand (at low tide)
and tented beer garden with live
jazz in July and August.
🏚 Q 🛏 🏵 🕻 🕽 ♿ ⇌ ♣

GLENROTHES

GLENROTHES SNOOKER CENTRE
Plot 7, Caskiebberran Rd (off A92)
☎ (01592) 642083
11-11; 11-midnight Thu-Sat;
12.30-11 Sun
**Alloa Arrols 80/-; Ind Coope
Burton Ale; guest beer** H
Comfortable leather armchairs
and sofas are a feature of the
plush lounge bar. Various rooms
house seventeen snooker tables.
& P

KETTLEBRIDGE

KETTLEBRIDGE INN
9 Cupar Road (A92 Glenrothes
road)
☎ (01337) 830232
11.30-2.30, 5-11 (4.30-midnight
Fri & Sat); 12.30-11 Sun
**Belhaven Sandy Hunter's Ale,
80/-, St Andrew's Ale; guest
beer** H
Welcoming country inn with
adjoining restaurant. Fifteen
years in the *Guide*. No bar food
Mon; restaurant closed Mon eve.
🏚 Q 🏵 🕻 🕽

KINGSBARNS

CAMBO ARMS HOTEL
5 Main Street
☎ (01334) 880226
11-11 (midnight Fri & Sat); 12.30-
11 Sun
**Belhaven 80/-, St Andrew's Ale;
guest beer** H
Family-owned, former coaching
inn dating back 400 years.
Renowned for its welcoming
atmosphere and good food, using
local produce. Eve meals in winter by arrangement only.
🏚 Q 🛏 🏵 🛏 🕻 🕽 & ♣ P

KIRKCALDY

HARBOUR BAR
471-473 High Street
☎ (01592) 264270
11-2, 5-11; 11-midnight Fri & Sat;
12.30-midnight Sun
Belhaven St Andrew's Ale; Fife Fyre; guest beers Ⓗ
Traditional, unspoilt local; home of Fyfe Brewery. Large murals depict the town's whaling history. Look out for the superb home-made pies. Q ⟊ ⊞ ⅄ ♣

LESLIE

BURNS TAVERN
187 High Street
☎ (01592) 741345
12-11; 11-midnight Wed-Sat;
12.30-midnight Sun
Beer range varies Ⓗ
Busy local with a plush lounge and a narrow bar leading to a games room. ⚏ ⇔ ⟅ ⊞ ♣ ☐

LEVEN

HAWKSHILL HOTEL
Hawkslaw Street
☎ (01333) 426056
11-midnight; 12-midnight Sun
Beer range varies Ⓗ
Comfortable, friendly hotel which hosts an annual beer festival. Excellent bar food and a restaurant.
⚏ ⟊ ❀ ⇔ ⟅ ⅅ ⅄ Å ♣ P ✄

LIMEKILNS

SHIP INN
Halketts Yard (off A985)
☎ (01383) 872247
11-11 (midnight Thu-Sat); 12.30-11 Sun
Belhaven 80/-, St Andrew's Ale, Five Nations, IPA Ⓗ
Small, friendly village local decorated with nautical and rugby memorabilia. Superb views over the Firth of Forth. ⟅ ⅄ ♣

LOCHORE

LOCHORE MINERS' WELFARE SOCIETY AND SOCIAL CLUB
3 Lochleven Road
☎ (01592) 860358
12-3.30, 6.30-11; 12-3.30, 6-midnight Fri; 11.30-midnight Sat;
12.30-11.30 Sun
Maclay 70/- Ⓗ
Old-style club with a warm, friendly atmosphere. Lounge, dance hall and a games room. Children's certificate. Q ⅄ ♣ P

LOWER LARGO

RAILWAY INN
11 Station Wynd
☎ (01333) 320239
11-midnight; 12.30-11 Sun
Beer range varies Ⓗ

Small bar and large, comfortable lounge. Two real ales available in summer, one in winter. Decorated with railway memorabilia, although only the viaduct remains above the pub. Handy for the beach. ⚏ ❀ ⟅ ♣

LUNDIN LINKS

COACHMAN'S (OLD MANOR HOTEL)
55 Leven Road
☎ (01333) 320368
11-3, 5-11 (winter); 11-11 (April-October); 12-3, 5-11 Sun
Beer range varies Ⓗ
Separate from the main hotel, this small bistro has been extended with a new conservatory and patio. Good food. Seafood and steaks are recommended at the separate restaurant. Q ⇔ ⟅ ⅅ P

ST ANDREW'S

AIKMAN'S (CELLAR BAR)
32 Bell Street
☎ (01334) 477425
11-3 (not winter), 5-midnight; 11-11.45 Sat; 6.30-midnight Sun
Belhaven 80/- Ⓗ
Basement bar below a small bistro. Long-standing favourite with town and gown. Regular mini beer festivals. meals can be brought down for the bistro. ⟅ ⅅ

LAFFERTY'S
99 South Street
☎ (01334) 474543
11-12; 11-11.30 Sat;
12.30-midnight Sun
Taylor Landlord; guest beers Ⓗ
Busy, small bar which continues to sell good ale though various changes of decor and theme. Food served all day till 9. ⟅ ⅅ

OGSTON'S BAR & BISTRO
116 South Street
☎ (01334) 473473
10am-midnight; 10am-1am Thu & Fri; 11am-midnight Sun
Beer range varies Ⓗ
Lively student pub with an Italian restaurant, with a good reputation, towards the rear. ⚏ ⟅ ⅅ

ST ANDREW'S

WHEY PAT TAVERN
1 Bridge Street
☎ (01334) 477740
11-12; 12-11.30 Sun
Theakston XB; guest beers Ⓗ
Comfortable, welcoming corner pub with an active social life. Good service. ⟅ ♣

ST MONAN'S

CABIN
16 West End
☎ (01333) 730327
11-midnight (1am Fri); 12.30-11 Sun
Belhaven IPA, 80/-, seasonal beers Ⓗ
Cosy, back-street local meets smashing seafood restaurant! Elegantly remodelled bar and lounge. The coservatory and patio at the rear look out over the harbour. Excellent reputation for food. Check for seasonal variations in opening hours.
Q ❀ ⟅ ⅅ ⊞ Å ♣ ☐

TAYPORT

BELL ROCK TAVERN
4-6 Dalgliesh Street (by harbour)
☎ (01382) 552388
11-midnight (1am Thu & Fri);
12.30-midnight Sun
Beer range varies Ⓗ
Busy local decorated with a strong theme of the sea, ships and history. Split-level bar with TV concealed. Two ales available. Children's certificate.
Q ⟊ ⟅ Å ♣

INDEPENDENT BREWERIES

Backdykes:
Thornton
Burntisland:
Burntisland
Fyfe:
Kirkcaldy

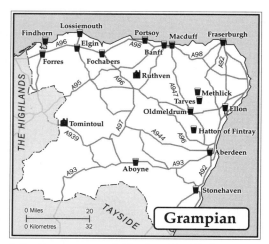

Authority areas covered: **Aberdeenshire UA, City of Aberdeen UA, Moray UA**

ABERDEEN

ARCHIBALD SIMPSON'S
3 King Street (opp Castlegate)
☎ (01224) 621365
11-midnight; 12.30-11 Sun
Caledonian Deuchars IPA, 80/-; Courage Directors; Theakston Best Bitter; guest beers H
Fine bank conversion by Wetherspoons retaining the main features of this listed building. Admire the friezes and other monetary hangovers. A long walk to the toilets upstairs.
Q ◖ ▶ ≉ ⊁ 冃

ATHOLL HOTEL
54 Kings Gate (Forest Rd jct)
☎ (01224) 323505
11-2.30, 5-11 (11.30 Fri & Sat); 12-2.30, 6.30-11 Sun
Beer range varies H
Traditional lounge bar in impressive west end hotel, very popular with its predominantly middle-aged clientele. Specialises in good value bar food. The walls are covered in pictures of Grampian landmarks.
Q ⇔ ◖ ▶ P

BLUE LAMP
121-123 Gallowgate
☎ (01224) 647472
11-midnight (lounge 1am Fri & Sat); 12.30-2.30, 7-11 Sun
Caledonian Deuchars IPA, 80/-; guest beers H
Small, intimate, public bar and a large, modern lounge which hosts live bands (mainly at weekends); free jukeboxes. Note for 1am drinking you must be in by midnight. Different beers are available in each bar. Wheelchair access to lounge only.
⊕ ⅋

CAMERON'S INN (MA'S)
6-8 Little Belmont Street (next to St. Nicholas churchyard)
☎ (01224) 644487
11-11.45; 12.30-11 Sun
Orkney Dark Island; guest beers H
Oldest inn in Aberdeen with the small public bar, unchanged for decades. Tiny listed snug, with impromptu live music some eves. The large modern lounge makes a great contrast. Food served in lounge Mon-Sat.
◖ ▶ ⊕ ≉ ♣

CARRIAGES
101 Crown Street (below Brentwood Hotel)
☎ (01224) 595440
11-2.30, 5-midnight; 6-11.30 Sun
Boddingtons Bitter; Caledonian Deuchars IPA; Castle Eden Ale; Courage Directors; Flowers Original; guest beers H
Very friendly, busy, city-centre bar offering an excellent and varied selection of ales (ten in all) plus bottled Belgian and German Weisse beers. Good food is served in both the bar and the restaurant (open eves). Limited parking.
⇔ ◖ ▶ ≉ P

HOWFF
365 Union Street (next to Bruce Miller's)
☎ (01224) 580092
11-11 (11.45 Thu-Sat); 11-11 Sun
Courage Directors H
Exceedingly steep steps lead to this warm and cosy cellar bar, which features an intricately carved bar and wood panelling. Plenty of alcoves to hide away in. Cheap and cheerful pub grub (not served Sun eve).
◖ ▶ ≉ ♣

MOORINGS
2 Trinity Quay (harbour front)
☎ (01224) 587602
11-midnight; 12.30-11 Sun
Caledonian Deuchars IPA, 80/-; Isle of Skye Red Cuillin; guest beers H
This haven for heavy rock 'n' real ale fans features guest beers predominantly from Scottish independents. With live music most weekends it can sometimes be a little noisy!
◖ ≉ ♣

OLD BLACKFRIARS
52 Castle Street (on Castlegate)
☎ (01224) 581922
11-midnight; 12.30-11 Sun
Belhaven 80/-, St Andrew's Ale; Caledonian Deuchars IPA, 80/-; Flowers Original; guest beers H
This former local CAMRA *Pub of the Year* is an excellent combination of old and new: imaginative use of stained glass displays behind the bar; plenty of nooks and crannies. Food served all day. The bar opens for coffee (with newspapers) at 10.30am except Sun.
◖ ▶ ⅋ ≉

PALM COURT HOTEL
81 Seafield Road (near Springfield Rd jct)
☎ (01224) 310351
11-11 (midnight Wed-Sat); 11-11 Sun
Caledonian 80/-; guest beer H
Small hotel converted from a Victorian house with rambling extensions and a huge conservatory which houses much of the bar.
⇔ ◖ ▶ P

TILTED WIG
55 Castle Street (opp Court House)
☎ (01224) 583248
12-midnight; 12.30-11 Sun
Alloa Arrols's 80/-; Ind Coope Burton Ale; Tetley Bitter; guest beers H
Refurbished Alloa 'Festival Alehouse' that is proud of its 'quality promise' deal. With the comfiest bar stools in town, great ale and sandwich deals and regular price promotions, it is home to legal eagles and fallen angels. Food served until late.
◖ ▶ ≉ ♣

UNDER THE HAMMER
11 North Silver Street
☎ (01224) 640253
5 (4 Fri, 2 Sat)-midnight; 6.30-11 Sun
Caledonian Deuchars IPA; guest beer H
Pleasant, one-room wine bar under the auction rooms. Table candles add to the intimate atmosphere.
Q ≉

ABOYNE

BOAT INN
Charleston Road (N bank of River Dee, by road bridge)
☎ (0133 98) 86137
11-2.30, 5-11 (midnight Fri); 11-midnight Sat; 11-11 Sun
Draught Bass; guest beer ℍ
Riverside inn with an emphasis on food in the lounge which features a log-burning stove and a spiral staircase leading to an upper drinking area. Popular with locals and tourists alike. Children welcome - ask to see the train in action. 🏨 ❀ ◖▶ ⊡ 🖫 Å P

BANFF

CASTLE INN
47 Castle Street
☎ (01261) 815068
11-12.30am including Sun
Courage Directors; guest beers ℍ
Two-roomed pub with a pleasantly refurbished lounge and a basic public bar offering pool and darts. Particularly popular with younger drinkers. ⊡ Å ♣

ELGIN

SUNNINGHILL HOTEL
Hay Street (opp Moray College)
☎ (01343) 547799
11-2.30; 5 (6.30 Sun)-11
Ind Coope Burton Ale; guest beers ℍ
Recently extended, family-run hotel, a long standing outlet for real ales. The predominantly mature clientele enjoys up to five beers and a varied bar menu. Also has a conservatory and a restaurant.
Q ❀ ✇ ◖▶ 🖫 Å ⇌ P 🖵

ELLON

TOLBOOTH
21-23 Station Road (near Town Square)
☎ (01358) 721308
11-2.30, 5-11 (midnight Fri); 11-11.45 Sat; 6.30-11 (closed lunch) Sun
Draught Bass; guest beers ℍ
Pub converted from a pair of semi-detached houses with a large conservatory, on a split level. Coffee and sandwiches sold all day, but no other food.
❀ 🖫 ♣

FINDHORN

CROWN & ANCHOR INN
Off A96, 4 miles from Forres
☎ (01309) 690243
11-11 (11.45 Thu, 12.30 am Fri & Sat); 12-11.45 Sun
Draught Bass; guest beers ℍ
Dating from 1739 and situated on the picturesque Findhorn Bay, this beamed two-bar inn serves

up to four guest beers and a wide variety of good food. Children welcome until 9pm.
🏨 ❀ ✇ ◖▶ 🖫 🖫 Å ♣ P

KIMBERLEY INN
Off A96, 4 miles from Forres
☎ (01309) 690492
11-11 (11.45 Thu, 12.30am Sat); 12.30-11.45 Sun
Beer range varies ℍ
Very popular, friendly, one-bar pub with a pool room, boasting bay views from the front patio. Good food at reasonable prices. Children's certificate until 8pm.
🏨 ❀ ✇ ◖▶ Å ♣

FOCHABERS

GORDON ARMS HOTEL
80 High Street
☎ (01343) 820508
11.30-2.30, 5-11 (12.30am Fri & Sat); 12.30-11 Sun
Caledonian Deuchars IPA; guest beers ℍ
200-year-old coaching inn on the west edge of the village, very popular with fishing guests; families welcome. A good range of malt whiskies available. Beer on tap in the smaller public bar only, but brought through to lounge or dining room. Petanque played.
Q ❀ ✇ ◖▶ 🖫 🖫 Å ♣ P

FORRES

CARISBROOKE HOTEL
Drumduan Road (½ mile off A96)
☎ (01309) 672582
11-11 (11.45 Tue & Thu, 12.30am Fri & Sat); 11-11 Sun
Boddingtons Bitter; Marston's Pedigree; guest beer ℍ
Cosy, friendly, two-bar, extended small hotel on the eastern outskirts of town. Families welcome. Regular barbecues. Three-crown accommodation.
🏨 ❀ ✇ ◖▶ 🖫 🖫 ♣ P

FRASERBURGH

WYND TOWER
57-63 High Street
☎ (01346) 511550
11-12.30am including Sun
Beer range varies ℍ
This family-run establishment situated in a former Co-op superstore has something for all the family with its games room, cafe, children's playroom (complete with bouncy castle) and a bar featuring three regularly changing guest beers. Eve meals at weekends.
🛏 ◖▶ 🖫 Å ♣

HATTON OF FINTRAY

NORTHERN LIGHTS
☎ (01224) 791261
11-2, 5-11 (1am Fri); 11-midnight Sat; 11-11 Sun

Beer range varies ℍ
Almost hidden down a back lane between houses in the village centre, this pub offers a choice of three guest beers and a wide selection of inexpensive traditional bar food. The conservatory is a quiet no-smoking area. The lounge also has an area for diners.
🏨 Q ❀ ✇ ◖▶ 🖫 🖫 ♣ P 🖵

LOSSIEMOUTH

CLIFTON BAR
4 Clifton Road (overlooking East Beach)
☎ (01343) 812100
11-2.30, 5-11 (11.45 Wed & Thu); 11-12.30am Fri & Sat; 12.30-11 Sun
Boddingtons Bitter; McEwan 80/-; Theakston Old Peculier; guest beer ℍ
Very popular free house on the east side of the town, reputed to be the oldest real ale establishment in the area.
🏨 🖫 Å ♣ P

SKERRY BRAE HOTEL
Stotfield Road (overlooking golf course)
☎ (01343) 812040
11-11 (11.45 Wed, 12.30am Thu-Sat); 11-11 Sun
Boddingtons Bitter; guest beer ℍ
Very popular hotel bar on the outskirts of town with views over the sea and golf course: an extended one-room bar with a pool table, no-smoking conservatory and a large outdoor balcony. Very good food. The big steaks are a challenge.
🏨 ❀ ✇ ◖▶ Å ♣ P 🖍

MACDUFF

KNOWES HOTEL
78 Market Street
☎ (01261) 832229
11-midnight; 12.30-11 Sun
Draught Bass; guest beer ℍ
Small, family-run hotel enjoying panoramic views of the Moray Firth. Get in early for the comfy chairs. Good quality bar food.
✇ ◖▶ Å ♣ P

METHLICK

GIGHT HOUSE HOTEL
Sunnybrae (B9170, ½ mile N of river)
☎ (01651) 806389
12-2.30, 5-midnight (1am Fri, 11.45 Sat); 12-11 Sun
Beer range varies ℍ
Attractive lounge bar in a former church manse, with two conservatories. The home-cooked meals use local produce.Two regularly changing beers. Has its own putting green, Petanque pit and children's play area.
🛏 ❀ ✇ ◖▶ 🖫 ♣ P

Established in 1983, Borve Brewery moved from its original site on the Isle of Lewis five years later to a former school on the mainland. The school is now a pub, with the brewhouse adjacent. Borve is one of a growing number of new Scottish breweries.

OLDMELDRUM

REDGARTH
Kirk Brae (off A947)
☎ (01651) 872353
11-2.30, 5-11 (11.45 Fri & Sat);
12.30-2.30, 5.30-11 Sun
Beer range varies Ⓗ
Well refurbished lounge bar with occasionally a beer on gravity dispense. Varied menu of home-cooked food. Fine views from the garden.
Q ☻ ❀ ⇌ ◑ ◗ ♣ P

PORTSOY

SHORE INN
Church Street (old harbour front)
☎ (01261) 842831
11-11 (12.30am Fri & Sat); 12.30-11 Sun
Beer range varies Ⓗ
18th-century seafaring inn nestling in a picturesque harbour. Features music on Fri and Sat evenings; meals until 9pm. Hosts the annual town festival in June. Tring memorabilia

commemorates the owners link to the brewery. Look out for the Watney's red barrel!
🏚 ◑ ◗ Å ♣

STONEHAVEN

MARINE HOTEL
Shorehead (harbour front)
☎ (01569) 762155
11-midnight including Sun
Caledonian Deuchars IPA; Taylor Landlord; guest beers Ⓗ
Wood-panelled bar which always stocks unusual guest beers. The picturesque harbour makes this a must in summer; there is outside seating is on the harbour wall. The family room is upstairs. Specialises in fish dishes; restaurant food is

also served in the bar.
🏚 ☻ ❀ ⇌ ◑ ◗ ⊞ Å ♣ ◔ 🗄

TARVES

ABERDEEN ARMS HOTEL
The Square
☎ (01651) 851214
11-2.30, 5-midnight (1am Fri); 11-11.45 Sat; 12.30-11 Sun
Caledonian 80/-; Flowers Original; guest beer Ⓗ
Small, family-run hotel in the village conservation area, boasting fine mirrors in the public bar. Children's certificate until 8pm.
🏚 ☻ ⇌ ◑ ◗ ⊞ ♣ P

INDEPENDENT BREWERIES

Borve:
Ruthven
Tomintoul:
Tomintoul

Authority areas covered: Highland UA, Orkney Islands UA, Shetland Islands UA, Western Islands UA

AVIEMORE

OLD BRIDGE INN
Dalfaber Road (S end of village, left along Ski Rd, then left, 300 yds)
☎ (01479) 811137
11 (12.30 Sun)-11 (midnight Fri & Sat)
Beer range varies🅷
Converted cottage, recently enlarged, popular with walkers, skiers and other outdoor enthusiasts. On the road to the Strathspey Steam Railway.
🏚 Q ✿ ◑ ▶ ❤ ▲ ≠ P

WINKIN OWL
Grampian Road (main street)
☎ (01479) 810676
11-midnight; 12.30-11 Sun
Alloa Arrol's 80/-; Marston's Pedigree; Tomintoul Stag 🅷
Well-established pub converted from a farm building years ago. Popular with walkers and skiers as well as locals. Good value food served all day. The 60/- is specially brewed for the pub by Tomintoul Brewery.
⛵ ✿ ◑ ≠ P ✂

AVOCH

STATION HOTEL
Bridge Street
☎ (01381) 620246
11-2.30, 5-11 (midnight Fri); 11-11.30 Sat (11-11 summer Mon-Fri); 12.30-11.30 Sun
Beer range varies 🅷
Busy local in a pleasant Black

Isle fishing village with a friendly atmosphere. Popular at weekends for good value food, served all day. Good variety of guest beers.
🏚 ✿ ◑ ▶ ❤ P ✂

CARRBRIDGE

CAIRN HOTEL
Main Road
☎ (01479) 841212
11.30-midnight (1am Fri & Sat); 12.30 (12 summer)-11 Sun
Beer range varies 🅷
A converted cottage adjoining the hotel serves as a locals' bar, which is popular with walkers, skiers and birdwatchers. Children's certificate. All the beers are from the Tomintoul Brewery.
🏚 ✿ ⇔ ◑ ▶ ≠ P

DINGWALL

NATIONAL HOTEL
High Street
☎ (01349) 862166
11-midnight (1am Thu & Fri, 11.30 Sat); 12.30-11 Sun
Iris Rose Roseburn Bitter, Gynack Glory, Black 5, seasonal beers; guest beers 🅷
Beers are from owners' new brewery in Kingussie. A popular hotel with a lounge bar in a modern comfortable extension. It serves coach parties, and is very busy on Ross County match days.
✿ ⇔ ⊟ ≠ P

EAVIE

MISTRA
At A966/B9057 jct on Orkney
OS365257
☎ (01856) 751216
6.30-11; 12-midnight Sat; 8-10.30 Sun
Beer range varies 🅷
Spartanly decorated howff above a shop. Real ale is from Orkney (summer only); large range of bottle-conditioned ales throughout the year.
🏚 ✿ ▲ ♣ P

FORT WILLIAM

GROG & GRUEL
66 High Street
☎ (01397) 705078
11 (12 winter)-midnight (1am Thu-Sat); 5-midnight (closed lunch) Sun
Beer range varies 🅷
Owned by the proprietors of the prize-winning Clachaig Inn. Home-made pasta and pizza and Tex-Mex meals are served in the restaurant upstairs. Very popular in the tourist season.
◑ ▶ ▲ ≠

GAIRLOCH

OLD INN
The Harbour (S end of village)
☎ (01445) 712006
11-midnight (11.30 Sat); 11-11 Sun
Beer range varies 🅷
Small highland hotel in a picturesque setting by a burn and an old road bridge. Popular all year round with sailors, walkers and climbers.
Q ✿ ⇔ ◑ ▶ ⊟ ▲ ♣ P

GLENCOE

CLACHAIG INN
On old road behind NT centre, 3 miles E of village
☎ (01855) 811252
11-11 (midnight Fri; 11.30 Sat); 11-11 Sun
Alloa Arrol's 80/-; Heather Fraoch Heather Ale; Ind Coope Burton Ale; Tetley Bitter; guest beers 🅷
Large building sheltering under rugged scenery. A lively bar with a stone floor and wooden benches, often filled with climbers fresh off the hills. A snug and lounge are provided for the more sedate. Beer festival in Feb.
🏚 ⛵ ✿ ⇔ ◑ ▶ ⊟ ⅙ P ✂

INVERIE

OLD FORGE
By ferry from Mallaig; no road access! ☎ (01687) 462267
11-midnight, including Sun
Draught Bass; guest beers
(summer) 🅷

Remotest pub in Britain! Access is either by ferry from Mallaig (one hour) or by foot from Kinloch-Hourn (16 miles). Used by hill walkers and yachtsmen and serves the small local community, complete with impromptu folk music; great atmosphere. Fine views of Loch Nevis. Food served all day.
🏨 Q 🍽 🌰 🍷 ▶ Å ♣

INVERNESS

BLACKFRIARS
93-95 Academy Street (400 yds from station) •
• ☎ (01463) 233881
11 (12.30 Sun)-11 (1am Thu & Fri, 11.45 Sat)
Courage Directors; Marston's Pedigree; McEwan 80/-; Theakston Best Bitter, Old Peculier; guest beers Ⓗ
Popular, town-centre pub, offering a good range of constantly changing guest beers; cask cider also available. Food served all day, up to 8pm (except Fri eve). Occasional live music.
🍷 ▶ ≈ ○

CLACHNAHARRY INN
17-19 High Street (A862, Beauly Road)
☎ (01463) 239806
11 (12.30 Sun)-11 (midnight Thu & Fri; 11.45 Sat)
McEwan 80/-; Tomintoul Culloden, Wildcat; guest beers Ⓗ
Family-run 17th-century coaching inn with spectacular views over the Caledonian Canal sea lock and the Beauly Firth beyond. Up to three beers available on gravity. Good bar meals. Families always welcome. House beer also sold.
🏨 🐂 🍽 🍷 ▶ 🍴 ♣ P

PHOENIX
108 Academy Street (400 yds from station)
☎ (01463) 233685
11 (12.30 Sun)-11 (12.30am Thu & Fri, 11.30 Sat)
Draught Bass; Caledonian Deuchars IPA, 80/-; Maclay Wallace IPA; guest beers Ⓗ
Busy, town-centre pub, the traditional public bar has a rare example of an island bar; also a lounge bar. Children's certificate. The house beers are brewed by Tomintoul and Caledonian. Eve meals in summer. 🍷 ▶ 🍴 ≈

ISLE OF SKYE

SLIGACHAN HOTEL
Sligachan (A850/A863 jct)
☎ (01478) 650204
9am-midnight (11 Sun)
Beer range varies Ⓗ
Excellent, family-run, 19th-century hotel next to the Cuillin Hills,

superb for walks and climbing. Good bar meals until 9pm. Families welcome (creche in summer). Seumas' bar boasts over 80 single malts. Entertainment some summer weekends; children's certificate. The beers are usually from Skye Brewery.
🏨 🐂 🍽 🍷 🍷 ▶ 🍴 Å ♣ P

KINGUSSIE

ROYAL HOTEL
High Street
☎ (01540) 661898
11 (12.30 Sun)-midnight (1am Thu-Sat)
Iris Rose Roseburn Bitter, Gynack Glory, Black 5, seasonal beers; guest beers Ⓗ
Large, extended, old coaching inn, still popular with modern coach parties. Live music most nights. Beer festival each November, now in its ninth year. Beers now come from Iris Rose Brewery at the back of the hotel.
🐂 🍽 🍷 🍷 ▶ 🍴 Å ≈ ♣ P ✂

KIRKWALL

BOTHY BAR (ALBERT HOTEL)
Mounthoolie Lane (behind Woolworth's)
☎ (01856) 876000
11-midnight (1am Thu-Sat); 12-11.30 Sun
Orkney Dark Island; guest beer Ⓗ
Public bar in a town-centre hotel with a massive open fire and a reputation for good quality food; locally caught fish a speciality. Try the scallops.
🏨 🍷 🍷 ▶ 🍴 Å P

NAIRN

INVERNAIRNE HOTEL
Thurlow Road (off A96, down Seabank Rd, third right)
☎ (01667) 452039
11-11.30 (12.30am Fri, midnight Sat); 11-11.30 Sun
Isle of Skye Red Cuillin; guest beer Ⓗ
Victorian seaside hotel with a lovely, wood-panelled bar with panoramic view of Moray Firth. A large fireplace adds to the friendly atmosphere; occasional live music. The garden path leads to the beach. Popular venue for high teas. Children's certificate.
🏨 Q 🍽 🍷 🍷 ▶ 🍴 P

ONICH

NETHER LOCHABER HOTEL
By S terminal of Corran ferry, 200 yds off A82
☎ (01855) 821235
11-2.30, 5-11; 12.30-2.30, 6.30-11 Sun
Draught Bass Ⓗ

Delightful wee bar tucked behind this family-run hotel.
Q 🍽 🍷 🍷 ▶ Å ♣ P

STRATHCARRON

STRATHCARRON HOTEL
On A890 by the station at the head of Loch Carron
☎ (01520) 722227
11-11, including Sun
Theakston Best Bitter; guest beers Ⓗ
Typical hillwalkers' pub, allowing full use of the hotel facilities for campers. Meals served all day. It enjoys a spectacular position, overlooking Loch Carron on the road to Skye.
🏨 🍽 🍷 🍷 ▶ Å ≈ ♣ P

STROMNESS

STROMNESS HOTEL
Victoria Street (200 yds from ferry terminal)
☎ (01856) 850298
Summer: 11-midnight (1am Thu-Sat); 12-11.30 Sun. Winter: 5-11 (1am Fri); 11-1am Sat; 6-11 Sun
Orkney Red McGregor; guest beer Ⓗ
Refurbished, first-floor lounge bar in an hotel overlooking the harbour and bay. Packed with visiting divers in summer and locals enjoying price promotions in winter. Hosts own beer festival in September. The guest beer is from Orkney. No real ale in the public bar.
🏨 🍽 🍷 🍷 ▶ Å ♣

ULLAPOOL

FERRYBOAT INN
Shore Street
☎ (01854) 612366
11 (12.30 Sun)-11
Beer range varies Ⓗ
Small, comfortable, lounge bar on the village waterfront with open views over Loch Broom. The accommodation has been recently refurbished. Handy for visitors to the Western Isles.
🏨 Q 🐂 🍷 🍷 ▶ Å

INDEPENDENT BREWERIES

Aviemore:
Aviemore

Iris Rose:
Kingussie

Isle of Skye:
Uig

Orkney:
Quoyloo

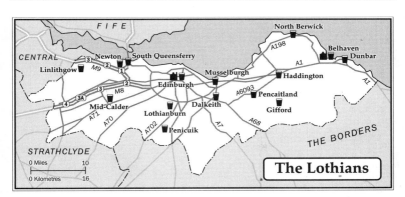

The Lothians

Authority areas covered: City of Edinburgh UA, East Lothian UA, Midlothian UA

BELHAVEN

MASONS ARMS
8 High Street (A1087, ½ mile W of Dunbar)
☎ (01368) 863700
11-2.30 (not Wed), 5-11 (not winter Tue, 1am Fri); 11-midnight Sat; 12.30-5 Sun
Guest beer Ⓗ
Friendly locals' bar close to the brewery with fine views to the Lammermuir Hills and an aviary in the back yard. The guest beer is usually from Belhaven. Meals Fri and Sat eves in the comfortable lounge. Lovely beaches nearby.
🏮 ▶ 🍺 Å ♣

DALKEITH

BLACK BULL
1 Lothian Street (behind Jarnac Court shopping precinct)
☎ (0131) 663 2095
11-11.30 (midnight Thu-Sat); 12.30-11.45 Sun
Caledonian Deuchars IPA; guest beers Ⓗ
An example of a 'Gothenburg' with a busy, vibrant, public bar boasting fine arched windows, cornice work and a well crafted gantry. Large TV for sport. The quieter lounge is modern in contrast and has a children's certificate. Disabled access is by a side door. Two guest beers.
🏮 ◖ 🍺 ♿ ♣

DUNBAR

VOLUNTEER ARMS
17 Victoria Street (between harbour and swimming pool)
☎ (01368) 862278
11-11 (1am Thu-Sat); 12.30-midnight Sun
Belhaven 80/-, St Andrew's Ale; guest beer Ⓗ
History of the local lifeboat and the area adorn the walls of this oak-beamed and panelled, friendly, boisterous bar near the har-

bour. An RNLI flag proudly flies in the front garden. Good local seafood; meals only available in winter if booked. Children welcome.
🏮 ◖ ▶ Å 🍺 ♣

EDINBURGH

BOW BAR
80 West Bow (between Royal Mile and Grassmarket)
☎ (0131) 226 7667
11-11.30; 12.30-11 Sun
Caledonian Deuchars IPA, 80/-; Blackdykes Malcolm's Golden Vale; Flying Firkin Aviator; guest beers Ⓐ
Traditional, one-room stand up bar with efficient, friendly service. Several extinct brewery mirrors and old cigarette ephemera cover the walls. Large selection of malt whisky; four guest beers; quality hot snacks.
🍺 (Waverley)

CAMBRIDGE BAR
20 Young Street (near Charlotte Sq) ☎ (0131) 225 4266
11-1am; closed Sun
Caledonian Deuchars IPA, 80/-; Harviestoun Schiehallion; Marston's Pedigree; guest beers Ⓗ
Slightly off the beaten track, on the north-west edge of the town centre. The building fabric is classic 'New Town' dating from 1775. The wooden floored interior has an eclectic knick-knack collection. Exciting guest beer range.
◖ ▶ ♣ 🍴

CARTER'S BAR
185 Morrison Street (near the Haymarket)
☎ (0131) 623 7023
12-1am (3am during festival); 12.30-1am Sun
Belhaven St Andrew's Ale; Caledonian Deuchars IPA, 80/-; guest beers Ⓗ
Friendly, street-corner bar near

the West End. The dark wood split-level interior allows downstairs customers to view the legs of those sitting in the gallery. Interesting breweriana and old photos. Good range of guest beers.
Q 🏮 ◖ 🍺 (Haymarket) ♣

CLOISTERS BAR
26 Brougham Street (between Tollcross and the Meadows)
☎ (0131) 221 9997
11 (12.30 Sun)-midnight (12.30am Fri & Sat)
Caledonian Deuchars IPA, 80/-; Courage Directors; Flying Firkin Aviator; Village White Boar; guest beers Ⓗ
Alehouse which reflects its previous use as a parsonage, with bare boards, church pews and a bar and gantry built with reclaimed wood from a redundant church. Rare old brewery mirrors decorate the walls. Imaginative meals and range of four guest beers.
Q ◖

CUMBERLAND BAR
1-3 Cumberland Street (off Dundas St in New Town)
☎ (0131) 558 3134
12-11.30 (midnight Thu-Sat); 12-11 (closed winter) Sun
Caledonian Murray's Summer Ale, Deuchars IPA, 80/- guest beers Ⓐ

Elegant, functional, New Town pub with half-wood panelling. Exquisite large ornate brewery mirrors on the walls accompany framed, decorative and illustrative posters. The wooden finish is enhanced by dark green leather seating. Six guest beers, usually including a mild.
Q ❀ ◖

GOLDEN RULE
30 Yeaman Place (off Dundee St)
☎ (0131) 229 3413
11-11.30; 12.30-11 Sun
Draught Bass; Caledonian Deuchars IPA, 80/-; Harviestoun Schiehallion; Orkney Dark Island; guest beers Ⓗ
Busy, friendly, street-corner local in a Victorian tenement. This comfortable, split-level lounge bar is often lively at weekends and can be smoky. Spicy snacks served all day. Good selection of guest beers.
≠ (Haymarket) ♣

GUILDFORD ARMS
1 West Register Street (behind Burger King, at E end of Princes Street)
☎ (0131) 556 4312
11 (12.30 Sun)-11 (midnight Thu & Sat)
Draught Bass; Belhaven 60/-; Caledonian Deuchars IPA; Harviestoun 70/-; Orkney Dark Island; guest beers Ⓗ
Busy, city-centre pub with ornate plaster work and ceilings, spectacular cornices and friezes, window arches and screens and an unusual wood-panelled gallery above the main bar. Six interesting guest beers; no food Sun.
◖ ≠ (Waverley)

HALFWAY HOUSE
24 Fleshmarket Close (near Waverley Stn rear entry)
☎ (0131) 225 7101
11 (12.30 Sun)-11.30 (midnight Thu, 1am Fri & Sat)
Beer range varies Ⓗ
Cosy, wee, L-shaped howff down an old town close. Often crowded, noisy and smoky, it features railway memorabilia. Three beers.
≠ (Waverley) ♣

HOMES BAR
102 Constitution Street, Leith
☎ (0131) 553 7710
12 (12.30 Sun)-11 (midnight Thu, 1am Fri & Sat)
Beer range varies Ⓗ
Traditional, one-roomed, no-frills, friendly, public bar. Decor includes antique tin boxes and a growing array of pumpclips. An interesting range of real ales are served from five custom handpumps. Folk music Fri and Sat eves. Toasties available lunchtime. ♣

KAY'S BAR
39 Jamaica Street (mews between India St and Howe St)
☎ (0131) 225 1858
11-midnight; 12.30-11 Sun
Boddingtons Bitter; Theakston Best Bitter; guest beers Ⓗ
Cosy, comfortable and friendly New Town bar displaying a clever use of barrels as decor and interesting furniture. Good, varied lunches. Over 50 single malt whiskies.
♨ Q ♣

LESLIE'S BAR ☆
45 Ratcliffe Terrace (Newington, 2 miles S of city centre)
☎ (0131) 667 5957
11 (12.30 Sun)-11 (12.30am Thu-Sat)
Draught Bass; Belhaven 80/-; Caledonian Deuchars IPA, 80/-; guest beer Ⓗ
Superb, busy Victorian pub with one of the finest interiors in the city. A snob screen separates the saloon and snug from the public bar. Snacks available.
♨ Q ⊞ ♣

OLD CHAIN PIER
32 Trinity Crescent (foreshore between Leith and Granton)
☎ (0131) 552 1233
11 (12.30 Sun)-11 (midnight Thu-Sat)
Black Sheep Best Bitter; Caledonian Deuchars IPA; Ind Coope Burton Ale; guest beers Ⓗ
Welcoming, cosy seafront bar on the site of the booking office of the old pier destroyed in 1898. It contains sailing artefacts and is a great place to watch ships and birds. Children welcome on the quarterdeck until 7pm. Eve meals in summer.
❀ ◖ ▶ ♣

PORT O'LEITH
58 Constitution Street, Leith
☎ (0131) 554 3568
9am (12.30 Sun)-12.45am
Caledonian 80/- Ⓐ
Characterful locals' bar with a nautical theme. The ceiling is bedecked with flags and posters. Note the collection of life belts in the window.

SHORE
3 Shore, Leith
☎ (0131) 553 5080
11-midnight; 12.30-11 Sun
Maclay 80/-, Kane's Amber Ale Ⓐ
Popular Leith harbour-front bar and restaurant. The wooden interior is little changed from its days as a docks boozer but the atmosphere is now 'new' Leith. The high ceiling and large mirror lend space to the otherwise small bar.
❀ ◖ ▶

STARBANK INN
64 Laverockbank Road (foreshore between Leith and Granton)
☎ (0131) 552 4141
11 (12.30 Sun)-11 (midnight Thu-Sat)
Belhaven Sandy Hunter's Ale, IPA, 80/-, St Andrew's Ale; Taylor Landlord; guest beers Ⓗ
Bright and airy, bare-boarded alehouse with three separate areas. The decor includes rare brewery mirrors, waiters' trays and water jugs. Children welcome until 8.30. Four interesting guest beers. Q ◖ ▶ ♣

WINSTONS
20 Kirk Loan, Corstorphine (off St Johns Road, A8)
☎ (0131) 539 7077
11-11.30 (midnight Fri & Sat); 12.30-11 Sun
Caledonian Deuchars IPA, 80/-; Ind Coope Burton Ale; guest beer Ⓗ
Not far from the zoo, this smart suburban lounge bar is well favoured by locals. The decor features golfing and rugby themes. No food Sun. Q ◖

GIFFORD

GOBLIN'HA HOTEL
Main Street
☎ (01620) 810244
11-2.30, 4.30-11; 11-midnight Fri & Sat; 11-11 Sun
Hop Back Summer Lightning; Marston's Pedigree; guest beers Ⓗ
Large village hotel with a functional public bar which has an oak-panelled counter. The lounge/cocktail bar has a comfortable seating area and a conservatory which looks out over the extensive garden with its play area. Cider in summer. Children welcome (certificate).
♨ ❀ ⇔ ◖ ⊞ ♣ ⌣

HADDINGTON

PHEASANT
72 Market Street
☎ (01620) 824428
11-11 (midnight Thu-Sun)
Caledonian 80/-; Ind Coope Burton Ale; Tetley Bitter; guest beers Ⓗ
Vibrant and sometimes noisy pub attracting younger folk. A long thin bar snakes through to a lounge/pool area where Basil the African Grey (surely a disguised Norwegian Blue) oversees, and joins in, the proceedings.
♨ ♣

WATERSIDE BISTRO
1-5 Waterside, Nungate
☎ (01620) 825647
11.30-2.30, 5-11 (midnight Fri & Sat); 12.30-11 Sun

Adnams Broadside; Belhaven 80/-; Caledonian Deuchars IPA; guest beer Ⓗ

Well-appointed bar, with a marble-topped counter, and extensive restaurant in an old building by the river. The bar can be used for meals when the restaurant is busy. Excellent menu. Children's certificate.
🏚 Q ⊛ ◖ ▶ P ⏦

LINLITHGOW

BLACK BITCH
14a West Port (near A803/A706 jct)
☎ (01506) 842147
11-midnight, including Sun
Caledonian Deuchars IPA; guest beer Ⓗ
Traditional pub whose name is derived from the town crest.
⊛ ⊞ ⇌

FOUR MARYS
69 High Street
☎ (01506) 842171
11 (12.30 Sun)-11 (midnight Thu-Sat)
Belhaven 70/-, 80/-; Caledonian Deuchars IPA; guest beers Ⓗ
Olde-worlde country inn which has an authentic atmosphere. Its decor reflects the town's history.
◖ ▶ ⇌

LOTHIANBURN

STEADING
118-120 Biggar Road (A702, near dry ski slope)
☎ (0131) 445 1128
11-midnight; 12.30-11 Sun
Belhaven 70/-, 80/-; Caledonian Deuchars IPA; Orkney Dark Island; Taylor Landlord; guest beers Ⓗ
Stone cottages converted into an attractive bar and restaurant, with conservatory extensions. Although it's a popular eating establishment there is a sizable bar area, nearly half of which is no-smoking, where only snacks are served.
🏚 Q ⊛ ◖ ▶ ⅙ P ⏦

MID-CALDER

TORPHICHEN ARMS
36 Bank Street
☎ (01506) 880020
11-11 (11.45 Thu-Sat); 11-11Sun
Caledonian Deuchars IPA, 80/-; Ind Coope Burton Ale; Marston's Pedigree; guest beers Ⓗ
Village local, originally a hotel dating back to 1778. Several rooms are now one L-shaped bar with public and lounge areas. Live music at weekends; occasional beer festivals. Children's certificate.
⊛ ◖ ♣ P

MUSSELBURGH

LEVENHALL ARMS
10 Ravensheugh Road (B1348 near racecourse roundabout)
☎ (0131) 665 3220
11.30 (3 winter)-11 (1am Fri & Sat); 12.30-11 Sun
Caledonian Deuchars IPA, 80/-; Ind Coope Burton Ale; guest beer Ⓗ
Busy pub, which is popular with locals, racegoers and visitors to the nearby golf course. The building dates from 1830 and houses a comfortable three-roomed pub. Formerly a stopping point for London stage-coaches and more recently it had a tram terminus outside.
⊞ ⅙ ⇌ (Wallyford) ♣ P

VOLUNTEER ARMS (STAGGS)
78-81 High Street (behind Brunton Hall)
☎ (0131) 665 9654
11-11 (11.30 Thu, midnight Fri & Sat); 11-2.30, 5-11 Tue & Wed; closed Sun
Caledonian Deuchars IPA, 80/-; guest beer Ⓗ
Run by the same family since 1858, this is a busy, traditional bar with dark wood panelling, defunct brewery mirrors and a superb gantry topped with old casks. A comfortable lounge to the rear has no real ale. Home of the FFARTS drinking society and current CAMRA national *Pub of the Year*.
⊛ ⊞ ⅙ ♣ P

NEWTON

DUDDINGSTON ARMS
13-15 Main Street (A904)
☎ (0131) 331 1948
11-2.30, 5-11; 11-11 Sat; 12.30-4, 7-11 Sun
Maclay 80/-; guest beer Ⓗ
Friendly village local which extends a warm welcome to visitors. Snacks only at weekends.
🏚 ◖ ♣

NORTH BERWICK

NETHER ABBEY HOTEL
20 Dirleton Avenue (A198, ½ mile W of centre)
☎ (01620) 892802
11 (12 Sun)-11 (midnight Thu, 1am Fri & Sat)
Beer range varies Ⓐ
Family-run, comfortable hotel in a Victorian villa with a large extended bar/restaurant area. The garden features a petanque court. Good selection of four real ales. An ideal base for exploring the East Lothian coast. Children's certificate.
🏚 ⊛ ⇴ ◖ ▶ ⊞ Ⱥ ⇌ P

PENCAITLAND

OLD SMIDDY INN
Main Street (A6093)
☎ (01875) 340368
11.30 (12 Sun)-11 (1am Fri & Sat)
Draught Bass; Caledonian 80/-; guest beers Ⓗ
Previously the village smithy and now a friendly country inn with a large, comfortable lounge bar and a noted restaurant. High teas are popular Sat and Sun. Glenkinchie distillery is nearby. Children's certificate. 🏚 ⊛ ◖ ▶ ♣ P

PENICUIK

CRAIGIEBIELD HOUSE HOTEL
50 Bog Road (between A701 and A766 W of centre)
☎ (01968) 672557
12-3, 5-midnight; 12-midnight Fri-Sun;
Caledonian Deuchars IPA; guest beers Ⓗ Ⓐ
Fine stone building with impressive gables. The small, comfortable lounge bar has prints of local and golfing interest. The beautiful dining room, with its real fire, is of particular architectural interest. 🏚 ⊛ ⇴ ◖ ▶ P

SOUTH QUEENSFERRY

ANCHOR INN
10 Edinburgh Road
☎ (0131) 331 3684
11-11.30 (midnight Thu, 1am Fri & Sat); 12.30-midnight Sun
Belhaven 80/-; Caledonian Deuchars IPA Ⓗ
Busy, one-roomed, comfortable locals' bar at the east end of the high street, close to the foreshore. The building dates from 1886; pictures of old South Queensferry decorate the walls.
Q ◖ ⇌ (Dalmeny) ♣

FERRY TAP
36 High St ☎ (0131) 331 2000
11.30 (12.30 Sun)-11.30 (midnight Thu, 12.30am Fri & Sat)
Draught Bass; Caledonian Deuchars IPA, 80/-; Orkney Dark Island; guest beer Ⓗ
A well-appointed, one-roomed L-shaped bar with an unusual barrel-vaulted ceiling in a 300-year-old building, decorated with brewery artefacts and ephemera.
Q ◖ ⇌ (Dalmeny) ♣

INDEPENDENT BREWERIES

Belhaven:
Belhaven
Caledonian:
Edinburgh

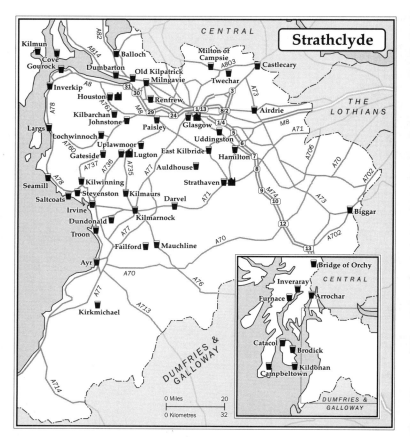

Strathclyde

Authority areas covered: Argyll & Bute UA, City of Glasgow UA, Dunbarton & Clydebank UA, East Ayrshire UA, East Dunbartonshire UA, East Renfrewshire UA, Inverclyde UA, North Ayrshire UA, North Lanarkshire UA, Renfrewshire UA, South Ayrshire UA, South Lanarkshire UA

Note: Licensing laws permit no entry after 12pm to pubs in Gourock, Houston, Johnstone, Kilbarchan, Inverkip, Lochwinnoch, Pasiley, Renfrew and Uplaw.

AIRDRIE

CELLAR BAR
79 Stirling Street
11-midnight; 12.30-5, 8-midnight Sun
Beer range varies Ⓗ
Single bar on several levels. In addition to the ever-changing guest beers (up to three ales) it offers a wide range of malt whiskies. Folk music performed Mon eves. 🎰 ≈

ARROCHAR

VILLAGE INN
On A814, ½ mile S of A83 jct
☎ (01301) 702279
11-midnight; including Sun
Maclay Wallace IPA; guest beers Ⓗ
Idyllic lochside inn with a warm,

friendly atmosphere, enhanced by candlelit tables. The front garden offers breathtaking views of the Cobbler mountain which towers menacingly above the head of Loch Long. Excellent food - try the famous village rib rack!
🏰 🎰 ⇔ ◖ ▶ Å P

AULDHOUSE

AULDHOUSE ARMS
12 Langlands Road
☎ (01355) 263242
2-11; 12-midnight Fri & Sat; 12.30-11 Sun
Belhaven 80/- Ⓗ
200-year-old, totally unspoilt village pub: a public bar with snugs off, decorated with old paintings, photographs and plates. The lounge and restaurant area is a

recent conversion of the adjacent house kept in the same style.
🏰 Q ⇔ ▶ ⊞ P ⊬

AYR

BURROWFIELDS
13 Beresford Terrace
☎ (01292) 269152
11-12.30am; 12.30-midnight Sun
Beer range varies Ⓗ
This cafe/bar on a corner site serves three guest beers regularly. A former insurance office, the bar has been well converted with wood panelling. Handy for the cinema and the station. ◖ ≈

CHESTNUTS HOTEL
52 Racecourse Road (A719 S of centre) ☎ (01292) 264393
11 (12 Sun)-midnight

Tetley Bitter; guest beers H
Comfortable lounge bar with a
vaulted ceiling and a large collection of water jugs. Excellent bar
meals. A garden play area; close
to the beach and two golf
courses.
🏾 Q ❀ 🛏 ◁ ▶ P

GEORDIE'S BYRE
103 Main Street (over river
towards Prestwick)
☎ (01292) 264925
11 (12.30 Sun)-11 (midnight Thu-
Sat)
Caledonian Deuchars IPA; guest
beers A
A friendly, traditional local, with
an excellent range of guest ales
from anywhere between Orkney
and Cornwall. 1996 Scottish
CAMRA Pub of the Year, and
twice winner of the local award.
🍺

OLD RACECOURSE HOTEL
2 Victoria Park (A719 S of
centre)
☎ (01292) 264393
11 (12 Sun)-midnight (12.30 Fri &
Sat)
Beer range varies H
An open, airy hotel lounge bar
with an unusual pot still-shaped
fireplace as a centrepiece. Close
to beach and two golf courses.
Good B&B.
🏾 ❀ 🛏 ◁ ▶ & ♣ P

TAM O'SHANTER
230 High Street
☎ (01292) 611684
11-12.30am; 12.30-midnight Sun
Beer range varies H
Town-centre bar which was formerly a Burns Museum. Two
guest ales are available regularly. The bar has been sympathetically restored with a flagstone
floor. Due to its small size it can
get noisy when the music is
turned on. & ≈

WELLINGTON'S
17 Wellington Square (behind
seafront)
☎ (01292) 262794
11-12.30am; 12.30-midnight Sun
Beer range varies H
Basement lounge bar in a
Georgian square near the beach.
Regular folk and quiz nights.
Student discount. Good bar meals
served 12-7 (12.30-6.30 Sun).
◁ ▶ ♣

BALLOCH

BALLOCH HOTEL
Balloch Road
☎ (01389) 752579
11-midnight (1am Fri & Sat); 11-
midnight Sun
Ind Coope Burton Ale; guest
beers H
Attractive hotel at the southern
end of Loch Lomond. Beers are

on tap in the lounge bar and can
be supplied to the public bar if
required. The landlord has won
two Master Cellarmanship
awards, 1996 and 1997; also
CAMRA regional Pub of the Year
1998
❀ 🛏 ◁ ▶ 🍺 & Å ≈ P

BIGGAR

CROWN HOTEL
109 High Street
☎ (01899) 220116
11.30 (12.30 Sun)-11 (midnight
Thu, 1am Fri)
Beer range varies H
Popular lounge bar in a small
hotel in the centre of an attractive Borders village.
🏾 Q ❀ 🛏 ◁ ▶ Å

BRIDGE OF ORCHY

BRIDGE OF ORCHY HOTEL
☎ (01838) 400208
12-11 (midnight Fri & Sat); 12-11
Sun
Caledonian 70/-, Deuchars IPA,
ERA , 80/- H
Isolated hotel on the main road
just before it climbs to Rannoch
Moor. A small renovated public
bar serving a good selection of
home-cooked food weekdays
(eve meals until 8.30).
🏾 Q 🐂 🛏 ◁ ▶ ≈ P

BRODICK

DUNCAN'S BAR
Kingsley Hotel, Shore Road
☎ (01770) 302531
11-midnight (winter 11-2.30,
closed eves Mon-Thu; 7-midnight
Fri & Sat; closed Sun)
Boddingtons Bitter; Theakston
XB; guest beers H
Large, comfortable bar at the
side of a seaside hotel. It is
sometimes busy in summer due
to students staying nearby.
Excellent views from the large
front garden across the bay to
Goat Fell. Eve meals and accommodation in summer.
🏾 Q 🐂 ❀ 🛏 ◁ ▶ & Å P

CAMPBELTOWN

COMMERCIAL INN
Cross Street
☎ (01586) 553703
11 (12.30 Sun)-1am
Caledonian Deuchars IPA; guest
beers (occasional) H
Friendly, family-run pub, very
popular with locals and most welcoming to visitors. 🍺

CASTLECARY

CASTLECARY HOUSE HOTEL
Main Street
☎ (01324) 840233
11 (12.30 Sun)-11 (11.30 Thu-Sat)

Draught Bass; Belhaven 70/-,
80/-, St Andrews's Ale;
Caledonian Deuchars IPA, 80/- H
Small, private hotel with three
drinking areas (most ales in
Castle lounge). The highly recommended restaurant serves high
teas. The village is on the site of
one of the major forts on the
Antonine Wall. Other Belhaven
and Caley beers are usually
available. 🛏 ◁ ▶ 🍺 & P

CATACOL

CATACOL BAY HOTEL
☎ (01770) 830231
11-midnight (1am Thu-Sat);
11-midnight Sun
Black Sheep Best Bitter;
Caledonian Deuchars IPA H
Seafront hotel on the northern
coast of the Isle of Arran, facing
across to Kintyre. Originally a
manse when built in the 19th
century, next to the Twelve
Apostles, an unusual listed terrace of houses.
🏾 Q 🐂 ❀ 🛏 ◁ ▶ Å P

COVE

KNOCKDERRY HOTEL
204 Shore Road (B833)
☎ (01436) 842283
11-midnight; 12.30-11 Sun
Beer range varies H
Splendid Victorian mansion on
the Rosneath Peninsular. The
large, comfortable lounge boasts
fine wooden panelling and views
across Loch Long. Good food at
all times. Snooker room.
🏾 Q ❀ 🛏 ◁ ▶ ♣ P

DARVEL

LOUDOUNHILL INN
On A71, 3 miles E of Darvel
☎ (01560) 320275
12-2.30 (not Wed), 5-11 (not Tue,
midnight Fri); 12-midnight Sat;
12.30-11 (12.30-2.30, 4.30-11
winter) Sun
Beer range varies H
Old coaching inn near Loudoun
Hill and an old battlefield site. It
has a refurbished lounge/restau-
rant and a conservatory.
Children's certificate.
🏾 ❀ 🛏 ◁ ▶ P

DUMBARTON

CUTTY SARK
105 High Street
☎ (01389) 762509
11 (12.30 Sun)-midnight (1am Fri
& Sat)
Orkney Dark Island; guest beer H
Split-level lounge bar hosting
occasional live folk music. The
guest ale tends to be chosen by
popular demand. Lunches Mon-
Thu, eve meals Fri and Sat (until
7.30).
❀ ◁ ▶ & ≈ (Central) 🍺

DUNDONALD

CASTLE VIEW
29 Main Street (B730 opp church)
☎ (01563) 851112
11 (12.30 Sun)-11
Beer range varies [H]
A former hotel in an historic village which has an impressive 14th-century castle. Recently refurbished to a relaxing bar area in what is otherwise mainly a restaurant.
Q ❀ ◖ ◗ P

EAST KILBRIDE

EAST KILBRIDE SPORTS CLUB
Torrance House, Strathaven Road
☎ (01355) 236001
12 (12.30 Sun)-11 (1am Fri & Sat)
Beer range varies [H]
Thriving sports and social club just inside Calderglen Country Park. The comfortable members lounge usually sells three guest beers from small breweries nationwide. CAMRA members admitted on production of a membership card.
❀ ◖ P

NEW FARM
Strathaven Road
☎ (01355) 267177
11-midnight; 12.30-11 Sun
Boddingtons Bitter; Caledonian 80/-; Flowers Original; guest beers [H]
Above average 'Brewers Fayre' having not only several dining areas (one no-smoking), but also a spacious bar. Usually two guest beers from the Whitbread portfolio and a bi-annual beer festival.
❀ ◖ ◗ ♿ P

FAILFORD

FAILFORD INN
On B743
☎ (01292) 541674
11-2.30, 4.30-11 (11-11 Sat); 12-11 Sun
Belhaven 80/- [H]
A low-ceilinged bar with an old tiled range. The garden and restaurant overlook the wooded gorge of the River Ayr and a walk through the gorge starts nearby. Limited parking. Children's certificate.
Q ❀ ◖ ◗ P

FURNACE

FURNACE INN
☎ (01499) 500200
12 (12.30 Sun)-midnight
Beer range varies [H]
Friendly, stone-walled local. Originally built about 1860 as a private house and post office, it was converted to a pub in 1987. Local CAMRA *Pub of the Year* 1998. Open 365 days a year - but no meals in winter.
❀ ◖ ◗ P

GATESIDE

GATESIDE INN
39 Main Road (B777, 1 mile E of Beith)
☎ (01505) 503362
11-2.30, 5-11; 11-midnight Sat; 12.30-11 Sun
Caledonian Deuchars IPA [P]
Cosy, country inn with a modernised interior in a small village near Beith. It has an eating area to the rear, and there are partial screens in the bar. Eve meals Thu-Sun
❀ ◖ ◗ P

GLASGOW

BLACKFRIARS
36 Bell Street
☎ (0141) 552 5924
11.30 (12.30 Sun)-midnight
Alloa Arrol's 80/-; [H] **Belhaven 60/-** [P] **Ind Coope Burton Ale; Tetley Bitter; guest beers** [H]
A lively pub, closely involved with many city-centre events and decorated with posters advertising local activities. Live bands three nights a week, function room downstairs. Guest Belgian beer on draught.
◖ ◗ ⇌ (Argyle St/High St)

BON ACCORD
153 North Street (near Mitchell Library, just off M8)
☎ (0141 248 4427
11-11.45; 12.30-11 Sun
Courage Directors; Marston's Pedigree; Theakston Best Bitter, XB; guest beers [H]
One of S&N's Victorian T&J Bernard houses, once the pioneer of real ale availability in Glasgow, it still represents a good range of independent ales.
◖ ◗ ♿ ⇌ (Charing Cross) ⊖ (St Georges Cross)

COUNTING HOUSE
2 St Vincent Place
☎ (0141) 248 9568
11 (12.30 Sun)-midnight
Caledonian Deuchars IPA, 80/-; Courage Directors; Theakston Best Bitter; Tomintoul Wild Cat; guest beers [H]
This listed building is the former Bank of Scotland HQ. Popular with professional and business people at lunchtime, it draws a mixed clientele otherwise. Fabulous architecture and surroundings; a basic Scottish history lesson is provided by the various paintings.
◖ ◗ ⇌ (Queen St) ⊖ (Buchanan St)

HOGSHEAD
1397 Argyle Street (opp. art gallery and museum)
☎ (0141) 334 1831
11 (12.30 Sun)-11 (midnight Fri & Sat)
Boddingtons Bitter; Whitbread Abroad Cooper; guest beers [H]
Traditional alehouse, part of the Whitbread chain, with quick friendly service. A popular, one-bar pub serving up to six guest beers. Proceeds from the weekly quiz go to charity, occasional beer festivals held. Eve meals finish at 7.
◖ ◗ ⇌ (Kelvin Hall) ⊖

STATE BAR
148 Holland Street
☎ (0141) 332 2195
11 (12.30 Sun)-midnight
Caledonian Deuchars IPA, 80/-; Courage Directors; Theakston Best Bitter; guest beers [H]
Renovated island bar with plenty of dark wood, stained glass panels and Glasgow folk pictures. Business people come at lunchtime (weekday meals) and a younger clientele in the eves for whom there are live bands twice weekly. ◖ ⇌ (Charing Cross)

STATION BAR
55 Port Dundas Road (near STV Studios)
☎ (0141) 332 3117
11 (12.30 Sun)-midnight
Caledonian Deuchars IPA; guest beers [H]
Recently refurbished local, boasting a fine McEwan's mirror and a recently exposed cornice ceiling. The pub is run by Glasgow CAMRA's current *Landlord of the Year*. Two guest beers; a must.
⇌ (Queen St) ⊖ (Cowcaddens)

STOAT & FERRET
1534 Pollokshaws Road (Haggs Road jct)
☎ (0141) 632 0161
12-11 (midnight Fri & Sat); 12-11 Sun
Alloa Arrol's 80/-; [H] **Belhaven 60/-;** [P] **Caledonian Deuchars IPA; guest beers** [H]
Corner pub where a large wood-floored bar area offers ample seating and standing room. Four guest ales, a guest draught Belgian beer, a good small foreign bottled beer selection, plus a fine choice of malts and wines. Children-friendly; well worth a visit.
◖ ◗ ♿ ⇌ (Shawlands/Pollokshaws W) ♣

TAP BAR AND COFFEE HUIS
1055 Sauchiehall Street (near art galleries)
☎ (0141) 339 8866
12 (12.30 Sun)-11 (midnight Fri & Sat)

Alloa Arrol's 80/-; Belhaven 60/-; Caledonian Deuchars IPA; guest beers Ⓟ

Formerly the Brewery Tap, the bar was refurbished and changed its name. Now a European cafe-bar with a friendly and efficient staff and fine views over Kelvingrove Park.
◖ ▶ ⊖ (Kelvinhall) ⌂

THREE JUDGES
141 Dumbarton Road (Byres Rd jct)
☎ (0141) 337 3055
11 (12.30 Sun)-11 (midnight Fri & Sat)
Maclay Broadsword, 80/-; guest beers Ⓗ

Traditional West End local serving 1,500 guest beers in six years and aiming for 2,000 by 2000. A regular local CAMRA award winner, this pub is both a locals' and visitors' haven.
⇌ (Partick) ⊖ (Kelvinhall) ⌂

GOUROCK

SPINNAKER HOTEL
121 Albert Road (A770)
☎ (01475) 633107
11-11.30 (12.30am Sat); 12.30-midnight Sun
Beer range varies Ⓐ

Small, family-run hotel on the coastal route, enjoying excellent views to Kilcreggan, Dunoon and beyond. An alcove bar and restaurant adjacent; a small bar on the upper floor (only open when busy) can be hired for functions. Bar snacks and coffee available all day. Good value B&B.
❀ ⇖ ◖ ▶ ⇌

HAMILTON

GEORGE
18 Campbell Street (near Bottom Cross)
☎ (01698) 424225
11 (12.30 Sun)-11.45
Beer range varies Ⓗ

Small, friendly, family-run pub in the town centre. It regained the CAMRA Lanarkshire *Pub of the Year* award in 1998 after a two-year gap. Difficult to find for a town-centre pub, though any rational drinker visiting Hamilton will make the effort.
◖ ▲ ⇌ (Central)

HOUSTON

FOX & HOUNDS
South Street
☎ (01505) 612448
11 (12 Sun)-midnight (1am Fri & Sat)
Houston Killellan, Barochan; guest beers Ⓗ

The award-winning Houston ales come from the adjoining brewery, and are available in all three

bars; guest ales in the lounge bar only. This popular pub in a rural setting bears a hunting theme throughout.
Q ◖ ▶ ⊟ P

INVERARY

GEORGE HOTEL
Main Street East
☎ (01499) 302111
11 (12 Sun)-midnight (1am Thu-Sat)
Beer range varies Ⓗ

Now in its fifth generation of family ownership, in an historic West Highland town. Culinary emphasis at the George is on fresh food and there is an extensive wine list.
⇖ Q ⛺ ❀ ⇌ ◖ ▶ ⊟ ♿ P

INVERKIP

INVERKIP HOTEL
Main Street (off A78, near Kip marina)
☎ (01475) 521478
11-2.30, 5-11 including Sun
Houston Barochan; Caledonian 80/-; Orkney Dark Island Ⓗ

Small hotel in an unspoilt village on the Clyde coast. A welcoming lounge bar with additional seating in two alcoves opposite. Regulars encourage community spirit with trips abroad, etc. A 'real' village pub; ale in the lounge bar only.
Q ⇖ ⇌

IRVINE

MARINA INN
110 Harbour Street
☎ (01294) 274079
11-midnight (1am Fri & Sat), (11-2.30, 6-midnight (5-1am Fri) winter); 12.30-midnight Sun
Belhaven St Andrew's Ale Ⓗ

Attractive harbourside lounge bar next to the Magnum Centre and the Scottish Maritime Museum. Emphasis on food at lunchtime and early eve, with an extensive menu. Beer price is higher than average for the area. Folk session Tue eve. Children's certificate.
❀ ◖ ▶ ♿ ⇌

SHIP INN
120-122 Harbour Street (by Magnum Leisure Centre)
☎ (01294) 279722
11-2.30; 5-11 (midnight Fri); 11-midnight Sat; 12.30-11 Sun
Theakston Best Bitter Ⓗ

Harbourside pub, the oldest licensed premises in town, renowned for its well-cooked, good value meals. A quiet atmosphere lunchtime and early eve, but rather lively later on. See the local scenes drawn on the vaulted ceiling. Children's certificate.
Q ❀ ◖ ▶ ♿ ⇌

TURF HOTEL
32-34 Eglinton Street
☎ (01294) 275836
7.30-10am; 11-midnight (1am Fri & Sat); 12.30-11 Sun
Beer range varies Ⓗ

Totally unspoilt, traditional Scottish bar in a recently listed building. Quite cosmopolitan at lunchtime, when quality lunches of amazing value are served (weekdays), it is more of a local at night. New opening hours mean you can have a pint with breakfast.
⇖ ◖ ⊟ ♣

JOHNSTONE

COANES
26 High Street
☎ (01505) 322925
11-11.30 (1am Fri, 12.30 am Sat); 11-11.30 Sun
Boddingtons Bitter; Caledonian Deuchars IPA, 80/-; Orkney Red Macgregor, Dark Island; guest beers

Friendly, town-centre local: the bar features fake beams and bric-à-brac, while a comfortable open-plan lounge offers a full a la carte menu of excellent food at competitive prices (closed Mon and Tue eves). Guest ales include those of Renfrewshire's only brewery, Houston.
◖ ▶ ⊟ ⇌

KILBARCHAN

TRUST INN
8 Low Barholm (off A737)
☎ (01505) 702401
11.30-11.30 (midnight Thu-Sat, 12.30 am Fri); 12.30-11 Sun
Beer range varies Ⓗ

Traditional rural village local in an area connected with the weaving industry. A comfortable lounge with cosy nooks, beamed ceiling and decorative brasses. Beers come from the Alloa range. The Glasgow-Irvine cycle path is close by. No food Sun.
◖ ▶ ⇌ (Milliken Pk)

KILDONAN

BREADALBANE HOTEL
W end of the shore, on the loop road
☎ (01770) 820284
11-midnight (1am Thu-Sat); 11-midnight Sun
Draught Bass Ⓗ

Long, whitewashed building in a quiet village in the south east corner of the Isle of Arran. A large bar with a fine stone fireplace and an enclosed verandah offers views of Ailsa Craig and the Firth of Clyde. Self-catering accommodation is also available.
⇖ ⛺ ❀ ⇌ ◖ ▶ ♿ ▲ P ⚥

KILMARNOCK

HUNTING LODGE
14-16 Glencairn Square (opp Safeway)
☎ (01563) 522920
11-3, 5-midnight; 11-1am Fri & Sat; 12-midnight Sun
Beer range varies Ⓗ
Seven handpumps dispense a changing range of beers in a large lounge bar with areas for games and dining. The venue for the local folk club (Thu), quizzes (Mon) and occasional Ceilidhs. Children's certificate.
◖ ▶ ♿ ⊬

KILMAURS

WESTON TAVERN
27 Main Street (A735)
☎ (01563) 538805
11 (12.30 Sun)-midnight
Beer range varies Ⓗ
Originally a manse, school and smithy in an historic area next to the 'Jougs', this pub dates back to circa 1500. The partly-tiled floor is a listed feature; note, too the craggy stoneworked bar and panelled games area. Rear lounge for families. Eve meals by request. Q ◖ ▶ ⊞ ♿ ⇌ ♣ P

KILMUN

COYLET HOTEL
Loch Eck (A815, 9 miles N of Dunoon)
☎ (01369) 840426
11-2.30; 5(6 winter)-11 (midnight Fri & Sat); 12.30-2.30, 6-11 Sun
Caledonian Deuchars IPA; McEwan 80/-; Younger No. 3 Ⓗ
Attractive lochside bar with open log fires; good fishing, touring and walking nearby. Excellent bar food using local produce (children welcome in the dining area). Setting for the film *The Blue Boy*. Close to local holiday caravan and lodges park.
🏨 ⇌ 🌳 ⇌ ◖ ▶ P

KILWINNING

CLAREMONT HOTEL
67 Byres Road
☎ (01294) 558445
12-2.30, 5-midnight; 12-1am Fri & Sat; 12-midnight Sun
Beer range varies Ⓗ
Attractive lounge bar in a small hotel next to the station. Also a traditional bar and a night club, neither with real ale. Pricey except during happy hours (5-7 Mon-Fri, during quiz Tue eve, and Sun afternoon). Children's certificate. ⇌ ◖ ▶ ⊞ ♿ ⇌ P

KIRKMICHAEL

KIRKMICHAEL ARMS
3 Straiton Road (B7045, 3 miles E of Maybole)
☎ (01655) 750375
11-2.30, 5-11; 11-11 Fri & Sat; 12.30-11 Sun
Beer range varies Ⓗ
Pub with a small, friendly public bar, a lounge and a restaurant set in a picturesque village at the heart of rural Ayrshire. Good home-made meals. Children's certificate.
🏨 Q ◖ ▶ ⊞

LARGS

CLACHAN
14 Bath Street (B7025)
☎ (01475) 672224
11-midnight (1am Thu-Sat); 12.30-11 Sun
Bateman XXXB; Ⓗ **Belhaven 80/-** Ⓐ
Single-bar pub with a games room, just off the main street, near the seafront and ferry terminal. Good selection of whiskies.
♿ ⇌ ♣

LOCHWINNOCH

BROWN BULL
33 Main Street (Largs Road, off A737)
☎ (01505) 843250
11 (12.30 Sun)-11 (midnight Fri & Sat)
Belhaven IPA, St Andrew's Ale; Boddingtons Bitter; Orkney Dark Island; guest beer Ⓗ
Extremely friendly, country pub in a small village, featuring a low ceiling and pictures by local artists. Folk music Fri. Close to Glasgow-Irvine cycle track.
🏨 🌳 ⇌

MAUCHLINE

LOUDOUN ARMS
12-14 Loudoun Street (B743, Ayr Road)
☎ (01290) 551011
11 (12 Sun)-midnight
Beer range varies Ⓗ
Popular, comfortable village bar and lounge with strong Robert Burns connections. Children's certificate.
🏨 ⇌ ◖ ▶ ⊞ ♣ P

MILNGAVIE

TALBOT ARMS
30 Main Street
☎ (0141) 956 3989
11 (12.30 Sun)-11 (midnight Thu-Sat)
Caledonian Deuchars IPA; Marston's Pedigree; guest beers Ⓗ
Busy, 100-year-old town-centre pub, named after a now-extinct breed of hunting dog. Popular with walkers setting off on (or finishing) the West Highland Way.
◖ Ⓐ ⇌

MILTON OF CAMPSIE

KINCAID HOUSE HOTEL
Birdston Road
☎ (0141) 776 2226
12-midnight (1am Fri); 12-midnight Sun
Beer range varies Ⓗ
Hotel with a public bar and a large conservatory for meals where children are welcome. Regular happy hours. Children's outdoor play area. The Carlsberg-Tetley's beers are from the Tapster's Choice range.
🌳 ⇌ ◖ ▶ ⊞ ♿ P

OLD KILPATRICK

ETTRICK
159 Dumbarton Road
☎ (01389) 872821
11 (12.30 Sun)-midnight (1am Fri & Sat)
Beer range varies
Traditional, late Victorian village local with a horseshoe-shaped public bar, named after the Ettrick shepherd and poet, James Hogg, a friend of Sir Walter Scott. Handy for those walking the Forth and Clyde canal tow-path. Smoking restrictions in lounge until 7pm.
🌳 ◖ ▶ ⊞ ♿ ⇌ (Kilpatrick) P ⊬

PAISLEY

BULL INN ☆
7 New Street (off pedestrianised High St)
☎ (0141) 848 1468
11-midnight; 12.30-11 Sun
Maclay Broadsword, 80/-, Wallace IPA; guest beer Ⓟ
Former coaching inn on the Paisley Heritage Trail, run as a Maclays managed house. Much of the original character has been retained but the pub now sports a collection of bric-à-brac more at home in a museum. Popular with young and old alike. Three snugs at the rear.
◖ ⇌ (Gilmour St/Paisley Canal)

GABRIELS
33 Gauze Street (Silk St jct)
☎ (0141) 887 8204
11-midnight (1am Fri, 12.45am Sat, 11.45 Sun)
Caledonian Deuchars IPA; Orkney Dark Island; guest beers
This often busy, town-centre pub has period decor and an oval island bar, plus a raised dining area serving excellent food. Infrequent pub beer festivals.
◖ ▶ ♿ ⇌ (Gilmour St)

WEE HOWFF
53 High Street
☎ (0141) 889 2095
11-11 (1am Fri, 11.30 Sat); closed Sun

Caledonian 70/-; Ind Coope
Burton Ale; guest beer Ⓗ
Small but perfectly formed local
near the university. The interior
has Tudor-style beams and pan-
elling. The only regular outlet for
Caley 70/- in the area.
⮞ (Gilmour St)

RENFREW

TAP & SPILE
Terminal Building, Glasgow
Airport (off M8, jct 28a)
☎ (0141) 848 4869
8-11 (1am Fri, 11.45 Sat); 12.30-
11 Sun
Beer range varies Ⓗ
Busy airport lounge bar in traditional Tap & Spile decor, including house merchandise.
Unfortunately, due to the location, the prices are also sky high.
The beer range increases in summer.
♿ ✂

SALTCOATS

HIP FLASK
13 Winton Street (near seafront)
☎ (01294) 465222
11-midnight (1am Thu-Sat);
11-midnight Sun
Belhaven St Andrew's Ale; guest
beer Ⓗ
Small, friendly café-bar, well
placed for both the town centre
and the beach. The raised seating area can double as a stage;
music and quizzes some eves.
Good value food (book eve
meals). Newspapers and magazines are supplied. Lively weekend eves. Children's certificate.
🍴 ◖ ▶

SEAMILL

WATERSIDE INN
Ardrossan Road (A78, S of village)
☎ (01294) 823238
11-midnight (1am Fri & Sat);
12.30-11 Sun
beer range varies Ⓗ
'Brewer's Fayre' house with a
bar that has more of a pub feel
than others. It sits right on the
beach and has wonderful sea
views from the restaurant and
garden. Food is available all day.
Guest beers are mostly from the
Whitbread range. Children's certificate. 🍴 ◖ ▶ ♿ ♣ P

STEVENSTON

CHAMPION SHELL INN
5 Schoolwell Street (off A738)
☎ (01294) 463055
11 (12.30 Sun)-midnight (1am
Thu-Sat)
Beer range varies Ⓗ
Refurbished bar/lounge in a listed building - the oldest inhabited
building in the 'Three Towns'. Its

name comes from an 18th-centu-
ry competition for drinking mead
from a shell. Two guest beers
come from a variety of sources.
Public car park opposite.
Q ◖ ▶ ♿ ♣

STRATHAVEN

WEAVERS
1 Green Street
5-12.15am (1.30am Fri); 2-
1.30am Sat; 7-12.15am Sun
Beer range varies Ⓗ
Comfortable pub, adorned with
pictures of Hollywood icons, situated in the centre of this attractive little town which was a major
centre of the 1820 radical upris-
ing and is now the home of
Strathaven toffee. Note the limited opening hours. P

TROON

ARDNEIL HOTEL
51 St Meddans Street (by station)
☎ (01292) 311611
11 (12 Sun)-midnight
Draught Bass; Caledonian
80/- Ⓗ
This hotel, bar and restaurant is
very popular with visiting golfers
and locals alike. The bar is
attractively decorated to ensure
a relaxed drinking atmosphere.
Conveniently situated for Troon's
golf courses, shops and the station.
🛏 ⇔ ◖ ▶ ♿ ♣ P ✂

McKAY'S ALE HOUSE
69 Portland Street (A759)
☎ (01292) 311079
11-12.30am; 12.30-midnight Sun
Boddingtons Bitter; Ⓗ Maclay
80/-; guest beers Ⓟ
Popular, town-centre lounge bar
serving five ales. The guest beers
rotate on a regular basis. The bar
can be busy weekend eves but a
friendly welcome is the norm.
Live music Sun.
🍴 ◖ ▶ ⮞

PIERSLAND HOUSE HOTEL
15 Craigend Road (B749 S of
centre)
☎ (01292) 314747
11-midnight, including Sun
Caledonian Deuchars IPA,
80/- Ⓗ
Popular, three-star hotel, overlooking Royal Troon golf course.
The hotel has a good reputation
for its food, which may restrict
space for drinkers. It is child-
friendly with gardens for adults
and youngsters alike. Croquet
played. Children's certificate.
🛏 Q 🛏 🍴 ⇔ ◖ ▶ ♿ ♣ P

TWECHAR

QUARRY INN
Main Street

☎ (01236) 821496
11 (12.30 Sun)-11.30 (1am Fri)
Maclay 70/-, Broadsword;
Tetley Bitter Ⓗ
Lively village local selling excellent Maclay's beers at very reasonable prices. Old pot-bellied
stoves at either end of the bar
make for a very cosy pint. Sky
sports shown.
🛏 ⊟ ♣ P

UDDINGSTON

ROWAN TREE ☆
60 Old Mill Road (next to
Tunnocks bakery)
☎ (01698) 812678
11-11.45; 12.30-11 Sun
Maclay 80/-, Wallace IPA; guest
beers Ⓗ
Formerly a coaching inn, now a
vibrant community pub with an
unspoilt, wooden interior, two
fireplaces and rare brewery mirrors. Haunted by the ghost of a
stable lad who died after being
kicked by a horse. CAMRA
Scottish *Pub of the Year* 1997. No
food Sun.
🛏 ◖ ♿ ⮞ P

UPLAWMOOR

UPLAWMOOR HOTEL
66 Neilston Road (off A736,
Barrhead-Irvine Road)
☎ (01505) 850565
12-3, 5-midnight; 12-midnight
Sat; 12-11 Sun
Draught Bass; Orkney Dark
Island Ⓗ
Village hotel, a comfortable
lounge and a large airy cocktail
bar/restaurant with a central
feature fireplace. Not easily
accessible, but well worth the
effort.
🛏 🚲 🍴 ⇔ ◖ ▶ ♿ P

INDEPENDENT
BREWERIES

Clockwork:
Glasgow

Heather:
Glasgow

Houston:
Houston

Lugton:
Lugton

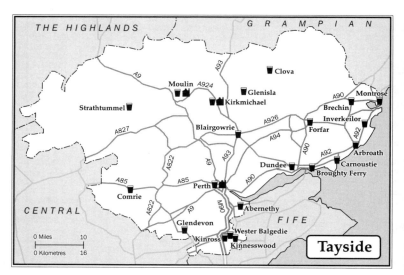

Authority areas covered: Angus UA, City of Dundee UA, Perth & Kinross UA

ABERNETHY

CREES INN
Main Street
☎ (01738) 850714
11-2.30, 5-11; 11-11 Sat; 12.30-11 Sun
Beer range varies Ⓗ
Comfortable village pub, in a listed former farmhouse, with lounge area and snug. Near Abernethy round tower. Four beers available, two Scottish.
🏚 Q ◖ P ⊁

ARBROATH

LOCHLANDS
14-16 Lochlands Street
☎ (01241) 873286
11-11; 11-12 Fri & Sat; 12.30-11 Sun
Beer range varies Ⓗ
Very popular local, with sports events usually showing on bar's TVs. Juke box in lounge. Bar snacks always available. 🍴 ≢ ♣

BLAIRGOWRIE

ROSEMOUNT GOLF HOTEL
Golf Course Road
☎ (01250) 872604
11-11 (11.45 Fri & Sat); 12-11 Sun
Inveralmond Independence; guest beer Ⓗ
Attractive and welcoming traditional hotel, popular with locals and visitors. Good base for golf, skiing or walking. Separate restaurant. 🍴 ◖ ▶ & P

STORMONT ARMS
101 Perth Street
☎ (01250) 873142
11-2.45, 5-11; 11-11 Fri & Sat; 12.30-2.30, 6.30-11 Sun

Beer range varies Ⓗ
Traditional, high-ceilinged bar with a modern lounge. Three beers on at all times.
🍺 ♣

BRECHIN

DALHOUSIE
1 Market Street
☎ (01356) 622096
11-11 Mon-Sat; 12.30-11 Sun
Beer range varies Ⓗ
Town-centre pub with extensive wood-panelling and old brewery mirror. One real ale.
🍺 ♣

BROUGHTY FERRY

FISHERMAN'S TAVERN
10-12 Fort Street
☎ (01382) 775941
11-midnight (1am Thu-Sat); 12.30-midnight Sun
Belhaven St Andrew's Ale; Boddingtons Bitter; Maclay 80/-; guest beers Ⓗ
This 1993 CAMRA *Pub of the Year* has an excellent atmosphere; it is cosy, low-ceilinged and welcoming. The only Scottish pub to have been in every *Guide* since 1975.
Q 🛏 🍴 ◖ ▶ ≢ ♣

OLD ANCHOR
48 Gray Street
☎ (01382) 737899
11-midnight; 12.30-11 Sun
Courage Directors; Theakston Best Bitter; guest beers Ⓗ
Busy, one-room bar with partitions. Decorated with a nautical theme.
🛏 ◖ ≢ (limited service) ⊁

CARNOUSTIE

STAG'S HEAD
61 Dundee Street
☎ (01241) 852265
11-midnight (1am Fri); 12.30-midnight Sun
Marston's Pedigree; Taylor Landlord; guest beers Ⓗ
Comfortable, friendly local with games room off the main bar. Summer beer festival and mini-fests twice a year. Barbecue and live music on summer weekends.
🛏 🕯 ◖ ▶ ≢ (Golf St, limited service) ♣ P

CLOVA

CLOVA HOTEL
Glen Cova (B955 15 miles N of Kirriemuir)
☎ (01575) 550222
11-midnight; 12.30-11 Sun
Beer range varies Ⓗ
Very friendly pub set amid stunning scenery. Busy at weekends with walkers, climbers and fishermen. Easter beer festival and monthly barbecues and ceilidhs in spring/summer. May Day features helicopter flights. (Camping facilities during beer festival.)
🏚 🛏 ◖ ▶ 🍺 🏕 ♣

COMRIE

ROYAL HOTEL
Melville Square
☎ (01764) 679219
11-11 Mon-Thu; 11-11.45 Fri & Sat; 12-11 Sun
Caledonian 80/, Deuchars IPA; guest beer Ⓗ
Coaching inn built in 1765 on the site of an earlier tavern which adopted the epithet Royal after

Queen Victoria stayed. Comfortable lounge bar and a public bar with pool table. As well as four-five real ales there are up to 170 single-malt whiskies. ᴘᴘ Q ❁ ⇔ ◖ ⊕ P

DUNDEE

DROUTHY NEEBORS
142 Perth Road
☎ (01382) 202187
11-12; 12-11 Sun
Belhaven IPA, 80/- , St Andrew's Ale; Orkney Dark Island; guest beers
Split-level bar, popular with students. One of Belhaven's theme pubs, with many Burns allusions. Up to four guest beers. ◖ ≢

FREELANCE & FIRKIN
13 Brown Street
☎ (01382) 227080
11-midnight; 12.30-11.30 Sun
Firkin Frisket, Freelance, Dogbolter, seasonal beers Ⓗ
Large, open-plan bar with bare floorboards, high ceilings and its own microbrewery (visits by arrangement). Meals 1-7.
◖ ▮ ⅋ ≢ P

FREW'S
117 Strathmartine Road
☎ (01382) 810975
11-11.45; 12.30-11 Sun
Draught Bass Ⓗ
Busy corner pub with two lounges (one based on the Queen Mary). The bar has an authentic Victorian feel — note the fine gantry and fireplace. Worthington White Shield is stocked. ⊕

HOGSHEAD
7-9 Union Street (opp city churches)
☎ (01382) 205037
11-midnight; 12.30-11 Sun
Boddingtons Bitter; Whitbread Abroad Cooper; guest beers Ⓗ
Friendly and very popular town-centre bar in a former bank. Up to six guest beers. Good food.
Q ◖ ▮ ⅋ ≢ ⌣

MICKEY COYLE'S
21-23 Old Hawkhill (behind university)
☎ (01382) 225871
11-11.30 (midnight Fri & Sat)
Boddingtons Bitter; Broughton Greenmantle; guest beers Ⓗ
Long, low-ceilinged lounge bar popular with university people. Two-three guest ales. Good bar meals and a variety of rums.
◖ ▮ ≢ ♣ P

SPEEDWELL BAR (MRS MENNIES) ☆
165-167 Perth Road
☎ (01382) 667783
11-midnight; 12.30-11 Sun
Beer range varies Ⓗ Ⓐ

Noted for its listed interior (1903) with mahogany and glass fittings and excellent Art Nouveau etched windows. Q ⊕ ▮ ⅋ ⅍

FORFAR

O'HARA'S
41 West High Street
☎ (01307) 464350
11-2.30, 5.30-11 (midnight Fri & Sat); 12.30-2, 6.30-11 Sun
Beer range varies Ⓗ
Upstairs small bar-bistro with helpful, friendly bar staff. Excellent lunchtime menu. Occasional music at weekends. One real ale.
ᴘᴘ ◖ ▮

GLENDEVON

TORMAUKIN HOTEL
☎ (01259) 781252
11-11; 12-11 Sun
Ind Coope Burton Ale; guest beers Ⓗ
Country hotel with real ale served in the rear lounge. Popular centre for golfers and walkers. The two guest beers come from Harviestoun.
ᴘᴘ Q ⌑ ⇔ ◖ ▮ Å P

GLENISLA

GLENISLA HOTEL
☎ (01575) 582223
11-11 (12.30am Fri, midnight Sat); 12.30-11 Sun
Boddingtons Bitter; Inveralmond Independence Ⓗ
Traditional coaching inn set in beautiful countryside, ideal for walkers and skiers. Wood-burning fire.
ᴘᴘ Q ⇔ ◖ ▮ Å P

INVERKEILOR

CHANCE INN
Main Street (off A92 coast road)
☎ (01241) 830308
12-2.30, 5-11; 12-11 Sat; 12.30-11 Sun
Wadworth 6X; guest beers Ⓗ
Eighteenth-century coaching inn noted for food (booking recommended). Lively bar with adjoining lounge/dining room where handpumps are installed. No food Mon.
⇔ ◖ ▮ ⊕ ⅋ ♣ P

KINNESSWOOD

LOMOND COUNTRY INN
Main Street
☎ (01592) 840253
11-11 (midnight Fri & Sat); 11-11 Sun
Draught Bass; Jennings Bitter; guest beer Ⓗ
Open-plan bar/restaurant with views over Loch Leven. A popular refuge in this part of Perthshire.
ᴘᴘ Q ⌑ ❁ ⇔ ◖ ▮ ⅋ P ⅍

KINROSS

KIRKLANDS HOEL
High Street
☎ (01577) 863313
11-2.30, 5-11 (11.45 Sat); 12.30-11 Sun
Maclay 80/-; guest beers Ⓗ
Small, comfortable hotel with a cosy public bar and lounge area.
Q ⇔ ◖ ⊕

MUIRS INN
49 The Muirs
☎ (01577) 862270
11-2.30, 5-11 (11.45 Fri); 11-11.45 Sat; 12.30-11 Sun
Beer range varies Ⓗ
Listed building dating back to the 1800s, originally a farmhouse. Comfortable lounge with its own 'wee still'. The compact bar area has eight handpumps: up to five ales are available. The pub has its own beer festival and malt whisky festival.
Q ❁ ⇔ ◖ ▮ ⊕ P

KIRKMICHAEL

ALDCHLAPPIE HOTEL
At A924/B950 jct
☎ (01250) 881224
11-3 (not Mon), 5.30-11.45; 12-3, 6.30-11 Sun
Beer range varies Ⓗ
Comfortable hotel in a former droving inn/farm dating from 1620. Good base for walkers, skiers and tourists. Its own microbrewery vies for the title of the smallest brewery in Britain. Meals end 8.45pm.
ᴘᴘ Q ⌑ ❁ ⇔ ◖ ▮ ⊕ ⅋ Å P

MONTROSE

GEORGE HOTEL
22 George Street
☎ (01674) 675050
11-2, 4.30-11; 11-11 Sat; 12-11 Sun
Beer range varies Ⓗ
Long, comfortable lounge with a four-handpump bar decorated with hop bines. The extensive menu is reasonably priced. Four of the bedrooms have four-poster beds. ⇔ ◖ ▮ ≢ P ⅍

MARKET ARMS
95 High Street
☎ (01674) 673384
11-midnight; 12.30-2.30, 6.30-11 Sun
Beer range varies Ⓗ
Large, basic, 1960s town-centre pub. Often busy and noisy. ≢ ♣

MOULIN

MOULIN INN
11-13 Kirkmichael Road (³/₄ mile NE of Pitlochry)
☎ (01796) 472196
11-11 Mon-Thu; 11-11.45 Fri & Sat; 12-11 Sun

423

Moulin Light; Braveheart; Ale of
Atholl; Old Remedial Ⓗ
Old country inn with adjoining
brewhouse. A welcoming watering hole in this part of rural
Perthshire.
🏨 ⛵ 🛏 ◐ 🍺 ᵔ Ⓐ P

PERTH

LOVAT HOTEL
90-92 Glasgow Road
☎ (01738) 636555
11.30-2.30, 5-11, including Sun
**Inveralmond Independence,
Ossian Ale, Lia Fail; guest
beers** Ⓗ
Busy, friendly hotel which offers
excellent bar suppers and holds
an annual beer festival. There is
a pool table in the back room.
Good base for touring Perthshire.
🛏 ◐ 🍺 ᵔ Ⓐ ⇌ P ⚥

MONCRIEFF ARMS
75 Princes Street
☎ (01738) 625670
11-11 Mon -Thu; 11-11.45 Fri &
Sat; 12.30-11 Sun
**Ind Coope Burton Ale; guest
beers** Ⓗ

Comfortable, open-plan lounge
bar with a pool table. The separate restaurant is very popular.
🛏 ◐ 🍺

OLD SHIP INN
Skinnergate Street (off High
Street)
☎ (01738) 624929
11-2.30, 5-11; 11-11.45 Fri & Sat;
closed Sun
**Caledonian Deuchars IPA; guest
beers** Ⓗ
One of the oldest licensed houses
in Perth, dating from 1665, has
four handpumps dispensing a
good choice of ales.
Q ◐ 🍺 ♣

STRATHTUMMEL

LOCH TUMMEL INN
On B8019 3 miles W of Queen's
View
☎ (01882) 634272
11-11; 12.30-11 Sun
Moulin Braveheart Ⓗ
Old coaching inn set amid mag-
nificent scenery overlooking Loch
Tummel. The bar is in the former
stables; the restaurant is the for-

mer hayloft. Closed from 1st
week after New Year until 1st
week in March.
Q ❀ 🛏 ◐ P

WESTER BALGEDIE

BALGEDIE TAVERN
At B919/A911 jct, near Kinross
☎ (01592) 840212
11-3, 5-11; 12.30-11 Sun
Ind Coope Burton Ale Ⓗ
Warm, friendly and atmospheric
rural tavern dating from 1534.
Features three separate seating
areas and a small bar. Families
welcome. Eve meals 6-9.
🏨 Q ❀ ◐ 🍺 P

INDEPENDENT BREWERIES

Aldchlappie:
Kirkmichael
Inveralmond:
Perth

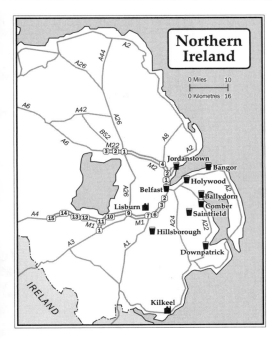

Northern Ireland

0 Miles 10
0 Kilometres 16

BALLYDORN

DAFT EDDY'S
Skeltrick Island (A2 from Comber, follow signs to Whiterock)
☎ (01238) 541615
11.30-11.30 (1.30am Fri & Sat); 12.30-10 Sun
Draught Bass; Theakston Best Bitter Ⓗ
Modern, two-bar building. The public bar has a tiled floor, an open range fire, a beamed ceiling and a quiet atmosphere. The lounge has an open fire and the patio and restaurant offer scenic views of Strangford Lough. Handy for the boating marina and club. Children welcome.
🏚 Q 🌣 🏵 🕽 🌓 ⊟ & P

BANGOR

ESPLANADE
12 Ballyhome Esplanade
☎ (01247) 270954
11.30-11; 12.30-10 Sun
Beer range varies Ⓗ
Comfortable seaside pub affording commanding views over Ballyhome Bay from the patio and lounge. Handpumps in the public bar only, but staff in the lounge will fetch real ale on request. Excellent food.
🏚 Q 🏵 🕽 🌓 ⊟

JENNY WATTS
41 High Street (Marina End)
☎ (01247) 270401
11-11; 12-10.30 Sun
Theakston Best Bitter Ⓗ
Open-plan, seaside pub dating from 1740; it features a stone floor and displays local memorabilia. Famous for its Sunday jazz lunch. 🏚 🏵 🕽 🌓 ⊟ ≈

BELFAST

BEATEN DOCKET
46-52 Great Victoria Street (opp Europa Hotel)
☎ (01232) 242986
9am-1am; 12-midnight Sun
Draught Bass; Cains FA; Caledonian Deuchars IPA; Tomintoul Laird's Ale; guest beers Ⓗ
At the heart of Belfast's Golden Mile this lively city-centre pub public bar has a lounge/restaurant upstairs serving traditional well-cooked meals. Music Fri and Sat eves.
🏚 🌣 ⊟ ≈ (Gt Victoria St) ✂

BITTLES BAR
70 Upper Church Lane
☎ (01232) 311088
11.30-11.30; 11.30-10.30 Sun
Draught Bass Ⓗ
Neat, corner bar with an unusual triangular shape and a relaxed, friendly atmosphere.
🕽 ≈ (Central)

BOTANIC INN
23-27 Malone Road
☎ (01232) 660460
11.30-midnight (1am Wed-Sat); 12.30-10 Sun
Cains Bitter; guest beers Ⓗ
Large pub in the university area of the city. It hosts traditional

music Tue eve and a real ale club. Tapas served 5-11pm. A very busy pub, especially with students.
🏚 🕽 & ≈ (Botanic)

CROWN LIQUOR SALOON ☆
44 Great Victoria Street (opp Europa Hotel)
☎ (01232) 249426
11.30-midnight (1am Fri & Sat); 12.30-10.30 Sun
Draught Bass Ⓗ
This bar is remarkable, not only for its decor, but for being jointly run by the NT and Bass. Belfast's most famous pub where a large crowd and a good atmosphere are ensured; very popular with tourists. 🕽 ≈ (Victoria St)

ERRIGLE
320 Ormeau Road
☎ (01232) 641410
11.30-1am; 11.30-10 Sun
Beer range varies Ⓗ
Boasting five bars with modern decor, one without TV. Children are allowed in the restaurant.
Q 🕽 🌓 ⊟ & ♣

KITCHEN BAR
16 Victoria Square
☎ (01232) 324901
11.30-11; closed Sun
Beer range varies Ⓗ
Popular, family-run, city-centre pub close to the main shopping area. The front and back bars both serve ale. Renowned for its high quality and good value lunches. Memorabilia from the old Belfast Theatre days.
🕽 ≈ (Central)

LAVERY'S GIN PALACE
12-16 Bradbury Place
☎ (01232) 328205
11.30-1am; 12.30-midnight Sun
Beer range varies Ⓗ
Large, open-plan pub with real ale in the public bar only. The back bar has a snug offering entertainment every night and, being next to Queens University, it is popular with students.
🕽 ⊟ ≈ (Gt Victoria St/Botanic)

MONICO BARS
17 Lombard Street (off High St)
☎ (01232) 323211
10-11; closed Sun
Cains FA; guest beers Ⓗ
Next to Whites Tavern in the heart of the busy shopping centre. Extensive snack and lunch menu. Range of comfortable relaxing lounges. 🏚 🕽 &

PORTSIDE INN
1 Dargan Road (100 yds from M2 jct)
☎ (01232) 370746
10-10 (1am Fri; 9 Sat); 10-6 Sun
Beer range varies Ⓗ
Established in 1990, this welcom-

ing, one-bar pub bears a seaside theme. Very popular for the full bar menu at lunchtimes; staff are extremely friendly. Within sight of the Harland and Wolff Shipyard, birthplace of the Titanic.
❀ ◑ ▶ ♿ P

WHITES TAVERN
2-4 Winecellar Entry (off High St)
☎ (01232) 243080
11.30-11; 1-7 Sun
Cains FA Ⓗ
Established in 1630 and one of Belfast's oldest pubs; originally a bonded warehouse, it maintains its true character with exposed beams and rough plaster walls. Excellent food on a home-cooked menu.
🚲 Q ◑

COMBER

NORTH DOWN HOUSE
101-103 Mill Street
☎ (01247) 872242
11.30-11.30; 12.30-10.30 Sun
Draught Bass Ⓗ
Situated on the old Ards Grand Prix circuit with its Tourist Trophy Restaurant and wine bar, this pub is steeped in the tradition of the famous TT motor car race.
Q ▶ ⊞ P

DOWNPATRICK

DENVIR'S HOTEL
14-16 English Street (near Down Cathedral)
☎ (01396) 612012
11-11; 12.30-11 Sun
Hilden Ale Ⓗ
17th-century coaching inn, just renovated and returned to its original form of three bars.
🚲 Q 🛏 🛋 ◑ ▶ ⊞ ♿ P

HILLSBOROUGH

HILLSIDE
21 Main Street
☎ (01846) 682765
12-11; 12-10 Sun
Cains Bitter; Whitewater Mountain Ale; guest beers Ⓗ
Long, narrow bar with a stone floor, dating back to the 1800s. Excellent pub food is served in an extension at the rear with a very popular, top quality restaurant upstairs. Local CAMRA *Pub of the Year* 1997.
🚲 Q ❀ ◑ ▶

PLOUGH
3 The Square
☎ (01846) 682985
11.30-11; 12.30-10 Sun
Theakston Best Bitter; Whitewater Mountain Ale Ⓗ
Traditional village pub, estab-

lished in 1758, boasting wood-panelled walls and ceiling beams. A comfortable, spacious U-shaped lounge and an excellent restaurant.
🚲 Q ❀ ◑ ▶ P

HOLYWOOD

DIRTY DUCK
2 Kennegar Road
☎ (01232) 425533
11-midnight (1am Thu-Sat); 11.30-midnight Sun
Beer range varies Ⓗ
Waterside pub on the shore of Belfast Lough where good food is served all day, including Sun until 8.30. Live music most nights.
🚲 ❀ ◑ ▶ ⇌

JORDANSTOWN

WOODY'S
607 Shore Road, Whiteabbey
☎ (01232) 863206
11.30-11; 1-10 Sun
Beer range varies Ⓗ
Comfortable upstairs bar with regular quiz nights and other entertainments. Weekday lunches. An attached off-licence stocks a range of bottled ales.
Q ◑ P

SAINTFIELD

WHITE HORSE
49 Main Street
☎ (01238) 510417
10-11; closed Sun
Beer range varies Ⓗ
Family-run pub with a comfortable, friendly atmosphere. A wide range of excellent food is served in the bar and downstairs restaurant. Annual beer festival (Nov).
🚲 Q ◑ ▶

Also available from CAMRA/Storey.

INDEPENDENT BREWERIES

Hilden:
Lisburn
Whitewater:
Kilkeel

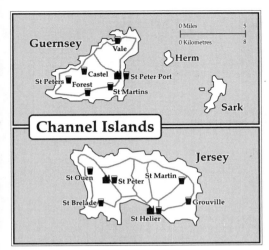

Guernsey

CASTEL

FLEUR DU JARDIN
Kings Mills ☎ (01481) 57996
11-11.45; 12-2, 6-10.30 Sun
Guernsey Sunbeam, seasonal beers H
Quality hotel in a pleasant setting, renovated in keeping with its farmhouse origins. Excellent bar meals and an adjoining restaurant. The public bar opens eves. 🏨 🐕 ➥ ◑ ▶ 🍺 P

FOREST

VENTURE INN
Rue de la Villiaze
☎ (01481) 63211
10.30-11.45; closed Sun
Randalls Patios Ale H
Established local not far from the airport. The functional, sports-oriented public bar contrasts with the comfortable lounge. Occasional brewery special brews are on offer.
🏨 🐕 ◑ ▶ 🍺 ♣ P

ST MARTINS

CAPTAIN'S HOTEL
La Fosse ☎ (01481) 38990
10-11.45; 12-11 (closed winter) Sun
Guernsey Sunbeam H
Single lounge bar with a genuine pub feel in an attractive hotel near Moulin Huet Bay and Pottery. Note the impressive beer engine. Evening meals are also served in the adjoining bistro-style restaurant.
🐕 ➥ ◑ ▶ P

L'AUBERGE DIVETTE
Jerbourg (next to Jerbourg Monument)
☎ (01481) 38485
10.30-11.45 12-3 Sun

Guernsey Braye (summer), Sunbeam H
Comfortable pub with two bars, close to cliff path walks. Magnificent views from the lounge and garden. Eve meals in summer.
🏨 🐕 ◑ ▶ 🍺 ♣ P

ST PETER PORT

COCK & BULL
No. 2 Lower Hautville
☎ (01481) 722660
11.30-2.30, 4-11.45; 11.30-11.45 Fri & Sat; closed Sun
Ringwood Best Bitter; guest beers H
Open, spacious bar on three levels, hosting occasional live music evenings. Eve meals served in summer. ◑ ▶

DRUNKEN DUCK
Charotterie
☎ (01481) 725045
11-11.45; 12-3.30 Sun
Beer range varies H
Small, two-roomed pub with a garish exterior. Occasional live music and quiz eves. ◑ ♣

SHIP & CROWN
Pier Steps, Esplanade
☎ (01481) 721368
10-11.45; 12-3.30, 6-11 Sun
Guernsey Sunbeam, seasonal beers H
Lively, large, single-bar town pub, popular with locals and tourists, boasting good views over the harbour. Local CAMRA *Pub of the Year* 1997. Eve meals in summer 5.30-8. ◑ ▶

ST PETERS

LONGFRIE INN
Route de Longfrie
☎ (01481) 63107
11-3, 6-11.45; 12-2.30, 6-10.30 Sun

Guernsey Sunbeam, seasonal beers H
Food and family-oriented hostelry, sometimes very busy. A well-equipped children's room, a large garden and a good varied menu are features.
🐕 🐾 ➥ ◑ ▶ P

VALE

CHANDLERS' HOTEL
Braye Road
☎ (01481) 44280
10.30-11.45; closed Sun
Randalls Patois Ale H
A lively locals' public bar contrasts with a cosy lounge. Good value bar meals include Thai and unusual specials. Frequent live music in upstairs function room. Skittle alley and shove ha'penny played. Q 🐕 ➥ ◑ ▶ 🍺 ♣ P

HOUMET TAVERN
'La Route de Picquerel', L'islet
☎ (01481) 43037
10.30-11.45; closed Sun
Guernsey Braye H
Popular pub with a pleasant outlook over picturesque Grande Havre Bay. The sole handpump is in the bar - ask for 'mild'. Very good reputation for bar meals (no eve meals Mon or Thu).
Q 🐕 ◑ ▶ 🍺 🅰 ♣ P

Jersey

GROUVILLE

PEMBROKE
Coast Road
☎ (01534) 855756
9-11.30; 11-11.30 Sun
Draught Bass; Boddingtons Bitter; Theakston XB (summer)**; guest beers** H
Large, welcoming, popular pub with a family atmosphere. Booking advised for Sun lunch. Excellent food; eat out on the large patio. Outside play area for children.
🏨 Q 🐕 ◑ ▶ 🍺 ♿ ♣ P

SEYMOUR INN
La Rocque
☎ (01534) 854558
10-11.30, including Sun
Guernsey Sunbeam; Jersey Ann's Treat H
Coastal pub directly opposite the beach, with a patio area and several small bars including a real ale bar. The good, no-nonsense food is well priced. It boasts a large range of pub games.
🏨 Q 🐕 🐾 ◑ ▶ 🍺 ♣ P

ST BRELADE

OLD SMUGGLERS INN
Ouaisne Bay
☎ (01534) 41510
11-11.30, including Sun
Boddingtons Bitter; guest beers H

17th-century granite pub offering various guest ales. In a romantic setting next to the beach, it hosts live music. Sun eve diners are well catered for with excellent food. 🏨 Q ⌒ ◖ ▶ ♣

ST HELIER

DOG & SAUSAGE
Hilary Street
☎ (01534) 30982
9.30-11.30, including Sun
Draught Bass Ⓗ
Small pub in a pedestrian shopping area with an outdoor area extending into the precinct. A welcome stop in a busy area of town, it is fashioned like a pre-war railway carriage. ❀ ◖

LAMPLIGHTER
Mulcaster Street (near bus station)
☎ (01534) 23119
10-.11.30; 11-11.30 Sun
Draught Bass; Boddingtons Bitter; Marston's Pedigree; Theakston Old Peculier; guest beer Ⓗ
The only gas-lit pub on Jersey, it serves a wide range of beers plus Bulmers traditional cider and good value, no-nonsense food. ◖ ♣ ⌣

PRINCE OF WALES TAVERN
Hilgrove Street
☎ (01534) 37378
10-11; 11-2 Sun
Adnams Bitter; Boddingtons Bitter; Marston's Pedigree Ⓗ
Traditional market pub off a cobbled street, with a surprisingly pleasant beer garden enclosed by warehouses. Note the ship's bell (but don't ring it).
❀ ◖ 🍺

SOUTHAMPTON
Weighbridge
☎ (01534) 20144
10-11.30; 11-11.30 Sun
Guernsey Sunbeam; guest beer Ⓗ
First stop from either the harbour or bus terminal, this is a workingman's pub with a witty welcome guaranteed and a good lunchtime menu. Jersey CAMRA *Pub of the Year 1997.*
Q ◖ 🍺 ♣

ST MARTIN

ANNE PORT BAY HOTEL
Anne Port Bay
☎ (01534) 852058
11-2.30, 5-11; 11-11 Sat & Sun
Draught Bass; Marston's Pedigree; Tipsy Toad Ale Ⓗ
Small, quiet hotel bar tucked away in the east of the island, enjoying a strong local following. For guest beers check the blackboard. Good B&B; visit the local craft centre incorporated in the hotel. Jersey CAMRA *Pub of the Year* 1996. ⌒ ❀ 🛏 P

ROYAL HOTEL
La Grande Route de Faldouet
☎ (01534) 856289
9.30-11.30; 11-11.30 Sun
Boddingtons Bitter; guest beers Ⓗ
Large, popular pub next to St Martin's church. It has a large children's play area and patio (families welcome). A quiet lounge contrasts with the busy public bar. The upstairs restaurant is popular with locals (real

ale provided here on request); excellent food.
🏨 Q ⌒ ❀ ◖ ▶ 🔥 🛇 ♣ ▲ ♣ P

ST OUEN

MOULIN DE LECQ
Grève de Lecq
☎ (01534) 482818
11-11.30, including Sun
Guernsey Sunbeam; Tipsy Toad Ale; guest beer Ⓗ
Converted 12th-century working watermill with a moving drive wheel behind the bar. The landscaped garden has a children's play area. Excellent food. Situated in pleasant valley leading to the beach.
🏨 Q ⌒ ❀ ◖ ▶ P ✂

ST PETER

STAR & TIPSY TOAD
La Route de Beaumont
☎ (01534) 485556
10-11.30; 11-11.30 Sun
Tipsy Toad Ale, seasonal beers Ⓗ
Tipsy Toad brew pub; a spacious and tasteful renovation. Good food and live music are features. Tours available; new brews are regularly introduced. This busy and popular pub caters well for families (outdoor play area).
🏨 ⌒ ❀ ◖ ▶ 🔥 ♣ ⌣ P

INDEPENDENT BREWERIES

Guernsey:
St Peter Port
Randalls:
St Peter Port
Jersey:
St Helier
Tipsy Toad:
St Peter

ISLE OF MAN INDEPENDENT BREWERIES

Bushy's:
Braddan
Okells:
Douglas
Old Laxey:
Laxey

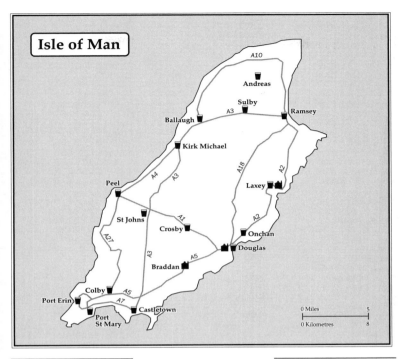

Isle of Man

ANDREAS

BALLAUGH

KIRK MICHAEL

PEEL

ST JOHNS

CROSBY

PORT ERIN

COLBY

CASTLETOWN

PORT ST MARY

SULBY

RAMSEY

LAXEY

ONCHAN

DOUGLAS

BRADDAN

0 Miles 5

0 Kilometres 8

ANDREAS

GROSVENOR
Kirk Andreas ☎ (01624) 880576
12-11 (midnight Fri & Sat); 12-3,
7-10.30 Sun
Cains bitter; Okells Bitter Ⓗ
Country pub with a bar and
restaurant (good home cooking).
Q ✿ ◖ ▶ 🍽 ᙭ ♣ P

BALLAUGH

RAVEN
Main Road (at Ballaugh Bridge
on TT course) ☎ (01624) 897272
11-11 (midnight Fri & Sat); 12-3,
7-10.30 Sun
**Okells Bitter; Marston's
Pedigree; guest beers** Ⓗ
Village pub and bistro on the
famous TT course, popular with
race fans. ᙭ ◖ ▶ ⚑ P

CASTLETOWN

CASTLE ARMS
The Quay (opp Castle Rushen)
☎ (01624) 824673
12-10.45 (midnight Fri & Sat);
12-3, 7-10.30 Sun
Okells Bitter; Theakston Best Bitter Ⓗ
Historic alehouse in the town centre, near the harbour. Lunchtime
bar meals; Thai food in the restaurant some eves. ◖ ≈ (IMR)

SHIP
Hope Street (harbourside)
☎ (01624) 824959
12-11 (11.30 Fri & Sat); 12-3,
7-10.30 Sun
Okells Bitter Ⓗ
Popular, town-centre pub. The
upper lounge overlooks the harbour. The bars are on the ground
floor.✿ ◖ ≈ (IMR)

SIDINGS
Victoria Road (by station)
☎ (01624) 823282
12-10.45 (midnight Fri & Sat);
12-3, 7-10.30 Sun
**Bush's Manannan's Cloak;
Marston's Pedigree; Theakston
Mild, Best Bitter; Wadworth 6X;
guest beers** Ⓗ
An interesting range of draught
beers is always to be found at
this pub, improved since its run-
down brewery days.✿ ◖ ≈ ♣

COLBY

COLBY GLEN
Main Road (A7) ☎ (01624) 834853
12-11 (11.30 Fri & Sat); 12-3 Sun
Okells Mild, Bitter Ⓗ
Convivial country inn with a var-
ied choice of excellent food.
✿ ◖ ▶ ⚑ ≈ (IMR) P

CROSBY

CROSBY
Main Road ☎ (01624) 852767
12-11 (11.30 Fri & Sat); 12-3,
7-10.30 Sun
Okells Mild, Bitter Ⓗ
Well-known pub on the TT course;
popular with locals and visitors
alike. Good food. ✿ ◖ ⚑ P

DOUGLAS

ALBERT
Chapel Row (next to bus station)
☎ (01624) 673632
11-11 (midnight Thu & Fri); 12-3,
7-10.30 Sun
Okells Mild, Bitter; guest beers Ⓗ
An excellent example of a Manx
harbourside pub, very much a
local and popular with fishermen.
This unmodernised pub is well
worth a visit. ᙭ ⚑ ≈ (IMR)

FORESTERS ARMS
St Georges Street (off Athol St)
☎ (01624) 676509
12-11 (11.30 Fri & Sat); 12-3,
7-10.30 Sun
Okells Mild, Bitter Ⓗ
Excellent, basic, well-run local, a
former Castletown house - note
the windows. This pub should be
visited before its refurbishment.
᙭ ⚑ ≈ (IMR) ♣

OLD MARKET INN
Chapel Row (near bus station)
☎ (01624) 675202
12-11 (midnight Fri & Sat); 12-3,
7-10.30 Sun
Bushy's Bitter; Okell's Bitter Ⓗ
A locals' pub that gives a warm
welcome and is very popular with
visitors. Very much a beer pub.
᙭ ⚑ ≈ (IMR)

RAILWAY HOTEL
Bridge Road (by station)
☎ (01624) 673157
12-11 (midnight Fri & Sat); 12-3,

429

7-10.30 Sun
Okells Mild, Bitter, seasonal beers H
Friendly pub where darts and pool are played. ◖⊞≢(IMR)♣

ROVERS RETURN
11 Church Street (behind Town Hall) ☎ (01624) 676459
12-11 (midnight Fri & Sat); 12-3, 7-10.30 Sun
Bushy's Bitter, seasonal beers; guest beers H
Part of Bushy's empire, it is very popular with locals and visitors alike. Good food. Outside seating and tables in summer (pedestrian area). ⚌ ⚌ ◖≢(IMR)

SADDLE INN
Queen Street (off North Quay) ☎ (01624) 673161
12-11 (midnight Fri & Sat) 12-3, 7-10.30 Sun
Cains Bitter; Okells Mild, Bitter, seasonal beers; guest beers H
Small, friendly, quayside pub popular with fishermen. ◖≢(IMR)♣

SAMUEL WEBB
Marina House, Marina Road ☎ (01624) 675595
12-11 (11.30 Fri & Sat); 12-3, 7-10.30 Sun
Courage Directors; Marston's Pedigree; Okells Bitter; Ruddles County; guest beers H
Pleasant staff, a friendly landlord and good selection of beers. Popular with race fans, locals and visitors.
⚇ ◖ ▶ ≢(IMR)⊖ (Church Rd)

TERMINUS TAVERN
Strathallan Crescent (Promenade) ☎ (01624) 624312
12-11 (11.30 Fri & Sat); 12-3, 7.30-10.30 Sun
Okells Mild,Bitter, seasonal beers H
Large, well-established, two-roomed Victorian town pub. Children welcome until 7.30. Eve meals Thu. No food Sun.
⛺ ◖ ⅋ ≢(Derby Castle)

WOODBOURNE HOTEL
Alexander Drive ☎ (01624) 621766
12-11 (midnight Fri & Sat); 12-3, 7-10.30 Sun
Okells Mild, Bitter H
Friendly hostelry, popular with locals.Has the island's only gentlemen-only bar.
⚇Q◖⊞♣

KIRK MICHAEL

MITRE HOTEL
Main Road ☎ (01624) 878244
12-11 (midnight Fri & Sat); 12-3, 7-10.30 Sun
Okells Bitter H
Reputed to be the oldest pub on the island, popular with locals and visitors. Excellent food, live music, folk music, and karaoke.
⚇ ⛺ ◖▶⊞⅋ A ♣ P

LOWER LAXEY

SHORE HOTEL
Old Laxey Hill (near harbour) ☎ (01624) 861509
12-2.30, 4.30-11 (midnight Fri &Sat); 12-11 summer; 12-3, 7-10.30 Sun
Okells Bitter; Old Laxey Bosun Bitter H
Extremely popular riverside pub with tables on the riverbank. Brews Bosun Bitter in the former restaurant. This is the island's third and latest brewery.
⚇ ⛺ A ≢(MER) P

ONCHAN

LIVERPOOL ARMS HOTEL
Baldrine (A2) ☎ (01624) 674787
12-11 (midnight Fri & Sat); 12-3, 7-10.30 Sun
Okells Bitter, seasonal beers H
Friendly, popular pub, near the electric tram stop. Good food.
⚇Q⛺◖▶⅋≢(MER) ♣ P

PEEL

ROYAL HOTEL
Athol Street (opp bus station) ☎ (01624) 842217
12-11 (midnight Fri & Sat); 12-3, 7-10.30 Sun
Okells Mild, Bitter H
Old pub with a long narrow bar and friendly locals. ⚇ ⛺ ♣

WHITE HOUSE
2 Tynwald Rd ☎ (01624) 842252
12-11 (midnight Fri & Sat); 12-3, 7-10.30 Sun
Bushy's Bitter; Flowers Original; Okells Mild, Bitter, seasonal beers; guest beers H
Popular, homely pub; good range of guest beers always on tap. Manx music Sat eve. Limited lunch menu. ⚇Q◖⚌A♣ P

PORT ERIN

FALCONS NEST HOTEL
Station Road (by the promenade) ☎ (01624) 834077
12-11 (midnight Fri & Sat); 7-10.30 Sun
Boddingtons Bitter; Castle Eden Ale; Flowers Original; Okells Bitter; Tetley Bitter; guest beers H
Friendly hotel by the beach with original features and comfortable bars. Good food.
⚇Q⚌◖▶⊞⅋≢(IMR)♣ P

PORT ST MARY

ALBERT HOTEL
Athol Street (near harbour) ☎ (01624) 832118
12-10.45, (midnight Fri & Sat); 12-3, 7-10.30 Sun
Draught Bass; Cains Mild; Okells Bitter H
Popular with locals and visiting yachtsfolk, the Albert is enjoying a new lease of life, free of brew-

ery tie. The original features remain unspoilt. ⚇ ⚌ ◖⊞♣

STATION HOTEL
Station Road ☎ (01624) 832249
12-11 (11.30 Fri & Sat); 12-3, 7-10.30 Sun
Okells Mild, Bitter H
Large, traditional Victorian ex-hotel. On a main bus route.
◖▶⊞⅋ A ≢(IMR)

RAMSEY

STANLEY HOTEL
West Quay (opp harbour swing bridge) (01624) 812258
☎ 12-11 (midnight Fri & Sat); 12-3, 7-10.30 Sun
Okells Bitter; guest beers H
Recently refurbished pub also known as the Cask House. A good range of beers is served by cheerful staff. A warm, harbour-side pub. ⊞⅋≢(MER)♣

SWAN
Parliament Square (near harbour) ☎ (01624) 814236
12-11 (midnight Fri & Sat); 12-3, 7-10.30 Sun
Okells Mild, Bitter H
On the TT course, this pub has a large lounge and bar areas, and a garden at the rear. Very good food. ⛺ ◖⊞⅋ A ≢(MER)♣

TRAFALGAR HOTEL
West Quay (harbourside) ☎ (01624) 814601
12-11 (midnight Fri & Sat); 12-3, 7-10.30 Sun
Bushy's Bitter; Cains Bitter; Old Laxey Bosun Bitter; guest beers H
1996 and '97 local CAMRA *Pub of the Year*, this friendly harbour-side pub is well known for its good food. Very much a locals' bar, but also busy with visitors.
⛺ ◖ ≢(MER)

ST JOHNS

FARMERS ARMS
☎ (01624) 801372
12-11 (midnight Fri & Sat); 7-10.30 Sun
Ind Coope Burton Ale; Old Laxey Bosun Bitter; Tetley Bitter; guest beers H
Next to the auction mart, so busy on market days with farmers. Very genial hosts; very good food. ⚇ ⛺ ◖▶♣ P

SULBY

SULBY GLEN HOTEL
On A3 (TT course, near the school) ☎ (01624) 897240
12-11 (midnight Fri & Sat); 12-3, 7-10.30 Sun
Bushy's Bitter; Okells Mild, Bitter H
Typical, friendly Manx pub on the TT course. Excellent food, live music, good accommodation.
⚇ ⛺ ⚌ ◖▶⊞⅋ A ♣ P

Independent breweries

HOW TO TO USE THE BREWERIES SECTION

Breweries are listed in alphabetical order. The Independents (including brewpubs) are listed first, followed by the Nationals and then the Pub Groups.

• Within each brewery listing, beers are listed by increasing order of strength.

• Beers which are available for less than three months of the year are listed in the brewery description as 'seasonal' or 'occasional'.

• Bottle-conditioned beers are also mentioned; these are bottled beers which have not been pasteurised and still contain yeast, allowing them to ferment in the bottle just like real ale does in the cask.

Symbols

Ō A brewpub: a pub which brews beer on the premises.

◆ CAMRA tasting notes, supplied by a trained CAMRA tasting panel. Beer descriptions which do not have this symbol are based only on limited tastings or have been obtained from other sources. Tasting notes are not provided for brewpub beers which are available in less than five outlets, nor for other breweries' beers which are available for less than three months of the year.

✿ A *Good Beer Guide Beer of the Year* in the last three years.

◧ One of the year's *Good Beer Guide Beers of the Year,* finalist in the *Champion Beer of Britain* contest held during the Great British Beer Festival at Olympia in August 1998 or in the Champion Winter Beer of Britain contest held in winter 1998.

⊙ The brewery's beer can be acceptably served through a tight sparkler or showerhead.

⊗ The brewery's beer should not be served through a tight sparkler or showerhead.

Abbreviations
OG stands for original gravity, the reading taken before fermentation of the amount of fermentable material in the brew. It is a rough indication of strength.

ABV is the alcohol by volume rating and is more reliable. It gives the percentage of alcohol in the finished beer. Many breweries now only declare ABV figures, but where OGs are available they have been included.

Shop
This means the brewery also has a shop; opening hours are given where available, but please check as they tend to be revised regularly.

Tours by arrangement
A number of breweries offer tours. The bigger the brewery, the more likely the tour is to be a regular event. Tours by arrangement means just that: if you intend to visit, discuss your arrangements with the brewery beforehand.

A quick-check list of new breweries is on page page 534

ABBEY

Abbey Ales Ltd, The Abbey Brewery, 2
Lansdown Road, Bath BA1 5EE
Tel (01225) 444437 Fax (01225) 444437
Tours by arrangement
Launched with a single cask ale at the Bath
Beer Festival in October 1997, Abbey is the
first brewery to open in Bath for 40 years. It
supplies over 40 outlets within a 20-mile
radius and has plans for a small tied estate.
Its first pub, the Belvedere Brewery Tap,
opposite the brewery, was opened in April
1998 and features a range of beers from
other micros as well as Bellringer.
Bellringer *(OG 1042, ABV 4.2%)* ▮

ABBEYDALE

Abbeydale Brewery, Unit 8, Aizlewood
Road, Sheffield, S. Yorkshire S8 0YX
Tel (0114) 281 2712 Fax (0114) 281 2713
⊛ When it opened in September 1996, this
brewery won immediate acclaim with one of the first
brews of its best bitter, Moonshine. Future
plans include brewing special beers and
experimenting with different flavourings.
Matins *(OG 1035, ABV 3.5%)*
Moonshine *(OG 1041, ABV 4.3%)*
Absolution *(OG 1051, ABV 5.3%)*
Black Mass *(OG 1065, ABV 6.7%)*
Last Rites *(OG 1100, ABV 10.5%)*

ABC

See Nationals, Carlsberg-Tetley.

ABINGTON PARK

Brewery closed.

ADNAMS

Adnams and Company PLC, Sole Bay
Brewery, East Green, Southwold, Suffolk
IP18 6JW
Tel (01502) 727200 Fax (01502) 727201
Shop 10-6 Mon-Sat Tours by arrangement (trade only)
⊗ East Anglia's seaside brewery, established
in 1890, whose local deliveries are still made
by horse drays. Real ale is available in all its
80 pubs, and it also supplies some 850 other
outlets direct, with the beers available
nationwide via agents. Gradual expansion is
planned for the tied estate. Seasonal beers:
Mild (OG 1035, ABV 3.2%, February), Old
(OG 1043, ABV 4.1%▮▯, December-
January), Oyster Stout (OG 1047, ABV
4.3%, March-April and October-
November), Tally Ho (OG 1075, ABV 7%,
December)▮.
Best Bitter *(OG 1036, ABV 3.7%)* ▯❧
An excellent drinking beer, with the characteristic Adnams aroma of hops, citrus fruits
and sulphur. The flavour is dry and hoppy,
with some fruit. The finish is long, dry and
hoppy.
Extra *(OG 1042, ABV 4.3%)* ▯❧ An
aroma of hops and citrus fruit leads
through to bitter orange and hops on the
palate, before a long, dry finish with some
hops and fruit.
Regatta *(OG 1042, ABV 4.3%)*
Pleasantly malty with a very long finish.
Broadside *(OG 1048, ABV 4.7%)* ❧
A mid-brown beer with a well-balanced

flavour of fruit, malt and hops on a bittersweet base. The aroma is fruity, with some
underlying malt and hops. Bitter fruit finish.

ALDCHLAPPIE

▯ Aldchlappie Hotel, Kirkmichael,
Perthshire and Kinross, PH10 7NS
Tel (01250) 881224 Fax (01250) 881373
Tours by arrangement
A microbrewery opened alongside this pub
in 1996, initially as an experiment to pro-
duce two beers (a combination of full mash
and malt extract) for its clientele of walkers
and skiers. The beer names follow a
Scottish/English history theme. Beers: 1707
(OG 1046, ABV 4.5%), 1314 (OG 1046,
ABV 4.5%).

ALL NATIONS

▯ All Nations, Coalport Road, Madeley,
Telford, Shropshire TF7 5DP
Tel (01952) 585747 Tours by arrangement
One of the very few brewpubs left before the
new wave, All Nations has, in fact, been
brewing for 200 years. Still known as Mrs
Lewis's, the inn has been in the same family
since 1934.
Pale Ale *(OG 1032, ABV 3%)*

ALLIED BREWERIES

See Nationals, Carlsberg-Tetley.

ALLOA

See Nationals, Carlsberg-Tetley.

ANCIENT DRUIDS

Ancient Druids, Napier Street, Cambridge
Ceased brewing.

ANN STREET

See Jersey.

ANSELLS

See Nationals, Carlsberg-Tetley.

ARCHERS

Archers Ales Ltd, Penzance Drive,
Churchward, Swindon, Wiltshire SN5 7JL
Tel (01793) 879929 Fax (01793) 879489
Shop 9-5 Mon-Sat, 9-12 Sat Tours by arrangement
⊗ Brewery set up in 1979 in the old Great
Western Railway works. Production of
Archers' beers was moved in 1996 into the
former weighbridge, now converted into a
traditional tower brewery. The company
supplies three tied houses and another 200
free trade outlets direct and via wholesalers.
Occasional/seasonal beers: Headbanger (OG
1065, ABV 6.3%), Marley's Ghost (OG
1068, ABV 7%, Christmas). Bottle-conditioned beer: Golden Bitter (OG 1046, ABV
4.8%).
Village Bitter *(OG 1035, ABV 3.6%)*
❧▮ A dry, well-balanced beer, with a full
body for its gravity. Malty and fruity in the
nose, then a fresh, hoppy flavour with balancing malt and a hoppy, fruity finish.
Best Bitter *(OG 1040, ABV 4%)* ❧
Slightly sweeter and rounder than Village,

with a malty, fruity aroma and a pronounced bitter finish.
Black Jack Porter *(OG 1046, ABV 4.6%)* ✦ A winter brew: a black beer with intense roast malt dominant on the tongue. The aroma is fruity and there is some sweetness on the palate, but the finish is pure roast grain.
Golden Bitter *(OG 1046, ABV 4.7%)* ✦ A full-bodied, hoppy, straw-coloured brew with an underlying fruity sweetness. Very little aroma, but a strong bitter finish.

ARKELLS
Arkell's Brewery Ltd, Kingsdown, Swindon, Wiltshire SN2 6RU
Tel (01793) 823026 Fax (01793) 828864
Tours by arrangement
⊗ Established in 1843 and now one of the few remaining breweries whose shares are all held by one family, with its managing director, James Arkell, a great-great-grandson of founder John Arkell. Gradually expanding its tied estate, mainly along the M4 corridor, and the brewery is committed to a continual programme of upgrading and refurbishment for its pubs. All 93 tied pubs serve real ale, which is also supplied direct to around 200 free trade accounts.
Occasional/seasonal beers: Yeomanry (OG 1045, ABV 4.5%), Peter's Porter (OG 1050, ABV 4.8%), Noel Ale (OG 1055, ABV 5.5%, Christmas) – these may not be available in all Arkell's pubs and may need seeking out.
2B *(OG 1032, ABV 3.2%)* ✦ A hoppy, pale beer with a hint of fruit and honey. A most refreshing lunchtime or session ale, with good body for its OG.
3B *(OG 1040, ABV 4%)* ✦ An unusal and distinctive bitter. The crystal malt gives a nutty taste which persists throughout and combines with bitterness in the aftertaste.
Kingsdown Ale *(OG 1052, ABV 5%)* ✦ 3B's big brother with which it is parti-gyled (derived from the same mash). A powerful roast malt/fruit flavour is followed by a lingering, dry aftertaste.

ARUNDEL
Arundel Brewery, Unit C7, Ford Airfield Estate, Ford, Arundel, W. Sussex BN18 0BE
Tel (01903) 733111 Fax (01903) 733381
Tours by arrangement
⊗ Set up in 1992, the town's first brewery in 60 years, Arundel produces beers from authentic Sussex recipes, without the use of additives. Its commitment to this tradition has led to steady growth and the brewery now supplies around 100 outlets, plus its single tied house, the Swan in Arundel. Old Knuckler was named after a legendary dragon, who terrorised townsfolk before being slain by a local hero. Arundel brews a single beer for Beards of Sussex (see Pub Groups). Occasional/seasonal beers: Footslogger (OG 1044, ABV 4.4%), Summer Daze (OG 1047, ABV 4.7%, June), Old Conspirator (OG 1050, ABV 5%, Guy Fawkes Night), Romeo's Rouser (ABV 5.3%, Valentine's Day), Old Scrooge (OG 1060, ABV 6%, Christmas).
Best Bitter *(OG 1040, ABV 4%)* ✦ A pale tawny beer with fruit and malt noticeable in the aroma. The flavour exhibits a good balance of malt, fruit and hops, with a dry, hoppy finish.
Gold *(OG 1042, ABV 4.2%)* A light golden ale with a malty, fruity flavour and a little hop in the finish.
ASB *(OG 1045, ABV 4.5%)* A golden brown beer with roast malt and hop flavour giving way to a fruity, hoppy, bittersweet finish.
Stronghold *(OG 1050, ABV 5%)* ✦ A good balance of malt, fruit and hops come through in this rich, malty beer.
Old Knuckler *(OG 1055, ABV 5.5%)* ✦ A dark, full-bodied beer. The flavour is a complex blend of sweet fruit and caramel maltiness, which balances a dry roast bitterness. This is mirrored in the aftertaste. Roast malt, fruit, caramel and some hops feature in the aroma. Brewed September-April.

For Beards:
Beards Best Bitter *(OG 1040, ABV 4%)* ✦ Hints of fruit and hops in the aroma lead into a sweet, malty beer, with a dry, hoppy aftertaste.

ASH VINE
Unit F, Vallis Trading Estate, Robins Lane, Trudoxhill, Somerset, BA11 3DT
Tel (01373) 300041 Fax (01373) 300042
Tours by arrangement
⊗ Ash Vine had been brewing at the White Hart pub in Frome for most of its 12 years, but moved early in 1998 to a new purpose-built brewery with twice its previous capacity. Over 50 free trade outlets are supplied with real ale, while bottled Hop and Glory is widely available in supermarkets. It also exports to Europe. Ash Vine also brews two beers for the small wholesaler Quality Cask Ales, tel: (01373) 473591. Bottle-conditioned beers: Penguin Porter (OG 1044, ABV 4.2%), Hop & Glory (OG 1052, ABV 5%).
Bitter *(OG 1037, ABV 3.5%)* ✦ A light gold bitter with a floral hop aroma. A powerful, bitter hoppiness dominates the taste and leads to a dry, and occasionally astringent, finish. An unusual and distinctive brew.
Challenger *(OG 1042, ABV 4.1%)* ✦ A mid-brown beer with a solid malt flavour balanced by a good hoppy bitterness and subtle citrus fruits. It can be sulphurous and slightly metallic.
Black Bess Porter *(OG 1044, ABV 4.2%)* ✦ A dark copper-brown, bitter porter with roast malt, hops and a sweet fruitiness. Roast malt and hop nose; dry, bitter finish. Bottled as Penguin Porter.
Hop & Glory *(OG 1052, ABV 5%)* ✦ A pale straw-coloured beer with a malt, fruit and hop aroma. The taste is bittersweet, with hops in abundance and some citrus fruits. Similar finish. A complex, rich and warming winter ale.

For Quality Cask Ales:
Munro's Mickey Finn *(OG 1047, ABV 4.5%)*
Six '5' Special *(OG 1068, ABV 6.5%)*

ASTON MANOR

Aston Manor Brewery Company Ltd, 173
Thimblemill Lane, Aston, Birmingham, W.
Midlands B7 5HS
Tel (0121) 328 4336 Fax (0121) 328 0139
Aston Manor ceased all brewing in early
1998 to concentrate on expanding produc-
tion of bottled ciders.

AVIEMORE

The Aviemore Brewery Co. Ltd, Unit 12
Dalfaber Industrial Estate, Aviemore PH22
1PY
Tel (01479) 812060 Fax (01479) 811465
Tours by arrangement
With the laudable intent of aiming for qual-
ity, not quantity, this new brewery opened in
July 1997 and currently serves six outlets. A
visitor centre is due to open early in 1999
with a shop.
Ruthven Brew *(ABV 4%)*
Wolfes Brew *(ABV 4.6%)*
Cairngorn Brew *(ABV 5%)* A
European-style lager.
Red Murdoch *(ABV 5.8%)*

B&T

B&T Brewery Ltd, The Brewery, Shefford,
Bedfordshire SG17 5DZ
Tel (01462) 815080 Fax (01462) 850841
Tours by arrangement
⊗ Banks & Taylor, founded in 1981, fell
into receivership in 1994 but was quickly
rescued under the name of B&T, with key
Banks & Taylor personnel retained to pro-
duce the same extensive range of beers,
including the monthly special brews. The
company now supplies around 60 outlets
direct, including two pubs of its own.
Occasional/seasonal beers: Midsummer Ale
(OG 1035, ABV 3.5%), Bedfordshire
Clanger (OG 1038, ABV 4%, March), Santa
Slayer (OG 1040, ABV, 4%), Madhatter
(OG 1042, ABV 4.2%, May), Maiden's
Rescue (OG 1042, ABV 4.2%, April),
Bodysnatcher (OG 1044, ABV 4.4%,
October), Guy Fawkes Bitter (OG 1045,
ABV 4.5%, November), Romeo's Ruin (OG
1045, ABV 4.5%, February), Emerald Ale
(OG 1050, ABV 5%, March), Juliet'ss
Revenge (OG 1050, ABV 5%, February),
Shefford Wheat Beer (OG 1050, ABV 5%,
July-August), Frostbite (OG 1055, ABV
5.5%, December-January), Bat Out of Hell
(OG 1060, ABV 6%, November), Skeleton
Special (OG 1060, ABV 6%). Bottle-condi-
tioned beer: Edwin Taylor's Extra Stout (OG
1045, ABV 4.5%). B&T also brews under
contract for Martin Elms Wines, tel. (01245)
478323 and Oliver Hare Wholesale, tel.
(01799) 508058.
Shefford Bitter *(OG 1038, ABV 3.8%)*
◆ A pleasant, well-hopped session beer with
a balance of malt and fruit aromas and
flavours.
Shefford Dark Mild *(OG 1038, ABV
3.8%)* ◆ A dark beer with a well-balanced
taste. Sweetish, roast malt aftertaste.
Dragonslayer *(OG 1045, ABV 4.5%)* ◆
A straw-coloured beer, dry, malty and
lightly hopped.
Edwin Taylor's Extra Stout *(OG
1045, ABV 4.5%)* 🗆✦⊛◎ A pleasant, bitter
beer with a strong roast malt flavour
Shefford Pale Ale (SPA) *(OG 1045,
ABV 4.5%)* ◆ A well-balanced beer, with

hop, fruit and malt flavours. Dry, bitter
aftertaste.
Shefford Old Strong (SOS) *(OG
1050, ABV 5%)* ◆ A rich mixture of fruit,
hops and malt is present in the taste and
aftertaste of this beer. Predominantly hopply
aroma.
Shefford Old Dark (SOD) *(OG 1050,
ABV 5%)* ◆ SOS with caramel added for
colour. Often sold under house names.
Black Bat *(OG 1060, ABV 6%)* ◆ A powerful, sweet, fruity and malty beer for winter.
Fruity, nutty aroma; strong roast malt aftertaste.
2XS *(OG 1060, ABV 6%)* ◆ A reddish beer
with a strong, fruity, hoppy aroma. The taste
is full-flavoured and the finish strong and
sweetish.
Old Bat *(OG 1070, ABV 7%)* ◆ A power-
ful-tasting, sweet winter beer, with bitterness
coming through in the aftertaste. Fruit is present in both aroma and taste.

For Martin Elms Wines:
Woodcocks IP *(OG 1036, ABV 3.6%)*

For Oliver Hare Wholesale:
Old Hand Cranker *(OG 1045, ABV
4.5%)*

BACKDYKES

Backdykes Brewing Company, The Dairy,
Mid Strathore Farm, Strathore Road,
Thornton, Fife KY1 4DF
Tel (01592) 775303 Tours by arrangement
◎ This brewery was set up in a former dairy
in 1995 and began production in January
1996. 'Malcolm's Severely Drinkable Ales'
(named after the King of Scotland responsi-
ble for the death of Macbeth) are supplied to
30-40 free trade outlets. There are plans to
bottle Help Ma Boab through a co-opera-
tive.
Malcolm's Ceilidh *(OG 1039, ABV
3.7%)* Sold south of the Border as Session.
Malcolm's Folly *(OG 1042, ABV 4%)*
Golden Vale *(OG 1045, ABV 4.4%)*
Malcolm's Premier *(OG 1046, ABV
4.3%)*
Help Ma Boab *(OG 1052, ABV 5%)*
Jockstrap *(OG 1071, ABV 6.5%)*

BADGER

Hall & Woodhouse Ltd, The Badger
Brewery, Blandford St Mary, Blandford
Forum, Dorset DT11 9LS
Tel (01258) 452141 Fax (01258) 459953
Shop 9-7 Mon-Sat, 10-2 Sun
Tours by arrangement
⊗ When Charles Hall founded the Ansty
Brewery in 1777, it prospered by supplying
beer to the troops fighting the French. In
1847, Charles's son took George
Woodhouse into partnership to create Hall
& Woodhouse, although the company
soon became known by its logo, featuring
a badger. The Badger name, however, has
only recently been adopted as its trading
name, with alterations made to the beer
range at the same time. Still largely family-
run, the brewery continues to broaden its
trading area and is always on the lookout
for new pubs in the South of England. All
205 of its houses take cask ale (although
some use cask breathers) and a further 300

outlets are supplied direct. The brewery
also owns the Gribble Inn brewpub in
Oving, W. Sussex (qv) and since the closure of Gibbs Mew brewery in September
1997 has been brewing two of that company's beers.
IPA *(OG 1036, ABV 3.6%)* A light,
smooth, thin-bodied bitter with a slightly
hoppy aftertaste or served with a creamy
head.
Dorset Best *(OG 1041, ABV 4.1%)* ❧ A
fine best bitter whose taste is strong in hop
and bitterness, with underlying malt and
fruit. Hoppy finish with a bitter edge.
Tanglefoot *(OG 1050, ABV 5.1%)*

For Gibbs Mew:
Deacon *(OG 1050, ABV 4.8%)*
The Bishops Tipple *(OG 1066, ABV
6.5%)*

BALLARD'S

Ballard's Brewery Ltd, Unit C, The Old
Sawmill, Nyewood, Petersfield, Hampshire
GU31 5HA
Tel (01730) 821301 Fax (01730) 821742
Shop 8.30-4.30 Mon-Fri
Tours by arrangement
⊗ Founded in 1980 at Cumbers Farm,
Trotton, Ballard's has been trading at
Nyewood (in W. Sussex, despite the postal
address) since 1988 and now supplies
around 60 free trade outlets. Occasional/sea-
sonal beers: Golden Bine (OG 1042, ABV
4.2%, spring), Nyewood Gold (OG 1050,
ABV 5%, summer), plus a Christmas ale
with a gravity to match the number of the
year. Bottle-conditioned beers: Wassail (OG
1060, ABV 6%), Blizzard (OG 1090, ABV
9.8%).
Midhurst Mild *(OG 1035, ABV 3.5%)*
A rarely seen, basic dark mild, brewed in
autumn and winter.
Trotton Bitter *(OG 1036, ABV 3.6%)* ❧
Complex for its gravity, this well-balanced
beer has an initial maltiness which fades to a
hoppy finish.
Best Bitter *(OG 1042, ABV 4.2%)* A
copper-coloured beer with a malty aroma. A
good balance of fruit and malt in the flavour
gives way to a dry, hoppy aftertaste.
Wild *(ABV 4.7%)* ❧ A dark brown beer,
produced for autumn and winter, by blend-
ing Mild with Wassail. Initial hints of fruit
give way to a malty flavour and a dry, hoppy
aftertaste.
Wassail *(OG 1060, ABV 6%)* ❧ A strong,
full-bodied, fruity beer with a predominance
of malt throughout, but also an underlying
hoppiness. Tawny/red in colour.

BANBURY

Banbury Micro Brewery, 14 Bettina
Crescent, Banbury, Oxon OX16 7FH
Tel (01295) 276087
Tours by arrangement
A tiny, part-time brewery, operating only at
weekends, in the owner's garage, Banbury
was set up in June 1997. It serves five local
outlets. Occasional beer: Old Vic (OG 1057,
ABV 6%, Christmas).
Two Ferrets *(OG 1034, ABV 3.4%)*
A summer beer.
Cross Bitter *(OG 1039, ABV 3.7%)*
Edgecutter Bitter *(OG 1042, ABV
3.9%)*

BANK TOP

Bank Top Brewery, Unit 1, Back Lane, off
Vernon Street, Bolton, Greater Manchester
BL1 2LD *Tel (01204) 528865*
Tours by arrangement
☺ John Feeney learned about the brewing
business at Sunderland University and then
at Thomas McGuinness Brewery. In 1995 he
set up this brewery, originally as a partner-
ship, but now runs it on his own. His award-
winning beers are supplied to 50 outlets
locally, and John has plans to acquire a free
house and move the brewery there. Seasonal
beer: Santa's Claws (OG 1050, ABV 5%,
Christmas).
Brydge Bitter *(OG 1038, ABV 3.8%)*
Fred's Cap *(OG 1040, ABV 4%)*
Gold Digger *(OG 1040, ABV 4%)*
Samuel Crompton's Ale *(OG 1042,
ABV 4.2%)*
Cliffhanger *(OG 1045, ABV 4.5%)*
Porter *(OG 1045, ABV 4.5%)*
Satanic Mills *(OG 1050, ABV 5%)*
Smokestack Lightnin' *(OG 1050,
ABV 5%)*

BANKS & TAYLOR
See B&T.

BANKS'S

The Wolverhampton & Dudley Breweries
PLC, PO Box 26, Park Brewery, Bath Road,
Wolverhampton, W. Midlands WV1 4NI
Tel (01902) 711811 Fax (01902) 329464
Tours by arrangement
☺ Wolverhampton & Dudley Breweries was
formed in 1890 by the amalgamation of
three local companies. Hanson's was
acquired in 1943, but its Dudley brewery
was closed in 1991 and its beers are now
brewed at Wolverhampton. The 100
Hanson's pubs keep their own livery. In
1992, W&D bought Camerons Brewery and
51 pubs from Brent Walker. In 1997 he total
estate for the whole group stood at 1,022
houses (377 of which are tenanted), virtually
all serving traditional ales, mostly through
electric, metered dispense. Its pubs offer a
'full pint guarantee' by serving the beer in
oversize glasses. The company also has 20
'Taphouses', cask alehouses which also sell
Taphouse Bitter, a general name given to
various Banks's brews prepared from different recipes. There is also extensive free trade
throughout the country, particularly in pubs
and clubs. In late 1997 it sold 147 tenancies
to Avebury Taverns for £16.4 million
(Wolverhampton and Dudley will continue
to supply them) and announced that 43
smaller managed pubs would be turned into
tenancies. A fifth of the company's managed
houses are branded Milestone Taverns,
Milestone Restaurants and Varsity
Taverns,and W&D has invested in new
theme pubs in 1997. Banks's also do a
monthly 'Festival Ale'.
Hanson's Bitter *(OG 1035, ABV 3.3%)*
Hanson's Mild *(OG 1035, ABV 3.3%)*
❧ A mid- to dark brown mild with a malty
roast flavour and aftertaste.
Mild *(OG 1036, ABV 3.5%)* ❧ A top-selling, amber-coloured, well-balanced, refreshing light mild.

Bitter *(OG 1039, ABV 3.8%)* ♠ A pale brown bitter with a pleasant balance of hops and malt. Hops continue from the taste through to a bittersweet aftertaste.

BARNFIELD

Barnfield Brewery, Unit 3F, Spa Field Industrial Estate, Slaithwaite, Huddersfield, W. Yorkshire HD7 5BB
Tel (01484) 845757
Tours by arrangement

☺ Brewery originally set up in February 1997 in premises formerly occupied by Wild's Brewery (now ceased trading), using equipment purchased from the Wortley Arms brewery in Sheffield, which closed in November 1996. The first beers were brewed using Wortley Arms recipes, and a further three beers were introduced after moving to Slaithwaite Industrial Estate. The brewery moved again in spring 1998 to the Packhorse Hotel in Slaithwaite to brew beers for that outlet and 40-50 others.
Bitter *(OG 1038, ABV 3.8%)* ♠ Smooth, creamy, copper-coloured bitter with well-balanced malt and hops; some fruit initially and a gentle, bitter finish.
Earls Ale *(OG 1043, ABV 4.3%)* A medium-bodied bitter with a malty and fruity character which leaves a clean and dry aftertaste.
Tribute Ale *(OG 1043, ABV 4.3%)*
Captain Kos *(OG 1046, ABV 4.6%)*
Countess *(OG 1053, ABV 5.3%)* A dark, full-bodied, strong bitter with a pleasant, fruity and hoppy taste; slightly bitter with a sweet finish.
Bloody Hell Fire *(OG 1060, ABV 6%)* A dark, full-bodied, strong ale with chocolate overtones and a slightly sweet finish.

BARNGATES

See Drunken Duck.

BARNSLEY

Barnsley Brewing Co. Ltd, Wath Road, Elsecar, Barnsley, S. Yorkshire S74 8HJ
Tel (01226) 741010 Fax (01226) 741009
☺ Established in 1994 as the South Yorkshire Brewing Company, Barnsley changed its name in 1996 and brews with an old yeast culture from the town's long-defunct Oakwell Brewery. Demand continues to grow, with over 200 outlets taking the beer.
Bitter *(OG 1038, ABV 3.8%)* ♠ ⬠ A pale brown creamy and smooth bitter with a hoppy and fruity aroma and an even balance of hops and malt in the taste and in the lasting bitter dry finish.
Oakwell *(OG 1039, ABV 4%)*
IPA *(OG 1041, ABV 4.2%)* A beer dominated by malt and hops, leading on to a hoppy finish. Yellowish in colour; flowery aroma.
Black Heart Stout *(OG 1046, ABV 4.6%)* ♠ A black stout with a hoppy aroma, and lots of roasted malt flavour throughout. Chocolatey, bitter finish. Hard to find.
Glory *(OG 1046, ABV 4.8%)*

BARUM

Barum Brewery, c/o The Reform Inn, Pilton,
Barnstaple, Devon EX31 1PD
Tel (01271) 329994 Fax (01271) 321590
Tours by arrangement
In 1996 the Combe Brewery in Ilfracombe was purchased and relocated to the Reform Inn in Barnstaple, followed a year later by the brewer himself. Now steadily growing, Barum serves the Reform and 50 outlets directly with its cask ales.
Special Edition *(OG 1036, ABV 3.5%)*
Gold *(OG 1040, ABV 4%)*
Original *(OG 1044, ABV 4.4%)*
Challenger *(OG 1056, ABV 5.6%)*
Barnstablasta *(OG 1066, ABV 6.6%)* A winter warmer.

BASS

See Nationals.

BATEMAN

George Bateman & Son Ltd, Salem Bridge Brewery, Wainfleet, Lincolnshire PE24 4JE
Tel (01754) 880317 Fax (01754) 880939
Tours by arrangement
☒ A family-owned and run brewery, established in 1874 by the grandfather of present chairman George Bateman. In the mid-1980s a family dispute threatened the brewery's future, but, after a three-year battle, George secured the brewery's independence and is now steadily expanding its sales area to cover nearly the whole of the UK. Around 200 outlets are supplied direct and Bateman owns 59 houses which all serve real ale. Occasional/seasonal beers: two seasonal ranges are produced: Jolly's Jaunts and Mystic Brews – a beer for each sign of the zodiac. Bateman also brews under contract for the non-brewing Sherwood Forest Brewery, tel: (0115) 911 8822.
Dark Mild *(OG 1033, ABV 3%)* ▣⬠ Ruby/black mild, with a creamy brown head, a fruit and nut nose leading to a complex mix of malt hop and fruit taste. The sweetness dies, but bitterness lingers in the aftertaste.
XB *(OG 1037, ABV 3.7%)* ♠ A well-balanced bitter, although dominated by the characteristic appley hop on taste and aroma. Malt is always in the background and lingers in the finish of this mid-brown bitter.
Hill Billy Bitter *(OG 1042, ABV 4.2%)*
Valiant *(OG 1043, ABV 4.2%)* ♠ Fruit and almonds, behind malt and hops on the aroma of this golden-brown beer, with a soft combination in the mouth where hops and bitterness stay longest.
Salem Porter *(OG 1049, ABV 4.7%)* ▣⬠♠ Liquorice on the nose, with a bitter, hoppy bite leading to a complex bitter aftertaste. The underlying liquorice fruit is present throughout.
XXXB *(OG 1050, ABV 4.8%)* ⬠♠ A complex, popular and durable dark tan combination of malt, hops and an almost banana back fruitiness. The malt features in the lingering, bitter finish, adding to its all-round drinkability. A classic.
Victory Ale *(OG 1060, ABV 5.7%)* ♠ Strong fruitiness on the aroma of this compex, powerful, chestnut beer leads to malt and hops in the finish. Difficult to find in the tied trade.

For Sherwood Forest:

Lionheart Ale *(ABV 4.2%)*

BATH

Bath Ales, c/o Barvick Engineering, Bow
Bridge Works, Henstridge, Somerset BA8
0HE
Tel (0117) 907 1797 Fax (0117) 909 5140
⊗ Founded in 1995 by two former Smiles
Brewery employees, using the same brewing plant as Henstridge Brewery (qv). Bath
supplies its own pub, plus around 150
other outlets, but not on a regular
basis.
SPA *(OG 1038, ABV 3.7%)* ◆ Yellow,
refreshing, dry bitter beer. Aroma is of pale
and lager malts and citrus hop. Medium
bodied, full flavoured with lots of malt and
good apple citrus floral hops. Long, pale,
malty bitter finish with some fruit.
Gem *(OG 1041/2, ABV 4.1%)* ◆🏠With
malty, fruity and hoppy aroma, this
medium-bodied bitter has a similar taste
and finish which is somewhat more dry
and bitter at the end. Amber coloured.
Barnstormer *(OG 1046, ABV 4.5%)* ◆
A mid-bodied, smooth, well-crafted ale.
Aroma is a combination of malt, a little
roast chocolate, hops and fruit. Mid-
brown in colour it has a well balanced mix
of malt/roast chocolate and bittersweet
fruit. Complex malt and bitter finish.

BATHAM

Bathams (Delph) Ltd, Delph Brewery, Delph
Road, Brierley Hill, W. Midlands DY5 2TN
Tel (01384) 77229 Fax (01384) 482292
☺ Small brewery established in 1877 and
now in its fifth generation of family ownership. Batham's sympathetic programme of
upgrading and refurbishment in its tied
estate has been rewarded by winning
CAMRA's 1996 Joe Goodwin Award for
pub refurbishment for the Vine (or Bull &
Bladder), one of the Black Country's most
famous pubs and the site of the brewery. The
company has nine tied houses and supplies
around 20 other outlets. Batham's also
bought the Britannia brewpub ('Sallie's') at
Upper Gornall, West Midlands, where the
continuation of brewing is under consideration. Occasional/seasonal beers: Britannia
Bitter (OG 1044, ABV 4.3%), AJ's Strong
Mild Ale (OG 1049, ABV 5%), XXX (OG
1064, ABV 6.3%, winter).
Mild Ale *(OG 1037, ABV 3.5%)* ◆ A
fruity, dark brown mild with a malty sweetness and a roast malt finish.
Best Bitter *(OG 1044, ABV 4.3%)*
🏠◆ A pale yellow, fruity, sweetish bitter,
with a dry, hoppy finish. A good, light,
refreshing beer when on form.

BAYNARDS

Baynards Brewhouse, The Thurlow Arms,
Baynards, Rudgwick, W. Sussex RH12 3AD
Tel (01403) 822459 Fax (01403) 822125
⊗ Established in February 1996 using
equipment transferred from the Cyder
House Inn at Shackleford. Beers: Station
House Brew (ABV 4.2%), Old Shunter
(ABV 4.8%), Tunnel Vision (ABV 6%
October-March).

BEARDS

See Arundel and Pub Groups.

BEARTOWN

Beartown Brewery, Unit 9, Varey Road,
Eaton Bank Industrial Estate, Congleton,
Cheshire CW12 1UW *Tel (01260) 299964*
Tours by arrangement
Congleton's links with brewing can be
traced back to 1272, when the town received
charter status. Two of its most senior offi-
cers at the time were Ale Taster and Bear
Warden, hence the name of this brewery, set
up in 1994 on land which once housed a silk
mill. Run on a part-time basis until late 1997
when one of the original partners left, it then
became a limited company and is now concentrating on building up local trade rather
than supplying wholesale customers as
before.
Ambeardextrous *(OG 1035, ABV
3.8%)* ◆ A mid-brown, well-balanced bitter
with coffee and chocolate notes.
Bear Ass *(OG 1038, ABV 4%)*
Bearskinful *(OG 1040, ABV 4.2%)* ◆
A tawny, malty beer, with a clean hop
finish.
Polar Eclipse *(OG 1045, ABV 4.8%)* ◆
A smooth and roasty, dark beer with chocolate notes and a dryish finish. Brewed winter
and spring.
Bruin's Ruin *(OG 1048, ABV 5%)* ◆
A smooth, darkish and well-balanced beer,
with a hint of roast, also just for winter and
spring.

BECKETT'S

Beckett's Brewery Ltd, 8 Enterprise Court,
Rankine Road, Basingstoke, Hampshire
RG24 8GE
Tel (01256) 472986 Fax (01256) 703205
Tours by arrangement
⊗ After 16 years working for Fuller's,
Richard Swinhoe took the plunge and set up
his own brewery in March 1997, the first in
Basingstoke for 50 years. Currently supply-
ing 30 outlets direct, future plans include the
purchase of a brewery tap and a range of
bottle-conditioned beers. The regular beer
range is complemented by 'Porterquack
Ales', a series of unusual small volume
beers.
Old Town Bitter *(OG 1037, ABV
3.75%)*
Original Bitter *(OG 1040, ABV 4%)* ◆
A mid-brown colour and a malty and hoppy
aroma. The taste is mainly malty and bitter,
as is the aftertaste.
Golden Grale *(OG 1045, ABV 4.5%)*
Fortress Ale *(OG 1050, ABV 5%)*

BEECHAM'S

☖ Beecham's Bar & Brewery, Westfield
Street, St Helens, Merseyside WA10 1PZ
Tel (01744) 623420
Tours by arrangement
Full mash brewery opened in 1997 as a
training facility for students at St Helens
College. The students not only learn to brew
but also how to be a successful licensee. The
public are welcome to use the bar which is
housed beneath the town's famous
Beecham's clock tower, in buildings donated
by the Beecham's Powders company. Bottled
beers are planned. Beers: Anniversary Ale
(OG 1045, ABV 4.5%), Celebration Bitter

Belhaven 80/- receives the Beer of the Year Award from Glasgow & West of Scotland CAMRA. The presentation was made by Ellen McSwiggen to Carl Heron of Belhaven. Belhaven has a history which goes back 800 years and is Scotland's oldest brewery. A management buyout rescued it in 1993 and it continues to brew its award-winning ales.

(OG 1045, ABV 4.5%), Stout (OG 1050, ABV 5.2%).

BEER ENGINE

◻ The Beer Engine, Sweetham, Newton St Cyres, Exeter, Devon EX5 5AX
Tel (01392) 851282 Fax (01392) 851876
⊠ Brewpub set up in 1983, next to the Barnstaple branch railway line. Two other outlets are supplied regularly and the beers are also distributed via agencies. Seasonal beers: Return Ticket (OG 1033, ABV 3.4%, a summer mild), Golden Arrow (ABV 4.6%, summer), Porter (ABV 4.7%), Whistlemas (ABV 6.7%, Christmas).
Rail Ale *(OG 1036, ABV 3.8%)* ◆ A straw-coloured beer with a fruity aroma and a sweet, fruity finish.
Piston Bitter *(OG 1043, ABV 4.3%)* ◆ A mid-brown, sweet-tasting beer with a pleasant, bittersweet aftertaste.
Sleeper Heavy *(OG 1054, ABV 5.4%)* ◆ A red-coloured beer with a fruity, sweet taste and a bitter finish.

BELCHERS

See Hedgehog & Hogshead.

BELHAVEN

Belhaven Brewery Group PLC, Brewery Lane, Dunbar, East Lothian EH42 1PE
Tel (01368) 86448 Fax (01368) 86448

Shop open during tours Tours by arrangement
⊛ With a tradition of brewing going back almost 800 years, Scotland's oldest brewery has had a chequered recent history. It was bought in 1989 by the London-based Control Securities PLC, but in 1993 its employees successfully engineered a management buyout of the brewery. It continues to produce award-winning beers, supplying all of its 69 houses, and an extensive free trade, with cask beer. 80/- was second in the Champion Beer of Scotland award in 1997. Four seasonal beers are produced each year to complement the permanent range.
60/- Ale *(OG 1030, ABV 2.7%)* ⬚◆ A fine, but sadly rare, example of a Scottish light: a reddish-brown beer dominated by malt throughout. Roast is evident, with fruit in the aftertaste. Characteristic Belhaven sulphury nose.
70/- Ale *(OG 1035, ABV 3.2%)* ◆ An underrated malty, bittersweet, pale brown beer in which hops and fruit are increasingly evident in the aftertaste. The Belhaven sulphury nose is noticeable.
Sandy Hunter's Traditional Ale *(OG 1038, ABV 3.6%)* ◆ A distinctive, medium-bodied beer named after a past chairman and head brewer. An aroma of malt, hops and characteristic sulphur greets the nose. A hint of roast combines with the malt
and hops to give a bittersweet taste and finish.

80/- Ale *(OG 1040, ABV 4%)* ♠ An incredibly robust, malty beer with the characteristic sulphury aroma. This classic ale has a burst of complex flavours and a rich, bittersweet finish.
IPA *(OG 1041, ABV 4%)*
St Andrew's Ale *(OG 1046, ABV 4.9%)* ♠ A bittersweet beer with plenty of body. There are malt and fruit in the taste, with a developing hop character leading to an increasingly bitter aftertaste. beware of the nitrokeg beer with the same name.

BELVOIR
Belvoir Brewery Ltd, Woodhill, Nottingham Lane, Old Dalby, Leicestershire LE14 3LX
Tel (01664) 823455 Fax (01664) 823455
Tours by arrangement
⊠ Brewery founded at the edge of the Vale of Belvoir by a former Theakston and Shipstone's brewer in 1995, with equipment largely obtained from the defunct Shipstone's Brewery. Occasional/seasonal beers: Peacock's Glory (OG 1047, ABV 4.7%), Old Dalby (OG 1050, ABV 5.1%), Owd Merry (OG 1059, ABV 6%, Christmas).
Whipping Golden Bitter *(OG 1036, ABV 3.6%)* Brewed for spring and summer.
Star Bitter *(OG 1039, ABV 3.9%)* A beer designed to replicate the bitter flavour of the old Shipstone's Bitter.
High Flyer *(OG 1041, ABV 4.1%)*
Beaver Bitter *(OG 1043, ABV 4.3%)* ♠ A light brown bitter, which starts malty in both aroma and taste, but soon develops a hoppy bitterness. Appreciably fruity.

BENSKINS
See Nationals, Carlsberg-Tetley.

BEOWULF
The Beowulf Brewing Company, Waterloo Buildings, 14 Waterloo Road, Yardley, Birmingham, W. Midlands B25 8JR
Tel (0121) 706 4116 Fax (0121) 706 0735
Tours by arrangement
Five-barrel brewery launched in old shop premises in February 1997 on a single bitter. It now produces three beers on a regular basis (with more in the pipeline) to supply over 100 outlets throughout the Midlands. Occasional/seasonal beers: Dragon Smoke Stout (OG 1046, ABV 4.7%), Grendel's Winter Ale (OG 1055, ABV 5.8%, winter).
Noble Bitter *(OG 1038, ABV 4%)*
Heroes Bitter *(OG 1046, ABV 4.7%)*
Mercian Shine *(OG 1048, ABV 5%)*

BERKELEY
Berkeley Brewing Co., The Brewery, Bucketts Hill, Berkeley, Gloucestershire GL13 9NZ *Tel (01453) 511799*
Tours by arrangement
This small operation was set up in an old farm cider cellar in 1994, but did not start brewing full-time until October 1996 when the beer range was expanded to include seasonal ales. Twenty-five free trade outlets are supplied. Seasonal beers: Late Starter (OG 1047, ABV 4.8%, October-November), Christmas Ale (OG 1048, ABV 4.9%, December), Old (OG 1052, ABV 5.3%,

January-February), Lord's Prayer (OG 1049, ABV 5, July-September).
Old Friend *(OG 1037, ABV 3.8%)* ♠ A hoppy aroma introduces this golden, fruity, hoppy beer which has a gentle hoppy, bitter finish.
Dicky Pearce *(OG 1042, ABV 4.3%)* ♠ A copper-coloured best bitter, with a hoppy aroma. A good balance of hop and malt in the mouth leads to a rich, bittersweet aftertaste.
Early Riser *(OG 1047, ABV 4.8%)* Available March-June.

BERROW
Berrow Brewery, Coast Road, Berrow, Burnham-on-Sea, Somerset TA8 2QU
Tel (01278) 751345 Tours by arrangement
⊠ Brewery founded in 1982 to supply pubs and clubs locally (about a dozen direct free trade outlets).
Best Bitter or 4Bs *(OG 1038, ABV 3.9%)* ♠ A pleasant, pale brown session beer, with a fruity aroma, a malty, fruity flavour and bitterness in the palate and finish.
Porter *(OG 1044, ABV 4.5%)*
Topsy Turvy (TT) *(OG 1055, ABV 6%)* ♠ A straw-coloured beer with an aroma of malt and hops, which are also evident in the taste, together with sweetness. The aftertaste is malty. Very easy to drink. Beware!

BIG LAMP
Big Lamp Brewers, Big lamp Brewery, Grange Road, Newburn, Newcastle-upon-Tyne NE15 8NL *Tel (0191) 2671687*
Tours by arrangement
☺ Set up in 1982 and changed hands at the end of 1990. Currently undergoing phased development, the brewery has acquired a second tied house, which is effectively the brewery tap at the company's new premises, a converted water pumping station where brewing commenced in February 1997. Fifty outlets currently supplied.
Bitter *(OG 1038, ABV 3.9%)* ♠⏏ A good, clean standard bitter with malt,hops and a hint of fruit. A good, hoppy aftertaste.
Prince Bishop Ale *(OG 1048, ABV 4.8%)* ♠ A rich, hoppy, golden beer with lots of fruit. A light, astringent aftertaste.
Summerhill or Mulligan's Stout *(OG 1048, ABV 4.8%)* ♠ A tasty, rich, ruby-red stout with a lasting rich roast character and a malty mouthfeel.
Premium *(OG 1052, ABV 5.2%)* ♠ A well-balanced, flavoursome bitter with a big nose and strong hop impact. The sweetness lasts into a mellow, dry finish.
Winter Warmer *(OG 1055, ABV 5.5%)*
Blackout *(OG 1100, ABV 11%)* ♠ A strong bitter, fortified with roast malt character and rich maltiness. Try it for its mouthfeel and lasting bitterness.

BIGFOOT
New Farm, Blyton Carr, Gainsborough, Lincolnshire *Tel 01427 628563*
Began brewing in February 1998.
Genesis *(ABV 3.8%)*
Big Foot Extra *(ABV 4.9%)*

BIRD IN HAND

⛫ Wheal Ale Brewery Ltd, Paradise Park, Hayle, Cornwall TR27 4HY
Tel (01736) 753974
Unusual brewery in a bird park, founded in 1980 as Paradise Brewery and now brewing intermittently. Beers: Paradise Bitter (OG 1040, ABV 3.8%), Miller's Ale (OG 1045, ABV 4.3%), Artists Ale (OG 1055, ABV 5.1%), Old Speckled Parrot (ABV 6.3%).

BISHOPS
Bishop's Brewery, 2 Park Street, Borough Market, London SE1 9AB
Brewing suspended.

BITTER END
⛫ Bitter End Brewing Company, 15 Kirkgate, Cockermouth, Cumbria
☺ Brewpub founded in 1995.
Cockersnoot *(OG1038, ABV 3.8%)* .
Skinners Old Strong *(OG1054, ABV 5.4%)*

BLACK BULL
Black Bull Brewery, Ashes Farm, Ashes Lane, Fenny Bentley, Ashbourne, Derbyshire DE6 1LD
Tel (01335) 350581 Fax (01335) 350581
Tours by arrangement
☺ Brewery opened as a part-time venture by a keen home brewer in 1994. He moved the brewery to a larger, converted building on his farm in summer 1996 to provide greater capacity to serve a steadily growing trade.
Dovedale Bitter *(OG 1036, ABV 3.6%)*
A light straw-coloured summer beer, partly hopped with American lager hops.
Best Bitter *(OG 1040, ABV 4%)*
A ruby-coloured, well-hopped bitter.
Anklecracker *(OG 1041, ABV 4.2%)*
A summer beer.
Raging Bull *(OG 1049, ABV 4.9%)*
A light copper-coloured beer, similar to the best bitter but stronger.
Jacobs Ladder (Dovedale Special) *(OG 1050, ABV 5%)* A stronger version of Dovedale.
Owd Shrovetide *(OG 1060, ABV 5.9%)*
A winter warmer, available October-February.

BLACK DOG
Black Dog Breweries, St Hilda's Business Centre, The Ropery, Whitby, N. Yorkshire YO22 4EU
Tel (01947) 821467 Fax (01947) 603301
Tours by arrangement
☺ Taking its name from Bram Stoker's Dracula (the vampire transformed himself into a black dog to land in Whitby), this new brewery opened in December 1997. It took over the premises of the former Whitby's Own Brewery which had closed a year earlier, but there is no other connection between the two companies. The beers, which are still being test marketed and may undergo name changes, are supplied to 30-40 outlets.
First Out *(OG 1040, ABV 4%)* A light, fruity bitter.
Whitby Abbey Ale *(OG 1036, ABV 3.8%)*
HM Bark *(OG 1042, ABV 4.2%)*
Monks *(OG 1043, ABV 4.4%)*
Rhatas *(OG 1047, ABV 4.6%)* A dark, malty bitter.

BLACK HORSE
Black Horse Brewery, Victoria Buildings, Burnley Road, Luddendenfoot, Halifax, W. Yorkshire HX2 6AA *Tel (01422) 885930*
Shop Tours by arrangement
☺ Brewery founded in 1995 at Walkleys Clogs centre in Hebden Bridge, sharing facilities with Eastwood's Brewery until its relocation to Luddendenfoot, when the two breweries parted company. Black Horse Brewery is now located in a former textile mill on the Rochdale Canal, and currently supplies around 20 outlets locally.
Best *(ABV 3.8%)*
Bitter *(1040, ABV 4%)* A well-balanced, golden beer with a light, hoppy taste and aroma.
Chestnut *(ABV 4.2%)*
Shire *(ABV 5%)* A single malt beer which is pale in colour, with a smooth, clean taste and light, hoppy aroma.
Black Stallion *(1053, ABV 5.3%)* A porter with a rich, roasted barley flavour and a distinctive taste.

BLACK HORSE & RAINBOW
See Liverpool.

BLACK SHEEP
The Black Sheep Brewery Plc, Wellgarth, Masham, Ripon, N. Yorkshire HG4 4EN
Tel (01765) 689227 Fax (01765) 689746
Shop 9-5 daily (Wed-Sun January-March) Tours
☺ Set up in 1992 by Paul Theakston, a member of Masham's famous brewing family, in the former Wellgarth Maltings, Black Sheep has enjoyed continued growth and now supplies a free trade of around 500 outlets in the Yorkshire Dales and in an 80-mile radius of Masham, but it owns no pubs. A limited number of wholesalers is also supplied. Most of the output is fermented in Yorkshire slate squares, although some Yorkshire stainless rounds have been added to cope with demand, which can exceed supply at peak times. There is a visitor centre, with a bar and bistro open 10am-11pm Tues-Sat; 10am-6pm Sun & Mon.
Best Bitter *(OG 1039, ABV 3.8%)* ⬧
A hoppy and fruit balanced beer with strong bitter overtones, leading to a long, dry, bitter finish.
Special Bitter *(OG 1046, ABV 4.4%)* ⬧
A well-rounded and warming bitter beer with a good helping of hops and fruit in the taste and aroma, leading to a moderately dry, bitter aftertaste.
Riggwelter *(OG 1056, ABV 5.9%)* ⬧
A fruity bitter, with complex underlying tastes and hints of liquorice and pear drops leading to a long, dry, bitter finish.

BLACKAWTON
Blackawton Brewery, Washbourne, Totnes, Devon TQ9 7UF
Tel (01803) 732339 Fax (01803) 732151
⊗ Situated just outside the village of Washbourne, this small family brewery was

founded in 1977 and is now the oldest in Devon. It originated in the village of Blackawton, but moved to its present site in 1981 and, although it changed ownership in 1988, it retains a loyal local following for its additive-free beers. These are served in around 50 free trade outlets, but Blackawton has no pubs of its own. Occasional beer: Dart Mild (OG 1036, ABV 3.6%). Bottle-conditioned beer: Devon Gold Export (OG 1045, ABV 5%, occasional).

Bitter *(OG 1037, ABV 3.8%)* ❧ Tawny in colour, with a bitter/fruity taste and a bitter aftertaste.

Devon Gold *(OG 1038, ABV 4.1%)* A straw-coloured summer brew, available April-October.

Shepherds Delight *(OG 1042, ABV 4.6%)* ❧ A wheat beer for springtime (available February-April): a pale brown beer with a complex bitter/fruity taste and finish.

44 Special *(OG 1044, ABV 4.5%)* ❧ A tawny, fruity-flavoured bitter with a slightly sweet taste and finish.

Nell Gwyn *(OG 1044, ABV 4.7%)* A dark wheat beer with citrus overtones, available October.

Winter Fuel *(OG 1048, ABV 5%)* A dark, spiced beer, available mid-November-end January

Headstrong *(OG 1049, ABV 5.2%)* ❧ A mid-brown, strong beer, with a pleasant, fruity, sweet taste and finish.

BLACKBEARD
See Fox & Hounds (Shropshire).

BLACKBURN
Blackburn Brewing Company, Cellar Bar, 41 King Street, Blackburn, Lancashire BB2 2DH *Tel (01254) 698111*
Tours by arrangement
☺ Opened in the autumn of 1996, this pub/brewery was built on two levels. The brewery on the ground floor supplies the Cellar Bar downstairs. It has since acquired a second pub and also supplies five or so other local outlets. The beers are more widely available via wholesalers.

BBC3 *(ABV 3.8%)* A dark beer, with a well-balanced hop and malt flavour which gives way to a chocolate aftertaste.

BBC2 *(ABV 4.1%)* A beer that makes the best use of crystal malt, with a good hop flavour.

BBC1 *(ABV 4.4%)* ❧ A pale amber brew beginning malty on the nose and tongue then developing a delicate but persistent hoppiness before a dry finish. Deceptively drinkable for its strength.

BLANCHFIELD
⌂ Blanchfields Brewery, The Bull, Bridge Street, Fakenham, Norfolk NR21 9AG *Tel (01328) 862560* Tours by arrangement
☒ Began brewing in November 1997 using a two and a half barrel plant. A wheat beer is planned.

Black Bull *(ABV 3.6%)*
Bull Best Bitter *(ABV 3.9%)*
Raging Bull *(ABV 4.9%)*

BLEWITTS

⌂ Blewitts Brewery, The Ship & Plough, The Promenade, Kingsbridge, Devon TQ7 1JD *Tel (01548) 852485*
☒ Established in 1991 and only brewing for the one pub. Best (OG 1038, ABV 3.8%), Wages (OG 1045, ABV 4.5%), Head Off (OG 1050, ABV 4%).

BLUE ANCHOR
⌂ Blue Anchor, 50 Coinagehall Street, Helston, Cornwall TR13 8EX
Tel (01326) 562821 Tours by arrangement
Historic thatched brewpub, possibly the oldest in the UK, originating as a monks' resting place in the 15th century. It produces powerful ales known locally as 'Spingo' beers. The brewery has just undergone complete refurbishment and the pub is also due for improvement, with careful attention to preserving its special character. A beer garden is to be added for 1999. Beers: Middle (OG 1050, ABV 5%), Best (OG 1053, ABV 5.3%), Special (OG 1066, ABV 6.6%), Easter and Christmas Special (OG 1076, ABV 7.6%).

BLUE COW
⌂ The Blue Cow Inn and Brewery, South Witham, nr Grantham, Lincolnshire NG33 5QB
Tel (01572) 768432 Fax (01572) 768432
☒ Landlord Dick Thirlwell installed a four-barrel brew plant himself in a converted outbuilding at his pub and started brewing here in March 1997. His full mash beers (stored in both casks and cellar tanks) were immediately appreciated by his customers, not least because of the low prices. Two other local outlets are supplied. Beers: Thirlwell's Best Bitter (OG 1040, ABV 3.8%), Thirlwell's Templars Tipple (OG 1042, ABV 4%), Thirlwell's Premium (OG 1045, ABV 4.2%).

BLUE MOON
The Blue Moon Brewery, Pearces Farm, Seamere, Hingham, Norfolk NR9 4LP
Tel (01953) 851625 Tours by arrangement
After nearly 20 years in the pub trade, former publican Peter Turner opted for a quieter life as a brewer. He opened the Blue Moon Brewery at his farm in January 1997 where he brews 200 gallons a week for over 50 local outlets. The farmhouse offers overnight 'bed and brewery' accommodation.

Easy Life *(OG 1038, ABV 3.7%)*
Dark Side *(OG 1041, ABV 4%)*
Sea of Tranquility *(OG 1042, ABV 4.5%)* ❧ A mid-brown beer with a malty start and hints of fruit but fairly thin in body with a long bitter finish.
Hingham High *(OG 1054, ABV 5.2%)*
Milk of Amnesia *(OG 1055, ABV 5.2%)*
Liquor Mortis *(OG 1064, ABV 6.2%)*

BODDINGTONS
See Nationals, Whitbread.

BODICOTE
See Plough Inn.

BORDER

Border Brewery Company, The Old Kiln, Brewery Lane, Berwick-upon-Tweed, Northumberland TD15 2AH
Tel (01289) 303303 Fax (01289) 306115
Tours by arrangement
☺ Do not confuse with the Wrexham brewery taken over and closed by Marston's; this operation opened in 1992 in an old kiln on the site of Berwick's original (defunct) Border Brewery, which was established in the 17th century. A change in ownership took place in 1994, with the company becoming a partnership. The output is slowly increasing, and the brewery supplies 150 outlets, including a single tied house. Occasional beer: Rudolph's Ruin (OG 1057, ABV 6%, Christmas).
Farne Island Pale Ale *(OG 1038, ABV 4%)* ❧ A pale brown, full-bodied, hoppy, fruit, bitter, taking its name from the Northumberland isle. A fine nose, pleasing taste and robust aftertaste.
Flotsam Bitter *(OG 1038, ABV 4%)*
Old Kiln Ale *(OG 1038, ABV 4%)* ❧ Good mouthfeel with balanced hops, malt and fruit highlighting the taste. Long, slightly sweet finish.
Noggins Nog *(OG 1041, ABV 4.2%)* ❧ Dark brown, robust ale. A good mix of hops and roast malt leaves an impressive chocolate character in the aftertaste.
Jetsam Bitter *(OG 1046, ABV 4.8%)*
SOB *(OG 1047, ABV 5%)* ❧ A malty ale with a resinous bitterness, finishing with a woody dryness.

BORVE

⚑ Borve Brew House, Ruthven, Huntly,
Moray AB54 4SG *Tel (01466) 760343* Tours by arrangement
☺ Established in 1983, Borve moved from its original site, on the Isle of Lewis, five years later, taking up residence in a former school on the mainland. The school is now a pub, with the brewhouse adjacent. Beers: Borve Ale (OG 1040, ABV 3.8%), Tall Ships (OG 1050, ABV 5.1%). Bottle-conditioned beers: as cask, plus Extra Strong (OG 1085, ABV 10%).

BRAINS

SA Brain & Co. Ltd, The Old Brewery, 49 St Mary Street, Cardiff CF1 1SP
Tel (01222) 399022 Fax (01222) 383127
Tours by arrangement
Traditional brewery which has been in the Brain family since Samuel Brain and his uncle Joseph bought the Old Brewery in 1882. In March 1997 the company merged with the other major Welsh brewer, Crown Buckley, to become the largest independent brewery in Wales, resulting in the closure of Crown Buckley's Llanelli site in early 1998, with the loss of 30 jobs. The Pontyclun site has become a packaging centre. The beers have been transferred to the Brain's brewery in Cardiff ; so far only Buckley's IPA has been dropped, but further brand rationalisation seems almost inevitable. The company owns 181 pubs (79 are tenanted), as well as having a sizeable free trade market, plus interests in hotel and leisure projects in Wales and the West Country.
Crown Buckley Pale Ale (CPA) *(OG 1033, ABV 3.4%)*
Buckley's Dark Mild *(OG 1034, ABV 3.4%)* 🗂
Brains Bitter *(OG 1035, ABV 3.7%)* ❧ A

Campaigners against the closure of Buckley's Brewery carried a mock coffin through the streets of Llanelli to mark the passing of 200 years of brewing history in the town. Buckley's beers are now being brewed in Cardiff after the company was taken over by Brains to form Brains Crown Buckley. The old brewery equipment is being dismantled.

pale bitter beer, somewhat hoppy, with a hint of malt followed by a dry, bitter finish. Known locally as light.

Brains Dark (OG 1035, ABV 3.5%) ☐❧ A dark brown mild with caramel just dominating a balanced mix of malt and hops with a bittersweet edge and a rounded finish. A beer which benefits from good cellarmanship.

Brains Mild Ale or MA (OG 1035, ABV 3.6%) A brewery mix of Dark and Bitter.

Buckley's Best Bitter (OG 1036, ABV 3.7%)

Crown Buckley Special Best Bitter (SBB) (OG 1036, ABV 3.7%)

Brains SA Best Bitter (OG 1042, ABV 4.2%) ☐❧ A noticeably bitter beer, well-balanced with malt, hops and fruit, followed by a mellow, dry aftertaste.

Buckley's Reverend James Original Ale (OG 1045, ABV 4.5%)

BRAKSPEAR

WH Brakspear & Sons PLC, The Brewery, New Street, Henley-on-Thames, Oxfordshire RG9 2BU *Tel (01491) 570200 Fax (01491) 410254*

Shop 9-6 Mon-Sat Tours by arrangement

⊗ Brewing took place before 1700 on this Henley site, but the Brakspear family involvement began only in 1799, when Robert Brakspear formed a partnership with Richard Hayward. It was Robert's son, William Henry, who greatly expanded the brewery and its trade. After years of closing small, unprofitable pubs in the Henley area, Brakspear is now displaying a greater determination to enhance its estate of 103 mostly tied pubs, which boasts many excellent, unspoilt hostelries, all serving traditional ales. The larger outlets are being converted to managed houses with 10 per cent of the estate to be under management by the end of 1998. Some 70 free trade outlets are supplied direct and trading arrangements with Whitbread and Scottish Courage mean that Brakspear's ales are available throughout southern England. A small bottling line was opened in 1998 and many of Robert Brakspear's original recipes have recently been decoded from the 'heiroglyphics' he used to protect them. The 1998 Vintage Ale, sold in stone bottles, is one such brew. Bottle-conditioned beer: Vintage Ale.

XXX Mild (OG 1032, ABV 3%) ❧ A thin beer with a red/brown colour and a sweet, malty, fruity aroma. The well-balanced taste of malt, hops and caramel has a faint bitterness, complemented by a sweet, fruity flavour. The main characteristics extend through to the bittersweet finish.

Bitter (OG 1035.5, ABV 3.4%) ☐❧ A well-hopped, moderately fruity session bitter with a spicy bitterness and good mouthfeel. Ends fruity, dry and pungently hoppy.

Regatta Gold (OG 1039.5, ABV 3.8 %) Available late summer. A light, crisp, refreshing beer brewed with Czech Saaz and German Hallertan Hops.

Dark Rose (OG 1041, ABV 4.1%) ❧ A rich, dark red-brown winter porter, available January-March with a strong chocolate and roast malt character hiding hints of whisky malt. An excellent mouthfeel and dry finish add up to a beer that makes winter

bearable.

Hop Demon (OG 1042, ABV 4.2%) A new spring beer, golden in colour and dry-hopped, giving an intense aroma. Slightly sweet, it has a bite of hops in the aftertaste.

XXXX Old Ale (OG 1043.5, ABV 4.3%) ❧ Red/brown in colour with good body. The strong, fruity aroma is well complemented by malt, hops and caramel. Its pronounced taste of malt, with discernible sweet, roast malt and caramel flavours, gives way to fruitiness. The aftertaste is of bittersweet chocolate, even though chocolate malt is not used.

Special (OG 1043.5, ABV 4.3%) ☐❧ A honey-coloured bitter, well-balanced with fruit and a good bitter hop character. Pale malt and hops lead through to an astringent finish.

Bee Sting (OG 1048, ABV 4.7%) Available early summer, a golden beer made with what, honey and some oats, giving a full flavour with initial honeyed sweetness soon followed by a crisp, dry finish. Very drinkable.

OBJ (OG 1049, ABV 4.8%) Available November-January. Red/brown in colour, with an intensely fruity/hoppy aroma. An initial sweetish taste, strong in fruit and hops, is followed by bitterness with some malt and a lasting hops/bitter aftertaste. A slightly lower gravity than in previous years, also with less sugar content, therefore less sweet than usual.

Reapers Reward (OG 1051, ABV 5%) An autumn beer, ruby red in colour, made with Crystal Amber malt and Crystal Rye.

BRAMCOTE

See Castle Rock.

BRANDY CASK

Brandy Cask Brewing Company, r/o 25 Bridge Street, Pershore, Worcestershire WR10 1AJ *Tel (01386) 555338 Fax (01386) 555338*

⊗ Brewing started in a refurbished bottle store behind the Brandy Cask pub in 1995, supplying that pub (which is a separate business) and 15 other local outlets, but not on a regular basis.

Whistling Joe (OG 1036, ABV 3.6%) ❧ A powerful hop aroma and a skilful balance between malt and hop tastes make this a very enjoyable bitter.

Brandy Snapper (OG 1039, ABV 4%) ❧ Sweet and hoppy flavours make this a very drinkable, straw-coloured beer.

John Baker's Original (OG 1046, ABV 4.8%) ❧ A warming, tawny drink that has a full array of flavours to attack the palate. Malty, fruity and sweetish.

BRANSCOMBE VALE

The Branscombe Vale Brewery, Great Seaside Farm, Branscombe, Devon EX12 3DP *Tel (01297) 680511*

Tours by arrangement November-March

⊗ Brewery set up in 1992 in two cowsheds owned by the National Trust, by former dairy workers Paul Dimond and Graham Luxton, who converted the sheds and dug their own well. The NT have recently built an extension for the brewery to ensure future growth. It currently supplies 50 outlets regularly. An own-label house beer (OG 1045, ABV 4.6%) is produced for several local pubs in east Devon and a bottle-conditioned beer (Olde Stoker, OG 1053, ABV 5.4%▧) should go on sale at the same time as this *Guide*. Seasonal beers: Anniversary Ale (OG 1045, ABV 4.6%, January-February), Yo Ho Ho (OG 1065, ABV 6%, Christmas, Champion Beer award).

Branoc *(OG 1037, ABV 3.8%)* ▧ ◥ A pale brown, well-balanced bitter. Malt and fruit aroma with distinct hop bitterness to the flavour and finish.

Hells Bells *(OG 1048, ABV 4.8%)* A new winter beer, brewed October-March.

Summa That *(OG 1049, ABV 5%)* ◥ Hop and fruit aroma to this golden beer, which has a bitter hop taste and finish. April-Oct.

BRECKNOCK

Brecknock Brewery Ltd, Unit 323-324 Ynyscedwyn Industrial Estate, Trawssffordd Road, Ystradgynlais, Swansea SA9 1DT
Tel (01639) 849888 Fax (01639) 849888
Tours by arrangement

This new brewery was opened in August 1997 by a former Coca-Cola employee, with a five-barrel plant purchased from the closed Stocks brewery in Doncaster. It currently supplies 120 outlets directly with the cask beers. Seasonal ales in production are Dark Mild (ABV 3.9%), Artic (ABV 4.6%), Iceberg (ABV 5.1%).

Valhalla Original *(OG 1037, ABV 3.8%)* **Valhalla Gold** *(OG 1043, ABV 4.3%)*
Valhalla Northern Lights *(OG 1048, ABV 4.8%)*
Valhalla Premier *(OG 1050, ABV 5%)*

BRETTVALE

Brettvale Brewing Company Ltd, 132 High Street, Bildeston, Suffolk IP7 7ED
Tel (01449) 741434 Fax (01449) 741719
Tours by arrangement

⊗ This brewery was set up with a five-barrel plant in old stables behind the King's Head in Bildeston. It now has a second tied house and there are plans for further acquisitions. Ten other local outlets are also supplied.

Best Bitter *(OG 1038, ABV 3.8%)*
Blondie *(OG 1041, ABV 4.1%)*
First Gold *(OG 1043, ABV 4.3%)*
Billy *(OG 1049, ABV 4.8%)*

BREWERY ON SEA

The Brewery on Sea Ltd, 24 Winston Business Centre, Chartwell Road, Lancing, W. Sussex BN15 8TU *Tel (01903) 851482*
⊗ This brewery was established in 1993 and increased its capacity in 1995 to around 55 barrels a week, some of which is taken by wholesalers, although up to 100 outlets are supplied directly. Beers are also brewed for East-West Ales, tel. (01892) 834040, and the brewery often produces beers for special occasions. Seasonal beers: Spinnaker Jester (ABV 4%, April-May), Mother's Daze (ABV 4.1%, Mother's Day), Big Fat Santa (ABV 4.2%, November-December), Old Flame (ABV 4.2%, February-March), Spinnaker Dragon (ABV 4.2%, St George's Day), Spinnaker Shamrock (ABV 4.2%, a green beer for St Patrick's Day), Shell Shock (ABV 4.3%, Easter), Snow Belly (ABV 4.4%, Christmas), Whale Ale (ABV 4.4%, May), Spinnaker Valentine (ABV 4.6%, February), Up in Smoke (ABV 4.8% Guy Fawkes Night), Candyman (ABV 5%, Hallowe'en), Wild Turkey (ABV 5.2%, winter).

Spinnaker Bitter *(OG 1036, ABV 3.5%)* ◥ A hoppy-tasting, smooth, basic ale.
Spinnaker Mild or Lancing Special Dark *(OG 1036, ABV 3.5%)* Dark in colour and rich in flavour.
Spinnaker Golden Lite *(ABV 3.8%)* The popularity of this summer brew now ensures its year-round availability. Golden brown in colour and flavoursome.
Spinnaker Classic *(OG 1040, ABV 4%)* ◥ The brewery's first beer: copper-coloured, with hints of malt in the aroma, giving way to a fruity flavour.
Timeless *(ABV 4.1%)* A classic summer ale.
Leaf Thief *(ABV 4.2%)* An autumn brew.
Rain Dance *(ABV 4.4%)* ◥ Originally a 'one-off' wheat beer, now permanently established. Very pale with a cereal aroma.
Spinnaker Buzz *(OG 1045, ABV 4.5%)* ◥▧ An amber-coloured beer primed with honey, which dominates the aroma. An initial sweetness gives way to an intriguing flavour mix of malt, honey and hops. Hoppy aftertaste.
Black Rock *(OG 1050, ABV 5.5%)* A dark beer with a good measure of roasted barley.
Special Crew *(OG 1050, ABV 5.5%)* A full-bodied bitter which gains its flavour and copper colour from a mix of pale and crystal malts.
Spinnaker Ginger *(OG 1050, ABV 5.5%)* Mid-light brown in colour, this beer contains pure ginger, making it highly aromatic.
Riptide *(OG 1060, ABV 6.5%)* A premium strong ale, fully fermented.
Tidal Wave *(OG 1065, ABV 7%)* A dry-tasting, strong, dark beer.

For East-West Ales:
Winter Widget *(OG 1043, ABV 4.5%)*
Wicked Widget *(OG 1045, ABV 4.7%)*

THE BREWERY
See Liverpool.

BREWSTERS

Brewsters Brewing Company Ltd, Penn Lane, Stathern, nr Melton Mowbray, Leicestershire LE14 4JA
Tel (01949) 81868 Fax (01949) 81868
Brewster is the old English term for a female brewer, derived from the times when women used to brew and sell most of the ale drunk in England; Sara Barton is a modern example. Formerly with Courage, she set up her own company in the Vale of Belvoir in January 1998 with equipment from the defunct Wylye Valley brewery. Around 20 outlets are supplied with the beers, which include seasonal offerings. Further permanent additions to the range are planned.
Bitter *(OG 1040, ABV 4.2%)*

BRIDGE OF ALLAN

⌂ Queens Hotel, 24 Henderson Street, Bridge of Allan, Central *Tel (01786) 833268*
⊗ Scottish ale house which began brewing in 1998. A visitor centre is due to be opening soon. Seasonal beer: Spring Ale (ABV 4.2%, April-May).
Bitter *(ABV 3.7%)*
Stirling Brig *(ABV 4%)*

BRIGG

⌂ Brigg Brewing Co, Queens Arms Hotel, Wrawby Street, Brigg, Lincolnshire DN20 8BS
Tel (01652) 653174 Fax (01652) 651614
Tours by arrangement
Bob Nicholson designed and built this new brewery himself to supply his own pub and four other outlets with his own recipe beers.
Bobs Bitter *(OG 1040, ABV 4%)* ◆
Balanced and a little thin for its gravity. Pale brown, the hop is slightly fruity in the taste, while bitterness gives way to a grainy malt in the finish.
Grannies Bitter *(OG 1044, ABV 4.4%)*
◆ Tawny brown, with a creamy head and a malty vanilla aroma that also dominates the taste, although the finish does bitter slightly. Quite a creamy, rich beer for its strength.

BRISTOL BREWHOUSE

See Ross.

BRITANNIA

See Batham.

BRITISH OAK

British Oak Brewery, Salop Street, Eve Hill, Dudley, West Midlands
Brewery closed.

BROOKLANDS

See Planets.

BROUGHTON

Broughton Ales Ltd, The Brewery, Broughton, Biggar, The Borders ML12 6HQ
Tel (01899) 830345 Fax (01899) 830474
Shop 9-5 Mon-Fri
Tours by arrangement (eves)
⊗ Founded in 1979, but went into receivership in 1995, this brewery was then taken over by Whim Brewery owner Giles Litchfield. Half the beer is bottled (not bottle-conditioned), much of it for export. A single tied house and 200 outlets in Scotland are supplied direct from the brewery, other customers throughout the UK are served by wholesalers. Seasonal/occasional beers: Reeket Yill (OG 1048, ABV 4.8%, a smoked winter, January).
Bramling Cross *(OG 1034, ABV 3.6%)*
This summer beer is the latest addition to the range.
IPA *(OG 1036, ABV 3.8%)* Brewed for spring and summer.
Greenmantle Ale *(OG 1038, ABV 3.9%)* ◆ A beer with a predominantly malty aroma, a malty taste with hints of fruit and hops, but little aftertaste. Somewhat lacking in character.
Special Bitter *(OG 1038, ABV 3.9%)* ◆
A dry-hopped version of Greenmantle Ale. An aroma of hop, with malt and fruit, leads into a pleasingly bitter beer balanced with more malt and fruit. The bitterness and fruit last into the aftertaste. Slightly lacking in body.
Merlin's Ale *(OG 1042, ABV 4.2%)* ◆
A much improved golden ale. A well-hopped, fruity flavour is balanced by malt. The finish is bittersweet and light, but dry.
80/- *(OG 1042, ABV 4.2%)*
Scottish Oatmeal Stout *(OG 1045, ABV 4.2%)* ◆ A rare winter pleasure, this wonderfully dry stout has a bitter aftertaste, dominated by roast malt. A distinctive malt aroma is followed by a prominent roast taste, with fruit evident throughout.
The Ghillie *(OG 1043, ABV 4.5%)* ◆
This superb ale assaults the nose with a strong aroma of hop. Hops continue to dominate the palate, with malt and fruit, and it ends in a hop-dominated, dry finish.
Black Douglas *(OG 1053, ABV 5.2%)*
A winter brew, dark ruby in colour.
Old Jock *(OG 1070, ABV 6.7%)* Strong, sweetish and fruity in the finish. Also sold as River Tweed Festival Ale.

MATTHEW BROWN

See Mansfield and Nationals, Scottish Courage.

ABEL BROWN'S

Abel Brown's Brewery, The Stag, 35 Brook Street, Stotfield, Hitchen, Herts
Ceased brewing.

TOM BROWN'S

See Goldfinch.

BRUNSWICK

⌂ The Brunswick Brewery Co. Ltd, 1 Railway Terrace, Derby DE1 2RU
Tel (01332) 290677 Fax (01332) 370226
Tours by arrangement
⊗ Purpose-built tower brewery attached to the Brunswick Inn, the first purpose-built railwaymen's hostelry in the world, which was partly restored by the Derbyshire Historic Building Trust and bought by the present owners in 1987. Brewing began in 1991 and a viewing area allows pub-users to watch production. The beers are supplied to the Inn and five other outlets directly. Numerous one-off beers are also produced. Beers: Recession Ale (OG 1033, ABV 3.3%), Triple Hop (OG 1040 ABV 4%), Mild Mild (OG 1037 ABV 3.7%), Second Brew (OG 1042, ABV 4.2%), Railway Porter (OG 1045, ABV 4.3%), Old Accidental (OG 1050, ABV 5%).

BUCHANAN

See Federation.

BUCKLEY

See Brains.

BUFFY'S

Buffy's Brewery, Mardle Hall, Rectory
Road, Tivetshall St Mary, Norfolk NR15
2DD *Tel* (01379) 676523
Tours by arrangement

⊗ Situated alongside a 15th-century house,
Buffy's started life as Mardle Hall Brewery
in 1993, but was forced to change its name
after a complaint from another brewery.
Work to double the brewery's capacity was
completed in 1997 enabling Buffy's to aim
for substantial market expansion. Fifty-free
trade outlets are now supplied, but the bulk
of the beer is sold via wholesalers. It plans to
start bottling beers in 1998. Seasonal beers:
Hollybeery (OG 1046, ABV 4.8%), Festival
9X (OG 1080, ABV 9%).

Bitter *(OG 1038, ABV 3.9%)* ❧ A good,
hoppy, well-balanced, tawny-coloured session beer, dry on the palate. Moreish, good
standard old-fashioned bitter.

Polly's Folly *(OG 1041, ABV 4.3%)* ❑
❧ Good balance of bitterness and fruit.
Lovely copper colour.

Mild *(OG 1042, ABV 4.2%)* A stronger
than average dark mild.

Polly's Extra Folly *(OG 1046, ABV
4.9%)* ❧ This is tje same basic brew as the
Polly's Folly, but tawny in colour with extra
strength.

Ale *(OG 1052, ABV 5.5%)* ❧ A pale brown
beer which is a smooth and hardy, strong
bitter throughout. Slightly warming and easy
to drink.

IPA *(ABV 4.7%)* ❧ Stronger than usual for
an IPA. An interesting, malty brew. A full-
flavoured light brown ale with full body and
excellent clean bitter finish.

Strong Ale *(OG 1062, ABV 6.5%)* ❧ This
superb, brown, full-bodied, rich, fruity,
strong ale has excellent, balance and is very
complex. A classic ale, but not for the faint-
hearted.

BULLMASTIFF

Bullmastiff Brewery, 14 Bessemer Close,
Leckwith, Cardiff CF1 8DL
Tel (01222) 665292

Small brewery set up in the Penarth dock-
lands in 1987 and moved to larger premises
in Cardiff in 1992. Bullmastiff now supplies
about 30 outlets locally, though much of the
production is sold in other parts of the country through wholesalers. Seasonal beers:
Mad Dog (OG 1073, ABV 7.3%,
Christmas), Spring Fever (OG 1043, ABV
4.3%), Summer Moult (OG 1043, ABV
4.3%), Southpaw (OG 1048, ABV 4.8%,
autumn).

Gold Brew *(OG 1039, ABV 3.8%)* ❧
Refreshing, hoppy aroma and flavour dominate a fine balance of malt and fruit with a
lasting, hoppy bitterness.

Best Bitter *(OG 1042, ABV 4%)* ❧ A
well-balanced beer with a hoppy, bitter and
fruity finish. A fine example of a best bitter.

Spring Fever *(OG 1043, ABV 4.3%)*
The spring beer.

Summer Moult *(OG 1043, ABV 4.3%)*
The summer beer.

Cardiff Dark *(OG 1044, ABV 4.2%)*

Thoroughbred *(OG 1046, ABV 4.5%)*
❧ A tasty, premium bitter with hops strong
in the aroma and flavour balanced by fruit
and malt with a bitter finish.

Southpaw *(OG 1048, ABV 4.7%)* Brewed
for the autumn.

Brindle *(OG 1050, ABV 5%)* ❧ A full-
bodied beer, well hopped throughout, with
malt and fruit followed by a lasting,
hoppy/bitter finish.

Son of a Bitch *(OG 1062, ABV 6%)* ❑
❧ A powerful beer with a complex blend of
hop, malt and fruit and a balancing bitterness. Warming, tasty, with a lasting, bitter
finish. A deserved award winner.

BUNCES

Bunces Brewery, The Old Mill, Netheravon,
Salisbury, Wiltshire SP4 9QB
Tel (01980) 670631 *Fax* (01980) 671 187
Shop 9-5 Mon-Fri, 10-1 Sat
Tours by arrangement

⊗ Tower brewery housed in a listed building
on the Wiltshire Avon, established in 1984
and sold to Danish proprietors in summer
1993. Its cask-conditioned beers are delivered to around 50 free trade outlets within a
radius of 50 miles, and a number of wholesalers are also supplied. Seasonal beers: Sign
of Spring (OG 1044, ABV 4.6%, March-
April), Rudolph (OG 1050, ABV 5%,
Christmas).

Benchmark *(OG 1035, ABV 3.5%)* ❧ A
pleasant, bitter ale of remarkable character,
which maintains one's interest for a long
time. The taste is malty, the aroma subtle
and the very long finish is quite dry on the
palate.

Pigswill *(OG 1040, ABV 4%)* A beer first
brewed for the Two Pigs at Corsham, now
more widely available.

Second to None *(OG 1044, ABV 4.6%)*
A summer wheat beer.

Danish Dynamite *(OG 1050, ABV 5%)*
A light golden, slightly fruity, dry strong ale
with hop and bitter balance.

Old Smokey *(OG 1050, ABV 5%)* ❧ A
delightful, warming, dark bitter ale, with a
roasted malt taste and a hint of liquorice surrounding a developing bitter flavour. Very
appealing to the eye.

Stig Swig *(OG 1050, ABV 5%)* A golden
autumn beer brewed with the herb sweet
gale, an old Viking beer ingredient.

BURNTISLAND

Burntisland Brewing Company, Burntisland
Brewery, 83 High Street, Burntisland, Fife
KY3 9AA *Tel* (01592) 873333
Shop 7-7 (7-2 Wed, 12-3 Sun) May-September; 8-6 in winter

☺ Brewery housed behind a delicatessen/off-
licence which began operation in 1996. It
was upgraded in 1997 and there are plans to
add a bottling line to produce more bottle-
conditioned beers. Some beer has been contract-brewed for Burntisland by
Harviestoun. Over 20 outlets are now supplied with the beers. Bottle-conditioned
beers: Alexander's Downfall (OG 1045,
ABV 4.3%), Dockyard Rivets (OG 1050,
ABV 5.1%).

Alexander's Downfall *(OG 1045,
ABV 4.3%)*

Dockyard Rivets *(OG 1050, ABV 5.1%)*
A real pilsner-style lager.

BURTON BRIDGE

Burton Bridge Brewery, 24 Bridge Street,
Burton-upon-Trent, Staffordshire DE14 1SY

Tel (01283) 510573 Fax (01283) 51559
Tours by arrangement (Tue evening)

☺ Brewery established in 1982, with one tied outlet at the front and another opened in January 1997. Conversion of the adjoining premises, an early 19th-century malt house, into a new brewhouse was completed later the same year. Guest beers are supplied to around 250 outlets virtually nationwide and other brewers beers are sold by them into the East and West Midlands. Additionally, Burton Bridge specialises in commemorative bottled beers to order. Seasonal beers: Spring Ale (OG 1047, ABV 4.7% March-April), Battle Brew (OG 1050, ABV 5%, July-August), Hearty Ale (OG 1050, ABV 5%, December-January). Bottle-conditioned beers: Burton Porter (OG 1045, ABV 4.5%), Empire Pale Ale (ABV 7.5%), Tickle Brain (ABV 8%).

Summer Ale *(OG 1038, ABV 3.8%)*
Only available during British Summer Time. A beer with a strong hop aroma and a dry, bitter finish.

XL Bitter *(OG 1040, ABV 4%)* ❦ A golden, malty, drinking bitter, with a faint, hoppy and fruity aroma. An excellent mix of flavours follows, with fruitiness dominating.

Bridge Bitter *(OG 1042, ABV 4.2%)* ❦ Amber-coloured and malty. Clean tasting with little aroma but superb, bitter, hoppy aftertaste.

Burton Porter *(OG 1045, ABV 4.5%)*
🍺❦ Dark ruby-red, with a faint aroma. The taste combines moderate liquorice flavour with hops and fruit; slightly sweet. Dry, astringent aftertaste.

Staffordshire Knot Brown *(OG 1048, ABV 4.8%)* An autumn beer.

Top Dog Stout *(OG 1050, ABV 5%)* ❦ A winter brew with a strong roast malt and fruit mix, developing into a potent malt and roast malt aftertaste.

Festival Ale *(OG 1055, ABV 5.5%)* ❦ A full-bodied, copper-coloured, strong but sweet beer. The aroma is hoppy, malty and slightly fruity. Malt and hops in the flavour give way to a fruity finish. Tremendous mouthfeel.

Old Expensive *(OG 1065, ABV 6.5%)*
❦ A barley wine of deep red hue, malty aroma but strong caramel taste leading to a hoppy, fruity bitter finish. Very tasty and satisfying, tremendous mouthfeel.

For Feelgood Bar and Catering Services:
Stairway to Heaven *(ABV 5%)*

For Lakeland Brewing Co:
Amazon *(ABV 4.5%)*
Great Northern *(ABV 5%)*
Winter Holiday *(ABV 5%)*
For Thomas Sykes Pub:
Thomas Sykes Ale *(ABV 10%)*

BURTONWOOD

Burtonwood Brewery PLC, Bold Lane, Burtonwood, Warrington, Cheshire WA5 4PJ
Tel (01925) 225131 Fax (01925) 229033
Tours by arrangement (charge)

☺ Family-run public company established in 1867 by James Forshaw. In the 1980s, Burtonwood embarked on a £6 million extension plan and a new brewhouse was completed in 1990. Burtonwood still has shares in, and remains a major supplier to, the Paramount pub group, and in fact manages the distribution of all products to the Paramount estate. It is enlarging its own tied estate, creating themed operations, such as Forshaws Ale Houses and Top Hat Taverns. Its 498 outlets include 100 pubs on a long lease from Allied Domecq. However, only half of Burtonwood's pubs take real ale. Burtonwood sold its free trade interests to Carlsberg-Tetley in 1996, but it still supplies around 100 other outlets direct. Some seasonal beers have occasionally been produced, and it brews two beers under contract for Whitbread.

Mild *(OG 1032, ABV 3%)* ❦ A smooth, dark brown, malty mild with a good roast flavour, some caramel taste and a hint of bitterness. Slightly dry finish.

Bitter *(OG 1037, ABV 3.7%)* ❦ A well-balanced, refreshing, malty bitter, with good hoppiness. Fairly dry aftertaste.

James Forshaw's Bitter *(OG 1039, ABV 4%)* ❦ A malty and hoppy, well-balanced bitter.

Top Hat *(OG 1046, ABV 4.8%)* ❦ Soft, nutty, malty and a little sweet. Fairly thin for its gravity.

The brewing scene at the Isle of Man brewery of Bushy's. The brewery began life in a pub in 1986, but the success of its ales meant expansion to its present site in 1990. All the beers are brewed to the stipulations of the Manx Brewers' Act of 1874.

David Bellamy knows a pint that's made from natural ingredients when he sees one. The naturalist is pictured at Butterknowle Brewery in County Durham. Since its founding in 1990, Butterknowle's beers have won awards and generated growth for the brewery. It now supplies 200 outlets nationwide and produces bottle-conditioned beers.

Buccaneer *(OG 1052, ABV 5.2%)* ❧
A pale golden, sweet and malty bitter, with subtle hop flavour. Its light taste belies its strength.

For Whitbread:
Higsons Bitter *(OG 1037, ABV 3.8%)*
Oldham Bitter *(OG 1037, ABV 3.8%)* ❧
A copper-coloured beer with an aroma of malt and fruit. The flavour is malty and bitter, with a bittersweet tinge and a dry, malty finish. A relic of the Oldham Brewery closed by Boddingtons.

BURTS

Burts (Sandown Brewery) Ltd, Sandown Brewery and Stillroom, 15 St Johns Road, Sandown, Isle of Wight PO36 8EN
Tel (01983) 408308 Fax (01983) 408337
Tours by arrangement
Founded in Newport in 1840 but went into receivership in 1992. The name and brands were bought by the Hampshire soft drinks firm Hartridges, owners of Island Brewery, who now use the Burts name for all their brewing operations. The Newport brewery was closed in 1996 and the brewing carried out at the new brew pub, Sandown Brewery & Stillroom, supplying five tied houses and 16 other outlets. The brewery and pubs were bought by Ushers in March 1998, which has 12 pubs on the island. Former owner Geoff Hartridge plans a new mainland micro and the expansion of his Winchester Ale Houses chain.

Nipper Bitter *(OG 1035, ABV 3.4%)* ❧
A thin, malty and fruity, golden brown session beer, with some astringency and acidity.

Parkhurst Porte *(OG 1038, ABV 3.8%)*
Vectis Premium Ale or VPA *(OG 1042, ABV 4.2%)* ❧ A refreshing, malty, bitter beer with a fruity nose.

Newport Nobbler *(OG 1044, ABV 4.4%)* ❧ A malty, fruity, light bitter with a clean finish and solid body. Pale straw in hue.

Codswallop *(OG 1050, ABV 5%)*
Crustache *(OG 1052, ABV 5.5%)*

BUSHY'S

The Mount Murray Brewing Co. Ltd,
Mount Murray, Castletown Road, Braddan,
Isle of Man IM4 1JE
Tel (01624) 661244   Fax (01624) 611101
Tours by arrangement

⊕ Set up in 1986 as a brewpub, Bushy's
moved to its present site in 1990, when
demand outgrew capacity. Its fifth tied
house opened in summer 1998 and the beers,
all brewed to the stipulations of the Manx
Brewers' Act of 1874, are also supplied to 20
other outlets. Occasional/seasonal beers:
Summer Ale (OG 1036, ABV 3.6%, July),
Celebration Ale (OG 1040, ABV 4%),
Piston Brew (OG 1045, ABV 4.5%, for the
TT races in May-June), Old Bushy Tail (OG
1045, ABV 4.5%), Old Shunter (OG 1045,
ABV 4.5%, August-September), Lovely
Jubbely Christmas Ale (OG 1052, ABV
5.2%).
Mild *(OG 1035, ABV 3.5%)*
Bitter *(OG 1038, ABV 3.8%)* ❧ An aroma
full of pale malt and hops introduces you to
a beautifully hoppy, bitter beer. Despite the
predominant hop character, malt is also evi-
dent. Fresh and clean-tasting.
Export Bitter *(OG 1038, ABV 3.8%)*
Manannan's Cloak *(OG 1040, ABV
4%)*

BUTCOMBE

Butcombe Brewery Ltd, Butcombe, Bristol
BS40 7XQ
Tel (01275) 472240 Fax (01275) 474734
Tours by arrangement (trade only)

✗ One of the most successful of the newer
breweries, set up in 1978 by a former
Courage Western MD, Simon Whitmore.
During 1992-93, the brewery virtually doubled in size (for the third time) and, after 18
years of brewing just a single beer, a second
ale went into production in 1996 after further plant development. Butcombe has
recently acquired a further two pubs, bringing its estate up to six houses (although none
are tied) and it also supplies 350 other outlets within a 50-mile radius of the brewery.
Bitter *(OG 1039, ABV 4%)* ▢❧ A malty
and notably bitter beer, with subtle peardrop
and citrus fruit qualities. Amber-coloured, it
has a hoppy, malty, citrus aroma and a long,
dry, bitter finish with light fruit notes.
Consistent.
Wilmot's Premium Ale *(OG 1048,
ABV 4.8%)* ❧ Full-bodied, with good malt,
strong hops and some fruit. Mid-brown in
colour, it has an aroma of hops, malt and
citrus/peardrop fruits; long, dry, bitter,
slightly spicy, resinous finish. Tasty.

BUTTERKNOWLE

Butterknowle Brewery, Old Schoolhouse,
Lynesack, Butterknowle, Bishop Auckland,
Co. Durham DL13 5QF
Tel (01388) 710109 Fax (01388) 710373
Launched in 1990, its award-winning ales
have resulted in growth for the brewery. It
now supplies 200 outlets nationwide regu-
larly. Occasional/seasonal beers: West
Auckland Mild (OG 1034, ABV 3.3%), First

Gold (ABV 3.8%). Bottle-conditioned beers:
Conciliation Ale (OG 1042, ABV 4.3%),
High Force (OG 1060, ABV 6.2%).
Bitter *(OG 1036, ABV 3.6%)* ❧ A light,
fruity pale ale with a good balance of
flavours. Fruity aroma; slight hoppy aftertaste.
Banner Bitter *(OG 1040, ABV 4%)* ▢❧
A good, moderately bitter-tasting, pale
brown beer. Lingering aftertaste; hoppy
aroma with fruity undertones.
Conciliation Ale *(OG 1042, ABV 4.2%)*
▢❧ Returning to its original form, this classic beer continues to impress. Well-balanced
and warming, it is decidedly bitter with a
long, fruity aftertaste which finishes dry and
bitter.
Black Diamond *(OG 1050, ABV 4.8%)*
❧ A rich malty/toffee/liquorice taste dominates this deep red/brown ale. Fruity aroma;
bitterness complements the initial sweetness
in the mouth.
Lynesack Porter *(OG 1050, ABV 5%)*
A dark, traditional porter.
High Force *(OG 1060, ABV 6.2%)*
A smooth strong ale, well-hopped, with
some fruity sweetness. A good depth of
flavour develops in the aftertaste. A multi-
dimensional beer.
Old Ebenezer *(OG 1080, ABV 8%)*
A splendid, rich and fruity, seasonal barley
wine: liquid Christmas cake with a potent
punch. Surprisingly moreish, if only in sips!

BUTTS

Butts Brewery Ltd, Northfield Farm,
Wantage Road, Great Shefford, Hungerford,
Berkshire RG17 7BY
Tel (01488) 648133 Fax (01189) 321840
Tours by arrangement

✗ Brewery set up in converted farm build-
ings in 1994 with plant acquired from
Butcombe. Butts now supplies 80 outlets,
mainly in Berkshire, but also in Oxfordshire,
Hampshire and Wiltshire. Occasional beer:
Golden Brown (OG 1050, ABV 5%).
Jester *(OG 1035, ABV 3.5%)*
Bitter *(OG 1040, ABV 4%)*
Blackguard *(OG 1045, ABV 4.5%)* A
new winter porter
Barbus Barbus *(OG 1046, ABV 4.6%)*

The Victorian brewhouse of Caledonian has survived fire and threats of closure. It uses the last three direct-fired, open coppers in Britain, one of which dates back to 1869 when the brewery was founded by George Lorimer and Robert Clarke. Its 80/- won the Champion Beer of Scotland Award in 1997.

CAINS

Robert Cain & Co. Ltd, The Robert Cain Brewery, Stanhope Street, Liverpool, Merseyside L8 5XJ
Tel (0151) 709 8734 Fax (0151) 709 8395
Tours by arrangement
⊕ Robert Cain's brewery was first established on this site in 1850, but was bought out by Higsons in the 1920s, then by Boddingtons in 1985. Whitbread took control of the Boddingtons breweries in 1990 and closed the site, switching the brewing of Higsons to Sheffield and later Castle Eden. The site was then bought by GB Breweries to brew canned beers, but with enthusiastic staff and CAMRA support, it soon moved on to cask ales. The company is now a division of the Brewery Group Denmark A/S. Cain's has five tied houses and there are plans to expand the estate to around 10 traditional Victorian alehouses. An arrange-ment has been made to badge some of Greenalls' pubs as Cain's pubs, offering the full range of Cain's beers. Around 400 outlets in Merseyside and the North-West also take the beers, which include a monthly guest beer. Occasional/seasonal beers: Red Fox (OG 1039 ABV 4%), Golden Summer Ale (OG 1040, ABV 4%), Mayflower Ale (OG 1044, ABV 4.5%), Styrian Gold (OG 1045, ABV 4.5%), Superior Stout (OG 1048, ABV 4.8%), Chocolate Ale (OG 1048, ABV 5%), Brewer's Droop (OG 1049, ABV 5%), Victorian Winter Ale (OG 1049, ABV 5%).
Dark Mild *(OG 1032, ABV 3.2%)* 🗇
🍺 A smooth, dry and roasty, dark mild, with some chocolate and coffee notes.
Brewery Bitter *(OG 1036, ABV 3.5%)*
A new bitter, brewed exclusively for Cain's-badged Greenalls pubs: a malty and smooth, light tan-coloured beer with a fragant nose.

Traditional Bitter *(OG 1039, ABV 4%)*
✦ A darkish, full-bodied and fruity bitter, with a good, hoppy nose and a dry aftertaste.
Formidable Ale (FA) *(OG 1048, ABV 5%)* ✦ A bitter and hoppy beer with a good, dry aftertaste. Sharp, clean and dry.

CALEDONIAN

The Caledonian Brewing Company Ltd, 42 Slateford Road, Edinburgh EH11 1PH
Tel (0131) 337 1286 Fax (0131) 313 2370
⊗ Described by Michael Jackson as a 'living, working museum of beer making', Caledonian operates from a Victorian brewhouse, using the last three direct-fired, open coppers in Britain, one of which dates back to 1869 when the brewery was founded by George Lorimer and Robert Clark. The site was taken over by Vaux of Sunderland in 1919, who continued to brew there until 1987, when, under threat of closure, it was acquired by a management buyout team. A disastrous fire in 1994 destroyed the historic maltings and necessitated a major rebuild. A new visitors' centre was incorporated. Caledonian has no tied estate, but around 400 free trade outlets are supplied directly, and the beers are increasingly available south of the border. Significant developments are now under way at the brewery to cope with extra production demands arising from winning the contract to brew Alloa beers for Carlsberg-Tetley this year, and its own beer range has also been rationalised. 80/- won the Champion Beer of Scotland award in 1997. Bottle-conditioned beer: Tempus Fugit (ABV 4.4%).
70/- Ale *(OG 1036, ABV 3.5%)* ✦ A traditional Scottish session beer, with malt to the fore in the aroma. The subtle, bitter-sweet taste has a balance of malt, fruit, and roast, with hop to the fore. The malt fades in the aftertaste. It can be hard to find.
Murrays Summer Ale *(OG 1036, ABV 3.6%)* ✦ A clean-tasting, thirst-quenching, golden session beer, with hop and fruit evident throughout. A bitter beer, balanced by malt in the taste and aftertaste.
Deuchars IPA *(OG 1038, ABV 3.8%)* ⊓
✦ An extremely tasty and refreshing, amber-coloured session beer. Hops and malt are very evident and are balanced by fruit throughout. The lingering aftertaste is delightfully bitter and hoppy.
80/- Ale *(OG 1042, ABV 4.1%)* ▊⊓✦ A predominantly malty, copper-coloured beer, well balanced by hop and fruit; a complex Scottish heavy with the hop characteristics of a best bitter.
Golden Promise *(OG 1048, ABV 5%)* An organic beer, pale in colour, with pronounced hop character. Floral and fruity on the nose.
Merman XXX *(OG 1050, ABV 4.8%)* ✦ A mid-brown beer, based on a Victorian recipe. This rich, malty, fruity beer has a thick, initially sweetish, taste which becomes increasingly complex, with roast, hops and a hint of caramel.
Edinburgh Strong Ale or ESA *(OG 1064, ABV 6.4%)* A complex mix of malt and hops without the cloying sweetness that beers of this strength can have. Most commonly available in bottles (not bottle-conditioned).

tioned).

CARMARTHEN BREWERIES

See Tomos Watkin.

CAMBRIAN

Cambrian Brewery, Units 17-18, Marian Mawr Enterprise Park, Dolgellau, Gwynedd
Brewery closed.

CAMBRINUS

Aspinalls Cambrinus Craft Brewery, Home Farm, Knowsley Park, Knowsley L34 4AQ
Tel (0151) 546 2226 Tours by arrangement
Intended as a part-time business, this brewery, has in fact been brewing full-time since it opened in July 1997. Set up in part of a farm building it currently supplies 50 outlets.
Occasional beers: Wreck of the Old 97 (OG 1045, ABV 4.5%), Celebrance (OG 1060, ABV 6.5%, Christmas).
Renaissance *(OG 1036, ABV 3.3%)*
Restorance *(OG 1036, ABV 3.6%)*
Deliverance *(OG 1042, ABV 4.2%)*
Lamp Oil *(OG 1048, ABV 5%)*
Dominance *(OG 1050, ABV 5.5%)*

CAMERONS

Camerons Brewery Company,Lion Brewery, Hartlepool TS24 7QS
Tel (01429) 266666 Fax (01429) 868195
Tours by arrangement
⊗ This major brewer of real ale, established in 1865, went through a period of neglect for some 17 years when it was owned by non-brewers. In 1992 it was bought by Wolverhampton & Dudley Breweries, in a deal that included the brewery, 51 pubs and the brands. With solid investment and a successful re-launch of the beers, Camerons is going from strength to strength. Lined, over-sized glasses are used in all its pubs. The company has 172 tied houses, most of which take real ale, and the beers are also widely available in the free trade.
Bitter 1036 *(OG 1036, ABV 3.6%)* A light bitter, but well-balanced, with hops and malt.
Strongarm *(OG 1042, ABV 4%)* ⊓✦ A well-rounded, ruby-red ale with a distinctive, tight creamy head; initially fruity, but with a good balance of malt, hops and moderate bitterness.

CANNON

Parker & Son Brewers Ltd, The Cannon, Cannon Street, Wellingborough, Northamptonshire NN8 4DJ
Tel (01933) 279629 Tours by arrangement
⊠ A family-run business which supplies the pub and five other free trade outlets, as well as Flying Firkin and other wholesalers.
Light Brigade *(OG 1036, ABV 3.6%)* A thin-bodied, amber/gold session beer, with a fruity malt aroma and apple fruitiness on the tongue. Faint, dry bitterness in the aftertaste.
Pride *(OG 1042, ABV 3.6%)* Cascade hops give tart fruitiness to the malt aroma. Hops finally overcome the intense malt of this amber brew in a well-balanced finish.
Florrie's Night-in-Ale *(OG 1048,*

ABV 4.8%) Winter only: hops and malt battle in an astringent fruitiness for dominance on the tongue. The bitter aftertaste finally wins through with dryness building. Light brown, with medium body.
Fodder *(ABV 5.5%)*
Old Nosey *(ABV 6%)*

CANNON ROYALL

♀ Cannon Royall Brewery, The Fruiterer's Arms, Uphampton, Ombersley, Worcestershire WR9 0JW
Tel (01905) 621161 Fax (01562) 74326
Tours by arrangement
⌧ This five-barrel plant was set up in 1993 in a converted cider house behind the Fruiterer's Arms pub. Besides the Fruiterer's Arms, 20 other outlets are supplied, and it is looking to acquire a tied house.
Fruiterer's Mild *(OG 1037, ABV 3.7%)*
🍺 A rich, black mixture of malt, roast and fruit flavours make this a joy to drink.
Arrowhead *(OG 1039, ABV 3.9%)* 🍺
A fruity and hoppy, golden brew that fills the mouth with flavour. Refreshing bitter finish.
Buckshot *(OG 1045, ABV 4.5%)* 🍺 Malt, hops and a juicy, fruity taste battle for prominence in this premium bitter.
Olde Merrie *(OG 1060, ABV 6%)* 🍺
A sweet and fruity old ale with plenty of malt flavour. For winter drinking.

CARTMEL

Cartmel Brewery, Unit 7, Fell View, Trading park, Shap Road, Kendal, Cumbria L~~~ 6NZ Tel (01539) 724085
☻ Set up by Nick Murray, in ~~~~~ at the Cavendish Arms, C~~~~~ ~, but later moved to K~~~~~ ow supplies around 4~~~~~, plus a few in Scotland.
Pride *(~~ ~~~ 3.5%)* 🍺 A beer with ~~~~~ el and sweet, complex f~~~~~ alt in the taste, with flowery h~~~~~ middle. Unbalanced bitter astringe~~~ the aftertaste. Lots of taste for a beer of this gravity.
Lakeland Gold *(OG 1038, ABV 4%)*
A golden beer with a light, clean taste, a hoppy aroma and a dry finish.
Thoroughbred *(OG 1044, ABV 4.5%)*
Winter Warmer *(OG 1050, ABV 5.2%)*

(BREWERY CLOSED)

CASTLE EDEN

See Nationals, Whitbread.

CASTLE ROCK

Castle Rock Brewery, Queensbridge Road, The Meadows, Nottingham NG2 1NB
Tel (0115) 985 1615 Fax (0115) 985 1615
Tours by arrangement
Situated next to the Tynemill pub chain's Vat and Fiddle pub, this new brewery operates with a 25-barrel plant purchased from the former Cambrian Brewery. It is looking for trading agreements with other breweries on a like-for-like basis. Brewers Phil Darby and Niven Balfour ran the former Bramcote brewery until forming a partnership with Tynemill for this new venture in September 1997.
Golliards Gold *(ABV 3.8%)* An

autumn beer.
Summer Daze *(ABV 3.8%)* A seasonal beer for summer.
Hemlock *(OG 1040, ABV 4%)*
Bendigo *(OG 1045, ABV 4.5%)*
Salsa *(ABV 4.5%)* A springtime brew.
Elsie Mo *(ABV 4.7%)*
Trentsman *(ABV 4.8%)*
Black Jack Stout *(ABV 4.9%)* A winter beer.

CAYTHORPE

Caythorpe Brewery, Hoveringham Brewers, 3 Gonalston Lane, Hoveringham, Nottinghamshire NG14 7JH
Tel (0115) 966 4376 Tours by arrangement
This new brewery is run as a 'semi-retirement project' by an ex-Home Brewery employee. Set up in 1997 at the rear of the Black Horse in Caythorpe (but under separate ownership), it supplies some 20 local outlets.
Light Horse Bitter *(ABV 3.7%)*
Dover Beck Bitter *(OG 1037, ABV 4%)*
Dark Horse Bitter *(OG 1039, ABV 4.3%)*

CHALK HILL

Chalk Hill Brewery, Rosary Road, Thorpe Hamlet, Norwich, Norfolk NR1 4DA
Tel (01603) 477077 Tours by arrangement
⌧ Run by former Reindeer brewpub owner Bill Thomas and his partners, Chalk Hill began production with a 15-barrel plant in 1993. It is looking forward to a bright future since taking on award-winning David Winter (ex-Woodforde's) as head brewer, and is developing plans for expansion and new brews. Chalk Hill supplies its own two pubs and 20 local free trade outlets. The beers are also available nationwide via beer agencies.
Tap Bitter *(OG 1036, ABV 3.6%)* 🍺
A pale-coloured, no-frills, lightweight beer with a long, bitter finish.
CHB *(OG 1042, ABV 4.2%)* 🍺 A pleasantly well-balanced, tawny-coloured session beer. Easily drinkable, with no outstanding flavours but a strong yeast aroma.
Dreadnought *(OG 1049, ABV 4.9%)* 🍺
Complex flavoured, red-coloured beer with lots of malt and fruit offerings, not to mention some toffee notes.
Flintknapper's Mild *(OG 1052, ABV 5%)* 🍺 An unbalanced, sweet, fruity mild with gentle aroma but little else.
Chalk Hill IPA *(ABV 5.3%)* A genuine IPA.
Old Tackle *(OG 1056, ABV 5.6%)* 🍺
In spite of its strength, thin and unbalanced; some fruit and malt.

CHARRINGTON

See Nationals, Bass.

CHERITON

♀ The Cheriton Brewhouse, Cheriton, Alresford, Hampshire SO24 0QQ
Tel (01962) 771166 Tours by arrangement
⌧ Purpose-built brewery, opened in 1993 by the proprietors of the Flower Pots Inn (next door). The brewery is now working close to

its weekly capacity of 50 barrels to supply 30-40 outlets as well as a second tied house. Occasional/seasonal beers: Beltane (OG 1045, ABV 4.5%), Turkey's Revenge (OG 1060, ABV 5.9%, Christmas).

Pots Ale *(OG 1037, ABV 3.8%)* ⌑
◆ Pale brown, with a hoppy nose. A well-balanced bitter and hoppy taste leads through to the aftertaste.

Best Bitter *(OG 1043, ABV 4.2%)*◨◆ A malty and fruity taste continues into the aftertaste. A dark brown beer with a malty and fruity nose.

Diggers Gold *(OG 1045, ABV 4.6%)*◨⌑
◆ A golden beer with a citric, hoppy aroma; bitter and hoppy in all respects. A dry finish.

Flower Power *(OG 1052, ABV 5.2%)*

CHESTER'S

See Everards and Nationals, Whitbread.

CHILTERN

The Chiltern Brewery, Nash Lee Road, Terrick, Aylesbury, Buckinghamshire HP17 0TQ
tel (01296) 613647 Fax (01296) 612419
Shop 9-5 Mon-Sat Tours by arrangement
⊠ Set up in 1980 on a small farm (and now the oldest working brewery in the county), Chiltern specialises in an unusual range of beer-related products, such as beer mustards, Old Ale chutneys, cheeses, liqueur chocolates and even hop cologne. These products are available from the brewery shop and from about 20 other retail outlets. Cask beer is regularly supplied to four free trade outlets and a couple of beers are brewed just for individual outlets. There is a small museum and self-catering accommodation in a converted barn. Bottle-conditioned beer: Bodgers Barley Wine (OG 1080, ABV 8%).

Chiltern Ale *(OG 1038, ABV 3.7%)* A distinctive, tangy light bitter.

Beechwood Bitter *(OG 1043, ABV 4.3%)* Full-bodied and nutty.

Three Hundred Old Ale *(OG 1050, ABV 5%)* A strong, rich, deep chestnut-coloured beer.

CHURCH END

Church End Brewery Ltd, Church Road, Shustoke, Warwickshire B46 2LB
*Tel (01675) 481567*Tours by arrangement; public tour Sat noon
Brewery founded in 1994 in an old coffin workshop next to the Griffin Inn. Now brewing to capacity, it supplies 50-60 outlets with a range of beers produced at different times of the year. A beer named after the latest car registration is also brewed.
Occasional beers: Mild Quaker (ABV 3.4%), Anchor Bitter (ABV 4%), Hooker Ale or Rusty Dudley (ABV 4.5%), Pews Porter (ABV 4.5%), Silent Night (ABV 4.5%, Christmas), Willie Brew'd (ABV 4.5%, Burns Night), Stout Coffin (ABV 4.6%), Shustoke Surpryes (ABV 4.8%), Cracker or Four King Ale (ABV 5%, Christmas), Father Brown (ABV 6%), Rest in Peace (ABV 7%).

Cuthberts *(OG 1038, ABV 3.8%)* ◆
A refreshing, hoppy beer, with hints of malt, fruit and caramel taste. Lingering bitter aftertaste.

Gravediggers *(OG 1038, ABV 3.8%)*

A premium mild. Black and red in colour, with a complex mix of chocolate and roast flavours, it is almost a light porter. Available in spring and summer.

Wheat-a-Bix *(OG 1042, ABV 4.2%)*
A wheat beer; clear, malty and very pale, combining German hops and English wheat.

What the Fox's Hat *(OG 1043, ABV 4.2%)* ◆ A beer with a malty aroma and a hoppy and malty taste with some caramel flavour.

Pooh Beer *(OG 1044, ABV 4.3%)* ◆
A bright golden beer brewed with honey. Sweet, yet hoppy; moreish.

Vicar's Ruin *(OG 1044, ABV 4.4%)*
A straw-coloured best bitter with an initially hoppy, bitter flavour, softening to a delicate malt finish.

Old Pal *(OG 1055, ABV 5%)* A strong, copper-coloured ale, full of rich, malty flavours. Three different types of hops are used; dry finish.

CITY OF CAMBRIDGE

City of Cambridge Brewery Ltd, 19 Cheddars Lane, Cambridge CB5 8LD
Tel (01223) 353939 Tours by arrangement
⊗ Brewery launched in May 1997 at the Cambridge Beer Festival where its first beer, Gyle Number One, took the Champion Beer award. It serves outlets within a 30 mile radius of Cambridge. Bottle conditioned ales occasionally produced, usually for special contract as commemorative or corporate editions.

Jet Black *(OG 1037, ABV 3.7%)* A rare example of the dark bitter class of beer, bursting with hop aroma.

True Blue *(OG 1038, ABV 3.8%)* A hoppy session beer.

Hobson's Choice *(OG 1041, ABV 4.1%)* ◨◆ A highly drinkable, golden brew with a pronounced hop aroma and taste, and a fruity, bitter balance in the mouth, finishing gently dry. Vegetable notes occur when young.

Atomsplitter *(OG 1047, ABV 4.7%)*

Bramling Traditional *(OG 1055, ABV 5.5%)*

MATTHEW CLARK

See Ushers.

CLARK'S

HB Clark & Co. (Successors) Ltd, Westgate Brewery, Westgate, Wakefield, W. Yorkshire WF2 9SW
Tel (01924) 373328 Fax (01924) 372306
Shop 8-5 Mon-Fri, 8-1 Sat and Sun
Tours by arrangement
⊛ Founded in 1905, Clark's ceased brewing during the keg revolution of the 1960s and 1970s, although it continued to operate as a drinks wholesaler. It resumed cask ale production in 1982. It now has six tied houses and its beers are widely available. Brews are produced throughout the year for special occasions, the beer name depending on the event. Black Cap was introduced in 1998.

Traditional Bitter *(OG 1038, ABV 3.8%)* ◆ A copper-coloured, well-balanced, smooth beer, with a malty and hoppy aroma, leading to a hoppy, fruity taste and a good, clean, strong malt flavour. Bitterness and dryness linger in the taste and aftertaste.

Festival Ale *(OG 1042, ABV 4.2%)* ❧
A light, fruity, pleasantly hopped premium bitter with a good fruity, hoppy nose. Moderate bitterness follows, with a dry, fruity finish. Gold in colour.

Burglar Bill *(OG 1044, ABV 4.4%)* ❧
A good, hoppy, fruity aroma precedes an enjoyable, strongly hoppy and fruity taste, with moderate bitterness and good malt character. A lingering, dry, hoppy finish follows. Dark brown in colour.

Rams Revenge *(OG 1046, ABV 4.6%)*
❧ A strong, dark brown ale with good body, a strong malt flavour and some caramel, balanced with a fruit and hop taste which does not linger.

Hammerhead *(OG 1056, ABV 5.6%)* ❧
Rich malt in the mouth, but with hop flavour and bitterness to balance. The malty, hoppy aroma is faint, but the finish is long, malty and dry. A robust, strong bitter.

Winter Warmer *(OG 1060, ABV 6%)* ❧
A dark brown, powerful strong ale. A strong, mouth-filling blend of roast malt, hop flavour, sweetness and fruit notes concludes with a satisfying finish of bittersweet roast malt.

Old Dreadnought *(OG 1080, ABV 9%)*
A strong, powerful, mid-brown beer, moderately malty with a good hop flavour. Easy to drink for its strength.

CLOCKWORK

◻ The Clockwork Beer Co., Graham Enterprises, 1153-5 Cathcart Road, Glasgow G42 9BH
Tel (0141) 649 0184 Fax (0141) 649 0643
Tours by arrangement

A husband and wife partnership bought this Glasgow pub in 1997, gutted it and rebuilt it to include a microbrewery where they plan to produce an interesting range of beers, including fruit beers, under the guidance of Bruce Williams of Heather Ales (qv). Beers: Key Amber (OG 1038, ABV 3.8%), Key Red (OG 1045, ABV 4.4%).

COACH HOUSE

The Coach House Brewing Company Ltd, Wharf Street, Howley, Warrington, Cheshire WA1 2DQ
Tel (01925) 232800
Fax (01925) 232700
⊕ Brewery founded in 1991 by four ex-Greenall Whitley employees. In 1995 Coach House increased its brewing capacity to cope with growing demand and it now delivers to outlets throughout England, Wales and Scotland, either direct or via wholesalers. The brewery also produces specially commissioned beers and brews three beers for non-brewing company John Joule of Stone, tel: (01785) 814909. Seasonal beers: Wizards Wonder Halloween Bitter (OG 1042, ABV 4.2% October), Cracker Barrel Bitter (OG 1046, ABV 4.6%, November), Dewi Sant Heritage Ale (OG 1047, ABV 4.7%, March), Regal Birthday Ale (OG 1047, ABV 4.7%, April), St Patrick's Leprechaun Ale (OG 1047, ABV 4.7%, March), St George's Heritage Ale (OG 1049, ABV 4.9%, April), Bootleg Valentines Ale (OG 1050, ABV 5%, February), Combine Harvester (OG 1052, ABV 5.1%, late summer), Burns Auld Sleekit (OG 1055, ABV 5.5%, January), Anniversary Ale (OG 1060, ABV 6%), Cheshire Cat (OG 1060, ABV 6%), Three Kings Christmas Ale (OG 1060, ABV 6%).

Flintlock Best Bitter *(ABV 3.7%)* A very pale, light beer.

Coachman's Best Bitter *(OG 1037, ABV 3.7%)* ❧ A well-hopped, malty bitter, moderately fruity with a hint of sweetness and a peppery nose.

Honeypot Bitter *(OG 1038, ABV 3.8%)*

Ostlers Summer Pale Ale *(OG 1038, ABV 4%)* ❧ Light, refreshing and very bitter, with a hint of pepper and a very dry finish.

Gunpowder Strong Mild *(OG 1039, ABV 3.8%)* ◻❧ Full-bodied and roasty dark mild with hints of pepper, fruit and liquorice, plus chocolate overtones. Malty aroma and full finish.

Dick Turpin *(OG 1042, ABV 4.2%)* Also sold under other names as a pub house beer.

Squires Gold Spring Ale *(OG 1042, ABV 4.2%)* ❧ A golden spring beer. New Zealand hops give intense bitterness which is followed by a strong chocolate flavour from amber malt. Uncompromising and characterful.

Innkeeper's Special Reserve *(OG 1045, ABV 4.5%)* ❧ A darkish, full-flavoured bitter. Quite fruity, with a strong, bitter aftertaste.

Gingernut Premium *(OG 1050, ABV 5%)*

Posthorn Premium Ale *(OG 1050, ABV 5%)* ◻❧ Well-hopped and very fruity, with bitterness and malt also prominent. Hoppy aroma and fruity aftertaste.

Taverners Autumn Ale *(OG 1050, ABV 5%)* ❧ A fruity, bitter, golden ale with a slightly dry aftertaste. A warming, autumnal ale.

Blunderbus Old Porter *(OG 1055, ABV 5.5%)* ❧ A superb winter beer. The intense roast flavour is backed up by coffee, chocolate and liquorice, and hints of spice and smoke. Very well-hopped with massive mouthfeel. An intense, chewy pint which is surprisingly refreshing and moreish.

For Joule:
Old Knotty *(OG 1037, ABV 3.7%)*
Old Priory *(OG 1044, ABV 4.4%)*
Victory Brew *(OG 1050, ABV 5%)*

COCK

◻ The Cock Tavern, Harborough Road, Kingsthorpe, Northamptonshire NN2 7AZ
Tel (01604) 715221
Brewpub opened in 1995 as The Hop House Brewery, after the refurbishment and renam-

ing of the Cock Hotel. In 1996 its parent company, Labatt Retail, sold out to Enterprise Inns, which then sold the pub on to McManus Taverns, a local pub chain. Only one beer is produced, which is also sold in some other McManus pubs. At the Cock itself, the beer is kept under blanket pressure. Beer: Bitter (ABV 4%).

COMMERCIAL
See Worth.

CONCERTINA
The Concertina Brewery, The Mexborough Concertina Band Club, 9A Dolcliffe Road, Mexborough, S. Yorkshire S64 9AZ *Tel (01709) 580841*
Brewery in the cellar of a club, which began production in 1993, brewing eight barrels a week and supplying about 25 occasional outlets. Occasional beers: Shot Firers Porter (OG 1040, ABV 4.5%), Fitzpatrick's Stout (OG 1043, ABV 4.5%), Bandsman Strong Ale (OG 1038, ABV 5.2%).
Best Bitter *(OG 1038, ABV 3.9%)*
This mid-brown bitter has lots of hops on the nose, a hoppy taste and a dry finish, plus gentle fruitiness throughout.
Old Dark Attic *(OG 1038, ABV 3.9%)*
A very dark brown beer with a fairly sweet, fruity taste.
One-eyed Jack *(OG 1038, ABV 4%)* Fairly pale in colour, with plenty of hop bitterness. Brewed with the same malt and hops combination as Bengal Tiger, but more of a session beer. Also known as Mexborough Bitter.
KW Special Pride *(ABV %)*
A smooth, medium-bodied premium bitter with a fine mixture of grain, fruit and hop in the mouth, followed by a balanced, mellow aftertaste. Easy drinking for a beer of its strength.
Bengal Tiger *(OG 1043, ABV 4.6%)*
Brewed in the style of an IPA; pale in colour, bitter and very hoppy.

CONISTON
The Coniston Brewing Co. Ltd, Coppermines Road, Coniston, Cumbria LA21 8HL
Tel (01539) 441133 Fax (01539) 441177
Tours by arrangement
Brewery set up in 1995 behind the Black Bull pub. The ten-barrel plant was built by Marston Moor and now supplies other local outlets (half on a regular basis). Seasonal beer: Blacksmith's Ale (OG 1049, ABV 5%, December–January).
Bluebird Bitter *(OG 1036, ABV 3.6%)*

A well-regarded beer named after Donald Campbell's Bluebird. Its pronounced, complex fruitiness is backed by a lingering, soft sweetness, and balanced by hoppy bitterness.
Opium *(OG 1040, ABV 4%)*
Old Man Ale *(OG 1043, ABV 4.4%)*
A ruby-red ale.
Blacksmith's Ale *(OG 1048, ABV 5%)*
A winter brew.

COTLEIGH
Cotleigh Brewery, Ford Road, Wiveliscombe, Somerset TA4 2RE
Tel (01984) 624086 Fax (01984) 624365
Tours by arrangement
Cotleigh, which started trading from a farmhouse in 1979, is now one of the most successful small breweries in the West Country. It is now housed in specially converted premises in Wiveliscombe, capable of producing 140 barrels a week. Cotleigh supplies around 150 outlets direct, mostly in Devon and Somerset, and the beers are also available across the country via wholesalers.
Two beers are produced exclusively for the Kent wholesalers East-West Ales Ltd, tel: (01892) 834040. Occasional beers (made available to customers on a monthly rota): Swift (OG 1030, ABV 3.2%), Nutcracker Mild (OG 1036, ABV 3.6%), Harvest Ale (OG 1040, ABV 4%), Hobby Ale (OG 1042, ABV 4.2%), Goshawk (OG 1043, ABV 4.3%), Peregrine Porter (OG 1045, ABV 4.4%), Golden Eagle (OG 1045, ABV 4.5%), Merlin Ale (OG 1049, ABV 4.8%), Osprey (OG 1050, ABV 5%), Monmouth Rebellion (OG 1050, ABV 5%), Snowy Ale (OG 1050, ABV 5%), Red Nose Reinbeer (OG 1060, ABV 5.6%, Christmas).

Harrier SPA *(OG 1035, ABV 3.6%)*
A straw-coloured beer with a very hoppy aroma and flavour, and a hoppy, bitter finish. Plenty of flavour for a light, low-gravity beer.
Tawny Bitter *(OG 1038, ABV 3.8%)*
A mid-brown-coloured, very consistent beer. A hoppy aroma, a hoppy but quite well-balanced flavour, and a hoppy, bitter finish.
Barn Owl Bitter *(OG 1045, ABV 4.5%)*
Old Buzzard *(OG 1048, ABV 4.8%)*
A winter brew: a dark, ruby beer tasting of roast malt balanced with hops. Roast malt continues in the finish, with bitterness.

For East-West Ales:
Aldercote Ale *(OG 1042, ABV 4.2%)*
Aldercote Extra *(OG 1046, ABV 4.7%)*

455

COTTAGE

Cottage Brewing Company, The Old Cheese Dairy, Lovington, Castle Cary, Somerset, BA7 7PS
Tel (01963) 240551 Fax (01963) 240383
Tours by arrangement

⊠ Brewery founded in West Lydford in 1993 and upgraded to a ten-barrel plant in 1994. Owned by an airline pilot, the company got off to a flying start, with Norman's Conquest taking the Champion Beer of Britain title at the 1995 Great British Beer Festival. Other awards followed and, on the strength of this success, the brewery moved to larger premises in September 1996, doubling the brewing capacity at the same time. The beer is served in 450 outlets nationally, with local deliveries made by the company's steam lorry and horse-drawn dray. The names mostly follow a railway theme. Seasonal beers: Goldrush (OG 1049, ABV 5%), Santa's Steaming Ale (OG 1055, ABV 5.5%, Christmas). Golden Arrow (OG 1044, ABV 5.4%) and bottle-conditioned Norman's Conquest (OG 1066, ABV 7%) are now brewed under contract by Hampshire (qv).

Southern Bitter *(OG 1037, ABV 3.7%)*
Wheeltappers Ale *(OG 1039, ABV 4%)*
Champflower *(OG 1043, ABV 4.2%)*
Golden Arrow *(OG 1044, ABV 4.5%)*
🗂
Somerset & Dorset Ale (S&D) *(OG 1044, ABV 4.4%)* Named after the Somerset & Dorset Railway: a well-hopped, malty brew, with a deep red colour.
Our Ken *(OG 1044, ABV 4.5%)*
Great Western Real Ale (GWR) *(OG 1053, ABV 5.4%)* Similar to S&D but stronger and darker, with a full-bodied maltiness.
Norman's Conquest *(OG 1066, ABV 7%)* 🗂🍴◣ A dark strong ale, with plenty of fruit flavour and a touch of bitterness.

COURAGE

See Nationals, Scottish Courage.

CRANBORNE

⚲ The Cranborne Brewery, Sheaf of Arrows, 4 The Square, Cranborne, Dorset BH21 5PR
Tel (01725) 517456 Tours by arrangement
⊠ This brewery, set up in a stable block behind the Sheaf of Arrows pub, went into production at Easter 1996, initially just to serve just that pub. It now supplies a further two outlets direct and there are plans for the beers to be distributed further afield. Beers: Quarrel (OG 1038, ABV 3.8%), Quiver (OG 1038, ABV 3.8%), Porter (ABV 4%), Summer Ale (ABV 4%), Seasonal Ale (ABV 6%).

CREWKERNE

⚲ Crewkerne Brewery, Crown Inn, 34 South Street, Crewkerne, Somerset TA18 8DB
Tel (01460) 72464 Tours by arrangement
Brewery established in December 1997 in the courtyard of the Crown Inn, a 16th-century coaching house. Eight outlets currently supplied.

Bartholemews *(OG 1033, ABV 3.4%)*
Crookhorn *(OG 1039, ABV 4%)*
Monmouth's Revenge *(OG 1055, ABV 5.8%)* 1998 CAMRA Award for Best Somerset Beer.

CROPTON

⚲ Cropton Brewery Co., Woolcroft, Cropton, near Pickering, N. Yorkshire YO18 8HH
Tel (01751) 417310
Fax (01751) 417310
Shop 10-5 daily, March-November
Tours by arrangement

☺ Brewery set up in 1984 in the cellar of the New Inn just to supply the pub. The plant was expanded in 1988, but by 1994 it had outgrown the cellar and a purpose-built brewery was installed behind the pub. Cropton's additive-free beers are now supplied to 40 outlets locally, plus nationwide via wholesalers. There is a visitor centre adjoining the pub which provides overnight accommodation. All the beers listed below are also available bottle-conditioned.

King Billy *(OG 1039, ABV 3.6%)* ◣ A refreshing, straw-coloured bitter, quite hoppy, with a strong, but pleasant, bitter finish that leaves a clean, dry taste on the palate.
Two Pints *(OG 1040, ABV 4%)* ◣ A good, full-bodied bitter, perhaps with a more balanced flavour than in previous years. Malt flavours initially dominate, with a touch of caramel, but the balancing hoppiness and residual sweetness come through.
Scoresby Stout *(OG 1044, ABV 4.2%)* 🗂◣ Truly a classic of the genre. A jet-black stout whose roast malt and chocolate flavours contrast with a satisfying bitter finish.
Uncle Sams *(OG 1044, ABV 4.4%)* ◣ A clean-tasting and refreshing premium pale ale. The overriding characteristic is the fruity bouquet yielded by authentic Stateside ingredients.
Backwoods Bitter *(OG 1049, ABV 4.7%)* ◣ A malty premium bitter, tawny-coloured and full-bodied. A long and satisfying, sweet finish contains an abundance of fruit flavours. Now with a lower ABV.
Monkmans Slaughter *(OG 1060, ABV 6%)*

CROUCH VALE

Crouch Vale Brewery Ltd, 12 Redhills Road, South Woodham Ferrers, Chelmsford, Essex CM3 5UP
Tel (01245) 322744 Fax (01245) 329082
Tours by arrangement (trade and CAMRA members)
⊠ Founded in 1981, Crouch Vale's business continues to grow steadily, and in recent years it has become one of the largest guest cask beer wholesalers in the Eastern coun-

Alan Edgar of the Cuckmere Haven Brewery was one of dozens of small brewers who lobbied Parliament in November. Members of the Society of Independent Brewers were calling for a sliding scale of duty which would benefit small companies who are being hit by the fact that duty rates in the UK are five times what they are across the Channel.

ties, supplying 250 outlets and beer festivals. The brewery's single tied house, the Cap and Feathers at Tillingham, was the CAMRA national Pub of the Year in 1989. The installation of four new fermenters in 1997 increased production by 15 barrels a week, and future plans include a bottle-conditioned beer. Occasional/seasonal beers: Essex Porter (OG 1051, ABV 5.1%), Fine Pale Ale (OG 1057, ABV 5.9%), Willie Warmer (OG 1060, ABV 6.4%).

Best Dark Ale *(OG 1036, ABV 3.6%)* A smooth, malty mild.

Woodham IPA *(OG 1036, ABV 3.6%)* ❧ An amber beer with a fresh, hoppy nose. A good session bitter with a well-balanced malt and hop taste leading to a fruit and hop finish.

Best Bitter *(OG 1040, ABV 4%)* ❧ The fruit in the aroma melts into a hoppy, malty taste before dominating the finish.

Millennium Gold *(OG 1042, ABV 4.2%)* ▯❧ A golden beer with a notable hop nose. The strong hop/fruit presence makes this a deceptively easy-drinking premium bitter.

Strong Anglian Special or SAS *(OG 1050, ABV 5%)* ❧ Well-balanced and full-bodied, this is a sharply bitter beer with a dry aftertaste.

CROWN BUCKLEY
See Brains.

CROWN HOTEL
See Scott's.

CROWN INN
▯ Munslow Brewhouse, The Crown Inn, Munslow, nr Craven Arms, Shropshire SY7 9ET
Tel (01584) 841205 Fax (01584) 841205
Tours during business hours
 Pub brewery established in 1994, using a two-barrel plant and the brewer's own recipes. Four other local outlets are supplied: Ironmaster (OG 1042, ABV 4.2%) is brewed solely for the Golden Ball in Ironbridge. Beers: Boy's Pale Ale (OG 1036, ABV 3.6%), Hundred Ale (OG 1041, ABV 4.1%).

CUCKMERE HAVEN
The Cuckmere Haven Brewery, Exceat Bridge, Cuckmere Haven, East Sussex BN25 4AB
Tel (01323) 892247
Tours by arrangement
⊠ This tiny brewhouse went into production in 1994 to serve the Golden Galleon pub (the brewery's owner), and now produces four regular beers for that outlet and five others on an occasional basis. There are plans to take over a pub in nearby Seaford to boost brewery production on a profitable level and make expansion of the brewery viable. Beers: Swallow's Return (OG 1039, ABV 4%, summer), Gents – Nil Taxation Ale (OG 1040, ABV 4%), Dark Velvet (OG 1045, ABV 4.7%, winter), Saxon Berserker (OG 1066, ABV 7.2%, occasional).

Saxon King Stout *(OG 1041, ABV 4.1%)*

Best Bitter *(OG 1042, ABV 4.2%)* ❧

Malty overtones in the aroma are joined by a hoppy biterness in the flavour.
Guv'nor *(OG 1045, ABV 4.6%)* ❦ A pleasant biter in which malt in the aroma gives way to a hoppy bitterness in the taste and aftertaste.
Golden Peace *(OG 1053, ABV 5.5%)* ❦ An amber-coloured, strong beer.

DALESIDE
Daleside Brewery Ltd, Camwal Road, Starbeck, Harrogate, N. Yorkshire HG1 4PT
Tel (01423) 880041
⊛ Formerly Big End brewery, founded in 1987, this company moved to new premises and changed its name in 1992. After years of gradual expansion it currently supplies 200 outlets, mainly on the A1 corridor from Newcastle to Kent, plus other outlets nationwide via wholesalers.
Occasional beers:
Barnstormer (ABV 4.5%),
Christmas Classic (ABV 4.5%), Witt Bier (ABV 4.5%, a wheat beer).
Nightjar *(OG 1038, ABV 3.7%)* ❦ A fruity, amber-coloured, medium-hopped beer with some sweetness. Leads to a sharp, slightly subdued, bitter, long finish.
Old Legover or Country Stile *(OG 1042, ABV 4.1%)* ❦ A well-balanced, mid-brown, refreshing beer which leads to an equally well-balanced, fruity and bitter aftertaste.
Old Lubrication *(OG 1042, ABV 4.1%)*
Green Grass Old Rogue Ale *(OG 1046, ABV 4.5%)*
Crack Shot *(OG 1047, ABV 4.5%)*
Monkey Wrench *(OG 1056, ABV 5.3%)* ▇❦ A powerful strong ale, mid-brown to ruby in hue. Aromas of fruit, hops, malt and roast malt give way to well-balanced fruit, malt and hoppiness on the tongue, with some sweetness throughout. A very flavoursome beer.
Morocco Ale *(OG 1057, ABV 5.5%)* ▇ ❦ A powerful, dark brew with malt and fruit in the taste. A very spicy beer in which ginger predominates and can at times overpower. This beer is becoming increasingly more widely available.

For AVS Wholesalers of Gravesend: Shrimpers *(ABV 4.1%)* A light, medium-brown session beer.

DARK HORSE
Dark Horse Brewing Co. (Hertford) Ltd, Adams Yard, off Maidenhead Street, Hertford SG14 1DR
Tel (01992) 509800 Fax (01992) 503598
Tours by arrangement
⊛ Brewery set up in the cellar of the White Horse free house in 1994, but moved in summer 1996 to its own premises, in converted Victorian stables in the town centre, giving scope for greatly increased output. It supplies its own two pubs, plus 23 other outlets in Hertfordshire, and further afield via wholesalers. Wetherspoons pubs also take the beers.
Occasional/seasonal beers: St Elmo's Fire (OG 1047, ABV 4.6%, a wheat beer), Black Widow Stout (OG 1050, ABV 4.6%).

Ale *(OG 1030, ABV 3.6%)*
A tasty light bitter, with a hint of roast grain. Slightly more malty than when first produced.
Mild *(OG 1039, ABV 3.8%)*
Sunrunner *(OG 1042, ABV 4.1%)*
A well-balanced, full-flavoured bitter, with fruit notes and a strong, bitter finish.
Fallen Angel *(OG 1042, ABV 4.2%)* ▇
Death Wish *(OG 1053, ABV 5%)*

DARK STAR
Dark Star Brewing Co. Ltd (incorporating Skinner's of Brighton), 55-56 Surrey Street, Brighton, E. Sussex BN1 3PB
Tel (01273) 701758 Tours by arrangement, for very small groups
⊗ Rob Jones, formerly of the Pitfield Brewery (qv), first brewed Dark Star at the London brewery. In 1994 it won the Champion of Champions award at the St Albans beer Festival. Brewery set up by Peter Skinner and Peter Halliday in 1994 in the cellar of their pub, the Evening Star. In 1995 they formed Dark Star Brewing Co. with Rob Jones (formerly of Pitfield Brewery), adding Rob's Dark Star beers alongside the Skinner's range. Both company names are used on the beers, but are not connected to Skinner's Cornish Ales (qv). There have been many different brews and styles to supplement the regular beers. The beers are supplied to Peter Skinner's two pubs (the other being the Gardener's Arms in Lewes), and occasionally to a few other outlets. Dark Star beers: Dark Side of the Moon (OG 1045, ABV 4.5%), Dark Star (OG 1050, ABV 5%), Black Hole (OG 1060, ABV 6%), Critical Mass (OG 1073, ABV 7.5%). Skinner's beers: Target Practice (ABV 3.4%), BSM (OG 1035, ABV 3.5%), Roast Mild (OG 1035, ABV 3.5%), Summer Ale (OG 1035, ABV 3.6%), Pale Ale (OG 1037, ABV 3.7%), Brighton Rock (OG 1040, ABV 4.1%), Penguin Stout (OG 1042, ABV 4.2%, winter), Golden Gate Bitter (OG 1043, ABV 4.3%), Old Familiar (OG 1050, ABV 5%), Cliffe Hanger Porter (OG 1055, ABV 5.5%), Pavilion Beast (OG 1060, ABV 6%).

DARKTRIBE
DarkTribe Brewery, 25 Doncaster Road, Gunness, Scunthorpe, Lincolnshire DN15 8TG
Tel (01724) 782324 Fax (01724) 782324
Tours by arrangement for CAMRA branches
⊗ Dave 'Dixie' Dean caught the brewing bug by helping out at the Iceni Brewery, and in June 1996 installed a small plant, made from converted dairy equipment, in his garage. He went into production in November with the first beer named after his dog; the later brews, which have already won awards, recall his former trade as marine engineer. Currently around 25 pubs take the beer. Occasional beers: Compass (OG 1039, ABV 4%), Gunness Stout (OG 1039, ABV 4.1%), Jolly Roger (OG 1043, ABV 4.5%), Gubernacula (OG 1044, ABV 4.5%), Dixie's Midnight Runner (OG 1057, ABV 6.5%).

Full Ahead *(OG 1037, ABV 3.8%)* A well-balanced session bitter with hop and fruit flavours and a dryish, bitter aftertaste.

Terrier *(OG 1041, ABV 4.2%)* A light, refreshing bitter ale with a gentle, malty, sustained bitter finish.

Galleon *(OG 1045, ABV 4.7%)* 🍷 A tasty, golden, smooth, full-bodied ale with a thirst-quenching, fruity aftertaste that lingers.

Twin Screw *(OG 1047, ABV 5.1%)* ◆ Ruby/red colour. A well-balanced if fruity nose leads to a rosehip taste backed by a hoppy bitterness that complements and overtakes the fruity sweetness in the dry finish.

DARLEY
See Ward's.

DARTMOOR
See St Austell and Nationals, Carlsberg-Tetley.

DARWIN
Darwin Brewery, Unit 5, Castle Close, Crook, Co. Durham DL15 8LU
Tel (01388) 763200 Fax (0191) 515 2531
Tours by arrangement
☺ Brewery founded in 1994 with a tiny half-barrel brewlength, as a research facility for the staff and students at the University of Sunderland. In summer 1997 Darwin took over Hodge's brewery for its mainstream production, while keeping the university's plant for student training and research. Production of the one Hodge's beer has been continued. Future plans include expansion of its trade (currently 10 outlets) and development of specialist bottled beers.

Evolution Ale *(OG 1042, ABV 4%)* A dark amber, full-bodied bitter with a malty flavour and a clean, bitter aftertaste.

Hodge's Original *(OG 1043, ABV 4%)* ◆ Smooth, with a soft, bitter taste and generally light character. Ending with a stronger, slightly fruity and bitter aftertaste.

Richmond Ale *(OG 1048, ABV 4.5%)*

Saints Sinner *(OG 1052, ABV 5%)* A rich, smooth-tasting, ruby-red ale with a fruity aroma and hop character in the taste.

Killer Bee *(OG 1054, ABV 6%)* A strong beer made with honey.

DAVENPORT ARMS
♨ Davenport Arms, Main Street, Worfield, Bridgnorth, Shropshire WV15 5LF
Pub brewery established in 1994. The plant was upgraded in 1995 and the range increased, with the beers now supplied direct to over 30 regular outlets within a 20-mile radius. Occasional beer: Hermitage Barley Wine (OG 1100, ABV 8.8%, Christmas).

JLK Pale Ale *(OG 1039, ABV 3.8%)*
Hopstone Bitter *(OG 1042, ABV 4%)*
Burcote Bitter *(OG 1049, ABV 4.5%)*
Reynold's Redneck *(OG 1056, ABV 5.5%)*

DAVENPORTS
See Nationals, Carlsberg-Tetley, and Pub Groups, Greenalls.

DAVIS'ES
See Grainstore.

DEEPING
Deeping Ales, 12 Peacock Square, Blenheim Way, Market Deeping, Lincolnshire PE6 8LW
Tel (01778) 345988 Fax (01778) 348750
Tours by arrangement
⊗ Set up in 1997 with a 10-barrel plant; 35 outlets currently supplied. Occasional beers: Session (OG 1037, ABV 3.7%, seen under various names); Glory (OG 1043, ABV 4.3%, a summer beer with a summer 1998 launch date), St George (OG 1045, ABV 4.5%, April-May), Snow (OG 1050, ABV 5%, a dark winter beer).

Red *(OG 1040, ABV 4.1%)* Ruby-coloured flagship ale.

Special *(OG 1048, ABV 4.8%)* A stronger version of Red.

Gunpowder *(OG 1051, ABV 5.2%)* After its success as a bonfire brew it is now a permanent beer.

DENT
Dent Brewery, Hollins, Cowgill, Dent, Cumbria LA10 5TQ
Tel (01539) 625326 Fax (01539) 625033
Tours by arrangement (minimum six people)
☺ Brewery set up in a converted barn in the Yorkshire Dales in 1990, originally to supply just three local pubs. It now has two tied houses and supplies 20 free trade outlets directly. Its own distribution company, Flying Firkin Distribution, tel: (01282) 865923, delivers all over northern England and is making some inroads into the South. All Dent's beers are brewed using the brewery's own spring water.

Bitter *(OG 1036, ABV 3.7%)* ◆ A well-balanced, light bitter with fruit and hops in the nose, supplemented by bitterness and malt in the taste. The increasingly bitter finish is quite short.

Ramsbottom Strong Ale *(OG 1044, ABV 4.5%)* ◆ This complex, chestnut-coloured beer has a warming, dry, bitter finish to follow its unusual combination of roast, bitter, fruity and sweet flavours. 'Rum and raisin' aroma.

T'Owd Tup *(OG 1058, ABV 6%)* ◆ A rich, fully-flavoured, strong stout with a roast coffee aroma. The dominant roast character is balanced by a warming sweetness and a raisiny, fruit-cake taste which linger on into the long aftertaste.

For Flying Firkin:
Aviator *(OG 1038, ABV 4%)* ◆ This medium-bodied amber ale is characterised throughout by strong citrus and hoppy flavours which develop into an enjoyable bitter finish.

Kamikaze *(OG 1048, ABV 5%)* 🍷◨ ◆ Hops and fruit dominate this full-bodied, golden, strong bitter, with a pleasant, dry bitterness growing in the aftertaste. Look also for citrus and honey in the nose, and a spicy finish.

DERWENT

Derwent Brewery, Units 2a-2b, Station Road Industrial Estate, Silloth, Carlisle, Cumbria CA5 4AG
Tel (0169 73) 31522 Fax (016973) 31523
Tours by arrangement
☺ Brewery set up in 1997 by two ex-Jennings employees at Cockermouth, and moved at the end of that year to larger premises in Silloth. Currently supplying around 70 customers direct, their aim is to build up trade in Cumbria, Lancashire, Yorkshire and the North-East.
Bitter

DERWENT ROSE

See Grey Horse.

DEVON

⚲ Devon Ales, Mansfield Arms, 7 Main Street, Sauchie, Alloa, Clackmannanshire FK10 3JR
Tel (01259) 722020 Fax (01259) 218409
Tours by arrangement
☺ Brewery founded in 1994 at CAMRA's 1993 Scottish Pub of the Year, the Mansfield Arms. It has since been expanded by the addition of two five-barrel fermenters. One other associated pub also takes the beer. Beers: Gold (OG 1037, ABV 3.8%, summer), Original (OG 1037, ABV 3.8%), Thick Black (OG 1040, ABV 4.1%), Pride (OG 1046, ABV 4.6%).

DONNINGTON

Donnington Brewery, Stow-on-the-Wold, Gloucestershire GL54 1EP
Tel (01451) 830603
⊗ This 13th-century watermill in idyllic countryside was bought by Thomas Arkell in 1827, and he began brewing on the site in 1865. It is still owned and run by the Arkell family and the millwheel is still used to drive small pumps and machinery. Donnington supplies its own 15 tied houses and a dozen free trade outlets.
XXX *(OG 1036, ABV 3.6%)* ▦◆ Thin in aroma but very flavoursome. More subtle than others in its class, it has some hops and traces of chocolate and liquorice in the taste and a notably malty finish. Worth seeking out.
BB *(OG 1036, ABV 3.6%)* ◆ A pleasant bitter with a slight hop aroma, a good balance of malt and hops in the mouth and a bitter aftertaste.
SBA *(OG 1040, ABV 3.8%)* Malt dominates over bitterness in the subtle flavour of this premium bitter, which has a hint of fruit and a dry malty finish.

DRUNKEN DUCK

⚲ Barngates Brewery at The Drunken Duck Inn, Barngates, Ambleside, Cumbria
Tel (0153 94) 36347 Fax (0153 94) 36781
Tours by arrangement
☺ Brewery opened in May 1997 at the famous Drunken Duck Inn, with assistance from Peter Yates of Yates Brewery. The brew plant is small, just one-barrel in length, but planning permission has been granted to move into a larger building with an eight-barrel plant during 1998, with the intention of supplying other

local pubs (only the Drunken Duck itself is currently supplied). Beers: Cracker Ale (OG 1038, ABV 3.9%), Chesters Strong and Ugly (OG 1048, ABV 4.9%).

DUFFIELD

⚲ The Duffield Brewing Co., The Thorold Arms, High Street, Harmston, Lincolnshire LN5 9SN *Tel (01522) 720358*
⊗ Tiny brewery, founded in November 1996 in the cellar of the Thorold Arms. It currently brews just nine gallons of a single beer at a time to serve the free house itself. Beers: Bitter (OG 1038, ABV 3.6%), Special Bitter (OG 1044, ABV 4.3%), Mulley's Irish Stout (OG 1044, ABV 4.4%), Extra Special Bitter (OG 1047, ABV 4.8%).

DURHAM

The Durham Brewery, Units 6D/E, Bowburn North Industrial Estate, Bowburn, Co. Durham DH6 5PF
Tel/Fax (0191) 377 1991
☺ Brewery established in 1994 and enjoying continued growth, with plans to double its weekly output to 30 barrels a week in the pipeline.
Magus *(OG 1038, ABV 3.8%)* ◆ A hoppy beer with very light aroma but background malt character. Ends dry with complex aftertaste.
White Gold *(OG 1040, ABV 4%)*
White Velvet *(OG 1042, ABV 4.2%)* ◆ Smooth, golden bitter with a tangy hop and fruit taste. Aftertaste lingers with a pleasant, fruity.
Celtic *(OG 1043, ABV 4.2%)* ◆ A mid-brown ale with a slight malty and fruity aroma. The aftertaste is predominantly dry and well-balanced.
Canny Lad *(OG 1045, ABV 4.5%)*
White Bishop *(OG 1046, ABV 4.8%)*
Pagan *(OG 1047, ABV 4.8%)* ◆ There's a decent balance of malt and hops in this premium ale. Slight sweetness in the mouth and a faint bitter aftertaste are preceded by a hint of fruit in the aroma.
Cuthberts Ale *(OG 1048, ABV 5%)*
Sanctuary *(OG 1056, ABV 6%)* An old ale for winter.

DYFFRYN CLWYD

Bragdyr Dyffryn Clwyd, Chapel Place, Denbigh LL16 3TU *Tel (01745) 815007*
Tours by arrangement
☺ Brewery founded by local pub landlord Ioan Evans in 1994. Its beers, which have bilingual pump clips, are sold in free houses in North Wales and some outlets in England direct, and are more widely available in England via wholesalers. More permanent beers are planned; seasonal beers are also produced.
Dr Johnson's Draught *(OG 1035, ABV 3.6%)* ▦◐◆ Clean tasting and fruity, with a lasting bitter aftertaste.
Cwrw Arbennig Porthmon or Drovers Special Ale *(OG 1042, ABV 4.2%)*
Pedwar Bawd or Four Thumbs *(OG 1048, ABV 4.8%)* ◐ ◆ A well-balanced, fruity and sweetish bitter with a hint of caramel. Dryish aftertaste.

EARL SOHAM

⚲ Earl Soham Brewery, c/o The Victoria, Earl Soham, Suffolk IP13 7RL
Tel (01728) 723455
Bew ⊗ Brewery set up behind the Victoria in 1984, initially to supply just that pub. It expanded to supply a second tied house (since sold to Everards) and other pubs. The company ceased brewing for a while in 1996, but has since acquired another tied house and sales to the free trade (eight outlets) are healthy. Seasonal beer: Jolabrugg (OG 1055, ABV 5%, Christmas).

Gannet Mild *(OG 1034, ABV 3.3%)*
An unusual, full-tasting mild with a bitter finish and roast flavours which compete with underlying maltiness.

Victoria Bitter *(OG 1037, ABV 3.6%)*
A characterful, well-hopped, malty beer with a tangy, hoppy aftertaste.

Sir Roger's Porter *(OG 1042, ABV 4.1%)* Full-flavoured dark brown malty beer with bitter overtones, and a fruity aftertaste.

Albert Ale *(OG 1045, ABV 4.4%)* Hops dominate every aspect of this beer, but especially the finish. A fruity, astringent beer.

EASINGWOLD

⚲ Easingwold Brewery, Station Hotel, Knott Lane, Raskelf Road, Easingwold, N. Yorkshire YO6 3NT
Tel (01347) 822635 Fax (01347) 823491
Tours by arrangement
⊗ Brewery set up in a stable block behind the Station Hotel in May 1996, supplying the hotel itself and beer festivals. Now a further seven local outlets take the beer. The range has expanded, with new brews following the railway theme.

Tender Mild *(OG 1035, ABV 3.4%)*
A thin, dark brown mild with traces of roast malt and chocolate flavours. A session beer.

Steamcock Bitter *(OG 1038, ABV 3.8%)* ♦ A sweet, malty bitter. The predominant aroma is of fruit. Maltiness is balanced by a slight bitterness in the aftertaste.

Express *(OG 1047, ABV 4.6%)* ♦ A full-bodied, well-balanced, amber-coloured premium bitter. Fruit and malt attack the nose and front of the tongue, joined later by a pleasant hoppiness and a strong, fruity, bittersweet aftertaste.

Pullman Porter *(OG 1050, ABV 5%)*
A porter featuring roast malts, with a hint of chocolate in the flavour and aroma, and a clean, dry finish.

EAST-WEST ALES

See Brewery on Sea and Cotleigh.

EASTWOOD'S

Eastwood's Brewery, Barge & Bank, Park Road, Elland, W. Yorkshire
Tel (01484) 656024
⊗ Originally set up in Huddersfield. Since then the beer range has been expanded and recipes refined. The company sells to 12 local outlets. The company is presently in the process of moving site. Beers: Best Bitter (ABV 3.9%), Reserve (ABV 4.3%), Nettlethrasher (ABV 4.4%), Black Stump (ABV 5.1%), Leveller (ABV 5.7%), Myrtle's Temper (ABV 7%).

ECCLESHALL

Eccleshall Brewery, George Hotel, Castle Street, Eccleshall, Stafford ST21 6DF
Tel (01785) 850300 Fax (01785) 851452
Tours by arrangement
⊗ Brewery opened in outbuildings behind the George Hotel in 1995. The brewery was extended two years later and further extensions are planned to cope with the demand (currently 450 outlets) for its award-winning 'Slaters Ales'. Seasonal beer: Hi Duck (OG 1041, ABV 4.1%, Easter).

Slaters Bitter *(OG 1035, ABV 3.6%)*
🍺♦ Malt and hops combine with a fruity flavour in this light amber beer.

Slaters Original *(OG 1040, ABV 4%)*
A distinctive, creamy amber beer.

Top Totty *(OG 1040, ABV 4%)* A new summer beer.

Slaters Premium *(OG 1044, ABV 4.4%)* Strong, but light and creamy, dry bitter, darker than the other brews.

Slaters Supreme *(OG 1044, ABV 4.7%)*
A well-hopped, dry bitter added to the range in 1997.

ELDRIDGE POPE

See Thomas Hardy and Pub Groups.

ELGOOD'S

Elgood & Sons Ltd, North Brink Brewery, Wisbech, Cambridgeshire PE13 1LN
Tel (01945) 583160 Fax (01945) 587711
Shop Tours by arrangement
⊗ Based in Georgian, riverside premises, converted in 1786 from a mill and granary and acquired by the Elgood family in 1877, this brewery is one of the few remaining to use open copper coolers. It supplies real ale to all but one of its 45 tied houses, to a free trade of around 200 outlets, and to other pubs throughout England and Wales via wholesalers. In 1998 the brewery gardens, newly remodelled in period style, opened to visitors; there is also a museum and shop. Seasonal beers: Barleymead (OG 1049, ABV 4.8%, September); North Brink Porter (OG 1056, ABV 5%), Reinbeer (OG 1061, ABV 5.9%, Christmas), Wenceslas Winter Warmer (OG 1076, ABV 7.5%, December).

Black Dog Mild *(OG 1037, ABV 3.6%)*
🍺♦ Black and ruby ale with a gentle, fruity aroma, then dry roast malt and hops and a lingering, dry roast finish.

Cambridge Bitter *(OG 1038, ABV 3.8%)* ♦ Pale, dry, session bitter, with a light, malty aroma, restrained hop and some fruit in the balanced palate, which ends notably dry.

Pageant Ale *(OG 1044, ABV 4.3%)*

Golden Newt *(OG 1046, ABV 4.6%)* ♦ Fragrant hops and orange fruit aromas introduce this golden bitter. Citrus, resiny hop fills the mouth, and the finish is delightfully bitter, with hops and fruit persisting.

Old Black Shuck *(OG 1046, ABV 4.5%)*
A new winter beer.

Greyhound Strong Bitter *(OG 1053, ABV 5.2%)* ♦ Full-bodied, tawny brew, with a mouthfilling blend of malty sweetness and fruit. Starts with berry fruits on the nose and ends surprisingly bitter.

MARTIN ELMS

See Nethergate.

ENVILLE

Enville Ales, Enville Brewery, Cox Green, Enville, Stourbridge, W. Midlands DY7 5LG
Tel (01384) 873728 Fax (01384) 873770
⊛ Brewery on a picturesque Victorian farm complex. Using the same water source as the original village brewery (closed in 1919), the beers also incorporate over three tons of honey annually (produced on the farm), using recipes passed down from the proprietor's great-great aunt. Enville's owner had originally intended to go into full-time bee-keeping with brewing as a sideline, but the position is now reversed; the brewery grows its own barley, too. Enville (in Staffordshire, despite the postal address) also runs the Victoria Pub Co. and supplies around 80 outlets with the beers.
Bitter *(OG 1038, ABV 3.8%)* ❧ A straw-coloured, hoppy and bitter beer which leaves a malty, moreish aftertaste.
Low Gravity Mild *(OG 1038, ABV 3.8%)*
Simpkiss Bitter *(OG 1038, ABV 3.9%)* ❧ A medium-bodied, golden bitter. The refreshing, hoppy taste lingers.
White *(OG 1042, ABV 4%)* ❧ A clean, well-balanced, golden, sweet bitter, light in flavour. An appealing beer.
Ale *(OG 1045, ABV 4.5%)* 🍺🍴❧ A pale gold, medium-bodied bitter. Light hops and sweet fruit in the taste; a hint of honey in the aroma and aftertaste.
Gothic *(OG 1054, ABV 5.2%)* ❧ Malt, hops and caramel combine with a strong roast malt taste in this dark, stout-like beer. Well-balanced, with lurking hints of honey. Available October-March.

EVENING STAR

See Dark Star.

EVERARDS

Everards Brewery Ltd, Castle Acres, Narborough, Leicester LE9 5BY
Tel (0116) 201 4100 Fax (0116) 281 4199
Tours by arrangement (CAMRA members)
⊠ Small, forward-looking, family-owned brewery, founded in Leicester in 1849 by William Everard, great-great-grandfather of the current chairman, Richard Everard. Production was transferred to Castle Acres in 1991. Its gradually expanding tied estate of 155 pubs includes many attractive, historic houses, and over 90 per cent of them sell cask ale (but with the occasional use of cask breathers). Everards also supplies ale to some 500 free trade accounts, and the beers (particularly Tiger) are available nationally via wholesalers, retailers and other brewers. Seasonal beers: Mild (OG 1036, ABV 3.3%), Equinox (OG 1048, ABV 4.8% autumn), Nutcracker

EVERARDS
ESTABLISHED 1849

Winter Ale (OG 1048, ABV 5%), which replaces Daredevil (ABV 7.1%).
Beacon Bitter *(OG 1036, ABV 3.8%)* 🍺❧ A refreshing, well-balanced, mid-brown session beer that has a malty, hoppy bitterness in the taste. This leads to a long, dry, bitter finish that is quite sulphurous. Indeed, sulphur is present throughout.
Tiger Best *(OG 1041, ABV 4.2%)* 🍺❧ Mid-brown and smooth, this bitter has a gentle aroma of malt, hops and fruit, leading to a well-balanced palate and dry finish.
Old Original *(OG 1050, ABV 5.2%)* ❧ The sulphurous, hop/malt aroma of this mid-brown brew leads to a complex taste dominated by a bitter maltiness. Fresh beer seems to be 'peppery' in the nose and throat!

For Whitbread:
Chester's Best Mild *(OG 1032, ABV 3.5%)*

EVESHAM

⛨ **SM Murphy Associates Ltd, The Evesham Brewery, The Green Dragon, 17 Oat Street, Evesham, Worcestershire WR11 4PJ**
Tel (01386) 443462 Fax (01386) 443462
Tours by arrangement
⊛ Brewery set up in 1992 in the old bottle store at the Green Dragon Inn in Evesham. The owner and licensee, Steve Murphy, who also owns another pub, currently supplies another four outlets direct. The brewery has become something of a tourist attraction, drawing thousands of visitors each year. 'Asum' in the beer names is the local pronunciation of Evesham. Seasonal beer: Santa's Nightmare (OG 1060, ABV 6%).
Asum Ale *(OG 1038, ABV 3.8%)* ❧ Smooth, multi-flavoured drink with plenty of fruitiness on the tongue. Very enjoyable throughout.
Asum Gold *(OG 1050, ABV 5.2%)* ❧ A copper-coloured premium bitter that has a distinctly sharp, fruity taste to satisfy the palate.

EXE VALLEY

Exe Valley Brewery, Lan d Farm, Silverton, Exeter, Devon EX5 4HF
Tel (01392) 860406 Fax (01392) 860406
Tours by arrangement
⊠ Founded as Barron Brewery in 1984 by Richard Barron, this company's name changed in 1991 with the expansion of the brewery, when Guy Sheppard became a partner. It operates from an old barn (using the farm's own spring water), using new plant installed in 1993 which trebled capacity. The brewery supplies 30 regular outlets and 30 more on an occasional basis within a 30-mile radius and other customers nationally via wholesalers.
Occasional beer: Barron's Dark (OG 1039, ABV 4.1%).
Bitter *(OG 1038, ABV 3.7%)* ❧ A light

brown beer with a fruity, malty aroma, a crisp, clean palate, a predominately fruit taste, with a bitter finish.

Devon Summer *(OG 1039, ABV 3.9%)* A fruity nose with a complex bitter/malt taste and finish. A seasonal beer.

Barron's Hopsit *(OG 1040, ABV 4.1%)* ◆ Straw-coloured beer with strong hop aroma, hop and fruit flavour and a bitter hop finish.

Dob's Best Bitter *(OG 1040, ABV 4.1%)* ◼◆ A light brown brew with a fruity nose and taste and a pleasant, bitter, hopped finish.

Spring Beer *(OG 1042, ABV 4.3%)* ◆ A straw-coloured beer with a malt and fruit aroma and taste before a bitter finish.

Autumn Glory *(OG 1044, ABV 4.5%)* ◆ Smooth, slightly smoky, malty, mid-brown beer.

Devon Glory *(OG 1046, ABV 4.7%)* ◆ Mid-brown, fruity-tasting pint with a sweet, fruity finish.

Sheppard's Crook *(OG 1046, ABV 4.7%)*

Exeter Old Bitter *(OG 1047, ABV 4.8%)* ◆ A well-balanced beer with a malt/fruit aroma and taste, and a complex, sweet, fruity finish.

Winter Glow *(OG 1058, ABV 6%)* ◆ A dark, fruity beer through the aroma, taste and aftertaste.

EXMOOR

Exmoor Ales Ltd, Golden Hill Brewery, Wiveliscombe, Somerset TA4 2NY
Tel (01984) 623798 Fax (01984) 624572
Tours by arrangement
⊗ Somerset's largest brewery was founded in 1980 in the old Hancock's brewery, which had been closed since 1959. It quickly won national acclaim, as its Exmoor Ale took the Best Bitter award at CAMRA's Great British Beer Festival, the first of many prizes. The brewery has enjoyed many years of continuous expansion and steadily increasing demand. Around 250 pubs in the South-West are supplied directly, and others nationwide via wholesalers and pub chains. Seasonal beer: Exmas (OG 1050, ABV 5%, November-December). Also brews Double Dragon.

Ale *(OG 1039, ABV 3.8%)* ◆ A pale brown beer with a malty aroma, a malty, dry taste and a bitter and malty finish. Very drinkable.

Fox *(OG 1043, ABV 4.2%)*

Gold *(OG 1045, ABV 4.5%)* ◆ Yellow/golden in colour, with a malty aroma and flavour, and a slight sweetness and hoppiness. Sweet, malty finish.

Hart *(OG 1049, ABV 4.8%)*

Stag *(OG 1050, ABV 5.2%)* ◆ A pale brown beer, with a malty taste and aroma, and a bitter finish. Slightly sweet. Very similar to Exmoor Ale and drinks as easily.

Beast *(OG 1066, ABV 6.6%)* ◼ A winter brew, available October-Easter.

FAR NORTH

⬯ Far North Brewery, Melvich Hotel, Melvich, by Thurso, Sutherland KW14 7YJ
Tel (01641) 531206 Fax (01641) 531 347
Currently brewing just for his own hotel on an irregular basis, Peter Martin has plans to expand his new brewery to supply other Highland outlets. Beer: Real Mackay (OG 1042, ABV 4.1%).

FARMERS ARMS

Mayhem Brewery, Lower Apperley, Gloucestershire GL19 4DR
Tel (01452) 780172 Fax (01452) 780307
⊗ Brewery opened in 1992 in a thatched barn in the grounds of the Farmers Arms, which also produces its own cider. In October 1996 it was taken over by Wadworth. The beers are available only at the pub.

Odda's Light *(OG 1038, ABV 3.8%)* ◆ A hoppy, refreshing, golden bitter with a clean, bitter taste and a lingering hint of malt followed by a bitter aftertaste.

Mayhem's Sundowner *(OG 1044, ABV 4.5%)* ◆ Malt predominates in this smooth, easy-drinking bitter with a slight bittersweet aftertaste.

FARMERS BOY

See Verulam Brewery.

FAT GOD'S

See Queen's Head.

FEATHERSTONE

Featherstone Brewery, Unit 3, King Street Buildings, King Street, Enderby, Leicestershire LE9 5NT
Tel (0116) 275 0952 Fax (0116) 275 0952
⊗ Small brewery which has moved site several times. It specialises in supplying custom beers to pubs for sale under house names, and turnover has grown considerably since it started in 1989. Four local outlets take the beers regularly. Occasional beer: Vulcan (OG 1049, ABV 5.1%, brewed to order).

Hows Howler *(OG 1036, ABV 3.6%)*

Best Bitter *(OG 1042, ABV 4.2%)*

Stage Ale *(OG 1045, ABV 4.8%)*

Kingstone Bitter *(ABV 7.2%)* A winter brew.

FEDERATION

Federation Brewery Ltd, Lancaster Road, Dunston, Tyne & Wear NE11 9JR
Tel (0191) 460 9023 Fax (0191) 460 1297
Tours by arrangement
⊚ Federation was founded as a co-operative by local clubs in 1919, to overcome the post-war beer shortage. After 50 years at John Buchanan's Brewery, expansion demanded a move to a green-field site at Dunston in the early 1980s. The brewery is still owned by local clubs, and their business accounts for the majority of the brewery's trade. Cask beers were reinstated in 1986, but only since the introduction of the Buchanan range in 1991 have sales taken off.

Buchanan's Best Bitter *(OG 1036, ABV 3.6%)* Very difficult to find, especially on top form, when it has a pleasant aroma, a bitter flavour and a well-balanced aftertaste, with a hint of fruit throughout. Really an ordinary bitter, not a best.

Buchanan's Original *(OG 1045, ABV 4.4%)* ◆ A rich, ruby-red bitter with a smooth, creamy taste and lingering mouthfeel. A robust malt character makes this a

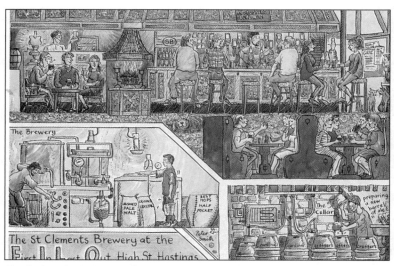

First In, Last Out began brewing ten years ago and this drawing depicts how brew-pubs operate (all the characters pictured are real!). The brewpub is a rapidly growing phenomeon. Some brewers have gone into partnership with pubs as this guarantees them an outlet in a time of rationalisation of beer lists by major purchasers.

better-than-average drinking bitter.
Rupert Tetlow Tummy Tickler
(ABV 4.7%)

FELDON

Feldon Brewery, Coach & Horses, 16 New Street, Shipston- on-Stour, Warwickshire CV36 4EN
Brewing ceased.

FELINFOEL

Felinfoel Brewery Co. Ltd, Farmers Row, Felinfoel, Llanelli, Dyfed SA14 8LB
Tel (01554) 773357 Fax (01554) 752452
Shop Mon-Thu 9-4.30, Fri 9-3
⊕ This renowned Welsh brewery was built by David John in 1878, when the village brewpub could no longer keep up with demand. Famously, it was the first brewery in Europe to can beer (in the 1930s). Still family owned, Felinfoel now supplies cask ale to most of its 80 houses (though some use top pressure) and to roughly 50 free trade outlets.
Bitter *(OG 1032, ABV 3.2%)* ✦ A pale brown, hoppy, fruity beer with a hint of sulphur and a trace of malt. Balanced hoppy and fruity finish.
Dark *(OG 1032, ABV 3.2%)* ✦ A dark brown/red mild, rather thin, with a slightly bitter flavour and aftertaste.

FENLAND

The Fenland Brewery, Unit 4, Prospect Way, Chatteris, Cambridgeshire PE16 6TY
Tel (01354) 696776 Fax (01354) 695852
Tours by arrangement
⊗ Research chemist Dr Rob Thomas set up his new brewery in Chatteris early in 1997, so opening the first brewery in the town for 65 years. With two awards already under its belt and some 30 outlets to supply locally, the brewery looks set to expand. Occasional

beers: Tall Tale Pale Ale (ABV 3.6%), Smokestack Lightning (ABV 4.2%), Fractale (ABV 4.5%). Bottle-conditioned beers: Sparkling Wit (ABV 4.5%), Doctor's Orders (ABV 5%).
FBB *(OG 1043, ABV 4%)* ✦ Pale copper brew with a good balance of mouth-filling hops, malt and fruit. Starts with berry fruits on the nose and ends dry with hops and malt.
Sparkling Wit *(ABV 4.5%)* A wheat beer for spring and summer.
Doctor's Orders *(OG 1051, ABV 5%)*
Rudolph's Rocket Fuel/Winter Warmer *(ABV 5.5%)* ✦ Strong, pungent ginger spice dominates the aroma and taste of this warming, winter brew. There is also fruit, cinnamon and a hint of roast malt in the mouth, but a surprisingly restained, bittersweet finish.

FERNANDES

Fernandes Brewery, The Old Malthouse, Savison Yard, Kirkgate, Wakefield, W. Yorkshire WF1 1VA
Tel (01924) 291709 Fax (01924) 369547
Shop 10-6 Mon-Wed, 10-8 Thu-Sat Tours by arrangement
⊕ This brewery was established in 1997 in the former malt kiln of the Fernandes & Co. Ale & Porter brewery, which ceased trading in 1919. The names of the beers are taken from lost Wakefield pubs.
Old Bridge Bitter *(OG 1040, ABV 4.1%)*
Wheatsheaf Wheat Beer *(OG 1040, ABV 4.1%)*
Wakefield Pride *(OG 1043, ABV 4.5%)*
Double Six *(OG 1055, ABV 6%)*
Empress of India *(OG 1055, ABV 6%)*

FIDDLERS

Fiddlers Ales Ltd, The Brewhouse, The Fox & Crown, Church Street, Old Basford, Nottinghamshire NG6 OGA
Tel/Fax (0115) 942 2002
Tours by arrangement
Using brand new plant originally destined for the USA, this brewery was installed in autumn 1996 and went into service in December. Initially brewing solely for the Fox & Crown, Fiddlers now supplies around 20 local outlets. Occasional/seasonal beers: Old Basford Pale Ale (OG 1052, ABV 5.2%), Ruby Ale (OG 1055, ABV 5.5), Old Fashioned Porter (OG 1065, ABV 6.6%).
Mild *(OG 1034, ABV 3.4%)*
Best Bitter *(OG 1037, ABV 3.7%)*
Summer Ale *(OG 1040, ABV 4.2%)* A seasonal offering.
Finest *(OG 1045, ABV 4.5%)*

FIRKIN
See Nationals, Carlsberg-Tetley.

FIRST IN, LAST OUT
⊡ FILO Brewery, 14-15 High Street, Old Town, Hastings, E. Sussex TN34 3EY
Tel (01424) 425079 Fax (01424) 447141
Tours by arrangement
The First In Last Out began brewing in 1985 and changed hands three years later. Restricted by space, it brews just for the one pub and beer festivals. The ABVs of the beers can vary. Beers: Crofters (OG 1040, ABV 4%), Cardinal (OG 1045, ABV 4.3%).

FLAGSHIP
The Flagship Brewery, Unit 2, Building 64, The Historic Dockyard, Chatham, Kent ME4 4TE
Tel (01634) 832828 **Tours by arrangement**
⊠ Brewery set up in 1995 in Chatham's preserved Georgian dockyard, now a major tourist draw. A visitor centre at the brewery features an exhibition about beer and the Navy, and a display of labels from defunct Medway breweries. Some 50 outlets are supplied direct, and other pubs throughout the UK take the beer via wholesalers. It is also due to start operating at an additional site, a brewpub, in autumn 1998. Occasional/seasonal beers: Victory Mild (OG 1036, ABV 3.5%), Frigging Yuletide (OG 1052, ABV 5.5%), Old Sea Dog Stout (OG 1052, ABV 5.5%), Nelson's Blood (OG 1056, ABV 6%).
Capstan Ale *(OG 1038, ABV 3.8%)*
A medium-dry beer with a balanced malt and hop flavour and hints of honey.
Spring Pride *(OG 1042, ABV 4%)* A seasonal beer.
Ensign Ale *(OG 1042, ABV 4.2%)* A fruity ale, with a good balance of malt and hops.
Spanker *(OG 1042, ABV 4.2%)* A version of Ensign.
Friggin in the Riggin *(OG 1045, ABV 4.7%)* A premium bitter with a smooth malt flavour and a bittersweet aftertaste.
Crow's Nest *(OG 1048, ABV 4.8%)*
A straw-coloured, sweet and fruity ale with a hoppy aroma.
Futtock Ale *(OG 1050, ABV 5.2%)* A fruity, ruby-coloured ale, with a roast malt aftertaste.

FLANNERY'S
Flannery's, 1 High Street, Aberystwyth, SY23 1JG *Tel (01970) 612334*
Tours by arrangement
Flannery's started brewing just for the pub's own consumption in May 1997 and by September was running at full capacity. Work started on a new brewhouse in January 1998 to house a 40-barrel plant to supply a second tied house and a growing number of other outlets (currently 30). Seasonal beer: Noidea (OG 1055, Christmas).
Granny Flans *(OG 1036, ABV %)*
A pale/golden brown beer with a dry, crisp hop aroma. Not too bitter, but surprisingly dry.
Celtic Ale *(OG 1042, ABV %)*
A complex malty and bitter taste with a hint of fruit.
Oatmeal Stout *(OG 1044, ABV %)* A balance of pale malt, roasted barley, chocolate malt and a special blend of oats. Its full character is brought out by the use of Irish North Down hops. Overall Champion Beer at the Narbeth beer festival.

FLOWER POTS INN
See Cheriton.

FLOWERS
See Nationals, Whitbread.

FLYING FIRKIN
See Dent.

FOUR RIVERS
Four Rivers Brewing Company Ltd, Hadrian Brewery, Unit 10, Hawick Crescent Industrial Estate, Newcastle-upon-Tyne, Tyne & Wear NE6 1AS
Tel (0191) 276 5302 Fax (0191) 276 5302
Tours by arrangement
☺ Brewery founded in October 1996 by former Tap & Spile executive Mike Wallbank and former Hadrian brewer Trevor Smith. In spring 1997 Four Rivers acquired the assets, site and trading names of the closed Hadrian Brewery. The old Hadrian brands have been revived and are sold alongside Four Rivers beers in around 50 pubs in the 'four rivers' trading area (bounded by the rivers Tyne, Wear, Tees and Humber). The company acquired its first pub in December 1997 and further acquisitions are planned. It brews a single beer for Pubmaster Celebration Alehouses. Seasonal beer: Emperor (ABV 5%).
Moondance *(OG 1038, ABV 3.8%)* ◆
Dry, bitter ale. Initial hop and fruit taste with hints of malt intensifies into a long, fruity aftertaste.
Hadrian Gladiator *(OG 1040, ABV 4%)* ◆ A good, amber session beer with a hoppy taste and bitter finish.
Hadrian Legion Ale *(OG 1042, ABV 4.2%)* ⬚
Rowan Ale *(ABV 4.2%)*
Hadrian Centurion *(OG 1045, ABV 4.5%)*
Hadrian Emperor Ale *(OG 1050,*

ABV 5%)

For Pubmaster:
Celebration Alehouse Bitter *(OG 1037, ABV 3.7%)*

FOX AND HOUNDS (BARLEY)
Barley Brewery, Barley, Hertfordshire
Ceased brewing.

FOX & HOUNDS
♥ Woody Woodward's Brewery, c/o The
Fox & Hounds, High Street, Stottesdon,
Shropshire DY14 8TZ *Tel (01746) 718222*
Tours by arrangement
☻ Brewing commenced at this pub in 1979
and was taken over 10 years later by Glen
Woodward. The beers are sold at the pub
and to the free trade via wholesalers. He also
brews under contract for the Blackbeard
Trading Company, tel: (01584) 872908. The
'wust' and 'bostin' in the beer names are
Black Country expressions meaning worst
and best. Beers: Lemon Ale (ABV 4%), Wust
Bitter (OG 1037, ABV 3.7%), Bostin Bitter
(OG 1043, ABV 4.2%), Wild Mild (OG
1043, ABV 4.2%), Gobstopper Bitter (OG
1060, ABV 6%, winter).

**For Blackbeard Trading: Brew
37** *(OG 1052, ABV 5.1%)*

FOX & HOUNDS (STRATHCLYDE)
See Houston.

FOXFIELD BREWERY
Foxfield Brewery, Prince of Wales, Foxfield,
Broughton-in-Furness, Cumbria CA 20 6BX
Tel (01229)716238
See Prince of Wales and Tigertops.

FRANKLIN'S
Franklin's Brewery, Bilton Lane, Bilton,
Harrogate, N. Yorkshire HG1 4DH
Tel (01423) 322345
☻ Brewery set up in 1980 and now run by
Leeds CAMRA founder-member Tommy
Thomas, supplying guest beers to eight pubs
in N. Yorkshire, plus beer festivals.
Occasional beers: Summer Blotto (OG 1047,
ABV 4.7%), Winter Blotto (OG 1047, ABV
4.7%).
Bitter *(OG 1038, ABV 3.8%)* ◆ A tremen-
dous hop aroma precedes a flowery hop
flavour, combined with malt. Long, hoppy,
bitter finish. A fine, unusual amber bitter.
DT's *(OG 1045, ABV 4.5%)*

FREEDOM
Freedom Brewing Company Ltd, The
Coachworks, 80 Parsons Green Lane,
Fulham, London SW6 4HU
Tel (0171) 731 7372 Fax (0171) 731 1218
Tours by arrangement
☒ Brewery opened in 1995, as the first dedi-
cated lager micro-brewer in the UK. Aiming
to put the taste back into the style, it brews
unpasteurised premium lagers following the
edicts of the German Beer Purity Law. The
beers are available in over 300 London bars.

FREEMINER
Freeminer Brewery Ltd, The Laurels, Sling,
Coleford, Gloucestershire GL16 8JJ
Tel (01594) 810408 Fax (01594) 810640
Tours by arrangement
☒ Established at the edge of the Forest of
Dean in 1992, Freeminer is now brewing to
full capacity. It has one tied house (the
Miners Arms in Sling) and supplies 60 free
trade outlets directly, plus others nationwide
via wholesalers. Freeminer is one of six partners in the Wessex Co-operative set up in
1995 by a group of West Country micros to
share bottling facilities. Currently 20 per
cent of Freeminer's output is bottled. Bottle-
conditioned beers: Bitter (OG 1038, ABV
4%), Speculation Ale (OG 1047, ABV
4.7%), Shakemantle Ginger Ale (OG 1050,
ABV 5%), Slaughter Porter (OG 1050, ABV
5%), Trafalgar IPA (OG 1060, ABV 6%),
Deep Shaft Stout (OG 1060, ABV 6.2%).
Bitter *(OG 1038, ABV 4%)* ◆ A light,
hoppy bitter with a wonderful hop aroma
and a very dry, hoppy finish. Very moreish.
Strip and At It *(OG 1038, ABV 4%)* ◆
A pale summer bitter with a refreshing,
hoppy taste and a smooth, hoppy finish with
a hint of bitterness.
Iron Brew *(OG 1044, ABV 4.2%)* A
ruby red bitter with a rich malt character
with some hopiness.
Speculation Ale *(OG 1047, ABV 4.8%)*
◆ An aromatic, chestnut-brown beer with a
smooth, well-balanced mix of malt and hops
and a predominantly hoppy aftertaste.
Celestial Steam Gale *(OG 1050, ABV
5%)* ◆ A pale, full-bodied ale. Bitterness is
immediately present, with some hoppiness in
the mouth and finish.
Gold Standard *(OG 1050, ABV 5%)*
A new addition to the range made with First
Gold hop variety.
Hopewell Special *(OG 1050, ABV 5%)*
An annual brew using the season's first hops.
Shakemantle Ginger Ale *(OG 1050,
ABV 5%)* ▦◆ A refreshing ginger ale
brewed for summer. Unfined, with a high
wheat content, it is like a European-style
wheat beer. Ginger dominates throughout,
mingled with a light hoppiness.
Slaughter Porter *(OG 1050, ABV 5%)*
◆ A dark, full-bodied ale, mainly produced
for spring and autumn. The roast malt
flavour is followed by a hoppy finish.
Deep Shaft Stout *(OG 1060, ABV
6.2%)* ◆ A black, complex stout. A roast
malt and bitter chocolate flavour hits you
immediately, followed by dry, bitter aftertaste.
Trafalgar IPA *(OG 1060, ABV 6%)* ◆
Pale, heavily hopped traditional IPA with a
pronounced bitterness. Hoppy nose, malt
and hops on the palage and a dry, hoppy finish.

FREMLINS
See Nationals, Whitbread.

FRIARY MEUX
See Nationals, Carlsberg-Tetley.

FROG ISLAND
Frog Island Brewery, The Maltings,

Westbridge, St. James Road, Northampton NN5 5HS *Tel (01604) 587772 Fax (01604) 750754* **Tours by arrangement**
⊠ Based in an old malthouse, once owned by the defunct Thomas Manning brewery, this company has been in operation since 1994 and is about to double the size of its plant. Frog Island is a local name for an area once prone to flooding. 150 free trade outlets are currently supplied. Personalised bottled beers are produced to order. Seasonal beers: Fuggled Frog Mild (OG 1035, ABV 3.5%, May), Head in the Clouds (OG 1044, ABV 4.4%, August). Bottle-conditioned beers: Fire Bellied Toad (OG 1048, ABV 5%), Croak & Stagger (OG 1058, ABV 5.6%).
Best Bitter *(OG 1040, ABV 3.8%)* A fairly complex beer, with malt, roast malt and fruit, plus a hint of sulphur, before a powerful kick of hop bitterness and astringency in the aftertaste. Pale brown in colour, and light on the tongue.
Shoemaker *(OG 1044, ABV 4.2%)* The Cascade hop citrus notes on the tongue are preceded by a huge malty aroma with passion fruit and roast characteristics. The malty aftertaste fades into a dry, nuttiness. Rich, pale brown and complex.
Fire Bellied Toad *(OG 1045, ABV 4.4%)*
Natterjack *(OG 1048, ABV 4.8%)* Deceptively robust, golden and smooth. Fruit and hop aromas fight for dominance before the grainy astringency and floral palate give way to a long, strong, dry aftertaste with a hint of lingering malt.
Croak & Stagger *(OG 1056, ABV 5.8%)* The initial honey/fruit aroma is quickly overpowered by roast malt then bitter chocolate and pale malt sweetness on the tongue. Gentle, bittersweet finish. A winter brew.

FROG & PARROT
See Nationals, Whitbread.

FROMES HILL
⬚ The Wheatsheaf Inn & Fromes Hill Brewery, Wheatsheaf Inn, Fromes Hill, nr Ledbury, Herefordshire HR8 1HT *Tel/Fax (01531) 640888* **Tours by arrangement**
⊠ Brewery founded in 1993, supplying the Wheatsheaf and four other outlets with beers produced with local hops. Beers: Buckswood Dingle (OG 1038, ABV 3.6%), Overture (OG 1042, ABV 4.2%).

FROME VALLEY BREWERY
Frome Valley Brewery, Mayfields, Bishop's Frome, Herefordshire via Worcestershire, WR5 5AS *Tel (01531) 640321*
Brewery founded in May 1997 and established in a former 18th-century hop kiln in the depth of the Frome Valley. It supplies the local pub and other outlets.

Frome Valley Premium Bitter *(OG 1038, ABV 3.8%)* A traditional beer, good bitterness, with a light aroma. Local hops and spring water used.

FRUITERER'S ARMS
See Cannon Royall.

FULLER'S
Fuller, Smith and Turner PLC, Griffin Brewery, Chiswick Lane South, Chiswick, London W4 2QB *Tel (0181) 996 2000 Fax (0181) 996 2079* **Shop 10-6 Mon-Sat Tours by arrangement**
⊠ Beer has been brewed on the Fuller's site for over 325 years, John Fuller being joined by Henry Smith and John Turner in 1845. Descendants of the original partners are still on the board today. In the early 1990s the brewery underwent a £1.6 million brewhouse redevelopment to cope with growing demand, and the installation of new mash tuns led to an increase in capacity of 50 per cent. Fuller's owns 210 pubs, roughly half of which are managed and half tenanted, and all serve its award-winning real ale. Fuller's also supplies 350 outlets within a 50-mile radius of Chiswick. Occasional/seasonal beers: Honey Dew (OG 1042, ABV 4.3%), Old Winter Ale (OG 1044, ABV 4.8%), Red Fox (OG 1044, ABV 4.3%). Bottle-conditioned beer: 1845 Celebration Ale (OG 1062, ABV 6.3%)◫⬚.
Chiswick Bitter *(OG 1034, ABV 3.5%)* ◆ A distinctively hoppy, refreshing beer, with underlying maltiness and a lasting bitter finish. Champion Beer of Britain 1989.
Summer Ale *(OG 1037, ABV 3.9%)* ◆ A refreshing, golden, hoppy bitter with balancing malt flavour. Available June-September.
London Pride *(OG 1040, ABV 4.1%)*◫◆ An award-winning beer with a good, malty base and a rich balance of well-developed hop flavours.
ESB *(OG 1054, ABV 5.5%)* ◫◆ A strong and aromatic beer of great character. The immediate, full-bodied maltiness gives way to a rich hoppiness in the finish.

FYFE
⬚ Fyfe Brewing Company, 469 High Street, Kirkcaldy, Fife KY1 2SN *Tel/Fax (01592) 646211* **Tours by arrangement**
⊛ Established in 1995 behind the Harbour Bar, this is Fife's first brew pub this century. Most of the output is taken by the pub, the remainder being sold direct to 20 local outlets and to the free trade via wholesalers. Seasonal beer: Cauld Turkey (OG 1060, ABV 6%, Christmas).
Rope of Sand *(OG 1037, ABV 3.7%)* ◆ Named after the legendary local Rope of Sand, this is a quenching bitter. Malt and fruit throughout, with a hoppy, bitter aftertaste.
Auld Alliance *(OG 1040, ABV 4%)* ◆ A very bitter beer with a lingering, dry, hoppy finish. Malt and hop, with fruit, are present throughout, fading in the finish.
Lion Slayer *(OG 1042, ABV 4.2%)*
Fyfe *(OG 1048, ABV 4.8%)* Golden,

GALES

George Gale & Co. Ltd, The Brewery,
Horndean, Hampshire PO8 0DA
Tel (01705) 571212 Fax (01705) 598641
Shop 10-5 Mon-Fri Tours by arrangement
⊗ Hampshire's major brewery, Gale's was
founded in 1847. The original building was
largely destroyed by fire and a new, enlarged
brewery was built on the site in 1869. This
was extended to incorporate a new brewhouse in 1983. A bottling line installed in
1997 is dedicated to packaging a new range
of bottle-conditioned, corked beers, while
retaining the Prize Old Ale which enjoys a
good export trade. Still family owned, the
company has grown slowly and steadily and
all 114 tied houses (which include some very
attractive old inns) serve real ale. Gale's also
supplies 550 free trade outlets directly, and
other pubs via the big breweries.
Occasional/seasonal beers: Trafalgar Ale
(OG 1041, ABV 4.2%, October),
Hampshire Glory (OG 1043, ABV 4.3%,
June), Harvest Ale (OG 1045, ABV 4.5%,
September), Force Eight (OG 1050, ABV
5%), Xmas Ale (OG 1056, ABV 5.5%).
Bottle-conditioned beer: Trafalgar Ale (OG
1090, ABV 9%), Prize Old Ale (OG 1095,
ABV 9%)◧⬚.
Butser Bitter *(OG 1034, ABV 3.4%)* ◆
A mid-brown chestnut beer. A slightly malty
and fruity aroma preludes a sweet taste, with
some fruit and malt. The aftertaste is sweet
and fruity with a little bitterness.
GB *(OG 1040, ABV 4%)* A medium-bodied, deep golden brown brew which is initially malty sweet, has a fruity middle period
with a hint of burnt orange and a dry hop
flower tasting bitter finish. Several of the
characteristics are ruined if served through a
sparkler.
Winter Brew *(OG 1044, ABV 4.2%)* ◆
A rich winter ale, containing Prize Old Ale.
Almost black in colour, it has a roast malt
aroma with fruit and caramel, all of which
are echoed in the taste and finish. Available
November-March.
HSB *(OG 1050, ABV 4.8%)* ◆ A mid-
brown beer with a fruity aroma. The full-
bodied, sweet and fruity taste, with some
maltiness, follows through to the aftertaste.
For those with a sweet tooth.
Festival Mild *(OG 1052, ABV 4.8%)* ◆
Black in colour, with a red tinge. The aroma
is fruity. A sweet, fruity and malty taste,
with some caramel, carries through to the
aftertaste, but with more bitterness.

GIBBS MEW

See See Badger, Ushers and Pub Groups.

GLENTWORTH

Glentworth Brewery, Glentworth House,
Crossfield Lane, Skellow, Doncaster,
S. Yorkshire DN6 8PL
Tel (01302) 725555 Fax (01302) 724133
◉ Brewery established in January 1996 in
former dairy outbuildings at the owners'
home. Deliveries are made direct to 100 out-
lets in Yorkshire, Lincolnshire, Derbyshire
and Nottinghamshire. Now brewing five-ten
barrels a week. Beers: Light Year (OG 1040,
ABV 3.9%), Northern Lights (OG 1040,
ABV 3.9%), Yorkshire Gold (OG 1043,

ABV 4.3%), Lightmaker (OG 1045, ABV
4.5%), Pot O'Gold (OG 1045, ABV 4.5%),
Full Monty (OG 1050, ABV 5%).
Dizzy Blonde *(ABV 4.5%)* ◆ A pale
brown, dry, premium bitter with a full body
and a satisfying and lasting bitterness. Good
hop aroma.
Old Flame *(ABV 4.5%)* ◆ Golden amber
premium beer with a good balance of malt,
hop and fruity flavours in both taste and finish.

GOACHER'S

P&DJ Goacher, Unit 8, Tovil Green
Business Park, Maidstone, Kent ME15 6TA
Tel (01622) 682112
Tours by arrangement
⊗ Kent's most successful small independent
brewer, set up in 1983 by Phil and Debbie
Goacher, producing all-malt ales with
Kentish hops for two tied houses and around
35 free trade outlets in the Maidstone area.
Special, a 75/25 per cent mix of Light and
Dark, is also available to pubs for sale under
house names.
Real Mild Ale *(OG 1033, ABV 3.4%)* ◧
A full-flavoured malty ale with a back-
ground bitterness.
Fine Light Ale *(OG 1036, ABV 3.7%)*
◧◆ A pale, golden brown bitter with a
strong, floral, hoppy aroma and aftertaste. A
very hoppy and moderately malty session
beer.
Best Dark Ale *(OG 1040, ABV 4.1%)*
An intensely bitter beer, balanced by a mod-
erate maltiness, with a complex aftertaste.
Now back to its original darker colour.
Crown Imperial Stout *(OG 1044, ABV
4.5%)* Brewed to celebrate Goachers' 15th
year - occasional brew.
Gold Star *(OG 1050, ABV 5.1%)* A pale
ale (now brewed all year)
Maidstone Porter *(OG 1050, ABV
5.1%)* A dark ruby winter beer with a roast
malt flavour.
Old Ale *(OG 1066, ABV 6.7%)* A black,
potent old ale, produced in winter only.

GODDARDS

Goddards Brewery, Barnsley Farm, Bullen
Road, Ryde, Isle of Wight PO33 1QF
Tel (01983) 611011 Fax (01983) 611012
⊗ Housed in a picturesque converted 18th-
century barn, on a farm near Ryde, this brewery went into production in 1993. Sales of its
award-winning beers have been rising steadily
and brewery capacity quadrupled in 1997,
although this is partly to allow for kegging
and the production of a new lager, Bazooka
(occasionally available cask-conditioned,
ABV 4%). A bottled (not bottle-conditioned)
version of Fuggle-Dee-Dum is produced using
equipment at King & Barnes. Around 40 outlets are supplied with the real ale.
Special Bitter *(OG 1039, ABV 4%)* ◧
◆ A refreshing, clean, easy-drinking bitter,
with a wonderful aroma of freshly-rubbed
hops that carries right through to a satisfying
aftertaste.
Fuggle-Dee-Dum *(OG 1048, ABV
4.8%)* ◧◆ An intensely flavoured, malty,
hoppy, strong ale that makes your mouth
water. Amber/brown in colour and full bodied.
Inspiration Ale *(OG 1052, ABV 5.2%)*
Winter Warmer *(OG 1052, ABV 5.2%)*

GOFF'S

Goff's Brewery Ltd, 9 Isbourne Way,
Winchcombe, Gloucestershire GL54 5NS
Tel (01242) 603383 Fax (01242) 603959
Tours by arrangement
⊗ Family concern which started brewing in
1994, using plant purchased from
Nethergate Brewery. Goff's now supplies
200 outlets.
Jouster *(OG 1040, ABV 4%)*▉▢◆ A very
drinkable, tawny-coloured ale, with a light
hoppiness in the aroma. It has a good balance of malt and bitterness in the mouth,
underscored by fruitiness, with a clean,
hoppy aftertaste.
White Knight *(OG 1046, ABV 4.7%)* ◆
A well-hopped bitter with a light colour and
full-bodied taste. Bitterness predominates in
the mouth and leads to a dry, hoppy aftertaste. Deceptively drinkable for its strength.
Black Knight *(OG 1053, ABV 5.3%)* ◆
A dark, ruby-red-tinted beer with a strong
chocolate malt aroma. It has a smooth, dry,
malty taste, with a subtle hoppiness, leading
to a dry finish. A classic winter porter.

GOLDFINCH

47 High East Street, Dorchester, Dorset DT1
1HU *Tel (01305) 264020*
⊗ Brewery established in 1987 at Tom
Brown's Public House, whose theme is
broadly based on *Tom Brown's Schooldays*.
A second tied house in Salisbury is also
called Tom Brown's. The brewery supplies
these two pubs and 15 other free trade outlets direct, plus others via wholesalers.
Tom Brown's Best Bitter *(OG 1039,
ABV 4%)* ◆⊛ A pale-coloured bitter which
is fruity in both aroma and taste, with hops
and some malt. The bittersweet taste gives
way to a predominantly bitter finish.
Flashman's Clout Strong Ale *(OG
1043, ABV 4.5%)* ◆ A tawny/mid-brown
beer with an attractive, honeyed aroma, and,
again, a bittersweet taste with malt and some
hops. Hoppiness continues through to give a
bitter edge to the aftertaste.
Midnight Blinder *(OG 1050, ABV 5%)*
◆ A ruby-red-coloured beer with an intense
fruit aroma. Malt, hops and fruit combine to
give the familiar bittersweet taste of
Goldfinch beers, leading into a marvellous
hoppy, bitter finish.

DOROTHYGOODBODY

See Wye Valley.

GOOSE EYE

Goose Eye Brewery, Ingrow Bridge, South
Street, Keighley, W. Yorkshire BD22 5AX
Tel (01535) 605807 Fax (01535) 605735
Tours by arrangement
⊚ After an absence of four years from the
brewing scene, Goose Eye was re-opened in
1991 in a converted carpet warehouse, and
the brewery has since then undergone a complete refurbishment. Around 50 free trade
outlets in North and West Yorkshire and
Lancashire take the beers, which are also
available through national wholesalers and
the Tap & Spile pub chain. Seasonal beer:
Christmas Goose (OG 1045, ABV 4.5%).
Bitter *(OG 1038, ABV 3.8%)* ◆ A fruity

aroma, hoppy fruit flavours and some malt
characterise this refreshing, gold-coloured
beer. The bitter finish is quite short.
Bronte *(OG 1040, ABV 4%)* ◆ A gold-
coloured bitter whose malty aroma is followed by a slightly sweet, malty taste, with
some hoppy and fruity notes. The aftertaste is
short.
Spellbound *(OG 1040, ABV 4%)*
Summer Jacks *(OG 1042, ABV 4.2%)*
A seasonal beer.
Wharfedale *(OG 1045, ABV 4.5%)* A
copper-coloured best bitter, becoming
increasingly hard to find.
Pommie's Revenge *(OG 1052, ABV
5.2%)* A light-coloured, full-bodied and
fruity, strong bitter.

GRAINSTORE

Davis'es Brewing Company Ltd, The
Grainstore Brewery, Station Approach,
Oakham, Rutland LE15 6QW
Tel (01572) 770065 Fax (01572) 770068
Tours by arrangement
⊗ This new brewery's rather strange company name comes from the fact that it was
founded by Tony Davis and Mike Davies.
After 30 years in the industry, latterly with
Ruddles, Tony decided to set up his own business after finding a derelict Victorian railway
building which had the potential of becoming
an ideal brewhouse and tap. The tap room
was opened first, in 1995, offering guest
beers, then a few months later the brewery
went into production. It now supplies 60
other outlets. Tupping Ale (OG 1042, ABV
4.2%) is brewed especially for the British
Charrolais Sheep Society.
Cooking *(OG 1036, ABV 3.6%)* ◆
A smooth, copper-coloured beer, full-bodied
for its gravity. Malt and hops on the nose;
malt and fruit to the taste, with a malty
aftertaste.
Triple B *(OG 1042, ABV 4.2%)* ◆
Initially, hops dominate over malt in both
the aroma and taste, but fruit is there, too.
All three linger in varying degrees in the
sweetish aftertaste of this tawny brew.
Springtime *(OG 1043, ABV 4.2%)* ◆
A new seasonal offering.
Gold *(OG 1045, ABV 4.5%)* A summer
beer.
Harvest IPA *(OG 1050, ABV 5%)*
An autumn brew.
Ten Fifty *(OG 1050, ABV 5%)* This full-
bodied, tawny beer is very hoppy and fruity
right into the aftertaste. A little malt on the
nose and in the initial taste, with an undying
sweetness and an increasing bitterness.
Winter Oats *(OG 1050, ABV 5%)*
A fourth seasonal beer.

GRAND METROPOLITAN

See Nationals, Scottish Courage, and Pub
Groups, Inntrepreneur.

GREEN DRAGON

See Evesham.

GREEN DRAGON (BUNGAY)

⚲ Green Dragon Free House & Brewery,
29 Broad Street, Bungay, Suffolk NR35 1EE
Tel (01986) 892681 Fax (01986) 892681

The Green Dragon at Bungay began life in a pub purchased from Brent Walker in 1991; it then moved into a converted barn across the car park. The ability to increase its capacity meant it could produce a larger range of ales as well as seasonal beers.

Tours by arrangement
⊠ The Green Dragon was purchased from Brent Walker in 1991 and the buildings at the rear converted to a brewery. In 1994 the plant was expanded and moved into a converted barn across the car park. The 100 per cent increase in capacity permitted the production of a larger range of ales, including seasonal and occasional brews, but the beers are only available at the pub itself and a couple of other outlets. Beers: Bigod Stout (OG 1037, ABV 3.7%), Chaucer Ale (OG 1037, ABV 3.7%), Bridge Street Bitter (OG 1046, ABV 4.5%), Dragon (OG 1055, ABV 5.5%).

GREEN JACK

Green Jack Brewing Co. Ltd, Oulton Broad Brewery, Harbour Road Industrial Estate, Lowestoft, Suffolk NR32 3LZ *Tel (01502) 587905*
Shop 5-11 (7-11 winter) Mon-Sat, 7-10.30 Sun (brewery tap) Tours by arrangement
⊠ Green Jack began production in 1993, on the site of the closed Forbes Brewery. It quickly built up a demand for its distinctively hoppy, award-winning ales and now supplies around 20 outlets direct, as well as its own three pubs. Wholesalers also take the beers. Occasional/seasonal beers: Mild (OG 1032, ABV 3%), Bramble Bitter (OG 1041, ABV 4% autumn), Honey Bunny (OG 1041, ABV 4% spring), Old Thunderbox (OG 1041, ABV 4%, winter), Summer Dream (OG 1041, ABV 4%), Norfolk Wolf Porter (OG 1050, ABV 5.2%). Bottle-conditioned beers Grasshopper: (OG 1043, ABV 4.2%), Swallow (OG 1047, ABV 4.8%, bottled Golden Sickle), Lurcher (OG 1052, ABV 5.4%).

Bitter *(OG 1037, ABV 3.5%)* ❧ A malty, light bitter with a fresh floral hoppiness.
Canary *(OG 1039, ABV 4.2%)*
Golden Sickle *(OG 1047, ABV 4.8%)* ❧ An uncomplicated light bitter, stronger than it tastes.
Lurcher Strong Ale *(OG 1052, ABV 5.4%)* ❧ A sharp-tasting, fruity, strong bitter.
Ripper *(OG 1077, ABV 8.5%)*

GREENE KING PLC

Greene King PLC, Westgate Brewery, Westgate Street, Bury St Edmunds, Suffolk IP33 1QT
Tel (01284) 763222 Fax (01284) 723803
Tours by arrangement
⊠ Greene King is East Anglia's largest brewery and was established in 1799. For years it ran a second brewery at Biggleswaide, which produced lager, but this was closed during 1997. Acquisitions of pubs from Allied have extended the company's estate into south-eastern England, whilst an additional 65 pubs acquired from Bass has strengthend its position in London. In 1996 the company bought the Magic Pub Company chain of 277 pubs for £197.5 million. Its total estate now stands at 1,083 houses, 460 of which are managed, 623 of which are tenanted. All Green King's tied houses take real ale, but many have a cask breather device fitted in the cellar which, happily, some licensees choose not to use. Green King also supplies some 2,500 free trade outlets. Group tours by arrangement. Martha Greene can be found in the company's pubs. Twelve 'King's Court' seasonal beers run through the year: Old Goat (ABV 4%, July), Resolution Breaker (ABV 4% January), King's Champion (ABV 4.2%, June), Mad Judge (ABV 4.2%, September, brewed with cranberries), Old Horny (ABV 4.3, October), Black

Baron (ABV 4.3%, October), Fantasy Ale (ABV 4.3%, August), March Madness (ABV 4.4%, March), Demon Eyes (ABV 4.5, May), Sorcerer (ABV 4.5%, April), Captain Christmas (ABV 4.6, November-December), Winter Ale (ABV 6.4, December).

XX Dark Mild *(OG 1036, ABV 3%)* ◆ Smooth and sweetish, with a bitter, slightly astringent aftertaste. Still under threat, due to low volumes.

Martha Greene Bitter *(ABV 3.1%)*
IPA *(OG 1036, ABV 3.6%)* ◆ A blandish session bitter. Not unpleasant, it has weak hop on the nose, with hop and bitterness in the taste, ending in an astringent, bitter finish.

Rayments Special *(OG 1040, ABV 4%)*
Abbot Ale *(OG 1048, ABV 5%)* 🗍◆ A medium-bodied, distinctive, fruity brew, with a pleasant bittersweet and hoppy aftertaste. A much improved brew since changes were made in 1995; it is now fermented longer and is late hopped with pellets instead of hop oil.

GREY HORSE

🗍 Derwent Rose Brewery, The Grey Horse, 115 Sherburn Terrace, Consett, Co. Durham DH8 6NE *Tel (01207) 502585*

Tours by arrangement

County Durham's newest micro-brewery is based in Consett's oldest surviving pub (150 years old in 1998). It produced its first brew in a former stable block behind the pub in November 1997; other occasional and celebratory beers are produced. Beers: Mutton Clog (ABV 3.8%), Steel Town (ABV 3.8%), Red Dust ABV 4.2%), Swordmaker (ABV 4.5%), Coast 2 Coast (ABV 5%), Derwent Deep (ABV 5%).

GRIBBLE INN

🗍 The Gribble Brewery, The Gribble Inn, Oving, nr Chichester, W. Sussex PO20 6BP *Tel (01243) 786893* **Tours by arrangement**
⊠ Brewpub owned by Hall & Woodhouse (Badger, qv) which has expanded to supply over 20 other local outlets. A new beer, Oving Bitter is also supplied to other Badger houses. Black Adder II is not to be confused with the beer from Mauldons, nor Pig's Ear with the brew from Uley.

Ewe Brew *(OG 1040, ABV 3.8%)*
Ale *(OG 1043, ABV 4.1%)*
Oving Bitter *(OG 1045, ABV 4.5%)*
Reg's Tipple *(OG 1050, ABV 5%)*
Black Adder II *(OG 1060, ABV 5.8%)*
Pig's Ear *(OG 1060, ABV 6%)* Available March-Sep.
Wobbler *(OG 1080, ABV 7.2%)* 🗍 A winter brew.

GRIFFIN INN

See Church End.

GUERNSEY

The Guernsey Brewery Co. (1920) Ltd, South Esplanade, St Peter Port, Guernsey GY1 1BJ
Tel (01481) 720143 Fax (01481) 710658
Shop 8-1, 2-5 Mon-Fri Tours by arrangement
⊠ One of two breweries on this Channel Isle, serving its stronger than average real ales in 13 of its 33 pubs. Originally opened as the

London Brewery in 1856, it became a Guernsey registered company in 1920 upon the introduction of income tax on the mainland. It was acquired in 1978 by Bucktrout Co. Ltd, a Guernsey wine and spirit company with several pubs on the island. In 1988 Bucktrout merged with Ann Street (now Jersey) Brewery and Guernsey real ale is still available in selected Jersey Brewery houses. Sadly, more beer is now being sold as keg, dispensed with mixed gas. Six free trade outlets in the Channel Isles are supplied with the real thing.

Braye Ale *(OG 1038, ABV 3.7%)* 🗍◆ Copper-red in colour, with a complex aroma of malt, hops, fruit and toffee. The rich, mellow flavour combines malt, fruit, hops and butterscotch, whilst the finish has malt and hops. Full-flavoured, surprisingly dry and hoppy.

Sunbeam Bitter *(OG 1045, ABV 4.6%)* ◆ Golden in colour, with a fine malt aroma. Malt and fruit are strong on the palate and the beer is quite dry for its strength. Excellent, dry malt and hop finish

Summer Ale *(OG 1055, ABV 5.5%)*
Winter Warmer *(OG 1060, ABV 5.8%)*

GUINNESS

See Nationals.

Save Independent Brewers

HADRIAN
See Four Rivers.

HALE & HEARTY
⚲ The Hale & Hearty Brewery, 104 Upper Hale Road, Farnham, Surrey GU9 0PB *Tel (01252) 735278* Tours by arrangement
⊗ Beers with a cricketing theme are produced at this brewery, set up in November 1996 behind the Ball & Wicket pub (its main customer). Seasonal beers and one-off brews (usually fruit-based) are also produced. Beers: Upper Ale (ABV 3.8%), Wicket Bitter (ABV 4.3%).

HALL & WOODHOUSE
See Badger.

HAMBLETON
Nick Stafford Hambleton Ales, The Brewery, Holme-on-Swale, Thirsk, N. Yorkshire YO7 4JE
Tel (01845) 567460 Fax (01845) 567741
Shop 8-5 Mon-Fri, 9-12 Sat
Tours by arrangement
⊛ Hambleton was set up in 1991 in a Victorian barn on the banks of the River Swale, but production soon outgrow the original premises and it moved in 1996 to the other end of the hamlet and was soon brewing 50 barrels a week. Bottling of the beers started in October 1997. The brewery supplies over 100 outlets in Yorkshire and the North-East directly, with other parts of the UK served by wholesalers. Hambleton brews beers under contract for the Village Brewer wholesale company, tel: (01325) 374887.
Bitter *(OG 1036, ABV 3.6%)* ❧
Rich, hoppy aroma rides through this light and drinkable beer. Taste is bitter with citrus and marmalade aroma and solid body. Ends dry with a spicy mouthfeel.
Goldfield *(OG 1040, ABV 4.2%)* ❧ A light amber bitter with good hop character and increasing dryness. A fine blend of malts gives a smooth overall impression.
Stallion *(OG 1040, ABV 4.2%)* ❧ A premium bitter, moderately hoppy throughout and richly balanced in malt and fruit, developing a sound and robust bitterness, with earthy hop drying the aftertaste.
Stud *(OG 1042, ABV 4.3%)* ❧ A strongly bitter beer, with rich hop and fruit. It ends dry and spicy.
Nightmare *(OG 1048, ABV 5%)* ⬥❧

Fully deserving its acclaim, this impressively flavoured beer satisfies all parts of the palate. Strong roast malts dominate, but hoppiness rears out of this complex blend.

For Village Brewer:
White Boar *(OG 1036, ABV 3.6%)* ❦
A light, flowery and fruity ale; crisp, clean and refreshing, with a dry-hopped, powerful but not aggressive, bitter finish.
Bull *(OG 1039, ABV 4%)* ❦ A fairly thin, but very well-hopped bitter, with a very distinct dryness in the aftertaste. Obviously from the Hambleton stable.
Old Raby *(OG 1045, ABV 4.8%)* ❦ A full-bodied, smooth, rich-tasting dark ale. A complex balance of malt, fruit character and creamy caramel sweetness offsets the bitterness nicely. A classic old ale.

HAMPSHIRE
Hampshire Brewery Ltd, 6-8 Romsey Industrial Estate, Greatbridge Road, Romsey, Hampshire SO51 0HR
Tel (01794) 830000 Fax (01794) 830999
Shop 9-5 Mon-Fri Tours by arrangement
⊗ Set up in 1992, the brewery outgrow its capacity in Andover and has now completed its expansion with a move to a larger site in Romsey. Pride of Romsey was launched to celebrate the move and is on course to become the brewery's leading brand. A bottling plant has been installed at the new site. It also brews Norman's Conquest for Cottage Brewery (qv). Bottle-conditioned beer: Pride of Romsey (OG 1050, ABV 5%).
King Alfred's *(OG 1038, ABV 3.8%)*
A mid-brown beer, featuring a malty and hoppy aroma. A malty taste leads to a hoppy, malty and bitter finish.
Ironside *(OG 1042, ABV 4.2%)* ❧ A beer with little aroma, but some malt. The taste has solid fruit with lasting hops and malt. The aftertaste is more bitter and malty. Pale brown in colour.
Lionheart *(OG 1042, ABV 4.2%)* A smooth, golden best bitter.
Pendragon *(OG 1048, ABV 4.8%)* A full-bodied and fruity premium ale.
Pride of Romsey *(OG 1050, ABV 5%)*
1066 *(OG 1062, ABV 6%)*

HANBY
Hanby Ales Ltd, New Brewery, Aston Park, Soulton Road, Wem, Shropshire SY4 5SD

HARVIESTOUN ORIGINAL 80/- CASK CONDITIONED ALE · Brewed in Dollar SCOTLAND

Tel (01939) 232432 Fax (01939) 232432
Tours by arrangement

⊗ Following the closure of Wem Brewery by
Greenalls in 1988, the former head brewer,
Jack Hanby, set up his own business. By
1990 he had moved into a new, larger brewhouse (which was improved in 1991).
Hanby supplies some 200 pubs directly and
others via wholesalers. In addition to the
extensive, award-winning, regular range, a
monthly 'special' is brewed. Occasional/sea-
sonal beers: Cherry Bomb (OG 1060, ABV
6%), Joy Bringer (OG 1060, ABV 6%).
Black Majic Mild *(OG 1033, ABV
3.3%)* ❦ A dark, reddish-brown mild,
which is dry and bitter with a roast malt
taste.
Drawwell Bitter *(OG 1039, ABV 3.9%)*
❦ A hoppy beer with excellent bitterness,
both in taste and aftertaste. Beautiful amber
colour.
All Seasons Bitter *(OG 1042, ABV
4.2%)*
Rainbow Chaser *(OG 1043, ABV
4.3%)* A pale beer brewed with pioneer
hops.
Shropshire Stout *(OG 1044, ABV
4.4%)* 🍴❦ A full-bodied, rich ruby stout,
with a very distinctive, chocolate malt, dry
flavour.
Wem Special *(OG 1044, ABV 4.4%)* A
pale, smooth, hoppy bitter.
Cascade *(OG 1045, ABV 4.5%)*
Scorpio *(OG 1045, ABV 4.5%)*
Premium Bitter *(OG 1046, ABV 4.6%)*
❦ Formerly Treacleminer, a pale brown
beer which is sweeter and fruitier than the
beers above. Slight malt and hop taste.
Old Wemian Ale *(OG 1049, ABV 4.9%)*
Golden-brown colour with an aroma of malt
and hops and a soft, malty palate.
Taverners Ale *(OG 1053, ABV 5.3%)*
Nutcracker Bitter *(OG 1060, ABV
6%)*❦
A warming, smooth, mid-brown beer, with
malt and hops coming through. Definitely
more bitter than sweet.

HANCOCK'S
See Nationals, Bass.

HAND IN HAND See Kemptown

HANSON'S
See Banks's

HARDY, THOMAS
**Thomas Hardy Brewing Ltd, Weymouth
Avenue, Dorchester, Dorset DT1 1QT**
Tel (01305) 250255 Fax (01305) 258381
Tours by arrangement

⊗ Founded by the Eldridge family as the
Green Dragon Brewery in 1837, this brewery
now operates as the Thomas Hardy Brewery,
following a management buyout in March
1997, leaving Eldridge Pope to concentrate
on pub ownership (see Pub Groups). Thomas
Hardy brews Eldridge Pope's beers under
contract, and also brews and packages for
other breweries (mostly bottled beers).
Bottle-conditioned beer: Thomas Hardy's
Ale (OG 1125, ABV 12%)🍴.

For Eldridge Pope:
Pope's Traditional *(OG 1036, ABV
3.8%)* ❦ Formerly Eldridge Pope Best
Bitter. A mixture of malt and hop with a
hint of fruit.
Hardy Country *(OG 1040, ABV 4.2%)*
❦ A dry, hoppy beer with faint undertones
of malt and fruit. The taste is smooth despite
a bitter edge which continues into the finish.
Royal Oak *(OG 1048, ABV 5%)* ❦ A
full-bodied beer with a distinctive banana
aroma and a mainly sweet, fruity taste. This
is balanced by malt and some hops and there
is a fruity finish to this smooth, well-
rounded brew.

For Cottage:
Norman's Conquest *(OG 1066, ABV
7%)* Bottle conditioned beer.

HARDYS & HANSONS
**Hardys & Hansons PLC, Kimberley
Brewery, Nottingham NG16 2NS**
*Tel (0115) 938 3611 Fax (0115) 945
9055* Tours by arrangement

☺ Established in 1832 and 1847 respec-
tively, Hardys & Hanson were two competitive breweries until a merger in 1931 produced the present company. The brewery is
today controlled by descendants of the original Hardy and Hanson families. The majority of its 255 tied houses take its award-winning real ales, mostly drawn by metered
dispense into oversized glasses, although
Kimberley Classic, and increasingly the
Bitter, are served by handpull. Around 60
other outlets are also supplied direct. A
range of seasonal ales, with a new beer every
two months, introduced in the spring of
1996 under the 'Cellarman's Cask' banner,
has proved very successful. Occasional/sea-
sonal beers: Crazy Crow (ABV 4.1%),
Crowing Cock (ABV 4.2%), Frolicking
Farmer (ABV 4.2%), Peddler's Pride (AV
4.3%), Guzzling Goose (ABV 4.4%) and
Rocking Rudolph (ABV 5.5%).
Kimberley Best Mild *(OG 1035, ABV
3.1%)* 🍴❦ A deep ruby mild, deliciously
dominated by chocolate malt. The fruitiness
and caramel sweetness are well balanced in
the taste, with a faintly hoppy finish.
Kimberley Best Bitter *(OG 1039,
ABV 3.9%)* 🍴❦ A beer with a flowery
hoppy and fruity nose, although malt is
never far away. Fruity hop is evident in the
taste and there is a consistent bitterness.
Kimberley Classic *(OG 1047, ABV
4.8%)* ❦ A brown beer with an amber hue.
Bitter throughout, it has a fruity hop nose,
with malt behind the hops in the taste and
aftertaste. It is not always easy to find (often
alternating with seasonals).

HARPENDEN
See Verulam.

HART
⚑ **Hart Brewery, Cartford Hotel, Cartford
Lane, Little Eccleston, Lancashire PR3 0YP**
Tel (01995) 671686 Tours by arrangement

☺ Brewery founded in 1994, in a small private garage, which moved to premises at the
rear of the Cartford Hotel in 1995. With a
ten-barrel plant, Hart is supplying a growing

number (currently around 100) of local free houses. A monthly beer is available along-side the regular range. Seasonal beers: Liberator (OG 1037, ABV 3.7%, September), Fyle Ale (OG 1040, ABV 4%, April), Criminale Porter (OG 1041, ABV 4%, October), Mayson Premier (OG 1042, ABV 4%, August), High Octane Gold Beach (OG 1043, ABV 4.2%, May), Excalibur (OG 1045, ABV 4.5%, June), Hart of Steel (OG 1045, ABV 4.5%, July), No Balls (OG 1045, ABV 4.5%, Christmas), Andrew's Cobblestone Stout (OG 1050, ABV 5%, February), Old Ram (OG 1050, ABV 5%, March), Amadeus (OG 1055, ABV 5.5%, November), Merrie Hart Stout (OG 1055, ABV 5.5%, January).

Cleo's Asp *(OG 1037, ABV 3.7%)* ◆
A smooth golden brew with a light, fruity aroma, a slow burst of fruit and hop flavours and a restrained, dry, hoppy finish. Very drinkable.

Beth's Arrival *(OG 1040, ABV 4%)*
Ambassador *(OG 1041, ABV 4.2%)*
This ruby-red beer is a little drier than others in the range. Brewed with crystal and chocolate malts and Kent Fuggles.

Squirrels Hoard *(OG 1042, ABV 4%)*
Brewed for the Cartford Hotel and CAMRA festivals. Pale and crystal malts produce a wonderfully nutty flavour.

Off Your Trolley *(OG 1045, ABV 4.5%)*
Nemesis *(OG 1046, ABV 4.5%)* A light amber-coloured beer with a refreshing flavour.

Road to Rome *(OG 1050, ABV 5%)*
Originally brewed for CAMRA's 25th anniversary, now a permanent addition to the range. A rich, ruby-red beer with a full malt flavour and a sweet aftertaste.

HARTLEYS
See Robinsons.

HARVEYS
Harvey & Son (Lewes) Ltd, The Bridge Wharf Brewery, 6 Cliffe High Street, Lewes, E. Sussex BN7 2AH
Tel (01273) 480209 Fax (01273) 483706
Shop 9.30-4.45 Mon-Sat Tours by arrangement (long waiting list)
⊗ Established in the late 18th century by John Harvey, on the banks of the River Ouse, this Georgian brewery was rebuilt in 1881. The Victorian Gothic tower and brewhouse remain a very attractive feature. A major development in 1985 doubled brewing capacity and production has since risen to more than 30,000 barrels per year. Still a family-run company, Harveys supplies real ale to all its 41 pubs and 600 free trade outlets in Sussex and Kent. One of the first breweries to introduce seasonal ales, it also frequently produces commemorative beers, which are sometimes available on draught. It opened its first London pub, the Royal Oak in Tabard Street, in summer 1997. Seasonal beers: Family Ale (OG 1020, ABV 2.2%, June), Knots of May Light Mild (OG 1030, ABV 3%, May), Southdown Harvest Ale (OG 1050, ABV 5%, September), 1859 Porter (OG 1053, ABV 4.8%, March), Tom Paine (OG 1055, ABV 5.5%, July), Firecracker (OG 1066, ABV 5.8%,

November), Christmas Ale (OG 1090, ABV 8.1%, December). Bottle-conditioned beer: 1859 Porter (OG 1053, ABV 4.8%)⬚.

Sussex XX Mild Ale *(OG 1030, ABV 3%)* ⬚◆ A dark, malty brew with slight malt and hops in the aroma and roasted malt and hops coming through in both the flavour and finish.

Sussex Pale Ale *(OG 1033, ABV 3.5%)* ⬚◆ An agreeable, light bitter with malt and hops dominating the aroma, whilst a hoppy bitterness develops throughout the taste, to dominate the finish.

Sussex Best Bitter *(OG 1040, ABV 4%)* ⬚◆ A medium-strength bitter with a good balance of malt and strong hops in the flavour, which develops into a bitter, hoppy aftertaste.

Sussex XXXX or Old Ale *(OG 1043, ABV 4.3%)* ◆ Brewed October-May: a rich, dark beer with a good malty nose, with undertones of roast malt, hops and fruit. The flavour is a complex blend of roast malt, grain, fruit and hops with some caramel. Malty caramel finish with roast malt.

Armada Ale *(OG 1045, ABV 4.5%)* ◆
A full-bodied beer in which hops are dominant throughout. Long, dry finish.

HARVIESTOUN
Harviestoun Brewery Ltd, Devon Road, Dollar, Clackmannanshire FK14 7LX
Tel/Fax (01259) 742141
⊗ Hand-built in a 200-year-old stone byre, by two home-brew enthusiasts in 1985, this small brewery operates from a former dairy at the foot of the Ochil Hills, near Stirling. A new custom-built brewing plant was installed in 1991 and Harviestoun now serves 70 outlets in central Scotland as well as wholesalers' customers throughout Britain. Occasional beers: Spring Fever (OG 1038, ABV 3.8%, March), Brooker's Bitter and Twisted (OG 1038, ABV 3.8%, April), Cutlass Sharp Bitter (OG 1039, ABV 3.9%, July-August), Freshers (OG 1039, ABV 3.9%, October), Summer Ale (OG 1040, ABV 4%, June-July), Autumn Ale (OG 1041, ABV 4.1%, September), Mayfest Wheat Beer (OG 1043, ABV 4.3%, May), Black Lager (OG 1044, ABV 4.6%, February), Good King Legless (OG 1045, ABV 4.5%, November-December), Auld Lang Syne (OG 1046, ABV 4.6%, January).

Waverley 70/- *(OG 1037, ABV 3.7%)*
◆ Light in body, with a malt, hop and fruit aroma. Malt, hops, some fruit and roast feature in the taste, before a dry finish.

Original 80/- *(OG 1041, ABV 4.1%)* ◆
This beer has malt, fruit and hops throughout, with a slight toffeeness in the taste. Faintly sulphurous aroma.

Montrose Ale *(OG 1042, ABV 4.2%)* ◆
A tawny-coloured beer with a complex aroma of malt, roast, caramel and fruit, which remain in the taste, giving way to a slight bitterness.

Ptarmigan 85/- *(OG 1045, ABV 4.5%)*
◆ A well-balanced, bittersweet beer in which hops and malt dominate. The blend of malt, hops and fruit produces a clean, hoppy aftertaste.

Schiehallion *(OG 1048, ABV 4.8%)* ⬚◆
A Scottish cask lager, brewed using a lager

yeast and Hersbrücker hops, and properly lagered. A fruity aroma, with hops and malt, leads to a malty, bitter taste with floral hoppiness and a bittersweet finish.
Old Manor *(OG 1050, ABV 5%)* A winter brew.

HEATHER
Heather Ale Ltd, Craigmill, Sandford Road, Strathaven, Lanarkshire ML10 6PB
Tel (01357) 529529 Fax (01357) 522256
⊛ Bruce Williams started brewing Fraoch (Gaelic for heather) in 1992 at the now closed West Highland Brewery in Argyll. He moved his production the following year to Maclay's Thistle brewery, then moved again in 1997 to the current site from where he supplies ten free trade outlets, although the bulk of beers are still brewed by Maclay. Heather Ale is made with flowering heather, following an ancient tradition – hence its seasonal nature. Pictish is brewed in November using the last crop of heather flowers.
Fraoch Heather Ale *(OG 1042, ABV 4.1%)* Available May-November; a beer with a floral, peaty aroma, a spicy, herbal, woody flavour and a dry finish.
Fraoch Pictish Ale *(OG 1052, ABV 5.3%)* Available December-April.

HEDGEHOG & HOGSHEAD
Belchers Brewery, 100 Goldstone Villas, Hove, E. Sussex BN3 3RX
Tel(01273) 324660
⊠ Brewpub chain established with two outlets (Hove and Southampton) in 1990 by David Bruce (of Firkin fame), who sold them in 1994 to Grosvenor Inns who then sold them to Senria (see Pub Groups). Only the Hove pub currently brews, but information is unclear. Beers: BiBi or Best Bitter (OG 1042, ABV 4.2%), Bootleg Bitter (OG 1052, ABV 5.2%).

HENSTRIDGE
Henstridge Brewery, Gibbs Marsh, Bow Bridge Works, Henstridge Trading Estate, Henstridge, Somerset BA8 0TH
Tel (01963) 363150 Fax (01963) 363864
⊠ After 15 years of making just about everything used in the brewing trade, David Vickery decided it was time to try making some beer himself; thus in 1994 Henstridge Brewery was born. It still brews just one beer for local outlets and pubs further afield via an agent. See Bath Brewery.
Vickery's Bill *(OG 1040, ABV 4%)*

HESKET NEWMARKET
Hesket Newmarket Brewery, Old Crown Barn, Back Green, Hesket Newmarket,

Cumbria CA7 8JG *Tel/Fax (016974) 78066*
Tours by arrangement, tel: (016974) 78288
⊛ Brewery set up in 1988 in a barn behind the Old Crown pub in an attractive North Lakes village. Its beers are named after local fells, with the notable exception of Doris's 90th Birthday Ale (Doris sadly died in 1995, aged 96). Around 20 pubs take the beers regularly and many more on an occasional basis. The brewery also produces house beers for local pubs. In summer 1998 it began production of a new ale, Pig's Ear. Occasional/seasonal beers: Show Ale (OG 1040, ABV 3.9%), Anniversary Ale (OG 1043, ABV 3.8%), Mediaeval Ale (OG 1045, ABV 4.3%), Kern Knott's Cracking Stout (OG 1057, ABV 5%), Ayala's Angel (OG 1080, ABV 7%, Christmas).
Great Cockup Porter *(OG 1035, ABV 2.8%)* A refreshing, chocolate-tasting beer.
Blencathra Bitter *(OG 1035, ABV 3.1%)* A predominantly bitter beer, from the start to the dry finish. Malty nose.
Skiddaw Special Bitter *(OG 1035, ABV 3.7%)* A golden session beer, despite its name.
Doris's 90th Birthday Ale *(OG 1045, ABV 4.3%)* A fruity premium ale.
Catbells Pale Ale *(OG 1052, ABV 5.1%)* An initially sweet, strongly aromatic beer developing a bitter finish.
Old Carrock Strong Ale *(OG 1064, ABV 5.6%)* A dark red, powerful ale.

HEXHAMSHIRE
Hexhamshire Brewery, The Brewery, Leafields, Hexham, North-umberland NE45 1SX *Tel (01434) 606577*
⊠ This brewery was set up in a redundant farm building in 1992, as a partnership. That partnership was dissolved in 1997 and the brewery is now solely owned by Mrs J. Brooker, with husband Geoff as head brewer. No adjuncts are used in the beers which are produced for its single tied house, the Dipton Mill Inn and 20 other outlets. Seasona beer: Old Humbug (ABV 5.5%).
Shire Bitter *(OG 1037, ABV 3.8%)* Thicker than expected: a bitter beer with a malty overtone.
Devil's Water *(OG 1041, ABV 4.1%)* A beer of mixed character and unexpected range of flavours. Malt dominates and bitterness gradually declines, giving a strong sweet finish.
Whapweasel *(OG 1048, ABV 4.8%)* This malty bitter has a lasting hoppiness and a smooth mouthfeel.

HIGH FORCE
High Force Hotel Brewery, Forest-in-Teesdale, Barnard Castle, Co. Durham DL12 0XH

Tel (01833) 622222 Fax (01833) 622264
Tours by arrangement
☺ Founded in 1995 and claims to be the highest brewery in Britain; at 1,060 feet it is situated by the High Force waterfall. The brewery won the Best Beer in Festival award at the Durham Beer Festival three years running, with Cauldron Snout. Cauldron Snout sausages are marinated in the beer and sold locally.

Teesdale Bitter (OG 1037, ABV 3.8%) ✦ A well-balanced session ale with lingering fruit character and spicy aftertaste,
Forest XB (OG 1041, ABV 4.2%) ✦ A smooth malty flavoured beer, with a solid bitterness and almond undertones to a spicy finish. Also available bottled.
Cauldron Snout (OG 1052, ABV 5.6%) ✦ A dark and creamy ale with a smooth roasted taste and a rich, solid body. Deceptively drinkable. Also available bottled.

HIGH PEAK
See Lloyds.

HIGHGATE
Highgate & Walsall Brewing Company Ltd, Sandymount Road, Walsall, W. Midlands WS1 3AP Tel/Fax (01922) 644453
Tours by arrangement
☺ Highgate, which celebrated its centenary in 1998, was an independent brewery until 1938 when it was taken over by Mitchells & Butlers and subsequently became the smallest brewery in the Bass group. It had been under threat of closure for some years until a management buyout brought it back into the independent sector in 1995. Some of the original equipment in the traditional Victorian tower brewery is still in use. Highgate now has seven tied houses and is aiming for an estate of 50. All the tied houses take the real ale and Highgate has an expanding free trade, with 70 outlets in the Midlands supplied direct and further afield via wholesalers. The company also has a contract to supply Bass.
Dark Mild (OG 1035, ABV 3.2%)◨◫✦ A dark brown, Black Country mild with a good balance of malt and hops, and traces of roast flavour following a malty aroma.
Bitter (OG 1039, ABV 3.7%)
Fox's Nob (OG 1039, ABV 3.6%)
Saddlers Best Bitter (OG 1043, ABV 4%) ✦ A very fruity, pale yellow bitter with a strong hop flavour and a light, refreshing bitter aftertaste.
Breacalis (OG 1043, ABV 4.3%)
A 'whisky' beer.

Black Pig (OG 1046, ABV 4.4%)
Old Ale (OG 1054, ABV 5.1%) ✦ A winter beer (November-January): a dark brown/ruby-coloured old ale, full-flavoured, fruity and malty, with a complex aftertaste which has hints of malt, roast, hops and fruit.

HIGHWOOD
Highwood Brewery Ltd, Melton Highwood, Barnetby, Lincolnshire DN38 6AA
Tel (01652) 680020 Fax (01652) 680729
Tours by arrangement
⊗ Located in a converted granary on the edge of the Lincolnshire Wolds, this brewery went into production in 1995 and is currently brewing around 40 barrels a week to supply 60 regular outlets, as well as its own two pubs. Seasonal beer: Bomber County (ABV 4.8%).
Tom Wood Best Bitter (OG 1036, ABV 3.5%) ◧✦ Dark amber and dominated by a fruity hop with an almost passion fruit tang to it. Bitter and hoppy throughout.
Lincolnshire Legend (OG 1039, ABV 4.2%) ✦ A coppery chestnut in colour, this is a bitter beer with citric hops on the nose and taste. Balanced by a good backbeat of malt, the orange fruitiness intensifies as the drink develops.
Shepherd's Delight (OG 1039, ABV 4%) ✦ Fruity on the nose, malt is strong in the taste, with a constant bitterness and waning fruit and hops in this amber brew.
Tom Wood Harvest Bitter (OG 1041, ABV 4.3%) ✦ A rounded beer with the hop in ascendancy as in the Bitter, although with less fruit evident. Malt is much more pronounced behind the hop. Amber in colour.
Old Timber (OG 1046, ABV 4.5%) ✦ Hoppy on the nose, but featuring well-balanced malt and hops otherwise. A slight, lingering roast/coffee flavour develops, but this is generally a bitter, darkish brown beer.

HIGSONS
See Cains and Nationals, Whitbread.

HILDEN
Hilden Brewery, Hilden House, Grand Street, Lisburn, Co. Antrim BT27 4TY
Tel (01846) 663863
☺ Mini-brewery beside a Georgian country house, set up in 1981 to counter the local Guinness/Bass duopoly. It presently supplies Hilden Ale to just a handful of pubs in Northern Ireland, with the full range of beers exported to some pubs in England. Occasional beers: Special (OG 1037, ABV

3.6%), Festival Ale (OG 1052, ABV 5.2%).
Great Northern Porter *(OG 1039, ABV 4%)* ❧ A beer with a rich, tawny colour and a pronounced malty aroma. Crystal malt is dominant in both the flavour and aftertaste.
Hilden Ale *(OG 1040, ABV 4%)* ❧ An amber-coloured beer with an aroma of malt, hops and fruit. The balanced taste is slightly slanted towards hops, and hops are also prominent in the full, malty finish. Bitter and refreshing.
Special Reserve *(OG 1048, ABV 4.6%)* ❧ Dark red/brown in colour and superbly aromatic – full of dark malts, producing an aroma of liquorice and toffee. Malt, fruit and toffee on the palate, with a sweet, malty finish. Mellow and satisfying, but not always available.

HOBSONS

Hobsons Brewery & Co., Newhouse Farm, Tenbury Road, Cleobury Mortimer, nr Kidderminster, Worcestershire DY14 8RD
Tel (01299) 270837
Tours by arrangement
⊗ Opened at Easter 1993 in a former sawmill, Hobsons (a Shropshire brewery, despite its postal address) is now located in a characterful building which was once a farm granary. The brewery is working close to its capacity of 60 barrels a week and supplying around 80 outlets with cask ale.
Best Bitter *(OG 1038, ABV 3.8%)* 🗇❧ A pale brown to amber, medium-bodied beer with strong hop character throughout. It is consequently bitter, but with malt discernible in the taste.
Town Crier *(OG 1045, ABV 4.5%)* A straw-coloured bitter.
Old Henry *(OG 1050, ABV 5.2%)*

HODGE'S BREWERY
See Darwin.

HOGS BACK

Hogs Back Brewery, Manor Farm, The Street, Tongham, Surrey GU10 1DE
Tel (01252) 783000 Fax (01252) 782328
Shop 9-6 Mon, Tue and Sat; 9-8.30 Wed-Fri; 10-4.30 Sun Tours by arrangement
⊗ This purpose-built brewery was set up in a restored farm building (circa 1768) in 1992 and the popularity of its ales – particularly the award-winning TEA – has resulted in a major plant change to double the production capacity. From small beginnings, with just a single beer, Hogs Back now brews nearly 20 beer types on a regular or occasional basis. Occasional/seasonal beers: Dark Mild (OG 1036, ABV 3.4%), Legend (OG 1038, ABV 4%), APB or A Pinta Bitter (OG 1037, ABV 3.5%), Legend (OG 1038, ABV 4%, September), Friday 13th (OG 1044, ABV 4.2%), Blackwater Porter (OG 1046, ABV 4.4%), BSA or Burma Star Ale (OG 1048, ABV 4.5%), YES or Your Every Success (OG 1048, ABV 5%), Fuggles Nouveau (OG 1052 ABV 5%), Goldings Nouveau (OG 1052, ABV 5%), UTOPIA (OG 1058, ABV 5.4%), OTT or Old Tongham Tasty (OG 1066, ABV 6%), Brewster's Bundle (OG 1076, ABV 7.6%), Santa's Wobble (OG

1077, ABV 7.5%, Christmas), A over T or Aromas over Tongham (OG 1091, ABV 9%), Wheat Your Whistle (4.8%, for the summer). Bottle-conditioned beers: TEA (OG 1044, ABV 4.2%), BSA (OG 1048, ABV 4.5%), Brewster's Bundle (OG 1076, ABV 7.4%), Wobble in a Bottle (OG 1077, ABV 7.5%), A over T (OG 1091, ABV 9%).
Hair of the Hog *(OG 1038, ABV 3.5%)*
TEA or Traditional English Ale *(OG 1044, ABV 4.2%)* 🗇❧ A pale brown, malty bitter with a developing hop balance. Slightly fruity.
Hop Garden Gold *(OG 1048, ABV 4.6%)* ❧ A malty, golden beer with a hoppy finish.
Rip Snorter *(OG 1052, ABV 5%)* ❧ A strong, malty and fruity, reddish-brown bitter with a slight hop flavour.

HOLDEN'S

Holden's Brewery Co. Ltd, Hopden Brewery, George Street, Woodsetton, Dudley, W. Midlands DY1 4LN
Tel (01902) 880051 Fax (01902) 665473
Shop 11-10 Mon-Sat, 12-3, 7-10 Sun
☺ Family brewery going back four generations. Holden's began life as a brewpub when Edwin and Lucy Holden took over the Park Inn (now the brewery tap) in the 1920s. With 21 pubs (the latest being a disused railway station), it is continuing to build up its tied estate. Some 15 other outlets are also supplied with Holden's real ales. Occasional/seasonal beers: Stout (OG 1035, ABV 3.4%), Old 'XL' Ale (OG 1069, ABV 6.8%, Christmas).
Mild *(OG 1037, ABV 3.7%)* ❧ A good, red/brown Black Country mild; a refreshing, light blend of roast malt, hops and fruit, dominated by malt throughout.
Bitter *(OG 1039, ABV 3.9%)* ❧ A medium-bodied, golden ale; a light, well-balanced bitter with a subtle, dry, hoppy finish.
XB or Lucy B *(OG 1041, ABV 4.1%)* ❧ Named after founder Lucy Blanche Holden, this is a sweeter, slightly fuller version of the bitter. Sold in different outlets under different names.
Special Bitter *(OG 1051, ABV 5.1%)* ❧ A sweet, malty, full-bodied amber ale with hops to balance in the taste and in the good, bittersweet finish.

HOLT

Joseph Holt PLC, Derby Brewery, Empire Street, Cheetham, Manchester M3 1JD
Tel (0161) 834 3285 Fax (0161) 834 6458
☺ Successful family brewery, celebrating its 150th annniversary in 1999 – not to be confused with Carlsberg-Tetley's Midlands division, Holt, Plant & Deakin. The tied estate has been gradually increased over the last 15 years or so, and now exceeds 120 houses, all serving real ale, with most of the pubs taking hogsheads (54-gallon casks), because the low prices result in a high turnover. The beers are also popular as guests and Holt supplies a free trade of around 75 outlets (plus another 40 or so via an agent).
Mild *(OG 1033, ABV 3.2%)* ❧ A very dark beer with a complex aroma and taste. Roast malt is prominent, but so are hops and fruit. Strong in bitterness for a mild,

with a long-lasting, satisfying after-taste.

Bitter *(OG 1039, ABV 4%)* ◆ A tawny beer with a good hop aroma. Although balanced by malt and fruit, the uncompromising bitterness can be a shock to the unwary.

HOLTS
See Nationals, Carlsberg-Tetley.

HOME
See Mansfield and Nationals, Scottish Courage.

HOME COUNTY
Home County Brewery, The Old Brewery, Station Road, Wickwar, Gloucestershire GL12 8NB
Tel (01454) 294045 Fax (01454) 294045
Shop Fr. eves
A second brewery, set up in November 1997, on the same site as the Wickwar Brewery in south Gloucestershire, with a five-barrel brewlength. Plans to expand premises soon. Supplies local free trade.

Wichen *(OG 1042, ABV 4.2%)* ◆ Amber/mid-brown coloured, it has a malty aroma with a little hop and fruit. Good, malty taste with a fullish body, some hops and fruit, and a quenching bitterness. Similar finish with malt and bitterness lasting longest.

Old Tradition *(OG 1048, ABV 4.8%)* ◆ Malty in both aroma and taste, with bitterness and only slightly sweetness. Red-brown in colour.

Country Pride *(OG 1051, ABV 5%)* ◆ Malt/fruit aroma, with hints of roast and caramel. Mid-bodied, similar taste with a dry, malt aftertaste. Red-brown in colour.

HOOK NORTON
The Hook Norton Brewery Co. Ltd, The Brewery, Hook Norton, Banbury, Oxfordshire OX15 5NY
Tel (01608) 737210 Fax (01608) 730294
Shop 9-4 Mon-Fri Tours by arrangement
⊗ Still family owned, Hook Norton is one of the most delightful, traditional Victorian tower breweries remaining in Britain. It retains much of its original plant and machinery, the showpiece being a 25-horse-power stationary steam engine which still pumps the Cotswold well water used for brewing. Work is in hand to convert an old maltings into a new visitor centre due to open on the brewery's 150th anniversary in 1999. The brewery boasts some fine old country pubs, with all 37 of its tied houses serving real ale, and some 250 free trade outlets also supplied direct. Seasonal beers: Haymaker (OG 1052, ABV 5%, July-

August), Twelve Days (OG 1058, ABV 5.5%, December-January).

Best Mild *(OG 1032, ABV 3%)* ◆ A dark, red/brown mild with a malty aroma and a malty, sweetish taste, tinged with a faint hoppy balance. Malty in the aftertaste. Highly drinkable.

Best Bitter *(OG 1035, ABV 3.4%)* ◆ An excellently-balanced, golden bitter. Malty and hoppy on the nose and in the mouth, with a hint of fruitiness. Dry, but with some balancing sweetness. A hoppy bitterness dominates the finish.

Generation *(OG 1041, ABV 4%)*

Old Hooky *(OG 1048, ABV 4.6%)* ◆ An unusual, tawny beer with a strong fruity and grainy aroma and palate, balanced by a hint of hops. Full-bodied, with a bitter, fruity and malty aftertaste.

Double Stout *(OG 1050, ABV 4.8%)* This dry, dark red-brown stout has masses of roast malt flavour but not too much depth of character. The finish is dry and powdery. Available February-June.

HOP BACK
Hop Back Brewery PLC, Unit 22 Batten Road Industrial Estate, Downton, Salisbury, Wiltshire SP5 3HU *Tel (01725) 510986*
⊗ Founded as a brewpub, the Wyndham Arms, in 1987, Hop Back switched most of its production to a new brewery at Downton in 1992. A new 50-barrel plant was installed in 1995 and in 1997 a further industrial unit was purchased to house the bottling plant. It now has six tied houses, including the Hop Leaf in Reading (see Reading Lion Brewery) and Hop Back also sells directly to 150 other outlets. Bottle-conditioned beers: Summer Lightning (OG 1049, ABV 5%), Thunderstorm (OG 1048, ABV 5%).

GFB *(OG 1034, ABV 3.5%)* ◆ A golden beer, with the sort of light, clean, tasty quality which makes an ideal session ale. A hoppy aroma and taste lead to a good, dry finish. Refreshing.

Crop Circle *(OG 1041, ABV 4.2%)*

Entire Stout *(OG 1043, ABV 4.5%)* ◆■▢ A rich, dark stout with a strong roasted malt flavour and a long, sweet and malty aftertaste. A vegan beer. Also produced with ginger.

Thunderstorm *(OG 1048, ABV 5%)* ■▢ A softly bitter, easy drinking wheat beer.

Summer Lightning *(OG 1049, ABV 5%)* ■▢◆ A very pleasurable pale bitter with a good, fresh, hoppy aroma and a malty, hoppy flavour. Finely balanced, it has an intense bitterness leading to a long, dry finish. Though strong, it tastes like a session ale.

HOP HOUSE
See Cock.

478

HOP LEAF
See Reading Lion.

HORSEBRIDGE
See Royal Inn.

HOSKINS
Tom Hoskins Brewery PLC, Beaumanor Brewery, 133 Beaumanor Road, Leicester LE4 5QE
Tel (0116) 266 1122   Fax (0116) 261 0150
Tours by arrangement
⊗ This brewery was set up around a 100 years ago by Jabez Penn in his own cottage, and became Hoskins Brewery some time after his son-in-law took control in 1901. A traditional tower brewery, it remained in family hands until 1983, when it was acquired and expanded by TRD Estates Ltd. Following the sale of eight pubs to Wolverhampton & Dudley in 1992, the brewery was taken over by Halkin Holdings in 1993, and in 1995 it was subject to a management buyout. Since then its tied estate has grown again to 14 houses, all stocking real ale and the beers have recently been relaunched. The brewery plans to increase its estate to 50 over the next four years. Seasonal beer: Old Nigel (OG 1060, ABV 5%, winter).

Bitter *(OG 1037, ABV 3.7%)* ❧ Tawny in colour this bitter-tasting beer has a grainy-malt flavour that precedes an astringent-bitter finish

Tom's Gold *(OG 1042, ABV 4.4%)* ❧ This dark-brown, tawny beer has malt, hops and fruit evident throughout, but is not very well balanced. Artificial flavours are present, with a sugary taste dominant.

Churchills Pride *(OG 1047, ABV 4.9%)* ❧ A sugary sweetness dominates this unbalanced, tawny beer. A metallic taste and aroma may indicate the use of cask breathers.

HOSKINS & OLDFIELD
Hoskins & Oldfield Brewery Ltd, North Mills, Frog Island, Leicester LE3 5DH *Tel (0116) 251 0532*
Brewery set up by two members of Leicester's famous brewing family, Philip and Stephen Hoskins, in 1984, after the sale of the old Hoskins Brewery. The company supplies over 15 outlets directly, and others nationwide via wholesalers. Occasional/seasonal beers: Tom Kelly's Christmas Pudding Porter (OG 1052, ABV 5%, Christmas), Reckless Raspberry (OG 1055, ABV 5.5%, a wheat beer with raspberries). Bottle-conditioned beer: 'O4' Ale (ABV 5.2%).

HOB Best Mild *(OG 1036, ABV 3.5%)*

⬚❧ An almost black coloured beer, with malt and hops in the taste. A former champion mild of Britain.

Brigadier Bitter *(OG 1036, ABV 3.6%)* An ordinary bitter.

HOB Bitter *(OG 1041, ABV 4%)* ⬚❧ A tawny-coloured best bitter with a sulpherous hoppy nose and dominated by a hoppy bitterness throughout. Not well balanced.

Little Matty *(OG 1041, ABV 4%)* A complex brown/red beer.

White Dolphin *(OG 1041, ABV 4%)* A fruity wheat beer.

IPA *(OG 1042, ABV 4.2%)* A well-hopped pale ale.

Tom Kelly's Stout *(OG 1043, ABV 4.2%)* A dark, dry stout.

Supreme *(OG 1045, ABV 4.4%)* A very light gold best bitter.

Tom Hoskins Porter *(OG 1050, ABV 4.8%)* Brewed using honey and oats.

EXS Bitter *(OG 1051, ABV 5%)* A malty, full-bodied premium bitter.

'O4' Ale *(OG 1052, ABV 5.2%)* A red/brown coloured, full-flavoured ale.

Ginger Tom *(OG 1053, ABV 5.2%)* A ginger beer.

Old Navigation Ale *(OG 1071, ABV 7%)* ⬚ A strong ruby/black beer.

Christmas Noggin *(OG 1100, ABV 10%)* A potent barley wine. Despite its name, available all year

HOUSTON
⬚ Houston Brewing Company, South Street, Houston, Renfrewshire PA6 7EN
Tel (01505) 612620   Fax (01505) 614133
Tours by arrangement
This microbrewery was set up in 1997 by Carl Wengel to supply his father's pub and restaurant, the Fox and Hounds. Attached to the pub itself, its beers (brewed to a secret recipe) are also available in a few other local outlets and nationwide via wholesalers.

Killellan *(OG 1037, ABV 3.7%)*

Barochan *(OG 1041, ABV 4.1%)*

HP&D
See Nationals, Carlsberg-Tetley.

HUDDERSFIELD
The Huddersfield Brewing Company, c/o Unit J, Shaw Park, Ivy Street East, Aspley, Huddersfield, W. Yorkshire HD5 9AF
Tel (01484) 300028 Fax (01484) 542709

If you launch a beer called Rampant Ram then you make sure everybody knows about it. Adam Hyde, financial director of the family-owned Hydes' Anvil, is the one with the wellies. The March beer was one of the company's seasonal brews.

Tours by arrangement

This new brewery was launched in November 1997 by Robert Johnson of Kitchen Brewery (qv). Operating from the same address it produces a completely different range of beers. One penny from each pint sold goes to local charities.

Town Bitter *(ABV 3.8%)* Dark tan in colour with a malty character ending with a good bitterness.

Huddersfield Pride *(ABV 4.4%)* Dark-straw in colour with a rich, malty flavour, medium bitterness, with a well-hopped nose finishing with a deep fruity aftertaste.

Wilson's Wobble Maker *(ABV 5%)* Golden-coloured with a smooth, malty manner from the German malt, a dry-hopped nose and a fruity flavour.

HUGHES

⚲ Sarah Hughes Brewery, Beacon Hotel, 129 Bilston Street, Sedgley, Dudley, W. Midlands DY3 1JE *Tel (01902) 883380*
Tours by arrangement
☺ Brewery re-opened in 1987 after lying idle for 30 years, to serve the village pub and a few other local houses, but now also supplying beers to more than 70 outlets in the free trade. A Victorian-style conservatory acts as a reception area for brewery tours. Bottle-conditioned beer: Dark Ruby Mild (OG 1058, ABV 6%).
Pale Amber *(OG 1038, ABV 4%)* A well-balanced beer, initially slightly sweet but with hops close behind.
Sedgley Surprise *(OG 1048, ABV 5%)*
❧ A bittersweet, medium-bodied, hoppy ale with some malt.
Dark Ruby Mild *(OG 1058, ABV 6%)*
🍺🗂❧ A near-black, strong ale with a good balance of fruit and hops, leading to a pleasant, lingering, hops and malt finish.

HULL

The Hull Brewery Co. Ltd, 144 English Street, Hull, E. Yorkshire HU3 2BT
Tel (01482) 586364 Fax (01482) 586365
☺ The name of the closed Hull Brewery was resurrected after a 15-year absence with a new brewery opened in 1989. It was, however, forced into liquidation in 1994 and the assets taken over by a local businessman, who formed a new company. It acquired its first (and only) tied house in 1995 (from Bass), and now supplies around 100 other pubs. Hull has an arrangement to brew Stocks' beers for Century Inns which took over and closed Stocks Brewery in 1996, although at the time of writing only Old Horizontal had actually been produced. A bottling plant was set up in 1997 allowing Hull to bottle any of its beers (not bottle-conditioned). Occasional beers: Knocker Dibb (OG 1041, ABV 4.1%), Old Millennium (OG 1043, ABV 4.3%), Millennium Gnome (OG 1045, ABV 4.5%), Smokehouse (OG 1045, ABV 4.5%), Merry Crimble (OG 1050, ABV 5%, Christmas), Coal Porter (OG 1052, ABV 5.2%).
Mild *(OG 1034, ABV 3.3%)* A smooth and malty dark mild with a long lasting aftertaste and a rich aroma of fruit, hops and roast malt. Served with a tight, creamy head.
Ellwood's Best Bitter *(OG 1038, ABV 3.8%)* A golden, straw-coloured session bitter, smooth and rounded, with subtle hints of hops and malt and a refreshing aftertaste.
Bitter *(OG 1039, ABV 3.8%)* A refreshing copper bitter, with a predominantly hoppy aroma. The initial bitter aftertaste leads to a pleasant, lingering maltiness. Complex.
Amber Ale *(OG 1040, ABV 4%)* ❧ A light brown beer with an unusual, dry, malty taste in which amber malt dominates. Slightly fruity aroma; dry, bitter finish. Some tartness can be evident.
Northern Pride *(OG 1042, ABV 4.2%)*
A distinctive, full-bodied beer, with a malty aroma.
The Governor *(OG 1046, ABV 4.4%)*
A full-bodied, amber-coloured premium ale; a deceptively powerful brew with a malty taste and a distinctive hop aroma.

Mickey Finn *(OG 1050, ABV 5%)*
A robust strong, deep copper-coloured ale with a good hop flavour.

For Centruy Inns:
Stocks Old Horizontal *(OG 1054, ABV 5.4%)*

HYDES' ANVIL

Hydes' Anvil Brewery Ltd, 46 Moss Lane West, Manchester M15 5PH.
Tel (0161) 226 1317 Fax (0161) 227 9593
Tours by arrangement
☺ Family-controlled, traditional brewery, first established at the Crown Brewery, Audenshaw, Manchester in 1863 and on its present site, a former vinegar brewery, since the turn of the century. It supplies cask ale to all its 60 tied houses and directly to 25 free trade outlets. A successful programme of seasonal beers was introduced in the mid-1990s, including Rampant Ram in March. Seasonal beers: Billy Westwoods bitter (OG 1030, ABV 3.2%), Anvil 4X Strong (OG 1065, ABV 6.8%, winter).
Mild *(OG 1032, ABV 3.5%)* ❧ A mild with a caramel and fruit aroma: quite sweet and fruity, with a pleasant aftertaste. Sold mainly in the company's Welsh pubs, but rare in the Manchester area.
Light Mild *(OG 1034, ABV 3.7%)* ❧
A lightly-hopped session beer, with malt and a refreshing fruitiness dominating before a brief, but dry, finish.
Bitter *(OG 1036, ABV 3.8%)* 🗂❧ A good-flavoured bitter, with a malty and fruity nose, malt and hop in the taste, with a fruity background, and good bitterness through into the aftertaste.

481

Moving Isle of Skye barrels across the water. The brewery is situated at the pier terminal for the Outer Hebrides and it now serves nine outlets on the island plus an increasing number of outlets in Scotland and England. Skye is one of several Scottish breweries which are finding an increasingly wide market for their distinctive ales.

ICENI

The Iceni Brewery, 3 Foulden Road, Ickburgh, Mundford, Norfolk IP26 5BJ
Tel (01842) 878922 Fax (01842) 879216
Tours By arrangement

⊠ Armed with redundancy money and a grant from the Rural Development Commission, but no brewing experience, Brendan Moore fulfilled a dream by setting up this small brewery in 1995. The beers, mostly named after Celtic queens and the Iceni tribe, are supplied direct to 40 outlets. Occasional beers: Curse of Macha (OG 1034, ABV 3.4%), Mild (ABV 3.9%), Festival Ale (OG 1045, ABV 4.5%), Queen Maev Stout (OG 1045, ABV 4.9%), Something Very Different (ABV 4.9%).
Boadicea Chariot Ale (OG 1038, ABV 3.8%) The original brew; a well-balanced session bitter with hop and fruit flavours and a dry aftertaste.
Fine Soft Day (OG 1040, ABV 4%)
Celtic Queen (OG 1040, ABV 4%) A light summer ale, packed with flavour.
Fen Tiger (OG 1041, ABV 4.2%)
Deidre of the Sorrows (OG 1042, ABV 4.4%) A gold-coloured ale, with a distinctively pleasant taste that lingers. Moreish; a firm local favourite.
Roisin Dubh (OG 1042, ABV 4.4%) Roisin Dubh translates as 'dark rose'. The beer is also dark in colour, with a slightly sweet taste. Very smooth.
It's a Grand Day (OG 1043, ABV 4.5%)
Gold (OG 1045, ABV 5%) A strong ale, sun gold in colour. Crisp taste; smooth and

deceptive for its strength.

IND COOPE
See Nationals, Bass, Carlsberg-Tetley.

INVERALMOND
The Inveralmond Brewery Ltd, 1
Inveralmond Way, Inveralmond, Perth PH1
3UQ
Tel (01738) 449448 Fax (01738) 449448
⊛ The first brewery in Perth for over 30
years, Inveralmond was established in April
1997 by former Ruddles, S&N and Courage
brewer Fergus Clark. With his ten-barrel
plant he now supplies over 100 outlets
directly and the beers are available throughout the UK.
Independence *(OG 1040, ABV 3.8%)*
An amber-red, sweetish beer with a hint of
spiciness in the aroma.
Ossian *(OG 1042, ABV 4.1%)*
Lia Fail *(OG 1049, ABV 4.7%)* The name
is the Gaelic title of the Stone of Destiny: a
malty, full-bodied brew with chocolate notes
and a balanced finish.

IRIS ROSE
⬚ Iris Rose Brewery, The Royal Hotel, High
Street, Kingussie PH21 1HX
Tel (01540) 661898 Fax (01540) 661061
Tours by arrangement
 Named after the brewer's wife and mother-
in-law, this new brewery opened in August
1997 originally just to brew for their own
three hotels. Demand for the beers has led to
them brewing practically full-time to supply
another four outlets and beer festivals. All
the beers are also available bottle-conditioned. Apart from the three regular beers,
monthly specials and beer festival specials
are also produced. Beers: Roseburn Bitter
(OG 1038, ABV 3.8%), Gynack Glory (OG
1042, ABV 4.4%), Black Five (OG 1049,
ABV 5%).

ISLAND
See Burts.

ISLE OF MAN
See Okells.

ISLE OF SKYE
The Isle of Skye Brewing Company (Leann
an Eilein), The Pier, Uig, Isle of Skye IV51
9XY
Tel (01470) 542477 Fax (01470) 542488
**Shop 10-6 Mon-Sun, May-October Tours by
arrangement**
⊛ Brewery set up in 1995 on an island
which has no tradition of real ale. It is
housed in purpose-built premises at the pier
terminal for the Outer Hebrides. Trade is
steadily expanding and should continue with
the addition of a new bottling hall, completed in 1998. The company serves 50 outlets directly (nine on the island itself), and
others via wholesalers across Scotland and
into England.
Young Pretender *(OG 1040, ABV 4%)*
⬥ Golden amber ale with a burst of fruit on
the nose and a light and fruity sweetness in
the mouth, ending with a surprisingly bitter

finish.
Red Cullin *(OG 1042, ABV 4.2%)* ⬚⬥
A burst of fruit with malt introduces this
reddish beer. A lingering, fruity sweet character ensues, with a developing, gentle dryness.
Black Cuillin *(OG 1045, ABV 4.5%)* ⬥
Avalanche *(OG 1050, ABV 5%)* A powerful, full-bodied, golden ale with a strong,
hoppy aroma and hop flavour with a
smooth, malty balance and hints of fruit.

ITCHEN VALLEY
Itchen Valley Brewery Ltd, Shelf House,
New Farm Road, Alresford, Hampshire
SO24 9QE
Tel (01962) 735111 Fax (01962) 735678
Tours by arrangement
⊗ This brewery produced its first beer in
July 1997 in a former factory warehouse. It
was the brainchild of two businessmen who
hatched the idea while acting as godfathers
at a christening – hence the name of their
first beer. It supplies 30 outlets direct.
Occasional beers: Red Roses (OG 1041,
ABV 4%), Father Christmas (OG 1055,
ABV 5.5%).
Godfathers *(OG 1042, ABV 3.8%)*⬚⬥ A
pale brown beer with a hoppy aroma. A
malty and bitter taste leads through to the
finish.
Fagin *(OG 1043, ABV 4.1%)*
Judge Jeffreys *(OG 1048, ABV 4.5%)*

JENNINGS
Jennings Bros PLC, The Castle Brewery,
Cockermouth, Cumbria CA13 9NE
Tel (01900) 823214 Fax (01900) 827462
Shop 9-4.45 Mon-Fri Tours by arrangement
⊛ Founded in 1828, and moved to its present site in 1874, where it still uses its own
well water, Jennings has gradually expanded
over the years (particularly during the
1920s). Although there is no longer any
family involvement, many of the company's
shares are owned by local people. Around
200 free trade outlets are supplied from its
own Leyland and Newcastle depots, and
many more via a network of wholesalers
throughout the UK. Real ale is also available
in most of its 114 tied houses. Seasonal
beers: New Season's Ale (OG 1044, ABV
4.6%, September), La'al Cockle Warmer
(OG 1062, ABV 6.5%, November-
December).
Dark Mild *(OG 1031, ABV 3.1%)* A
dark, mellow, malty, sweet mild.
Bitter *(OG 1035, ABV 3.6%)* ⬥ A distinctive, red/brown brew with a hoppy, malty
aroma. A good, strong balance of grain and
hops in the taste, with a moderate bitterness,
develops into a lingering, dry, malty finish.
Cumberland Ale *(OG 1040, ABV 4%)*
⬥ A light, but hoppy, bitter, with a creamy
taste and smooth mouthfeel. The aroma can
be sulphury, but the taste ends crisp and dry
with a spicy bitterness.
Cocker Hoop *(OG 1047, ABV 4.8%)* ⬥
A full-flavoured, malty beer with a pronounced hop flavour and a complex bitter
aftertaste.
Sneck Lifter *(OG 1055, ABV 5.1%)*
A very dark bitter, with a rich, full malt
flavour, followed by a smooth and mellow
mixture of malt and hop in the after

taste.

JERSEY

Ann Street Brewery Co. Ltd t/a Jersey
Brewery, 57 Ann Street, St Helier, Jersey JE1
1BZ
Tel (01534) 31561 Fax (01534) 67033
Tours by arrangement
☒ Jersey (which was formerly known by its
parent company's title of Ann Street) began
brewing cask beer again in 1990 after a
break of 30 years. It has 50 tied houses, of
which 12 take real ale, including beers
from its sister company, Guernsey
Brewery.
Old Jersey Ale *(OG 1035, ABV 3.6%)*
◆ An attractive tawny/copper colour, this
bitter ale packs an immense depth of malt
flavours, the crystal malt giving hints of barley sugar. The malty bitterness is quite
intense in the aftertaste.
Ann's Treat *(OG 1050, ABV 5%)*
Winter Ale *(OG 1070, ABV 7.5%)* ◆
Very dark brown, with hues of copper, this
is a complex beer, full of roast barley and
malt flavours, giving glimpses of chocolate,
coffee and butterscotch. Quite bitter for its
strength and very rewarding.

JOHN O'GAUNT

John O'Gaunt Brewing Co. Ltd, Unit 4B
Rural Industries, John O'Gaunt,
Melton Mowbray, Leicestershire
LE14 2RE
Tel (07071) 223876 Fax (01664) 454777
Tours by arrangement
☒ This brewery was set up by Celia Atton
next to the Stag and Hounds pub at nearby
Burrough on the Hill (erstwhile home of the
Parish Brewery). The Post Office address is
as above. The first beer, Robin a Tiptoe, was
named after a local landmark; a third brew
is planned. Some 20 local outlets are sup-
plied.
Robin a Tiptoe *(OG 1043, ABV 3.9%)*
Cropped Oak *(OG 1047, ABV 4.4%)*

JOLLYBOAT

The Jollyboat Brewery Ltd, 4 Buttgarden
Street, Bideford, Devon EX39 2AU
Tel (01237) 424343 **Tours by arrangement**
☒ Brewery established in 1995 and currently
supplying over 30 local outlets, plus wholesalers. Plunder and Mainbrace are now
available bottled.
Buccaneer *(OG 1038, ABV 3.7%)* A pale
brown summer bitter with a pleasant presence of hops and bitterness from the nose
through to the aftertaste.
Mainbrace Bitter *(OG 1041,
4.2%)* ◆ Golden-coloured brew with malt
and hops on the nose. A well balanced malt
and bitter taste and finish.
Plunder *(OG 1048, ABV 4.8%)* ▨◆ A
good balance of malt, hops and fruit are present right through this red/brown-coloured
beer with a bitter finish.
Contraband *(OG 1055, ABV 5.8%)* A
porter available November-March.

JONES & MATHER

Jones & Mather Ales Ltd, Unit 2, North
Street Trading Estate, Brierley Hill,
W Midlands DY5 3QF

Brewery closed.

JOULE

See Coach House.

JUDGES

Judges Brewery, Unit 15A, Boughton Road
Industrial Estate, Boughton Road, Rugby,
Warwickshire CV21 1BU.
Tel (01788) 535356 **Tours by arrangement**
☒ Brewery set up in 1992 in a Warwickshire
village, but moved in 1995 to a larger site in
Rugby, doubling capacity. Its beers are sold in
about 12 local outlets on a regular basis, plus
another 100 in the Midlands as guests.
M'lud *(OG 1034, ABV 3.3%)* A medium
dark mild.
Barristers Bitter *(OG 1036, ABV 3.5%)*
▨◆ A well-balanced, pale-coloured session
beer; light and easily drinkable.
Grey Wig *(OG 1040, ABV 4%)* A blend
of Barristers and Old Gavel Bender.
Magistrate's Delight *(OG 1045, ABV
5%)* A reddish-brown, balanced ale.
Old Gavel Bender *(OG 1048, ABV 5%)*
◆ A beer with a complex hop, fruit and malt
aroma, with some caramel. There's a perfect
bittersweet balance in the taste, but no significant aftertaste.
Solicitor's Ruin *(OG 1054, ABV 5.6%)*
◆ Dark, strong and full-tasting: a very well-
hopped beer, with a smooth, sweetish, trea-
cly taste, and a bitter finish.

JUWARDS

Juwards Brewery, Unit 14G, c/o Fox
Brothers & Co. Ltd, Wellington, Somerset
TA21 0AW *Tel (01823) 667909*
☒ Juwards is a one-man band, owned by
Ted Bishop, former brewer at Cotleigh and
Ash Vine. Set up in 1994 in an old wool mill,
50 per cent of its production is sold to
wholesalers, while Juwards itself supplies 10
local outlets direct.
Bitter *(OG 1039, ABV 3.8%)*
Golden *(OG 1043, ABV 4.3%)*
Winter Brew *(OG 1043, ABV 4.3%)* A
seasonal porter.
Premium *(OG 1047, ABV 4.8%)*

KELHAM ISLAND

Kelham Island Brewery, 23 Alma Street,
Sheffield, S. Yorkshire S3 8SA
Tel (0114) 249 4804 Fax (0114) 249 4803
Tours by arrangement
☺ The brewery was due to move to a new
site in October 1998. Started as a brewpub
at the Fat Cat pub in 1990, this operation
moved in 1998 to new, purpose-built
premises next to the Kelham Island
Industrial Museum, from where it serves
over 60 outlets in Derbyshire,
Nottinghamshire and S. Yorkshire. Seasonal
beer: Red Rudolph (OG 1051, ABV 5%,
Christmas).
Bitter *(OG 1038, ABV 3.8%)* ◆ A clean
and crisp, pale brown beer of character. The
nose and taste are dominated by refreshing
hoppiness and fruitiness which last, along
with a good bitter dryness, in the aftertaste.
Golden Eagle *(OG 1043, ABV 4.2%)* ◆
An excellent hoppy, fruity best bitter. The
aroma is strong in hops with a slight fruitiness which gets stronger in the taste and in

the finish, which is moderately bitter.
Gatecrasher *(OG 1045, ABV 4.4%)*
A light, golden beer with a well-rounded, clean, fruity palate. It is bittered with English hops, with American hops added for aroma.
Hercules *(OG 1049, ABV 4.8%)*
Wheat Bier *(OG 1051, ABV 5%)* A new summer beer.
Pale Rider *(OG 1053, ABV 5.2%)* ◆
A well-bodied, straw-pale ale, with a good fruity aroma and a strong fruit and hop taste. Its well-balanced sweetness and bitterness continue in the finish.
Bête Noire *(OG 1056, ABV 5.5%)* 🗍◆
A dark ruby winter beer with little aroma. Malt and caramel, along with some fruitiness and dryness, are in the taste, which also has plum notes and chocolate, and develops into a dry, but sweet, aftertaste.
Grande Pale *(OG 1068, ABV 6.6%)*
A strong, full-bodied pale ale with a mellow hop aroma. A winter brew.

KELTEK

Keltek Brewing Company Ltd, Chandela House, Cardrew Industrial Estate, Redruth, Cornwall, TR15 1SS
Tel (01872) 530814 Fax (01872) 530814
⊠ Keltek was set up in Tregony in 1997 as a part-time venture and is due to move to a new purpose-built brewery at its new address in Redruth by autumn 1998. This will allow them to keep up with demand from wholesalers and ten local outlets, and for bottle-conditioned beers to be produced on a more regular basis. It also brews monthly 'specials' and house beers for pubs. Bottle-conditioned beers: Golden Lance (OG 1036, ABV 3.8%), King (OG 1050, ABV 5.1%), Trelawney's Revenge (ABV 7%).
Even Keel *(ABV 3.5%)*
Golden Lance *(OG 1036, ABV 3.8%)*
A pale golden beer.
Magik *(OG 1040, ABV 4.2%)* A fairly dark, strongly flavoured ale.
Nektar *(ABV 4.3%)* A new honey beer.
King *(OG 1050, ABV 5.1%)* A pale strong bitter.
Bishop Trelawney's Revenge *(ABV 7%)* A very dark, complex, sweetish ale.

KEMPTOWN

♥ **Kemptown Brewery Co. Ltd, Hand in Hand, 33 Upper St James's Street, Kemptown, Brighton, E. Sussex BN2 1JN**
Tel (01273) 699595 **Tours by arrangement**
⊠ Brewery established in 1989 (the oldest in Brighton), built in the 'tower' tradition behind the Hand in Hand, which is possibly the smallest pub in England with its own brewery. It takes its name and logo from the former Charrington's Kemptown Brewery 500 yards away, which closed in 1964. Six free trade outlets are supplied.
Brighton Bitter *(OG 1035, ABV 3.5%)*
◆ A refreshing, dry beer, with malt and hops in the flavour and a dry, hoppy finish.
Bitter *(OG 1041, ABV 4%)* ◆ Hops in the aroma lead into a soft, malt flavour with bitterness, which fades in the aftertaste.
Ye Old Trout *(OG 1045, ABV 4.5%)*
Staggering in the Dark (SID) *(OG 1057, ABV 6.7%)* ◆ A dark, almost black, beer with a vinous nose and a complex flavour, with roast and bitterness giving way

to a dry finish.
Old Grumpy *(OG 1063, ABV 6.2%)*
Available November-February.

KENT

Kent Brewery Ltd, Home Farm, Betteshanger, Deal, Kent CT14 0NT
Tel (01304) 614624 **Tours by arrangement**
⊠ A new brewery, set up in January 1998 in converted stables on the farm. Founded and run by ex-licensees. Brewing on a 28-barrel plant, using only Kentish hops and concentrating on local trade (about 75 outlets); distribution is from the brewery and not via wholesalers.
Swifty *(ABV 3.6%)* A full-flavoured classic ale with a distinctive hoppy finish.
Delight *(ABV 4%)* A strong blend of fruit and hops on the nose, followed by a hoppy bitterness and a dry aftertaste.
Crafty One *(ABV 4.6%)* A full-bodied, fruity-tasting premium ruby bitter with a dry, satisfying, hoppy aftertaste.
Crafty One *(ABV %)*
BSB *(OG 1050, ABV 5%)*

KING & BARNES

King & Barnes Ltd, The Horsham Brewery, 18 Bishopric, Horsham, W. Sussex RH12 1QP
Tel (01403) 270470 Fax (01403) 270570
Shop 11-7 Mon-Fri, 9-7 Sat Tours by arrangement
⊠ Long-established brewery, dating back almost 200 years and in the present premises since 1850. It is run by the King family, which united with the Barnes family brewery in 1906. A continuing programme of investment in brewery plant and machinery has meant its 'Fine Sussex Ales' are always in demand and that brewers such as Salopian are entrusting K&B with production of their bottled beers. All 57 tied houses take real ale, which is supplied direct to more than 200 other outlets. Seasonal/occasional beers: Summer Ale (OG 1039, ABV 3.8%, June-July), Best Bitter (OG 1041, ABV 4.1%), Valentine (OG 1042, ABV 4%, February), Amber Malt Ale (OG 1043, ABV 4.3%, May), Oatmeal Stout (OG 1045, ABV 4.5%, March), Slayers (OG 1045, ABV 5%, a rye lager), Challenger (OG 1047, ABV 4.7%), Ghost Blaster (OG 1047, ABV 4.5%), Harvest Ale (OG 1047, ABV 4.5%, September), Old Duck (OG 1047, ABV 4.7%), Horsham Ale (OG 1049, ABV 4.7%), IPA (OG 1051, ABV 5.2%), Christmas Ale (OG 1064, ABV 6.5%). Bottle-conditioned beers: Kings Crystal (OG 1040, ABV 4.1%), Faygate Dragon (OG 1047, ABV 4.7%), Single Hop Ale (OG 1047, ABV 4.7%), Festive (OG 1051, ABV 5.3%), IPA (OG 1051, ABV 5.3%), Worthington White Shield (OG 1052, ABV 5.6%), Coppercast (OG 1057, ABV 5.5%), Old Porter (OG 1058, ABV 5.5%), Cornucopia (OG 1069, ABV 6.5%).
Mild Ale *(OG 1034, ABV 3.5%)* 🗍◆ A well balanced, smooth, dark brown mild. A good crystal malt character is supported by undertones of roast malt and blackcurrant, leading to a dry finish.
Sussex *(OG 1034, ABV 3.5%)* ◆ While hops are still most apparent in the finish of this mid-brown bitter, they are not as evi-

dent throughout the beer as they used to be.

Broadwood *(OG 1042, ABV 4.2%)* ◆
A tawny-coloured, well-balanced beer from aroma to finish, with hops winning through in the end.

Old Ale *(OG 1045, ABV 4.5%)* ▮🍴◆
A dark brown, well-rounded old ale with an excellent balance of fruit, together with chocolate and roast malts. A classic, complex beer.

Festive *(OG 1050, ABV 5%)* ▮🍴◆ A redbrown beer with a fruity aroma. The flavour is also fruity and malty but with a noticeable hop presence. Malt and fruit dominate the aftertaste.

KITCHEN

The Kitchen Brewery, Unit J, Shaw Park Industrial Complex, Ivy Street East, Aspley, Huddersfield, W. Yorkshire HD5 9AF
Tel (01484) 300028 Fax (01484) 542709
Tours by arrangement
⊛ Brewery founded in 1996 by CAMRA member Robert Johnson in the pickling shed at the Shaw Park Industrial Complex, with a

five-barrel plant which uses steam as a heat source. It also houses the new Huddersfield Brewing Company (qv). The beers, whose names are derived from Robert's first career as a chef, are on sale in local pubs and in pubs in Northamptonshire (Robert's home county). The beer range varies every two months with the addition of new special brews. Seasonal beer: Plum Duff (ABV 5.2%, Christmas).

Commi *(ABV 3.6%)* Smooth, with a lightly aromatic character. A citrus beginning and fruity flavour are followed by a dry bitterness.

Aperitif *(ABV 4%)* A smooth, malty beer with a fruity flavour, mild bitterness and a well-balanced, lightly-hopped sweetness. Light brown in colour.

Syllabub *(ABV 4.2%)* A summer beer with a highly aromatic, dry-hop nose, a very dry flavour and moderate bitterness. Light amber in colour.

Waitress *(ABV 4.2%)* A smooth and aromatic beer with a slightly citrus beginning and a fruity flavour, ending with dry bitterness. Very light in colour.

A close shave: White Shield is saved by King & Barnes who take on the contract to brew it. Above is Bill King of K&B with Phil Haworth. Opposite is Bill (minus moustache) with David Crofton of Bass.

Celebration *(ABV 4.5%)*
Porter *(ABV 4.8%)* A dark, winter porter with a very smooth, creamy, malty, liquorice flavour. Lightly hopped, with a subtle spice note.
Potage *(ABV 4.7%)* A spring beer, straw-coloured, with a rich, malty flavour. Well-hopped nose; deep, fruity aftertaste.
Chef's Cut *(ABV 5%)* A light amber beer, mild, smooth and malty, with a citric, dry-hop note and some fruity flavour.

LAKELAND

Lakeland Brewing Company, 1 Sepulchre Lane, Kendal, Cumbria LA9 4NJ
Tel (01539) 734528
⊗ Brewery formerly based at the Masons Arms pub (see also Strawberry Bank), but now a completely separate business, serving over 20 local outlets. Lakeland's beers are currently brewed on 'borrowed' equipment, but the brewery was due to move in 1998. All beers are named after novels by local author Arthur Ransome. All the beers are also available bottle-conditioned. Beers: Amazon (OG 1046, ABV 4%), Great Northern (OG 1052, ABV 5%), Winter Holiday (OG 1052, ABV 5%), Damson Ale (OG 1055, ABV 5.5%).

LARKINS

Larkins Brewery Ltd, Larkins Farm, Chiddingstone, Edenbridge, Kent TN8 7BB
Tel (01892) 870328 Fax (01892) 871141
Tours by arrangement (winter weekends)
⊗ Larkins brewery was founded in 1986 by the Dockerty family (who are farmers and hop growers), with the purchase of the Royal Tunbridge Wells Brewery. Brewing was transferred to a converted barn at the family farm in 1989 and an additional copper and fermenter were acquired in 1991 to keep up with the growing local free trade. The additive-free beers can now be found in around 60 pubs and tourist venues in the South-East. Mostly Kent hops are used,
some from the farm itself.
Traditional Bitter *(OG 1035, ABV 3.4%)* A tawny-coloured beer.
Chiddingstone Bitter *(OG 1040, ABV 4%)* A malty and slightly fruity, bitter ale, with a very malty finish. Copper-red in colour.
Best Bitter *(OG 1045, ABV 4.4%)* ◆ Full-bodied, slightly fruity and unusually bitter for its gravity. Dangerously drinkable!
Porter *(OG 1054, ABV 5.2%)* ◆ Each taste and smell of this potent black winter beer reveals another facet of its character. An explosion of roasted malt, bitter and fruity flavours leaves a bittersweet aftertaste.

LEANN AN EILEIN

See Isle of Skye.

LEATHERBRITCHES

♡ Leatherbritches Brewery, Bently Brook Inn, Fenny Bentley, Ashbourne, Derbyshire DE6 1LF *Tel (01335) 350278 Fax (01335) 350422*
☺ Leatherbritches Brewery is housed behind the Bently Brook Inn, just north of Ashbourne, a pub owned by the parents of brewery founder, Bill Allingham. Founded in 1994, it soon outgrew its initial capacity of five barrels a week and has been expanded. Around 30 other local outlets take the beer, as do the three pubs owned by Steamin' Billy company, of which Bill owns 50 per cent. Bottle-conditioned beers: Stout (ABV 4%), Bespoke (ABV 5%).
Goldings *(ABV 3.6%)*
Belt 'n' Braces *(ABV 3.8%)* A light-coloured, hoppy session beer; a dry finish.
Steamin' Billy Mild *(ABV 3.8%)*
Belter *(ABV 4%)*
Stout *(ABV 4%)* A beer with a dominant chocolate flavour, smooth and fruity, with a long, satisfying finish.
Ashbourne Ale *(ABV 4.5%)*
Steamin' Billy Bitter *(ABV 4.5%)* A dry-hopped version of Ashbourne Ale.
Hairy Helmet *(ABV 4.7%)*
Bespoke *(ABV 5%)* A rich, well-balanced, fruity, full-bodied premium bitter.
Scrum Down Mild *(ABV 5.3%)*
Tarebrain (ABV 5.8%)

LEDBURY

Ledbury Brewing Co. Ltd, 5 The Southend, Ledbury, Herefordshire HR8 2EY
Tel (01531) 635031 Fax (01531) 635032
⊗ This brewery was first established in 1841 and was re-opened in the original building, some 75 years after its closure in 1921. After a change in management in September 1997, the brewery is currently building up its local trade with 65 outlets supplied directly. The beer range has been almost completely revised, while maintaining the production of a new 'special' beer, often of an experimental nature, each month. Seasonal beer: Xmas Ale (OG 1060, ABV 6.5%).
Challenger *(OG 1038, ABV 3.8%)* ◆ Bitterness is evident on the tongue in a rich, malty taste.
Clarkson's Progress *(OG 1038, ABV 4%)*
Northdown Winter *(OG 1039, ABV 4.2%)*

Clarkson's Best Bitter *(ABV 4.2%)*
Cluster *(OG 1042, ABV 4.6%)*

LEES

JW Lees & Co. (Brewers) Ltd, Greengate
Brewery, Middleton Junction, Manchester
M24 2AX
Tel (0161) 643 2487 Fax (0161) 655 3731
Tours by arrangement
☺ Family-owned brewery, founded in 1828
by John Willie Lees and now employing
sixth-generation family members. In 1995
Lees took on its first full-time cooper for
almost 30 years (half its cask beer is still
delivered in traditional oak casks). A new
range of seasonal beers is being developed.
All the brewery's 175 pubs (most in northern
Manchester) serve real ale, which is also supplied to 150 other outlets directly. Seasonal
beers: Jumbo Star Ale (OG 1043, ABV
4.5%), Ruff Yed (OG 1048, ABV 5%),
Scorcher (OG 1038, ABV 4%), Archer Stout
(OG 1046, ABV 4.6%).
GB Mild *(OG 1032, ABV 3.5%)* ◆ Malty
and fruity in aroma. The same flavours are
found in the taste, but do not dominate in a
beer with a rounded and smooth character.
Dry, malty aftertaste.
Bitter *(OG 1037, ABV 4%)* ◆ A pale beer
with a malty, fruity aroma and a distinctive,
malty, dry and slightly metallic taste. Clean,
dry Lees finish.
Moonraker *(OG 1073, ABV 7.5%)* ◆
A reddish-brown beer with a strong, malty,
fruity aroma. The flavour is rich and sweet,
with roast malt, and the finish is fruity yet
dry. Available only in a handful of outlets.

LEITH HILL

▽ RD & AJ Abrehart, T/A The Leith Hill
Brewery, The Plough Inn, Coldharbour
Lane, Coldharbour, Dorking, Surrey RH5
6HD *Tel/Fax (01306) 711793*
⊗ Without any previous brewing experience, the licensees of the Plough started
brewing at their pub in 1996, 'through
necessity, due to increasing overheads', using
a 'micro-micro' (half barrel) plant.
Expansion is planned when finances allow.
Spring water from Leith Hill (the highest
point in South-East England) is used in production. Beers: Crooked Furrow (OG 1040,
ABV 4.2%), Tallywhacker (OG 1056, ABV
5.6%).

LEYLAND

Leyland Breweries Ltd, Unit 78, Lawrence
Leyland Industrial Estate, Irthlingborough
Road, Wellingborough, Northamptonshire
NN8 1RT
Tel (01933) 275215 Fax (01933) 273225
⊗ Established by the merger of the former
Nene Valley and Nix Wincott breweries and
the beers are labelled either 'Nene',
'Wincott' or 'Leyland' when on sale. Future
plans include acquiring a chain of pubs.
Beers: Old Cock Up Mild (OG 1032, ABV
3.5%), This Bitter (OG 1034, ABV 3.6%),
Unicorn Bitter (OG 1036, ABV 3.6%), Two
Henrys Bitter (OG 1038, ABV 3.9%),
Leyland Gold (OG 1042, ABV 4.2%),
Griffin (ABV 4.4%), Leyland Happy Go
Lucky (OG 1046, ABV 4.6%), Old Black
Bob (OG 1047, ABV 4.7%), Winky's
Winter Warmer (ABV 4.7%), THAT (OG

1048, ABV 5%), Rawhide (OG 1050, ABV
5%), Midas (ABV 5.2%), Winky Wobbler
(OG 1072, ABV 7.5%), Medusa Ale (OG
1080, ABV 8%). Occasional beer: Trojan
Bitter (OG 1038, ABV 3.8%).

LICHFIELD

Lichfield Brewery, John Thompson Inn,
Ingleby, Derbyshire, DE7 1HW *Tel (01332)
863033* **Tours by arrangement**
☺ Established in 1992, the brewery moved
in June 1998 to new premises at the John
Thompson Inn across the Derbyshire border.
Still fully independent and under a new part-
nership, the brewery moved to increase
capacity and range. Over a hundred outlets
are supplied either directly or via agencies.
Seasonal beer: Mincespired (OG 1060, ABV
5.8%, Christmas).
Bellringer Mild *(OG 1037, ABV 3.7%)*
Steeplechase *(OG 1037, ABV 3.7%)*
A summer beer.
Inspired *(OG 1040, ABV 4%)* ◆ Dark
brown, malty beer with hops and some fruit
aroma and bitter finish.
Sheriff's Ride *(OG 1042, ABV 4.2%)*
A seasonal brew for autumn.
Resurrection Ale *(OG 1043, ABV 4.3%)*
Formerly a spring beer, now in the perma-
nent range.
Steeplejack *(OG 1045, ABV 4.5%)* ◆
Pale brown, with a distinct aroma of malt
and hops, tingles the palate and leaves a ple-
sant, dry finish.
Cavalier *(OG 1047, ABV 4.7%)* Pale,
hoppy, refreshing, aromatic brew.
Gargoyle *(OG 1050, ABV 5%)* Full bod-
ied, fruity yet bitter strong ale.

LIDSTONE'S

Lidstone's Brewery, Coltsfoot Green,
Wickhambrook, Newmarket, Suffolk CB8
8UW *Tel 01440 820232*
Tours by arrangement
Brewery started by a former solicitor in April
1998. Currently supplying the free trade in
Lincoln and North Yorkshire. The plan is to
move the brewery to a free house.
Bitter *(OG 1038, ABV 3.7%)*
Summer Ale *(OG 1041, ABV 4.1%)*
Best Bitter *(OG 1048, ABV 4.5%)*

LINFIT

▽ Linfit Brewery, Sair Inn, 139 Lane Top,
Linthwaite, Huddersfield, W. Yorkshire
HD7 5SG *Tel (01484) 842370*
Tours by arrangement
☺ Nineteenth-century brewpub (CAMRA
national Pub of the Year 1997) which
recommended brewing in 1982, producing
an impressive range of ales for sale here and
in the free trade as far away as Manchester
(27 regular outlets). New plant installed in
1994 has almost doubled its capacity.
Occasional/seasonal beers: Smoke House Ale
(OG 1040, ABV 5.3%), Pringbok Bier (OG
1055, ABV 5.7%), Xmas Ale (OG 1082,
ABV 8.6%). Bottle-conditioned beer:
English Guineas Stout (OG 1050, ABV
5.5%).
Mild *(OG 1032, ABV 3%)* ◆ Roast malt
dominates this straightforward dark mild
which has some hops in the aroma and a
slightly dry flavour. Malty finish.

Bitter *(OG 1035, ABV 3.7%)* ❧ A refreshing session beer. A dry-hopped aroma leads to a clean-tasting, hoppy bitterness, then a long, bitter finish with a hint of malt.
Ginger Beer *(OG 1040, ABV 4.2%)*
Swift *(OG 1040, ABV 4.2%)* ❧ Inviting hop aroma followed by a strong, hop bitterness, with a long, satisfying, bitter finish. Previously Summer Ale.
Special *(OG 1041, ABV 4.3%)* ❧ Dry-hopping provides the aroma for this rich and mellow bitter, which has a very soft profile and character: it fills the mouth with texture rather than taste. Clean, rounded finish.
Janet Street Porter *(OG 1043, ABV 4.5%)* A smooth, dry porter with a bitter, roasted malt character.
Autumn Gold *(OG 1050, ABV 4.7%)* ❧ Straw-coloured best bitter with hop and fruit aromas, then the bittersweetness of autumn fruit in the taste and the finish.
English Guineas Stout *(OG 1050, ABV 5.3%)* ❧ A fruity, roast aroma preludes a smooth, roasted malt, chocolatey flavour which is bitter but not too dry. Excellent appearance; good, bitter finish.
Old Eli *(OG 1050, ABV 5.3%)* A well-balanced premium bitter with a dry-hopped aroma and a fruity, bitter finish.
Baht Ale *(OG 1053, ABV 5.5%)*
Leadboiler *(OG 1063, ABV 6.6%)* ❧ Powerful malt, hop and fruit in good balance on the tongue, with a well-rounded bitter-sweet finish.
Enoch's Hammer *(OG 1080, ABV 8.6%)* ❧ A straw-coloured beer with malt, hop and fruit aromas. Mouth-filling, smooth malt, hop and fruit flavours with a long, hoppy bitter finish. Dangerously drinkable.

LITTLE AVENHAM
The Little Avenham Brewery, Arkwright Mill, Hawkins Street, Preston, Lancashire PR1 7HS
Brewery Closed.

LIVERPOOL
The Liverpool Brewing Company, The Brewery, 21-23 Berry Street, Liverpool L1 9DE *Tel (0151) 709 5055*
⊛ Brewery with a five-barrel plant, set up in 1990 to brew solely for what was the Black Horse & Rainbow pub, although this was sold and renamed The Brewery in 1996. The beer is stored in casks and cellar tanks and the brewing equipment can be viewed both from inside the pub and from the street. There has been much experimentation with different grains and hop types, resulting in Celebration staying the course, joined by five new beers which have helped increase sales to their own four outlets as well as to a handful of free houses.
Young Stallion *(OG 1038, ABV 3.6%)*
Red *(OG 1041, ABV 3.8%)*
Blondie *(OG 1044, ABV 4.1%)*
First Gold *(OG 1044, ABV 4.2%)*
Rocket *(OG 1045, ABV 4.3%)*
Celebration *(OG 1040, ABV 4.8%)*

LLOYDS
Lloyds Country Beers Ltd, John Thompson Brewery, Ingleby, Derbyshire DE73 1HW
Tel (01332) 863426 **Tours by arrangement**

⊠ Lloyds is the separate business set up to sell the beers brewed at the John Thompson Inn (qv) to the free trade. Despite problems in establishing a brand image in the guest beer market, and faced with a fluctuating demand, it still supplies around 150 outlets, mainly in the Midlands. Its single-hop brews, produced on a monthly basis, have been very well received. It is also brewing the beers of the High Peak Brewery, until suitable premises are found for that company.
Derby Bitter or JTS XXX *(OG 1042, ABV 4.1%)* Full and fruity.
IPA (Ingleby Pale Ale) *(OG 1045, ABV 4.5%)* A new summer beer.
Scratching Dog *(OG 1045, ABV 4.5%)*
Vixen Velvet *(OG 1045, ABV 4.5%)* A winter porter.
VIP (Very Important Pint) *(OG 1048, ABV 4.7%)* A heavier, darker version of the bitter.

For High Peak:
Peak Pale *(ABV 3.8%)*
Bagman's Bitter *(OG 1045, ABV 4.5%)*
Cracken *(ABV 5.5%, Christmas)*

LONDON BEER COMPANY
See Pitfield.

LUGTON
⌖ Lugton Inn & Brewery, Lugton, Ayrshire KA3 4DZ
Tel (01505) 850267 Fax (01505) 850509
Tours by arrangement
⊛ This brewpub is Ayrshire's only brewery, producing additive-free beers, just for the pub itself, from hops grown without the use of pesticide. In March 1998 it became a founder member of Scotland's Craft Beer Co-op, initially with four other breweries, who share the bottling line (not for bottle-conditioned beers) set up at Lugton. Beers are kept under top pressure. Beers: Black (OG 1036, ABV 3.4%), Gold (OG 1050, ABV 5%), John Barleycorn (OG 1050, ABV 5%).

LWCC
See Mansfield.

M&B

See Nationals, Bass.

MACLAY

Maclay Group plc, Thistle Brewery, Alloa FK10 1ED *Tel (01259) 216511*Tours by arrangement (for trade customers only)
☺ Founded in 1830 and moved to the present Victorian tower brewery in 1869, Maclay still uses traditional brewing methods and direct-fired coppers, with the beers produced using solely bore-hole water (the only Scottish brewery to do so) without any adjuncts. It is the last independent regional brewery in Scotland to remain in family ownership. Brewery modernisation has led to an upturn in sales with a wider distribution than ever before. Maclay has 34 tied houses, 20 of which serve real ale, which is also supplied direct to 100 other outlets. A range of seasonal ales is produced. Beers are brewed for Heather Ales under contract.
60/- *(OG 1035, ABV 3.4%)*
70/- *(OG 1037, ABV 3.6%)* ▆◆ A well-rounded, malty, fruity, clean-tasting beer. There is malt in the nose and a dry, but sweet, finish.
Broadsword *(OG 1039, ABV 3.8%)* ◆ A golden-coloured beer, with a lingering dry finish. Malt and fruit are dominant in the aroma, with a hop character developing in the bittersweet taste and becoming dominant in the bitter aftertaste.
80/- *(OG 1041, ABV 4%)* ◆ A rich, creamy, bittersweet beer, well worth seeking out; plenty of malt and fruit, balanced with bitterness in a lingering dry finish.
Kane's Amber Ale *(OG 1041, ABV 4%)* ◆ Brewed to commemorate the contribution of the late Dan Kane to Scottish brewing: a malty, fruity, bittersweet, amber-coloured beer with a good hop character. Perhaps not as bitter as when first launched.
Wallace IPA *(OG 1046, ABV 4.5%)* ◆ An aroma of malt, hops and fruit preludes a strong malty, hoppy taste with fruit still in evidence. These flavours linger in a bittersweet, hoppy aftertaste.

MALLARD

Mallard Brewery, 15 Hartington Avenue, Carlton, Nottingham NG4 3NR
Tel/Fax (0115) 952 1289
Tours by arrangement
⊗ Phil Mallard started his brewery in September 1995 and now has more than 40 regular customers, spread over 40 counties. Seasonal beer: Quismas Quacker (OG 1060, ABV 6%, Christmas).
Duck & Dive *(OG 1036, ABV 3.7%)*
A light single-hopped beer made from the new dwarf hop First Gold. A bitter beer with a very hoppy nose, good bitterness on the palate and a dry finish.
Best Bitter *(OG 1038, ABV 4%)* ◆ Golden brown, fruity and hoppy to the nose, with malt more apparent in the taste than anywhere else. The fruity hop carries through to a bitter, dry finish.
Duckling *(OG 1039, ABV 4.2%)* A crisp refreshing bitter with a hint of honey and citrus flavour. Dry hopped.
Waddlers Mild *(OG 1039, ABV 3.7%)* A dark ruby mild with a fruity chocolate

flavour in the moth and a fruity finish.
Drake *(OG 1044, ABV 4.5%)* A full bodied premium bitter, malt and hops on the palate and a fruity finish.
Friar Duck *(OG 1048, ABV 5%)* A pale full malt beer, hoppy with a hint of blackcurrant flavour.
Owd Duck *(OG 1048, ABV 4.8%)* ◆ Intensely roasty, this ruby/brown drink has moderate undertones of fruit and faint hops throughout.
DA *(OG 1059, ABV 5.8%)* A dark, sweetish winter ale.

MALTON

Malton Brewery Company Ltd, Suddaby's Crown Hotel, Wheelgate, Malton, N. Yorkshire YO17 0HP
Tel (01653) 697580 Fax (01653) 691812
Tours by arrangement
☺ Malton began brewing in 1985 in a stable block at the rear of the Crown Hotel (but is a separate business). The additive-free beers are supplied to around 35 free trade outlets directly and pubs further afield via wholesalers. Future plans include offering beer enthusiasts special stays at the hotel linked to a working day at the brewery. Bottled beers are also in the pipeline.
Pale Ale *(OG 1034, ABV 3.3%)*
Double Chance Bitter *(OG 1038, ABV 3.8%)* ◆ A clean-tasting, amber bitter in which hops predominate. Little malt character, but hop and fruit flavours lead to a smooth, bitter finish.
Pickwick's Porter *(OG 1042, ABV 4.2%)* ◆ A dry, nutty porter with an abundance of malt and roast aromas and flavours. The grainy malts combine with autumnal fruit flavours into a dry finish.
Crown Bitter *(OG 1045, ABV 4.5%)* ◆ A strong, malty pale ale, well-balanced by hop aromas and fruit flavours.
Winter Special *(OG 1052, ABV 5.2%)* A new seasonal beer.
Owd Bob *(OG 1055, ABV 6%)* ▆◆ A deep ruddy-brown coloured ale with a rich, warming feel. Powerful malt, roast, hops and fruit attack the nose and palate. The sweet finish, with malt and roast malt flavours, is balanced by a late trace of bitterness.

MAN IN THE MOON

The Man in the Moon Brewery, Unit L1, Elms Park Farm, Bitteswell, nr Lutterworth, Leicestershire LE17 4RA
Tel (0116) 2750275 Tours by arrangement
⊗ This brewery opened in 1996, and has since moved to a new site, redeveloped its product range and enjoyed rapid expansion. Currently supplying 12 free trade outlets directly, it has plans to acquire a couple of pubs of its own.
Harvest Moon *(OG 1038, ABV 3.7%)*
Eclipse *(OG 1041, ABV 4.1%)*
Ivory Stout *(OG 1040, ABV 4.1%)*
Werewolf *(OG 1050, ABV 5%)*

MANSFIELD

Mansfield Brewery PLC, Littleworth, Mansfield, Nottinghamshire NG18 1AB
Tel (01623) 625691 Fax (01623) 658620
Shop Tours by arrangement

☺ Founded in 1855, Mansfield has developed into one of the major regional brewers, with a tied estate of some 486 houses (three-quarters of which sell real ale). It returned to cask beer production in 1982 after a break of ten years. The purchase of Hull's North Country Brewery in 1985 and subsequent acquisitions from the Scottish Courage group have helped to bring Mansfield's award-winning ales, all fermented in traditional Yorkshire squares, to a wider audience. In 1997/8 the 263-strong tenanted estate underwent a £3 million refurbishment and upgrading programme. Sizeable club and free trade outlets are supplie. Mansfield produces a number of contract brews for Scottish Courage (Younger's Scotch, MB Lion Mild, MB Lion Bitter, Home Mild), Webster's (Pennine Bitter) and LWCC wholesalers in Manchester, tel: (0161) 707 7878. Four Season's cask bitter (3.6% ABV) is produced for the Beer Seller, and Tavern Classic (3.5% ABV) for Tavern Wholesale.
Riding Mild *(OG 1035, ABV 3.5%)* ◥
Chocolate malt on the nose leads to blackcurrant fruit on the taste, with hops finishing. However, the chocolate malt continues throughout this ruby-black beer.
Riding Bitter *(OG 1035, ABV 3.6%)* ◥
A beer first aimed at Mansfield's Yorkshire market. Mid-brown and moderately bitter, it is dominated by an aromatic, fruity hop, but with malt always present.
Mansfield Bitter *(OG 1038, ABV 3.9%)*
◥ This mid-brown bitter is well balanced in taste but has hops to the fore on the nose and malt lingering in the aftertaste, although some bitterness is discernible.
Old Baily *(OG 1045, ABV 4.8%)* ▣◥
Malt dominates over moderate hop in this discernibly Scotch-style brew. Generally more bitter than sweet, it has a pleasant fruitiness on the nose. Complex and rewarding when on form.
For Scottish Courage:
Matthew Brown Lion Mild *(OG 1030, ABV 3.1%)*
Matthew Brown Lion Bitter *(OG 1034, ABV 3.5%)*
Home Mild *(OG 1036, ABV 3.6%)*

MANSFIELD ARMS
See Devon.

MARBLE
⌂ The Marble Brewery, 73 Rochdale Road, Manchester M4 4HY
Tel/Fax (0161) 819 2694 Tours by arrangement
Opened in December 1997 behind the Marble Arch free house, this new brewery supplies that tied house and a rapidly growing number of free trade outlets.
Bitter *(OG 1040, ABV 4%)*
IPA *(OG 1046, ABV 4.6%)*
Totally Marbled *(OG 1050, ABV 5%)*
Dobber Strong *(OG 1065, ABV 6.5%)*

MARCHES
Marches Ales, Unit 6, Western Close, Southern Avenue Industrial Estate, Leominster, Herefordshire HR6 0QD
Tel (01568) 611084 Tours by arrangement
⊗ The Solstice Brewery of Kington was

taken over by Paul Harris in 1995 and moved to this new purpose-built brewery, which takes its name from its location at the edge of the Marches. Demand for the beers has led to expansion of the brewery. The beer range has also been expanded to include seasonal brews and house beers brewed exclusively for the Black Horse in Leominster. Free trade has grown to 80 outlets.
Lempster Ore *(OG 1036, ABV 3.8%)*
Best Bitter *(OG 1038, ABV 3.8%)*
Forever Autumn *(OG 1040, ABV 4.2%)*
◥ Hop fruitiness predominates in a complex array of flavours, to give a rich aftertaste.
Gold *(OG 1043, ABV 4.5%)*
Sunshine 855 *(OG 1044, ABV 4.5%)*
A summer beer.
Priory Ale *(OG 1046, ABV 4.8%)*
Available October-March.
Lord Protector *(OG 1046, ABV 4.7%)*
Jenny Pipes Blonde *(OG 1050, ABV 5.2%)*
Earl Leofric's Winter Ale *(OG 1072, ABV 7.2%)*

MARSTON MOOR
Marston Moor Brewery, Crown House, Kirk Hammerton, York, N. Yorkshire YO5 8DD *Tel/Fax (01423) 330341*
☺ Small but expanding brewery, set up in 1983 and moved to the rear of its first tied house, the Crown, in 1988. This pub was closed in 1993 after the acquisition of the Beer Exchange at Woodhouse in Leeds. The company currently brews 1,000 barrels a year and supplies around 50 free trade outlets. It also installs brewing plants and acts as a consultant to mini-brewers, both here and abroad; to date it has helped set up 25 breweries in the UK. Bottle-conditioned beer: Brewers Droop (ABV 5%).
Cromwell Bitter *(OG 1036, ABV 3.6%)*
◥ A golden beer with hops and fruit in strong evidence on the nose. Bitterness as well as fruit and hops dominate the taste and long aftertaste.
Brewers Pride *(OG 1042, ABV 4.2%)* ◥
A light but somewhat thin, fruity beer, with a hoppy, bitter aftertaste.
Merrie Maker *(OG 1044, ABV 4.5%)*
Brewers Droop *(OG 1049, ABV 5%)*
A pale, robust ale with hops and fruit notes in prominence. A long, bitter aftertaste.
Trooper *(OG 1049, ABV 5%)*

MARSTON'S
Marston, Thompson & Evershed PLC, Shobnall Road, Burton upon Trent, Staffordshire DE14 2BW
Tel (01283) 531131 Fax (01283) 510378
Shop 10-2 Tours by arrangement
☺ The only brewery still using the Burton Union system of fermentation (for its stronger ales), Marston's reinforced its commitment to this method in 1992 with a £1 million investment in a new Union room. Real ale is available in all the company's 868 pubs, which stretch from Yorkshire to Hampshire. The Head Brewer's Choice scheme (noted as HBC in *Good Beer Guide* pub entries) offers a range of new brews to selected outlets for two weeks at a time. Marston's also enjoys an enormous free trade, thanks to trading agreements with

The Marston's team at the World Barrel Rolling Competition, which is held annually at the Burton Festival. The 36-gallon oak casks and bobbin sticks are made by Marston's cooperage. Marston's Pedigree is one of the best-selling cask ales in the UK.

many regional and national brewers. In 1998 Pedigree overtook Draught Bass to become Britain's top-selling best bitter, according to a survey carried out for the *Publican*. Bottle-conditioned beer: Oyster Stout (OG 1045, ABV 4.5%)⊡.
Bitter *(OG 1037, ABV 3.8%)* ✎ An amber/tawny session beer which can often be sulphury in aroma and taste. At its best, a splendid, subtle balance of malt, hops and fruit follows a faintly hoppy aroma and develops into a balanced, dry aftertaste.
Pedigree *(OG 1043, ABV 4.5%)* ✎ Sulphurous aroma giving way to hops. Tastes hoppy and fruity and leaves a bitter aftertaste; moreish.
Owd Rodger *(OG 1080, ABV 7.6%)* ▣⊡✎ Strong, dark red, fruity barley wine. Sweet start with a liquorice character develops into fruit and hops and finishes with a spicy, dry, lingering aftertaste.

For Tesco:
Tesco Select Ales IPA *(OG 1048, ABV 5%)*
Tesco Select Ales Porter *(OG 1048, ABV 5%)*

For Wetherspoons:
Sundance *(OG 1048, ABV 5%)* An IPA-style beer.

MASH & AIR
40 Charlton Street, Manchester M1 3HW
Tel (0161) 661 6161 Fax (0161) 661 6060
'Brew restaurant' founded in 1997 in converted mill, specialising in tutored beer-tasting lunches, with beers brewed to accompany various meals. Tours (with a meal) Sat. All beers are conditioned and stored in cellar tanks using a cask-breather-type CO2 system. Beers: Peach (ABV 5%), Mash (ABV

5.1%), Mash Wheat (ABV 5%), Blackcurrant Porter (ABV 5.3%), India Pale Ale (ABV 5.3%), Scotch (ABV 6%). An outlet was set up in London in 1998.

MASONS ARMS
See Lakeland and Strawberry Bank.

MAULDONS
Mauldons Brewery, 7 Addison Road, Chilton Industrial Estate, Sudbury, Suffolk CO10 6YW
Tel (01787) 311055 Fax (01787) 311055
Tours by arrangement
⊗ Company set up in 1982 by former Watney's brewer Peter Mauldon, whose family had its own local brewery in the late 18th century. Its extensive beer list changes frequently and is supplied to 150 free trade outlets in East Anglia, as well as pubs further afield via wholesalers. Seasonal beers: Broomstick Bitter (OG 1040, ABV 4%, Hallowe'en), Mother's Ruin (OG 1040, ABV 4%, Mothering Sunday), George's Best (OG 1045, ABV 4.4%, St George's Day), Love Potion No. 9 (OG 1045, ABV 4.5%, St Valentine's Day), Bah Humbug (OG 1049, ABV 4.9%, Christmas), Mr McTavish (OG 1050, ABV 5%, January), Gunpowder Blast (OG 1063, ABV 6%, Guy Fawkes Night), Christmas Reserve (OG 1066, ABV 6.6%).
May Bee *(OG 1037, ABV 3.7%)* Softer than the Best Bitter, with added honey. Available in summer.
Moletrap Bitter *(OG 1037, ABV 3.8%)* ✎ Previously Best Bitter, a well-balanced session beer with a crisp, hoppy bitterness balancing sweet malt.
Original Porter *(OG 1042, ABV 3.8%)* ✎ A black beer with malt and roast malt flavours dominating. Some hop in the finish.

Midsummer Gold (OG 1040, ABV 4%)
A light-coloured summer beer.
Mid Autumn Gold (OG 1041, ABV 4.2%)
A seasonal offering.
Eatanswill Old XXXX (OG 1042, ABV
4%) ❦ Taking its name from the title given
to Sudbury by Dickens in Pickwick Papers,
this is a winter ale of deep red and brown
hue, with well-balanced fruit and malt plus a
slight sweetness on the palate, ending in a
pleasant roast bitterness.
Squires Bitter (OG 1044, ABV 4.2%) ❦
A best bitter with a good, malty aroma and a
reasonably balanced flavour, which leans
towards malt. Hops come through late and
crisply into the aftertaste.
Midwinter Gold (OG 1045, ABV 4.5%)
A winter beer.
Suffolk Pride (OG 1050, ABV 4.8%) ❦
Formerly Suffolk Punch, a full-bodied,
strong bitter. The malt and fruit in the
aroma are reflected in the taste and there is
some hop character in the finish. Deep
tawny/red in colour.
Black Adder (OG 1053, ABV 5.3%) ❦
A dark stout. Roast malt is very strong in the
aroma and taste, but malt, hop and bitterness
provide an excellent balance and a lingering
finish. Champion Beer of Britain 1991.
White Adder (OG 1053, ABV 5.3%) 🍺 ❦
A pale brown, almost golden, strong ale. A
warming, fruity flavour dominates and
lingers into a dry, hoppy finish.
Suffolk Comfort (OG 1065, ABV 6.6%)
🍺 A clean, hoppy nose leads to a predominantly malty flavour in this full-bodied beer.
Dry, hoppy aftertaste.

MAYHEM

⊗ See Farmers Arms.

MAYPOLE

Maypole Brewery, North Laithes Farm,
Wellow Road, Eakring, Newark,
Nottinghamshire NG22 0AN
Tel (01623) 871690 Tours by arrangement
⊗ Brewery established in 1995 in an 18th-
century converted farm building, with equip-
ment purchased from Springhead Brewery.
Its name comes from the permanent giant
maypole which is a feature of neighbouring
Wellow. One beer, Lion's Pride (OG 1038,
ABV 3.9%) is brewed just for the Red Lion
opposite the maypole. Currently supplying
around 40 outlets, Maypole also brews one-
off beers for festivals and other events.
Seasonal beer: Donner and Blitzed (OG
1048, ABV 5.1%, a stronger version of
Poleaxed for Christmas).
Celebration (OG 1040, ABV 4%) ❦
A ruddy-brown bitter in which malt dominates. Some fruity hop in the nose and taste,
with an initial sweetness that dries into a bitter
finish where the fruit and hops meet the malt.
Mayfair (OG 1037, ABV 3.8%)
Centenary Ale (OG 1041, ABV 4.2%)
A light-coloured bitter with a fruity nose and a
dry aftertaste. There are hints of vanilla in this
crisp, refreshing, moreish beer. Full-bodied.
Flanagan's Stout (OG 1043, ABV 4.4%)
Brewed initially for St Patrick's Day: a full-
bodied, rich stout. An initial burnt malt dryness gives way to a smooth, mellow, lingering aftertaste with hints of liquorice, dark
chocolate and coffee.

Mayday (OG 1045, ABV 4.5%) 🍺❦ A
tawny best bitter, with malt and a hint of
dates on the nose. The taste is predominantly
fruit and malt again, which becomes more
bitter and hoppy in the finish.
Mae West (OG 1044, ABV 4.6%)
A blonde, 'Belgian-style' summer beer. Citrus
flavours predominate in the nose and taste. A
deceptively drinkable beer for its strength.
Poleaxed (OG 1046, ABV 4.8%) A tawny,
smooth beer. Damsons come out in the nose
and taste which give way to a slightly burnt
aftertaste. A full-bodied, warming beer
which is easily drinkable.
Old Homewrecker (OG 1047, ABV 4.7%)
A smooth winter porter. Initial maltiness gives
way to a bittersweet aftertaste. Black in colour.

McEWAN

See Nationals, Scottish Courage.

McGUINNESS

⎔ Thomas McGuinness Brewing Company,
1 Oldham Road, Rochdale, Greater
Manchester OL16 1UA
Tel/Fax (01706) 711476 Tours
☺ Small brewery established in 1991 behind
the Cask & Feather pub by the late Thomas
McGuinness and brewer Eric Hoare. It currently supplies real ale to its own pub and six
other local outlets direct and nationwide via
wholesalers. 'Personalised contract brewing'
was introduced in 1996 for pubs wanting to
use their own brand name on beers of a
requested colour and strength. Seasonal
beers: Winter's Revenge (ABV 4.6%,
January-March), Egg Nobbler's Strong Ale
(ABV 4.6%, Easter), Christmas Cheer (ABV
4.6%, winter).
Feather Plucker Mild (OG 1034, ABV
3.4%) A dark brown beer, with roast malt
dominant in the aroma and taste. There's a
touch of bitterness, too.
Best Bitter (OG 1038, ABV 3.8%) ❦ Gold
in colour with a hoppy aroma: a clean,
refreshing beer with hop and fruit tastes and
a hint of sweetness. Bitter aftertaste.
Utter Nutter (OG 1038, ABV 3.8%)
Special Reserve Bitter (OG 1040, ABV
4%) ❦ A tawny beer, sweet and malty, with
underlying fruit and bitterness, and a bittersweet aftertaste.
Junction Bitter (OG 1042, ABV 4.2%) ❦
Mid-brown in colour, with a malty aroma.
Maltiness is predominant throughout, with
some hops and fruit in the taste and bitterness coming through in the finish.
Autumn Glory (ABV 4.6%) Available mid-
September-mid-January.
Summer Tipple (ABV 4.6%) Available
May-September.
Tommy Todd's Porter (OG 1050, ABV
5%) 🍺❦ A winter warmer, with a fruit and
roast aroma, leading to a balance of malt
and roast malt flavours, with some fruit. Not
too sweet for its gravity.

McMULLEN

McMullen & Sons Ltd, The Hertford
Brewery, 26 Old Cross, Hertford SG14 1RD
Tel (01992) 584911 Fax (01992) 500729
Tours by arrangement
⊗ Hertfordshire's oldest independent brew-
ery, founded in 1827 by Peter McMullen.

The Victorian tower brewery, which houses the original oak and copper-lined fermenters still in use today, was built on the site of three wells. Cask ale is served in all McMullen's 145 pubs in Hertfordshire, Essex and London (although nearly all use cask breathers), and also supplied directly to 75 free trade outlets. Seasonal beers are brewed for a limited period under the banner of McMullen Special Reserve.

Original AK *(OG 1033, ABV 3.7%)*◻◈
A pleasant mix of malt and hops leads to a distinctive, dry aftertaste. Well-attenuated.
Country Best Bitter *(OG 1041, ABV 4.3%)* ◈ A full-bodied beer with a well-balanced mix of malt and hops throughout and fruit flavours coming through later.
Gladstone *(OG 1041, ABV 4.3%)* ◻◈
A beer with a hoppy, fruity aroma, a full-bodied, mainly malty flavour and a sweetish, fruity aftertaste.
Strongheart *(OG 1065, ABV 7%)* ◻◈
A sweetish, rich, dark, winter beer, full of fruit and hop aromas and flavours.

MERIVALES

Merivales Ales Ltd, Warden Brewery, Manor Farm, Chipping Warden, near Banbury, Oxfordshire OX17 1LH
Tel/Fax (01295) 710204
Tours by arrangement
Company set up in 1994 with a tiny brew-plant at Edgcote, it moved in 1996 to a lovely old tithe barn (in Northamptonshire, despite the postal address), with eight times the capacity. After a few hiccups, the brewery is now fulfilling its targets and supplying some 15 outlets regularly with its beers, plus around 30 others on an intermittent basis.
Haywain *(OG 1034, ABV 3.4%)* Brewed March-September.
CHB or Choice Hopped Bitter *(OG 1039, ABV 3.9%)*
Chaser *(ABV 4.5%)*
Twister *(OG 1051, ABV 5.1%)*

MERRIMANS

Merrimans Brewery, Old Fart Ltd, Weston Square, Beeston, Leeds
Brewery closed.

MIDDLETON'S

The Wheatsheaf, 67 Manor Road, St Helens, Bishop Auckland, Co. Durham
Brewing ceased.

MIGHTY OAK

Mighty Oak Brewing Company, 9 Prospect Way, Hutton Industrial Estate, Brentwood, Essex CM13 1XA *Tel/Fax (01277) 263007*
Tours by arrangement
⊗ Brewery launched in August 1996, constructed largely from equipment purchased from the defunct Whitworth Hall Brewery in Co. Durham. Mighty Oak has a potential capacity of around 50 barrels a week. It supplies about 80 outlets, mostly within a radius of 20 miles, and including some Whitbread Hogshead pubs. Occasional beers: Heartswood Bitter (ABV 3.8%), Ale Dancer (ABV 4.2%), Bingle Jells (ABV 5.2%, Christmas).

Barrackwood IPA *(OG 1038, ABV 3.6%)*
A new golden, predominently malty, beer.
Burntwood Bitter *(OG 1041, ABV 4%)*
A very well-balanced mix of hops, malt and fruit; mid-brown in colour.
Twenty Thirst Bitter *(OG 1044, ABV 4.4%)* Initially brewed for South-West Essex CAMRA's 21st anniversary: an amber-coloured and fairly fruity beer, yet still with good bitter content.
Bitter *(OG 1047, ABV 4.8%)* Red-brown in colour and fairly full-bodied. Malty, with a balancing bitterness.

MILDMAY

The Mildmay Brewery, Holbeton, Plymouth, Devon PL8 1NA.
⊗ Ceased brewing in September 1997 . The contracts for supplying beer to Jolly's wholesalers – Mildmay Colours and 50/1 – were taken on by Skinners of Cornwall.

MILLWRIGHT'S ARMS

The Millwright's Arms, Coten End, Warwickshire CV34 4NU
Tel (01926) 49695 Tours by arrangement
Brewpub which started brewing its own guest beer at the end of 1997. Planning to bew different ales and increase the range.
Jimmy Ridddle *(OG 1040, ABV 3.8%)*
The Full Malty *(OG 1047, ABV 4.9%)*

MINERVA

See Nationals, Carlsberg-Tetley.

MITCHELL'S

Mitchell's of Lancaster (Brewers) Ltd, 11 Moor Lane, Lancaster, Lancashire LA1 1QB
Tel (01524) 63773 Fax (01524) 846071
Tours by arrangement
☺ The only surviving independent brewery in Lancaster (est. 1880), wholly owned and run by direct descendants of founder William Mitchell. In 1997 it increased its tied estate by acquiring 26 new pubs, bringing the total up to 78; all but one of them sell real ale. The estate now covers east Lancashire, from Blackburn northwards to south Cumbria and North Yorkshire. The beers are also available nationwide in the free trade. Occasional/seasonal beers: Lakeland Reserve (OG 1036, ABV 3.6%, July-August), Spooner (OG 1044, ABV 4.5%), Conqueror (OG 1049, ABV 5%), Brewer's Pride (OG 1052, ABY 5.2%), Old Faithful (OG 1052, ABV 5.2%), Guy Fawkes (OG 1048, ABV 4.8), Christmas Cracker (OG 1056, ABV 5.5%).
Dark Mild *(OG 1035, ABV 3.3%)* A light-flavoured malty beer, with hints of liquorish and a dry finish.
Bitter *(OG 1036, ABV 3.8%)* A pale gold beer, a light hoppy aroma, a malty hoppy taste with some fruit notes, clean tasting with a good long finish.
Lancaster Bomber *(OG 1044, ABV 4.4%)* A dark golden bitter with some hop aroma; a rich, full palate of nicely balanced hops and malt.

MITCHELLS & BUTLERS

See Nationals, Bass.

MOLE'S

Mole's Brewery (Cascade Drinks Ltd),
5 Merlin Way, Bowerhill, Melksham,
Wiltshire SN12 6TJ
Tel (01225) 704734
Fax (01225) 790770
Tours by arrangement
⊗ Brewery established in 1982 by former
Ushers brewer Roger Catté. It brews traditional cask-conditioned beer primarily for
the local trade (around 200 outlets), delivered by its own wholesale company within a
100-mile radius of Melksham. The beers are
also available in 14 of its 15 tied houses and
nationwide via other brewers and wholesalers. Expansion during 1997 increased
capacity to 250 barrels a week. Seasonal
beers: Molegrip (OG 1047, ABV 4.7%),
Moél Moél (OG 1060, ABV 6%,
Christmas), Holy Moley (OG 1047, ABV
4.7%), Barley Mole (OG 1042, ABV 4.2%).
Bottle-conditioned beer: Brew 97 (OG 1050,
ABV 5%).
Tap Bitter *(OG 1035, ABV 3.5%)* ◆ A pale
brown beer with a trace of malt in the
aroma. A gentle, malty, dry flavour with
apple and pear fruits follows, then a bitter
finish.
Best Bitter *(OG 1040, ABV 4%)* ◆ A pale
brown/golden-coloured beer with a light
malt aroma. The taste is clean, dry and
malty, with some bitterness and delicate floral hop. A well-balanced, light and subtle
ale.
Landlords Choice *(OG 1045, ABV 4.5%)*
A deceptively strong dark, smooth, hoppy
bitter.
Brew 97 *(OG 1050, ABV 5%)* ◆ A mid-
brown, full-bodied beer with a gentle malt
and hop aroma. The rich flavour is malty,
with fruit, hop and traces of vanilla. A wonderfully warming, malty ale.

MOOR

Moor Beer Company, Whitley Farm,
Ashcott, Bridgwater, Somerset
TA7 9QW
Tel/Fax (01458) 210050
Shop 9-5 (when brewery is open) Tours by
arrangement
⊗ Farmer Arthur Frampton and his wife
Annette set up this brewery in a former
workshop on their dairy farm in 1996. The
business took off quickly, mainly due to the
large number of free houses in the area. The
dairy cows were soon replaced by Gloucester
Old Spot pigs who happily munch through
the used malt. The plant has been upgraded
to ten barrels and the beer range increased;
there are plans afoot for bottling. The brewery supplies over 40 regular outlets, plus
another 40 with guest beers. Occasional/sea-
sonal beer: Santa Moors (OG 1052, ABV
5%).
Withy Cutter *(OG 1041, ABV 3.8%)*
A lightly malty, pale brown beer with a
moderate bitter finish.
Merlin's Magic *(OG 1044, ABV 4.3%)*
Amber-coloured, malty and full-bodied,
with fruit notes.
Peat Porter *(OG 1045, ABV 4.4%)*
Chandos Gold *(OG 1052, ABV 5%)*
A straw-coloured, hoppy strong ale.
Old Freddy Walker *(OG 1074, ABV
7.3%)*

MOORHOUSE'S

Moorhouse's Brewery (Burnley) Ltd.,
4 Moorhouse Street, Burnley, Lancashire
BB11 5EN *Tel/Fax (01282) 422864*
Tours by arrangement
⊗ Long-established (1865) producer of hop
bitters, which in 1978 began brewing cask
beer. A succession of owners failed to
develop the company until it was taken over
in 1985 by Bill Parkinson, since when it has
grown considerably, opening the first of six
tied houses in 1987. A modern brewhouse
was installed in 1988 and more fermenting
vessels were added in 1991 to keep up with
demand. Moorhouse's supplies real ale to
around 190 free trade outlets, and brews a
single beer under contract for Yates Brothers
Ltd., tel (0161) 273 3336.
Black Cat *(OG 1036, ABV 3.4%)* ▨
Premier Bitter *(OG 1036, ABV 3.7%)* ◆
Pale brown in colour, this characterful brew
has a superb hop flower aroma, with some
fruit and malt. Dry, hoppy finish.
Pendle Witches Brew *(OG 1050, ABV
5.1%)* ▢ ◆ A good hoppy aroma leads
through to a full-bodied, malty sweetness,
with a trace of hop bitterness.
Owd Ale *(OG 1065, ABV 6.2%)* A winter
beer brewed November-January.

For Yates Brothers:
Peter Yates 1884 *(OG 1040, ABV 4.1%)*

MORDUE

Unit 21A, West Chirton North Industrial
Estate, Shiremoor, Tyne & Wear NE29 8SF
Tel/Fax (0191) 2961879 Tours by
arrangement
⊗ Before winning the Champion Beer of
Britain award at the Great British Beer
Festival in 1997, the brewery had a capacity
of 30 BBL a week. A new site opposite the
old brewery has now opened and a new 20
BBL brewlength brewing plant has been
installed. The brewery plans to buy its first
pub in 1998. Mordue has already purchased
Heaton Drink off-licence, which has five
handpulls (four Mordue and one guest) and
over 100 different bottled beers, mainly
microbreweries and Belgian beers. Around
100 outlets are currently supplied. Seasonal
beers: Summer Tyne (ABV 3.6%), Spring
Tyne (ABV 4%), Headmasters Xmas
Sermon (ABV 5.2%), Wallsend Brown Ale
(ABV 4.5%).
Five Bridge Bitter *(ABV 3.8%)* ◆
A fruity, amber beer with more than a hint
of hops. The bitterness carries on in the
aftertaste. A superb session beer.
Geordie Pride *(ABV 4.2%)* ◆ A well balanced, hoppy bitter with a long, butter finish.
An amber hue and a hoppy, fruity aroma.
Workie Ticket *(ABV 4.5%)* ▢ ◆ A tasty,
complex beer with malt and hops throughout and a long, satisfying bitter finish. Well
worthy of the title Champion Beer of Britain
1997. Now available in 500ml bottles.
Black Midden Stout *(OG 1046, ABV
4.6%)* Named after the treacherous rocks in
the tynemouth Estuary, it is a rich and tasty
example of its type.
Radgie Gadgie *(ABV 4.8%)* ▨◆ A strong,
easy-drinking, northern ale, with balanced
hops, fruit and malt and a long, lingering
finish. Soon to be available in bottles.

MORLAND

Morland PLC, The Brewery, Ock Street, Abingdon, Oxfordshire OX14 5BZ
Tel (01235) 553377 Fax (01235) 540508
Tours by arrangement
⊗ Established in 1711, Morland is the second oldest independent brewer in the UK. In 1992 it survived a takeover bid by Greene King and in 1995 it purchased the small pub company Unicorn Inns, owner of the Newt & Cucumber mini-chain, as well as the Wig & Pen chain and 24 Exchange Diners from Allied Domecq. In 1997 Morland acquired the major regional Ruddles brewery from its Dutch owner, Grolsch, but far from continuing to brew the once famous Ruddles brands (and Wilson's Original Mild for Scottish Courage) at Langham in Leicestershire, Morland decided to shut down the brewery. Most of Morland's 410 pubs serve real ale, but in some cases the licensee uses cask breathers. The company also supplies around 250 free trade outlets around the Thames Valley and Surrey. Last year a £5 million investment in the brewery expanded production facilities in Abingdon.
Independent IPA *(OG 1036, ABV 3.4%)*
Ruddles Best Bitter *(OG 1037, ABV 3.7%)* ▯

Original Bitter *(OG 1039, ABV 4%)* ◆ A light amber beer with malty, hoppy nose and a hint of fruitiness. Distinct, but lightish, malt and hops carry over to the flavour and leave a sweet but dry, hoppy aftertaste.
The Tanners Jack *(ABV 4.4%)*
Ruddles County *(OG 1049, ABV 4.9%)* ▮
Old Speckled Hen *(OG 1052, ABV 5.2%)* ◆ Morland's most distinctive beer, deep tawny/amber in colour. A well-balanced aroma of malt and hops is followed by an initially sweet, malty, fruity taste which soon allows dry hop flavour through.

For Scottish Courage:
Wilson's Original Mild *(OG 1032, ABV 3%)*

MORRELLS

Morrells Brewery Ltd, The Lion Brewery, St Thomas' Street, Oxford OX1 1LA
Tel (01865) 792013 Fax (01865) 791868
Tours by arrangement
⊗ The oldest brewery in Oxford has been owned or managed by the Morrell family since they acquired it in 1782. Of its 131 pubs, over 50 are within the city limits and all but one of them serve cask ale, though

Garry and Matthew Fawson of Mordue celebrate winning CAMRA's Champion Beer of Britain award at the Great British Beer Festival. Their brew, Workie Ticket, is called after the Geordie dialect phrase for a loafer — but it's hard work brewing great beer.

some employ blanket pressure. Around 180 other outlets are supplied directly from the brewery. As this *Guide* went to press Morrells had been put up for sale. Seasonal beer: College Ale (OG 1073, ABV 7.4%, winter).

Oxford Bitter *(OG 1036, ABV 3.7%)* ❦
Golden in colour and light in body, but not in flavour, with a good aroma of hops complemented by malt and fruitiness. An initial dry hop bitterness is well-balanced by malt, which gives way to a refreshing, slightly sweet fruitiness. Bittersweet, hoppy finish.

Oxford Mild *(OG 1037, ABV 3.7%)* A full-bodied dark mild.

Varsity *(OG 1041, ABV 4.3%)* ❦
A tawny/amber beer. Malt, hops and fruit are the main features in both aroma and taste but are well balanced. The slightly sweet, malty, fruity start fades away to a distinctive, bittersweet finish.

Graduate *(OG 1048, ABV 5.2%)* ❦ An intense malt and roast malt aroma carries through to the taste and is complemented by a moderate hoppiness. Pleasant, bitter finish.

MOULIN

◊ RTR Catering Ltd, Moulin Hotel & Brewery, Kirkmichael Road, Moulin by Pitlochry PH16 5EW *Tel (01796) 472196 Fax (01796) 474098*
Shop 11-4, Thu-Mon Tours by arrangement
☺ Opened in 1995 at the Moulin Hotel, the brewery has since moved next door to the Old Coach House. Supplies six outlets. Bottle-conditioned beer: Ale of Atholl.

Light *(ABV %)* ❦ Thirst-quenching, straw-coloured session beer, with a light, hoppy, fruity balance ending with a gentle, hoppy sweetness.

Ale of Athol *(ABV %)* ❦ A reddish, quaffable, malty ale, with a solid body and a mellow finish.

Braveheart *(ABV %)* ❦ An amber bitter, with a delicate balance of malt and fruit and a Scottish-style sweetness.

Old Remedial *(ABV %)* ❦ A distinctive and satisfying dark brown old ale, with roast malt to the fore and tannin in a robust taste. Deserves to be more widely available.

MUNSLOW
See Crown Inn.

NAGS HEAD
◊ Nags Head, Abercych, Boncath, Pembrokeshire SA37 0JH
Tel (01239) 841200
☺ Pub brewery producing just one brew on an occasional basis largely for its own consumption. Beer: Old Emrys (ABV 4.1%).

NENE VALLEY
See Leyland.

NETHERGATE
Nethergate Brewery Co. Ltd, 11-13 High Street, Clare, Suffolk CO10 8NY
Tel (01787) 277244 Fax (01787) 277123
Tours by arrangement (trade and CAMRA groups)
☒ Small brewer of award-winning beers, set

up in 1986, which continues to use traditional methods and no additives. The Umbel beers are infused with coriander seeds, recalling an ancient brewing style, and other brewers have now followed Nethergate in adding herbs and spices to their beers. A single tied house and 180 free trade outlets are now supplied, most in East Anglia. Two beers are produced for the wholesaler Martin Elms Wines: tel. (01245) 478323. Seasonal/occasional beers: Priory Mild (ABV 3.5%), Augustinian Ale (ABV 4.8%), Christmas Ale (OG 1048, ABV 4.8%)

IPA *(OG 1036, ABV 3.6%)* ❦ An apple crisp, refreshing session beer, hoppy throughout, without fully masking the malt. Lingering, bitter aftertaste.

Umbel Ale *(OG 1039, ABV 3.8%)* ⬚❦
Wort is percolated through coriander seeds to give a wonderful, warming, spicy fruit tang to both the taste and aroma. The hops are strong enough to make themselves known and a strong, bitter malt finish hits late.

Bitter *(OG 1039, ABV 4%)* ❦ A dark bitter in which delightful malt and hop aromas give way to a well-balanced palate. Rich malts and powerful bitterness dominate the flavour, ending in a strong, bitter finish.

Golden Gate *(OG 1045, ABV 4%)* ❦
A golden bitter using three hop varieties, giving it a fresh aroma and a hoppy finish. Malt and hops are balanced in the taste.

Old Growler *(OG 1055, ABV 5.5%)* ▣⬚❦
A complex and satisfying porter, smooth and distinctive. Sweetness, roast malt and fruit feature in the palate, with bitter chocolate lingering. The finish is powerfully hoppy.

Umbel Magna *(OG 1055, ABV 5.5%)*
▣⬚❦ The addition of coriander to the Old Growler wort completes the original 1750s recipe for this very distinctive dark beer. The powerful spiciness only adds to this porter's appeal.

For Martin Elms Wines:
Porters Suffolk Bitter *(ABV 3.5%)*
Porters Sidewinder *(ABV 4.5%)*

NICHOLSON'S
See Nationals, Carlsberg-Tetley.

NIX WINCOTT
See Leyland.

NORTH DOWNS
See Weltons.

NORTH YORKSHIRE
North Yorkshire Brewing Co., Pinchinthorpe Hall, Pinchinthorpe, Guisborough, N. Yorkshire TS14 8HG
Tel (01287) 630200 Shop 9-5 Tours by arrangement
☺ Brewery founded in 1990 and moved in 1998 to Pinchinthorpe Hall, a moated, listed medieval ancient monument near Guisborough which has its own spring water. The site also includes a visitor centre, restaurant and overnight accommodation. Over 100 free trade outlets are currently supplied.

O'Hanlon's is that rare thing: a genuine, independent Irish pub. The brewery is in Vauxhall, South London, and the pub is situated in Clerkenwell, North London. The brewery supplies some 25 other outlets.

Prior's Ale *(OG 1036, ABV 3.6%)* ◈ Light, very refreshing and surprisingly full-flavoured for a pale, low gravity beer, with a complex, bittersweet mixture of malt, hops and fruit carrying through into the aftertaste.

Archbishop Lee's Ruby Ale *(OG 1040, ABV 4%)* A full-bodied, northern beer with a malty aroma and a balanced malt and hops taste, with vanilla notes.

Golden Ale *(OG 1046, ABV 4.6%)* ◈ A well-hopped, lightly malted, golden premium bitter, using Styrian and Goldings hops.

Lord Lee's *(OG 1048, ABV 4.7%)* ◈ A refreshing, red/brown beer with a hoppy aroma. The flavour is a pleasant balance of roast malt and sweetness which predominates over hops. The malty, bitter finish develops slowly.

Castles Bitter *(OG 1038, ABV 3.8%)* A session bitter.

County *(OG 1040, ABV 4%)* A smooth, hoppy bitter.

Secret Kingdom *(OG 1043, ABV 4.3%)* A very dark, malty beer.

Best Bitter *(OG 1045, ABV 4.5%)* A full-bodied bitter.

Bomar Bitter *(OG 1049, ABV 5%)*

Duke of Northumberland Premium Ale *(OG 1049, ABV 5%)* A dark-malted premium bitter.

NORTHUMBERLAND

The Northumberland Brewery Ltd, Earth Balance, West Sleekburn Farm, Bomarsund, Bedlington, Northumberland NE22 7AD
Tel/Fax (01670) 822112 Tours by arrangement
☺ This brewery went into production on an industrial estate in 1996, but the ecology-conscious owners moved after a year to a purpose-built, solar-powered brewery on the 220-acre, environmentally sustainable Earth Balance community site, where there is a brewery tap. The beers, which are totally organic, are supplied to an extensive free trade.

Santa's Secret *(OG 1047, ABV 4.7%)* Seasonal beer: Christmas.

O'HANLON'S

O'Hanlon's Brewing Company Ltd, 114 Randall Road, Vauxhall, London SE11 5JR
Tel (0171) 793 0803 Tours by arrangement
☺ Brewery set up in 1996 initially to supply John O'Hanlon's own pub in Clerkenwell, but has expanded to serve around 25 other outlets direct, with others taking the beers via wholesalers. Seasonal beers: Spring Gold (ABV 3.6%), Summer Gold (ABV 3.6%), Blakeley's Autumn Ale (ABV 3.8%), Maltsters Weiss (ABV 4%), Damson Ale (ABV 4.5%), Blakeley's Best No. 2 (ABV 5.2%), Christmas Ale (ABV 5.2%).

Dry Stout *(OG 1041, ABV 4.2%)* Black malt and roasted barley give this rich stout a dense black colour. Hop bitterness and a smooth lingering finish are features.

Blakeley's Best No. 1 *(OG 1044, ABV 4.2%)* A premium ale in which roasted barley helps give a more complex flavour. A late addition of hops in the kettle provides a hoppy nose and finish.

Myrica Ale *(ABV 4.2%)* Flavoured with organic honey and bog myrtle.

Red Ale *(OG 1044, ABV 4.5%)* ❧ A typical Irish red ale. Well balanced with a good, dry, hoppy finish.

OAKHAM

Oakham Ales, 80 Westgate, Peterborough, Cambridgeshire PE1 1RD *Tel/Fax (01733) 358300* Tours by arrangement

❌ Established in 1993 in industrial units on a Rutland trading estate, Oakham found a new owner in 1995. A move to the above address, a former unemployment office in Peterborough, was due to take place in summer 1998, the premises split between the brewery and a brewery tap to accommodate up to 700 people. The design is based on an American-style brew pub, with the brewery visible from the bar through glass panels. New plant, increasing the brew length to 35 barrels makes this one of the largest brewpubs in Britain. Oakham also supplies two other associated pubs, plus over 60 free houses. Occasional beers: Periwig OPA (OG 1043, ABV 4.3%, Five Leaves Left (OG 1045, ABV 4.5%).

Jeffrey Hudson Bitter or JHB *(OG 1038, ABV 3.8%)* ⬛❧ Delightful, thirst-quenching, straw-coloured brew with a distinctive, fresh, floral and grassy hop character on the nose and palate.

White Dwarf *(OG 1043, ABV 4.3%)*

Bishops Farewell *(OG 1046, ABV 4.6%)* ❧ Yellow, with impressive, floral hops and peach fruit aroma and taste. Smooth and fairly full bodied, with a long, dry finish.

Helterskelter *(OG 1050, ABV 5%)* A summer offering.

Mompessons Gold *(OG 1050, ABV 5%)* Available March-October.

Old Tosspot *(OG 1052, ABV 5.2%)* Robust, copper-coloured, balanced brew with malt on the nose. The taste has hops, malt, with a sweet fruitiness and a lingering, dry, bitter finish. Replaces Mompessons Gold in the winter months.

OAKHILL

Oakhill Brewery, The Old Maltings, Oakhill, nr Bath, Somerset BA3 5BX *Tel (01749) 840134* Shop

❌ Situated high in the Mendip Hills in Somerset, this brewery was set up by a farmer in 1984 in an old fermentation room of the original Oakhill Brewery (established in 1767 and burnt down in 1924). By the mid-1990s the brewery had outgrown its original premises and moved in 1997 to the old maltings building in Oakhill which had been newly renovated, with a brewing capacity of over 300 barrels a week. It now supplies five tied houses and over 200 free trade outlets direct.

Bitter *(OG 1036, ABV 3.5%)*

Best Bitter *(OG 1040, ABV 4%)* ❧ A clean-tasting, tangy bitter, with a good hop content and citrus fruit and malt balance. Dry finish; light hop aroma. Very quenching.

Black Magic Stout *(OG 1045, ABV 4.5%)* ❧ A black/brown bitter stout with roast malt and a touch of fruit in the nose. Smooth roast malt and bitterness in the taste, with mellow coffee and chocolate.

Mendip Gold *(OG 1045, ABV 4.5%)*

Yeoman Strong Ale *(OG 1050, ABV 5%)* ❧ A strong, pale brown, full-bodied bitter, with a floral hop palate and notable fruitiness. Dry, bitter, lasting finish.

Mendip Ticket *(OG 1063, ABV 6.3%)* A winter warmer.

OAKWELL BREWERY

Oakwell Brewery, Barnsley, South Yorkshire Supplies free trade pubs in the RBNB chain plus some free trade outlets. Beers: Oakwell Bitter; Old Tom.

OKELLS

Okell & Son Ltd, Falcon Brewery, Kewaigue, Douglas, Isle of Man IM2 1QG *Tel/Fax (01624) 661120* Tours by arrangement

☺ Founded in 1874 by Dr Okell and formerly trading as Isle of Man Breweries, this is the main brewery on the island, having taken over and closed the rival Castletown brewery in 1986. The brewery moved in 1994 to a new, purpose-built plant at Kewaigue. All beers are produced under the unique Manx Brewers' Act 1874 (permitted ingredients: water, malt, sugar and hops only). All but seven of the company's 55 pubs sell real ale and over 40 free trade outlets are also supplied directly. Seasonal beers: Spring Ram (OG 1042, ABV 4.2%), Olde Skipper (OG 1045, ABV 4.5%, May), St Nick (OG 1050, ABV 4.5%, Christmas).

Mild *(OG 1034, ABV 3.4%)* ❧ A genuine, well-brewed mild ale, with a fine aroma of hops and crystal malt. Reddish-brown in colour, this beer has a full malt flavour with surprising bitter hop notes and a hint of blackcurrants and oranges. Full, malty finish.

Bitter *(OG 1035, ABV 3.7%)* ❧ A golden beer, malty and superbly hoppy in aroma, with a hint of honey. Rich and malty on the tongue, it has a wonderful, dry, malt and hop finish. A complex but rewarding beer.

OLD BARN

Old Barn Bewery, The Industrial Estate, Tow Law, County Durham *Tel/Fax (01388) 819991* Established in August1998, with the first brew supplied to the Durham Beer Festival. It now supplies Fitzgerald's pub chain, occasionally the Durham Beer Company, and 30-plus free houses in a 20-mile radius of Tow Low. It also supplies pubs with their own personalised and named beer. A Millennium Ale is planned and will be bottle-conditioned. Beers: Antistress (ABV 3.6%), Sheepdog (ABV 4.4%), Collywobble (ABV 4.7%); the last two available as bottle-conditioned ales.

OLD BEAR

⬚ Old Bear Brewery, 6 Keighley Road, Cross Hills, Keighley, N. Yorkshire BD20 7RN *Tel (01535) 632115* Tours by arrangement ☺ Brewery founded in 1993 by former

Goose Eye Brewery owner Bryan Eastell, next to the pub in which he is a partner, producing beers brewed with local spring water. Five other free trade outlets are also supplied. Occasional beers: Ursa Minor (OG 1044, ABV 4.6) Ursa Major (OG 1056, ABV 5.8%), Old Grizzly (ABV variable).
Bitter *(OG 1038, ABV 3.9%)* ◥ A refreshing and easy-to-drink bitter. The balance of malt and hops gives way to a short, dry, bitter aftertaste.

OLD CHIMNEYS

Old Chimneys Brewery, The Street, Market Weston, Diss, Norfolk IP22 2NZ
Tel (01359) 221411 Tours by arrangement
☒ Tiny craft brewery opened in 1995 by former Greene King/Broughton brewer Alan Thomson, producing beers mostly named after local endangered species. Despite the postal address, the brewery is in Suffolk. It currently supplies 30 outlets directly and, in addition to the beers listed, a number of house beers are brewed to individual customers' requirements. Occasional/seasonal beers: Bittern Bitter (OG 1039, ABV 4.1%, summer), Great Raft Bitter (OG 1042, ABV 4.2%, winter), Polecat Porter (OG 1042, ABV 4.2%), Black Rat Stout (OG 1044, ABV 4.4%), Golden Pheasant (OG 1045, ABV 4.7%, summer), Natterjack Premium Ale (OG 1050, ABV 5%, winter), Winter Cloving (OG 1078, ABV 7.5%, winter).
Military Mild *(OG 1035, ABV 3.4%)* ◥
A moreish dark mild, with good body for its gravity. Light roast bitterness features, with a crisp, dry, malt and hop aftertaste.
Swallowtail IPA *(OG 1036, ABV 3.6%)* ◥ An interesting session bitter, with hop dominating over a toffee, nutty flavour.

OLD COTTAGE

Old Cottage Beer Co., Unit 3, Hall House Industrial Estate, New Hutton, Kendal, Cumbria LA8 0AN *Tel/Fax (01539) 724444*
☺ Brewery launched in March 1996, with a single cask ale brewed using local spring water, with specials produced on request. The company was restructured early in 1998 and now supplies 70 outlets direct.
Red Pyke *(OG 1036, ABV 3.6%)* ◥
A gold/amber-coloured session beer with a distinct, overriding caramel aroma and a malty middle, but poor balance. Dry, bitter, astringent aftertaste.
Pheasant Plucker *(OG 1038, ABV 3.8%)*
Barleycorn *(OG 1040, ABV 4%)* A dark brew with hops and malt in the taste.
Flasher *(OG 1040, ABV 4%)*

OLD FORGE

Pett Brewing Company, The Old Forge Brewery, C/o The Two Sawyers, Pett, Hastings, E Sussex TN35 4HB *Tel* (01424) 813030) Tours by arrangement
Brewery established in 1995 in a restored old village forge. Its output is still increasing, with 50 local outlets supplied regularly. Occasional/seasonal beers: White Christmas (OG 1060, ABV 6%), Heavy Petting (ABV 8%, January-February)
Brothers Best *(OG 1037, ABV 3.9%)* ◥
A hoppy, amber-coloured, session beer.
Pett Progress *(OG 1043, ABV 4.6%)* ◥
A mid-brown beer makred by its maltiness, which dominates the aroma and taste. Caramel comes through in the aftertaste.
Pett Genius *(OG 1043, ABV 4.6%)*
A stout.
Summer Eclipse *(OG 1048, ABV 5%)*
Ewe Could Be So Lucky *(ABV 6%)*
Light in colour for a strong bitter, with fruit predominant in the aroma and taste before a hoppy, bittersweet finish
.

OLD LAXEY

♻ Old Laxey Brewing Co. Ltd, Old Laxey Hill, Laxey, Isle of Man IM4 7AD.
Tel (01624) 862451 Tours by arrangement
☺ The island's newest brewery is set behind the Shore Hotel, which sold the first cask of Bosun Bitter in March 1997. Five other local free houses are also supplied with the beer.
Bosun Bitter *(OG 1038, ABV 3.8%)*

OLD LUXTERS

Old Luxters Vineyard Winery & Brewery, Hambleden, Henley-on-Thames, Oxfordshire RG9 6JW
Tel (01491) 638330
Fax (01491) 638645
Shop 9-5.30 Mon-Fri, 11-5.30 Sat-Sun
Tours by arrangement
☒ Buckinghamshire brewery (despite the postal address) set up in 1990 in a 17th-century barn by David Ealand, owner of Chiltern Valley Wines. Apart from the brewery and vineyard, the site also houses a fine art gallery and a cellar shop. The brewery supplies a few local free trade outlets and pubs further afield via wholesalers. Occasional brews are produced to order for other independent breweries, and these are often also supplied bottle-conditioned. Bottle-conditioned beers: Barn Ale (OG 1048, ABV 5.4%), Dark Roast Ale (OG 1047, ABV 5.0%). Dark Roast Ale is also occasionally available in draught (OG 1047, ABV 5.0%).
Barn Ale Bitter *(OG 1038, ABV 4%)*
A fruity, aromatic, fairly hoppy, bitter beer.
Barn Ale Special *(OG 1043, ABV 4.5%)*
◥ The original Barn Ale: predominantly malty, fruity and hoppy in taste and nose, and tawny/amber in colour. Fairly strong in flavour: the initial, sharp, malty and fruity taste leaves a dry, bittersweet, fruity aftertaste. It can be slightly sulphurous.

OLD MILL

Old Mill Brewery Ltd, Mill Street, Snaith, Goole, E. Yorkshire DN14 9HU
Tel (01405) 861813 Fax (01405) 862789
Tours by arrangement

⊛ Small brewery opened in 1983 in a 200-year-old former malt kiln and corn mill. A new brewhouse was installed in 1991 to increase the brewlength to 60 barrels and the brewery is slowly building up the tied estate (currently 15 houses). The innovation of selling some beers in plastic, non-returnable handicasks has meant that the beer can now be found nationwide. Around 200 free trade outlets are also supplied direct from the brewery.

Traditional Mild *(OG 1035, ABV 3.4%)* ◆ A satisfying roast malt flavour dominates this easy-drinking, quality dark mild.

Nellie Dean *(OG 1035, ABV 3.5%)*

Traditional Bitter *(OG 1038, ABV 3.9%)* ◆ The Old Mill character has returned to this beer, though bitterness remains at a premium. It has a malty nose and initial flavour, with hops hiding until the lingering finish.

Old Curiosity *(OG 1043, ABV 4.5%)*

Bullion *(OG 1045, ABV 4.7%)* ◆ The malty and hoppy aroma is followed by a neat mix of hop and fruit tastes within an enveloping maltiness. Dark brown/amber in colour.

Blackjack *(OG 1050, ABV 5%)*

OLD PINT POT

⌂ Old Pint Pot Brewery, Adelphi Street, Salford, Greater Manchester M3 6EM
Tel (0161) 839 1514
⊛ Brewing commenced in summer 1996 at this Salford pub, which is part of the locally-based Honeycomb Leisure group. The one beer has no constant name or strength, but it is a full mash brew and is cask-conditioned. It is sold here and in one other pub.

OLDERSHAW

Oldershaw Brewery, 12 Harrowby Hall Estate, Grantham, Lincolnshire NG31 9HB
Tel/Fax (01476) 572135
Tours by arrangement (small groups)
⊗ Experienced home-brewer Gary Oldershaw and his wife set up this new brewery at their home in January 1997. Grantham's first brewery for 30 years, Oldershaw now supplies 40 local free houses. Occasional/seasonal beers: Sunnydaze (OG 1040, ABV 4%, a summer wheat beer), Caskade (OG 1041, ABV 4.2%, spring and summer), Topers Tipple (OG 1044, ABV 4.5%, autumn and winter).

Harrowby Bitter *(OG 1036, ABV 3.6%)*

Newton's Drop *(OG 1040, ABV 4.1%)*

Ermine Ale *(OG 1040, ABV 4.2%)* A pleasant session bitter.

Old Boy *(OG 1047, ABV 4.8%)* A full-bodied beer with a fine bitter taste.

OLDHAM

See Burtonwood.

ORIGINAL

See Nationals, Bass.

ORKNEY

The Orkney Brewery, Quoyloo, Stromness, Sandwick, Orkney KW16 3LT
Tel (01856) 841802 Fax (01856) 841754
Tours by arrangement
⊛ Set up in 1988 by former licensee Roger

White. Cask ales now represent 90 per cent of sales. The brewery was completely modernised in 1995 with new buildings replacing a single cramped room. The beers are available nationwide via wholesalers.
Seasonal/occasional beers: Island Pale (OG 1040, ABV 4%), White Christmas (OG 1057, ABV 6%).

Northern Light *(OG 1038, ABV 3.8%)*

Raven Ale *(OG 1038, ABV 3.8%)* ◆ A pale brown beer in which fruit predominates. Roast is evident in the aroma and taste, and hop in the taste and aftertaste. Initially sweet, but with a satisfying dry, bitter aftertaste.

Dragonhead Stout *(OG 1040, ABV 4%)* ◆ A strong, dark malt aroma flows into a complex, dry roast and caramel flavour. The roast malt continues to dominate the aftertaste and blends with chocolate and fruit to develop a strong, dry finish. Hard to find.

The Red MacGregor *(OG 1040, ABV 4%)* ◆ Smooth tasting, full-bodied, tawny red ale with a powerful smack of malt to start and a long, bitter and malty finish.

Dark Island *(OG 1045, ABV 4.6%)* ⬚◆ Dark, beautifully balanced and full of roast malt and fruit. A bittersweet taste leads to a long-lasting, roasted, slightly bitter finish. Full-bodied and deceptively drinkable.

Skullsplitter *(OG 1080, ABV 8.5%)*

OTTER

Otter Brewery, Mathayes, Luppitt, Honiton, Devon EX14 0SA
Tel (01404) 891285 Fax (01404) 891124
⊗ Named after its situation at the head-springs of the River Otter, the brewery began operation in 1990 under David McCaig, formerly of Whitbread. Steady growth over the following eight years has meant the need for a plant that can produce 30 barrels, with a capacity of 135 barrels a week. No further expansion is planned. The brewery also bottles its own beers. All beers are brewed with local spring water and yeast culture. The brewery breathes a family business character, and the view is that this will never change. Seasonal beer: Otter Claus (ABV 5%, Christmas).

Bitter *(OG 1036, ABV 3.6%)* ⬚◆ Tawny-coloured, having a malty nose and taste, a developing hop balance and a bitter finish.

Bright *(OG 1039, ABV 4.3%)* ◆ Malt and fruit aroma in this malty tasting, straw-coloured brew with a bitter finish.

Ale *(OG 1043, ABV 4.5%)* ⬚◆ A pleasant, mid-brown beer. A malt aroma and flavour with a bitter taste and finish.

Head *(OG 1054, ABV 5.8%)* ◆ Fruit and malt aroma and flavour to this mid-brown beer with a bitter attertaste.

OUTLAW

See Rooster's.

PALMERS

JC & RH Palmer Ltd, The Old Brewery, West Bay Road, Bridport, Dorset DT6 4JA
Tel (01308) 422396 Fax (01308) 421149
Shop 9.30-6 Mon-Thu, 9.30-8 Fri-Sat
Tours by arrangement
⊗ Thatched brewery, founded in 1794, situated by the sea in former mill buildings. The company is managed by the great-grandsons of brothers John Cleeves and Robert Henry Palmer, who acquired the brewery in the late 19th century. The company has 60 tenanted houses, the latest being a newly-built thatched pub, their first in Taunton. All its pubs serve real ale, although top pressure and cask breathers are widely in use. A further 100 free trade outlets are supplied directly, and Palmers' beers reach a wider audience throughout the south via wholesalers. Its occasional beer, Tally Ho!, was withdrawn early in 1998, to be relaunched.
Bridport Bitter *(OG 1032, ABV 3.2%)*
◆ A light beer with a hoppy aroma, a bitter, hoppy taste with some malt, and a bitter aftertaste.
Best Bitter or IPA *(OG 1040, ABV 4.2%)* ◆ A beer that is hoppy and bitter throughout. Fruit and malt undertones give some balance to the aroma and taste, and there is a lingering bitter aftertaste.
200 *(OG 1054, ABV 5%)* ◆ Full-bodied, caramel sweetness and fruity aroma are balanced with a dry finish, not excessively bitter. A deep-copper ale, originally brewed to mark the brewery's 200th anniversary.

PARADISE

See Bird in Hand.

PARISH

▽ Parish Brewery, The Old Brewery Inn Courtyard, High Street, Somerby, Leicestershire LE14 2PZ
Tel (01664) 454781
Tours by arrangement
⊗ The first brewery to be established in Somerby since the 16th century, Parish started life at the Stag & Hounds, Burrough on the Hill, in 1983. It moved to the Old Brewery Inn in 1991, acquiring a new 20-barrel plant. Parish is listed in the *Guinness Book of Records* as brewer of the strongest beer in the world – Baz's Super Brew (ABV 23%), brewed as a one-off in 1995. A slightly weaker bottled version (not bottle-conditioned) of Baz's Bonce Blower is now brewed by Bateman for London-based beer agency Jacktar Ltd, which has licensed the name from Parish. It currently supplies 20 local outlets.
Mild *(OG 1035, ABV 3.5%)*
Special Bitter or PSB *(OG 1038, ABV 3.8%)*
Farm Gold *(OG 1038, ABV 3.8%)*
Somerby Premium *(OG 1040, ABV 4%)* ⌷
Wild John Bitter *(OG 1048, ABV 4.7%)*
Poachers Ale *(OG 1058, ABV 6%)*
Baz's Bonce Blower or BBB *(OG 1100, ABV 11%)*

PARKER

See Cannon.

PASSAGEWAY

Passageway Brewing Company, Unit G8, Queens Dock Commercial Centre, Norfolk Street, Liverpool, Merseyside L1 0BG
Tel (0151) 708 0730 Fax (0151) 709 0925
Tours by arrangement
☺ Adventurous brewery established in 1994 which experiments with continental beer styles. Yeast from a Belgian monastic brewery is used, and some water from St Arnold's well in Belgium is added to the copper during each brew of St Arnold (named after Belgium's patron saint of brewers). Occasional/seasonal beers: Canticle (OG 1043, ABV 4.5%), Seasonal Wood Smoked Porter (OG 1048, ABV 5%), Advent (OG 1067, ABV 7%, Christmas).
Docker's Hook *(OG 1036, ABV 3.6%)*
◆ A mid-brown, full-bodied ale. Banana fruitiness dominates the palate and aftertaste.
Redemption *(OG 1038, ABV 4%)* ◆ A dry, tart and clean beer brewed with rye.
St Arnold *(OG 1048, ABV 5%)* ⌷◆ Deep ruby in colour, this is a very bitter and fruity beer, yet not sweet. Hop, roast malt, chocolate and liquorice flavours also fight for attention in the taste and dry aftertaste. A complex, heavy beer, reminiscent of a Belgian brown ale. Highly drinkable.
The Fab Four *(OG 1040, ABV 4.2%)*
Genuine Blonde Wheat Beer *(OG 1040, ABV 4.2%)*
Dubbel *(OG 1058, ABV 6%)*
Tripel *(OG 1068, ABV 7%)*

PEMBROKE

Pembroke Brewery Co., Eaton House, 108 Main Street, Pembroke SA71 4HN
Tel (01646) 682517 Fax (01646) 682008
Tours by arrangement
⊗ Brewery founded in 1994 in former stables behind the proprietors' house. The plant was re-designed the following year to allow for smaller runs and greater flexibility. Pembroke supplies a single tied house, the Station Inn (a converted railway building at Pembroke Dock) which features a new brew each week, and other outlets via distributors for whom it produces numerous 'specials'.
Darklin Mild *(OG 1035, ABV 3.5%)*
Sound Whistle *(OG 1038, ABV 3.8%)* A summer beer.
Dimond Lager *(OG 1040, ABV 4.1%)*
Main Street Bitter *(OG 1040, ABV 4.1%)*
Golden Hill Ale *(OG 1044, ABV 4.5%)*
Old Nobbie Stout *(OG 1048, ABV 4.8%)*
Off the Rails *(OG 1051, ABV 5.1%)*
Signal Failure *(OG 1060, ABV 6%)* A winter brew.

PETT

See Old Forge.

PHOENIX

Oak Brewing Co. Ltd, Phoenix Brewery, Green Lane, Heywood, Greater Manchester OL10 2EP *Tel (01706) 627009*
Tours by arrangement
☺ Company established as Oak Brewery in 1982 in Ellesmere Port. It moved in 1991 to

The heart of the matter: the brewing scene at Pilgrim Ales in Reigate.

Heywood and changed its name in 1996. Phoenix now supplies over 150 free trade outlets in the North-West and W. Yorkshire. Seasonal beers: Black Shadow Mild (ABV 4%, April), Jovian (ABV 4.2%, January), St George's Cross (ABV 4.3%, April), Shamrock (ABV 4.2%, February), March Hare (ABV 4.4%, February), Mayfly (ABV 4.5%, April), Midsummer Madness (ABV 4.5%, May), Firecracker (ABV 4.7%, October), Massacre (ABV 4.7%, January), Resurrection (ABV 4.7%, March), Spooky Brew (ABV 5%, October), Porter (ABV 5%, November), Sticky Wicket (ABV 5.4% June), Humbug (ABV 7%, November).

Bantam Bitter *(ABV 3.5%)* Darker and drier than Hopwood Bitter below, with a slight nutty finish.

Oak Best Bitter *(ABV 3.9%)*

Hopwood Bitter *(ABV 4.3%)*

Old Oak Ale *(OG 1044, ABV 4.5%)* ◆ A well-balanced, brown beer with a multi-tude of mellow fruit flavours. Malt and hops balance the strong fruitiness in the aroma and taste, and the finish is malty, fruity and dry.

Thirsty Moon *(ABV 4.6%)* A beer with a slight malty character and a full and crisp hop finish.

Bonneville *(ABV 4.8%)* A very malty beer with a short hop finish.

Double Dagger *(OG 1050, ABV 5%)* ◆ A pale brown, malty brew, more pleasantly dry and light than its gravity would suggest. Moderately fruity throughout; a hoppy bit-terness in the mouth balances the strong graininess.

Wobbly Bob *(OG 1060, ABV 6%)* ⬛◆ A red/brown beer with a malty, fruity aroma. Strongly malty and fruity in flavour and quite hoppy, with the sweetness yielding to a dryness in the aftertaste.

PILGRIM

Pilgrim Ales, The Old Brewery, West Street, Reigate, Surrey RH2 9BL

Tel (01737) 222651 Fax (01737) 225785
⊠ Set up in 1982, and moved to Reigate in 1985, Pilgrim has gradually increased its capacity and its beers have won both local and national awards, although sales are mostly concentrated in the Surrey area (around 60 outlets). Occasional/seasonal beers: Saracen (OG 1047, ABV 4.5%), Autumnal (OG 1045, ABV 4.5%, September-October), Excalibur (OG 1045, ABV 4.5%, March-May), The Great Crusader (OG 1063, ABV 6.5%, June-August), Pudding (OG 1075, ABV 7.3%, November-January). Bottle-conditioned beers: Progress (ABV 4.3%), Springbock (ABV 5.2%), Pudding (ABV 6.8%).

Surrey Bitter *(OG 1037, ABV 3.7%)* ◆ A clean, well-balanced session bitter. Hop flavour comes through in the finish.

Porter *(OG 1040, ABV 4%)* ◆ This porter, with a rich mouthfeel, has a good balance of dark malts, with berry fruit flavours declining to a short finish.

Progress *(OG 1040, ABV 4%)* ◆ Reddish-brown in colour, with a predomi-nantly malty flavour and aroma, although hops are also evident in the taste.

Saracen *(OG 1047, ABV 4.5%)* ⬛◆ Roast malt dominates the aroma of this black stout, but hops balance the roast malt flavour, leading to a bitter finish. Tasty.

Crusader *(OG 1047, ABV 4.9%)* ◆ A light, golden beer with a good marriage of malt and hops from aroma through to fin-ish. Very drinkable.

Talisman *(OG 1049, ABV 5%)* ◆ A strong ale with a mid-brown colour, a fruity, malt flavour and a faint hoppiness.

Springbock *(OG 1050, ABV 5.2%)* A Bavarian-style wheat beer.

PIONEER

See Rooster's.

PITFIELD

Pitfield Brewery, The Beer Shop, 14 Pitfield Street, Hoxton, London N1 6EY
Tel (0171) 739 3701 Shop 11-7 Mon-Fri, 10-4 Sat Tours by arrangement
⊗ First established in 1982, Pitfield brands were contract-brewed for a while at Brewery on Sea until Pitfield re-opened with new equipment in new premises next to the Beer Shop in July 1996. It supplies six outlets direct as well as the shop. Special bottles for events can be produced to order. All the draught ales are available in bottle-conditioned form and an additional bottle-conditioned beer, Eco Warrior (OG 1045, ABV 4.5%) is also produced, using organic ingredients.
Bitter *(OG 1036, ABV 3.7%)* ◆ Hoppy bitter with an underlying maltiness. The flavour tails off quickly in the finish.
Golden Otter *(OG 1040, ABV 4%)*
Shoreditch Stout *(OG 1040, ABV 4%)*
Amber Ale *(OG 1042, ABV 4.2%)*
Hoxton Heavy *(OG 1048, ABV 4.8%)*
Black Eagle *(OG 1050, ABV 5%)*

PLANETS

� HG Wells Planets Brewery, Crown Square, Woking, Surrey GU21 1HR
Tel (01483) 727100 Fax (01483) 712701
⊗ Brewery opened in 1996 in a leisure complex, supplying its full mash beers only to the house bars initially, although now selling to the free trade under the name of Brooklands Brewery. At the leisure complex the beers are kept under a blanket of gas in cellar tanks. Beers: Bobbies Bitter (OG 1042, ABV 4.2%), HG's Ale (OG 1052, ABV 5%).

PLASSEY

Plassey Brewery, The Plassey, Eyton, Wrexham LL13 0SP
Tel (01978) 780922 Fax (01978) 780019
Shop 11-5 daily Tours by arrangement
☺ Brewery founded in 1985 on the 250-acre Plassey Estate, which also incorporates a touring caravan park, craft centres, a golf course, three licensed outlets for Plassey's ales, and a brewery shop. A new viewing gallery was added in 1997. Thirty free trade outlets also take the beers. A bottling plant was installed in 1997. Bottle-condtioned beer: Fusilier Ale (OG 1046, ABV 4.6%).
Bitter *(OG 1041, ABV 4%)* ☐◆ A well-balanced, hoppy, straw-coloured beer with a citrus fruitiness.
Welsh Stout *(OG 1046, ABV 4.6%)* ☐◆ A dry, roasty stout, sweetish; a long, dry finish.
Royal Welch Fusilier *(OG 1046, ABV 4.5%)*
Ruddy Rudolph *(OG 1047, ABV 4.6%)*
Cwrw Tudno *(OG 1048, ABV 5%)* ◆ More fruity than the bitter; well-balanced, with a good, dry aftertaste.
Dragon's Breath *(OG 1060, ABV 6%)* ☐ A fruity, strong bitter, smooth and quite sweet, though not cloying, with an intense, fruity aroma. A dangerously drinkable winter warmer.

PLOUGH INN

⊽ Bodicote Brewery, Plough Inn, 9 High Street, Bodicote, Banbury, Oxfordshire

Ian Dale of Plassey, one of the breweries flying the flag for Welsh beer. In May, Simon Buckley of Tomos Watkin in Llandeilo called for more all-round support for Welsh-produced beers.

OX15 4BZ *Tel (01295) 262327*
Tours by arrangement
⊗ Brewery founded in 1982 at the Plough, No. 9 High Street (hence the beer name), which has been in the same hands since 1957. Two other outlets are also supplied with its full mash beers. Two very popular week-long beer festivals are held each year in February and August. Beers: Bodicote Bitter (OG 1035, ABV 3.3%), Three Goslings (OG 1041, ABV 4%, summer), No. 9 (OG 1045, ABV 4.4%), Old English Porter (OG 1047, ABV 4.7%, winter), Triple X (OG 1059, ABV 6.6%, Christmas).

POOLE

⊽ The Brewhouse Brewery, 68 High Street, Poole, Dorset BH15 1DA
Tel (01202) 682345
⊗ Brewery established in 1980 by David Rawlins who opened the Brewhouse pub in 1983. The brewery now has a capacity of 75 barrels a week and serves over 15 outlets direct and a widespread free trade through wholesalers. Occasional beers: Bedrock Bitter (OG 1042, ABV 4.2%), Double Barrel (OG 1053, ABV 5.5%).
Best Bitter or Dolphin *(OG 1038, ABV 3.8%)* The brewery's original session bitter: amber-coloured and well balanced.
Holes Bay Hog *(OG 1044, ABV 4.5%)* Light amber in colour, this beer is brewed from pale malt and malted wheat, and has a distinctive, dry-hopped character and a refreshing aftertaste.
Bosun Bitter *(OG 1045, ABV 4.6%)* The brewery's top selling beer. A rich, amber-coloured beer with a smooth, crisp, powerful malty flavour and a pronounced hoppy aftertaste.

For Hogshead
Hedgehog *(ABV 5.2%)* Available from July 1998.

PORTER

♥ Porter Brewing Co. Ltd, Rossendale Brewery, The Griffin Inn, Hud Rake, Haslingden, Lancashire BB4 5AF
Tel/Fax (01706) 214021
Tours by arrangement
⊕ The Griffin Inn was refurbished and re-opened, complete with microbrewery, by new owner David Porter in 1994. A third tied house was acquired in 1996 and a fourth is planned; all the pubs serve real ale and several other local outlets also take the beer. Occasional/seasonal beers: Timmy's Ginger Beer (OG 1042, ABV 4.2%), Sleighed (OG 1064, ABV 6.5%, December-January), Celebration Ale (OG 1068, ABV 7.1%, July-August).
Dark Mild *(OG 1033, ABV 3.3%)* A true dark mild, with a slight maltiness and a good hint of roast in the finish.
Bitter *(OG 1037, ABV 3.8%)* A dark beer for a standard bitter, with a good, sharp, northern bitterness that lingers through to the back of the throat, and a dry finish.
Rossendale Ale *(OG 1041, ABV 4.2%)* An initial slight, malty sweetness leads through to a deep, fruity taste and a linger-ing fruity finish.
Porter *(OG 1050, ABV 5%)* A rich beer with a slightly sweet, malty start, counter-balanced with sharp bitterness and a very noticeable roast barley dominance.
Sunshine *(OG 1050, ABV 5.3%)* An intensely hoppy and bitter golden ale, full-bodied with some malt, a robust mouthfeel and a lingering bitterness.

PORTERS
See Nethergate.

POWELL
See Wood.

PRINCE OF WALES
♥ Foxfield Brewery, Prince of Wales, Foxfield, Broughton in Furness, Cumbria LA20 6BX *Tel (01229) 716238*
⊕ The owners of Tigertops Brewery (qv) bought the Prince of Wales pub in September 1996 and started brewing in the garage there 12 months later. It supplies a number of other free houses and festivals. Beers: Mild (OG 1037, ABV 3.3%), Fleur de Lys (OG 1038, ABV 3.6%), White Coombe (OG 1047, ABV 4.5%), Black Coombe (OG 1052, ABV 5%), Vixen's Vengeance (OG 1065, ABV 6.2%).

PRINCETOWN
Princetown Breweries Ltd., The Brewery, Tavistock Road, Princetown, Devon PL20 6QF
Tel (01822) 890789 Fax (01822) 890719
Tours by arrangement
⊗ Brewery established in 1994 by a former Gibbs Mew and Hop Back brewer. It sup-plies five pubs owned by a sister company and 12 other local outlets. Bottle-condi-tioned beer: Jail Ale (ABV 4.8%).
Dartmoor IPA or Best Bitter *(OG 1040, ABV 4%)*
Dartmoor Royal Stout *(OG 1046, ABV 4.5%)*

Jail Ale *(OG 1048, ABV 4.8%)* ❧ Hops and fruit predominate in the flavour of this mid-brown beer which has a slightly sweet aftertaste.
Dartmoor Gold *(OG 1050, ABV 5%)*

QUALITY CASK ALES
See Ash Vine.

QUAY
The Quay Brewery, Lapin Noir Ltd, Brewers Quay, Hope Square, Weymouth, Dorset DT4 8TR *Tel (01305) 777515*
Tel/Fax (01305) 777515
Shop 9-5.30 daily Tours by arrangement
⊗ Brewery set up in summer 1996 in the old Devenish and Groves brewery buildings, ten years after the closure of Devenish. Although Greenalls owns the complex, the brewery is totally independent and is open to visitors as part of the Timewalk attraction. A Victorian Tastings Bar and shop opened in Easter 1997. It has quickly developed local trade, with 20 outlets taking the beers. Occasional/seasonal beers: Groves Oatmeal Stout (OG 1049, ABV 4.7%, winter), Silent Knight (OG 1060, ABV 5.9%, a dark wheat beer). Bottled-conditioned beers: Groves Oatmeal Stout (OG 1049, ABV 4.7%), Old Rott (OG 1050, ABV 5%), Silent Knight (OG 1060, ABV 5.9%).
Weymouth Harbour Master *(OG 1036, ABV 3.6%)* ❧ Well balanced, nut-brown session beer, sweetish, but not cloy-ing, thanks to the dry finish. May be badged by pubs as a house beer.
Weymouth Special Pale Ale (SPA) *(OG 1038, ABV 4%)* ❧ While having the malt and caramel taste and dryness of the house style, a bitter finish marks this golden beer out in the brewery's range.
Weymouth JD 1742 *(OG 1040, ABV 4.2%)* ❧ Clean, refreshing taste, with both bitterness and sweetness in moderation, after a fruity aroma. Bitterness develops in the fin-ish, with a slight tang of yeast.
Bombshell Bitter *(OG 1044, ABV 4.5%)* ❧ Cleaner tasting than might be expected from the deep copper colour and fruity aroma. Caramel sweetness dominates the taste.
Old Rott *(OG 1050, ABV 5%)* ❧ Warming finish despite a rather light caramel and malt taste. Hint of sulphur and yeastiness throughout.

QUEEN'S HEAD
♥ Fat God's Brewery, The Queen's Head, Iron Cross, Evesham, Worcestershire WR11 5SH
Tel (01386) 871012 Fax (01386) 871362
Tours by arrangement
⊗ Pub brewery (in Warwickshire, despite the postal address) opened in summer 1997, with its first beer named after the prevailing weather conditions that night! The full mash beers are now supplied to ten other outlets and seasonal brews are planned. In 1998 voted Community Pub of the Year by Brewers & Licensed Retailers Association.
Fat God's Bitter *(OG 1036, ABV 3.6%)* ❧ Balanced between maltiness and hopiness, this mainly hoppy beer leaves a clean, dry aftertaste.
Kim's First Brew (KFB) *(OG 1039,*

ABV 3.9%) ◆ This beer does not overpower the palate with strong flavours, but its subtle, hoppy taste is very thirst-quenching.
Thunder and Lightning (OG 1043, ABV 4.3%) ◆ Malt is the main taste in this premium bitter. Hops are there in the mouth, but the final impression is one of malt.
Merrie Miller's Winter Wobbler (OG 1049, ABV 4.9%)

RAINBOW

⚲ Rainbow Inn & Brewery, 73 Birmingham Road, Allesley Village, Coventry, W. Midlands CV9 5GT Tel (01203) 402888
Tours by arrangement
⊠ Pub brewery, housed in former stables, which opened in 1994 just to serve its own customers. The brewery was expanded in March 1997. Beers: Piddlebrook (OG 1040, ABV 3.8%), Firecracker (OG 1052, ABV 5%), Santa's Spice (OG 1056, ABV 5.5%, Christmas).

RANDALLS

RW Randall Ltd, Vauxlaurens Brewery, St Julian's Avenue, St Peter Port, Guernsey GY1 3JG Tel (01481) 720134 Fax (01481) 713233 Shop 9.30-5.30 Mon-Sat Tours by arrangement
⊠ The smaller of Guernsey's two breweries, purchased by PH Randall from Joseph Gullick in 1868. Successive generations have continued to run the business, except during the period of the German occupation, when it ceased brewing until after the war. Randalls owns 22 pubs (18 of which are tied), but only three serve real ale. Do not confuse with Randalls Vautier of Jersey, which no longer brews. Occasional beers: Mild (OG 1035, ABV 3.4%), Stout (OG 1050, ABV 6%). Bottle-conditioned beers (available occasionally): Mild (OG 1035, ABV 3.4%), Bitter (OG 1046, ABV 5%).
Patois Ale (OG 1046, ABV 5%) ◆ Amber in colour, with a hoppy aroma. Bitter and hoppy both in the palate and finish.

RAT & RATCHET

⚲ The Rat & Ratchet Brewery, 40 Chapel Hill, Huddersfield, W. Yorkshire HD1 3EB Tel (01484) 516734 Tours by arrangement
⊕ Well-known alehouse which began brewing in 1994 to supply just itself and occasional beer festivals. The beer range varies, the aim being to have at least one Rat beer available most of the time.

RAVEN

See Winfields.

RCH

RCH Brewery, West Hewish, nr Weston-super-Mare, Somerset BS24 6RR Tel (01934) 834447 Fax (01934) 834167
Tours by arrangement
⊠ Brewery originally installed by previous owners in the early 1980s behind the Royal Clarence Hotel at Burnham-on-Sea, but since 1993 brewing has taken place on a commercial basis in a former cider mill at West Hewish. RCH now supplies 50 outlets

directly and the award-winning beers are available nationwide through its own wholesaling company which also distributes beers from other small independent breweries. Bottle-conditioned beers: Pitchfork (OG 1043, ABV 4.3%), Old Slug Porter (OG 1046, ABV 4.5%) ⚲, Firebox (OG 1060, ABV 6%).
Hewish IPA (ABV 3.6%) ◆ A light, hoppy bitter with some malt, subtle sweetness and fruit, all of which lasts well into the finish. Floral, citrus hop aroma. Pale brown/amber-coloured.
PG Steam (OG 1039, ABV 3.9%) ◆ Floral hop aroma with some malt. Medium-bodied, hoppy and bitter, with some malt, fruit, and sweetness. Finish is similar, with less fruit. A complex, multi-layered ale. Pale brown in colour.
Pitchfork (OG 1043, ABV 4.3%) ❦◆ Yellow/gold pale bitter with a floral, citric hop aroma with pale malt. Hops predominate in a full-bodied similar taste. which is slightly sweet and fruity. Finish is just as good, if longer. Very tasty,
Old Slug Porter (OG 1046, ABV 4.5%) ◆ Good aroma of chocolate, coffee and roast malt, with some hops. Tastes similar: fullish bodied, with blackcurrant and black cherry fruits. Long, mellow, bittersweet finish. Dark red/brown and appetising.
East Street Cream (OG 1050, ABV 5%) ◆ Enigmatic in taste and aroma, this malty, hoppy, fruity, bitter and sweet ale has flavours which all vie for dominance. Pale brown in colour, it is a well-crafted ale, full bodied and worthy of respect.
Firebox (OG 1060, ABV 6%) ◆ Mid-brown, medium bodied, smooth and full flavoured. Fine combination of malt, floral citrus hop and cherry fruit bittersweet flavours. Equally strong finish, which is more dry and bitter.

READING LION

⚲ Reading Lion Brewery, The Hop Leaf, 163-165 Southampton Street, Reading, Berkshire RG1 2QZ Tel (0118) 931 4700
Tours by arrangement
⊠ Brewery opened by Hop Back Brewery in 1995 at the Hop Leaf pub, a former Inntrepreneur house, becoming Reading's first real ale brewery since Courage closed the old Simonds site in the late 1970s. The five-barrel plant came from the Wyndham Arms in Salisbury and beers are stored in both casks and cellar tanks (no blanket pressure). The beers, which vary, are brewed on an occasional basis, mainly for the pub, with occasional brews for other Hop Back pubs and the free trade.

REBELLION

Rebellion Beer Company, Unit J, Rose Industrial Estate, Marlow Bottom Road, Marlow, Buckinghamshire SL7 3ND Tel/Fax (01628) 476594 Shop 8-6 Mon-Fri, 9-4 Sat
Tours by arrangement (CAMRA branches only)
⊠ Opened in 1993, Rebellion helps to fill the gap left in Marlow by Whitbread's closure of the Wethered brewery in 1988. Due to move in summer 1998 to a new site in order to increase the brewing capacity, Rebellion currently supplies 120 outlets

directly with others served via wholesalers. Beers (including a range of seasonal brews) are also produced for Scanlon's Brewery tel: (01895) 256270, which ceased production in summer 1997. Seasonal beers: Overdraft (OG 1044, ABV 4.3%, January-March), Roasted Nuts (ABV 4.6%, Christmas). Bottle-conditioned beer: Mutiny (OG 1052, ABV 5%).

IPA *(OG 1039, ABV 3.7%)* A very clean, refreshing pale ale. A sweet malt character dominates the palate, before a crisp, dry finish. A good session beer.

Smuggler *(OG 1041, ABV 4.1%)* Different hops are added at four stages during the brewing process, resulting in a bittersweet beer with a fresh, fruity late hop flavour and aroma.

Blonde Bombshell *(OG 1043, ABV 4.3%)* A summer brew, brewed using only pale and lager malts, giving the beer a light, golden colour.

Mutiny *(OG 1046, ABV 4.5%)* A reddish, full-bodied beer, with a well-balanced malt and hop taste. Goldings are added for a late hop charge to give a lasting aftertaste.

Red Oktober *(OG 1048, ABV 4.7%)* An autumn beer in the style of a German altbier. Brewed using crystal and rye malts and continental hops, it has a deep reddish hue.

Zebedee *(OG 1048, ABV 4.7%)* The spring offering: light in colour, crisp and refreshing with a delicate floral aroma.

Old Codger *(OG 1054, ABV 5%)* A heart-warming winter ale with a full, dark-roasted malt character. The hops give contrast, but do not overpower the richness of the malt.

For Scanlon's:
Spike *(OG 1046, ABV 4.5%)* (plus occasional other brews)
Brunel Premier Ale *(OG 1048, ABV 4.8%)*

RECTORY

Rectory Ales Ltd, Streat Hill Farm Outbuildings, Streat Hill, Streat, Nr Hassocks, E. Sussex BN6 8RP
Tel (01273) 891378 **Tours by arrangement**
Unusual brewery founded in 1996 by the Rector of Plumpton, Godfrey Broster, to generate profits for the maintenance of the three churches in his parish. Financial help from parishioners purchased the equipment and further capital injection increased brewing capacity by 100 per cent. A move to a larger site took place in spring 1997 and the brewery now supplies 12 local outlets. Seasonal beer: Christmas Cheer (ABV 4.5%, December-January).

Parson's Porter *(ABV 3.6%)*
Rector's Pleasure *(ABV 3.8%)*
Light Relief *(ABV 4.5%)*
Rector's Revenge *(ABV 5.4%)*

RED CROSS

Red Cross Brewery, Perryfields Lane, Bromsgrove, Worcestershire B61 8QW
Tel/Fax (01527) 871409
Tours by arrangement
Red Cross started brewing in 1993 in the old bull pen of Red Cross Farm, a 17th-century yeoman farmhouse. The beer is available in five local outlets, including the Hop Pole Inn in Bromsgrove, an M&B pub, formerly run by the Red Cross brewer.

Anniversary Ale *(OG 1040, ABV 4%)*
Nailer's Oh Be Joyful (OBJ) *(OG 1040, ABV 4.2%)* A light-coloured, sweet bitter which puts plenty of hops in the mouth, to leave a refreshing aftertaste.
Old Knee Jerker (OKJ) *(OG 1049, ABV 4.9%)* A darker, maltier ale than OBJ but with the characteristic intense hop flavours.

RED LION HOTEL

Willows Lane, Greenhowarth, Accrington, Lancs BB5 3SJ Tel (01254) 233194
Steven Pickles began brewing in February 1998 in the cellar of the pub on equipment he made himself.

Picks Bedlam Bitter *(OG 1038, ABV 3.9%)*
Picks Morrgate Mild *(OG 1035, ABV 3.5%)* A dark mild.

RED LION HOTEL

Red Lion Hotel, Long Bridge Street, Llanidloes, Powys SY18 6EE
Tel (01686) 412270 Fax (01686) 413573
Tours by arrangement
Brewery set up in a garage adjoining the Red Lion in 1995, brewing just for the pub itself and beer festivals. Beers: Cobbler's Thumb (OG 1044, ABV 4.4%), Cobbler's Last (OG 1095, ABV 10%, Christmas).

RED SHED

Red Shed Brewery, 10 Flixton Road, Kimberley, Nottingham NG16 2TJ
Tel (0115) 938 5360 **Tours by arrangement**
A part-time venture for psychiatric nurse, Mike Lynch, this brewery was set up in his garden shed in October 1997 (to coincide with the Nottingham Beer Festival) with a tiny 1.5 barrel plant. Currently supplying a dozen local outlets, he would like to expand and brew full time. Seasonal beer: Rudolph's Red Nose (OG 1046, ABV 5.5%).

Pot the Red Ale *(OG 1030, ABV 4%)*
Red Devil *(OG 1032, ABV 4.2%)*
Red Alert *(OG 1040, ABV 4.8%)*
Red Light *(OG 1042, ABV 5%)*

RED SHOOT

Toms Lane, Linwood, Hampshire
Brewpub owned by Wadworth.

REEPHAM

Reepham Brewery, Unit 1, Collers Way, Reepham, Norfolk NR10 4SW
Tel (01603) 871091 **Tours by arrangement**
Family brewery, founded in 1983 with a former Watney's research engineer, with a purpose-built plant in a small industrial unit. Reepham now supplies its award-winning ales to around 20 local outlets. Recent developments have included the production of a wheat beer, a raspberry ale and a low gravity beer for drivers. Occasional beers: Strong Ruby Ale (OG 1048, ABV 4.5%), Bittern (OG 1050, ABV 5%).

Granary Bitter *(OG 1038, ABV 3.8%)* A most pleasant, gold-coloured, malty beer, with hints of smoke and fruit with a long finish.

Rapier Pale Ale *(OG 1043, ABV 4.3%)*
🍺 An excellent, rounded, well balanced, amber-coloured beer with smoky overtones and a malty, fruit finish.

Norfolk Wheaten *(OG 1045, ABV 4.5%)*

Velvet Stout *(OG 1045, ABV 4.5%)* 🍺
The fruity, malt aroma of this darkish brown winter stout gives way to a sweet, mellow taste explosion of malt, roast malt, fruit and hops. This subsides to a pleasant aftertaste with hints of liquorice.

Brewhouse *(OG 1055, ABV 5.5%)*
A strong winter ale.

RESTALRIG

Restalrig Village Brewery Ltd, Unit 5b Loaning Road, Restalrig, Edinburgh *Tel* (0131) 468 6969 *Fax* (0131) 468 7071
Tours by arrangement
⊛ Set up by two ex-Courage employees in the summer of 1997, this new brewery is capable of brewing 100 barrels per week, for its rapidly growing market (currently 70 outlets). Future plans include the production of bottle-conditioned beers. Occasional beer: Three Bears Ale (OG 1041, 4.1% ABV, for Rugby Internationals).

Lemon Weiss *(OG 1037, ABV 3.6%)*
A lemon wheat beer for summer.

Leith IPA *(OG 1038, ABV 3.8%)*

80/- *(OG 1043, ABV 4.4%)*

Dr Geoffrey's Original Ale *(OG 1052, ABV 5.2%)*

Highwayman *(OG 1075, ABV 7.2%)*
A winter beer.

RIDLEYS

TD Ridley & Sons Ltd, Hartford End Brewery, Chelmsford, Essex CM3 1JZ
Tel/Fax (01371) 820316
Tours by arrangement
⊠ Ridleys was established by Thomas Dixon Ridley in 1842, and is still family-run. It is building up its tied estate (currently supplies 66 tenanted pubs, aiming to have 80 houses by the millennium. It also supplies 300 other outlets. Ridley also bottles Mackeson for Whitbread. Seasonal beer: Winter Winner (OG 1057, ABV 5.5%).

IPA *(OG 1034, ABV 3.5%)* 🍺 Refreshing and hoppy throughout, well-balanced by a persistent maltiness and delicate fruit in the flavour, with a lingering bitteness.

Mild *(OG 1034, ABV 3.5%)* 🗂🍺 A very dark mild, with a light aroma of roast malt and subdued hop. Quite bitter for a mild, with roast malt and fruit in the taste and a balanced, dry finish with hops and roast malt.

ESX Best *(OG 1047, ABV 4.3%)* 🍺
Harmonious malt and hops dominate the taste of this best bitter, with a hint of fruit. Hops just gain over malt in the finish.

Spectacular *(OG 1047, ABV 4.6%)*
A pale, straw-coloured beer with a flowery nose. It has a delicate malty flavour and a rather bitter aftertaste.

Witchfinder Porter *(OG 1047, ABV 4.3%)* 🍺 A dark ruby, bittersweet winter beer, with strong roast malt and light hoppiness.

Rumpus *(OG 1049, ABV 4.5%)* 🍺
A tawny, malty beer with a developing fruiti-

ness and a bittersweet balance, becoming dryer, with hops in the finish.

RINGWOOD

Ringwood Brewery Ltd, Christchurch Road, Ringwood, Hampshire BH24 3AP
Tel (01425) 471177 Fax (01425) 480273
Shop 9.30-5 Mon-Fri 9.30-12 Sat
Tours by arrangement
⊠ Ringwood was set up in 1978 and moved in 1986 to attractive 18th-century buildings, formerly part of the old Tunks brewery. A new brewhouse was commissioned at the end of 1994, and a new fermenting room completed in 1995. Demand for the beers is growing steadily in the free trade (400 accounts) and the brewery also supplies two tied houses. Bottle-conditioned beer: Fortyniner (OG 1049, ABV 4.9%).

Best Bitter *(OG 1038, ABV 3.8%)* 🍺
A well-balanced golden brown beer. A malty and hoppy aroma leads through to a malty taste with some sweetness. Malty and bitter finish, with some fruit present.

True Glory *(OG 1043, ABV 4.3%)* 🍺
A malty aroma leads to a hoppy taste with malt and fruit, followed by a malty, hoppy and fruity aftertaste. Copper-coloured.

XXXX Porter *(OG 1048, ABV 4.7%)* 🗂🍺
An aroma of roasted malt leads to a rich, roasted malt taste with coffee and fruit. The aftertaste is malty and bitter. Almost black

> The Essex brewery of Ridleys was established by a miller, Thomas Ridley, on the banks of the River Chelmer in 1842. Curiously, the idea belonged to his wife – but then she came from a Chelmsford brewing family. The brewery is still family-run.

in colour with a slight ruby-red tinge. Available October-March.

Fortyniner *(OG 1049, ABV 4.9%)* 🍺 Pale brown in colour. A malty and fruity aroma leads to a well-balanced taste of malt and hops. Fruity finish.

Old Thumper *(OG 1056, ABV 5.6%)* 🍺 A mid-brown beer. A fruity aroma preludes a sweet, malty taste with some fruit. Surprisingly bitter aftertaste, with malt and fruit.

RISING SUN

The Rising Sun Inn, Shraley Brook, Audley, Stoke-on-Trent, Staffordshire
Ceased brewing.

RIVERHEAD

🍺 Riverhead Brewery Ltd, 2 Peel Street, Marsden, Huddersfield, W. Yorkshire HD7 6BR *Tel (01484) 841270*
Tours by arrangement
☺ Brewpub which opened in 1995, after two years' work converting an old corn merchant's/grocery store. The pub is on two floors, with a window onto the brewing area. The brewery also supplies ten local outlets and seasonal and special brews are produced.

Sparth Mild *(OG 1036, ABV 3.6%)* 🍺 A light-bodied, dry, mild, with a dark ruby colour. Fruity aroma with roasted flavour and a dry finish.

Butterley Bitter *(OG 1038, ABV 3.8%)* 🍺 A dry, amber-coloured hoppy session beer.

Deer Hill Porter *(OG 1040, ABV 4%)*

Cupwith Light Bitter *(OG 1042, ABV 4.2%)* 🍺 Fruity and hoppy golden best bitter, with a dry, bitter finish.

Black Moss Stout *(OG 1043, ABV 4.3%)* 🍺 Roast malt and fruit aromas from a lightly-hopped dry stout with a chocolatey finish.

March Haigh Special Bitter *(OG 1046, ABV 4.6%)*

Redbrook Premium Bitter *(OG 1055, ABV 5.5%)* 🍺 A rich and malty strong beer, with malt and fruit aroma and sweet, fruity aftertaste.

RIVERSIDE

Riverside Brewery Ltd, The Gatehouse, Pallion Shipyard, Pallion, Sunderland, Tyne & Wear SR4 6LL
Tel/Fax (0191) 514 3212
Tours by arrangement
☺ Company which began commercial brewing in December 1996, based on the concept of self brew (for private members) and corporate bottled beers. During 1997 the commercial side expanded, brewing cask ales for pubs (supplying six on a regular basis) and festivals, as well as a range of bottle-conditioned beers for Beaumont Wines off licence, and others for Binns Department Store in Darlington. In May 1998 Riverside progressed from brewing with malt extract to full mash beers. Bottle-conditioned beers for Beaumont Wines: Tommy Hepburn (OG

1038, ABV 3.8%), WP Roberts (OG 1045, ABV 4.5%), Alex Wilkie (OG 1048, ABV 4.8%), Ellen Wilkinson (OG 1048, ABV 4.8%)1926 (OG 1048, ABV 4.8%), 1984 (OG 1049, ABV 4.9%), Scottish Ale (OG 1049, ABV 4.9%), English Ale (OG 1059, ABV 5.9%), Scottish Ale (OG 1049, ABV 4.9%), plus a series of beers based on steam trains. Bottle-conditioned beers for Binns Department Store: Anti-Perpendicular (OG 1048, ABV 4.8%), Red Devil (OG 1048, ABV 4.5%), Rachels Relish (OG 1048, ABV 4.8%), Sweet and Stout.

Belly Buster Bitter *(OG 1038, ABV 3.8%)*
Publican Bitter *(OG 1042, ABV 4.2%)*
Anti-Perpendicular *(OG 1048, ABV 4.8%)*
Rachels Relish *(OG 1048, ABV 4.8%)*
Red Devil *(OG 1048, ABV 4.5%)*

ROBINSON'S

Frederic Robinson Ltd, Unicorn Brewery, Stockport, Cheshire SK1 1JJ
Tel (0161) 480 6571 Fax (0161) 476 6011
Shop 9-5.30 Mon-Fri 9-1 Sat
Tours by arrangement
☺ Major Greater Manchester family brewery, founded in 1838. Robinson's has grown through various pub and brewery acquisitions over the years, including Hartleys of Ulverston in 1982. The Hartleys brewery was closed in 1991 and only Hartleys XB is still brewed (at Stockport). Robinson's supplies real ale to all its 413 tied houses (most in southern Manchester and Cheshire), and to the free trade outlets.

Hatters Mild *(OG 1033, ABV 3.3%)* ◆
A light mild with an unpronounced malty aroma and a refreshing dry, malty flavour. Short bitter/malty aftertaste.

Old Stockport Bitter *(OG 1035, ABV 3.5%)* ◆ A beer with a refreshing taste of malt, hops and citrus fruit, a characteristic fruity aroma, and a short, dry finish.

Hartleys XB *(OG 1040, ABV 4%)* ◆
Robinson's copy of Hartley's XB is far from the beer once brewed in Ulverston. It is an overtly sweet and malty bitter with a bitter citrus peel fruitiness and a hint of liquorice in the finish.

Best Better *(OG 1041, ABV 4.2%)* ◆
A pale brown beer with a malty, hoppy nose. There are malt, hops and bitterness in the flavour and the aftertaste is short and bitter.

Frederics *(OG 1050, ABV 5%)* A golden, full-bodied, premium bitter. A hoppy nose leads through to a full, hoppy taste, softened by malt in the finish. Rarely found in the Robinson's estate, it is mainly a free trade beer.

Old Tom *(OG 1079, ABV 8.5%)* ▮◖◆
A full-bodied, dark, fruity beer. The aroma is fruity and mouthwatering; the aftertaste is bittersweet, with an alcoholic kick.

ROCKINGHAM

Rockingham Ales c/o 25 Wansford Road, Elton, Cambridgeshire PE8 6RZ
Tel (01832) 28880722
Part-time microbrewery set up in 1997 in a converted building on an isolated farm near Blatherwyke, Northamptonshire (business

address as above). Several local pubs and a handful of outlets in the Midlands are supplied with the beers which are brewed on a rota basis, supplemented with specials brewed to order. Seasonal beers: Sanity Clause (OG 1042, ABV 4.1%, Christmas), Old Herbaceous (OG 1046, ABV 4.5%, winter).

Elton Pale Ale *(OG 1040, ABV 3.9%)*
Forest Gold *(OG 1040, ABV 3.9%)*
A1 Amber Ale *(OG 1041, ABV 4%)*
Fruits of the Forest *(OG 1042, ABV 4.1%)*

ROOSTER'S

Rooster's Brewery, Unit 20, Claro Court Business Centre, Claro Road, Harrogate, N. Yorkshire HG1 4BA. *Tel (01423) 561861*
☺ Brewery set up in 1993 by Sean Franklin, formerly of Franklin's Brewery. The plant was expanded in 1994 and again in 1997 to cater for the increased demand for the award-winning beers. Winner of the Brewing Award 1997 from the British Guild of Beer Writers. A subsidiary label, Outlaw (previously known as Pioneer), produces a different, experimental beer every two months for the guest beer market; three of these have proved so popular that they have been moved into Rooster's permanent range. Occasional/seasonal beers: Jak's (OG 1039, ABV 3.9%), Nector (ABV 5.8%, Christmas).

Special *(OG 1038, ABV 3.9%)* ▮◆ A yellow-coloured beer with an intense fruity/floral aroma, which is carried through the taste where it is joined by a well-balanced bitter taste.

Ringo *(OG 1042, ABV 4.3%)* ◆ Flowery and aromatic, hops and fruit come through the taste in abundance. Has a hoppy, bitter aftertaste and a golden hue.

Scorcher *(OG 1042, ABV 4.3%)* ▮◆
Golden, aromatic and fruity, with balancing bitterness. The fruitiness is carried through into the aftertaste, where the bitterness tends to increase. A well-balanced beer.

White Cloud *(OG 1042, ABV 4.3%)*
A wheat beer switched from the Outlaw range.

Yankee *(OG 1042, ABV 4.3%)* ◆ A straw-coloured beer with a delicate, fruity aroma leading to a well-balanced taste of malt and hops with a slight evidence of sweetness, followed by a refreshing, fruity/bitter finish.

Cream *(OG 1046, ABV 4.7%)* ◆ A pale-coloured beer with a complex, floral bouquet leading to a well-balanced refreshing taste. Fruit lasts throughout and into the aftertaste.

Rooster's *(OG 1046, ABV 4.7%)* ◆ A light amber beer with a slightly hoppy nose. Strong malt flavours,with a slight toffee character, precede an unexpected hoppy finish.

ROSE STREET

See Nationals, Carlsberg-Tetley.

ROSS

◘ Ross Brewing Company, The Bristol Brewhouse, 117-119 Stokes Croft, Bristol BS1 3RW
Tel (0117) 942 0306 Fax (0117) 942 8746

Shop 9-5.30 Mon-Sat Tours by arrangement
⊠ Set up in Hartcliffe in 1989, Ross was the first brewery to brew with organic Soil Association barley, initially producing bottle-conditioned beers only. The brewery later moved to the Bristol Brewhouse pub and now no longer produces bottled beers. Ross brews for its tied house, but the range includes many occasional beers. The brewery shop is at Brewers Droop, 36 Gloucester Road, Bishopston, Bristol. Beers: Hartcliffe Bitter (OG 1045, ABV 4.5%), SPA (OG 1050, ABV 5%), Saxon Ale (OG 1055, ABV 5.5%), Uncle Igor (ABV 21%).

ROSSENDALE
See Porter.

ROTHER VALLEY
Rother Valley Brewing Company, c/o Buckland Hill Ltd, Station Road, Northiam, E. Sussex TN31 6QT. *Tel (01797) 252922*
⊠ Rother Valley Brewing Company was established in Northiam in 1993 and now looks set to remain there as plans to move to Sedlescombe have been scrapped. The brewery uses locally grown hops and malt in the production of its popular beers, which are taken by around 30 local outlets. Occasional beer: Spirit Level (OG 1045, ABV 4.5%, Christmas).
Lighterman *(OG 1032, ABV 3.2%)*
Level Best *(OG 1040, ABV 4%)*
Blues *(OG 1045, ABV 5%)*

ROYAL CLARENCE
See RCH.

ROYAL INN
⚑ Royal Inn & Horsebridge Brewery, Horsebridge, Tavistock, Devon PL18 8PS
Tel (01822) 870214 **Tours by arrangement**
⊠ Fifteenth-century pub, once a nunnery, which began brewing in 1981. The brewer, Simon Woods, has stayed in his post since 1984 through changes of ownership, to supply just the single outlet. Beers: Tamar Ale (OG 1039, ABV 3.9%), Right Royal (OG 1050, ABV 5%), Heller (OG 1060, ABV 6%).

RUDDLES
⊠ See Morland.

RUDGATE
Rudgate Brewery Ltd, 2 Centre Park, Marston Business Park, Rudgate, Tockwith, York, N. Yorkshire YO5 8QF
Tel (01423) 358382 **Tours by arrangement**
☺ Brewery founded in 1992, located in an old armoury building on a disused airfield. It supplies 150 outlets with the beers which are fermented in open square vessels. A new range of seasonal beers has been launched. Occasional beer: Rudolf's Ruin (OG 1060, ABV 5.4%, Christmas).
Viking *(OG 1038, ABV 3.8%)* ✦ An initially warming and malty full-bodied beer, with hops and fruit lingering into the aftertaste.
Battleaxe *(OG 1042, ABV 4.2%)* ✦ A well-hopped bitter with slightly sweet initial

taste and light bitterness. Complex fruit taste gives a memorable aftertaste to this drinkable ale.
Mild *(OG 1044, ABV 4.4%)*
Black Beauty Stout *(ABV 4.5%)* The new autumn beer.
Maypole *(ABV 4.5%)* The spring offering.
Mirage *(ABV 4.6%)* A summer beer.

RYBURN
⚑ Ryburn Brewery, c/o Ram's Head, Wakefield Road, Sowerby Bridge, Halifax, W. Yorkshire HX6 2AZ
Tel (01422) 835413   Fax (01422) 836488
☺ Founded in 1990 in a former dye works, this brewery is now in its fourth home, beneath its single tied house. Business efforts are now being concentrated on supplying that pub, with very limited sales outside (currently just two regular outlets).
Best Mild *(OG 1033, ABV 3.3%)* ✦ More akin to a thin, sweet stout than a dark mild, this dark brown beer has a 'rum and raisin' aroma, a slightly fruity, burnt taste and a short, dry finish.
Best Bitter *(OG 1038, ABV 3.6%)* ✦ A thin beer, initially sweet with some bitterness in the aftertaste.
Rydale Bitter *(OG 1044, ABV 4.2%)* ✦ A lightly hopped, sweet bitter with a growing dry, bitter finish.
Luddite *(OG 1048, ABV 5%)* ✦ This sweetish, black stout is dominated throughout by a roast maltiness. The finish is dry and quite bitter.
Stabbers *(OG 1052, ABV 5.2%)* ✦ A fruity sweetness competes with bitterness and malt and leads to a dry aftertaste in this golden amber, strong bitter. There is some background sulphur throughout.
Coiners *(OG 1060, ABV 6%)* ✦ Fruit, a syrupy sweetness and some background bitterness characterise this strong bitter and develop into a short but increasingly dry finish.

STOREY BOOKS

S&N
See Nationals, Scottish Courage.

SADDLEWORTH
◻ Saddleworth Brewery, Church Inn, Uppermill, Saddleworth, Greater Manchester OL3 6LW *Tel (01457) 820902*
☻ Pub brewery opened in January 1997 and presently only supplying the pub itself and some beer festivals. The full mash beers are kept in casks. Beers: More (ABV 3.8%), Bert Corner Bitter (ABV 4%), Shaft Bender (ABV 5.4%).

ST AUSTELL
St Austell Brewery Co. Ltd, 63 Trevarthian Road, St Austell, Cornwall PL25 4BY
Tel (01726) 74444 Fax (01726) 68965
**Shop 9.30-4.30 Mon-Fri in the visitors' centre
Tours by arrangement**
☒ St Austell was set up in 1851 by maltster and wine merchant Walter Hicks. It remains a family business, selling real ale to all its 160 pubs. A further 600 free trade outlets are supplied directly from the brewery. St Austell brews under contract for Carlsberg-Tetley, re-creating beers from the closed Furgusons Plympton brewery.
Bosun's Bitter *(OG 1032, ABV 3.1%)* ◆
A refreshing session beer, sweetish in aroma and bittersweet in flavour. Lingering, hoppy finish.
XXXX Mild *(OG 1039, ABV 3.6%)* ◆
Little aroma, but a strong, malty character. A caramel-sweetish flavour is followed by a good, lingering aftertaste which is sweet, but with a fruity dryness. Very drinkable.
Tinners Ale *(OG 1039, ABV 3.7%)* ◆
A deservedly popular, golden beer with an appetising malt aroma and a good balance of malt and hops in the flavour. Lasting finish.
Trelawny's Pride *(OG 1045, ABV 4.4%%)* ◆ A beer which if served through a swan neck and sparkler is robbed of aroma and taste and keeps aftertaste to a minimum.
Hicks Special Draught or HSD *(OG 1051, ABV 5%)* ◆ An aromatic, fruity, hoppy bitter which is initially sweet and has an aftertaste of pronounced bitterness, but whose flavour is fully-rounded. A good premium beer.
Winter Warmer *(OG 1060, ABV 6%)* ◆ A red/brown beer, available November-February. Full-bodied, it has a pronounced malty aroma which leads into a palate featuring strong malt and hop flavours.

**For Carlsberg-Tetley:
Dartmoor Best Bitter** *(OG 1038, ABV 3.9%)*

ST GILES IN THE WOOD
St Giles in the Wood Brewery, Unit 2 Hatchmoor Industrial Estate, Great Torrington, Devon EX38
Tel (01805) 625242
This new West Country brewery was set up using ex-Sutton Brewery plant by publican Steve Lock early in 1998. Apart from supplying his own three pubs and around 50 other local outlets, he contract brews for one regional brewer and has plans for bottling.

Although St Peter's bottled beers are not bottled-conditioned, their ales can be sampled at over 75 outlets, including the Good Beer Guide-listed Jerusalem Tavern in Clerkenwell, London EC1.

Best Bitter *(OG 1045, ABV 4.2%)*
Premium *(OG 1054, ABV 5.3%)*

ST PETER'S
St Peter's Brewery Co. Ltd, St Peter's Hall, St Peter, South Elmham, Bungay, Suffolk NR35 1NQ
Tel (01986) 782322 Fax (01986) 782505
☒ The beers are produced using a pure source of water, pumped from 300 feet below the brewery, to supply five tied houses in the Waveney Valley and one in London, plus 70 other outlets direct. The beer range has expanded to eight cask ales, including speciality fruit and wheat beers, and plans are in hand to further develop the bottled (not bottle-conditioned) beers.
Fruit Beer *(OG 1035, ABV 3.6%)*
Mild *(OG 1035, ABV 3.6%)*
Wheat Beer *(OG 1035, ABV 3.6%)*
Best Bitter *(OG 1037, ABV 3.6%)*
Extra *(OG 1043, ABV 4.4%)*
Golden Ale *(OG 1044, ABV 4.7%)*
Honey Porter *(OG 1049, ABV 5.1%)*
Strong *(OG 1049, ABV 5.1%)*

SALOPIAN
The Salopian Brewing Company Ltd, The Brewery, 67 Mytton Oak Road, Shrewsbury, Shropshire SY3 8UQ
Tel/Fax (01743) 248414 **Shop
Tours by arrangement**
☒ The first brewery in Shrewsbury in 30 years began production in 1995 in a former dairy in Copthorne on the outskirts of the town. Brewer Martin Barry, formerly of the Snowdonia Brewery, produces a wide range of beers. After a brief period of voluntary liquidation in 1997 the brewery was restarted in January 1998 by Martin Barry and Wilf Nelson, a former wine merchant.

More emphasis is now placed on cask ale production and sales, and about 30 outlets are supplied. However, the well-received bottle-conditioned beers (produced at King & Barnes) are still produced: they are available from the brewery shop and nationally via Oddbins and selected independent wholesalers. Occasional beers: Manchester Festival Beer (OG 1043, ABV 4.3%), Parsons Progress (OG 1045, ABV 4.5%), Lemon Bitter (OG 1045, ABV 4.5%), White Wheat Beer (ABV 4.7%). Bottle-conditioned beers (produced at King & Barnes): Gingersnap (OG 1047, ABV 4.7%), Minsterley Ale (OG 1045, ABV 4.5%), Snapdragon Spiced Beer (OG 1045, ABV 4.5%), Jigsaw Black Wheat (OG 1048, ABV 4.8%), Puzzle White Wheat (OG 1048, ABV 4.8%), Firefly Smoked Malt (OG 1050, ABV 5%), Ironbridge Stout (OG 1050, ABV 5%), Dragonfly Oat Beer (OG 1050, ABV 5%), Goodall's Gold)OG 1050, ABV 5%), Answer (OG 1050, ABV 5%, lager).

Bitter (OG 1035, ABV 3.5%) A hoppy, fruity bitter

Proud Salopian (OG 1040, ABV 4%) A dark, malty bitter using four hop strains. Formerly known as Monkmoor.

Choir Porter (OG 1045, ABV 4.5%) A smooth, traditional porter.

Minsterley Ale (OG 1045, ABV 4.5%) A premium bitter using three kinds of hops.

Ironbridge Stout (OG 1050, ABV 5%) A red-coloured, very malty strong ale.

Golden Thread (OG 1050, ABV 5%)

Jigsaw (OG 1050, ABV 5%)

Puzzle (OG 1050, ABV 5%)

Hollybush Winter Ale (OG 1060, ABV 6%)

SCANLON'S

Rebellion Beer Company, Unit J, Rose Industrial Estate, Marlow Bottom Road, Marlow, Buckinghamshire SL7 3ND
Tel (01895) 256270
Scanlon's ceased brewing in summer 1997, transferring all its beer production to Rebellion Brewery (qv), leaving it free to concentrate on selling the beer to pubs.

SCATTOR ROCK BREWERY

Scattor Rock Brewery, 5 Gridleys Medow, Christow, Exeter EX6 7QB
Tel (01647) 252120
Brewery founded in July 1998 and situated within Dartmoor National Park. The brewery's name was taken from the local tor, which has now been quarried. Occasional planned beers: Scattor Brain (ABV 4.8%), Scatty Bitter (ABV 3.8%).

Teign Valley Tipple (ABV 4%) Mid-brown and well balanced.

Newton 'n' Abbott (ABV 4.6%) A pale ale.

Devonian (ABV 5%) Premium beer, brown-coloured, slightly fruity, hoppy.

SCOTT'S

Scott's Brewing Co., Crown Street East, Lowestoft, Suffolk NR32 1SH
Tel (01502) 537237 Fax (01502) 515288
⊗ Founded in 1988, in former stables at the rear of the Crown Hotel, Scott's is on the site of a brewery owned by William French

400 years ago. Two maturation tanks have been added recently which, following an agreement with Courage to use some of their casks, has enabled Scott's to increase their supplies to the five pubs owned by their parent company Scott's Inns and to 100 free trade outlets. Seasonal beers: Festival Staggers (OG 1062, ABV 6%), Santa's Quaff (OG 1064, ABV 6.1%, a Christmas ale).

Golden Best (OG 1033, ABV 3.4%) ◆
A golden beer with a reasonable balance of malt and (pungent) hop, the latter dominating the aftertaste.

Blues & Bloater (OG 1036, ABV 3.7%)
◆ This pleasant, malty, fruity beer has some hop bitterness in the aftertaste.

East Point Ale or EPA (OG 1040, ABV 4%) A mid-strength, best bitter of medium colour; dry to the palate throughout, with a hoppy flavour.

Strong Mild (OG 1043, ABV 4.4%)
A dark, ruby mild ale, smooth and full-bodied, with medium chocolate flavours.

Hopleaf (OG 1045, ABV 4.5%) A light and dry bitter, with Challenger hops added late in the boil to impart an aromatic, lasting dry finish.

William French (OG 1048, ABV 5%)
◆
A full and beautifully-balanced beer. A faint, malty aroma leads into strong malt and hop flavours, with considerable fruitiness. Full and balanced aftertaste, too.

Dark Oast (ABV %) ◆ Red/brown in colour, with less body than its gravity would suggest. The taste has roast malt as its main characteristic, with hoppiness prominent in the aftertaste.

SCOTTISH & NEWCASTLE
See Nationals, Scottish Courage.

SELBY
Selby (Middlebrough) Brewery Ltd., 131 Millgate, Selby, N. Yorkshire YO8 0LL
Tel (01757) 702826
⊗ Old family brewery which resumed brewing in 1972 after a gap of 18 years but which is now mostly involved in wholesaling. Its beers, which are brewed on an occasional basis, are available, while stocks last (only in bulk), through its Brewery Tap off-licence in Selby (open 10-2, 6-10, Mon-Sat) and not at the company's single pub. They are also sold as guest beers into the local free trade. Beers: No. 1 (OG 1040, ABV 4%), No. 3 (OG 1040, ABV 4%), Old Tom (OG 1065, ABV 6.5%).

SHARDLOW
Shardlow Brewery Ltd, British Waterways Yard, Cavendish Bridge, Leicestershire DE72 2HL *Tel (01332) 799188*
Tours by arrangement
⊗ This brewery opened in 1993 in the old kiln house of the original Cavendish Bridge Brewery (closed in the 1920s), and moved in December 1996 to new premises, at the same site on the River Trent, opposite Shardlow Marina. The new brewery is situated on two floors of former stables which retain some original features. Shardlow supplies 30 free trade outlets.

Chancellor's Revenge (OG 1036,

ABV 3.6%)
Avon Ale *(ABV 3.8%)*
Bitter *(OG 1042, ABV 4.1%)* A pleasingly dry bitter.
Abu Derby *(OG 1042, ABV 4.1%)*
New Brewery Bitter *(OG 1042, ABV 4.1%)*
Reverend Eaton's Ale *(OG 1046, ABV 4.5%)* A medium strong beer with a sweet aftertaste.
Whistle Stop *(OG 1050, ABV 5%)* A strong and malty beer.

SHARP'S

Sharp's Brewery, Pityme Industrial Estate, Rock, Wadebridge, Cornwall PL27 6NU
Tel (01208) 862121 Fax (01208) 863727
⊠ Established in 1994, Bill Sharp's brewery currently supplies 300 outlets and has recently completed an expansion.
Cornish Coaster *(OG 1038, ABV 3.6%)*
◆ A smooth, easy-drinking beer, golden in colour, with a fresh hop aroma and dry malt and hops in the mouth. The finish starts malty but becomes dry and hoppy.
Doom Bar Bitter *(OG 1040, ABV 4%)*

Shepherd Neame fought to take the UK government to the European Court of Justice for its failure to harmonise alcohol duty rates. Cheap imports and bootleggers are devasting the British drinks industry.

◆ A rich, golden brown beer with a hint of barley. Dry malt and hops in the mouth. The malty finish becomes dry and hoppy. Fresh hop aroma.
Own *(OG 1044, ABV 4.4%)* ◆ A deep golden brown beer with a delicate hops and malt aroma, and dry malt and hops in the mouth. Like the other beers, its finish starts malty but turns dry and hoppy.
Special Ale *(OG 1053, ABV 5.2%)* ◆ Deep golden brown with a fresh hop aroma. Dry malt and hops in the mouth; again, the finish is malty but becomes dry and hoppy.

SHEPHERD NEAME

Shepherd Neame Ltd, 17 Court Street, Faversham, Kent ME13 7AX
Tel (01795) 532206 Fax (01795) 538907
Shop 9-5
⊠ Kent's major independent brewery is believed to be the oldest continuous brewer in the country (since 1698), but records show brewing commenced as far back as the 12th century. The same water source is still used today, steam engines are employed and the mash is produced in two teak tuns which date from 1910. A visitors' reception hall is housed in a restored medieval hall (tours by arrange-ment). The company has 390 tied houses in the South-East, nearly all selling cask ale, but ten-ants are encouraged to keep beers under blan-ket pressure if the cask is likely to be on sale for more than three days. Over 500 other outlets are also supplied directly. 1698 Commemorative Ale has been available on draught since March and is set to continue until the end of 1998. Seasonal beers: Early Bird Spring Hop Ale (ABV 4.5%, March-May), Goldings Summer Hop Ale (ABV 4.7%, June-August (note: this uses Styrian Goldings, a fug-gle-type hop and is not the same as last year's Canterbury Jack (ABV 4.5%) or Goldings Harvest Ale (ABV 5%), both of which used East Kent Goldings). Late Red Autumn Hop Ale (ABV 4.3, Sept-Nov). Bottle-conditioned beer: Spitfire (OG 1047, ABV 4.7%)▮◻.
Master Brew Bitter *(OG 1037, ABV 3.7%)* ◆ A very distinctive bitter, mid-brown in colour, with a very hoppy aroma. Well-balanced, with a nicely aggressive bitter taste from its hops, it leaves a hoppy/bitter finish, tinged with sweetness.
Best Bitter *(OG 1041, ABV 4.1%)* ◆ Mid-brown, with less marked characteristics than the bitter. However, the nose is very well-bal-anced and the taste enjoys a malty, bitter smokiness. Malty, well-rounded finish. It also appears under the name Canterbury Jack.
Spitfire Premium Ale *(OG 1047, ABV 4.7%)* A commemorative brew (Battle of Britain) for the RAF Benevolent Fund's appeal, now a permanent feature.
Bishops Finger *(OG 1052, ABV 5.2%)* A well-known bottled beer, introduced in cask-conditioned form in 1989.
Original Porter *(OG 1052, ABV 5.2%)* ▮◆ A rich, black, full-bodied winter brew. The good malt and roast malt aroma also has a fine fruit edge. The complex blend of flavours is dominated by roast malt, which is also present in a very dry aftertaste.

For Kaltenberg: Bottle condi-tioned beer:
Prinzregent Luitpold Weissbier
(ABV 5%)

SHERWOOD FOREST
See Bateman.

SHIP & PLOUGH
See Blewitts.

SHIPSTONE'S
See Nationals, Carlsberg-Tetley, and Pub Groups, Greenalls.

SHOES
Shoes Brewery, Three Horse Shoes Inn, Norton Canon, Hereford HR4 7BH
Tel (01544) 318375
Landlord Frank Goodwin had long been a home-brewer, but decided in 1994 to brew on a commercial basis for his pub. The beers are brewed from malt extract and stored in casks under mixed gas. Beers: Norton Ale (OG 1039, ABV 3.5%), Canon Bitter (OG 1042, ABV 4.2%).

SHUGBOROUGH
See Titanic.

SIX BELLS
Six Bells Brewery, Church Street, Bishop's Castle, Shropshire SY9 5AA
Tel (01588) 638930 Fax (01588) 630132
Tours by arrangement
⊠ Brewery based in a trust-owned building at the Six Bells pub, which is now the brewery tap, but run as a separate business. Production began in January 1997 and now around 25 pubs within a 30-mile radius take the beers. Wholesalers are also supplied.
Big Nev's *(OG 1037, ABV 3.8%)* A pale, fairly hoppy bitter.
Cloud Nine *(OG 1043, ABV 4.2%)* Pale, well hopped with a citrus finish. Available Spring to October.
Spring Forward *(OG 1045, ABV 4.6%)* Originally a spring beer but now permanent: dry, hoppy and darkish in colour.
Old Recumbent *(ABV 5.2%)* Well hopped winter ale available october to Spring.

SKINNER'S
Skinner's Fine Cornish Ales, Riverside View, Newham, Truro, Cornwall TR1 2SU
Tel (01872) 271885 Fax (01872) 271886
⊠ Brewery founded in July 1997 by Steve and Sarah Skinner, formerly of the Tipsy Toad brewery in Jersey. The beer names are mostly based on characters from Cornish folklore. Do not confuse the brewery with Skinner's of Brighton (see Dark Star).
Best Bitter *(ABV 3.7%)*
Spriggan Ale *(ABV 3.8%)* ❧ A light golden hoppy bitter. Well balanced with a smooth bitter finish.
Betty Stogs Bitter *(ABV 4%)* ❧ A pale amber mid-strength bitter with hoppy overtones.
Cornish Knocker Ale *(ABV 4.5%)* ❧ A strong, clean tasting golden ale. Distinctive flowery aroma with a lasting finish.
Figgy's Brew *(ABV 4.5%)* ❧ A classic dark premium strength bitter. Full flavoured with a smooth finish.
Skilliwidden Ale *(ABV 5.1%)* ❧ A rich ruby ale flavoured with chocolate malt. Finely balanced and robust hoppy character.

SKINNER'S OF BRIGHTON
See Dark Star.

SLATERS
See Eccleshall.

SMILES
Smiles Brewing Co. Ltd, Colston Yard, Colston Street, Bristol BS1 5BD *Tel (0117) 929 7350 Fax (0117) 925 8235*
Tours by arrangement
⊠ Establshed in 1977 to supply a local restaurant, Smiles commenced full-scale brewing a year later. Under the ownership of Ian Williams, who acquired the company in 1991, the tied estate has since increased to 15 houses, all selling real ale, and there are plans to add more. Noted for its good, traditional pubs (winners of three CAMRA Pub Design awards), the brewery also supplies over 250 other outlets. Monthly beers: Bristol Porter (ABV 4.7%, January), Old Tosser (ABV 4.3, February), March Hare (ABV 4%, March), April Fuel (ABV 4.8%, April), May Fly (ABV 4.5%, May), Zummer Vat Ale (ABV 4%, June), Maiden Leg Over ABV 3.5%, July), Glorious 12th (ABV 3.8%, August), Wurz Ale Gone (ABV 4.1%, September), Old Russ Ale (ABV 4.4%, October), Roman Cand Ale (ABV 5.5%, November), Holly Hops (ABV 5.5%, December).
Golden Brew *(OG 1039, ABV 3.8%)* ❧ Replacing Brewery Bitter in 1996 this has a nicely balanced, pale malt, hop and fruit aroma, which continues in a bittersweet light/medium-bodied taste. Similar finish. Refreshing yellow/golden ale.
Best Bitter *(OG 1040, ABV 4.1%)* ❧ Pale brown, well-balanced; mid-bodied, bittersweet ale with malt, hops and fruit. Taste characteristics continue to the finish, which is slightly more bitter.
Heritage *(OG 1051, ABV 5.2%)* ❧ Renamed from Exhibition, this is a complex. red-brown, medium to full-bodied fruity ale, with an aroma of malt, subtle roast-chocolate and hops. Lasting, bittersweet finish.

For Greenalls:
Cheshire Cat *(OG 1046, ABV 4.5%)*
Occasional

SAMUEL SMITH
Samuel Smith Old Brewery (Tadcaster), High Street, Tadcaster, N. Yorkshire LS24 9SB
Tel (01937) 832225 Fax (01937) 834673
Tours by arrangement
Small company operating from the oldest brewery in Yorkshire, dating from 1758 and once owned by John Smith. Unlike John Smith's, however, Sam's is still family owned and fiercely independent. The beer is brewed from well water without the use of adjuncts and all cask beer is fermented in Yorkshire stone squares before being racked into wooden casks made by the brewery's own

cooper. Real ale is sold in most of its 200-plus tied houses, but, sadly, many of Sam's London pubs no longer stock cask beer.
Old Brewery Bitter (OBB) *(OG 1040, ABV 4%)* ◆ Malt dominates the aroma, with an initial burst of malt, hops and fruit in the taste which is sustained in the aftertaste.

JOHN SMITH'S
See Nationals, Scottish Courage.

SNOWDONIA
Snowdonia Brewery, Snowdonia Park Hotel, Waunfawr, Gwynedd
Tel (01286) 650733 Tours by arrangement
Began brewing in summer 1998 using a two-barrel brewlength plant installed by the Bitter End brewpub in Cockermouth.
Session Bitter *(OG 1042, ABV 4.2%)*
Experimental Ale *(OG 1050, ABV 5%)*
Haf *(OG 1050, ABV 5%)* A summer ale.
Dafydd Du *(OG 1050, ABV 5%)* A porter.

SP SPORTING ALES
SP Sporting Ales Ltd, Cantilever Lodge, Stoke Prior, Leominster, Herefordshire HR6 0LG *Tel/Fax* (01568) 760226
⊠ Small brewery opened in April 1996 and now supplying over 65 outlets. Its main beer, Dove's Delight, is sold under various names. The brewery is due to be expanded.
Winners *(ABV 3.5%)*
Dove's Delight *(OG 1040, ABV 4%)*

SPIKES
Spikes Brewery, The Wine Vaults, 43-47 Albert Road, Southsea, Portsmouth, Hampshire PO5 2SF *Tel* (01705) 864712
Tours by arrangement
⊠ Brewery installed above the Wine Vaults pub in 1994 with a four-barrel plant, but this was changed to a two-and-a-half-barrel plant in September 1996. It currently only supplies the Wine Vaults (which is not a tied house), but there are plans to bottle beer for the American market. Beers: Anorak Ale (OG 1033, ABV 3.3%), Impaled Ale (OG 1036, ABV 3.6%), Stinger (OG 1045, ABV 4.5%), Southsea Bitter (OG 1045, ABV 4.6%), Golden (OG 1052, ABV 5.2%).

SPRINGHEAD
Springhead Brewery, Unit 3, Sutton Workshops, Old Great North Road, Sutton-on-Trent, Newark, Nottinghamshire NG23 6QS
Tel (01636) 821000 *Fax* (01636) 821150
⊠ Springhead started out as the country's smallest brewery, set up in the owner's home, but moved to larger premises in 1994. In 1997 brewing was temporarily halted but the brewer succeeded in attracting backers who follow his goals of brewing for a discerning public which is no longer satisfied by mass produced keg beers. Brewery tours available lunchtime or evenings by arrangement, in the new visitors centre.
Hersbrucker Weizenbier *(OG 1035, ABV 3.6%)* A wheat beer with a gentle aroma, light, refreshing with a dry finish. Available March to September.

Surrender *(OG 1035, ABV 3.6%)* A burnished copper coloured bitter with a stunning combination of malt and hops. Long dry finish. Wonderfully refreshing.
Hole-in-Spire *(OG 1038, ABV 4%)* A dark but not too heavy porter.
Bitter *(OG 1040, ABV 4%)* A clean tasting, easy drinking hoppy beer. Also available bottle-conditioned.
Puritans Porter *(OG 1040, ABV 4%)* A porter - ominously dark, not heavy. Smooth with a lingering finish of roasted barley.
Roundhead's Gold *(OG 1042, ABV 4.2%)* Golden light, made with wild flower honey. Refreshing but not too sweet with the glorious aroma of Saaz hops. Also available bottle-conditioned.
Goodrich Castle *(OG 1044, ABV 4.4%)* Brewed following a 17th century recipe using rosemary. Pale ale, light on the palate with a bitter finish and a delicate flavour.
The Leveller *(OG 1046, ABV 4.8%)* ⬚ Dark, smoky, intense flavour with a toffee finish. Brewed in the style of Belgian Trappist ales. Also available bottle-conditioned.
Roaring Meg *(OG 1052, ABV 5.5%)* ⬚ 'The Big Blonde'. Smooth and sweet with a dry finish and citrus honey aroma. Also available bottle-conditioned.
Cromwell's Hat *(OG 1060, ABV 6%)* As smooth as silk, robust with a hint of juniper and cinnamon. Available October to March. Also available bottle-conditioned.

STANWAY
Stanway Brewery, Stanway, Cheltenham, Gloucestershire GL54 5PQ
Tel (01386) 584320
⊠ Small brewery founded in 1993 with a five-barrel plant, which confines its sales to the Cotswolds area (around 25 outlets). Seasonal beer: Lords-a-Leaping (OG 1045, ABV 4.5%, winter). Only the bitter can be acceptably served through a sparkler.
Stanney Bitter *(OG 1042, ABV 4.5%)* ◆ A light, refreshing, amber-coloured beer, dominated by hops in the aroma, with a bitter taste and a hoppy, bitter finish.

STEAM PACKET
⬚ The Steam Packet Brewery, The Bendles, Racca Green, Knottingley, W. Yorkshire WF11 8AT *Tel/Fax* (01977) 674176
☺ Pub brewery which began producing beers for its own bar in 1990 but which has expanded to supply 50 outlets regularly (and more on an occasional basis), mainly in the North-West. New brews (including fruit beers) are regularly added to the range.
Gamekeeper Bitter *(OG 1036, ABV 3.6%)* ◆ A bitter and dry, light brown beer, with little aroma. Good, malty taste, but an unbalanced, weak aftertaste. Little hop content.
Blow Job or Bitter Blow *(OG 1038, ABV 3.8%)* ◆ A gold-coloured beer with a harsh, bitter, strongly fruity taste which echoes the aroma. The moderately malty flavour doesn't last and there is an underlying sourness throughout.
Ginger Minge *(OG 1039, ABV 4%)* ⬚◆ A wonderfully refreshing and clean-tasting ginger beer with a good hop and fruit taste and well-balanced ginger flavour. The bitter-

sweet aftertaste doesn't linger and gives way to gingerness.

Porter *(OG 1040, ABV 4%)* ❧ A dark porter with a strong malt content and a lingering woody flavour.

Brown Ale *(OG 1045, ABV 4.5%)* ❧ A malty brown ale, with a hoppy, fruity nose and a good balance of caramel, malt, hops, sweetness and bitterness in the taste, which fades slightly in the finish.

Poacher's Swag *(OG 1050, ABV 5%)* ❧ A full-bodied, sweetish mid-brown beer, with a moderately fruity aroma, leading to a bitter, slightly fruity and malty taste, and a very dry astringency which dominates the aftertaste. Some yeastiness.

Craam Stout *(OG 1050, ABV 5%)* ❧ A strong blend of roast malt and malt abounds in this beer, with a moderate hoppiness and some fruit, leading to a lingering, dry, bitterness. Black in colour. Note: the OG varies.

STEAMIN' BILLY

See Leatherbritches.

STOCKS

See Hull and Pub Groups, Century Inns.

STONES

See Nationals, Bass.

STONY ROCK

Stony Rock Brewery, Leek Road, Waterhouses, Stoke-on-Trent, Staffordshire ST10 3LH *Tel (01538) 308352*
Tours by arrangement
✗ This new brewery opened in March 1997, operating on a very small scale at the owners' farm and selling to around 20 outlets on a fairly regular basis. Plans include the acquisition of a pub or brewery tap. Occasional beer: Old Fossil (OG 1065, ABV 6.7%, brewed to a medieval recipe).

Cavern *(OG 1042, ABV 4.2%)* A full-flavoured, dry bitter.

STRAWBERRY BANK

⚲ Strawberry Bank Brewery, Masons Arms, Cartmel Fell, Grange-over-Sands, Cumbria LA11 6NW
Tel (0153 95) 68486 Fax (0153 95) 68780
Tours by arrangement
☺ Strawberry Bank is the new name of the brewery at the famous Masons Arms, the Lakeland brewery (qv) having moved out. The beer range has also been revised. Beers: Ned's Tipple (OG 1040, ABV 4%), Blackbeck (OG 1045, ABV 4.5%), Damson Ale (OG 1060, ABV 6%), Rulbuts (OG 1060, ABV 6%).

STRONG

See Nationals,Whitbread.

SULWATH

Sulwath Brewers Ltd, Gillfoot Brewery, Southerness, Kirkbean, Dumfries & Galloway DG2 8AY *Tel (01387) 255849*
Tours by arrangement

☺ Work started on this new brewery at Gillfoot farm at the end of 1995. Owned by a retired banker and a former dairy farmer, it supplies three regular outlets, plus ten others in South-West Scotland on an occasional basis. Occasional beer: JPJ Special (ABV 5%, originally brewed to commemorate the 250th anniversary of the birth of John Paul Jones in a cottage near the brewery).

Knockendoch *(OG 1045, ABV 3.8%)*
Criffel *(OG 1047, ABV 4.6%)*

SUMMERSKILLS

Summerskills Brewery, Unit 15, Pomphlett Farm Industrial Estate, Broxton Drive, Billacombe, Plymouth, Devon PL9 7BG
Tel (01752) 481283 **Tours by arrangement**
✗ Originally set up in a vineyard in 1983, but closed after two years, Summerskills was re-launched by new owners in 1990 with plant from the old Penrhos brewery. Production of its award-winning beers continues to grow at a steady rate, with 35 free trade outlets supplied directly and others nationally via wholesalers. Occasional/seasonal beers: Menacing Dennis (OG 1044, ABV 4.5%), Turkey's Delight (OG 1050, ABV 5.1%, Christmas). Bottle-conditioned beers: Best Bitter (OG 1042, ABV 4.3%), Indiana's Bones (OG 1056, ABV 5.6%).

BBB *(OG 1037, ABV 3.7%)* ❧
Best Bitter *(OG 1042, ABV 4.3%)* ❧ A mid-brown beer, with plenty of malt and hops through the aroma, taste and finish. A good session beer.

Tamar Best Bitter *(OG 1042, ABV 4.3%)* ❧ A tawny-coloured bitter with a fruity aroma and a hop taste and finish.

Whistlebelly Vengeance *(OG 1046, ABV 4.7%)* ❧ A red/brown beer with a beautiful malt and fruit taste and a pleasant, malty aftertaste.

Ninjabeer *(OG 1049, ABV 5%)* ❧ A dark gold beer, with a strong, fruity aroma and a predominantly fruity taste and aftertaste. Very drinkable. Brewed October-April.

Indiana's Bones *(OG 1056, ABV 5.6%)* ❧
🗂 A mid-brown beer with a good balance of fruit and malt in the aroma and taste, and a sweet, malty finish.

SUTTON

Sutton Brewing Company, 31 Commercial Road, Coxside, Plymouth, Devon PL4 0LE
Tel (01752) 255335
Tours by arrangement
✗ This brewery was built alongside the Thistle Park Tavern, near Plymouth's Sutton Harbour, in 1993. It went into production the following year to supply that pub and one other. It now sells to over 50 outlets in and around Plymouth, and a bigger plant and additional fermenters have been installed to cope with demand. Occasional/seasonal beers: Hopnosis (OG 1045, ABV 4.5%), Weetablitz (OG 1050, ABV 5%, summer), Sleigh'd (OG 1058, ABV 5.8%, Christmas).

Dartmoor Pride *(OG 1038, ABV 3.8%)*
XSB *(OG 1042, ABV 4.2%)* ❧ Amber nectar with a fruity nose and a bitter finish.
Gold *(OG 1044, ABV 4.4%)* ❧ Predictably gold-coloured, this is an extremely bitter-tasting beer, right through to the aftertaste.

Jinja *(OG 1045, ABV 4.5%)* ◆ 1056, ABV
5.5%) Brewed November-February; a dark
brown beer with a distinct roast malt aroma,
taste and finish.
Eddystone Light *(OG 1050, ABV 5%)*
Old Pedantic *(OG 1050, ABV 5%)*
Knickadroppa Glory *(OG 1055, ABV
5.5%)*
Plymouth Porter *(OG 1056, ABV 5.5%)*
Winter Warmer *(OG 1059, ABV 6%)*

SWALE

The Swale Brewery Co., Unit 1, D2 Trading
Estate, Castle Road, Eurolink,
Sittingbourne, Kent ME10 3RH
Tel (01795) 426871 Fax (01795) 410808
Tours available
⊠ Swale was opened in 1995 in the village
of Milton Regis by experienced home-
brewer John Davidson. It moved to a new
home in Sittingbourne in 1997. The cask
ales, including seasonal and special beers,
are now supplied to around 50 free trade
outlets and the bottle-conditioned ales are
proving equally successful. Indian Summer
Pale Ale was Champion of Champions at the
St Albans Beer Fsetival in 1997. Bottle-conditioned beers: Old Dick (OG 1052, ABV
5.2%), Kentish Gold (ABV 5%).
Kentish Pride *(OG 1039, ABV 3.8%)*
A clean-tasting, light brown-coloured ale,
dry-hopped with East Kent Goldings.
Copperwinkle *(OG 1040, ABV 4%)*
A copper-coloured bitter, predominantly
hoppy through to the finish.
Indian Summer Pale Ale *(ABV 4.2%)*
Won Champion Beer of Kent in 1997, origi-
nally a seasonal beer for autumn, now
brewed all year round.
Old Dick *(OG 1052, ABV 5.2%)* A
strong, dark winter bitter, with a smooth
taste. Brewed around Christmas.

SWALED ALE

Swaled Ale, West View, Gunnerside,
Richmond, N. Yorkshire DL11 6LD
Tel (01748) 886441
⊠ Founded in 1995 as a part-time venture,
Swaled Ale, churning out just two barrels a
week, serves a couple of outlets in N.
Yorkshire plus a few others on request. The
beers are named after local mines. Beers:
Priscilla (OG 1038, ABV 3.8%, also sold
under pub house names), Old Gang Bitter
(OG 1043, ABV 4.4%).

SWANSEA

⏚ Swansea Brewing Company, Joiners Arms,
Bishopston, Swansea, SA3 3EJ *Tel (01792)
290197*
☺ Founded in April 1996, this is the first
commercial brewery in the Swansea area for
almost 30 years. It doubled its capacity
within the first year and now produces one
regular beer and four others on an occasional basis for a small number of free trade
outlets in Swansea and South Wales.
Occasional beers: Three Cliffs Gold (ABV
4.7%), Pwlldu XXXX (ABV 4.9%), The
Original Wood (ABV 5.2%), St Teilo's
Tipple (ABV 5.5%).
Bishopswood Bitter *(ABV 4.3%)* A
mid-brown beer with a fine balance of malt
and fruit leading to a bitter finish.

TALLY HO!

⏚ Tally Ho! Country Inn and Brewery, 14
Market Street, Hatherleigh, Devon EX20
3JN *Tel (01837) 810306 Fax (01837)
811079*
Tours by arrangement
⊠ The Tally Ho! revives the 200-year tradi-
tion of brewing on the same site. Its beers are
produced from a full mash, with no addi-
tives, and, as well as sales at the pub itself,
beer agencies now take the beers. Seasonal
beers: Master Jack's Mild (OG 1040, ABV
3.5%, May), Jollop (OG 1064, ABV 6.8%,
December). Bottle-conditioned beers:
Hunter's (OG ABV 5.1%), Crebers Ale
(ABV 6.2%).
Pot Boilers Brew *(OG 1036, ABV
3.5%)* ⏚
Tarka's Tipple *(OG 1042, ABV 4%)*
Nutters Ale *(OG 1048, ABV 4.6%)*
Thurgia *(OG 1056, ABV 6%)*

TAYLOR

Timothy Taylor & Co. Ltd, Knowle Spring
Brewery, Keighley, W. Yorkshire BD21
1AW
Tel (01535) 603139 Fax (01535) 691167
☺ Independent family-owned company
established in 1858 and moved to the site of
the Knowle Spring in 1863. Its prize-winning
ales, which use Pennines spring water, are
served in all 28 of the brewery's pubs as well
as 300 other outlets. The company no longer
runs the Ale Shop off-licence in Raglan
Road, Leeds, although they still supply it.
the company put four pubs up for sale in
February 1998, are refurbishing a number of
others to be managed houses, and are looking to acquire others.
Golden Best *(OG 1033, ABV 3.5%)*
⏚⏚⏚◆ A clean-tasting and refreshing amber-
coloured mild with fruit in the nose, a light
hoppiness in the taste, a hoppy, bitter finish

The spendid copper brewing equipment at
the Tally Ho! brewpub in Hatherleigh,
Devon. The brewery also produces bottle-
conditioned beers – which is growing area
for many brewers in the UK.

and background malt throughout. A good session beer.

Dark Mild *(OG 1034, ABV 3.5%)* ✦ The hops of the underlying Golden Best combine with a caramel sweetness in this thin, dark brown beer with a bitter aftertaste.

Porter *(OG 1041, ABV 3.8%)* ✦ Sweetness and caramel can dominate this beer if it is served too young. However, when mature, the sweetness is balanced by fruity flavours and bitterness in the finish.

Best Bitter *(OG 1037, ABV 4%)* ▦◖✦ Hops and a citrus fruitiness combine well against some background malt in this very drinkable amber bitter. Bitterness increases down the glass and lingers in the aftertaste.

Landlord *(OG 1042, ABV 4.3%)* ▦✦ An increasingly dry, bitter finish complements the pungent hoppiness and complex fruitiness of this full-flavoured and well-balanced beer. Some background malt. Instantly recognisable. Champion Beer of Britain 1994.

Ram Tam (XXXX) *(OG 1043, ABV 4.3%)* ✦ A dark brown winter beer with red hints. Caramel dominates the aroma and leads to sweetish toffee and chocolate flavours in the taste, well-balanced by the hoppy fruitiness of the underlying Landlord. Increasingly dry and bitter finish.

TAYLOR WALKER
See Nationals, Carlsberg-Tetley.

TEIGNWORTHY
Teignworthy Brewery, The Maltings, Teign Road, Newton Abbot, Devon TQ12 4AA
Tel (01626) 332066
Shop 10-3 weekdays at Tuckers Maltings
Tours by arrangement
✲ Brewery founded in 1994 with a 15-barrel plant by former Oakhill and Ringwood brewer John Lawton, using part of the historic Victorian malthouse of Edward Tucker & Sons. A new bottling plant was installed in 1996 and extra capacity is presently being installed to give a maximum weekly output of 45 barrels. About 60 other outlets take the beer. Seasonal beers: Xmas Cracker (OG 1060, ABV 6%, Christmas). Bottle-conditioned beers: as cask beers.

Reel Ale *(OG 1039, ABV 4%)* ✦ Pale brown bitter with a malty nose. Hop bitter taste and aftertaste predominate.

Spring Tide *(OG 1043, ABV 4.3%)* ✦ A tawny-coloured beer with a malty nose and a hoppy, bitter taste and finish.

Beachcomber *(OG 1045, ABV 4.5%)* ✦ Available in summer: a pale brown beer with a fruity, malty taste and a bitter finish.

Maltster's Ale *(OG 1049.5, ABV 5%)* ✦ Available Oct-April: a mid brown, full-flavoured beer with a hint of chocolate turning to vanilla. Strong malt aftertaste.

TEME VALLEY
⌸ **Teme Valley Brewery, The Talbot at Knightwick, Knightwick, Worcestershire WR6 5HP**
Tel (01886) 821235 Fax (01886) 821060
Tours by arrangement
The Clift family have lived in the Teme Valley for 150 years and in August 1997 put in their own microbrewery into the family-

owned Talbot at Knightwick Inn. All brews are made only with the choicest hops from their own farm. Three other outlets are supplied.
Seasonal beers: Wot (ABVV 6%), Christmas; Hops Nouvelle (ABV 4.1%), Sep-Oct.

The Other T'Other *(ABV 3.5%)* ✦ A light bitter for easy drinking. Very hoppy on the nose but it fails to fulfill its promise.

This *(ABV 3.7%)* ✦ Sharp, well balanced session beer. A dry, crisp aftertaste make this a very quaffable drink.

That *(ABV 4.1%)* ✦ A thick, syrupy drink which is not as strong as its taste would suggest. A dry, malty aroma leads to a dry, fruity taste.

Wot *(ABV 6.2%)* ✦ A nutty tasting beer that seems to have everything. If you don't find a flavour you like, just take another sip and you'll find it eventually.

TENNENT
See Nationals, Bass.

THEAKSTON
See Nationals, Scottish Courage.

THOMPSON'S
Thompson's Brewery, London Hotel, 11 West Street, Ashburton, Devon TQ13 7DT
Brewery closed.

THREE HORSESHOES
See Shoes.

THREE TUNS
⌸ **The Three Tuns Brewing Co. Ltd, Salop Street, Bishop's Castle, Shropshire SY9 5BW**
Tel/Fax (01588) 638023
Tours by arrangement
✲ Historic brewpub, with a four-storey Victorian tower brewhouse, which first obtained a brewing licence in 1642. Much of the Victorian equipment is used, as is the 17th-century timber-framed malt store adjoining the brewery. Fifteen outlets now take the beer, and a brewery museum is planned. Seasonal beers: Old Scrooge (OG 1064, ABV 6.5%, Christmas). Bottle-conditioned beer: Clerics' Cure (OG 1048, ABV 5%, bitter), Old Scrooge (OG 1064, ABV 6.5%, stout).

Sexton *(OG 1037, ABV 3.7%)*
XXX Bitter *(OG 1042, ABV 4.3%)*
Offa's Ale *ABV 4.9%)*
Robert's Winter Special *(OG 1056, ABV 5.8%)*

THWAITES
Daniel Thwaites Brewery PLC, PO Box 50, Star Brewery, Blackburn, Lancashire BB1 5BU
Tel (01254) 54431 Fax (01254) 681439
Tours by arrangement
☺ One of the oldest family-run Lancashire firms, founded by excise officer Daniel Thwaites in 1807 and still brewing at the Star Brewery. About 80 per cent of its 500 pubs serve real ale. A substantial free trade (over 450 outlets) is also supplied. Investment in technology has now produced

a very modern brewhouse and Thwaites' commitment to cask ales is an ongong process. The Connoisseur Cask Ale Collection of monthly brews was superseded in 1997 by a new range of seasonal beers: Bloomin' Ale (ABV 4%, spring), Morning Glory (ABV 3.8%), summer, Golden Charmer (ABV 4.5%, autumn), Winter Warmer (ABV 5.5%).

Mild *(OG 1032, ABV 3.3%)* ◗ A rich, dark mild presenting a smooth, malty flavour and a pleasant, slightly bitter finish.

Bitter *(OG 1035, ABV 3.6%)* ◗ A gently-flavoured, clean-tasting bitter. Malt and hops lead into a full, lingering, bitter finish.

Chairman's Premium Ale *(OG 1042, ABV 4.2%)*

Daniel's Hammer *(OG 1047, ABV 5%)*

TIGERTOPS

Tigertops Brewery, 22 Oakes Street, Flanshaw Lane, Flanshaw, Wakefield, W. Yorkshire WF2 9LN *Tel (01229) 716238*
Tours by arrangement (at Foxfield Brewery)
☺ Microbrewery established in 1995 by two CAMRA enthusiasts. The three-barrel plant supplies several local free houses, other microbreweries as well as their own beer festivals. Owners Lynda and Stuart Johnson have bought their own pub, the Prince of Wales in Foxfield, Cumbria, and have set-up their original one-barrel equipment there, with plans to install a three-barrel set-up by the end of 1998. Occasional beer: Internettle (OG 1034, ABV 3.3%, a nettle beer).

Mild *(OG 1037, ABV 3.3%)*

Fleur-de-Lys *(OG 1038, ABV 3.6%)* A refreshing, amber-coloured session bitter with good hop character and a balancing sweetness.

White Coombe *(OG 1047, ABV 4.5%)*

Black Coombe *(OG 1052, ABV 5%)*

Vixens Vengeance *(OG 1065, ABV 6.2%)*

TIPSY TOAD

♀ The Tipsy Toad Brewery, St Peter's Village, Jersey JE3 7AA
Tel (01534) 485556 Fax (01534) 485559
Tours by arranngement
⊗ Brewpub launched by Steve Skinner in 1992. Taken over by Jersey Brewery in December 1997. Under new head brewer Patrick Dean, the Tipsy Toad is hoping to expand sales throughout the Channel Islands, with the Jersey Brewery distributing the beers through their tied estate. Several new seasonal beers are planned. In November 1997 the two brewpubs, the Star and the Townhouse, were put up for sale. Seasonal beers: Festive Toad (OG 1077, ABV 8%).

Tipsy Toad Ale *(OG 1038, ABV 3.8%)*

Jimmy's Bitter *(OG 1042, ABV 4.2%)*

Horny Toad *(OG 1050, ABV 5%)*

Dixie's Wheat Beer *(OG 1041, ABV 4%)*

Naomh Pádraig's Porter *(OG 1045, ABV 4.4%)*

TISBURY

Tisbury Brewery Ltd, Church Street, Tisbury, Wiltshire SP3 6NH
Tel (01747) 870986 Fax (01747) 871540

⊗ Housed in the old village workhouse, converted by maltster Archibald Beckett in 1868 but rebuilt after a fire in 1885, this brewery ceased production in 1914. It re-opened as Tisbury Brewery in 1980 but this foundered, leaving the premises to be taken over by Wiltshire Brewery, which brewed here until closing the site in 1992. This new Tisbury Brewery took over the building and began production in April 1995. It now provides beer for over 100 outlets, using the slogan 'The small brewery with the big taste'. Plans to treble production capacity by 1999. Seasonal beers (all OG 1045, ABV 4.5%): Old Mulled Ale; Fanfare; Ale Fresco; Real Nut Ale.

Best Bitter *(OG 1038, ABV 3.8%)* A golden/amber-coloured beer with a malty nose. The malty taste has hints of fruit and hop. Full-bodied for its strength.

Archibald Beckett *(OG 1043, ABV 4.3%)* A very malty, full-bodied, dark amber bitter with some caramel on the nose. Strong hop flavours come through in the taste.

Nadderjack Ale *(OG 1043, ABV 4.3%)* A golden, full-bodied, well-balanced bitter with a spicy hop finish.

Old Wardour *(OG 1048, ABV 4.8%)* A full-bodied, mahogany-hued beer with a faintly burnt nose. Malty and slightly sweet, it has a delicate fruitiness and a final hop bite.

TITANIC

The Titanic Brewery, Unit G, Harvey Works, Lingard Street, Burslem, Stoke-on-Trent, Staffordshire ST6 1ED
Tel (01782) 823447 Fax (01782) 812349
Tours by arrangement
☺ Named in honour of the Titanic's Captain Smith, who hailed from Stoke, this brewery was founded in 1985 and taken over by its present owners after initial difficulties. It moved to larger premises in 1991 and installed new brewing plant in 1995. In 1996 Titanic began brewing for demonstration purposes on the log-fired Victorian micro-brewery in the Staffordshire County Museum at Shugborough Hall. The company now supplies over 200 free trade outlets, as well as two pubs of its own (which also sell other independents' guest beers). Bottle-conditioned beers: Stout (OG 1046, ABV 4.5%), Captain Smith's (OG 1054, ABV 5.2%), Christmas Ale (OG 1080, ABV 7.8%). Shugborough Brewery: Longhorn (OG 1057, ABV 5.5%, Dec-Feb), Horsepower (OG 1046, ABV 4.5%, March-May), Redcap (OG 1044, ABV 4.3%, June-August), Saddleball (OG 1044, ABV 4.3%, Sep-Nov). Shugborough brews are also available bottle-conditioned in the same periods.

Best Bitter *(OG 1036, ABV 3.5%)* ◗ A crisp, clean, refreshing bitter with a good balance of fruit, malt and hops. Bitter finish.

Lifeboat Ale *(OG 1040, ABV 3.9%)* ◗ A fruity and malty, dark red/brown beer, with a fruity finish.

Premium *(OG 1042, ABV 4.1%)* ◗ An impressive, well-balanced pale brown bitter with hops and fruit in the aroma which develop into a full flavour and a dry, hoppy finish.

Red Cap *(ABV 4.3%)* Available June-

August.
Horse Power *(ABV 4.5%)* Available
March-May.
Stout *(OG 1046, ABV 4.5%)* A dark com-
bination of malt and roast with some
hops. Strongly flavoured and well-
balanced.
White Star *(OG 1050, ABV 4.8%)* ❦ A
bittersweet amber ale with a very fruity taste
and a long fruit aftertaste.
Saddleback *(ABV 5%)* Available
September-November.
Captain Smith's *(OG 1054, ABV 5.2%)*
❦ A full-bodied, dark red/brown beer,
hoppy and bitter with malt and roast malt
flavours, and a long, bittersweet finish.
Longhorn *(ABV 5.5%)* A dark brew, full-
flavoured with a rich bittersweet finish.
Available October-January.

TOLLY COBBOLD

**Tollemache & Cobbold Brewery Ltd, Cliff
Road, Ipswich, Suffolk IP3 0AZ**
Tel (01473) 231723 Fax (01473) 280045
Shop Tours by arrangement for groups
⊠ One of the oldest breweries in the country, founded by Thomas Cobbold in 1723.
In 1989 Brent Walker took over the company, closed the Cliff Brewery and transferred production to Camerons in
Hartlepool. But a management buyout
meant Tolly Cobbold Ipswich-brewed ales
were back on sale in 1990. It brews only
cask-conditioned ales. The new company
acquired no pubs from Brent Walker, but
secured a long-term trading agreement with
Pubmaster (the company which runs former
Brent Walker pubs), and now supplies
around 400 outlets. It opened a brewery tap
in 1992 and owns six other outlets. Tours
for groups (daily) have become a major
attraction. The Bottlers Room, contains the
largest public display of commemorative
bottled beers. Shop open lunchtimes in the
tourist season. It introduces a new bottled
beer annually: 1998's is Old Strong Porter,
its first porter for many years. Seasonal beers
include Valentine's Ale, St George's Best,
and Christmas Ale.
Mild *(OG 1032, ABV 3.2%)* ⌂❦ A tasty
mild with fruit, malt and roast malt characters. Pleasing aftertaste. It tends to lose
complexity when forced through a
sparkler.
Bitter *(OG 1035, ABV 3.5%)* ❦ A light,
mid-brown-coloured malty beer lacking bitterness.
Original Best Bitter *(OG 1038, ABV
3.8%)* ❦ A slightly stronger bitter with
assertive hop character throughout. The finish is bitter, but with a good balancing maltiness. Disappointingly hard to find.
IPA *(OG 1040, ABV 4.2%)* A best bitter,
full of citrus fruit flavours and flowery hoppiness.
Old Strong Winter Ale *(OG 1050,
ABV 5%)* ❦ Available November to
February. A dark winter ale with plenty of
roast character throughout. Lingering and
complex aftertaste.
Tollyshooter *(OG 1050, ABV 5%)* ❦
A reddish premium bitter with a full, fruity
flavour and a long, bittersweet aftertaste.
Good hop character, too. Named after the
Sir John Harvey-Jones TV series,
Troubleshooter, in which Tolly featured.

Conquest *(OG 1051, ABV 5%)*

TOMINTOUL

**Tomintoul Brewery Co. Ltd, Mill of
Auchriachan, Tomintoul, Ballindalloch,
Banffshire AB37 9EQ**
Tel (01807) 580333 Fax (01807) 580358
☺ Brewery opened in November 1993 in an
old watermill, in an area renowned for malt
whisky and salmon. Around 80 outlets are
currently supplied and wholesalers take the
beer into England and Northern Ireland.
Seasonal ales: Scottish Bard (OG 1044, ABV
4.4%),Grand Slam (OG 1047, ABV 4.7%),
Caillie (OG 1040, ABV 4%), Trade Winds
IPA (OG 1049, ABV 4.5%), Black Gold (OG
1048.5, ABV 4.4%), Witches' Cauldron (OG
1049, ABV 4.9%), Saint's Ale (OG 1043,
ABV 4.5%), Santa's Sledgehammer (OG
1058, ABV 6.3%). Stag is now available bottled, but not bottle-conditioned.
Laird's Ale *(OG 1038, ABV 3.8%)* ❦
A worthy addition to the list of Scottish 70/-
session ales. A well-balanced brew with
some hops in the lingering fruity finish.
Stag *(OG 1039.5, ABV 4.1%)* ❦ A powerful, malty nose with less hop character on
the palate than in the early brews. This
tawny brew has a lingering, malty, gently
bitter aftertaste.
Nessie's Monster Mash *(OG 1044,
ABV 4.4%)* ❦ A mahogany-coloured, full,
malty brew with a creamy mouthfeel leading
to a satisfying, fruity finish.
Culloden *(OG 1046, ABV 4.6%)* ❦ Not as
hoppy as the other Tomintoul beers, but
packed full of maltiness on the palate and
with a creamy, roast finish. A smooth, full-
bodied mid-brown brew.
Wild Cat *(OG 1049.5, ABV 5.1%)* ❦
A deep amber, old-ale-style brew, but with a
good balance of hops on the palate and an
intense, hoppy, fruity finish. Goes well with
stovies and oatcakes in front of a real open
fire in winter.

TOMLINSON'S

**Tomlinson's Old Castle Brewery, Units 5 &
6, Britannia Works, Skinner Lane,
Pontefract, W. Yorkshire WF8 1H4**
Tel (01977) 780866 **Shop 10-3 Mon-Fri
Tours by arrangement**
☺ Established in 1993, the award-winning
brews take their names from various local
historical connections. Over 60 outlets are
now supplied. Occasional beers: Femme
Fatale (OG 1043, ABV 4.5%), Fractus XB
(OG 1045, ABV 4.5%), Double Helix (OG
1055, ABV 5.5%). Bottle-conditioned beer:
Three Seiges (OG 1058, ABV 6%).
Hermitage Mild *(OG 1036, ABV 3.7%)*
⌂
Sessions *(OG 1038, ABV 4%)* ❦ A dry,
bitter beer with a light, hoppy, smoky aroma
leading to a well-hopped and slightly fruity
taste and aftertaste, which is also dry. Light
brown/copper in colour.
De Lacy *(OG 1044, ABV 4.6%)* ❦
An enjoyable amber, bitter, dry beer with a
good, hoppy, fruity nose and a well-balanced strong hop and fruit taste with some
sweetness. Dry, slightly yeasty aftertaste.
Deceitful Rose *(OG 1048, ABV 5%)* ⌂❦
Superbly dry, hoppy, straw-coloured beer in
the style of an India Pale Ale. Very bitter and
dry in the taste and finish, with a clean, hoppy

and slightly fruity flavour which lingers.
Richard's Defeat *(OG 1050, ABV 5%)*
❧ A dark brown porter in which roast
flavour, malt and hops all have a strong
presence through to the finish.
Three Sieges *(OG 1058, ABV 6%)*
A liquorice beer, brewed in winter.

TOWNES

⌂ Townes Brewery, Speedwell Inn,
Lowgates, Chesterfield, Derbyshire S43 3TT
Tel (01246) 472252
Tours by arrangement
⊗ Established in 1994 by Alan Wood, bring-
ing brewing back to Chesterfield after nearly
40 years, the brewery relocated in October
1997 to its first tied house, the Speedwell Inn,
Chesterfield's first brewpub this century.
Around 25 outlets are supplied. Future plans
include installation of a small bottling plant.
Sunshine *(OG 1036, ABV 3.6%)* A light-
coloured session beer with a full fi
nish.
Golden Bud *(OG 1038, ABV 3.8%)*
Colliers *(OG 1040, ABV 4%)* A new
brown ale.
Spireite *(OG 1040, ABV 4%)*
GMT *(OG 1040, ABV 4%)* A pale, spicy ale
with a malty base and a hoppy finish.
Available winter only.
IPA *(OG 1045, ABV 4.5%)* A well-
balanced, strong pale ale. Available summer
only.

TRAQUAIR

Traquair House Brewery, Traquair Estate,
Innerleithen, Peeblesshire EH44 6PW
Tel (01896) 831370 Fax (01896) 830639
Shop 2-5.30, April-Oct Tours by arrangement
☺ This 18th-century brewhouse is in one of
the wings of Traquair House (over 1,000
years old) and was rediscovered by the 20th
Laird, the late Peter Maxwell Stuart, in
1965. He began brewing again using the
original equipment (which was intact, having lain idle for over 100 years). The brewery has been run by Peter's daughter,
Catherine Maxwell Stuart, since his death in
1990. All the beers are oak-fermented and
60 per cent of production is exported
(mostly bottled Traquair House Ale and
Jacobite Ale). About five outlets take the
cask beer. Occasional/seasonal beers:
Festival Ale (OG 1045, ABV 4%), Fair Ale
(OG 1055, ABV 6%).
Bear Ale *(OG 1050, ABV 5%)* ❧ A powerful, malt/fruit aroma precedes a deep, rich
taste bursting with fruit, which lingers and
subtly changes into a long-lasting, dry finish.

TRAVELLERS INN

⌂ Travellers Inn, Pen y Cefn, Caerwys,
North Wales CH7 5BL
Tel (01352) 720251 Fax 01352 721066
Pub brewery which opened in April 1997,
producing full mash beers only for sale

Traquair House is over 1,000 years old and the imposing setting for the Traquair House Brewery; the old brewing equipment had lain idle for over 100 years. Traquair is well known for its bottled-conditioned beer, Traquair House Ale.

Glory Ale (OG 1070, ABV 7.2%).
Finest Summer Ale *(OG 1037, ABV 3.7%)* Available May-September; a refreshing summer ale with a proportion of wheat malt in the mash.
The Ridgeway Bitter *(OG 1039, ABV 4%)* ☐◆ A beer with a pleasant mix of flowery hops, malt and fruit flavours before a dryish aftertaste.
Old Icknield Ale *(OG 1049, ABV 5%)* A beer with a distinct, hoppy flavour and a dry, bitter aftertaste.

TRIPLE FFF BREWING COMPANY
Triple fff Brewring Company, Magpie Works, Unit 3, Station Approach, Four Marks, Alton, Hants GU34 4HN
Tel/Fax (01420) 561422
 Established in October 1997 by Graham Trott and Alan Norris with a five-barrel plant.
Moondance *(OG 4.2, ABV %)* Uses Northdown, FirstGold and Cascade hops.
Comfortably Numb *(ABV %)* Uses Styrian hops.

TRUEMAN'S
Sam Trueman's Brewery, Henley House, School Lane, Medmenham, Buckinghamshire SL7 2HJ
Tel (01491) 576100 Fax (01491) 571764
⊗ Henley House is a business training centre set in an idyllic spot near Marlow. Its brewery was set up in 1995 to produce real ale for delegates attending courses. Now has five-barrel equipment to supply a limited number of outlets and what it terms 'bona fide wholesalers' after problems with late-paying wholesalers. No plans to increase range. Bottle-conditioned beers: Northdown Bitter (ABV 4.7%), True Gold Lager (ABV 5.5%), Percy's Downfall (ABV 6%).
Best *(OG 1036, ABV 3.5%)*
Tipple *(OG 1041, ABV 4.2%)* Available autumn.
Gold *(OG 1050, ABV 5%)* Available summer.
Percy's Downfall *(OG 1084, ABV 8.2%)* Available Christmas.

within the pub itself. One of thre smallest breweries in Wales, its two-and-a-half barrel plant is on display in the pub.
Roy Morgan's Original Ale *(OG 1042, ABV 4.2%)*
Old Elias Strong Pale Ale *(OG 1052, ABV 5%)*

TRING
The Tring Brewery Company Ltd, 81-82 Akeman Street, Tring, Hertfordshire HP23 6AF
Tel (01442) 890721 *Fax (01442) 890740*
Tours by arrangement
⊗ Established in 1992, this 32-barrel brewery brings brewing back to Tring after over 50 years. The brewery supplies 30-60 outlets. Occasional beers are produced. Seasonal beer: Death or Glory Ale (OG 1070, ABV 7.2%, brewed October 25 to commemorate the Charge of the Light Brigade in 1854 and sold December-January). Bottle-conditioned beer: Death or

TYNLLIDIART ARMS
Tynllidiart Arms, Capel Bangor, Aberystwyth, Ceredigion
Brewing ceased at the site in spring 1998, although Flannery's Brewery of Aberystwyth are producing an uprated version of Rheidol Reserve (ABV 4.8%) as their premium bitter.

ULEY

Uley Brewery Ltd, The Old Brewery, Uley,
Dursley, Gloucestershire GL11 5TB
Tel (01453) 860120

⊗ Brewing at Uley began in 1833 at Price's
Brewery and after a long gap the premises
were restored and Uley Brewery opened
1985. It serves over 40 free trade outlets in
the Cotswolds area. Seasonal beers: Pigor
Mortis (OG 1062, ABV 6%, October-
November), Severn Boar (OG 1062, ABV
6%, December-January).

Hogshead Bitter *(OG 1036, ABV 3.5%)*
◆ A pale-coloured, hoppy session bitter
with a good hop aroma and a full flavour
for its strength, ending in a bittersweet aftertaste.
Bitter *(OG 1036, ABV 3.5%)* ◆ A copper-
coloured beer with hops and fruit in the
aroma and a malty, fruity taste, underscored
by a hoppy bitterness. The finish is dry, with
a balance of hops and malt.
Old Ric *(OG 1046, ABV 4.5%)* ◆ A full-
flavoured, hoppy bitter with some fruitiness
and a smooth, balanced finish. Distinctively
copper-coloured.
Old Spot Prize Ale *(OG 1050, ABV
5%)* ◆ A distinctive full-bodied, red/brown
ale with a fruity aroma, a malty, fruity taste,
with a hoppy bitterness, and a strong, balanced aftertaste.
Pig's Ear Strong Beer *(ABV %)* ◆ A
pale-coloured beer, deceptively strong.
Notably bitter in flavour, with a hoppy,
fruity aroma and a bitter finish.

USHERS

Ushers of Trowbridge PLC, Directors
House, 68 Fore Street, Trowbridge,
Wiltshire BA14 8JF *Tel (01225) 763171
Fax (01225) 774289*
Tours groups by arrangement

⊗ This famous West Country brewery was
founded in 1824, but lost its identity after
being swallowed up by Watney (later
Grand Met) in 1960. A successful management buy in purchasing the brewery and
433 pubs from Courage in 1991 gave
Ushers back its independence. It has since
invested in pubs and plant, with over £7
million alone spent on the brewery, and a
new Ushers Cellar Master Award scheme
has been introduced to promote good beer
care and dispense. Ushers was launched on
the Stock Exchange in 1997. In November
1997 it began work on a £4 million investment programme to cope with brewing
contracts. By summer 1998 it was due to
have increased its capacity by 100,000 barrels and to be able to brew a further
100,000 at little extra cost. It now supplies
real ale to nearly all its 580 houses (most
tenanted and all in the South, South-West
and South Wales) and also to Scottish
Courage/Grand Met Inntrepreneur pubs.
Keg and bottled products are brewed for
Scottish Courage and other international
breweries, although there has been a cut in
demand for Ushers brands from Scot Co.
Beer is also produced for the Matthew
Clark (formerly Freetraders) wholesaling
company, Gibbs Mew and a number of
supermarket own-label beers. Seasonal
beers: Plus January Sale (OG 1031, ABV
3%, January), 1824 Particular (OG

1062.5, ABV 6%, December), St George
and the Dragon Ale (OG1040, ABV 4%).
Best Bitter *(OG 1037.5, ABV 3.8%)* ◆
An amber/pale brown, light bitter with malt
and hoppy bitterness in the flavour followed
by a dry, bitter finish.
Spring Fever *(OG 1040, ABV 4%)*
Available March-June.
Summer Madness *(OG 1040, ABV 4%)*
Available June-September.
Autumn Frenzy *(OG 1041, ABV 4%)*
Available September-December.
Winter Storm *(OG 1041, ABV 4%)*
Available December-February.
Founders Ale *(OG 1046, ABV 4.5%)* ◆
A pale brown beer with a bitter hop taste,
balanced by sweet maltiness and faint citrus
fruit. Predominantly bitter finish.

**For Matthew Clark (Freetraders):
Chadwick's** *(OG 1037, ABV 3.7%)*

For Gibbs Mew: *(ABV %)* ◆
Wiltshire Traditional *(OG 1036, ABV
3.5%)*
Salisbury Best Bitter *(OG 1042, ABV
4.1%)* ◆ A rather chewy, sweet ale, decidedly lacking in bitterness. All the same, a
pleasant beer.

**For Yates Wine Lodges:
Peter Yates Bitter** *(OG 1040, ABV
4.1%)*

VALE

Vale Brewery Company, Thame Road,
Haddenham, Buckinghamshire HP17 8BY
Tel (01844) 290008 Fax (01844) 292505
Tours by arrangement
⊗ After many years working for large
regional breweries and allied industries,
brothers Mark and Phil Stevens opened a
small, purpose-built brewery in
Haddenham. This revived brewing in a vil-
lage where the last brewery closed at the end
of World War II. The plant was expanded in
November 1996 and now has a capacity of
40 barrels. All beer is traditionally brewed
without using adjuncts, chemicals, or preser-
vatives and have gaied a strong local identity
and following. Around 200 local outlets
now take the beers.
Notley Ale *(OG 1032/33, ABV 3.3%)*
A well-hopped session beer.
Wychert Ale *(OG 1038, ABV 3.9%)*
A full-flavoured beer withnutty overtones.
Hadda's Summer Glory *(OG
1039/40, ABV 4%)* A seasonal beer.
Edgar's Golden Ale *(OG 1042/43,
ABV 4.3%)* ⬠ A full-bodied golden ale made
with fuggle and Golding hops.
Hadda's Autumn Ale *(OG 1044, ABV
4.5%)* A seasonal beer.
Hadda's Spring Gold *(OG 1049, ABV
5%)* A seasonal beer.
Good King Senseless *(OG 1050, ABV
5.2%)* A seasonal (winter) beer.

VAUX

Vaux Breweries Ltd, The Brewery,
Sunderland, Tyne & Wear SR1 3AN
Tel (0191) 567 6277 Fax (0191) 514 0422
Tours by arrangement
⊛ First established in 1837 and now one of
the country's largest regional brewers, Vaux

remains firmly independent. It owns Ward's of Sheffield, but sold off Lorimer & Clark in Edinburgh to Caledonian in 1987. Real ale is sold in over 500 of its 860 houses (which include those run by Wards and Vaux Inns Ltd.) and is also provided to its 400 free trade customers. Vaux Waggle Dance (OG 1047, ABV 5%) is produced at Ward's (qv), whilst Vaux Mild is Ward's Mild rebadged. As sponsors of Sunderland AFC Vaux produced Wear Best (OG 1038, ABV 3.9%), a dry-hopped bitter, for the new stadium; it is available there and in selected Vaux Inns. Hopes to have 30 of its Henry Bramwell Heritage Ale Houses by the end of 1998, for which it brews Henry Bramwell Heritage Ale (OG 1038, ABV 3.9%).

Lorimer's Best Scotch *(OG 1036, ABV 3.6%)* ◗ A replica of the original Scottish Scotch. Aroma is often lacking, but, when fresh, there can be a subtle hop character to balance a sweet and malty taste.

Lambton's *(OG 1038, ABV 3.8%)*

Vaux Bitter *(OG 1038, ABV 3.9%)* ◗ A light and drinkable bitter with low bitterness and some fruit evident. Aroma is easily lost, but can be hoppy.

Samson Smoth *(OG 1041, ABV 4%)* A light ale with a distinctive, full bodied flavour brewed to give a smoother finish and creamy head.

Double Maxim *(OG 1048, ABV 4.7%)* ◗ A smooth brown ale, rich and well-balanced, with lasting fruit and good body.

Moonlight Mouse *(ABV 4.7%)* A seasonal beer for autumn.

St Nicholas's Christmas Ale *(ABV 5%)* A seasonal beer.

VENTNOR

Ventnor Brewery Ltd,119 High Street, Ventnor, Isle of Wight PO38 1LY
Tel (01983) 856161 Fax (01983) 856404
Tours by arrangement
⊗ Founded in 1840 by John Corbould it was bought by J. Burt in 1866 and still called Burt's, although it was sold to Phillips in 1906. Having survived German bombing and being rebuilt in the 1950s, the brewery closed in 1981 and the trade name was sold to Hatridges. Its new ownership resurrected brewing here in 1995 under the original name of the Ventnor Brewery. It now serves 70-100 pubs, including one tied house. Currently establishing a distribution line with Hall & Woodhouse.

Ventnor Dark Mild *(ABV 3.3%)* An autumn beer.

Ventnor Volunteer Bitter *(OG 3.5, ABV %)* A summer beer.

Golden Bitter *(OG 1040, ABV 4%)* ◗ A truly, well-balanced, straw-coloured bitter with an excellent rich and creamy mouthfeel and lasting maltiness.

Kangaroo Bitter *(ABV 4.8%)*
XAV *(OG 1050, ABV 5%)* ◗ Primarily a winter beer, strong, dark and bursting with roast flavour. Roast malt and hops feature in the aroma. Good, solid body.

VERULAM

♬ Verulam Brewery, 132 London Road, St Albans, Hertfordshire AL1 1PQ *Tel (01727) 766702*
⊗ Brewery housed behind the Farmers Boy pub in St Albans, having been moved here in 1997 from the Red Cow in Harpenden, where it traded as Harpenden Brewery. Both these pubs take the beer. A cask-conditioned lager, VB Lager, is also brewed. Beers: Special (OG 1037, ABV 3.8%), IPA (OG 1040, ABV 4%), Farmers Joy (OG 1043, ABV 4.5%).

VIKING

Viking Ales Ltd, t/a Viking Brewery, 5 Blenheim Close, Pysons Road, Broadstairs, Kent CT10 2YF
Brewery closed.

VILLAGE

See Hambleton.

WADWORTH

Wadworth & Co. Ltd, Northgate Brewery, Devizes, Wiltshire SN10 1JW
Tel (01380) 723361 Fax (01380) 724342
Shop Mon-Fri, 9-5 Tours by arrangement
⊗ Market town brewery set up in 1885 by Henry Wadworth. Though solidly traditional (with its own dray horses), it continues to invest in the future and to expand, producing up to 2,000 barrels a week to supply a wide-ranging free trade in the South of England, as well as its 226 outlets (163 tied). All the pubs serve real ale and 6X remains one of the South's most famous beers, with national distribution now achieved via the Whitbread guest ale portfolio. Wadworth also owns two brew pubs: the Farmers Arms (qv) and the Red Shoot (qv). Seasonal beers: Old Timer (OG 1055, ABV 5.8%, December-January), Valentine's Oat Malt Ale (OG 1043, ABV 4.5% February), Easter Ale (OG 1043, ABV 4.5%), Malt & Hops (OG 1043, ABV 4.5%, September).

Henry's Original IPA *(OG 1035, ABV 3.8%)* ◗ A golden brown-coloured beer with a gentle, malty and slightly hoppy aroma, a good balance of flavours, with maltiness gradually dominating, and then a long-lasting aftertaste to match, eventually becoming biscuity. A good session beer.

6X *(OG 1040, ABV 4.3%)* ◗ Copper-coloured ale with a malty and fruity nose and some balancing hop character. The flavour is similar, with some bitterness and a lingering malty, but bitter finish. Full-bodied and distinctive.

SummerSault *(OG 1038, ABV 4%)* Now available all year, a pale, fragrantly hoppy, refreshing beer made with Saaz lager hops.

Farmers Glory *(OG 1046, ABV 4.5%)* ◗ This dark beer can be delightfully hoppy and fruity, but varies in flavour and conditioning. The aroma is of malt and it should have a dryish, hoppy aftertaste.

WARD'S

Ward's Brewery, Ecclesall Road, Sheffield, S. Yorkshire S11 8HZ
Tel (0114) 275 5155 Fax (0114) 272 5582
Tours by arrangement
⊗ Established in 1840 by Josiah Kirby, Ward's has been a subsidiary of Vaux of Sunderland since 1972. Since the closure of

525

the neighbouring Thorne brewery in 1986, it has also produced Darley's beers. Real ale is available in 160 of the brewery's 220 tied houses and around 300 free trade outlets are supplied directly. Seasonal beers: Boxing Hare Spring Ale (ABV 4.7%, March). How's Your Father Summer Ale (ABV 4.6%, July, wheat beer).

Vaux Mild (OG 1034, ABV 3.4%) ❧
Also known as Darley's Dark Mild. This beer's rich dark brown and red hue promises more than is delivered. A strong malt nose precedes a roast malt taste, with hints of chocolate. The dry finish can be tinged with sweetness, if it lasts long enough.

Thorne Best Bitter (OG 1037, ABV 3.8%) ❧ Recently improved, this malty-nosed, mid-brown beer has a hoppy bitterness but is well-balanced throughout, including well into the finish.

Best Bitter (OG 1038, ABV 5%) ❧
The rich, malty aroma of this pale brown bitter has been toned down, but it still has a malty base and a bittersweet aftertaste.

Waggle Dance (OG 1049, ABV 5%) ❧
A beer brewed with honey, gold in colour. A malty drink with a gentle bitterness and a dry, malty finish. Better for not being as sweet as before.

WARDEN
See Merivales.

WARWICKSHIRE
Warwickshire Brewery, Princes Drive, Kenilworth, Warwickshire
Brewery closed.

WATKIN, TOMOS
Tomos Watkin & Sons Ltd, The Castle Brewery, 113 Rhosmaen Street, Llandeilo, Carmarthenshire SA19 6EN
Tel (01558) 824140 Fax (01558) 824098
Tours by arrangement
☺ Brewery established by Simon Buckley (formerly of Buckley and Ushers breweries), adopting the name of a Llandovery brewery which ceased production in 1928. Brewing commenced in December 1995 and Tomos Watkins is now recognised as Wales's largest small brewer, supplying over 50 outlets. The brewery is currently being expanded and a new bottle-conditioned range, including its stout, is due to be launched in September 1998. The brewery now owns seven pubs, all serving cask ale, and hopes to aquire 13 more during 1998/1999. An attached craft centre opened in spring 1996. Seasonal beers are occasionally produced for the brewery's own pubs. Seasonal beers: Cwrw Haf (1042, ABV 4.7%, summer), Cwrw Santa (OG 1046, ABV 4.6%, Christmas). Bottle-conditioned beer: Merlin Stout (OG 1042, ABV 4.2%).

Watkin's Whoosh (OG 1037, ABV 3.7%)

Brewery Bitter (OG 1041, ABV 4%) ❧
An amber-coloured beer with a short-lived hoppy and malty aroma. Hops, malt and a hint of fruit in the mouth lead to a building bitterness which overpowers sweetness in the aftertaste.

Cwrw Caio (OG 1040, ABV 4%)
OSB (OG 1045, ABV 4.5%) ❧ An amber ale with fruit and hops in the aroma and taste, leading on to a malty, dryish finish.

Canon's Choice (OG 1047, ABV 4.7%)
Merlin's Stout (OG 1042, ABV 4.2%)

WEATHEROAK
Coach and Horses Inn, Weatheroak Hill, Alvechurch West Midlands B48 7EA
Tel (0498) 773894
This joint venture between Weatheroak and Phil and Sheila Meads, proprietors of the Coach and Horses, produced its first beer in January 1998. A second fermenter was added in April and there are plans to add new beers as time progresses.

Weatheroak Ale (ABV 4.1%) ❧
The brewery's first brew is a good balance of malt and hops which produces a beer with a hoppy but clean bitter taste, with a long, dry aftertaste.

Hopwood Ale (ABV 4.1%)
Chestnut Ale (ABV 4.1%)

WEBSTER'S
See Mansfield, and Nationals, Scottish Courage.

WEETWOOD
Weetwood Ales Ltd, Weetwood Grange, Weetwood, Tarporley, Cheshire CW6 0NQ
Tel (01829) 752377
☺ Brewery set up at an equestrian centre in 1993, with the first brew on sale in March of that year. Around 40-50 regular customers are now supplied.

Best Bitter (OG 1038, ABV 3.8%) ❧
A clean, dry and malty bitter with little aroma. Bitterness dominates the finish.

Eastgate Ale (OG 1044, ABV 4.2%)
Old Dog Bitter (OG 1045, ABV 4.5%)
❧ A fuller-bodied version of the bitter: fruitier, with a hint of sweetness.

Oasthouse Gold (OG 1050, ABV 5%)
A golden, sweeitsh, fruity bitter.

WELLS
Charles Wells Ltd, The Eagle Brewery, Havelock Street, Bedford MK40 4LU
Tel (01234) 272766 Fax (01234) 279000
Tours by arrangement
✖ The largest, independent, family-owned brewery in the country established in 1876 and still run by descendants of the founder. The brewery has been on this site since 1976 and 290 of its tied 300 pubs serve cask ale, though about 50 per cent apply cask breathers. Wells also supplies around 600 other outlets direct. A bottling line was added in 1996. Its export market of 23 countries earned it a Queen's Award for Export in 1997. Seasonal ales: Summer Solstice (OG 1041, ABV 4.1%, available June), Josephine Grimbley (OG 1041, ABV 4.1%), available September.

Eagle IPA (OG 1035, ABV 3.6%) ❧
A refreshing, pale brown session bitter. Good samples have fresh, flowery hop with citrus fruit and a dry bitter finish, but the use of tight sparkers often seems to produce blander results.

Bombardier Premium Bitter (OG 1042, ABV 4.3%) ❧ Gentle citrus hop is balanced by traces of malt in the mouth, and this pale brown best bitter ends with a lasting dryness. Sulphur often dominates the

aroma, particularly with younger casks.
Fargo *(OG 1050, ABV 5%)* ♦ A winter beer to search for. Hops, fruit and sulphur are prominent on the nose, followed by a bitter, citrus fruit flavour with a little malt to add a slight sweetness. Hops and fruit in the long, dry finish.

WELSH BREWERS
See Nationals, Bass.

WELTONS
Weltons North Downs Brewery Ltd, Unit 24 Vincent Works, Vincent Lane, Dorking, Surrey RH4 3HQ *Tel (01306) 888655*
⊠ The brewery was conceived, designed and built by Ray Welton, a former beer whole-saler, and installed in a renovated milking parlour on Rugge Farm in Capel near Dorking in October 1995. August 1997 saw a major step forward with the move of the brewery to a factory unit in Dorking. 140 outlets are regularly supplied directly. Occasional beers: Easter Special (ABV 4.1%, March), May Gold (ABV 4.1%, May, a wheat beer), Tam O'Shanter (ABV 4.1%, January), Burning Wicket (ABV 4.4%, July), Coronation Ale (ABV 4.4%, May and June), Winter Old (ABV 4.5% December), Passion Ale (ABV 4.5%, February), Midsummer Passion (ABV 4.5%, June), St George's Special (ABV 4.6%, April), Bloody Bosworth Bitter Battle (ABV 4.6%, August), Guy Fawkes Revenge (ABV 4.6%, November), Wenceslegless (ABV 4.8%, December), IPA (ABV 4.9%), Abinger Hammer (ABV 5.2%, March and May), Wellington's Cannon (ABV 5.4%), Dr French's Old Remedy (ABV 5.5%, November), Nelson's Cannon (ABV 5.6%, October) Other one-off brews will also be available.
Dorking Pride *(ABV 2.8%%)* Light and nutty with more body than you would expect for its strength.
Best Bitter *(OG 1038, ABV 3.8%)* ⬚ A fruity golden copper coloured beer with hops on the aftertaste.
Old Cocky *(OG 1043, ABV 4.3%)* Full flavoured with a malty and fruity aroma with hops developing in the flavour and dominating the aftertaste.
Summer Special *(OG 1048, ABV 4.8%)* A complex light golden beer, with deep malt fruitiness on the tongue, followed by hops and a deep aroma.
Tower Power *(OG 1050, ABV 5%)* Strong bitter brewed in honour of the famous building on nearby Leigh Hill, this beer is brewed in February, April, July and September.
Old Harry *(OG 1051, ABV 5.2%)* Easy drinking, golden copper-coloured beer with both malt and hop flavours. Available October to January.

WEST BERKSHIRE
The West Berkshire Brewery Company, Pot Kiln Lane, Frilsham, Yattendon, Berkshire RG18 0XX *Tel/Fax (01635) 202638*
Tours by arrangement only
⊠ Brewery established in 1995 in converted farm buildings in the grounds of the Pot Kiln pub, although the businesses are separate.

Began on a five-barrel plant, but has since added 12-barrel FV. Over 30 outlets take the beers regularly and they guest in other pubs. A small bottling plant may be added. Brick Kiln Bitter (OG 1042, ABV 4%) is only available at the Pot Kiln. Occasional beers: Hartslock No. 1 (OG 1045, ABV 4.2%), Longdog (OG 1045, ABV 4.3%), Berkshire Dark (OG 1046, ABV 4.4%). Loughbite (OG 1048.5, ABV 4.4%) is brewed for the Little Ale Cart wholesaler in Loughborough. Specials have included Two Moons (bottle-conditioned and cask), Spiced Porter, and Wheat Beer.
Skiff *(OG 1037.5, ABV 3.6%)* A beer with a flowery, almost herbal, aroma, and rounded bitter flavours which are more pro-nounced than expected for its gravity.
Good Old Boy or Old Tyler *(OG 1042, ABV 4%)* A well-balanced, fruity and hoppy beer with some sweetness in the fin-ish.
Dr Hexter's Wedding *(OG 1043, ABV 4.1%)* There are hints of grapefruit in this pale coloured beer, with strong hop aromas and a long, bitter finish.
Graft Bitter *(OG 1045, ABV 4.3%)* ♦ A well balanced beer, with fruit aromas, a malty character and a bitter finish.
Dr Hexter's Healer *(OG 1051, ABV 5%)* There is a slight sweetness, with subtle citric aromas, although hops predominate in this rich, refreshing bitter.

WETHERED
See Nationals, Whitbread.

WHEAL ALE
See Bird in Hand.

WHEATSHEAF INN
See Fromes Hill.

WHIM
Whim Ales, Whim Farm, Hartington, Buxton, Derbyshire SK17 0AX
Tel (01298) 84991 Fax (01298) 84702
⊠ Brewery opened in 1993 in redundant outbuildings at Whim Farm by Giles Litchfield who, in 1995, purchased Broughton Brewery (qv). There are plans for the two breweries to distribute each other's beers in their local areas. The brewery is now brewing to capacity (25-30 barrels a week). Whim's beers, meanwhile, are avail-able in 50-70 outlets, and the brewery owns the Wilkes Head in Leek, Staffordshire. Some one-off brews are produced. A loose sparkler would benefit Special Ale, Old Izaak and Black Christmas. Occasional beers: Snow White (OG 1043, ABV 4.5% a wheat beer), Old Izaak (OG 1050, ABV 5%, seasonal), Black Christmas (OG 1065, ABV 6.5%). Bottle-conditioned beer: Black Bear Extra Stout (ABV 6.5%).
Arbor Light *(OG 1035, ABV 3.6%)* Very light-coloured bitter, sharp and clean with lots of hop character and a delicate light aroma.
Magic Mushroom Mild *(OG 1037, ABV 3.8%)* Ruby-black in colour, well bal-anced with a complex mix of flavours and a sweet finish.

Hartington Bitter *(OG 1038, ABV 4%)*
A light, golden-coloured, well-hopped session beer. A dry finish with a spicy, floral aroma.
Hartington IPA *(OG 1038, ABV 4%)*
Pale and very light-coloured, smooth on the palate allowing malt to predominate. Slightly sweet finish combined with distinctive light hop bitterness. Well rounded.
Special Ale *(OG 1047, ABV 4%)* Full bodied amd fruity combined with a complex hop flavour. Well-balanced bitterness and rich aroma. A summer replacement for Old Izaak, but may be available all year round.

WHITBREAD
See Nationals.

WHITE
White Brewing Company, The 1066 Country Brewery, Pebsham Farm Industrial Estate, Pebsham Lane, Bexhill, E. Sussex TN40 2RZ *Tel (01424) 731066*
⊗ Brewery founded in May 1995 by husband and wife David and Lesley White to serve local free trade outlets and some wholesalers, brewing five to ten barrels a week. Visits by appointment only.
1066 Country Bitter *(OG 1040, ABV 4%)*

WHITEWATER
Whitewater Brewing Co., 40 Tullyframe Road, Kilkeel, Newry, Co. Down BT34 4RZ *Tel/Fax (013967) 26370*
Tours by arrangement
⊛ Brewery founded in May 1996 on a farm outside Kilkeel with a five-barrel brew length and 40-barrel conditioning capacity. It now supplies around 12 outlets in Northern Ireland, and other outlets throughout the British Isles as wholesalers, with beers which have already won beer festival prizes, including first at Belfast in 1996 and 1997.
Best Bitter *(OG 1038, ABV 3.7%)*
Solstice Pale Ale *(OG 1041, ABV 4%)*
Glen Ale *(OG 1043, ABV 4.2%)*
Mountain Ale *(OG 1043, ABV 4.2%)*
Belfast Special Bitter *(OG 1046, ABV 4.5%)*
Bee's Endeavour *(OG 1048, ABV 4.8%)*
Explosive Ale *(OG 1058, ABV 5.8%)*
Eirann Stout *(OG 1044, ABV 4.3%)*

WICKWAR
The Wickwar Brewing Co., Arnolds Cooperage, The Old Cider Mill, Station Road, Wickwar, Gloucestershire GL12 8NB *Tel/Fax (01454) 294168*
Tours by arrangement
⊗ Brewery launched on the 'Glorious First of May 1990' (guest beer law day) by two Courage tenants with the aim of providing guest ales for their three tenancies. The business proved so successful that they dropped the pubs to concentrate on directly supplying their other regular outlets (now totalling around 150). The brewery operates from the cooper's shop of the old Arnold, Perret & Co brewery. Bottle-conditioned beer: Station Porter (ABV 6.1%).
Coopers' WPA *(OG 1036.5, ABV 3.5%)*
🍺 A yellow/gold, well-balanced, light, refreshing brew with hops, citrus fruit, peardrop flavour and notable malt character. Bitter, dry finish.
Brand Oak Bitter (BOB) *(OG 1038.5, ABV 4%)* 🍺 Amber-coloured, BOB is a distinctive blend of hops, malt and apple/pear citrus fruits. The slightly sweet taste turns into a fine, dry bitterness with a similar malty lasting finish.
Olde Merryford Ale *(OG 1048, ABV 4.8%)* 🍺 An amber/pale brown, full-flavoured, well-balanced ale, with malt, hops and cherry fruit throughout. Slightly sweet, with a long-lasting, malty, dry fruity finish. Enjoyable.
Station Porter *(OG 1059.5, ABV 6.1%)*
🍺🏆🍺 Classic, smooth, dark brown ale. Roast malt, coffee and rich fruit aroma. Similar, complex and spicy, rich, bittersweet taste and a long, smooth, warming roast finish. Available October-December. CAMRA Silver Award,1996/7, 1997/8.

JAMES WILLIAMS
See Pub Groups.

WILLY'S BREWERY
⌂ Willy's Brewery Ltd, 17 High Cliff Road, Cleethorpes, Lincolnshire DN35 8RQ *Tel (01472) 602145 Fax (01472) 603578*
⊛ Seafront pub brewery opened in 1989, also supplying a second local outlet and some free trade. Old Groyne is popular as a guest beer through wholesalers. Tours by arrangement.
Original Bitter *(OG 1038, ABV 3.8%)*
🍺 A fruity hop on the nose and in the taste, with a slight tang of the nearby sea in the dry aftertaste. Malt is there in a supporting role in this light brown bitter.
Burcom Bitter *(OG 1044, ABV 4.2%)* 🍺 Sometimes known as 'Mariner's Gold', although the beer is dark ruby in colour. It is a smooth and creamy brew with a sweet chocolate-bar maltiness, giving way to an increasingly bitter finish.
Weiss Buoy *(OG 1045, ABV 4.5%)*
A cloudy wheat beer.
Coxswains Special Bitter *(OG 1050, ABV 4.9%)*
Old Groyne *(OG 1060, ABV 6.2%)* 🍺 An initial sweet banana fruitiness blends with malt to give a vanilla quality to the taste and slightly bitter aftertaste. A copper-coloured beer with some almost Trappist ale qualities.

WILSON'S
See Mansfield.

WINFIELDS
⌂ Winfields Brewery, The Raven, Bedford Street, Portsmouth, Hampshire PO5 4BT *Tel (01705) 829079*
⊗ Very small pub brewery

set up in 1995, just serving the pub itself and only brewing occasionally. Beers: Mild (ABV 3.5%), Bitter (ABV 3.7%), Stout (ABV 3.8%), Winter Brew (ABV 4.5%).

WOLF

The Wolf Brewery Ltd, 10 Maurice Gaymer Road, Attleborough, Norfolk NR17 2QZ *Tel (01953) 457775 Fax (01953) 457776* **Tours by arrangement**

⊠ Brewery founded by the former owner of the Reindeer Brewery in 1996, using a 20-barrel plant housed on the site of the old Gaymers cider orchard. About 90 customers take the beer.

Hare of the Dog *(ABV 3.8%)* ◆ Pale gold, crystal clear ale. Dry, crisp and hoppy, and develops into a light, refreshing well-balanced bitter finish.

Best Bitter *(OG 1040, ABV 3.9%)* ◆ A full-flavoured, pale brown, well-balanced session beer with a delicious hop finish.

Coyote *(OG 1042, ABV 4.3%)* ◆ An amber, distinctive, complex, full-flavoured beer. Well balanced, with a long, bitter, hoppy finish.

Granny Wouldn't Like It *(OG 1060, ABV 4.8%)* ▮◆ A copper-coloured rich, full-bodied, fruity beer, with lots of malt notes and fruitcake hints.

WOLVERHAMPTON & DUDLEY

See Banks's and Camerons.

WOOD

Wood Brewery Ltd, Wistanstow, Craven Arms, Shropshire SY7 8DG *Tel (01588) 672523 Fax (01588) 673939* **Tours by arrangement**

⊠ A village brewery, founded by the Wood family in 1980, in buildings adjacent to the Plough Inn. The brewery has enjoyed steady growth in recent years and now supplies around 200 other outlets (locally, and fur-

ther afield via wholesalers). Sam Powell beers have been brewed here since 1991. One pub is owned at present, but more may be acquired. Seasonal beers: Saturnalia (OG 1040, ABV 4.2%, January), Get Knotted (OG 1047, ABV 4.7%, February), Hopping Mad (OG 1048, ABV 4.7%, March-April), Anniversary Ale (OG 1051, ABV 5%, April), Christmas Cracker (OG 1061, ABV 6%, November-December). Bottle-conditioned beers: Shropshire Lad (OG 1051, ABV 5%), Hopping Mad (OG 1047, ABV 4.7%), Christmas Cracker (OG 1061, ABV 6%, November-December).

Wallop *(OG 1032, ABV 3.4%)*
Sam Powell Best Bitter *(OG 1033, ABV 3.4%)*
Sam Powell Original Bitter *(OG 1036, ABV 3.7%)*
Summer That! *(OG 1038, ABV 3.9%)* Available May-September.
Parish Bitter *(OG 1040, ABV 4%)* ◆ A blend of malt and hops with a bitter aftertaste. Pale brown in colour.
Special Bitter *(OG 1041, ABV 4.2%)* ◆ A tawny brown bitter with malt, hops and some fruitiness.
Shropshire Lad *(OG 1045, ABV 4.5%)*
Sam Powell Old Sam *(OG 1047, ABV 4.6%)*
Wonderful *(OG 1047, ABV 4.8%)* ◆ A mid-brown, fruity beer, with a roast and malt taste.

WOODBURY

Home Farm Cottage, Great Witley, Worcs WR6 6JJ *Tel (01299) 896219* **Tours by arrangement** Nominal four-barrel brewery set up in summer 1997. Supplies 20 pubs in the Worcester to Stourbridge area.
White Goose *(OG 1039, ABV 3.8%)*
Old House Bitter *(OG 1045, ABV 4.3%)*
Monumental Bitter *(OG 1051, ABV 5%)*

WOODFORDE'S

Woodforde's Norfolk Ales (Woodforde's Ltd), Broadland Brewery, Woodbastwick, Norwich, Norfolk NR13 6SW *Tel (01603) 720353 Fax (01603) 721806* **Shop Seasonal hours: phone for details Tours**

⊠ Founded in late 1980 in Drayton, near Norwich, Woodforde's moved to a converted farm complex, with greatly increased production capacity, in the picturesque Broadland village of Woodbastwick in 1989. Water is from its own borehole and the beer is made from East Anglian malt and whole hops. It brews an extensive range of beers and runs three tied houses, with some 250 other outlets supplied on a regular basis. The

529

company launched its own range of home brew kits in 1996, allowing drinkers to brew Wherry, Norfolk Nog and Headcracker at home. Occasional beers: Old Bram (OG 1043, ABV 4.1%), John Browne's Ale (OG 1043, ABV 4.3%), Mother-in-Law's Tongue (ABV 4.3%, for Mother's Day), Phoenix XXX (ABV 4.8%), Norfolk Stout or Emerald Ale (OG 1042, ABV 4.3%). Bottle-conditioned beers: Wherry Best Bitter (OG 1038, ABV 3.8%), Great Eastern Ale (OG 1043, ABV 4.3%), Nelson's Revenge (OG 1045, ABV 4.5%), Norfolk Nog (OG 1049, ABV 4.6%), Baldric (OG 1052, ABV 5.6%), Headcracker (OG 1069, ABV 7%), Norfolk Nips (OG 1085, ABV 8.6%). Available exclusively at Woodforde's Visitor Centre.

Broadsman Bitter *(OG 1035, ABV 3.5%)* ◣ Fruity aroma follows through with fruit flavours but lacks depth or complexity. Copper coloured, with a slightly soapy finish.

Mardler's Mild *(OG 1035, ABV 3.5%)* ◣ Red/brown in colour, this mild disappoints as the fruity nose fails to follow through to the flavour. Hints of roast with a quick finish. Thin and watery mouthfeel.

Wherry Best Bitter *(OG 1038, ABV 3.8%)* 🍴🍶◣ This award-winning, amber beer has a distinctly hoppy nose and a well-balanced palate with pronounced bitterness and, usually, a flowery hop character. A long-lasting, satisfying, bitter aftertaste. Champion Beer of Britain 1996.

Great Eastern Ale *(OG 1043, ABV 4.3%)* A refreshing, pale-coloured bitter with a slightly sweetish, malty taste. A well-balanced example of the new generation of pale beers.

Nelson's Revenge *(OG 1045, ABV 4.5%)* ◣ A light-brown-coloured, fruity, hoppy beer; a robust combination of flavours, but lacking depth, with a quick, bitter-sweet finish.

Norfolk Nog *(OG 1049, ABV 4.6%)* ◣ Dry, fruity, dark red old ale. Quite a sweet, fruity flavour with roast notes and hints of chocolate. A good, old-fashioned old ale.

Baldric *(OG 1052, ABV 5.6%)* ◣ Fruit and malt aroma leads to a complex, well-balanced, full-bodied ale, with a sweet fruit flavour but a quick finish. Amber in colour.

Headcracker *(OG 1069, ABV 7%)* 🍴🍶◣ This pale brown barley wine has a sweet fruit aroma leading to a dry, malty flavour, then on to a peardrop finish.

WOODHAMPTON

Woodhampton Brewing Company,

Aymestrey, Herefordshire HR6 9ST
Tel (01568) 770503 Fax (01568) 709058
Tours by arrangement
⊠ Opened in May 1997 at Woodhampton Farm, brewing 15 barrels a week, initially to supply the local Riverside Inn. The brewery now supplies around 20 local pubs with its full range plus seasonal beers, all of which are produced from locally-grown hops and hillside spring water. Expansion is planned for 1999.

Old Rooster *(OG 1039, ABV 3.6%)*
Jack Snipe *(OG 1043, ABV 4.1%)*
Kingfisher Ale *(OG 1047, ABV 4.4%)*
Ravens Head Stout *(OG 1049, ABV 4.5%)*

WOODY WOODWARD'S

See Fox & Hounds, Shropshire.

WORFIELD BREWING COMPANY

⬙ The Davenport Arms, Worfield, Bridgnorth, Shropshire WV15 5LF
Tel (01746) 716320
Set up in 1994, this brewery now sells beer wholesale to 25-30 free trade outlets. It holds two annual beer festivals and four beers are always available at the pub. There are special brews occasionally, e.g. such as Hermitage barley wine, ABV 8.8%.

JLK Pale Ale *(OG 1037, ABV 3.8%)*
Hopstone Bitter *(OG 1040, ABV 4%)*
Burcote Premium Bitter *(OG 1050, ABV 4.7%)*
Reynolds Redneck *(OG 1060, ABV 5.5%)*

WORLDHAM

Worldham Brewery, Smiths Farm, East Worldham, Alton, Hampshire GU34 3AT
Temporarily ceased brewing.

WORTH

Worth Brewery, Worth Way, Keighley, W. Yorkshire BD21 5LP
Tel (01535) 611914 Fax (01535) 691883
Shop Mon-Fri, 10am-noon Tours by arrangement
☺ Formerly Commercial Brewing Company, set up in a former garage, this brewery's first beer was produced in 1992. Worth has hosted four CAMRA Keighley beer festivals. It supplies 20 outlets and owns two pubs, with plans to acquire more. Occasional/seasonal beers: Knobwilter (OG 1049), ABV 5.2%, spring-summer), Beckside Mild (ABV 3.6%), Worth Porter (OG 1045, ABV 4.5%), Santa's Toss (OG 1080, ABV 8%, December). Bottle-condi-

DOROTHY GOODBODY'S SEASONAL ALES
WYE VALLEY BREWERY HEREFORD

tioned beers: Storm Export (ABV 4%), Worth Gold (ABV 5%), Worth Porter (ABV 4.5%), Neary's Extra Stout (ABV 5%), Knobwilter wheat beer (ABV 5.2%), Old Toss (ABV 6.5%), Santa's Toss (ABV 8%).

Alesman *(OG 1036, ABV 3.7%)* ♦ Fruity and with a hoppy bitteress throughout, this clean-tasting and well-balanced, amber beer provides an excellent example of a standard 'quaffing' bitter.

Wild Boar *(OG 1041, ABV 4%)* ♦ A reasonably full-bodied bitter in which a faint aroma leads to malt and hops flavours and a pronounced bitter aftertaste.

Worth Gold *(OG 1050, ABV 5%)* A golden strong bitter with a citrus fruity nose, a fruity, hoppy, bitter, taste and a long, dry, bitter aftertaste.

Best Bitter *(OG 1045, ABV 4.5%)* ♦ A long, dry bitter finish rounds off this aggressively hoppy, golden amber ale. Citrus dominates the aroma. Distinctive and satisfying.

Old Toss *(OG 1065, ABV 6.5%)* ♦ A full-bodied and warming, dark old ale. Roast and fruit flavours dominate over background sweetness, malt and hops. Burnt aroma; long, bitter finish.

WORTHINGTON

See Nationals, Bass.

WYCHWOOD

Wychwood Brewery Company Ltd, The Eagle Maltings, The Crofts, Corn Street, Witney, Oxfordshire OX8 7AZ
Tel (01993) 702574 Fax (01993) 772553
Shop 9-5, Mon-Fri Tours only for CAMRA branch visits

⊗ Set up as Glenny Brewery in 1983, in the old maltings of the extinct Clinch's brewery, this brewery moved to a new site in 1987 and was radically revamped during 1992, when nine pubs were acquired (leased from Allied or Inntrepreneur) by its sister company Hobgoblinns Ltd. The company now runs 30 managed pubs (ten FOT, the rest tied), in various towns across the South and South-West, all restyled in the bare boards and breweriana idiom, most renamed Hobgoblin and all taking real ale. Wychwood also supplies about 70 other outlets. As a consequence of the extra demand, the brewery moved back to the old Clinch's site in 1994. Now brewing over 500 barrels a week. In two years, Hobgobin is a top best-selling bottled ale in the UK. Seasonal beer: Black Wych Stout (OG 1050, ABV 5%, Christmas) plus various themed beers brewed to coincide with sporting events.

Shires XXX *(OG 1036, ABV 3.7%)*

Fiddlers Elbow *(OG 1040, ABV 4%)* Brewed May-September, a straw-coloured beer containing barley and wheat malts.

Special *(OG 1042, ABV 4.2%)* ♦ Formerly Wychwood Best: a mid-brown, full-flavoured premium bitter. Moderately strong in hop and malt flavours, with pleasing, fruity overtones which last through to the aftertaste.

Old Devil *(OG 1042, ABV 4.2%)* A bitter beer featuring honey, with a dry, fruity finish (October only).

The Dog's Bollocks *(OG 1052, ABV 5.2%)* A full-bodied, hoppy, golden brew, incorporating Styrian hops and wheat.

Hobgoblin *(OG 1055, ABV 5.5%)* ♦ Powerful, full-bodied, copper-red, well-balanced brew. Strong in roasted malt, with a moderate, hoppy bitterness and a slight fruity character. (September-March).

WYE VALLEY

Wye Valley Brewery, 69 St Owen Street, Hereford HR1 2JQ
Tel (01432) 342546 Fax (01432) 266553
Tours occasionally, by arrangement

⊗ Began production in 1985 and moved to its present address a year later. New plant was installed in 1992 to increase capacity and cater for a rapidly growing free trade, now 500 outlets. The company also has two pubs of its own and produces seasonal beers under the Dorothy Goodbody name. Bottle-conditioned beers: Brew 69 (OG 1055, ABV 5.6%), Wholesome Stout (ABV 4.6%), Winter Tipple (ABV 5.3%), Golden Ale (ABV 4.2%), Father Christmas Ale (ABV 8%, December, also available on draught at Christmas).

Bitter *(OG 1036, ABV 3.5%)* ♦ A beer whose aroma gives little hint of the bitter hoppiness which follows right through to the aftertaste.

Dorothy Goodbody's Wonderful Springtime Bitter *(OG 1040, ABV 4%)* Available March-May; a full, malt-flavoured beer with bitterness and a hop aroma.

Hereford Pale Ale or HPA *(OG 1040, ABV 4%)* ♦ A pale, hoppy, malty brew with a hint of sweetness before a dry finish.

Dorothy Goodbody's Golden Summertime Ale *(OG 1042, ABV 4.2%)* Available June-August; a golden ale with a light malt flavour.

Supreme *(OG 1045, ABV 4.3%)* ♦ A rich, fruity, malt aroma leads to a sweet, malt and fruit taste which lingers to the finish.

Dorothy Goodbody's Autumn Delight *(OG 1045, ABV 4.5%)* BV 4.5%). Available September-November; a dry, full-flavoured beer with a deep colour.

Classic *(OG 1046, ABV 4.5%)* Not sold at the Barrels, the brewery tap.

Dorothy Goodbody's Wholesome Stout *(OG 1046, ABV 4.6%)* ♦ A very smooth and satisfying stout without a bitter edge to its roast flavours. The finish combines roast grain and malt.

Dorothy Goodbody's Warming Wintertime Ale *(OG 1049, ABV 4.9%)* ♦ Available December-February. A sweet winter ale with a fruity, hoppy taste and a rich, fruity aftertaste.

Brew 69 *(OG 1055, ABV 5.6%)* A pale premium beer named after the brewery's street number. Its hoppy taste has a hint of malt; slightly bitter aftertaste.

WYRE PIDDLE

Wyre Piddle Brewery, Unit 21, Craycombe Farm, Fladbury, Evesham, Worcestershire WR10 2QS *Tel (01386) 860473*

⊗ Brewery established by a former publican and master builder in a converted stable in 1992. The brewery owns five pubs and around 85 outlets take the beer, in locations throughout the southern Midlands. The brewery relocated and upgraded its equipment in 1997. For the Green Dragon,

Young's drayhorses make an appearance with Young's chairman John Young at the re-opening of the refurbished Crown in Burnt Ash, South-East London; licensees Phil and Michelle Cope are also pictured. Young's drayhorses have been a familiar sight on the streets for over 400 years, but had to be withdrawn from their delivery round after being attacked by a raging motorist in 1997. But they began delivering again in February 1998.

Malvern: Dragon's Downfall (ABV 3.9%), Dragon's Revenge (ABV 4%). For Severn Valley Railway: Royal Piddle (ABV 4.2%). Bottle-conditioned beer: Piddle in the Hole (ABV 4.6%).

Piddle in the Hole *(OG 1039, ABV 3.9%)* ✎ The strong, malty flavours are balanced by a strong, bitter counter-taste which leaves a dry, lingering aftertaste.

Piddle in the Wind *(ABV 4.2%)* ✎ This drink has a superb mix of flavours. A nice hoppy nose through to a lasting after-taste makes it a good, all-round beer.

Piddle in the Snow *(ABV 5.2%)* ✎ A dry, strong taste all the way through draws your attention to the balance beween malt and hops in the brew. A glorious way to end an evening's drink.

Piddle in the Sun *(ABV 5.2%)* ✎ Citrus spice dominates this dry and bitter beer. It ends with a dry background of fruit.

YATES

Yates Brewery, Ghyll Farm, Westnewton, Aspatria, Cumbria CA5 3NX
Tel (016973) 21081
⊛ Small, traditional brewery set up in 1986

by Peter and Carole Yates in an old farm building on their smallholding, where a herd of pedigree goats makes good use of the brewery's by-products. Brewing award-winning beers to their capacity of 34 barrels a week during summer and other peak times, they also serve around 20 free trade outlets and own one pub. House beers are produced for a couple of other pubs. Seasonal beer: Best Cellar (OG 1052, ABV 5.5%, Christmas).

Bitter *(OG 1034, ABV 3.7%)* ✦ Pale straw, golden bitter with a fresh natural malt taste and a complex hoppy bitterness, rising in the aftertaste with lactic overtones. Best served through a tight sparkler. Exemplary balance. Wonderful, very highly regarded indeed.

Premium *(OG 1048, ABV 5.2%)*
Available at Christmas and a few other times of the year. Straw-coloured, with a strong aroma of malt and hops, and full-flavoured, with a slight toffee taste. The malty aftertaste becomes strongly bitter.

Best Cellar *(OG 1052, ABV 5.4%)*

YORK

York Brewery Co. Ltd, 12 Toft Green, Micklegate, York, N. Yorkshire YO1 1JT
Tel (01904) 621162 Fax (01904) 621216
Shop 9-8 Mon-Sat, 4-8 Sun Tours daily; no disabled access

⊕ Began production in 1996, the first brewery in the city for over 40 years. The plant came from the closed Lion's brewery in Burnley and was installed in a site on the York Tourist Trail, within the city walls. The brewery was planned with the visitor very much in mind and there are plans to extend the Visitors Centre and tap room, extend the facilities and provide food. Over 300 pubs take the beer. Bottle-conditioned beer: Stonewall (OG 1037, ABV 3.7%).

Stonewall *(OG 1037, ABV 3.7%)* ✦
A light amber bitter with little maltiness but strong hop and fruit aromas and flavours. Clean-tasting, its hoppiness leads to a dry, bitter finish.

M'Lud *(OG 1040, ABV 4%)*
Yorkshire Terrier *(ABV %)* ✦ A golden premium bitter with a balance of malt and hops to the fore, giving way to an assault of fruit, hops and, finally, an astonishingly dry, bitter finish.

Last Drop Bitter *(OG 1045, ABV 4.5%)*

YORK TAVERN

York Tavern, 1 Leicester Street, Norwich, Norfolk NR2 2AS   Not brewing at present.

YORKSHIRE GREY

See Nationals, Scottish Courage.

YOUNG'S

Young & Co.'s Brewery PLC, The Ram Brewery, High Street, Wandsworth, London SW18 4JD
Tel (0181) 875 7000 Fax (0181) 875 7100
Shop 10-6, Mon-Sat Tours Daily tours of the brewery and stables. Tel: (0181) 875 7005
⊠ Beer has been continuously brewed here

The Great British Beer Festival, held in August at Olympia, is the Campaign for Real Ale's biggest event, a showcase for fine beers, lagers and ciders.

since 1581, making it the oldest site in Britain for beer production. The present brewery was founded in 1675 and bought by Charles Young & Anthony Banbridge in 1831; the business was continued by the Young family and, although it became a public company in 1898, it remains very much a family affair. Young's were the only London brewer to eschew the keg revolution in the 1970's. Young's brew award-winning beers in the traditional manner and also produce up to four seasonal beers. Even its keg lagers are brewed to the Rheinheitsgebot. More than 1,000 free-trade outlets are supplied throughout Britain, concentrated in London and the South-East. Young's growing tied estate stands at over 180 pubs. The Bill Bentley's wine bar chain and Cockburn & Campbell wine importers are also part of the business. The brewery has outlawed pour-backs in its tied houses and recommends use of cask breathers only if its smallest casks cannot be consumed within three days. Bottle-conditioned beer: Special London Ale (ABV 6.4%).

Bitter *(OG 1036, ABV 3.7%)* ✦ An amber, distinctive beer. A strong, hoppy bitterness is followed by a delightfully astringent and hoppy, bitter aftertaste. An underlying malt balance is present throughout.

Special *(OG 1046, ABV 4.6%)* ⬒✦
A strong, full-flavoured, bitter beer with a powerful hoppiness and a balancing malt flavour. Hops persist in the aftertaste.

Ram Rod *(OG 1050, ABV 5%)* ✦ A malty aroma leads to a strong malt flavour and a slightly sweet, malty aftertaste. There is only a faint hint of hops throughout in this mid-brown beer.

Winter Warmer *(OG 1055, ABV 5%)* ✦
A dark reddish-brown ale with a roast malt aroma and flavour, leading to a sweet, fruity finish. A hint of caramel throughout. Available October-March.

533

New breweries

ENGLAND

CAMBRIDGESHIRE
Rockingham, Elton

CUMBRIA
Foxfield Brewery, Broughton-in-Furness
Prince of Wales, Broughton-in-Furness

DEVON
Barum, Barnstaple
St Giles In The Wood, Torrington
Scatter Rock, Christow

DORSET
Red Shoot, Linwood

DURHAM
Grey Horse, Consett
Old Barn, Tow Law

GLOUCESTERSHIRE
Abbey, Bath
Home County, Wickwar

HAMPSHIRE
Triple FFF Brewing Company, Alton

HEREFORDSHIRE
Frome Valley

KENT
Kent Brewery, Deal

LANCASHIRE
Red Lion Hotel, Accrington

LEICESTERSHIRE
John O'Gaunt, Melton Mowbray

LINCOLNSHIRE
Bigfoot, Gainsborough
Brigg, Brigg
Willy's Brewery, Cleethorpes

MANCHESTER
Marble, Manchester

MERSEYSIDE
Cambrinus, Knowsley

NORFOLK
Blanchfield, Fakenham

NORTH YORKSHIRE
Black Dog, Whitby

NOTTINGHAMSHIRE
Castle Rock, Nottingham
Caythorpe, Hoveringham
Red Shed, Kimberley

SHROPSHIRE
Worfield Brewing Company, Bridgnorth

SOMERSET
Crewkerne, Crewkerne

SUFFOLK
Lidstone's, Newmarket

WARWICKSHIRE
Millwright's Arms, Cotton End

WEST MIDLANDS
Weatheroak, Alvechurch

WEST YORKSHIRE
Huddersfield, Huddersfield

WORCESTERSHIRE
Teme Valley, Knightwick
Woodbury, Great Wortley

SCOTLAND

CENTRAL
Bridge of Allan, Bridge of Allan

HIGHLANDS AND ISLANDS
Aviemore, Aviemore
Far North, Melvich
Iris Rose, Kingussie

LOTHIAN
Restalrig, Restalrig

STRATHCLYDE
Clockwork, Glasgow
Houston, Houston

WALES

WEST WALES
Brecknock, Ystradgynlais

NORTH-WEST WALES
Snowdonia, Waunfawr

Over 40 new breweries are listed in the main Independents section. We are continually hearing about new breweries, particularly brewpubs.

Our list is as up to date and as comprehensive as we can make it, although one needs the pyschic talents of Doris Stokes to keep up with all the changes.

Breweries which have come to our attention since main listings were compiled include:

Balta Sound, Unst, Shetland Isles
Cask & Cutler (brewpub), Sheffield
Dukeries Brewery, Langold, Nottinghamshire
Gt Finborough, Suffolk
St George's Brewery, Bush Lane, Callow End, Malvern WR2 4TF
Soho Brewing Company, London

Notes on new breweries

National breweries

BASS

Bass Brewers Ltd, 137 High Street, Burton upon Trent, Staffordshire DE14 1JZ
Tel (01283) 511000 Fax (01283) 513326
Founded in 1777, Bass is Britain's second largest brewer, with some 23 per cent of all beer production. Its merger with Carlsberg-Tetley was blocked in June 1997. However, Bass then bought C-T's large modern brewing complex in Burton, saving 540 jobs.

It then announced the closure of two of its real ale breweries: Neepsend in Sheffield , where William Stones launched his ale in 1860, and Cardiff, which produces Hancock's HB. Sheffield will remain in operation until the start of 1999 and Cardiff until the start of 2000, unless buyers can be found. Ironically, Welsh Brewers had just been re-equipped to produce Worthington and Hancock's cask ales, as well as Allbright – supposedly Wales's biggest selling beer. The closure was announced the week after Hancock's had won the award as Bass's most productive brewery.

Bass will concentrate on producing lager, such as Carling, which last year became the first UK beer to sell more than three million barrels.

Bass also announced it was to axe Worthington White Shield (🍷) , the biggest selling bottle-conditioned beer in the country. Bass claimed it wasn't selling enough of the classic ale, although the beer did suffer a lack of investment compared to the £7.9 million spent on Carling. But a strong campaign led by CAMRA ended successfully with King & Barnes taking on the contract to produce White Shield (see Independents).

Meanwhile, a survey in the *Publican* claimed that Draught Bass had been ousted by Marston's Pedigree as the country's top-selling cask ale.

Bass seems to be repositioning itself as a leisure corporation rather than a brewer. Its tenanted pubs operation (1190 tenanted, and 238 managed which were being converted into leased pubs) was sold to restaurant gurus Hugh Osmond (of Pizza Express fame) and Roger Myers (former Pelican Group head) – they had already bought 850 pubs from Nomura-backed Phoenix Inns. Bass would focus on its managed pubs operations, said Bass Taverns CEO Tim Clark, consisting of 1,500 outlets, mainly of Harvester, Vintage Inns, Toby and All Bar One formats.

Bass's sites at Alton, Belfast and Tadcaster produce only keg beer. There is a cask ale facility at Glasgow and this has attempted a few brews in recent years, though with little success.

ALLSOPP

Samuel Allsopp Brewery Company, 107 Station Street, Burton-upon-Trent, Staffordshire DE14 1BZ
Tel (01283) 502284 Fax (01283) 502209
Specialist cask brewery on the site of the main Burton complex. Reviving the old Allsopp's name, the brewery was re-opened in 1994 to produce limited edition, mid-high strength beers for Carlsberg-Tetley's Tapster's Choice 'guest' beer scheme (each available for about six weeks). These have included Single Malt Ale (ABV 4.1%), Harvest Ale (ABV 4.2%, summer), Sam's Stout (OG 1040, ABV 4.2%), IPA (OG 1041, ABV 4.2%), Old Ruby (OG 1041, ABV 4.2%), Double Diamond Cask (OG 1041.5, ABV 4.3%), Summer Golden Ale (ABV 4.4%), Treason Ale (OG 1046, ABV 4.7%), Devil's Kiss (OG 1050.5, ABV 5.2%), Sam's Porter (ABV 5.2%), Triple Diamond (ABV 5.3%) and Winter Warmer (OG 1052, ABV 5.5%). Bought by Bass following the failure of the proposed merger with Carlsberg-Tetley, Bass has since anncounced it was considering closing the brewery.

For HP&D:
HP&D Mild *(OG 1036, ABV 3.7%)* ☺
Entire *(OG 1043, ABV 4.4%)* ☺

BIRMINGHAM

Cape Hill Brewery, PO Box 27, Smethwick, Birmingham, W. Midlands B16 0PQ
Tel (0121) 558 1481
One of the largest cask beer production centres in the country
M&B Mild *(OG 1034.5, ABV 3.2%)* 🍷 ☺
A dark brown quaffing mild with roast and malt flavours. Dry, slightly bitter finish.
M&B Brew XI *(OG 1039.5, ABV 3.8%)*
🍷 ☺ A sweet, malty beer with a hoppy, bitter aftertaste.

BURTON

Burton Brewery, Station Street, Burton-upon-Trent, Staffordshire DE14 1JZ
Tel (01283) 511000
The original home of Bass, producing one of Britain's most famous ales.
Draught Bass *(OG 1043, ABV 4.4%)* 🍷 ☺
Hoppy aroma and taste; fruity with a dry, bitter, spicy finish. Swan-neck dispense loses much distinction of this classic amber beer.
Stones Bitter *(ABV 3.7%)*

CARDIFF (Welsh Brewers)

The Brewery, Crawshay Street, Cardiff CF1 1TR
Tel (01222) 233071 Fax (01222) 372668
Tours by arrangement
The Hancock's brewery (founded in 1884) which was taken over by Bass Charrington in 1968 and which is now threatened with closure (see above). Occasional beer: Hancock's IPA (OG 1038, ABV 3.6%).
Worthington Dark Mild *(OG 1034.5, ABV 3%)* 🍷 ☺ A dark brown, creamy mild with a somewhat caramel and malty flavour, followed by a faint, balanced finish.
Hancock's HB *(OG 1037, ABV 3.6%)* 🍷☺
A pale brown, slightly malty beer whose initial sweetness is balanced by bitterness but lacks a noticable finish. A consistent if inoffensive Welsh beer.
Worthington Best Bitter *(OG 1038, ABV*

3.6%) ◆ ⊛ A pale brown bitter of thin and unremarkable character.

MUSEUM

Museum Brewing Company, The Bass Museum, PO Box 220, Horninglow Street, Burton-upon-Trent, Staffordshire DE14 1YQ
Tel (01283) 511000 Fax (01283) 513509
Shop and tours: see below
⊛ Active brewery housed within Bass's pop- ular museum, producing around 50 barrels a week of beers for sale on site and in other outlets. The beer recipes are taken from the Bass archives but the brewery enjoys a sub- stantial degree of independence within the Bass empire. A range of IPAs in the ABV range of 4.9-5.4% is also produced for sale as pub house beers. Museum open 10-5 (last entries 4); shop open 10-6, all week. The bar on site is open until 7 for visitors already inside. Occasional beers: Quaffing Ale (ABV 3.5%), No. 6 Mild Ale (OG 1037, ABV 3.9%), Offilers Bitter (OG 1038, ABV 4%), 'E' (OG 1044, ABV 4.8%), Masterpiece IPA (OG 1048, ABV 5.4%), Premium Pale Ale (ABV 6.5%). Bottle-conditioned beers: Masterpiece IPA (OG 1048, ABV 5.4%), P2 (OG 1072, ABV 8%), No. 1 Barley Wine (OG 1105, ABV 10.5%).
P2 Imperial Stout *(OG 1072, ABV 8%)* A black, sweetish, complex stout.
No.1 Barley Wine *(OG 1105, ABV 10.5%)* A dark ruby winter beer brewed in summer and fermented in casks for six months.

SHEFFIELD

Cannon Brewery, 43 Rutland Road, Sheffield, S. Yorkshire S3 8BE
Tel (0114) 272 0323 Fax (0114) 272 6442
Tours by arrangement
The original home of William Stones Ltd, dating from at least 1860. It was taken over by Bass in 1968 and following much invest- ment in recent years, became the company's specialist cask beer brewery. Not only is it faced with the axe, but Stones Bitter has been reduced in strength from 3.9% to 3.7%.
Mild *(OG 1032, ABV 3.1%)* ◆
A pleasant, smooth, dark mild with a faint aroma of caramel, which leads to a caramel and roast rich taste, with complementing sweetness and bitterness. A good, long, satis- fying, roast malt and caramel-sweet finish.
Toby Cask *(OG 1032, ABV 3.2%)* ◆ ⊛
An amber-coloured mild: a lightly-flavoured blend of malt, sweetness and bitterness. At its best, it has a delicate, pleasing, flowery taste, but can too often be bland. A disap- pointing, short, sweetish finish and little aroma.
Worthington Draught Bitter *(OG 1038, ABV 3.6%)* This supplements supplies from the Cardiff brewery.
Stones Bitter *(ABV 3.7%)*

Bass BrewPubs
Original Brewing Company, Bass Leisure Entertainments Ltd, New Castle House, Castle Boulevard, Nottingham NG7 1FT
Tel (0115) 924 0333 Fax (0115) 924 0657
Tours by arrangement

⛳ Chain of microbreweries housed in ten-pin bowling alleys. The first opened in Leicester in 1995, with a brewery visible to the public on the first floor. The company has since opened four further breweries at bowling centres.
The full mash beers are kept under CO2 in casks and cellar tanks. Beers: Xmas Cask Lager (OG 1043, ABV 4%), VSP (OG 1045, ABV 4.4%), Disciples' Brew (OG 1049, ABV 5%), 4 Xmas (OG 1061, ABV 6.2%, Christmas).

Current breweries:

Hollywood Bowl (Basildon)
Festival Leisure Park, off Cranes Park Road, Basildon, Essex SF14 3DG
Tel (01268) 530462

Hollywood Bowl (Bolton)
Middlebrook Sports Village, 25-27 The Linkway, Horwich, Bolton BL6 6JA
Tel (01204) 692999

Hollywood Bowl (Bracknell)
The Point, Skimpedhill Lane, Bracknell, Berkshire RG12 1EN
Tel (01344) 867700

Hollywood Bowl (Cardiff)
Atlantic Wharf, 1 Hemmingway Road, Cardiff CF1 5JY
Tel (01222) 471444

Hollywood Bowl (Coatbridge)
Showcase Leisure Park, Bawbridge Road, Bargeddie, Coatbridge, Strathclyde G69 7TX
Tel (01236) 425222

Hollywood Bowl (Finchley N12)
Finchley Leisure Park, Finchley High Road, North Finchley, London N12 0GL
Tel. (0181) 446 1958 Fax (0181) 446 0292.

Hollywood Bowl (Leicester)
Meridian Leisure Park, Braunstone, Leicester LE3 2WX
Tel (0116) 263 1234 Fax (0116) 263 1102

Hollywood Bowl (Leeds)
Cardigan Field Road, off Kirkstall Road, Leeds
Tel (0113) 2799111

Hollywood Bowl (Stevenage)
Unit 5, Stevenage Leisure Centre, Six Hills Way, Stevenage, Hertfordshire SG1 2NY
Tel (01438) 747777

Hollywood Bowl (Watford)
Woodside Leisure Park, Kingsway, Garston, Watford, Hertfordshire WD2 6NB
Tel. (01923) 682929 Fax (01923) 682442

CARLSBERG-TETLEY

Carlsberg-Tetley Brewing Ltd, 107 Station Street, Burton-upon-Trent, Staffordshire DE14 1BZ
Tel (01283) 512222 Fax (01283) 502357
Formerly Britain's third largest brewing con- cern, Carlsberg-Tetley's story can be traced back to 1961 when Ansells, Tetley Walker and Ind Coope joined forces to become

Allied Breweries.

In 1992 Allied merged with Danish lager giant Carlsberg and Carlsberg-Tetley was born. In 1996 Tetley Walker's Warrington brewery and the Plympton brewery in Plymouth were closed. In 1996, the Holt, Plant & Deakin brewery in the Black Country brewed its last.

In November 1997 C-T announced 'the worst holocaust in British brewing', said CAMRA's monthly paper, *What's Brewing*, with the announced closure of three breweries and the loss of 1,500 jobs.

The threatened Ind Coope brewery was bought by Bass, but C-T continues to brew Ind Coope Burton Ale.

The Alloa Brewery and the Wrexham Lager Brewery were not so lucky.

The Alloa Brewery dates back to 1810, and the brewing takes place in a classic European-style brewing hall, opened in 1956. It was diversifying into real ale which kept the brewery going after the demise of Skol. There were once nine breweries in Alloa: after the closure of Alloa Brewery, only the Thistle Brewery of Maclay and Co will remain.

The Wrexham Lager Brewery was founded in 1882 by a group of Germans working in North Wales. It became a part of Allied, brewing the keg lagers such as Castlemaine XXXX. Wrexham Lager, apart from a touch of wheat to gives it a good head, conforms to the strictures of the German 'Reinheitsgebot', the 16th-century pure beer law.

Carlsberg-Tetley is effectively only a brewing company. The former Allied pubs, which are mostly still tied to Carlsberg-Tetley beers, are held by Allied Domecq. Local brewery liveries still decorate many of the pubs, with the old brewing names of Tetley, Peter Walker, Friary Meux, Benskins, ABC, Halls and Ansells still in evidence.

In London, the Taylor Walker division is complemented by the small Nicholson's chain of upmarket pubs.

The Firkin chain of brewpubs was acquired from Stakis Leisure in 1991 and has been rapidly expanded.

There have also been many pub disposals, with hundreds of Allied pubs sold or leased to regional breweries and pub chains, some with the Carlsberg-Tetley beer tie still in place. The current Allied stock stands at around 4,000 pubs.

Allied Domecq tried to wriggle out of its guest beer obligations in 1997 by offering to supply its tenants with a range of guest ales itself. A-D also operates Festival Ale Houses.

ALLOA
Carlsberg-Tetley Alloa Ltd, Alloa Brewery, Whins Road, Alloa, Clackmannanshire FK10 3RB
Tel (01259) 723539
The company's Scottish arm, established in 1819. It fell to Ind Coope & Allsopp's in 1951, becoming part of Allied in the 1961 merger. Over £2.5 million has been invested in the site in recent years, but less than half of Alloa's 310 pubs sell real ale. The intention to close the brewery was announced in 1997. Occasional beer: Arrol's 90/- (ABV 4.9%).
Arrol's 80/- *(OG 1041, ABV 4.4%)* ◆ ⊛

A fruity Scottish heavy, dominated by malt, fruit and hops, with increasing hoppiness in the aftertaste. Well worth seeking out when in top form.

BURTON
Carlsberg-Tetley Burton Brewery Ltd, 107 Station Street, Burton-upon-Trent, Staffordshire DE14 1BZ
Tel (01283) 531111
Brewery established by the merger of the adjoining Allsop's and Ind Coope breweries in 1934. It provides beer for the Ansells, Ind Coope Retail and Nicholson's trading divisions of Allied Domecq. These 'local' beers are largely derived from two mashes: ABC and Friary from one, Benskins and Nicholson's from the other. Voted Champion Beer of Britain in 1990, Ind Coope Burton Ale, a pioneer amongst big brewery real ales, is still brewed by C-T after the sale of Ind Coope to Bass.
Ansells Mild *(OG 1033, ABV 3.4%)* ◆⊛
A dark red/brown beer full of caramel taste and a roast bitterness balancing hops and fruit.
ABC Best Bitter *(OG 1035, ABV 3.7%)* ⊠
A light, refreshing bitter, owing much of its character to dry hopping but with malt and fruit on the tongue.
Ansells Bitter *(OG 1035, ABV 3.7%)* ◆⊛
Clean, bright taste. Refreshing, with an aroma of apples and hoppy taste, changing to a mouthwatering sharpness.
Benskins Best Bitter *(OG 1035, ABV 3.7%)* ◆ ⊠ A predominantly hoppy beer with fruit and malt flavours. It can be a very suppable pint but sometimes suffers from an astringent aftertaste.
Friary Meux Best Bitter *(OG 1035, ABV 3.7%)* ◆⊠ Malt just dominates over hops in the aroma and flavour of this beer, and a strange, fruity taste lurks in the background.
Nicholson's Best Bitter *(OG 1035, ABV 3.7%)*⊠
Ind Coope Burton Ale *(OG 1047, ABV 4.8%)* ◆ ▉ ⏢ ⊛ Full, hoppy taste and aroma throughout. Fruity, with an astringent finish which takes some time to come through. A classic, moreish, unspoilt beer.

For Greenalls:
Greenalls Mild *(OG 1032, ABV 3.3%)*
◆⊛ A thin and undemanding dark mild with a hint of liquorice. More fruity than its Warrington predecessor.
Shipstone's Mild *(OG 1034, ABV 3.4%)*
Davenports Traditional Bitter *(OG 1037, ABV 3.7%)*
Greenalls Bitter *(OG 1036, ABV 3.8%)*
◆⊛ A thin, dry bitter which lacks balance. As with the mild, fruitiness has increased.
Shipstone's Bitter *(OG 1037, ABV 3.9%)*
Thomas Greenall's Original Bitter *(OG 1045, ABV 4.6%)* ⊛ Now just a higher gravity version of Greenalls Bitter. A fruity bitter with a hint of sweetness.

For Little Pub Company:
Little Lumphammer *(OG 1039, ABV 3.5%)*

TETLEY
Carlsberg-Tetley Brewing Ltd, Joshua Tetley & Son, PO Box 142, The Brewery, Leeds,

W. Yorkshire LS1 1QG
Tel (0113) 259 4594
Yorkshire's best-known brewery, the site covers 20 acres and includes a brewhouse opened in 1989 to handle the increased demand for Tetley Bitter (Carlsberg-Tetley's biggest cask ale brand). Nineteen new Yorkshire square fermenting vessels were commissioned in 1996, making the brewery the largest cask ale site in the group. A £6 million visitor centre and museum, Tetley's Brewery Wharf, opened in 1994. Seasonal beers: Autumn Ale (ABV 4.7%), Walker Winter Warmer (OG 1060, ABV 6.2%).
Tetley Dark Mild *(OG 1032, ABV 3.2%)*
❦ A reddish, mid-brown smooth beer with a light malt and caramel aroma. A well-balanced taste of malt and caramel follows, with good bitterness and a satisfying finish.
Tetley Mild *(OG 1032, ABV 3.2%)* ❦
A mid-brown, smooth beer with a light malt and caramel aroma. A well-balanced taste of malt and caramel follows, with good bitterness and a dry, satisfying finish.
Walker Bitter *(OG 1033, ABV 3.6%)*❦ ⊛
A nutty and fruity light bitter with a dry aftertaste. Now fuller-flavoured than previously.
Walker Best Bitter *(OG 1036, ABV 3.7%)*
❦ ⊛ A fruity and dry beer with an aggressive bitterness. As with the Walker Bitter, fuller-flavoured than before.
Tetley Bitter *(OG 1036.5, ABV 3.7%)* ❦⊛
A variable, light, dry, bitter with a slight malt and hop aroma, leading to moderate bitterness with a hint of fruit,ending with a dry, bitter finish. Amber in colour.
Imperial *(OG 1042, ABV 4.3%)* ❦ ⊛
A complex, creamy, copper-coloured beer. A light malt and fruit nose is followed by a well-rounded taste of malt, hops and fruit, leading to a short-lived dry, bitter finish.

For HP&D:
HP&D Bitter *(OG 1036, ABV 3.7%)*

Allied Domecq Brewpubs:

FIRKIN
The Firkin Brewery, Allied Domecq Inns, 107 Station Street, Burton-upon-Trent, Staffs DE14 1B7
Tel (0113) 200 2000 Fax (0113) 200 2041
⛫ Pub brewery chain founded by David Bruce in 1979, re-launching the brewpub concept in what used to be run-down national brewers' houses. The pubs were refurbished in a back-to-basics fashion and were given in-house breweries, tucked away behind viewing windows. In 1988 Bruce sold all the pubs to Midsummer Leisure (later European Leisure), which, in turn, sold them to Stakis Leisure in 1990. Since 1991, the chain has been owned by Allied Domecq. Many of the pubs are of historic interest and Allied has angered many by its crass mishandling of these buildings. There are now some 185 Firkins, but only 51 brew on site. The remainder are supplied by the brewpubs. Four basic brews are available, usually sold under house names, a 1034 OG/3.4% ABV mild, 1036 OG/3.5% ABV bitter, a stronger bitter at 1043/4.3%, and Dogbolter (OG 1057, ABV 5.6%). Some pubs offer extra one-off brews, including summer and winter ales, and also seen are Stout (OG 1047, ABV

4.6%) and Golden Glory (OG 1051, ABV 5%). All the brews are full mash and most pubs now offer some cask-conditioned beer with no additional gas applied. However, cellar tanks with mixed gas breathers are still used in some outlets. It is the intention of Allied to move all Firkins over to cask.

Current brewpubs:

Faculty & Firkin, Holt Street, Aston University Campus, Gosta Green, Birmingham, W. Midlands B7 4BD
Tel (0121) 359 6597

Fahrenheit & Firkin, Chobham Road, Woking, Surrey GU2 1HR
Tel (01483) 714484

Falcon & Firkin, 360 Victoria Park Road, Hackney, London E9 7BT
Tel (0181) 986 0102

Fantail & Firkin, 87 Muswell Hill Broadway, Muswell Hill, London N10 3HA

Faraday & Firkin, 66A-66C Battersea Rise, London SW1 1EQ

Fathom & Firkin, 20 Chapel Road, Worthing, W. Sussex BN11 1BJ
Tel (01903) 204431

Feast & Firkin, 229 Woodhouse Lane, Leeds, W. Yorkshire LS2 3AP
Tel (0113) 244 5076

Fedora & Firkin, Chapel Street, Luton, Bedfordshire LU1 2SE
Tel (01582) 452130

Felon & Firkin, 26-30 Great George Street, Leeds, W. Yorkshire LS1 3DL Tel (0113) 245 3198

Fermenter & Firkin, 480 Dudley Road, Wolverhampton, W. Midlands WV2 3AF
Tel (01902) 454834

Ferret & Firkin, 114 Lots Road, Chelsea, London SW10 0RJ
Tel (0171) 352 6645

Fiddler & Firkin, 14 South End, Croydon, Surrey CR0 1DL
Tel (0181) 680 9728

Fielder & Firkin, 346 High Street, Sutton, Surrey SM1 1PR
Tel (0181) 642 9018

Fieldmouse & Firkin at the Fighting Cocks, St Mary's Row, Moseley, Birmingham, W. Midlands B13 0HW
Tel (0121) 449 0811

Finch & Firkin, 467 Smithdown Road, Liverpool, Merseyside L15 5AE
Tel (0151) 733 5267

Finings & Firkin, 91 Station Road, Langley, Oldbury, Warley, W. Midlands B69 4LU
Tel (0121) 552 5386

Finnesko & Firkin, 10 Dereham Road, Norwich, Norfolk NR2 4AY
Tel (01603) 617465

Firecracker & Firkin, 2-4 Brighton Road, Southgate, Crawley, W. Sussex RH10 3JT
Tel (01923) 553196

Firefly & Firkin, 38 Holdenhurst Road, Bournemouth, Dorset BH8 8AD
Tel (01202) 293576

Fish & Firkin, 53 Alexandra Street, Southend-on-Sea, Essex SS2 6ES
Tel (01702) 392174

Fizgig & Firkin, St Anne's Well, Lower North Street, Exeter, Devon EX4 9DU
Tel (01392) 437667

Flag & Firkin, Station Road, Watford, Hertfordshire WD1 1ET
Tel (01923) 242184

Flamingo & Firkin, 1-7 Beckett Street, Derby DE1 1HT
Tel (01332) 297598

Flare & Firkin, 225 Holburn Street, Aberdeen AB10 1BP
Tel (01224) 585836

Fledgling & Firkin, Parliament Square, Hertford SG14 1EX
Tel (01992) 509287

Flicker & Firkin, 1 Dukes Street, Richmond, Surrey TW9 1HP
Tel (0181) 332 7807

Flounder & Firkin, 54 Holloway Road, Holloway, London N7 8HP
Tel (0171) 609 9574

Fly & Firkin, 18 Southfield Road, Middlesbrough, N. Yorkshire TS1 3BZ
Tel (01642) 253093

Flyer & Firkin, 54 Blagrave Street, Reading, Berkshire RG1 1PZ
Tel (01734) 569151

Flyman & Firkin, 166-170 Shaftesbury Avenue, London WC2H 8JB
Tel (0171) 240 7109

Font & Firkin, Union Street, Brighton, E. Sussex BN1 1HB
Tel (01273) 747727

Footage & Firkin, 137 Grosvenor Street, Manchester M1 7BZ
Tel (0161) 273 7053

Ford & Firkin, 15 High Street, Romford, Essex RM1 1JU

Forger & Firkin, 55-56 Woodridge Road, Guildford, Surrey GU1 4RF
Tel (01483) 578999
Forester & Firkin, 3 Eastgate Street, Stafford, ST16 2NQ
Tel (01785) 250755

Fort & Firkin, The Promenade, Windsor, Berkshire SL4 1QX
Tel (01753) 622273

Foundry & Firkin, 240 West Street, Sheffield, S. Yorkshire S1 4EU

Tel (0114) 279 5257

Fowl & Firkin, 1-2 The Butts, Coventry, W. Midlands CV1 3GR
Tel (01203) 231457

Fox & Firkin, 316 Lewisham High Street, Lewisham, London SE13 3HL
Tel (0181) 690 8343

Freelance & Firkin, 13 Brown Street, Dundee DD1 SED

Fresher & Firkin, 16 Chesterton Road, Cambridge CB4 3AX
Tel (01223) 324325

Friar & Firkin, 120 Euston Road, Euston, London NW1 2AL
Tel (0171) 388 0235

Friesian & Firkin, 87 Rectory Grove, Clapham, London SW4 0DR
Tel (0171) 622 4666

Fringe & Firkin, 2 Goldhawk Road, Shepherd's Bush, London W12 8QD
Tel (0181) 749 0229

Fuggle & Firkin, 14 Gloucester Street, Gloucester Green, Oxford OX1 2BN
Tel (01865) 248959

Fuzz & Firkin, 2 Albert Road, Southsea, Portsmouth, Hampshire PO5 2SH
Tel (01705) 827137

Phantom & Firkin, Leicester Road, Loughborough, Leicestershire LE11 2AG
Tel (01509) 262051

Pharoah & Firkin, 88-90 High Street, Fulham, London SW6 3LF
Tel (0171) 731 0732

Philanthropist & Firkin, 11-13 Victoria Street, St Albans, Hertfordshire AL1 3JJ
Tel (01727) 847021

Philatelist & Firkin, Drill Hall, East Street, Bromley, Kent BR1 1QQ
Tel (0181) 464 6022

Philosopher & Firkin, 288 Cowley Road, Oxford OX4 1UR
Tel (01865) 244386

Phoenix & Firkin, 5 Windsor Walk, Camberwell, London SE5 8BB
Tel (0171) 701 8282

Photographer & Firkin, 23-25 High Street, Ealing, London W3 6ND
Tel (0181) 567 1140

Physician & Firkin, 58 Dalkeith Road, Edinburgh EH16 5AD
Tel (0131) 662 4746

MINERVA
Minerva Hotel (Allied Domecq Leisure), Nelson Street, Hull, E. Yorkshire HU1 1XE
Tel (01482) 326909
Tours by arrangement
♩ Full mash operation, set up in 1985 and refurbished in 1995. The pub's own beer is

stored under a nitrogen gas blanket pressure in cellar tanks (although the other ales on sale are cask-conditioned). Special brews are produced for special occasions. Beers: Sea Fever Ale (OG 1040, ABV 4%, August-September), Pilots Pride (OG 1042, ABV 4.2%), Midnight Owl (OG 1045, ABV 4.5%, December-February).

ROSE STREET
Rose Street Brewery, 55 Rose Street, Edinburgh EH2 2NH
Tel (0131) 220 1227
☼ Founded in 1983 and run by Alloa Brewery, supplying a handful of other Alloa outlets with beers produced from malt extract. Beers: Auld Reekie 80/- (OG 1042, ABV 4.1%), Auld Reekie 90/- (OG 1054, ABV 5.3%).

GUINNESS
Guinness Brewing GB, Park Royal Brewery, London NW10 7RR
Tel (0181) 965 7700 Fax (0181) 963 5120
Guinness, for a few years, was the only national brewery which did not produce real ale. There had been no cask beer for decades when, in 1993, at a time when interest in bottle-conditioned beers was reviving, the company decided to axe its naturally-conditioned, bottled stout, Guinness Original. (Guinness Original is still on sale, but only in a brewery-conditioned, pasteurised version, which lacks the complexity and freshness of the bottle-conditioned beer.) The porter apart, all Draught Guinness sold in the UK is keg. In Ireland, Draught Guinness (OG 1038, brewed at Arthur Guinness, St James's Gate, Dublin 8) is not pasteurised but is served with gas pressure. In 1997 it was announced that Guinness was to merge with Grand Metropolitan.

SCOTTISH COURAGE
Scottish & Newcastle PLC, 111 Holyrood Road, Edinburgh, Lothian EH8 8YS
Tel (0131) 556 2591 Fax (0131) 558 1165
Scottish & Newcastle was formed in 1960, as a merger between Scottish Brewers Ltd (the former Younger and McEwan breweries) and Newcastle Breweries Ltd. In 1995 S&N agreed to purchase Courage from its Australian owner, Foster's. Courage had been a brewer with no pubs since 1991, following the sale of its pub estate to Inntrepreneur Estates (see Pub Groups), a company Foster's jointly owned with Grand Metropolitan. The government allowed the S&N takeover to go through without reference to the Monopolies and Mergers Commission, despite the fact that it created Britain's largest brewing company, with nearly 30 per cent of the market in beer production. The consequences for the UK industry were obvious. Brewery rationalisation took place, with the loss of hundreds of jobs and fears for the future of many beer brands. Home Brewery in Nottingham was top of the closures list, along with the Fountain Head brewery at Halifax.
This left the company with five major UK cask ale breweries, plus keg beer plants in Manchester, Reading and Mortlake (a joint venture with American giant Anheuser-Busch known as The Stag Brewing Company and producing Budweiser). The company also owns the Beamish & Crawford brewery in Cork, Ireland.
Scottish & Newcastle (Retail) operates over 2,600 pubs nationwide, around 1,900 being managed houses and some 80 per cent selling cask beer. Some 400 houses are currently themed, and this is an area the company wants to develop in future. These include the T&J Bernard and Barras & Co. ale houses and the Rat & Parrot and the Old Orleans chains. Scottish Courage also continues to have a massive presence in the free trade (particularly through McEwan and Theakston brands and Newcastle Brown Ale), and also dominates many free houses through the loan-tie system of offering financial loans in return for beer sales.
In 1998 it closed the Abington in Northampton and the Greyhound in Streatham brewpubs.

BRISTOL
Scottish Courage Brewing Ltd, The Courage Bristol Brewery, Counterslip, Victoria Street, Bristol BS1 6BX
Tel (0117) 929 7222 Fax (0117) 927 6150
Established in 1702, this brewery was owned and run by the George family from 1788 until 1961, when it was acquired by Courage. Now Scottish Courage's only real ale brewery in the South, it lays claim to being the world's largest dedicated real ale brewery and is very keen to promote its heritage. Though its main beers, Courage Best and Directors, are very well promoted nationally, Georges Bitter Ale sales are confined mostly to the West Country and South-East Wales. These three beers are all diluted versions of the same original high-gravity brew. A new range of occasional beers has been introduced, based on recipes from the Courage archives and there are plans to focus on the heritage of the brewery by opening a visitor's centre. Occasional/seasonal beers: Old Chopper (OG 1040, ABV 4.1%), Navigator (OG 1043, ABV 4.4%), Rocketeer (OG 1046, ABV 4.5%), Directors Winter Warmer (OG 1055, ABV 5.5%).
Georges Bitter Ale *(OG 1032, ABV 3.3%)* ◆ ⊠ An amber, light-bodied session bitter, with a slight malt grain taste, a hoppy aroma and a lasting, dry, bitter finish with some malt, grain and hops. Light, tasty and refreshing.
Courage Best Bitter *(OG 1038, ABV 4%)* ◆ ⊠ Medium-bodied, dry and bitter with good malt, grain, moderate hop oil and a balancing sweetness. Pale brown, with a malt/hop aroma, it has a dry, bitter finish, with malt grain and a hint of fruit.
Courage Directors *(OG 1045, ABV 4.8%)* ◆ ⊠ A well-balanced, full-bodied, mid-brown malty ale, with grain, hops, malt and fruit in the nose. In the mouth it is dry and bitter with malt, grain, fruits and hops/hop oil, and a touch of balancing sweetness. Similar, lengthy finish, if less sweet.

FOUNTAIN
Fountain Brewery, 159 Fountainbridge,

Edinburgh EH3 9YY
Tel (0131) 229 9377 Fax (0131) 229 1282
The Scottish production centre, formerly the
home of William McEwan & Co. Ltd.,
founded in 1856. Its beers are sold under
two separate names – McEwan and
Younger, depending on the trading area.
Occasional beers: Gillespie's Porter (OG
1042, ABV 4.2%), McEwan Export (OG
1043, ABV 4.5%), Raeburn's Edinburgh Ale
(OG 1042, ABV 4.7%), McEwan 90/- (OG
1052, ABV 5.5%).
**McEwan 70/- or Younger Scotch
Bitter** *(OG 1036, ABV 3.7%)* ❦⊛ A well-
balanced, sweetish brew, becoming more
and more rare.
McEwan 80/- or Younger IPA *(OG
1042, ABV 4.5%)* ❦⊛ A thin-bodied beer
with a cloying metallic aftertaste. Once a
classic, now bland and sweet with some
maltiness.

JOHN SMITH'S
**Scottish Courage Brewing Ltd, John Smith's
Brewery, Tadcaster, N. Yorkshire LS24 9SA**
Tel (01937) 832091 Fax (01937) 833766
Tours by arrangement
A business founded at the Old Brewery in
1758 and taken over by John Smith (brother
of Samuel Smith – see Independents) in
1847. The present brewery was built in 1879
and became part of the Courage empire in
1970. Major expansion has taken place since
the formation of Scottish Courage, with 11
new fermentation vessels installed. Imperial
Russian Stout (■) was axed in 1998.
Webster's Green Label Best *(OG 1032,
ABV 3.2%)* ⊛
Webster's Yorkshire Bitter *(OG 1035,
ABV 3.5%)* ⊛
Bitter *(OG 1036, ABV 3.8%)* ❦ ⊛Copper-
coloured beer balanced, but with no dominant features. Hoppy, short, finish.
Magnet *(OG 1040, ABV 4%)* ❦ ⊛
An almost ruby-coloured beer with a com-
plex aroma of hops and malt and citrus fruit.
Malt dominates the taste and aftertaste in
this warming beer.

THEAKSTON
**T&R Theakston Ltd, Wellgarth, Masham,
Ripon, N. Yorkshire HG4 4YD**
Tel (01765) 689544 Fax (01765) 689769
Shop   Tours by arrangement
Founded in 1827 and based at this brewery
since 1875. Theakston became part of S&N
in 1987. More than £1 million has been
spent on this brewery in the 1990s, reflecting
the 'national' status its brews have been
given by Scottish Courage, yet most of
Theakston's production now takes place in
Newcastle. The same pump clips are used for
Masham and Newcastle beers, so the consumer is not told whether the beer actually
comes from Theakston's brewery.
Occasional beers: Hogshead Bitter (OG
1040, ABV 4.1%), Lightfoot (ABV 5.2%),
Masham Ale (OG 1065, ABV 6.6%).
Mild Ale *(OG 1035, ABV 3.5%)* ❦⛉ ⊛ A
rich and smooth mild ale with a creamy
body and a rounded liquorice taste. Dark
ruby/amber in colour, with a mix of malt
and fruit in the nose and a dry, hoppy aftertaste.
Black Bull Bitter *(OG 1037, ABV 3.9%)*

❦ ⊛ Dry and hoppy bitter with moderate
fruit and bitterness initially but ends dry
with a spicy atsringency.
Best Bitter *(OG 1038, ABV 3.9%)*❦ ⊛
A dry and metallic bitter with light hop character when fresh. Older samples lose character and end watery and pale..
XB *(OG 1044, ABV 4.6%)* ❦ ⊛A sweet
tasting bitter with background fruit and
spicy hop. Some caramel character gives this
ale a malty dominance.
Old Peculier *(OG 1057, ABV 5.7%)*
❦⛉⊛ Strong, fruity character dominates in
this malty,roasted ale. Dark malts and
liquorish blend into a rainbow of flavour,
balancing a smooth sweetness in young
casks but tasting dry when older.

TYNE
**Tyne Brewery, Gallowgate, Newcastle-
upon-Tyne, Tyne & Wear NE99 1RA**
Tel (0191) 232 5091 Fax (0191) 261 6297
The home of Newcastle Breweries Ltd,
formed in 1890 as an amalgamation of five
local breweries. In recent years it brewed little real ale, until most of Theakston's production was transferred here, but no indication is given at the point of sale or in
advertising that Theakston beers are brewed
in Newcastle (for tasting notes see
Theakston).
Theakston Mild Ale *(OG 1035, ABV
3.5%)*
Theakston Best Bitter *(OG 1039, ABV
3.8%)*
Newcastle Exhibition *(OG 1040, ABV
4.4%)*
Theakston XB *(OG 1045, ABV 4.6%)*
Theakston Old Peculier *(OG 1057, ABV
5.7%)*

Scottish Courage
Brewpubs:

ABINGTON PARK
**Abington Park Brewery Co.,
Wellingborough Road, Northampton**
Closed.

GREYHOUND
**Greyhound Brewery Company Ltd, 151
Greyhound Lane, Streatham Common,
London**
Closed.

ORANGE
**The Orange Brewery, 37/39 Pimlico Road,
Pimlico, London SW1W 8NE**
Tel (0171) 824 8002
Tours by arrangement
⛫ Brewery opened in 1983 and refurbished
in 1995. The full mash brews are stored in
cellar tanks and are kept under blanket pressure. Beers: SW1 (OG 1039, ABV 3.8%),
Porter (OG 1045, ABV 4.3%), SW2 (OG
1049, ABV 4.8%), Victoria Lager (OG
1049, ABV 5.5%), Spiritual Reunion (OG
1058, ABV 6.1%, a winter brew containing
orange blossoms).

YORKSHIRE GREY
**The Yorkshire Grey Brewery, 26 Theobalds
Road, Holborn, London WC1X 8PN**
Tel (0171) 405 8287 Fax (0171) 831 2359

♻ Brewpub on the corner of Gray's Inn Road which was extensively refurbished in 1995. The beers are now produced from full mashes but a CO2 blanket is applied to the cellar tanks which store the finished products. Numerous one-off and occasional beers are brewed each year. Beers: Barristers Best (OG 1040, ABV 3.8%), Summer Horne Wheat Beer (ABV 4.1%, occasional), QC Best Bitter (OG 1046, ABV 4.5%), Birthday Bevvy Porter (ABV 4.6%, occasional), Patently Oblivious (ABV 4.6%, occasional), Harvest Festival Ale (ABV 4.7%, occasional), Lordship Supreme Old Ale (OG 1050, ABV 5%).

WHITBREAD

The Whitbread Beer Company, Whitbread PLC, Porter Tun House, Capability Green, Luton, Bedfordshire LU1 3LS
Tel (01582) 391166 Fax (01582) 397397
The smallest of the national brewers, Whitbread has been the most active in the real ale market in the first half of the 1990s. In the 1970s and 1980s, Whitbread wielded a sharp axe and numerous small breweries went: Strong's of Romsey, Wethered of Marlow, Fremlins of Faversham, Chester's of Salford and Higsons of Liverpool were all shut down. In the first half of the 1990s Whitbread seemed to re-discover cask-conditioned beer and invested heavily in its real ale portfolio. The retail side of the company turned dozens of pubs into Tut 'n' Shive and Hogshead alehouses to support this initiative and there were also some noteworthy special brew promotions, involving limited edition beers brewed in Cheltenham and Castle Eden. By the latter half of 1990s began to switch its emphasis back to keg products. Many of the various regional beers which survived brewery closures by transferring to other breweries have now been discontinued altogether, and the only cask beer enjoying substantial financial support is Boddingtons Bitter.
In October 1997 Whitbread embarked on a major clearout of nine minor cask ale brands, in an effort to help its major brands hang to their market share. These included Chester's Bitter, originally from Salford, Bentley's Yorkshire Bitter, Wethered's Bitter and Fremlin's. The company said it was making alternatives available from other brewers, but it cleared the way for the major brands.
The Hogshead chain has been successful: it plans to have 250 open by 2001. In 1998 Whitbread's house newspaper announced the establishment of a new pub chain – the Real Pub Company, aimed at 'people who want a quiet pint down a traditional local'. Trading agreements with regional brewers like Wadworth and Marston's now help fill out Whitbread's cask portfolio. In addition to the cask ale breweries, the company operates keg beer factories in Magor in South Wales and Samlesbury in Lancashire. Whitbread also announced the closure of the Flowers brewery in Cheltenham (see page 127) and the closure of Castle Eden in Durham (see page 104) unless they were sold by 1 October 1998.
Whitbread's 3,850 pubs are controlled by two divisions: Whitbread Inns (managed houses) and Whitbread Pub Partnerships (pubs leased out, usually on 20-year terms).

BODDINGTONS

Strangeways Brewery, PO Box 23, Strangeways, Manchester M60 3WB
Tel (0161) 828 2000 Fax (0161) 828 2213
Tours by arrangement
Established in 1778 and acquired by Whitbread when the Boddingtons company, which had already taken-over and closed Oldham Brewery, retreated to pub owning and other leisure enterprises. Now Whitbread is pushing Boddingtons Bitter relentlessly nationwide and the beer takes up 90 per cent of the brewery's already expanded production capacity. To create room, Oldham Best (OB) Bitter (OG 1037.5, ABV 3.8%) has been transferred to Burtonwood Brewery (see Independents).
Boddingtons Mild *(OG 1032, ABV 3.1%)* ♦ ⊗ A thin, dark mild with a sweet caramel and malt flavour, and a short aftertaste. It has now disappeared from many tied houses.
OB Mild *(OG 1032, ABV 3%)* ♦ ⊗ Reddish-brown beer with a malty aroma. A smooth roast malt and fruit flavour follows, then a malty and surprisingly bitter aftertaste.
Boddingtons Bitter *(OG 1034.5, ABV 3.8%)* ♦ ⊗ A pale beer in which the grainy malt, hop and bitter character can be spoiled by a rather cloying sweetness.

CASTLE EDEN

Castle Eden Brewery, PO Box 13, Castle Eden, Hartlepool, Co. Durham TS27 4SX
Tel (01429) 836007
Originally attached to a 17th-century coaching inn, the old Nimmo's brewery (established in 1826) was purchased by Whitbread in 1963. It found a niche within the Whitbread group and went on to produce some of the company's better quality beers. Whitbread announced in 1998 that the brewery would close that October (see page 104) should a buyer not be found. All beers will be transferred to Boddingtons in Manchester. The beers listed below were those being brewed in July 1998.
Castle Eden Ale *(OG 1042, ABV 4.2%)#* ♦☐⊗ A light, creamy, malty, sweet ale with fruit and a mellow, dry bitterness to finish. Easily marred by poor cellarmanship.
Fuggles Imperial IPA ⊗ *(OG 1055, ABV 5.5%)* Pale but robust beer which oozes hops and has a citrus flavour.

FLOWERS

The Flowers Brewery, Monson Avenue, Cheltenham, Gloucestershire GL50 4EL
Tel (01242) 265415 Fax (01242) 265404
The Flowers brewing operation and title were transferred from Stratford-upon-Avon in 1968 and the brewery became the centre for Whitbread cask ale in the South when it absorbed production from other breweries as they closed. Cheltenham was due to close (see page 127) unless a buyer was found before 1 October. All beers were due to be transferred to Boddingtons, Manchester.
Flowers IPA *(OG 1036, ABV 3.6%)* ⊗ A light, spicy, floral hop aroma precedes malty bitterness in the taste. Citrus hop finish.
Trophy Bitter *(OG 1036, ABV 3.8%)* ⊗

A mellow balance of hop, malt and grain flavours follows a malty and light, floral hop aroma. Dry hop finish.
Whitbread Best Bitter *(OG 1036, ABV 3.6%)* ⊠ A beer with light malt and nut aromas, with a hint of hops. Some malt in the mouth, before a malt, nuts and light fruit finish.
The Abroad Cooper Summer Ale *(ABV 4.1%)* ⊠ Spring/autumn.
Flowers Original *(OG 1044, ABV 4.4%)* ⊠ A fresh lemon/blackcurrant dry hop aroma leads to a distinctive, balanced taste of malt, fruit and hops, before a long, hoppy bitter finish.
The Abroad Cooper *(OG 1049, ABV 5.1%)* ◆ ⊠ A dark red/copper-coloured beer with a fruity aroma. A sweet malt taste is followed by a slight bitter aftertaste. Autumn/winter.

Whitbread Brewpubs:

ALFORD ARMS Alford Arms Brewhouse, Frithsden, Hertfordshire.
Brewery closed temporarily.

FELLOWS, MORTON & CLAYTON
Fellows, Morton & Clayton Brewhouse Company, 54 Canal Street, Nottingham NG1 7EH
Tel (0115) 950 6795 Fax. (0115) 955 1412
Ω This pub began brewing in 1980 and still uses malt extract. Some strong seasonal beers are also produced (6%+). Beers: Fellows Bitter (OG 1041, ABV 3.9%), Clayton's Strong Ale (OG 1052, ABV 5%).

FOX & NEWT
Fox & Newt, Leeds, W. Yorkshire.
Brewery closed.

FROG & PARROT
Frog & Parrot, 64 Division Street, Sheffield, S. Yorkshire S1 4SG
Tel (0114) 272 1280
Paying tours available
Ω Malt extract brewpub which began production in 1982. Beers are kept in casks and are sometimes available in a handful of other pubs. Beers: Do's Brew (ABV 3.9%), Reckless (OG 1045, ABV 4.6%), Conqueror (OG 1066, ABV 6.2%), Armageddon (ABV 6.9%), Roger & Out (OG 1125, ABV 12.5%). Bottle-conditioned beer: Roger & Out (OG 1125, ABV 12.5%).

LASS O'GOWRIE
Lass O'Gowrie Brewhouse, 36 Charles Street, Manchester M1 7DB
Tel (0161) 273 6932
Tours by arrangement
Ω Victorian pub, revamped and re-opened as a malt extract brewpub in 1983 and now part of the Hogshead division. The brewery in the cellar is visible from the bar and the beer is now stored in casks. Beers: LOG 35 (OG 1035, ABV 3.8%), LOG 42 (OG 1042, ABV 4.7%), Centurion (ABV 5%, occasional), Graduation (ABV 5.1%, occasional).

OLD COURT The Old Court Brewhouse, Queen Street, Huddersfield, W. Yorkshire HD1 2SL *Tel (01484) 454035*

Ω Malt extract brewpub opened in 1994 in Huddersfield's former County Court. The building's character has been retained and the brewing copper, protruding from the lower ground floor into the ground floor public bar, provides an unusual talking point. Beers: Coppers' Ale (ABV 3.4%), M'Lud (ABV 4%), 1825 (ABV 4.5%), Maximum Sentence (ABV 6%).

Notes on nationals

Pub groups

It was the 1990 Beer Orders which really boosted the pub groups sector. At first they were mostly run by ex-big brewery middle management and largely tied to their former employers. But the sector has proved to be dynamic and fast moving. Huge pub empires have risen and fallen and more are appearing all the time. Wether this instability will be good for the sector and the standards of the pubs within is arguable.

The sector as a whole consists of 20,000 pubs. As the big brewers prepare to dump their remaining tenanted estates Britain's hard-won guest beer law could be dead if action isn't taken now. Mike Benner, CAMRA's Head of Campaigns, said CAMRA would lobby hard to have the guest ale right extended to cover large pub chains.

The 11,000-odd pubs owned by the regional brewers are now almost the only traditional tied houses left. The free trade and pub chains are increasingly price dominated and microbreweries and regionals are consequently losing out.

And every time a free trader sells up the odds are that a regional brewer or non-brewing pub chain snaps up the premises.

One wholesaler, who specialises in supplying the free trade with ales from micros and regional brewers, says, 'With no guest ale provision in pub chains, my market is being more and more restricted.'

However, not all pub chains ignore the wishes of drinkers. Inn Business has said: 'While the retail pub market has become highly competitive, with new entrants and a whole plethora of new concept brands and mega brands, there is no doubt that there remains a place in the consumers' heart and minds for that traditional local pub.'

And Bernard White of Crowded House says people are turning their backs on large, branded pub/restaurants.

In 1998 CAMRA won an extension of the guest ale right: from April 1998 eligible pubs will be allowed to stock one bottle-conditioned ale.

But the number of eligible pubs has been shrinking.

In December, Allied Domecq asked the Office of Fair Trading to release it from the guest ale entitlement.

What's Brewing carries news of the pub groups sector every month.

ALLIED DOMECQ

See Nationals, Carlsberg-Tetley

AMBISHUS

214-216 Wellingborough Road, Northampton, NN1 4EE
Tel (01604) 637670 Fax (01604) 620744
Has 40 pubs, including ten recently purchased from Wetherspoon, which included some of the earliest Wetherspoons pubs in London which no longer fitted the corporate bill. Ambishus is now quoted on the Alternative Investment Market, the so-called junior investment market. Formerly called Sirenia.

AVEBURY TAVERNS

20 Station Road, Gerrards Cross, Bucks SL9 8EL
Tel (01753) 482600
Set up with the backing of Japanese bank Daiwa, emulating on a much smaller scale the pub-buying amitions of rival Nomura. It bought its first 147 pubs from Wolverhampton & Dudley, but is tied to them for beer supply.
This expanded in early 1998 with the purchase of more than 222 pubs from Bass and 62 fromWhitbread. It currently has 470 leased and tenanted pubs. Avebury chairman Rodney Mann is a member of the Mann brewing family.

ASCOT ESTATES

See Mayfair Taverns

BEARDS

Beards of Sussex Ltd, West End, Herstmonceux, E. Sussex BN27 4NN
Tel (01323) 832777 Fax (01323) 832833
Former brewing company (founded in 1797) which opted out of production in 1959. After contracting out its beers to Harveys from 1960 to 1986, Beards then abandoned brewing altogether and became a cask ale wholesaler as well as a pub company. The wholesaling division was sold off in 1994 and Beards currently runs 46 traditional pubs in Sussex (11 managed, 34 tenanted and one joint venture with Whitbread/Beefeater), which can sell any beers from the wide list offered by the Beer Seller wholesaler and from Scottish Courage. A new beer, Beards Best Bitter, is now brewed for the company by Arundel Brewery (see Independents). In July 1998 Beards was bought by Greene King, adding 43 pubs to its estate.

CAFE INNS

Café Inns PLC, 3 St Thomas's Road, Chorley, Lancashire PR7 1HP
Tel (01257) 262424 Fax (01257) 260497
Established in 1987 and now running 85 outlets (73 tenanted, 12 managed) in the North-West. The figure includes one restaurant and two coffee shops. Pubs sell beers from Bass and Scottish Courage.

CATMERE

Catmere Ltd, Station Road, Scunthorpe, North Lincolnshire DN15 6PY
Tel (01724) 861703, Fax (01724) 861708

Catmere owns ten sites – nine managed, one tenanted, mostly in the free trade, but it plans to expand to 12 sites in 1998. Its guest ales are supplied by Bass, Courage, Mansfield and the Beer Seller. One of its outlets, the Honest Lawyer, at Scunthorpe, has regional and microbrewery cask ales at any one time, changing on a daily basis.

CENTURY INNS

Century Inns PLC, Belasis Business Centre, Coxwold Way, Billingham TS23 4EA
Tel (01642) 343426 Fax (01642) 345603
Formed in 1991 by Camerons employees who bought 195 pubs from Bass. The intention was to establish a pub estate for a buy-out of the Camerons brewery, but this was scuppered by Brent Walker. The number of pubs now stands at 500, 96 managed and the rest traditionally tenanted (three-year agreements), with the management side growing. The pubs are located down the North-Eastern side of the country, from Tyneside to Lincolnshire. The company's cask-conditioned beers are supplied by Bass, Scottish-Courage and Carlsberg-Tetley and, to a small extent, Whitbread, including a selection from their cask beer ranges. All outlets are given the opportunity to buy from the above brewers; tenenated houses' choices are confined to these, though the managed pubs also take some beers from smaller breweries. Six pubs are branded 'Dr Brown's' and feature a strong food emphasis and live music. In summer 1996, Century took over and closed Stocks Brewery in Doncaster. Some Stocks beer is now produced under contract by Hull (see Independents). In summer 1997 Century bought Pubmaster's managed house division, including 44 Tap & Spile branded pubs. However, Century have appointed the Beer Seller wholesaler to supply its Tap & Spile chain, and as a result many microbreweries will deliver via the wholesaler, and not direct. CAMRA fears that many of these micros will now disappear from the chain's suppliers' list.
Century also have five continental café bars, four under the BieRRex name (formerly owned by Pubmaster), and 30 outlets forming part of the country tavern diversion. Real ale features, but food accomodation and take precedence.

CM GROUPS

See Commer Inns

TOM COBLEIGH

Tom Cobleigh PLC, Phoenix House, Oak Tree Lane, Mansfield, Nottinghamshire NG18 4LF
Tel (01623) 638800 Fax (01623) 638820
Established in 1992 with two pubs. Since then the estate has grown to 70 across north and central UK. The company was taken over by Rank in October 1996 but the direction of the business appears unaltered. There are expansion plans for a further 20 outlets in 1998, taking the brand to a national arena. The pubs aim to conform to the company's slogan of 'unspoilt pubs for nice people'. Licensees choose beers from a head office range of national and regional ales, with Bass and Scottish Courage the main suppliers. A list of rotating guest beers is also offered. The tenanted estate of 18 pubs was acquired from Whitbread in 1994, though these are signed as belonging to The Nice Pub Company.

COMMER INNS

CM Group Ltd, Magnet House, Station Road, Tadcaster, N. Yorkshire LS24 9JF
Tel (01937) 833311 Fax (01937) 834236
Pub chain in North-East England. The pubs were initially leased, then acquired, from Whitbread. Commer Inns, the tenanted operation, has 40 outlets, and Commer Management, the managed side, has 45. In November 1997 it bought six West Yorkshire pubs from Jolly Taverns of Bradford. Supplies come from Whitbread, Scottish Courage, Bass, Carlsberg-Tetley and Old Mill. Independent Pub Chain of the Year finalists in 1997. All cask ales on suppliers' lists are available to tenants.

CONQUEST INNS

Conquest Inns Ltd, 1st floor, 172 Bullsmoor Lane, Enfield, Middlesex EN1 4SE
Tel (01992) 717718 Fax (01992) 717788
Conquest Inns are a subsidiary of the Jersey Brewing Company and operate an estate, mainly tenanted, of 50 pubs. Most of the pubs are in the South-East, but the company is looking to expand at the rate of 20 pubs a year. Beers come from Bass and Scottish Courage, and the company has no definitive policy on cask ale, leaving the choice to tenants.

CROWDED HOUSE INNS

Formed with the purchase of 40 former Beefeater pub/restaurants fromWhitbread for £36 million in May 1998. Indications are that it plans to return the pubs to their original, pre-Beefeater names and shy away from any kind of theming/branding. Bernard White, company chief, says that consumers are turning their backs on large, branded pub and restaurant chains and that only pub chains with discreet branding (apart from the branded pubs that are already successful) will succeed.

JT DAVIES

JT Davies & Sons Ltd, 7 Aberdeen Road, Croydon, Surrey CR0 1EQ.
Tel (0181) 681 3222 Fax (0181) 760 0390
Wine merchants now controlling 35 tenancies and eight managed houses in the South-East. Its main suppliers are Bass and Scottish Courage, with some beers taken from Fuller's and Harveys.

DAVY

The Davy Group, 59-63 Bermondsey Street,

London SE1 3XF
Tel (0171) 407 9670 Fax (0171) 407 5844
Wine merchants and shippers since 1870,
Davy's has been opening wine bars/restau-
rants in the London area since 1965, taking
previously unlicensed properties (largely
basements) and creating a Dickensian, sawdust, nooks-and-crannies type of establishment. Its Davy's Old Wallop (ABV 4.8%) is
a re-badged brew of undeclared origin
(though Courage Best and Directors fit the
bill). These are usually served in pewter or
copper tankards. The company currently
runs around 50 outlets, including a few pubs.

DISCOVERY INNS

See Enterprise Inns.

ELDRIDGE POPE

Eldridge, Pope & Co. PLC, Weymouth
Avenue, Dorchester, Dorset ST1 1QT
Tel (01305) 251251 Fax (01305) 258300
Founded as the Green Dragon Brewery in
1837, Eldridge Pope finally divorced itself
from brewing in 1996 when it split into two
wings, the brewing side becoming known as
Thomas Hardy Brewery (see Independents).
The company now runs 200 pubs, 124 man-
aged, the rest tenanted.

ENTERPRISE INNS

Enterprise Inns Ltd, Friars Gate, Stratford
Road, Solihull, W. Midlands B90 4BN
Tel (0121) 733 7700 Fax (0121) 733 6447
Midlands-based company founded in 1991
with the purchase of 372 pubs from Bass.
The total now stands at around 1,150, following the purchase of John Labatt Retail in
1996 and Discovery Inns in May 1997. It
also bought Gibbs Mew in February 1998
for £48 million, further increasing its stock.
About half the pubs are run on a 21-year
lease basis and the remainder are tenanted,
with beers provided by Bass, Whitbread,
Carlsberg-Tetley, Scottish Courage and
Wolverhampton & Dudley. Licensees were
not allowed to buy beers outside the company. The pubs are situated across the country, with the exception of Scotland. The Hop
House brewpub in Kingsthorpe,
Northamptonshire (see Independents) has
now been sold. Boss Ted Tuppen said he
believed retailers would want greater freedom of operation. 'I want to get the brands I
want, not the brands my suppliers dictate,'
he told *What's Brewing*. He also sees his tenants being free to order whatever they need
for their businesses to succeed.

FAMOUS PUB COMPANY

Famous Pub Company PLC, 510 Hertford
Road, Enfield, Greater London EN3 5SS
Tel (0181) 805 4055 Fax (0181) 805 0115
Expanding pub company established with
the purchase of 37 pubs from Whitbread in
February 1996. The company currently
owns 44 pubs in London and the Home
Counties; 42 are owned freehold and ten-
anted and two are managed. Many of the

pubs are Grade II listed. Supplied by
Courage and Whitbread, the cask ales range
includes major brewers and some regional
brewers, such as Morland, Adnams and
Greene King.
The estate now totals some 45 pubs, all traditionally tenanted (one-year contracts) and
supplied with beer by Whitbread. Some tenants are allowed a guest beer.

FITZGERALD

Sir John Fitzgerald Ltd, Café Royal
Buildings, 8 Nelson Street, Newcastle-upon-
Tyne, Tyne & Wear NE1 5AW
Tel (0191) 232 0664 Fax (0191) 222 1764
Long-established, family-owned, property
and pubs company. Its pubs convey a 'free
house' image, most offering a decent choice
of cask beers, including guest ales. All 29
pubs are located in the North-East.

GIBBS MEW

Anchor House, Netherhampton Road,
Salisbury, Wiltshire SP2 8RA.
Tel. (01722) 411911 Fax 01722 411486
Established in 1898, Charrington bought a
stake in the company in the 1960s, which
the Gibbs family bought back in 1972. In
1992, with CAMRA support, it saw off new
predators Brierly Investments. In 1994 it
bought the Centric Pub Company (197
pubs) and in 1995 it exchanged the Castle
Leisure Complex in Cardiff for the six pubs
formerly owned by Harmony Leisure Group.
In September 1997 the company closed its
Anchor House brewery to concentrate on its
estate. In February 1998 it was bought by
Enterprise Inns. The company owns 330
pubs, around 300 tied; most of those are in
the South of England around 200 serve cask
conditioned beer. Wiltshire Traditional and
Salisbury Best Bitter are brewed by Ushers
and Badger (Hall & Woodhouse) brew
Deacon and Bishop's Tipple.

GRAND PUB COMPANY

The biggest pub firm in Britain came into
being after Inntrepreneur and Spring Inns
was bought by Japanese banking giant
Nomura for £1.2 billion. Nomura makes
more money than Honda and Toyota and is
one of the most powerful financial organisa-
tions in the world; in 1997 it also bought the
William Hill betting chain. *What's Brewing*
city columnist John Reynolds explained that
the pub chains offer Noumra security when
it wants to borrow money to expand. 'The
purchase of Inntrepreneur is no more than a
means to an end,' he commented. CAMRA
has called on the company not to limit customer choice in a scramble for discounts.
Both Inntrepreneur and Spring Inns licensees
had signed supply agreements before the
takeover, while Phoenix Inns (part of
Inntrepreneur) are free of tie. Inntrepreneur
said those agreements would remain in
place.
The bulk of Bass's sale of tenanted houses
was set to go to Nomura.
Inntrepreneur landlords who had withheld
rent claiming that their beer ties were illegal

lost their case in the High Court in August. The Inntrepreneur estate will be split in two, hiving off 2,600 into a new company owned by one of its own bankers.

GRAY

Gray & Sons (Chelmsford) Ltd, Rignals Lane, Galley Wood, Chelmsford, Essex CM2 8RE
Tel (01245) 475181 Fax (01245) 475182
Former brewery which ceased production at its Chelmsford brewery in 1974 and which now supplies its 49 tied, tenanted pubs in Essex with cask beers from Greene King (chiefly IPA and Abbot Ale) and Shepherd Neame (Master Brew Bitter or Spitfire), as well as various guest ales from Tavern.

GREENALLS

Greenalls Group PLC, PO Box 2, Greenalls Avenue, Warrington, Cheshire WA4 6RH
Tel (01925) 651234 Fax (01925) 444734
Former brewing giant which destroyed many fine independent breweries before turning its back on brewing in 1991. In the 1980s Greenalls took over and closed the Wem, Davenports, Simpkiss and Shipstone's breweries. Since the closure of its own Warrington brewery, Greenalls brands have been brewed by Carlsberg-Tetley, and are now produced at Burton-upon-Trent.
The company now operates around 2,500 pubs, about 1,200 of which are tenanted and 790 of which are managed. The Boddingtons acquisition included the Liquid Assets wholesaling arm and this, together with Greenalls own Tavern distribution company, has made Greenalls the country's largest beer wholesaler. Pubwise, Whitbread beers can be found in the former Devenish estate, and these are also sold in the former Boddingtons pubs. Guest beers across the country include Tetley Bitter, Stones Bitter, Worthington Bitter and, in a few outlets, ales from Adnams, Greene King, Young's and Coach House. Some Liverpool pubs have been re-branded as Cains pubs and sell Cains beers. There are guest ale programmes in various outlets. Various theme outlets have been established, including Irish pubs, Jungle Bungles, Ale & Hearty food pubs and Porters Ale Houses.

HONEYCOMBE LEISURE

This 20-year-old company owns 32 managed houses and was expected to announce plans for flotation.

HEAVITREE

Heavitree Brewery PLC, Trood Lane, Matford, Exeter, Devon EX2 8YP
Tel (01392) 258406 Fax (01392) 411697
West Country brewery (established 1790) which gave up production in 1970 to concentrate on running pubs. The current estate (largely in Devon) stands at 116: 11 managed, and the rest tenanted or leased out (on ten- or 21-year contracts). The pubs are tied to taking beers from the Whitbread Cask Collection, with some products from Bass and Eldridge Pope.

INN BUSINESS

Inn Business Group PLC, The Firs, Whitchurch, Nr Aylesbury, Bucks HP22 4TH
Tel (01296) 640000 Fax (01296) 640070
Inn Business currently runs around 500 traditional pubs under its 'local's local' banner in Southern England (some in the Midlands and the North-East), following the acquisition of Marr Taverns and Sycamore Taverns in 1996. the company says its assets were 'primarily invested in the timeless value of the traditional local'.
The pubs are predominantly tenanted, but also include traditional food and alehouse managed outlets. Beers come from Whitbread, Bass, Carlsberg-Tetley and Scottish Courage, and include the guest beers these supply. The Hooden Horse branded pubs offer spicy food and real ales, with beers including those from Hook Norton, Goacher's, King & Barnes and Pilgrim.

INN KENT GROUP

Inn Kent Group Ltd, Victoria Hotel, 141 Week Street, Maidstone, Kent ME14 1RE
Tel (01622) 661782 Fax (01622) 661717
Pub group formed in 1991 as Inn Kent Leisure, with an enterprising guest beer and price promotion policy in some of its 27 pubs, mainly in Kent. Otherwise beers come from Scottish Courage and Whitbread.

INNTREPRENEUR

Inntrepreneur Pub Company Ltd, Mill House, Aylesbury Road, Thame, Oxfordshire OX9 3AT.
Tel (01844) 262000 Fax (01844) 262332
Inntrepreneur and Spring Inns had combined estates of around 4,000 pubs in England and Wales. Inntrepreneur was the pub-owning company formed by Courage (Foster's) and Grand Metropolitan as part of a pubs-for-breweries swap in 1991. In the deal, Courage bought up all Grand Met's (Watney's) breweries, with most of Courage's pubs taken over by Inntrepreneur. Inntrepreneur has led the way with the long lease (20 years) as a replacement for the traditional tenancy, a move which saw many valued former Courage tenants leave the trade. In 1995, the company belatedly changed tack and installed a new management team to switch the emphasis from property investment to pub operating. After the sale of 1,410 pubs to a holding company, Spring Inns, in 1996, Inntrepreneur had 2,906 pubs (228 tenanted, 18 managed and the rest on long leases). New supply arrangements, introduced in March 1998, provide access for publicans to a range of cask ales from the leading brands of national suppliers as well as regional brands (Charles Wells, Marston's, Greene King, Wolverhampton and Dudley, Young's and others).
The pubs will still be tied to products approved by Inntrepreneur, although the company is looking to broaden its portfolio

of beers. Existing publicans will retain their guest beer rights, but it was thought that new publicans signing leases after this date will have no guest beer entitlement.
In October 1997 Inntrepreneur was bought by Nomura (See Grand Pub Company).

MAYFAIR TAVERNS
Mayfair Taverns Ltd, The Old Malt House, St John's Road, Banbury, Oxfordshire OX16 8HX
Tel (01295) 275012 Fax (01295) 278677
Company established with a management buyout from Ascot Estates and the purchase of 251 Ascot pubs in April 1996 (Ascot's remaining pubs are being gradually disposed of as the company winds down). The pubs are spread throughout most of the UK, as far north as Bradford and Manchester, and are either three-year tenanted or leased out on 20-year contracts. Beers are supplied entirely by Scottish Courage and Carlsberg-Tetley.

MERCURY TAVERNS
Mercury Taverns PLC, Mercury House, Amber Business Village, Amington, Tamworth, Staffordshire B77 4RP
Tel (01827) 310000 Fax (01827) 310530
Company running 160 pubs (31 managed, the rest tenanted), scattered from Cumbria and the North-East to South Wales and into London and the South-East. Brewers Marston's and Wolverhampton & Dudley jointly acquired two-thirds of the company in 1996, supplying their beers to the pubs, but they have since sold their shares inthe company. Part of the group is the Irish-themed Dublin Pub Company. The company was bought by Pubmaster in June 1998 for £35.

MILL HOUSE INNS
Century House, Westcott Venture Park, Westcott, Bucks HP18 0TG
Tel (01296) 652600 Fax (01296) 652626
Consists of 44 managed pubs, nationwide, bought from Phoenix Inns. They are leased 'free of tie'. There is a supply agreement with Bass.

NICE PUB COMPANY
See Tom Cobleigh.

OLD ENGLISH PUB COMPANY
The Old English Pub Company PLC, 3 Reliant House, Oakmere Mews, Oakmere Land, Potters Bar, Hertfordshire EN6 5DT
Tel (01707) 665175 Fax (01707) 664767
Six-year-old company now running 101 coaching inns and 53 pub/restaurants and looking for120 by the turn of the century. All the pubs are managed and are largely centred in Southern England and the Midlands, from East Anglia and the northern home counties across to Gloucestershire. Typically old-fashioned in style, they all have restaurants and about

half offer accommodation. All sell cask ale, the main range coming from Scottish Courage, with guests supplied by the Beer Seller wholesaler. Old English has had a full stock market listing since May 1997 and in November 1997 announced results with every trading figure 100 per cent up on the previous year.

PARAMOUNT
Paramount Plc, Suite H3, Steam Mill Business Centre, Steam Mill Street, Chester CH3 5AN
Tel (01244) 321171 Fax (01244) 317665
Founded in 1987, Paramount has undergone a complete restructuring of the board, sloughing off partners and disposing lease-holds. It now owns outright all 163 pubs under its control (52 are under the 'Real Inns' banner) and the estate is comprised entirely of tenancies. Distribution is centrally controlled, with beers from Burtonwood, Bass, Whitbread and Scottish Courage. One hundred and six pubs take cask ale permanently, and three ale houses with a wide range of beers are also operated. In addition, a pilot scheme is being trialled in 12 houses which take a different independent guest ale each week.

PHOENIX
Phoenix Inns Ltd., Beechwood Place, Thame Business Park, Wenman Road, Thame, Oxfordshire OX9 3XA
Tel (01844) 262200 Fax (01844) 262237
Prevously, the company operated around 1,300 former Inntrepreneur Estates pubs in England and Wales, of which just under 800 were leased out, the rest being tenanted. Since May 1997 the company sold 845 pubs to Grovebase Properties Ltd (see Punch) and has undertaken other disposals on a piece-meal basis; disposal plans will continue on this basis until the company has a core estate. Currently, 224 pubs are on free-of-tie agreement, around 200 are on short-term12-month agreements, and the remainder on 20-year leases. In 1997 Phoenix was bought by Nomura (see Grand Pub Company).

PUB ESTATE COMPANY
The Pub Estate Company Ltd, 3-5 Ashfield Road, Chorley, Lancashire PR7 1LH
Tel (01257) 238800 Fax (01257) 233918
Company established with the purchase of 230 pubs from S&N and now consolidated by taking its sister companies, The Second and Third Pub Estate Companies, under its wing. It currently has 335 pubs (28 managed, the rest tenanted or leased) which are based in the North of England and Scotland. According to their existing contracts, the pubs variously sell beers from Scottish Courage, Carlsberg-Tetley, Bass or Whitbread, but some do have guest beer rights. The company's aim is to convert all pubs to its own three-year lease which would offer no guest beer entitlement and would mean all pubs being served by a favoured supplier, probably Scottish Courage.

PUBMASTER

Pubmaster Ltd, Greenbank, Hartlepool
TS24 7QS
Tel (01429) 266699
Fax (01429) 278457
Company formed in 1991 to take over the
pub estate of Brent Walker (ex-Camerons
and Tolly Cobbold pubs). In 1992, 734
houses were leased from Allied, and other
acquisitions have been made from
Whitbread and Bass.
Pubmaster currently runs about 1,600 pubs
across the country, 1,500 of which are tenanted (three-year contracts). In June 1998 it
bought Mercury Taverns. Other, non-
branded Pubmaster pubs stock beers from
Bass, Carlsberg-Tetley, Whitbread and some
regional independents.

PUNCH TAVERNS

Formed by a team led by Hugh Osmond, of
Pizza Express and Grovebase Properties
fame, and Roger Myers, with the purchase
of the Bass leased estate in April 1998 when
Punch announced plans for a stock market
floation. The chain includes the Punch
Tavern in Fleet Street, where the magazine
was invented in 1841 and which acts as the
company's flagship outlet. Punch now plans
to spend about £40 million upgrading the
pubs it has bought.
It has scrapped the guest beer provision in all
the pubs, replacing it with a supply deal
involving specific nationals and regionals,
but claims tenants are still free to take extra
beers if they want to...

RANDALLS VAUTIER

Randalls Vautier Ltd, PO Box 43, Clare
Street, St Helier, Jersey JE4 8NZ
Tel (01534) 887788
Fax (01534) 888350
Brewery which ceased production in 1992. It
now runs 30 pubs (14 managed, the rest ten-
anted with three-year agreements) on Jersey
which sell beers from Bass, Whitbread,
Scottish Courage and Marston's. Not to be
confused with Randalls of Guernsey (see
Independents).

REGENT INNS

Regent Inns PLC, 10 Ely Place, London
EC1N 6RY
Tel (0171) 405 8855
Fax (0171) 242 3103
Founded in 1980 and now owning 90 man-
aged pubs in London and the Home
Counties, and growing by 25 pubs a year.
Expansion into the Midlands and the North
is taking place. The majority of the pubs are
unbranded and allowed to retain their own
identities and are not tied to any supplier.
Most pubs feature a wide range of national,
local and seasonal cask ales chosen by the
manager.
The company has contracts with Bass,
Scottish Courage and Whitbread, plus half a
dozen regional breweries, but licensees can
also take beer from the Beer Seller wholesaler. Branded pubs include Walkabout Inns
and Jongleurs.

RYAN

Ryan Elizabeth Holdings PLC, Ryan
Precinct, 33 Fore Street, Ipswich, Suffolk IP4
1JL
Tel (01473) 217458 Fax (01473) 258237
This company's 54 pubs in East Anglia
(many bought from national brewers) are
mostly leased to individual operators on 35-
year contracts, although eight are managed.
The pubs are generally free, but some have a
tie to Bass. A subsidiary company, Elizabeth
Hotels, operates indpendent bars/pubs in its
hotels with a local community focus, offering four to five real ales and live entertainment. Main beer supplier is Bass National
Sales, but Adnams, Greene King, Tolly
Cobbold and Nethergate also supply products.

SIRENIA

See Ambishus

SCORPIO INNS

Scorpio Inns Ltd, Commerce House, Abbey
Road, Torquay, Devon TQ2 5PJ
Tel (01803) 296111 Fax (01803) 296202
Pub group formed in 1991 and now running
100 pubs leased from Whitbread (nearly all
tenanted). These stock beers from Whitbread
and Bass and are located in South Wales, the
Bristol and Hereford areas and along the M4
corridor to Swindon.

SFI GROUP

SFI Group, Headley House, Headley Road,
Grayshott, Hindhead, Surrey GU26 6TU
Tel (01428) 602300 Fax (01428) 602301
Established in 1986, the SFI Group – formerly Surrey Free Inns – is now AIM listed
and runs around 40 pubs and café bars in
London and the South of England. The number is set to increase, with further acquisitions planned for the first part of 1998. The
popularity of its Litten Tree pubs and Bar
Med café bars has made this a high-flying
share on the stock market. The focus is on
stylish food in the daytime and an 'entertainment' atmosphere in the evening. Products
are from national brewers, according to
local preferences.
Cask ale is a feature of the Litten Trees, and
there is a guest ale where demand is sufficient. All the pubs are managed and SFI
hopes to have 80 by the end of 1999, all in
Southern England. Not all are branded:
around 20, such as the Ostrich Inn at
Colnbrook, near Heathrow, have kept their
own identity.

SLUG & LETTUCE

The Old Schoolhouse, London Road,
Shenley, Hertfordshire WD7 9DX
Tel (01923) 855837 Fax (01923) 857992
Formerly Grosvenor, this group runs 48 (43
managed, five tenanted) pubs in the South-
East, all under the Slug & Lettuce name.
Everything else has now been sold to
Ambishus.

SYCAMORE INNS
See Inn Business

TRENT TAVERNS
Trent Taverns Ltd, PO Box 1061, Gringley
on the Hill, Doncaster, S. Yorkshire
DN10 4ED
Tel (01777) 817408 Fax (01777) 817247
Company set up by a former S&N
employee. Its 84 tenanted pubs in the
Midlands and the South are mostly leased
from Whitbread, with some freehold acquisitions. They sell beers from the Whitbread
and Scottish Courage lists, including
regional brewers' cask ales sold through
them.

WETHERSPOON
JD Wetherspoon PLC, Wetherspoon House,
Central Park, Reeds Crescent, Watford,
Hertfordshire WD1 1QH
Tel(01923) 477777 Fax (01923) 219810
Expanding independent pub retailers,
founded by Tim Martin, which opened its
first pub in 1979 and went public in 1992. It
currently owns over 230 managed pubs,
with rapid plans for expansion. 'Our aim is
to have 500 pubs by the end of 2001, and we
are well on target,' said Tim Martin in
December 1997. No music is played in any
of the pubs, all offer no-smoking areas and
food is served all day. In October 1997 it
introduced oversized, lined glasses in all its
pubs. Two standard beers from Scottish
Courage are available to managers:
Theakston Best Bitter and Courage
Directors. Each pub also has one regional ale
(from the likes of Fuller's, Banks's, Cains
and Wadworth) and at least two guest ales.
Announcing the company's latest results in
March 1998 (a 37 per cent rise in pre-tax
profits), Tim Martin said that managers of
Wetherspoon pubs would be given more
freedom to chose their guest ales, and less
would be supplied by the chain's principal
supplier, Scottish Courage. There are beer
festivals in spring and January and
Weatherspoons also supported CAMRA's
1998 National Mild Day.

WHARFEDALE TAVERNS
Wharfedale Taverns Ltd, Croft House,
Audby Lane, Wetherby, W. Yorkshire LS22
4DN
Tel: (01937) 580805 Fax (01937) 580806
Company set up in 1993 by former Tetley
employees to lease 90 pubs from that company. The company currently owns 17 pubs,
mainly in Yorkshire. It also runs 40-50 other
houses on varying agreeements from
national brewers and larger pub companies.
Fifty-five houses are managed and seven are
tenanted. It is looking to acquire a further 10
freehold properties during 1998/1999, having bought five pubs from Great Yorkshire
Inns in late 1997. It is developing its
'Wharfedale Traditional Taverns' concept:
four houses are under this banner and all
future acquisitions will fit into this brand.

The main beers come from Carlsberg-Tetley
and John Smith's; guest beers are from
Carlsberg-Tetley's 'Tapster's Choice'.

WHITE ROSE INNS
White Rose Inns PLC, Chantrell House,
1 Chantrell Court, The Calls, Leeds,
W. Yorkshire LS2 7HA
Tel (0113) 246 1332 Fax (0113) 246 1350
Group with 30 tenancies and six managed
houses in Yorkshire. The main supplier is
Carlsberg-Tetley.

WILLIAMS
James Williams (Narberth), 7 Spring
Gardens, Narberth, Pembrokeshire SA67 7BP
Tel (01834) 860318 Fax (01834) 862202
Privately-owned concern, founded in 1830
and operating 55 pubs in South-West Wales
(53 tenanted, 2 managed). Tenants have
been chiefly supplied by Brains Crown
Buckley, Tomos Watkin, Bass, Carlsberg-
Tetley and Whitbread. Worthington Bitter; a
house ale, James Williams IPA, brewed by
Brains Crown Buckley, is also available.
Over the last year regional brands have also
been taken, including beers from Adnams,
Banks, Bateman, Jennings, Felinfoel and
Shepherd Neame amongst others. The company has a regular, extensive guest, cask-
conditioned beer policy.

WIZARD INNS
City Gate, 17 Victoria Street, St Albans AL1
3JJ
Tel (01727) 792200 Fax (01727) 792210
Former CAMRA national chairman Chris
Hutt, former boss of Midsummer Inns and
Unicorn Inns, purchased 30-40 former
Phoenix Inns pubs to set up this new company. Nomura, the Japanese bank which
owns Grand Pub Company, has a £9.5 million stake. Wizard Inns will operate traditional, unbranded pubs. The plan involved
buying out sitting lessees and running the
pubs under managers.

YATES'S
Yates's Wine Lodges Ltd, Peter Yates House,
Manchester Road, Bolton, Greater
Manchester BL3 2PY
Tel (01204) 373737 Fax (01204) 388383
Company founded in Oldham in 1884 by
wine merchant Peter Yates. It now runs 70
managed pubs, in locations from Scotland to
London, and is planning to open a further
25 by mid-1999. Most are branded, styled in
Victorian fashion and feature bold, vivid
colours in their decor. Beers are mainly from
Whitbread, Scottish Courage and Bass, with
some regional ales also featured.
Boddingtons Bitter is sold at one price,
'smashing the North-South beer price
divide', says the company. But regional variations remain on all other products sold in
its pubs. CAMRA's view is that price cutting
by national chains which can buy beer at
huge discounts threatens the individuality of
traditional tenancies and free houses.

Other notable pub chains

Operated by, or divisions of, brewing companies or pub groups

All Bar One (Bass)
Artist's Fare (Morland)
Barras & Co. (Scottish Courage)
Bar Central (Grosvenor Inns)
Beefeater (Whitbread)
Bert's Bars (Alloa)
BieRRex (Century Inns)
Big Steak (Allied Domecq)
Bill Bentley's Wine Bars (Young's)
Bootsy Brogan's (Glendola Leisure)
Brewer's Fayre (Whitbread)
Café Rouge (Whitbread)
Calendars (Allied Domecq)
Countryside Hotels (Greene King)
Dave & Busters (Bass)
Dr Brown's (Century Inns)
Dublin Pub Company (Mercury Taverns)
Edwards (Bass)
Exchanges (Taylor Walker)
festival Ale Houses (Carlsberg-Tetley)
Firkin (Allied Domecq)
Fork & Pitcher (Bass)
Forshaw's (Burtonwood)
Harvester (Bass)
Harvey Floorbangers (Regent Inns)
Henry's Café Bars (Greenalls)
Henry's Tables (Greenalls)
High Street Taverns (Grosvenor Inns)
Hobgoblinns (Wychwood)
Hogshead Ale Houses (Whitbread)
Hooden Horse (Inn Business)
Hudsons (Greenalls)
Hungry Horse (Greene King)
It's a Scream (Bass)
JJ Moon's (Wetherspoon)
Jongleurs (Regent Inns)
Jungle Bungle (Greenalls)

King's Fayre (Greene King)
Lacon Inns (Adnams)
Landlord's Table (Mansfield)
Maxwells (Allied Domecq)
Milestone Restaurants and Taverns (Wolverhampton & Dudley)
Millers Kitchen (Greenalls)
Mr Q's (Allied Domecq)
Newt & Cucumber (Morland)
O'Neills (Bass)
Pickled Newt (Greene King)
Pitcher & Piano (Marston's)
Pizza Hut (Whitbread)
PJ Pepper (Whitbread)
Porters Ale Houses (Greenalls)
Quincey's (Greenalls)
Rat & Carrot (Greene King)
Rat & Parrot (Scottish Courage)
Roast Inns (Greenalls)
Scruffy Murphy's (Allied Domecq)
Shamus O'Donnell's (Enterprise Inns)
Spoofers (Regent Inns)
T&J Bernard's (Scottish Courage)
Tap & Spile (Century Inns)
TGI Friday (Whitbread)
Toby Restaurants (Bass)
Tut 'n' Shive (Whitbread)
Vantage Inns (Burtonwood)
Vintage Inns (Bass)
Walkabout Inns (Regent Inns)
Wayside Inns (Whitbread)
Wig & Pen (Morland)
Wirral Taverns (Enterprise Inns)

Note: There are now over 400 companies in the pub groups sector, right down to companies with only two or three pubs.

The beers index

Your quick guide to the real ales of the UK. Over 2,000 beers are highlighted.

Ⓐ
A1 Amber Ale: Rockingham
Abbot Ale: Greene King
ABC Best Bitter: Carlsberg-Tetley
Abinger Hammer: Weltons
The Abroad Cooper: Whitbread
Absolution: Abbeydale
Abu Derby: Shardlow
Advent: Passageway
AJ's Mild Ale: Batham
Albert Ale: Earl Soham
Aldercote Ale: Cotleigh (East-West Ales)
Aldercote Extra: Cotleigh (East-West Ales)
Ale Dancer: Mighty Oak
Ale Fresco: Tisbury
Ale of Atholl: Moulin
Alesman: Worth
Alexander's Downfall: Burntisland
Alex Wilkie: Riverside (Beaumont Wines)
All Seasons Bitter: Hanby
Amadeus: Hart
Amazon: Burton Bridge (Lakeland)
Ambassador: Hart
Ambeardextrous: Beartown
Amber Ale:
 Hull
 Pitfield
Amber Malt Ale: King & Barnes
Anchor Bitter: Church End Andrew's
Cobblestone Stout: Hart
Anklecracker: Black Bull
Anniversary Ale:
 Beechams
 Branscombe Vale
 Coach House
 Hesket Newmarket
 Red Cross
 Wood
Ann's Treat: Jersey
Anorak Ale: Spikes
Ansells Bitter: Carlsberg-Tetley
Answer: King & Barnes (Salopian)
Ansells Mild: Carlsberg-Tetley
Anti-Perpendicular: Riverside (Binns)
Antistress: Old Barn
Anvil 4X Strong: Hydes' Anvil
A over T: Hogs Back
APB: Hogs Back
Aperitif: Kitchen
Aquarius: Bateman
Arbor Light: Whim
Archbishop: North Yorkshire
Archer Stout: Lees
Archibald Beckett: Tisbury
Arctic: Brecknock
Aries: Bateman
Armada Ale: Harveys
Aromas Over Tongham: Hogs Back
Arrol's 80/-: Alloa (Carlsberg-Tetley)
Arrol's 90/-: Alloa (Carlsberg-Tetley)
Arrowhead: Cannon Royall
Artists Ale: Bird in Hand
ASB: Arundel
Ashbourne Ale: Leatherbritches
Asum Ale: Evesham

Asum Gold: Evesham
Atomsplitter: City of Cambridge
Augustinian Ale: Nethergate
Auld Alliance: Fyfe
Auld Lang Syne: Harviestoun
Auld Reekie 80/-: Rose Street (Carlsberg-Tetley)
Auld Reekie 90/-: Rose Street (Carlsberg-Tetley)
Autmnal: Pilgrim
Autumn Ale:
 Tetley (Carlsberg-Tetley)
 Harviestoun
Autum Frenzy: Ushers
Autumn Glory:
 Exe Valley
 McGuinness
Autumn Gold:
 Linfit
 O'Hanlon's
Avalanche: Isle Of Skye
Aviator: Dent (Flying Firkin)
Avon Ale: Shardlow
Ayala's Angel: Hesket Newmarket

Ⓑ
B: Thwaites
Backwoods Bitter: Cropton
Bagman's Bitter: Lloyds (High Peak)
Bah Humbug: Mauldons
Baht Ale: Linfit
Baldric: Woodforde's
Bandsman Strong Ale: Concertina
Banner Bitter: Butterknowle
Bantam Bitter: Phoenix
Barbus Barbus: Butts
Barleycorn: Old Cottage
Barleymead: Elgood's
Barley Mole: Mole's
Barn Ale: Old Luxters
Barn Ale Bitter: Old Luxters
Barn Ale Special: Old Luxters
Barn Owl Bitter: Cotleigh
Barnstablaster: Barum
Barnstormer: Bath, Daleside
Barochan: Houston
Barrack Wood IPA: Mighty Oak
Barristers Best: Yorkshire Grey (Scottish Courage)
Barristers Bitter: Judges
Barron's Dark: Exe Valley
Barron's Hopsit: Exe Valley
Bartholomews: Crewkerne
Bat Out of Hell: B&T
Battleaxe: Rudgate
Battle Brew: Burton Bridge
Baz's Bonce Blower: Parish
BB: Donnington,
BBB: Summerskills
BBC1: Blackburn
BBC2: Blackburn
BBC3: Blackburn
Beachcomber: Teignworthy
Beacon Bitter: Everards
Bear Ale: Tranquair
Bear Ass: Beartown
Beards Best Bitter: Arundel (Beards)
Bearskinful: Beartown

Beast: Exmoor
Beaver Bitter: Belvoir
Beckside Mild: Worth
Bedfordshire Clanger: B&T
Bedrock Bitter: Poole
Beechwood Bitter: Chiltern
Bee's Endeavour: Whitewater
Bee Sting: Brakspear
Belfast Special Bitter: Whitewater
Bellringer: Abbey
Bellringer Mild: Lichfield
Belly Buster: Riverside
Beltane: Cheriton
Belter: Leatherbritches
Belt 'n' Braces: Leatherbritches
Benchmark: Bunces
Bendigo Bitter: Castle Rock
Bengal Tiger: Concertina
Beskins Best Bitter: Carlsberg-Tetley
Berkshire Dark: West Berkshire
Bert Corner Bitter: Saddleworth
Bespoke: Leatherbritches
Best Cellar: Yates
Best Dark Ale:
        Crouch Vale
        Goacher's
Bete Noire: Kelham Island
Beth's Arrival: Hart
Betty Stogs Bitter: Skinner's
BiBi: Hedgehog & Hogshead
Big Fat Santa: Brewery on Sea
Big Foot Extra: Bigfoot
Bigod Stout: Green Dragon
Billy: Brettvale
Billy Westwood's Bitter: Hydes' Anvil
Bingle Jells: Mighty Oak
Birthday Bevvy Porter: Yorkshire Grey
        (Scottish Courage)
Bishopswood Bitter: Swansea
Bishops Farewell: Oakham
The Bishop's Finger: Shepherd Neame
The Bishop's Tipple: Badger (Gibbs
        Mew)
Bishop Trelawney's Revenge: Keltek
Bitter Blow: Steam Packet
Bittern: Reepham
Bittern Bitter: Old Chimneys
Bitter 1036: Camerons
Black: Lugton
Black Adder: Mauldons
Black Adder II: Gribble
Black Baron: Greene King
Black Bat: B&T
Black Bear Stout: Whim
Blackbeck: Strawberry Bank
Black Beauty Stout: Rudgate
Black Bess Porter: Ash Vine
Black Bull: Blanchfield
Black Bull Bitter: Theakston (Scottish
        Courage)
Black Cat: Moorhouse's
Black Christmas: Whim
Black Coombe: Prince of Wales,
        Tigertops
Black Cuillin: Isle of Sky
Blackcurrant Porter: Mash & Air
Black Diamond: Butterknowle
Black Dog Mild: Elgood's
Black Douglas: Broughton
Black Eagle: Pitfield
Black Five: Iris Rose
Black Gold: Tomintoul
Blackguard: Butts
Black Heart Stout: Barnsley
Black Hole: Dark Star

Blackjack: Old Mill
Black Jack Porter: Archers
Black Jack Stout: Castle Rock
Black Knight: Goff's
Black Lager: Harviestoun
Black Magic Stout: Oakhill
Black Magic Mild: Hanby
Black Mass: Abbeydale
Black Midden Stout: Mordue
Black Moss Stout: Riverhead
Blackout: Big Lamp
Black Pig: Highgate
Black Rat Stout: Old Chimneys
Black Rock: Brewery on Sea
Black Shadow Mild: Phoenix
Blacksmith's Ale: Coniston
Black Stallion: Blark Horse
Black Stump: Eastwood
Blackwater Porter: Hogs Back
Black Widow Stout: Dark Horse
Black Wych Stout: Wychwood
Blakeley's Autumn Ale: O'Hanlon's
Blakeley's Best No. 1: O'Hanlon's
Blakeley's Best No. 2: O'Hanlon's
Blencathra Bitter: Hesket Newmarket
Blizzard: Ballards
Blondie:
        Brettvale
        Liverpool
Bloomin' Ale: Thwaites
Blonde Bombshell: Rebellion
Bloody Bosworth Bitter Battle:
        Weltons
Bloody Hell Fire: Barnfield
Blow Job: Steam Packet
Bluebird Bitter: Coniston
Blues: Rother Valley
Blues & Bloater: Scott's
Blunderbus Old Porter: Coach House
Bobs Bitter: Brigg
Boadicea Chariot Ale: Iceni
Bobbie Bitter: Whitbread
Bobbies Bitter: Planets
Boddingtons Bitter: Whitbread
Boddingtons Mild: Whitbread
Bodgers Barley Wine: Chiltern
Bodicote Bitter: Plough Inn
Bodysnatcher: B&T
Bomar Bitter: Northumberland
Bombardier Premium Bitter: Wells
Bomber County: Highwood
Bombshell Bitter: Quay
Bonneville: Pheonix
Bootleg Bitter: Hedgehog & Hogshead
Bootleg Valentines Ale: Coach House
Borve Ale: Borve
Bostin Bitter: Fox & Hounds
Bosun Bitter: Old Laxey Poole
Bosun's Bitter: St Austell
Boxing Hare Spring Ale: Ward's
Boy's Pale Ale: Crown Inn
Bramble Bitter: Green Jack
Bramling Cross: Broughton
Bramling Traditional: City of
        Cambridge
Brand Oak Bitter: Wickwar
Brandy Snapper: Brandy Cask
Branoc: Branscombe Vale
Braveheart: Moulin
Braye Ale: Guernsey
Breacalls: Highgate
Brew 37: Fox & Hounds (Blackbeard
        Trading)
Brew 69: Wye Valley
Brew 97: Mole's

Brewer's Droop:
    Cains
    Marston Moor
Brewers Pride: Marston Moor, Mitchells
Brewery Bitter:
    Cains
    Watkin
Brewhouse: Reepham
Brewster's Bunder: Hogs Back
Brick Kiln Bitter: West Berkshire
Bridge Bitter: Burton Bridge
Bridge Street Bitter: Green Dragon
Bridport Bitter: Palmers
Brigadier Bitter: Hoskins & Oldfield
Bright: Otter
Brighton Bitter: Kemptown
Brighton Rock: Dark Star (Skinner's)
Brindle: Bullmastiff
Britannia Bitter: Batham
Broadside; Adnams
Broadsman Bitter: Woodforde's
Broadsword: Maclay
Broadwood: King & Barnes
Bronte: Goose Eye
Brooker's Bitter and Twisted:
    Harviestoun
Broomstick Bitter: Mauldons
Brothers Best: Old Forge
Brown Ale: Steam Packet
Bruin's Ruin: Beartown
Brydge Bitter: Bank Top
BSA: Hogs Back
BSB: Kent
Buccaneer:
    Burtonwood
    Jollyboat
Buchanan's Best Bitter: Federation
Buchanan's Original: Federation
Buckley's Best Bitter: Brains
Buckley's Dark Mild: Brains
Buckshot: Cannon Royall
Buckswood Dingle: Fromes Hill
Bull: Hambleton (Village Brewer)
Bull Best Bitter: Blanchfield
Bullion: Old Mill
Burcom Bitter: Willy's Brewery
Burcote Bitter: Davenport Arms
Burcote Premium Bitter: Worfield
Burglar Bill: Clark's
Burma Star Ale: Hogs Back
Burning Wicket: Weltons
Burns Auld Sleekit: Coach House
Burntwood Bitter: Mighty Oak
Burton Porter: Burton Bridge
Butser Bitter: Gale's
Butterley Bitter: Riverhead

C

Cairngorm Brew: Aviemore
Cailie: Tomintoul
Cambridge Bittter: Elgood's
Cancer: Bateman
Candyman: Brewery on Sea
Canny Lad: Durham
Canon Bitter: Shoes
Canon's Choice: Watkin
Canticle: Passageway
Capricorn: Bateman
Capstan Ale: Flagship
Captain Kos: Barnfield
Captain Smith's: Titanic
Captain Christmas: Greene King
Cardiff Dark: Bullmastiff
Cardinal: First Inn, Last Out
Cascade: Hanby

Caskade: Oldershaw
Castles Bitter: Northumberland
Catbells Pale Ale: Hesket Newmarket
Cauldron Snout: High Force
Cauld Turkey: Fyfe
Cavalier: Lichfield
Cavern: Stony Rock
Celebration:
    Beechams
    Kitchen,
    Liverpool
    Maypole
Celebrance: Cambrinus
Celebration Ale:
    Bushy's
    Fullers,
    Porter
Celebration Alehouse Bitter: Four
    Rivers
Celestial Steam Gale: Freeminer
Celtic: Durham
Celtic Ale: Flannery's
Celtic Queen: Iceni
Centenary Ale: Marypole
Centurion: Lass O' Gowerie
    (Whitbread)
Chadwick's Fines: Ushers (Matthew Clark
    Freetraders)
Chairman's Premium Ale: Thwaites
Challenger:
    Ash Vine
    Barum
    King & Barnes
    Ledbury
Champflower: Cottage
Chancellor's Revenge: Shardlow
Chandos Gold: Moor
Chaser: Merivales
Chaucer Ale: Green Dragon
CHB:
    Chalk Hill
    Merivales
Chef's Cut: Kitchen
Cherry Bomb: Hanby
Cheshire Cat:
    Coach House (Greenalls)
    Smiles
Chester's Best Mild: Everards
    (Whitbread)
Chester's Strong and Ugly: Drunken
    Duck
Chestnut: Black Horse
Chestnut Ale: Weatherbrook
Chiddingstone Bitter: Larkins
Chiltern Ale: Chiltern
Chiswick Bitter: Fullers
Chocolate Ale: Cains
Choir Porter: Salopian
Christmas Ale:
    Berkeley
    Harveys',
    King & Barnes
    Nethergate,
    O'Hanlon's
    Titanic,
    Tolly Cobbold,
Christmas Cheer: McGuinness Rectory
Christmas Classic: Daleside
Christmas Cracker: Mitchells, Wood
Christmas Goose: Goose Eye
Christmas Noggin: Hoskins & Oldfield
Christmas Reserve: Mauldons
Churchills Pride: Hoskins
Clarkson's Best Bitter: Ledbury
Clarkson's Progress: Ledbury

Classic: Wye Valley
Clayton's Strong Ale: Morton & Clayton (Whitbread)
Cleo's Asp: Hart
Cleric's Cure: Three Tuns
Cliffe Hanger Porter: Dark Star (Skinner's)
Cliffhanger: Bank Top
Cloud Nine: Six Bells
Cluster: Ledbury
Coal Porter: Hull
Coachman's Best Bitter: Coach House
Coast 2 Coast: Grey Horse
Cobbler's Last: Red Lion
Cobbler's Thumb: Red Lion
Cocker Hoop: Jennings
Cockersnoot: Bitter End
Codswallop: Burts
Coiners: Ryburn
College Ale: Morrells
Colliers: Townes
Combine Harvester: Coach House
Comfortably Numb: Triple FFF Brewing
Commi: Kitchen
Conciliation Ale: Butterknowle
Conqueror: Mitchells
Conquest: Tolly Cobbold
Contrabrand: Jollyboat
Cooking: Grainstore
Coopers' WPA: Wickwar
Coopers' Ale: Old Court (Whitbread)
Copperwinkle: Swale
Coppercast: King & Barnes
Cornish Coaster: Sharp's
Cornish Knocker Ale: Skinner's
Cornucopia: King & Barnes
Coronation Ale: Weltons
Countess Ale: Barnfield
Country Best Bitter: McMullen
Country Pride: Home County
Country Stile: Daleside
County: Northumberland
Courage Best Bitter: Scottish Courage
Courage Directors: Scottish Courage
Coxswains Special Bitter: Willy's Brewery
Coyote: Wolf
Cracken: (High Peak) Lloyds
Cracker: Church End
Cracker Ale: Drunken Duck
Cracker Barrel Bitter: Coach House
Crackshot: Daleside
Crafty One: Kent
Crazy Crow: Hardy's & Hansons
Cream: Rooster's
Cream Stout: Steam Packet
Crebers Ale: Tally Ho!
Criffel: Sulwath
Criminale Porter: Hart
Critical Mass: Dark Star
Croak & Stagger: Frog Island
Crofters: First in, Last Out
Cromwell Bitter: Marston Moor
Cromwells' Hat: Springhead
Crooked Furrow: Leith Hill
Crookhorn: Crewkerne
Crop Circle: Hop Back
Cropped Oak: John O'Gaunt
Cross Bitter: Banbury
Crowing Cock: Hardys & Hansons
Crown Bitter: Malton
Crown Imperial Stout: Goacher's
Crown Pale Ale: Brains
Crow's Nest: Flagship
Crusader: Pilgrim

Crustache: Burts
Culloden: Tomintoul
Cumberland Ale: Jennings
Cupwith Light Bitter: Riverhead
Curse of Macha: Iceni
Cuthberts: Church End
Cuthberts Ale: Durham
Cutlass Sharp Bitter: Harviestoun
Cwrw Arbennig Porthmon: Dyffryn Clwyd
Cwrw Cai: Watkin
Cwrw Haf: Watkin
Cwrw Santa: Watkin
Cwrw Tudno: Plassey

D

DA: Mallard
Dafydd Du: Snowdonia
Damson Ale:
    Lakeland
    O'Hanlon's
    Strawberry Bank
Daniels Hammer: Thwaites
Danish Dynamite: Bunces
Dark Horse: Caythorpe
Darking Pride: Weltons
Dark Island: Orkney
Darklin Mild: Pembroke
Dark Mild:
    Bateman
    Blackawton
    Brecknock
    Cains
    Highgate
    Hogs Back
    Jennings
    Mitchell's
    Porter
    Taylor
Dark Oast: Scott's
Dark Rose: Brakspear
Dark Roast Ale: Old Luxters
Dark Ruby Mild: Hughes
Dark Side: Blue Moon
Dark Side Of The Moon: Dark Star
Dark Star: Dark Star
Dark Velvet: Cuckmere Haven
Dark Mild: Blackawton
Dartmoor Best Bitter: St Austell
Dartmoor Gold: Princetown
Dartmoor IPA: Princetown
Dartmoor Pride: Sutton
Dartmoor Royal Stout: Princetown
Davenports Traditional Bitter: Greenalls (Carlsberg-Tetley)
Deacon: Badger (Gibbs Mew)
Death or Glory Ale: Tring
Death Wish: Dark Horse
Deceitful Rose: Tomlinson's
Deep Shaft Stout: Freeminer
Deer Hill Porter: Riverhead
Deidre of the Sorrows: Iceni
De Lacy: Tomlinson's
Delight: Kent
Deliverance: Cambrinus
Demon Eyes: Greene King
Derby Bitter: Loyds
Derwent Deep: Grey Horse
Deuchars IPA: Caledonian
Devil's Kiss: Carlsberg-Tetley
Devil's Water: Hexhamshire
Devon Glory: Exe Valley
Devon Gold: Blackawton
Devonian: Scatter Rock Brewery
Devon Summer: Exe Valley

Dewi Sant Heritage Ale: Coach House
Dick Turpin: Coach House
Dicky Pearce: Berkeley
Diggers Gold: Cheriton
Dimond Lager: Pembroke
Directors: Scottish Courage
Directors Winter Warmer: Scottish
 Courage
Disciples' Brew: Original (Bass)
Dixie's Midnight Runner: Dark Tribe
Dixie's Wheat Beer: Tipsy Toad
Dizzy Blonde: Glentworth
Dob's Best Bitter: Exe Valley
Dobber Strong: Marble
Docker's Hook: Passageway
Dockyards Rivets: Burntisland
Doctor's Orders: Fenland
The Dog's Bollocks: Wychwood
Dogbolter: Firkin (Carlsberg-Tetley)
Dolphin: Poole
Dominance: Cambrinance
Donner and Blitzed: Maypole
Doom Bar Bitter: Sharp's
Doris's 90th Birthday Ale: Hesket,
 Newmarket
Dorothy Goodbody's Autumn Delight:
 Wye Valley
Dorothy Goodbody's Father Christmas
 Ale: Wye Valley
Dorothy Goodbody's Golden
 Summertime Ale: Wye Valley
Doroth Goodbody's Warming
 Wintertime Ale: Wye Valley
Dorothy Goodbody's Wholesome
 Stout: Wye Valley
Dorothy Goodbody's Wonderful
 Springtime Bitter: Wye Valley
Dorset Best: Badger
Do's Brew: (Frog & Parrot) Whitbread
Double Barrel: Poole
Double Chance Bitter: Malton
Double Dagger: Pheonix
Double Diamond Cask: Carlsberg-
 Tetley
Double Dragon: Exmoor
Double Helix: Tomlinson's
Double Maxim: Vaux
Double Six: Ferandes
Double Stout: Hook Norton
Dovedale Bitter: Black Bull
Dovedale Special: Black Bull
Dover Beck: Caythorpe
Dove's Delight: SP Sporting Ales
Dragon: Green Dragon
Dragonfly: King & Barnes (Salopian)
Dragonhead Stout: Orkney
Dragon's Breath: Plassey
Dragon's Downfall: Wyre Piddle (Green `
 Dragon)
Dragon's Revenge: Wyre Piddle (Green
 Dragon)
Dragonslayer: B&T
Dragon Smoke Stout: Beowulf
Drake: Mallard
Drawwel Bitter: Hanby
Dreadnought: Chalk Hill
Dr French's Old Remedy: Weltons
Dr Geoffrey's Original Ale: Restalrig
Dr Hexter's Healer: West Berkshire
Dr Hexter's Wedding: West Berkshire
Dr Johnson's Draught: Dyffryn Clwyd
Drovers: Dyffryn Clwyd
Dry Stout: O' Hanlon's
DT's: Franklin's
Dubbel: Passageway

Duck & Dive: Mallard
Duckling: Mallard
Duke of Northumberland Premium Ale:
 Northumberland
Dynamite: Greyhound (Scottish Courage)

E
'E': Museum (Bass)
Eagle IPA: Wells
Earl Leofric Winter Ale: Marches
Earls Ale: Barnfield
Early Riser: Berkeley
Easter Ale: Wadworth
Easter and Christmas Special: Blue
 Anchor
Easter Special: Weltons
Eastgate Ale: Weetwood
East Point Ale: Scott's
East Street Cream: RCH
Easy Life: Blue Moon
Eatanswill Old XXXX: Mauldons
Eclipse: Man in the Moon
Eco Warrior: Pitfield
Eddystone Light: Sutton
Edgar's Golden Ale: Vale
Edgecutter Bitter: Banbury
Edinburgh Strong Ale: Caledonian
Edwin Taylor's Extra Stout: B&T
Egg Nobbler's Strong Ale: McGuinness
1859 Porter: Harveys
1825 Old Court (Whitbread)
1824 Particular: Ushers
80/-:
 Broughton
 Restalrig
80/- Ale:
 Belhaven
 Caledonian
 MaClay
Eireann Stout: Whitewater
Ellen Wilkinson: Riverside (Beaumont
 Wines)
Ellwood's Best Bitter: Hull
Elsie Mo: Castle Rock
Elton Pale Ale: Rockingham
Emerald Ale:
 B&T
 Woodforde's
Emperor Ale: Four Rivers
Empire Pale Ale: Burton Bridge
Empress of India: Fernandes
English Ale: Riverside (Beaumont
Wines)
English Guineas Stout: Linfit
Enoch's Hammer: Linfit
Ensign Ale: Flagship, Carlsberg-Tetley
 (HP&D)
Entire Stout: Hop Back
EPA: Scott's
Equinox: Everards
Ermine Ale: Oldershaw
ESB: Fuller's
Essex Porter: Crouch Vale
ESX Best: Ridleys
Even Keel: Keltek
Evolution Ale: Darwin
Ewe Brew: Gribble
Ewe Could Be So Lucky: Old Forge
Excalibur: Hart, Pilgrim
Exeter Old Bitter: Exe Valley
Exmas: Exmoor
Experimental Ale: Snowdonia
Explosive Ale: Whitewater
Export Bitter: Bushy's
Express: Easingwood

EXS Bitter: Hoskins & Oldfield
Extra:
> Adnams
> St Peter's
Extra Special Bitter: Duffield

F

The Fab Four: Passageway
Fagin: Itchen Valley
Fair Ale: Traquair
Fallen Angel: Dark Horse
Family Ale: Harveys
Fanfare: Tisbury
Fantasy Ale: Greene King
Fargo: Wells
Farmers Glory: Wadworth
Farners Joy: Verulam
Farm Gold: Parish
Farne Island: Border
Fat God's Best Bitter: Queen's Head
Father Brown: Church End
Father Christmas: Itchen Valley
Father Christmas Ale: Wye Valley
Faygate Dragon: King & Barnes
FBB: Fenland
Feather Plucker Mild: McGuinness
Fellows Bitter: Fellows, Morton & Clayton
> (Whitbread)
Femme Fatale: Tomlinson's
Fen Tiger: Iceni
Festival 9X: Buffy's
Festival Ale:
> Banks's
> Burton Bridge
> Clark's
> Hilden
> Iceni
> Traquair
Festival Mild: Gale's
Festival Stagger: Scott's
Festive: King & Barnes
Festive Toad: Tipsy Toad
Fiddlers Elbow: Wychwood
Figgy's Brew: Skinner's
Fine Light Ale: Goacher's
Fine Pale Ale: Crouch Vale
Fine Soft Day: Iceni
Finest: Fiddlers
Finest Summer Ale: Tring
Fire Bellied Toad: Frog Island
Firebox: RCH
Firecracker:
> Harveys,
> Phoenix
> Rainbow
Firefly Smoked Malt: King & Barnes
> (Salopian)
First Gold:
> Brettvale
> Butterknowle
> Liverpool
First Out: Black Dog
Fitzpatrick's Stout: Concertina
Five Bridge Bitter: Mordue
Five Leaves Left: Oakham
Flanagan's Stout: Maypole
Flasher: Old Cottage
Flashman's Clout Strong Ale:
> Goldfinch
Fleur-de-Lys: Prince of Wales,
> Tigertops
Flintknapper's Mild: Chalk Hill
Florrie's Night-in-Ale: Cannon
Flotsam: Border
Flower Power: Cheriton

Flowers IPA: Whitbread
Flowers Original: Whitbread
Fodder: Cannon
Footslogger: Arundel
Force Eight: Gale's
Forest Gold: Rockingham
Forest XB: High Force
Forever Autumn: Marches
Formidable Ale: Cains
Fortress Ale: Beckett's
44 Special:
> Blackawton
> Hogs Back
Fortyniner: Ringwood
Founders Ale: Ushers
4B's: Berrow
Four King Ale: Church End
Four Thumbs: Dyffryn Clwyd
Four Seasons: Mansfield (Beer Seller)
Fox: Exmoor
Fox's Nob: Highgate
Fractale: Fenland
Fractus XB: Tomlinson
Fraoch Heather Ale: Heather
Fraoch Pictish Ale: Heather
Frederics: Robinson's
Fred's Cap: Bank Top
Freshers: Harviestown
Friar Duck: Mallard
Friary Meux Best Bitter: Carlsberg-
> Tetley
Friday 13th: Hogs Back
Friggin in the Riggin: Flagship
Frigging Yuletide: Flagship
Frolicking Farmer: Hardys & Hansons
Frostbite: B&T
Fruit Beer: St Peter's
Fruiterer's Mild: Cannon Royall
Fruits of the Forest: Rockingham
Fuggle-Dee-Dum: Goddards
Fuggled Frog: Frog Island
Fuggles Imperial IPA: Whitbread
Fuggles Nouveau: Hogs Back
Full Ahead: Darktribe
Full Monty:
> Glentworth
> Millwright's Arms
Fusilier Ale: Plassey
Futtock Ale: Flagship
Fyle Ale: Hart
Fyfe: Fyfe

G

Galleon: Dark Tribe
Gamekeeper Bitter: Steam Packet
Gannet Mild: Earl Soham
Gargoyle: Lichfield
Gatecrasher: Kelham Island
GB: Gales
GB Mild: Lees
Gem: Bath
Gemini: Bateman
Generation: Hook Norton
Genesis: Big Foot
Gents-nil Taxation Ale: Cuckmere
> Haven
Genuine Blonde Wheat Beer:
> Passageway
Geordie Pride: Mordue
George's Best: Mauldons
Georges Bitter Ale: Scottish Courage
Get Knotted: Wood
GFB: Hop Back
The Ghillie: Broughton
Ghost Blaster: King & Barnes

Gillespie's Malt Stout: Scottish Courage
Ginger Beer: Linfit
Ginger Minge: Steam Packet
Gingernut Premium: Coach House
Gingersnap Wheat beer: King & Barnes (Salopian)
Ginger Tom: Hopkins & Oldfield
Glastone: McMullen
Glen Ale: Whitewater
Glory: Deeping
GMT: Townes
Gobstopper Bitter: Fox & Hounds
Godfathers: Itchen Valley
Gold:
    Arundel
    Barum
    Bath
    Devon
    Exmoor
    Grainstore
    Iceni
    Marches
    Sutton
    Trueman's
Gold Brew: Bullmastiff
Gold Digger: Bank Top
Golden: Juwards, Spikes
Golden Ale:
    St Peter's
    Wye Valley
Golden Arrow:
    Cottage
    Beer Engine
Golden Best: Taylor
Golden Best Bitter: Scott's
Golden Bine: Ballard's
Golden Bitter:
    Archers
    Ventnor
Golden Brew: Smiles
Golden Brown: Butts
Golden Bud: Townes
Golden Charmer: Thwaites
Golden Eagle:
    Cotleigh
    Kelham Island
Golden Gate: Nethergate
Golden Gate Bitter: Dark Star (Skinner's)
Golden Glory: Firkin (Carlsberg-Tetley)
Golden Grale: Beckett's
Golden Hill Ale: Pembroke
Golden Lance: Keltek
Golden Newt: Elgood's
Golden Otter: Pitfield
Golden Peace: Cuckmere Haven
Golden Pheasant: Old Chimneys
Golden Promise: Calendonian
Golden Sickle: Green jack
Golden Summer Ale: Cains
Golden Thread: Salopian
Goldfield: Hambleton
Goldings: Leatherbritches
Goldings Nouveau: Hogs Back
Goldrush: Cottage
Gold Standard: Freeminer
Gold Star: Goacher's
Golliards Gold: Castle Rock
Goodalls Gold: King & Barnes (Salopian)
Good King Legless: Harviestown
Good King Senseless: Vale
Good Old Boy: West Berkshire
Goodrich Castle: Springhead

Goshawk: Cotleigh
Gothic Ale: Enville
The Governor: Hull
Graduate: Morrells
Graduation: Lass O'Gowrie (Whitbread)
Graft Bitter: West Berkshire
Granary Bitter: Reepham
Grande Pale: Kelham Island
Grand Slam: Tomintoul
Grannies Bitter: Brigg
Granny Flans: Flannery's
Granny Wouldn't Like It: Wolf
Grasshopper: Green Jack
Gravediggers: Church End
Great Cockup Porter: Hesket Newmarket
The Great Crusader: Pilgrim
Great Eastern Ale: Woodforde's
Great Northern: Burton Bridge (Lakeland)
Great Northern Porter: Hilden
Great Raft Bitter: Old Chimneys
Great Western Real Ale: Cottage
Green Grass Old Rogue Ale: Daleside
Greenmantle Ale: Broughton
Grendel's Winter Ale: Beowulf
Greyhound Strong Bitter: Elgood's
Grey Wig: Judges
Griffin: Leyland
Groves Oatmeal Stout: Quay
Gubernacula: Dark Tribe
Gunness Stout: Dark Tribe
Gunpowder: Deeping
Gunpowder Blast: Mouldrons
Gunpowder Strong Mild: Coach House
Guv'nor: Cuckmere Haven
Guy Fawkes: Mitchell's
Guy Fawkes Bitter: B&T
Guy Fawkes Revenge: Weltons
Guzzling Goose: Hardys & Hansons
Gynack Glory: Iris Rose

Ⓗ

Hadda's Autumn Ale: Vale
Hadda's Spring Gold: Vale
Hadda's Summer Glory: Vale
Hadrian Centurion: Four Rivers
Hadrian Emperor Ale: Four Rivers
Hadrian Gladiator: Four Rivers
Hadrian Legion Ale: Four Rivers
Haf: Snowdonia
Hair of the Dog: Hogs Back
Hairy Helmet: Leatherbritches
Hammerhead: Clark's
Hampshire Glory: Gale's
Hancock's HB: Bass
Hancocks IPA: Bass
Hanson's Bitter: Banks's
Hanson's Mild: Banks's
Hardy Country Bitter: Hardy (Elridge Pope)
Hare of the Dog: Wolf
Harrier SPA: Cotleigh
Harrowby Bitter: Oldershaw
Hart: Exmoor
Hartcliffe Bitter: Ross
Hartington Bitter: Whim
Hartington IPA: Whim
Hartleys XB: Robinson's
Hart of Steel: Hart
Hartslock No.1: West Berkshire
Harvest Ale:
    Calsberg-Tetley
    Cotleigh
    Gale's

King & Barnes
Harvest Festival Ale: Yorkshire Grey
(Scottish Courage)
Harvest IPA: Grainstore
Harvest Light: Old Cottage
Harvest Moon: Man in the Moon
Hatters Mild: Robinson's
Haymaker: Hook Norton
Haywain: Merivales
HBC: Marston's
Head: Otter
Headbanger: Archers
Head Brewer's Choice: Marston's
Headcracker: Woodforde's
Head in the Clouds: Frog Island
Headmaster's Xmas Sermon: Mordue
Head Off: Blewitts
Headstrong: Blackawton
Heart of Oak: Cannon Royall
Heartswood Bitter: Mighty Oak
Hearty Ale: Burton Bridge
Heavy Petting: Old Forge
Hedgehog: Poole (Hogshead)
Heller: Royal Inn
Hells Bells: Branscombe Vale
Help Ma Bob: Backdykes
Helter Skelter: Oakham
Hemlock Bitter: Castle Rock
Henry Bramwell Heritage Ale: Vaux
Henry's Bitter: Leyland
Henry's Original IPA: Wadworth
Hercules: Kelham Island
Hereford Pale Ale: Wye Valley
Heritage: Smiles
Hermitage Barley Wine: Worfield
Hermitage Mild: Tomlinson's
Heroes Bitter: Beowulf
Hersbrucker Weizenbier: Springhead
Hewish IPA: RCH
HG's Ale: Planets
Hicks Special Draught: St Austell
HiDuck: Eccleshall
High Flyer: Belvoir
High Force: Butterknowle
High Octane Gold Beach: Hart
Highwayman: Restalrig
Higsons Bitter: Burtonwood
(Whitbread)
Hilden Ale: Hilden
Hill Billy Bitter: Bateman
Hingham High: Blue Moon
HOB Best Mild: Hoskins & Oldfield
HOB Bitter: Hoskins & Oldfield
Hobby Ale: Cotleigh
Hobgoblin: Wychwood
Hobson's Choice: City of Cambridge
Hodge's Original: Darwin
Hogshead Bitter:
Theakston (Scottish Courage)
Uley
Hole-in-Spire: Springhead
Holes Bay Hog: Poole
Holey Moley: Mole's
Hollybeery: Buffy's
Holybush Winter Ale: Salopian
Home Bitter: Mansfield (Scottish
Courage)
Home Mild: Mansfield (Scottish
Courage)
Honey Bunny: Green Jack
Honey Dew: Fuller's
Honey Porter: St Peters
Honey Pot Bitter: Coach House
Hooker Ale: Church End
Hop & Glory: Ash Vine

Hopewell Special: Freeminer
Hop Garden Gold: Hogs back
Hopleaf: Scott's
Hopnosis: Sutton
Hopping Mad: Wood
Hops Nouvelle: Teme Valley
Hopstone Bitter:
Phoenix
Worfield
Hopwood Ale: Weatheroak
Hopwood Bitter: Phoenix
Horny Toad: Tipsy Toad
Horse Power: Titanic
Horsham Ale: King & Barnes
Hows Howler: Featherstone
How's Your Father: Ward's
Hoxton Heavy: Pitfield
HSB: Gale's
Huddersfield Pride: Huddersfield
Humbug: Phoenix
Hundred Ale: Crown Inn
Hunter's Ale: Tally Ho!

Ⅰ

Iceberg: Brecknock
Impaled Ale: Spikes
Imperial: Tetley (Carlsberg-Tetley)
Imperial Russian Stout: Scottish
Courage
Ind Coope Burton Ale: Carlsberg-Tetley
Independence: Inveralmond
Independent IPA: Morland
Indian Summer Pale Ale: Swale
Indiana's Bones: Summerskills
Ingleby Pale Ale: Lloyds
Innkeeper's Special Reserve: Coach
House
Inspiration: Goddards
Inspired: Lichfield
Internettle: Tigertops
Iron Brew: Freeminer
Ironbridge Stout: King & Barnes
(Salopian)
Ironmaster: Crown Inn
Ironside: Hampshire
Island Pale: Orkney
It's a Grand Day: Iceni
Ivory Stout: Man In The Moon

J

Jack Snipe: Woodhampton
Jacob's Ladder: Black Bull
Jail Ale: Princetown
Jak's: Rooster's
James Forshaw's Bitter: Burtonwood
Janet Street Porter: Linfit
Jeffery Hudson Bitter: Oakham
Jenny Pipes Summer Ale: Marches
Jester: Butts
Jetblack: City of Cambridge
Jetsam: Border
Jigsaw: King & Barnes (Salopian)
Jigsaw Black Wheat: Salopian
Jimmy's Bitter: Tipsy Toad
Jimmy Riddle: Millwright's Arms
Jinja: Sutton
JLK Pale Ale: Worfield
Jock Strap: Backdykes
John Baker's Original:
Brandy Cask
Lugton
John Barleycorn: Lugton
John Browne's Ale: Woodforde's
Jolabrugg: Earl Soham
Jollop: Tally Ho!

Jolly Roger: Dark Tribe
Josephine Grimbleby: Wells
Joules Bitter: Museum (Bass)
Jouster: Goff's
Jovian: Phoenix
Joy Bringer: Hanby
JPJ Special: Sulwath
JTS XXX: Lloyds
Judge Jeffries: Itchen Valley
Juliet's revenge: B&T
Jumbo Star Ale: Lees
Junction Bitter: McGuinness

K

Kamikaze: Dent (Flying Firkin)
Kane's Amber Ale: Maclay
Kangaroo Bitter: Ventnor
Kentish Gold: Swale
Kentish Pride: Swale
Kern Knott's Cracking Stout: Hesket Newmarket
Key Amber: Clockwork
Key Red: Clockwork
Killellan: Houston
Killer Bee: Darwin
Kimberly Best Bitter: Hardys & Hansons
Kimberly Best Mild: Hardys & Hansons
Kimberly Classic: Hardys & Hansons
Kim's First Brew: Queen's Head
King: Keltek
King Alfred: Hampshire
King Billy: Cropton
Kingfisher Ale: Woodhampton
King's Champion: Greene King
Kingsdown Ale: Arkell's
Kingstone Bitter: Featherstone
Knickadroppa Glory: Sutton
Knobwilter: Worth
Knockendoch: Sulwath
Knocker Dibb: Hull
Knots of May Light Mild: Harveys
KW Special Pride: Concertina

L

La'al Cockle Warmer: Jennings
Lairds Ale: Tomintoul
Lakeland Gold: Cartmel
Lakeland Reserve: Mitchell's
Lambton's: Vaux
Lamp Oil: Cambrinus
Lancaster Bomber: Mitchell's
Lancing Special Dark: Brewery on Sea
Landlord: Taylor
Landlords Choice: Mole's
Last Drop Bitter: York
Last Rites: Abbeydale
Leadboiler: Linfit
Leaf Thief: Brewery on Sea
Lee's Ruby Ale: North Yorkshire
Legend: Hogs Back
Leith IPA: Restalrig
Lemon Bitter: Salopian
Lemon Weiss: Restalrig
Leo: Bateman
Lempster Ore: Marches
Level Best: Rother Valley
Leveller: Eastwood's, Springhead
Leyland Gold: Leyland
Leyland Happy Go Lucky: Leyland
Lia Fail: Inveralmond
Liberator: Hart
Libra: Bateman
Lifeboat Ale: Titanic

Light Brigade: Cannon
Lighterman: Rother Valley
Light Horse: Caythorpe
Lightmaker: Glentworth
Light Mild: Hyde's Anvil
Light Relief: Rectory
Light Year: Glentworth
Lincolnshire Legend: Highwood
Lionheart: Hampshire
Lionheart Ale: Bateman (Sherwood Forest)
Lion's Pride: Maypole
Liquor Mortis: Blue Moon
Little Matty: Hoskins & Oldfield
LOG 35: Lass O'Gowrie (Whitbread)
LOG 42: Lass O'Gowrie (Whitbread)
London Pride: Fuller's
Longdog: West Berkshire
Longhorn: Titanic
Lord Lee's: North Yorkshire
Lord Protector: Marches
Lords-a-Leaping: Stanway
Lordship Supreme Old Ale:
Lord's Prayer:
    Berkeley
    Yorkshire Grey (Scottish Courage)
Lorimer's Best Scotch: Vaux
Loughbite: West Berkshire
Lovely Jubbely Christmas Ale: Bushy's
Love Potion No.9: Mauldons
Low Gravity Mild: Envile
Lucy B: Holden's
Luddite: Ryburn
Lurcher Strong Ale: Green Jack
Lynesack Porter: Butterknowle

M

MA: Brains
Mad Dog: Bullmastiff
Madhatter: B&T
Mad Judge: Greene King
Mae West: Marypole
Magic Mushroom Mild: Whim
Magik: Keltek
Magistrate's Delight: Judges
Magnet: John Smith's (Scottish Courage)
Magus: Durham
Maiden's Rescue: B&T
Maidtone Porter: Goachers
Mainbrace Bitter: Jollyboat
Main Street Bitter: Pembroke
Malcolm's Ceilidh: Backdykes
Malcolm's Folly: Backdykes
Malcolm's Golden Vale: Backdykes
Malcolm's Premier Ale: Backdykes
Malt & Hops: Wadworth
Maltster's Ale: Teignworthy
Malster's Weiss: O'Hanlon's
Manannan's Cloak: Bushy's
Manchester Festival Beer: Salopian
M&M Brew XI: Bass
M&B Mild: Bass
March Haigh Special Bitter: Riverhead
March Hare: Phoenix
March Madness: Greene King
Mardler's Mild: Woodforde's
Marley's Ghost: Archers
Martha Greene Bitter: Greene King
Mash: Mash & Air
Mash Wheat: Mash & Air
Massacre: Pheonix
Master Brew Bitter: Shepherd Neame
Master Jack's Mild: Tally Ho!
Masterpiece IPA: Museum (Bass)

Matins: Abbeydale
Matthew Brown Lion Bitter: Mansfield (Scottish Courage)
Matthew Brown Lion Mild: Mansfield (Scottish Courage)
Maximum Sentence: Old Court (Whitbread)
May Bee: Mauldons
Mayfair: Maypole
Mayfest: Harviestoun
Mayflower Ale: Cains
Mayfly: PhOEnix
May Gold: Weltons
Mayhem's Odda's Light: Farmers Arms
Mayhem's Sundowner: Farmers Arms
Maypole: Rudgate
Mayson Premier: Hart
McEwan 70/-: Scottish Courage
McEwan 80/-: Scottish Courage
McEwan 90/-: Scottish Courage
McEwan Export: Scottish Courage
Medieval Ale: Hesket Newmarket
Medusa Ale: Leyland
Menacing Dennis: Summerskills
Medip Gold: Oakhill
Medip Ticket: Oakhill
Mercian Shine: Beowulf
Merlin Ale: Cotleigh
Merlin's Ale: Broughton
Merlin's Magic: Moor
Merlin Stout: Watkin
Merman XXX: Caledonian
Merrie Hart Stout: Hart
Merrie Maker: Marston Moor
Merrie Miller's Winter Wobbler: Queen's Head
Merry Crimble: Hull
Mickey Finn: Hull
Midas: Leyland
Mid Autum Gold: Mauldons
Middle: Blue Anchor
Midhurst Mild: Ballard's
Midnight Blinder: Goldfinch
Midnight Owl: Minerva (Carlsberg-Tetley)
Midsummer Ale: B&T
Midsummer Gold: Mauldons
Midsummer Madness: Phoenix
Midsummer Passion: Weltons
Midwinter Gold: Mauldons
Mlld Mild: Brunswick
Mild Quaker: Church End
Military Mild: Old Chimneys
Milk of Amnesia: Blue Moon
Millennium Gnome: Hull
Millennium Gold: Crouch Vale
Miller's Ale: Bird In Hand
Mincespired: Lichfield
Minsterley Ale: King & Barnes (Salopian)
Mirage: Rudgate
M'lud: Judges
M'Lud: York
Moel Moel: Mole's
Mole Grip: Mole's
Moletrap Bitter: Mauldons
Mompessons Gold: Oakham
Monkey Wrench: Daleside
Monkmans Slaughter: Cropton
Monks: Black Dog
Montrose Ale: Harviestoun
Monmouth Rebellion: Cotleigh
Monmouth's Revenge: Crewkerne
Monumental Bitter: Woodbury
Moondance:

Four Rivers
Triple FFF
Moonlight Mouse: Vaux
Moonraker: Lees
Moonshine: Abbeydale
More: Saddleworth
Morning Glory: Thwaites
Morocco Ale:
Daleside
Whitewater
Mother-in-laws Tongue: Woodforde's
Mother's Daze: Brewery on Sea
Mother's Ruin: Mauldons
Mountain Ale: Whitewater
Mr McTavish: Mauldons
Mulley's Irish Stout: Duffield
Mulligan's Stout: Big Lamp
Munro's Mickey Farm: Quality Cask Ales (Ash Vine)
Murrays Summer Ale: Caledonian
Mutiny: Rebellion
Mutton Clog: Grey Horse
Myrica Ale: O'Hanlon's
Myrtle's Temper: Eastwood's

Ⓝ

Nadderjack Ale: Tisbury
Nailer's Oh Be Joyful: Red Cross
Naomh Pádraig's Porter: Tipsy Toad
Nathaniel's Special: Fox & Hounds
Natterjack: Frog Island
Natterjack Premium Ale: Old Chimneys
Navigator:
Dark Tribe
Scottish Courage
Neary's Extra Stout: Worth
Nector: Rooster's
Ned's Tipple: Strawberry Bank
Nektar: Keltek
Nell Gwyn: Blackawton
Nellie Dene: Old Mill
Nelson's Blood: Flagship
Nelson's Cannon: Welton
Nelson's Revenge: Woodforde's
Nemesis: Hart
Nessie's Monster Mash: Tomintoul
Nettlethrasher: Eastwood's
New Brewery Bitter: Shardlow
Newcastle Exhibition: Scottish Courage
Newport Nobbler: Burts
New Seasons Ale: Jennings
Newton 'N' Abbot: Scatter Rock Brewery
Newton's Drop: Oldershaw
Nicholson's Best Bitter: Carlsberg-Tetley
Nightjar: Daleside
Nightmare: Hambleton
1926: Riverside (Beaumont Wines)
1984: Riverside (Beaumont Wines)
Ninjabeer: Summerskills
Nipper Bitter: Burts
No Balls: Hart
Noble Bitter: Beowulf
Noidea: Flannery's
Noel Ale: Arkell's
Noggins Nog: Border
Norfolk Nips: Woodforde's
Norfolk Nog: Woodforde's
Norfolk Stout: Woodforde's
Norfolk Wheaten: Reepham
Norfolk Wolf Porter: Green Jack
Norman's Conquest:
Cottage

Hampshire
Hardy
North Brink Porter: Elgood's
Northdown Bitter: Trueman's
Northdown Winter: Ledbury
Northern Light: Orkney
Northern Lights: Glentworth
Northern Pride: Hull
Norton Ale: Shoes
Notely Ale: Vale
No. 1: Selby
No. 1 Barley Wine: Museum (Bass)
No. 3: Selby
No. 6 Mild: Museum (Bass)
No. 9: Plough Inn
Nutcracker Bitter: Hanby
Nutcracker Mild: Cotleigh
Nutcracker Winter Ale: Everards
Nutters Ale: Tally Ho!
Nyewood Gold: Ballard's

©

'O4' Ale: Hoskins & Oldfield
Oak Best Bitter: Phoenix
Oakwell: Barnsley
Oasthouse Gold: Weetwood
Oatmeal Stout:
    King & Barnes
    Flannery's
OBB: Samuel Smith
OBJ: Brakspear
OB Mild: Whitbread
Odda's Light: Farmers Arms
Offilers Bitter: Musuem (Bass)
Offilers Mild: Museum (Bass)
Off the Rails: Pembroke
Off Your Trolley: Hart
Old: Berkeley
Old Accidental: Brunswick
Old Ale:
    Goachers
    Highgate
    Harveys,
    King & Barnes
Old Bailey: Mansfield
Old Basford Pale Ale: Fiddlers
Old Bat: B&T
Old Black Bob: Leyland
Old Black Shuck: Elgood's
Old Boy: Oldershaw
Old Bram: Woodforde's
Old Brewery Bitter: Samuel Smith
Old Bridge Bitter: Fernandes
Old Bushy Tail: Bushy's
Old Buzzard: Cotleigh
Old Carrock Strong Ale: Hesket
    Newmarket
Old Chopper: Scottish Courage
Old Cock up Mild: Leyland
Old Cocky: Weltons
Old Codger: Rebellion
Old Conspirator: Arundel
Old Curiosity: Old Mill
Old Dalby: Belvoir
Old Dark Attic: Concertina
Old Devil: Wychwood
Old Dick: Swale
Old Dog Bitter: Weetwood
Old Dray Bitter: Worldham
Old Dreadnought: Clark's
Old Duck: King & Barnes
Old Duke: York Tavern
Old Ebenezer: Butterknowle
Old Eli: Linfit
Old Elias Strong Pale Ale: Travellers

Inn
Olde Merrie: Cannon Royall
Old Friend: Berkeley
Old Emrys: Nag's Head
Old English Porter: Plough Inn
Olde Skipper: Okells
Olde Stoker: Branscombe Vale
Old Expensive: Burton Bridge
Old Faithful: Mitchell's
Old Familar: Dark Star (Skinner's)
Old Fashioned Porter: Fiddlers
Old Flame:
    Brewery on Sea
    Glentworth
Old Fossil: Stony Rock
Old Freddy Walker: Moor
Old Gang Bitter: Swaled Ale
Old Gavel Bender: Judges
Old Grizzly: Old Bear
Old Growler: Nethergate
Old Groyne: Willy's
Old Grumpy: Kemptown
Oldham Bitter: Burtonwood
    (Whitbread)
Old Hand: B&T (Oliver Hare)
Old Harry: Weltons
Old Herbaceous: Rockingham
Old Henry: Hobsons
Old Homewrecker: Maypole
Old Hooky: Hook Norton
Old Horny: Greene King
Old House Bitter: Woodbury
Old Humbug: Hexhamshire
Old Icknield Ale: Tring
Old Izaak: Whim
Old Jersey Ale: Jersey
Old Jock: Broughton
Old Kiln: Border
Old Knee Jerker: Red Cross
Old Knotty: Coach House (Joule)
Old Knuckler: Arundel
Old Legover: Daleside
Old Lubrication: Daleside
Old Man Ale: Coniston
Old Manor: Harviestown
Old Merryford Ale: Wickwar
Old Millennium: Hull
Old Mulled Ale: Tisbury
Old Navigation Ale: Hoskins & Oldfield
Old Nigel: Hoskins
Old Nobbie Stout: Pembroke
Old Nosey: Cannon
Old Oak Ale: Pheonix
Old Original: Everards
Old Pal: Church End
Old Peculier: Theakston (Scottish
    Courage)
Old Pedantic: Sutton
Old Porter: King & Barnes
Old Priory: Coach House (Joule)
Old Raby: Hambleton (Village Brewer)
Old Ram: Hart
Old Recumbent: Six Bells
Old Remedial: Moulin
Old Ric: Uley
Old Rooster: Woodhampton
Old Rott: Quay
Old Rugby: Carlsberg-Tetley
Old Scrooge:
    Arundel
    Three Tuns
Old Sea Dog Stout: Flagship
Old Shunter:
    Baynards
    Bushy's

Old Slug Porter: RCH
Old Smokey: Brunces
Old Speckled Hen: Morland
Old Speckled Parrot: Bird in Hand
Old Spot Prize Ale: Uley
Old Stockport Bitter: Robinson's
Old Strong Winter Ale: Tolly Cobbold
Old Tackle: Chalk Hill
Old Thumper: Ringwood
Old Thunderbox: Green Jack
Old Timer: Wadworth
Old Tom:
    Oakwell
    Robinson's
    Selby
Old Tongham Tasty: Hogs Back
Old Toss: Worth
Old Tosspot: Oakham
Old Town: Beckett's
Old Traditional: Home County
Old Tyler: West Berkshire
Old Vic: Banbury
Old Wardour: Tisbury
Old Wemian Ale: Hanby
Old Winter Ale: Fuller's
Old 'XL' Ale: Holden's
One-eyed Jack: Concertina
Opium: Coniston
Original:
    Barum
    Beckett's
    Devon
Original AK: McMullen
Original Best Bitter: Tolly Cobbold
Original Bitter:
    Morland
    Willy's Brewery Co.
Original 80/-: Harviestoun
Original Porter:
    Mauldon
    Shepherd Neame
The Original Wood: Swansea
OSB: Watkin
Osprey: Cotleigh
Ossian: Inveralmond
Ostlers Summer Pale Ale: Coach House
The Other T'Other: Teme Valley
OTT: Hogs Back
Otter Claus: Otter
Our Ken: Cottage
Overdraft: Rebellion
Overture: Fromes Hill
Oving Bitter: Gribble Inn
Owd Ale: Moorhouse's
Owd Bob: Malton
Owd Duck: Mallard
Owd Merry: Belvoir
Owd Rodger: Marstons
Owd Shrovetide: Black Bull
Own: Sharp's
Oxford Bitter: Morrells
Oxford Mild: Morrells
Oyster Stout: Marston's

Ⓟ

P2 Imperial Stout: Museum (Bass)
Pagan: Durham
Pageant Ale: Elgood's
Pale Amber: Hughes
Pale Rider: Kelham Island
Paradise Bitter: Bird in Hand
Parish Bitter: Wood
Parkhurst Porter: Burts
Parson's Porter: Rectory

Parsons Progress: Salopian
Passion Ale: Weltons
Patently Oblivious: (Yorkshire Grey)
    Scottish Courage
Patios Ale: Randalls
Pavilion Beast: Dark Star (Skinner's)
Peach: Marsh & Air
Peacock's Glory: Belvoir
Peak Pale: (High Peak) Lloyds
Peddlars Pride: Hardys & Hansons
Peat Porter: Moor
Pedigree: Marston's
Pedwar Bawd: Dyffryn Clwyd
Pendle Witches Brew: Moorhouse's
Pendragon: Hampshire
Penguin Porter: Ash Vine
Penguin Stout: Dark Star (Skinner's)
Percy's Downfall: Truemans
Peregrine Porter: Cotleigh
Periwig OPA: Oakham
Peter's Porter: Arkell's
Peter Yates Bitter: Ushers (Yates Wine
    Lodge)
Peter Yates 1884: Moorhouse's (Yates
    Brothers)
Pett Genius: Old Forge
Pett Progress: Old Forge
Pews Porter: Church End
PG Steam: RGH
Pheasant Plucker: Old Cottage
Phoenix XXX: Woodforde's
Picks Bedlam Bitter: Red Lion Hotel
Picks Morrgate Mild: Red Lion Hotel
Pickwick's Porter: Malton
Piddlebrook: Rainbow
Piddle in the Hole: Wyre Piddle
Piddle in the Snow: Wyre Piddle
Piddle in the Sun: Wyre Piddle
Piddle in the Wind: Wyre Piddle
Pigor Mortis: Uley
Pig's Ear:
    Gribble
    Hesket Newmarket
Pig's Ear Strong Beer: Uley
Pigswill: Bunces
Pilots Pride: Carlsberg-Tetley
    (Minerva)
Pinta Bitter: Hogs Back
Pisces: Bateman
Piston Bitter: Beer Engine
Piston Brew: Bushy's
Pitchfork: RCH
Plum Duff: Kitchen
Plunder: Jollyboat
Plus January Sale: Ushers
Plymouth Porter: Sutton
Poachers Ale: Parish
Poacher's Swag: Steam Packet
Polar Eclipse: Beartown
Poleaxed: Maypole
Polecat Porter: Old Chimneys
Polly's Extra Folly: Buffy's
Polly's Folly: Buffy's
Pommie's Revenge: Goose Eye
Pooh Bear: Church End
Pope's Traditional: (Eldridge Pope)
    Hardy
Porters Sidewinder: (Martin Elms Wines)
    Nethergate
Porters Suffolk Bitter: Martin Elms Wines
(Nethergate)
Posthorn Premium Ale: Coach House
Potage: Kitchen
Pot Black: Tigertops
Pot O'Gold: Glentworth

Pots Ale: Cheriton
Pot the Red Ale: Red Shed
Premier Bitter: Moorhouse's
Premium:
    Big Lamp
    Blue Cow
    Juwards
    St Giles in the Wood
    Titanic
    Yates
Premium Bitter: Hanby
Pride:
    Cannon
    Cartmel
    Devon
Pride of Romsey: Hampshire
Prince Bishop Ale: Big Lamp
Priors Ale: North Yorkshire
Priory Ale: Marches
Priory Mild: Nethergate
Priscilla: Swaled Ale
Prize old Ale: Gales
Progress: Pilgrim
Proud Salopian: Salopian
PSB: Parish
Ptarmigan 85/-: Harviestoun
Publican Bitter: Riverside
Pudding: Pilgrim
Pullman Porter: Easingwold
Puritans Porter: Springhead
Puzzle: Salopian
Puzzle White Wheat: King & Barnes
    (Salopian)
Pwlldu XXXX: Swansea

Ⓠ
QC Best Bitter: Scottish Courage
    (Yorkshire Grey)
Quaffing Ale: Bass (Museum)
Quarrel: Cranbourne
Queen Maev Stout: Iceni
Quismas Quacker: Mallard
Quiver: Cranborne

Ⓡ
Rachels Relish: (Binns) Riverside
Radgie Gadgie: Mordue
Raeburn's Edinburgh Ale: Scottish
    Courage
Raging Bull: Black Bull
Rail Ale: Beer Engine
Railway Porter: Brunswick
Rainbow Chaser: Hanby
Rain Dance: Brewery on Sea
Ram Rod: Young's
Ramsbottom Strong Ale: Dent
Rams Revenge: Clark's
Ram Tam: Taylor
Rapier Pale Ale: Reepham
Raven Ale: Orkney
Ravens Head Stout: Woodhampton
Rawhide: Leyland
Rayments Special: Greene King
Real MacKay: Far North
Real Mild Ale: Goacher's
Real Nut Ale: Tisbury
Reapers Reward: Brakspear
Recession Ale: Brunswick
Reckless: (Frog & Parrot) Whitbread
Reckless Raspberry: Hoskins &
    Oldfield
Rector's Pleasure: Rectory
Rector's Revenge: Rectory
Red: Deeping, Liverpool
Red Ale: O'Hanlon's

Redbrook Premium Bitter: Riverhead
Red Alert: Red Shed
Red Cap: Titanic
Red Cullin: Isle of Skye
Red Devil:
    Red Shed (Binns)
    Riverside
Redemption: Passageway
Red Fox:
    Cains
    Fullers
Red Light: Red Shed
The Red MacGregor: Orkney
Red Murdoch: Aviemore
Red Nose Reindeer: Cotleigh
Red Oktober: Rebillion
Red Pyke: Old Cottage
Red Roses: Itchen Valley
Red Rudolph: Kelham Island
Reeket Yill: Broughton
Reel Ale: Teignworthy
Regal Birthday Ale: Coach House
Regatta: Adnams
Regatta Gold: Brakspear
Reg's Tipple: Gribble
Reinbeer: Elgood's
Renaissance: Cambrinus
Reserve: Eastwood's
Resolution Breaker: Greene King
Rest In Peace: Church End
Resurrection: Phoenix
Restorance: Cambrinus
Resurrection Ale: Lichfield
Return Ticket: Beer Engine
Reverend Eaton's Ale: Shardlow
Reverend James Original Ale: Brains
Reynold's Redneck: Worfield
Rhatas: Black Dog
Richard's Defeat: Tomlinson's
Richmond Ale: Darwin
Ridgeway Bitter: Tring
Riding Bitter: Mansfield
Riding Mild: Mansfield
Riggwelter: Black Sheep
Right Royal: Royal Inn
Ringo: Rooster's
RIP: Church End
Ripper: Green Jack
Rip Snorter: Hogs Back
Riptide: Brewery on Sea
Road to Rome: Hart
Roaring Meg: Springhead
Roasted Nuts: Rebellion
Roast Mild: Dark Star (Skinner's)
Robert's Summer Special: Three Tuns
Robert's Winter Special: Three Tuns
Robin a Tiptoe: O'Guant
Rocket: Liverpool
Rocketeer: Scottish Courage
Rocking Rudolph: Hardy & Hansons
Roger & Out: (Frog & Parrot) Whitbread
Roisin Dubh: Iceni
Romeo's Rouser: Arundel
Romeo's Ruin: B&T
Rooster's: Rooster's
Rope of Sand: Fyfe
Roseburn Bitter: Iris Rose
Rossendale Ale: Porter
Roundhead's Gold: Springhead
Rowan Ale: Four Rivers
Royal Oak: (Eldridge Pope) Hardy
Royal Piddle: (Severn Valley Railway)
    Wyre Piddle
Royal Welch Fusilier: Plassey
Roy Morgan's Original Ale: Travellers

Inn
Ruby Ale: Fiddlers
Ruddles Best Bitter: Morland
Ruddy Rudolph: Plassey
Rudolf's Ruin: Border, Rudgate
Rudolph: Brunces
Rudolph's Rocket Fuel: Fenland
Ruff Yed: Lees
Rulbuts: Strawberry Bank
Rumpus: Ridleys
Rupert Tetlow Tummy Tickler:
    Federation
Rusty Dudley: Church End
Ruthven Brew: Aviemore
Rydale Bitter: Ryburn
Rye Beer: King & Barnes

Ⓢ
SA Best Bitter: Brains
Saddleback: Titanic
Saddlers Best Bitter: Highgate
Sagittarius: Bateman
St Andrew's Ale: Belhaven
St Arnold: Passageway
St Elmo's Fire: Dark Horse
St George: Deeping
St George and the Dragon: Ushers
St George's Best: Tobby Cobbold
St George's Cross: Phoenix
St George's Heritage Ale: Coach House
St George's Special: Weltons
St Nicholas's Christmas Ale: Vaux
St Nicks: Okells
St Patrick's Leprechaun Ale: Coach
    House
Saint's Ale: Tomintoul
Saints Sinner: Darwin
St Teilo's Tipple: Swansea
Salem Porter: Bateman
Salisbury Best Bitter: (Gibbs Mew)
    Ushers
Salsa: Castle Rock
Sam Powell Best Bitter: Wood
Sam Powell Old Sam: Wood
Sam Powell Original Bitter: Wood
Samson: Vaux
Sam's Porter: Carlsberg-Tetley
Sam's Stout: Carlsberg-Tetley
Samuel Crompton's Ale: Bank Top
Sanctuary: Durham
Sandy Hunter's Traditional Ale:
    Belhaven
Sanity Claus: Rockingham
Santa Moors: Moor
Santa's Claws: Bank Top
Santa Slayer: B&T
Santa's Nightmare: Evesham
Santa's Quaff: Scott's
Santa's Secret: Northumberland
Santa's Sledgehammer: Tomintoul
Santa's Spice: Rainbow
Santa's Steaming Ale: Cottage
Santa's Toss: Worth
Santa's Wobble: Hogs Back
Saracen: Pilgrim
Satanic Mills: Bank Top
Saturnalia: Wood
Saxon Ale: Ross
Saxon Beserker: Cuckmere Haven
Saxon King Stout: Cuckmere Haven
SBA: Donnington
SBB: Brains
Scatter Brain: Scatter Rock Brewery
Scatty Bitter: Scatter Rock Brewery
Schiehallion: Harviestown

Scorcher:
    Lees
    Rooster's
Scoresby Stout: Cropton
Scorpio: Hanby
Scotch: Mash & Air
Scottish Ale: (Beaumont Wines)
    Riverside
Scottish Bard: Tomintoul
Scottish Oatmeal Stout: Broughton
Scratching Dog: Lloyds
Scrooge: Rebellion
Scrum Down Mild: Leatherbritches
Sea Fever Ale: Carlsberg-Tetley
    (Minerva)
Sea of Tranquility: Blue Moon
Seasonal Ale: Cranbourne
Seasonal Wood Smoked Porter:
    Passageway
Second Brew: Brunswick
Second to None: Brunces
Secret Kingdom: Northumberland
Sedgley Surprise: Hughes
Session: Deeping
Session Bitter: Snowdonia
Sessions: Tomlinson's
1707: Aldchlappie
Severn Boar: Uley
Sexton: Three Tuns
Shaft Bender: Saddleworth
Shakemantle Ginger Ale: Freeminer
Shamrock: Phoenix
Sheepdog: Old Barn
Shefford Bitter: B&T
Shefford Dark Mild: B&T
Shefford Old Dark: B&T
Shefford Old Strong: B&T
Shefford Pale Ale: B&T
Shefford Wheat Beer: B&T
Shell Shock: Brewery on Sea
Shepherds Delight:
    Blackawton
    Highwood
Sheppard's Crook: Exe Valley
Sheriff's Ride: Lichfield
Shipstone's Bitter: Carlsberg-Tetley
    (Greenalls)
Shipstone's Mild: Carlsberg-Tetley
    (Greenalls)
Shire: Black Horse
Shire Bitter: Hexhamshire
Shires XXX: Wychwood
Shoreditch Stout: Pitfield
Shot Firers Porter: Concertina
Show Ale: Hesket Newmarket
Shrimpers: Daleside (AVS)
Shropshire Lad: Wood
Shropshire Stout: Hanby
Shustoke Surpryes: Church End
Signal Failure: Pembroke
Sign of Spring: Bunces
Silent Knight: Quay
Silent Night: Church End
Simpkiss Bitter: Enville
Single Hop Ale: King & Barnes
Single Malt Ale: Carlsberg-Tetley
Sir Roger's Porter: Earl Soham
Six '5' Special: Ash Vine (Quality Cask
    Ales)
70/-:
    Belhaven
    Caledonian
    Maclay
60/- Ale:
    Belhaven

Maclay
6X: Wadworth
Skeleton Special: B&T
Skiddaw Special Bitter: Hesket
	Newmarket
Skiff: West Berkshire
Skilliwidden Ale: Skinners
Skinners Old Strong:
	Bitter End
	Orkney
Skullsplitter: Orkney
Slaters Bitter: Eccleshall
Slaters Original: Eccleshall
Slaters Premium: Eccleshall
Slaters Supreme: Eccleshall
Slaughter Porter: Freeminer
Slayers: King & Barnes
Sleeper Heavy: Beer Engine
Sleigh'd: Sutton
Sleighed: Porter
Smokehouse: Hull
Smoke House Ale: Linfit
Smokestack Lightnin': Bank Top
Smokestack Lightning: Fenland
Smuggler: Rebellion
Snapdragon: King & Barnes (Salopian)
Sneck Lifter: Jennings
Snow: Deeping
Snow Belly: Brewery on Sea
Snow White: Whim
Snowy Ale: Cotleigh
SOB: Border
Solicitor's Ruin: Judges
Solstice Pale Ale: Whitewater
Something Very Different: Iceni
Somerby Premium: Parish
Somerset & Dorset Ale: Cottage
Son of a Bitch: Bullmastiff
Sorcerer: Green King
Sound Whistle: Pembroke
Southdown Harvest Ale: Harveys
Souther Bitter: Cottage
Southpaw: Bullmastiff
Southsea Bitter: Spikes
SPA: Ross
Spanker: Flagship
Sparkling Wit: Fenland
Sparth Mild: Riverhead
Special Ale:
	Sharp's
	Whim
Special Bitter: Wood
Special Crew: Brewery on Sea
Special Edition: Barum
Special London Ale: Young's
Special Reserve: Hilden
Special Reserve Bitter: McGuinness
Spectacular: Ridleys
Speculation Ale: Freeminer
Spellbound: Goose Eye
Spike: Rebellion (Scanlon's)
Spinnaker Bitter: Brewery on Sea
Spinnaker Buzz: Brewery on Sea
Spinnaker Classic: Brewery on Sea
Spinnaker Dragon: Brewery on Sea
Spinnaker Ginger: Brewery on Sea
Spinnaker Golden Lite: Brewery on Sea
Spinnaker Jester: Brewery on Sea
Spinnaker Mild: Brewery on Sea
Spinnaker Shamrock: Brewery on Sea
Spinnaker Valentine: Brewery on Sea
Spireite: Townes
Spirit Level: Rother Valley
Spiritual Reunion: (Orange) Scottish
	Courage

Spitfire: Shepherd Neame
Spitfire Premium Ale: Shepherd Neame
Spooky Brew: Phoenix
Spooner: Mitchell's
Spriggan Ale: Skinner's
Spring Ale: Burton Bridge, Bridge of
	Allan
Spring Beer: Exe Valley
Springbock: Pilgrim
Springbok Bier: Linfit
Spring Fever:
	Bullmastiff
	Harviestoun
	Ushers
Spring Forward: Six Bells
Spring Gold: O'Hanlon's
Spring Pride: Flagship
Spring Ram Ale: Okells
Spring Tide: Teignworthy
Spring Time: Grainstore
Spring Tyne: Mordue
Squires Bitter: Mauldons
Squires Gold Spring Ale: Coach House
Squirrels Hoard: Hart
Stabbers: Ryburn
Staffordshire Knot Brown: Burton
	Bridge
Stag:
	Exmoor
	Tomintoul
Stage Ale: Featherstone
Staggering in the Dark: Kemptown
Stainton Bitter: Middleton's
Stairway to Heaven: Burton Bridge
	(Feelgood Bar & Catering)
Stallion: Hambleton
Stanney Bitter: Stanway
Star Bitter:
	Belvoir
	Stanway
Station House Brew: Baynards
Station Porter: Wickwar
Steamcock Bitter: Easingwold
Steamin' Billy Bitter: Leatherbritches
Steamin' Billy Mild: Leatherbritches
Steel Town: Grey Horse
Steeplechase: Lichfield
Steeplejack: Lichfield
Stickey Wicket: Phoenix
Stig Swig: Bunces
Stinger: Spikes
Stirling Brig: Bridge of Allan
Stocks Old Horizontal: (Century Inns)
	Hull
Stones Bitter: Bass
Stonewall: York
Streatham Strong: (Greyhound) Scottish
Courage
Storm Export: Worth
Stout Coffin: Church End
Strip and At It: Freeminer
Strong: St Peter's
Strong Ale: Buffy's
Strong Anglian Special: Crouch Vale
Strongarm: Camerons
Strongheart: McMullen
Stronghold: Arundel
Strong Mild: Scott's
Strong Ruby Ale: Reepham
Stud: Hambleton
Styrian Gold: Cains
Suffolk Comfort: Mauldons
Suffolk Pride: Mauldons
Summa That: Branscombe Vale
Summer Ale:

Burton Bridge
Bushy's
Cranbourne
Dark Star (Skinner's)
Fiddlers
Fullers
King & Barnes
Guernsey
Harviestoun
Lidstone's
Summer Abroad Cooper: Whitbread
Summer Blotto: Franklin's
Summer Daze:
    Arundel
    Castle Rock
Summer Dream: Green Jack
Summer Eclipse: Old Forge
Summer Gold: O'Hanlons
Summer Golden Ale: Carlsberg-Tetley
Summerhill: Big Lamp
Summer Horne Wheat Beer: Scottish
    Courage (Yorkshire Grey)
Summer Jacks: Goose Eye
Summer Lightning: Hop Back
Summer Madness: Ushers
Summer Moult: Bullmastiff
Summer Sault: Wadworth
Summer Solstice: Wells
Summer Special: Weltons
Summer That: Wood
Summer Tipple: McGuinness
Summer Tyne: Mordue
Sunbeam Bitter: Guernsey
Sundance: Marston (Wetherspoon)
Sunnydaze: Oldershaw
Sunrunner: Dark Horse
Sunshine: Porter, Townes
Sunshine 855: Marches
Superior Stout: Cains
Supreme: Wye Valley
Surrender: Springhead
Surrey Bitter: Pilgrim
Sussex: King & Barnes
Sussex Best Bitter: Harveys
Sussex Pale Ale: Harveys
Sussex XX Mild Ale: Harveys
Sussex XXXX: Harveys
SW1: (Orange) Scottish Courage
SW2: (Orange) Scottish Courage
Swallow: Green Jack
Swallows Return: Cuckmere Haven
Swallowtail IPA: Old Chimneys,
Sweet and Sour: (Binns) Riverside
Swift:
    Cotleigh
    Linfit
Swifty: Kent
Swordmaker: Grey Horse
Syllabub: Kitchen

T
Talisman: Pilgrim
Tall Ships: Borve
Tall Tale Pale Ale: Fenland
Tally Ho!: Adnams
Tallywhacker: Leith Hill
Tamar Ale: Royal Inn
Tamar Best Bitter: Summerskills
Tam O'Shanter: Weltons
Tanglefoot: Badger
Tanners Jack: Morland
Tap Bitter:
    Chalk Hill
    Mole's
Target Practice: Dark Star (Skinner's)

Tarka's Tipple: Tally Ho!
Taurus: Bateman
Tavern Classic: Mansfield (Tavern
    Wholesale)
Taverners Ale: Hanby
Taverners Autumn Ale: Coach House
Tawny Bitter: Cotleigh
TEA: Hogs Back
Teesdale Bitter: High Force
Teign Valley Tipple: Scatter Rock
    Brewery
Templars Tipple: Blue Cow
Tempus Fugit: Caledonian
Tender Mild: Easingwold
Ten Fifty: Grainstore
1066: Hampshire
1066 Country Bitter: White
Terrier: Dark Tribe
Tesco Selected Ales IPA: Marston's
    (Tesco)
Tesco Selected Porter: Marston's
    (Tesco)
THAT: Leyland
That: Teme Valley
Theakston Best Bitter: Scottish
    Courage
Theakston Mild Ale: Scottish Courage
Theakstone Old Peculier: Scottish
    Courage
Theakston XB: Scottish Courage
Thick Black: Devon
Thirlwell Best Bitter: Blue Cow
Thirsty Moon: Phoenix
1314: Aldchlappie
This: Teme Valley
This Bitter: Leyland
Thomas Greenall's Original Bitter:
    Carlsberg-Tetley (Greenalls)
Thomas Hardy's Ale: (Eldridge Pope)
    Hardy
Thomas Sykes Ale: Burton Bridge
    (Thomas Sykes)
Thorne Best Bitter: Ward's
Thoroughbred: Bullmastiff, Cartmel
3B: Arkells
Three Bears Ale: Restalrig
Three Cliffs Gold: Swansea
Three Goslings: Plough Inn
Three Hundreds Old Ale: Chiltern
Three Kings Christmas Ale: Coach
    House
Three Seiges: Tomlinson's
Thunder and Lightning: Queen's Head
Thunderstorm: Hop Back
Thurgia: Tally Ho!
Tickle Brain: Burton Bridge
Tidal Wave: Brewery on Sea
Tiger Best Bitter: Everards
Timeless: Brewery on Sea
Timmy's Ginger Beer: Porter
Tinners Ale: St Austell
Tipple: Trueman's
Tipsy Toad Ale: Tipsy Toad
Toby Cask: Bass
Tollyshooter: Tolly Cobbold
Tom Brown's Best Bitter: Goldfinch
Tom Kelly's Christmas Pudding Porter:
    Hoskins & Oldfield
Tom Kelly's Stout: Hoskins & Oldfield
Tommy Hepburn: (Beaumont Wines)
    Riverside
Tommy Todd's Porter: McGuinness
Tom Paine: Harveys
Tom's Gold: Hoskins
Tom Wood Best Bitter: Highwood

Tom Wood Harvest Bitter: Highwood
Tom Wood Old Timber: Highwood
Tom Wood Shepherd's Delight:
    Highwood
Top Dog Stout: Burton Bridge
Topers Tipple: Oldershaw
Top Hat: Burtonwood
Topsy Turvy: Berrow
Top Totty: Eccleshall
Totally Marbled: Marble
T'Owd Tup: Dent
Tower Power: Weltons
Town Bitter: Huddersfield
Town Crier: Hobsons
Trade Winds IPA: Tomintoul
Traditional Bitter:
    Cains
    Clark's
    Larkins
    Old Mill
Traditional English Ale: Hogs Back
Traditional Mild: Old Mill
Trafalgar Ale: Gale's
Trafalgar IPA: Freeminer
Treason Ale: Carlsberg-Tetley
Trelawney's Revenge: Keltek
Trelawney's Pride: St. Austell
Trentsman: Castle Rock
Tribute Ale: Barnfield
Tripel: Passageway
Triple B: Grainstore
Triple Diamond: Carlsberg-Tetley
Triple Hop: Brunswick
Triple X: Plough Inn
Trojan Bitter: Leyland
Trooper: Marston Moor
Trophy Bitter: Whitbread
Trotton Bitter: Ballard's
True Blue: City of Cambridge
True Glory: Ringwood
True Gold Lager: Trueman's
Tunnel Vision: Baynards
Tupping Ale: Grainstore
Turkey's Delight: Summerskills
Turkey's Revenge: Cheriton
Twelve Days: Hook Norton
Twenty Thirst Bitter: Mighty Oak
Twin Screw: Dark Tribe
Twister: Merivales
2B: Arkells
Two Ferrets: Banbury
200: Palmers
Two Pints: Cropton
2XS: B & T

U

Umbel Ale: Nethergate
Umbel Magna: Nethergate
Uncle Igor: Ross
Uncle Sams: Cropton
Unicorn Bitter: Leyland
Up In Smoke: Brewery on Sea
Upper Ale: Hale & Hearty
Ursa Major: Old Bear
Ursa Minor: Old Bear
Utopia: Hogs Back
Utter Nutter: McGuinness

V

Valentine: King & Barnes
Valentine's Ale: Tolly Cobbold
Valentine's Oat Malt Ale: Wadworth
Valhalla Gold: Brecknock
Valhalla Northern Lights: Brecknock
Valhalla Original: Brecknock

Valhalla Premier: Brecknock
Valiant: Bateman
Varsity: Morrells
Vaux Bitter: Vaux
Vaux Mild: Ward's
Vectis Premium Ale: Burts
Velvet Stout: Reepham
Ventnor Dark Mild: Ventnor
Ventnor Volunteer Bitter: Ventnor
Vicar's Ruin: Church End
Vickery's Brew: Henstridge
Victoria Bitter: Earl Soham
Victoria Lager: (Orange) Scottish
    Courage
Victorian Winter Ale: Cains
Victory Ale: Bateman
Victory Brew: Coach House (Joule)
Victory Mild: Flagship
Viking: Rudgate
Village Bitter: Archers
Vintage Ale: Brakspear, Old Luxters
VIP: Lloyds
Virgo: Bateman
Vixens Vengeance: Prince of Wales,
    Tigertops
Vixen Velvet: Lloyds
VSP: Bass (Original)
Vulcan: Featherstone

W

Wages: Blewitts
Waggle Dance: Ward's
Waddlers Mild: Mallard
Waitress: Kitchen
Wakefield Pride: Fernandes
Walker Best Bitter: Carlsberg-Tetley
Walker Bitter: Carlsberg-Tetley
Walker Mild: Carlsberg-Tetley
Walker Winter Warmer: Carlsberg-
    Tetley
Wallace IPA: Maclay
Wallop: Wood
Wallsend Brown Ale: Mordue
Wassail: Ballard's
Watkin's Whoosh: Watkin
Waverley 70/-: Harviestoun
Weatheroak Ale: Weatheroak
Webster's Green Label Best:
    Ruddles
    Scottish Courage
Webster's Yorkshire Bitter:
    Mansfield
    Scottish Courage
Weetablitz: Sutton
Weiss Buoy: Willy's
Wellington's Cannon: Weltons
Welsh Stout: Plassey
Wem Special: Hanby
Wenceslas Winter Warmer: Elgood's
Wenceslegless: Weltons
Werewolf: Man in the Moon
West Auckland Mild: Butterknowle
Weymouth Harbour Masters: Quay
Weymouth JD 1742: Quay
Weymouth Special Pale Ale: Quay
Whale Ale: Brewery on Sea
Whapweasel: Hexhamshire
Wharfedale: Goose Eye
What the Fox's Hat: Church End
Wheat-a-Bix: Church End
Wheat Beer: St Peter's
Wheat Bier: Kelham Island
Wheatsheaf Wheat Beer: Fernandes
Wheat your Whistle: Hogsback
Wheeltappers Ale: Cottage

Wherry Best Bitter: Woodforde's
Whippling Golden Bitter: Belvoir
Whistle Belly Vengeance:
    Summerskills
Whistlemass: Beer Engine
Whistle Stop: Shardlow
Whistling Joe: Brandy Cask
Whitby Abbey Ale: Black Dog
White: Enville
White Adder: Mauldons
White Bishop: Durham
White Boar: Hambleton Village
    (Brewer)
White Christmas:
    Old Forge
    Orkney
White Cloud: Rooster's
White Coombe: Prince of Wales,
    Tigertops
White Dolphin: Hoskins & Oldfield
White Dwarf: Oakham
White Gold: Durham
White Goose: Woodbury
White Knight: Goff's
White Star: Titanic
White Velvet: Durham
White Wheat Bear: Salopian
Wholesome Stout: Wye Valley
Wichen: Home County
Wicked Widget: Brewery on Sea (East-
    West Ales)
Wicket Beer: Hale & Hearty
Wild: Ballard's
Wild Boar: Worth
Wild Cat: Tomintoul
Wild John Bitter: Parish
Wild Mild: Fox & Hounds
Wild Turkey: Brewery on Sea
William French: Scott's
Willie Brew'd: Church End
Willie Warmer: Crouch Vale
Wilmot's Premium Ale: Butcombe
Wilson's Original Mild: Morland
    (Scottish Courage)
Wilson's Wobble Maker: Huddersfield
Wiltshire Traditional: (Gibbs Mew)
    Ushers
Winky's Winter Warmer: Leyland
Winky Wobbler: Leyland
Winners: SP Sporting Ales
Winter Ale: Greene King, Jersey
Winter Blotto: Franklin's
Winter Brew:
    Gale's
    Juwards,
    Winfields
Winter Cloving: Old Chimneys
Winter Fuel: Blackawton
Winter Glow: Exe Valley
Winter Holiday: Burton Bridge
    (Lakeland)
Winter Oats: Grainstore
Winter Old: Weltons
Winter's Revenge: McGuinness
Winter Special: Malton
Winter Storm: Ushers
Winter Tipple: Wye Valley
Winter Warmer:
    Big Lamp
    Cartmel
    Clark's
    Goddards
    Guernsey
    St Austell
    Sutton

Thwaites
Young's
Winter Widget: Brewery on Sea (East-
    West Ales)
Winter Winner: Ridleys
Witches Cauldron: Tomintoul
Witchfinder Porter: Ridleys
Witham Wobbler: Blue Cow
Withy Cutter: Moor
Witt Bier: Daleside
Wizards Wonder Halloween Bitter: Coach
    House
Wobble in a Bottle: Hogs Back
Wobbler: Gribble
Wobbly Bob: Phoenix
Wolfes Brew: Aviemore
Wonderful: Wood
Woodcocks IP: B&T (Martin Elms)
Woodham IPA: Crouch Vale
Workie Ticket: Mordue
Worth Gold: Worth
Worthington Dark Mild: Bass
Worthington Draught Bitter: Bass
Worthington White Shield: Bass
Worth Porter: Worth
Wot: Teme Valley
WP Roberts: (Beaumont Wines) Riverside
Wreck of the Old '97: Cambrinus
Wust Bitter: Fox & Hounds
Wychert Ale: Vale

X
XAV: Ventnor
XB:
    Bateman
    Holden's
    Scottish Courage (Theakston)
XL Bitter: Burton Bridge
Xmas Ale:
    Gales
    Ledbury
    Linfit
Xmas Cracker: Teignworthy
XSB: Sutton
XX Dark Mild: Greene King
XXX:
    Batham
    Donnington
XXXB: Bateman
XXX Bitter: Three Tuns
XXX Mild: Brakspear
XXXX Mild: St Austell
XXXX Porter: Ringwood

Y
Yankee: Rooster's
Ye Olde Trout: Kempton
Yeomanry: Arkkell's
Yeoman Strong Ale: Oakhill
YES: Hogs Back
Yo Ho Ho: Branscombe Vale
Yorkshire Gold: Glentworth
Yorkshire Terrier: York
Younger IPA: Scottish Courage
Younger No.3.: Scottish Courage
Younger Scotch Bitter: Scottish Courage
Young Pretender: Isle of Skye
Young Stallion: Liverpool
Your Every Success: Hogs Back

Z
Zebedee: Rebellion

Readers' recommendations
Suggestions for pubs to be included or excluded

All pubs are surveyed by local branches of the Campaign for Real Ale. If you would like to comment on a pub already featured, or any you think should be featured, please fill in the form below (or copy it), and send it to the address indicated. Your views will be passed on to the branch concerned. Please mark your envelope with the county where the pub is, which will help us to sort the suggestion efficiently.

Pub name:

Address:

Reason for recommendation/criticism:

Pub name:

Address:

Reason for recommendation/criticism:

Pub name:

Address:

Reason for recommendation/criticism:

Your name and address:

Please send to: [Name of county] Section, Good Beer Guide, 230 Hatfield Road, St Albans, Hertfordshire AL1 4LW, UK

Other Storey Titles You Will Enjoy

The Good Beer Guide to Belgium and Holland, by Tim Webb. A comprehensive CAMRA/Storey travel guide to the best cafés and bars of this unique beer rich region. Includes beer tasting notes on the diverse styles as well as maps and food recommendations. 288 pages. Paperback. ISBN 1-58017-103-6.

Brew Your Own British Real Ale, by Graham Wheeler and Roger Protz. Features more than 100 homebrew recipes for recreations of well-know beers such as Bass, Fuller's, Guinness, and more. Many recipes were created with the help of the brewers themselves and reveal some long-guarded secret ingredients. 196 pages. Paperback. ISBN 1-58017-102-8.

The Beer-Taster's Log: A World Guide to More Than 6,000 Beers, by James D. Robertson. This is the most complete reference available on domestic and international beers, with review of more than 6,000 beers including ratings on aroma, balance, visual appearance, flavor, and more. 624 pages. Paperback. ISBN 0-88266-939-7.

The Beer Enthusiast's Guide: Tasting & Judging Brews from Around the World, by Gregg Smith. Smith offers beer lovers a complete course in tasting, judging, and appreciating all types of beer from around the world. Readers will learn about brewing history, evaluation techniques, ingredients, and beer styles and characteristics. Also included are a listing of microbreweries and supply shops and a study guide for the Beer Judge Certification Program. 144 pages. Paperback. ISBN 0-88266-838-2.

The Beer Directory: An International Guide, compiled by Heather Wood. A worldwide beer-lovers' directory with more than 4,500 listings of large and small breweries, places to enjoy good beer, stores that sell good beer, places of historical beer interest, festivals, celebrations, magazines and publications, organizations, and even beer-oriented travel groups and agencies. 224 pages. Paperback. ISBN 0-88266-903-6.

CloneBrews: Homebrew Recipes for 150 Commercial Beers, by Tess and Mark Szamatulski. With this unique collection of recipes for 150 international brand-name beers, homebrewers can "clone" their favorite beers at home and enjoy them at a fraction of their retail price. 176 pages. Paperback. ISBN 1-58017-077-3.